PRAISE FOR *PERJURY: THE HISS-CHAMBERS CASE*

"The definitive account."

—*Reader's Catalog*

"A historic event. . . . Stunningly meticulous, a monument to
the intellectual ideal of truth stalked to its hiding place."

—GEORGE WILL, *Newsweek*

"Lucidly written, impressively researched, closely
argued. . . . The result is formidable."

—IRVING HOWE, *New York Times Sunday Book Review*

"So far as any one book can dispel a large historical
mystery, this book does it, magnificently."

—GARRY WILLS, *New York Review of Books*

"The most exciting piece of history in recent memory."

—WILLIAM F. BUCKLEY

"The most objective and convincing account we have of
the most dramatic court case of the century."

—ARTHUR SCHLESINGER, JR

"The most dispassionate, step-by-step account of [the case]."

—GEOFFREY WARD, *American Heritage*

"Devastatingly complete and detailed . . . an impressively
unemotional blockbuster of fact."

—ALFRED KAZIN, *Esquire*

"I do not envy Weinstein's critics their task any more than I would want to
be a defense counsel who had listened for three days while a professor read
Weinstein's book aloud to the jury and who now had to rise for rebuttal."

—MURRAY KEMPTON

"[Weinstein] has gone as far as any historian could to establish the formal
validity of the verdict. . . . His treatment of the resulting material strikes one as
both judicious and properly skeptical; he writes of it with clarity and restraint.
. . . Weinstein's contribution, then, is major and I would say definitive."

—JOHN KENNETH GALBRAITH

"Allen Weinstein has come up with the facts . . . [he] not only amasses new
and old evidence, [he] demolishes arguments of government conspiracy."

—PETER S. PRESCOTT, *Newsweek*

"Impressive . . . [Weinstein] makes persuasive use of this material
in a narrative that is lucid, dramatic and even handed."

—ROBERT KIRSCH, *Los Angeles Times Book Review*

PERJURY

Allen Weinstein

PERJURY
The Hiss-Chambers Case

Third Edition

HOOVER INSTITUTION PRESS

STANFORD UNIVERSITY   STANFORD, CALIFORNIA

The Hoover Institution on War, Revolution and Peace, founded at Stanford University in 1919 by Herbert Hoover, who went on to become the thirty-first president of the United States, is an interdisciplinary research center for advanced study on domestic and international affairs. The views expressed in its publications are entirely those of the authors and do not necessarily reflect the views of the staff, officers, or Board of Overseers of the Hoover Institution.

www.hoover.org

Hoover Institution Press Publication No. 567

Hoover Institution at Leland Stanford Junior University,
Stanford, California 94305-6010

First edition 1978
Second edition 1997
Third edition 2013
19 18 17 16 15 14 13   7 6 5 4 3 2 1

Manufactured in the United States of America

The paper used in this publication meets the minimum Requirements of the American National Standard for Information Sciences—Permanence of Paper for Printed Library Materials, ANSI/NISO Z39.48-1992. ∞

Cataloging-in-Publication Data is available from the Library of Congress.
ISBN: 978-0-8179-1225-3 (pbk. : alk. paper)
ISBN: 978-0-8179-1226-0 (e-book)

For Adrienne
with love and gratitude

"What pleased me most in this affair," the Assistant [Commissioner] went on, talking slowly, "is that it makes such an excellent starting-point for a piece of work which I've felt must be taken in hand—that is, the clearing out of this country of all the foreign political spies, police, and that sort of—of—dogs. In my opinion they are a ghastly nuisance; also an element of danger. But we can't very well seek them out individually. The only way is to make their employment unpleasant to their employers. The thing's becoming indecent. And dangerous, too, for us, here."

Mr. Vladimir stopped again for a moment.

"What do you mean?"

"The prosecution of this Verloc will demonstrate to the public both the danger and the indecency."

"Nobody will believe what a man of that sort says," said Mr. Vladimir, contemptuously.

"The wealth and precision of detail will carry conviction to the great mass of the public," advanced the Assistant Commissioner gently.

"So that is seriously what you mean to do?"

"We've got the man; we have no choice."

—JOSEPH CONRAD
The Secret Agent

CONTENTS

PART FIVE: CONSEQUENCES

PART SIX: MEMORY

                   Photo Section follows after page 396

ACKNOWLEDGMENTS

I began research on *Perjury: The Hiss-Chambers Case* in 1973, continued to work steadily on it prior to its initial publication in 1978, and have pursued my interest in the case up through the present. After four decades spent "living" with Hiss-Chambers, however, it would be impossible to thank every individual who has contributed to my understanding of the episode and its main characters.

Many of the country's leading historians, archivists, museum directors, and librarians opened their research collections and their memories to me. I thank all of them. I remain indebted to the American Civil Liberties Union for filing a lawsuit in 1973 on my behalf demanding release of the FBI's Hiss-Case records. Two years later, the ACLU won its case, thereby opening up thousands of pages of research materials to me and other scholars.

I had the privilege of working on the initial edition of *Perjury* with the late Ashbel Green of Knopf, one of the great editors in publishing. Two other distinguished editors worked on the book's second edition, Robert Loomis and Geoff Shandler, both with Random House at the time. Throughout the process, I benefited from literary agent Robert Barnett's wise council. In addition, I owe a special, personal thanks to several other friends for their timely encouragement, including editors Harold Evans and James Wade, historians Timothy Naftali, Ronald Radosh, and Alyce Radosh, and my long-time assistant Donna Gold.

Regarding the new edition of *Perjury*, I have received unwavering support from the Hoover Institution Press's managing editor Jennifer Presley, book production manager Barbara Arellano, copy editor Keith Tidman, graphic designer Jennifer Navarrette, and other Hoover Institution Press consultants and staff who made this unique project come alive again.

I'm especially grateful for the first-rate support provided by my two assistants in Washington, Evin Rose Lipman and Lauren Vilbert. Both not only helped prepare *Perjury*'s new edition, but have assisted also on a number of my other projects with unfailingly good cheer.

Obviously, none of the individuals mentioned are responsible for any errors that might turn up in the book.

Finally, I owe a deep debt of gratitude for *Perjury*'s continued existence to Andrew and David Weinstein. They know why.

INTRODUCTION

Once upon a time, when the Cold War was young, a senior editor of *Time* accused the president of the Carnegie Endowment of having been a Soviet agent. The *Time* editor made his charge stick, aided by an obscure young congressman from the House Un-American Activities Committee, a tough federal prosecutor, and the director of the FBI. As a result, the Endowment president spent forty-four months in jail and became a cause célèbre; the magazine editor resigned and died a decade later, still obsessed with the case; the prosecutor became a federal judge; the director of the FBI lived to guard the republic against real or imagined enemies for another twenty-five years; and the young congressman left obscurity behind to become the thirty-seventh president of the United States.

The original edition of *Perjury* opened with that capsule summary, which evokes the fantastic and virtually improbable qualities of a timeless espionage novel. In fact, when the Hiss-Chambers case broke open, its main characters and events seemed more appropriate to spy fiction than to the realities of American life in the late 1940s. And although more than a half-century has passed since the jury at Alger Hiss's second trial pronounced him guilty of perjury, the case remains controversial and the verdict leaves questions unanswered. Did Hiss become an undercover Communist while serving as a New Deal official? Did he turn over classified State Department files to Whittaker Chambers, a self-confessed former underground agent for the Communist Party? Or did Chambers, for obscure and malevolent reasons, deliberately set out to frame and destroy a respected public official?

Public debate over the case has resumed regularly in the generation since this book's appearance in 1978. Alger Hiss's late-1970s appeal for a new hearing based upon allegations of unfair prosecution tactics at his original trials was denied in July 1982.* Hiss's accuser, Whittaker Chambers, died in 1961, but Alger Hiss continued to profess his complete innocence of Chambers's allegations until his death in 1996. Richard Nixon's return to prominence as a policy advocate during the 1980s brought periodic reminders in the American and global media

---

*See Chapter XVI.

of Nixon's initial fame as Hiss's main pursuer in the televised 1948 House committee hearings.

Memoirs by two leading Soviet intelligence chieftains, published in the past decade, both asserted Hiss's complicity as an agent. Another former Soviet official-turned-historian, urged on by an appeal from a longtime Hiss supporter, at first announced in 1992 that his review of KGB files had turned up nothing on Hiss. Reminded that Chambers had accused Hiss of working *not* for the KGB's "civilian" espionage predecessor agency but for Soviet *military* intelligence and amid widespread international focus on his assertion, the official (possibly after reviewing military intelligence files) recanted his earlier statement and claimed to have been pressured by Hiss's advocate to issue it.

A Hungarian historian, after reviewing interrogations of a friend and colleague of Hiss's during the 1930s, Noel Field (opened in Budapest for her inspection in 1993), announced that Field had not only admitted his own role in Soviet espionage but had implicated Alger Hiss as a confederate. Most recently, in 1996, release of the National Security Agency's "VENONA" intercepts of cables sent by Soviet spymasters from Washington and New York to Moscow during World War II tagged one agent—referred to only by his alias "ALES"—as "probably Alger Hiss." Hiss had been identified years earlier in the memoirs of defecting Soviet agent Oleg Gordievsky using the same alias, and this author's research in Soviet KGB archives on another book project also turned up major new evidence on Alger Hiss's and Whittaker Chambers's involvement in Soviet espionage, described in this new edition of *Perjury.*

Thus has "the case" continued to make headlines and attract considerable media attention in the years since this book was first published. This new edition incorporates evidence available only in the past two decades and brings the essential public story of the episode up to the present.

The Hiss-Chambers case caused widespread political damage and much human suffering. Although nothing written at a distance of more than five decades can undo its effects, perhaps this analysis can explain the passion that the case still arouses. Few Americans in that earlier period failed to react: Republicans invoked Hiss's presumed treachery to accuse the Democrats of condoning Communism-in-government during the New Deal–Fair Deal era. Moreover, in the decades that followed Alger Hiss's trials, Whittaker Chambers's life and ideas— widely publicized in his best-selling memoir (*Witness*) and in other writings— shaped and reinvigorated the conservative movement in the United States.

Many liberals, in turn, viewed the assault on Hiss as the spearhead of a right-wing attempt to discredit the Roosevelt-Truman domestic and foreign policies. "Without the Alger Hiss case," Earl Latham noted in a study of the Washington spy probes, "the six-year controversy that followed might have been a much tamer affair, and the Communist issue somewhat more tractable." But the Hiss case "revolutionized public opinion" and left in its wake the legacy of McCarthyism.

Within a month of Hiss's conviction, the British atomic spy Klaus Fuchs had been arrested and Senator Joseph R. McCarthy had delivered his first Communism-in-government speech at Wheeling, West Virginia, an event that launched his political career. Julius and Ethel Rosenberg were convicted at their New York trial in March 1951, further reinforcing public anger at real and alleged internal security lapses during the previous decade. Richard Nixon's leadership in the HUAC probe of Hiss-Chambers restored the committee's prestige and gave Nixon the reputation of a successful spy hunter, helping him gain a Senate seat in 1950 and the vice presidential nomination two years later.

Right-wingers turned Hiss into a symbol of the supposed treason that lay behind New Deal policies, particularly in the State Department. Those, like the 1952 Democratic presidential candidate, Adlai E. Stevenson, who had believed in Alger Hiss prior to his conviction, found themselves on the defensive. "A native American, a man groomed for national leadership," in the words of Joseph Goulden, had been "shown to be susceptible to subversion for a foreign power." That someone of Hiss's background would become a Soviet agent seemed as improbable to many Americans as Harold "Kim" Philby's exposure as a veteran Russian operative would later appear to many in Great Britain.

The symbolic lines were sharply drawn. For some, Alger Hiss's close association with New Deal radicals and with the wartime policy of Soviet-American *entente* corroborated his guilt. For others, Hiss's activities confirmed his innocence. But the clash of symbols did little to encourage efforts to analyze the evidence closely. Rather, it tended to confirm preconceptions. This attitude of partisan exhortation has characterized almost every early book written on the case, with the notable exception of Alistair Cooke's.

Those politically and temperamentally disposed to support Hiss generally relied on a welter of conspiracy theories, which shared an underlying theme: that Whittaker Chambers perjured himself. Beyond that, the scripts invariably alternated between named and nameless plotters.

For over two decades after his release from prison, Alger Hiss tried to renew interest in the case. His efforts proved unsuccessful until, thanks to the Watergate crisis and the downfall of his former nemesis, Richard Nixon, Hiss regained public prominence. This time a new generation of Americans, unfamiliar with the complex facts of the case, responding both to the renewed publicity and to a post-Watergate penchant for conspiracies, hearkened to the claims of innocence expressed by Hiss in lectures, press conferences, and radio and television appearances.

Even before, many of the active left-liberals growing up in the Silent Fifties were well disposed to believe Hiss's version of events. His innocence was a matter of faith, if only because Chambers, Nixon, Hoover, and others on the anti-Communist right were his political enemies. Hiss's fate symbolized for young liberals the quintessence of McCarthyism, its paranoid fear of any public figure to the left of Dwight Eisenhower.

My interest in the case began in 1969, as part of a larger, yet uncompleted study of the Cold War and American society. I published an article on Hiss-Chambers and concluded that both men had probably lied; that Hiss hid facts concerning his personal relationship with Chambers, while the latter had falsely accused Hiss of Communist ties and espionage. I urged that the FBI files on the case be opened to provide the additional evidence needed to answer any unresolved questions. The proposal produced only one immediate result: the FBI opened a file on me. J. Edgar Hoover read a *Washington Post* account of my suggestion and wrote in its margin: "What do we know about Weinstein . . . ?"

In 1972, with support from the American Civil Liberties Union, I filed a lawsuit under the Freedom of Information Act to obtain FBI and Justice Department records on the case. *Weinstein v. Kleindienst, Gray, et al.,* after three years of court struggle and many meetings with FBI and Justice Department officials, resulted in the release of over thirty thousand pages of classified FBI files and thousands of pages of additional Justice Department records. (Even Hoover's "do-not-file files" on Hiss-Chambers surfaced.) During this same period my requests also brought to light extensive and formerly closed records from the CIA, the State Department, and the Immigration and Naturalization Service, all bearing on the Hiss-Chambers case.

But my analysis and conclusions have not been drawn solely from FBI and other once-classified government records. I have sought and gained access to many previously undiscovered, unavailable, or unconsulted sources of documentary and oral evidence, both in this country and abroad. Visits to over two dozen public archives uncovered important new material and verified numerous details about the case from the papers or recollections of Adolf Berle, Malcolm Cowley, David Dallin, Ralph de Toledano, Allen Dulles, John Foster Dulles, Jerome Frank, Felix Frankfurter, Josephine Herbst, Stanley K. Hornbeck, Gardner Jackson, Karl Mundt, Richard Nixon, Lee Pressman, Francis B. Sayre, Edward R. Stettinius, Jr., Harry S. Truman, Harry Dexter White, and others.

Much new evidence came from individuals close to either Hiss or Chambers who—in many cases—had refused previous requests for interviews from other researchers. Over eighty people who had special knowledge of the case or its protagonists gave interviews. They included every shade in the political spectrum: Soviet agents and congressional Red-hunters, close friends and advisers of both Chambers and Hiss, spies and former Communists, liberals and conservatives, and members of both the Hiss and Chambers families (including a half-dozen interviews with Alger Hiss, five meetings with Priscilla Hiss, and one with

Donald Hiss). These interviews began in 1973 and continued into mid-1977, a process that involved travel to every corner of the United States and to England, Germany, Hungary, Israel, Italy, and Mexico. More than forty of these people had never spoken openly about the case.

The revelations of five participants in Soviet intelligence work in the United States and Europe during the 1930s—Joszef Peters, Nadya Ulanovskaya, Maxim Lieber, Paul Willert, and Hede Massing—proved particularly instructive. Peters headed the American Communist Party's underground work during the thirties, Ulanovskaya and her husband ran Russian military espionage in the United States from 1931 to 1934, and Lieber was for a time a close associate of Chambers in secret activities. With the exception of Peters, they gave either significant new information about the case or pertinent corroboration of Chambers's account of Soviet espionage in the United States during the 1930s, as did several others who had been approached by Chambers but refused to turn spy, and who talked to me.

I interviewed "J. Peters" (the first Westerner to do so) in Budapest in 1975. By all accounts, Peters was the liaison between the American Communist Party's underground branch and the Soviet agents who led their own separate groups in the United States during the 1930s and 1940s.

The story of Soviet espionage in the United States between 1931 and 1934 unfolded in rich detail during three days of talks in Jerusalem with Nadya Ulanovskaya, whose husband had been head of the Red Army's Fourth Branch intelligence unit, based in New York. Ulanovskaya was also an agent at the time and knew Esther and Whittaker Chambers well: Nadya and Alexander (the husband) appear in *Witness* as the Russians "Elaine" ("Maria") and "Ulrich." Besides confirming the accuracy of Chambers's account of the Soviet network in New York during the early 1930s, Ulanovskaya provided new information about its personnel and activities, and about another key figure in the Hiss-Chambers drama: Boris Bykov, who headed Red Army intelligence in America from 1936 to 1939 and was Chambers's superior during the years prior to his defection in 1938. Nadya recounted a Moscow meeting in 1939 at which Bykov gave important details about Chambers's break and about the nature of Russian espionage in Washington. (Three key witnesses from the FBI files also substantiate Bykov's activities and the work of Chambers's Washington spy ring: Henry Julian Wadleigh, William Edward Crane, and Felix Inslerman.)

Maxim Lieber further confirmed Chambers's story, recalling his orders from Bykov and Peters in mid-1938 to track down Chambers (a defector by then), and telling of the latter's role in Russian intelligence work earlier in the thirties. Paul Willert, who performed anti-Nazi courier work for the German Communist Party during the same period (before becoming a British agent in the Second World War), described his encounter with Chambers in 1938 when he (Willert) headed American operations for Oxford University Press. Willert gave Chambers translating work prior to the latter's break with the Communist Party in April 1938, and later that year warned Chambers that a Comintern agent had arrived from Europe looking for him. With Willert's help, I have identified that agent (Chambers tagged him incorrectly). Other interviews that corroborated aspects of Chambers's underground work included talks with Hermann Field (Noel's brother), Czech historian Karel Kaplan, Ella Winter (Lincoln Steffens's widow), former publisher David Zabladowsky, and four of Chambers's friends during this period—Robert Cantwell, Felix Morrow, Professor Meyer Schapiro, and his wife, Dr. Lillian Schapiro.

Professor Kaplan left Czechoslovakia in 1976 with a significant archive on modern Czech history collected during his eight years (1960–68) as an archivist for the Communist Party's Central Committee. He had read the long interrogations of both Noel and Herta Field by Czech and Hungarian security officials, and in two long interviews in Munich, he described to me the material in those files that dealt with Alger Hiss.

Meyer and Lillian Schapiro gave me copies of Whittaker Chambers's letters to them, never before shown to a researcher, which clarified a number of questions about the man's years as a Communist agent and defector. The late Sylvia Salmi, widow of the anti-Communist radical journalist Herbert Solow, another of Chambers's friends, made her husband's invaluable papers available for the first time at her home in a Mexican village. They include an extraordinary cache of previously unsuspected material: a collection of letters from Chambers written during the months after his defection, a memo Solow prepared and had notarized in late 1938 outlining Chambers's career in the Communist underground (based upon over a dozen interviews with Chambers from 1932 to 1938), a detailed card file on Soviet agents in the United States compiled by Solow (lengthier and more accurate for the 1930s than the FBI's), and two unpublished articles on Russian espionage in America that Chambers wrote only months after his break, articles that he had instructed Solow to destroy and therefore did not consult himself at the time of the case. Solow's files contain hard evidence that Chambers saved government documents stolen by Washington officials.

Two friends of Chambers from the 1920s, both then Communists, political cartoonist Jacob Burck and Samuel Krieger, who arranged for Chambers's initial membership in the "open" Communist Party, fleshed out a portrait of the agent as a young man, while later intimates at *Time*—T. S. Matthews, Henry Grunwald, Samuel Welles, Robert Cantwell, and Duncan Norton-Taylor among them—helped clarify Chambers's stormy years on the magazine. Interviewed in England, Matthews generously allowed me to read his unpublished memoir on Chambers. Other private records used in the book include *Time*'s archives, examined through the courtesy of its publishers, which document both Whittaker Chambers's career as a journalist and his complex relationship with Henry

Luce. Among the individuals who permitted me access to their own material on the case or its protagonists, most of which had never been released before, are Sidney Hook, Isaac Don Levine, Mrs. Mary Mundt, Robert Stripling, and Alden Whitman.

Esther Chambers, who lived in seclusion, was the only major member of the Hiss or Chambers families to decline an interview.* However, her son, John, a Washington journalist, answered questions about his father's past on several occasions.

Alger Hiss's friends and associates proved as informative as Chambers's. Two of the psychiatrists associated with Hiss's trial defense, Doctors Viola Bernard and Henry Murray, offered revealing glimpses into Hiss's behavior. Five lawyers who worked on the Hiss defense and the widow of a sixth—Helen Buttenwieser, Claude B. Cross, John F. Davis, Mrs. Chester Lane, William L. Marbury, and Robert von Mehren—discussed their client and the nature of his trial strategy with me. Several typewriter experts hired by the Hiss defense after the second trial added facts not given to previous researchers, as did Manice de F. Lockwood, a close friend of Alger Hiss's, who acted as an unpaid investigator for decades.

Priscilla Hiss commented on the case, though obliquely, in a series of luncheon meetings. "A curtain has descended," Mrs. Hiss told me at our first meeting, "and I don't remember the period. I don't want to remember it." Nevertheless, her remarks on the case were instructive. Another member of the family, Alger Hiss's stepson, Dr. Timothy Hobson, saw me at his Northern California home and offered shrewd insights on the lives and character of the Hisses. Donald Hiss, Alger's brother, met me for a talk at the Washington law firm of Covington, Burling, from which he had retired.

I went over numerous details of the case with Alger Hiss on six occasions between 1973 and 1976, once joined by his son, Anthony. The extensive and revealing Hiss defense files—divided among four lawyers' offices in Baltimore, Boston, and New York during the period I studied them—were a major source of new information.

The role of Richard Nixon in the case and the full story of his rise to political prominence, which the late Mr. Nixon hid and distorted for the past half-century, has been reconstructed in this book for the first time from a variety of sources: HUAC's chief of staff at the time, Robert Stripling; committee investigator Donald Appell; lawyer Nicholas Vazzana, who probed the case for *Time* in 1948; Father John Cronin, who first told Nixon about Alger Hiss's alleged Communist ties; and journalist Isaac Donald Levine all contributed new information that

---

*Others who refused my requests for interviews (or left such requests unanswered) included three alleged onetime members of the Communist Party's Washington "Ware Group"—Nathan Witt, John Abt, and Jessica Smith Abt; also Judge Thomas Murphy and Julian Wadleigh.

helped piece together the story. Nixon's aide Franklin Gannon listened politely as I outlined my findings during a 1975 visit to San Clemente. But the former president would not see me, although at a chance 1987 meeting, Nixon spoke in complimentary terms about this book despite the fact that its findings challenge in critical particulars his own oft-repeated version of his role in the case.*

A number of others helpful to the original edition of *Perjury* appear in the Acknowledgments section. Regarding the book's present edition, several of those most helpful in providing information and insights include Russian friends, only some of whom appear (for obvious reasons) among those described in the Acknowledgments. I am especially grateful to leading officials of the Russian Intelligence Service (SVR), including its former director, Yevgeny Primakov, General Vadim Kirpichenko, General Yuri Kobaladze (head of its press bureau, with primary responsibility for dealing with inquisitive Western scholars and journalists), and Oleg Tsarev, retired colonel and avid historian. Over numerous meetings, lunches, and dinners between 1993 and 1996 they shared their perspectives on matters related to Soviet intelligence work in America (which often disagree sharply with those found in *Perjury*). Each of these encounters added immeasurably to this historian's education in multiarchival history.

My coauthor on *The Haunted Wood,* a more general history of Soviet espionage, Alexander Vassiliev, Russian journalist and briefly a KGB operative in his earlier years, has brought a keen intelligence and diligent research habits to the craft of collaboration that has affected not only our joint study but this edition of *Perjury*. Closer to home, the writer Sam Tanenhaus, while researching his biography of Whittaker Chambers, shared generously his insights into issues of evidence that have emerged only recently, including the Volkogonov episode, Anna Schmidt's revelation of the Noel Field interrogations, and a number of other issues related to the case.

Among still others who have contributed to whatever merit resides in the new edition of *Perjury* and are acknowledged accordingly elsewhere in the book, one friend and guide to the labyrinth of Soviet espionage efforts in the United States—former senior editor at Crown, James O'Shea Wade—brought both wise counsel and inside information to various elements in this book as well as to *The Haunted Wood*. Finally, along with other scholars, I am grateful to the CIA and NSA historians and archivists—Michael Warner, Lou Benson, Brian Latell, and the others—whose skillful editing and diligence has placed the entire corpus of

---

*Beginning in 1969, I sought unsuccessfully to gain access to HUAC records dealing with the case, helped by Representatives Claude Pepper and Robert Drinan. But in 1976 the House Judiciary Committee sealed the now-defunct committee's records for fifty years. Much new documentation on HUAC's Hiss-Chambers inquiry, however, came from previously untapped papers at the Truman Library, from the Karl Mundt archives, and from the papers of Ralph de Toledano at the Hoover Institution (Stanford University).

intercepted Soviet cables from the World War II years, including some of interest to this book, into the public domain with a remarkable measure of balance and sensitivity.

With the new evidence blended into the "old," most of the troubling questions about the Hiss-Chambers case can be answered. Not surprisingly, the story that emerges, although as dramatic as the conspiracy theories, provides one new dimension: It actually happened.

—ALLEN WEINSTEIN
Washington, D.C.
December 2012

Part One
ORIGINS

If Arthur Croom was the man of the near future, Gifford Maxim was the man of the far future, the bloody, moral, apocalyptic future that was sure to come. Once Laskell's sense of the contradiction between his two friends had been puzzling and intense. But now it was possible to hold Gifford Maxim and Arthur Croom in his mind with no awareness of contradiction at all. He was able to see them both as equally, right was perhaps not the word, but valid or necessary. They contradicted each other, the administrator and the revolutionary and perhaps eventually, one would kill the other. Yet now Laskell saw how they complemented each other to make up the world of politics.

—*Lionel Trilling*, The Middle of the Journey

I

HUAC:
A MONTH OF HEADLINES

AUGUST 3, 1948: THE WITNESS

What was HUAC up to this time? A new "mystery witness," perhaps, or some other bald move timed to make the next day's front pages? Whatever the purpose, the House Un-American Activities Committee had reserved the Ways and Means Committee's more spacious hearing room only minutes earlier. A large contingent of Washington reporters, summoned on short notice to the unexpected public session, wondered what surprise the unloved and unpredictable committee had concocted for that hot summer morning.

Three Republican congressmen and three Democrats, all opponents of the Truman administration, attended the session. Representing the Republican majority were Karl E. Mundt of South Dakota, John McDowell of Pennsylvania, and a first-term Californian named Richard M. Nixon. The Democrats seated on the dais were John Rankin of Mississippi, J. Hardin Peterson of Florida, and F. Edward Hébert of Louisiana. Chairman J. Parnell Thomas, under suspicion of having received kickbacks from his employees (a crime for which he would be indicted that year and later convicted), did not appear on August 3.

Thomas's predicament was only the latest threat to the committee's standing. John Rankin, who spiked most hearings with Negrophobic, anti-Catholic, and anti-Semitic tirades, and the other members of HUAC had trouble distinguishing between alleged Communist activities and participation in the New Deal. HUAC, first charged in 1938 with probing all varieties of domestic political extremism, had zeroed in—whether under Democratic or Republican chairmen—on the Democratic Party's liberal left more than on avowed Communists or fascists.[1]

Its well-publicized hearings seldom bore any apparent relationship to the drafting of legislation. The committee's 1947 hearings on "subversion" in the motion-picture industry, for example, although producing indictments of the Hollywood Ten, ended by generating considerable opposition to HUAC's ruthless headline-hunting style, persuading many liberals as well as those on the left that they had seen the authentic face of a modern political witchhunt. Even some conservatives in Congress and in the press corps began to attack the committee for exceeding its original mandate, and one reporter, Bert Andrews of the New York *Herald Tribune,* won a Pulitzer Prize for a series of articles critical of its

Hollywood hearings. HUAC's tarnished reputation made it vulnerable by mid-1948, and Truman aides drafted a bill to abolish the committee if the November election restored Democratic control of Congress.[2]

Lying low, the group planned no major new probes before the election. "As a committee, we are getting some 'panning' from our colleagues on the floor and others," Acting Chairman Mundt wrote Thomas in late July 1948. "This will require some careful handling and some thorough planning." Only at the last minute did the committee decide to hear a witness who had testified days earlier before a Senate investigating subcommittee.

Elizabeth Bentley—fortyish, plump, sharp-nosed, and a former courier for Communist agents—had first approached the FBI in 1945. Director J. Edgar Hoover had deluged Truman, Attorney General Tom Clark, and others in 1945 and 1946 with memos detailing Bentley's allegations of widespread Soviet espionage, but the administration had taken no action, perhaps because the informant offered no corroboration for her story.[3]

At the outset of Truman's 1948 presidential campaign, however, Bentley's well-publicized appearances before congressional committees revived the "Communism-in-government" issue. Dubbed the "Red Spy Queen" by the press, Bentley told HUAC on July 31 that from 1938 to 1945 she had made contact with almost two dozen Washington officials, Communists, and left-sympathizers, who—according to the witness—had delivered secret documents to her for transmission to Russian agents.*

Bentley named names—including some prominent government aides, first mentioned publicly at her HUAC appearance and not in earlier congressional testimony. Lauchlin Currie, who had served as a top assistant to President Franklin Roosevelt, was one; and Harry Dexter White, former assistant secretary of the Treasury, chief architect of the World Bank, and, after 1946, director of the International Monetary Fund, was another. Although Bentley ranged more widely in her charges before HUAC than during Senate testimony, she offered only her version—her word—and Truman dismissed the accusations as false and politically motivated. Still, public interest in Bentley's appearances persuaded Thomas, Mundt, and HUAC's chief investigator, Robert E. Stripling, a Democratic holdover from the chairmanships of Martin Dies and John Rankin, of her usefulness. Staff members searched for evidence to reinforce Bentley's tale of a Communist spy ring widespread in government and produced statements by a not-too-cooperative witness whom committee investigators had interviewed in March. That witness became the surprise of August 3.[4]

---

*Recently released material from the KGB archives amply confirms the substance of Bentley's testimony. See Allen Weinstein and Alexander Vassiliev, *The Haunted Wood: Soviet Espionage in America* (New York: Random House, 1999), *passim.*

Whittaker Chambers had led three lives since attending Columbia: as an "open Party" Communist journalist and a freelance translator during the late 1920s and early 1930s; as a Communist underground agent during the mid-thirties; and, since 1939, as a writer and editor for *Time*. During the March session Chambers had asked that he not be subpoenaed,* and summoning him on August 2 to corroborate Bentley seems to have been Karl Mundt's idea. Mundt, in turn, acted on the suggestion of a New York *World-Telegram* reporter, Frederick Woltman, who had learned of Chambers's past from ex-radical friends and from the FBI.[5]

The forty-seven-year-old Chambers made an unimpressive appearance in executive session on the morning of the 3rd. "He was short and pudgy," Richard Nixon later wrote. "His clothes were unpressed; his shirt collar was curled up over his jacket. He spoke in a rather bored monotone [and] seemed an indifferent if not a reluctant witness."

Chambers asked permission to read an opening statement, and after quickly skimming it, Robert Stripling agreed. The witness proceeded listlessly through the few pages of text until one committee member perked up at the names Chambers mentioned and interrupted: "Hell, why is this in executive session? This should be in the open!" Anticipating good publicity, HUAC adjourned to hold a public hearing in the Ways and Means Committee room.[6]

In the witness chair Chambers, his voice continually trailing off, read once more the statement explaining his decision to leave the Communist Party:

> Almost exactly nine years ago—that is, two days after Hitler and Stalin signed their pact [in August 1939]—I went to Washington and reported to the authorities what I knew about the infiltration of the United States Government by Communists.

After defecting in 1938, Chambers asserted, he had "lived in hiding, sleeping by day and watching through the night with gun and revolver within easy reach." He then described his reasons for thinking that the Communists might try to kill him:

> For a number of years I had myself served in the underground, chiefly in Washington, D.C. The heart of my report to the United States Government [in 1939] consisted of a description of the apparatus to which I was attached. It was an underground organization of the United States Communist Party developed, to the best of my knowledge, by Harold Ware, one of the sons of the Communist leader known as "Mother Bloor." I knew it at its top level, a group of seven or so men, from among whom in later years certain members of Miss Bentley's

---

*Among the interrogators in March had been HUAC Research Director Benjamin Mandel, a former Communist who had originally enrolled Whittaker Chambers in the Communist Party (CP) during the mid-1920s, a fact neither Mandel nor Chambers mentioned in August.

organization were apparently recruited. The head of the underground group at the time I knew it was Nathan Witt, an attorney for the National Labor Relations Board. Later, John Abt became the leader. Lee Pressman was also a member of this group, as was Alger Hiss, who, as a member of the State Department, later organized the conference at Dumbarton Oaks, San Francisco, and the United States side of the Yalta Conference.[7]

Reporters present realized that they had their "lead" for the next day's papers. Witt and Abt, also named by Bentley, were middle-rank bureaucrats and had long since left the government. So had Pressman, who was now general counsel of the Congress of Industrial Organizations (CIO). But Alger Hiss in such company was news. Since leaving the State Department, Hiss had become president of the Carnegie Endowment for International Peace. The next day's papers used variants of the headline "TIME EDITOR CHARGES CARNEGIE ENDOWMENT HEAD WAS SOVIET AGENT," which did not reflect the qualifying sentences Chambers had used to describe the "ring":

> The purpose of this group at that time was not primarily espionage. Its original purpose was the Communist infiltration of the American Government. But espionage was certainly one of its eventual objectives.[8]

Eager for additional details—and names—Stripling and the committee members intensified their questioning. Had Chambers named all the members of this secret New Deal Communist cell? No, the witness responded; he had singled out only the most prominent ones—Witt, Abt, Pressman, and Alger Hiss. "Other members of the group were . . . Donald Hiss [Alger's younger brother], Victor Perlo, [and] Charles Kramer (originally Charles Krivitsky)," all low-to-middle-rank functionaries at the time within the New Deal. The Ware Group, he explained, had met either at the apartment of Henry Collins, another member, or at the violin studio of Harold Ware's sister, Helen. Collins collected the dues. Ware's superior was a man named "J. Peters" ("to the best of my knowledge, the head of the whole underground United States Communist Party"), who visited the group "from time to time." Peters had been the object of a deportation hearing in 1947, but, according to Stripling, neither immigration authorities nor HUAC (which had become interested in Peters during the 1947 Hollywood Ten hearings) had been able to locate him.

After breaking, Chambers said, he had discussed his activities with Assistant Secretary of State Adolf A. Berle in September 1939 and later repeated his story several times to FBI and State Department agents who sought him out. Stripling wanted to know about encounters with Washington underground contacts after fleeing the party. Chambers told of one with Alger Hiss:

MR. CHAMBERS: . . . I went to the Hiss home one evening at what I considered considerable risk to myself and found Mrs. Hiss at home. Mrs. Hiss is also a member of the Communist Party.

MR. MUNDT: Mrs. Alger Hiss?

MR. CHAMBERS: Mrs. Alger Hiss. Mrs. Donald Hiss, I believe, is not. . . . Mr. Hiss came in shortly afterward, and we talked and I tried to break him away from the party. As a matter of fact, he cried when we separated, when I left him, but he absolutely refused to break. . . . I was very fond of Mr. Hiss.

MR. MUNDT: He must have given you some reason why he did not want to sever the relationship.

MR. CHAMBERS: His reasons were simply the party line.

Chambers then said he had also visited Harry Dexter White to urge him to break with Communism. Again, as in the case of Hiss, Chambers reported failure. White and Hiss, he testified, had been separated—at the orders of J. Peters—from further direct contact with the Ware Group's operations in 1936 and placed in a parallel apparatus that reported through Chambers to Peters. The party had concluded that these two officials were "going places in the Government . . . were an elite group . . . and their position in the Government would be of very much more service to the Communist Party" than as members of a larger secret group. "I should make the point that these people were specifically not wanted to act as sources of information," the witness observed, thus denying that Hiss, White, or any of the others had ever committed espionage.[9]

Most committee members did not anticipate the great press attention and public interest that would overwhelm HUAC in the next twenty-four hours. Only Nixon knew beforehand of Chambers's charges against Alger Hiss.

In mid-1948 the freshman congressman from Whittier, California, was little known outside his own district. Richard Nixon—lawyer, Navy veteran, congressional candidate by virtue of a newspaper ad—had replaced his Democratic predecessor, Jerry Voorhis, as a member of HUAC. He had absented himself from the committee's more controversial hearings, such as the Hollywood investigation in Los Angeles. His major public concern prior to Chambers's appearance involved joint sponsorship of the Mundt-Nixon Bill to outlaw the Communist Party, HUAC's pet measure earlier that year. Although Nixon recalled that the committee had not initially considered Chambers's testimony "especially important," HUAC rarely decided to move immediately from executive to public session without reasonable assurance of good press coverage. Nixon further insisted that he "considered for a moment the possibility of skipping the public hearing altogether, so that I could return to my office and get out some mail."

Nixon's recollection is not perfectly clear. He did attend the session, and although he claimed that his thoughts wandered to "other subjects," he participated actively in the questioning. "This was the first time I had ever heard of either Alger or Donald Hiss," Nixon incorrectly wrote in 1962. He had actually been briefed extensively on the allegations against the Hisses and other Ware Group members for the preceding year and a half.[10]

Shortly after Nixon entered Congress, a Republican colleague, Charles Kersten of Wisconsin, took him to Baltimore for the first of several meetings with a Catholic priest named John Cronin, who specialized in collecting data on Communist infiltration. He had access to FBI files and, in 1945, produced a confidential report to the American Catholic bishops, "The Problem of American Communism," in which he listed the names of many actual and alleged Communists—including Alger Hiss. The priest's briefings of Nixon and Kersten included long discussions of Soviet espionage in America and mentioned the presence of "certain Communists . . . in the State Department." Hiss figured prominently in Cronin's report to the bishops, a copy of which Nixon read. But during his interrogation of Chambers, and in subsequent HUAC hearings, Nixon never mentioned Cronin's assistance, or his own prior knowledge of the charges.

Alger Hiss learned about Chambers's HUAC accusations on the evening of August 2, when a reporter phoned him for comment on leaks from a committee source about the impending testimony. Afternoon papers and news broadcasts covered Chambers's appearance at length, and most stories emphasized the statements about Hiss, who immediately sent a telegram to J. Parnell Thomas:

MY ATTENTION HAS BEEN CALLED BY REPRESENTATIVES OF THE PRESS TO STATEMENTS MADE ABOUT ME BEFORE YOUR COMMITTEE THIS MORNNING BY ONE WHITTAKER CHAMBERS. I DO NOT KNOW MR. CHAMBERS AND, SO FAR AS I AM AWARE, I HAVE NEVER LAID EYES ON HIM. THERE IS NO BASIS FOR THE STATEMENTS ABOUT ME MADE TO YOUR COMMITTEE. I WOULD APPRECIATE IT IF YOU WOULD MAKE THIS TELEGRAM A PART OF YOUR COMMITTEE'S RECORDS AND I WOULD FURTHER APPRECIATE THE OPPORTUNITY OF APPEARING BEFORE YOUR COMMITTEE TO MAKE THESE STATEMENTS FORMALLY AND UNDER OATH. I SHALL BE IN WASHINGTON ON THURSDAY [AUGUST 5] AND HOPE THAT THAT WILL BE A CONVENIENT TIME FROM THE COMMITTEE'S POINT OF VIEW FOR ME TO APPEAR. ALGER HISS.

A copy of the wire went to the chairman of the Carnegie Endowment's Board of Trustees, John Foster Dulles, the man primarily responsible for having brought Alger Hiss to the organization.

The previous day Hiss had returned from a month's vacation in Peacham, Vermont, where his wife stayed with their seven-year-old son, Tony. Priscilla Hiss remained unaware of the uproar, Alger Hiss recalled in a 1975 interview with the author, until he phoned her late on the afternoon that Chambers testified. "I gave her the news as soon as I got through the newspaper calls, sometime around 5 PM. . . . I told her just what I planned to do [to testify before HUAC]. I said, 'Don't worry, little one. This will all blow over. I will handle it.' . . . I 'pooh-poohed' it." Hiss remembered the incident differently—and more casually—at the time. "As we have no telephone in Peacham and make use of the general store for long-distance calls,"* he wrote Dulles on August 5, "I have not had a chance to talk directly to Priscilla though I wrote her as soon as I learned of Chambers' testimony."[11]

The conflict between these versions sharpens when compared to the recollections of Edmund F. Soule, Hiss's longtime Peacham landlord, neighbor, and friend. Soule was returning to Peacham by train in August 1948. During a New York City stopover that afternoon he

> saw Alger's name in a paper, with this accusation by Chambers. . . . I remember taking the train (perhaps the Montrealer) to Montpelier, being met, and bringing this dreadful news to Prossy [Priscilla Hiss's nickname], who was up in Peacham, staying with my Mother and the baby boy Tony. . . . I can remember getting back to Peacham and hearing Prossy try to remember who this Whittaker Chambers was. Either to Mother or both of us she said something like: "Wait a minute . . . I remember a dreadful man named Crosley or something like that . . ." and that was her identification of the creature.

Presumably, Mrs. Hiss's recollection of "Crosley" was based on the photographs of Chambers in the afternoon paper brought by Soule. "She, as I remember it, seemed to be casting over in her mind what could be remembered," Soule later wrote, "and sort of thoughtfully, quietly, slowly said something like: 'Yes . . . I remember an awful man we knew once' . . . and went on a bit like that, speculating, 'Could that be the person?'" Mrs. Hiss, despite her initial shock of recognition, could recall almost nothing else about Crosley when questioned by HUAC on August 18. Hiss later acknowledged only "a slight sense of familiarity about some of his press photographs."[†12]

The committee went ahead without waiting for Hiss. Karl Mundt began the next day's session on August 4 by reading Hiss's telegram and scheduling his appearance for the following morning. The first witness was a Russian-born former government official, Nathan Gregory Silvermaster, who had been described by Bentley as a leading underground Communist in Washington and organizer of what HUAC began referring to as "the Silvermaster Group."

Silvermaster dismissed Bentley's "false and fantastic" charges, denouncing his accuser as a "neurotic liar." When Robert Stripling posed the committee's standard opening question—"Are you now or have you ever been a member of

---

*Yet when asked to arrange to have Mrs. Hiss testify during a subsequent appearance before the committee on August 16, Hiss replied: "I think I should try to reach her on the telephone." HUAC, Hearings, August–September 1948, p. 973. (In subsequent footnotes these hearings will be referred to as HUAC, I, and those held in December 1948 as HUAC, II.)

†It would be almost two weeks before Alger Hiss first mentioned the name "Crosley" to HUAC (on August 16) and acknowledged some familiarity in the press photographs of Chambers.

the Communist Party?"—Silvermaster invoked the Fifth Amendment. He also refused to state whether he knew Bentley or others whom she had implicated.*[13]

Later, Stripling introduced into the record a memorandum prepared by his staff that dealt with the career of another alleged Communist spymaster, "J. Peters," whom Chambers had mentioned. The memo described Peters's role as a former Comintern (Communist International) representative in the United States and his CP fund-raising activities in Hollywood. It did not mention specific links between Peters and espionage, however, despite the extensive list of aliases at the head of the memo: "RECORD OF J. PETERS, ALSO KNOWN AS J. PETER, J. V. PETERS, ALEXANDER GOLDBERGER, ROBERTS, STEVE LAPIN, PETE STEVENS, STEVE MILLER, ISADOR BOORSTIN, STEVEN LAPUR, ALEXANDER STEVENS." Peters was using the last of these aliases when Immigration and FBI agents located and subpoenaed him later that month.[14] By the time the morning session wound down, Whittaker Chambers, called originally only to support Bentley's story, had clearly upstaged the "Red Spy Queen."

Alger Hiss had spent the day at his desk. Messages of support—letters, phone calls, and telegrams—flowed in from friends and former associates in government. One such message, a copy of a letter sent to Hiss's brother, Donald, by a Baltimore attorney named William L. Marbury, declared confidently that "if you and Alger are party members, then you can send me an application." Marbury offered his services, and later that day he received a call from Alger asking him to come the next day to Donald Hiss's Washington office in the prestigious law firm of Covington, Burling, Rublee, Acheson, and Shorb.

After working on his opening statement to the committee, Hiss left early that evening for Washington. There he obtained and scanned (with the help of his brother, Donald, and a well-known mutual friend) a transcript of Chambers's testimony: "I had the benefit of Dean Acheson's advice last night," Hiss wrote Dulles the following day, "as I was trying to compose my own thoughts."

Four men met in Donald Hiss's office on the morning of August 5 for a last-minute discussion of Alger's appearance before HUAC: the Hiss brothers, Acheson, and Marbury. Alger asked Acheson and Marbury to accompany him to the hearing. Acheson declined, perhaps fearing possible embarrassment to Truman, who nominated him to be secretary of state later that year. Another friend, Joseph E. Johnston, a lawyer from Birmingham, Alabama, joined Hiss and Marbury at the hearing room. As it turned out, Hiss required very little help from his friends that day.[15]

---

*A committee investigator, Louis J. Russell, read into the record Silvermaster's Civil Service Commission investigatory file, which stated flatly that there was "considerable testimony . . . indicating that [since 1920] the applicant was an underground agent for the Communist Party," citing material in FBI and Naval Intelligence records. HUAC, I, pp. 612–19.

AUGUST 5: THE QUARRY

The audience packed into the caucus room of the Old House Office Building had to put up with some grandstanding by Congressmen Rankin and McDowell and the appearance of an unimportant witness before Alger Hiss took the oath. "He repeated, 'So help me God' twice," Robert Stripling remembers, "which was a little frosting on the cake I'd never heard before."[16]

Hiss's physical appearance contrasted strikingly with that of his corpulent and rumpled accuser. Hiss was handsome and relaxed. From the beginning of his testimony, he smiled frequently and displayed none of Chambers's nervous mannerisms. Hiss began by reading a statement denying "unqualifiedly" the charges made by Chambers:

> I am not and never have been a member of the Communist Party. I do not and never have adhered to the tenets of the Communist Party. I am not and never have been a member of any Communist-front organization. I have never followed the Communist Party line, directly or indirectly. To the best of my knowledge, none of my friends is a Communist. . . . To the best of my knowledge, I never heard of Whittaker Chambers until 1947, when two representatives of the Federal Bureau of Investigation asked me if I knew him and various other people, some of whom I knew and some of whom I did not know. I said I did not know Chambers. So far as I know, I have never laid eyes on him, and I should like to have the opportunity to do so.

Hiss then outlined his relationships with others whom Chambers had mentioned as New Deal Communists. Henry Collins had been a boyhood friend whom he later knew socially at Harvard Law and during the New Deal. Lee Pressman had also been a law-school classmate and coworker on the *Harvard Law Review*; he and Pressman had both served on the legal staff of the Agricultural Adjustment Administration as assistants to general counsel Jerome Frank, later a federal judge. Hiss had seen Pressman "only occasionally and infrequently" since 1935. Nathan Witt and John Abt were also members of the AAA legal staff: "I knew them both in that capacity. I believe I met Witt in New York a year or so before I came to Washington [in 1933]." He had also met Charles Kramer at the AAA, but had seen the last three persons only "infrequently" since 1935. Hiss did not remember ever knowing Victor Perlo. "Except as I have indicated, the statements made about me by Mr. Chambers are complete fabrications," his statement concluded. "I think my record in the Government service speaks for itself."[17]

Nevertheless, Hiss outlined that record for the committee. He graduated from Harvard Law School in 1929 and, at the recommendation of Felix Frankfurter (a Supreme Court Justice in 1948 but a Harvard law professor in 1929), he clerked for Justice Oliver Wendell Holmes. After a few years of practice in Boston and New York, Hiss held several New Deal posts, working first for the AAA, next for the Senate's Nye Committee investigation of the munitions industry, and briefly for the Justice Department under the immediate supervision of Stanley Reed, another U.S. Supreme Court Justice in 1948. Hiss joined the State Department in 1936 and rose quickly; he attended the Yalta Conference as a member of the American delegation and, in 1945, presided at the UN organizing meeting in San Francisco. He left State in 1947 for the Carnegie Endowment.

"I had no respect for Mundt, for Thomas, Rankin (I thought he was evil), for most of the others," Hiss later said.[18] On that August 5, however, he hid his scorn, handling each question directly, if sometimes cautiously, and displaying a far greater skill at sparring with Stripling and committee members than had been demonstrated by most of his predecessors in the HUAC witness chair. Thus when Stripling pressed Hiss about his claim never to have seen Chambers, Hiss stated that the name meant "absolutely nothing" to him. Stripling produced a photo of Chambers taken earlier that week, pointing out that people who remembered the latter from the 1930s said he was much heavier today. Hiss responded that he preferred to meet Chambers in person. He had studied all available newspaper photos and, if Stripling's was an accurate picture of Chambers, "he is not particularly unusual looking. He looks like a lot of people, I might even mistake him for the [acting] chairman of this Committee." When the laughter in the hearing room died down, Mundt responded: "I hope you are wrong in that."

Mundt had earlier confessed puzzlement over Hiss. What "possible motive" could Chambers have had for falsely "mentioning Donald Hiss and Alger Hiss in connection with these other six" (Witt, Pressman, Perlo, Kramer, Abt, and Ware), especially when there "seems to be no question about [their] subversive connections?" Hiss claimed to be equally baffled:

> MR. HISS: I wish I could have seen Mr. Chambers before he testified.
> MR. RANKIN: After all the smear attacks against this committee and individual members of this committee in *Time* Magazine, I am not surprised at anything that comes out of anybody connected with it. (Laughter.)

Hiss denied flatly all of Chambers's assertions, including the story about visiting him after the break with the party. To all of these charges Hiss's response was adamant: "I am testifying the exact opposite." He acknowledged that in June 1947 two FBI agents had interrogated him:

> They asked me a number of questions not unlike the points Mr. Chambers testified to. . . . They asked me if I knew the names of a number of people. One of those names was Chambers. I remember very distinctly because I had never heard the name Whittaker Chambers.

"That was the first occasion I had ever heard the name," Hiss would reiterate to one of his lawyers the following year. "I did not [recognize it] and I told them so. That was all there was to the reference to him."

But Chambers's was not simply one name out of the many casually dropped by the agents. On June 2, 1947, Hiss signed a statement prepared by the FBI agents that contained the following specific denial: "I am not acquainted with an individual by the name of Whittaker Chambers. No individual by that name has ever visited my home on any occasion so far as I can recall." The statement also described Hiss's recollections of Pressman, Witt, Ware, Kramer, Collins, Abt, and other old acquaintances. The only other individuals mentioned in the document whom Hiss claimed not to know were Nathan Gregory Silvermaster, Richard Post, and a man named "Gene" or "Eugene."[19]

Hiss also described an earlier meeting with the FBI in 1946—this one at his request while he was still at the State Department. Secretary of State Byrnes had summoned him shortly after Hiss returned from attending a UN conference in London. Byrnes said that several congressmen were about to denounce him as a Communist. Hiss denied the charge, and Byrnes suggested that he see J. Edgar Hoover personally in order to clear up the situation. Hiss could not arrange an appointment with Hoover, but on March 25, 1946, spoke instead to one of the director's top aides.[20] Chambers's name did not come up.* Hiss failed to mention this interview—and the charges made against him in 1946—to Dulles or other Carnegie Endowment board members during the discussions that preceded his selection as the Endowment's president.

Committee members questioned Hiss closely on the possible source of the FBI's accusations, although it seemed increasingly clear that Chambers's 1939 conversation with Berle had triggered the matter. Hiss held firm, denying that his wife and his brother had been or were Communists. His forceful testimony, bolstered by his credentials as a public servant, seemed to sway some committee members in his favor. Stripling acknowledged the obvious to Mundt: that "there is very sharp contradiction here in the testimony" and that Chambers should "be brought back before the committee and clear this up." Diametrically opposed testimony had come, as Karl Mundt pointed out, "from two witnesses whom normally one would assume to be perfectly reliable":

> They have high positions in American business or organizational work. They both appear to be honest. They both testified under oath. Certainly the committee and the country must be badly confused about why these stories fail to jibe so completely.

Nixon, who had said very little up to that point, then suggested a simple way to resolve the problem. He proposed "that the witnesses be allowed to confront each other so that any possibility of a mistake in identity may be cleared up. . . . I

---

*The reasons for this and the entire story of Hiss's last year at State are described in Chapter X.

think if there is mistaken identity on Mr. Chambers' part he will be able to recall it when he confronts Mr. Hiss."

Hiss had already asked for such a confrontation. But before the committee could consider the idea, Stripling began to question the witness on his knowledge of the people named by Bentley and Chambers. Hiss could not remember whether he had ever visited the St. Matthews Court apartment in Washington in which, according to Chambers, the Ware Group assembled. Nixon asked if Hiss knew Harold Ware, and Hiss acknowledged an acquaintanceship during his years in the Department of Agriculture. It stemmed from Ware's work as a "specialist" on "large scale wheat farming with combines and tractors and that sort of thing" in the Soviet Union (Ware had organized several collective farms during the 1920s at Lenin's personal invitation):

MR. HISS: My recollection is he came into my offices in the Department of Agriculture, as many callers did, on several occasions [in connection with the large-scale wheat-farming project].*

MR. NIXON: Your testimony in effect is that your acquaintance with Mr. Ware was only casual in the course of your employment.

MR. HISS: That is correct.

MR. NIXON: And not otherwise.

MR. HISS: And not otherwise.[21]

Questioning then focused on the controversy that led to the purging of "radicals" on the AAA's legal staff in 1935. The victims included Hiss's boss, Jerome Frank; Frank's assistant, Gardner ("Pat") Jackson, a crusading newspaperman during the Sacco-Vanzetti case and later an organizer of the CIO; and Lee Pressman—but not Hiss, despite his identification with the others in this group.[†] Stripling then ran Hiss through a list of several dozen names of alleged Communists named by Bentley and Chambers, asking which ones Hiss knew. John Abt? Yes. Lauchlin Currie? "I know [him] very well and have a high regard for him"—at which point Mundt interjected: "Do you have a high regard for Lee Pressman?" Hiss remained unruffled: "I knew Pressman first at law school and

---

*Hiss acknowledged in a 1975 interview with me a less casual interest in Harold Ware, both professionally and personally. He remembered that the magazine Ware had edited for the Communist Party at the time was widely read and respected in the Department of Agriculture. Hiss compared it "to a little magazine that we used to read in the Far Eastern Division, Amerasia, which caused a lot of stink. . . . It [Ware's magazine] was extremely well-written, . . . and the analysis made sense." And "Hal married someone I'd known from the twenties, Jessica Smith," a party member like Ware, and the families' movements apparently intersected on occasion in Washington during the mid-'30s. Hiss recalled that Ware's son and his own stepson, Timothy Hobson, once attended the same children's camp. Following Ware's death in an automobile accident in 1935, Jessica Smith married Hiss's AAA colleague John Abt. Author's interviews with Alger Hiss, June 21 and October 4, 1975. (In subsequent footnotes, unless otherwise indicated, all interviews referred to were also conducted by the author.)

†The reasons for the AAA purge, and Hiss's escape, are discussed in Chapter IV.

I have seen very little of him recently. I liked him and admired him as a law student, and knew him and admired him as a fellow lawyer in the Agricultural Adjustment Administration." Nathan Gregory Silvermaster? "Not to the best of my knowledge." Harry Dexter White? "I do know Mr. Harry D. White."

The roll call concluded, Mundt and Rankin briefly took up Hiss's role at Yalta and his work in organizing the first United Nations conference. The witness denied the charge made by journalist Isaac Don Levine, editor of the anti-Communist monthly *Plain Talk,* that he had drafted the section of the Yalta agreement that gave Russia three votes in the UN General Assembly—"I opposed the particular point"—but Hiss would not condemn what was done at Yalta. With some words of praise for the witness from Rankin and Mundt, the session ended.

After the hearing, Hiss received congratulations from spectators and reporters for having emerged with both his reputation and his composure intact. Rankin and McDowell joined the admiring group, and before leaving the committee room, both shook his hand. Most of the newsmen evidently felt that HUAC had been seriously embarrassed, that the investigation should be quashed, and that the committee should apologize to Hiss for having heard Chambers in public without first verifying his story. Mary Spargo of *The Washington Post,* according to Nixon, expressed the consensus concerning Hiss's cool and effective testimony: "This case is going to kill the Committee unless you can prove Chambers' story."[22]

At Harry Truman's press conference that morning, a reporter had asked: "Mr. President, do you think that the Capitol Hill spy scare is a red herring to divert the public attention from inflation?" Truman agreed with the questioner that congressional probes such as HUAC's were being used by the Republican "do-nothing" Congress to disguise its legislative failures. Many newspapers juxtaposed prominently Hiss's denials and Truman's "red herring" label (the term supposedly a direct quote from HST) during the next twenty-four hours.

Hiss's performance heartened HUAC's Democratic opponents and, at the same time, halted the momentum generated by the testimony of Bentley and Chambers. Donald Hiss, emboldened by his brother's appearance, wrote the committee on August 5 demanding to be heard in order to deny Chambers's accusations against *him.* One Alabama congressman informed Hiss's friend Joseph Johnston that "he had talked to several members of the committee and with other Congressmen who were there and that . . . they all felt that the burden of suspicion had been fully transferred to Chambers."[23]

When the committee met in executive session that afternoon—"in a virtual state of shock," according to Nixon—most members agreed that the investigation should be dropped. Mundt warned that HUAC's reputation would be further tarnished "unless the Committee was able to develop a collateral issue which would take it off the spot and take the minds of the public off of the Hiss case." A bipartisan consensus emerged at this point. "Let's wash our hands of the whole mess," Hébert suggested, while one of the Republican members complained: "We've been had! We're ruined." Hébert underscored the sense of desperation by insisting that the only suitable course of action was to send the Chambers and Hiss testimony to Attorney General Tom Clark, the committee's foremost administration critic, and "ask him to determine who was lying."

That proposal proved unpalatable to HUAC's Republican members and to Rankin, thus allowing Nixon a chance to propose an alternative plan. Supported only by Stripling, Nixon argued that "although the Committee could not determine who was lying on the issue of whether or not Hiss was a Communist, we could at least determine which was lying on the issue of whether or not Chambers knew Hiss." Nixon then persuaded Mundt to appoint him head of a subcommittee to question Chambers privately in New York. From that moment, the case became the responsibility of Nixon, Stripling, and the HUAC staff. Other committee members, acquiescing warily to the Californian's proposal, receded gratefully into secondary roles.[24]

Why did Nixon ask for the assignment? What impelled him to disregard the unanimous opinion of his elders on the group and go on with the inquiry?

Two factors apparently influenced his decision to press on. Nixon had good reason to doubt Hiss's veracity, although he wrote to John Foster Dulles the following month that "if at the beginning I had any prejudice one way or the other, it was more likely that I favored Hiss rather than Chambers, due to the fact that I have close friends in Washington who were also friendly with Donald and Alger Hiss."* But Nixon made no mention of having had earlier briefings by Father John Cronin, a Catholic priest, on communist infiltration in the federal government. He had kept that information from his HUAC colleagues while arguing that the hearings should be continued. Nixon had persuaded them to place the investigation in his hands and neglected to inform them that his arguments were based not on suspicions or hunches, but upon considerable advance knowledge of the information on Hiss in government security files.

Second, despite Nixon's disclaimer, he had already developed an intense personal dislike of Alger Hiss on the basis of that morning's encounter. Hiss, in psychohistorian Bruce Mazlish's blunt summary, "was everything Nixon was not." Raised in an upper-middle-class Baltimore atmosphere, Hiss had glided with honors and scholarships through college and law school, ascending in apparently premeasured stages from Justice Holmes's chambers to the Carnegie Endowment's presidency. Nixon's background—as the child of struggling and unsuccessful parents whose failures in life brought to mind the most anguished of Sherwood Anderson's *Winesburg, Ohio* villagers—contrasted painfully. Furthermore, "Hiss, the embodiment of Eastern values," Mazlish noted,

---

*No such "friends" are mentioned in any of Nixon's subsequent writings or comments on the case.

had "treated Nixon . . . like dirt"—or so Nixon believed. The witness's repressed contempt for the committee had not escaped Nixon's easily bruised sensibilities as it apparently had those of his more complacent colleagues. "His manner was coldly courteous and, at times, almost condescending," Nixon would later write about Hiss's Ivy League disdain and his own response. "He was rather insolent toward me. . . . His manner and tone were insulting in the extreme."[25]

Robert Stripling shared Nixon's belief that Hiss had lied to the committee that day. Stripling also felt that Nixon's reaction transcended the question of the witness's credibility and reflected, from the beginning, a private sense of grievance. "Nixon had his hat set for Hiss" from their first exchanges, Stripling observed in a 1975 interview with the author. "It was a personal thing. He was no more concerned about whether or not Hiss was [a Communist] than a billy goat!" This negative and emotional response to Hiss contributed to Nixon's decision to keep the inquiry alive."[26]

Meanwhile, after his triumph that morning, Hiss had gone on the offensive. His future at Carnegie, given the unfavorable publicity after Chambers's testimony, depended upon John Foster Dulles's firm backing. Dulles, on the other hand, had his own problems to consider in dealing with the matter. As the leading foreign-policy adviser of, and probable secretary of state–designate to the Republican presidential nominee, Thomas E. Dewey, Dulles could ill afford to have his name linked with a well-known New Deal Democrat and now alleged high-level Communist, whatever the truth of Chambers's accusations. Marbury informed Dulles that same day that everyone in the hearing room was convinced after Hiss's testimony that Chambers's charges "were wholly false." Since Dulles hardly knew Marbury—or Joseph Johnston, who sent a similar letter several days later—the burden of persuasion felt upon Hiss himself.

That afternoon, at his brother Donald's office, Hiss wrote a two-page, single-spaced letter to "Foster," enclosing a copy of his opening statement to the committee because "it may or may not be included in the morning papers as denials seldom get the same coverage as sensational charges do." Hiss asked that Dulles send copies of the statement to other members of the Endowment board, and praised Dulles for his "counsel and calm judgment [which] have been invaluable to me." After mentioning that Dean Acheson had helped him prepare the opening statement, and after bringing in the names of Marbury and Johnston—presumably so that Dulles could identify them when their letters arrived—Hiss described the case's impact on his family. He planned to join Priscilla that weekend in Vermont, "as the shock must have been a very great one." Hiss noted also that his mother and sister had been staying with him that week, "so that I was able to be personally with them during the very first unpleasant hours following Chambers' testimony." Finally the letter came to the point, a plea for compassion and endorsement from the man who held Hiss's career in his hands:

I am quite conscious, surprisingly enough, of a very definite sense of relief from the oppressive feeling of being completely unable to come to grips with the source of all the ugly rumors that have been floating around for months, I think it is now clear that they all stem from the same single source. . . .

I regret indeed any embarrassment or anxiety this whole unpleasant affair may have caused you. . . . I regret to say that your name was brought in in the course of my testimony obviously with political intent. I trust that you will find my answers to the questions involving you not too distasteful.

With gratitude and respect,

Ever sincerely,
Alger

If Dulles responded to Hiss's explanation and plea for support, the letter has not survived. Answering a request made the following day by Philip C. Jessup, a fellow Endowment board member and friend of Hiss's, that the board formally "express their confidence in the President," Dulles remained noncommittal. He avowed that he had just finished reading the transcript of Hiss's testimony and had heard from another board member and friend of Hiss's, James T. Shotwell, about the "excellent impression" Hiss had made. Dulles, however, appreciated the political dangers involved for him in a blanket endorsement of Hiss at this uncertain moment; he flatly rejected Jessup's suggestion. "It seems to me better," he responded coolly, "to defer decision until after the present Hearings have been concluded."[27]

AUGUST 7: THE CHASE

From his Columbia days in the early 1920s onward, Whittaker Chambers had worked diligently to separate personal life from career obligations. Even during his years as a Communist underground agent he not only succeeded in creating a family life for his wife and two children that was reasonably detached from his work as a courier, but he managed to maintain friendships with non-Communists without the knowledge of CP superiors. Since joining *Time* in 1939 he had divided his week almost equally between days of intense activity in New York—often working through the night—and days of retreat in Westminster, Maryland, where he and his wife farmed with the aid of their children and hired hands. The schedule was grueling; twice during these years—in 1942 and 1945—he suffered heart attacks and spent months of enforced rest at the farm. But it allowed him the privacy and close connection with family that he believed essential to emotional well-being.

Chambers had "resolved not to read any news stories about my testimony, or to listen to radio broadcasts," and so, he claimed, it was only through a phone call from a committee investigator that he learned of Alger Hiss's testimony. Chambers offered to return to Washington for another round of questioning, but instead was asked to appear at the Federal Court House in New York City on Saturday, August 7, to meet with the HUAC subcommittee.

Nixon immediately laid bare the central issue at the executive session:

> Mr. Chambers, you are aware of the fact that Mr. Alger Hiss appeared before this committee . . . in public session and swore that the testimony which had been given by you under oath before this committee was false. The committee is now interested in questioning you further concerning your alleged acquaintanceship with Mr. Alger Hiss so that we can determine what course of action should be followed in this matter in the future.

When had he known Hiss? Roughly "between the years 1935 and 1937." Did he know him under his real name? Yes. During that period did Hiss know him as Whittaker Chambers? "No, he did not." (Hiss had stated repeatedly on August 5 that he did not know "a man named Whittaker Chambers.") By what name had Hiss known Chambers? "He knew me by the party name of Carl." Regarding Hiss and the Communist underground:

MR. NIXON: This entire [underground] group with which you worked in Washington did not know you by your real name? . . . All knew you as Carl?

MR. CHAMBERS: That is right . . .

MR. NIXON: I understood you to say that Mr. Hiss was a member of the party.

MR. CHAMBERS: Mr. Hiss was a member of the Communist Party.

MR. NIXON: How do you know that?

MR. CHAMBERS: I was told that by Mr. Peters . . . [who] was head of the entire underground, as far as I know . . . [of] the Communist Party in the United States.

MR. NIXON: Do you have any other evidence, any factual evidence, to bear out your claim that Mr. Hiss was a member of the Communist Party?

MR. CHAMBERS: Nothing beyond the fact that he submitted himself for the two or three years that I knew him as a dedicated and disciplined Communist.

MR. NIXON: Did you obtain his party dues from him?

MR. CHAMBERS: Yes, I did . . . [for] two or three years, as long as I knew him.

MR. NIXON: Party dues from him and his wife?

MR. CHAMBERS: I assume his wife's dues were there; I understood it to be . . . Mr. Hiss would simply give me an envelope containing party dues which I transferred to Peters. I didn't handle the money.

MR. NIXON: How often?

MR. CHAMBERS: Once a month. . . . I must also interpolate there that all Communists in the [Ware] group in which I originally knew him accepted him as a member of the Communist Party.

MR. NIXON: Could this have possibly been an intellectual study group?

MR. CHAMBERS: . . . Its primary function was not that of an intellectual study group . . . [but] to infiltrate the Government in the interest of the Communist Party. . . . No members of that group to my knowledge ever had party cards, nor do I think members of any such group have party cards.

MR. NIXON: The reason is—

MR. CHAMBERS: The reason is security, concealment.[28]

Nixon then asked a series of questions about the Hisses' private lives, aimed at testing whether Chambers had ever known them well. Specifically, Nixon later noted, he had tried to determine, "What should one man know about another if he knew him as well as Chambers claimed to know Hiss?"

Responding to queries from subcommittee members and staff—Nixon, Hébert, Stripling, and Ben Mandel—Chambers apparently remembered a great deal. More than a decade had passed since his described friendship with the Hisses, and Chambers later admitted inaccuracies in his original August 3 testimony and in some statements at the August 7 hearing. Thus he met Hiss in 1934, not '35, and his defection from Communism came in 1938 rather than in '37. The Hisses, furthermore, were not teetotalers, nor was Alger's stepson, Timothy Hobson, a "puny little boy."

For the most part, however, Chambers displayed remarkable familiarity with the domestic arrangements of the Hisses, considering the decade-long gap in their association. He provided the subcommittee with numerous homey details: nicknames (his memory of "Hilly" for Alger and "Prossy" for Priscilla was later acknowledged as correct, although the Hisses and some friends disputed "Dilly" as Priscilla's other nickname), eating habits, pets, hobbies, mannerisms, relatives, vacation trips, the location and exteriors of their houses, descriptions of their furniture. As Nixon would write in a February 1949 memo:

> Either he knew Hiss or . . . he had made a very thorough study of Hiss's life for the purpose of being able to testify against him. The second theory required, of course, that Chambers must have had a motive, and as Chambers himself put it to me in private conversation, the motive must have been so strong that it would lead him to act in such a manner as to destroy his own career in the process.[29]

Had Chambers ever stayed overnight in Hiss's home?

MR. CHAMBERS: Yes. I stayed overnight for a number of days . . . from time to time . . . I have stayed there as long as a week. . . . I made that kind of informal headquarters.

MR. NIXON: . . . what was the financial arrangement?

MR. CHAMBERS: There was no financial arrangement.

MR. NIXON: You were a guest?

MR. CHAMBERS: Part of the Communist pattern.

Chambers professed a continued fondness for Hiss himself, although not for his wife: "Hiss is a man of great simplicity and a great gentleness and sweetness of character, and they lived with great simplicity. . . . Mrs. Hiss is a short, highly nervous, little woman."

The HUAC members listening to Chambers recognized that he might have obtained much of his information about Hiss not from direct contact but by researching his life. Still, "some of the answers," Nixon later observed, "had a personal ring of truth about them beyond the bare facts themselves." Two episodes in particular soon proved especially damaging to Hiss's denials of the reputed relationship. Asked whether Hiss had any hobbies, Chambers responded:

> Yes, he did. They [Alger and Priscilla Hiss] both had the same hobby—amateur ornithologists, bird observers. They used to get up early in the morning and go to Glen Echo, out the canal, to observe birds. I recall once they saw, to their great excitement, a prothonotary warbler.

Congressman McDowell, himself an ornithologist, interrupted to ask, "A very rare specimen?" To which Chambers replied: "I never saw one. I am also fond of birds."[30]

The second incident concerned Communist involvement. Nixon had asked whether the Hisses had a car, and Chambers described an old Ford—"black and . . . very dilapidated . . . [with] hand windshield wipers. I remember that because I drove it one rainy day and had to work those windshield wipers by hand." Chambers also said Hiss purchased a new Plymouth two-seater sedan in 1936. Hiss then "insisted" upon turning over the old Ford "to the open Party so it could be of use to some poor organizer in the West or somewhere." Although this action violated "all the rules of underground organization," Hiss prevailed against Chambers's—and J. Peters's—"better judgment." Chambers's memory of the episode became vague at this point, since he had not taken part personally in the transfer process. He could say only that either Hiss or J. Peters had left the Ford at a Washington service station or car lot owned by a Communist, and that the latter "took care of the rest of it for him. I should think the records of that transfer would be traceable." Although he could not offer specific details, Chambers's testimony about a Ford car allegedly transferred by Hiss to the Communist Party gave committee investigators a major lead in their attempt to resolve the contradictory testimony.

By the time Nixon adjourned the session, Chambers's disclosures and the mass of detail he had provided about the Hisses had restored the committee's faith in his credibility. "Would you be willing to submit to a lie detector test on this testimony?" Nixon asked near the end. "Yes, if necessary," replied the witness. "You have that much confidence?" "I am telling the truth."[31]

AUGUST 9–13: THE SKIRMISHING

Nixon's three-member subcommittee resumed hearings in Washington on August 9. Joining the chairman that morning were not only Hébert and McDowell but also Thomas and Mundt, who—along with other committee members—had been briefed on Chambers's executive-session testimony. Mundt also had been given additional information bearing on the current hearings, material that he chose not to share with his colleagues.

Shortly after Hiss's appearance on August 5, Mundt heard from a "very troubled" State Department friend, John Peurifoy, assistant secretary of state for security affairs. Peurifoy, according to Mundt, told him:

> Karl, I don't know what to do. I'm torn between loyalty and duty. . . . Frankly, all I am I owe, in this town, to Dean Acheson . . . and I don't want to do him a disservice. And still, I'm a good American. And I know that what you are saying and insinuating about Alger Hiss is true, because I have access to [Hiss's] security files in the State Department. . . . Would it be helpful to you if you could see those security files?

Peurifoy brought Mundt the files in the middle of the night, and after the two men "spent two or three hours" going over them, Mundt's indecision faded. "The evidence was there," he later said, that "Hiss was involved with those Communist activities and Communist agents." Emboldened by the dossiers, he rejoined the HUAC inquiry the following Monday.[32]

The committee's first witness that day was Victor Perlo, an economist named by Chambers as a member of the CP underground. Perlo, who now worked for Henry Wallace's Progressive Party, invoked the Fifth Amendment whenever Nixon and Stripling asked about his associations in Washington or about his possible involvement in underground activities. Elizabeth Bentley returned to assert that during the Second World War Perlo had supplied her with classified information, which she had passed on to Russian contacts. She described a series of meetings with Perlo in Washington and New York, insisting that the two secret networks with which she worked at the time had been headed by Perlo and Nathan Gregory Silvermaster. Perlo claimed the protection of the Fifth when asked about these charges.*

On August 11 Elizabeth Bentley testified that in the summer of 1945, after breaking with the party, she told her story to the FBI for the first time and was instructed to maintain contact with Russian agents. In October 1945, while under FBI surveillance, Bentley received a package containing $2,000 on a New York street from someone she knew only as "Al," later identified by the bureau as

---

*Neither Perlo nor the committee knew at the time that the witness's former wife, Katherine Perlo, had corroborated Bentley's charges against her ex-husband in an anonymous letter—later acknowledged by Mrs. Perlo—sent to the FBI several years earlier. Katherine Perlo accused her husband of engaging in espionage and named others in the group, her list of names being comparable to Bentley's later one. Perlo's involvement and that of Silvermaster's received further corroboration from the recently released VENONA intercepts of Soviet intelligence cables and, independently, from newly available KGB archives, both bodies of evidence cited in Weinstein and Vassiliev, *The Haunted Wood, passim.*

Anatol Gromov, first secretary of the Russian Embassy. Gromov, protected by diplomatic immunity, subsequently left the country.[33]

Another in the long list of alleged Communists fingered by Bentley, a former government economist named Abraham George Silverman pleaded self-incrimination when asked on August 11 whether he knew her and if he was a Communist. He denied any complicity in espionage. While questioning Silverman, the committee focused on Bentley's testimony and neglected to ask the witness if he had known Whittaker Chambers. (Chambers had not yet indicated his connection with Silverman but would do so at a subsequent meeting of HUAC.) Silverman proved more forthcoming—though still not entirely so—in several interviews with Alger Hiss's attorneys the following spring:

> Silverman knew Whittaker Chambers during the general period 1935–37 in Washington [states one of their March 1949 memos]. He does not remember the circumstances under which he met Chambers and recalls him as just one of the people he happened to know. From time to time he had lunch with Chambers . . . they talked about art and music. . . . Silverman does not remember whether he helped Chambers to get a job [for the National Research Council in late 1937]. He thinks it is possible that he may have done so. . . . He thought he might have even called Irving Kaplan [head of the council] and says that he knew Kaplan. . . .

But Silverman escaped questioning by HUAC about these and other dealings with Chambers.[34]

Harry Dexter White, who appeared before HUAC on August 13, had taught international economics at Harvard before joining the Treasury Department during the New Deal. He acknowledged to the committee that he had known Silvermaster "pretty well" for the past decade but denied having been a Communist or being "even close to becoming one," and said he could not recall ever having met either Bentley or Chambers, "judging from the pictures I have seen in the press." White called the charge that he had helped obtain "key posts for persons I knew were engaged in espionage work to help in that work . . . unqualifiedly false." Press and spectators were sympathetic toward the cheerful, mild-mannered White, and when he finished reading his prepared statement, they broke into a sustained round of applause.*[35]

Stripling began with the familiar roll call of alleged Communists or fellow travelers—Silverman, Currie, Pressman, Alger and Donald Hiss, and others—asking which of them White knew. Finally he asked whether White knew "anyone in 1935 or 1936 who went under the name of Carl, C-a-r-l." "I do not recollect any such name," White responded. "I may have; it is a long time ago." White

---

*White lied to the committee. His extensive and complex involvement with American and Russian agents for Soviet intelligence emerges plainly from both the VENONA intercepts and from KGB archives, cited in Weinstein and Vassiliev, *passim.*

then denied—"to the best of my recollection"—having known Chambers under that name. He also denied that Chambers had visited White after defecting in order to urge him to cease associating with the CP underground.

Later, as White testified that he had played ping-pong in Nathan Silvermaster's basement, Chairman Thomas interrupted:

> Just a minute, right there. . . . One thing I cannot reconcile, Mr. White, you send me a note and you say that: "I am recovering from a severe heart attack. I would appreciate it if the chairman would give me five or ten minutes after each hour." For a person who had a severe heart condition, you certainly can play a lot of sports.

White's face fell, according to news reports, as he replied:

> I did not intend that this note should be read aloud. I do not know any reason why it should be public that I am ill, but I think probably one of the reasons why I suffered a heart attack was because I played so many sports, and so well. The heart attack which I suffered was last year. . . . I hope that clears that up, Mr. Chairman.

Before he finished, spectators began applauding again. Chairman Thomas could not resist making a foolish crack, one he would regret within several days, if only for political reasons, when White suffered a fatal heart attack: "I would say that you had an athlete's heart."

The witness defended Silvermaster eloquently against the charge of Communist association: "You cannot erase seven or eight years of friendship with a man that way unless I see evidence, unless the court declares that he is, and until they prove he is guilty, I believe he is innocent." White had interceded to help Nathan Silvermaster fight removal from government service in 1942 after satisfying himself that his friend was not a Communist, and he stood by his record in the Treasury on security matters, declaring he had never knowingly employed a Communist.

When Thomas asked whether any of White's friends could be members of the Communist Party, the witness became visibly exasperated: "How can I answer that, Mr. Congressman? . . . (a) There are Communists; (b) I have friends; (c) those friends might be Communists. I mean, that is silly."

Henry Collins, executive director of the American-Russian Institute and a friend of Alger Hiss from childhood, told HUAC that he could not recognize news photos of Chambers and (using the same formulation employed earlier by Hiss) that he had never known "a man by the name of Whittaker Chambers." When asked by Stripling if he was acquainted with an individual named "Carl" in 1935, however, Collins invoked the Fifth Amendment. (By the time Collins appeared before a federal jury in December, he recalled having met Chambers during the mid-thirties.)[36]

The witness agreed he had lived at St. Matthews Court in Washington in the apartment building at which Chambers said the Ware Group had met. But Collins declined on grounds of self-incrimination to state whether he had met alleged members of that group there, such as Abt, Hiss, Pressman, or Peters. He also refused to say whether he had ever been a member of the Communist Party.

Although Chambers had accused him only of secret Communist membership, not of spying, Collins took pains to deny—both in his prepared statement and in his testimony—that he had taken part in any form of espionage for a foreign power. But Collins was later implicated in espionage by a former State Department official, Laurence Duggan, who told the FBI on December 10, 1948, that Collins, whom he had known since 1934, approached him in June 1938 "to assist in furnishing information ... Duggan states he could not recall the words of Collins, but the obvious import was that he wanted information furnished to the Soviets." Duggan said he had turned down Collins's request.*[37]

When he appeared before HUAC, Donald Hiss said he did not know Whittaker Chambers either by that name or under the pseudonym of "Carl, or any other name." He rejected "categorically" Chambers's assertion of meetings at Henry Collins's apartment. According to the witness, he had never met Harold Ware or J. Peters, and his contacts with people such as Pressman, Abt, and Witt had been either at the Harvard Law School, where he and Witt were classmates for a time, or in connection with government service during the New Deal. He stated that he had never been a member of the Communist Party or of any front organization and was not "in sympathy with the principles of the Communist Party."[38]

Had his brother, Alger, ever known Chambers under the name of "Carl"? Nixon asked Donald Hiss. "Not to my knowledge," he replied, referring the question directly to his brother.† Donald said he had not discussed the case with Alger since the latter's appearance before HUAC—a questionable assertion since it was to Donald's office that Hiss returned after his August 5 appearance and there that he wrote his letter to John Foster Dulles—and Nixon observed that "we will have to ask your brother that question ourselves." Both Mundt and Nixon commented on the obvious conflict in the testimony of Chambers and

---

*Letters written in 1934 by John Hermann, another member of the underground Ware Group, confirm that the group met—among other places—at Collins's St. Matthews Court apartment. See Chapter IV, p. 151.

†Joseph Johnston, who accompanied Hiss to the August 5 hearing, recounted the following bit of hearsay to William Marbury the following month: "Dean Kimball of Covington, Burling [Donald Hiss's law firm] was in the office a few days ago ... when the subject of the Hiss case arose. He said that Maynard Toll [another friend] told him recently of a conversation he had had with Donald Hiss a number of years ago, I believe around 1939 or 1940, in which Donald said that Alger's wife, Priscilla, was a 'red-hot Communist.'" When I interviewed him, however, Donald Hiss repeated his statement that neither Alger nor Priscilla had been a Communist. See Johnston to Marbury, September 17, 1948, and Marbury to Johnston, September 22, 1948, Hiss Defense Files; also Interview, Donald Hiss, September 29, 1975.

Hiss. Mundt asked whether Donald could think of a "conceivable motive" for Chambers having lied to the Committee, but the witness could not provide any.

Despite the flurry of public hearings that week, Nixon, Stripling, and the HUAC staff devoted most of their time to checking out Chambers's executive-session testimony. In his February 1949 memo Nixon said: "It was during this period that I finally reached a definite conclusion that Hiss was not telling the truth on the issue of whether he knew Chambers, and I would say that my visits to Chambers were the major factor which convinced me on this point." He made at least two unpublicized visits to Chambers at Westminster that week, encounters that "did not, in themselves, furnish many specific leads or new evidence, [but] did serve to convince me that Chambers actually did know Hiss and that he had not manufactured the story for the purpose of destroying Hiss." Nixon later wrote that he was struck by Chambers's willingness to submit to a lie-detector test, contrasted with Hiss's later rejection of the idea; by Hiss's insistence on being furnished transcripts of his HUAC testimony after each appearance while Chambers declined to see his; and by the latter's willingness to appear always without legal counsel. Another factor greatly impressed Nixon: Chambers's conversations about Hiss during those visits—"He was talking about someone he knew rather than someone whose life he had studied."

Not relying on his judgment alone in deciding upon Chambers's veracity, Nixon showed the transcript of Chambers's then-secret August 7 testimony to William P. Rogers, chief counsel for the Senate Internal Security Subcommittee (which had first heard Elizabeth Bentley),* to Congressman Charles Kersten, and to New York *Herald Tribune* reporter Bert Andrews. All three agreed, after reading the testimony, that Chambers knew Hiss and all counseled pursuing the investigation.[39]

On August 11 Nixon met secretly with John Foster Dulles and his brother, Allen, at the Roosevelt Hotel in New York City, hoping to deter the former from issuing a public endorsement of Hiss. But Dulles had already begun to disengage himself from Hiss, who had not informed him—prior to assuming the Carnegie Endowment presidency—about the continuing rumors of his Communist ties or about his 1946 interview with the FBI. Dulles had found himself in the uncomfortable position of having to defend Hiss against persistent complaints by rightwing anti-Communists. Moreover, it had become clear by the time of Nixon's visit that leading Republicans in Dewey's entourage had grown concerned over the possible effects of the Hiss affair on the presidential race. Thus, Karl Mundt worried that the Hiss-Chambers imbroglio—which he described as "a very unsavory situation"—might injure Dewey's campaign. Mundt kept Dewey's

---

*Rogers later became attorney general under Eisenhower and, still later, secretary of state in the Nixon administration.

campaign manager, Herbert Brownell, Jr., informed about developments in the case through periodic letters. According to Mundt, the HUAC probe was then "in such a fluid state, it may break loose in any direction." He urged that Dewey "not commit himself in any way which might prove tremendously embarrassing . . . if the outcome of this tangled web of evidence should take a surprising and nation-rocking turn."[40]

The Dulles brothers were understandably eager for any light Nixon could shed on the confusing drama then unfolding. Their caller unwrapped the Chambers transcript—as he had done with Rogers, Kersten, and Andrews—and, after studying it, Foster and Allen Dulles agreed on the situation. "Go ahead," Nixon quoted John Foster Dulles as saying. "There's no question that Hiss apparently in this case has lied to the Committee, and you've got to press it [the investigation]." Allen Dulles's later, separate statement confirms his brother's reaction.[41]

Nixon has been aptly described (in James David Barber's phrase) as an "active-negative type," a personality that ordinarily displays twin sets of impulses—"the struggle to control aggression, and the pursuit of power, prestige, and status." Both compulsions emerged during the early weeks of the Hiss-Chambers case. On the one hand, Nixon nursed a suppressed but intensely personal antagonism toward Alger Hiss, his witness turned quarry. On the other, he had begun to identify closely with his fellow Red-hating Quaker, Whittaker Chambers, and with key figures in the Republican Party's national leadership. Nixon knew full well the political benefits to be derived from "breaking" the case, if only by resolving to the satisfaction of a curious public the mystery of whether Chambers really knew Alger Hiss. Robert Stripling cautioned him that week, "You're in the big leagues now."[42] But the reminder seemed unnecessary for a man whose phone calls were now as often from "Foster," "Herb," and "the Speaker" (Republican Joe Martin) as from his California constituents.

Nixon ended his preparations that weekend with two additional visits to Westminster, in which he took Bert Andrews and Robert Stripling separately to see Chambers, if only to confirm his belief in Chambers's honesty. Andrews, a Pulitzer Prize-winning reporter, and Stripling were fast becoming two of Nixon's three main advisers on the case; the other was Chambers himself. Stripling's visit was unnecessary since he already distrusted Hiss, but Andrews's suspicion of the man intensified after his talk with Chambers. Having isolated himself from family and friends as he worked on the case that week, Nixon spent his time taking long walks, avoiding meals, and refusing sleep. This pattern of behavior, he would later write, was a normal symptom for him of intense preparation for political battle.[43]

Nixon's "vigil" ended abruptly on August 16, when Alger Hiss appeared before HUAC in executive session. The committee's telegram requesting his presence had arrived the previous Friday while Hiss was preparing to leave for a Vermont weekend. He tried to reach William Marbury, but the Baltimore attorney had left on a month's assignment in Europe. "The discontinuity of counsel," he would write Marbury on August 31, "has been one of my most serious disadvantages. I know well that no man should attempt to be 'his own lawyer.'"

When he learned of Marbury's absence, Hiss "made hurried attempts" to contact friends at the well-known New York law firm of Cahill, Gordon, but the attorneys there had gone for the weekend. He left a message, and, in response, several of the firm's lawyers met him on his train Monday morning as it passed through New York City on the way from Vermont to Washington. Cahill, Gordon declined to represent him, however, Hiss later wrote, "due to a conflict of another government interest," and he finally arranged for a friend, a Washington attorney named John F. Davis, to accompany him before the committee that day. Curiously, Hiss later wrote that he had gone unrepresented: "As at the first hearing, I saw no occasion for having counsel with me."[44]

AUGUST 16: THE TRAP

At the executive session Hiss repeated his earlier claim to have heard Chambers's name mentioned for the first time at his 1947 FBI interview and then only casually, as "one of fifteen or twenty . . . of whom I had never heard." He also denied knowing any person named "Carl" or J. Peters. As for Henry Collins's apartment, he had gone there only on social occasions. Lee Pressman and others whom Chambers had accused of participating in the Ware Group might have been present while he was in Collins's apartment, although he had "no recollection of it." Nixon then produced two photographs of Chambers and asked again if Hiss knew the man "either as Whittaker Chambers or as Carl or as any other individual." Hiss wavered slightly, admitting that the picture "is not completely unfamiliar." He asked again for an opportunity to confront Chambers, and Nixon agreed that this should occur soon. Hiss also said he would arrange for his wife's testimony, to corroborate his own. Nixon, in turn, stressed the committee's desire to avoid an open session and "any publicity" until the conflicts between Hiss's account and Chambers's had been explored thoroughly in private, asking that Mrs. Hiss appear before the subcommittee the next day, perhaps in New York if more convenient. The witness promised to phone her and, if possible, make arrangements.[45]

But Hiss bridled at Nixon's next request, that his stepson, twenty-two-year-old Timothy Hobson, whom Chambers claimed to have met, also appear—even though he was in New York. Hiss explained that Hobson, who had served briefly in the Navy, was living apart from his parents. "He is being what people in Vermont call not only independent, but 'indegoddamnpendent.'" He also said that

Hobson had been consulting a psychiatrist and that he did not know his stepson's current address.

At that point Alger Hiss admitted to having "been angered and hurt" by the committee's apparent willingness to consider his own testimony and that of Chambers on an equal footing despite his (Hiss's) reputation. He asked that Chambers—who was "apparently endeavoring to destroy me"—be brought before HUAC immediately to state "his alleged knowledge of me." Otherwise, Hiss said, he would be testifying to "personal facts about myself which, if they came to his [Chambers's] ears, could sound very persuasive to other people that he had known me at some prior time."

When Stripling said that at the executive session Chambers had "sat there and testified for hours . . . [and] rattled off details like that," Hiss seemed unnerved. "He has either made a study of your life in great detail," Stripling went on, "or he knows you." Again Hiss was shown a recent photograph of Chambers, Stripling pointing out that he was "much heavier now than he was in 1937 or 1938." But although Hiss agreed that the face was "definitely not an unfamiliar face," he still claimed to "see Mr. Mundt" and a "lot of other people" in it. "Now, here is a man who says he spent a week in your house," Thomas broke out. "Do you recognize him?" "I do not recognize him from that picture. . . . I want to hear the man's voice," Hiss retorted.

Moments later Hiss suddenly announced: "I have written a name on this pad in front of me of a person whom I knew in 1933 and 1934 who not only spent some time in my house but sublet my apartment. . . . I do not recognize the photographs as possibly being this man. If I hadn't seen the morning papers with an account of statements that he knew the inside of my house, I don't think I would even have thought of this name." (Later Hiss would state that he had first thought of "this name" after Chambers's initial appearance before HUAC.) Hiss urged the committee not to ask him for the individual's name or for personal facts about himself, lest these be quietly leaked, demanding instead "to see Chambers face to face and see if he can be this individual." On one point Hiss was adamant: "He was not named Carl and not Whittaker Chambers." Hiss denied spending a week with the unnamed person in the apartment he sublet to him—only "a day or two . . . when he moved in."[46]

After Hiss complained that HUAC had known Chambers would bring out his name when it went into public session on August 3, Hébert, misrepresenting the fact, denied the charge. "And whichever of you is lying," the Louisiana Democrat exploded, "is the greatest actor that America has ever produced."

Despite his evident reluctance, Hiss now began providing the committee with the details of his personal life for which they had asked. The members inquired about family maids, and Hiss named Martha Pope, who had worked for them in Washington in 1933, and another maid obtained through an agency, whose name he could not recall and who "wasn't very satisfactory." He would check with his wife, but could not remember offhand the names of other domestics who had worked for the family during the mid-1930s and therefore might have seen Chambers.

Throughout the session Alger Hiss's memory on the subject of maids proved surprisingly uneven. Although he gave the names of three former servants (two only by first name), none of whom he had seen since the thirties, he omitted from his testimony before the committee that day and later in the month the name of Claudia ("Clytie") Catlett, who had worked for his family from 1935 to 1938, or through most of the period (1934–38) that Chambers claimed to have known Hiss. Stranger still, the Hiss families—Alger's and Donald's both—had maintained contact with Claudia Catlett and her family since the late thirties, the only one of Alger and Priscilla's former maids about whom this could be said. The Hisses had even gone to a Catlett family wedding during the early 1940s. Although Hiss in a later statement would categorize her erroneously as "sporadically" employed by his family, Claudia Catlett worked full-time and daily for the Hisses for more than three years. Also, her two older sons performed occasional odd jobs at the house. Catlett was obviously in the best position of any Hiss maid to identify Chambers as a visitor to the Hiss homes, but Hiss did not mention her name to HUAC.[47]

There seemed to be some important reason—although difficult to discern in August 1948—for Alger Hiss to have misled HUAC about Claudia Catlett, telling the House committee nothing about her. When the FBI finally located Catlett early in 1949, she proved to be one of two Hiss maids who remembered meeting Chambers. Claudia Catlett later confirmed on the witness stand the FBI account of her meeting with Chambers at bureau headquarters on February 1, 1949, at which time she

> recognized him and associated him with Hiss residence at 2905 P Street, Northwest [where they lived from June 1935 to June 1936]. She says that she may have seen him at the other addresses [in 1936–38], but does not recall it and would not have paid any attention to him after seeing him for the first time. . . . Chambers and Catlett spent considerable time recalling incidents of mutual knowledge pertaining to the Hisses.*

---

*Claudia Catlett also provided a tantalizing, if uncertain, comment related to Chambers's claim that he visited the Hisses at Christmastime 1938 after his break. According to the FBI report of her February 1, 1949, interview, "Catlett recalls an incident whereby an unidentified man inquired for Alger or Priscilla Hiss when the Hisses resided on Volta Place, Northwest [1938] during Christmas season. Catlett recalls that the Hisses were away and that the man came there twice in the evening inquiring for them. She is unable to state that this man was Whittaker Chambers, but definitely recalls incident as she considered a visit of this nature unusual."

But if Catlett remembered Chambers in 1949, her former employer had more difficulty calling her to mind under questioning by HUAC the previous August 16.[48]

During a recess that morning Hiss had apparently either searched his memory
again or reconsidered his position; he began with another abrupt announcement:

> The name of the man I brought in—and he may have no relation to the whole
> nightmare—is a man named George Crosley. I met him when I was working
> for the Nye committee. He was a writer. He hoped to sell articles to magazines
> about the munitions industry.
>
> I saw him, as I say, in my office over in the Senate Office Building, dozens of
> representatives of the press, students, people writing books, research people. It
> was our job to give them appropriate information out of the record, show them
> what had been put in the record. This fellow was writing a series of articles,
> according to my best recollection, free-lancing, which he hoped to sell to one
> of the magazines.
>
> He was pretty obviously not successful in financial terms, but as far as I
> know, wasn't actually hard up.

Hiss's memories of "George Crosley," once he had introduced the name,
proved almost as detailed as Chambers's earlier recollections of Hiss: Crosley
had blond hair, "blonder than any of us here," he was married with "one little
baby" at the time he sublet Hiss's apartment, his wife was a "strikingly dark
person," while Crosley himself was "shortish." His most memorable physical
feature? "Very bad teeth," Hiss recalled. "That is one of the things I particularly
want to see Chambers about. . . . [Crosley] did not take care of his teeth. . . . They
were stained."[49]

Although earlier Hiss had testified to knowing Crosley "in 1933 and 1934,"
he now said that the latter had rented his apartment in June 1935. Not only had
the Hisses loaned the Crosleys some furniture until the subtenant's moving van
arrived but, according to Hiss, they had shared their apartment with the Crosleys
for several days.* When Stripling asked about the type of car Chambers owned

---

*The matter of Alger and Priscilla Hiss's various Washington, D.C., residences during the
1930s, all in the Northwest section, would figure prominently in the events that followed and
requires summary:

Dates	Hiss Residence
1933–July 1934	3411 O Street, N.W.
July 1934–June 1935	2831 28th Street, N.W.
June 1935–June 1936	2905 P Street, N.W.
June 1936–Dec. 1937	1245 30th Street, N.W.
December 1937–1943	3415 Volta Place, N.W.

Chambers said that he met the Hisses at the 28th Street residence and saw them for the last
time in December 1938 at Volta Place.

when he rented the Hisses' apartment, the witness confirmed at least the bare details of his accuser's earlier testimony by replying:

> No kind of automobile. I sold him an automobile. I had an old Ford that I threw in with the apartment [in June 1935] and had been trying to trade it in and get rid of it. I had an old, old Ford we kept for sentimental reasons. We got it just before we were married in 1929. . . . [An] early A model with a trunk on the back. . . . Dark blue. It wasn't very fancy but it had a sassy little trunk on the back.

Had Hiss "sold" Chambers the car? Nixon asked. The witness replied:

> I threw it in. He wanted a way to get around and I said, "Fine, I want to get rid of it. I have another car, and we kept it for sentimental reasons, not worth a damn." I let him have it along with the rent.

Pressed by Nixon on the Ford transfer, Hiss insisted that without receiving extra compensation he had "charged the rent and threw the car in at the same time . . . in addition." After all, Hiss pointed out, the Ford was simply "sitting in the streets in snows for a year or two" while he and Priscilla "were using the other car." The "other car," Hiss testified, was a Plymouth four-door sedan that he had purchased presumably before he gave his Ford to Crosley in June 1935. He did not remember having provided Crosley with a bill of sale: "I think I just simply turned it over to him." Neither could Hiss produce a written lease—then or later—for the apartment he sublet to Crosley.

Additional details followed in rapid order. Crosley had stayed overnight "a couple of times," driven with Hiss to New York City at one point, and seen him "several times" after his sublease expired in September 1935, at which time Crosley told him he was moving to Baltimore.

But Hiss could evoke very little of his conversations with "George Crosley" except for those on Nye Committee affairs, about which they had talked "backwards and forwards": "He purported to be a cross between Jim Tully, the author, and Jack London. He had been everywhere." Obviously seeking the names of those who could validate the conflicting claims of one or the other man about the relationship, Nixon returned several times to the question of Hiss's servants during this period. But the witness stuck to his earlier testimony, which omitted the name of his daily maid for the 1935–38 period, Claudia Catlett.

Hiss verified some aspects of Chambers's testimony about his personal life, including the fact that his family had vacationed during the thirties on Maryland's Eastern Shore, that they had owned a cocker spaniel, and that Hiss had sold spring water as a boy growing up in Baltimore. When asked about his hobbies, the witness stepped into a carefully set trap:

MR. NIXON: What hobby, if any, do you have, Mr. Hiss?
MR. HISS: Tennis and amateur ornithology.

MR. NIXON: Is your wife interested in ornithology?

MR. HISS: I also like to swim and also like to sail. My wife is interested in ornithology, as I am, through my interest. Maybe I am using too big a word to say an ornithologist because I am pretty amateur, but I have been interested in it since I was in Boston. I think anybody who knows me would know that.

MR. MCDOWELL: Did you ever see a prothonotary warbler?

MR. HISS: I have right here on the Potomac. Do you know that place?

THE CHAIRMAN: What is that?

MR. NIXON: Have you ever seen one?

MR. HISS: Did you see it in the same place?

MR. MCDOWELL: I saw one in Arlington.

MR. HISS: They come back and nest in those swamps. Beautiful yellow head, a gorgeous bird.

Mr. Collins is an ornithologist, Henry Collins. He is a really good ornithologist, calling them by their Latin names.*[50]

The inquiry about Hiss's hobbies had been a loaded one, and the witness, presumably unaware of Chambers's earlier testimony on this point, confirmed something a casual acquaintance might not be expected to know. But Hiss's antennae may have sensed danger: his gratuitous reference to Henry Collins supplied the committee with the name of another ornithologist whom Chambers had also accused of Communist involvement.

Parrying Nixon's invitation to submit to a lie-detector test, Hiss argued with the congressman about the validity of such probes, Nixon and Stripling having already consulted on the matter with Leonardo Keeler, the country's leading polygraph expert. Hiss asked for additional time to consult with legal experts before making a decision on the proposal.

Although Crosley failed to pay most of his rent, according to the witness, he brought over a rug at one point which he said some wealthy patron had given him: "I have still got the damned thing." Despite Crosley's inability to meet the rent payments, Hiss said he gave the man "a couple of loans," until deciding finally that he would never be able to collect the debts, "that I had been a sucker and he was a sort of deadbeat; not a bad character, but I think he just was using

---

*Collins tried to divert attention to himself on the matter of a prothonotary warbler the following month, when he told Hiss's lawyer, Edward G. McLean, on September 22: "Collins also mentioned that his record of a bird walk which he took on August 19, 1934, with Hiss, Mrs. Hiss and a few friends shows that they saw a prothonotary warbler at that time. This was the first time Collins had ever seen one. The walk was on the south bank of the Potomac and was not near the C. & O. canal. This may have been the occasion to which Hiss referred in his testimony." If Chambers recalled correctly having learned of this sighting from the Hisses—he remembered their "great excitement" when telling him—then he was already in contact with the couple in August 1934, months before Hiss said he met "George Crosley." "Further Information from Mr. Collins," September 22, 1948, Hiss Defense Files.

me as a soft touch." Thus, at their last meeting, he and "George Crosley" had exchanged "hard words," with Hiss telling his debtor that he never expected him to pay the money he owed, that the writer had "simply welshed from the beginning." But when Nixon asked if this seemed "sufficient motive" for Chambers, assuming that he was Crosley, to lie about Hiss, the witness pointedly observed that no "normal man" would hold a grudge in that fashion.

The grueling three-and-a-half-hour session concluded with arrangements to hear Mrs. Hiss in executive session in New York and to schedule a public confrontation between Hiss and Chambers in Washington—Hiss's preference—on August 25. The nine-day delay, however, seemed altogether too long for Richard Nixon. Although he apparently went along with the plan during the hearing itself, Nixon displayed his unique theatrical talents in the twenty-four hours that followed.

Biographers of Richard Nixon invariably comment on his belief that timing in politics constitutes a form of acting, an effort to control or shift the flow of events through careful self-dramatization at critical moments. Once the male lead in his Whittier College fraternity's production of *The Trysting Place,* Nixon would later provide some memorable moments of national melodrama, but his view of politics as theater, even soap opera, received its first tryout during HUAC's Hiss-Chambers investigation. Frequently Nixon would describe the probe—in Bruce Mazlish's phrase—"as if it were a sort of stage play."

In later writings Nixon portrayed the episode theatrically, with himself sometimes playing the role of chief critic, at other times that of a Pirandello-like director stage-managing the performances in full view of the audience. Early in the hearings, for example, Nixon privately gave Chambers's testimony a favorable critical review ("I did not feel that it was an act") while panning Hiss, who "had put on a show" and "overacted."[51] Nixon's request to head the HUAC subcommittee and his exertions over the ten days preceding Hiss's August 16 appearance showed clearly his determination to direct the drama personally.

His next move, therefore, followed in logical sequence. Rather than allowing things to slide toward the public confrontation scheduled for August 25, Nixon decided to "control" events. Without consulting other committee members, he phoned Chambers. Although no record of their talk survives, Nixon presumably grilled him further on Hiss's testimony and on Nixon's belief that Hiss had known Crosley was Chambers when he testified. That evening, Nixon and Stripling spent several hours reviewing Hiss's testimony and at some point the congressman decided to push ahead the meeting in order to prevent Hiss from gaining "nine more days to make his story fit the facts." At 2:00 AM Nixon phoned Stripling with instructions to arrange "for the confrontation scene" in New York City the following afternoon. Hiss, who had left the August 16 session with "a sense of having accomplished something," was soon to learn differently.[52]

AUGUST 17: THE CONFRONTATION

Haste and some deception characterized arrangements for the Hiss-Chambers meeting of August 17. That morning Hiss received a call from Donald T. Appell, a committee investigator, who said, according to Hiss, only that Congressman McDowell wished to speak to him briefly late that afternoon. Chambers had gone to HUAC's Washington headquarters in the morning, according to his memoir, because he "felt a curious need to . . . see the Committee." More likely, Nixon had instructed the *Time* editor to appear and he accompanied the committee staff by train to New York. That afternoon McDowell himself called Hiss and invited him to come to Room 1400 of the Commodore Hotel. McDowell, Nixon, and "one other" person would be present, Hiss's caller said, an unmistakable indication that the summons was for official committee business. Harry Dexter White had died of a heart attack the previous day, and Hiss suspected that the unexpected meeting was an effort to divert public sympathy for White by shifting attention to his own case. (Nixon actually had arranged the session the previous night, before news of White's death reached him.)[53]

When Hiss arrived at Room 1400, accompanied by his friend Charles Dollard, president of the Carnegie Corporation, they found Nixon and McDowell in the company of Stripling and other staff members (Parnell Thomas would arrive shortly). The encounter began on an acrimonious note, and Hiss remained irritable, angry, and defensive throughout the hour-and-forty-minute session. Nixon announced that the committee had moved up the time for his meeting with Chambers in order to allow Hiss to determine at this early point whether his accuser was in fact George Crosley. Hiss asked permission to make a statement before the proceeding got under way. McDowell agreed, and Hiss launched into an attack on the committee for leaking segments of his previous day's testimony to the press. The two congressmen denied responsibility for the leaks, and after this initial bickering Nixon ordered Chambers brought in from the adjoining room, where, unknown to Hiss, he had been waiting.[54]

Nixon directed both principals to rise: "Mr. Hiss, the man standing here is Mr. Whittaker Chambers. I ask you now if you have ever known that man before." Hiss responded cautiously: "May I ask him to speak? Will you ask him to say something?" Chambers gave his name, at which point Hiss inquired, "Are you George Crosley?"

MR. CHAMBERS: Not to my knowledge. You are Alger Hiss, I believe.
MR. HISS: I certainly am.
MR. CHAMBERS: That was my recollection.

Hiss then asked the HUAC members if Chambers's voice pattern had been somewhat deeper during earlier testimony and, although stating that he thought the latter was George Crosley, asked that Chambers continue talking. The *Time* editor began reading from a copy of *Newsweek* handed to him by Nixon. Hiss—who had asserted earlier that Crosley's most identifiable feature was a set of bad teeth— then posed a series of questions about dental work done on Chambers since the 1930s (the latter acknowledged that his teeth had been in abysmal shape during the period he claimed to have known Hiss).

Still not positively identifying Crosley, Hiss said that Chambers was *probably* the man he had known, "but he looks very different in girth and in other appearances—hair, forehead, and so on, particularly the jowls." At that point Nixon and Stripling began a series of questions that contrasted Hiss's version of the relationship—Crosley as a "freelance writer," apartment rental, car transfer, gift of a rug, and other details—with the facts supplied earlier by Chambers. Hiss now said he had seen Crosley "ten or eleven times," never socially but only in the course of Nye Committee business, throughout 1935.

Despite the denial of a social relationship, Hiss repeated his earlier testimony that Crosley had stayed overnight at his home on occasions other than the sub-letting of his apartment, and he reiterated that he had driven Crosley to New York once (date unknown). Stripling seemed bemused by the witness's apparent inability to make a positive identification:

> I certainly gathered the impression when Mr. Chambers walked into the room and you walked over and examined him and asked him to open his mouth, that you were basing your identification purely on what his upper teeth might have looked like.
>
> Now, here is a person that you knew for several months at least. You knew him so well that he was a guest in your home. . . . You gave him an old Ford automobile, and permitted him to use, or you leased him your apartment, and in this, a very important confrontation, the only thing that you have to check on is this denture; is that correct? There is nothing else about this man's features which you could definitely say, "This is the man I knew as George Crosley," that you have to rely entirely on this denture; is that your position?

Hiss responded angrily:

> I am not given on important occasions to snap judgments or simple, easy state-ments. I am confident that George Crosley had notably bad teeth. . . . I saw him at the time I was seeing hundreds of people. Since then I have seen thousands of people. . . . if this man had said he was George Crosley, I would have no dif-ficulty in identification.[55]

But Hiss had recognized the sarcasm in Stripling's remarks and immediately asked permission to ask Chambers "some further questions to help in identifica-tion." After all, "he may have had his face lifted." With the approval of Nixon and McDowell, Hiss began interrogating his adversary, who raised no objection to this unusual procedure.

Although Chambers denied at this time having ever used the name "George Crosley" and denied that he had sublet Hiss's 28th Street apartment on a rental basis, he again noted that the Chambers family had spent three weeks living there when the Hisses moved to their new P Street home. Asked by Hiss to reconcile the two statements, Chambers responded, "Very easily, Alger," and brought their conflicting stories into sharp relief. Hiss had insisted "Crosley" was only a casual acquaintance—"He meant nothing to me"—but Chambers ("Carl") stressed a more intimate bond: "I was a Communist and you were a Communist." Nixon interrupted, demanding further clarification, and Chambers reiterated his basic testimony:

> I came to Washington as a functionary of the American Communist Party. I was connected with the underground group of which Mr. Hiss was a member. Mr. Hiss and I became friends. To the best of my knowledge, Mr. Hiss himself suggested that I go there [to the 28th Street apartment], and I accepted gratefully.

At this point, after some additional questioning of Chambers, an overwrought Hiss announced:

> Mr. Chairman, I don't need to ask Mr. Whittaker Chambers any more questions. I am now perfectly prepared to identify this man as George Crosley.[56]
> Stripling: "Will you produce for the committee three people who will testify that they knew him as George Crosley?" Hiss agreed "if it is possible," pointing out that since he had known Crosley in 1935, the only people who also might have known him "with certainty" were three associates on the Nye Committee staff, including Stephen Raushenbush, the staff director. "I shared seeing the press with Mr. Raushenbush," Hiss noted. But extensive later inquiries by the FBI and (separately) by Hiss's attorneys failed to produce a single other member of the Nye Committee staff—including Raushenbush—who had met George Crosley or Whittaker Chambers under any name.

Although they discussed politics "quite frequently," Hiss said he had not known Crosley was a Communist. He reminded the subcommittee that the political atmosphere in Washington was "quite different" in the New Deal period from what it was in 1948; whether or not Crosley had been a Communist "was of [no] significance to me," since "it was my duty to give him information, as I did any other member of the press." Now, complained Hiss in a rare rhetorical outburst, more than a decade later he had been summoned to the Commodore to "discover that the ass under the lion's skin is Crosley." Hiss announced that he was finished questioning Chambers/Crosley and could identify him positively "on the basis of his own statement that he was in my apartment at the time when I say he was there. . . . If he had lost both eyes and taken his nose off, I would be sure."

Suddenly Hiss rose and began walking in Chambers's direction, stating loudly and "for the record" that he challenged his accuser

MR. HISS: . . . to make those same statements out of the presence of this committee without their being privileged for suit for libel, I challenge you to do
so, and I hope you will do it damned quickly. I am not going to touch him
[addressing Louis Russell of the HUAC staff]. You are touching me.

MR. RUSSELL: Please sit down, Mr. Hiss.

MR. HISS: I will sit down when the chairman asks me.

MR. RUSSELL: I want no disturbance.

MR. HISS: I don't—

MR. MCDOWELL: Sit down, please.

MR. HISS: You know who started this.

When testimony resumed after a recess, Hiss asked McDowell, who was serving as chairman, to obtain from Chambers "for the record his response to the
challenge that I have just made to him." By this time Hiss had lost considerable self-control. For the next few minutes he argued with Stripling and Nixon
over the legal question of whether Chambers's voluntary statement to Assistant Secretary of State Adolf Berle in 1939 was "privileged" testimony or might
serve as the basis for a libel action. Nixon and Stripling felt it could be used
for this purpose. Hiss said that his own counsel had advised him differently,
and he demanded a transcript of his earlier testimony. Once more he claimed
not to have known Chambers as "Carl" or to have paid Communist Party dues
(as Chambers alleged) either to J. Peters or to Henry Collins: "Not even for the
Audubon Society did I pay dues to Henry Collins." Nor did he know very much
about Crosley's characteristics other than his bad teeth. Unconvinced, McDowell
reminded the witness that

[of] all the newspaper men that you were in contact [with] in your highly
important job with the Nye Committee . . . you must have formed some sort of
an affection for this man to go through all the things that you did to try to [have
him] occupy your home, take over your lease, and give him an automobile.

But Chambers reiterated that he had not represented himself to Hiss as a free-
lance writer, and Hiss conceded he had never seen anything written by Crosley
during their dozen or more contacts. All he could remember, vaguely, was that
Crosley "was given to talking in quite a cultivated manner . . . about a variety of
subjects . . . [capping] any story with a story of his own." Hiss recalled one such
story: Crosley's claim to have worked in laying rails for Washington's first street
railway—which Chambers acknowledged having told Hiss, although not under
the name George Crosley.

The tense confrontation had left the participants emotionally drained. Hiss
protested again the committee's action in springing this unexpectedly quick
meeting with Chambers, while Stripling and Nixon persisted in their familiar
queries. Hiss asked if the group intended to publicize the session, "because I am
interested in my own protection." He was told that the August 25 open session

before the full committee would take place as scheduled, with both Hiss and Chambers appearing as witnesses. Hiss said that his wife was already on her way from Vermont, and Nixon offered to remain in New York and take her testimony on the following day at her convenience. The hearing then concluded, as it had begun, acrimoniously.

> MR. HISS: May I come with her?
> MR. MCDOWELL: Yes.
> MR. HISS: Thank you. Am I dismissed? Is the proceeding over?
> THE CHAIRMAN: Any more questions to ask of Mr. Hiss?
> MR. NIXON: I have nothing.
> THE CHAIRMAN: That is all. Thank you very much.
> MR. HISS: *I don't reciprocate.*
> THE CHAIRMAN: Italicize that in the record.
> MR. HISS: I wish you would.*

Nixon's stage management had worked. The Commodore confrontation proved dramatically the essential point he had set out to demonstrate: that, whatever the relationship and under whatever name, Hiss and Chambers knew each other.

In their rush to inform the press, Nixon, McDowell, and Thomas all apparently dispensed with dinner that evening. Although the session ended at 7:15 PM, the early editions of the morning papers published front-page stories based on telephone conversations with the trio. Nixon provided the information for *The New York Times* account—headlined "ALGER HISS ADMITS KNOWING CHAMBERS; MEET FACE TO FACE"—which contained a summary of the confrontation and of Chambers's previous testimony. The *Times* also printed an account of a hastily called press conference at Hiss's apartment that evening, at which he reiterated both his earlier testimony about George Crosley and his feeling that there was "something funny" about the committee's having moved up the meeting date.[57]

Sharing the Commodore Hotel suite with Nixon that evening was Donald Appell, who remembers the congressman asking him to spend the night because he did not wish to be alone. Late that evening Nixon placed a phone call to Bert Andrews, and while the two men spoke, Appell went to bed. He awoke in the night to discover Nixon still discussing the case with Andrews and, after checking his watch, realized that the call had already lasted for over three hours.[58]

---

*Charles Dollard, who had accompanied Hiss to the Commodore meeting, later told Hiss's attorneys "that Alger behaved very badly, was very irritable. He could not tell whether Alger really recognized Chambers before he admitted it or not. Dollard thought that both McDowell and Nixon were trying to be fair. He also thought that they would not have called Priscilla if Alger had not practically insisted on it." "Memorandum of Conference with Charles Dollard . . . ," Jan. 21, 1949, Hiss Defense Files.

When Priscilla Hiss appeared at the suite the following morning accompanied by her husband and Charles Dollard, the mood in Room 1400 had lightened considerably. Only Nixon and Appell were present to take her testimony, and their manner was almost serene. Mrs. Hiss had to wait while Nixon briefly interrogated a New York *World-Telegram* reporter, Nelson Frank, who had known Chambers in the "open" CP when both wrote for *The Daily Worker* and later, in 1932, while Chambers helped edit *The New Masses*. Asked if he recognized Chambers, whom he had not seen from 1932 to 1944, from press photographs, Frank replied:

> Oh, yes. The face was definitely the same. I was quite surprised by the amount of weight he had put on . . . [but] I would say his basic appearance, certainly of his face, was very much the same. . . . His teeth had always been noticeably bad . . . [and] he had got himself a nice set of teeth. . . . There was no doubt in my mind [however]. . . . As soon as I looked at the face, I knew him.

Such casual and immediate recognition of Chambers at first sight from photos, even after many years had passed, proved the rule among the latter's old Communist associates, underground contacts, and even brief acquaintances. Alger Hiss's inability to recall the man definitely for two weeks, under whatever name, despite Hiss's claim to have scrutinized press photos closely during that period, was the sole exception.[59]

Priscilla Hiss's testimony took only ten minutes. Whether because he lacked sleep or because, as he later said, he felt "spent physically, emotionally and mentally," Nixon was an almost inert examiner. He ran Mrs. Hiss through the briefest account of her relationship with George Crosley. She said that she met Crosley in 1934, although she professed only the foggiest memory of that encounter. She confirmed that Crosley had stayed in their apartment for two or three days in the summer of 1935 before the Hisses moved to a new home, but, as for Crosley himself, "I have a very dim impression of a small person, very smiling person—a little too smiley, perhaps. I don't recollect the face, but a short person." Priscilla Hiss told Nixon nothing about having identified Chambers as Crosley for Edmund Soule on August 3. Nor did she remember either the trip to New York with Crosley mentioned by Alger Hiss or the last time she had seen the man, except for an "impression . . . of being perhaps a little put off" because he was "a sponger."[60]

Despite Priscilla Hiss's perfunctory answers, Nixon did not question sharply or insist on more responsive testimony, as he had done earlier with her husband. Instead, he brought the session to a close in a manner that contrasted starkly with the previous night's fireworks:

MR. NIXON: I appreciate your coming.
MRS. HISS: I am glad it has been so quiet, because that was really what I had a
    strong distaste for. I would like to thank you for our just being together.
MR. HISS: I greatly appreciate your courtesy, Mr. Nixon.

Later that day Hiss wrote to Parnell Thomas, again expressing his deep reservations about submitting to a lie-detector test. His own inquiries had persuaded him that the polygraph machine measured only "changes in certain physical indices of emotion" whose interpretation lay entirely within the "subjective discretion of the operator of the machine." In short, it had no scientific validity and no federal agency—including the FBI, Hiss argued—accepted its results.[61]

The committee resumed its inquiry on August 20, with three of Hiss's New Deal associates—John Abt, Lee Pressman, and Nathan Witt—in executive session. President Truman, during a press conference the previous day, had again denounced HUAC's spy probes for infringing on the Bill of Rights, but a discernible shift in opinion toward the hearings had begun to take place, even among many moderates and liberals, spurred, of course, by the revelation that Hiss had admitted knowing Chambers/Crosley. "Get to the Bottom," demanded a New York *Herald Tribune* editorial that morning. The *Tribune,* critical of the committee in the past, now pronounced that the group, "whatever its past or present sins, is really trying to get to the bottom of a matter which is of serious public consequence."

Abt, Pressman, and Witt did little to assist in this search for evidence; all three declined on grounds of self-incrimination to answer questions about their own alleged Communist activities or about their knowledge of such involvement on the part of either Hiss or Chambers. Abt and Pressman were then leading officials in Henry Wallace's Progressive Party campaign; Witt practiced law in New York City. Hiss had testified to social contacts with all three and also to having worked with them at the AAA, but he denied knowing that any of them was a Communist. The proceeding lasted little more than an hour, and it is doubtful that Nixon had expected any more from the uncooperative witnesses than what they provided for the record—and for the following day's headlines: repeated reliance on the Fifth.*[62]

---

*Two years later almost to the day, Pressman testified again before HUAC, this time voluntarily and more fully about his Communist involvements. Nixon was also present that day. The Korean War was then in progress, and Pressman had broken publicly with the left-wing American Labor Party shortly before his appearance. Although he did not plead self-incrimination before the committee, he sparred constantly with its members, who felt that he was still being far from candid. Pressman named himself, John Abt, Henry Collins, Charles Kramer, and Nathan Witt as members of the Ware Group during the 1933–35 period. He also confirmed having met J. Peters at the time.

But the witness insisted the Ware Group had been a Marxist "study group" and not one that pilfered government documents. Moreover, he had never met Whittaker Chambers and, as for Alger Hiss, "for the period of my participation in that group . . . [he] was not a member of the group." Although Pressman qualified his assertion by avowing that he had "no knowledge" of Hiss's political beliefs or affiliations, his testimony helped neutralize a public statement made earlier that year by another Ware Group member, Nathaniel Weyl (unnamed by Pressman but self-confessed), that Hiss had been an active member of the group. Significantly, Pressman could

Nixon held a final one-man executive session on August 24, at which he interrogated a half-dozen witnesses to corroborate important aspects of Chambers's
testimony. Martha Pope, who worked as a maid for the Hisses intermittently
between 1930 and 1935, could not recall seeing the Chambers family either at the
28th Street apartment they had sublet or at the house on P Street to which the
Hisses had moved. Photographs of Whittaker and Esther Chambers and their
baby daughter taken at the time did not change her testimony. Mrs. Pope's recollections, however, damaged Hiss's story in one respect. She told of having worked
for the Hisses at their P Street home for four or five months before leaving—in
other words, well into the fall of 1935—and having seen only the Ford car "all the
time that I worked for them," not the new Plymouth, although Hiss said he gave
the Ford to Chambers in June 1935 at the time he sublet at 28th Street.[63]

The transfer in ownership of that 1929 Ford with the "sassy little trunk" had
brought the four remaining witnesses to the Old House Office Building that
afternoon, three of them officials of Washington's then largest auto dealership,
the Cherner Motor Company. A search by the HUAC staff of District of Columbia
Motor Vehicle Bureau records had turned up the certificate of title to the car, and
that document directly contradicted Hiss's testimony about casually giving the
automobile to Chambers in June 1935 as part of the apartment rental. It established that Hiss had signed over title to the car to Cherner Motor Company more
than a year later, on July 23, 1936. (Hiss would later concede the genuineness of
his signature on the title transfer but would alter his original story to account
for the later disposal.) The reverse side of the certificate indicated that Cherner
Motor, in turn, sold the car for $25 to a William Rosen that same day. (Rosen
would be identified by committee investigators shortly after as a member of the
Communist Party.)

All three auto-dealership officials who testified—Joseph Cherner, Samuel
Mensh, and Henry Gertler—said they had no knowledge of the 1936 transaction.
Nor did they know of those apparently involved—Hiss, Rosen, or J. Peters—
except for the person whose address was listed below Rosen's signature on
the Ford title-transfer certificate, Benjamin Bialek, suspected by HUAC of

---

not recall the names of any Ware Group members other than the four he mentioned, whose Communist involvement at the time had long been the subject of public comment. His testimony, in
short, was cooperative but within sharp limits that restrained total candor—perhaps about Hiss
and certainly about Chambers.

Both Pressman and Witt aided Hiss in 1948 and 1949 while the latter's attorneys sought
information to disprove Chambers's story. Both men told Hiss's attorneys "that the story about
the first apparatus which had allegedly met in Henry Collins' house [i.e., the Ware Group] was
completely false," a statement that Pressman—though not Witt—revised in his 1950 HUAC testimony. For Pressman's August 28, 1950, HUAC testimony, see HUAC, "Hearings Regarding Communism in the United States Government—Part 2," 81st Cong., 2nd Sess., pp. 2844–2901. Also see
"Re Lee Pressman (and Nathan Witt)," March 7, 1949, Hiss Defense Files.

CP involvement.* Joseph Cherner (and his two brothers, Leon and Henry) admitted knowing Bialek, but not as a Communist. Joseph Cherner also testified that his company kept no records going back to 1936, only to discover that HUAC staff members had found entries for the month of the Ford transfer while examining the company's books, but no listing of the transaction. Cherner then agreed that the entire process—taking in a car without any purchase payment and selling it the same day—seemed "very unusual." Although Samuel Mensh identified his signature on the title assignment to Rosen, he pointed out that he signed titles for such sales in batches of up to a dozen and rarely knew all the buyers.[64]

An attorney at the Department of Justice who had notarized the document there in 1936, W. Marvin Smith, then identified his signature. Like Mensh before him, however, Smith could not recall the incident. Questioned by Nixon and Mundt, Smith stated he would not have notarized the transfer had Alger Hiss not signed the form in his presence. Moreover, Smith thought the assignment to Cherner would already have been filled out when Hiss signed because he (Smith) made it a practice never to notarize blank assignments on such documents.[†65]

That evening, August 24, the day before HUAC's scheduled public confrontation between himself and Whittaker Chambers, Alger Hiss released to the press the text of a long letter he had just sent to Chairman Thomas. It not only detailed Hiss's irritation at his inability to deflect further pursuit by the committee, but also presented the lines of his future legal and public defense. The accusations against him went "beyond the personal," Hiss wrote, since these charges were being publicized in order "to discredit recent great achievements of this country in which I was privileged to participate." Thus Hiss linked his own misfortunes directly to his services in the New Deal, at the Yalta Conference, and in the founding of the United Nations. He called Mundt, in particular, "trigger quick to cast such discredit," and claimed that the congressman had already declared him guilty in the press.[66]

As for Chambers, Hiss called him a "self-confessed liar, spy, and traitor": "It is inconceivable that the men with whom I was intimately associated during those fifteen years (in all three branches of government) should not know my true character far better than this accuser." He asked, in effect, why—if Chambers spoke the truth—no one had caught him (Hiss) out during this long period, or why his actions as an official had not revealed evidence of Communist association.

Outlining in detail his career and his associates, Hiss thereby played what was clearly his strongest suit—a defense by reputation. He dwelt on the "living personages of recognized stature under whom or in association with whom

---

*Bialek's family members deny that their father had any ties to the Communist Party.

†W. Marvin Smith committed suicide later that year, but no direct connection to his HUAC testimony has ever been proved.

I worked in the government." The list was a formidable one, a veritable catalogue of establishment figures in American politics and government, all of whom
would presumably verify Hiss's integrity. It included three former secretaries of
state—Cordell Hull, Edward Stettinius, and James Byrnes; two prominent U.S.
senators—Tom Connally and Arthur Vandenberg; former Under Secretary of
State Dean Acheson; Supreme Court Justice Stanley Reed; Judge Jerome Frank
and Chester Davis, his superiors at the AAA; former Senator Gerald Nye, head of
the munitions investigation for which Hiss served as a chief attorney; John Foster
Dulles and a dozen others, including Eleanor Roosevelt, with whom Hiss had
served at international conferences; and his State Department superiors, Francis
Sayre and Stanley Hornbeck.

The roster included generals and admirals, Republicans, Democrats, and
independents, "with whom and under whom I worked intimately." All were
"persons of unimpeachable character." Let them be his judges, Hiss demanded
of Thomas; had any of them ever found him wanting in the "highest adherence
to duty and honor"? Many of those listed would in fact stand behind Hiss in
his subsequent efforts to demonstrate innocence, either privately or by testifying as character witnesses. Sayre and Hornbeck, for example, both praised his
integrity while at State, although Sayre questioned important aspects of Hiss's
story and Hornbeck acknowledged receiving warnings of his possible Communist ties from French intelligence sources (by way of the American ambassador
to France), probably in 1940. Stettinius and Acheson, both personal friends of
Hiss, but not Byrnes, would also vouch for his fidelity as a departmental official;
Justice Reed would testify publicly to his good character, while Mrs. Roosevelt
supported his cause faithfully in her newspaper columns.

But others named had doubts, sometimes grave ones, about Alger Hiss's reliability. Both Frank and Chester Davis believed Hiss to have been closely linked
with the coterie of Communist lawyers within AAA, and neither would appear as
a character witness. Byrnes had cooperated closely with the State Department's
security investigation of Hiss in 1946; he told the FBI that he would have fired
him outright except for the mandatory Civil Service Commission hearing, which
would have revealed confidential Bureau sources on the affair. (State Department and FBI memos show that Byrnes and J. Edgar Hoover worked together to
ease Hiss out of the department in 1946.) Nye told the FBI he thought Hiss had
been a Communist when he worked for the munitions investigating committee
during the 1934–35 period (the time when Hiss and Chambers met) and declined
to cooperate with Hiss's lawyers. Several others—including all of the military
officers—also refused to come forward in the months ahead, and Dulles eventually disowned Hiss completely. Even Hornbeck came to believe that Hiss had lied
about his ties with Chambers. But when Hiss released his letter to the press on
August 25, the morning of his public confrontation with Chambers, newspaper

readers could only believe that the Carnegie Endowment president enjoyed the wholehearted support of all these prominent figures.

Hiss provided in the letter his first response to the often-asked question of why Chambers had made such charges if they were untrue. He denounced Chambers as "a self-discredited accuser whose names and aliases are as numerous and as casual as his accusations." Hiss's explanation, simply, was that Chambers was unbalanced.

> Is he a man of consistent reliability, truthfulness and honor: clearly not. He admits it, and the committee knows it. Indeed, is he a man of sanity? Getting the facts about Whittaker Chambers, if that is his name, will not be easy. My own counsel have made inquiries in the past few days and have learned that his career is not, like those of normal men, an open book. His operations have been furtive and concealed. Why? What does he have to hide? I am glad to help get the facts.

The tone and contents of his letter to Thomas indicated that Hiss had recovered completely from the attack of nerves suffered during the subcommittee meeting at the Commodore Hotel.

AUGUST 25: THE TELEVISED CLIMAX

For the first time at a congressional hearing, television cameras were in place to record the confrontation of August 25. Chairman Thomas reviewed the previous three weeks' testimony, mentioning the August 17 encounter at the hotel between Hiss and Chambers, and pointedly observing: "As a result of this hearing, certainly one of these witnesses will be tried for perjury."[67]

Alger Hiss was accompanied to the witness table by attorneys John F. Davis and Harold Rosenwald of New York, a friend and former Harvard Law School classmate. Robert Stripling asked Whittaker Chambers to stand and, for the record, asked Hiss whether he had ever seen the man. Hiss and Chambers faced one another, and the former identified his antagonist as "George Crosley," whom he "first knew . . . sometime in the winter of 1934 or 1935 . . . [and last saw] sometime in 1935." The identification, however, was doubly qualified by the statement "according to my best recollection, not having checked the records." Chambers was sworn as a witness at that point and agreed that he knew the person facing him as Alger Hiss, whom he met "about 1934" and last saw "about 1938."

The questioning did not go well for Hiss. He admitted not having been able to identify Chambers previously on the basis of press photographs. He complained about his inability to refresh his recollection by access to the appropriate records, particularly with respect to the District of Columbia's Motor Vehicle Bureau file on the 1929 Ford, which, Hiss asserted, had been taken by the Committee. Stripling noted that his investigators had subpoenaed only a photostatic copy of the car's certificate of title; the original should still be in the file.

A question about the lease between Hiss and "Crosley" drew from the witness a reminder that he had never testified there was such a written document, only "a sublease orally arranged." Hiss had since learned that the dates originally given to the committee were in error—he had left the 28th Street apartment and begun residence at P Street earlier than he remembered in previous testimony, but he could not give precise dates until he reviewed the records.

The HUAC investigators, however, had done their homework. Stripling produced letters from local realtors detailing Hiss's various leases, although Hiss challenged the significance of this information: "The important charges are not questions of leases, but questions of whether I was a Communist." Nixon retorted: "The issue in this hearing today is whether or not Mr. Hiss or Mr. Chambers has committed perjury before this committee, as well as whether Mr. Hiss is a Communist."[68] If it could be shown that either Hiss or Chambers had deliberately lied, Nixon suggested, not simply on what Hiss called "housekeeping details" but about the nature of their relationship, then the committee might have some general yardstick by which to measure "the truth or falsity" of conflicting statements.

Debating this point, Hiss said it did not appear to him "a very rational basis for determining credibility," but Nixon reminded him that when a witness is found to be lying on material questions raised during a court proceeding, his credibility on other questions becomes suspect. The committee had already shown, Nixon went on, that Hiss knew Chambers; the question now was "how well you knew Chambers and whether you knew him as a Communist." The interrogation about leases had shown that, whatever else was true, Chambers and his family could have sublet the former Hiss apartment for a maximum of two months, May and June 1935, and not—as Hiss had claimed earlier—for the entire summer, nor even during the normal July-August summer period.

Having established Hiss's inaccuracy on this housekeeping detail, Stripling turned to the question of verifying Crosley's identity. Again Hiss mentioned his three Nye Committee associates, but in the months ahead he was able to find only one person to identify Chambers as George Crosley, a New York publisher of pornographic literature named Samuel Roth, who proved to be of little use to Hiss for two reasons: The nature of his business had produced several jail sentences, and he claimed knowledge of the pseudonym almost a decade before Hiss met "Crosley." Roth asserted that Chambers had published under his own name several poems on sexual themes in one of his periodicals in 1926 and 1927; subsequently, according to Roth, Chambers had submitted another group of poems for publication with an accompanying letter requesting that they be printed under the name "George Crosley." But Roth had not saved Chambers's letter, and he had returned "Crosley's" poems unpublished the following year.[69]

No one else could remember the elusive Mr. Crosley. Stripling pointed out that HUAC probes had failed to turn up a single article written under the name "George Crosley" in the Library of Congress's bibliographic files, and no one in publishing (except Roth) came forward. Again Hiss testified that Crosley had told him he hoped to sell his articles on the Nye Committee to the *American* magazine—here and in later testimony Hiss was definite about Crosley mentioning that particular publication. Yet, unknown to the committee, a friend of Hiss's, Beverly Smith, had published a long account of the Nye Committee's work in the May 1935 issue of the *American* at precisely the time when Hiss claimed to have discussed the subject of such an article with Crosley. Furthermore, Smith's piece, a portrait of Nye's career and of the munitions investigation, was the second such article to appear in the *American* in as many months. The April 1935 issue contained an article by General Hugh S. Johnson, head of the National Recovery Administration, criticizing the Nye group's focus on profits made by munitions makers. Unaware of these articles, Stripling and Nixon missed a chance to raise the question of why—as a lawyer and Nye Committee official—Hiss had failed to check out Crosley's credentials concerning the placing of an article in the *American* with Smith, an old friend of the Hiss family.[70]

The issue of Hiss's transfer of the Ford became the focus of much questioning. Committee members now pursued the witness avidly and, for the first time, with barely disguised disbelief. Again Hiss's "best recollection" was that he had given the Ford to Chambers as part of the transaction involving the apartment sublet at 28th Street—that the two deals were "simultaneous"—and that he owned "both a [new] Plymouth and this old Ford" at the time, the Ford "of no use, deteriorating, being left outdoors." Stripling: "Well, as a matter of fact, Mr. Hiss, you sold the [Ford] car a year later, did you not?" Stripling then produced a photostat of the D.C. Motor Vehicle Bureau's certificate of title for Hiss's 1935 Plymouth sedan, which listed the owner's address as 2905 P Street, N.W., and contained the following information: "How secured: Conditional sale; date, September 7, 1935, purchased from the Smoot Motor Co., Inc." Hiss had purchased the Plymouth, in other words, four months after allegedly subletting the 28th Street apartment to Crosley, and two months after Crosley's last possible date of residence there.[71] The apartment sublease and Hiss's disposition of the Ford, in short, occurred at different times, not simultaneously as Hiss had asserted.

Nixon pointed out that the June 1935 ads in the Washington *Evening Star* showed the "lowest-cash value" for 1929 Ford roadsters to be $59—more for trade-ins—and not the $25 value earlier cited by Hiss. The witness reiterated that because of his "sentimental attachment" to the Ford, he preferred to give it to Crosley, a casual acquaintance, rather than to sell the old Model A or trade it to a dealer.

Stripling noted Chambers's previous testimony that Hiss had purchased a new car "in 1936 probably" and that Hiss had allegedly disposed of the Ford to a Communist organizer through a Washington service station or car-lot owner. It was then that Stripling introduced the July 23, 1936, D.C. certificate of title showing that Hiss had assigned the Ford to the Cherner Motor Company.

Exempting the three Cherner Motor officials from any responsibility for the transfer (although presumably someone at the company had taken part in the dummy transaction), Stripling said: "The point we are making is that Mr. Hiss, according to this document, delivered the Ford automobile to the Cherner Motor Company on July 23, 1936. On that same date this car was sold or transferred to one William Rosen, but there is no evidence in the sales records of this particular transaction."

Although Hiss could not recall having signed the certificate, nor writing in the name and address of the Cherner Motor Company, he conceded "that also looks not unlike my own handwriting." When Stripling and Nixon reminded the witness that W. Marvin Smith had testified he notarized the signature, Hiss agreed that "with the evidence that has been shown to me" the signature was indeed his. But he persisted in disclaiming "present recollection of the disposition of the Ford."

That afternoon Hiss adjusted his testimony to take into account the newly revealed 1936 certificate of title. After giving Crosley the car in 1935, he speculated, "at some later stage he or someone else [possibly] came to me and said 'You disposed of a car, there remains a technical transaction to be completed,'" but Hiss said he did not remember such an event. He also stressed the possibility that the Ford "may have bounced back or it may have been a loan." Hiss now recalled vaguely having seen Crosley "not more than a couple of times—two, three times" after his 28th Street subtenancy, and he said also that Crosley might have stayed with him once after that time when he could not obtain a hotel room.

The boundaries of the relationship between the two men kept expanding as the day wore on. Hiss stated that Crosley, after receiving the Ford in mid-1935, might have given it to someone else who in turn approached Hiss in July 1936 to conclude a "formal" transfer. But the witness no longer doubted that he had indeed signed the certificate of title transfer that month. If he had allowed someone else to use the car for over a year while retaining title, Nixon rejoined, Hiss would still have been liable in the event of an accident involving the vehicle. Surely as a lawyer "who stood extremely high in his class at Harvard Law School," Nixon observed, he would have recognized that fact? "I certainly did not realize it," Hiss responded.

Reviewing Hiss's testimony about the Ford from his earliest appearance before HUAC, Nixon noted that until that day the witness "had conveyed the impression that the transfer was outright, that he didn't get the car back, that it was not a loan, since he had used the words 'sold,' 'got rid of.'" This earlier testimony about a car transfer in May or June 1935 had now been discredited, Nixon continued, and "if Mr. Hiss did give Mr. Crosley a car at any time, he gave it to him after September . . . 1935 when he had both of his cars . . . at a time . . . after Mr. Hiss had learned that Mr. Crosley was not financially responsible and that he had not paid his rent."[72]

Raising the general issue of Hiss's "credibility," Mundt asked him when he first informed John Foster Dulles about his 1946 FBI interview. Hiss had been elected president of the Endowment in December 1946 and began work there on February 1, 1947. "At that time, Mr. Mundt, the FBI had not come to interview me," replied Hiss. But the 1946 interview took place in March, eight months before his selection by the Carnegie Endowment board. As for Dulles, Hiss remembered "a conversation shortly after I had been elected but before I had assumed office . . . in which he said that he had heard reports that people had called me a Communist. We discussed those reports at that time. . . . Sometime in December 1946." Hiss acknowledged that Dulles and not he had raised the subject: "Mr. Dulles called me and said he had had a report. I said, 'I thought that had been laid to rest,' and I discussed it with him then."

Dulles would later recall a different sequence of events. He confirmed a phone conversation with Hiss in January 1947, held after Dulles had first received the disquieting reports: "Hiss replied," according to Dulles, "that there had been some rumors which, however, he had completely set to rest at Washington. . . . I do not recall that Hiss then mentioned the FBI, but he might have done so, although I recall he treated the matter very lightly."[73] In Dulles's account, in other words, a version later confirmed by Hiss, the latter said nothing about any charges of Communist ties made against him until after he had been selected president of the Carnegie Endowment.

But when Republican Congressman Walter Judd had raised the same charges against Hiss in several letters to Dulles the following year, 1948, the latter asked Hiss for an explanation. Again Hiss had "categorically denied any Communist association or sympathy," but in explaining the basis of these rumors to Dulles, he described his former associates at the Harvard Law School and in the Department of Agriculture far differently than he did to HUAC later that year:

> Hiss says that when he first came to New York [in 1932], [Dulles wrote to Judd] he wrote for and helped to edit a little paper on labor decisions [for the International Juridical Association, a Communist-front organization] and that some of his associates [Hiss specifically mentioned Lee Pressman in a confidential memo on the conversation filed by Dulles at the time] were labor people who he now knows may have been or may have become Communists.

In his confidential file memo on the talk, Dulles also noted a point he mentioned when writing to Judd: that Hiss "also said that when he was in the Department of Agriculture there were there some persons who might have had some Communist sympathy, but he had with them only casual acquaintance." In all of his appearances before HUAC, Hiss never alluded to such personal knowledge or belief that any of his former colleagues and friends—not "casual acquaintances"—in either the International Juridical Association or the AAA might have had Communist connections. On the contrary, Hiss several times specifically disclaimed such awareness, both to HUAC and to the FBI.[74]

The committee members no longer bothered disguising their doubts concerning Hiss's veracity, Hébert, for example, insisted he had difficulty in understanding a man of Hiss's "intellect and . . . ability who gives to casual people his apartment, who tosses in an automobile, who doesn't know the laws of liability, who lends money to an individual just casually, [yet] is so cautious" in responding to the committee's questions. Mundt made a long statement about his own attitude toward the hearings, telling Hiss he had been "inclined to be in your corner" and accept his statements "at face value" in the beginning—an assertion confirmed in Mundt's earlier letters to Republican officials—"despite the fact that . . . I had frequently heard the name of Alger Hiss bandied about as having possible Communist connections in years past." Mundt described these rumors as "rather common scuttlebutt . . . around Washington." Previous testimony, according to Mundt, had produced several "points in agreement":

> You knew this man [Chambers]; you knew him very well. You knew him so well that you even trusted him with your apartment; you let him use your furniture; you let him use or gave him your automobile. You think that you probably took him to New York. You bought him lunches in the Senate Restaurant. You had him staying in your home. . . . and made him a series of small loans. There seems no question about that.[75]

Three basic points of disagreement existed between Hiss and Chambers, Mundt continued, none of which the committee could then resolve definitely: Was Hiss a Communist? Did he belong to the underground Ware Group? And had he known Chambers as "Carl" or as "George Crosley"? But where the committee had been able to obtain "verifiable evidence," Mundt noted that Chambers's testimony "has stood up. It stands unchallenged," and on some of the other points of contention Hiss's testimony "is clouded by a strangely deficient memory." Hiss responded: "Chambers has, by his own testimony, been peddling* to various Government agencies for ten years or so stories about me. During that time he has had an opportunity to check on all sorts of details about my personality."

---

*Only his original visit to Berle—at Isaac Don Levine's request—was voluntary on Chambers's part. For the entire decade after that meeting, in which Berle chose to ignore Chambers's allegations of Communist involvement by various officials including Alger Hiss, Chambers was an extremely reluctant witness when summoned by the FBI for interviews or, in 1948, by HUAC. See pp. 55–58, on the Berle interview.

Reminding the committee that facts such as his interest in ornithology could be found in *Who's Who*, Hiss further implied that Chambers had also consulted *Time*'s file on him for background data. He challenged specifically one piece of his accuser's testimony: that he had enrolled his stepson in less expensive schools in order to donate child-support funds from Mrs. Hiss's former husband to the Communist Party. He promised to "examine other points" and to produce witnesses who knew Chambers as Crosley.

When Hiss demanded that Chambers state—among other things—whether he had ever been charged or convicted of a crime, or whether he had ever been treated for mental illness, Hébert broke in to observe that whenever a former Communist testified before HUAC, "a typical Communist smear is . . . to say he is insane or an alcoholic or something else is wrong with them." According to Hébert, he had already asked Chambers whether he was an alcoholic or had ever been treated psychiatrically, in or out of an institution, "and he replied in the negative." Apparently the rumors about Chambers and mental illness, noted Hébert, "came from *Time* magazine by his own associates," but when Nixon asked whether Hiss had any hard evidence, the witness backed down: "I have made no such charge." Hiss said he was only "seeking information," although he admitted having received "reports made by individuals . . . members of the press . . . so far only hearsay" concerning Chambers's mental health.[76]

After avowing that he last saw Crosley "sometime in 1935," Hiss qualified the statement. He did not believe there had been any contact with Crosley in 1936 (the year of the Ford car transfer) and he was "reasonably positive" he had not seen the man in 1937, although it was "conceivable and possible" that he might have. But Hiss insisted he had never met Crosley at the 30th Street house in which he had lived from June 1936.

Nixon asked caustically whether the witness meant to imply that Chambers, if indeed he had been "George Crosley," had charged Hiss with Communist ties because of an unpaid debt of approximately $150. Such a trivial obligation, Hiss countered, could not "possibly motivate any normal person to make such a charge." Hiss stressed the word "normal," and—before stepping down—at Nixon's insistence, he gave the various sources of rumors he had heard about Chambers's alleged mental instability.

The day had gone badly for Hiss, and Chambers's testimony that afternoon, which also covered familiar ground, reinforced his difficulties. The two principals, by this time, had completely reversed their earlier roles before the committee. Hiss's performance had been nervous and emotional, while Chambers now appeared relaxed, calmly answering the questions put to him. Under Stripling's gentle prodding, he reviewed his career as a Communist, both in the "open" Party and in the underground before defecting "in early 1938." Stating that he had met Hiss while in the underground "a number of times . . . let's say

20 times" during a period that began "probably in 1934" and continued until 1938, Chambers denied that he had sublet Hiss's 28th Street apartment. "There was no talk of a sublease," he insisted; Hiss had merely suggested that he use the apartment.[77]

Chambers termed Hiss a "devoted and at that time a rather romantic Communist" because of his willingness to violate the traditional separation between secret and open Communist parties in the Ford transaction. Chambers asserted, with some exaggeration, that he had seen Hiss "constantly" in 1936 and 1937—actually, he remembered only twenty meetings overall between 1934 and 1938—and maintained further that he had stayed at Hiss's home overnight several times during this period.

Describing in detail his final visit to the Hiss household in December 1938 to try and persuade Hiss to leave the Communist underground, Chambers called Hiss "the closest friend I ever had in the Communist Party."* When Nixon asked about his reasons for testifying against Hiss, Chambers provided this melancholic explanation:

> The story has spread that in testifying against Mr. Hiss, I am working out some old grudge, or motives of revenge or hatred. I do not hate Mr. Hiss. We were close friends, but we are caught in a tragedy of history. Mr. Hiss represents the concealed enemy against which we are all fighting, and I am fighting. I have testified against him with remorse and pity, but in a moment of history in which this Nation now stands, so help me God, I could not do otherwise.

He then identified a photograph of J. Peters, whom he told of seeing for the last time "shortly before I broke. It was in the early 1938 period." Hébert asked, finally, whether he had any motives for lying about Hiss. Chambers denied that he had any, pointing out that he was "jeopardizing . . . not just my position on *Time* . . . [but] my position in the community" through appearing before HUAC. He called Hiss's testimony "80 percent at least fabrication."

Shortly before the nine-and-one-half-hour session adjourned, Chambers tried to explain the appeal that Communism held for educated people such as himself and Hiss during the Depression decade:

> Marxism, Leninism offers an oversimplified explanation of the causes [of world economic crisis] and a program for action. The very vigor of the project particularly appeals to the more or less sheltered middle-class intellectuals, who feel that there the whole context of their lives has kept them away from the world of reality.[78]

---

*Although this claim may have revealed more about the loneliness of Whittaker Chambers's underground life than about his intimacy with the Hisses, there is substantial evidence to support Chambers's claim that the two couples enjoyed a close, ongoing relationship in 1937 and 1938.

AUGUST 26: THE MYSTERIOUS FORD

The following day, August 26, the committee held an executive session to question William Rosen, first of ten witnesses to be subpoenaed over the next two weeks in an effort to clarify the circumstances surrounding the 1936 Ford transfer. Rosen, sixty-four years old in 1948, ran a small dry-cleaning shop in the District of Columbia and said he had lived there only since 1941. He claimed to have resided in New York City in 1936 but pleaded the Fifth Amendment when asked whether he had ever visited Washington that year. A subsequent witness, Irvin Farrell, said that Rosen and his wife had run a dry-cleaning store in Washington in 1935 and 1936, a shop Farrell patronized. But Rosen would not respond to questions about possible Communist affiliations or his knowledge of the Ford transfer.*[79]

Stripling asked the witness how the purchase of a 1929 automobile could possibly incriminate him, and Rosen answered: "It might bring out something else and it may involve me in answers that might incriminate me after." He declined to state if he had been a Communist organizer in 1936 but did not claim his privilege when asked if he knew J. Peters: "Never heard of him, never seen him, don't know him." Rosen also testified that he had never met Alger Hiss, although such a meeting had not been the point at issue in the Ford transfer. The witness refused to say whether he knew Benjamin Bialek, whom the committee suspected of having arranged the 1936 transaction.

After a Labor Day recess, Addie Rosen stated that she did know Bialek, although she disclaimed any close relationship. Rosen denied that her husband had been in Washington in 1936, that he had ever purchased an auto from Cherner, or that he had ever owned a 1929 roadster. She denied knowing anything about the Ford transfer. Stripling had come prepared with data that seemed to confirm Mrs. Rosen's Communist Party membership, but the witness declined to answer any questions on the subject.

Next day, Rosen—the threat of a contempt citation hanging plainly over him—decided to answer some questions about which he had previously refused to testify. He acknowledged now a distant acquaintanceship with Benjamin Bialek but still declared he had not been in Washington in 1936. Admitting to

---

*The committee advised a subsequent witness, Henry Cherner, a former partner in Cherner Motors, that their handwriting experts were "pretty certain" he had written Rosen's name on the title transfer. Cherner denied this, but admitted: "I have had people sign titles and then I would fill the address in. I have done that many a time. Whether I did it in this particular case, I wouldn't say." He said he did not know William Rosen and stressed that the signature on the Ford title certificate was not his. HUAC, I, pp. 1319–28; see also pp. 1227–29 for Henry Cherner's earlier testimony.

CP membership from 1923 to 1929, Rosen said he had not been a Communist in 1936 but refused to answer whether or not he was still a party member. Nor would he say if he knew anything about the 1936 Ford transaction except that "this thing" had already "ruined my life, has ruined my livelihood, has ruined me." Although he asserted that no one from the Communist Party had "instructed" him to testify, Rosen refused to say whether Baltimore Party officials had contacted him concerning his August 26 appearance before HUAC.[80]

Although the complete story of the Ford transaction will probably never be known, Rosen's lawyer spelled out the essential details for the benefit of one of Hiss's attorneys during a remarkably candid meeting on March 9, 1949. In a memorandum filed that day, Edward G. McLean wrote:

> Emmanuel Bloch, attorney for William Rosen,* told me the following [facts] today. Rosen does not know Hiss. Rosen did lend himself to a dummy transaction concerning the Ford car. Apparently Rosen did not sign the title certificate dated July 23, 1936. It is not clear whether Rosen knew at that time that his name would be used in this transaction. However, at some later date, a man came to see Rosen and told him that the title certificate to the Ford was in Rosen's name and asked Rosen to sign an assignment of it to some other person. Rosen did this. The man who came to see Rosen is a very high Communist. His name would be a sensation in this case. The man who ultimately got the car is also a Communist. Bloch implied that Rosen was a Communist too but did not say so expressly.[81]

McLean's memo tends to verify Chambers's account of how the 1929 Ford roadster with the "sassy little trunk" left Alger Hiss's ownership to be transferred by "a very high Communist" (J. Peters?) to another party member. It cannot be established beyond doubt that Hiss knew of the Ford's ultimate destination while signing the title transfer. But his claim to have disposed of the automobile in mid-1935 as part of the 28th Street apartment "sublease" remains as improbable today as it was in its first telling.

AUGUST 27: THE HISS-CHAMBERS FARM

The HUAC hearings took still another surprising turn two days after the public confrontation. The Baltimore *News-Post* published on August 27 an account of real-estate transactions surrounding Chambers's purchase in 1937 of thirty-eight acres and a dilapidated farmhouse near Westminster, Maryland. A year before, in 1936, Alger and Priscilla Hiss had signed a bill of sale to buy that same property.

---

*Bloch, later widely known as attorney for Julius and Ethel Rosenberg, also represented J. Peters for a time in 1948.

The *News-Post* carried long accounts of the Carroll County farmhouse, which had been known in 1936 as "the Shaw place" after the owner, who died that year. The newspaper quoted from the correspondence exchanged by Edward W. Case, a real-estate agent involved in both transactions, separately, with the Hisses and Chambers. After Stripling and Nixon heard rumors of the dramatic development from *News-Post* reporters, a HUAC investigator rushed to Case's Westminster office to subpoena the correspondence. By the time agents from the FBI's Washington field office reached Case several days later, only two letters on the negotiations remained in his files, both inadvertently held back from HUAC's Appell.[82]

That night, Nixon's subcommittee asked Chambers about the Westminster farm. Although his memory was fuzzy about some of the details regarding Hiss's interest in the property, Chambers confirmed the basic outline of the *News-Post*'s account. "Mr. Hiss and I had talked about how much each of us would like to have a small place in the country somewhere," Chambers stated. Sometime soon after this conversation (Chambers could not recall the date) Hiss spotted Case's advertisement of the Shaw place, went to inspect it, and made a down payment or deposit:

> He then at some time took Mrs. Hiss up there, and Mrs. Hiss did not like the place and did not like the countryside. I heard her say . . . some such expression like "a nasty, narrow valley." . . . Then, Hiss called off his arrangement with the realtor. Then, some time later, according to my recollection almost a year, but I could be mistaken, I appeared on the scene; that is, I got in touch with Case—I left out an important thing—I made one trip up there with Alger Hiss . . . and saw this place.

They drove there in the 1929 Ford, according to Chambers, which would have meant that the trip took place prior to July 1936. But he did not stay overnight in Westminster with Hiss and did not meet Edward Case that day. Since the farmhouse front door required only a skeleton key to open (Case later said he had probably given Hiss a key in exchange for the deposit), such an encounter was unnecessary. Chambers remembered meeting Case for the first time "a good deal later" when he himself went to inspect farm properties, long after Hiss had withdrawn his deposit. Hiss did not know Chambers had purchased the Shaw place: "I did not want him to know it, because I bought the house under my name, and didn't want him to know my real name."

Such behavior puzzled the subcommittee, and, somewhat exasperated, Chambers lectured them briefly on the nature of underground work:

> Americans are not conspiratorial by nature and tradition, and they cannot understand how conspirators work. Now this whole set-up here [in the 1930s] was conspiratorial. 1 . . . I had two compartments, Whittaker Chambers on one side, which is my more or less private compartment, and Carl in these

[Communist] groups here, and I did not want to make any bridge between them. . . .[83]

Chambers thought the realtor had shown him several other Westminster properties before bringing him to the Shaw place. This would suggest an unconscious irony in his having bought the very farm earlier rejected by Hiss. But Case's files indicate that Chambers set out to buy the Shaw place. Thus Chambers's own version of these events was far less helpful to his general claim of close friendship with Hiss, as seen through their mutual knowledge of a specific Maryland farm, than the Case documents themselves.

Chambers's basic story squared with the facts of the two Westminster sales as unearthed by the *News-Post,* and it proved far more accurate than Priscilla Hiss's when she reacted to the press accounts. "Mrs. Hiss does not recall this transaction," a Hiss lawyer observed in a memorandum written at the time. "She has frequently looked at old farms in various parts of the country but never bought any. She does not recall signing the contract to buy this one but recognized the picture of her signature on the contract in the newspaper."*[84]

Priscilla Hiss in fact had initiated the Westminster transaction herself with a November 1935 letter to Edward Case. The realtor's records showed that the Hisses did not pursue the inquiry until April 4, 1936, when Alger drove to Westminster to see the Shaw place. After an exchange of letters with Case, Hiss returned—this time with Priscilla—on April 13, when they left a $20 deposit. That same day Hiss wrote Case, enclosing both a signed buy-and-sell agreement to purchase the property for $650 and a check for an additional $100, the agreed-upon down payment. In the weeks that followed, Hiss wrote several additional letters to the realtor as it became clear that Case was having problems clearing title to the property because of Mrs. Shaw's heirs' reluctance to sell for $650.

If Chambers did visit the farm with Hiss, it would probably have been sometime in mid-April. Hiss's letters to Case indicate he made additional trips to the property during this period, and on at least one of these, Hiss expressly noted that he did not see Case.[85]

In late April, Case informed Hiss that Mrs. Shaw's sister, a Mrs. Shirkey, executrix of the estate, refused to sell the property for less than $850, and Hiss expressed his disappointment at the news in an April 25 letter. After determining that Shirkey would not reduce her demands, he wrote Case again on May 13 asking for return of his $120 deposit: "I am not interested in the higher figure." A final letter from Hiss to Case on May 28, 1936—"I am not interested in the Shirkey place at this time"—confirmed this decision. Once again Hiss asked that Case refund the deposit money and "terminate the negotiations completely."

---

*Neither the committee nor the press knew of Mrs. Hiss's flawed memories of the farm purchase at the time.

The letter also bore indications that Hiss had paid unsupervised visits to the farmhouse. Case delayed returning Hiss's deposit until July 14, 1936—and then refunded only $100, for reasons that remain unclear.

There the matter rested until the following February, when Case received a letter from Chambers inquiring about a property remarkably similar to the "Shirkey place." The letter carries the date February 3, 1936, but since Case had no recollection of meeting Chambers before the Hiss negotiation had fallen through, the letter was probably misdated, a conclusion accepted by all parties in 1948: Hiss's lawyers, the FBI, newsmen, HUAC staff members, Chambers, and Case. A September 10, 1948, FBI report stated that the February 3 letter "indicates that Chambers may have had some prior knowledge of the Shaw Place prior to the time he actually wrote this letter," and the 1937 document suggests familiarity with "the house, the purchase price and the locale" of Hiss's abortive farm purchase. It was addressed to Case and signed "J. W. Chambers, c/o Reuben Shemitz, Attorney" (Esther Chambers's brother), giving Shemitz's New York place of business as its return address.

The realtor answered later that month, and a February 26, 1937, notepad entry indicated that he had heard from Chambers again, by which time Case had already mentioned to Chambers the Shaw/Shirkey place. Case's notation was scribbled on an October 9, 1936, standard desk-pad page (presumably used for scrap notes by then), and it read in its entirety:

> Feb. 26. Jay Chambers
> 3310 Auchentoroly Terrace about 10 a. [acres] $650, to be out next week
> Pd Alger Hiss $100.00 refund on Deposit Pd. by him on the I. Estella
> Shaw Place
> July 14, 1936—by
> Edward W. Case

Chambers moved to his Auchentoroly Terrace apartment in Baltimore during the fall of 1936, providing further confirmation for dating this memo in 1937. Moreover, Case's reference to returning Hiss's deposit on the Shaw place the previous July linked on the same memo to "Jay Chambers's" impending visit suggested that the realtor intended showing the same place to his new customer. Case's interview with the FBI in early September 1948 also indicated that Chambers had asked to see that identical property:

> Continuing, Case stated that . . . on March 12, 1937 Chambers appeared at his office in Westminster, driving "an old brown car." Chambers and Case thereafter went to the Shaw property that same day, returned to Case's office, at which time an Agreement of Sale was drawn up. Case made available his cashbook which contains the following notations:
> "March 12, 1937, sale of Shaw place, $40." (deposit)
> "April 10, 1937. Mr. Chambers acc. Place, $285."

The last entry actually referred to *Esther* Chambers having paid Case $285 toward the total purchase price of $650 (apparently the owners had backed down by then from their earlier demand for $850). Mrs. Chambers served as the legal purchaser of the Westminster farm, a logical step, since Whittaker intended to resume his underground work and pseudonym once the farm had been bought. The sequence of events strongly suggests that Chambers had seen the Shaw place prior to his March 1937 visit.[86]

The Hisses went to Westminster in mid-October 1948 at the insistence of their attorney. They chatted amicably with Edward Case but learned little new, although they did pay a visit to the farmhouse. Their reactions to the home once purchased by their nemesis (the Chambers family had moved to a larger farm in the area) echoed in an uncanny way the couple's initial response to Chambers himself: "Various changes have been made: a brick wall under the porch, a new chimney, some imitation brick siding. Mrs. Hiss could not remember it. Mr. Hiss found the view and something about the porch familiar."[87]

AUGUST 27: THE JUDGMENT

When the Westminster farm story broke, Nixon and his HUAC colleagues were preparing to leave Washington for fall campaigning. Before the committee disbanded, it published on August 27 an "interim report" on the Bentley-Chambers spy probe—along with the transcripts of both executive- and open-session testimony—under the title *Hearings Regarding Communist Espionage in the United States Government.* The report summarized the testimony of its two star witnesses on Communist infiltration into the federal government and concluded with HUAC's obligatory denunciation of the White House and the attorney general for refusing to cooperate with its inquiries.[88]

But the document's marrow consisted of a long section entitled "Hiss-Chambers Testimony," which termed Hiss's testimony as "vague and evasive" and Chambers's as "forthright and emphatic." HUAC left little doubt as to credibility: "The verifiable portions of Chambers's testimony have stood up strongly; the verifiable portions of Hiss's testimony have been badly shaken." Hiss's unpersuasive recollections concerning the Ford transactions were particularly damaging, in the committee's view, and raised doubts "as to other portions of his testimony." The committee concluded that Hiss "was not completely forthright" in testifying at first that he could not recognize Chambers (Crosley) from photographs on August 5. Furthermore, he could not have associated with Harold Ware, Nathan Witt, John Abt, Henry Collins, Lee Pressman, and Whittaker Chambers—"all of whom are either known or admitted members of the Communist Party"—without suspecting their affiliation. In short, "the burden is upon Hiss to establish that . . .

[he] knew Crosley as a free-lance writer rather than as the admitted Communist functionary, which Chambers actually was during that period."

The month of headlines surrounding the Hiss-Chambers probe had restored much luster to the committee's public reputation. A Gallup poll in September 1948 showed that four out of five Americans approved HUAC's latest espionage inquiry and felt it should be continued. President Truman's "red herring" charge did not apparently find much support among voters, since a comparable majority—three out of every four (including 71 percent of the Democrats surveyed)—believed that there was "something to these spy investigations" and that it was not "a case of playing politics." Important newspapers normally critical of HUAC—such as *The Washington Post, The New York Times,* and the New York *Herald Tribune*—agreed editorially that the Hiss-Chambers probe had produced significant unanswered questions.[89]

On August 27 Whittaker Chambers appeared on the radio program *Meet the Press.* His questioners displayed considerable skepticism about Chambers's accusations, and three of them—Lawrence E. Spivak, editor of *The American Mercury,* Tom Reynolds of the Chicago *Sun-Times,* and Edward Folliard of *The Washington Post*—seemed to favor Alger Hiss (Reynolds was a good friend). The fourth panelist was Nat Finney of Cowles Publications; James B. Reston of *The New York Times* served as moderator.

Folliard began with the pivotal question. He reminded Chambers that his HUAC testimony concerning Hiss had been privileged—"protected from lawsuits." Since Hiss had challenged his accuser to make the same charges publicly, Folliard asked: "Are you willing to say now that Alger Hiss is or ever was a Communist?" Chambers replied: "Alger Hiss was a Communist and may be now." Reynolds pointed out that these assertions were "quite useful . . . to the Republicans," and wondered if Chambers had any party affiliations. He did not.[90]

To Spivak's question of why the American public should believe his story as an ex-Communist when Communists are known to lie for their cause, Chambers responded: "I can simply try to produce facts which will on investigation stand up." Folliard wanted to know if he was prepared to go to court to defend these charges, to which Chambers observed laconically: "I do not think Mr. Hiss will sue me for slander or libel." Chambers was asked whether Hiss, as an alleged Communist, had committed overtly treasonous or disloyal acts, but he responded: "I am only prepared at this time to say he was a Communist." He reminded his interrogators that he had told the committee that Hiss and others in the underground group of government officials had been brought together not "for the purpose of espionage, but for the purpose of infiltrating the government and influencing government policy by getting Communists in key places." The network's aim was not espionage but policymaking, in short, "something very much more important than spying."

The interview with Chambers laid the groundwork for a slander or libel action by Hiss. Despite the latter's earlier urgent demands for such a public accusation, however, he did not take his adversary into court until late September. The delay in filing suit puzzled his partisans, delighted disbelievers, and allowed the conclusions of HUAC's August 1948 report to circulate unchallenged.

AUGUST 30: THE EVASIONS

The HUAC subcommittee experienced one final day of high drama that month when it resumed business on August 30 in New York City to hear two men: Alexander Stevens (alias J. Peters, etc., etc.), reputed chief of the American Communist underground, and former Assistant Secretary of State Adolf A. Berle. Stevens proved predictably uncooperative, while Berle responded to all questions. Yet each, for different reasons, told the committee less than he knew of the Hiss-Chambers affair: Both Peters, the Communist zealot, and Berle, the New Deal partisan, either evaded answering or distorted their testimony when confronting the subcommittee.

Immigration and Naturalization Service agents had been investigating Stevens for almost a year on the grounds that he had entered the United States illegally. "J. Peters," a small and chunky fifty-four-year-old man in a baggy suit, with wire-frame glasses, a huge shock of brown hair, and a mustache, would be aptly described in *Time* as a "Groucho Marx likeness." He then lived in the Bronx under the name "Isidore Boorstein." Peters had been arrested on October 8, 1947, charged with violating a 1918 statute for failing to list his Communist membership on the various applications for residence and other forms he submitted during several trips in and out of the United States between 1924 and 1939 (he never became an American citizen).[91]

Peters, who also used the name Joszef Peters, recalls that the FBI sent four agents to arrest him in 1947. He was released on $5,000 bond, and the INS probe of his activities proceeded slowly until Whittaker Chambers injected his name into the HUAC hearings. Only then did immigration agents intensify their investigation of the Hungarian-born Communist.

The witness declined to answer questions concerning the Communist Party, his use of aliases,* whether he had ever acted as a representative in the United States of the Communist International, whether he had participated in an underground apparatus in Washington during the 1930s aimed at infiltrating the federal government, or whether he knew Whittaker Chambers. Answering

---

*FBI laboratory analysis had verified the fact that "Alexander Stevens" had also signed a series of documents—including internal Communist Party memos—not only under that name but also as "Alexander Goldberger," "J. Peter," and "J. Peters." FBI Laboratory Report, August 27, 1948.

these questions, Peters avowed, "might degrade and incriminate me." Stripling then asked Chambers, who had been watching from another part of the room, to stand and confront the witness. Peters refused to state if he had known Chambers either under that name or as "Carl," if he had seen Chambers in Hiss's presence in Washington, or if he had ever met Chambers at Henry Collins's apartment from 1934 to 1938.[92]

Chambers said that he had met Peters first at the *Daily Worker* office in 1928. For his part, Peters would not say if he had known Hiss and then responded "Same answer" when read a catalogue of those named as Communists in the Bentley-Chambers hearings. He agreed that he knew Earl Browder but refused to admit that he had ever been in Washington. He declined to say whether he had furnished confidential government documents to Soviet agents, whether he knew William Rosen, or whether he knew anything about the transfer of Hiss's 1929 Ford.

After their first meeting Chambers saw Peters again in late 1932 or early 1933 when Max Bedacht, who recruited him for secret work, handed over the fledgling agent to Peters's direction. Describing the latter's close association with Harold Ware and the group of young government officials assembled by Ware in 1934, Chambers said that Peters had worked actively with the Washington Communist underground during the mid-thirties and, in the process, had come to Washington often. Peters, according to Chambers, had introduced him to every member of the secret cell, including Alger Hiss, whom he claimed to have met first in 1934 while in the company of Peters and Ware. Chambers repeated his earlier claim—apparently confirmed by William Rosen's attorney, Emmanuel Bloch—that Peters had arranged the transfer of Hiss's 1929 Ford to an "open Party" organizer in 1936.[93]

Portraying himself as a close associate of his superior's in their underground work, Chambers detailed various trips taken with Peters. In these meetings Peters had introduced to Soviet agents, including an operative named "Ewald"— a Latvian who was arrested in Russia in late 1937 during the Great Purge while traveling under two false American passports in the names "Robinson" and "Rubens." Chambers was alluding to a case that made headlines in the United States early in 1938, when Ewald's American-born wife was also arrested in Moscow and held on espionage charges along with her husband.* According to Chambers, Peters had been involved in obtaining spurious passports for the Rubenses and for other Communists. Also Peters had occasionally spoken in the 1934–35 period at meetings of the Washington underground apparatus (one key member of the Ware Group, Lee Pressman, subsequently confirmed this).

J. Peters remains one of the least-known and most intriguing figures in the history of American Communism, a gray eminence who held important posts

---

*The Robinson/Rubens case, which would figure significantly in the Hiss-Chambers conflict later that year, is described more fully in Chapters VII and IX.

for twenty-five years at both the "open" organizational level and in the party's "secret work." His widely used 1934 handbook, *The Communist Party: A Manual on Organization*, is still in print. Several witnesses at his deportation hearings, including the ex-Communist Louis Budenz, testified to Peters's great influence within the world Communist movement. Andrew Smith, a skilled worker who had moved to the Soviet Union in 1932, produced several letters of introduction written by Peters that year, certifying Smith's reliability as a CP member and signed "J. Peters, Acting Representative, CP USA, E.C.C.I." (The latter abbreviation stood for "Executive Committee, Communist International.") Several witnesses present at the time placed Peters at the Lenin School in Moscow, which trained underground agents for service elsewhere in the world.[94]

He went into partial eclipse during the Second World War, when Earl Browder tried to replace a separate Communist organization with a more broadly based antifascist coalition of leftist political forces within the United States. With Browder's downfall and expulsion from the party in 1946, old revolutionary stalwarts such as Peters regained importance within American Communism.

When I met him in Budapest in 1975, then in his eighties, Joszef Peters retained the charm and forcefulness that former Communist associates such as Chambers and Budenz recognized while testifying against him. David Dallin's account of *Soviet Espionage* described Peters as

> indefatigable . . . an outstanding leader, man of many aliases and a multitude of clandestine assignments, who remained at his American post from 1933 to 1941. His era was marked by great exploits [and] . . . [he was] the most active, energetic, and resourceful man in those obscure depths of the underground where Soviet espionage borders on American Communism.

After deportation from the United States in 1949, Peters went to Hungary. For many years he edited *The International Review*, the official Communist compendium of foreign press opinion. He was also a high official of the Hungarian State Publishing House, "in charge of books on international problems."[95]

Despite the heavy weight of available evidence, Peters insisted to me that he served in the United States only as an ordinary CP functionary and was never involved in "secret work." He said he never met Whittaker Chambers except possibly once early in the 1930s at the *New Masses* office. He also denied having been involved in Communist espionage in the United States, either as head of the entire underground or in any other capacity.

But Maxim Lieber, one of Chambers's closest friends and a sometime associate in the underground, identified Peters as "the head of the whole Communist espionage apparatus in this country." Not only Lieber but others who sympathized with Alger Hiss and exhibited no fondness for Whittaker Chambers in 1948 also confirmed Peters's participation in "secret work." Thus, although Peters also insisted that he had never met David Zabladowsky during the 1930s, the latter—whom Chambers knew from Columbia days—told a Senate subcommittee in 1952 that at Chambers's request he had delivered a message to Peters sometime in 1936, knowing that the latter was an espionage agent. Peters similarly denied having known Lee Pressman as a member of the Ware Group, although Pressman testified before HUAC in 1950 to several such encounters with Peters at cell meetings in 1933 and 1934.[96]

"Alexander Stevens" had guarded his knowledge of Chambers and the Communist spy networks behind a Fifth Amendment wall while testifying before the committee. Adolf A. Berle, Jr., who replaced Stevens in the witness chair, proved more voluble. But Berle's recollections of his 1939 meeting with Chambers and its aftermath were surprisingly inaccurate. A distinguished economist, lawyer, scholar, and coauthor (with Gardner Means) of the pathbreaking 1932 study *The Modern Corporation and Private Property,* Berle had been an original member of Roosevelt's New York "Brain Trust" before turning to diplomacy. He continued to serve FDR during the New Deal, becoming assistant secretary of state in 1938. Among Berle's other duties, Roosevelt assigned to him supervision of intelligence matters within the State Department and elsewhere in the government. For this reason the president's appointments secretary, Marvin McIntyre, had referred Isaac Don Levine to Berle when Levine (acting on Whittaker Chambers's behalf) sought an audience for Chambers with the president.

Berle's memory of his conversation with Chambers and Levine differed from their earlier testimony before the committee. Berle asked the group to excuse any "discrepancies in detail" between his version of that meeting and the previous accounts: "I am testifying from recollection about something that happened nine years ago . . . please lay it [any discrepancy] to faulty memory and not lack of desire to tell the story." (Actually, Berle kept a diary, which contained a long entry on the 1939 visit, and which he had every reason to consult before testifying.) Berle referred to his informant as "Whittaker K. Chambers"—apparently believing that the pseudonym "Karl," which Chambers had used throughout their talk, was actually the man's middle name. He did not think Levine had accompanied Chambers to the interview, "but that may be an absence of memory." He believed the visit took place in late August, not September 2, and confirmed that "Karl wished to disclose certain information about Communist activities in Washington."[97]

According to Berle, Karl said he had been "a member of the underground Communist group from 1934 to [the] end of 1937," after which he had defected and gone into hiding for a year "in fear of some sort of reprisal. . . . [He] was obviously under some emotional strain." Karl told him about the Communist Party's efforts "to develop a group of sympathizers" within the government, but there was never in his informant's story "any question of espionage. There was no espionage involved in it. He stated that their hope merely was to get some people who would be sympathetic to their point of view." To achieve this, Berle remembered, the CP's "sympathizers" within the New Deal had formed "a study group of some sort" to learn about Russia and Communism. Chambers, however, "did not make the direct statement that any of these men [Berle then specifically recalled mention of the names of Alger and Donald Hiss, Lee Pressman, and Nathan Witt] were members of the Communist Party." Berle had asked Chambers why he didn't go to the FBI with the information. "He didn't want to spend the rest of his life with this hanging around his neck," his guest had replied; "he wanted to tell the story, and then he wanted to disappear . . . and not do anything further about it."

Had Berle tried to verify Chambers's leads? Stripling asked. In reply, the diplomat noted that Pressman was out of the government by then and Witt's associations were well known—even in 1939. But he had inquired about "the two Hiss boys." Berle specifically remembered asking Dean Acheson about them "when Acheson became the Assistant Secretary of State and Alger Hiss became his executive assistant" (Acheson became assistant secretary in 1941, two years after Chambers's visit, and it was actually Donald Hiss who worked closely with Acheson in the department). Acheson told Berle that he had known the "Hiss boys" "from childhood and he could vouch for them absolutely." Also, Berle said, he checked with Justice Felix Frankfurter—date unmentioned—who gave them "an exactly similar endorsement."

Reminding Berle that HUAC's major interest in his testimony was the light it might shed on Alger Hiss's conduct at State, Stripling asked him if he had been "ever at any time suspicious of Mr. Hiss." Berle then conceded to having been "worried" and launched into a long explanation of his differences with "Mr. Acheson's group . . . with Mr. Hiss as his principal assistant" over what Berle felt was its "pro-Russian point of view." He admitted that these differences influenced his "biased view" of Hiss, since he (Berle) "got trimmed in the fight," was relieved as assistant secretary of state in late 1944, and was sent to Brazil as American Ambassador—he resigned the following year—which "ended [his] diplomatic career." Noting that pro-Russian sympathies within the government had not been unusual during the wartime period of Soviet-American alliance, Berle said, "Frankly, I still don't know whether this is the boy [Alger Hiss] that got in deep and then pulled clear, or what goes on here." In defense of the fact that he did not begin checking seriously on Chambers's allegations against the Hiss brothers until the United States had entered the Second World War, Berle insisted that "Chambers did not state to me that he [Hiss] was a member of the Communist Party; merely that this was a group that was hoping to be sympathetic; so that was all you had to go on."

THE BURLE MEETING

If accurate, Berle's testimony would obviously dampen considerably the over-heated climate of HUAC's investigation by suggesting to the committee, the press, and the public that Chambers's "revelations" in 1939 had been small pota-toes, hardly worth fussing over, and certainly nothing that involved the ques-tion of underground Communist Party cells capable of influencing government policy or committing espionage. But the FBI later produced a copy of Berle's 1939 memorandum on Chambers's visit, which he had retained for four years before sending it to the bureau in 1943.

His four-page series of notes, titled "Underground Espionage Agent," con-tradicted almost every specific point Berle made in his HUAC testimony.[98] It contained a list of individuals mentioned by "Karl" during their conversation, including major Communist espionage agents and underground government con-tacts as well as "sympathizers." The names included not only the Hiss brothers, Pressman, and Witt, but also J. Peters; Philip Rosenbliett (a leading New York underground Communist); Alexander Trachtenberg (a member of the American Communist Executive Committee); "Volkov" (the head of CP West Coast espi-onage operations); Harold Ware and other alleged members of his "group"— Frank Coe, John Abt, Jessica Smith, Charles Krivitsky, Marian Bachrach; and other names which had not yet been mentioned by Chambers but which would figure in the case shortly—Franklin Victor Reno (sometimes known as Vincent Reno) and Philip Reno, Elinor Nelson, Julian Wadleigh, Noel Field (named only briefly in August 1948), and Hedda Gumperz (Hede Massing). Laurence Duggan was described by Chambers in Berle's notes as a "Fellow Traveler," and Isaac Don Levine's notes on the meeting (but not Berle's) also record Henry Dexter White's name as one that entered the discussion.

Nor did Berle's 1939 memorandum describe a collection of Communist sym-pathizers casually connected in an innocuous "study group." It proceeded name by name, department by department, to show that Chambers had stressed actual espionage already committed rather than the mere possibility of future action or secret involvement with Communism. Terms such as "head of Underground Trade Union Group," "Underground connections," in "Underground Appara-tus," and similar references recurred in the notes, which described—among other things—the alleged theft of Navy plans for new "Super-battleships" as well as Vincent Reno's secret work with "Aerial bomb sight Detectors." Only when the FBI requested his memo in 1943, having learned about it during an interview with Chambers the previous year, did Berle provide a copy to the bureau. But he never filed the memo, before or afterward, with either State Department security officers or military intelligence agencies, despite its references to military espio-nage. The memo concluded with a section on the Hiss brothers that clashed with

Berle's 1948 testimony that "Karl" had described the pair merely as Communist Party "sympathizers," and with his subsequent casualness over confirming this information to HUAC

Donald Hiss
(Phillipine [sic] Adviser)
Member of C.P. with Pressman & Witt—
Labor Dep't.—Asst. to Frances Perkins—
Party wanted him there—to send him as arbitrator in Bridges trial—
Brought along by brother—

Alger Hiss
Ass't. to Sayre—CP—37
Member of the Underground Com.—Active
Baltimore boys—
Wife—Priscilla Hiss—Socialist—
Early days of New Deal

In his testimony to the HUAC subcommittee, Berle stated that he was testifying from memory alone, apparently suggesting (unpersuasively, for a man who kept well-ordered files) that he had not retained a copy of his 1939 memorandum. But there was also his diary, and the first entry after his visit with Levine and Chambers belied Berle's assertion to HUAC that he did not know Chambers had been a highly placed Communist espionage agent:

> Saturday night [September 2] I had, to me, a singularly unpleasant job. Isaac Don Levine in his contact with the Krivitsky matter* had opened up another idea of the Russian espionage. He brought a Mr. X around to my house. . . . Through a long evening, I slowly manipulated Mr. X to a point where he had told some of the ramifications hereabout; and it becomes necessary to take a few simple measures. I expect more of this kind of thing, later. A good deal of the Russian espionage was carried on by Jews; we know now that they are exchanging information with Berlin; and the Jewish units are furious to find out that they are, in substance, working for the Gestapo [Chambers and Levine had come to see Berle only days after the signing of the Nazi-Soviet Pact]. To bed at 1:00 AM.[99]

Berle's memory lapse was to some extent intentional. "I hope what I said was sedative," he confided to his friend (and Alger Hiss's onetime superior at the AAA) Judge Jerome Frank in a September 9, 1948, letter. "This was the intention but it is hard to get sanity into a super-charged emotional atmosphere. It seems the great question was not whether there was treason to the United States, but

---

*General Walter Krivitsky, a leading Western European agent for Soviet Military Intelligence, had defected the previous year and—through Levine and others—begun providing American and British authorities with information on Russian espionage rings in both countries.

whether Alger Hiss goes to heaven when he dies—and I cannot contribute anything to that decision."[100]

Having followed the case closely in the press, Berle expressed grave doubts privately, both in his diary and later to Hiss's attorneys, about the latter's veracity. The Hiss-Chambers confrontation on August 17 brought this response in a diary entry on September 3:

> My private opinion is that Hiss was pretty deep in something or other in the early days; nevertheless I am not prepared to think that he maintained these obligations after he got into a position of influence. In other words, he was not a traitor. The Committee hearings do seem to suggest that he is a liar—but this is a matter he can settle with St. Peter.

His major concern in 1948—at a time when Berle was a Liberal Party leader in New York working for Truman's election—was to defuse, if possible, the influence of anti-Communist sentiment and of the case itself in that election year. "I hated to appear to be in the 'red-baiting business,'" he noted when composing a diary entry on his HUAC testimony. Also Berle appeared to be settling old scores with his chief adversary at State, Dean Acheson, whom he believed instrumental in forcing his ouster as assistant secretary. Berle clearly tried to lay Alger Hiss at Acheson's doorstep, even though Donald—and not Alger—was the closer of the two to Acheson within the department. Furthermore, Berle's suggestion to HUAC that he had been purged by a pro-Soviet faction at State is a distortion of his differences with Acheson, who shared Berle's suspicions of the Russians' postwar intentions.[101]

Alger Hiss himself complained privately about the inaccuracies of Berle's account of State Department politics, thereby opening an inquiry that provided a suggestive footnote to the testimony. Historian James Shotwell, a trustee of the Carnegie Endowment and a fervent Hiss supporter, had taken over day-to-day administration of the Endowment, to allow Hiss more time to prepare his defense. After reading press accounts of Berle's testimony, Shotwell asked Hiss to prepare a document recording his positions within the State Department and elsewhere in the government. Hiss gave Shotwell, among other notes, a memorandum on his relations with Berle, correcting errors he had detected, including those previously mentioned about Berle's confusion of Alger and Donald Hiss when discussing Dean Acheson's assistant.

The most significant portion of Hiss's memo concerned its assertion that

> In January or February 1944, when I was about to be assigned to United Nations matters, Mr. Berle and his executive assistant, Mr. Fletcher Warren, now our Ambassador to Paraguay, invited me to join Mr. Berle's special staff working on intelligence matters. I declined because of my greater interest in United Nations work and because it was apparent to me that my superiors in the Department wanted me to do the United Nations work.[102]

The intelligence post involved, among other things, liaison between the State Department and both the FBI and military intelligence services. If Hiss recalled correctly, then Berle had by then quashed any suspicion of Hiss as a possible subversive, and the assistant secretary's failure to mention this to HUAC would be only one more instance of his "faulty memory."

Later that year William Marbury asked a friend, James Bruce, the American Ambassador to Argentina, to serve as an intermediary in raising the question with Warren, whose memory of the incident Marbury wished to check before consulting Berle directly. Bruce complied with Marbury's request and received, in turn, a letter from Fletcher Warren denying having made any such offer to Hiss. Berle also rejected Hiss's assertion.

Adolf Berle's difficulties with the Hiss case in 1948 derived from the perfunctory manner in which he had dealt with Chambers's information in 1939. Thus, according to Hiss, one of his wife's old engagement books showed that the Hisses "had dinner in the Berles' house . . . in November, 1939, a relatively few weeks after Chambers had told his lurid tale. There was certainly no difference in Mr. Berle's attitude on that occasion."[103]

The memorandum on Berle was only one of many such reports that Hiss prepared for his attorneys. He had begun gearing up to start legal action against Chambers, and almost daily he received information from friends and sympathizers—facts, rumors, and mixtures of the two—concerning his adversary's background. Even Hiss's friends agreed that his performance at the HUAC hearings had severely damaged his credibility and, therefore, his reputation. Keeping his job and avoiding indictment for perjury depended upon his ability to demonstrate his innocence satisfactorily.

As one part of this process, Hiss began collecting data on Chambers's past, much of which involved allegations of homosexuality, insanity, imposture, and criminal behavior. The sources varied widely and ranged from some of Chambers's old enemies at *Time* to such well-known journalists as Walter Lippmann and Joseph Alsop. Many New York, Boston, and Washington psychiatrists—according to Hiss's friends and contacts—were reported to have treated Chambers for mental disorders. Upon investigation, these rumors failed to produce much solid information, but they preoccupied the energies of Hiss's hired investigators and volunteer sleuths.[104]

Many of the gamiest stories came from within the Communist movement via Hiss's old friends Henry Collins and Lee Pressman, both of whom had collaborated with his lawyers from the time the HUAC hearings ended in early September. Later there would be even closer links between the Hiss defense and this circle. Thus when one of Hiss's attorneys approached J. Peters's lawyer, Carol Weiss King, seeking information from Peters, he was clearly taken aback by her response. The meeting with Mrs. King, which took place in January 1949, was duly recorded in a memo by a Hiss attorney, Harold Rosenwald:

She said that a liaison had been established between the proper persons and Hiss's attorneys and that the proper persons would let us know in due course whether any information would be forthcoming from Stevens [Peters]. I asked her whether she knew anything bearing upon the suspected homosexuality of Chambers. She said that we would get any information that might be forthcoming through the same channels. I told her that I was not aware of any such liaison between Hiss' attorneys and the Communist Party. She smiled knowingly and mysteriously and refused to be more specific in describing the so-called liaison arrangement. . . . She said that Hiss had been very foolish in his conduct toward the Government, first in having so vigorously denied that he knew Chambers. . . .[105]

Shortly after HUAC issued its interim report, Alger Hiss circulated a fourteen-page "open letter" to the committee. HUAC members had already begun leaving Washington for their home districts, persuaded that their work on the Hiss-Chambers inquiry was over. It was now up to the Justice Department or, if Hiss filed suit, the courts to determine who had committed perjury. Richard Nixon returned to Whittier in mid-September, where he faced no problems in the November election, having captured both the Democratic and Republican nominations for his district (a feat then possible under California's cross-filing system). But Nixon used the campaign to regale crowds with his version of the Hiss case, from initial testimony to final confrontation. Karl Mundt plunged into the South Dakota Senate race and, similarly, enjoyed unusual voter recognition for the committee's well-publicized August hearings (Mundt won easily in November). J. Parnell Thomas would soon have his own "case" to prepare as charges circulated during the campaign that he had received kickbacks from his staff (Thomas was subsequently indicted, convicted, and served nine months in jail).

An exciting four-way battle for the presidency had crowded the Hiss-Chambers case off the front pages by mid-September, and Hiss's supporters grew impatient awaiting his legal response to Chambers's *Meet the Press* interview. In this context, Hiss's fourteen-page "open letter" to HUAC can be understood as his "interim report" on the hearings—a reaction to the committee's August 27 document—and as a precursor to his lawsuit against Chambers. The letter assailed HUAC: "No American is safe from the imagination of such a man, so long as your committee uses the great powers and prestige of the United States Congress to help sworn traitors to besmirch any American they may pick upon."[106]

Describing Chambers as "a confessed traitor," "this character," "this self-same erratic," unstable, unreliable, and (at four points in the statement) "somewhat queer," Hiss contrasted his own unblemished record with Chambers's past "in the sewers, plotting against his native land, for thirteen years." He demanded due process: "The Anglo-Saxon method of ascertaining the truth has for centuries made use of the ancient rule of evidence that by their works shall ye know them." Hiss's denials were categorical: "I have [never] done the slightest thing

or said the slightest word to further Communism." He railed at the committee for its unwillingness to summon as character witnesses those with whom
he had worked in the government for over a decade to check his "credibility
and reliability" against that of Chambers, whom "preliminary inquiry shows [to
be] a man who is a combination of Guy Fawkes, the Mr. Hyde in Dr. Jekyll and
Mr. Hyde, and characters out of all the mystery and spy stories anybody ever
read." Once people understood the man in his various guises—"Mr. Carl-David-
George-Jay-John Chambers-Crosley-Kelly . . . and other aliases"—Hiss argued,
then Chambers's motives for slandering him would emerge.

Rarely has the issue of personal identity agitated the national political scene
so abruptly and with so great an impact. With each man insistent that candor
and full disclosure meant vindication for him, evidently the facts could not be
resolved satisfactorily until more was known about their public and private lives.
What had they done (or not done) together during the Depression decade?

II

ALGER AND WHITTAKER: THE CRUCIBLE OF FAMILY

Alger Hiss and Whittaker Chambers were born three years, two hundred miles, and a world apart. Both came from once prosperous families that had experienced financial and emotional reverses in their parents' lifetime. Both families lived in respectable but undistinguished neighborhoods—Chambers's in the Long Island town of Lynbrook and Hiss's in Baltimore. Both boys lacked strong paternal guidance in their younger days: Hiss's father died before Alger was three, and Chambers's father was separated from his wife and children for several years. A succession of suicides and other deaths in the Hiss and Chambers families afflicted the lives of both Alger and Whittaker as they grew to manhood.

The two boys responded differently to the respective disruptions in their family lives. Hiss, from the start, became an exemplary young man concerned with the approval of his peers and elders, later obtaining recognition and social standing. He achieved scholastic honors at Johns Hopkins and Harvard Law (aided by scholarships), was on the staff of the *Harvard Law Review,* and served as a clerk for Justice Holmes. At Harvard, Alger became a protégé of Professor Felix Frankfurter, who arranged the post with Holmes for the bright and deferential Hiss (whose brother, Donald, would later follow him both to Harvard Law and to a Holmes clerkship). Although the deaths of his older brother, Bosley, and his sister, Mary Ann, shook Hiss profoundly during the late 1920s, the first signs of rebellion against his Baltimore family and his own measured advance toward a conservative career in law came in 1929 while he was working for Justice Holmes. Unexpectedly, Alger married Priscilla Fansler Hobson, whose far more adventurous and socially conscious nature deeply affected Hiss's own latent sympathies for progressive causes (Hiss had been at Harvard during the campaign to save Sacco and Vanzetti from execution, a drive that Felix Frankfurter had helped lead). Hiss's mother disapproved of her son's decision to marry Priscilla, and, for reasons that remain unclear, Hiss changed earlier plans to practice law in Baltimore (he had taken the Maryland bar exam after graduating from Harvard). On short notice, he went instead to Boston, where he worked for a leading law firm.

In 1932 Hiss followed Priscilla to New York, settling into a job at another staid and conservative law firm in Manhattan. Thirteen million Americans were unemployed during the Depression winter of 1932–33, and the problems of the disadvantaged and dispossessed affected Alger and Priscilla deeply, all the more perhaps because of their own relatively comfortable exemption from the suffering. While Priscilla completed a book on the fine arts in America, Alger helped corporations untangle their legal problems with patents and antitrust legislation. The couple spent their nonwork hours involved in a variety of radical groups and causes. This double life continued for Hiss, defending corporations during the day while writing pro-labor articles for a radical lawyers' group at night, and for his wife until the spring of 1933, when they left for Washington after Alger accepted a post in the New Deal bureaucracy.

Both Hiss and Chambers struggled to achieve as young men. But while Alger sought approval assiduously and, for the most part, successfully, Whittaker rebelled and displayed a growing alienation from family and bourgeois values. At first, Chambers avoided the realities of his unstable family through absorption in books, particularly romantic novels such as those of Victor Hugo. But as he moved into adolescence, his vicarious delight in heroic fiction gave way increasingly to a desire to write his own adventures—and perhaps to experience a few. At Columbia College he became friendly with several aspiring writers and artists, among them Lionel Trilling, Clifton Fadiman, and Meyer Schapiro, but Chambers fled college after two years to begin a vagabond's *Wanderjahr*. After traveling across the country, he returned to Columbia in 1924, but left within a few months. By his own admission, the decision he made to join the Communist Party in 1925 seemed an expression of both personal bitterness and yearning for some believable scheme of values. Following the suicide of his brother, Richard, in 1926, Chambers spent months crippled by grief, only to plunge back into CP activities, more dedicated than before to the party's creed.

Throughout the 1920s Whittaker was involved in a series of love affairs with women and possibly in one homosexual relationship, in all cases with people who shared his radical beliefs. He served on the staff of *The Daily Worker* until 1929, when he drifted away from the CP in a controversy involving two leadership factions. He also gained a minor reputation in New York during these years as a skilled translator of German books (his translation of *Bambi* appeared in 1928) and as a poet.

He rejoined the Communist Party in 1931 after publishing several short stories in *The New Masses* that proved popular among radicals. That same year Chambers became an editor of the magazine and married a young socialist artist, a quiet and demure woman named Esther Shemitz, who tempered some of his flamboyant affectations. Chambers left *The New Masses* in late 1932, after having been recruited for the Communist underground.

The Hisses and the Chamberses lived in New York City during that worst year of Depression and despair, but did not meet until 1934. Even in 1932, however, the lives of Communist activists such as Whittaker and Esther Chambers and of liberals sympathetic to the CP had begun intersecting. For both Alger Hiss and Whittaker Chambers, the road to Union Square—where in 1932 Chambers edited *The New Masses* while the Hisses attended lectures at the socialist Rand School—commenced in a series of sometimes tragic family experiences that neither man had absorbed entirely.

Marriage to Esther Shemitz represented for Whittaker the start of a recommitment to the integrity of his own family, or what was left of it—wife, mother, and, shortly, children—although it would be a decade before he managed to discipline the homosexual urges that disrupted his adolescence and early manhood. Hiss's marriage had a similarly remodeling effect upon Alger's personality. Just as Esther imposed a measure of order upon Whittaker's unruly disposition, Priscilla Hiss brought to bear a degree of idealistic adventurousness upon her husband's rigidly disciplined and calculated ambitiousness. The mixture proved beneficial to both marriages, and it laid the groundwork for the relationship that would evolve two years later between these two dissimilar individuals, Alger Hiss and Whittaker Chambers.

"STRIVE AND SUCCEED": THE EARLY LIFE OF ALGER HISS

"I was born on November 11, 1904, in Baltimore, Maryland," begins the series of "autobiographical notes" Alger Hiss prepared for his attorneys in 1948. "My father died when I was about three, leaving my mother to bring up a family of five children—three boys and two girls, all of whom were older than I except my brother Donald who is two years my junior." The facts are there—but only barely. His father, Charles Alger Hiss, killed himself by cutting his throat with a razor on April 7, 1907, at his Linden Avenue home. Charles Hiss, formerly a Baltimore dry-goods importer and jobber, was then forty-two, out of work, and burdened with the support not only of his own wife and children but also of his deceased brother's six children, whom Charles had helped financially until suffering his own reverses.[1]

Alger, who was two and a half at the time, knew nothing about the manner of his father's death until he was a teenager, but overnight his closely knit family became matriarchal and extended. Although Charles's more successful brother George, a cotton manufacturer in North Carolina, sent some money, the day-to-day management of the Hiss children came under the supervision of Charles's sister Eliza (Lila), who moved into the household. Other aunts, uncles, and cousins assisted over the years, with Alger Hiss's mother, Mary, known to her family and friends as "Minnie," technically but seldom actually in charge.

Minnie Hiss was devoted to her children but also to club meetings, belonging to many of Baltimore's civic and women's groups, and sandwiching in her parental obligations with the help of Aunt Lila and a cook. Hiss later described the type of household his mother ran, apparently long on domestic efficiency and spurs to achievement while somewhat bereft of warmth: "My mother's energy was fantastic. She did run the house well and checked on our clothes, manners, health, and eating habits as thoroughly as if she did naught else. . . . She was definitely a good manager. We always had a cook but Mother supervised the shopping, the choice of menus, and the preparation of meals." And one of Hiss's biographers learned about Minnie that "[s]he urged [her children] to exhibit their virtues, talents, and knowledge, and to be nice and especially pleasant to important people. For years in advance she planned their college education."[2]

Whittaker Chambers later recalled Alger telling him that "his relations with his mother were affectionate but not too happy. She was, perhaps, domineering."* Hiss's complaint over Chambers's characterization of Minnie only served to confirm it: "My relations with my mother have always been close and cordial." Hiss would later recall a happy and active "family environment," filled with the socializing of his siblings: "Friends of my older sisters and of my older brother [Bosley] were frequently in the house. Both my sisters and my older brother were musical and my older brother, in particular, was a specially gifted and charming person with great interest in literature. I have always read a great deal since my very early days and was no doubt encouraged in this way by my brother's interests and tastes."[3]

During the summers the Hisses vacationed at an aunt's home on Maryland's Eastern Shore—"a three-hundred-acre place with an old house built when the farm was subdivided early in the nineteenth century." While there, "Donald and I . . . lived the lives of boys on a farm, with all that that implies. At about thirteen or fourteen years of age I went to a boys' camp in Maine for two summers (where I first met Henry Collins, a fellow-camper). Right up until my marriage, however, I continued to pay regular visits to my Aunt's place and spent several summers there while at college or law school."†

Under Minnie's and Aunt Lila's ministerings, Hiss led an extremely sheltered and happy childhood. He attended the Episcopal church, went to the Baltimore public schools, and, after graduating from high school and spending an additional

---

*William Marbury also recalls Minnie Hiss as "a domineering type." Interview, February 24, 1975.

†"Alger Hiss was the child of shabby gentility," Murray Kempton wrote, "and he and his mother made the best use of it they could. The Hisses were not a distinguished family run down. In his final tragedy, his friends and enemies would join in exaggerating the nobility of his origins. When disaster came to him, he was listed in the Washington Social Register, but his mother was not in its Baltimore edition. . . . They were not a family of special social prestige, but the Baltimore in which Alger Hiss grew up was still enough of a Southern city . . . [so that] in the circumstances of her life, society felt a particular sympathy for Alger Hiss's mother; among the shabby-genteel, the women tend to be stronger than the men; the average runs alarmingly toward widows with promising sons. . . . And Alger Hiss appears to have been the sort of boy who made a special impression on older people, and for the very good reason that he deserved to." Part of Our Time . . . (New York: Dell, 1967, paperback ed.), p. 17.

year (1921–22) at Powder Point Academy in Duxbury Massachusetts, entered Johns Hopkins, from which his brother Bosley previously had graduated. "As a youngster I attended Sunday School regularly," Hiss chronicled in 1948,

> and the children always accompanied Mother to church. Bill Marbury's family sat in the pew behind us. I was a member of the Boy Scout troop. . . . At college I acted as assistant scout master for my own church's troop. . . . In the past couple of weeks the present Rector of my old church took occasion to inform the congregation that the records of the church showed the public service which I had rendered in Sunday School and Scout work."[4]

The years at Johns Hopkins continued Hiss's unbroken record of moral excellence, social approbation, and overall achievement. Again in his description of his years at Hopkins (he was in the class of 1926):

> . . . I participated rather fully in student activities, being editor of the college newspaper, president of the dramatic club, and president of the Student Council. I was also on the track squad where I was an indifferent quarter-miler. I was in the ROTC all four years and in my senior year was the cadet commander. As our family financial resources were moderate I applied for and received scholarships each year at college and [later] at law school. I was elected a member of Phi Beta Kappa and the Tudor and Stuart Club [a prestigious Hopkins society].

"Alger was almost universally admired from the beginning of his college career," recalled William Marbury. "It was said at Johns Hopkins that 'Alger had a mortgage on Gilman Hall [the Administration building].'" Other than his "indifferent" stint at track, Hiss left behind him a string of academic and extracurricular successes at Hopkins. Alger's first and only known personal failure of any consequence during these years had actually come the year before he graduated: his unsuccessful courtship of a pretty and vivacious Bryn Mawr graduate, Priscilla Fansler.[5]

They had met on board a ship headed for Europe in June 1924—Alger was nineteen and Priscilla a year older—and saw a great deal of each other in London at the start of their tours and in September, before returning home. During that summer Priscilla toured England while Hiss wandered through France with a friend. He later recalled having been extremely fond of Priscilla and protective toward her that summer, according to his biographer, although the interlude apparently made far less of an impression upon her.

While Hiss returned to his junior year at Hopkins that fall, Priscilla began graduate studies in literature at Yale. They corresponded, and the following Easter she visited friends in Baltimore who also knew the Hisses. At some point during this visit, according to Hiss, Priscilla told him that she was engaged to Thayer Hobson, a fellow graduate student at Yale, who later became a New York publisher. An oft-told and well-known story among Hiss's friends concerned the time during this period that Alger and Priscilla supposedly traveled all night back and forth on the ferry between New York City and Hoboken—Hiss having journeyed up from Hopkins—while Alger tried (and failed) to persuade her not to marry Hobson. Hiss caught pneumonia soon after this, according to William Marbury, apparently from the evening chill.[6]

But Hiss rebounded quickly, becoming engaged to a graduate student at Hopkins for a time but breaking off the relationship during his first year at Harvard Law. After Priscilla's marriage during the summer of 1925, the Hobsons moved to New York, where she gave birth to a son, Timothy, on September 19, 1926. Shortly after that, the couple separated. For two years Priscilla worked for a new weekly newsmagazine named *Time* as "office manager," editing copy and helping to run the office staff. She left in 1928 to resume graduate work in literature and received an M.A. from Columbia in the summer of 1929.[7]

In later years Hiss credited his entrance into law school to the advice of a family friend, who counseled law as an avenue toward a career in diplomacy. Whatever interest in the foreign service Hiss might have brought to Harvard quickly became sidetracked, and his letters from the period discuss his ambition to practice law in large private firms—as well as other goals—while remaining silent on diplomacy. Thus he wrote his Harvard mentor, Felix Frankfurter, in 1930: "A phrase in a recent letter of yours about academicians taps a strong current in me. After four or five years of [private] practice I should like most seriously to consider teaching, assuming I were given the offer."

At Harvard, Hiss was academically and socially prominent. During his second year he won election to *Law Review* (on which he served for two years) and became a member of Lincoln's Inn, the eating club.* A number of his colleagues on *Law Review* later became friends—Richard Field, Edward McLean, Harold Rosenwald, and Lee Pressman among them.† His years at Harvard, Hiss later felt, had broadened his attitudes toward people, albeit with an inescapable self-consciousness:

> Ideologically I was at college rather a snob, socially and intellectually [he later told Meyer Zeligs]. I had already at Johns Hopkins lost the somewhat anti-Semitic snobbishness of my mother's background and outlook. I had good friends at Hopkins who were Jewish. I had many Jewish friends. I worked on the *Law Review* with a Negro student without any feeling on my part.[8]

Among his Jewish friends was the teacher to whom he became closest, Felix Frankfurter, who, along with Lee Pressman, helped turn Hiss's interest toward labor law (Hiss contributed to a *Law Review* "Note" on the constitutionality of

---

*His teachers at Harvard included not only Frankfurter but Francis B. Sayre, under whom Hiss would serve in the State Department.

†The first three worked on Hiss's defense at the time of the case.

"yellow-dog contracts"). Pressman recalled for Murray Kempton those years at Harvard when the two fellow members of *Law Review* became friends:

> I remember Alger Hiss best of all for a kind of distinction that had to be seen to be believed. If he were standing at the bar with the British Ambassador and you were told to give a package to the Ambassador's valet, you would give it to the Ambassador before you gave it to Alger.
>
> He gave you a sense of absolute command and absolute grace and I think Felix felt it more than anyone. He seemed to have a kind of awe for Alger.[9]

Hiss became Frankfurter's protégé at the height of the professor's and his wife, Marion's, efforts to save Sacco and Vanzetti. Mrs. Frankfurter later edited the two doomed men's letters for publication, and Felix wrote a widely cited book arguing that they had been unfairly convicted and were probably innocent. Despite the enormous campaign mounted by their defenders, Sacco and Vanzetti were executed in August 1927. Oddly, Hiss never commented publicly on the impact of the case upon his own evolving social convictions.*

Shortly after Hiss arrived at Harvard in September 1926, his older brother died, an event that deeply affected Alger. Bosley Hiss had worked as a reporter for the *Baltimore Sun* while Alger studied at Hopkins. Bosley rebelled against the tight, straitlaced Victorian moral code to which Alger and the other Hisses— under Minnie's tutelage—subscribed:

> . . . I have always considered that I learned even more from Bosley's mistakes in the area of emotional judgment [Hiss informed Zeligs]. He was undisciplined in habits of sleep, diet, and drink and was to my mind too casual in sexual matters. I thought I could see the injury he brought to himself or was storing up and suspected that he was hurting others. His close cronies were more glaring examples of frivolous and destructively living young men.[10]

In 1923 Bosley had contracted a degenerative kidney ailment, Bright's disease, malignant and crippling. He remained an invalid in Baltimore for a time, quarreled with his mother, and left Linden Avenue for the Rye, New York, home of a friend, Margaret Owen, a woman twenty years older, who married him as his death approached.

Under these circumstances, with Bosley and Minnie still estranged, Alger came to live with and nurse his brother at Rye during the summer of 1926, between his Hopkins graduation and his entrance into Harvard. "My stay was a family arrangement," Hiss recalls. "I was and regarded myself as the family's deputed representative sent to help one of us who needed just the kind of practical aid I was qualified to supply. I reported regularly to them by letter an account

---

*Nor, although they mention the event, did Hiss's biographers ask for his reaction. For the impact of the Sacco-Vanzetti case on the radical development of Hiss's friend Noel Field, see Chapter VI.

of my stewardship." After settling in at Harvard for the year, Hiss received a call from Margaret in late October reporting Bosley's further deterioration. Alger rushed down to Rye to resume his "stewardship," this time accompanied by his sister Mary Ann, who lived in Boston with her husband. Donald and Minnie hurried up from Baltimore, and with his family at his bedside Bosley died on November 3, 1926. "His charm and precocious talents were enhanced and frozen by his lingering illness and early death," Alger later reminisced. "To this extent he became, after his death, somewhat 'legendary.'"

The years at Harvard were bridged by tragedy for Hiss: Bosley's death at the beginning and the suicide of his sister Mary Ann (Mrs. Elliot Emerson) only weeks before his graduation. Minnie Hiss had encouraged her girls to seek marriages with successful and socially prominent "catches," just as she had spurred her boys on to fame and achievement in their own names.

After graduating from Smith College in 1920, Mary Ann married a Bostonian seventeen years her senior. A wealthy member of a distinguished family, Elliot Emerson lost most of his money early in the 1920s and spent the rest of the decade trying to recover it, borrowing from Mary Ann's family (among others) in the process. These futile efforts and other marital tensions led to periodic separations, and to Mrs. Emerson's suffering two long periods of acute depression and several shorter stays in private mental sanitoriums. Despite frequent visits to the Emersons during his three years at Harvard, Alger later stated that he knew nothing about his sister's mental illness or about her having been institutionalized. To him, Mary Ann's suicide came as "a sudden, irrational act" which he was "unable to comprehend." After a middle-of-the-night argument with her husband in May 1929, Mary Ann Hiss Emerson swallowed a bottle of Lysol.[11]

The following month, Hiss graduated and left to spend the summer in Europe, and when he returned in the fall, he began clerking for Justice Oliver Wendell Holmes, Jr. Soon after assuming the post, he sent Frankfurter a progress report:

> I'd been intending to drop you a note this summer but my brother and I had such a peaceful quiet summer. . . .
>
> Donie and I sat us down in Normandy at a charming but plumbingless little inn and swam and tennissed and read prodigiously. . . . Our evenings were composed of beer drinking and litr'y discussion with Monet's grandson followed by early retiring. . . .
>
> The justice is perfectly charming. . . . [Holmes] seems extremely well and strong and amazingly interested in his work. His zest for life is boundless; he takes a keen interest in his personal appearance . . . and enjoys his intellectual bouts with Justice Brandeis . . . et al. to the full.
>
> Being with the Justice by day and with evenings well taken care of by my first tackle [?] of domesticity (Charlie and I have a cute apartment) [Charles Willard, a law-school classmate] and week-ends free to romp off to the fields of Maryland and Virginia. I am indeed a beamish boy.

Please give my very best to Mrs. F. The two tiny flies in the vanishing cream are the loss of the Sunday afternoon teas at your home and the fact that all Washington's music is in the afternoon.[12]

Less than two months after writing to Frankfurter, and with almost no warning to either his friends or his family, Alger Hiss married Priscilla Fansler Hobson.

Most surprised of all concerning this sudden leap into matrimony was Justice Holmes. Frankfurter selected Holmes's law clerk each year, and the tradition had been that the young man remained unmarried for that period. Hiss later insisted that Holmes quickly became reconciled to the situation. As evidence of this, he told a biographer about Holmes's wedding present—Hiss's choice—a copy of the justice's collected speeches. Holmes inscribed the volume "To Alger Hiss," but when Hiss said, "Oh, that's not enough! Write something more," the "reconciled" Holmes wrote: "Et ux" (and wife).[13]

Hiss assured Frankfurter that all was well in a December 13 letter, two days after his marriage:

Dear Mr. Frankfurter,

I learned some ten hours before my marriage from a chance remark . . . that the Justice had definitely stipulated that his secretaries be unmarried. Of course, I had appreciated what must be [at] the bottom of this rule—the secretary's personal affairs must never impinge upon a "scintilla" of the Justice's time or energy, and I—rather, we—laid meticulous plans to that end. As part of these plans the Justice was not informed until the last moment (the evening before the wedding). He has not shown any annoyance or foreboding. He both gave me his blessing the evening of the ceremony and his "welcome into the brotherhood" the following morning. Today he had us both to luncheon. (Of course, these are consonant, I well realize, with disapproval hidden behind the Justice's charm.)

It never occurred to me that he had a definite "rule of law" on the point.[14] I do see the wisdom of such a rule, however. I had been going to New York Saturday afternoon all fall to the Justice's knowledge and apparent amusement. He often chaffed me about the "dangers" I was headed for but I in no wise sensed any fiat negative to marriage qua marriage—of inconsiderateness which might reasonably grow out of a secretary's marrying he did gently complain, I suppose. The knowledge that Shulman and Justice Stone's 1928–29 secretary were both married undoubtedly made me feel that it was a question of my own integrity as to whether I should permit anything to affect my devotion to the Justice. I don't believe my getting married has altered my sense of values in that direction. . . .

Such moments of personal crisis invariably elicited from Hiss the claim that he was either unaware or unprepared for the occasion.[15]

After being told of Priscilla's divorce from Hobson, Hiss had renewed contact with her during the spring of 1929, shortly before his sister's suicide. Although they saw one another several times in those months, Priscilla made it clear that she was deeply involved with another man. After Hiss's return from the summer in Europe, he contacted Priscilla only to discover that she was about to enter a New York hospital for an abortion. Priscilla's lover, according to Alger, was a New York newspaperman named William Brown Meloney, who refused to marry. Her son, Timothy Hobson, was then three years old, Alger's age at the time his father died.[16]

His protectiveness took hold. Alger began traveling to New York to see Priscilla each weekend, though his October 1929 letter to Frankfurter mentions only spending his weekends "romping in the fields." Priscilla shared Hiss's interest in theater and music, and she matched his knowledge of law with her own scholarly command of literature. By that time she was already a talented and experienced writer-editor and had apparently told Alger of her intention to pursue a career after their marriage.

Minnie Hiss thought Alger's plan to marry Priscilla Hobson a disaster for her son, apparently because of Priscilla's divorce, career plans, and outspokenness. Minnie refused to attend the ceremony, thoughtfully sending Alger a telegram instead that stated: "Do not take this fatal step." The telegram "arrived on their wedding day," according to John Chabot Smith, "and Alger was naïve enough to show it to Priscilla. She never forgave her mother-in-law for that; and she is still angry at Alger about it today."[17]

Nor did Priscilla favorably impress many of Alger's Baltimore friends, who thought her "too radical and too intellectual." Key figures in that society, notably Hiss's mother, his brother Donald, and his closest friend, William Marbury, all felt uncomfortable with her. Priscilla, in turn, did not care much for Alger's Baltimore friends, regarding them (according to Smith) as "part of his 'undergraduate' experience, which he grew out of once he was a married man." Minnie Hiss and her daughter-in-law remained on guardedly "cordial" terms during the years that followed. Donald, according to a 1949 statement by his lawyer, had little use for his brother's wife, objecting to her "on personality rather than on political grounds. . . . One reason he did not like Priscilla was that he considered her conversation too highbrow and believed that Alger and Priscilla associated with too intellectual a group." As for Marbury, he would say only (to me in a 1975 interview) that Priscilla "was not a popular woman. Alger's friends didn't like her very much. But I didn't know Priscilla well enough to form a judgment on her."[18]

An incident that epitomized the feeling of tension on both sides occurred shortly after the marriage. Hiss took his bride to a party at the William Marburys and, as he tells the story, circulated among his friends while Priscilla remained aloof. After they left, she accused him of "disloyalty" for having enjoyed himself while "abandoning" her for the evening. At subsequent parties Hiss remained close to Priscilla.[19]

The unhappiness Priscilla Hiss felt in Alger's Baltimore circle changed things considerably. Initially Hiss had intended to work with a Baltimore law firm after completing his duties for Holmes. "My present plans call for settling in Baltimore," he wrote Frankfurter on February 27, 1930. "I hope Venable, Baetjer and Howard are going to decide to take on another man after ten years! New York did lure us but I'm still strong on State's rights." Hiss passed the Maryland Bar exam in June, indicating that he still sought a job in the state at that time. Meanwhile he had turned down other possibilities. In March his friend Richard Field had arranged an invitation for Hiss to join a Boston firm, and Alger wrote Frankfurter on March 20: "I am seriously considering going with [the] firm though what Dick Field calls my 'sentimental affection' for Baltimore is strong. I must decide in a day or so but at present am far from any determination."

But Frankfurter apparently played a leading role in Hiss's decision to reject Field's offer, since four days later Alger wrote his mentor again: "Priscilla and I liked Mr. Brown [a head partner in Field's firm], and even Mrs. Brown, less than you had prophesied. . . . I have just written a letter of refusal to Mr. Brown and a most difficult one to Dick Field. I hope I was sufficiently adroit so that Dick doesn't know what your advice was. Please realize how deeply Priscilla and I appreciate Mrs. Frankfurter's and your kindness and rare sympathy."[20]

It was not because of pressure from Priscilla that he did not settle in Baltimore in 1930, Hiss has said, but because he failed to obtain an adequate position. "Two leading firms" in the city, he noted, had offered him only an opportunity to read law "without charge," but without pay, in their offices. Only then did he make other arrangements. That Hiss could not have received a good offer from a leading Baltimore firm after clerking for Justice Holmes, and with Frankfurter's backing, seems extraordinary, however, and there is no evidence to suggest that he seriously sought a position there during the spring of 1930. In any event, Frankfurter had other plans for his protégé, as indicated in a letter from Hiss:

> Your far too flattering letter to Mr. John Lord O'Brian [Assistant Attorney General and head of the Justice Department's Anti-Trust Division] led him to see me last week. He seemed to think that there was no doubt he could use me next fall and discussed mainly the question of where he could place me in the lists the Comptroller General had made up. My next step appears to be the "passing of the bar." I think I can arrange to be in Washington on June 17, 20 and 21 and only hope I can manage as easily to pass the examination then given.
>
> I found Mr. O'Brian most charming and am deeply grateful for your letter to him and "'hint" to me.

Despite this endorsement—Frankfurter described Hiss to O'Brian as "not only a first rate lawyer, but a man of unusual cultivation, charm, and prematurely solid judgment"—Hiss subsequently turned aside the Justice Department post. O'Brian had already offered him one in more definite terms than indicated by

Hiss's letter to Frankfurter. Hiss's method of handling the situation recalled the evasive manner in which he had dealt with other uncomfortable situations, such as the decision to marry while clerking for Holmes. He simply never contacted O'Brian again. "It is my recollection," O'Brian wrote Frankfurter in 1938, "that in the winter or spring [of 1930] he applied to me for a position in the Anti-Trust Division for the following autumn. After some discussion, I told him I would appoint him. I thought he was coming down, but never heard anything further from him, except that some time during the autumn, I learned indirectly, that he had changed his plans and taken a position in Boston."[21]

Whatever his reasons, Hiss decided to ignore O'Brian's offer. Instead, that summer William Marbury, who had begun practicing law in Baltimore, wrote friends in Boston on Alger's behalf and helped to land him a job with Choate, Hal and Stewart, an important firm. Marbury later recalled that the choice of Boston apparently represented a compromise for both Alger and Priscilla between his earlier desire to settle in Baltimore and her yearning to return to New York. Hiss began working for Choate, Hall and Stewart in October 1930 after completing his obligations to Justice Holmes. The couple lived in Cambridge, close to the Frankfurters and to Alger's other law-school friends.[22]

JAY VIVIAN CHAMBERS: DISORDER AND EARLY SORROW

"I was born in Philadelphia, Pennsylvania, on April 1, 1901, as Jay Vivian Chambers," begins a deposition Chambers gave the FBI in 1949. "My parents were Jay Chambers and Laha Whittaker Chambers. . . . [My] parents had only two children, myself and my brother Richard Godfrey Chambers . . . [who] was probably born in 1904." As in Alger Hiss's autobiographical notes, the "facts" are there— but only barely. Chambers's memoir, *Witness*, tells us more:

> I was born in Philadelphia on April 1, 1901. When my father, Jay Chambers, who was then a young staff artist on the New York *World*, received the startling news, he crumpled the telegram and threw it into a waste basket. He did not believe it and he did not think that April Fool jokes were in good taste. . . .
>
> Mine was a dry birth and I weighed twelve pounds and measured fourteen inches across the shoulders. I had to be taken with instruments. After this frightful delivery, Dr. Dunning sat for several hours beside my mother, holding together the edges of a torn artery. . . . [H]e thought that she was certainly dying. . . . My mother overcame her memory [of the agonizing childbirth] sufficiently to bear a second son, my brother, Richard Godfrey. But my terrible birth was fixed indelibly in her mind. Throughout my boyhood and my youth, she repeated to me the circumstances of that ordeal until they were vivid to me. They made me acutely unhappy, and her repetition of them made me even unhappier (for it seemed to imply a reproach). But I never told her so.

Chambers's mother apparently exaggerated both his birth size and perhaps her degree of trauma, but her account reflected the tensions that characterized life in the Chambers family.[23] Shortly after his birth Jay Vivian and family moved to Brooklyn, New York. After several years they settled in Lynbrook, then a small fishing and farming village with a few hundred inhabitants on Long Island's south shore, eighteen miles from New York City. Their home was ramshackle and spartan, lacking central heat, electricity, and running water; the coalstove-heated kitchen "was the only really warm room in the house," and, Chambers recalled, "like most country people . . . we lived chiefly in the kitchen. In summer, we moved partly out of doors." The inlets, farms, and villages of southern Long Island would provide Whittaker with many of his happiest memories as a young man—"I used to go off for long rambles by myself through the woods and became very much interested in nature"—but his family life offered few such pleasures. Jay and Laha quarreled frequently.[24]

For one thing, the Chambers family did not fit the Lynbrook mold. Jay Vivian was born into a family of newspapermen: Jay Sr. worked initially for the *World* but later became a successful illustrator for a New York City advertising firm. On weekends he prowled along the coves and fields around Lynbrook with his paints and canvases. Laha had once been a professional actress but held no job while raising her two sons (afterward she worked for New York City's Welfare Department for a number of years). "My parents were the intellectuals of that period," Chambers later observed, ". . . aware of the new ideas and . . . the latest books. I was brought up in an atmosphere of no religion at all. I was quite young when I asked my mother if God made the world. She said, 'You are just picking up ideas from people.' The world was formed, she said, by gases which solidified. Her attitude, impressed upon me, was that intelligent people just don't discuss religion."[25]

At the same time, his parents and grandparents were all Republicans, and Chambers initially adopted this creed, supporting Calvin Coolidge while a college student in 1920. Despite the family's political conservatism, some of their Lynbrook neighbors were put off by the Chamberses, who not only failed to attend church but also, in Laha's case, spoke several languages other than English, read a great deal, and even painted pictures. "My family was regarded by the community as 'peculiar.' . . . we were called the 'French family,' that being apparently the most radical term that they could think of."[26]

But life in the "French Quarter" of Lynbrook was neither radical nor placid. Both Jay and Laha bore deep scars from their families' rapid descent down the ladder from their upper-middle-class beginnings; both had abandoned earlier personal ambitions.

My grandfather Whittaker [Laha's father] was a schoolteacher, a writer, an inventor and a manufacturer. He was, I think, the Superintendent of Schools in Milwaukee at one time. He founded the first magazine in the Northwest. . . . He made and lost a fortune. About the time my mother came of age, they lost their money. She had to go to work. She went on stage with a stock company and traveled all over the country. . . . Her family was then extremely poor. My grandparents opened a small restaurant. My mother waited on tables. There she met my father.

Subsequently Laha's father began teaching French in the New York schools, "was accused falsely of drinking," according to Chambers, lost his job, and "died soon after of cancer."

"Grandfather Chambers" fared somewhat better professionally but not personally. He became a political reporter in Philadelphia and married "a very shallow, cranky woman." Soon he began drinking heavily:

> My grandfather was a terrific lady's man and she [his wife] knew it. . . . When my grandfather was drinking he was hard to handle. You could hear him coming at a distance and the sound of his voice was enough to frighten children. He terrified my father to a point where he was very much under the thumb of his mother. He became very quiet, shy and introspective. . . . [After studying art and going to work for a New York newspaper] he married my mother, and according to my mother's story, my grandfather did as much as possible to wreck the marriage.

Grandfather Chambers vacationed in Lynbrook every summer, Chambers would remember. "This consisted of taking me and my brother with him on a tour of saloons. This used to put my mother in a frightful state of mind."[27]

But Chambers associated his mother, Laha, with whatever pleasure he derived from his family. Jay remained, if not indifferent toward his sons, "then uncommunicative to the point of seeming mute." He generally kept silent on the few trips on which the boys accompanied him: to a New York studio that he maintained, or to museums, or on painting expeditions near their Lynbrook home. "Once in a long while, he would utter one word: 'Don't'—when my brother and I were doing something that he did not like." Jay Sr. declined the name "Papa" along with the role, insisting that the boys call him "Jay."

With Laha, Jay was as withdrawn and sullen most of the time as with his sons: "My earliest recollections are of my mother pacing up and down the rooms in Lynbrook carrying on imaginary and dramatic conversations with my father. There was an air of tenseness over the house. About 1908, my mother and father separated. He went to live in New York City and we stayed in Lynbrook—my mother and the two children. My father gave us, I think, $8.00 a week to live on. To eke that out my mother raised chickens, baked cakes and grew vegetables. I developed a small route in the town selling these things."[28]

"I sent him away," Laha announced to her two boys—seven and four years old—that first night, and she proceeded to move their cots into her bedroom.

Each night for the next three years they all slept uneasily together, with the bedroom door bolted and a heavy dresser placed against it. For a time Laha kept an ax under the bed, and each night they listened anxiously whenever noises came from the distance.

Jay had moved to Brooklyn to live with his lover and their circle of artist friends. Jay's mother left her husband in Philadelphia and moved into a nearby apartment in Brooklyn to help keep house for him, but she also visited Lynbrook frequently, much to the irritation of Laha. Although Jay Vivian (Whittaker) despised "Grandmother Chambers," he agreed later that she had been the first to describe to him the Quaker faith, which she practiced and to which he was converted during the 1940s. Yet Chambers recalled those three years as happy ones for his mother—and probably for himself and his younger brother—despite their poverty: "Without my father, our home, though divided, was tranquil."[29]

Just as Alger Hiss learned only during his teens that Charles Hiss had killed himself, Whittaker Chambers did not discover the true reason for his own father's absence until much later. Jay had left his family to pursue a love affair with a male friend. Presumably Chambers heard about it from Laha, who never forgave her husband's bisexuality, even after Jay returned to Lynbrook in 1911:

> About three years after my parents separated, my father came back home, but he was in disgrace. The first night he went away nothing had been said to us children. My mother said he wasn't coming back anymore when I asked. This gave me a feeling of sickness which I can still feel. My mother never attacked my father to us children, but she was able to convey to us that we shouldn't like him. I couldn't stand the way he made her suffer.
>
> When he came back, he lived entirely in his own room. When he came in the evening [from working in New York City], I used to carry up a tray of supper to him. He often made efforts to conciliate me, but I resented them. On Sundays, he had all his meals in his room. I don't think he ever came into the lower part of the house. That condition lasted until [1926]. . . . During a great many of these years, I scarcely spoke to him at all.[30]

Even without such talks, Jay contributed to his son's education. The Lynbrook home was filled with the books, prints, recordings, and other aesthetic evidences of Jay's and Laha's common passion for the arts. His father's tastes ran heavily toward Oriental and mystical themes, both in his commercial sketches and in personal collections (which included five illustrated editions of the *Arabian Nights* in Jay's room), capped by a passion for Pre-Raphaelite painters and writers. "Our house was a peeling outpost of what my father and mother would have summed up as 'culture' . . . visible in the overflowing bookcases and bookshelves, which were everywhere, and . . . visible in the pictures that covered the walls."[31]

Not often do we remember with exactitude the influences that shaped our childhood perceptions. Chambers later displayed a phenomenal recall of those years, although perhaps not always an accurate one.[32] He described summer

visits by his "Grandfather Chambers," for example, spent mainly in Long
Island taverns where the Philadelphia newspaperman discoursed on politics
and world affairs while Jay Vivian and Richard Godfrey wolfed down the bar's
"free lunch." His earliest memories of listening to discussions of national and
international affairs, Chambers claimed, dated from those taproom tours with
his grandfather.

If Grandfather Chambers provided the public conversation of his youth,
Grandfather Whittaker's collection of two hundred books, stored in the family
attic in Lynbrook, supplemented his family's own library and introduced him to
the book that most influenced the boy's malleable intellect, "the Bible of my boyhood," Victor Hugo's *Les Miserables:*

> It taught me two seemingly irreconcilable things—Christianity and revolution.
> It taught me first of all that the basic virtue of life is humility. . . . It taught me
> justice and compassion. . . . That was the gist of its Christian teaching. It taught
> me revolution, not as others were to teach me—as a political or historical
> fact—but as a reflex of human suffering and desperation. . . . [I]t corresponded
> exactly to a need I felt within myself.[33]

These influences on Whittaker's youth would play their part in Chambers's
later life. But Grandmother Whittaker's (and Laha's) contribution to his education was more immediately fruitful: a gift for languages and the encouragement
to study them. By the time Jay Vivian had graduated from high school, he was
already fluent in French and German and had begun plowing through language
grammars in other tongues: Spanish, Italian, Gaelic, Arabic, Persian, Hindi,
Romanian, and Russian—thereby laying the groundwork for his later work as
a translator.

A European-born Lynbrook woman named Dorothea Maude Mont Ellen,
daughter of a German orchestra leader and a friend of Laha's, encouraged
Chambers's cultural interests, and he would later call her "the dominant force in
the early years of my adolescence":

> She had the mind of a highly cultured European. . . . She spoke Italian and
> French fluently . . . taught me German and French and used to talk German
> with me. She gave me my first understanding of music but most important she
> was a European and made me aware of the old European tradition of culture
> as a continuing process. At a later stage when I was exposed to European influ-
> ences such as Marx, Lenin, Tolstoy, etc., I was prepared for them. . . . She was a
> very isolated person in [Lynbrook] too. . . . [But] my friendship with Mrs. Ellen
> was not an "affair" and there was no scandal.

Apart from his relationship with Dorothea Ellen, Chambers's high-school
years passed uneventfully. He received excellent grades in English and foreign languages, but only adequate ones in other subjects, and he worked hard

at competitive sports, particularly wrestling and handball, also playing on the school basketball team. But Chambers remained a loner and made few friends in his own age group. Family pressures increased as his graduation approached, with Jay insisting that his son make plans to work while Laha urged Jay Vivian to consider entering college. Chambers and his younger brother, Richard, drifted apart while Laha and her younger son drew closer. The commitments that serve to counteract the normal narcissism and alienation of a thoughtful adolescent seemed almost entirely absent in Chambers's case as he prepared to leave high school and "choose" a life: "By degrees I told myself: I am an outcast. My family is outcast. We have no friends, no social ties, no church, no organization that we claim and that claims us, no community." For a time Jay Vivian was determined to join the Army and fight in World War I, but when his graduation came in the spring of 1919, that option no longer existed.

By graduation Chambers had decided to leave Lynbrook. At the ceremonies themselves, he performed a minor but unmistakable act of rebellion against an unsatisfying family (his parents were in the audience) and what he perceived as a community that had excluded him. Because of his talent with language, he had been chosen as "class prophet." Mixed in among the obvious assignments of future roles for classmates, he predicted that one girl would become a prostitute. The principal, outraged, withheld Chambers's diploma for a time. Meanwhile, Laha obtained a job for her restless son in a Lynbrook bank, where Jay Vivian, fighting constantly with his fellow employees, lasted only a few weeks.[34]

Laha's finding him this boring job as a bank clerk proved the final indignity for Chambers and determined his next step. One day, without warning, he boarded a train for Baltimore and ran away from home.

WHITTAKER: THE ESCAPE FROM LYNBROOK

Chambers left with a companion, a Lynbrook friend named Anthony Muller. After a weekend in a Baltimore fleabag hotel, the two young men obtained jobs as day laborers in Washington, D.C. The Baltimore company handling the work maintained rooms for their laborers in local hotels, and Chambers, who used the first of his many pseudonyms, Charles Adams, later called this period his "introduction to the proletariat."* The laborers were "an international mob, many of whom spoke a foreign language." After four months the work ended. Chambers and Muller moved on to New Orleans, where, unable to find jobs in the postwar

---

*Chambers wrote regularly to Laha during these months but did not tell her his Washington address or alias. She and Grandfather Whittaker alerted the Washington police, but the young runaway was never found.

slump, they lived in poor quarters on short rations in the French Quarter. Occupying the next room was a prostitute nicknamed "One-Eyed Annie," and many other residents were from the area's lower depths.

Still calling himself Charles Adams, Chambers tried to ship out as a seaman, but, lacking the necessary papers, he was turned away. Finally, after several frustrating months of unemployment, Muller enlisted in the Marines and Jay Vivian wrote his family asking for money to return home.

After reaching Lynbrook late in 1919, Chambers struck a bargain with his family: He would work for his father's Manhattan advertising firm as a file clerk for the next half-year and then enter college in the fall of 1920. Because his father "was worried if he introduced me as his son the firm people would think he was favoring me," Jay passed off the boy as "Charles Whittaker," marking Chambers's first use of his mother's family name, and his second pseudonym. Most people at Seaman and Company apparently learned after a while about the relationship between "Whittaker" and Jay.

A young copywriter at the advertising firm, a Williams College graduate, urged "Charles" to enter Williams in August and not Columbia, as he intended. Laha also seemed "enthusiastic for Williams," according to her son. Her cosmopolitanism, it seemed, had limits: "She had always been against Columbia because of the number of Jews and because it was such a big place." Chambers traveled to Williams in September, passed an entrance exam, and had his furniture and personal possessions shipped up. But he left after a single day, having "decided Williams was not for me. I was sure my parents could not stand the expense." He took a train to New York, went immediately to Columbia even before returning home, and managed to enroll. For the entire school year Chambers lived in Lynbrook while commuting daily to Columbia.[35]

Columbia College during the 1920s was a haven for talented young men with literary or artistic interests, many of them Jews, and Chambers quickly joined forces with a group that shared his cultural concerns and more than matched him intellectually. Upon entering the school, "Whit" (as most of his Columbia friends called him) found Mark Van Doren, the poet and literary critic, assigned as his faculty adviser. Van Doren soon became a friend as well, as did a number of fellow students who went on to impressive careers as writers, scholars, and public figures. The list of classmates with whom Chambers became friendly at Columbia included art historian Meyer Schapiro, literary critic Lionel Trilling, writer-editor-radio personality Clifton Fadiman, theatrical critic John W. Gassner, poet Louis Zukofsky, and journalists Charles Wagner and Herbert Solow. Among others with whom he fraternized were the poet Langston Hughes, the philosopher Mortimer Adler, prosecutor Frank Hogan, and two men—David Zabladowsky and Irving Kaplan—who later figured in Chambers's experience as an underground Communist.[36]

Although Alger Hiss made and retained friends from each of his youthful social worlds—Baltimore, Johns Hopkins, and Harvard Law—Chambers drew only from his Columbia circle (other than from later Communist associates) for his close relationships during the 1920s and 1930s. That first year, each day he and about a dozen other undergraduates—mainly commuters like himself—would eat their bagged lunches together in the college gym:

> They lived an intense, intellectual life, almost wholly apart from the life of the campus [he later reminisced]. They were a cohesive group, bound together by a common origin, a common flight from a common fear, and a common poverty. . . . They were Jewish, of course, but my inexperience in such matters may be judged from the fact that for a long time, I supposed that Schapiro was an Italian name.
>
> All of them were intensely serious. Not that they did not laugh. They laughed a great deal. Their humor was at times highly intellectual. At other times, their humor was extremely earthy. . . .
>
> Their seriousness was organic. It was something utterly new in my experience. It sprang from a struggle in which to gain an inch was the achievement of a lifetime. . . . My strange luncheon companions were *ernste Menschen* [serious men]—and with good reason, for most of them were sitting there as a result of a struggle with a warping poverty impossible for those who have not glimpsed it to imagine. . . . They came from a stock that, after God, worshipped education and the things of the mind. They were there, in most cases, by acts of superhuman sacrifice and contrivance on the part of their families. To me, that seriousness was deeply impressive. . . . It spoke directly to a seriousness within myself, that sprang from no such struggle as theirs, but partook of a similar organic attitude toward life.

Less charitably, Chambers would tell the FBI in 1949: "From these young zealots I had my first exposure to Marxists' ideas. We used to have long and violent arguments in which they tried to convert me to Marxism." The "conversion" efforts during Whittaker's first two and a half years at Columbia, if they occurred at all, proved unsuccessful. Instead—largely through the influence of Van Doren and of friends such as Schapiro, Zukofsky, and Fadiman—Chambers "converted" to an apolitical aestheticism. Van Doren, a liberal humanist, apparently tempered the fuzzy mysticism with which Chambers had toyed prior to entering Columbia: "I wrote some religious poetry which I showed to Van Doren. . . . He said that . . . 'it contained a pathological [pathetic?] fallacy,' which I had never heard of until then [and which], according to Van Doren, was that 'God operates in nature.'"[37]

Van Doren and Whittaker's student friends also gently spoofed "Whit's" residual Republicanism. Chambers had been a fan of Calvin Coolidge ever since, as governor of Massachusetts in 1919, Coolidge received unearned credit for stopping the Boston police strike. He also wrote as English-class themes for Van Doren editorials expressing his conservative political views: "Mark asked me into his office after class. He praised my editorial writing, but he wondered, with his infectious chuckle, whether the Russian Revolution was really as bad as I supposed, or whether Calvin Coolidge was as good." Van Doren later recalled Chambers going "about the University [in 1920] putting up posters for Mr. Coolidge. This caused some comment because people at Columbia did not take an active part in political campaigns in those days."

Moving into a Columbia dormitory room for his sophomore year in the fall of 1921, Chambers shifted his primary allegiance from the bag-lunch Marxists to another group of predominantly Jewish students, most from "comfortable homes, but [who also] shared the same general view of life as my locker room friends. They were also *ernste Menschen*." Most would become writers (a few painters), and in their company—Schapiro's, Trilling's, Fadiman's, Zukofsky's, Wagner's, Gassner's, and Solow's, to name only the most prominent—Chambers began to write poems and short stories, many of them for *The Morningside,* the Columbia literary magazine that he later helped edit. Fadiman subsequently summarized the assessment of Whittaker's Columbia friends: "[H]e considered Chambers at that time a brilliant poet and . . . he thought it was too bad that Chambers did not in later life concentrate on his writing because he felt that if Chambers had done so, he would [have become] a renowned literary figure. . . ."[38]

But Chambers remained restless at Columbia, cutting classes frequently and spending much time in the gym playing handball or wrestling. When not writing, he read prodigiously in several European literatures, especially Russian and German, which he read in the original. Like many of his Columbia classmates, Chambers had become a humanistic "free-thinker," alienated from formal religion. He rejected ideologies of every description—Christianity, Communism, even Republicanism and his beloved Cal Coolidge, who would soon become president. Chambers's behavior became erratic by 1922, and he developed an addiction to sometimes-brutal pranks and a passion to shock.

In November 1922 this newly acquired and calculated playfulness led to removal from Columbia. Chambers had become editor-in-chief of *The Morningside* that term. In the first issue produced under his direction, and with Van Doren's approval, Whittaker published under the pseudonym "John Kelly" a one-act drama called *A Play for Puppets,* containing a simple story line and mildly scatological verses. Two Roman centurions guard Christ's tomb. They swap tales of Mark Antony and Caesar, discuss the delights of lovemaking, and one centurion observes that Jesus "never lay with a woman." Angels come to announce Christ's resurrection, but Jesus declines to leave with them. He claims to be only a simple carpenter's son, until the "Voice of God" calls him. "CHRIST (meekly following angel off right): I am the truth, the way, and the light." The centurions resume their conversation—the old one fearful about losing the body, the young one reflecting on his woman. Van Doren said at the time—and later—that he thought the playlet excellent: It "dealt with Christ as a human being, that He did not want to be resurrected and wanted to be allowed to sleep and that this was somewhat in the Anatole France tradition."[39]

Running through *A Play for Puppets* is a theme that characterized Chambers's writing and reflections before his commitment to Communism later in the decade: the destruction of an individual's goodness (as embodied in Jesus) by both established society and organized religion—and a yearning for life's termination. Thus the "Voice of Christ" intones: "Who is breaking my sleep? . . . What is God? . . . Heaven? Let me sleep. I am weary. . . . Do not men live and do not men die? I wish to sleep. . . . Roll back the stone and go thy way. It is very quiet in the earth and I will sleep."

Yet Chambers may not have intended to expose his personal discontent so directly, nor perhaps did he anticipate the drastic reaction of university authorities to *A Play for Puppets*. Van Doren had approved its publication, and Chambers had used the "John Kelly" pseudonym in an apparent effort to defuse criticism. Still, the image of a Christ figure left so weary by life that he preferred peaceable death to resurrection related intimately to Whittaker's sketch earlier that year in *The Morningside* of "Everett Holmes," the dead hero of the autobiographical story to which Chambers assigned—with heavy-handed irony—the title "The Damn Fool": "He wasn't a Bolshevik. He was a Puritan, perhaps. That is a radical, of course. He was an extremist," a friend says of the deceased Holmes. "A man's praise was the one thing he had never had, and now he fought and lived [in the anti-Bolshevik armies] in the tremendous energy of their devotion." The two men debate Holmes's death. One calls him "a damn fool": "What he did gives weakness a false appearance of glory. He wasn't glorious. How many weary miles did he tramp to escape himself." The other, apparently the authorial voice, is wry but more sympathetic: "He gained some things, though, I think. I did not say he was glorious. He was a strange chap." A flip and all-pervasive cynicism, an unserious amoralism, permeated Whittaker's writings and his behavior during this period.[40]

After New York newspapers began publicizing his "blasphemous" issue of *The Morningside*, Chambers resigned from its editorial board, and two months later, after conferring with a college dean over the incident, he withdrew "voluntarily" from Columbia. "I'm leaving for good," Chambers told a friend after meeting with Dean Herbert Hawkes. "He wants all copies of *Morningside* confiscated and an apology. It can't be done and I'm leaving college." "We go," the friend's present-tense recollection continues, "to a Chinese restaurant on 110th Street to talk things over. But it seems that all we do is laugh things over. Whittaker was never happier. Something ha[s] been released in him and his usual wit has an edge of fire, Promethean fed with Shavian shavings."[41]

After leaving Columbia, Chambers began an experimental, rootless, creative, but disintegrating period in his life. It lasted almost a decade before stabilizing in 1931 with marriage, readmission to the Communist Party, and an editorship at *The New Masses*. At first, the withdrawal did not noticeably affect his ties to Columbia. Whittaker continued to meet regularly with friends, sleep over often in their dormitory rooms, and take part in their revels. Shortly after the furor over *A Play for Puppets,* Chambers began drinking heavily for the first time—and after his initial encounter with whiskey in his dorm room, "I tore the place apart."

His evident restlessness led Van Doren, who had not succeeded in quieting the attacks on his pupil by Columbia faculty colleagues and administrators, to suggest that Whittaker go abroad. "Why don't you go to Soviet Russia?" Chambers later remembered Van Doren urging him. "The Russian Revolution is like Elizabethan England. All the walls are falling down. You should go and see it." In Meyer Schapiro's room at Columbia, Chambers met a young man named Sender Garlin who was then working for Russian-American Relief, an organization that sought to alleviate the famine then afflicting the Soviet Union. He made one effort that spring—whether inspired by Van Doren, by Garlin, or independently—to join the relief program for Russia's famine organized separately by the American Friends Service Committee. Whittaker recalled having been received warmly in Philadelphia by Quaker officials when he first applied, but the Quakers rejected him after learning about the *Play for Puppets* incident.

While in Philadelphia, Chambers stayed at his grandfather's house. One night the police phoned to report his grandfather's illness. Whittaker rushed to the address and found him dead: "It was in the house of this 'other woman' that my grandfather died." Whittaker arranged with the editor of the paper for which the elder Chambers had worked to write a story stating "that he died en route to his own residence and had gone to the nearest house for aid."[42]

When Chambers traveled to Europe in the summer of 1923, it was not to help feed starving Russians, but to wander through Germany and Belgium with two Columbia friends, Meyer Schapiro and Henry Zelinsky. The trio lived in Berlin for a month, then proceeded to Brussels and—in Whittaker's case—to Paris before returning to the United States in September.

His experiences in Europe that summer had drawn him initially toward Communism, Chambers later argued, as a result of firsthand observation of the physical devastation and economic distress wrought by World War I. He recalled returning to live in his parents' Lynbrook home, where he read widely in Fabian socialist, Marxian socialist, and other classic schools in the literature of modern social protest, if only to try to comprehend the "crisis" he believed to be overtaking the West. He concluded, in Spenglerian fashion, that an America seemingly dedicated to sexual revolt, bootleg whiskey, and campus hijinks was in fact a "dying world . . . without faith, hope, character, understanding of its malady or will to overcome it."[43]

Despite Chambers's version, the historical record indicates that observations of European decay, explorations of socialist classics, and reflections on Communist ideology played only supporting roles, at best, in Whittaker Chambers's decision to join the American Communist Party. He appeared preoccupied at the time— his letters suggest—not with political but with aesthetic concerns and with his own dwindling literary output.

During the year following his return from Europe in the fall of 1923, Chambers wrote little and preserved even less. His decision to join the Communist Party in 1925 was apparently triggered by an inability to resolve a series of emotional crises stemming from personal and family experiences.

Drifting away from Lynbrook, he took a position at the main branch of the New York Public Library, supervising the Newspaper Room in the evenings. This left his days free for writing and allowed him the further luxury of using the library as a base of operations for reading and study. Although Chambers met a number of Communists working there, he made no move to join the CP for a time. Instead, he alternated periods spent living in Lynbrook (his mother was "at me to complete my college course") with periods spent living with a friend, James Green,* a fellow Columbia College dropout. The two men first shared a room in Manhattan, and during the summer of 1924 they set up a large tent in a hollow between the dunes at Atlantic Beach on Long Island's southern shore, not far from Lynbrook. Green worked in Manhattan and would come out on weekends, while Chambers would also spend weekdays in the tent, commuting to New York to work at the library each evening: "[I] spent most of the time there by myself. It was in that tent that I [studied] Fabian Socialism."

James Green often brought his younger brother, Lewis,† then in his final year of high school in Lynbrook, out to Atlantic Beach. Over the next few years Chambers's friendship with James cooled, but he became close to Lewis Green. Sometime during that period he also met and fell in love with a married woman. It happened when Atlantic Beach "began to develop, so we crossed Broad Channel across from Atlantic Beach and began to camp there. Presently other campers began to cluster around us. One of these was a Mrs. Mainland and her children. Mrs. Mainland was a Socialist." The lady whom Chambers dubbed "Mrs. Mainland" and met sometime in 1924 (he obviously did not use her real name) soon became important to Whittaker, although what little is known about her comes indirectly from a few of Chambers's 1924 letters to Meyer Schapiro and Mark Van Doren. To Schapiro during midsummer Chambers enthused:

> I have spent the whole day with a noble woman and her two beautiful children, a boy and a girl. What more can a man want? Indeed I want little else. . . . I might as well tell you the truth, Meyer. I'm tangled with another woman. Now, it is alright. The happiest I have known: the happiest I have been for a long time. But it should not have come now. Too many sleepless nights and

*A pseudonym.
†A pseudonym.

days gentle and libidinous. There is a satisfaction in the happiness itself. I feel
wrung and heavy. And it all seems bound up [Here Schapiro's copy of the letter
breaks off.] . . . .

To Van Doren, Chambers wrote in September that he had decided to return to
Columbia in the fall: "I have an unconventional partner in this world for whom
I care very much, and it is she who is urging me to this reversal. . . . She argues
(and in this I think she is right) that my present job ideally permits me to study. I
shall keep it and pay my own way. And I am happy to do what she wishes."[44]

Chambers did not last out the term. He did poorly on several midterm exams,
stopped attending classes entirely around Thanksgiving, and by semester's
end had dropped most of his courses. But he continued working at the library.
Why he failed to follow through on his earlier enthusiasm for returning to
school—"I have seldom felt so eager and so active," he had written Van Doren
in September—remains obscure. Chambers and his "unconventional partner"
apparently broke off by the following year, by which time Whittaker had begun
another love affair. Meyer Schapiro recalled Chambers getting drunk once in late
1924 and speaking about a mistress he had in Brooklyn (Atlantic Beach?) who
had recently borne his child, a son named Richard (presumably after Chambers's
younger brother, Richard Godfrey).* But, apart from some fragmentary traces of
the relationship with "Mrs. Mainland," she disappeared from Chambers's life
without further mention to friends.[45]

Even without the breakup of a love affair, the closing months of 1924 proved
excruciatingly difficult for Whittaker because of events connected with the
three generations of his family then living in Lynbrook. "In that period I used
to wander a great deal at night, brooding on my family," he later wrote, "which
seemed to represent in miniature the whole crisis of the middle class." Caught in
Whittaker's "miniature crisis" were his violent, senile grandmother; his reclusive
father; his possessive mother; and his suicidal brother.

Grandmother Whittaker, who had lived with Laha's family since her husband's death in 1920, needed almost constant attention. "It was feared that she
might kill one of us," Chambers recalled, "so it was arranged that I used to sit up
at night and watch her."

> She had delusions that someone was trying to asphyxiate her with gas and
> was poisoning her food; therefore, she took to cooking in her own room. She
> kept the door to her room shut and locked and sat in there at night scream-
> ing unpleasantries about my father. Frequently I was sent to take knives away
> from her and to step between her and my father when she threatened him with
> scissors. . . .

---

*That fall Chambers published a story in the December 1924 *Morningside* about a
mother and her son "Robert" who goes off to war and dies. The story bore a dedication: "In
Memory of R.G."

But Laha made no move to institutionalize her mother. Grandmother Whittaker's behavior may have seemed to Laha fit punishment for her husband's transgressions and not much stranger than most other aspects of life at her house.*

"One night around midnight," late in 1924, "I suddenly came upon my grandmother standing alone at a trolley stop" in East Rockaway. Chambers often wandered through this area, if only because Mrs. Mainland apparently lived nearby. "I thought she [his grandmother] was living in New York [after having earlier run away from Lynbrook]. She did not show any surprise at seeing me. She said something about someone calling to her and asked me if I couldn't hear the voice. I urged her to go home but presently she took a trolley to Brooklyn and it was a short time after that she was picked up in Jersey City." Grandmother Whittaker lived at the Jersey City YWCA until she landed in the psychiatric ward of a local hospital one night, having run into the street in her nightgown crying that "those old Jews had drilled a hole in her ceiling and started to pump gas into her room."[46]

When Chambers was not disarming his grandmother—"the small scars on my hand," he would write, "are where the scissors missed my father and caught me"—he found himself acting as custodian for his brother, who at Christmas 1924 had returned from his first months in college, thoroughly disoriented. According to Chambers, "Richard had been a completely different character from me . . . gentle, merry and athletic." But his brother now seemed quite different. He drank heavily, "had become an atheist and . . . a complete skeptic in every field, apparently as a result of reading works by French Enlightenment rationalists," or so Whittaker believed.

Although Chambers later described Richard's newfound cynicism in terms similar to his own earlier experiences at Columbia, in his own case there had existed a community of friends with whom to share this postadolescent confusion. Richard's disillusionment cut directly to the source of their mutual despair, not the "social crisis" but the wrenching nature of their family life. "Look around you," Whittaker quotes his brother, "look at people. Every one of them is a hypocrite. Look at the world. It is hopeless. . . . Look at marriage. Look at Mother and Jay. What a fraud! Look at the family. Look at ours! . . . We're hopeless people. We can't cope with the world. . . . We're too gentle to face the world." Chambers argued with Richard that the Communists "have found a way out," but Richard ridiculed the Marxist dream as well.[47]

Whatever compassion Whittaker then felt toward Richard was inevitably mixed with resentment. His younger brother had supplanted him as their mother's favorite "problem child." Whittaker was already twenty-three, working full-time, had returned to school, and seemed content. Richard, on the other

---

*Grandmother Whittaker was finally committed to a sanatorium several months before her death in 1929.

hand, needed as much attention as Grandmother Whittaker, and Laha dispatched her older son to accompany Richard on his nightly tours of Long Island speakeasies. Chambers recalled many evenings spent watching Richard and his cronies get drunk while he (Chambers) would sit nearby talking politics with radical immigrant workers. Often Richard would propose that they commit suicide together, but Whittaker claimed that he rejected such a pact each time his brother suggested one.

For a time, early in 1925, Richard curbed his suicidal impulses. He fell in love with a Lynbrook girl and began sneaking her at night into a little house no larger than a toolshed that he had built for himself in back of his parents' home. Jay Sr. learned about the trysting and one night, when Richard returned home drunk, began pummeling his son. Whittaker walked in on the scene and "turned on my father. We had a fight in which I beat my father up. It was after this that my brother married the girl."

First, however, Richard tried to kill himself. "One night he did not meet me at the train as he usually did before an evening's carousing, and that worried me. On some hunch, I looked into the little house and found him with the gas on, unconscious. I carried him into the big house and brought him back to consciousness. He cursed me for bringing him back to life."[48]

Whittaker Chambers's precise reasons for becoming a Communist in 1925 are unknown. But his decision came during a period that included many elements of personal failure: the collapse of his love affair, the inability to complete his term at Columbia, and an even greater degree of private anguish. A skein of interrelated family dramas preoccupied Whittaker during the months prior to his joining the Communist Party, each drama complicating the others. The cumulative strain of managing his unbalanced family—with his grandmother's violent seizures, Richard's nightly binges and periodic suicidal urges, Laha's neurotic harangues, and Jay's single brutal outburst—undoubtedly took its toll.

Which of these episodes set off the final "crisis" of Whittaker's family, which of these unresolvable problems drove him to try to cauterize his emotional wounds at the social level, remains impossible to determine. But Chambers's earliest commitment to Communism apparently represented an effort to extricate himself from Lynbrook and from a family melodrama that had become unbearable. By providing him with a sense of purpose at this confused and disturbing moment, Whittaker's decision to commit himself represented a desperate effort at restoring some sanity to his life. "It was inevitable," he wrote Mark Van Doren in March 1925. "On February 17, I joined the Communist Party. Now I am busy from morning till night, and at night too, but I am also happy and healthy with a feeling of singular mental well being."[49] Chambers hardly exaggerated. His involvement in the Communist Party over the next year and a half probably kept him alive, especially after the family tragedy that he most feared and most expected finally occurred.

ALGER AND PRISCILLA: MOVING LEFT

Neither of the Hisses talked much, publicly, about their years in Boston and New York between 1930 and 1933. At Choate, Hall and Stewart, Hiss assisted John Hall in preparing an important and complicated case involving the Gillette Safety Razor Company. Priscilla had worked as a librarian during their final months in Washington, but she apparently found no job in Cambridge and settled into uneasy domesticity caring for Alger and Timothy. Hiss's circle of Cambridge friends included few women who could match Priscilla's lively intelligence. She became friendly with the few, such as Marion Frankfurter, who could.

Boston, however, was clearly Alger's world and not hers, as one of Hiss's biographers noted: "'I'm not sure,' the wife of one of Alger's close friends recalled, 'that anyone knew Priscilla very well.' Almost all of 'their' friends were his friends. Priscilla felt alone and left out." Harvey Bundy, a Choate partner, confirmed this estimate of Priscilla by Alger Hiss's Boston circle: "The office liked him very much when he was here [at Choate]. They didn't like his wife much—Priscilla. . . . She was a kind of wild-eyed do-gooder. I don't know. They didn't trust her. . . . She seemed to have some of the aspects of a *femme fatale*." Alger appeared content in Boston-Cambridge. Practicing corporate law with a major firm presented a challenge, and he also found himself renewing friendships, such as the one with Felix Frankfurter, begun several years earlier.[50]

But Priscilla would not settle for a subordinate role as "Alger Hiss's wife." After brief involvement in social work, she received a grant from the Carnegie Corporation, collaborating with her sister-in-law, Roberta Fansler, an art historian, to study research in the fine arts.* Priscilla promptly moved to New York in the fall of 1931, taking an apartment in the building near Columbia University where her sister-in-law and brother lived. Although the Hisses gave up their Cambridge apartment, Alger remained in Boston for more than six months, staying with the Richard Fields during the week and commuting to New York on weekends. But during the spring of 1932, with completion of his work on the Gillette case, he resigned from Choate and obtained a job with Cotton and Franklin, a New York corporate-law firm.[51]

While in Cambridge, Hiss had renewed an earlier interest in labor law and social reform, according to his biographer, reading for the first time writings by Karl Marx, Robert Owen, and Sidney Webb. Despite Hiss's well-paying job and comfortable lifestyle, which included live-in maids and child care for Timothy, evidences of social misery surfaced in most neighborhoods of Depression-era Boston and New York. In Manhattan, Priscilla had become deeply involved in

---

*Their book, *Research in Fine Arts in American Colleges and Universities*, appeared in 1934.

both the humanitarian and the organizational aspects of Socialism. She joined the Columbia-area branch of the Socialist Party in 1930 even before having moved to New York, according to their records. Both she and her brother registered as Socialists on the 1932 Morningside Heights voting rolls, and Priscilla attended meetings while donating to the party. Shack colonies known as Hoovervilles lined Riverside Drive only blocks from her building, and the Socialist Party opened soup kitchens along Broadway that coexisted with those run by the Salvation Army. Priscilla apparently worked as a volunteer in one such dispensary. "Hiss had no objection to all this," according to John Chabot Smith; "he thought it quite right and proper, and he attended some of the meetings with his wife to hear about the Socialists' proposals for relief of the poor and reform of the economic system."[52]

In New York, Hiss's legal work dealt largely with his firm's defense of the Radio Corporation of America, which was involved in antitrust litigation, and it kept him busy many evenings and weekends. Although Priscilla continued to collaborate with Roberta Fansler on the fine-arts project, the Hisses moved from Morningside Heights during the spring of 1932 to a more attractive and fashionable apartment on Central Park West. In the little free time available to him, Hiss worked with a group of attorneys interested in labor law, including both liberals and Communists, in a newly formed organization known as the International Juridical Association. The group included several other Harvard Law people such as Lee Pressman and Nathan Witt. "In the winter of 1932–33," Hiss later wrote, "I must have attended three or four meetings of contributors or editors, and my name may even have appeared on the masthead if there was any listing of editors and contributors. As on the [law] review we divided up recent cases [in labor law] for reading and analysis and discussed the articles which should be prepared. I wrote two or three articles myself though I do not remember the topics."[53]

The association published a bulletin devoted mainly to labor-law and civil-liberties cases, and it served as a meeting ground for some young lawyers interested in social reform, many of whom, like Hiss, spent their days working in corporate practice. Hiss resigned from the IJA when he left for Washington in 1933. Another member of the group, Jerome R. Hellerstein, recalled in speaking to a Hiss attorney:

> The members of the Association in 1932 were men of "liberal" points of view. Some few of them were probably out and out Communists. These included Carol King and Joseph Brodsky, who was then attorney for the Communist Party. However, there were many other liberals who were not Communists. . . . Lee Pressman and Nat Witt also were active in the group. They were not Communists, at least at that time. . . . Alger's only contribution was to write a few articles for the bulletin and to attend a few of the open forum meetings.

Hellerstein recalls one meeting at the New School related to foreclosure of farm mortgages at which Alger made a speech. . . . Hellerstein says that the Association was not Communist dominated. . . . [He] knew Alger fairly well in 1932, visited at his house in New York, met and liked Priscilla. He knew that she was a member of the Socialist party. He, Hellerstein, was not.[54]

But one of the Communists mentioned by Hellerstein, Carol King, did not share, in later discussions with Hiss's attorneys, his assessment of the IJA.

. . . Mrs. King thought that Hiss made a mistake in denying membership in any Communist Front organization [in HUAC testimony]. She said that the International Judicial Association is on the Attorney General's list, that this seems rather silly since the organization was dissolved in 1911, but that Hiss was a member of it [in 1932–33] and that his name appeared on the letterhead of the National Committee of this organization. She said that she knew Alger and Priscilla Hiss and liked them very much.[55]

It is doubtful that Hiss became either a Socialist or a Communist during this period. But, influenced both by Priscilla's Socialism and by the more radical perspectives of friends such as Pressman and King on the IJA, Alger's beliefs shifted leftward.

Priscilla's Socialist commitment seemed much stronger than Alger's at the time. It went beyond merely voting and provisioning soup kitchens into organizing new coalitions of American radicals. While Alger spent his free hours working for the IJA, Priscilla helped found a new group called the American Labor Associates, an organization of dissidents from the traditional parties of the left, which described itself as "a cooperative, nonprofit making research, study, publishing, and distributing organization, created . . . to study, analyze, and interpret factual developments and the movement of ideas in the American social order and their bearings on the course and the aims of the labor movement."[56]

During the spring of 1932 the ALA held several meetings to gain supporters and raise funds for a monthly magazine. The group's "Advisory Board," listed on the American Labor Associates' letterhead, included Communists, Socialists, and nonaffiliated radicals—including Priscilla Hiss. On June 15, 1932, the ALA held a planning session. The agenda for discussion, a document entitled "Next Steps in Radicalism: An Outline," included standard militant rhetoric of the time such as this passage:

Revolutions do not, by themselves, come out of depressions, however severe. . . . Two basic pre-conditions of a revolutionary overturn are essential: the existence of *an organized purposive revolutionary movement*, and a *revolutionary situation* with a progressive impairment of the governmental machine of the ruling class.

The document concluded that "the task of revolutionary radicals in this situation seems to be that of building a revolutionary movement. . . ." "Radicals" were urged to "be active in the conservative unions, the Socialist Party, the Communist organizations . . . and in various lay organizations where social and economic issues come to a head."[57]

One participant at the American Labor Associates' agenda meeting was a nonmember, the radical philosophy teacher Corliss Lamont, who wrote Sidney Hook:

> Enclosed is agenda of meeting I attended Wed. night. Persons checked on letterhead present, as well as others making about 40 in all. . . . Discussion was interesting *and futile.* I don't see how you can get 40 people of this type to agree on a program for a magazine.

Among the names checked on the ALA letterhead by Lamont, indicating that she attended the meeting, was Priscilla Hiss's.[58] Her active membership in the ALA and her work within the Socialist Party indicate a strong commitment to radical social change during the 1932–33 Depression years when the Hisses lived in New York. Both Alger and Priscilla had already been considerably "radicalized," in short, long before the election of a Democratic reform administration caused the couple to move from New York City to Washington.

WHITTAKER: THE PRODIGAL COMMUNIST

"Is there still a Communist Party?" Clifton Fadiman asked when Whittaker told him about his ideological conversion. When Chambers decided to join the Communist Party in 1925, most of his friends and former Columbia classmates were apolitical and interested mainly in the arts and their own careers. None of them could even help Whittaker make contact with a CP member to arrange for his own initiation; to them the party seemed a haven largely for foreign-speaking immigrant workers and not an appropriate place for an educated American WASP with literary talent such as their brooding, secretive friend. But Whittaker's habit of self-dramatization had long since become familiar to Columbia intimates, and most viewed this move toward Communism as merely his latest "mystification," in Meyer Schapiro's word. Schapiro, Fadiman, Trilling, Zukofsky, Van Doren, and the others to whom Chambers announced his plan found it odd but unsurprising.

It was Sender Garlin who put him into contact, Chambers said, with the small and elusive Communist Party. "Garlin arranged for me to be introduced to Charles [actually Sam] Krieger, whom I later learned used the alias, Clarence Miller," a CP member then working for a Yonkers newspaper. "Krieger brought me to my first Communist Party meeting, which was held in a loft at about West 57th Street and the North River. The Branch at this address was known as the English-speaking Branch," indicating the preponderance of immigrants in the party at that time, at least in New York. "I was admitted to membership . . . at this first meeting." A few days later Chambers received his Communist Party card at the group's New York headquarters in Union Square from a man named "Bert Miller."* In the month that followed, Chambers tried unsuccessfully to recruit two Columbia friends for the party, Zukofsky and Gassner, and took them to meetings of the English-speaking branch.[59]

Sam Krieger, who served as Chambers's sponsor, provided the author with a firsthand account of Whittaker's early Communist days. He recalled contacting Chambers first at the Public Library's Newspaper Room:

> [After] bringing him into the Communist Party, I maintained a relationship with him that was also of a social nature, because that was also part of recruiting someone: you made sure that that person got an education in the ways and the habits of Communist Party members and that person fitted into the activities or life of the Communist Party members. So that in addition to just going to Party meetings with Whittaker, I had to make sure that he read certain books at the time and that he acquired basic knowledge of the important material that went into the thinking of Communist Party members—for instance, a knowledge of Marx, Engels, Lenin—and that he engaged also—in addition to reading, or perhaps attending some workers' school or study group—that the new recruit undertook to do some sort of important day-to-day work . . . physically, like distribute the paper *The Daily Worker,* or sell literature. . . . In this case, Whittaker undertook to distribute *The Daily Worker* to newsstands and collect the unsold copies. . . . And I think he enrolled in a workers' school.

Encouraged by Krieger, Chambers joined a study group run by the Socialist economist Scott Nearing at the Rand School. Nearing's seminar studied "The Law of Social Revolution," and Krieger and his wife belonged to the group. Krieger and Chambers had drawn close—along with party work, they shared a common passion for handball at the Yonkers YMCA—but Chambers lost contact with his sponsor shortly afterward.[60]

Chambers continued to live in Lynbrook during his apprenticeship as a Communist, but family problems did not lessen. During the summer of 1925 he left his job at the library and spent six weeks hitchhiking across the country to Seattle. Chambers later recalled joining the IWW while in the West, having hitched for a time on his way out with a Wobbly: "He gave me instructions on how to jump freight trains. In those days each train was ruled by an IWW man and there

*Chambers met "Bert Miller" twenty-three years later under his real name, Ben Mandel, as HUAC's research director.

was a distinct advantage in having an IWW card." But Whittaker did not involve himself in union work and spent some of his time on the trip writing poetry. Two of the poems later appeared in *The Nation* through the help of Van Doren, then the magazine's literary editor.[61]

Back in New York, Chambers resumed Communist Party activities, went to work again at the library, and again fell in love with a married woman, Gertrude Zimmerman Hutchinson, the wife of a journalist named Kenneth Hutchinson, who met Chambers that fall at the library. Her husband found out about the affair:

> He and I took a long bus ride one evening [Chambers recalled], at which time he asked me to lay off his wife, which I did. However, she wouldn't lay off me. She used to come up to the library at night and hang over my desk until I finally got rough and told her it was over. This lasted for some months. She later became a Communist, and having separated from Hutchinson in about 1925,* she rented a very small house in Whitestone, Long Island. She was working then on the Encyclopedia Britannica. One night, she either came to the library or I met her by chance, and she suggested that I go to her home with her. Thereafter, I moved in with her in this Whitestone house. I lived there with her for about a year.[†62]

Despite his involvement with Gertrude Hutchinson, Whittaker spent part of the next summer on another westward swing, this time in style. He recalled buying a Ford roadster and driving to Montana with Lewis Green, known as "Bub." Chambers had planned initially to visit a friend in Seattle, but the tourists ran out of money in Montana and turned back. Neither man has left an account of their experiences, but both later denied a homosexual relationship, although they acknowledged in remarkably similar terms that "if there was such a relationship he [Green] never realized it; it was never a physical relationship but it might have been . . . psychological. . . ." Green's family (brother James excepted) strongly disapproved of Bub's association with Chambers, six years his senior.[63]

Chambers's androgynous sexual enthusiasms during this period emerged in a skillful poem, "Tandaradei," which appeared in June 1926 in a small quarterly called *Two Worlds* run by a young publisher of erotica named Samuel Roth.

---

*Chambers erred throughout this FBI statement by a year, which meant that her separation occurred in 1926.

†Chambers became successively involved with three Jewish women during this period: Gertrude Zimmerman Hutchinson, 1925–29; Ida Dales, 1929–31; and Esther Shemitz, whom he married in 1931. Jacob Burck, a friend and fellow Communist at the time, speculated about Chambers's predilection for Jewish women. Chambers told Burck that he had been circumcised when he was six because of an infection. But the explanation probably has much more to do with propinquity than anatomy or ethnicity; most of Chambers's friends at this time, male or female, were Jewish.

"Tandaradei" blurs all distinction between male and female, describing the actions of two lovers who could be of either sex—or of both.[64]

At about the time Chambers and Gertrude Hutchinson resumed their love affair, Whittaker's brother complicated matters further. First, he married his Lynbrook girlfriend, who had apparently become pregnant, and settled in Rockville Centre, a nearby town. Laha and Jay Sr. did not attend the wedding. Richard, unemployed, continued drinking, and the marriage quickly fell apart. Richard returned to his "little house" in Lynbrook, where Whittaker foiled a second suicide attempt. Chambers still returned to Lynbrook each evening after working until the library closed. Richard would meet him at the train to pour out his latest troubles. One night Whittaker remained late in New York, and when he reached the Lynbrook train station, his brother was not there.

Richard had apparently waited briefly, then driven to a nearby wharf from which "he could look in the direction of the place his wife was staying." He then left and returned to the Rockville Centre apartment, drank a quart of whiskey, turned on the gas stove, and stuck his head in the oven. "I heard the telephone ring the next morning," Whittaker remembered, "and then a frightful scream from my mother. I knew what had happened. We went over right away. . . . We took the body back home to Lynbrook. Both my parents were prostrated so the funeral arrangements were left to me."[65]

Richard's suicide proved to be the most painful and enduring emotional event of Whittaker's life. He was guilt-stricken, possibly because of his absence the previous night or, more likely, because of his refusal to agree to the suicide pact Richard had proposed earlier, despite an obvious attraction to suicide as a solution to his own woes. Chambers remained inconsolable and immobilized in Lynbrook for two months.

Apparently Richard had discussed the suicide pact again with Whittaker shortly before his final—and successful—attempt on his life, since Chambers wrote a poem the day before his brother's death, which he titled simply "Sept. 8, 1926":

> The moving masses of cloud, and the standing
> Freights on the siding in the sun,
> Alike induce in us that despair,
> Which we, brother, know there is no withstanding . . .
>
> . . . And you know, brother, it is the same with cessation;
> You know how perfect must be
> The moves of anything
> Designing its return to cessation.
>
> You know it is the perfection of the motion in me I am waiting.
> Not lack of love, or love of the motion of beings

Or things, or the sun's generation, that keeps me,
*But my perfection for death I am waiting.**

By early November, Whittaker's grief began to subside, and his thoughts turned increasingly (almost as consolation) to the prospect of rededicating his life to Communism. But, as Chambers revealed in a letter he sent to Meyer Schapiro, who was then studying abroad, the idea of suicide stayed with him.[66]

Sam Krieger recalled Chambers speaking incessantly about his brother's death once he resumed contacts with Communist friends late in 1926: "The only thing that kept him going was that he was now a member of the Communist Party, and . . . otherwise he didn't know what he'd have to live for." Chambers also remembered that friends in the CP like Harry Freeman or Sender Garlin, "who were then working on *The Daily Worker,* to get me out of my mood . . . urged me to go with them on that paper," and although he did begin writing news articles for the *Worker,* Whittaker had by no means settled his future course.

He haunted his brother's Rockville Centre home and Lynbrook gravesite in free moments, tramped the Long Island coastal countryside, and thought constantly about death:

> Well, I will go on [he wrote Schapiro in mid-December]. There are still a hundred ways of living: I will go to sea perhaps, or I will drop underground where no one knows me, or I will go to South America or I will stay here and develop with the working class movement, or I must finally make a name as a writer. In the evening I smile at all that, and know that little of it is me . . . tho death seems infinitely near: there is no soul and there is no eternity. . . . I really do not expect to take my own life within this month or this year (tho, of course, the horrible thought comes up: this is his year, and if you can postpone it now you never can die so near him again) but I am so organically indifferent that there is real doubt.[67]

Chambers had begun reading extensively again, mainly in the literature of revolutionary social theory, with Schapiro sending him a number of books unavailable to him in the United States.

Late in 1926 Whittaker apparently moved from Lynbrook into Gertrude Hutchinson's Whitestone home. But there are signs that Chambers's relationship with Hutchinson had become cooler than his emotional involvement with

---

*When Chambers published this poem in the February 1931 issue of *Poetry,* he changed the title to "October 21, 1926," a month and a half after Richard's death, and he also altered the final stanza significantly:

> *You know it is the cessation of the motion in me I am waiting:*
> *And not lack of love, or love of the sun's generation, and the motion*
> *Of bodies, or their stasis, that keeps me—but my perfection for death I am waiting.*

Lewis ("Bub") Green, who shared a love of camping, canoeing, and the outdoors. Gradually he supplanted his older brother James as Chambers's intimate. There were stark family resemblances between Bub's family situation and Whittaker's. Lewis Green later recalled that he and Whittaker became "particularly close friends after Chambers's brother committed suicide and [my] mother died in about 1924 [actually 1926]."[68]

Whittaker, in short, became drawn increasingly to Bub at the very moment he felt most guilty over Richard's suicide. But in the years that followed, however far their relationship may have extended, Chambers exhibited toward Green more than an older brother's normal protectiveness. The two men were together constantly for the next year or two, not only on their camping trips and horseback-riding Sundays but also in the company of Whittaker's Communist friends, whom Bub met on excursions to *The Daily Worker* (which Chambers began to help edit in 1927) and elsewhere. Several of Whittaker's friends in radical circles, also in their twenties, shared his enthusiasm for the outdoors, and both Green and Chambers later recalled running into many of them while camping out near Atlantic Beach. There Green met Sender Garlin and Mike Intrator, another of Whittaker's CP friends, while Chambers said that nearby tents were occupied by his friend and classmate Jack Rush (whose sister, Pauline, had married Clifton Fadiman) and by two young radical artists, a writer named Grace Lumpkin and her painter friend Esther Shemitz.

But Green's home deteriorated during the period he spent with Chambers; his father remarried, "got mixed in embezzlement, . . . and he completely disappeared." This led to Lewis's unhappy six months as a plumber's apprentice, after which he entered, first, CCNY (in 1927) and, a year later, NYU, where Chambers helped pay his tuition for one semester "with the proceeds from one of my translations." Although Chambers considered his ties with Bub best described as a "father-and-son relationship," he admitted later that the "homosexual aspect of this relationship was secret to both of us for years, but apparently not a secret to others. It was first brought to my attention during . . . a drunken party . . . probably in 1927 at the apartment of [name omitted]. At that time, I overheard [name omitted] remark . . . that there was a homosexual relationship between [Bub] and myself. This statement horrified me."[69]

Sometime in 1927 Green moved in with Chambers and Gertrude Hutchinson in her small Whitestone, Long Island, house. Both Green and Chambers later confirmed that Mrs. Hutchinson had sexual relations with both men. Chambers apparently told his next lover, Ida Dales, that he had initiated the communal sex, "feeling that Green needed" such experience, but that "eventually it became a rather intolerable and tense situation" and Chambers "had insisted upon breaking [it] up. . . ."[70]

Whittaker's long association with Gertrude Hutchinson ended abruptly in 1929 when a mutual friend introduced him to another young Communist activist named Ida Dales, with whom he soon set up housekeeping in an East Rockaway apartment. Lewis Green also broke with Hutchinson at about that time, and he married the following year. Ida Dales may have played a role in disrupting Bub's friendship with Whittaker: Green recalled "that he had very little to do with Ida . . . because he did not like her, considering her a very unattractive woman and a rude individual."*[71]

Professionally, the years that followed Richard's death proved remarkably productive for Whittaker, both as a journalist and as a translator. His assignments on *The Daily Worker* became increasingly important ones until by 1929 he had become news editor, teaching journalism courses at the CP's "Workers School." He also expressed his devotion to Communism in a series of revolutionary poems, but his literary talents found more lasting expression (although Chambers would not have thought so at the time) in eight books that he translated from the French and German, published between 1928 and 1932. The best known and most popular of these, his translation of Felix Salten's children's classic, *Bambi*, its first version in English, appeared in 1928. Clifton Fadiman, who worked for the publishing house of Simon and Schuster at the time, helped arrange several of Chambers's translating jobs, among them novels by the important German writers Heinrich Mann and Franz Werfel.[72]

But Whittaker accepted the translation commissions primarily to supplement the small salary he received from the *Worker*. Although he maintained ties with Fadiman and other Columbia friends, Chambers denigrated their efforts to build lives and careers outside of the Communist Party:

Dear Meyer,

The young men of our generation are going to pieces in America [Chambers wrote Schapiro in 1927]; perhaps it is well that you escape to Egypt; yet why do you? Those who have no minds or character, only fads & education & inclination sail off to Europe every summer. . . . And I? What do I do? More & more, too long to tell. . . . Your generation is falling to pieces. In the last 3 or 4 months there have been from 10–19 suicides; all youths, school-boys & girls. Commenting on it in the *New Masses*, Mike Gold wrote: "There are only two positive philosophies in the U.S. today—the philosophy of Capitalist Imperialism & the philosophy of the Communists; and the younger generation has been taught to scoff at both." Of course it goes deeper than that, but there is a germ of truth there.[73]

---

*Later Green and his wife saw a great deal of Chambers in 1931 after he married Esther Shemitz, but his earlier intimacy with Whittaker was never restored. "He . . . at first found Esther Shemitz friendly although later she appeared to be antagonistic toward him, possibly because she felt that Chambers was too fond of him." Although the two men corresponded and saw one another occasionally during the 1930s, their contacts tapered off after Chambers joined the Communist underground.

Whatever meaning Chambers extracted from his life at this point—apart from his relationships with Gertrude Hutchinson, Lewis Green, and (later) Ida Dales—came entirely from life on the *Worker* and from his ponderous poems, such as "March for the Red Dead" published in the *Worker* on May 23, 1927 ("For the dead, the dead, the dead, we march, comrades, workers"), or an equally self-conscious "proletarian" anthem, "Before the End," that appeared in the July 9, 1927, issue of *News Magazine Supplement* ("Before the end, Comrade, before the end / How many of us alive today will stand / Helpless to press a sentenced comrade's hand / Knowing we look our last upon a friend, / Comrades, before the end?").

"I have gone quite over [to] the revolutionary movement," Chambers wrote Schapiro in April 1927 about his devotion to Communism. "This was inevitable, and it is even surprising that the process took so long." He dreamed about a future role of importance within the CP:

> If I cannot be a leader of one kind or another, I shall certainly belie my quali-
> fications, be less useful than I should, a failure, in fact. . . . I am what is, in the
> Party, called a *literate,* and the *literates,* willy-nilly struggle as they may against
> it, make up a leading van, just as the Party as a whole leads the van of the labor
> movement; leads when it properly functions.

That same month the Public Library fired its leading Communist "literate" as a book thief. An inspection of his locker on April 13 turned up eight NYPL books, and in a subsequent search of his Lynbrook home, inspectors found fifty-six books he had stolen years earlier from Columbia. "I have lost my job in the Library," Chambers wrote Schapiro several weeks later;

> locker raided: radical books & handbills discovered. And, what is worse, books
> smuggled from other departments. Hence a *technical* charge based on *character*
> & discharge. But nothing *criminal* could be charged. So I have been barred from
> the Library, may not use it, a real misfortune. . . . For me [however] the loss is
> not so serious. I had arranged with Kip to leave the Library in September &
> enter an automobile training school, to learn mechanics. The break, says Kip,
> came only 2 months too soon.[74]

But Chambers never pursued this technical training. Instead he began full-time activity at *The Daily Worker* and accepted the first of his translating assignments, with Fadiman's help. The books he stole from Columbia, when returned, led Whittaker's old nemesis, Dean Hawkes, to inscribe on Chambers's college transcript on April 25: "Should not be allowed to register in any part of the university," an injunction that would only have amused the young "revolutionary" had he known about it. Chambers spent the next two years concerned mainly with translations, writing for the *Worker,* and a deteriorating relationship with Gertrude Hutchinson.

The stock-market collapse made 1929 a decidedly unhappy year for many Americans. But for Chambers the signs were somewhat more mixed. The *ménage à trois* in Whitestone broke down, and there ensued a two-year disruption of his membership in the Communist Party. The deaths of his father and grandmother that year left only the more sympathetic Laha surviving of Whittaker's troubled Lynbrook family. At the same time, Whittaker began the happier phase of a two-year love affair with Ida Dales.

Since 1927 Chambers had "sat in the workers' councils" as an important staff member of *The Daily Worker*. Despite his recollection that its chief editor, Robert Minor, was "constantly out of his office and the job of running the 'Daily Worker' . . . [was] left to me," this description seems an exaggeration. Communist journalists who worked on the paper at the time recalled Whittaker, whose writing they admired, as a copy editor and specialist in rewriting stories and "workers' correspondence." Whatever his true role on the paper, Chambers ended it, leaving the *Worker*—and the CP—sometime in 1929 during a battle between the party's then-dominant leadership group, led by Jay Lovestone and Benjamin Gitlow, and an insurgent wing that included William Z. Foster and Earl Browder. The rebels, although comprising only a minority of the membership, took over the party's leadership through the support of Soviet Party chiefs. Chambers had not been closely identified with the "Lovestoneites," but after the expulsion of Lovestone and his followers in 1929 he found himself under attack (especially by a brother-in-law of Browder's also on the *Worker*). He drifted away from the paper and the party in disgust that same year.[75]

Before leaving the *Worker*, Chambers had met Ida Dales, then twenty-eight like himself and employed in a Communist organization as a stenographer. Their affair began sometime that summer, and the couple moved in September 1929 into an East Rockaway apartment. Dales would recall "that she had intended to marry him and she believed that was his intention also. . . . Their relationship lasted for about one and one half years." The month after they met, Jay Sr. died of chronic hepatitis. Whittaker's father had been a heavy drinker since 1926; Richard's death had apparently destroyed his remaining interest in life. Grandmother Whittaker had been placed in a mental institution earlier that year, where she soon died, so that Jay's death left Laha alone in the Lynbrook house.

At Laha's invitation, Whittaker and Ida moved into the home with her in November and remained there for "three or four months." The two women apparently fought a great deal, or so Chambers told his friends Jacob and Esther Burck. Then Ida became pregnant. She and Chambers moved out, "taking an apartment on East 12th Street, New York City [where] she submitted to an abortion." Afterward Chambers and Dales returned to East Rockaway, where they remained until the relationship ended—at Whittaker's insistence—"in late 1930 or early 1931." Chambers told the Burcks at this time that he had broken with Ida Dales because she couldn't get along with his mother and because she didn't wish to have a child. He said nothing about the abortion. "No need was so strong in me as the need to have children," Chambers later wrote of this year in his life.[76]

Sometime in 1930 Chambers began seeing Esther Shemitz, who quickly supplanted Ida Dales in his affections. "I told Ida . . . of this fact and we then parted." (Chambers may already have been living with Esther at that time.) Ida later described Whittaker as "a truthful person but a rather strange personality. She thought of him as a romantic person, highly emotional, and unrealistic, [and] during the period she lived with Chambers she had thought that he had some tendency toward homosexuality." Apparently Chambers told Dales the entire story of his Whitestone years with Green and Hutchinson prior to meeting her.[77]

His two years of formal separation from the Communist Party proved neither unhappy nor wrenching ones for Chambers, both because of his active love life and because of his ability to maintain ties with many Communist friends. One of them, Mike Intrator, a supporter of Lovestone, had been expelled in 1929, and Chambers spent a great deal of time with him during this period. Other intimates, such as Jacob and Esther Burck, remained sympathetic and receptive to Whittaker despite his alienation from the CP's new leadership. Burck then worked as a cartoonist for *The New Masses,* and he maintained a studio apartment on 14th Street, where he sculpted and painted. Chambers spent many evenings with the Burcks during his years of ostracism, often showing up at mealtime, and regularly proclaiming his devotion to Communism although as a member of the unrecognized "loyal opposition." Whittaker also began writing short stories sometime in 1930, and Burck served as intermediary with Walt Carmon, editor of *The New Masses,* to arrange their publication, a circumstance that led directly to Chambers's return to the Communist Party.[78]

Initially some Communists on *The New Masses,* including the cartoonist William Gropper, protested Carmon's decision to publish the work of a "Lovestoneite renegade" (the magazine was ostensibly an independent radical organ at the time, although dominated by Communist writers). But Carmon printed the four stories submitted by Chambers in 1931: "The titles of these stories were 'Can You Make Out Their Voices?,' 'The Death of the Communists,' 'You Have Seen the Heads,' [and] 'Our Comrade Munn.' The themes . . . [Chambers recalled] were the situation among the poor farmers in the middle west, the struggle of the Chinese Communist, how a Communist organizer should conduct himself, and a kind of religious appraisal of what a devoted Communist should be."

The four stories attracted considerable attention among American radicals. International Publishers, the official Communist publishing house, issued "Can You Make Out Their Voices?" in pamphlet form, and it was soon translated into a number of languages. Hallie Flanagan, then the head of Vassar's Playwriting Laboratory, turned the story into a play, which radical theater groups around the world performed regularly during the 1930s. Another of the stories, "Our Comrade Munn," also was translated, dramatized, and widely produced.

More important to Chambers's future in the CP, however, was the reaction of a leading Soviet critic in the Moscow publication *International Literature*, who rhapsodized about "Can You Make Out Their Voices?": "It gives a revolutionary exposition of the problem of the agricultural crisis and correctly raises the question of the leading role of the Communist Party in the revolutionary farmers' movement. . . . For the first time [in American writing], it raises the image of the Bolshevik."

Before year's end, Chambers had made his peace with Communist Party officials, meeting first with Alexander Trachtenberg—the party's leading cultural "commissar"—and with an even more important (if mysterious) figure, Charles Dirba, head of the CP's Central Control Commission, which screened members for ideological deviations. Because of the popularity his short stories enjoyed among party members, and considering Chambers's evident talent as a writer, Dirba apparently forgave Whittaker's past indiscretions and approved his selection as an editor of *The New Masses*. The magazine's July 1931 issue announced his new status and contained a somewhat embroidered and distorted biography alongside a picture of Chambers.*[79]

Both footloose bachelors at the time, Whittaker and Mike Intrator struck up friendships with Esther Shemitz and Grace Lumpkin, who shared a small house in Greenwich Village where Grace wrote her novels and Esther painted. The two women had become friends a few years earlier while they worked for a Quaker magazine called *The World Tomorrow*. Both participated in a number of Communist-sponsored causes during the late twenties and early thirties, although neither joined the CP. *The World Tomorrow* had a pacifist and mildly Socialist orientation. Among the magazine's editors were two women who would soon become leading Communists, Grace Hutchins and Anna Rochester, and who became friendly with Esther Shemitz. With Rochester's help, Esther obtained a job with the Soviet government-affiliated Amtorg Trading Company, where she worked for three years after leaving the pacifist magazine. While at Amtorg, Esther joined the John Reed Club, participated in Communist rallies, and became involved in a 1930 Passaic strike demonstration, where she remembered being "beaten up during an ensuing riot."[80]

It was "at, or after this demonstration," Esther thought, that she initially encountered Whittaker Chambers. But Shemitz and Lumpkin, whose 1932 novel, *To Make My Bread*, made her famous among radicals, may have met Chambers and Intrator earlier on an Atlantic Beach outing. They became a foursome in 1930. Esther and Whittaker married on April 15, 1931, and Lumpkin and Intrator were wed the same year.

---

*At about the same time Chambers joined a local branch of the Communist-dominated John Reed Club of radical writers and artists.

The two couples shared cramped quarters in the women's 11th Street house for several months until the *ménage à quatre* began to attract criticism from friends. Some of these suspected that both Whittaker and Mike Intrator had been homosexuals prior to their marriages. "You are all living in a sea of shit," Jacob Burck told Chambers at this time, to which Whittaker responded laconically: "You, too." Whether because of tensions inherent in living at such close quarters or because of their friends' disapproval, Whittaker and Esther moved early in 1932 to a farmhouse at Glen Gardner, New Jersey, owned by a friend named Franklin Spier. Chambers commuted into Manhattan to work at *The New Masses*. But he remained at the magazine only a few months longer. At that point he received and accepted an invitation to join the Communist underground.[81]

Whittaker Chambers and Alger Hiss had at least one thing in common in 1932 that distinguished them from millions of Americans: they were both working. At times that fact apparently discomfited the Hisses, as when a friend of Alger's remarked how pleasant the day seemed, only to have Priscilla snap back that it might be a nice day for people with homes and servants, but it wasn't a very nice day for the sharecroppers in Oklahoma! "Priscilla denies that she would ever have said such a thing," according to a Hiss biographer, "and Alger doesn't remember being present at the time, but he says it would have been perfectly in character for her, and in those days he might have said the same thing."[82]

Satisfactorily married and with a promising career in corporate law ahead of him, Hiss apparently assuaged uneasiness over the Depression's suffering by devoting many of his free hours to the International Juridical Association. His wife found sufficient time—apart from caring for Timothy and researching the fine-arts book—to immerse herself more deeply than Alger in the organizational network of New York radicalism, both of the traditional Socialist and the innovative American Labor Associates varieties. Whittaker Chambers's commitment to revolutionary Socialism went deeper still, especially after seven years of close and turbulent association with the Communist movement. Esther Shemitz Chambers, although content to remain detached from her husband's CP work, also remained a quietly faithful, if somewhat nondenominational, radical with Socialist, pacifist, and Communist elements mingled in her background.

All four young people (Esther was senior at thirty-two) shared with millions of their generation yearning to transcend mere personal or professional fulfillment, whether in families or careers, for more active roles as reformers in the rapid transformation of American society.

To radicals especially, 1932 seemed both a terminal year and a turning point in their dreams. Millions were jobless and undernourished. A Bonus Army of World War I veterans had been dispersed by federal troops in Washington. The country's capitalists had proved impotent in the face of continued economic collapse. The

Hoover administration lived out its final months despised by America's impoverished majority and incapable of providing relief for the needy. Old authorities crumbled, and widespread social despair encouraged the belief—at least among the more militant—that no amount of piecemeal change could restore the nation's battered economic structure and the bruised morale of its people.

It seemed to some a moment for revolutionaries impatient to serve, if not themselves, then "the sharecroppers of Oklahoma" and similarly desperate Americans. "Ah, what an age it is / When to speak of trees is almost a crime / For it is a kind of silence about injustice," ran Bertolt Brecht's verses about this era. "You, who shall emerge from the flood / In which we are sinking, Think— / When you speak of our weaknesses, / Also of the dark time / That brought them forth."[83] The following year, in that dark time, Alger Hiss joined the New Deal and Whittaker Chambers entered the Communist underground.

III

THE UN-SECRET AGENT

A NEW LIFE

When he disappeared to become a member of the Communist underground in the spring of 1932, Whittaker Chambers and his bride were still living in the New Jersey farmhouse. Glen Gardner was two hours' commuting time from New York and Chambers's work at the *New Masses* editorial post. Before dropping out of sight, he and Esther had remodeled a barn on the farm property where they lived during the transition period between Whittaker's brief tenure as a recusant "open Party" *New Masses* editor and his recruitment for secret work. Esther Shemitz's quiet demeanor contrasted comfortably with the flamboyant excesses toward which Chambers tended at moments of crisis. The couple settled into easy domesticity, and in the years that followed—despite their frequent changes in residence while Whittaker served in the underground—Esther managed to create a peaceful and stable family environment, one for which Chambers yearned if only to counterbalance the violent, unhappy memories of the Lynbrook maelstrom.[1]

Late in the spring of 1932 Chambers received a phone call from someone he had never met, Max Bedacht, head of the International Workers Order, an important party affiliate, and a member of the American Communist Central Committee. Bedacht summoned Chambers to his office and announced that he had been "co-opted" for secret work with a "peculiar institution" of the party—"I remember the expression 'peculiar institution,' because it has a [special] meaning in American history"—and he gave Chambers a day to think it over. Understandably, Esther "strongly opposed" the change. But the next morning, according to Chambers's FBI deposition, when he reported his refusal to Bedacht, "he told me that I had no choice."[2]

The new post required that Chambers separate himself from *The New Masses* and disappear from "open" Communist circles. Before the recruit could object further, Bedacht led him away from CP headquarters into the nearby 14th Street subway station, where they met a friend of Chambers's from their *Daily Worker* days, John Loomis Sherman, who also had been expelled in 1929 as a Lovestoneite. Chambers recalled that at their last meeting after the expulsion he had tried to comfort Sherman, who "sat down at his typewriter and cried." Yet Chambers felt somehow that "it was perhaps John Sherman who suggested me for underground activity."

Later that day Sherman introduced Chambers to a Russian named "Herbert," who questioned him closely about his earlier separation from the party and his subsequent views on doctrinal questions. ("Herbert" was later identified as Valentin Markin, a relative of the Soviet leader V. M. Molotov; Markin died in New York in 1934 under still-unsettled circumstances.) In the days that followed, Chambers met another Russian named "Ulrich," a man "who thereafter became my superior. And it was he who explained to me my function," which at the time involved acting as liaison between the American Communist Party underground and the Russian espionage network in New York.[3]

Several factors made Whittaker Chambers an attractive prospect for such secret work. First, he was a well-educated and highly literate native American CP member at a time when foreign-born immigrant workers still comprised the bulk of party membership. Chambers could mingle easily with all classes of Americans outside the party. Moreover, his keen intelligence, despite a weakness for self-dramatization, apparently commended him to his Russian underground superiors such as Herbert and Ulrich far more than to the party's more prosaic and doctrinaire American functionaries. By this time the Soviet Union had the final say on all such matters within American Communism.

His separation from the CP between 1929 and 1931, despite its consolations, had shaken Chambers: "I was determined that I would never again leave the Communist Party no matter what I thought, but would simply accept discipline and go along whether I believed in it or not." But this "good soldier" explanation subsequently adopted by Chambers obscures a large portion of the truth, or so the evidence suggests: namely, that he welcomed and relished the new assignment as an opportunity to demonstrate his talents while serving as a front-line "soldier of the revolution." His friend Jacob Burck described Chambers to the author as a "writer who preferred to live his novels rather than to write them," and in the years that followed, Whittaker Chambers became probably the most un-secret agent in the annals of American espionage, a spy (in Burck's phrase) "who basked in the cold."[4]

In July 1932 Chambers left his *New Masses* office for the last time to begin a six-year career as an underground courier. He used the alias "Karl" most frequently during these years, although his contacts also knew the husky, intense young man under a variety of other pseudonyms. Ella Winter, then the wife of journalist Lincoln Steffens and a friend of many left-wing notables, met Chambers in 1933 as "Harold Phillips," while the literary agent Maxim Lieber, who also knew Chambers's true identity, worked with him for a time on an underground project as "Lloyd Cantwell."[5] Others who circulated around the periphery of American Communism during the Depression decade recognized the brown-haired agent as "David Breen," "Arthur Dwyer," "Bob," and still other aliases.

The furtive life of a secret CP functionary evidently excited Chambers at the beginning, especially when contrasted with his mundane writing and editing chores at *The New Masses*. Along with other Communists, Chambers considered the goal of a "Soviet America" within reach in the foreseeable future. Fifteen million Americans were unemployed in 1932, and many thousands wandered the highways, train tracks, and countryside in search of food, shelter, work, and purpose. Although most Americans remained firmly committed to providing reform and relief through the normal processes of government, a million of them broke political ranks that year to vote for either the Socialist presidential candidate, Norman Thomas, or the Communist nominee, William Z. Foster. In such times one radical writer's ability to regard his "secret work" as important and constructive seems more comprehensible.

OUR MAN IN MANHATTAN

Few among Chambers's older New York friends and associates, either from Columbia days or among "open" Communists, remained in the dark. Many individuals from all parts of the American Left—Communists, Lovestoneites, Trotskyites, and Socialists—were soon "witting" to the nature of Chambers's new role in the underground. Since most of "Karl's" assignments until mid-1933 were in the New York City area, Chambers frequently had opportunity to dramatize his new vocation with elaborate displays of nonrecognition whenever he chanced upon friends or acquaintances in public places. One leading Communist official indicated this awareness when he told a New York journalist that "we all knew Chambers' picture was turned to the wall, but with honor." Ella Winter remembered one of these occasions. While walking along a Manhattan street with a friend during the mid-thirties, Chambers, who had previously tried—and failed—to recruit her for the underground using the name "Harold Phillips," suddenly came into view. "Don't take any notice of that man," her friend, a leading film distributor, quickly cautioned her. "That was Whittaker Chambers, who is doing secret work for the Party."[6]

During his six years as an agent Chambers successfully led several lives, each detached from the others. First, his normal one within the CP's espionage network. Second, a family life with Esther and two children. Third, a series of detours into homosexual encounters. And, fourth, his secretive efforts to maintain close links with non-Communist friends outside the party's orbit. Chambers managed to juggle these conflicting lives without noticeable damage to his primary roles as a husband, father, and Communist agent.

Throughout the period, he tried to maintain close and regular contacts with friends whose political loyalties brought them into opposition to the Stalinist-dominated CPUSA. Chambers often removed himself momentarily from his responsibilities as a party courier to visit people such as Meyer and Lillian Schapiro, Robert Cantwell, Herbert Solow, and Mike Intrator, all of whom knew generally about the nature of his work for the CP without being privy to the details.* Chambers "took breathers" from his espionage assignments in short, much as he had fled prosaic literal editing for the underground. When the Moscow purges went public in 1936, these extra-party associations would prove costly to him, but in the early years there seemed no harm in the practice. Often Chambers described the work proudly to these friends, persons whose company also provided the chance to discuss literary or artistic interests unrelated to CP work or party slogans.[7] But if he relished his newly acquired notoriety among old friends, in the process he recklessly cast off the normal degree of anonymity necessary for effective espionage. Thus Herbert Solow described Chambers's behavior:

> During my absence in Europe [in 1932], Chambers had left the *New Masses*. On my return he told me he was back in the Party but that he was engaged in special work of a confidential nature. Later he told me he was a member of the Russian, not of the American CP. . . . One day he asked me to lend him $400 because, he said, funds had been delayed. He repaid me at the appointed time, a few days or a week. Another time he told me to take his key and enter his apartment before him, as he thought enemies might be there. I did so, thinking the business rather silly. I questioned him at this time and he told me that he was engaged in counterespionage for the Soviets against the Japanese.

Chambers also told Mike Intrator and Grace Lumpkin about his new assignment, shortly after becoming an underground Communist. He appeared so proud of the role, in fact, that Meyer Schapiro remembered Chambers visiting old Columbia friends far more frequently than during the late twenties: "He had found valuable work and had regained a sense of dignity."[8]

This disdain for normal security precautions when communicating with his New York circle reached a high point when during a short stay in Moscow (the precise length of the trip remains unknown) Chambers sent postcards to friends in the United States in April 1933, including Jacob Burck and Meyer Schapiro. Whittaker and Esther Chambers traveled to the Soviet Union, using fraudulent passports, presumably so that he could train as an agent at the Lenin School or receive extensive briefing by the Soviet Military Intelligence (Fourth Branch) officials to whom Chambers had been assigned shortly after joining the underground.[†]

---

*Chambers told Franklin Spier that he was doing "highly secretive work," but refused to disclose any details of the work since he did not want his friends involved, according to Spier. FBI Interview #3059, March 14, 1949. "Around the Movement, he [Chambers] was the best known of underground agents that the Party had." James T. Farrell to the author, April 14, 1978.

†Felix Inslerman, a photographer who later worked with Chambers microfilming stolen documents, took a similar trip to Russia for training in espionage in 1935. After leaving the CP in 1938, Chambers wrote several articles about his work in helping to prepare faked passports for use by agents wishing to travel abroad secretly for Comintern meetings and other purposes.

Chambers could not resist writing to the Schapiros in order to congratulate them upon the birth of their child, and one of the two postcards sent (both bearing postmark cancellations from the Soviet Union) reads: "4/22/33 Moscow. Esther and I send our best to the new baby. A Soviet blessing on it. [signed] David [one of Chambers's middle names] and Esther." This card was in Esther's handwriting, while the second one, written by Whittaker, had a picture on its front of Maxim Gorky holding two children and read: "Best wishes to all three of you. Whit." Jacob Burck remembers receiving a card from Chambers in Moscow about the same time, but did not save his.[9]

For the remainder of his life Chambers never admitted having been in the Soviet Union. Occasionally he even feigned ignorance of Russian, a language in which he was fluent. And Mrs. Chambers still disavows any knowledge of their mission to Moscow. Further confirmation of the trip, however, comes from Robert Cantwell, Chambers's friend, who was then on *The New Republic*'s book-review staff. In mid-1933 Chambers asked Cantwell if he could review a new book, *The White Armies of Russia.* The review appeared in the magazine's July 19, 1933, issue under the pseudonym "Hugh Jones." In the credit line Chambers described himself: "Hugh Jones is an engineer who recently returned from an extended visit to Russia."[10]

That "Hugh Jones" was really Whittaker Chambers was confirmed by Lincoln Steffens. Apparently Steffens had corresponded with Chambers in 1933 about preparing a biography of Edward B. Filene, the Boston department-store magnate, radical progressive, and Steffens's patron. Eventually, Robert Cantwell took the assignment and lived for a period with Steffens and Ella Winter in Carmel, California, though he never published the biography. But Steffens had written Chambers in June 1933 congratulating him on his short stories in *The New Masses:*

> How you can write! And your stuff—Whenever I hear people talk about "proletarian art and literature," I'm going to ask them to shut their minds and look at you. I hope you are very young, though I don't see how you can be. I hope, too, that you are daring, that you have no respect for the writers of my generation and you know as I do that you can do it. Now I will put on my hat again.[11]

Although already in the underground, Chambers contacted Steffens on Thanksgiving Day 1933 during a visit Steffens paid to New York City:

> Whittaker Chambers called up this morning; said he heard I would like to see him and offered to call [Steffens wrote his son that evening]. I suggested lunch

---

I found copies of the articles, which Chambers believed destroyed, in Herbert Solow's files. In 1940 the Communist Party leader in the United States, Earl Browder, was convicted of using such passports, known in the trade at the time as "boots." Nadya Ulanovskaya, interviewed in 1978 after publication of *Perjury,* questioned whether Chambers had actually been to Russia. Chambers's biographer, Sam Tanenhaus, also questions the above analysis.

with me here. He had been cheered by a copy of my letter to him. Really appreciated it because nobody had ever before given him a hand. "Not the other left writers, not the other men on the Masses?" I ask—

He: Never a word. We don't do that for one another. I said that was a Red fault; there must be "warm spots." He agreed; he himself tries now to be a warm spot. But it is not the spirit of the Party. I said I got that at the Masses yesterday; they listened, but were unresponsive, and I thought, got or took nothing. "There you are known," he said. They told me they had a very impressive, suggestive talk from you and that's why I am here; because they were so impressed, especially North [Joseph North, a Communist writer and friend of Chambers]. . . .

In September 1934 Steffens wrote a long letter to Chambers, beginning "Dear Mr. Hugh Jones." Doubtless Robert Cantwell, at some point during his months with Steffens, described the "Hugh Jones" review and explained Chambers's present work and use of pseudonyms.

A number of those who came to know him as "Karl"—including Alger and Priscilla Hiss, according to Chambers—believed that he was either a German or a Russian because of the slight accent and foreign intonation that he affected, an easy partial disguise for a skilled linguist like Whittaker to adopt. "[Ludwig] Lore, [John] Abt and others who have met [him in the underground] think he is a Russian," Solow's notarized 1938 memo quotes Chambers as stating. "He once went to Lore's and met there a group including Alphonse Goldschmidt. The latter mistook him for somebody else and said, 'Why, Col. Dietrich, the last time I saw you, you were on the General Staff in Moscow.' He let the impression stick in that group." Chambers taught himself to write and speak several languages, including German, Russian, Spanish, and—according to his friends—more difficult ones such as Hungarian and Chinese. Julian Wadleigh, who later confessed to passing State Department documents to Chambers in 1937–38, described a dinner with "Karl" in a Washington Chinese restaurant where the latter read the entire menu aloud in what appeared to be Chinese.[12]

THE SECRET LIFE OF WHITTAKER CHAMBERS

Underground work or not, the Chamberses wanted a normal family life. The strains and tensions must have been profound for them both. Two children were born in these years, Ellen in 1933 and John in 1936. Esther understood clearly that her husband was performing secret, perhaps illegal tasks for the CP; her name was often changed to match his own aliases. Thus, "David Breen's wife became Edna Breen," and, according to Whittaker and Esther, they presented themselves to Alger and Priscilla Hiss as "Carl" and "Liza." The Chambers family lived in many places during this period, and Esther made the best of her husband's irregular schedule. Often he was gone for days at a time, presumably on assignments about which he rarely confided.* While at home, Chambers was an attentive husband (according to Esther) and, as his letters at the time indicate, an evidently doting father.[13]

Not only did Chambers withhold from his wife detailed knowledge of his underground activities, but he also kept from her any awareness of his other secret life away from home, his intermittent homosexual encounters. Even when confessing these to the FBI in February 1949, fearing that defense lawyers would pounce on the issue at Alger Hiss's forthcoming perjury trial, Chambers did so reluctantly and with shame. But Chambers denied the many rumors circulating in 1949 about possible sexual relations between himself and Hiss:

> This is completely untrue [he stated to the FBI]. At no time, did I have such relations, or even the thought of such relations with Hiss or with anybody else in the Communist Party or connected with Communist work of any kind. I kept my secret as jealously from my associates in the C.P. as I did from everyone else. I tell it now only because, in this case, I stand for truth. Having testified mercilessly against others, it has become my function to testify mercilessly against myself.[14]

When she was questioned by the FBI in 1949, his former mistress Ida Dales had no direct recollection of any homosexual activities on Whittaker's part. Nor did Grace Lumpkin or others. Apparently it was only after Chambers began underground work that his new *modus operandi* allowed him the opportunity to test in a more secretive fashion the other side of his sexual nature. The story is told most fully in Chambers's 1949 statements to the FBI:

> In 1933 or 4, a young fellow stopped me on the street in N.Y. and asked me if I could give him a meal and lodgings for the night. I fed him and he told me about his life as a miner's son. I was footloose, so I took him to a hotel to spend the night. During the course of our stay at the hotel that night I had my first homosexual experience. There he . . . taught me an experience I did not know existed. At the same time, he revealed to me, and unleashed, the . . . tendency of which I was still unaware. It was a revelation to me. As a matter of fact it set off a chain reaction in me which was almost impossible to control. Because it had been repressed so long, it was all the more violent when once set free.
>
> I do not know the identity of the young man I spoke of, nor does he know my true identity. I have never seen him since the first night I met him. For three or four years, I fought a wavering battle against this affliction. Since that time [in 1933 or 1934], and continuing up to the year 1938, I engaged in numerous

---

*Esther Chambers insisted during the Hiss trials that she had never realized Whittaker was engaged in espionage work.

homosexual activities both in New York and Washington, D.C. At first I would engage in these activities whenever by accident the opportunity presented itself. However, after a while the desire became greater and I actively sought out the opportunities for homosexual relationships. I recall that incidents of this nature took place in the Hotel Annapolis and the Hotel Pennsylvania in Washington, D.C. I registered in these hotels under assumed names which I cannot now recall. I know that other incidents took place in hotels in New York City which I cannot now remember, but concerning which I might state that they were the typical "flea bag" type of hotel one finds in certain parts of Manhattan. I never had any prolonged affair with any one man and never visited any known places where these type of people were known to congregate. I generally went to parks and other parts of town where these people were likely to be found.

I am positive that no man with whom I had these relations during this period ever knew my true identity, nor do I at this time recall the names of any of them.[15]

When he left the Communist Party in 1938, according to Chambers, he "managed to break myself of my homosexual tendencies and since that time I have been a model husband and father." He described his homosexuality as his "darkest personal secret," one that he had never divulged either to his family or to friends, "particularly those in the Communist Party." Nor had he even mentioned the subject previously to his wife or attorneys, he told the FBI, raising it "for the first time to anyone today [because] . . . in all probability this subject matter will be brought to light [during the Hiss trial]." How had he managed to cease homosexual activities in 1938? "With God's help," he said, after "embracing, for the first time, religion."

But Chambers's memory may have tricked him on this point. Although he defected from the Communist underground in 1938, his formal affiliation with Episcopalianism came several years later and his 1937–39 letters do not indicate interest in religion. The implication remains clear: that Chambers persisted in forming casual homosexual attachments after he broke with Communism when (even though in hiding) he made a number of brief, sometimes puzzling trips to New York City, ostensibly in connection with efforts to obtain money and translating jobs. It is possible that only after he began work at *Time* in April 1939 and either formed or renewed close (but nonsexual) friendships with several of his religiously minded colleagues, men such as Samuel Welles and Robert Cantwell, did Chambers finally break all ties with his only remaining underground activity, that restless "cruising" of city streets for male partners which had both attracted and tormented him during the 1930s.[16]

ULRICH AND HIS CIRCLE:
THE WORLD OF SOVIET INTELLIGENCE

No evidence has emerged to contradict Chambers's assertion that he never mixed the Communist Party's secret work with his private homosexual encounters. Long periods away from home gave him time enough for both, although during the early months after joining the underground he maintained a crowded schedule spent learning the personnel and practices of his new associates. The Sherman-"Herbert" spy network appears crude and haphazard when contrasted with the CP's far more extensive—and more professional—secret operations in Washington during the New Deal years and the Second World War. In the 1932–34 period there was a good deal of bustling about Manhattan to conspiratorial meetings using passwords and the other paraphernalia of an espionage operation—but little in the way of results, as the Russians later acknowledged when they recalled, first, "Herbert" and, later, his successor, Alexander Petrovich Ulanovski ("Ulrich"). Herbert and Ulrich did not get along. Although Herbert was an ordinary Bolshevik bureaucrat seconded for some reason to the *apparat*, Ulrich had led a complex life, common among Soviet espionage agents at the time. Many had begun their secret work during the early 1920s when the Bolsheviks treated new, ideologically suspect recruits from Menshevik or Social Revolutionary ranks more tolerantly. Many Russian underground workers abroad had developed loyalties not to Stalin, but to other Bolshevik leaders such as Trotsky, Bukharin, or Zinoviev, those who had lost out in the power struggle.

Some thought they had managed to detach themselves from the fratricidal battles within the Soviet leadership. Ulrich, as Chambers remembered him, fitted this latter description. He described the Russian to the FBI in 1949 as well read and someone who detested Stalin, claiming to have been in Siberian prisons with him prior to the Revolution:

> Ulrich was rather skeptical in his opinions of the Communist Party and in his activities, in that he did not always believe in the infallibility of the Party. He had been a Partisan leader in the Crimea and Southern Russia during the Civil War and [later] . . . had done underground work in the Argentine and also in China during the "Borodine days."*[17]

When first introducing him to Ulrich, John Sherman informed Chambers that the latter would be his superior and that Sherman—who then moved to the West Coast to recruit other underground volunteers—would no longer maintain contact. Ulrich's agents met regularly at a brownstone house in the West Fifties

---

*The reference is to Michael Borodin, an important Bolshevik representative to the Chinese Nationalist government—and to the Chinese Communist Party—during the 1920s.

known to group members as "the Gallery." The apartment's owner remained unknown to Chambers since there was no name on the doorbell, nor did he meet anyone there except for the Russians Herbert and Ulrich.

During these months of apprenticeship Chambers did little more for the group than to pass messages back and forth between the Russians and Max Bedacht concerning the movements of couriers. Chambers claimed to have had two meetings during this period also, through Ulrich, with a Finn named Arvid Jacobsen, who was later arrested and convicted in a major trial of Soviet agents in Finland during the 1930s. A few months after he joined Ulrich's group, Whittaker and Esther Chambers took their trip to the Soviet Union.

By the time they returned, the group had moved headquarters from "the Gallery" to an apartment on Gay Street in Greenwich Village:

> The Gay Street apartment [Chambers later told the FBI] was used primarily during the time that I visited there, as the base of operations for a communications system between the underground in the United States and Europe. This consisted of a receipt in the United States of communications carried by couriers who were seamen and stewards attached to the various ships of the North German Lloyd SS Line and the Hamburg American Line, and the forwarding of communications to Germany [then only recently fallen under Nazi domination]. These incoming communications consisted of microfilm and letters containing secret writing. However, the material delivered in the United States to these couriers for transmission to Germany took the form of microfilm only.

There was an innocuous message—the same one—on each of the letters received, and members of Ulrich's ring would dissolve the paper in a chemical solution in order to make the underlying message appear. These messages and also those on the microfilm were in Russian and presumably were meant for Ulrich or Herbert.*

Others joined the group to transmit messages between the German seamen and the American network, usually meeting in New York cafeterias or on Manhattan streets. This courier system aboard German ships operated throughout 1932 and 1933, according to Chambers, but was quickly broken up by the Gestapo, which, after Hitler's seizure of power, arrested a number of Communist seamen. Ulrich communicated for a time also with an American soldier in the Canal Zone, Corporal Robert Osman, who in 1933 confessed to providing plans of American installations in the Zone to Soviet agents.[18]

Few of the many operations engaged in by Chambers's underground unit proved particularly fruitful. Ulrich's orders from Red Army intelligence chiefs were to concentrate on industrial espionage—the theft of technical materials related to military production—but only a handful of the numerous attempts in

---

*A third Russian known only as "Charley" generally handled the exposure and enlarging of the microfilm.

which Chambers and his cohorts participated during the 1932–34 period turned up such documents. One scheme that did pan out, directed not by Ulrich but by J. Peters, involved contacts with CP sympathizers who worked for the Electric Boat Company of New London, Connecticut, the leading American manufacturer of submarines. A Communist employee there claimed that he could ferret away "any amount of blue prints on submarines and would do so if it was desired." Chambers had been taught by "Charley" to photograph documents by this time, and he took pictures of a first batch of material delivered by the New London contact only to discover that "none of the prints turned out." Thereafter an experienced photographer from the group went along on journeys to New London.

The scheme quickly fell apart when a company worker named Clayton B. Darrow confessed his role in it to the local American Legion chapter. In addition, Darrow spoke to FBI agents on May 2 and July 3, 1934. His account confirmed Chambers's story: "In 1932 Darrow was instructed . . . to remove a blue-print from the plant for photostating which he claimed he did. Darrow was later brought to NYC [to meet two] . . . individuals at a hotel in the neighborhood of 125th Street." Similar efforts by Chambers's network to obtain plans for American military equipment elsewhere in 1933 and 1934, usually from Communist sympathizers working at military installations, failed to produce much of value.[19]

Ulrich shifted operations again in late 1933, this time to an apartment in Brooklyn's Brownsville section owned by a member of the ring named Joshua Tamer. The Tamer apartment was the scene of an all-night party arranged by Ulrich that Chambers recalled vividly for the FBI in 1949. Although Chambers had a low tolerance for alcohol and, after defecting from the party, became a teetotaler, on this occasion he and Ulrich both drank more than their share, with embarrassing results:

> During the course of the evening Ulrich and [his wife] Elaine began questioning me as to my views on the Communist situation in Germany. I remember that I "damned" Stalin's policy in Germany and as a result incurred the displeasure of Elaine who advanced on me rather belligerently. As a result I pushed her lightly with my hand and she fell to the floor. By midnight everyone was out cold.
>
> When I woke the next morning I thought that I had ruined myself as a Communist because of my denouncement of Stalin . . . and my actions toward Elaine. However, when Ulrich arose he patted me on the back and said, "You are all right, Bob" [Chambers's pseudonym at the time]. This action on his part gave me the impression that Ulrich's opinion also deviated somewhat from the Party line. Elaine, however, did not speak to me for some months thereafter.[20]

For undetermined reasons, Ulrich and Elaine began disbanding their operations early in 1934 and transferring agents such as Chambers to the control of other underground leaders like Peters. Although Ulrich did not explain the move, Chambers believed that Ulrich's recall to the Soviet Union came as the result of bickering among Russian agents and the failure of Ulrich's efforts to infiltrate an Army arsenal, one of the group's flawed projects. Elaine had recently given birth, and Philip Rosenbliett, an underground associate, told Chambers that there had been some difficulty in obtaining the passport and visas needed to take the baby out of the country. "I remember that Ulrich's last words to me," Chambers informed the FBI in 1949, "were spoken in a semi-humorous slightly sinister manner, and were to the effect that 'Remember, Bob, you can be shot by them or you can be shot by us.'"

Until the mid-1970s, there existed only partial confirmation of Chambers's story of his years in Ulrich's network. FBI files corroborated his account of incidents such as the abortive espionage efforts at the Electric Boat Company in New London and elsewhere, but even the bureau could produce no other member of his earliest network to confirm the basic account, something they could more readily do for the period after 1935 when Chambers shifted most of his secret work to the Baltimore-Washington area. But Ulrich's wife, "Elaine," whose real name is Nadezhda (Nadya) Ulanovskaya and who emigrated to Israel in the 1970s, later came forward. Chambers had heard about her once a number of years after he left the party, and he recounted the incident to the FBI in 1949:

> ... about 1947 ... "Time" magazine's Bureau Chief in Moscow, Mr. Craig Thompson, wrote a letter to a Foreign News writer at "Time," Mr. John Barkham. In this letter, Mr. Thompson sent greetings to me and added "Nadya also sends greetings." ... When Mr. Thompson returned to New York sometime thereafter, I asked him who Nadya was and he told me she was a Russian woman employed in the Time Bureau to do part-time translations from Russian. The description he gave me of this woman and her husband convinced me that they were Ulrich and Elaine. Nadya had told Mr. Thompson that she knew me personally but did not go into details of underground work in the United States. Nadya's name in the Time Bureau was Ulanova. Lenin's real name was Ulanov. This I presume is what Elaine meant when she said that Ulrich was Lenin. ... Thompson also told me that the Ulanovs had become bitterly anti-Soviet and lived in constant fear of being shot or sent to Siberia.[21]

At the time Chambers gave the FBI this deposition in 1949, the Ulanovs had already been arrested, convicted, and sent to a Siberian labor camp.

Nadya Ulanovskaya confirmed for the author in 1975 the substance of Chambers's account of his underground activities from his recruitment up to the time when Ulrich and Elaine returned to Russia in early 1934. After reading Chambers's memoir and his deposition to the FBI, she commented:

> All of it I find perfectly in order. ... When I read his book I found in it some inaccuracies but they were of a minor character, obviously unintentional, such as addresses, dates, etc. I didn't in some cases agree with his judgment of people that we both knew. But all of that is irrelevant to the case. On the whole, the

book is fairly accurate in that part of it which describes events of which I had a firsthand knowledge.

Scoffing at the dangers involved in conducting an espionage ring in the United States during the early 1930s, at a time when no effective American counterintelligence agency existed, Nadya said: "If you wore a sign saying 'I am a spy,' you might still not get arrested in America when we were there."[22]

The Ulanovskis went on family picnics and swimming parties with Esther and Whittaker Chambers after the two couples became friends. Chambers would hold forth on his contempt for "bourgeois" culture, which irritated Nadya, who had quickly developed a fondness for the United States and its ordinary "bourgeois" citizens. As for Chambers's own character, "I knew him as a most disinterested and honest man, very kind and gentle, incapable of inflicting pain on any living creature."[23]

Others have also corroborated Chambers's role as an underground courier during those same years. Ella Winter, for example, recalled for the author having been approached in her New York hotel room in 1933 by "Harold Phillips," whom she later identified as Chambers. Phillips asked Winter to transport a large sum of money from New York to California for the underground—"only cash, not a check"—but, on the advice of her friend in the CP, Robert Minor, she declined. "Don't get mixed up with their spy rings," she quotes Minor as telling her.*[24]

Contacting Winter several more times with additional requests, Chambers once asked that she go to Washington and search through the desk of her friend William Bullitt, whom President Roosevelt had just appointed as the first American Ambassador to the Soviet Union. Winter was supposed to take from his desk any papers she felt would be of interest to the CP. She went to Washington to congratulate Bullitt on his appointment, but, although she later told Chambers about the trip, would not steal any papers.[25]

But Chambers would not give up on Ella Winter. She recalled that he badly wanted to meet a friend of hers who, in 1934, held a high post on the Nye Committee. (Chambers met Alger Hiss at that same time when Hiss first began working for the Committee.) The Nye Committee's work interested the Communist underground primarily because of the opportunities offered for military or industrial espionage through access to the files of some of America's leading arms manufacturers, such as the Du Pont Corporation. Thus Robert Cantwell was offered $25,000 to write a favorable book about the Du Ponts by Chambers's associate John Sherman in hopes that Cantwell could then infiltrate the company's records.[26]

Although Ella Winter agreed to introduce Chambers to her friend on the Nye Committee, she refused to accede to the conspiratorial preparations on which

---

*Chambers then took the money to California himself, according to FBI informant William Edward Crane.

"Harold Phillips" insisted, such as meeting in an out-of-the-way New York location, using a password, and similar routine procedures for underground agents. Chambers broke off further contact with Winter, perhaps at the instructions of superiors, who must have realized belatedly that she was far more useful as an open sympathizer with the party, as a writer, as Lincoln Steffens's wife, and as a successful fund-raiser for the Communists' West Coast labor-organizing efforts.[27]

Periodically during the mid-thirties "Karl" would also approach friends such as Herbert Solow, Meyer Schapiro, and even Lionel and Diana Trilling to serve as "letter drops" for underground messages or to provide other assistance. More often than not, these friends declined to cooperate, especially since relations between Communists and most others on the American Left had soured by 1934, a rift symbolized by the efforts of a CP goon squad that year to break up a Socialist rally in Madison Square Garden.[28]

A Columbia friend who agreed to help Chambers at one point was David Zabladowsky, who testified in 1952 before the Senate Internal Security Subcommittee that he had delivered a message in 1936 from Chambers to J. Peters. When asked if he knew that Peters was an espionage agent, Zabladowsky replied: "Yes, in a sense I did. I knew that Whittaker Chambers was, but very specifically on a certain matter, which was underground work against Germany, or against Hitler." Zabladowsky also testified that, at Chambers's request, he subsequently delivered an envelope containing material connected with an illegal Communist passport ring to a man whose name he could not remember.*[29]

In avowing that opposition to Hitler and to Nazi Germany had "triggered" a brief involvement with Soviet espionage, Zabladowsky was hardly unique. The Communist Party, in America and in many European countries, cited the growing menace of fascist militarism as one of its strongest arguments for engaging the loyalties of many non-Communists, and the services of some in "secret work" during the 1930s. At a time when Western European governments seemed determined to appease both Hitler and Mussolini, until the Nazi-Soviet Pact of 1939, some justification existed for arguing that the Russians stood almost alone in urging militant opposition to the so-called "anti-Comintern powers"—Germany, Italy, and Japan.

Strikingly, Soviet espionage agents in the United States during the thirties gave a good deal of attention to Japan as well as to the European fascist regimes. Even during his earliest days as a Communist agent in 1932 Chambers performed counterespionage work against Japanese agents on the East Coast. He

---

*But who was identified in letters written by Chambers after his break as a Latvian named "Ewald" by his Soviet underground associates, and whose story figured both in Chambers's decision to defect and in Alger Hiss's involvement with Chambers. See the Robinson/Rubens case materials in Chapters VII and IX. ("Ewald" later used both of those other pseudonyms.)

told Herbert Solow in 1933 "that some Jap spies had been caught in an aircraft plant on L.I. by the American counter-espionage [presumably military intelligence agents], and I understood from what he said that his organization had been instrumental in helping the Americans catch those Japs." Throughout the 1930s Russian military leaders feared a possible Japanese invasion along the Soviet Union's sparsely defended eastern frontier. In this connection, it is important to recall that Chambers worked not for the "civilian" GPU but directly for the Soviet Army's Fourth Branch military intelligence unit. Thus Robert Cantwell also remembered Chambers's talk about encounters with Japanese agents, as well as his special interest in military installations such as the New London naval base, where Chambers claimed to have engaged in espionage.[30]

Despite his use of pseudonyms, secret passwords, and the like, Chambers never really treated seriously the element of secrecy itself during the time he took part in supposedly "secret work" in New York City, and along the East Coast from 1932 to early 1934. He maintained contacts with friends outside the underground and even outside the party, and he recounted choice tidbits of his network's lore to them. Only when J. Peters ordered Chambers to move to the Baltimore-Washington area in 1934, after Ulrich's departure, did he conduct himself more appropriately as an agent, although even then he continued to visit non-CP friends during frequent trips to New York on business matters.

J. PETERS AND THE SOVIET SPY RING IN JAPAN

Peters became an increasingly important figure in Chambers's life once Ulrich and Elaine had returned to Moscow. Max Bedacht had instructed Chambers in 1933 to regard Peters as his primary contact with the American CP, although the new recruit continued to meet with both men for a time that year. Somewhat confused, Chambers had approached Ulrich and asked which of the two, Bedacht or Peters, he should deal with. The Russian cited a Turkish proverb: "When dealing with wolves, choose the one who has eaten." He meant Bedacht, who at the time was more influential within the party than Peters, but Chambers found the latter "very friendly and helpful." After Bedacht's departure for other assignments later that year, Chambers maintained contact between his Russian superiors and the American Communist underground network for the next five years exclusively through J. Peters, whose headquarters was in the CP's office building near New York's Union Square.*[31]

---

*Peters's leading role in such secret work was confirmed at the time of the Hiss case not only by Chambers but by many other witnesses summoned to testify at his deportation hearings and also by people who had met him in his underground guise, such as David Zabladowsky and Lee Pressman. Additional and more convincing corroboration of Peters's work as an agent during the

It was Peters who introduced Chambers to still another Russian agent in 1934 after Ulrich had left; with this man, known only as "Bill," he maintained irregular contact until 1936. That year "Bill" was replaced by Chambers's final Russian spymaster, a man he later identified as Colonel Boris Bykov. Sometime in 1934 Chambers learned that all of his Russian supervisors came from the Fourth Branch and not the GPU.

That same year Peters also introduced Chambers to the head of the Soviet underground cell in Washington, Harold Ware, so that the latter could use Chambers as a courier between his group and Peters's New York headquarters. Before Chambers moved permanently to Washington in mid-1934, however, "Bill" outlined plans that attracted him far more than did Peters's scheme. As Chambers told it, Bill "stated that he was going to England to head a Soviet apparatus which would be located in London." He urged Chambers to accompany him and "further suggested that I should provide myself with a cover such as representative of a legitimate American firm." After discussing the proposition with Peters, the latter "brought me together with Maxim Lieber, whom I had previously known in the John Reed Club."[32]

Then gaining a reputation in radical literary circles as an authors' representative, Lieber was an open Communist Party member and proved agreeable to the plan devised by Bill, Peters, and Chambers. "It was arranged that the apparatus would finance the opening of a branch in London for Lieber's firm. I [Chambers] was to be the head of the office as Lieber's representative and would do a regular job of seeing authors and preparing manuscripts received by Britons for Lieber."

Plans for the scheme dragged on throughout 1934 and early 1935, with Peters even obtaining for Chambers a false passport in May 1935 in the name "David Breen." (Peters also arranged to have the name of Chambers's daughter changed on her Atlantic City, New Jersey, birth certificate from Ellen Chambers to "Ursula Breen" to facilitate obtaining her passport.) Lieber, in turn, accompanied Chambers to the British Consulate in New York, where he "certified that I was the individual who was to represent him in London. As a result I was given a resident visa." Although Bill's hopes for an English operation fell through and were eventually abandoned, Chambers used the name "David Breen" at his various residences in 1935.[33]

But the plan followed an earlier scheme in 1934—also involving Chambers and Lieber, this time assisted by John Sherman. After leaving New York in 1933,

---

1930s came from FBI testimony by one of his operatives, William Edward Crane; from my interviews with Maxim Lieber, whom Peters assigned to occasional underground jobs; and from the recollections of Nadya Ulanovskaya, with whose husband, Ulrich, Peters had shared leadership of the spy network from 1931 to 1934. Hope Hale Davis also confirmed Peters's role in the underground. Recently available VENONA intercepts and KGB archives put the question of Peters's espionage career beyond dispute. See Weinstein and Vassiliev, *The Haunted Wood, passim.*

Sherman had worked for the CP on the West Coast, primarily in attempts to gain information concerning Japan. He received orders, presumably from Russian superiors, to move his base of operations to Japan itself and returned East searching for a legitimate business cover behind which he could set up a Japanese espionage network.* Bill assigned Chambers to the task of helping Sherman to devise such a *modus operandi* and, at the same time, to procure an American-born Japanese assistant who could work with Sherman in Japan, preferably one with connections to high political circles there.

The task proved formidable, and Chambers turned almost immediately to Lieber for a solution. Since the idea of an English branch of Lieber's agency seemed stalled, Chambers proposed (the idea may have come from Sherman) that the three men use Lieber's reputation to establish in Japan a news-gathering organization called the American Feature Writers Syndicate. Sherman and his assistant could then proceed to Japan under the guise of legitimate foreign correspondents, and Lieber from his agency's New York office would handle the sale and distribution of whatever genuine news stories they produced in Japan. Lieber agreed, and in August 1934 the plan went into operation.[34]

Chambers, Sherman, and Lieber registered the American Feature Writers Syndicate as a business enterprise in New York State. Only Lieber used his real name. Chambers signed the incorporation papers as "Lloyd Cantwell" and gave Lieber's office as his address. Sherman signed as "Charles F. Chase" (Peters promptly obtained a false passport for Sherman in that name on September 24, 1934, and "Chase" soon left for Japan). Peters also provided between $5,000 and $10,000, which Chambers deposited in a Chemical Bank branch near Lieber's office for use in financing the latter's expenses on the operation and to reimburse "correspondents" for any stories filed from Japan. Lieber had "AMERICAN FEATURE WRITERS SYNDICATE" inscribed on his office door and negotiated with CP sympathizers who worked for *The American Mercury,* the New York *Post,* and other possible users of the stories Sherman sent back, some of whom commissioned articles on the spot (although only the New York *Post* actually printed any of the pieces). Chambers even found a Japanese-American assistant for "Chase," a promising young painter and open-party member named Hideo Noda, who was related to the Japanese imperial family.

During the early 1930s Lieber had gained prominence in the New York publishing world by bringing to public attention the writings of previously unknown young clients such as Erskine Caldwell, Josephine Herbst, and Albert Halper. He was probably the country's foremost agent specializing in social-realist writers

---

*Soviet military intelligence units devised several such plans for establishing spy rings in Japan during the mid-1930s, the most spectacularly successful of which—led by Richard Sorge—was finally broken up by Japanese counterintelligence only during the Second World War. Sorge, parenthetically, began his career as an agent working as Ulrich's assistant in a Shanghai network in 1929.

who were themselves politically radical. The occasional use of this well-known authors' representative in secret Communist operations seemed quite normal in the more casual and freewheeling atmosphere within which Soviet intelligence expanded operations in the United States during the 1930s.

Although in a 1975 interview with the author Lieber excoriated Chambers's later decision to testify against fellow members of the CP underground ("the only thing I bear against him was that he exposed a lot of honest, decent, dedicated people"), he remembered fondly his personal association with Chambers. The Hiss-Chambers case brought Lieber to the attention of the FBI, and it ruined his literary agency.[35]

Maxim Lieber confirmed the essential account of the relationship between himself and Chambers that the latter first publicly described in 1948. "We were all Communists," Lieber noted, and "[besides] I regarded him as a friend." The literary agent and the CP courier shared common interests in literature, music, and chess during the many visits Chambers paid to Lieber's Manhattan apartment and to his Pennsylvania farm between 1934 and 1938. "Some things are romanticized in *Witness* [Chambers's memoir]," Lieber stated, "but most of it—as I know of the incidents—is true." Furthermore, "Chambers, Chase, and I set up that Syndicate [on orders from Peters]. We *did* organize it, as Chambers said. In fact, I had hopes of getting an agent contact in London from the [earlier] deal or in Japan, but nothing worked out." Lieber agreed that the American Communist Party engaged in espionage during this period, as Chambers detailed. "There were cells in Washington, no question. The ninth floor, for example, [of] the Party's Central Committee [CP headquarters in New York, where J. Peters had his office] knew of my relations with Chambers. So did Peters. Peters knew."[36]

Lieber also attested to Chambers's version of how the entire Japanese network scheme was scrubbed in 1935, apparently as a result of an error on "Bill's" part. The Russian contacted Chambers, said that there had been "arrests" in Tokyo, and fretted that "Chase" might have been among those taken into custody. Bill instructed Chambers to close down the American Feature Writers Syndicate immediately, and that same day the latter "destroyed all the stationery, closed out the bank account, and took the name off Lieber's door." Lieber, for his part, remembered handling these details: "Whittaker came in one day, very agitated, and he said, 'You must break up your organization. Get rid of your secretaries.'" The liquidation process, in which both probably took part, proved even simpler, since the syndicate had no secretaries of its own but merely shared office space with Lieber's literary agency. Chambers received the remaining cash in the bank account, while Lieber resumed his normal business.[37]

Pleased with his efficient termination of the syndicate, Chambers met with Bill again the next day, only to learn that the Russians had been mistaken: "[T]he whole thing was an error and there had been no arrests." It turned out that several Soviet agents who knew about the Japanese network had been arrested in

Europe, but to Bill even this seemed sufficient reason to halt operations in Tokyo and order both Sherman and Noda back to the United States. On his way to Moscow, John Sherman stopped in New York, where Chambers obtained (again through J. Peters) another false passport for him, after which he left for the Soviet Union.

On the heels of "Chase"/Sherman's departure, Hideo Noda reappeared in New York in late 1935 and immediately contacted both Chambers and their mutual friend, Noda's benefactor Meyer Schapiro. The latter, a Socialist and anti-Stalinist, regretted his earlier introduction of the impressionable Noda to Chambers. He now urged "Ned" to abandon underground work, leave the Communist Party, and resume normal life as a painter. Noda repeated this conversation to Chambers several days later. After listening to the account, Chambers, despite instructions from Bill to arrange for Noda's transfer to another Soviet apparatus in France, urged the painter to follow his mentor's advice. Noda "seemed to me to be in the wrong occupation," Chambers would tell the FBI in 1949. Besides, "maybe Schapiro is right." Shortly after this conversation Peters told Chambers that Noda had denounced him as a Trotskyite, the most serious accusation possible within CP circles at the time. But the disbelieving Peters, according to Chambers, brushed aside the charge, and Noda left for France. Within a year he was ordered back to Japan to work with a new network, and he died there of natural causes in 1939.[38]

The earlier Japanese spy ring, the American Feature Writers Syndicate, had been a fiasco, and Noda and Sherman between them gained little if any information of value during an eight-month period. "Chase" wrote several articles that eventually appeared in the New York *Post*, but otherwise turned out to be a remarkably indifferent operative. "Chase never did much work," Chambers told Herbert Solow in 1938, who promptly transcribed the conversation. "He let Ned [Noda] waste his time. He [Chase] played handball, and won the Jap medal ["Charles Chase" did win the Japanese championship handball tournament held in 1935 at the Tokyo YMCA], which they mailed to the New York business address [Lieber's] after the journalist left Tokyo for Moscow."[39]

THE MOVE TO WASHINGTON

With the collapse of the American Feature Writers Syndicate, Chambers could devote full-time energies to new responsibilities in the Baltimore-Washington area. He had moved his family there in August 1934, shortly after Peters introduced him to Harold Ware at a New York restaurant. The three Soviet agents discussed Chambers's future duties in Washington as a courier between Peters in New York and the Ware Group in Washington. Chambers described the meeting to the FBI in 1949: "I understood that most of the members of this group were employed in 'New Deal Agencies.' According to what Peters told me, it was his 'dream' to penetrate the 'old line agencies,' such as the Navy, State, Interior, etc. I was to learn the setup and the personnel of the present apparatus [Ware's group, whose members worked mainly for the more recent—and perhaps temporary— New Deal agencies such as the AAA] and attempt to build a parallel apparatus . . . using certain members of the Ware Group at first and then branching out. Consequently, about the end [of the summer] or in the fall of 1934, I made my first trip to Washington, D.C., where I met Harold Ware by pre-arrangement."[40]

Commuting frequently between Washington and New York during these months, Chambers informed Peters of genuine progress in gaining underground recruits for this "parallel apparatus." During trips to New York he also continued to visit his non-Communist friends and kept in touch with them, in addition, by mail, discussing mainly personal or family news. One letter confided to the Meyer Schapiros that he (Chambers) had just been awarded a "high honor" by the Soviet government for his services as an agent, an award he later identified to Herbert Solow as "the Lenin Order." Despite his idiosyncrasies as an underground operative, Chambers—that most un-secret agent—had apparently earned the respect of his colleagues and superiors.[41]

The clearest token of J. Peters's confidence in this writer-turned-spy was his willingness to entrust his own pet project to Chambers's hands: the organization into a "sleeper apparatus"—agents in place awaiting orders at some future time—of Washington's most promising Communist or pro-Soviet government officials. Peters would not be disappointed by the results. Once based in Washington, amid new surroundings and unfamiliar contacts, Chambers adopted a more circumspect pattern of behavior, the type normally expected of secret agents. It could even be argued that, in this sense, "Karl" became a secret agent (as opposed to an underground one) for the first time when he moved to Washington. Although Chambers often visited New York City during his remaining years in the apparatus, he served Soviet intelligence from mid-1934 to 1938 primarily as an organizer among convert Communists within Washington and as a conduit for their stolen documents.

IV

THE WARE GROUP
AND THE NEW DEAL

LEE PRESSMAN AND THE AAA

Alger Hiss had been in Washington for sixteen months by the time Whittaker Chambers settled into an apartment forty miles away on Baltimore's St. Paul Street in August 1934. Hiss had joined the legal staff of Jerome Frank, general counsel to the Agricultural Adjustment Administration, the New Deal's controversial "Triple A." Frank, a successful New York and Chicago corporation lawyer, was also a legal scholar of some accomplishment and a friend of Felix Frankfurter. Frank had shelved a law practice that brought in more than $50,000 to take the AAA post paying one-sixth that sum.

He determined to bring into the agency as his staff an equally dedicated corps of young attorneys from major law schools and prominent law firms. "What we need," Frank once said, "are brilliant young men with keen legal minds and imagination." The fact that most of the recruits had little or no knowledge of agrarian problems troubled him not at all. Frank believed that his young men of talent could quickly acquire such information on the job. Among those answering Frank's summons were a future Supreme Court justice (Abe Fortas), an eventual presidential candidate (Adlai Stevenson), a future Nuremberg war-crimes prosecutor (Telford Taylor), three members of Harold Ware's underground CP group (John Abt, Lee Pressman, and Nathan Witt)—and Alger Hiss.[1]

Frank's invitation flattered Hiss—Felix Frankfurter had recommended him—but he felt reluctant to leave New York and private practice. He declined Frank's initial offer, only to receive a telegram from Frankfurter early in April urging acceptance because of the "national emergency." According to Hiss, he treated this request from his mentor "as an order [he] couldn't refuse." After informing his superiors at Cotton and Franklin and receiving their good wishes, he resigned and left for Washington.

Some later asserted that Lee Pressman, a man close to the Communist Party even earlier while practicing law in New York and a charter member of the Ware Group, had influenced Hiss's decision, but Hiss always denied that Pressman played any role in the matter: "I had not seen him [at the time] . . . the fact that Jerome and Pressman had worked together as lawyers was something I didn't know about. . . . My call came directly from Jerome."[2]

Pressman, in fact, did play a role. Frank later recalled that either Frankfurter or Thomas Corcoran, Frankfurter's former student and a New Deal presidential aide, had initially recommended Hiss for an AAA post. But on April 10 Frank wrote to Pressman in New York confirming his previous invitation to join the AAA and adding: "You might be thinking of some other chaps to come down here. What would you think of Hiss? . . . Also what about Witt?" Hiss may indeed have had an earlier call from Frank—and even have received the telegram from Frankfurter that he remembered—but he also discussed accepting the AAA post with Pressman. "I have talked to Alger Hiss and Nat Witt who are considering the matter," Pressman wrote Frank on April 12, two days after receiving the latter's inquiry. Pressman and Frank were then close friends, and their exchange of letters in April 1933 indicates that Hiss's old law-school classmate did participate in Hiss's decision.[3]

Yet when Pressman testified before HUAC in August 1950 about his membership in the underground Ware Group and his relationship with Hiss, he either had forgotten his 1933 conversation with Hiss in New York or he chose to distort it. Hiss's conviction for perjury was then awaiting appeal, and Pressman apparently intended to use his testimony to aid that appeal, since he denied that Hiss was a member of the Ware Group "for the period of my participation." Pressman named only a trio of recruits to the group other than himself, all colleagues in the AAA, John Abt, Charles Kramer, and Nathan Witt.* The earlier Communist associations of all three men were widely commented upon at this time, but in Pressman's account the Ware Group comprised only these New Deal officials. Pressman's lack of candor was also suggested by this comment which he volunteered "to lay low, I hope once and for all, many distortions of truth":

> It has been asserted time and time again by some people that I was responsible . . . for getting Alger Hiss a job in triple A. I state as a fact, and the public records will bear me out, that . . . I had nothing whatsoever—and when I say nothing whatsoever I mean precisely that—nothing whatsoever to do with the employment of Alger Hiss in the triple A.

Whatever the facts, Alger Hiss's arrival in Washington delighted Frank, Frankfurter, and Pressman. "With a few fellows like Alger Hiss," Frankfurter wrote to Frank in June 1933, "you can really 'show 'em.'"[4]

Driving his young legal staff at a relentless pace, Frank quickly gained its loyalty and admiration by maintaining that same demanding schedule himself. "The young men, dazzled by his example," noted Arthur Schlesinger, Jr.,

---

*Pressman had lied about such membership in the Ware Group in his interviews with Hiss's lawyers in 1948 and 1949. He also denied to them that he had ever met Whittaker Chambers, something he later admitted. Pressman still insisted to HUAC in 1950, however, that he had met Chambers in 1936 and not earlier during the Ware Group years.

"worked twenty hours a day, slept on couches in their offices and hastily briefed themselves on the agricultural life." No one worked harder and more effectively for the Frank team than Alger Hiss. "He has too much spirit for his bodily strength," Beverly Smith wrote about Hiss in the *American Magazine* in February 1934, "and is in danger of working himself to death." Smith's article, "Uncle Sam Grows Younger," described a number of the more influential junior officials in the New Deal, and Jerome Frank's assistants—Hiss, Pressman, Fortas, and others—figured prominently in that account. But Frank's hard-driving manner, emulated by his staff, did not endear the general counsel's group to those in the farm-lobby wing of AAA:

> The old agrarians looked on Frank's office [wrote Schlesinger] as if it were a menagerie—"an entirely new species to me," said [George] Peek. The farm specialists had long constituted a club, where everybody knew everybody else, and they resented this upsurge of strange urban types. There were too many Ivy League men, too many intellectuals, too many radicals, too many Jews. Nor were they helped when (according to a familiar story) Lee Pressman, attending a meeting to work out a macaroni code, asked belligerently what the code would do for the macaroni growers. . . .[5]

In "the early part of 1934" Pressman had been recruited to Communism by Harold Ware himself at a time when Ware was organizing Washington's first underground CP cell. Ware had worked in the Soviet Union organizing collective farms during the 1920s at Lenin's invitation and had returned to the United States—also on the instructions of the Russian CP—to play a leading role in efforts to organize American farm workers. Somehow he became a consultant to the Department of Agriculture during the Coolidge administration, a post he held until the closing days of the Hoover presidency, when—in the fall of 1932—he and his mother involved themselves in farm strikes and protests. Ware returned to Washington in 1933 with several aides, including novelist John Herrmann, and immediately began recruiting younger New Deal officials for the Communist Party. Open avowal of their new beliefs, although not cause for dismissal, would probably have denied members promotion even in the reform-minded Roosevelt administration. Therefore, the group maintained secrecy, meeting for a time at a music studio owned by Ware's sister. It was there that Chambers first encountered the group in 1934.[6]

Because leading officials at the Department of Agriculture and AAA opposed Communist efforts to unionize small farmers and farm workers, Pressman and other fledgling members of the Ware Group who worked at these two agencies had to disguise their radicalism. These idealistic young bureaucrats felt ambivalent about holding government positions. They enjoyed a sense of shared excitement about their work and about their newfound influence over the lives of Americans through early New Deal programs such as the AAA. At the same time, they chafed over the continued restraints upon their actions imposed by their more conservative superiors.[7]

As the top-ranking AAA official within the Ware Group, Pressman probably helped recruit others for the network.* His interviews with the FBI in 1950 did confirm the Ware Group's existence and shed some light on its operations. Pressman told the bureau that Ware, who "floated" around the Agriculture Department in 1934, inquired one day if he would be interested in joining "a Communist group." The group itself was small, he claimed, "and, at the outset, included Harold Ware, John Abt, Nathan Witt, and himself." (Pressman added Kramer's name to its membership while testifying before HUAC in 1950.) During his period with the Ware Group, Pressman stated, "these were the only people who attended meetings and belonged," except for J. Peters. After Ware's death in a 1935 car crash, according to Pressman, Peters "showed up, announced that he was taking Ware's place, and continued, thereafter, to act more-or-less as the leader of the group." Its activities, whether under Ware or Peters, consisted (in Pressman's portrayal) primarily of discussing Communist literature and collecting party dues—in sum, it was a Marxist study group of four junior AAA officials and two prominent CP functionaries.[8]

Other members recalled the group as a much larger secret network of government functionaries who met not only to engage in discussions of Marxist-Leninist theory and practice, but to prepare themselves for more important roles within the New Deal and even, on occasion, to filch documentary material. This portrait of the group emerges not only from Whittaker Chambers's account, but is confirmed by another member of the cell, Nathaniel Weyl, and by novelist Josephine Herbst, formerly the wife of John Herrmann, Harold Ware's chief assistant in the CP underground from 1933 to 1935.[9]

Pressman stated in 1950 that Alger Hiss had not been a member of the Ware Group during his tenure as a member; "it was quite possible," he told the FBI, "that Alger Hiss might have been a member of this group but, if this was true, it would have been prior to the time he, Pressman, became associated with the Harold Ware group."

Pressman also "stated [to the FBI that] neither Alger or his attorneys have contacted him since the accusations," an untruth, since in fact he played a demonstrated role in Hiss's campaign to discredit Chambers, serving as a regular and

---

*He denied that allegation when interviewed by the FBI about underground activities two days after he first acknowledged such involvement in his August 1950 testimony before HUAC. Pressman's statement to the FBI, like his earlier comments to the committee, was not completely candid. His statements contained certain facts that are corroborated by other evidence but also a number of distortions and untruths, and he omitted most details of his period as a self-confessed Communist. Recently available VENONA intercepts and KGB files confirm Pressman's role in the Ware Group.

semiofficial conduit of rumors or facts concerning Chambers from the Communist Party to Hiss's lawyers.*[10]

Discussing his experiences as a Communist with the FBI only after the Korean War had begun, Nathaniel Weyl spoke to the bureau on November 27, 1950, after which he "went public" with the material in magazine articles and at Senate Internal Security Subcommittee hearings. Weyl's comments about Hiss remained difficult to assess. Although he named Hiss to the FBI in 1950 as a member of the Ware Group, that same year he published a book about internal subversion called *Treason,* containing several sympathetic references to Hiss. This undermines the credibility of his later assertion that he had known Hiss as a fellow member of the Ware Group, although Weyl's 1950 FBI interview still remains fascinating for its description of the group itself, its personnel and activities.[11]

Weyl (who also worked in the AAA at the time, although in a lesser post than Pressman's or Hiss's) portrayed a cell of secret New Deal Communists far more extensive than Pressman's tiny band. He had been a party member in New York City before coming to Washington in 1933, where Harold Ware contacted him with instructions to join the underground CP group then being formed. Weyl complied and regularly attended its meetings, naming the following as members of Ware's secret organization during the 1933–34 period: Lee Pressman, Alger Hiss, John Abt, Nathan Witt, Henry Collins, John Donovan, Victor Perlo, and Charles Framer (all but Collins and Donovan worked at AAA).

Weyl had "a fairly clear recollection of Alger Hiss and Lee Pressman being present together at some of these meetings." Those attending used their real names and not pseudonyms, since most knew one another from their daily work at the AAA. Discussions ranged into Marxist theory, agricultural problems, and various current policy issues. Ware traveled frequently between Washington and New York, personally collected CP dues from group members, and distributed Communist literature.

In midsummer 1934, according to Weyl, he left the Ware Group in order to organize agricultural workers for the Communist Party throughout the Midwest, so that his knowledge of the group's activities is limited to 1933–34. Later Weyl said that he never met at Ware Group meetings either Chambers, who first took up residence in the area in August 1934, or Peters, whose direct involvement in the group began only after Chambers reached the city.[12]

Yet Weyl told the FBI in November 1950 that he "met Alger Hiss at the meetings of the Ware group and his knowledge of the activities of Alger Hiss was confined to the activities of that group [Weyl was not employed in the same section

---

*An equally prominent role in Hiss's efforts to impeach Chambers fell to Henry H. Collins, Hiss's friend and an underground Communist agent (by the testimony of Chambers, Nathaniel Weyl, and Laurence Duggan).

of the AAA as Hiss]. . . . In his discussion with Alger Hiss, he found him to be intelligent, well informed and very sure of himself upon all occasions." If Weyl is correct, Hiss was a member of the Ware Group as early as the summer of 1933.[13]

JOSEPHINE HERBST: WITNESS TO THE WARE GROUP

A leading novelist in the 1930s, Josephine Herbst was a Socialist and her husband, John Herrmann, a Communist. They lived relatively independent lives. In 1933 Herrmann came to Washington at Harold Ware's invitation to assist in implementing the latter's plans for a secret CP network. The Herbst-Herrmann marriage had run aground by then. Herrmann drank heavily, Herbst disapproved of his underground work, and the woman who would later become Herrmann's second wife had already appeared on the scene. Josephine Herbst left John Herrmann—and Washington—in the fall of 1934, but not before she had met and spent a good deal of time with Whittaker Chambers, whom she knew as "Carl."

When the Hiss case broke in 1948, friends of Herbst who knew about these earlier contacts with Chambers got in touch with Hiss's lawyers, Edward McLean and Harold Rosenwald. Herbst told them about the Ware Group, about Whittaker Chambers, and about contacts between members of the group and Alger Hiss. But she withheld from the FBI that same year almost all of this information and claimed, instead, to have known Chambers only briefly in 1934 and without any real awareness of any Communist activities. At the same time she sent a letter to her ex-husband through his relatives, warning Herrmann about the FBI's interest in his activities and outlining exactly what she had revealed about the 1933–34 period, as well as what she had told Hiss's lawyers.* Whether

---

*Miss Herbst's letter (Herbst mss, Yale University) was written on February 6, 1949, moments after the FBI agents had left her home, and it indicated the concern she still felt for protecting her former husband:

> They are looking for you in connection with the business in Washington in the thirties. What they want is information about Hal's group and it is to throw light on the Alger Hiss case. . . . They will probably succeed in finding you. I have given them no information as to your present whereabouts as I don't know. . . .
>
> I did have to make some explanation of facts that they had already got hold of. My explanation was this. . . . I said you were writing at the time. . . . That you had gotten interested in farm problems in the fall of 1932. . . . That you were tinkering with various ideas for a play, for a novel based on the farm situation and that you were in Washington for some research. That you had got in touch with Hal Ware basically for that reason in connection with his farm research program and magazine. That you were writing in Washington. They knew that Carl had visited that apartment and I admitted that I had seen him there. My explanation of it was that you probably knew people that he would like to know. I admitted that I understood he was working for CP but did not know in what capacity. . . . Said that your connection with Carl or Chambers had been for the purpose of getting material, in my opinion. . . . I said I had not tried to find out anything about Carl and did not attempt to question you and did not know whom you saw in Washington. Said to my recollection you had known Ware but it had come about through your interest in farm problems.

or not Herrmann received the letter remains uncertain. But when the FBI finally located and interviewed him in Mexico in 1950, Herrmann denied that he had ever been a Communist, that he had ever belonged to the Ware Group or knew any of its members, that he knew either Chambers or Hiss—and even that he knew Harold Ware more than casually as an editor of a farmers' publication. But his letters to Herbst written from Washington in 1934 and Herbst's own interviews with Hiss's lawyers tell a different story.[14]

Sympathizing strongly with Alger Hiss at the time of the case, Josephine Herbst offered to testify on his behalf and gave his lawyers a candid account of her knowledge concerning Hiss, Chambers, and the Ware Group. Harold Rosenwald summarized a January 8, 1949, interview with Herbst in the first person:

> In July of 1934 I was living with my husband John Herrmann in an apartment on New Hampshire Avenue in Washington, D.C. . . . [M]y husband was a member of a group headed by Mr. Harold Ware. This was a group of people holding small and unimportant positions in various branches of the Government and was organized for the purpose of collecting information for the use primarily of the Communist Party in New York City.[15]

According to Herbst, its members "took great pride in their sense of conspiracy." She thought "that the ultimate purpose that the Party had in setting up 'cells' of this kind . . . was to provide for an organization capable of using influence and obtaining information in the event of a world or national crisis." Her "understanding" was that the Ware circle "had contacts in the War Department" but not at State, at least not in 1934. "On one occasion, I saw in my apartment certain documents that had been taken from Government offices by members of the 'cell' and brought to the apartment for transmission to New York." Herbst apparently read the material and portrayed its contents as "thoroughly innocent and innocuous" information, sometimes originals and in other cases "copies made by the individual cell member."* Although Herbst said that the stolen documents had been sent only to CP headquarters in New York and that "no direct contact existed between our group and Soviet authorities," she did not know of Chambers's work for the Red Army's Fourth Branch.

I did not give any names. I did not identify any of the people named. I did not name names when Hiss's lawyers saw me but did try to give them information about the period. Told them in my opinion a man like Chambers could have stolen material. Thought Hiss not guilty as charged. . . . I would have said about you that I knew nothing if I could have got away with it. I do not believe in this wholesale naming business that has been going on by the repentant sinners.

It is probably to your advantage not to avoid seeing these people. You may want to say something about Hal's activities if you knew. Anyhow he can't be hurt. He's dead. . . .

*Since Herbst left Washington for months at a time in 1934, she could neither verify nor refute Chambers's assertion that he photographed government documents in Herrmann's apartment.

Introduced to Chambers "simply as 'Carl' " in the summer of 1934, Herbst described him as "a heavy, tall, thickset man with a heavy opaque face, thick skin and mournful eyes . . . not too carefully groomed . . . kindly, but rather melancholy." After Herbst and Chambers became friends, "he spoke to me of his difficulties and told me that his wife and child lived in New Jersey. . . . He always seemed to be in anxiety and fear and always on the run." Herbst learned that Chambers "was a courier and that his job was to make contacts high within the United States Government." Because his underground responsibilities "were of a far graver and more professional nature," and because his government contacts were often officials in high positions not openly identified with Communist activities, Chambers—according to Herbst—"had absolutely no direct contact with members of our group." Herbst knew the names of five such "high" officials—"as high as the position then held by Mr. Alger Hiss"—with whom Chambers had contact, but, again, she refused to name names.

"Alger Hiss did meet 'Carl,'" Herbst told Rosenwald. "'Carl' told me of such a meeting and said Alger Hiss was 'a very cagey individual' and quite uncommunicative but friendly, polite and very charming and that Mrs. Hiss, whom 'Carl' also met, was very charming." The meeting between Chambers and Hiss took place in either July or August 1934, Herbst noted, confirming Chambers's own memory of the date. "I believe this impression was gained by information from Harold Ware and one other person. . . . [E]verything I know about them [Alger and Priscilla Hiss] was told to me by 'Carl,' Harold Ware or someone else." Herbst "had the impression" that Hiss had not yet become involved in CP activities at this initial meeting with Chambers. Herbst met Chambers at John Herrmann's apartment when only Herrmann was present. Sometimes when "Carl" came, "I was instructed to leave."

In her interview with McLean, Herbst gave a clear description of the "parallel apparatuses" that Peters had directed Chambers to organize in Washington: "There were ten to fifteen persons in the cell [the Ware Group] and five other persons holding high Government positions [the second network of government employees]." Herrmann, she avowed, had come to Washington at Ware's request "to work for the party . . . because of his thoroughly respectable front" as a writer on farm problems. She told McLean that Herrmann was probably a party member and that their marriage had foundered partly because of her opposition to "the secret conspiratorial nature of their work which I considered childish." Chambers sympathized with her views—this emerges also in letters exchanged between Herbst and Herrmann in 1934—and she last saw "Carl" in April 1935 at the New York apartment of their mutual friend Joseph North of *The Daily Worker*. Despite not having seen Chambers for thirteen years at the time she spoke to Rosenwald in 1949, Herbst had recognized him immediately from press photographs.

The letters Herrmann wrote her in 1934 contain several references to Ware, Chambers, and their activities, although some are guarded by references to "H" (Harold Ware) and "K" ("Karl").[16]

Early in 1935 the group moved its headquarters from the violin studio to a new location, where Herrmann set up residence: the Washington apartment of Henry Collins at 1213 St. Matthews Court. In March 1935 Herrmann wrote Herbst from Collins's apartment complaining about news that had spread among their Communist friends on their separation and Herrmann's involvement with another woman: "It has percolated through the whole organization by now thanks to your girl friends and Hal, K and plenty of others think I am what you tell them I am." In that same letter Herrmann advised her: "I am leaving here Monday. When you come wire or write me ahead of time care Henry Collins 1213 St. Mathews [sic] Court, N.W., and I'll meet you. I have two apts. in mind to take, dont know yet which it will be but am surely leaving this goddamned place." Another letter from that same period mentions that a friend of Collins would soon be arriving in Havana, where Herbst had gone on a reporting assignment: "Larry Duggan from the State Department . . . will look you up, very liberal but not entirely of a mind to come with us. He is a friend of many of our friends and might be of help to you." Herrmann's statements confirm Duggan's intimacy with those close to the Communist movement at the time, but also his reluctance to join in completely.[17]

According to Josephine Herbst, Ware, Herrmann, and the others in their group had been stealing government papers, although she considered most of the material innocuous, "busy work" to engage the energies of New Deal converts to Communism. "I am still seeing the same people and getting material but have got to whip it into shape," Herrmann wrote her in June 1934. "Otherwise the stuff I do will certainly not amount to what it should." Oddly enough, Chambers recalled no such espionage work being done in 1934 by members of the Ware Group, whose major functions, he believed, were to recruit more Communists within the government and to influence government policies.*[18]

But Herbst pointed out to Hiss's attorney Harold Rosenwald that she had lived in Herrmann's Washington apartment only from July to September 1934 and hence could not speak about Chambers's possible use of the quarters for espionage work—his and not the Ware Group's—at other times (Chambers remembered occasional use of the place for photographing documents, including those given to him by Alger Hiss). Another intimate of Hiss's also entered Rosenwald's questioning of Josephine Herbst:

---

*After interviewing extensively among former and present members of the Communist Party, an investigator for Alger Hiss concluded in an unsigned memo in the defense files on the "Political History of Whittaker Chambers" that the Ware Group had indeed engaged in "low-grade espionage work" and that "some sort of information gathering did go on."

She seemed startled by the mention of the name of Henry Collins and stated that she knew him in 1941 when she worked for the government. She intimated that Henry Collins knew all about the 1934 activities and could tell us everything if he wished to. She did not know much about Abt, Witt, or Perlo. She stated very definitely that she never met Alger or Priscilla Hiss. She said that Chambers and John Herman [sic] discussed Hiss and that they regarded Hiss as an important prospect to solicit for the purpose of getting papers. This was a task that was to be handled by Chambers because it was his function to make contacts with more important people in the government service. Herman was engaged with Harold Ware in organizing cells composed of minor government employees. Herman would not have been allowed to approach anyone as important as Alger Hiss.

She said she knew of George Silverman. She stated that she believed him to be a Communist and that Chambers and Herman had called him on the telephone from her apartment. . . .[19]

Thus three members of the Communist underground—Chambers, Herrmann, and Ware—all told Josephine Herbst in mid-1934 that they were already in touch with Alger Hiss, trying to recruit him for espionage—more than six months before Hiss claimed to have met Chambers under more innocuous circumstances. Although Herbst clearly wanted to help Hiss in 1948 and 1949 while discussing this information with his attorneys, her recollections would have been ruinous for him if made public.

ALGER AND WHITTAKER:
THE WARE GROUP AND THE NYE COMMITTEE

At the time the case broke, Hiss declared he had barely known Harold Ware during the mid-thirties. In August 1948 a former associate at AAA, Robert Cruise McManus, who had become a fervent anti-Communist in the intervening years, met with Hiss to discuss their years at the agency. McManus was about to publish a pamphlet accusing Hiss of having been a Communist at the time and wanted first to give him a chance to rebut the evidence collected. Hiss claimed, among other things, that he had never heard of Harold Ware's "front," Farm Research Inc., or its influence among radical AAA and Agricultural Department officials. "He says," McManus wrote, "he never knew of the Farm Research publication, 'Facts for Farmers,' despite the fact that it was well known in left-wing agricultural circles. . . ." But Hiss contradicted assertions he made in 1948 both about lacking knowledge of Ware's work while he (Hiss) was at the AAA and about their personal contacts having been minimal.* According to Whittaker Chambers, it was Ware who first introduced him to Alger Hiss.[20]

---

*In this connection, see especially the first footnote on p. 24 in Chapter I.

Even when present at the time, Chambers did not usually take part in the Ware Group's meetings. He recalled that John Abt, Donald Hiss, Charles Kramer, Victor Perlo, Henry Collins, Lee Pressman, Nathan Witt, and Harold Ware were either present for that first meeting he attended or he met them "at one time or another at one of those meetings in Collins's apartment." Chambers also claimed to have learned from Peters and Ware "that Alger Hiss was a member and a leader of this group and had been almost from its beginning," although "Carl" did not recall meeting Hiss at his first session. Ware Group members, said Chambers, knew about his role. Chambers recalled meetings where as many as twelve people were present, and, like Josephine Herbst, he estimated the group's total membership at "from ten to twenty members."[21]

Chambers claimed that members of Communist underground units in Washington—the Ware Group and the second one that he himself established with Alger Hiss as its charter recruit—paid CP dues. He "knew it," Chambers told the FBI in 1949, "from the fact that I was a courier . . . and I took dues to J. Peters." Rigorous collection of dues had both economic and psychological importance: Obviously, it helped finance the CP, and it also provided new Communists, especially those with no background or connections in the "open" party, with "the sense of being of real service and of underlining their loyalty." Chambers gave several contradictory accounts of this aspect of his work in 1948 testimony before HUAC, claiming that on occasion he had collected dues from Alger Hiss and that at other times Henry Collins or J. Peters handled this chore. He apparently tried to reconcile these conflicting accounts by noting that sometimes Collins (as treasurer of the Ware Group) gave him the dues for transmittal to Peters and that once Hiss himself passed him an envelope with money for Peters as a dues payment. There is no independent corroboration for any of these claims.

Transferring Hiss from the Ware Group to the second apparatus came, according to Chambers, as a result of Hiss's transfer within the government. In July 1934 he shifted from AAA to an important new post on the legal staff of the Nye Committee, then investigating the impact of foreign and domestic munitions makers upon American policy during and after the First World War (the phrase "merchants of death" enjoyed popularity at the time). "It was my understanding," Chambers told the bureau about his first meeting with Hiss a month after the change, "that at the time of my first going to Washington, Alger Hiss was separated from [the Ware Group] because of his just getting a new position with the Nye Committee. I had previously discussed Alger Hiss with J. Peters and Harold Ware. It had been decided that he should become the first member of the parallel Apparatus. . . . During the [first] meeting with Alger, Harold Ware, Peters [Chambers remained uncertain about Peters's presence there] and myself, it is my recollection that the nature of the new organization being developed was made known to him and he was perfectly agreeable to it." Chambers said that Peters was "in and out of Washington all of the time that I was there." "Carl" remembered Peters giving several talks to Ware Group members: "On one occasion the topic [was] . . . 'The Theory of Underground Organizations and the Nature of Parallel Apparatuses.'" (Lee Pressman also stated that Peters had served on occasion as a guest lecturer to the group.)*

Hiss may have transferred to the Nye Committee with help from Pressman. Hiss says that his shift from AAA to the committee (officially considered a loan of his services) had been arranged by two senators, Bone and Pope, who served on the Nye Committee and on the Senate Agricultural Committee. Jerome Frank said that either Gardner Jackson of AAA or Dorothy Detzer, an important Washington peace activist, had recommended Hiss for the post. Jackson remembered Gerald Nye offering *him* the position of committee chief of staff. After turning it down, Jackson recommended Stephen Raushenbush for the job.[22]

At this point, according to Jackson, Lee Pressman entered the picture:

> Lee came to me and said, "You know Alger Hiss on our legal staff [Jackson had been a good friend of Hiss's sister]. Since you were able to get Steve [Raushenbush], don't you think it would be a good idea if Alger were appointed counsel for that group?"
>
> I said, "I don't know Alger very well."
>
> Lee said, "He'd be ideal."
>
> So he was appointed counsel, loaned by the Triple A.

Jackson did not remember speaking directly to Hiss about the move but felt certain that Hiss knew of Pressman's inquiry on his behalf.[23]

Hiss and Chambers agreed that they had first met while Hiss worked for the Nye Committee, though they disputed the circumstances and the date. Chambers said that he met Hiss in mid-1934, an assertion supported by Josephine Herbst's statements to Hiss's defense lawyers, and that Alger Hiss was already a member of the Ware Group. Hiss stated that he knew Chambers as a freelance newspaperman named George Crosley who came to the Nye Committee for information for magazine articles on the munitions investigation. Although none of Hiss's Nye Committee associates could recall "Crosley," evidence suggests that Hiss

---

*The subject was an important one for Peters, since—as Chambers pointed out to the FBI—it concerned his "dream" of infiltrating the older government agencies with "sleeper" agents. "The purpose of the new parallel apparatus, which I was to organize," Chambers said, "was to take members from Apparatus A [the Ware Group] and other people with the idea of advancing them in the Government, particularly in the old line agencies, primarily, at this time, for the sake of penetration and to influence policy." The Nye Committee, of course, was scarcely an "old line" executive department, but it did offer the Communist Party a superb channel into State Department records and into the private files of leading American manufacturers of military equipment such as the Du Pont Company. That the CP had a keen interest in such records does not require Chambers's word alone for support. See Weinstein and Vassiliev, *passim.*

may have been accurate as to the name Chambers used. Chambers said in 1949 that he could "not definitely recall" the name he employed in associating with the Hisses in 1934 and 1935, and that it was "entirely possible'" that he used "George Crosley" rather than "Carl," his alias with other Ware Group members.* Moreover, Chambers told the FBI that during this period of underground service "I probably passed myself off as a free lance writer or newspaperman." Certainly if the two men were ever seen by outsiders, Hiss would require some cover story for his association with Chambers. But Herbst's account confirms a mid-1934 meeting date, rather than early 1935, as Hiss maintains.[†24]

Profoundly ironic in the light of his later experiences with HUAC was the fact that Hiss—flushed with the success of the Nye Committee's public hearings— was eager in 1934 to extend the powers of such committees in compelling information and documents. Hiss's questioning of Du Pont Company officials and of financier Bernard Baruch brought him a great deal of newspaper coverage, and in subsequent correspondence he tried to draw from a Columbia Law School professor the concession that congressional committees had extremely broad investigative authority over their witnesses. Also, in December 1934, Hiss wrote to Abe Fortas, who had only recently moved to an investigative post at the new Securities and Exchange Commission, arguing that attorney-client privileges were strictly limited to courtroom situations: "There is, therefore, no reason for a legislative committee [such as Nye's] to respect the attorney-client privilege," Hiss contended, "and there may be no reason for an administrative commission [such as the SEC] to respect such a privilege."[25]

Once contact had been made, according to Chambers, Hiss stole from the committee some confidential State Department documents that Chambers then photographed either at Hiss's home or at John Herrmann's apartment. Josephine Herbst said that Ware, Herrmann, and Chambers had discussed recruiting Hiss for the apparatus partly in connection with soliciting theft of such material, but Hiss ridiculed Chambers's accusation. Since the latter never produced Nye Committee materials—these, presumably, would have been forwarded to Peters in New York—there is no way of either confirming or rebutting the charge

---

*If Chambers's assignment was to separate Hiss from the group into a parallel apparatus, it might have seemed more logical to choose a different alias for his contacts with Hiss from the one under which other Ware Group members knew him.

†Hiss sometimes placed his first meeting with "Crosley" in 1934 during HUAC testimony, but this may have simply involved faulty calculation at the time. Hiss's memoir, however, has this to say about seeing Chambers's photographs at his first appearance before HUAC on August 5, 1948: "I would in any colloquy that morning with Chambers unquestionably have been able, as I was two weeks later when I did see him, to recognize him as the free-lance writer George Crosley whom I had met fourteen years before, in the early days of the New Deal." If he met "Crosley" fourteen years earlier, that would mean August 1934, precisely the month Chambers said that they met.

convincingly. Hiss's denial was supported in December 1949 by Joseph C. Green, State Department liaison with the munitions committee from 1934 to 1936. Green stated that the department had not given the Nye Committee secret documents, and that it always gave copies and never original documents.[26]

But the State Department did provide the committee with copies of a number of confidential documents, particularly those dealing with negotiations between the United States and foreign governments on the sale of munitions. Moreover, the department "extracted an understanding that investigators should make no exact copies of communications in diplomatic codes and that the committee would publish no document without State Department authorization." That agreement was often breached by committee members and staff, usually provoking protests from Secretary of State Hull and his aides, but it reflected the concern felt by the department—and by Roosevelt himself—that the Nye Committee could easily endanger American foreign relations by careless handling of diplomatic exchanges. John Wiltz, leading scholar of the committee's work, could not resolve the "possible discrepancy" between Green's deposition and the apparent facts at his [Wiltz's] disposal,* especially the existence of confidential memos in the committee's hands and the record of complaints made by the State Department about the periodic release of such controversial secret documents by the committee. The record, Wiltz concluded, did "not give a complete account and the memories of the participants are hazy.†[27]

THE HISSES AND THE CHAMBERSES: ANATOMY OF A FRIENDSHIP

Alger Hiss and Whittaker Chambers did not hit it off at their first meeting in August or September 1934, a point confirmed by Josephine Herbst. Chambers was uncertain as to whether the meeting had taken place in a Washington restaurant, Hiss's apartment, or elsewhere in the city, but by the time he wrote *Witness*

---

*Wiltz's conclusions about Hiss's role in the committee's work also differed markedly from the accounts of later writers—both favorable and hostile to Hiss—at the time of the case: "In truth, Hiss was no large figure in the investigation, just a bright, personable lawyer who recently had joined government employ." John Wiltz, *In Search of Peace*, p. 223. Hiss's own defense files provide evidence confirming the Nye Committee's use of secret government documents. The committee's "preliminary report," Numbered Copy #11, in Hiss's files, includes the following statement on its cover page: "Based on Confidential State Department Documents" (the report quotes a number of these, stamped "CONFIDENTIAL" in the margin) and notes "Attached documents stamped 'Confidential' are not under any circumstances to be released or quoted until after State Department permission has been secured."

†Gerald Nye, when interviewed by John Wiltz, "with every reason to defend his own committee, later said he believed Hiss had used his committee position for espionage in the way Chambers had described." *Op. cit.*, p. 53.

Chambers had settled on Hiss's apartment. He described a "pawing and aim-less" conversation during which he spoke of his own beliefs as a Communist while Priscilla Hiss "watched me intently." Like Herbst, he considered Hiss with-drawn on that occasion: "There was a polite but complete short circuit. I left shortly after, feeling that it had been pretty awful."[28]

But Chambers said he returned for another try a few nights later. By then the mood had changed entirely: "There were welcoming smiles and Alger was gra-cious in the way which is his particular talent." According to Chambers, Hiss apologized for his aloofness the previous evening and explained that he had not known "what to make of me," finally concluding that Chambers was not an American Party member but an underground Russian or Volga German who had mastered English. There is no direct confirmation of this initial encounter, however, and Chambers never resolved completely the contradictions in his tes-timony regarding details of the meeting.

The two men agreed, however, on a few things, although Hiss (who initially acknowledged meeting Chambers in 1934) finally settled on a January 1935 meeting date. Hiss insisted that "George Crosley" had a particular interest in the Nye Committee's aircraft-industry hearings of September 1934 and the Du Pont Company hearings that December. After their initial encounter, according to Hiss, "I saw him four or five times thereafter at the Senate Office Building or for lunch nearby." Chambers testified to a greater number of meetings, mainly private ones or with other members of the Ware Group. Hiss was reasonably consistent in his general impressions of Chambers, whatever the circumstances of their meeting. "He spoke knowingly of publishing and of literary matters," Hiss wrote in a memo for his attorney in late 1948,

> and appeared perfectly convincing in the role of a free-lance writer. He appeared well read and gave circumstantial accounts [which Hiss never elaborated upon] of prior free-lance writing exploits. . . . His stories were on the "tall" side. . . . He said he had travelled extensively in Europe and claimed to know German literature. I remember him as entertaining rather than the reverse . . . on the vain side judging from his tall stories. . . . I have a vague impression of boastful hints of sexual exploits but no hint of any unnatural sex interests [an important observation in light of Hiss's claim in later years that Chambers had been a spurned homosexual, the rejection of whose friendship by Hiss inspired Chambers's desire for revenge].[29]

Hiss admitted giving Chambers his 28th Street apartment during the early sum-mer of 1935—a rental, he said, not a free loan as Chambers asserted. Chambers's family stayed with the Hisses for several days at their P Street apartment in 1935. On one occasion Priscilla and Esther were sitting in the garden of that apartment when two friends of Mrs. Hiss came to visit (Mrs. Chambers remembered them, but garbled the name of one), and Priscilla also testified to several other meetings with either Whittaker or Esther Chambers or both, but not after 1935. Hiss drove

Chambers to New York once in 1935, possibly also with Mrs. Hiss, although she had no memory of the incident. Moreover, Hiss listed several other meetings with Chambers stretching into the spring of 1936 (he subsequently told the grand jury that he might have seen Chambers in the fall of that year). To his attorneys Hiss said that Chambers (Crosley) had probably not been present in July 1936 when he signed the certificate of title transferring the Ford car; if he had, "I think I would have recalled it." Later Hiss was less certain of this.[30]

Although Hiss spoke of making small loans to Crosley, Chambers described only one such transaction—in November 1937—involving a $400 loan from the Hisses that he used to purchase an automobile. But Hiss denied making that one and called Chambers a casual and irritating acquaintance who welshed on rent payments, pestered him for small loans, and kept returning to his Nye Committee office with additional questions related to freelance articles on the committee for the *American Magazine*.

Portraying both a more intimate and a more secretive relationship, Chambers tabulated a far greater number of meetings with the Hisses during this period and sketched out a friendship solidly grounded on Alger Hiss's involvement in the Communist underground. The Chambers family lived on St. Paul Street in Baltimore until the late spring of 1935. During these months, Chambers told the FBI early in 1949, "my wife has reminded me that Priscilla and Alger Hiss once visited there [St. Paul Street] for dinner." It was from that address that Chambers moved his family into the Hisses' 28th Street apartment, and Whittaker remembered Alger helping him pack up "some of the baby things on his 'old Ford'" and driving him to Washington. His family occupied the Hiss apartment at the invitation of the Hisses and rent-free, Chambers asserted. Moreover, the arrangement included the loan of some furniture from the Hisses, which the Chamberses kept—and produced in 1949 for Hiss's lawyers.[31]

Esther and Whittaker Chambers also said they visited the Hisses' family pediatrician with their daughter, Ellen, while in Washington, an episode the Hisses categorically denied. Esther claimed that Priscilla Hiss accompanied her to see Dr. Margaret Nicholson, who also treated the Hisses' child Timothy Hobson. According to Mrs. Chambers, the visit took place at "the end of September or early October of 1935" as part of a scheduled office visit by Mrs. Hiss and Timothy. According to Dr. Nicholson's records, the only office visit paid by Mrs. Hiss and Timothy during these months was on September 3, 1935. But Mrs. Chambers's and Ellen's presence on that occasion was implied by a letter Dr. Nicholson wrote to Esther, described in a 1949 FBI memo, "asking whether Mrs. Chambers would waive her rights so that Hiss could have access to her records."[*32]

---

*That same memo "stated that one month ago [February 1949] Dr. Nicholson talked to Ellen Chambers and told her that investigators had seen her and she wanted to know if Hiss [apparently a transcribing error, since the reference in context meant Chambers] would waive privileges

One of Chambers's recollections a decade later proved striking and, if true, suggested a strong measure of social intimacy with Alger Hiss during the Ware Group years:

> Mr. Hiss at some point, I presume it was in this general period [1934–35], told me something about Nat Witt's background, the fact that he had been at one time a taxi driver, and had in the course of once driving a passenger somewhere enlisted her interest in him, and she had helped him through schooling in some period.

But Hiss proved more precise about gender and other details in describing apparently that same incident in 1975, one that would have been appropriately told only to a mutual friend or acquaintance of Witt or Frankfurter (neither of whom "George Crosley" would have had any occasion to discuss with Hiss): "You know Nat was in a taxicab, driving a taxicab when Felix [Frankfurter] was going to the Harvard Club or something. Nat had to earn money to go to law school. And he [Witt] recognized him, and as he was depositing him [Frankfurter] he said something about it. And he said, 'I want to go to Harvard Law School. I'm working.' They became close from then on."[33]

Chambers's account of social intimacy with the Hisses during their years together in the underground was further corroborated in 1949 by Edith Murray, a maid who worked for the Chambers family in Baltimore in 1936. Evidence has also come to light confirming Chambers's 1948 contention that Mrs. Hiss visited his family in Smithtown, Pennsylvania, for ten days during the summer of 1935. This second incident involved Chambers's occasional collaborator in secret work, Maxim Lieber.

In August 1935 Chambers and Lieber decided to rent a summer place on the Delaware River in Smithtown. Lieber leased a cottage and became a regular visitor. The Chambers family lived there in August and September 1935 while Whittaker made occasional trips to Washington or New York.

He testified in 1948 that Priscilla Hiss stayed with his family in Smithtown for ten days in August and that Lieber saw her there. He also said that Alger Hiss drove from Washington in his old Ford to pick up Priscilla at the end of this visit. The Chambers family used the names "David and Edna Breen"—the same ones listed on Whittaker's passport—during their months at Smithtown, calling their daughter Ellen "Ursula Breen." Chambers testified that J. Peters had obtained a false Atlantic City birth certificate for Ellen under that name (the FBI turned up the document in 1949). Also, Chambers and his wife opened bank accounts in

---

to examine the documents." FBI Report #2272, March 1, 1949. Dr. Nicholson testified at Hiss's second trial in 1949, but only about certain dates on which she had seen Timothy Hobson as a patient, not on the question of whether she had ever treated Ellen Chambers or "Ellen Breen" in her office. Dr. Nicholson turned down my request for an interview. (Esther Chambers said that she had used the "Ellen Breen" name for her daughter during the visit.)

New Hope, Pennsylvania, under the Breen name, and Whittaker kept the copy of a New York birth certificate for the real David Breen (who had died in infancy) that Peters gave him. Apparently, then, they planned to leave for England after the Smithtown interlude until "Bill's" scheme fell through.[34]

Maxim Lieber later admitted renting the cottage and sharing it with the Chambers family, but did not recall a visit by Mrs. Hiss or having ever encountered Alger or Priscilla Hiss. But when Hiss's lawyers interviewed Lieber in 1948, he did recall such a meeting. One Hiss investigator, identified in a January 21, 1949, defense report only as "Licht," but apparently a Communist like Lieber, went to interview the agent.* "Licht says that he has had a talk with Lieber," the January 1949 memo states, "who says that he does know Hiss but does not propose to admit it."[35]

Fearing involvement in the Hiss-Chambers dispute, Lieber, although sympathetic toward Hiss, did little to help the defense attorneys. He denied having known Chambers well or having been involved with him in the Communist underground during the thirties. But one report by Harold Rosenwald filed in November 1948 contains this exchange: "At one point, [Lieber] said, 'Suppose I were to testify that Mrs. Hiss did visit me for ten days, how would that help you?'" Such testimony would, of course, have hurt Hiss's cause badly. "I replied that I would answer [Lieber's] question if [he] would tell me whether or not she had come there. This he refused to do. However, at one point, he made the following statement: 'I wouldn't know Mrs. Hiss if she were to come in this office and spit in my tea'!"† Equally intriguing is a comment made by Alger Hiss in 1972 to the writer Robert Alan Aurthur, a former client and friend of Lieber's. At the time of the case Alger and Priscilla Hiss denied completely Chambers's assertion that they had been in Smithtown and had met Lieber. Aurthur reported in an *Esquire* article that when he mentioned Lieber's name to Hiss, "Abruptly Alger interrupted. 'I never met him,' he said sharply. Suddenly there was a moment of silence. Then Alger came to the rescue. . . . 'But I never knew Lieber,' Alger reiterated. 'It's possible my wife may have met him.'"†[36]

---

*"Licht" had been providing Hiss's investigators with material from the private files of the Communist publications *The Daily Worker* and *The New Masses*, presumably for the period Chambers worked on each.

†Lieber denied making either statement—the one to Licht or the one to Rosenwald —when I showed him the defense memos in 1975. In the context of his anxieties in 1948 over the Hiss-Chambers case, however, the statements speak for themselves.

‡Another witness to Mrs. Hiss's alleged Smithtown visit, Joseph Boucot, who rented the cottage to Lieber and "David Breen," provided contradictory evidence in statements to Hiss's attorneys, to the FBI, and at Hiss's trial. Avowedly sympathetic toward Hiss, Boucot initially identified Hiss as a visitor, then shifted to a statement that he had seen neither of the Hisses at Smithtown. For Boucot's admission that he saw Hiss, told to a Hiss investigator by Boucot's wife, see Horace W. Schmahl to William L. Marbury, December 6, 1948, and Schmahl's November 16, 1948, report on his Smithtown investigation, Hiss Defense Files. For Boucot's reversal, see his February 18, 1949, FBI interview.

Another occasion in the mid-thirties provides strong eyewitness corroboration to social meetings between the two families. From fall 1935 to spring 1936 Esther and Whittaker lived in a Eutaw Place apartment in Baltimore, using the names "Mr. and Mrs. Lloyd Cantwell." They had employed a maid at the time named Edith, Chambers told the FBI in 1949, whose last name he could not remember. If found, she might verify visits by the Hisses to the apartment.

After a long search the FBI located a Baltimore woman named Edith Murray who had worked for the Cantwells at Eutaw Place. The agents showed Murray a miniature portrait that Esther Chambers had painted of her in 1935, and she identified it and the Cantwells immediately and without prompting. "So I said . . . 'Is Mr. Cantwell back in Baltimore? Are they looking for me to work for them?'" she told the agents, according to her later testimony at Hiss's trial. Murray had suffered a nervous breakdown in 1942 and since that time had not read daily newspapers. Thus she claimed to know nothing about the case. The FBI agents showed her pictures of Alger and Priscilla Hiss and, in response to questioning, she indicated in vague terms that they had visited the Cantwells' Eutaw Place apartment, Priscilla on at least four occasions but Alger only once. Several days later the FBI took Murray to the Chamberses' farm, where she named them as the Cantwells and engaged in a long discussion of her memories of the Baltimore apartment. Murray was clearly as friendly to her former employers as Hiss's former employees remained toward his family. She signed a deposition in which she said that in 1935 she had been told Cantwell was a "traveling salesman" and therefore "away most of the time." The couple "had few friends," moreover, and "practically no visitors while I was employed by them."[37]

Edith Murray singled out one visitor, "a lady from Washington, D.C. who had a little boy about 12 or 14 years old":

> This Lady came to visit Mrs. Cantwell three or four times but never brought her little boy along and I only learned she had a little boy through conversation. On one occasion in April or May of 1936 [Esther Chambers had previously mentioned such an occasion to Hiss's libel-suit lawyers in 1948 and later in an FBI deposition] this Lady from Washington . . . stayed with the Cantwells' daughter that day, overnight and until about noon the following day, while Mrs. Cantwell went to New York City. I definitely remember on the second day preparing and eating both breakfast and lunch with the Lady from Washington, who did not leave until Mrs. Cantwell returned. . . . Mrs. Cantwell was about two or three months pregnant at the time and said she went to New York City to be examined by a doctor. . . . From the way they treated each other, I would say that Mrs. Cantwell and the Lady from Washington were good friends.
>
> I do not recall the name of the Lady from Washington but may be able to recognize her if I see her in person.

Edith Murray also spoke of a man associated with the lady from Washington—"tall, slender . . . about 30 years of age, who was also very polite and nice."

She could not state "definitely" if he ever visited the Cantwells, but "it seems to me that they came to visit the Cantwells together one evening just before I left for the night." The FBI agents showed her a photograph of Alger Hiss, whom they named for her, and she stated that it "looks something like" the person in question. She identified similarly a picture of Priscilla Hiss as looking "very much like" the lady from Washington.[38]

FBI agents spent some time discussing the best manner to arrange a situation in which Edith Murray could observe the Hisses, knowing that the defense would attack the identification if it appeared coached, which the defense later did at Hiss's second trial. Finally, in November 1949, the bureau brought Murray to New York City's Federal Court House, where—according to her later testimony—the following scene ensued:

> Well, I just stood out in the hall, and it was a crowd of people. They asked me did I see anybody in the crowd that I knew, and I looked around, and I didn't see anyone at this time, and stood there and stood there; so, then, after a while, in the back of me where I was standing was an elevator, in the back of me, like, and I looked around, and then I see Mr. and Mrs. Hiss come over, and right away I knew them.

Although the credibility of Edith Murray was promptly challenged by Hiss's lawyers, the FBI interviews confirm (in a way that her trial testimony alone does not) that Murray's recollections concerning Priscilla Hiss, the "Lady from Washington," seemed genuine and unrehearsed. The Cantwells did not receive many visitors. Those who came stood a reasonable chance of being remembered.[39]

The weight of available evidence establishes clearly that Esther and Whittaker Chambers, under whatever names, enjoyed a degree of friendship and intimacy with Alger and Priscilla Hiss that the latter persistently denied.

In 1948 and thereafter Hiss tried to dismiss the details Whittaker and later Esther remembered about the Hisses as mere "housekeeping details," many of them inaccurate. But although Esther and Whittaker Chambers erred on some points, often—as in the case of the Ford car, the prothonotary warbler, and Nathan Witt's taxicab passenger—the most improbable incidents or points of detail recounted by Chambers were partly or wholly substantiated. Thus, Hiss stated in 1948 that he had been a regular churchgoer during the 1930s (Chambers had thought otherwise). Several ministers whom Hiss contacted seeking corroboration disputed the claim in statements to the FBI. One clergyman, the Rev. J. Gillespie Armstrong, said "he felt [Hiss's letter] was an attempt to put words into his mouth concerning Hiss' attendance at church." Armstrong told agents that he wrote Hiss stating "that although he visited him at his home perhaps twice in his capacity as a parson, he does not in fact recall Hiss ever having attended his church during the period mentioned."[40]

An even starker instance concerned Chambers's assertion that Hiss was deaf in one ear. Hiss derided the charge as nonsense and claimed that his hearing was perfect. But one of his lawyers, John F. Davis, wrote to him on October 18, 1948, with this account of a meeting with Hiss's former ear specialist:

> I talked today with Dr. Trible with respect to the tests of your hearing which he made from time to time. He says that on the occasions when he made the tests your eustachian tubes were inflamed affecting your hearing, particularly in the low registers. I asked him whether he ever tested your hearing when it was not impaired by that obstruction, and he stated that his records do not disclose that he did. Since it does not appear that his records would be helpful, I did not ask him for a letter.

But Hiss wrote to William Marbury on November 1, having obtained the services in the meantime of another specialist: "I am enclosing also a copy of Dr. Fowler's certification as to my hearing. . . . Dr. Fowler was good enough to say that he would be glad to change the form to suit our needs. . . . He is said to be an outstanding authority on ears."[41]

The portrait provided by Chambers of the Hisses' lives, habits, and domestic arrangements displayed ample familiarity, considering the fact that the two couples had not seen one another for over a decade. To accept the Hisses' avowal that they had befriended the Chambers family only briefly in 1935, one must believe that Alger and Priscilla Hiss, so formal and correct in their private lives, casually offered a chance acquaintance the use of their 28th Street apartment and furniture for two months during the summer of 1935, threw in as a gift a used automobile (an assertion contradicted by the evidence concerning actual transfer of the Ford), and even provided guest quarters in their new P Street home for several days before the Chamberses moved into the 28th Street apartment.[42]

In addition, the Hisses agreed that they held almost a dozen meetings with the "Crosleys" before and after these events in the summer of 1935.* Chambers's 1936 purchase of the same Westminster farm property on which the Hisses had previously placed a deposit strikingly reinforces the Chamberses' account of the close association between the couples. More significantly, although Hiss could not produce a single person at the Nye Committee or elsewhere in Washington during the mid-thirties to substantiate his testimony of knowing "George Crosley" as a free-lance journalist, Josephine Herbst's depositions lend credence

---

*In 1949 the Chamberses showed Hiss's attorneys a number of items that they claimed had been given to them by the Hisses during the 1930s. These included several old tables and chairs, an old chest, a worn rug, and a few books. Among the books was a 1928 volume on *Feeding the Child from Two to Six* (Timothy Hobson was two in 1928) and a book of bird pictures, color plates published in Massachusetts. Memorandum, "Personal Property Allegedly Given to Chambers by the Hisses," March 26, 1949, Hiss Defense Files.

to Chambers's account of having dealt with Hiss from the beginning in mid-1934 as a fellow member of the Communist underground. Dr. Nicholson's call to Ellen Chambers in 1949 implied a visit to her office by Mrs. Chambers in 1935. The sometime comments of Maxim Lieber concerning Priscilla Hiss's ten-day stay at Smithtown in August 1935 and Edith Murray's testimony about Mrs. Hiss's visits to the Chambers family in Baltimore (including one overnight visit) contradict the Hisses' assertion that they never saw the "Crosleys" socially. A mound of available evidence requires disbelief in short, for Hiss's version of the relationship with "Crosley" to be credited.

THE AAA PURGE

While working for the Nye Committee in February 1935, Alger Hiss became involved in a national controversy concerning his activities and associates at the AAA. Jerome Frank, Lee Pressman, and almost all of the others connected with the agency's nonagrarian "reform" wing (but not Hiss) were suddenly removed by the AAA's farm-wing administrator, Chester Davis. Hiss has consistently obfuscated his role in these events for reasons that bear on Chambers's charges.[43]

Once word of the purge had spread, Jerome Frank's associates gathered in Frank's office to ruminate. Frank had requested an appointment for them with Henry A. Wallace, and late that afternoon word came that the secretary would meet with Frank and a second representative. They chose Hiss, the only one who had not been fired. Pressman was amused by their efforts, considering them all naïve to continue having faith in Wallace, but Frank and Hiss went off to argue the case. Wallace greeted them warmly but nervously, saying, "Jerome, you've been the best fighter I've had for my ideas, but I've had to fire you. The farm people are just too strong. I've got to go along and you've got to go."[44]

Those fired were closely identified with Frank's urban reformist group within AAA. Only one such person escaped the purge: Alger Hiss. The reasons for Hiss's survival are obscured by conflicting accounts, including his own.*

Hiss downgrades his role in drafting a pro-sharecropper opinion on a cotton contract that provoked the purge. He told his attorneys in 1948 that Telford Taylor, another AAA staffer, acted as "the chief draftsman" of that document and that he simply worked "directly with Tel in revising the final drafts." In fact Hiss was the active force behind the opinion, not merely a "technical" legal adviser on

---

*But Hiss remained at the Nye Committee and never returned to work at the AAA. He later resigned as of May 1935 to join the Nye Committee payroll briefly before accepting a post at the Justice Department in August 1935. Davis neither fired him nor, apparently, sought his resignation.

its final stages. Jerome Frank made this clear in a memo, written in defense of his actions, which indicated his continued respect for Hiss, but noted that "the [AAA] files disclosed . . . that that opinion signed by Mr. Frank Shea [who was out of Washington while the cotton-contract opinion was being drafted] and approved by Mr. Alger Hiss and me had been most carefully considered and worked over by Mr. Hiss."* Frank stressed the point during his confrontation with Chester Davis shortly before the purge: "Mr. Hiss supervised the Benefit Contract Section and the Brief and Opinion Section of the Legal Division, both of which were concerned with this problem. *I therefore relied largely on his advice in the matter* [emphasis added]." In several memos prior to his firing, Frank advised Davis that "Mr. Hiss had carefully considered and approved the opinion." Describing Hiss as "not only an unusually brilliant lawyer but an eminently well balanced person of the highest integrity," Frank rejected in his arguments with Davis and Wallace the notion that either he or Hiss had devised the pro-sharecropper opinion disingenuously because they thought the outcome "desirable as a matter of social policy."[45]

Jerome Frank—whom Roosevelt soon appointed to the Reconstruction Finance Corporation—changed his opinion of Hiss. Within weeks after he was fired by Davis, Frank recalled, Hiss and Pressman came to his Georgetown home:

> I can still remember Hiss and Pressman in that living room. I don't know whether Hiss or Pressman spoke up. They said they came to consult me. Hiss had been offered the position of general counsel from which I had been fired [presumably chief AAA counsel, since Frank's separate office had been abolished]. They wanted to ask what I thought of his taking it. This was just a little while after my discharge. I said, "Look, you know me. You've seen . . . how much I enjoy having young people get ahead. . . . Nothing would delight me more than to see Alger advance rapidly, but that isn't this case. Obviously, this purge occurred because of a difference in policy. If you, having been identified with me and being associated with the action that immediately provoked this, take my place, it will appear that this fellow Frank is just an unpleasant man personally. He doesn't know how to keep his fingernails clean. He spits on the carpet. He's bad-mannered. That's all there is to it [the purge]. It has no significance. I wouldn't have volunteered this, but since you've asked me, I think it would be outrageous." . . . it seemed to me that I had shown him [Hiss] himself in a mirror and he crumpled. He shrank.
>
> "Well," he said, "if that's the way you feel about it—"
>
> I said, "Yes, I do."
>
> So he didn't take it. I'm not sure he was offered it from actual knowledge, but I can't believe he would have come to me if it hadn't been. His lawyer

---

*Frank's memo, prepared as a last-ditch argument for Wallace and Davis, can be found in his papers at Yale. Frank apparently decided not to send it, and the only draft is a handwritten one.

[presumably Edward McLean, who came to interview Frank in 1948] later confirmed that he was offered it.

Hiss later denied both Frank's story and having received the offer.[46]

One crucial detail puzzled Frank and continues to confuse students of the AAA purge. When commenting in later years on the pro-sharecropper opinion, Frank observed: "That opinion bore the name of Hiss. Mine was merely an approval of Hiss's opinion. How could he [AAA administrator Davis], since Hiss was primarily responsible, fire other people and retain Hiss?" Frank later refused Hiss's request that he testify as a character witness at his first trial.[47]

According to Hiss, some of those purged pressed him to resign, but he declined because of the "personal interchange with Mr. Davis," with whom he believed he could still work. The explanation is odd, since Hiss resigned soon afterward. In Hiss's account, Chester Davis summoned him into his office shortly after returning from the field to discover the Frank directive and demanded to know how Hiss "could have approved such a 'dishonest' opinion, and I replied by telling him that he had my resignation as I could not act as lawyer for anyone who would question my integrity." Davis, according to Hiss, then denied that he meant to question Hiss's integrity, apologized, and asked Hiss to remain. Hiss withdrew his resignation, he said, after cooling off and after further apologies from Davis, who "explained that he was under great pressure and had spoken hastily and carelessly."

Shortly after the purge Wallace and Davis held a press conference to explain their actions, at which Davis—when asked about Hiss—remarked: "There has been no suggestion of Mr. Hiss's resignation, except in the press, as far as I know." Whether because of Davis's personal fondness for Hiss, or Wallace's desire to retain one symbol of the Frank group within AAA, or simply because he was absent from the daily AAA scene on Nye Committee assignment, Alger Hiss's resignation did not come immediately (as those who had been purged hoped it would) but several months later.*[48]

Chester Davis, like Jerome Frank, declined to testify at Hiss's trial as a character witness despite several defense requests: "I . . . am convinced that my testimony will do Alger no good," he wrote William Marbury in March 1949. Nor would Gardner Jackson, who came to believe later that he had been

---

*According to Chester Davis, Jr., his father told him "that he was fully aware that Alger Hiss was deeply involved in the matter [writing the tenant farmer opinion—A.W.]. He did not fire Hiss. Instead he called him in and told him that he wanted his resignation within a decent interval. By decent he meant within a time period that would not obviously link Hiss with the purge. . . . His special handling of Hiss reflected only the concern of an older man about blighting the career of a particularly able and promising young man." Chester Davis, Jr., to the author, May 3, 1978.

duped by Lee Pressman, Nathan Witt, and Alger Hiss.* In searching for some leading figure from this period in Hiss's life to attest to his good character at his trials (Nye and Raushenbush also refused), Hiss's lawyers turned to the Legal Division's leading civil service bureaucrat, a career employee named Philip Wenschel, who had worked closely with Hiss during 1933–35, but he too declined.[49]

Hiss's move to the Justice Department in August 1935, one of the "old line" centers of government that J. Peters had expressed a desire to infiltrate, fitted nicely (according to Chambers's FBI deposition) into the CP's plans. Hiss had managed to escape the AAA purge that cut short the government career of the CP's other prominent representative within the agency: Lee Pressman left the New Deal to resume private practice in New York, joining the newly organized CIO and rising to become its general counsel.

The AAA purge and Harold Ware's death had disrupted the activities of the Washington underground network, and after a struggle for leadership, the group reformed (according to a great deal of later evidence) under the leadership of economist Victor Perlo. Hiss had been separated from this group the previous year, according to Chambers, but he remained on friendly terms with at least one of its members, Henry Collins.[50]

The existence of the Perlo Group and of its members was confirmed not only by defectors like Chambers but also by someone in a unique position to know its inside workings—Mrs. Perlo. Katherine Wills Perlo wrote an anonymous letter to the White House in 1944, and among those she named as past or present members of the Perlo Group were John Abt, Henry Collins, Charles Kramer, and Nathan Witt, plus others identified through FBI investigation, such as George Silverman and Frank Coe. Hope Hale Davis, another former member, observed in 1978 that "about Victor Perlo himself and his underground activities there can be no doubt. I attended a unit meeting (we did not use the term 'cell') once a week for more than two years, and Vic was present surely at more than seventy of them. He was my first unit leader. . . ."[†51]

Busy with other tasks as a courier throughout 1935, Chambers no longer fraternized with the Perlo Group as had been his custom with Harold Ware's underground friends. Through J. Peters, Chambers met David Carpenter (real last name: Zimmerman), a photographer working in Washington for the network. Zimmerman, in turn, introduced Chambers to Julian Wadleigh, William Ward Pigman, and Vincent Reno, all of whom Chambers said later turned over government materials to him. Both Wadleigh and Reno confessed their role in such

---

*Alger Hiss portrayed Gardner Jackson to me, in the course of a 1975 interview, as a heavy drinker whose testimony on the AAA period was unreliable.

†On the "Perlo Group," see Weinstein and Vassiliev, *passim.*

espionage to the FBI in 1948 as well as their knowledge of both Carpenter and Chambers as underground Communist contacts.

Early in 1936 Peters made what Chambers said his superior described as "an interesting suggestion": that the American Communist underground in Washington sell documents to the Soviet spy rings and use the funds acquired that way to finance activities of the American CP! Chambers recalled that the resident Russian agent, "Bill," reacted negatively, but agreed to examine some samples. Chambers then obtained some materials from Julian Wadleigh and Ward Pigman at this time (Wadleigh—but not Pigman—confirmed this) and photographed them for Bill at the home, according to Chambers, of either John Herrmann or Alger Hiss. But Bill remained indifferent to the scheme, and it died after a half-dozen such transmissions. Bill's successor, Colonel Bykov, who arrived in mid-1936 after Bill's disappearance, reacted much more favorably to such espionage.[52]

Occasionally Chambers's work took him outside of the Baltimore-Washington area.* He told of one 1935 train trip to the West Coast to deliver a money belt containing more than $10,000 to an underground Communist leader in San Francisco. It was on this trip that he first met William Edward Crane, whom he remembered using the pseudonym "Keith." Both Crane and Chambers told the FBI that they came to know one another quite well during the course of underground assignments over the next few years, and although their accounts of the relationship differed in some details, the stories meshed and corroborated one another on important questions. Crane took Chambers to meet a veteran Communist Party organizer named Isaac Volkov, a close friend, and Chambers later described Volkov's activities in his 1939 meeting with Adolf Berle:

West Coast—Head: "The Old Man"—Volkov is his real name—daughter a Comintern courier. He knows the West Coast underground—Residence: San Francisco or Oakland—

Interviewed separately by the FBI and without prior knowledge of Chambers's deposition, Crane confirmed the latter's West Coast visit and its purpose. Volkov, according to Crane, had praised Chambers for his earlier *New Masses* stories, a sure sign that the "old man" knew the real name and background of "Lloyd Cantwell"/"Carl"/"George Crosley" or whatever pseudonym Chambers had used on the trip.[53]

---

*In the fall of 1936 Chambers met Lee Pressman one final time in New York City. Adolf Berle's notes in 1939 record Chambers's version of the encounter: "[Chambers] Introduced him [Pressman] to Mack Moren, buying arms for Spanish (Loyalist) Gov't.—Pressman—as [CIO] counsel—helped Moren—made a flight to Mexico with him; forced down at Brownsville, Tex. in late '36 or early '37. . . ." Pressman confirmed almost all of Chambers's story, except for the plane crash, in a 1950 interview with the FBI.

During the fall of 1936, "George Crosley's" benefactor, Alger Hiss, began a new job as assistant to Assistant Secretary of State Francis B. Sayre. While Hiss settled into his new responsibilities at this vitally important "old line" department, Soviet Military Intelligence dispatched Colonel Boris Bykov to the United States as a replacement for its previous chief resident agent.* It was Bykov who revived J. Peters's earlier scheme to exploit fully the CP's government contacts in Washington for espionage purposes. The results would soon trigger the most dangerous phase of Whittaker Chambers's career as a Soviet courier and of Alger Hiss's secret life in the Communist underworld.

---

*Four members of the Communist underground during the 1930s other than Chambers—Maxim Lieber, Julian Wadleigh, William Edward Crane, and Nadya Ulanovskaya—have identified Bykov as the Russian agent they met, knew, or worked with during this period

Part Two

ESPIONAGE

In 1948, in a Philadelphia bar during the Progressive Party convention, which adopted Henry Wallace as a presidential candidate, a Russian forgot and talked. He said: "In England, now that the war is over and espionage trials take place in open court, persons detected in espionage on behalf of the Soviet Union are instructed by whichever of our organizations it is which has been using them, to plead guilty and to admit to the police their participation in the particular crime of which they are accused, and nothing more. In the United States such persons are at present instructed to proceed in precisely the opposite way and deny everything. This is a compliment to England. . . . In the United States, where legal proceedings are likely to be prolonged and confused, and all sorts of considerations may prevent the truth from appearing, it is worthwhile putting up a plea of not guilty, no matter how absurd this may be in view of the real facts."

—Rebecca West, The New Meaning of Treason

"'In your time it was kinderspiel [child's play],' Boris told us. He said, 'We have agents at the very center of government.'"

—Boris Bykov, to Nadya and Alexander Ulanovski, Moscow, 1939

V

PERJURY: A QUESTION OF DOCUMENTS

SEPTEMBER 27, 1948: THE SLANDER SUIT

In September 1948 government security officers speculated wildly that Alger Hiss planned to flee the country. The chief of naval intelligence, who apparently started the rumor, alerted his counterpart at the new Central Intelligence Agency that Hiss "may be preparing to leave the United States, possibly for the Far East." The CIA, in turn, dispatched a precautionary memo to the secretary of state about the unconfirmed report, asking that the agency "be notified . . . of Mr. Hiss's destination, if and when a passport is granted him."

On September 26 the rumor became public when HUAC investigators (having heard the news) promptly leaked it to Walter Trohan of the Chicago *Tribune.* "HISS PREPARING TO QUIT COUNTRY, PROBERS ADVISED," began Trohan's account, which quoted committee sources for the allegation that Hiss "has been taking a series of inoculations . . . of a type which would indicate that Hiss planned to go to the southwest Pacific or to the Soviet Union." Pointedly, Trohan recalled that "Hiss has not sued Chambers for libel or slander although the latter waived immunity of his testimony before the congressional committee by openly charging [on *Meet the Press*] Hiss was a member of the pre-war Communist underground in the capital."[1]

The day after the story appeared, Hiss filed a $50,000 slander suit against Chambers in U.S. District Court in Baltimore, Maryland. The action charged the *Time* editor with having made "untrue, false and defamatory" accusations against Hiss on *Meet the Press,* including such statements as "Alger Hiss was a Communist and may be now," remarks that had "damaged his professional reputation and office, brought him into public odium and contempt and caused him great pain and mental anguish."

Chambers replied laconically to the action: "I welcome Mr. Hiss' daring suit. I do not minimize the audacity or the ferocity of the forces which work through him. But I do not believe that Mr. Hiss or anybody else can use the means of justice to defeat the ends of justice."[2]

On October 8 Hiss filed a second slander action against Chambers, this time for $25,000, on the basis of that statement. Hiss claimed that his good faith in filing the earlier suit had been impugned. In Chambers's legal reply to the original suit, made later in October, he reiterated the charges against Hiss and made the additional accusations that Hiss had "committed perjury" in denying Chambers's HUAC testimony about their relationship.[3]

By mid-October the Justice Department was in a quandary. George Morris Fay, U.S. attorney for the District of Columbia, and John Beacher, an assistant to Attorney General Clark, had agreed that there was insufficient evidence to indict either Hiss or Chambers for perjury based on their conflicting testimony before HUAC: "Unless new evidence is uncovered, there would be no perjury trial." The Justice Department's decision to avoid involvement left the case squarely in the hands of the federal judge in Baltimore who would try Hiss's pending slander suit.[4]

The decision to sue Chambers had not been made easily, nor impulsively. For over a month Hiss's friends and associates gave him conflicting advice. The debate often became heated, with Hiss himself stymied for a time both because of disagreements over strategy and because of an embarrassment of legal riches, so many of his former associates having offered to serve either as advisers or directly as counsel. Hiss wrote William Marbury on August 31 about his legal situation. The day before, he had obtained the services of Debevoise, Plimpton and McLean, a major New York firm, "on a regular full-time overall basis" to conduct his defense. "Ed McLean was in my class at Law School . . . and has been primarily a trial lawyer. He . . . is the member of the firm who will devote full time to my problems—which are numerous":

> I am planning a suit for libel or defamation if we can get enough unprivileged material together to warrant it [Hiss wrote Marbury]. I also want to file affidavits from a number of people with whom and for whom I worked closely while in government service. There are a number of other witnesses to run down . . . [and] a number of relatively promising leads. . . . The number of volunteer helpers is considerable . . . but the real job was to get general overall counsel. . . . we must move swiftly as so far the committee with its large investigative staff and considerable resources has been able to seize the initiative continuously and regularly. . . .[5]

Edward McLean remained cautious about jumping into legal action against Chambers, despite the *Meet the Press* interview. John F. Davis, director of the Hiss investigations in Washington, sent McLean a *Washington Post* editorial critical of Hiss and pointed out that "these editorials reflect the general reaction of people who are or have been friendly to Alger. I have been deluged with complaints from people with whom I am in contact in Washington. All feel that he is doing his case great damage, some feel doubts on the real issue, and a few have even expressed the opinion that Alger is trying to protect Mrs. Hiss." Davis urged immediate filing of a suit for defamation. McLean, in turn, cautioned Davis against counterproductive haste: "Alger's real friends must realize that it takes a little time to make the necessary preparations for such a suit and that it is better to be prepared before starting."[6]

But McLean arranged to hire private investigators in New York to supplement the volunteer efforts of Davis and others in Washington. Several Carnegie Endowment trustees—notably Dulles, John W. Davis, and Arthur Ballantine—urged Hiss and McLean not to rush into court before a case had been thoroughly prepared. Marbury, however, criticized this course of action: "I told him [Hiss] that I considered that very bad advice," he wrote on September 15, "in spite of the eminence of the source." Marbury had also decided to offer his own services to Hiss to fight the lawsuit against Chambers.[7]

The belief that Hiss should move briskly to sue received support from other friends of Hiss such as Judge Charles Wyzanski of Boston and Supreme Court Justice Felix Frankfurter, and from some of Marbury's associates on the Harvard Corporation, including Grenville Clark and President James Conant, who had become anxious about the broader implications of Hiss's plight. "Although I don't know him at all," Clark wrote Marbury on September 18, "I am greatly interested in the case as a personal human problem and also because of its importance as a public matter. This is for the reasons mentioned by James B. Conant, i.e., that if Hiss, assuming the falsity of the allegations against him, can nevertheless be successfully smeared and ruined, nobody is safe and great public harm will be done." One thing puzzled Clark:

> You quote Hiss as saying that he is planning "a suit for libel or defamation if we can get enough unprivileged material to warrant it." I didn't hear the Chambers broadcast, but from J. B. Conant's account of it, it would seem to have included plenty of unprivileged material on which to base a suit. So this statement of Hiss rather surprises me.[8]

Grenville Clark appears to have been the source for a suggestion later adopted by the Carnegie trustees: Hiss should receive a leave of absence from the Endowment while he fought the slander action, if only to preclude pressures for his resignation: "As long as he retains his title as President . . . I shouldn't think such an arrangement would hurt him." Marbury, Clark, and Conant corresponded about the suit throughout September, and Marbury soon became the driving force behind the group of advisers urging quick legal action to confront Chambers. By mid-month the matter was settled. Marbury wrote Clark on the 22nd that Hiss wished to bring the suit in Baltimore rather than in New York, if only "so that he may be judged by the people who have had an opportunity to know him the longest and the best." Marbury was inclined to agree, and since both he and his partner had a considerable amount of trial experience, "if this case is tried here, this firm would, of course, take the lead in the trial."

His friends disagreed. Clark had suggested obtaining a distinguished senior trial lawyer for the suit, and ex-Secretary of War Robert Patterson recommended

Lloyd Paul Stryker, as had others close to Hiss. But Marbury pointed out the difficulty of retaining such prominent figures on short notice. "As for funds," he noted, "Hiss tells me that a number of people have offered to help and that two of his friends have suggested that they be permitted to act as trustees in this connection to accept contributions from his friends. Hiss had refused to do this but, under my persuasion, has reluctantly changed his mind."

When Hiss decided to sue in Baltimore, direction of the case passed from Edward McLean to Marbury, who began weaving together the many investigative strands. Marbury felt even better about the decision to sue once Trohan's silly but possibly damaging *Tribune* article appeared on the 26th: "[It] shows why he had no choice except to file the suit."[9]

Immediately Marbury sought the support of the Carnegie trustees. "Now that you have crossed the Rubicon on the slander suit," John W. Davis wrote, responding to a long letter from Marbury, "I wish you and Hiss every success."

But John Foster Dulles just as quickly and quietly moved to protect himself. He met with Nixon in August, and in September he received the congressman's long memorandum outlining the evidence HUAC had compiled against Hiss. Dulles did not tell Hiss about either the meeting or the memo. Hiss wrote to Dulles, then in Paris as an American delegate to a U.N. meeting, informing him about having filed the slander suit. He received, in return, a brief and noncommittal note, far different from the more sympathetic reactions of Davis and other trustees: "Dear Alger: I have your letter of September 27th. I have seen in the press that you had filed suit against Chambers and I am glad to have a copy of the Bill of Complaint." Earlier that month, before the committee concluded its inquiry, Dulles had urged Hiss to resign as president to "relieve the Endowment of embarrassment," but Hiss recognized the further damage to his reputation such a move would create. He asked to remain until after the HUAC hearings had ended, but promised to resign later.

By mid-September Dulles and John W. Davis arrived at a compromise acceptable to the other trustees. James T. Shotwell would assume active administrative direction of the Endowment while allowing Hiss to remain as president—Hiss to divide his time between Carnegie work and his defense efforts. Shotwell believed Hiss innocent and worked hard to fortify other trustees in that conviction. Dulles remained in Paris, conveniently removed from reporters' questions about Hiss. Shotwell wrote him on October 20 that he had "had good long talks" with several Endowment trustees—Thomas Watson of IBM, John W. Davis, David Rockefeller, General Dwight Eisenhower, and others. "They all agreed with me on two main things: One,—no action by the Trustees with reference to Mr. Hiss in the immediate future, that is to say while his [slander] case is up in court. The strongest expression of feeling on this came in my talk with General Eisenhower, but everyone agreed that it would prejudice the case itself if we were to take any action one way or another while it was undecided."

The trustees also agreed that they must meet soon after Dulles returned to the United States in order to chart a future course of action for the Endowment. By then perhaps Hiss's suit against Chambers would have produced results to guide their actions, "one way or another."[10]

One of Hiss's friends, a prominent Quaker named Clarence Pickett, made an intriguing effort to mediate the dispute with Chambers. Shortly before Hiss filed suit, Chambers met with Pickett, director of the American Friends Service Committee, in Philadelphia on September 21. The encounter represented the only attempt made throughout these months to resolve the conflict without a bruising confrontation. But Chambers, according to Hiss's memo of Pickett's visit, "gave no indication of being willing to modify his story. . . . Pickett, acting entirely on his own initiative, asked Chambers if he would be willing to see me. Chambers asked what the objective would be and then said that he would be glad to but that he did not think much would come of it."[11]

THE HISS DEFENSE PROBES

The Hiss investigative records were filling up with a staggering mass of "raw" data from the private detectives hired by McLean in New York, the investigations by John F. Davis in Washington, and the volunteer inquiries of friends and sympathizers received by Hiss, McLean, or Marbury. McLean focused his efforts—and those of investigators under his control—on collecting information on Chambers. His detectives began working in late August and were assigned specific "objectives," as listed in one of the investigator's initial reports:

1. To obtain background information on Chambers and his family.
2. To determine whether Chambers had ever been hospitalized in a mental institution.
3. To determine if Chambers had ever used the name of George Crosley.
4. To obtain information concerning purchase of a property at Westminster, Maryland, by Chambers, and in which property it is alleged that Chambers and Hiss had a mutual interest.[12]

Two personal questions—whether Chambers had ever been treated for a mental illness and whether Chambers had been (or still was) a homosexual—became the focus of much of this investigative work. The searchers took their cues from Hiss himself, whose statement to J. Parnell Thomas had referred to Chambers's "instability," hinted broadly at an earlier period of mental derangement, and applied the word "queer" (a pejorative colloquialism for a homosexual then as today) no less than four times in describing Chambers. Demonstrating that Chambers had been either mentally ill or a homosexual might have damaged irreparably his credibility as a witness, even though it would not in itself have disproved Chambers's allegations. Although the defense had received reports by late August of Chambers's alleged commitment to a mental institution, Hiss himself appears to have initiated the rumors of his accuser's homosexuality, first in his August 1948 comments about Chambers being "queer." Only in October did defense investigators begin reporting rumors of such homosexual behavior.[13]

From the beginning, moreover, Hiss directed his attorneys and detectives toward a psychiatric explanation of Chambers's alleged perjury. Thus, on August 28, the New York investigator began scanning records at Westchester County's mental hospital (formerly known as Bloomingdale Sanitorium) "upon receipt of information from the client in this case [Hiss] to the effect that Chambers may have been hospitalized" there. Two days later, August 30, the same detective searched for the address of a *New York Times* librarian named Jean Tomlinson, also "upon receipt of information from the client in this case that [she] had knowledge of a commitment of Chambers to a mental institution." The detective had checked out a leading New York psychiatrist, Dr. Lawrence Kubie, who had allegedly treated Chambers, or so several friends told Hiss. None of the leads panned out, although Alger Hiss wrote his brother, Donald, that, according to a friend who had spoken to the psychiatrist, "Dr. Kubie said that he feels so strongly about my case that he would not have allowed considerations of professional ethics to play any part in his actions. He most certainly never has treated Chambers."[14]

Much of the pre-libel-suit investigation of Chambers that took place during the fall of 1948 concerned the details of his family, youth, and life as a Communist. But unconfirmed allegations continued to trickle in about Chambers's period or periods in a mental hospital and about supposedly recurrent emotional difficulties. One such report came in September from Henry Collins, Hiss's boyhood friend and an alleged Ware Group member. "Collins has not obtained any further definite information as to the Washington psychiatrists who have treated Chambers from time to time. He says that a Dr. Benjamin Weininger, a Washington psychiatrist, might be able to provide information on this subject. He [Weininger] is said to be a good friend of Lauchlin Currie." Other allegations of Chambers's instability and homosexuality came at this time and later from Communists who knew him during the 1920s and '30s, notably Sender Garlin, Grace Hutchins, A. B. Magill, and Joseph Freeman.[15]

Harold Rosenwald obtained several leads concerning Chambers's private life from A. J. Liebling of *The New Yorker*. Liebling played much the same role of adviser and tipster for Hiss's lawyers that Bert Andrews of the *Herald Tribune* played for Nixon. In researching stories on the case, Liebling borrowed some letters Chambers had sent during the 1920s to Mark Van Doren. Without first getting Van Doren's permission, he gave the letters to Rosenwald along with Van

Doren's copies of Chambers's *Play for Puppets* and other material the Columbia professor had kept that dealt with his former student.*

Although unhappy when he learned about Liebling's transfer of the documents to Hiss's lawyer, Van Doren cooperated with Hiss's attorneys. He told what he knew of Chambers during the 1920s and, less intimately, during the thirties. "I asked Van Doren if he knew who the unconventional partner was to whom Chambers referred in his letter to Van Doren," Harold Rosenwald wrote on November 15. "He said that she had a nickname something like 'Bub.' I asked him if he was sure about the sex of the partner. He said that he had assumed it was a woman but he could not be sure and that Proust had written a long love story about a man and a woman and the woman actually was a man. He admitted the possibility that Chambers took a bit out of Proust's book."[16]

But Hiss's investigators could not verify the rumors that most attracted them— those dealing with Chambers's alleged homosexually and mental instability—as they prepared to take pretrial depositions from Esther and Whittaker Chambers in early November.

Unlike McLean, Marbury also made an effort to probe the Hisses' past. He asked Alger and Priscilla to prepare detailed descriptions of various aspects of their lives, if only to counter Chambers's portrait of them as "romantic communists." At the same time, Marbury tried to squelch the single damaging rumor that had spread among many of Hiss's friends—they believed him innocent, but thought he was probably covering up for Priscilla:

> The report about Priscilla Hiss [Marbury wrote Joseph Johnston on September 22] is typical of many which have been going around, and I have tried running them down with the usual result. . . . Her reputation for radicalism apparently stems from the fact that in 1932 she voted for Norman Thomas.
>
> As you know, she used to be very free in expressing her opinion on all kinds of topics, frequently with much vehemence. At times her self-assertion was annoying, simply because she dominated the conversation and never gave me a chance to discuss things with Alger. Aside, however, from a rather romantic

---

*Liebling became a good friend of the Hisses and the defense lawyers during the year that followed, raising questions in the minds of government prosecutors at Hiss's trial—and also in the minds of several journalistic colleagues—as to whether he had abandoned his normal role of recording events in his column on "the press" for an advocate's position in the case. "A couple of nights after the evening when I made Alger and Priscilla laugh with excerpts from my *Time* pieces," Liebling wrote Harold Rosenwald on December 31, 1949, "*Colliers* informed me that the stuff wasn't what they wanted—I was obviously biased against *Time*. . . . That time I called you I had received a telegram from Tom O' Neill [of the *Baltimore Sun*] saying: 'Government at Hiss trial suggested today you used subterfuge of preparing New Yorker profile of Whittaker Chambers to gather derogatory information regarding him when you were really acting as agent for defense lawyers, specifically McLean and Rosenwald stop appreciate comment wired collect.' I sent him the telegram of which I enclose a copy [denying] any such suggestion. . . ." Liebling to Rosenwald, December 31, 1949. For Liebling on the Hiss case, see *The New Yorker*, July 23, 1949, among other stories.

New Dealism, I do not remember any particular political tinge through her conversation, nor have I been able to find anyone else who had a different experience.[17]

Despite the comprehensiveness of Hiss's reports to Marbury on his youth and aspects of his government career, the Baltimore attorney remained impatient over the reluctance of his friend and client to discuss certain matters. Marbury wrote Hiss a few days before the first scheduled pretrial interrogation of Chambers, complaining about his failure to document important aspects of his story. Marbury believed that Hiss enjoyed widespread sympathy and support among his former government associates. But some of those he had written asking to help—people such as Jerome Frank, Chester Davis, and James Byrnes—refused to provide character references. Nor had Hiss obtained any cooperation from Mrs. Hiss's former husband, Thayer Hobson, in assisting his legal efforts.*[18]

The several investigations being conducted on Hiss's behalf prior to the libel suit turned up a mixed brew of facts, rumors, and potentially verifiable data about Chambers. Hiss, as usual, provided some of the most intriguing items. Thus he wrote Marbury on October 18: "Friday another anonymous communication listed additional alleged pseudonyms . . . [for Chambers, including] David Breen during the period 1935–36, Robert Caldwin [Cantwell?] and Bendt [no first name given]." In mid-August Hiss had received another "anonymous communication" from a caller who claimed to have known Chambers as "George Crosley." Another unknown informant, according to Hiss, provided some of Chambers's most important underground aliases and Baltimore addresses at the time, indicating that the person had known Chambers—and known him extremely well— in the Communist underground of the thirties.[19]

Offers of legal aid to Hiss proved even more numerous than his anonymous benefactors. Richard Field had agreed to act as chief fund-raiser for his slander-suit expenses. Not only did Field raise money, but also he obtained the free services of a friend's Boston law firm for any investigative work Hiss's attorneys wanted done in that city. Marbury and McLean had already indicated to their client that they would be charging him only expenses, not legal fees, for their services. And Hiss also received substantial unpaid help from two Washington firms: Covington, Burling, Rublee, Acheson, and Shorb, Donald Hiss's law firm, and the partnership for which Donald's attorney, Hugh Cox, worked—Cleary,

---

*More significantly, although Marbury never learned about this, Hiss had turned down a suggestion made in late 1948 by his friend Dr. Carl Binger, a psychiatrist who was assisting defense efforts in New York, that Binger question him after injecting scopalomine, a "truth serum." Hiss had exercised his constitutional rights earlier in declining HUAC's invitation to submit to a lie-detector test, but his refusal to be questioned by the friendlier and more professional Dr. Binger while under the influence of scopalomine was never mentioned publicly by him. The incident was described to me in an interview with a psychiatrist and family friend closely connected with Hiss's defense efforts.

Gottlieb, Friendly and Cox. The latter firm paid for a good portion of Hiss's investigative expenses. Marbury wrote Donald Hiss in October: "I wish that Dean [Acheson] would check this and let me know," and there were other instances when Acheson—soon to be secretary of state—aided Hiss's attorneys. The following month another partner at Covington, Spencer Gordon, wrote Marbury: "We are working on questions of evidence. Particularly we are working on (1) whether persons who worked with Hiss in the State Department can testify as to what he did which was anti-Russian, and (2) to what extent testimony can be put in to show mental incompetency of Chambers. We have done quite a bit of work on these points and shall soon have something to send you. I am, however, shipping the enclosed along to give you something to look at." What Gordon had sent was a memorandum entitled "Notes on Method of Presenting Evidence in *Hiss v. Chambers*," a guide to Marbury's handling of the Baltimore lawsuit.[20]

But McLean had his own ideas on conducting the pretrial depositions:

> I have given considerable thought to the Chambers deposition [he wrote Marbury on November 1]. I am very clear in my own mind that we should take him over the entire history of his dealings with Alger. I would start at the very beginning and ask him when he first met Alger, where, who was present, what was said, etc., and proceed in the same fashion with each and every meeting as far as he can recall. He was not asked about these matters in any such detail before the Committee, and I think that if we do, we will obtain information which may be of great help to us later on. . . . It is not my thought that we attempt to impeach him, but only to get him on record as to every last detail of his story as far as Alger is concerned.[21]

THE BALTIMORE DEPOSITIONS

When he interrogated Chambers in Baltimore, Marbury followed this course. McLean and Harold Rosenwald were also present in Marbury's office on Hiss's behalf, while Chambers was represented by his newly acquired counsel, Richard F. Cleveland (youngest son of President Grover Cleveland) and William D. Macmillan of the Baltimore firm of Semmes, Bowen and Semmes. *Time* magazine's counsel, Harold Medina, Jr., also assisted in Chambers's defense against the libel action. Marbury led Chambers through a detailed recitation of his unhappy family life, youth, and Communist Party experiences. The dates Chambers assigned to events often proved slightly wrong, especially attempts to date events in the 1920s. But Chambers volunteered much information later used by Hiss's lawyers in an unsuccessful effort to impeach him as a liar, a psychopath, an alcoholic, a homosexual, and a deviant in other ways. For example, he raised the name of Samuel Roth, who had published "Tandaradei"; he described his connection in the CP during the 1920s with Benjamin Mandel; and he outlined his love affair with Ida Dales.[22] Sometimes he interjected explanations of Communist Party practices, procedures, and dogmas to clarify aspects of his personal experience for the benefit of lawyers largely unfamiliar with the CP and its ways.

So detailed were Marbury's questions and Chambers's responses that Chambers had only begun to describe his underground work with the Ware Group when the November 4 interrogation ended. By then he had mentioned Hiss's name only once, as a Ware Group member, but before adjourning the session Marbury called upon him to "produce tomorrow, if he has any, any correspondence, either typewritten or in handwriting . . . from any member of the Hiss family . . . which he has received at any time . . . any papers signed by Mr. Hiss which may be in his possession—I would like to have those. And I hope you will accept this as a notice to produce."[23]

Next morning Marbury asked Chambers if he had brought papers with him. Chambers's attorney William Macmillan responded on behalf of his client: "Mr. Chambers has advised us that he has not explored all of the sources where some conceivable data might be. . . . We will make search and will make response." After Marbury obtained Macmillan's agreement that Chambers might be questioned regarding such written material, should any be produced, the probing resumed.[24]

The interrogation soon turned to the matter of Hiss's alleged involvement in the CP underground, first in the Ware Group and then in the parallel apparatus described by Chambers. Marbury pressed the witness for details of all his alleged meetings with Hiss. Chambers, responding, provided an account not only of dealings with Alger Hiss but of his and Esther Chambers's meetings with Priscilla during the mid-1930s. The two women, Chambers insisted, had become close friends at the time (although this had meant a breach in normal procedure for people in the CP underground, who were forbidden to fraternize with one another).

Chambers ran into some difficulty in explaining just what the Hisses did as party members once they had been separated into a parallel apparatus, since, according to his own testimony, they were forbidden to engage in activities with other members such as the regular meetings held by the Ware Group. He mentioned Hiss's transfer of the Ford car, one occasion when Hiss purportedly took State Department documents while working for the Nye Committee, and, after Hiss began working at State, "occasionally [giving] the Communist Party bits of information which he thought might be useful to them." When Marbury pressed for details, Chambers expanded the scope of his accusations against Hiss significantly:

Q. You mean he handed you a document.
A. I frequently read State Department documents in Mr. Hiss's house.

Q. Well, now, what kind of documents?

A. [One] told the story about the New York outlets* of an international or Russian [espionage] ring in England.

. . . .

Q. Now, what other State Department documents did you see? You say you frequently saw State Department documents?

A. Yes, Mr. Hiss very often brought a brief case with documents home, and I used to read those that were interesting. They were not very interesting, most of them. I think they were chiefly on trade agreements, and one thing and another. The most interesting ones were Mr. Messerschmidt's reports from Vienna, which were rather long and talky.†

. . . .

Q. You mean [reports from Vienna] addressed to the Secretary of State?

A. I have forgotten. Very likely.

Q. And what was the subject matter of those reports?

A. That was the period I would think either just before or just after the German invasion of Austria, and the reports were fairly lively accounts of conditions in Vienna, and in the vicinity of Vienna.

Q. Were they of special interest?

A. No, they were not of special interest.

Q. Well, what documents that were of interest to the Communist Party or to the Soviet Government . . . did you ever obtain from Mr. Hiss . . . ?

A. I would not say that I ever obtained any documents from him . . . [except for two that dealt with espionage matters].

Q. At any rate, at present, you cannot recollect any others, or the subject matter of any others?

A. I don't at the moment, no.

Q. Now, what other papers did you see besides this Messerschmidt report that you have told us about?

---

*A Greenwich Village store, the Phantom Red Cosmetic Company, which turned out—as Chambers testified—to have been a cover for a Communist espionage ring. In a February 4, 1938, memorandum to the FBI, the State Department described an English agent of this "company," presumably the memo Chambers recalled being shown by Hiss. The memo, written by Pierrepont Moffat, chief of the Division of European Affairs, and marked "Strictly Confidential," goes on to note that the arrested agent also "had dealings with the Charak Furniture Company." In November 1938, seven months after breaking with the CP, Chambers told Herbert Solow: "The man Brandes who was a courier for the outfit arrested in England, traveled as a salesman for the Charak Furniture Co. and the Phantom Red Cosmetic Co." Solow Memo, Herbert Solow Papers, Hoover Institution (Stanford University), p. 14.

†Chambers erred here. The Vienna dispatches typed on the Hiss Woodstock came from an American diplomat in Vienna named Wiley and told at times of his conversations with an Austrian Foreign Ministry official named Schmidt. George S. Messersmith (not Messerschmidt) was an assistant secretary of state at this time.

A. The others I have told you were chiefly accounts of trade agreements, or commercial figures of one kind or another relating to exports and imports, and this and that.

Q. These were of no interest to you?

A. They were of no interest. I simply read most of them out of curiosity, to see what kind of things were written about in such places. . . . I never transmitted a State Department document from Mr. Hiss to the Communist Party.[25]

The primary purpose of Hiss's parallel apparatus, Chambers again stated later that day, was not to acquire such information but to move up rapidly within the government.

Conceding he might have used the alias "George Crosley," Chambers said that he could not recall when, admitting to several other aliases during the thirties. After he described at length his break with the Communist Party, which he placed "sometime in the early spring of 1938," the session ended. Marbury could barely contain his delight. "The result was really amazing," he informed a Boston friend on November 11. "Chambers not only confirmed everything which we had heard which was derogatory to him but testified to other matters of which we had had no previous knowledge. I should add, however, that we have received no confirmation of the fact that Chambers has ever been confined to a mental hospital or treated for a mental disease. . . . That is only one of the surprising aspects of this amazing case."[26]

Greater surprises were in store for Marbury. Shortly before the November 4 deposition Chambers reviewed his testimony with Richard Cleveland. Cleveland paused suddenly, his eyes drifted off, and Chambers asked:

"You feel, don't you, that there is something missing?"

"I was discussing the case with my wife last night," he said, "and we both agreed that there was something missing."

"There *is* something missing," I said. "I am shielding Hiss."

Cleveland glanced at me over his half-glasses as he sometimes did.

"Espionage," I said.[27]

On November 14 Chambers sent a telegram to his nephew Nathan Levine in Brooklyn. Whittaker and Esther Chambers rarely saw their New York relatives in the Shemitz family by that time, and Chambers's wire—sent from Baltimore's railroad station—took Levine by surprise. It read: "ARRIVING AROUND ONE. PLEASE HAVE MY THINGS READY. (signed) WHIT."

The entire procedure smacked of Chambers's love of "mystification." He had phoned Levine on November 12, telling him that he would be coming to Brooklyn in a day or two "to obtain [the] envelope stored with Levine years before." His nephew seemed puzzled. Then, when Chambers wired from the railroad station, he signed his recognizable nickname "Whit" for Levine's identification, but the telegram itself listed the sender as "W. Simpson, 27 Oak St.,

Greenmount, Maryland" (a town near Westminster). Chambers's belief that Hiss's private detectives had been snooping around Pipe Creek Farm, and might even have been following him, probably accounted for this brief reversion to cloak-and-dagger tactics.[28]

When he reached New York, Chambers went directly to Levine's Brooklyn home and from there "accompanied Levine to the home of his mother," also in Brooklyn.

> Levine and I then went to the bathroom in this house where [he] reached into a dumbwaiter shaft and pulled out a large envelope that was covered with dust and dirt. He handed it to me and I took it to the kitchen where I opened the envelope and made a cursory examination of the material contained therein. Levine joined me after a short time and although he saw the miscellaneous assortment of material on the table, he did not examine any of it.
>
> He then drove me . . . to Pennsylvania Station where I took the train and arrived at my farm . . . either late that night or early the next morning. I again examined this material at my farm and found that it contained the following material:
>
> 4 small sheets of paper on which appeared the handwriting of Alger Hiss.
>
> 65 typewritten documents which I had received from Hiss in the early part of 1938.*
>
> 4 sheets of yellow paper bearing the handwriting of Harry Dexter White which was given to me by White in early 1938.
>
> 2 short strips of developed film.
>
> 3 cans containing rolls of undeveloped film.
>
> 1 small piece of paper, approximately 3" × 5".[29]

The material, if genuine, indicated that Hiss had lied in claiming not to have seen Chambers (under whatever name) after mid-1936 and, more important, that Hiss had been engaged in espionage.

Returning to Westminster, Chambers hid the material even from Esther. The following day, November 15, Chambers informed his attorneys about part—but not all—of the material, telling them only about the sixty-five typed documents and Hiss's four handwritten memos. According to Cleveland, Chambers said "that until he opened the envelope on Nov. 14 . . . he did not recall its exact contents or that the documents were so extensive."[30]

The two lawyers accompanied Chambers to Westminster, where he gave them the documents, still saying nothing about the cans and strips of microfilm. "I went to Levine's house to get the small pieces of paper containing Hiss's handwriting," Chambers told the FBI the following month, "and had forgotten about the documents and the film until they were turned over to me." According

---

*The sixty-five typewritten sheets summarized or copied completely seventy State Department cables and one War Department report.

to Chambers's later account, he remained undecided about whether to introduce the new evidence, which transformed a case of perjury into a far more serious matter of espionage. Probably Chambers could not have withheld the material for long, whatever his wishes, if only because Cleveland and Macmillan (and through them, presumably, *Time*'s attorney, Harold Medina, Jr.) were also privy to the information.[31]

But the documents received no mention the following day, November 16, when the pretrial depositions resumed with Esther Chambers's testimony. She told of their contacts with the Hisses, who knew her only as "Liza" and her husband only as "Carl." Esther Chambers, who had risen at 5:30 that morning to handle her farm chores before coming to Baltimore, appeared nervous and tired throughout the day's proceedings as she described an intimate friendship with Priscilla Hiss. At one point Marbury asked for and received a set of notes that Mrs. Chambers had been consulting for her testimony. Esther explained that she and her husband had reviewed their lives together during the 1930s in order to pin down the salient details.[32]

Both Chambers and his wife returned to Baltimore on November 17, and he told Macmillan and Cleveland that he felt "obliged" to hand over the documents. But first Marbury completed his questioning of Esther Chambers. He led the witness through a long and evidently painful recitation of the circumstances surrounding her husband's break with Communism. Esther spoke of the family's poverty after Whittaker's defection: "I remember at one point I did not have— well, we had taken most of everything down to the pawnshop that we had, and there was not gasoline for the car, and my husband was living—"[33]

At this point Esther Chambers broke down and wept for several minutes before recovering her composure. Marbury then renewed his call for "any letters or books or notes and so on, papers of any kind, from Priscilla Hiss," reminding Esther of his earlier request to Chambers for such material. Mrs. Chambers brought out two books on child care that she claimed Mrs. Hiss had given her, but as it turned out that neither book had an identifying inscription, Marbury impatiently brushed them aside.[34]

When the deposition continued after lunch, Marbury proved less brusque than bewildered as Whittaker Chambers resumed his testimony and began by handing over not a pair of baby books but a bundle of transcribed 1937–38 State Department documents.

THE BALTIMORE DOCUMENTS

It was not the best afternoon in William Marbury's life. He hadn't even begun questioning Whittaker Chambers when Macmillan announced that his client wished to make a statement. And for the remainder of the afternoon Chambers dominated the proceeding:

> In response to your request to produce papers from Mr. Hiss, I made a search, and I have certain papers in Mr. Hiss's handwriting and certain other papers. . . .
>
> I was particularly anxious, for reasons of friendship, and because Mr. Hiss is one of the most brilliant young men in the country, not to do injury more than necessary to Mr. Hiss.
>
> Therefore, I have carefully avoided testifying to certain activities of Mr. Hiss at any place or any time heretofore.
>
> I found when I looked at the papers which I had put by, certain documents which I had forgotten I had put by. I thought I had destroyed them. I supposed that the documents I had put away were the handwriting specimens of Mr. Hiss. The documents I refer to reveal a kind of activity, the revelation of which is somewhat different from anything I have testified about before. I first saw those documents last Sunday evening. I first brought them to the attention of my counsel on Monday. I was incapable of deciding at that time whether or not to present them in evidence. My counsel very strongly urged me, in the nature of the case, that I had practically no other choice. . . . The result of my turmoil, which is merely the last act of the turmoil that has been going on for a decade, was the decision to give you the material.[35]

Richard Cleveland indicated the pile of documents on the table: "We don't want the originals to leave our possession [but] we are prepared . . . to leave with you a photostatic set of the various documents."

Although flustered by this unexpected turn of events, Marbury regained his composure and asked to see the materials "before they are put in evidence." Technically, Macmillan pointed out, the materials would not be placed in evidence until Marbury presented them at the slander trial itself. Hiss's attorney finally expressed his irritation at having been trapped in this awkward situation (had he known in advance that such documents existed, Marbury later avowed, neither he nor any other lawyer would have advised Hiss to file a slander suit): "We asked you to produce them. I think we are entitled to examine them, and then if we want to put them in evidence we will, and if not, we will not." Before the day had ended, Marbury advised Hiss that he (Marbury) should contact the Justice Department immediately to inform them about the material.[36]

The documents, sixty-five pages of typed State Department cables and other dispatches, and four handwritten notes, covering a period from January 5 to April 1, 1938, were labeled, and Chambers resumed his statement:

> I have been careful to make a distinction in testifying as to Mr. Hiss's activities with the Communist Party, but in the year 1937, a new development took place in the Washington apparatus. Sometime in 1937, I think [Chambers later changed the date to late 1936], about the middle of the year, J. Peters introduced

me to a Russian [whom] . . . I subsequently learned from Walter Krivitsky . . . was one Colonel Bykov . . . Bykov was extremely interested in the Washington apparatus about which he questioned me endlessly . . . I should think in August or the early fall of 1937 I arranged a meeting between Alger Hiss and Colonel Bykov. For that purpose, Mr. Hiss came to New York, where I met him. . . . Colonel Bykov . . . raised the question of procuring documents from the State Department, and Mr. Hiss agreed . . . Colonel Bykov also raised the question of Donald Hiss's procuring documents. Alger Hiss said that he was not sure that his brother was sufficiently developed yet for that function—and . . . Donald Hiss never at any time procured any documents. Nevertheless, he was a member of the apparatus which I headed. Following that meeting Alger Hiss began a fairly consistent flow of such material as we have before us here. The method was for him to bring home documents in his brief case, which Mrs. Hiss usually typed. I am not sure that she typed all of them. Alger Hiss may have typed some of them himself. But it became a function for her and helped to solve the problem of Mrs. Hiss's longing for . . . Communist activity. Nevertheless, there occasionally came to Mr. Hiss's knowledge, certain things, or he saw certain papers which he was not able to bring out of the Department for one reason or another . . . [and] notations, in his handwriting are notes of such documents, such information, which he made and brought out in that form.[37]

Had he ever previously testified that Hiss had committed espionage? Marbury asked Chambers. The witness said he had never told the FBI or HUAC or anyone about it. Concern for Hiss had kept him silent: "Any informing of such matters was bound to injure them [his former Communist associates], but there are degrees of injury. And I did not think that it was proper to inflict that injury on Alger Hiss. It was given to me to find the strength to break with the Communist Party. And there is always a possibility that others who are still Communists will also find that strength. . . ."[38]

In the weeks ahead, Chambers offered several versions of his motives for having suddenly turned over what soon came to be known as "the Baltimore documents." Although he told Marbury that a feeling of compassion for the Hisses, supposedly his closest friends within the Communist Party, had kept him silent about Hiss's spying until then, he told Nixon and HUAC staff members another story early in December. To the House probers Chambers asserted that the Hiss defense's investigation into his alleged mental instability and deviance had changed his course of action. Convinced that "Hiss was determined to destroy me—and my wife, if possible," Chambers retaliated by producing the documents. He stressed Marbury's aggressive questioning of Esther Chambers on November 16 and 17 as the decisive factor, according to both Nixon and Robert Stripling, the "incident [that] made his decision for him."* But Esther testified

---

*Chambers asserted in his memoir that while his wife testified in Baltimore on November 16 he remained on his Westminster farm contemplating suicide, the first of several sets of similar

for the first time in Baltimore two days after Chambers recovered the packet of documents in New York, so that anger at his wife's treatment certainly did not provoke him into searching for the material.

Although compassion for the Hisses and protectiveness toward his wife may have influenced Chambers's behavior, the most likely factor goading him into turning over documentary evidence was Chambers's well-grounded fear that, lacking such evidence, a Baltimore jury would accept Hiss's testimony over his own. And if he lost the suit, Chambers would be hard-pressed to defend himself against something he had feared for an entire decade: indictment by the Justice Department.

Soon after Hiss filed suit, the federal grand jury in New York then investigating allegations of Communist espionage in government had subpoenaed Chambers. His appearance before that grand jury on October 14 proved to be a milestone for Chambers. One juror asked if he could "give one name of anybody who, in [his] opinion, was positively guilty, of espionage against the United States? Yes or no." Chambers equivocated: "Let me think a moment and I will try to answer that. I don't think so but I would like to have the opportunity to answer you tomorrow more definitely. Let me think it over overnight." The next day Chambers asked that same juror:

A. . . . I assume that espionage means in this case the turning over of secret or confidential documents.
Q. Or information—oral information.
A. Or oral information. I do not believe I do know such a name.[39]

His answer left Chambers liable to a perjury indictment if he later changed his story and charged espionage, even against Alger Hiss. Yet the question of espionage hovered in the air that day, and Chambers circled cautiously around it as he testified to the grand jury. On October 15, when he returned, Chambers first mentioned meeting a Russian later identified as Boris Bykov, but he skirted the question of whether he had information that Bykov had engaged in espionage.

The fact that he had committed perjury before the grand jury in October preyed on Chambers, and he registered his fear of indictment the following month when Richard Nixon visited Westminster. Nixon had not seen Chambers since early September, and he found the *Time* editor "in a mood of deep depression." Truman's belief that the Hiss-Chambers case was a "red herring"—and his upset victory in November—could mean the curtailing of future congressional probes into Communist activities. J. Parnell Thomas's indictment by a federal grand jury on November 8 certainly added to Chambers's uncertainties concerning the

---

reflections at critical moments during the month ahead. So intense was his agony over trying to decide whether or not to reveal the documents, he remembered, that for a time that day suicide seemed a reasonable option. *Witness,* pp. 737–38, 744–47.

future of HUAC at the time he spoke to Nixon. Pointing out that his depositions in the Hiss suit would resume in mid-November, Chambers expressed concern that the Democratic election triumph would inevitably strengthen both public and governmental support for Hiss. But he failed to rekindle Nixon's interest in the case, and the California congressman returned to Washington to work on other matters in the following weeks.[40]

Unless Chambers could prove his charges against Hiss to the satisfaction of the Baltimore slander-suit jury—and only additional evidence would enable him to do so—then he, and not Hiss, might face indictment by the grand jury acting at the Justice Department's request. Chambers's decision to retrieve the material he had entrusted to Levine in 1938 resulted directly from this desire to save himself from legal action, and the typed documents matched Chambers's description at the earlier deposition of State Department materials he had read in Hiss's home.

Once past his initial surprise Marbury recognized what appeared to be Hiss's handwriting on the four notes—the lawyer asked for time to examine the documents. Marbury questioned Chambers concerning the nature of his alleged work in the Communist espionage network.

Soon after the others had left his office, where the deposition had been held, Marbury phoned Hiss, telling him about the documents turned over by Chambers. The lawyer recommended—and Hiss agreed—that the material should be given immediately to the Department of Justice. The following day Marbury showed the photostatic copies to Hiss in New York and, as Marbury told FBI agents several days later, "Hiss admitted that the sixty-five letter-sized typewritten documents appear to be authentic copies of State Department documents and that four of the five smaller sheets [actually, three of the four] appear to be in his handwriting. Hiss denied having given any of this material to Chambers and wondered who stole same from the State Department and from his desk in the State Department and gave it to Chambers."[41]

After first telling Chambers's lawyers his plans and obtaining their consent, Marbury notified Judge W. Calvin Chesnut, who would preside at the slander suit, about the documents. Chesnut did not object to the material being turned over to Justice, and on November 19 Marbury phoned Solicitor General Philip Perlman, who referred the call to Alexander M. Campbell, head of the Justice Department's Criminal Division. Marbury asked for an immediate meeting, and that afternoon Campbell arrived at Baltimore with two aides. Also present at the meeting were Cleveland, Macmillan, and Harold Medina, Jr. Marbury told Campbell about the documents and Chambers's new testimony at the November 17 deposition. Cleveland informed Campbell that the photostatic copies which he possessed would be made available to the FBI (the originals had been sent to New York for inspection by a documents examiner), and all the attorneys present agreed, Campbell wrote several days later, "with the approval of the court to delay any further proceedings in this civil action for a period of two weeks in order that the Department of Justice might take whatever action it deems appropriate." All the lawyers recognized that Alger Hiss's civil suit for slander had now been overshadowed by the inevitable criminal investigation of possible perjury and espionage that lay ahead.[42]

Four days passed before Campbell told the FBI about these developments. A memo titled "Testimony of Whittaker Chambers Before Grand Jury" makes it evident that during these four days Campbell discussed the new evidence with his superiors at Justice, presumably including Attorney General Clark, who decided to direct the FBI's investigation toward a particular outcome. Democrats had been skeptical of Chambers from the moment he became HUAC's star witness in August. Coincidentally, on November 18 Democratic National Chairman J. Howard McGrath, who would shortly replace Clark as attorney general, announced after meeting with President Truman that HUAC faced "a dismal future" or "no future at all if it continues to act as it has in the past." Clark had asked the FBI that month whether Chambers had ever been in a mental institution. He "was advised that there is nothing indicated in the Bureau files . . . which would indicate that Chambers had been hospitalized." Campbell wrote Hoover on November 23 pointing out the discrepancies between Chambers's testimony to the grand jury in October—when he denied having knowledge of espionage by Hiss or receiving any government documents—and his November 17 deposition.

Campbell issued precise orders: "It is desired that an immediate investigation be conducted so that it can be determined whether Chambers has committed perjury. In this connection the photostatic copies of these documents should be obtained together with a copy of the deposition given by Chambers." Campbell also directed the FBI to interrogate Hiss—but not to initiate a perjury investigation against him—and perhaps arrange to have Hiss questioned before the grand jury as well. Since the jury's term would expire on December 15, Campbell ordered that the FBI probe "be given expeditious attention."[43]

Not every official at Justice agreed with the departmental decision to seek an indictment of Chambers alone. Thomas Donegan, the department's representative at the grand jury, met with Assistant FBI Director D. M. Ladd on the morning of November 23 (Donegan had worked as an FBI agent earlier in his career). Later that afternoon he phoned Ladd with new information that Ladd immediately passed on to Hoover. Donegan described Campbell's meeting with Marbury and the other lawyers in Baltimore, noted Chambers's documentary evidence, and reported that Campbell's aides were then drafting the November 23 letter that Hoover received later that day. "The purpose of Mr. Donegan's being in Washington today," Ladd noted, "was at the specific request of Mr. Campbell who now wants to institute perjury charges against Chambers. . . ." Hoover scrawled at the bottom of this memo: "Interesting but I wonder why they don't move against Hiss also."[44]

THE INVESTIGATORS

During the ten days that followed Campbell's memo to Hoover, the FBI spent much time gathering evidence for a grand jury indictment of Chambers. Hoover and other bureau officials felt no particular sympathy for the man, whose testimony had seriously embarrassed the FBI. Ladd prepared a special six-page memorandum for Hoover outlining the bureau's handling—mishandling, rather—of both Chambers's information and Berle's 1939 notes. Ladd seemed particularly disturbed that prior to 1945 no one had bothered to check on Chambers's 1942 statements and those in Berle's notes about Alger Hiss. The HUAC investigation had vexed Hoover since August, especially when FBI agents brought to the director's attention stories such as the August 19 account of a Nixon press conference: "FBI ACCUSED OF FAILURE IN HISS PROBE/HOUSE INVESTIGATOR [NIXON] CITES G-MEN'S FRUITLESS 4-YEAR HUNT."[45]

His decision to submit the documents to his lawyers and, through them, to Hoover's Justice Department superiors, rather than directly to the FBI, was merely Chambers's latest affront. But even after Hoover received Campbell's orders to prepare a perjury case against Chambers, his agents were stymied for a few days. Chambers's deposition had not yet been transcribed, and, lacking this crucial testimony, the FBI delayed scheduled interviews with both Hiss and his accuser. Hoover vented his irritation over the muddle in comments meant only for his assistant directors and scrawled on the sides of memos. "Such matters as the new developments in the Hiss-Chambers matter" were critical, he pointed out on December 1; "I should be advised *at once*. I was embarrassed by not being [illegible] informed. H." Hoover instructed Baltimore FBI agents on the 24th to collect the copies of documents and the deposition, and to investigate both at once, in order to interview Hiss and Chambers before expiration of the two-week moratorium (beginning November 19) agreed on by attorneys in the slander suit.[46]

Finally, the Baltimore FBI office received copies of Chambers's documents from Richard Cleveland, who told them the originals had been sent to New York to be examined by Ordway Hilton, a leading documents examiner hired by *Time*. Hilton determined that all but one of the pages had been typed on a Woodstock typewriter. Only on the 26th did Campbell's office—at the FBI's request—order the court reporter to transcribe Chambers's November 17 deposition, and the testimony reached the FBI three days later. By then the FBI had opened a case file on Chambers (but not Hiss) under the subject listings: "PERJURY; ESPIONAGE; INTERNAL SECURITY."[47]

While the FBI prepared perjury-indictment data on Chambers, Hiss's law-yers continued their own vigorous investigation. McLean, who had discharged one set of private detectives in mid-October, hired the New York firm of John G. Broady, which had assigned one of its leading operatives, Horace W. Schmahl, to the case. Broady's time and Schmahl's did not come cheaply, and Marbury sent McLean an out-of-pocket check for $750 "as a refresher" on November 22 (Broady had submitted an interim bill of almost $1,300 to McLean three days ear-lier for the previous month's investigation). Marbury would receive a check for that entire amount on December 2 from Hugh Cox, Donald Hiss's lawyer. Cox did not indicate who had picked up the tab.[48]

During most of November Schmahl collected information about Chambers's past. He was not assigned until early December to look into the November 17 "Baltimore documents." This evident complacency on the part of Hiss and his lawyers toward Chambers's new evidence—they did not even have their own documents examiner study the material for almost three weeks after receiving it—suggests strongly that at least some of those involved in Hiss's legal efforts had been told informally by Justice Department friends that Justice intended to seek an indictment of Chambers alone. Cox had particularly close links within the department, as several memos to Marbury during this period reveal; so did Donald Hiss's partners, including Dean Acheson.[49]

Hiss's attorneys proceeded meanwhile with their psychiatric explanation of Chambers's alleged perjury. Several psychiatrist friends of Hiss, notably Dr. Carl Binger and Dr. Viola Bernard, volunteered their services late in 1948. Dr. Binger's wife, Clarinda Garrison, daughter of New York civil-liberties lawyer Lloyd Garrison, also worked at the Dalton School, where Priscilla Hiss then taught. The Hisses and the Bingers had been friendly before the case. Dr. Bernard would later become close to the Hisses, but was brought into the case originally by a New York attorney named Louis Weiss, a partner of Lloyd Garrison in the firm of Paul, Weiss, Rifkind and Garrison, and a brother of Carol Weiss King, J. Peters's attorney and an old friend of the Hisses.[50]

But the strongest advocate of a psychiatric defense against Chambers's accu-sations at the slander suit was Harold Rosenwald, who had been Hiss's class-mate at Harvard Law School. On October 25, even before taking Chambers's first deposition, Rosenwald submitted to the other attorneys a memorandum on evidentiary problems that began:

> We would like to prove that Chambers has had neuroses which cause him to make false accusations that persons are Communists. Our theory would be that, as an abnormal reaction from his own experiences as a Communist, he has become imbued with a passion for denouncing and persecuting indiscrimi-nately persons who may be Communists and others who are not and never have been Communists.

Rosenwald's memo became a veritable casebook for the psychiatric arguments made on behalf of Hiss and against Chambers from that point to the present.[51]

"In support of this theory," Rosenwald noted, "we would want to introduce the following evidence." There followed allegations by the defense investigator (later proved incorrect) that insurance-company doctors had examined Chambers's application for life insurance and found that "he has had a 'series of neuroses' complicated by abnormal sexual appetites" (Chambers's insurance agents knew nothing about his earlier homosexuality); that Chambers told persons he would lie on behalf of his anti-Communist beliefs; and, most important: "On the issue of Chambers' veracity, we would like to show specific instances of lies told, or misstatements made, by Chambers both in relation to the subject matter of this case and in other matters." As for Hiss, Rosenwald reiterated his client's earlier HUAC defense by reputation: "We would like to show [his innocence] by the testimony of his superiors and associates in government service, his actions and statements, official and otherwise, and his views and attitudes on diplomatic and political issues affecting Russia."

In late November, at the suggestion (according to Hiss) of newspaperman Joseph Alsop and in an effort to understand what they believed to be Chambers's efforts to destroy Hiss, Rosenwald added to the defense's psychiatric dossier an analysis of Franz Werfel's *Class Reunion,* a novel that Chambers had translated in 1929. Bolstered by the information Chambers had divulged about himself earlier that month, Rosenwald developed the argument in a November 23 memo, which described in detail Werfel's melancholic story of two former Gymnasium classmates, Dr. Ernst Sebastian and Franz Adler, who confront one another in a courtroom after twenty-five years. By then Sebastian has become an examining magistrate and Adler, brought before him, has been arrested and accused of murdering a prostitute. Sebastian recognizes Adler and adjourns the proceedings for the moment. That evening Sebastian attends the twenty-fifth reunion of his Gymnasium class and his mind drifts into tortured reminiscences of his boyhood relationship with Adler. Sebastian returns home and writes out the story of that relationship, in which obsessive jealousy of Adler's brilliance and talents as a student led Sebastian to plagiarize poems in order to demonstrate his superiority over Adler.*[52]

Sebastian had plotted to humiliate his fellow student and managed to turn Adler into a figure of ridicule among their classmates. Then, after he persuaded Adler to change the grades on his (Adler's) poor grade sheet, the two boys had been caught in the act by a teacher. They decided to commit suicide by the use of "illuminating gas"—in short, in a manner similar to Chambers's brother, Richard.

---

*Rosenwald acknowledged, however, that the novel did not strongly suggest homosexuality as a factor in Sebastian's behavior, and that—as drawn by Werfel—the victim, Adler, closely resembled Chambers physically, not Hiss.

But Sebastian changed his mind at the last minute and rescued them. Sebastian then stole money to purchase Adler's fare to America and talked Adler into fleeing, an event that persuaded people Adler alone had been guilty of falsifying the grade report.

His deception and abuse of Adler prey on Sebastian that evening as he writes the account twenty-five years later. Guilt-stricken, he returns to court the next day to resume examining Adler. But, unable to contain himself any longer, Sebastian walks down from the judge's platform and begins confessing to his former classmate the wrong he had committed toward him a quarter-century earlier.

Harold Rosenwald concluded his summary of the book for the other Hiss lawyers with a quote from *Class Reunion:* "'It looked as if a life and death struggle were about to begin but Sebastian's arms slid down from Adler's body. Adler caught him as he was falling and supported him by the shoulders like a wounded man.' The story ends at this point," Rosenwald noted, "and we can only guess whether or not Adler murdered the prostitute."

But the story does *not* end at that point. It continues for another six pages. The novel's surprise ending goes unmentioned in Rosenwald's version of *Class Reunion:* The man in the dock is the *wrong* "Franz Adler." Confused and embarrassed by Sebastian's confession, Adler shrinks back until the examining magistrate recognizes the error. Sebastian apologizes to the court clerk for having made this scene—"I mistook this Franz Adler for a former schoolmate of mine"—and tells the clerk in a burst of magnanimity to try and set Adler free "just as soon as anything new turns up."[53]

The novel's closing pages should "confirm," if anything, Chambers's ("Sebastian's") account of having withheld the stolen documents out of compassion for Hiss (i.e., "Adler"), not Rosenwald's notion of a vengeful "Sebastian." But, of course, *Class Reunion* confirms nothing, any more than comparison of scenes from *Bambi,* which Chambers translated the year before *Class Reunion,* would demonstrate that the translator was a gun-shy deer. Missing from Rosenwald's memo, and from all subsequent references to *Class Reunion* by psychiatrists and lawyers attempting to use the novel as a model for Chambers's allegedly scheming revenge against Hiss, is the recognition that Chambers did not personally choose any of the dozen or so books he translated during the 1920s and 1930s. He received them on commission from publishers, and none of them necessarily provides a key to the "psychopathology" of its translator.

Undaunted, Rosenwald resumed his promotion of a psychiatric defense in a December memo:

> There is attached hereto a memorandum concerning a book translated by Whittaker Chambers in 1929.
> The general theory set forth in this memorandum has been fully confirmed by a prominent psychiatrist in New York City. The psychiatrist explains the motivation of Chambers in making his accusations against Hiss on the ground

that Chambers had a close and probably homosexual relationship with his younger brother who committed suicide in September 1926 and that Chambers had a subconscious impulse to be reunited with his brother in death.

Chambers had a homosexual attraction toward Alger Hiss which caused him to identify himself with Hiss to desire to possess him and to destroy him. The psychiatrist is convinced that Chambers is acting out the part of Sebastian in "Class Reunion."

Other writings of Chambers support this theory. He has written one blatantly homosexual poem, another poem concerning his desire to be reunited with his brother in death and his preparation for death by perfecting himself, and an article for Life Magazine called "The Devil" which is apparently autobiographical [!], in which he plainly shows his own frustration and envy of other persons.[54]

A psychiatric defense fascinated some but not all of Hiss's lawyers, and when McLean wrote Marbury on November 29 urging that the FBI be told about *Class Reunion* when Hiss went for his interview, Marbury agreed reluctantly. He had consulted a Baltimore expert on psychiatric evidence, Dr. Esther Richards, who shared his doubts: "While she thought that Chambers's history was that of a psychopathic personality, she recognized the difficulty of breaking his story down in such a way as to carry conviction to a court and jury. Frankly, she gave me little reason to hope that our problem could be solved with the aid of psychiatric advice."[55]

More than any other of Hiss's attorneys, Marbury sensed the gravity of the situation created by Chambers's documents. When he met with Alger and Priscilla Hiss in Baltimore on November 28, Marbury warned them that Hiss faced possible, even probable, indictment. He seemed especially struck by Hiss's failure to turn up either his old typewriter—whose make Hiss said he could not remember—or papers typed on it for comparison with the stolen documents. "I am troubled by the fact that your inability to explain what became of the typewriter which Prossie had in 1938 might be construed as an attempt to cover up something," Marbury wrote Hiss on December 3, having asked Hiss to look for the machine almost two weeks earlier. "This inference could be rebutted by a voluntary production on your part of papers which were typed by her on that particular machine. I think that she should make every effort to locate some such papers." Marbury enclosed a copy of a letter written by the American diplomat Fletcher Warren denying Hiss's claim that Warren and Berle had wanted him to join their wartime work within the State Department on security matters.[56]

When he wrote this letter, Marbury could not know that the chances of Hiss's indictment had increased dramatically that same day. On the evening of December 2 Chambers drove from Washington to his Westminster farm accompanied by two HUAC investigators, Donald Appell and William Wheeler. Chambers walked into a garden patch on the farm and removed the top from a hollowed-out pumpkin. He reached inside and pulled out two strips of developed film and canisters containing three rolls of undeveloped film, one of which later proved to be light-struck and blank. The developed film contained State Department documents from the same period as the typed and handwritten material Chambers had turned over on November 17. The two rolls of undeveloped film held Navy Department documents from early 1938.[57]

Chambers also handed over to the HUAC investigators a March 1938 personal note—unmentioned on November 17—that Cleveland had tossed back at him. The committee kept the item confidential for several months, since it apparently dealt with an extramarital, heterosexual love affair in which Chambers had then been involved.[58]

No similar restraint governed their treatment of the remaining material. Newspapers throughout the country published front-page stories about HUAC, Chambers, and what headline writers erroneously but alliteratively termed "pumpkin papers."

Again the committee had made the FBI investigation seem bumbling and inept. Despite a clear telephone warning from Nixon on December 1 that Chambers probably possessed additional documents that HUAC was about to subpoena, a warning that reached Hoover's desk, the FBI took no action to obtain whatever material Chambers might still have. Hoover informed no one at Justice about Nixon's warning. Departmental officials concerned with the case—Donegan, Campbell, Peyton Ford, and others—held a morning conference that day during which they phoned the Bureau and ordered that Chambers be interrogated immediately. Campbell pointedly reminded the agent to whom he spoke "that there is an indication in the [November 17] statement of Chambers that he has other documents," and that he "should be questioned with respect to such a possibility and an effort should be made to obtain from him any other documents that he might have which are governmental in character."[59]

By the time FBI agents questioned Chambers on the evening of December 3 in Baltimore, HUAC already had the "pumpkin papers" and other material from his cache. The fact that Justice Department officials had received Chambers's typed and handwritten documents two weeks earlier, kept secret until then, was also widely publicized on December 3, and all parties to the arrangement rushed to draft self-serving statements about the evidence. Late that afternoon Richard Cleveland phoned Campbell, and the harassed Justice Department official, "apparently trying to find out the significance of the developments," agreed that Chambers was no longer the sole person under investigation: "Mr. Campbell . . . said that at present no holds were barred and 'let the chips fall where they may.'"[60]

As usual, Hoover complained that he was the last person to learn things in the case. Another of his haiku-like remonstrances covered a bureau memo, this one on December 4 announcing Campbell's change of heart and other "new developments":[61]

> What are the facts?
> Was there any pumpkin involved at all?
>   H
> Here again I heard nothing
> of this for several days. I should
> have been advised *at once.*
>   H

"Make certain such angles as can be developed in [Chambers's December 3] statement are given prompt and vigorous attention," Hoover wrote on another December 4 memo. "Also in future I want to be kept more promptly advised. H."

But Assistant Director Louis B. Nichols had reported Congressman Nixon's December 1 phone call to Hoover's aide Clyde Tolson, pointing out that Nixon "specifically urged that we not tell the Attorney General that we were told of this information [about additional documents] as the Attorney General undoubtedly would try to make it impossible for the Committee to get at the documents. He also asked that the Bureau not look for the documents themselves." Nichols concluded: "It looks like the only thing we could do would possibly be to inquire of Alexander Campbell if he has any documentary evidence without revealing the reason for our inquiry or our source." Hoover's scribbled response: "Do so & let me know result. H." Tolson's scrawled comment on December 2: "This is being done by Dept. order."[62]

Hoover, in short, had no one to blame but himself. He withheld this vital information from his superiors at Justice and thereby lost one crucial day, which was all that HUAC needed in order to obtain Chambers's microfilm for its own purposes. Nixon and, more particularly, the committee's chief of staff, Robert Stripling, acted with remarkable speed.

THE "PUMPKIN PAPERS"

The web of secrecy surrounding the Baltimore documents turned over by Chambers on November 17 began to unravel on December 1. That morning two Washington newspapers published stories referring to the case, both apparently using information provided by Justice Department officials. The first item, a *Washington Post* column by Jerry Kluttz, announced that "some very startling information on who's a liar is reported to have been uncovered" in the Hiss-Chambers slander action. The second, a United Press story in the Washington *Daily News,* was headlined: "HISS AND CHAMBERS PERJURY PROBE HITS DEAD END." The writer quoted unnamed Justice Department senior officials as stating that the department was "about ready to drop its investigation" of possible perjury prosecution in the case "unless additional evidence is forthcoming." Both Stripling and Nixon read the stories that morning, and they exchanged ideas on the telephone about the obvious conflict between the two items and their possible meanings.[63]

Sometime that morning Nicholas Vazzana, a lawyer employed by Harold Medina, Jr., to investigate leads connected with Hiss's lawsuit, walked into the committee's offices and asked to see Stripling. Committee staffers knew Vazzana because of previous visits to obtain information from their Hiss-Chambers file. Vazzana had been summoned to Richard Cleveland's office on November 17, the day Chambers turned over the documents, and found a scene "of almost total confusion." The lawyers filled him in on the contents of the documents, and later Vazzana learned that Justice Department officials had warned everyone to avoid public mention of the new evidence. Vazzana decided, after reading the Washington newspapers on December 1, to inform Stripling that the *Post* was right and United Press wrong; that "new evidence" in the case did exist. "I just didn't want the case to die," Vazzana later said, and he determined to revive HUAC's interest as a means of pressuring the Justice Department.[64]

Since Vazzana seemed pleased, Stripling asked why, to which the investigator replied: "Can't talk or I might be held in contempt of court." Stripling then suggested that the attorney see Nixon with him, and in the congressman's office Stripling again broached the question. "I can't discuss it with either of you," Vazzana replied. "But I suppose I can tell you it has something to do with the Hiss-Chambers libel suit, and it concerns documents." After parrying questions from both men about these hints of new evidence, Vazzana finally told Nixon and Stripling everything about the November 17 scene in Baltimore. He mentioned specifically Chambers's delivery to Hiss's attorneys of the sixty-five pages of typed documents and the four memos in Hiss's handwriting, but he told the pair: "I am under an admonition from the Justice Department not to reveal their actual contents."

The decision to inform the committee about the Baltimore documents, Vazzana insists, was his alone. He had consulted neither Chambers nor Medina before visiting Stripling. Both he and Stripling remember spending over two hours in Nixon's office while Vazzana answered questions about Chambers's Baltimore depositions and the documents. Before Vazzana left, Nixon and Stripling had far more than the morning's newspaper rumors to consider: they had the entire story. Nixon and his wife were scheduled to leave on a ten-day Caribbean cruise on December 3, and Vazzana remembered Nixon asking him: "Do you think I should still go on vacation?" "That's your decision, Mr. Nixon," Vazzana replied, "not mine."

Nixon and Stripling lunched together shortly after Vazzana left and, according to Stripling, the congressman appeared nervous and highly irritable. Stripling was surprised, since he felt that Vazzana's visit—which he believed had been contrived either by Chambers or his lawyers as a means of alerting HUAC to the documents—offered them a chance to "break" the Hiss case and break it quickly. The new evidence, if confirmed, also changed the nature of the case from HUAC's perjury concern to the more serious charge of espionage. Still, Nixon seemed shaken, according to Stripling, for reasons that were not readily apparent.

Undoubtedly Nixon felt angry at Chambers. The man whom he considered a friend had not confided in him about the documents, either before or after submitting them on November 17. Nixon repeatedly turned down Stripling's proposal that they drive to Westminster that afternoon and confront Chambers about the new evidence. "I'm so god-damned sick and tired of this case," Stripling quotes Nixon responding. "I don't want to hear any more about it and I'm going to Panama. And the hell with it, and you, and the whole damned business!" Stripling recalls sitting silently after this outburst, while Nixon "cussed me out real good."

But Nixon was the logical committee member to deal with Chambers, and not simply because of their personal rapport. HUAC remained under Republican control until the new Congress met, and none of the other Republicans on the committee—Mundt, McDowell, and Chairman Thomas—was in Washington at the time. If Stripling could not persuade Nixon to take action, the matter would probably be held over until the next Congress, by which time Stripling would have left government employ. He insisted that the case could be broken once the committee revealed the existence of the Baltimore documents and possibly turned up additional papers at Chambers's home, but Nixon remained adamant: "Hell, I'm not going to Westminster. I'm going to Panama, and you can do what you damn want to, but I'm through with it."

In silence, the two men walked back to their offices. Stripling ordered a car to take him to Westminster and, one final time, phoned Nixon's office urging him to come. "Goddamn it," he remembers Nixon exploding, "if it'll shut your mouth, I'll go."

The drive was expectably tense, and the two men hardly looked at each other. Arriving at Westminster late that afternoon, they showed Chambers copies of the two news stories. Chambers turned away momentarily, stood silently for a minute, and then, according to Nixon's memoir (Chambers's and Stripling's later accounts of the incident basically agree), quietly remarked:

> In a deposition hearing two weeks ago, I produced some new evidence in the case—documentary evidence. It was so important that Hiss's attorneys and mine called the Justice Department. Alex Campbell, Chief of the Criminal Division, came to Baltimore and took the documents back to Washington. Before he left he warned everybody present to say nothing whatever about these documents and that if we did divulge any information, we would be guilty of

contempt of court. So, I can't tell you what was in the documents. I will only say that they were a real bombshell.

Chambers, when pressed by his two visitors for further details,* revealed that he had kept photostatic copies of the documents and, more important, that he possessed "another bombshell in case they try to suppress this one."† Nixon told Chambers not to surrender this second "bombshell" to "anybody except the Committee."

While driving back to Washington with Stripling, Nixon considered postponing his vacation: "I explained my predicament to Stripling and told him that . . . if necessary, [I] could fly back to Washington if he felt I had to. Taking no chances, however, I stopped off at the committee office and signed a *subpoena duces tecum* on Chambers for any and all documents in his possession relating to . . . the charges he had made against Hiss. Stripling said he would have the subpoena served on Chambers the next day."[65]

FBI files and subsequent accounts by both Stripling and Bert Andrews suggest that Nixon confused the sequence of events, beginning with the drive back to Washington. "As Mr. Nixon and I got into the car," Stripling recalled, "Mr. Nixon said, 'Well, what do you think he's got?' I said, 'I don't know what he has, but whatever he has, it'll blow the dome off the Capitol. Certainly you're not going to Panama now?' And he said, 'I don't think he's got a damned thing. I'm going right ahead with my plans.'" Nixon gave Stripling no order that evening to serve a subpoena on Chambers, nor, as Stripling remembers it, did the two men return to HUAC headquarters. Stripling urged him at least to give the FBI Chambers's information, but the investigator assumed that any future action by HUAC would have to await Nixon's return to Washington or the arrival of a more interested committee member.[66]

When he left Stripling at his own House office, Nixon phoned Bert Andrews, the New York *Herald Tribune* reporter. Andrews rushed over to Nixon's office, where he was told about the visit to Chambers, the documents Chambers had already handed over, and those he presumably still held in Westminster. "You were too nice to Chambers," Andrews remembered telling Nixon. "'Did you just

---

*Chambers's memoir described this incident in almost identical terms but omitted Nixon's presence completely. *Witness*, pp. 751–52.

†Chambers told the FBI two days later that he had withheld the microfilm only until he had developed the three remaining rolls and had a chance to examine their contents. Considering the two weeks that had passed since he turned over the typed and handwritten materials, however, this explanation seems highly suspect. More likely, his comments to Nixon and Stripling more accurately reflected his feelings. Given Chambers's distrust of the Justice Department and of Hiss's top-level connections, he had apparently withheld the microfilm for future release as a protective measure, still another form of "life preserver" should the typed documents be suppressed or should Justice decide to indict him.

ask for anything he had? Or did you slap a subpoena on him?' Nixon said he hadn't really thought of a subpoena. I told him: 'Look, before you leave town get hold of Bob Stripling. Tell him to serve a blanket subpoena on Chambers to produce *anything* and *everything* he still has in his possession.' . . . 'I'll think it over,' Nixon said. We parted about 12:30 AM, December 2."[67]

If Andrews reported this conversation correctly, Nixon did not think the matter over for very long. He phoned Louis B. Nichols of the FBI that same evening to tell him, "on a strictly personal and highly confidential basis," about the visit to Chambers and the documents in Chambers's possession. According to Nichols's memo of the call the following morning, December 2, Nixon said

> That he was going to Panama where he would be at the Tivoli Hotel and that he would return to Washington on December 15, that on December 18 he plans to reopen the Alger Hiss-Whittaker Chambers matter. Nixon stated that he understood that the Department of Justice told the FBI that there was no violation involved and that consequently no further action was to be undertaken by the FBI. . . . Nixon stated it was his intention to subpoena these documents [the ones still in Chambers's possession] at the hearings on December 18 and the purpose of his call, which he reiterated was strictly personal and highly confidential, was merely to apprise the Bureau so that the FBI would not be caught off base. He stated they [HUAC] were handling the matter so that there will be no criticism of the FBI and he particularly urged that we do nothing about the information which he has just furnished as he feels the statute of limitations has run.[68]

It is difficult, as usual, to pin down Nixon's actions or thoughts. Whether he spoke to Nichols before Andrews's visit and then decided to serve the subpoena immediately, or whether he changed his mind after speaking to Nichols, remains uncertain. But by morning Nixon had decided to take Andrews's advice about the subpoena but not Stripling's about canceling his trip.* He phoned Stripling at home and asked him to be at the committee office by eight in the morning. Stripling got caught in traffic, and by the time he arrived Nixon had left to catch a train to New York.[69]

At nine AM Nixon phoned again, this time using the train's radio-telephone. He ordered Stripling to serve the subpoena on Chambers that day, which Stripling had planned to do even before receiving the call. At almost that exact moment Bert Andrews filed a cablegram to John Foster Dulles in Paris, obviously based upon the previous evening's conversation with Nixon, cautioning Dulles: "NEW INFORMATION MAKES ME STRONGLY BELIEVE YOU SHOULD PERSONALLY GET OFF HOOK ON OUR ENDOWMENT FRIEND."[70]

---

*According to William "Fishbait" Miller, doorkeeper of the House, Nixon confided shortly before leaving on the boat trip that he expected to be summoned back because of dramatic developments in the Hiss-Chambers probe.

Nixon—always the calculator, seldom the zealot—would not be stampeded. He hoped to follow up Chambers's statement about having documents while minimizing political risks and without taking personal responsibility for the consequences. If Chambers's second bombshell fizzled, or if it exploded in Stripling's face, Nixon would be in Panama, far from the scene of carnage. He might be embarrassed but not discredited. If, on the other hand, Stripling obtained important new evidence from Chambers, the congressman could arrange to return. Also, Nixon may still have been furious at Chambers for keeping mum about the documents. What political advantage, Nixon might well have asked himself, could be gained by abruptly intruding into the Justice Department's probe without first obtaining more information, especially when it now involved espionage, not perjury alone? Given these unsettled circumstances, the cautious Nixon removed himself from the fast-breaking train of events by boarding a slow boat to Panama.*

After receiving Nixon's call that morning, Stripling telephoned Chambers at Westminster to ask when next he planned to be in Washington. As it happened, Chambers was about to leave for a Loyalty Hearing Board appearance concerning another State Department employee whom he had accused of Communist ties. Stripling requested that he stop in at the HUAC offices, which Chambers did before going to the hearing. Stripling served him with a blanket subpoena at that time and Chambers acknowledged that he had documentary material at his farm. Late that afternoon Chambers returned to the HUAC office to learn that Stripling could not accompany him to the farm, but that Appell and Wheeler, HUAC staffers, would make the trip.[71]

According to Donald Appell, Chambers told the two investigators about the microfilms as they drove to Westminster, so that his march into the pumpkin patch was a piece of prepared melodrama. Appell kept the microfilms in his home that night and turned them over to Stripling the following morning. The entire episode was staged, since Chambers later admitted to FBI agents that he had kept the film hidden in his farmhouse after getting it back from Levine and not till the morning of December 2 did he wrap the bundle carefully and place it in the hollowed-out pumpkin.[72]

When later tested, the microfilm, the typed documents, and the handwritten notes all fitted snugly into the brown manila envelope that Chambers turned over on November 17, but there is at least fragmentary evidence suggesting Chambers may have found the microfilm on a second visit to Nathan Levine later in November.[73]

---

*When writing his memoir, *Six Crises,* Nixon omitted, distorted, or papered over many of the details of his behavior during this two-day period in December. He emerges from that book as a decisive and forthright investigator rather than the cautious, irascible, indecisive, and fearful sleuth described by Stripling, Vazzana, and Appell.

Chambers obviously feared indictment after Campbell had ordered that news of the Baltimore documents be kept secret while Justice and FBI went on investigating. Moreover, Nixon's polite but unproductive visit to Westminster in mid-November probably persuaded Chambers that he could expect little help from HUAC.* Chambers's initial visit to Levine, therefore, was an act of desperation.

He apparently did not expect to find more than a few scraps containing Alger Hiss's handwriting, memos he vaguely recalled having ferreted away a decade earlier. When, unexpectedly, he found so much typed and handwritten material in the package Levine had placed in his mother's dumbwaiter, Levine recalled his uncle shouting "either 'holy cow' or some exclamation, 'I didn't think that this still existed,' or 'was still in existence.'"[74]

His search for material at the Levine home on November 14 was perfunctory. After retrieving the package, according to both men, Chambers left almost immediately for Baltimore. Did Chambers return to Brooklyn at some later date to rummage more systematically among his belongings?

In testimony to the FBI, Levine suggested that a second encounter with Chambers may have occurred after the November 14 visit. Thus Levine told the FBI that he turned the package over to Chambers "on November 21, 1948, when he and Chambers were at the Barnet Levine residence [Levine's mother's home]." This statement puzzled the bureau: "Levine is undoubtedly mistaken as to this date, inasmuch as the documents were produced by Chambers at the pretrial examination on November 17, 1948."[†75]

The FBI interviewed Levine again on December 5, by which time he had probably had a chance to coordinate his story with Chambers's. When the agents asked to inspect the basement area from which he had claimed Chambers took the envelope, "Levine then admitted that the material was not taken from the basement but rather from a dumbwaiter shaft in his parents' home; that he had placed it there about nine years ago . . . and that he had given it back to Chambers when the latter visited New York City about two weeks ago."[‡] Levine stuck to the phrase "two weeks ago," meaning approximately November 21, when he talked to the FBI.

---

*With the Justice Department and FBI working to indict him and HUAC spinning its wheels, those who have argued that high-level accomplices in government may have helped forge the microfilm and typed documents for Chambers have always confronted difficulties in identifying the prime initiator (or initiators) in their conspiracy theories.

†When the FBI first interviewed Levine on December 4, he denied that Chambers had ever left with him for safekeeping any personal property, specifically any documents or other written material. But immediately after stating this Levine confessed the facts of his uncle's visit, setting the date as "about two weeks ago."

‡If Levine was correct about the date, then Chambers gave him the material in 1939, not 1938. This lends support to evidence that Chambers originally placed it for safekeeping with an ex-Communist friend named Ludwig Lore only to take it back and give it to Levine.

Chambers had wired Levine on the 14th and gone to New York, where he picked up the envelope stored in Mrs. Levine's dumbwaiter. On the 17th he turned over this material at the slander-suit deposition, and two days later he learned that the Justice Department had impounded it. Fearful of what lay ahead, Chambers may have decided to make a more systematic search of Levine's mother's house for additional material that might corroborate his account of working as a Communist courier. Levine had told him on the 14th that the basement contained books and other materials that might be Chambers's. On the next Sunday, November 21, a date that Levine cited to the FBI, Chambers may have returned to Brooklyn and searched through the materials in Barnet Levine's basement, finding there another folder that contained the three undeveloped rolls and two developed strips of microfilm (Levine testified before HUAC in December that he had caught a glimpse of papers in the envelope Chambers took from the dumbwaiter on November 14, but he said nothing about microfilm).[76]

Later that month Chambers visited Meyer and Lillian Schapiro, whom he had seen several times earlier in November. Chambers had already told the Schapiros about having found the typed and handwritten documents and turned them over in Baltimore. On or around the Thanksgiving Day weekend Chambers displayed to the Schapiros the rolls of microfilm, which he described as "the clinching evidence." "This will vindicate me," he told the couple, and Schapiro remembered Chambers appearing "elated by [the microfilm], not sad, like a kid planning something mischievous." Chambers's evident "gleefulness" troubled Schapiro, who recognized that release of the microfilm would undoubtedly publicize the espionage element in the case and make it a much greater spectacle. Schapiro also believed that releasing the microfilm, which Chambers said he contemplated doing once details had been worked out, might "vindicate" Chambers but only at the price of destroying Alger Hiss, a price Schapiro believed too high under the circumstances. After Chambers's departure, Schapiro spent several days brooding about the visit and finally wrote his friend urging him not to release the microfilm. Chambers never answered the letter.[77]

By the time Chambers turned over the material to HUAC on December 2, he may have decided to compress two separate visits to Levine's house into one November 14 trip. This had the virtue of turning his fortuitous later discovery of the microfilms in the Levine basement into a calculated decision on his part to withhold them as "life preservers."

The Washington news stories that sent Nixon and Stripling dashing to Westminster probably forced an abrupt change in schedules. Before then, Chambers may have planned to introduce the microfilms either at a slander-suit deposition or in an interview with the FBI. With HUAC's interest in the case revived, however, Chambers placed himself implicitly under the committee's protection by surrendering the new documents to its investigators rather than volunteering the material to a less than friendly Justice Department.

After Appell delivered the microfilms to Stripling, Stripling sent two terse cables to Nixon aboard the S.S. *Panama* urging his immediate return: "SECOND BOMBSHELL OBTAINED BY SUBPOENA," and "CASE CLINCHED, INFORMATION AMAZING. HEAT IS ON FROM PRESS AND OTHER PLACES, IMMEDIATE ACTION APPEARS NECESSARY. CAN YOU POSSIBLY GET BACK?" Bert Andrews also wired several times. Nixon radioed Stripling to request a government seaplane to fly him from the boat near Cuba back to the mainland, and he reached Miami on December 5.[78]

Meanwhile, Stripling had also contacted Mundt in South Dakota, who agreed to fly back to Washington. After consulting with Mundt and other committee members, Stripling issued an incorrect statement declaring grandiloquently that the microfilms "have been the object of a 10-year search by agents of the United States Government" and, more accurately, that they "provided definite proof of one of the most extensive espionage rings in the history of the United States."[79]

Questioned by reporters about the contents of the films, Stripling talked exuberantly but inaccurately about "the ones we have developed so far [making] a stack of letter-sized documents 3 or 4 feet high." Actually, the total number—including blank panels—barely filled an inch-high stack. The microfilms, Stripling noted, were of State and Navy Department documents. To suggest their importance, he mentioned one 1938 cable from Ambassador William Bullitt that seemed to be in extremely secret code, and another State Department cable that was marked "Strictly confidential for the Secretary." Stripling hinted that possession of these cables would have allowed a foreign power to break America's most confidential diplomatic codes. He avoided a question as to whether Alger Hiss's name was mentioned in any of the documents—in fact, three State Department cables on one strip of developed film had come from Hiss's office—but Stripling added, when asked about Justice Department interest in Chambers, "I think the most important thing is—who made these things available to Mr. Chambers."

That same evening, December 3, Hiss issued a statement in New York. After consulting with Marbury, he confirmed the fact that Chambers had turned over other documents in the course of his slander-suit deposition "which I considered of such importance that I directed my attorney to place them at once before the Department of Justice. This has been done and I have offered my full cooperation to the Department of Justice and to the grand jury in a further investigation of this matter."[80]

Once more, as at other critical junctures in the case, Hiss and his lawyers turned to Dean Acheson for assistance. Already slated to become secretary of state, Acheson apparently retained a keen and cooperative interest in these defense maneuvers. "I enclose two sets of photostats of the documents," McLean wrote Marbury on December 3, "one for you and one for Mr. Acheson." McLean then added a quite remarkable question concerning a State Department security officer's 1945 interview with Chambers: "Do you suppose that Mr. Acheson would have any way of getting a look at it?" Whether or not Acheson, once he rejoined State, provided the Hiss defense with confidential departmental information in the midst of the Justice Department probe has never been determined, but some officials at State complained to the FBI the following year about such practices by the secretary.[81]

It had been a most extraordinary day. HUAC and Chambers had obviously placed the FBI, the Justice Department, and Alger Hiss on the defensive. Chambers's new allegations—and the typed documents and microfilmed "pumpkin papers" turned over as supporting evidence—completely overshadowed his earlier testimony to HUAC in August. Whether or not Hiss had known Chambers as a fellow Communist during the 1930s now seemed almost inconsequential. Looming far more importantly now was the question: Had Alger Hiss, trusted adviser to presidents and Supreme Court justices, been a Soviet espionage agent?

VI

THE DUAL LIFE

SOVIET ESPIONAGE AND THE POPULAR FRONT

Earl Browder, who led the American Communist Party throughout the Depression decade, acknowledged that there existed "a Communist apparatus in Washington during the thirties." Deeply involved in "secret work" himself, Browder knew the general outlines and many of the details of and participants in Soviet espionage in the United States, if only because both GPU and military intelligence agents called frequently for help from figures within the American Communist Party leadership such as Browder and J. Peters. There is no evidence that Browder ever met either Chambers or Hiss during the 1930s, however, although he probably knew through Peters and others about Chambers's work and about his subsequent defection.[1]

But Browder's testimony about the two men must be evaluated cautiously, if only because of his reticence in discussing the CP's "secret work" publicly, even after his expulsion in 1946. Neither Browder's surviving papers nor his published writings reveal details or descriptions of the "Communist apparatus.*[2]

But until the mid-1930s Russian intelligence was surprisingly haphazard and casual in taking advantage of opportunities for espionage in the United States. One problem the Soviets faced prior to American diplomatic recognition in 1933 was lack of an Embassy cover for agents. The Ware Group, for example, concentrated on recruiting Washington bureaucrats rather than on stealing documents. Instances of industrial espionage by Ulrich's ring in 1932–34 were often bungled, almost ludicrous capers. Nor did the Soviet *apparat* in this country perform successfully during these years in its efforts to branch out into espionage abroad—such as the botched attempt by Chambers, Lieber, and Sherman to organize the American Feature Writers Syndicate, or when Chambers, as "David Breen," spent months in 1935 planning to set up a similar network in England that never materialized.

Three factors help explain the haphazard record: the poor quality of Russian agents involved, the bickering between GPU and military intelligence agents,

---

*Only recently have the details of Browder's own career as a Soviet spymaster emerged. See Harvey Klehr, John Earl Haynes, and Igorevich Firsov. *The Secret World of American Communism* (New Haven: Yale University Press, 1995), pp. 231–48; also see the numerous references to Browder in the VENONA intercepts of Soviet agent traffic between the United States and the Soviet Union released by the CIA and NSA in 1995–96.

and the Soviet belief, until 1935, that the United States might best be used not as a major base for spying but as a launching pad for operations elsewhere in the world (and as a source of false passports for agents).

> From 1933 to 1935 [wrote David Dallin] Moscow refrained from sending important underground men to head its military intelligence in the United States. "Bill," a Red Army officer, did come over from Russia, but his main task was to prepare in the United States a new intelligence apparat for England. So strict was the hands-off policy that when Whittaker Chambers photographed and offered him papers procured by Harry Dexter White from the Treasury Department, "Bill" was not interested in them, and "did not wish me to continue with such work." Somewhat later Henry Julian Wadleigh obtained documents from the State Department and Abel Gross brought material from the Bureau of Standards, which Chambers photographed, but again "Bill" rejected the tempting offers. How painful this decision must have been for a secret intelligence officer!

As Dallin pointed out, this condition applied to the military intelligence units, with which Chambers was connected, but not to the GB (later called the GPU and, still later, the KGB), which—though often ineptly led—remained active in the American espionage field at this time.[3]

The situation changed dramatically in 1935 and 1936, even for Chambers's unit, when Russian intelligence leaders began to reassess the potential benefits of information acquired in the United States, particularly in Washington, where Communists and others close to the party had moved into a small number of government posts. The federal establishment had almost no effective security checks in the 1930s, and the position of the United States as an uncommitted world power with a strong diplomatic network in every major country made it a valuable listening post for foreign spies. Once the Soviet Union had concluded, in 1935, that its previous assessment of Nazi Germany had been too contemptuous and that the Nazis' successful consolidation of power had made Germany—along with Japan—a leading threat to the future security of the U.S.S.R., Chambers's underground cohorts began an intensive effort to seek out government sources of information.

No longer did German Communists predict freely that Hitler's regime would shortly be overthrown by a workers' uprising. Nazi success, more than any other single factor, forced the Soviet Union to reevaluate its relationships with "bourgeois democracies" such as England, France, and the United States. Thus Stalin signed the Franco-Soviet treaty of May 1935 with the right-wing French government of Pierre Laval, foreshadowing Soviet efforts to stir up sentiment for similar "collective security" arrangements among Western powers.

The Communist International Seventh World Congress met in Moscow during July and August 1935, and Bulgarian Communist Georgi Dimitrov gave the key speech, setting the stage for the Popular Front. In analyzing the new policy,

Dimitrov commented on American conditions. Unsurprisingly, he found fascism latent in the United States, but Dimitrov castigated CP policies during the early New Deal years. Communists had spent much of their energy attacking the New Deal as proto-fascist or merely reformist, when the party, according to Dimitrov, should have been concentrating instead on opposition to "the most reactionary circles of American finance capital, which are attacking Roosevelt" and which "represent first and foremost the very force which is stimulating and organizing the fascist movement in the United States." Although Dimitrov did not urge open support for FDR by the CPUSA, he did propose creation of a broadly based "Workers and Farmers Party," within which Communists would play a leading role. The new party might seek short-run reformist goals, and, above all, it would try to develop "a common language with the broadest masses"—in short, an American "Popular Front." Earl Browder and other American CP leaders in the audience cheered Dimitrov, despite the fact that his proposals totally reversed their previous tactics in responding to the New Deal, and they immediately proclaimed their support for the new policy.*[4]

ROMANTIC ANTIFASCISM: NOEL FIELD AND HIS FRIENDS

While the Popular Front lasted (1935–39), some in the West served the cause of antifascism by spying for the Soviet Union or for local Communist parties, sometimes for the same reasons that impelled young radical idealists to fight for the Republican government in the Spanish Civil War.† Even before war broke out in Spain, several people who would later figure in the Hiss-Chambers story had already begun engaging in "secret work." Professional Soviet agents in the United States such as J. Peters and "Herbert" (Valentin Markin) exploited every opportunity for recruiting sympathetic young "antifascist" government officials who appeared to be on the verge of promising careers. One leading Soviet diplomat, Alexander Orlov, a defector during the late 1930s, later wrote of such recruitment:

---

*J. Peters had just published an official and orthodox *Manual* on party organization and tactics, which was promptly disavowed by the CP and by Peters himself. When a radical publishing house issued a new edition of the manual in 1975, I sent a copy to Peters in Budapest, who replied: I can't say that I am happy about having it reprinted. In fact I regard it in the light of a provocation and if I could do anything to prevent further reprints I would." Joszef Peter to the author, March 4, 1976.

†"Indeed, there were times when Hiss himself was tempted to join the International Brigade, John Chabot Smith wrote about Hiss's response to that "foreign legion" of Communists and others on the left fighting for Loyalist Spain, including an American unit, the Abraham Lincoln Brigade, "although he never considered the possibility very seriously. His duties at the State Department were his contribution to the cause of better international relations, even if it was less romantic than fighting in Spain. He was getting a little old for such things—thirty-two in November 1936. And he had family responsibilities to keep him home." Smith, *Alger Hiss: The True Story*, p. 104.

This was the main theme on which the NKVD "residenturas" based their appeal to young men who were tired of a tedious life in the stifling atmosphere of their privileged class. And when the young men reached the stage when their thinking made them ripe for joining the Communist Party, they were told that they could be much more useful to the movement if they stayed away from the Party, concealed their political views, and entered the "revolutionary underground."[5]

One agent reached by this appeal in the United States, Noel Field, later provided an autobiographical fragment that shed light on his journey toward Communism. Field's memoir, which gave few specifics about Soviet espionage, provided a rare glimpse not only into Field's personal odyssey but also into the factors that led a person of his background toward involvement in a spy's life:

> . . . It was at this time twenty-five years ago that my wife and I sat beside the radio in our tiny Washington apartment and with waning hope followed the last-minute efforts to save the lives of Sacco and Vanzetti. . . . I have remained true to the beliefs that began to take shape, oh, how vague and how slowly, during the ghastly wake, when hope changed into despair. Many an inner conflict had to be fought out and overcome before the pacifist idealist—a typical middle-class intellectual and son of a middle-class intellectual—could become the militant communist of later years and of the present. . . . The shock of the Sacco-Vanzetti executions drove me leftward. In my free time, I began reading the works of Marx and Lenin. . . . The Great Depression stimulated further searching. I watched and sometimes took part in radical meetings and demonstrations, sought contact with left-wingers of different shades [while working for the State Department]. . . . A dual life, reflecting a dual personality struggling to overcome the conflict between old and new loyalties.
>
> I sought to resolve the contradictions by abandoning government service and continuing to work for peace in . . . the Secretariat of the League of Nations. Travels in Europe—including France of the Popular Front and the Soviet Union, and four stirring months spent in Republican Spain—resolved my wife's and my lingering hesitations, and by the time the second world war broke out, we had advanced from emotional anti-fascists to communists in thought and action. . . .[6]

Noel Field was recruited for espionage work by the German writer Paul Massing, who came to the United States in 1934 after escaping from a Nazi concentration camp. Massing's wife, Hede, had formerly been married to Gerhard Eisler, a leading Soviet underground agent and Comintern representative in the United States during the late 1930s. The Massings then worked as couriers for a Soviet spy ring run from Paris by Ignatz Reiss, a leading Russian intelligence operative. Noel Field and his wife, Herta, met the Massings at a dinner party arranged by a mutual friend, Marguerite Young of *The Daily Worker*. The two couples saw much of each other, and the Fields became intrigued by Massing's dangerous life.

Although, according to Hede Massing, Field resisted her efforts to persuade him to steal documents from the State Department, he moved closer and closer to Communist involvement through their friendship. Finally, in 1936, in an apparent effort to resolve what he himself had called a "dual life," Field turned down a pivotal post at the State Department's German desk. The Massings had urged him to take it on the grounds that he could greatly aid the Soviet Union by passing along American knowledge of German affairs. Instead, Field joined the League of Nations's disarmament secretariat in Geneva (he had been a specialist in the subject at State), partly for the curious reason (according to Flora Lewis) "that as an international civil servant he would not have anyone to betray if he also worked on the side as a Soviet agent."* He then began spying for the Russians.[7]

Working as a Soviet agent proved a troubling and unsatisfying experience for Noel Field in many ways, or so he told his Hungarian and Czech interrogators after being arrested in 1949. His first contact man in Geneva was Ignatz Reiss, who promptly defected in 1936 with a bitter attack on Stalin's rule. Reiss was later murdered by the GPU after being tricked into a public meeting, one which Field claimed to have helped arrange. Replacing Reiss was another high-ranking GPU "Resident" in Europe, Walter Krivitsky, who contacted Field in 1937, instructing him to travel to Paris on an assignment related to Soviet interest in the League's work. Immediately Krivitsky defected.[8]

Disturbed because there were no subsequent meetings with Russian superiors, Field and his wife journeyed to Moscow in late 1937 to request further assignments. The Russian purges were then approaching their brutal climax, and the Massings had been recalled to Moscow by their GPU handlers for questioning. Soviet security organs in that fear-ridden atmosphere had become as concerned with proving the reliability of their own professional agents, especially those abroad, as with obtaining secret information. From the Fields' hotel room, Hede Massing dramatically phoned GPU headquarters to demand that exit visas for herself and her husband be delivered at once to the room. The Russians complied, and the Massings returned to the United States, where they soon defected.[9]

Under the circumstances, GPU officials in Moscow were rather leery about using Field again, suspecting him of being a double agent. Not until 1941 did another Russian operative contact the Fields, this time in Geneva, instructing Noel to write an account of all his previous meetings with the Massings, Reiss, and Krivitsky. Field prepared the report, but no one picked it up. During the war Field continued passing information, mainly through Eastern European Communists he met in the course of his new job at Unitarian Relief. When Field next made formal arrangements to become an undercover agent, however, he

---

*Flora Lewis's Red Pawn provides a great deal of insight not only into Field but also into the lives of others like him who worked within the New Deal, including Field's friend Alger Hiss.

negotiated with Americans working for Allen Dulles's Office of Strategic Services (OSS) unit, although Dulles eventually rejected his overtures.[10]

After the war Field applied for "open" membership in the Swiss Communist Party, but his sponsor—the head of that party—was expelled for deviations from a fast-changing Moscow line. Thus when Field left to visit Eastern European countries as a freelance journalist in 1948 and 1949, at a time when Stalin had already excommunicated Tito's Yugoslavian CP and had become extremely wary of Communist nationalists elsewhere in Eastern Europe, Russian suspicions that Field functioned regularly on behalf of Western intelligence agencies were reasonable although not accurate.[11]

Noel Field's closest friend in Washington was Laurence Duggan, a specialist in Latin American affairs at State. Duggan told the FBI in 1948 that two other friends, Henry H. Collins, Jr., and Frederick Vanderbilt Field (no relation to Noel), had tried to recruit him for Communist espionage work in 1936–38. According to Chambers, who knew of these approaches to Duggan, Frederick Field advised that Duggan was already connected with an underground apparatus, the one in which Noel Field had been involved, whose contact person was Hede Gumperz Massing.*

Hede Massing had also tried to get Duggan to supply information. He would not provide documents, according to Mrs. Massing, but did agree—although the arrangements fell through—to give useful information orally from time to time. Duggan told the FBI he had never been involved in Communist activities and had not had contacts of this nature with Mrs. Massing; he may or may not have provided information to CP intelligence agents during the 1930s, but he did not report either Frederick Field or Henry Collins to his superiors at State after they approached him to commit espionage.[12]

During the winter of 1935–36 Noel and Herta Field met Alger and Priscilla Hiss at parties given by mutual friends such as Laurence Duggan. There were a number of such informal links among young New Dealers with both the right "social views" and the appropriate background. Flora Lewis described this circle:

> A friend [of Alger and Donald Hiss] later remembered a picnic by the swimming pool of his estate where a number of these government starlets had come to relax and chatter. There were the Hiss boys, Alger's onetime roommate Henry H. Collins, Noel Field, Laurence Duggan. "They all came from Harvard or Princeton or Yale, and highly respected families," the friend said, "a group of young aristocrats, polished, athletic, vigorous looking, lively and full of interests. You could see in a moment that they were real gentlemen. At the time, they all seemed to be young liberals, just good pacifists with the courage to speak out against what was wrong and with nothing to hide."[13]

---

*Mrs. Massing used her maiden name in secret work, and Chambers's letters from the 1930s show that he knew her as "Hedda Gumperz."

The Hisses and the Fields, probably introduced by the Duggans, struck it off from almost their first meeting.*

The conflict between governmental responsibilities and evolving radical beliefs affected both men. How best could they serve the cause of social reform? What ways of fighting fascism were open to them? On a more personal note, how could one resolve the contradictory imperatives of what Field later described as his "dual life" and "the conflict between old and new loyalties"? Field debated these contradictions for himself in Washington at a time when his friends included Alger Hiss, Henry H. Collins, Jr., who later served as both government official and Soviet agent, and Laurence Duggan, who, according to his own testimony, was approached by Collins to spy for Russia but declined. Prior to the AAA purge, Hiss's closest associates at the agency included Lee Pressman, Nathan Witt, and John Abt, all of whom presumably shared Field's dilemma. The problem of personal commitment, of loyalties divided between the liberal New Deal and more radical, even revolutionary socialist values, was endemic for this circle of reform-minded young government bureaucrats.

In Field's case, he tried to finesse the dilemma, first (during the late thirties) by combining a life as an international civil servant with underground work. This pattern continued during the war when Field, nominally an official of the Unitarian war-relief organization, worked covertly both for the American OSS (briefly) and for his Soviet superiors.[14]

Just before Noel Field left the United States for Geneva, an incident allegedly took place involving Field, Hede Massing, and Alger Hiss. Massing told the FBI in 1948 that in early 1935 Noel Field, reluctant to steal State Department documents himself, said he preferred to work instead with another person at State who was in the underground. Massing asked to meet this man, and subsequently the Fields introduced her to Alger Hiss at a dinner party held at their apartment (Priscilla was not present). Massing recalled drawing Hiss aside and engaging in the following banter:

> I said to Mr. Hiss, "I understand that you are trying to get Noel Field away from my organization into yours," and he said, "'So you are this famous girl that is trying to get Noel Field away from me," and I said, "Yes." And he said, as far as I remember, "Well, we will see who is going to win," at which point I said, "Well, Mr. Hiss, you realize that you are competing with a woman," at which either he or I said, the gist of the sentence was, "Whoever is going to win we are working for the same boss."[15]

---

*Herta Field recalled in 1949 that Alger Hiss "had been many times [a] guest" in the Field home during the winter of 1935–36 prior to Field's departure for Geneva. It seems improbable that the two families became close during the months that both men, Field and Hiss, were reevaluating their careers—Field having resigned from State only four months before Hiss joined the department—without discussing the dilemma that led Field to forsake Washington for Geneva.

The Fields were pleased, Massing remembered, that she and Hiss had gotten along so well. It was after this meeting with Hiss, Hede Massing would later testify, that Field agreed at first to remain in her apparatus but then, almost immediately, accepted the League of Nations post.*

Dorothy Detzer, the peace activist and friend of Hiss during his period on the Nye Committee, told the FBI in January 1949 that Hede Massing had confided to her in 1946 that Alger Hiss had been involved in an underground network during the mid-1930s. If Detzer remembered correctly, her testimony indicates that Hede Massing had been discussing Hiss's role in the CP years before the case broke. According to Detzer, she had applied for a UN post in 1946 and her application was held up, she learned, at Hiss's State Department desk. This surprised Detzer, since "she had regarded Alger Hiss as an old friend." Detzer mentioned this to an acquaintance at State, G. Howland Shaw, who remarked: "There are some who say Alger is a Communist."†16

Startled by Shaw's allegation, Detzer mentioned the incident in a visit the following week to Hede Massing, who (according to an FBI report) described Hiss's unfavorable response to Detzer's application as

> understandable . . . in view of the fact that Detzer had been so out-spoken in her anti-Communist and anti-Stalinist philosophy. Massing then in confidence related to Dorothy Detzer her previous Comintern espionage activities. In this conversation she related that her job had been to contact officials in the State Department and other government agencies and endeavor to develop them as informants for her Comintern apparatus. She stated she had been successful in developing and "delivering" Noel Field and at the same time mentioned Alger Hiss as being connected with this apparatus. . . . [Detzer] is certain his name was mentioned along with Noel Field.

Massing apparently told Detzer in 1946 that she had already given this information to the FBI, although bureau files do not reflect any knowledge of Massing's story about Hiss until late 1948.

Alger Hiss completely denied Massing's allegations. He claimed he had never met her and pointed out that he had not yet joined the State Department at the time of the alleged meeting. But he was an active participant in the regular meetings

---

*Massing recalled a luncheon meeting several days later with her underground superior, "Fred," in New York City at which he "came straight to the point and said, 'This man, Giss,'—when he was excited, he used the Russian 'G' instead of 'H'—and I said, 'You mean Hiss.' He whispered, 'Yes,' raising his finger in a silencing gesture. 'You forget him. Forget him completely! Don't mention him ever! Don't speak about him to Noel or to Herta or to Paul. Never see him again. Stay away from him and forget him. You and I will never speak about him, either.'" Massing claimed to have understood immediately the major source of "Fred's" concern. Not only had she met a member of another underground network but she had even conversed with him about "working in a parallel apparatus. This was strictly taboo. . . ." *This Deception,* p. 179.

†Shaw later testified as a character witness for Hiss.

of an informal group that called itself the Foreign Policy Association, made up largely of State Department officials, including Field and Duggan along with a half-dozen liberal, non-Communist internationalists such as Charles Yost.* The association was a favorite meeting place for New Deal officials, radicals and liberals alike, who were interested in foreign policy and predisposed toward Wilsonian concepts of collective security at a time when official government policy and the country's public temper were still strongly isolationist. Hiss said he attended the association's meetings for a year or two during the mid-thirties and categorized its dinner meetings as a kind of "supper club," noting somewhat strangely "that Lee Pressman represented labor in this supper club and possibly Mordecai Ezekiel represented the Department of Agriculture." Pressman had already joined the staff of the new CIO by then, while Ezekiel was a mainstream New Deal liberal. In the relaxed "Popular Front" atmosphere of the Foreign Policy Association's dinners, Hiss and his wife first became friendly with Noel and Herta Field.[17]

What degree of intimacy developed between the Hisses and the Fields remains uncertain. Although Flora Lewis's biography of Field describes a number of gatherings at the Hiss home and the Field apartment, both Alger and Priscilla Hiss later portrayed their association with the Fields as far more casual.[†]

Accounts of the four people involved vary considerably. When Noel Field wrote to Hiss in 1957, after his release from a Hungarian prison, he commented on Hede Massing's story: "Speaking of perjury, it was, of course, not until I came out of jail that I learned of the part played in your second trial by false testimony of a perjured witness with regard to a purported meeting and a conversation, neither of which ever took place, either within or without the confines of our Washington apartment." He called Hede Massing's account of meeting Hiss at the Field residence an "outrageous lie" and a "complete untruth." Field said nothing, however, about the exact nature of his 1935–36 relationship with the Hisses. Hiss testified accurately in 1949 that Field had been a friend, although not an intimate. Two months before learning of Hede Massing's testimony, Hiss wrote a memorandum for his lawyers about Noel Field in October 1948, describing a series of meetings with Field at the Foreign Policy Association's dinners— "more in the nature of social functions at which the emphasis was on serious conversation rather than purely on small talk." Hiss did not mention visiting the Field household or any contact between the two couples outside of the association's meetings during the 1935–36 period.[18]

When Mrs. Hiss testified before a New York grand jury in December 1948 (she had not yet learned about Hede Massing's testimony), she was asked about knowing the Fields:

---

*Yost became Ambassador to the United Nations during the Nixon administration.
†The two couples met infrequently after the spring of 1936, usually for an occasional dinner when the Fields returned from time to time to the United States.

I said I did know them. I was then asked were they close friends? I said, they were not very close but they were friends.

They asked how many times did I see them [the Fields] and I said several times, that I thought we had been there to dinner once or twice and had them to dinner once or twice. They said, could Alger ever have gone there to dinner without me? [This was undoubtedly a reference to Massing's testimony.] I said I didn't remember anything of that kind happening.[19]

Herta Field was reached in Geneva the following year, in July 1949, by a Swiss attorney representing Hiss. She acknowledged she had followed the case through reports in *The New York Times*. Herta knew of Hede Massing's claim to have met Hiss at the Fields' apartment, and the lawyer described her reaction:

> Mrs. Field immediately said that Mrs. Massing and Alger Hiss had never met in her apartment. She confirmed that both had been many times her and her husband's guests, but declared that they never were invited together. . . . [H]er apartment was very small and therefore they had never large parties. They necessarily seldom included more than four to six persons.
>
> She continued that even if her recollection should be wrong in this point [i.e., about Hiss and Mrs. Massing having been guests together for dinner] she was definitely sure that no such conversation as I had mentioned had ever taken place in her apartment. The small size of it would have excluded a private talk between Mrs. Massing and Alger Hiss.*[20]

But confirmation of Alger Hiss's relationship with Field in the Communist underground came recently from a unique source, Professor Karel Kaplan, a Czech historian and member of the Dubcek government's 1968 commission that investigated the political purge trials of the late Stalin era, in which Noel Field figured prominently. Kaplan read through the interrogations of Field by both Czechoslovakian and Hungarian security officials, the first of which came in 1948 when Field—months before his arrest—applied for extension of his Czech visa. In all of these interrogations, according to Kaplan, Field named Alger Hiss as a fellow Communist underground agent in the State Department during the mid-thirties: "Field said that he had been involved [while at the State Department] and that Hiss was the other one involved" after he joined the department. One major reason Field gave to his interrogators for not having returned to the United States in 1948 was to avoid testifying in the Hiss-Chambers case. Herta

---

*Hiss's lawyer, Flora Lewis, and Hermann Field (in an interview with the author) all agree that at the time Herta Field made this statement she was far more concerned about the possibility of trouble for herself and Noel with American officials (because of the Hiss case) than with the Russians. The Swiss attorney, Wilhelm Staehelin, quoted Mrs. Field during the same interview on July 25, 1949, as worrying that the "'publicity' would make life very difficult for her and her husband in America," and at a second meeting with Herta in August, shortly before she flew to Prague in search of her husband. Staehelin noted: "She confirmed again however her willingness to cooperate and apparently realized that she was partly in the same boat as Alger Hiss."

Field's interrogations, Kaplan noted, also mentioned Hiss's role as a Washington Communist when she knew him in the 1935–36 period.[21]

The Hisses made an effort in 1948 to minimize their earlier friendship with the Fields. If Herta Field's statement is correct, however, Alger had visited the Field home "many times" in the winter of 1935–36.

Additional confirmation and specific citation of these interrogations came from Hungarian historian Maria Schmidt, who examined these files in 1992 while researching a larger study of the post–World War II Eastern European purge trials in which Field figured as both victim and witness. In a 1993 *New Republic* article and more extensive unpublished paper, Schmidt quoted from the contents of these still-unreleased interrogations of Field and from Field's handwritten statements to his questioners in 1954 prior to his release from prison. After his release, Field and his wife settled in Budapest where, among other contacts, Schmidt's research asserts that he maintained friendly contact with another exiled local resident, J. Peters, head of the U.S. Communist Party's secret work during the 1930s.

Field freely conceded his prior involvement in espionage for the Soviet Union in 1954 statements made to Hungarian State Security officers, according to Schmidt, who quotes extensively from the Interior Ministry files on Noel Field: "From 1927 gradually I started to live an illegal life completely separate from my official life . . . [committing] espionage for the Soviet intelligence service. When I undertook this task, my wife was also present."*

Field left no doubt in his so-called rehabilitation statements to the Hungarian Interior Ministry's interrogators that Alger Hiss had also been active in working for the Soviets during this period: "[I]n Fall 1935 Hiss at one point called me to undertake espionage for the Soviet Union. . . . I informed him that I was already doing such work."† Field was unusually talkative for an agent, according to his 1954 confessional in Budapest while awaiting release, identifying various friends and associates whom he had told about underground activity including Hiss: "In 1935 I revealed myself for Alger Hiss," tacit confirmation of Hede Massing's account of this episode.‡

Similar unequivocal statements regarding that episode emerged from Schmidt's scrutiny of Field's 1954 statements, for example: "In the Summer of 1935 Alger Hiss tried to recruit me into the Soviet intelligence and I committed the unforgivable indiscretion that I told him he was too late with his offer. . . . I immediately told Hedda Gumperz [Hede Massing] what had happened. I received a stern rebuke from her." Elsewhere in the same deposition: "Alger Hiss

---

*Quoted in Maria Schmidt, "Behind the Scenes of the Show Trials of Central-Eastern Europe," unpublished paper (Budapest, 1993), p. 22.
†*Ibid.*
‡*Ibid.*, p. 23. See also *ibid.*, p. 25, on the Hiss-Field link.

also wanted to recruit me for espionage for the Soviet Union. . . . [I] carelessly told him that I was already working for the Soviet intelligence. . . . I knew, from what Hiss told me, that he was working for the Soviet secret service."*

Defenders of Hiss's innocence, interestingly, have not challenged the validity of Schmidt's quotations from Noel and Herta Field's interrogations by Hungarian Interior Ministry officials in 1954. Rather, they have questioned the accuracy of Field's assertions, arguing that such statements were made under extreme duress while interrogators held over the Fields power to deny their release from prison.† Such critics have also pointed out that, once released and resident in Budapest, Hiss and Field exchanged letters in 1958 in which Field denied having met with Hiss and Hede Massing in his apartment in 1935, a meeting he confirmed in his 1954 interrogations.

What possible reason Hungarian Communist security officials would have had in 1954 to pressure Noel Field to perjure himself in recounting his relationship with Alger Hiss remains—to say the least—extremely puzzling.

Laurence Duggan proved evasive when describing his relationship with Noel Field and Alger Hiss. Acknowledging that he had been a close friend of the Fields during the thirties, Duggan also told the FBI that he had probably met Hede Gumperz Massing but "cannot recall circumstances. May have been through Noel Field." He denied, however, that she had ever tried to recruit him for Soviet intelligence work, as she later testified. As for Hiss, Duggan would say only that he was "pretty certain that Alger Hiss knew Noel Field."[22]

This last, vague statement of Duggan's was not candid. Hiss and Duggan in fact had corresponded and talked earlier that same year about the possibility of finding employment for Field in the United States, including magazine outlets in this country for articles on conditions in Eastern Europe that Field wished to write. Both had been in contact with Field, who was in Europe at the time. Moreover, in October 1948 Hiss asked Duggan's wife, Helen, for Field's current address before writing him about Chambers, whom he described to Field as "unbalanced and . . . given to hallucinations." Hiss's memos to his lawyers show that he kept in touch with Duggan throughout the latter's last months about the charges raised by Massing and Chambers that Duggan apparently cooperated for a time with Soviet intelligence, a charge Duggan denied.[23]

---

*Ibid., p. 26.

†Those interested in the controversy should consult, in addition to Maria Schmidt's unpublished article, previously cited, the following: Maria Schmidt, "The Hiss Dossier: A Historian's Report, *The New Republic,* November 8, 1993; Sam Tanenhaus, "Hiss Case 'Smoking Gun'?" *The New York Times,* October 15, 1993; and—challenging the validity of Noel Field's statements concerning Alger Hiss's role as a Soviet agent—Ethan Klingsberg, "Case Closed on Alger Hiss?," *The Nation,* November 8, 1993.

Helen Duggan proved more forthcoming when she talked to Hiss's attorney the month after Duggan's death:

> ... Priscilla and Alger were "left" [wrote the lawyer], as I gathered were the Duggans and most of their friends. She became indignant when I mentioned this and pointed out with some heat that there was a great difference between being leftish and being a Communist agent or actually a traitor. . . . She thinks it most improbable that [Hiss] could have been disloyal. Last fall she told her brother that if Alger were disloyal, "the same could be true of Laurence." She mentioned this merely as showing how improbable it was. She admits also that she told Alger last fall that "we may be in it next."
>
> Duggan . . . told her [after his interview with the FBI] that it was concerned primarily with Noel Field and that from what the agents told him, he was satisfied that at some time during the years, Noel had become a Communist agent.[24]

That Alger Hiss knew of Field's dilemma about committing himself wholeheartedly to "secret work," and that they discussed it during Hiss's "many visits" in the winter of 1935–36, remains probable but impossible to prove. If Hiss was himself a Communist supporter at the time, Field may have been the last person in a comparable government position with whom Hiss could exchange beliefs, hopes, and fears concerning such future work on behalf of the Soviets. By the time Hiss joined the State Department in September 1936, Field was already in Europe, but there were people remaining in Hiss's own circle of close friends who shared his commitment to a "dual life."

NKVD agent records from the 1930s, recently opened to the author for use in a new book on Soviet espionage in the United States, show several 1936 meetings in Washington involving Alger Hiss, Noel Field, Laurence Duggan, and Hedda Gumperz (Hede Massing). The descriptions of these meetings in NKVD files confirm accounts by Gumperz and Chambers in the 1940s.

Hedda Gumperz (whose underground name then was "Ryzhaya" or "Redhead") confirmed Noel Field's version of Alger Hiss's approach to him in the following April 1936 dispatch to Moscow:

> Our friend "Ernst" [one of Noel Field's code names in dealings with Soviet intelligence at the time] the day before his departure to Europe told me the following story that he will communicate to our friends abroad personally. Alger Hiss turned to him approximately a week before "Ernst's" departure to Europe. Alger told him that he was a Communist and that he was connected with an organization working for the Soviet Union and that he knew that "Ernst" himself had certain connections. But Alger was afraid that they were not solid enough and that probably his knowledge was being used poorly.

Then he openly suggested that "Ernst" should make a report to him on London's Conference. According to "Ernst," they were close friends; that is why he did not refuse to talk to him about this topic, but told Alger that he already had made a report on that conference. When Alger, whom I had met through "Ernst," as you may remember, kept insisting on the report, "Ernst" was forced to tell him that he needed to consult his "connections."

The next day, after having thought it over, Alger said that he no longer insisted on the report, but he wanted "Ernst" to talk to Larry and Helen [Duggan] about him and let them know who he was and give him [Alger] access to them. "Ernst" again mentioned that he had contacted Helen and Larry. However, Alger insisted that he talk to them again, which "Ernst" ended up doing. "Ernst" talked to Larry about Alger and, of course, about having told him "about the current situation" and that "their main task at the time was to defend the Soviet Union" and "that they all needed to use their favorable positions to help in this respect." Larry became upset and frightened, and announced that he needed some time before he would make that final step; he still hoped to do his normal job, he wanted to reorganize his department, try to achieve some results in that area, etc.

Evidently, according to "Ernst," he did not make any promises, nor did he encourage Alger in any sort of activity, but politely stepped back. Alger asked "Ernst" several other questions; for example, what kind of person would succeed him, and if "Ernst" would like [Alger] to contact him. He also asked to help him to join the State Department, which apparently "Ernst" did.

When I pointed out to "Ernst" his terrible discipline and the danger he put himself into by connecting these three people, he did not seem to understand. He thought that just because "Alger was the first to open his cards, there was no reason for him to keep a secret." Besides, Alger announced that he was doing it for "us" and he lived in Washington, D.C. . . . and, finally, because I was going to go out of country for a while, he thought it would be a good idea to establish a contact between us.*

At the time, Gumperz was also engaged in an effort to cultivate both Laurence and Helen Duggan for her network. Thus she was greatly troubled by this apparently casual interweaving of agents involved in separate networks, in which Alger Hiss (known then to his underground colleagues by the code name "Lawyer") continued to play an unwanted role as exuberant recruiter of fellow New Dealers. A Soviet "illegal" in New York, Bazarov, soon to be replaced by the legendary spymaster Isaac Akhmerov, also complained about this unseemly socializing among active agents in an April 26, 1936, communication to his superiors in Moscow. Bazarov expressed special concern that, a few months earlier, Hedda Gumperz and Alger Hiss had apparently introduced themselves to one another in their capacity as Soviet operatives, as Hedda Gumperz Massing would testify

---

*NKVD personnel file on Laurence Duggan, Archive of the Russian Intelligence Service (Moscow), Case 36857, Book 1, pp. 21, 23.

a decade later. "I think, after this story," Bazarov wrote, "we should not speed up the recruitment of '19' [Laurence Duggan's code name] and his wife. Evidently, [a] persistent Hiss will continue carrying on his initiative."*

Gumperz's Soviet supervisors strongly criticized her management of the situation, for example, in this May 3, 1936, communication:

> We do not understand "Ryzhaya's" [Gumperz's] motives in meeting "Lawyer" [Alger Hiss's code name at the time]. As we understand, it happened after we gave our last directives about "Lawyer," after our instruction that "Lawyer" is the Neighbors' [GRU, or Soviet Military Intelligence] agent and needed to be left alone.†

In a cable to Moscow on May 18, 1936, newly arrived NKVD "resident" Isaac Akhmerov added yet another dimension to the sensitivity shown toward "Lawyer" by his Soviet handlers:

> "Ryzhava" met "Lawyer" only once during her stay in the country [Gumperz had left for Europe by then]; it was last winter. "Nord" [code name for Bazarov, Akhmerov's predecessor] agreed to this meeting. When you informed us that he was connected with the Neighbors, we did not see "Lawyer" anymore . . . .‡

If Hedda Gumperz's having stumbled accidentally across Alger Hiss as a fellow agent generated concern in 1936 among his Soviet handlers, two years later "Lawyer" caused them even greater anxiety when a fledgling recruit to the Soviet networks, Michael Straight (code-named "Nigel"), tried to recruit *him.* Akhermov described the episode and its aftermath in a June 28, 1938, memorandum to Moscow:

> Unfortunately, according to the conditions of his work, "Nigel" established contact with Hiss. "Nigel" mentioned him earlier to me, indicating that he was an interesting person who occupied a responsible position, etc. He also said that ideologically Hiss was a very progressive man. I didn't show my interest in him, but, on the other hand, I can't tell him to stop seeing Hiss. If I tell him that, he might guess that Hiss belongs to our family. There is another danger: *bratskiy* [American Communist Party's underground agents] or Neighbors' [Soviet Military Intelligence] resident (I am not quite sure with whom Hiss is connected) can ask Hiss to start working on "Nigel's" recruitment.

Akhmerov is referring to the fact that Straight had already been recruited, something not necessarily known to Hiss, who had displayed keen interest in recruiting other agents two years earlier. Akhmerov's memo continued:

Ibid., p. 22.

†*Ibid.*

‡*Ibid.,* p. 25.

I am sure that "Nigel" would refuse to cooperate with them, if they try to recruit him, but in this case "Nigel" would find out Hiss's nature. . . . I am writing about all this as a possibility that you should take into consideration and, if you have an opportunity, influence the Neighbors' station chief if he starts recruiting "Nigel" through Hiss. . . .*

The following month, on July 31, 1938, Akhmerov clarified his understanding of Hiss's role in the Soviet underground in this cable to Moscow:

"Storm" [Joszef Peters's code name at the time] let out a secret during one of our conversations: Hiss used to be a member of *bratskiy* organization [i.e., the Ware Group period from 1935 to 1936] who had been implanted into "Surrogat" [code name for the State Department at the time] and sent to the Neighbors later. He told me about it when I was hunting for Hiss. In one of our discussions, "Nikolai" [code name for Peter Gutzeit, a Soviet agent in the U.S. at the time] told me that it was possible that at present the Neighbors are not connected with Hiss, most likely because of some organizational difficulties [most likely a reference to the defection earlier in 1938 of Hiss's courier, Whittaker Chambers].†

Until the "Neighbors," or Soviet Military Intelligence, opens its archives, these insights into Alger Hiss's career as an agent during the 1930s, drawn from NKVD records, are likely to be the best available from Soviet records of that era.

HENRY COLLINS AND THE "COVER PERSONALITY" DILEMMA

Henry Collins worked for Soviet spy rings in Washington throughout the 1930s and perhaps later, beginning with the Ware Group and continuing at least through his 1938 effort to recruit Laurence Duggan. Collins remained throughout the 1930s and 1940s an intimate friend of both Alger and Priscilla Hiss. Few of Alger Hiss's boyhood friends had taken to his wife, as Hiss himself acknowledged, but Priscilla and Collins became friends.[25]

Shifting government posts several times during the New Deal, Collins moved from the National Recovery Administration in 1935 to the Labor Department, where he worked for several divisions until 1940, when he began a three-year stint with several congressional committees. After another three years in the Army, he worked briefly in 1946 for the Reconstruction Finance Corporation and for the State Department. Collins served for three weeks in 1947 on the staff of a Senate subcommittee, but he was forced to resign when an inconclusive 1942

---

*Ibid., p. 83.
†Collins's lawyer at the grand jury appearance was Nathan Witt.

FBI check on him came to the committee's attention. In February 1948 Collins became executive director of the pro-Soviet American-Russian Institute. He told Hiss's attorney in September 1948 that "he does not know Chambers and never saw him anywhere. Specifically, he never saw him with Hiss." Three months later Collins was subpoenaed to appear before the grand jury and changed his earlier testimony.*

Collins's memo of the appearance, prepared for Hiss's lawyers, contained his recollection of this exchange:

QUESTION: Did you ever know a man named Whittaker Chambers?
ANSWER: I think I knew a man who now goes under the name of Whittaker Chambers in Washington about '34 or '35. My impression is that someone brought him to a cocktail party I was giving: and I did see him on one or two occasions subsequently either at my place or elsewhere in Washington. My acquaintance with him was casual, so casual, that I have forgotten what name he was using at that time.
QUESTION: Where was your apartment at that time?
ANSWER: 1213 St. Matthews Court, N.W.

In the same round of questioning, Collins said he knew Pressman, Witt, Abt, and Ware. He denied knowing, however, that any of them had engaged in Communist activities during the thirties, and he also denied "unqualifiedly" all of the charges made by Chambers about Collins's Communist involvement.[26]

On all these questions, Collins lacked candor. John Herrmann's letters to Josephine Herbst showed that Herrmann had moved his base of operations in the Ware Group to Collins's apartment ("c/o Collins, 1213 St. Matthews Court, N.W., Washington, D.C."). And when Hiss's attorney questioned her in April 1949 about the Ware Group's composition, Herbst "seemed startled at the mention of the name of Henry Collins. . . . She intimated that Henry Collins knew all about the 1934 activities and could tell us everything if he wished to." Later in the decade Collins had approached Laurence Duggan about participating in Soviet espionage. Victor Perlo's estranged wife, Katherine, had listed Collins among the members of Perlo's underground Communist group in her anonymous letter to the FBI in 1944, and Whittaker Chambers later testified at length about Collins's contribution to the party's "secret work" during the thirties.[27]

Thus there exist independent sources of testimony that Collins was an active member of the Communist underground throughout the 1930s and perhaps into the Second World War. During this period he remained close to both Alger and Priscilla Hiss and met them frequently at their home. Was the connection purely social or did Collins represent for Hiss the last of his associates from the Ware

---

*Ibid., Case 58380, Book 1, pp. 73–74.

Group with whom he could share both aspects of a "dual life": not only the Communist "secret work" to which both men were committed but also the personal experiences of their Baltimore childhoods and of a subsequent friendship that lasted for decades?

The psychological dilemma of such agents, especially those holding respected "cover" positions as agents-in-place, remains acute. Kim Philby presented the problem succinctly when he wrote that the "first duty of an underground worker is to perfect not only his cover story but also his cover personality." A less successful agent than Philby, Klaus Fuchs, who passed atomic secrets to the Russians until his arrest in 1950, described his own experiences in developing a "cover personality"' this way:

> In the course of this work I began naturally to form bonds of personal friendship and I had to conceal from them my inner thoughts. I used my Marxist philosophy to establish in my mind two separate compartments. One compartment in which I allowed myself to make friendships, to have personal relations, to help people and to be in all personal ways the kind of man I wanted to be and the kind of man which, in a personal way, I had been before with my friends in or near the Communist Party. I could be free and easy and happy with other people without fear of disclosing myself because I knew that the other compartment would step in if I approached the danger point. I could forget the other compartment and still rely on it. It appeared to me at the time that I had become a "free man" because I had succeeded in the other compartment to establish myself completely independent of the surrounding forces of society. Looking back at it now the best way of expressing it seems to be to call it a controlled schizophrenia.[28]

"Controlled schizophrenia": The best and most successful secret agents have always perfected such a compartmentalized personality. Examples from the annals of Soviet intelligence include Richard Sorge in Japan fooling both Germans and Japanese with his cover role as a Nazi newsman; Fuchs, a highly trusted British atomic scientist in the secret laboratories of both the United States and his own country; and Philby himself, almost reaching the top in British intelligence before his two associates—Guy Burgess and Donald Maclean, the one a neurotic homosexual and the other an alcoholic—stripped away Philby's protective cover.

Only one American accused of Soviet espionage, Alger Hiss, fits this profile and led a public life that resembled the rigidly compartmentalized personality described by Fuchs. Noel Field would remain throughout the 1930s and 1940s suspended uneasily between the demands of a life in Soviet intelligence and his yearnings for a more open role as a Communist. Laurence Duggan, according to his own testimony, declined invitations by friends to engage in espionage, but never broke off the friendships or reported those who had tried to recruit him.

Hiss, far more self-confident than either of his friends, rarely experienced such uncertainty.

Few Westerners who became Soviet agents for ideological reasons during the 1930s acted as the result of an abrupt and decisive change in beliefs. Most underwent a gradual process of conversion to Communist activism under the influence of their own experiences, their friends, and the pressure of events. "How did it all begin?" Kim Philby asked in his memoirs. "My decision to play an active part in the struggle against reaction was not the result of sudden conversion." Nor is Philby unique. "My past," Noel Field wrote from a Hungarian jail, "was contradictory on the surface, yet there is a guiding line [toward Communism] from early childhood."[29]

In Alger Hiss's case, in Washington he became closely associated with members of the Ware Group while working for the AAA and the Nye Committee. By that time the pattern of a "dual life" described by Field, Philby, and other Russian agents had already been established in New York City.

By 1936 Hiss's background made him a logical candidate for recruitment by the CP underground during its "Popular Front" phase. Would Henry Collins have approached Duggan about such work, for example, and not discussed the possibilities with Hiss, a much closer friend? What reasons did Noel Field offer Hiss for turning down the German desk at State to leave for Geneva at a time when Hiss was about to enter the department? Hiss insists that he learned nothing about Field's Communist beliefs or his plans, and he also denies any knowledge of Collins's Communist involvement. Did Pressman, Witt, Abt, Kramer, Ware, and all his other acquaintances never discuss the subject of Communism with Hiss? According to Alger Hiss, none of them—nor Collins or Field—ever did.*

HISS JOINS THE STATE DEPARTMENT

Why Alger Hiss joined the State Department in September 1936 has never been satisfactorily explained, although it probably reflected—among other factors—his growing concern over world affairs. Hiss says he left the Nye Committee in August 1935 because of an increasing sense of estrangement from the isolationist aims of Senator Nye, his colleagues on the group, and most committee staff members. Such isolationist sentiment in Congress resulted in tough neutrality legislation to prevent sales of American munitions to European belligerents.

---

*Hiss told me that the only person with whom he ever held a discussion of Communism while serving in the government during the thirties was an AAA colleague, Abe Fortas. Interview, Alger Hiss, September 20, 1974.

Hiss quit the Nye group, according to his biographer, because he "didn't like the way the Committee was attacking Wilsonian idealism and America's allies in the [First World] war. . . . [The committee was] spreading the idea that it was the Wall Street bankers who had got America into the war, and American boys had been sent overseas to die for the bankers and their loans. Hiss wanted no part of that. . . ."

Yet earlier the biographer himself had described Hiss's role in investigating excess wartime profits made by the Du Pont Company and Bernard Baruch's negligence in investigating the situation: "his [Hiss's] point being that the company . . . forced the payment of huge profits, while the company had assumed none of the risk. It was a cover-up, a fraud on the public, and Bernard Baruch and the War Industries Board had been part of it, in Hiss's view." Hiss then questioned Baruch closely about his own financial interests during the First World War to debunk the notion that he had been the "unselfish" government servant "he pretended to be," and to show "he had been making profits from investments of his own in companies that were benefiting from his policies" as head of the War Industries Board.[30]

Alger Hiss, in short, had been one of those directly responsible for developing the "war profiteers" argument with which the Nye Committee became identified, despite his effort in the late forties to erase that identification: "I lost interest in the work of the committee when they commenced to go more and more into the question of America's entering the First World War," Hiss told his lawyers in 1949. "It seemed to me that their objective was to distort the real reasons why the United States went into the First World War and to encourage isolationist sentiment."[31]

If Hiss held these views while he worked for Nye in 1934 and 1935, there is no evidence that he ever informed the committee, its staff, or his friends, or that he dissented at all from its aims and activities. He kept to himself any policy disagreements he may have felt with the Nye Committee's isolationism. Hiss left the AAA payroll in April 1935 and for the next four months lived on a much-reduced salary paid by the committee. Moreover, he continued to work on a part-time basis for the committee while on the Justice Department payroll in late 1935 and 1936. He departed finally because the group was "nearing the end of its life." Far from disagreeing with its impending investigation of the Morgan banking interests, Hiss helped prepare that inquiry and seemed concerned—when he wrote to William Marbury in mid-June 1935—only about future job prospects:

> I have been living under the shadow of banishment—the Committee's chief remaining task is in the investigation of the World War banking story. Naturally, all of this is being done in New York and all our forces are there. I was prepared to go up for the summer as long ago as May 1 and finally went up for a few days last week. . . . Until that is settled—and our final appropriation, the preparing of various reports now almost completed, etc. are delaying that settlement—we shall be pretty uncertain of our week to week plans.[32]

During the months that followed, Hiss managed to land himself an important job at the Justice Department working for Solicitor General Stanley Reed, partly through William Marbury's timely assistance. Marbury arranged for the Maryland senators, George Radcliffe and Millard Tydings, to write letters to Reed recommending Hiss. Reed himself was impressed by Hiss's qualifications after several meetings with the applicant, and Hiss was hired in August 1935 as a "special attorney" in the Department of Justice attached to the solicitor general's office, with particular responsibility for legal problems connected with the Department of Agriculture.[33]

Hiss spent his first five months at Justice helping to prepare the legal brief in *United States v. Butler,* the suit on which rested the constitutionality of a major AAA policy, a processing tax on producers of commodities. The Supreme Court ruled the tax unconstitutional in January 1936, and the decision marked the death knell for Hiss's former agency. With his work on *Butler* completed, Hiss turned his attention to other matters connected with agriculture and to another major New Deal policy initiative then threatened with a court challenge: Secretary of State Cordell Hull's reciprocal foreign-trade agreements. Under that policy the United States had begun negotiating bilateral commercial agreements with other countries for reciprocal tariff arrangements. This approach represented a significant departure from the more extreme protectionist-tariff views of the early New Deal, and American manufacturers opposed to the program unleashed a series of court challenges.

The time spent developing the government's constitutional arguments for reciprocal trade agreements brought Hiss into frequent contact with the State Department official responsible for administering the program, Assistant Secretary of State Francis B. Sayre, who had taught Hiss at Harvard Law School, and with Sayre's assistant, John S. Dickey, later president of Dartmouth College. Dickey had attended Harvard Law with Donald Hiss before coming to the State Department with Sayre in 1934. His decision to return to private law practice in Boston created the opening in Sayre's office that Alger Hiss filled.[34]

Both Sayre and Dickey were puzzled concerning Hiss's willingness to shift from Justice to State at a substantial cut in salary. "He [Dickey] thought we should explain," Hiss's lawyers wrote after an October 27, 1949, interview with Sayre, "why Alger Hiss would leave a $7,500 position in the Department of Justice to accept $5,600 in the State Department. It was pointed out to him that Alger Hiss had been receiving $6,000 in the Justice Department until the end of July 1936 [when his salary became $7,500], after both the State Department and Alger Hiss had agreed upon the terms of his new employment. He seemed to know that Mr. Hiss had wanted to work in the field of international relations."* Whatever

---

*According to William Marbury, Hiss had confided an interest in working in the State Department years earlier, and John Chabot Smith wrote that, for Hiss, diplomatic service had been boyhood dream.

his motives, Hiss received confirmation of the State Department appointment from Sayre in May.[35]

A final point of confusion concerned the relations between Hiss and his predecessor as Sayre's assistant, John S. Dickey. At the time of the case Hiss described Dickey to his attorneys as "a very close personal friend . . . sharing my general views on most political and economic questions more closely than most anyone else I know." But Hiss's lawyer learned while interviewing Dickey in January 1949 that he had rarely seen Hiss in the years after leaving Sayre's employ and, while expressing a high opinion of Hiss's "intelligence and ability," denied any claim of friendship. Moreover, Dickey would not testify as a character witness for Hiss, feeling that since he contradicted his successor on vital points of evidence concerning Sayre's office procedures, his testimony could only injure Hiss. Also, Dickey "pointed out that if Alger was engaged in espionage, the office of assistant secretary would be the best possible place to work."[36]

THE BOKHARA RUGS

Alger Hiss's transfer to State in September 1936 coincided with the arrival in the United States of Boris Bykov to direct Chambers's unit of Soviet Military Intelligence. Chambers later recalled that Bykov knew little English and even less about the functioning of Russian underground work in this country.

Eager to increase the flow of information from Chambers's Washington contacts in the government, Bykov "discussed the possibility of giving them something to put them in a productive frame of mind. [He] first proposed that we offer them money. However, I [Chambers] objected to this, stating that they probably would be shocked and disturbed by such an offer since they were members of the Communist Party and this would be somewhat contrary to established Communist Party principles. Bykov then suggested that these selected people be given some expensive present. I again objected to this proposal. Bykov, however, insisted." The new Russian "Resident's" unfamiliarity with the ideological roots of Communist commitment for New Deal officials who engaged in secret work led to an incident that later provided a tangible link between the Soviet underground and four "selected people."[37]

These gifts were Bokhara rugs, which Bykov directed Chambers to give to four important underground contacts within the federal bureaucracy: A. George Silverman of the Railroad Retirement Board, Harry Dexter White in the Treasury Department, and Julian Wadleigh and—according to Chambers—Alger Hiss in the State Department. Bykov "also instructed me to inform [all four] that these rugs had been woven in Russia and were being given to them as gifts from the

Russian people in gratitude to their American comrades."* Chambers feared that his associates would not "swallow this speech," but he obeyed orders.

Since Chambers knew nothing about Oriental rugs, he took Bykov's money to Meyer Schapiro, who could get them for him wholesale. Schapiro arranged the purchase with a rug dealer in New York in December 1936 and had the rugs shipped by Railway Express the following month to Silverman in Washington.† Silverman kept one for himself and delivered another to his friend Harry Dexter White. "The third rug was given to Henry Julian Wadleigh," Chambers later noted, but "I have completely forgotten the details concerning the delivery of the rug from the Silverman house to Wadleigh." According to Chambers, one night in January 1937 Silverman drove the fourth Bokhara to a restaurant on the Baltimore Pike near College Park, Maryland, where Chambers and Hiss were parked. Hiss and Silverman knew nothing about each other's underground work, and they waited in their cars while Chambers transferred the rug to Hiss's car, after which they drove away.

Chambers recalled having seen the Bokhara while visiting the Hisses at their 30th Street house later in 1937. The rug was kept rolled up "in a closet or small room which was located just off the basement room," and Hiss took the rug out—"It was bright red and had an oriental design in black"—unrolled it briefly to show to Chambers, and returned it to its storage place.[38]

In 1948 Hiss said he had received in late 1935 a red rug from "George Crosley," who described it as a gift that had "been given to him by a wealthy patron," as "part payment" for Crosley's earlier rental of his apartment. Hiss denied Chambers's version of the incident: the drive to a Maryland restaurant to get the Bokhara and also Chambers's insistence that he later visited the Hiss household at 30th Street, where Hiss displayed the rug briefly. "The incident never took place," Hiss told his lawyers in March 1949. He had never seen Crosley after mid-1936 and, specifically, had no contact with the man as late as 1937. Moreover, when he received the rug from Crosley in 1935, Hiss said, he and his wife "were then living on P Street and we opened it in Mr. Crosley's presence and we immediately used it. . . . We have used the rug ever since and we have it today." The rug, according to Hiss, had never been kept in a closet.[39]

George Silverman, another recipient of a Chambers Bokhara, told Hiss's attorneys that he had not been involved in Communist "secret work" during

---

*In an article on Soviet espionage techniques, entitled "Welcome, Soviet Spies!," that Chambers wrote in November 1938, or within two years after arranging for the purchase of the rugs at Bykov's orders, he referred specifically to the gift of such rugs to prospective agents being encouraged: "A favorite gift during these courtships is a big handsome carpet from Soviet Turkmenistan."

†The rugs cost Chambers approximately $220 each and retailed at a much higher price. Even a casual inspection would have shown that the rug's value was almost exactly the total amount Chambers allegedly owed Hiss in rent money—$225. HUAC, I, pp. 982–83.

the 1930s. According to Silverman, he and Chambers first met when the latter "came to his office at the Tariff Commission, introduced himself as a free lance writer, gave his name as Whittaker Chambers, and indicated he was interested in information about the trade agreements program."* The two men, Silverman remembered, saw each other frequently from 1935 until 1938 on a social basis, often having lunch and sometimes dinner together to discuss "art and literature and music." Silverman, like Hiss, claimed that Chambers borrowed money from him occasionally and explained the Bokhara rugs (Silverman received two, one for Harry Dexter White) as an effort by Chambers to repay his debts. Sometime before the fall of 1937—"Chambers's testimony as to the date of December 1936 might well be correct"—Silverman recalled Chambers asking if the four rugs from "an importer friend" could be delivered to Silverman's house. Silverman offered to buy two of the Bokharas and (in Silverman's version) paid Chambers $300, also wiping out a $75 debt. "Silverman kept one of the rugs himself," he told Hiss's lawyers. "He still has it. He gave the other as a present to Harry White." Chambers took the remaining two rugs.[40]

Hiss's maid Claudia Catlett confirmed Chambers's version of how the Hisses stored one of the two Bokharas taken from Silverman. She told both the FBI and Hiss's attorneys in 1949 that the rug had been kept at 30th Street exactly as Chambers remembered: "I recall seeing a red rug with a fringe on it in the Hiss's [sic] house on 30th," read Mrs. Catlett's signed statement for the bureau. "This rug was in a closet next to the kitchen in the front part of the basement. The rug was rolled up and tied. . . . The Hisses did not use this rug in the house on 30th Street and I don't know when or where they got it." When questioned by the FBI about the date the Hisses acquired the rug, Mrs. Catlett replied:

> They may have had the rug while living on P Street [in 1935, as Hiss claimed] as there was a room there in which things were stored. That room was locked and I never went in it. I recall asking Mrs. Hiss why she didn't use this rug and, as well as I can recall at this time, she told me that it was because it did not belong to her. Later on when they moved to the Volta Place house [in 1938] this rug was put on the floor in Tim Hobson's room.

More damaging still, the FBI turned up proof in 1949 that the Hisses had paid a monthly fee to keep the Bokhara in storage during 1937 and 1938, not retrieving it for use in their Volta Place home until long after Chambers's defection.[41]

Additional corroboration exists concerning Chambers's story of the four rugs. Meyer Schapiro purchased the Bokharas from Edward H. Touloukian of the Massachusetts Importing Company in Manhattan on December 23, 1936. Schapiro

---

*But the previous month Silverman had reported to Hiss's lawyers that he "does not remember the circumstances under which he met Chambers and recalls him as just one of the people he happened to know." Harold Rosenwald, "Memorandum re A. George Silverman," March 21, 1949, Hiss Defense Files.

paid Touloukian with a check for $600 and $276.71 in cash, using funds provided by Chambers. The rugs were shipped to Schapiro's Manhattan home (since the importing company was a carpet wholesaler selling only to retailers, Schapiro had presented Touloukian with a letter from a friend in the rug business in order to complete the transaction). Schapiro, in turn, shipped the four rugs to someone in Washington whose last name he could later recall only as "Silver—."[42]

Although Hiss insisted he received his rug from Chambers in late 1935, not only Silverman but another person named as a recipient, Julian Wadleigh, told of acquiring a Bokhara early in 1937. Both Wadleigh and his ex-wife, in separate depositions, told the FBI in 1949 that he had "received no recompense for his [underground] work other than a new nine by twelve Persian rug . . . about 1937." The rug "was presented to him as a New Years gift in 1937 or 1938 by Whittaker Chambers." After comparing his recollections with those of his former wife, both agreed that the rug had actually been brought by "Harold Wilson" (David Carpenter) and not "Carl" (Chambers), but that the gift had been made in early 1937.[43]

In summary, from the available evidence these facts emerge: Four Bokharas were purchased for Chambers in December 1936 and shipped to George Silverman in Washington. All four individuals whom Chambers mentioned as recipients—Silverman, White, Wadleigh, and Hiss—acquired Bokharas, and three of them apparently received their rugs early in 1937. Only Hiss, among the four, claimed to have been given his rug much earlier, sometime in late 1935. Hiss's maid Claudia Catlett confirmed Chambers's story of having seen the rug rolled up in a basement closet of Hiss's 30th Street home, where he lived from June 1936 to December 1937—and where he said Chambers had never been. Mrs. Catlett's statement and the storage-company records conflicted with Hiss's assertion that the rug had been used continuously since its receipt and that it had never been rolled up in a closet or stored away.[44] A rug expert, acting on behalf of Hiss's attorney, inspected Hiss's rug in 1949. He declared it to be a Bokhara whose "dimensions were for all intensive [sic] purposes the same as those indicated on the sales slip" that Meyer Schapiro received for the four rugs purchased in December 1936.[45]

THE HISS-CHAMBERS RELATIONSHIP, 1937–38

Alger and Priscilla Hiss said they had not seen Whittaker and Esther Chambers after mid-1936. The brief relationship between the two couples, according to the Hisses, had ended in 1935—except for an occasional visit by Chambers the following year to borrow money, to obtain Hiss's signature on the Ford title transfer, and to deliver the Bokhara rug (an episode Hiss thought occurred in 1935). But Whittaker and Esther Chambers countered that they had seen the Hisses regularly throughout 1937 and early 1938, socially as well as in the course of Hiss's dealings with Chambers in the Communist underground.

Available evidence concerning delivery of the Bokhara rugs in January 1937 weakens Hiss's categorical denial that he met with Chambers at that time. More-over, there exists additional evidence that the two couples remained in close and friendly communication for more than a year after Hiss received the rug. Testimony suggests that Priscilla Hiss visited Esther Chambers in Baltimore while taking a course at the University of Maryland during the summer of 1937; that a Chambers maid recalled Alger Hiss, and perhaps Priscilla, visiting the Chamberses in Baltimore at this time; that Alger Hiss informed Chambers about his brother Donald's government work; that the Hisses depleted their small savings account with a $400 withdrawal in November 1937 in order to loan the Chamberses money to buy an automobile; and that the Hisses' friend and family pediatrician encountered Chambers under highly unorthodox circumstances in the Hisses' home during a house call in January 1938. Some of Chambers's later recollections concerning meetings with the Hisses in 1937 and 1938 could not be verified a decade later, but any one of these five incidents, added to the Bokhara-rug gift, confirms beyond reasonable doubt an active relationship between the two couples.

Esther Chambers described several visits from Priscilla Hiss while "Mrs. Hiss was enrolled at [Baltimore's] Mercy Hospital to study nursing." Mrs. Chambers remembered the episode having taken place while she and her husband lived at Eutaw Place, a residence that the Chamberses left during the spring of 1936. But Mrs. Hiss took her course in medical technology at the University of Maryland's Baltimore branch—not at Mercy Hospital—during the 1937 summer session, a time when the Chambers family also lived in Baltimore but at Auchentoroly Ter-race. Esther recalled a number of meetings with Priscilla during this brief period:

> . . . it was at that time . . . that I did see quite a good deal of her. I probably met her at the Fountain Shop, as I say, at Hutzler's [Department Store], and she came to the house to stay with the baby one night. And she came to the house several times during that period, mainly through the afternoon, the early after-noon, that she would have to get home in time to have dinner for Alger.[46]

Priscilla insisted that she did not see Esther that summer and that in fact she had never been interested in nursing, but had intended to complete the inorganic-chemistry course at the University of Maryland as preparation for entry into medical school. She denied having taken a nursing course at Mercy Hospital or anywhere else.

Hiss also dismissed Esther's account: "The undisputed facts . . . are: My wife never contemplated a nursing course. She never so much as started the contemplated medical-technology course. She never took any course at Mercy Hospital—or anywhere else in 1935 or 1936. She did in fact take a chemistry course in Baltimore at the University of Maryland in the summer of 1937, a year after I had last seen Chambers. . . ." Hiss suspected that the source of Esther's information was "that during the two days Mrs. Chambers was at P Street in the spring of 1935 my wife in Mrs. Chambers' hearing spoke of her objective of eventually studying medical technology at Mercy Hospital."[47]

Other evidence—including Priscilla Hiss's 1937 correspondence and two 1948 accounts of the episode written by Hiss—contradicts the Hisses' later version of events and supports Mrs. Chambers's claim. Priscilla Hiss, according to these documents, decided not in 1935, as Hiss asserted, but only in mid-1937 to pursue courses in "medical technology"—that is, nursing—rather than attempt to become a doctor. Moreover, she applied first at Mercy Hospital to take such courses, presumably the source of Esther Chambers's confusion about Priscilla's studies during that summer. On May 25, 1937, Priscilla wrote the director of admissions at the University of Maryland's Baltimore campus, W. M. Hillegeist, applying for admission to the summer courses in chemistry given by the School of Pharmacy, which would begin two weeks later. She had written Bryn Mawr the previous day to send Hillegeist her undergraduate transcript.

To explain these last-minute requests, she linked her decision to take the course directly to a program then being offered at Mercy Hospital: "I am extremely anxious to take the course [in inorganic chemistry] and obtain the necessary credits for Mercy Hospital's training course in medical technology. . . . I realize that this is extremely short notice for your office." Priscilla had originally applied for the program at Mercy Hospital, as Esther Chambers recalled, but had been referred to the University of Maryland, as shown in the following 1948 letter from Alger Hiss to his lawyer about his wife's application forms:

Here are the Mercy Hospital papers that Pros had run across when she was trying to reconstruct her activities from 1934 to date:
    She thinks she talked to someone at Mercy Hospital and took the blanks. Her original interest from Bryn Mawr on had been pre-med work. After Tim's illness [Timothy Hobson had been struck by a car while bicycle-riding on February 19, 1937; he spent four months confined to a bed with a fractured leg and walked on crutches for some months after that] she was moved to re-examine the possibilities & Dr. Nicholson (our Catholic woman pediatrician) & others recommended taking a laboratory technician's course as more practical in view of her age & family duties.
    Pros is quite sure that once she found that she would have to take inorganic to take the technician's course and that she needed only to add organic to college physics & get into George Washington Medical School she lost interest in the technician's course.[48]

Further confirmation comes from a June 1, 1937, letter to Mrs. Hiss from Sister M. Celeste of Mercy Hospital: "Regarding your summer course in Chemistry, if in organic chemistry, you acquire eight (8) credits, we will consider your application for September entrance in our School for Medical Technicians." Priscilla decided on a career in that field not in 1935, as Hiss later claimed, but, according to his own letter, after Timothy Hobson's serious accident in February 1937, and she filled out the application in late May. Hiss acknowledged this in a memo about Priscilla prepared for his attorneys in 1948 when he wrote: "In the summer of 1937, following Tim's recovery from a serious accident the preceding winter, Priscilla's mind turned toward medicine. . . ." Therefore, Esther Chambers would have had no way of knowing about these plans had she not seen Priscilla Hiss sometime during the summer of 1937. Chambers, in this connection, displayed familiarity with Hobson's accident when questioned by Hiss's attorneys in November 1948, an equally puzzling circumstance unless he had seen the Hisses that same year. Although wrong about the date, Esther and Whittaker Chambers recalled the circumstances surrounding Priscilla Hiss's daily trips to Baltimore during the summer of 1937, indicating an awareness of her last-minute decision to enter a Mercy Hospital medical-technician's program—a decision Priscilla did not make until late May 1937.[49]

According to Chambers, not all of his visits with the Hisses came as a result of such day trips. He told of one automobile trip with Alger and Priscilla Hiss in August 1937 to visit Harry Dexter White at the latter's Peterborough, New Hampshire, summer home. Chambers said the Hisses picked him up in Washington and, en route to Peterborough, stopped overnight at a tourist home in Thomaston, Connecticut. The next day, after visiting White briefly, they remained in Peterborough for a summer-theater performance of "She Stoops to Conquer," after which the trio spent the night at a guesthouse in the town, probably one named Bleak House. They drove back the following day.

The FBI's investigation showed that the play had been presented by the Peterborough Players, August 10–15, 1937. But the Bleak House register turned up no guests during that period whose handwriting fitted either of the Hisses or Chambers. Nor could Hiss's registration card be found at any Thomaston-area guesthouse.

The Hisses denied making the drive with Chambers and insisted that they had spent the first two weeks of August on vacation with Timothy Hobson in Chestertown, Maryland. They said they never left Chestertown during this entire vacation, but the records of Dr. Margaret Nicholson showed that Priscilla Hiss and Tim visited her Washington office on August 16. Several Chestertown friends of the Hisses testified in 1949–50 that the couple had been in residence there throughout August 1937, although in two cases it became evident that the witnesses' memories had been refreshed by extensive coaching from Hiss and his lawyer. A fellow tenant at the Hisses' Chestertown apartment house, there for the entire summer, stated he had never met or seen either Alger or Priscilla Hiss despite the fact that he rented the only other apartment on the same floor as the Hisses. The evidence for the Hisses' constant residence in Chestertown during August 1937, in short, is mixed and inconclusive.[50]

Harry Dexter White's widow told Hiss's lawyers in 1949 that the Whites had been in residence in Peterborough in August 1937 and, although she did not know of any such visit as the one described by Chambers, "she could not be certain that Chambers did not make a brief call upon her husband when she was away from home for a short time."

The FBI never followed up one extremely promising post-trial lead while checking out the story. Dorothy Detzer told the bureau that a Washington friend named Alma Kerr told her in 1950 that she [Kerr] "is a close friend of the daughter of a woman who owned an inn where Hiss stayed while on a trip with Whittaker Chambers. . . . [But] the owner of the inn [had] told the FBI that she had no record of Hiss staying there, whereas in fact she did recall Hiss as he was a very good-looking, personable, and polite young man. As she desired no publicity, the owner of the inn had withheld the above information from the FBI."[51]

Evelyn Morton, the maid who worked for the Chambers family in Baltimore, both at Auchentoroly Terrace in 1937 and on Mount Royal Terrace in 1938, "tentatively identified" photographs of Alger and Priscilla Hiss in 1952 as people who had visited the Chamberses once at the latter apartment (although initially she could not identify Priscilla's photo). According to Mrs. Morton, "Hiss came to Chambers's apartment one night when Chambers returned from New York." She was the second of Chambers's maids from the thirties to have recalled the Hisses visiting Chambers in Baltimore, despite their insistence that they had never been at any of the "Crosleys'" homes.[52]

In 1939 Chambers also proved well informed about the career of Hiss's brother, Donald, who he claimed had also been a member of the Communist underground (Donald later insisted that he had never met Chambers during the thirties even as "George Crosley"). Chambers described Donald to Adolf Berle in September '39 as "(Phillipine [sic] Adviser)—Member of C.P. with Pressman & Witt—Labor Dep't.—Asst. to Frances Perkins—Party wanted him there—to send him as arbitrator in Bridges trial." These accusations pose three important but distinct questions. First, was Chambers telling the truth about Donald Hiss's involvement with Communism? Second, assuming that Donald Hiss was not a Communist and that he had never met Chambers, from whom did Chambers learn such private details about Donald Hiss's career? Third, did Chambers present the facts concerning Donald Hiss and the Bridges trial accurately? Only the second and third of these questions bear on the issue of whether or not Alger Hiss saw Whittaker Chambers in 1937 and 1938, because the probable answer to question number two, if Donald truthfully denied any relationship with Chambers, was that the information came from his brother, Alger.

The Bridges trial mentioned by Berle was not a court case, but a hearing then under way in San Francisco, one of many efforts to deport Harry Bridges, the Australian-born leader of the West Coast longshoremen's union. The case was highly controversial, since Bridges's supporters argued that the government had acted against him only because of the union official's aggressive union leadership and his left-wing politics. At the same time, congressional conservatives denounced Secretary of Labor Frances Perkins unfairly for her alleged reluctance to move against Bridges, whose future remained in dispute until a December 1939 report by Harvard Law School Dean James M. Landis—appointed hearing officer in the case by Perkins—found no grounds for deportation.[53]

Donald Hiss denied he had ever been involved in the Bridges hearings while working for the Labor Department. He transferred from the Solicitor's Office at the Department of Labor, where he had worked since June 1936, to the post of assistant to the legal adviser in a newly created office of Philippine Affairs at the State Department in November 1937. The shift was arranged through the intervention of Francis B. Sayre, who was largely responsible for organizing the new department (a crucial area of concern because of the growing tension with Japan). Donald had been recommended originally by John Dickey for the post of Sayre's assistant obtained by Alger, and because of Sayre's involvement it is safe to assume that Alger knew the details of Donald's appointment and may even have played a role in arranging it.

Donald Hiss later testified to a federal grand jury in December 1948 that he had never prepared memoranda on the Bridges case because "I had never worked on the Bridges case." He had been in California in August 1937 holding a Labor Department hearing on another case, and in September, while returning by ship through the Panama Canal, he had received a wire from Washington asking him to contact the department. Only the following month did he learn that the department's solicitor, Gerard Reilly, had telegraphed him earlier, urging Donald to conduct the Bridges investigation while there. When Reilly failed to reach Donald, he left for California himself to handle the inquiry. Upon Reilly's return, according to Donald Hiss, he said that any further investigation of Bridges would be done by the Labor Department's field offices on the West Coast or by the Immigration and Naturalization Service. Thus Donald insisted, "I had never worked on the Bridges case at any time."[54]

But after he joined the State Department through Sayre's intervention in February 1938, events followed that seem extremely puzzling even in Donald Hiss's version:

. . . I had been in the Department of State a matter of two or so months [when] Mr. Reilly lunched with me and told me that he was going to request the loan of my services from the State Department to conduct the hearing on the Bridges case. I remember distinctly telling Mr. Reilly that it would be absurd to send me to hold the hearing on the Bridges case. Some lawyer of national reputation should be selected as the hearing officer and I did not possess such qualifications. . . . I then reported this conversation with Mr. Reilly to my superior, Mr. Jacobs, in the State Department and as I recall it, expressed no interest in the possibility of holding such a hearing, but preferred to continue in the work in which I was then engaged and had just acquired some real background. Thereafter the matter was handled by the Secretary of Labor or Mr. Reilly and the higher officers in the State Department.

Donald insisted that the only person other than Jacobs to whom he mentioned the matter was his wife. He did not recall discussing it with his brother, but since "the Office of Philippine Affairs reported through the Division of Far Eastern Affairs to Mr. Sayre, the Assistant Secretary . . . it might have been discussed by Mr. Jacobs with Mr. Sayre and with my brother."[55]

Why should Reilly request Donald Hiss's transfer from State to conduct the Bridges hearing if he had "never worked on the Bridges case" during his period at the Labor Department? Moreover, if Donald himself had objected to the move in conversation with Reilly, why did Secretary of Labor Frances Perkins make a formal request for Donald's services on the Bridges case in April 1938? The answer, despite Donald Hiss's denial, was that knowledgeable officials at Labor considered him the department's expert on the Bridges case. Thus, whatever his personal reservations about leaving his new post at State, and whatever truth lies in Chambers's allegations about involvement in Communism, there is a discrepancy between Donald Hiss's later insistence that he had never been involved in the Bridges case and the following letter from Secretary of Labor Frances Perkins to Francis B. Sayre dated April 22, 1938:

I have your letter of April 11 with regard to Mr. [Donald] Hiss and can understand your difficulties in arranging for his temporary detail to this Department in view of the opposition of his superiors in the Division of Philippine Affairs.

As you perhaps have heard, the hearing in the Bridges case has been continued pending the disposition by the Supreme Court of a petition for a writ of certiorari in another immigration case involving the same legal problem. Should the Court's decision make it necessary to hold further hearings in the Bridges matter, I should appreciate it at that time if you could arrange matters in your Department *so that Mr. Hiss could be assigned to the case again. As you know, his transfer to the State Department was a source of serious concern to the legal staff here as he was the only member fully cognizant of the various aspects of this important immigration case* [italics added].

If the case is marked up for hearing again, I hope to be able to give you ample notice so that arrangements which will not inconvenience his division can be made in advance.*[56]

So confident was Perkins of State's cooperation in releasing Hiss that she informed INS Commissioner J. L. Houghteling, who told the INS district commissioner in San Francisco on April 15, 1938, that "Donald Hiss . . . will preside at the Bridges hearing. He has been appointed an acting Immigration Inspector for this purpose." At the time Houghteling wrote, State had not yet turned down Perkins's request for Hiss's services. But Perkins's letter to Sayre stipulated that Donald Hiss was the Labor Department's foremost expert on the Bridges case— a fact he later denied—whether or not he had ever "worked on it" formally. Furthermore, Sayre's personal handling of the request from Labor for Donald's services indicated that Alger Hiss, Sayre's assistant, must have known about the matter. Considering Bridges's popularity and importance among American Communists, the selection of a presiding officer for his deportation hearing would not only have been of keen interest to CP officials but also a choice bit of gossip for an underground agent like Chambers.[57]

Frances Perkins's letter contradicts Donald Hiss's assertion that he was not involved with the Bridges case while at Labor. Whether his claim that he never met Whittaker Chambers is equally unreliable cannot easily be determined. But Sayre's handling of the Labor Department request for Donald's services meant that Alger, Sayre's only assistant, got the facts either from his boss or from his brother—or both. In any case, Chambers's description of these events to Berle in 1939, especially in the light of Perkins's letter, indicates familiarity with the facts of the situation that could have been acquired from talks with one or another Hiss brother in the period from late 1937 to April 1938.

Chambers claimed in 1949 that not only had he received classified information from Hiss, but also, in November 1937, Hiss made him a $400 loan, which he used toward the purchase of an automobile. Hiss said no, explaining that his wife had withdrawn $400 to purchase furnishings for a new home the couple rented the following month. Certain facts are undisputed. Priscilla Hiss withdrew $400 from the Hisses' joint savings account at the Riggs National Bank in Washington on November 19, 1937, leaving a balance in the account of $40.46. Four days later Chambers traded in a 1934 Ford and paid an additional $486.75 in cash for a 1937 Ford to a Randallstown, Maryland, dealer. He never informed his Communist superiors about the automobile's make, according to Chambers, and needed such an unfamiliar car to facilitate the break he planned.

---

*When this letter was made public in 1957, Donald Hiss dismissed it in writing to Alger Hiss's then-lawyer, Chester T. Lane, with a reference to Secretary Perkins's "unfortunate phraseology." Donald Hiss to Lane, April 17, 1957, Hiss Defense Files.

When Hiss's lawyers first questioned Esther Chambers about purchasing the car, she stated that although she did not know who had provided the cash, she thought it had been Chambers's mother: "Mother comes in there some place. I don't know. Mother did help us out at various times. She probably gave us the money for that. . . . I think so. I am not certain. These things were taken care of by him, and I don't know." Hiss argued later that Chambers had been coached by the FBI in a falsehood about the $400 loan: "It seems clear that among the things Chambers learned in the course of his three and a half months or more of daily conferring with the FBI [in early 1949] . . . was the fact that our savings account showed a withdrawal of $400 during the period of time that he claimed to have known me." Chambers's acknowledgment that he recalled the loan for the first time in 1949 "when I was going over this whole history with the F.B.I." bolstered Hiss's charge at first glance.[58]

But the sequence of events surrounding Chambers's initial recollection of the loan shows that he did not parrot information previously gained by the FBI. The FBI Washington field office submitted a subpoena from a New York grand jury for records of the Hisses' savings and checking accounts at the Riggs National Bank on January 30, 1949. The records were photographed by an FBI agent on February 7 and the originals were returned to Riggs. The records were not sent to New York, where Chambers was then being interrogated by agents of that FBI field office, but remained in the Washington field office.[59]

Without apparent prompting, Chambers first told the agents a version of the car loan from Hiss on February 14. While planning his defection, he decided a car was "essential" and persuaded Bykov that he needed a new auto. But Bykov did not have the $500 Chambers needed, and the Russian suggested that he borrow the money from Alger Hiss and it "would be paid back." Chambers recalled asking Hiss for the money and later receiving it: "Has recollection that Priscilla Hiss said she had to close out her account to get the money for him," the FBI's New York office wired Washington. "This would have been in early nineteen thirty eight. Chambers believes her account would have been in the Riggs National Bank, Main office or Dupont Branch." He remembered buying his 1937 Ford a few days after Hiss gave him $500 and "admits he never paid Hiss back." The agents in New York asked that the Baltimore field office check the Schmidt Motor Company and Maryland Bureau of Motor Vehicles for corroborating records, while it requested that Washington "check for bank accounts of Priscilla Hiss to determine if she made any such withdrawal in early 1938."[60]

Initially in February 1949 Chambers remembered the episode vaguely and inaccurately. He recalled borrowing $500 from the Hisses—not $400—and placed the transaction in early 1938 rather than in November 1937. Moreover, he recalled Priscilla Hiss stating that the loan forced her to close out the Hiss account when in fact she only withdrew ninety percent of its funds. "No particular significance had been attached to this withdrawal of $400 by the Washington Field Office prior to February 14, 1949," a later FBI report noted. Immediately after the tele-type from the New York office was received, however, "an analysis was made of the savings account of Priscilla Hiss and complete information concerning the $400.00 was furnished to the New York Office by teletype dated March 2, 1949. At the date of this teletype there was no information in the Washington Field Office files indicating that any prior information or documents had been furnished to the New York Office regarding this transaction."[61]

Neither the FBI agents in New York nor Chambers, in other words, had received information about the $400 withdrawal or about the Riggs National Bank documents at the time Chambers first mentioned the incident on Febru-ary 14. Nor had the Randallstown auto dealer been contacted yet for his records. Otherwise, there was no particular reason for Chambers to have made such obvious errors in his statement about the purchase. He could have said simply that he borrowed $400 from the Hisses and purchased his new auto in Novem-ber 1937. Further investigation by the FBI turned up these details and corrected Chambers's earlier inaccuracies.

The FBI also scrutinized the Hisses' assertion that Priscilla Hiss had with-drawn the money on November 19, 1937, to purchase certain items for a new home they had rented at 3415 Volta Place, N.W., and into which they moved on December 29. The Hisses said that such withdrawals were normal practice for them when they changed their residences,* although they acknowledged pay-ing for major purchases on most occasions not in cash but either by check (they also had a joint checking account at Riggs) or by using one of several credit accounts they maintained with Washington department stores, where many of the items were bought. Also, the Hisses lost bank interest on the $400 by the withdrawal.

The Hisses said they purchased many things for the move, but, a decade later, understandably could not supply receipts or delivery slips. Verifying the items themselves proved impossible by the late 1940s.[†62]

But the circumstances surrounding Hiss's rental of the Volta Place house raise serious questions concerning his account of the $400 withdrawal. Hiss thus explained his acquisition of the house:

> Throughout the fall of '37 we looked for a larger house. Sometime early in November we selected the Volta Place house as the house we desired and com-menced negotiations for it.

---

*Riggs National Bank records showed that although the Hisses had opened their account in November 1936, their first withdrawal—the $400—came a year later, and their next one three months after that.

†The Hisses asserted that Priscilla had purchased most of the items for Volta Place with the $400, although she was then also studying chemistry and physics at George Washington Univer-sity, in addition to carrying out her normal household duties. She failed to complete her courses, withdrawing from them on December 15.

> About the 18th of November, very closely before the date of this withdrawal, we had a commitment from Mr. Gilliat, the broker, the real estate broker with whom we had dealt for some years, and from whom we had rented the 30th Street house. . . . We had a commitment from him that he was confident that the price which we were prepared to pay would be satisfactory to the owner of the Volta Place house.

The next day, November 19, according to the Hisses, on the strength of this "commitment" from Gilliat, Priscilla withdrew the $400 to purchase furnishings for the new house.[63]

Both the realtor, J. H. B. Gilliat, and the owner of the house provided evidence that shows the Hisses did not acquire the Volta Place home—and may not even have learned of it—until a couple of weeks after Mrs. Hiss's $400 withdrawal. Moreover, on the day the Hisses rented the residence, December 8, Mrs. Hiss borrowed $300 from the Riggs National Bank, which she deposited immediately in her checking account (the loan was secured by a $1,000 Treasury Bond, which removed any necessity to explain its purpose to the bank). Gilliat told the FBI in 1949 "that the first listing of this property [3415 Volta Place, N.W.] in his files was on December 8, 1937, when $100 was received from Alger or Priscilla Hiss for the rental of this property for a one-month period ending January 31, 1938."*[64]

On September 1, 1937, Hiss had signed with Gilliat for a one-year renewal of his lease on the 30th Street apartment, and the realtor recalled only that Hiss's request for the broker to find him a more spacious residence "was probably made . . . a few days prior to signing the lease in December of 1937." Although Hiss claimed that Gilliat had assured him that the $100 rental he offered for the Volta Place house was acceptable to the owners, Gilliat challenged this assertion: "He said that he did not believe he ever made any type of commitment to Hiss concerning either the availability [or the price] of the Volta Place house. . . ." Gilliat pointed out that his policy had always been to avoid such commitments until he had been "specifically authorized by the owners to do so."

The Volta Place home was owned by an ailing woman named Catherine F. Flanagan, whose daughter, Gladys, handled the rental arrangements. The Flanagans lived in the house until the end of October and early the following month listed it with several brokers, including Gilliat. Gladys Flanagan Tally also denied having made any "commitment" to Hiss through Gilliat in mid-November. Had the Flanagans accepted Hiss's offer at the time (which was $10 less than the monthly rental they had asked), it seems unlikely that they would have taken an advertisement in *The Washington Post* on December 5, announcing the house for rent, and allowing prospective renters to inspect the premises that same day:

---

*Gilliat was apparently off by a week, since Hiss and Catherine Flanagan, the owner, signed a lease for the Volta Place rental—with Gilliat witnessing the document—on December 2.

Georgetown, 3415 Volta Place, N.W.; remodeled house with attic; automatic heat; insulated; walled garden; terrace; sun deck; two stairways; open fire-places; large living room; open for inspection Sunday from 10 AM to 6 PM.

Since the house had been vacant from early November, Mrs. Tally returned to Washington to show it to those answering the ad. "To the best of her recollection Gilliat called her on December 6, 1937, mentioning that he had prospective tenants; that they were a young couple and the man was prominently placed but that she did not recall Gilliat on this date mentioning the Hisses by name."[65]

Gilliat first phoned her about the Hisses' interest in the Volta Place home after Mrs. Tally returned to Washington to handle inquiries about her advertisement. Gilliat's records show that although Hiss signed a lease on December 2, he left a $100 binder on the new home only on December 8. Several days later Mrs. Tally visited Priscilla Hiss at their 30th Street residence to discuss the features of the Volta Place home. On December 21 Mrs. Hiss wrote the Potomac Electric Power Company requesting that service at Volta Place be started beginning December 29, and in January the Hisses moved to their new home.[66]

Some informal commitment from Gilliat concerning the Volta Place residence probably preceded Mrs. Tally's December 5 advertisement by a few days, since a sublet arrangement for the 30th Street house prepared by Gilliat's firm was signed by Hiss and one Edward D. Hollander on December 2. But there is no proof that the Hisses had inspected the Volta Place house in November and abundant evidence that both Gilliat and the Flanagans believed Volta Place was still on the market prior to the arrangements made with the Hisses in early December. Moreover, Mrs. Hiss's reasons for borrowing $300 for the couple's checking account so soon after her $400 withdrawal are unknown. Although Chambers proved to be slightly wrong about both the amount and the date of the loan he recalled receiving from the Hisses to buy a new car, the fact that only four days separated Priscilla Hiss's $400 withdrawal and the purchase of his automobile remains an extraordinary coincidence. Other than believing Chambers, there exists no plausible explanation for how the Hisses spent the money that they withdrew three weeks before they rented the Volta Place home.[67]

Evelyn Morton, the Chamberses' maid, was not the only person to link the two couples directly in 1937. The family pediatrician, Dr. Margaret Nicholson,* saw Chambers in the Hisses' 30th Street home in January 1937 during a house call to attend Timothy Hobson. Chambers claimed later that he and Esther had been

---

*Dr. Nicholson's story was told to me by Claude Cross, Hiss's attorney at the second trial, and subsequently confirmed by Alger Hiss when I questioned him about the incident. Cross said he was present when Hiss's attorney John F. Davis returned from interviewing Dr. Nicholson, who had been subpoenaed as a government witness at Hiss's second trial for perjury and had contacted Hiss asking to see him on an urgent matter.

guests of the Hisses on New Year's Eve, December 31, 1936, at the 30th Street house, and that only the two couples had been present. Hiss was able to show that Priscilla Hiss and Timothy Hobson were visiting relatives in Chappaqua, New York, in late December when Timothy came down with chicken pox. Whether or not the "party'" took place cannot be determined, but Dr. Nicholson's records show that she made house calls at 30th Street to treat Timothy on January 2, 3, and 6, 1937. Therefore, Mrs. Hiss and her son evidently returned to Washington sometime between December 30 and January 2.*[68]

After completing one house call in January, Dr. Nicholson returned to her car only to discover that she had left her gloves behind. She went back to the house and rang the doorbell. Mrs. Hiss was home at the time, but not her husband. A heavy-set, "very gruff" man whom Dr. Nicholson had never met before answered the door and blocked her entrance. The doctor had not seen the man earlier while treating Timothy. The stranger asked what she wanted. She explained about the gloves, but he refused to allow her to reenter the house. "You may not come in!" Puzzled and presumably angry, Dr. Nicholson returned to her car and waited. A few minutes later the man came out of the front door and joined a second man who had been waiting near the house. They walked quickly away. From newspaper photographs in 1949 Dr. Nicholson recognized the man who had answered the door as Whittaker Chambers.†[69]

Believing that Alger and Priscilla Hiss were Communists who transmitted stolen documents requires less explanation in some ways than accepting the facts of their close relationship with Esther and Whittaker Chambers. A devotion to radical social reform and to militant antifascism might very well have turned a rising young bureaucrat into the paths of espionage. But would such devotion sustain a friendship of this character?

How can we explain the link between Chambers and the Hisses, a couple as reserved in their private relationships as they were ambitious in their respective

---

*Harold Rosenwald dispatched Davis to "try to find out from Dr. Nicholson whatever it may have been that she wanted to tell us." Davis returned with the story repeated to me by Cross. In a telephone conversation on August 1, 1974, Dr. Nicholson declined to discuss the matter. Davis told me that although the incident "probably happened," he has no recollection of his talk with Dr. Nicholson, nor is there a memo of the conversation in the Hiss Defense Files. Harold Rosenwald to John F. Davis, January 6, 1950; interview with John F. Davis, August 29, 1974; interview with Claude Cross, July 15, 1974; interviews with Alger Hiss, September 11, 1974, and June 21, 1975. Dr. Nicholson, according to Cross, told Davis she feared being questioned at the trial about having seen Chambers in the Hiss household, but, as it turned out, her testimony was limited only to confirming certain dates on which she treated Timothy.

†Alger Hiss told me that there was a memo of John F. Davis's interview with Dr. Nicholson in the Defense Files—I found no such memo—and that he recalled Davis coming to tell Cross and himself about her recollections. Hiss stated that Chambers had come undoubtedly "to sponge off Priscilla or ask us for help again. He was always doing that." Interview with Alger Hiss, September 11, 1974. Hiss said of the missing memo: "I remember the memo very well. And of course Claude had it before." Interview with Alger Hiss, June 21, 1975.

career goals? Whatever personal attraction Chambers may have held for the Hisses, it could not have come from his physical presence: perpetually disheveled, unkempt, and displaying a mouth full of rotting teeth. But Chambers spoke as a representative of world revolution, offering to a select handful of rising New Deal bureaucrats, and at remarkably little cost in time or energy, the fascination of dual lives as romantic conspirators. "Karl" stood for noble (and dangerous) ends: the defeat of fascist tyranny abroad and of liberal capitalist "tyranny" in America. Apparently, for the Hisses, he also offered some respite from the bourgeois super-respectability demanded of them by their backgrounds, their public associations, and their secret ideological commitments.

VII

SPIES AND BUREAUCRATS: THE STOLEN DOCUMENTS

THE CONSPIRATORS

When Whittaker Chambers's friend and former superior, "Ulrich" (Alexander Ulanovski), encountered Boris Bykov accidentally on a Moscow street in 1939, his first question was: "Are you still alive too?" Ulanovski did not like Bykov, but was genuinely surprised and delighted that he also had managed to survive the purges of 1936–39, since most of their colleagues had been arrested and either imprisoned or executed in the traumatic years of Stalinist terror.[1]

Impulsively, since it remained dangerous to converse with any but trusted friends, Bykov invited Alexander and Nadya to his home. They were old military-intelligence associates and had met first in Berlin in 1921 when Bykov worked for the Cheka, predecessor of the GPU. Several months earlier Bykov had returned from a two-year tour in the United States as Fourth Branch "Resident," Ulanovski's former post, and he could not resist bragging to the Ulanovskis about his "tremendous" accomplishments. He had agents "close to Roosevelt," Bykov asserted, placed strategically in the State, Treasury, and War departments, allegedly influencing policies and providing documents. When they left, Nadya and Alexander, impressed by their host's stories, still speculated on how much more effective the American operation might have become in those years had the "Resident" been someone other than Boris Bykov, whom the Ulanovskis considered a cowardly, free-spending opportunist, insensitive and unintelligent and easily distracted.

Colonel Boris Bykov, the chief agent for Russian Military Intelligence in the United States during the late 1930s, received low marks as a spymaster from every agent who worked with him and who later discussed his activities: Chambers, Maxim Lieber, William Edward Crane, Julian Wadleigh, and General Walter Krivitsky. A stocky, average-sized man in his forties with reddish-brown hair, Bykov took command of agents like Chambers who had worked formerly for J. Peters and for the hapless "Bill," Bykov's Russian predecessor.[2]

It quickly became apparent to Chambers that Bykov outranked J. Peters and that further reports would go directly to the Russian. "At my first and earlier meetings with Bykov," Chambers told the FBI in 1949, "we discussed the possibilities existing in Washington and just which individuals would be of the most value." Julian Wadleigh confirmed Chambers's recollection that Bykov was concerned about increasing the flow of information from within the American government. During a dinner with Bykov, the Russian "lectured to him about being more social-minded and urged him to meet more people and widen his acquaintance. Wadleigh repeated that the unknown subject [Bykov] told him his superior in Moscow thought Wadleigh should deliver more material than he had been doing and again gave instructions to procure any information which would enlighten them concerning the war which Germany and Japan were preparing against the Soviet Union."[3]

The Red Army's fears of a combined attack by Japan on the eastern borders and by Nazi Germany in the west determined the priorities of Soviet Military Intelligence. In Japan, as Richard Sorge, the leading Russian intelligence agent, confessed after his arrest, his orders were explicit: "It would not be far wrong to say that it was [my] sole object . . . to observe more closely Japan's policy toward the U.S.S.R. . . . and at the same time, to give very careful study to the question of whether or not japan was planning to attack the U.S.S.R." This responsibility, Sorge wrote after his capture, "entailed the obtaining of very broad military intelligence because the Japanese military, in order to justify their increased budget demands, were pointing to the Soviet Union as Japan's principal enemy."

The Soviets considered the United States—because of its long history of involvement in Pacific affairs, its close relationship to China, and its growing distrust of Japan—the other major source of Pacific intelligence. "The importance of activity in this field increased," observed one student of Soviet espionage in the United States during the mid-1930s, "as Soviet-Japanese relations deteriorated and 'border incidents' took on the proportions of an undeclared war." From the start of his association with Chambers, therefore, Bykov gave top priority to obtaining information from government contacts, notably in the State and Treasury departments—data regarding American economic policies toward Japan and about Japanese military actions, especially as these affected the Sino-Japanese War.[4]

Bykov asked to meet not only Wadleigh but also other contacts within the New Deal from whom Chambers received documents and information. Thus he met Alger Hiss by prearrangement at a Brooklyn movie theater early in 1937, according to Chambers, shortly after the Bokhara rugs had been delivered.* The three men walked through the streets of Brooklyn, took a subway to Manhattan, and had dinner at a restaurant in Chinatown. Chambers translated while Bykov, who spoke little English, talked in German:

---

*Chambers said he arranged a similar meeting between Bykov and Henry Collins during this period and encounters between the Russian agent and both Harry Dexter White and George Silverman.

Bykov spent some time explaining to Alger the seriousness of Fascism and its danger to Russia and the necessity of aiding Russia in every way and the importance of intelligence work in such aid. . . . Bykov specifically discussed with Hiss the possibility of the latter's bringing out documents from the State Department which might be copied and the originals returned. . . . As a result of this conversation, Alger agreed to bring out State Department documents. I recall that Bykov indicated that he was generally interested in anything concerning Germany and the Far East. . . .

It is my further recollection that it was understood that specific documents were not to be secured, nor were any secured, but rather Alger Hiss was to obtain any documents, on the particular subjects mentioned, or any others that Hiss would think as being of interest and which in the normal course of State Department business would come into his hands.[5]

Although Chambers is the only source for this conversation, Julian Wadleigh described receiving a similar pep talk from Bykov. This meeting apparently took place some time after the Hiss-Bykov encounter, since Wadleigh remembered the Soviet agent speaking English "well" but "with a distinct Russian accent":

After the introduction, we went to a restaurant for dinner. . . . [Bykov] lost no time in getting down to business. The people in Moscow, he told me, were not satisfied with the material I was turning in. They believed that a man who had access to what they received from me must also have access to many other valuable documents which I had not delivered. . . . I was really astonished to hear this. . . . The selection of documents for circulation to the Trade Agreements Division in the State Department was rather haphazard, and this was the reason for the spotty character of my contribution.

I assured [Bykov] that I was not holding anything back . . . [and] said: "Perhaps I don't really understand enough about what kind of material you want. Can you tell me anything about that?"

"We want everything," he replied, "that bears on the preparations the Germans and Japanese are making for war against us." He said this with an air of finality. . . .[6]

Others from whom Chambers later said he received documents in the fifteen months that followed these talks included Harry Dexter White (who often made contact with Chambers through A. George Silverman), Vincent Reno, who worked at the Aberdeen Proving Grounds, and William Ward Pigman of the National Bureau of Standards. Although Chambers knew other Washington bureaucrats involved in espionage, he claimed to have received documents primarily from these five officials.* Wadleigh and Reno later admitted complicity in the Russian

---

*When Chambers defected in April 1938, he took with him as evidence of underground complicity material received from at least four of these men.

spy ring—stealing documents, which they turned over to Chambers and other confederates. Hiss and White denied involvement, although damaging documentary evidence undermined the credibility of both men. Pigman also said he had never cooperated with Chambers. Through the activities of Chambers and his government sources, significant and secret information passed into Russian hands.[7]

Normally, Chambers would deliver information received from the bureaucrats-turned-spies to Bykov, who maintained headquarters in New York City, but who occasionally visited Washington. Although Walter Krivitsky would later tell Chambers of Bykov's constant fear of being shadowed by counterintelligence agents, Chambers soon found himself subject to the same apprehension. In an unpublished article written shortly after he cut his ties to the CP in 1938, Chambers described Bykov's anxieties about a meeting between himself, Chambers, and a Russian agent named "Ewald," in the arcades of Rockefeller Center's RCA Building. Chambers, who described Bykov in this account as "a neurasthenic Russian," later asked for his superior's impressions of the meeting with Ewald:

> The Russian, who spoke hardly a word of English, threw up his hands. "*Schrecklich,*" he said, "*überall nur Geheimpolizei und Ewald, Geheimpolizei und Ewald!*" "Terrible, everywhere nothing but secret police and Ewald, secret police and Ewald!" No doubt, the "secret police" were only the usual loiterers in the Rockefeller corridors, but the average Russian cannot be made to believe that things are not done everywhere as they are in Moscow—a credulousness which is played upon, incidentally, by certain paid Soviet sources whose lurid reports can be spotted instantly as fiction by any American, but are highly valued by the Russians who are convinced that Americans simply do not understand such things.[8]

Nor was Chambers contemptuous only of Bykov. Not since Ulrich's departure in 1934 had the Russians sent competent agents to oversee their American operations. Despite the creation in Washington of the Ware Group and of an important parallel apparatus under J. Peters's direction, Chambers looked back upon his earliest years in the underground nostalgically and with a measure of romanticized distortion, asserting inaccurately in his article that "the Soviet's spy organization was at its peak" in 1934.* Clearly, what attracted Chambers to the older patterns of Russian espionage was the sense of fraternity among its practitioners: "Prior to 1929, all Soviet secret agents of the single American apparatus used to meet together weekly in a big room and hold a regular party meeting, discussing the work of their unit in common. This was clubby, but by

---

*The article—and an accompanying one—are unique in their contemporary "inside" portrait of Soviet espionage techniques in the United States.

all traditions of espionage, amateurish and absurd. Nevertheless, during this period Soviet espionage worked without fatalities. And not because it was idle. Quite the contrary."[9]

But in 1929, according to Chambers, a restructuring of the spy network led to increased powers for the Soviet agent-in-charge, a decline in group discussion, and an insistence upon more rigorous procedures. American agents now kept in touch with one another only through the Soviet chief, were known to one another only by pseudonyms, and, "in so far as the work permitted, they were kept in ignorance of each other." Concentrating powers in the hands of Soviet "Residents" had not increased the effectiveness of intelligence work, however, at least not in Chambers's version: "Unfortunately, Soviet Chiefs since 1929 have been nearly always, not so much stupid, as abysmally ignorant of what they have to do and how to do it: hence the consistently descending curve of Soviet Intelligence abroad."

About J. Peters, whom Chambers called "Sandor" in the article ("a former Austrian army officer illegally resident in the United States"), he wrote in quite different terms: "[He] is one of the few American Communists who is at once decent and intelligent. 'Sandor' is the organizer of most of the illegal activities of the Communist Party in America." Peters, according to Chambers, "makes his reports to [Earl] Browder in person every day in the year except when either of them is traveling." As for Peters's work while on the road, he "is busy organizing the Party 'underground' in what Communists call 'strategic places'—to mention only the least strategic, the Post Office (mails are very important); the Labor Department (and not through Frances Perkins); the Treasury Department (from which a well-placed comrade every week sends the Party a really useful digest of information)." In this way "'Sandor' . . . sits, in the person of his underground Communists, in the councils of the American Government, [and] is in a position to, and has, more than once influenced Government decisions."[10]

But J. Peters had not controlled the changes in Russian intelligence practices in the United States during the mid-thirties when, according to Chambers, the old Soviet "espionage unit . . . was split up, its functions parceled out among several autonomous groups, each with its own chief, while the old agents were forbidden by command (usually ignored) to know one another in future. This was the celebrated system of 'parallel apparatuses,' the glamour word of 1935 in the Soviet secret services." Despite Chambers's objections to the system, it was under Bykov's direction and as a courier to one of the parallel apparatuses in Washington that he became most effective as a spy.

Chambers worked closely in 1936–38 with three photographers who, for security reasons, did not know of one another's existence, although all of them copied documents provided by the participating government officials. Most often he dealt with Felix Inslerman, in Baltimore, who in 1954 provided an account of his work to the FBI and to a congressional committee. Inslerman worked in 1935 with an Estonian named "Bill"—apparently the same person whom Chambers identified as Bykov's predecessor—and Bill introduced Inslerman to "Bob," Chambers's pseudonym at the time. That same year, at Bill's orders, Inslerman visited the Soviet Union, where he was trained in the use of a Leica camera and in writing code.[11]

After returning to the United States in December 1935, Inslerman worked for the underground, first, in New York City and, after the summer of 1936, in Baltimore. According to Chambers, he first brought Inslerman documents for photographing with his Leica—"a miniature camera [that] takes pictures on 35 millimeter film"—in late 1936 (Inslerman recalled having begun work-ing with Chambers the following year).* Also, Inslerman later said he photo-graphed documents on "five different occasions," while Chambers remembered many more.

Some of the material, Inslerman said, had come from the State Department: "I recall the name of [Ambassador] Grew.... And [Ambassador] Bullitt."† Chambers's instructions after delivering a batch of documents, according to Inslerman, "were to photograph them and the following day return the docu-ments back to him as well as the film.... The documents usually had to be returned by the following morning.... I delivered them to Bob... in Washington, except on the first occasion, when he came to my home." Inslerman had meetings in both Washington and Baltimore with "Bob," who also paid Inslerman for his work. He last photographed documents for Chambers, Inslerman said, "some-time in either late spring or early summer of 1938," after which Inslerman's other contacts in the CP underground told him that "Bob" had defected.‡[12]

Occasionally Chambers used another member of the ring to reproduce docu-ments. William Edward Crane, a trained and experienced California photogra-pher, had been brought East for secret work in 1934 by John Sherman. Crane told the FBI in 1949 that he worked on a part-time basis "with Chambers in New York, Washington, and Baltimore, but only recalls doing photographic work in New York and Baltimore" at Bykov's orders. Once, in Baltimore, Crane "photo-graphed Treasury Department and State Department documents every night for a week straight," he said. Concerning the contents of this material, Crane recalled

---

*Inslerman's lawyer, Louis Bender, told Hiss's attorney in 1949: "Bender is convinced, pre-sumably on the basis of his own client's statement to him, that Chambers was in fact engaged in stealing government documents in 1937 and 1938." FBI documents examiner Frederick E. Webb testified in 1949 at Hiss's perjury trial—a point conceded by the defense—that Inslerman's Leica had been used to photograph the State Department microfilm strips turned over by Chambers.

†The only cables from those diplomats that appeared in the material saved by Chambers and handed over in 1948 had either been typed on Alger Hiss's Woodstock or—in one case—involved a microfilmed "information copy" initialed by Hiss.

‡Inslerman received a dramatic warning letter from "Bob" after that time, described in Chap-ter IX.

only the name of one high State Department official, George Messersmith, about whom he said Chambers had talked.*[13]

Prior to mid-1937 Chambers either reproduced documents himself or used the services of a Communist photographer named David Zimmerman (who at times used the English translation of his name, "David Carpenter"). Carpenter remained a Communist in later years, unlike Inslerman and Crane, both of whom left the party. Chambers said he worked with Carpenter, who had been a professional agent for years, during the 1937–38 period, and the two men divided the task of meeting with government contacts to obtain material.

Carpenter's responsibilities included handling such sources as Ward Pigman and Julian Wadleigh, and Chambers normally met with Alger Hiss, Victor Reno, and Harry Dexter White. Sometimes Chambers contacted Carpenter's sources as well. When Wadleigh confessed his espionage activities to the FBI in December 1948, for example, he identified both men: Chambers as a person whom he had known as "Carl," and Carpenter as "Harold Wilson."[14]

While working for State in 1935 or 1936, Wadleigh told the FBI, he became friendly with "Harold Wilson." Alarmed at the growing power of Nazi Germany, of militarists in Japan, and of Fascist Italy, Wadleigh, a Socialist, became disturbed that the American government was not "actively involved" in opposing these governments. Wadleigh therefore told "Harold," a Communist, that he wanted to do "something active to fight against the rise of Fascist and reactionary powers." At this point "'Harold' invited me to supply information on economic conditions in Germany and Japan which he said he knew from the nature of my work I would be able to supply."[15]

Beginning sometime in 1936, Wadleigh handed over to "Harold" regularly, once a week, "documents which came to my desk [at Trade Agreements] in the course of my work. I selected those items that contained significant economic information on Germany and Japan and other items of special interest." Although Wadleigh could not recall the precise date, sometime in 1937 "Harold" took him to Baltimore to meet his superior, "Carl Carlson"—Whittaker Chambers. Although names were never mentioned, both informed Wadleigh that "they had contacts with other people of the same kind as myself [if only] because of their knowledge of events and personalities in the State Department. . . ."

Wadleigh's description of procedures used in passing documents matched Chambers's:

On evenings when I was scheduled to meet "Harold," I would go through the documents on my desk, make an appropriate selection, and take it out in a

---

*Messersmith's was the one name mentioned by Chambers in October 1948 when questioned in pretrial depositions by Hiss's lawyer, William Marbury, about the type of State Department files he claimed to have read in Hiss's home. At that point Chambers had not yet mentioned either an espionage link to Hiss or the theft of classified documents. FBI Report, March 4, 1949, #2706.

briefcase which I would hand to "Harold" when meeting him. I would meet "Harold" the next day on my way to work and bring the documents back. I was given to understand by "Harold" that he photographed the documents using a Leica camera. I believe that on one or more occasions I may have handed the papers to "Carl."

Late in 1938, after Wadleigh's return from Turkey where he had gone in March to negotiate a trade agreement, "Carl" met him for lunch "and informed me he had, as he put it, 'deserted.' Naturally I was alarmed." Wadleigh himself broke decisively with his other CP underground contacts by 1940.

His employment in State's Trade Agreements Division, which was under the direct supervision of Assistant Secretary Francis B. Sayre, brought Wadleigh into "fairly frequent contact" with Alger Hiss "to discuss matters of official business." The two men, however, had no personal contact outside their departmental responsibilities, and Wadleigh declared later that he knew nothing about Hiss's alleged involvement in "Carl's" underground work.*[16]

Vincent Reno also told the FBI in 1948 and 1949 about his espionage activities during the mid-thirties.† Reno had become a CP member in Richmond, Virginia, during the spring of 1933. In the summer of 1935 he moved to Washington, where he received "a confidential and important assignment" from the party to organize cells and recruit members in military posts. He remained a CP organizer without much success until the spring of 1937, when he met Chambers and Carpenter in Baltimore.[17]

Although Carpenter had told Reno that his new assignment would be "espionage work for the Soviet Union," Chambers—whom Reno knew as "Carl"—suggested that "a nicer word was 'intelligence' work." Reno had been hired recently as a mathematician at the Aberdeen Proving Grounds specializing in "calculus on a bomb sight," and "Carl" suggested that he collect "any and all important information pertaining to developments in Army Ordnance. . . ." Although Reno admitted having transmitted "small batches of material" four or five times to Chambers, which Inslerman photographed, he apparently had little contact with secret documents at Aberdeen. Instead, Reno began relying upon published material as the source of information he gave to "Carl," much of it concerning bombsights but not the classified Norden bombsight. Perhaps erroneously, Chambers later recalled Reno having given him material on this new and top-secret piece

---

*Wadleigh's former wife, Marian (then Mrs. Carroll Daugherty), confirmed her ex-husband's role in the CP underground when she spoke to the FBI in 1949. Mrs. Daugherty also said that Wadleigh told her in the spring of 1938 that "Carl" had broken with the underground. FBI Report, February 9, 1949, #1910.

†Adolf Berle's notes of his 1939 conversation with Chambers mentioned Reno as an agent: "*Vincent Reno*—Now at Aberdeen Proving Grounds—Computer—Math Assist. to Col. Zorning/ (Aerial bomb sight Detectors) Formerly CP organizer under alias 'Lance Clark.'"

of equipment. Reno a decade later minimized his own theft of secret documents handed over to Chambers, possibly fearing indictment, but in fact his contributions to Soviet knowledge of American weaponry appeared minor at best.

Whatever his precise usefulness as a spy, Reno described "possibly four to seven . . . meetings" with Chambers during a four- to nine-month period beginning in June 1937, when they first met. "The arrangement terminated possibly early in 1938 not by pre-arrangement," Reno told the FBI, "but Carl just didn't show up for a specified meeting. . . . Furthermore, [Reno] had gathered the impression from Carl on one or two of the later meetings that Carl planned either to go abroad or that Carl was pulling away from that type of activity."

For all of his thievery from the Aberdeen Proving Grounds, Reno claimed he had never received more than $30 from Carl. His motives for spying, in short, had been ideological, like Wadleigh's, and not financial. Reno believed, as did others in Chambers's circle of government contacts, that by cooperating in the theft of documents he would strengthen the Soviet Union and thereby strike a personal and effective blow in the struggle against fascism. He said he discontinued involvement in Communist activities shortly after he saw Chambers/Carl for the last time.[18]

Later confessions by Reno, Wadleigh, and Crane connected all three men to Chambers's Washington spy ring. Several government officials who denied participation in espionage were linked to the group's operations by documents that Chambers ferreted away and turned over a decade later. From January to April 1938, as Chambers planned his defection, he withheld and hid handwritten, typed, and microfilmed documents stolen by contacts in at least three government agencies. The material implicated Harry Dexter White, Alger Hiss, and possibly Julian Wadleigh and Ward Pigman. These documents represented a small percentage of what Chambers claimed to have transmitted to Bykov between December 1937 and April 1938, and after defecting in the spring of 1938 he threatened to expose his former associates in Soviet intelligence, using this documentary evidence of espionage.

THE WHITE MEMORANDUM

Whittaker Chambers's packet of "life preservers" included a four-page handwritten memorandum on lined yellow paper of Treasury and State Department activities. The memo seemed exactly the type of summary Chambers had described in his 1938 article, although it had been written over a period of weeks rather than at a single sitting. Handwriting experts from the FBI laboratory and the Veterans Administration identified the memo a decade later as having been written by Harry Dexter White.[19]

That Chambers mentioned White to Adolf Berle in 1939 seems apparent from Isaac Don Levine's envelope listing those named among Chambers's former sources in the government, although Berle never recorded White in his memo, which listed two other Treasury officials. Berle identified the weekly "digest of information" described by Chambers with one of these men: *"Treasury / Schlomer Adler* [Sol Adler?] / Counsel's Office / Sends weekly reports to C.P. (Gen. Counsel's Office) / Frank Coe / Now teaches at McGill. . . ."* But Chambers told the FBI in June 1945 that the nature of Adler's "weekly reports" differed markedly from the type of material later found in the four-page White memo. Adler had been in "close contact with [J.] Peter [sic]," Chambers said, and "made reports of a financial nature to Peter."[20]

The first accusations that White had been involved in passing Treasury Department information to the Communists came to the FBI not from Chambers but from Elizabeth Bentley. She described White's alleged role in wartime espionage in terms similar to Chambers's. According to Bentley, White not only passed along confidential data but also helped place influential Communists in sensitive positions within Treasury:

> For all this [Bentley later wrote] he was essentially a timid man and, as Greg [Nathan Gregory Silvermaster] put it, "he doesn't want his right hand to know what his left is doing." To keep him peaceful, Greg had to tell him that his material was going to one man in the American Communist Party's Central Committee, and nowhere else. Although he [White] indubitably knew that it was in reality going to Moscow, he didn't care to think about such things. After the [defection of] . . . Whittaker Chambers, White had promised his wife, who was not a Communist and disliked his revolutionary activities, that he would stay out of espionage in the future, and he lived in terror that she would find out that he had broken his word.

Neither Chambers nor Bentley ever accused White of CP membership. Both said that White seemed too fearful to join the party, even though he passed information to party couriers or through intermediaries. Chambers's relationship with White, he later recalled, "was never especially close. I had the impression that he did not like me nor did I especially like him."[21]

The Harry Dexter White memorandum may have been delivered to Chambers in two segments. The first three pages concern events that occurred in January 1938 (although January 10 and January 19 are the only dates mentioned), and the third page ends with a brief sentence on its reverse side. The fourth page picks up with an entirely different Treasury Department matter, dated February 15. The memo is crammed with news of important government business and with

---

*During a 1977 visit to the People's Republic of China, an economist who had worked in the New Deal asked to meet some local economic planners. Among those he met were Sol Adler and Frank Coe.

scraps of interesting trivia. It describes, among other things, Treasury Secretary Henry Morgenthau's attitudes toward actions being considered by the department; a confidential conversation between Morgenthau and President Roosevelt over economic policies toward Japan; a secret mission to England by an American naval captain to discuss a possible joint trading boycott of Japan by the two countries; Secretary Morgenthau's reading habits; Treasury reactions to future aggressive moves by Japan in the Far East; State Department attitudes toward European tensions; and even Ambassador Bullitt's reports on conversations with French officials.[22]

It is difficult to fathom any purpose in the line of official duties for which White could have put together this disparate collection of news in a single memo. The document flits from subject to subject, as these excerpts indicate:

> 1/10/38. Taylor tried to press the Secretary (indirectly through Feis to Hull to Sec.) to hurriedly accept an offer from Hungary of settlement of her 2 million dollar debt to U.S. Govt. [Herbert Feis, an adviser to Morgenthau; Cordell Hull, Secretary of State] . . . Sec. [Morgenthau] reading Red Star Over China and is quite interested.[23] . . . About 1 month ago, the Pres. asked Sec. M. to secretly place as many obstacles in the path of imports from Japan as possible under existing regulations . . . State Dept. believes British moves toward Italy and Germany will reduce substantially European fear of war in the near future. If Japan repeats another incident like the Panay incident Treasury machinery is all ready to embargo Japanese imports into U.S. & freeze her dollar resources. This was done at the Pres. wishes. *It remains unknown outside of Treasury* [italics added].
>
> Bullitt just cabled to Sec. (copy not available) comment by Herriot, Blum, Reynaud to him. [All were leading French politicians.] Herriot says that if he were premier he would quickly strengthen ties to U.S.S.R. & reassure Czech that France will at once come to her military aid if Germany enters Czech . . . (via Cochrane) [a State Department official] Bachman of the Swiss. Nat Bank said 2/15/38 that the Japanese have recently put out a feeler to some of his banks for industrial development in Manchouko [sic]. . . .

These portions of the White memorandum suggest the reliable and important quality of the information. The memo described key presidential decisions taken concerning future relations with Japan that "remain[ed] unknown outside of Treasury," the confidential mission of a military officer sent to England, secret State Department cables from Ambassador Bullitt in Paris ("copy not available," presumably for microfilming, observed White), and valuable information on the economic resources of Japan and China—all in four pages. By any standard of espionage, Chambers had good reason to call this Treasury Department transmission "a really useful digest of information." Moreover, the type of material on which White reported in the memo closely resembled the subjects covered by the State Department documents—typed, microfilmed, and handwritten—that Chambers said he collected from Alger Hiss and then ferreted away.

Under Secretary of the Treasury Edward H. Foley, Jr., told the FBI in June 1949 that the data on the four sheets of lined yellow paper in White's handwriting had originated in Treasury Department documents, the release of which at the time to any "unauthorized person . . . would have been of help during [the] pertinent period to [an] unfriendly power." Foley added that even a casual glance at the information indicated that "most of this material is highly confidential and in many instances involves our relations with friendly foreign powers."[24]

A major study by David Rees sifted the evidence for White's alleged involvement in Communist spying. Rees concluded that, "on the whole, the story of the witnesses [Chambers and Bentley] regarding White was correct." In summing up his assessment, Rees noted:

> We have also seen that, as well as the silent evidence of the documents produced by Chambers, the so-called White Memorandum, his [Chambers's] story and that of Elizabeth Bentley were partly corroborated by each other. For Chambers had mentioned White . . . to the State Department security officer, Ray Murphy, in 1945, before Miss Bentley went to the authorities. We have also noted the comments of Professor [Herbert] Packer [in his book *Ex-Communist Witnesses*] that "it seems most reasonable to assume that what probably happened was what appears to have happened, namely that Miss Bentley and Chambers, independently and without knowledge of each other's stories," named White to the authorities at two different times. And that, Professor Packer concluded, "'is corroboration of a kind that cannot lightly be dismissed." . . . The writer [Rees] considers that the arguments against the credibility of Miss Bentley and Chambers on the central issue regarding White are not sustained.*[25]

THE NAVY DEPARTMENT MICROFILM

Before breaking with the spy ring in 1938, Chambers withheld not only White's memorandum but also two strips and three rolls of microfilm, two rolls of which contained documents from the Navy Bureau of Aeronautics. Chambers later told the FBI "that he obtained no information directly from [the] Navy Department and had no source of information at that department. Further . . . he believes that [the] Navy Department documents [were] furnished to him by Ward Pigman,

---

*White's complicity in Soviet espionage was confirmed in 1995–96 with release of the VENONA intercepts, in which White figures prominently as an American source of classified information for the Soviets. During the years in which he cooperated with the NKVD, White was assigned various code names, specifically "LAWYER," "RICHARD," and "REED." See also Weinstein and Vassiliev, *The Haunted Wood*, for a description of White's relationship with Soviet intelligence agents, both American and Russian.

then employed in [the] Bureau of Standards, [who] abstracted Navy documents from files of [the] Bureau of Standards and furnished them to Chambers," who had them photographed before returning them. According to Chambers, David Carpenter reproduced all of the material Pigman delivered, usually getting it directly from Pigman, although occasionally Chambers made the pickup himself. Normally, Carpenter delivered the microfilmed rolls to Chambers, who took them to Bykov in New York.[26]

The Navy Department documents on the two microfilmed rolls, all prepared in December 1937 and January 1938 under the direction of Rear Admiral A. B. Cook, then chief of the Bureau of Aeronautics, were technical memos, some of which were not secret and may even have been placed at the time in the Bureau of Standards library (Chambers obviously had no way of knowing this when his source delivered the material). A few of the memos could hardly have interested any foreign power. One, for example, provided instructions on the proper method of painting fire extinguishers. But other documents on the two rolls concerned new technical data on aircraft fuel systems, parachutes, radio transmitters, fuel-pressure settings, carburetors, inertia starters, and other major elements in current American aircraft equipment. Although the Navy Department memos were unclassified and were distributed to the Bureau of Standards, where Chambers's contact obtained them, such up-to-date military information was sought by the Russians, and neither Chambers nor Carpenter—who dealt (according to Chambers) with Pigman—had the scientific background to evaluate the data's importance. Apparently Pigman (or someone else) fobbed off unclassified material on Chambers more successfully than Vincent Reno, who recalled once having given "Carl" a standard manual on Army ordnance, in which the latter expressed little interest.[27]

Ward Pigman later said he had never passed documents to Chambers, did not even know the man, and did not participate in any form of espionage. He admitted having known David Carpenter (as "David Zimmerman") during the midthirties, when Pigman belonged to a radical union of government employees in Washington, D.C., called the Federation of Architects, Engineers, Chemists and Technicians, but could not say a decade later if Zimmerman had been a union official "or just what his connection was." Pigman admitted to the FBI that he "may have seen Zimmerman on one or two occasions from 1936 until Pigman went to Europe in the summer of 1938, but he recalls no instance." Although Pigman insisted that they had never met, he told Alger Hiss's lawyer after a grand jury appearance in December 1948 that Chambers "apparently described the inside of [his] house."

But Pigman's involvement in the spy ring remains unproved, and there was no independent confirmation for Chambers's claim that Pigman had provided documents for the two rolls of Navy Department microfilm."[28]

ALGER HISS'S HANDWRITTEN NOTES

Most of the materials that Chambers saved as "life preservers" were confidential State Department documents he said he received from Alger Hiss. According to Chambers, Hiss had provided the spy ring with many more documents. The batch he retained represented only a portion of the transmissions from Hiss between January and April 1938.

"The method of transmitting this material was as follows," Chambers later told the FBI. "Alger Hiss would bring home original documents from the State Department over night as 'a matter of custom.' On the agreed night, I would go to the 30th Street house and Alger would then turn over to me a zipper case containing these documents." Chambers remembered photographing the documents himself at first at the Baltimore apartment that David Carpenter rented: "Subsequently . . . the photographic work was taken over by Felix [Inslerman]. . . . After photographing the documents, I would return them on the same night to Alger Hiss in Washington. I usually traveled between Washington and Baltimore by Pennsylvania Railroad."[29]

Felix Inslerman's confession confirmed Chambers's testimony concerning his role as an underground CP photographer. In 1948 Chambers took Baltimore FBI agents to the apartment building in which Inslerman had lived during the 1937–38 period, even before the bureau had found and identified Inslerman.* Once Felix began working with Chambers, he would drive to Washington by prearrangement and pick up the material to be reproduced, normally returning it to Chambers later that evening in Baltimore. Chambers would then travel back to Washington and return the documents to Hiss.

Generally, Chambers said, he received such packets from Hiss "once a week or once in every ten days." Hiss "produced documents regularly from early 1937 until April, 1938." Chambers started acquiring both typed and handwritten information from Hiss in addition to the microfilmed documents, he asserted, because of Bykov's insistence on "more complete coverage." Hiss's deliveries of documents for microfilming each week or ten days allowed Chambers access only to those materials "that happened to cross his [Hiss's] desk on that day, and a few that on one pretext or another he had been able to retain on his desk." If Hiss brought home a briefcase each night filled with items of interest to the Russians, these could then "be typed in the Hiss household, either in full or in summary. Then, when I next visited him, Alger would turn over to me the typed copies, covering a week's documents, as well as the brief case of original documents that

---

*Since Wadleigh, Chambers's other source at State, worked directly with David Carpenter, Chambers recalled that only Hiss's transmissions—not Wadleigh's—went to his other photographer, Felix Inslerman.

he had brought home that night." Chambers would have the originals repro-duced and returned to Hiss: "The typed copies would be photographed and then returned to me by Felix. I would destroy them."[30]

The handwritten notes represented a third method of delivery, which began—according to Chambers—because of Hiss's efforts to inform him about important departmental documents that came into his hands only briefly, "often only long enough to read them." "He took to making penciled copies of such documents or notes of their main points, which he wrote down hastily on State Department memo pads. These he turned over to me also, usually tearing off the State Depart-ment's letterhead lest I forget." Chambers saved the White memorandum and four of Alger Hiss's scribbled notes when he began collecting "life preservers" in early 1938. Later that year, after defecting, Chambers wrote Meyer Schapiro that he had sent a warning to his former underground associates, enclosing "photo-graphic copies of handwritten matters the appearance of which would seriously embarrass them."[*31]

Although Hiss later claimed that Chambers could have fished the four memos out of a wastebasket in his office, none showed evidence of having been crumpled up or tossed away when Chambers turned them over in 1948. All were nearly folded in half. Three of the notes dealt with military matters and one with an American couple arrested in the Soviet Union, a story then on the front pages of American newspapers. None of the four memos related to questions of trade agreements or international economics that concerned Hiss and Sayre. Two of the original State Department cables summarized in the handwritten memos did contain sec-tions relating to international trade, but Hiss did not bother transcribing them.[32]

There is even more compelling evidence that Hiss passed the handwritten summaries to Chambers early in 1938 as the latter claimed. After breaking with the CP later that year, Chambers recorded one of the notes almost verbatim in one of his articles on Soviet espionage. Also, Hiss's superior, Francis Sayre, later denied having been interested in the subject matter of these memos in 1938—Hiss said he had copied them to brief Sayre—and Sayre could not understand why he had even been sent the original copy of the most damaging of these notes, the one transcribed by Chambers in his 1938 article.

Three handwritten notes summarized March 1938 cables. The first of these, a March 2 dispatch from the American Embassy in Paris to Secretary Hull about

---

*Chambers also alerted the CP about his intention to expose State Department espionage later in 1938 in a letter he sent via Inslerman, who copied portions of the document before passing it along to his underground superiors. See Chapter IX for a complete account of this episode. That same year, another major Soviet agent, Alexander Orlov, used the same strategy to keep himself and his family from being killed by Soviet pursuers. After defecting, Orlov wrote directly to Stalin via intermediaries detailing his knowledge of Soviet espionage activities: "I would publish everything I knew, he warned, should there be retribution against his family." See John Costello and Oleg Tsarev, *Deadly Illusions* (New York: Crown, 1993), pp. 305–12.

the U.S. response to the Sino-Japanese War, concerned recent orders placed by China for thirty late-model French fighter-bomber pursuit planes of the type called "Potez-63," the information having come from the American military attaché in Paris. (Unlike the other three handwritten memos, this note by Hiss broke off in mid-sentence with the phrase "a light bomber pursuit." This suggests that Chambers may have delivered its second page to Bykov, thinking it too important to withhold from his Russian superior without calling attention to his own impending defection, had Bykov learned its contents in some other way, since the March 2 cable went on to describe Soviet financing and shipment of airplanes and war matériel to China.)[33]

A second section of the March 2 message from Paris, cabled later that same day, was of even greater concern to the Soviet Union. It reported the conclusion of the French Ambassador to Japan that, although the Russian government intended "to refrain from taking any more direct or aggressive interest in the China-Japanese conflict . . . he nevertheless has the 'feeling' that the Japanese may be preparing for a move against the Russian maritime provinces." Although the informant in the French Foreign Office did not agree, the cable cited the view of unnamed "Japanese army chiefs . . . that they will be able to wage a successful war against Russia while holding the Chinese in check on their flank with little difficulty."

But the original of that same March 2 cable began with information of immediate and utmost concern to Sayre and Hiss that dealt with the reaction of European governments whose nationals had loaned money to China, and the probable impact on such loans of Japanese decisions to place customs duties from occupied Chinese ports in Japanese banks. Hiss did not copy this, thereby omitting the only important part of the cable that would be of interest to an American specialist in international economic relations.[34]

The transcription Hiss made of the second cable, a March 3 dispatch from London to Secretary Hull, also omitted the single passage that related directly to American policymakers at State. The cable recorded a private talk between the American naval attaché in England and a British admiral, Lord Chatfield, about British naval maneuvers. Hiss summarized thoroughly that portion of the wire that concerned the question of whether Chatfield intended to move ahead with plans for constructing new battleships and cruisers that year. Although the second page of Hiss's note on the March 3 cable was blank except for completing the sentence carried over from the first page, the cable itself went on to mention the only information of conceivable interest to a State Department official in Washington: that both the Foreign Office and Chatfield wished further discussions on the subject with American authorities before proceeding with their plans.[35]

The third handwritten note—dated March 11—concerned the Sino-Japanese War. Again, it omitted a long section of the original cable that dealt with Sayre's primary concern in the conflict, its impact upon international economic relations. According to the Hiss transcription:

> Mar. 11 Gauss U.S. consul at Shanghai cabled that military observers estimated that over 70,000 reinforcements with considerable quantities of heavy artillery have landed at Woosung during past 2 weeks. Over 50% are believed destined for southern Tainpu front, rest to be distributed between Wuhu, Hangchow & along the lines of communication.

But after disclosing this purely military information, which Hiss copied, the cable discussed the arrival in Shanghai of a Japanese minister named Tani, who had been assigned to coordinate his country's diplomatic work in Central and North China. The minister brought news of vital importance to makers of America's international economic policy, whatever its reliability. Tani, according to Japanese newsmen cited by Gauss, reported Japan's intention "to respect fully foreign rights and interests in China." Referring specifically to Anglo-Japanese relations, the cable quotes Tani as observing that "there can be no friction between Japan and Britain unless Japan infringes British trade interests and vested rights in the Orient. . . . Japan must pay careful attention to this point so as not to violate Britain's rights and interests."[36]

The analogy to *America's* "rights and interests" did not have to be spelled out by the U.S. consul at Shanghai, especially since Tani also praised the emergence of Neville Chamberlain's "appeasement" policies in England as "the replacement of idealism by realism" in British diplomacy. The signal seemed clear: The United States should stop supporting the Chinese government and accept Japanese conquests in China as the price for protection of American economic interests there. Since Sayre's office was then deeply involved in State Department consultations on future American trading policies toward Japan, the omission of this key portion of Gauss's March 11 cable in Hiss's transcription—and similar omissions in the two earlier handwritten notes—becomes inexplicable if the memos had been prepared for Sayre.

The earliest of the four cables jotted down by Hiss, dated January 28, 1938, seemed, on its face, mysterious:

M 28
Tel from Mary Martin widow of Hugh Martin formerly employed for special work by Legation at Riga
   Remember well Rubens while working for Hugh, be strict if needed,
   Write Lib. Cong., Law Div.

"M" presumably meant "Moscow," the cable's heading, since it had been sent to Secretary Hull in Washington by the American chargé d'affaires in the Soviet Union, Loy Henderson, informing Hull that he had received the telegram he quoted from "Mary Martin." Hiss copied the complete Henderson cable.[37]

The January 28 dispatch from Henderson to Hull concerned an American woman who had been arrested in Moscow after complaining to foreign newsmen that her husband had been arrested previously. On January 25, *The New York Times* printed one of several stories on the case, stating that the matter had become of concern to the United States government. Hull directed American officials in Moscow to see the woman in prison.

The episode referred to in the January 28 cable by Mary Martin involved a Soviet agent in the United States known to Chambers as "Ewald," who had been ordered back to Moscow in 1937 at the height of the purges. "Adolf A. Rubens" took his American-born wife, Ruth Boergers, with him, apparently gambling that his superiors would not dare imprison or execute him with his wife there to complain to the American Embassy and to newsmen. Ewald and his wife used two sets of false American passports on their journey from the United States to the Soviet Union, passports made out to couples named "Robinson" and "Rubens."

But Ewald's gamble failed. He was arrested soon after arriving in Russia, charged with espionage for the Nazis. After his wife began making the rounds of hotels frequented by American newsmen to complain about her husband's arrest, she, too, was apprehended. At this point, in December 1937, the case began making headlines. Loy Henderson demanded to see Mrs. Rubens in order to verify her U.S. citizenship.[38]

Henderson's cable referred to a telegram he had received from Mary Martin, the widow of a former leading American intelligence agent (hence its reference to "special work") in Riga, Latvia, then an independent country, and the United States's nearest and most important listening post for Soviet affairs during the 1920s, before the establishment of U.S.-Soviet diplomatic relations. Mrs. Martin apparently intended to inform Henderson that Rubens was a Soviet agent whom she had known earlier in Riga. Her warning—"be strict"—cautioned the diplomat against becoming involved on the arrested agent's behalf, despite Mrs. Rubens's American citizenship.[39]

Several weeks after cabling State the contents of Mary Martin's telegram, Henderson finally managed to interview Mrs. Rubens in prison. He sent the State Department a long report of the meeting, one of at least eight cables dealing with the Robinson/Rubens case that were sent to Washington during the three months beginning December 1937. None of these—including the January 28 Mary Martin telegram transcribed by Hiss—had any relationship to Francis Sayre's work on international economic agreements. The Communist underground, on the other hand, would have been intensely interested, since this episode had caused a serious and abrupt deterioration in Soviet-American relations. The following year Adolf Berle's notes of his interview with Chambers about Russian espionage included this statement just below an entry on Alger Hiss: "When Loy Henderson interviewed Mrs. Rubens his report immediately went back to Moscow. Who sent it?—Such came from Washington." There exists not only Alger Hiss's exact copy of Loy Henderson's January 28 telegram to suggest the answer to Berle's question, but equally compelling evidence that Hiss's transcription (delivered to Chambers) reached Soviet intelligence at the time.

One of several articles that Chambers wrote on Soviet espionage in the United States in November 1938, "The Faking of Americans: 1. The Soviet Passport Racket," devotes a great deal of attention to the activities of the agent "Ewald" (Mr. Robinson/Rubens). The manuscript described Ewald's work in the collection and preparation of fake American passports (known as "boots") for Soviet agents and discussed what happened to Ewald after he returned to the Soviet Union.[40]

In one remarkable passage of his article Chambers not only recorded almost verbatim the Mary Martin cable transcribed by Alger Hiss but also explained the reasons for Soviet interest in Henderson's dispatch.*[41]

Chambers was obviously familiar with the Mary Martin wire, presumably through Hiss's copy of that cable. And so similar are Henderson's February 10 dispatch concerning his interview with Mrs. Rubens and Chambers's description of that interview in his 1938 article that it is reasonable to conclude that Chambers had read Henderson's cable on the episode. Chambers's nearly exact quotation of Loy Henderson's January 28 telegram confirms that among the "handwritten matters" he possessed when he wrote his warning letter to former comrades in Soviet espionage that same year was the Mary Martin cable he said had been given him by Alger Hiss.[42]

The facts are highly significant: Alger Hiss transcribed Henderson's confidential Mary Martin telegram in January 1938, although the dispatch had nothing to do with his duties for Sayre; Chambers restated the memo practically verbatim in an article later that year (along with material from other secret cables sent by Henderson during the same period); and in 1948 Chambers turned over Hiss's verbatim copy of the Mary Martin cable along with summaries of three other secret State Department documents, all in Hiss's handwriting.[†]

When later confronted with the four memos, Hiss acknowledged having written the three partial summaries, but initially said that the Mary Martin transcription was not in his handwriting. He stuck by this in discussions with his attorneys until the spring of 1949, when FBI laboratory experts and Hiss's own handwriting examiners confirmed that he had transcribed Henderson's cable.[43]

Hiss explained that he frequently wrote memos to himself, such as the four turned over by Chambers, to brief Sayre on departmental dispatches passing

---

*Chambers also discussed the Robinson/Rubens case at this time with Herbert Solow, who prepared a notarized memo of his discussions with Chambers on November 28, 1938.

†Recently released NKVD files for that period indicate the importance to Soviet authorities in Moscow of the Robinson/Rubens case and of foreign response to the matter. See Klehr et al., *The Secret World of American Communism*, pp. 95–96, and Weinstein and Vassiliev, *passim*.

through the office. When asked by his attorney whether there was any military information in the four handwritten notes, Hiss replied: "Only in the sense that they refer to munitions to China from France." In fact the three memos other than the Mary Martin cable were entirely concerned with military information. Asked why he had drawn the matters described in the three March 1938 memos to Sayre's attention, Hiss told his attorneys that although Sayre's area of responsibility lay in international economics, "he was interested in subsidiary matters as they affected neutrality, the Philippines or the League of Nations." Moreover, he "was naturally very much interested in the developments of the Sino-Japanese war as they affected the military security of the Philippines." Although these "interests" of Sayre might conceivably account for Hiss's having scribbled notes on the cables that dealt with the Potez-63 planes (March 2) and Japanese reinforcements in China (March 3), they did not account for the Admiral Lord Chatfield (March 3) and Mary Martin (January 28) memos. Hiss was vague on the Chatfield cable: "The answer, I think, is that the higher officers of the department were kept generally informed of over-all developments." As for Mary Martin, Hiss answered simply that he had not written that particular memo. But his own documents examiners stated that he had.[44]

When questioned in 1948 and 1949 by the FBI and by Hiss's attorneys, Sayre proved unhelpful to the defense. Although he stated that he did not believe Hiss had been a Soviet agent, Sayre said he had not asked Hiss to prepare briefing memos such as the four handwritten notes: "Sayre did not admit that he recalled having seen written memoranda prepared by Hiss like the samples produced by Chambers." But Sayre "did not deny that such memoranda were written."

According to Sayre, he did not remember discussing military information with Hiss, had little interest in such matters, and did not understand why copies of departmental cables on the Robinson/Rubens case—in which he had *no* interest whatsoever—had been sent to his office. On the last point, Sayre told the FBI "that he was always disturbed by the Robinson cable [the Mary Martin wire transcribed by Hiss] as the handwritten note on this cable [Hiss's transcription] seemed to be of a personal nature and he could not understand why he was on the distribution list for this cable or why the note would be made on it or especially why an exact copy should have been made." Sayre repeated the last point to Hiss's attorney in October 1949 in categorical terms: "He does not recall giving any specific instructions to Alger Hiss to abstract telegrams." In a subsequent conversation with the defense lawyer, Sayre rejected Hiss's claims more explicitly, stating about the handwritten notes that he "does not recall that it was Alger's duty to 'sift' cables and digest them and make oral report on [their] contents . . . ."[45]

Under close questioning by Hiss's attorney in the same interview, Sayre began to shift his recollections slightly: "Alger did make handwritten memos on documents which Sayre asked him to read. These would be brief opinions, recommendations for action, etc. They would not be summaries of the contents." When asked at a December 1948 HUAC hearing by Richard Nixon: "Did Mr. Hiss, at his home, have as one of his duties the paraphrasing of these documents and bringing them back to you in this way [as handwritten memos]?" Sayre bluntly disavowed Hiss's assertions: "The answer is 'No.'" And the next month he told Hiss's attorney "that the handwritten notes are too complete to be summaries which Alger would have prepared for him. . . . Would not have been part of Alger's duty to prepare such summaries for Sayre. Never knew of Alger dictating such summaries."[46]

Two secretaries worked for Sayre and Hiss, Anna Belle Newcomb and Eunice A. Lincoln. Newcomb later recalled that Hiss "would sometimes attach brief handwritten summaries of cables to the cable and send it in or take it in to Sayre. . . . Newcomb thinks these memoranda were left on the cables when they came out of Sayre's office and were returned with the cable to be destroyed along with the cable." Sayre agreed that this was possible, but, when told of Newcomb's statement, he could not remember the practice. However, when shown copies of Hiss's handwritten notes, Anna Belle Newcomb observed: "The handwritten notes, Exhibits 2, 3 and 4, do not look like the sort of summaries that Alger made. She thinks they are too detailed. She does not recall that Sayre was interested in cables relating to military information."[47]

According to Eunice A. Lincoln, however, Sayre was correct and Newcomb wrong: "It was certainly not the practice for Hiss to attach summaries of telegrams to the telegrams themselves that Sayre was to see. Miss Lincoln does not recall ever seeing any summaries of telegrams, handwritten or otherwise." Moreover, she never saw Hiss report verbally to Sayre on the contents of departmental cables, nor did she see Hiss "refresh his recollection from handwritten notes in making such reports."[48]

Hiss conferred with Sayre once in February 1949 and tried to "refresh" his former superior's recollection of Hiss's version of the handwritten notes. The results emerge best in Hiss's lawyer's account of the meeting:

> Sayre said that he had never seen such notes while Alger worked for him. Alger said he would not expect him to have seen them, that Alger would have had them for his own use. Sayre said that he did not think that the information in the notes was anything that he would have been interested in. Alger pointed out that Sayre was interested in disarmament, in the London Naval Treaty, neutrality matters and matters pertaining to the Philippines. . . . Sayre was noncommittal but did admit that he was interested in following disarmament and neutrality matters.[49]

Nor did Hiss's predecessor, John S. Dickey, prove helpful. When questioned by Hiss's attorney in January 1949 about the practice of briefing Sayre through handwritten notes, Dickey made it clear that if Sayre had asked Hiss to brief him using such notes, the practice conflicted with Sayre's instructions to Dickey. Like Hiss, Dickey read all incoming mail and cables, selecting those he felt Sayre would want to see. Occasionally he appended a short note to a departmental cable, commenting generally and briefly on its contents: "'This is interesting' or 'This relates to such and such.'" But Dickey seldom reported orally to Sayre on such documents, as Hiss claimed to have done. Moreover, "Dickey did not write out summaries of cables. Sayre did not ask him to abstract dispatches or cables and he did not do so. Specifically, he did not make summaries of cables such as the handwritten notes in our case." According to Dickey, "Sayre was not interested in military matters and Dickey would not normally have sent him cables on such matters." In any event, "he would not have abstracted or summarized them," as in Hiss's four handwritten notes. In the end, Dickey felt he should not testify in 1949 on Hiss's behalf "because of vulnerability on cross examination as to the practices in Sayre's office, particularly with respect to not making summaries of documents."[50]

THE STATE DEPARTMENT MICROFILM

Included in the material Chambers turned over in 1948 were two strips of developed microfilm that contained fifty-eight separate prints. The microfilm consisted mainly of memoranda dealing with German-American trade negotiations, and the FBI laboratory established in 1949 that the two strips had been photographed and exposed by Felix Inslerman's 35-milimeter Leica camera.* Although the covering document on the first strip is a two-page letter to Francis Sayre on the trade negotiations, dated January 8, 1938, from Harry C. Hawkins, then chief of State's Trade Agreements Section, the letter and four enclosures attached to it may have been taken by Wadleigh (who worked in Trade Agreements) and not Hiss. The letter from Hawkins to Sayre and the enclosed memo by another departmental official, Charles F. Darlington, urged that State consider more sympathetically a reciprocal trade agreement with Nazi Germany on a number of grounds. News that key officials at State proposed a policy of closer economic cooperation with Germany during a period of increasing tension in Europe would probably have been of interest to all European countries, including the Soviet Union. The documents appended to Hawkins's letter included a sixteen-page letter, dated December 31, 1937, from Darlington to Hawkins; Darlington's four-page proposed memorandum to the German government on future trade; a fourteen-page

---

*FBI laboratory tests also confirmed that the fifty-eight panels on the two strips had been developed at the same time on a single photographic run. FBI Laboratory Report Februrary 23, 1949; FBI Report, Agents Sizoo to Harbo, December 13, 1949; testimony of Agent Frederick L. Webb, Second trial, pp. 1301–08.

aide-mémoire (in German) sent by Nazi officials to the State Department earlier in 1937; and a twelve-page State Department *aide-mémoire* on the question of German trade, dated July 21, 1937.[51]

Several of these documents—including the covering letter by Hawkins—were carbon copies rather than originals, and they did not bear Sayre's characteristic boxed date stamp, found on the remaining microfilmed documents. The FBI suggested in 1949 that it was "highly probable . . . that a carbon as well as an original copy of this memorandum, was sent to Mr. Sayre, which would account for the possession by Hiss of a carbon copy, rather than an original." Francis Sayre agreed, in talking to Hiss's lawyers, "that he might have wanted to have carbon copies of these [German trade] papers to send to [other divisions of State], or he might have preferred to send the original file to them" and keep a carbon for himself.[52]

Francis Sayre wavered but, in the end, he decided the documents had come from another office. For one thing, the microfilmed carbon did not have a corrected letter inserted on the original he had received from Hawkins. For another, Sayre did not read German and he felt that, had the German government document been his copy, "the English translation would certainly have been sent to him along with the Aide-Memoir [sic]."[53]

But Wadleigh later denied that he had stolen the memos on German trade agreements for Chambers: "There is a possibility that I may have handed this [material] to Chambers, but I think it is most improbable that I did. . . . To the best of my recollection I did not see these particular documents, and I did not work on this German Trade Agreement at the time when these documents were prepared."* Hiss also denied handing over the trade-agreement file—or any other documents—to Chambers.[54]

Although most of the evidence suggests that Wadleigh delivered the material on German trade agreements, sharing the second strip of microfilm with these documents are three January 1938 State Department cables—ten pages in all—that bear Sayre's office date stamp and Alger Hiss's initials. None of the three "information copies" of confidential dispatches, some portions of which were cabled in code, had been sent to Wadleigh's Trade Agreements Section.[†]

---

*John Chabot Smith mistakenly asserted that "It took long hours of cross-examination to draw this admission from" Wadleigh, whose testimony about the German trade agreements remained consistent in 1948–50 throughout FBI interrogations and Hiss's two perjury trials. Smith, *op. cit.* p. 347. Hiss summarizes the argument for Wadleigh's complicity in his memoir, *In the Court of Public Opinion,* pp. 251–59.

†State Department practice at the time involved distributing both "action" and "information" copies of incoming material. After the message was decoded and typed on a stencil, an "action" copy would be run off first on yellow paper and routed to the office primarily concerned with the data. "Information" copies would then be run off on white paper and sent to any departmental office that might have some interest in the cable The "action" copy would later be returned to the filing room for retention. Although "information" copies would normally be returned also for

The sequence of events surrounding these three January 13 cables weakens Hiss's claim that he did not supply Chambers with any of the microfilmed material. The information copies did come from Sayre's office, and Hiss's initials indicate familiarity with the documents. But State Department routing slips proved that no copies of these cables had been sent to Wadleigh's department. Also, Sayre was away from the office on January 14, 1938, when Hiss initialed the three cables.[55]

"In accordance with Department practice," Hiss later wrote, "I had initialed the cables to show that I had seen them and had finished with them." But Sayre told the FBI "that the documents which bore his office stamp January 14, 1938 were stamped into his office on a day on which he was not working," which made it particularly curious that Hiss avowed he had disposed of the important dispatches without waiting until the next working day to show them to his superior:

> [Sayre] then took a diary out of his desk for the year 1938 and showed [FBI] agents where on January 14, which was a Friday, he was on leave. On Saturday, the 15th and Sunday, the 16th, he was likewise not working. . . . He stated that he did not know why he was off on the 14th, where he went or what significance the date has. He said he had no idea whatsoever on the matter.

The two secretaries confirmed his recollection that they always stamped documents immediately upon their arrival. The three cables reached Sayre's office on the 14th in his absence, therefore, and apparently were read quickly by Hiss.[56]

All three dealt with the Sino-Japanese War.[57] Two of the three cables concerned aspects of the war of immediate, even urgent interest to the Soviet Union. A January 11 message from an American official in Hankow conveyed to the War Department an assessment by Colonel Joseph "Vinegar Joe" Stilwell of the fighting, and included coded passages about Chinese Communist strategy. A one-page January 13 cable from "Sokobin" in Tsingtao, also to the War Department, briefly described Japanese Army supplies and actions.

The third cable, a four-part January 13 message from Ambassador Bullitt in Paris to Secretary Hull, marked "STRICTLY CONFIDENTIAL FOR THE SECRETARY," also contained information of potential importance to Russian policymakers. Bullitt discussed a meeting that morning with the recently resigned Chinese Ambassador to Moscow, Tingfu Tsiang, who had stopped in Paris on his way back to China to assume a cabinet post. The information Tsiang provided Bullitt concerned the former's assessment of Russian intentions toward the Sino-Japanese War. Tsiang "was convinced that the Soviet Union would refuse to

---

burning, this requirement was seldom enforced. A messenger would usually pick up the "information" copies from each departmental office weekly, but (according to a departmental official who later described the 1937–38 procedures for the FBI) "no record was ever kept of those returned and destroyed or of those that remained outstanding." FBI Report, March 22, 1949, #2720.

enter the . . . conflict under any and all conditions," if only because of "internal difficulties" within Russia, a discreet reference to Stalin's massive purge, which was
then in progress. The Chinese diplomat described his recent conversations with
Soviet Foreign Minister Litvinov, who, despite repeated assurances that his country would declare war on Japan, finally acknowledged to Tsiang that Russia "had
no intention whatsoever of going to war with Japan under any circumstances."
Still, Tsiang praised the Soviet Union for its "generous" support of the Chinese
military effort through shipments of munitions and supplies, receiving payment
often in minerals and not gold. According to Tsiang's information, Germany and
Italy also continued to send China "large quantities of military supplies," and the
German military mission in China continued to work "loyally and efficiently" in
helping Chiang Kai-shek "direct the Chinese [Nationalist] armies."

Whether or not Soviet intelligence would have considered Bullitt's information significant cannot be known, although it was certainly a dispatch worth
photographing for later evaluation. The microfilmed copies of Bullitt's message
and the other two cables all bore Sayre's date stamp and Alger Hiss's initials.
How had Chambers acquired the three cables? In 1948, Hiss explained blandly:

> It was possible at all times in 1938 for anyone to come into the reception
> room [in Sayre's office] and take documents off the reception desk. During
> lunch hour, one of the two girls was supposed to be on duty at all times but
> discipline was not strict in this. There must have been many times when there
> was no one in the reception room.
>
> Hiss says that almost any respectable looking colored man would have been
> considered to be a messenger and could actually have taken the documents
> while the secretaries were present without risk of suspicion. There were no
> security regulations as to the handling of such documents.[58]

Both Eunice Lincoln and Anna Belle Newcomb insisted that they "staggered
their lunch hours so that one of them was always in the outer offices at lunch
time," and that "no one, not even department officials, was ever allowed in
Sayre's or Hiss's office alone." Hiss's assertion that "any respectable looking colored man" could have taken the documents was also disputed by the secretaries
themselves. Newcomb described office procedure for handling confidential documents: "These came from the code room in a locked box. Miss Lincoln opened
the box, took out the documents and stamped them immediately. . . . Miss Lincoln
kept the empty box until the office was finished with the documents, often several days. When both Sayre and Alger were finished with it, the document was
put back in the box and returned to the code room. . . ." Newcomb pointed out,
moreover, that all desks were cleared at night, and their contents locked up. The
last person to leave the office locked the door and left the only key with a guard
at State's main exit.[59]

But, says Hiss, if the cables were actually microfilmed in 1938, then someone—
presumably Chambers or perhaps Wadleigh—stole them from Sayre's office or,

later, from the State Department burning room: "Some official may intentionally or inadvertently have placed his own batch of papers on top of them and later have picked up the eight [actually ten] mimeographed sheets with his own, carrying them off to the Trade Agreements Division," according to Hiss. "Or they may have come to Chambers via a messenger or clerk responsible for some step in the disposal of discarded papers." Hiss argues therefore that Chambers or someone else may have sneaked into Sayre's office on the afternoon of January 14 *after* Hiss had initialed the three cables and, unobserved by the two secretaries or Hiss (all presumably off to lunch), flipped through the piles of departmental documents in the office until he located three of interest to the Soviet Union. Recognizing that the cables would be missed by Hiss—who had initialed them—unless replaced, Chambers or his confederate returned either on Monday or, at the earliest, Saturday morning (having had the documents microfilmed in the meantime) and somehow replaced them.[60]

Even those who believe that Hiss did not give the microfilmed cables to Chambers have recognized how farfetched this explanation sounds. They have argued instead that the "true story" is far simpler: The documents in question were reproduced not in 1938 but a decade later, during the successful effort to "frame" Alger Hiss. This argument for belated skullduggery is based on the theory that the two strips of State Department microfilm were manufactured during the mid-1940s or, in any case, not before 1938. But tests run both by the companies that manufactured the strips and by the FBI, along with other evidence previously unavailable, prove the speciousness of the "faked microfilm" argument: The two strips in question were manufactured in 1936 and 1937.*

The FBI's laboratory experts cut small strips from the film's margins in December 1948 to be tested by both the Du Pont Company, which had produced the roll containing the German trade documents, and Eastman Kodak, which had manufactured the other four rolls. The agents learned that Du Pont—but not Eastman Kodak—apparently used identical code markings on all its films in a regular sequence, so that the imprinted code number (#428) appeared on Du Pont film manufactured in December 1936 and in June 1944. But Du Pont laboratory officials also told the bureau on December 21, 1948, "after examining the film . . . that it is a coarse grained film and that [95 percent] of film made by Du Pont after 1939 is of the fine grain type, . . . [and furthermore] that fine grain film should have been used for this purpose [copying documents], and that fine grain film has been manufactured by Du Pont only since and not prior to 1939." Moreover, the other strip of State Department microfilm—containing the last of the German trade-agreement documents and the three cables initialed by Hiss—was an Eastman Kodak roll. Officials of that company told the FBI on

---

*The various "faked microfilm" theories are analyzed in the Appendix.

December 21, 1948, after examining a piece of the film, that the roll from which it came had been manufactured in 1937.[61]

Although the two rolls of microfilm containing Bureau of Standards documents had also been produced by Eastman Kodak, no challenge has been credibly raised to their authenticity, only to the espionage value of their contents. Eastman Kodak representatives also told the FBI that the type of "aluminum containers with flat slip-on covers" in which the three rolls of 35-millimeter film—other than the two State Department strips—had been stored were manufactured only between 1935 and 1940 or '41.[62]

Another important element in verifying the microfilms emerged from the FBI laboratory's analysis. The bureau's experts concluded that the two rolls containing State Department documents—the one manufactured by Du Pont having thirty-six separate panels, a normal packaging size for retail outlets at the time; and the other produced by Eastman Kodak with the final twenty-two panels of microfilm—were both shot in a single run at the same time, with the Leica camera that belonged to Felix Inslerman.[63]

The faked-microfilm theory runs into an immediate difficulty. If the State Department documents were placed on microfilm at some later date to implicate Hiss, why did the photographer use two different rolls produced by two different companies for the single run, stringing out the German trade-agreement material from one roll to the other? It would have been simpler and more credible to use only one roll of microfilm for all the incriminating documents, thereby minimizing the possibility that the fraud—if there was fraud—would be discovered. Also, why include a long set of documents that Julian Wadleigh could have obtained more easily than Alger Hiss, if the intent was to throw suspicion upon Hiss? For that matter, why include only three cables and not a number of other documents with Sayre's date stamp (and perhaps Hiss's initials), assuming, as one must, that only people with access to such State Department files could have organized the faked-microfilm conspiracy?

Most likely Hiss gave Chambers the January 14, 1938, cables and Wadleigh probably provided the German trade-agreement documents. Hiss's complicity cannot be excluded there, if only because the three cables and the trade-agreement memos formed part of the same photographic run on Inslerman's Leica. But available evidence supports Chambers's December 1948 statement to the FBI that both Hiss and Wadleigh apparently contributed material found on the two strips of microfilm.[64]

WOODSTOCK N230099: THE TYPED DOCUMENTS

The handwritten memos and two strips of microfilm that he ferreted away, according to Chambers, were only a small fraction of the memos and reproduced material he had received from Hiss during the early months of 1938. Most incriminating of all, Chambers also turned over in November 1948 a cache of sixty-five typed sheets containing (except for one sheet) State Department summaries or complete copies of original documents from State dating from January 5 to April 1, 1938:

> These documents were given to me for delivery to [Bykov]. . . . Alger Hiss was well aware that Colonel Bykov was the head of a Soviet underground organization. It is possible that some of the 65 [typed] documents . . . were photographed and copies of the photographs were turned over to Colonel Bykov. I didn't destroy the documents because I was preparing to break with the Party in about April, 1938. Some of the documents supplied by Hiss were copied on a typewriter in Alger Hiss's home by him or his wife, and then turned over to me.

Chambers never claimed to have known whether Alger or Priscilla Hiss served as typist, only that one of the two typed the material transmitted by Hiss himself.*[65]

All of the stolen documents turned over by Chambers dated from the January–April 1938 period, when he was preparing to defect.[66] The earliest typed State Department cables were on a single page containing three messages from Ambassador Bullitt to Hull, a January 5 dispatch and a January 12 pair sent only two days before Bullitt's long cable that appeared on the microfilm. All three summaries related to European affairs (later typed summaries were divided into "Europe" and "Far East"), two of the three were marked "STRICTLY CONFIDENTIAL FOR THE SECRETARY," and the January 5 summary dealt with only the first part of a four-part cable.† The January 12 dispatches covered Franco-German-Italian moves over the imminent German annexation of Austria, a theme that preoccupied European diplomats during these months and recurred in later typed summaries.

---

*Taken literally, a statement by Hiss to Stanley K. Hornbeck in 1949 can be read as an admission that he had given Chambers the retyped documents but not the microfilm. Mrs. Hornbeck described the scene to a friend, who told the FBI: "When Hiss arrived [at the Hombeck home in 1949] her husband [Hornbeck] stopped him in the hall and said: 'Alger, I have a blunt question which I am going to ask you right here and now . . . did you or did you not take the documents as charged? Answer me yes or no.' Hiss paused for a moment looking directly at [Hornbeck] and replied: 'If I had done it, I would have taken the originals and not the copies like Wadleigh did.'" FBI Report, December 21, 1949, #4494.

†Presumably the other three parts—which arrived later in the day—were not available to the person who stole the document's first part. Otherwise, it is difficult to understand why the typed summary did not include reference to Bullitt's report of a statement by a leading French Foreign Office personage: "His latest information from Russia was that the Russian Government would continue supplying arms and munitions to Chiang Kai-Shek but positively would not become involved in the war." The first part. however, which was transcribed, did include French assessments of British and American attitudes toward war with Japan.

Later tests conducted both by the FBI and by documents experts working for Hiss showed that the sixty-five pages of State Department documents had been typed on the Hisses' Woodstock typewriter, Serial Number N230099, except for a January 7, 1938, one-page summary of a report on the "Sino-Japanese Situation" issued by the War Department's Military Intelligence Division.[67]

The typed War Department material concerned supply matters, troop movements, and other military developments in the Far Eastern war. FBI lab tests showed that this document—unlike the pages typed by a Woodstock on tissue-thin, commonly sold paper—had been composed on a Royal, using paper with a government watermark. Thus the summary had presumably been typed by someone at the State Department. But departmental records showed that the War Department report had been sent only to State's Far Eastern Division. Chambers, however, said that he had received the document from Hiss, although, while testifying in 1950, he named Harry Dexter White as a possible source.[68]

Since the evidence indicated that Hiss had no access to this document and since it had not been typed on his Woodstock, Hiss later argued that Chambers's claim that he handed over all the other typed State Department material had no merit: "Demonstration that any one of the documents copied or summarized on a Woodstock typewriter did not come to my desk would undo Chambers's entire story about the typing . . . [which] must then have been undertaken, whenever it was done, only to incriminate me." But shortly after Chambers turned over the typed summaries and copies of complete documents, Edward C. McLean came to a less sweeping conclusion: "It seems quite apparent that Chambers obtained this memorandum from a source different from the sources of all the others."*[69]

Hiss and his supporters have suggested that Chambers—or a confederate like Julian Wadleigh—might have stolen at least some of the documents by simply wandering into the State Department and taking them. Thus John Chabot Smith theorizes that Chambers, using an expired identity card from another government agency, procured the material that he later typed (necessarily on a Woodstock almost identical in typeface to Hiss's) by rummaging unhindered through the extra copies of documents awaiting destruction in the department's Division of Communication and Records, sifting out those documents that bore Hiss's initials. But Alger Hiss would have enjoyed much easier access than Chambers to these departmental burn-baskets. Hiss had to acquire only two of the cables that went to neighboring offices and the War Department document—all of the others had gone to Sayre's office—while Chambers would have had the far greater and more improbable task of acquiring seventy-one documents over a

---

*Hiss noted in the margin next to McLean's comment: "Doesn't follow. Simply didn't have to type it myself & in passage of time thought it was one of Woodstock papers." Undated, ca. January 1949, Hiss Defense Files.

four-month period (all but three from Hiss's office) and then retyping them on the Hiss Woodstock.[70]

The papers retyped on that machine either verbatim or in summary contained seventy-one separate items. Sixty-eight of these cables had been routed to Francis Sayre's office at some point. But since three of the State Department documents did *not* reach Sayre's office, Hiss has asserted that he could not have obtained these and taken them home to be retyped on his Woodstock, and that the entire batch of pages typed on that machine therefore—including the sixty-eight cables to which he did have access—must have been "forged" by Chambers or his confederate. Although Hiss might have acquired the two stray cables from other offices in the department, the question remains unsettled since there is no hard evidence on the matter.*

These two cables aside, even Hiss's attorney Edward McLean expressed concern over the bulk of the typed documents, just as Francis Sayre was troubled by the contents and format of Hiss's four handwritten notes. The sixty-five pages of typed material, McLean wrote, "are very similar in form to the handwritten notes, and would appear to be typed copies of such handwritten memos. From the fact that these memoranda are similar in their structure to the handwritten memos admittedly written by Hiss, it would appear that the typed memos had originally been written by Hiss."[71]

The typed pages—along with the State Department microfilm and handwritten memos—apparently represent material Chambers picked up and culled out on five different occasions between mid-January and early April, with an interval of approximately two weeks after each batch. The earliest collection, possibly on or after January 14, would have included the microfilm (containing the three cables stamped with that date in Sayre's office), the three typed Bullitt summaries on "Europe," and the January 12 War Department summary.

The next batch of typing included four pages crammed with neatly divided cables from January 22 to February 2 labeled "Europe" (subdivided by country) and "Far East," as well as Hiss's handwritten copy of Henderson's January 28 Mary Martin cable. The dates in question indicated that Chambers's pickup came on or after February 2. Several of the sixteen cables summarized in the four pages had been marked "CONFIDENTIAL" or "STRICTLY CONFIDENTIAL" in the originals, and some had been sent in code. Sayre's office received "information copies" of all but one of the cables. Twelve of the sixteen concerned military and diplomatic aspects of the Sino-Japanese War. The others dealt with

---

*"But it is nonsense to suppose that a resolute and experienced operator occupying a senior post in the Foreign Office can have access only to the papers that are placed on his desk in the ordinary course of duty. I have already shown that I gained access to the files of British agents in the Soviet Union when I was supposed to be chivvying Germans in Spain." Kim Philby, *My Silent War* (New York: Grove, 1968), p. 181.

future British arms purchases in the United States, battlefield and home-front conditions in Spain, British concern about Japanese naval expansion, and French hopes for reconciliation with Germany. The summary of this last cable, a January 25 dispatch from Bullitt of a conversation with the French foreign minister, concerned only the first part of that dispatch. The cable's second part, transmitted separately, contained information about a talk with the Soviet ambassador to France, indicating that the person who took the cable did not have its final portion at hand.

The third group of typed cables retained by Chambers totaled twenty-six and were dated between February 11 and 18. Information copies of the originals had been sent to Sayre's office in all but one case: a verbatim typed copy of Sayre's own memorandum of a delicate February 18 conversation involving Secretary Hull, the Czechoslovakian minister, and himself. Seven of the twenty-six concerned the Sino-Japanese War, and the purpose of making the summaries seemed obvious: "One and one-half pages. Deals with occupation of University of Shanghai by Japanese," Hiss's lawyer wrote in 1949 about a February 11 cable. "Summary selects only one sentence, that relating to an airfield which is only incidentally mentioned in the cable. Shows that the summarizer was looking for military information."[72]

Most of the remaining cables had been taken from dispatches by American envoys in Europe—Bullitt in Paris, Wiley in Vienna, Gilbert in Berlin, Phillips in Rome—and concerned the Austrian crisis that then threatened European peace and was the chief diplomatic issue of the moment. German pressure on Austria in mid-February forced the country's government to capitulate to Hitler's demands and appoint pro-Nazis to key posts in the Austrian cabinet.

The events of that week and discussions with the major figures would prove profoundly important for the future of Central Europe and for the chances of European peace. American diplomats chronicled them in long and highly confidential dispatches—often presented in their entirety and not summarized—that were retyped on Hiss's Woodstock. These included six cables from Vienna, four from Berlin, five from Paris, one from Rome.

The mid-February packet of typed cables also contained a message from London that foreshadowed Hiss's March 3 handwritten note. The message reported that "Admiral Lord Chatfield talked informally but at some length yesterday with Captain Willson concerning escalation under the London Treaty. Based on this conversation it appears probable that the Admiralty will favor for this Year's programme raising the battleship limit to about 39,000 tons and making no change in cruiser limits. Captain Willson forwarded a full report by mail to the Navy Department in yesterday's pouch via Queen Mary. Johnson." In the light of this document, it seems probable that Hiss's later handwritten note represented an effort to follow up the earlier typed summary of Chatfield's comments on British naval development.

Perhaps the most incriminating document in this third batch is the retyped copy of Sayre's memorandum of a February 18 conversation with Hull and Vladimir Hurban, the Czech minister in Washington. Hurban was attempting to alert American diplomats to the dangers of German expansionism in Central Europe, a subject of critical importance to the Soviet Union. Copying Sayre's account of Hurban's conversation with Hull may have seemed to Hiss a logical addition to the cables that dealt with the Austrian crisis. Sayre's February 18 memo described Hurban's effort to persuade Hull of the dangers of German aggression in Central Europe and—implicitly—to plead for American economic pressures upon Germany.*[73]

The fourth collection of typed documents, spread out over a two-month period, concerned Japanese economic plans for the conquered Chinese territory of Manchuria (Manchukuo). The key item in this packet, a January 6 letter from Richard F. Boyce, American consul at Yokohama, enclosing a translated copy of the Japanese report on their "New Economic Organization of 'Manchukuo,'" reached Sayre's office on February 16. It remained there until March 11, when the State Department routing slips show that the report went to another assistant secretary (although Hiss's 1949 marginal notes on his lawyer's analysis of the routing argued concerning this sequence: "Doesn't follow. May have been in unauthorized hands on way to [the other assistant secretary]"). Both Hiss and Sayre had initialed Boyce's letter enclosing the report, indicating that both men had read the document.[74]

Transcribing the long report completely on Hiss's Woodstock took thirteen single-spaced, narrow-margined pages. Accompanying Boyce's report when it reached Sayre's office on February 16 were four other documents, three of which were also retyped and given to Chambers. The crucial one assessed Japanese plans, especially as they affected American investors in Manchukuo. Written by a specialist in the State Department's Far Eastern Division, and filling three single-spaced retyped pages in Chambers's copy, it was called "The Significance of the Establishment of the Manchukuo Heavy Industries Development Company."

Not until mid-March did these documents leave Sayre's office. The other sections at State had shuttled the Manchukuo dossier back and forth quickly, with none holding the material more than a few days, in some cases only a day. But the packet remained in Sayre's office for more than three weeks, in part perhaps because of the time it took in the evenings to retype so many pages of technical economic material.

---

*Both Sayre and Hiss's lawyers argued that Wadleigh might have stolen the Hurban memo, since a copy went to Trade Agreements. But the argument breaks down immediately, since the copy turned over by Chambers in 1948 was not on microfilm but on one of the sixty-four sheets typed on Hiss's Woodstock. See "Memo for von Mehren, June 27, 1949, Hiss Defense Files.

The fifth and final collection of State Department documents transcribed on the Hiss Woodstock reached Chambers sometime in early April—the last cable in this batch was dated April 1 and Chambers defected two weeks later. Some of the nineteen cables had been retyped in full. All but one came from wires received at State between March 28 and April 1, and the general organization appears more haphazard than for earlier batches. European, Far Eastern, and Latin American cables were mixed together almost randomly, often only one to a page, with most of the page left blank. Eight of the nineteen—which included coded sections—concerned Japanese economic affairs or the fighting in China. One summary of a March 23 cable from the American Consul at Dairen included only one sentence from a one-and-a-half-page cable: "The sentence picked out by the summary is only incidental in the cable," Hiss's lawyer concluded in 1949, "and seems to indicate that the summarizer was interested in military information only." Hiss's two handwritten notes dealing with the Sino-Japanese War and with Chinese acquisition of French planes—March 11 and March 2 telegrams—may also have been delivered to Chambers with this last batch of typed material.[75]

Two late-March cables from Rome concerned Italian (and possibly French) involvement in the Spanish Civil War. Six dispatches from American envoys in Europe dealt with possible German military and diplomatic moves, one of them updating Hull's earlier discussion with Hurban about German moves in Central Europe while another concerned British naval expansion, the subject of Hiss's handwritten "Lord Chatfield" memo. An April 1 dispatch concluded the stolen material Chambers had hidden during the first four months of 1938.

The contents of the stolen State Department documents cannot be considered peripheral or unimportant—certainly not to professional diplomats at the time—when viewed in the context of major issues then dominating world affairs: the Sino-Japanese War, the German takeover of Austria, the Spanish Civil War, possible German aggression in Czechoslovakia, Japanese threats to American interests in Asia, the response of other major powers in Europe and Asia toward the Soviet Union.

There appeared considerable linkage, moreover, between the major areas of concern in the three sorts of material saved by Chambers (typed, microfilmed, and handwritten)—for example, in the dispatches on military aspects of the Sino-Japanese War, or in the discussions with Lord Chatfield over British naval expansion. Hiss's lawyer noted how much the typed summaries of confidential documents resembled his client's handwritten summaries in format. And Sayre, among others, later pointed out another valuable feature of the stolen material to a foreign power: "Possession of the dispatches in secret code," he told Hiss's attorney in 1949, "would enable the Russians to break the code if they could also get the original code telegram which presumably could be obtained from the telegram office." He pointed out that "the Bullitt dispatch is in a secret code for the most part."[76]

But were the stolen documents typed on the Hisses' Woodstock and, if so, by whom? After exhaustive testing in 1948 and 1949, the FBI's laboratory experts and three different documents examiners hired over a year's time by Hiss's lawyers reached the same conclusion: The sixty-four pages of summaries and complete copies of 1937–38 State Department materials, other than the War Department summary, had been typed on the machine then owned by the Hisses, Woodstock N230099. Moreover, these experts agreed that the typing matched specimens from the mid-thirties that the Hisses acknowledged had been typed by Priscilla; in other words, she apparently copied the documents, since her husband has always insisted that he could not type and that his wife handled all such work in the family.[77]

Although Hiss and others have argued that Chambers somehow gained access to the Woodstock typewriter during this period—or to a virtually identical machine—several of Hiss's own documents experts, after examining samples of Chambers's typing, agreed that he could not have typed them. The FBI confirmed this after its own independent study of Chambers's typing samples.*[78]

After the recovery of the Hiss Woodstock in 1949, both FBI and defense experts again tested the stolen documents, this time matching them with typing samples taken from the machine itself. In addition, the FBI compared the stolen papers with material typed on the Woodstock during the 1940s, after it left the Hisses' possession, and with additional letters typed by Priscilla Hiss in the 1930s. Tests on all three sets of material confirmed the earlier opinions of both FBI and defense specialists: that the stolen documents had been typed on the Hiss machine. One defense expert stated flatly that Priscilla Hiss had typed all of the stolen documents (always excepting the War Department summary), while a second examiner hired by Hiss's lawyers skirted that view but avoided judgment by observing that "the only pronounced difference between the known Hiss samples and the Baltimore papers [the stolen documents] is that the Baltimore papers are all singly spaced whereas most of the Hiss samples are double spaced." The third defense expert hired during Hiss's trials, while agreeing that the State Department documents had been typed on Woodstock N230099, believed that the same person did not compose both the stolen materials and the "Hiss standards" of the 1930s. The FBI affirmed only that the Hiss machine had typed the stolen documents; it did not attempt to identify the typist.[79]

The Hisses apparently gave the Woodstock to Claudia Catlett's family in 1938, shortly after Chambers's defection. Since the machine was then in good working order—as documents typed on the Woodstock by Priscilla Hiss in 1937

---

*All of the letters and articles written by Chambers during 1937–39 that I have located were typed on the same machine, a Remington portable.

and by the Catletts and others as late as 1947 showed—the circumstances under which the Hisses disposed of the machine may have been connected with fear of incrimination after Chambers broke.[80]

Most often, and at their most candid, Claudia Catlett and her sons, Raymond and Perry, remembered getting the machine after April 1938. Although Hiss's lawyers—with difficulty—persuaded Perry Catlett, at least (but not Raymond or Claudia), to stick to a December 1937 date, there is no solid evidence supporting the Hisses' belated assertion that Woodstock N230099 changed hands earlier than April 1938.*

FBI experts and most defense documents examiners agreed that the stolen documents had been typed on that machine. Moreover, those same analysts specifically excluded the possibility of Whittaker Chambers having been the typist, a theory that would require him to have made at least five visits to the Catlett home. The Hisses rejected the notion that any of the Catletts had conspired with Chambers, and the idea that he passed unnoticed on a series of visits to the Catletts' home for lengthy typing sessions remains almost as bizarre as most subsequent "forgery by typewriter" theories.

Most probably the Catletts received the Woodstock at the time they and the Hisses first recalled the transfer having taken place, sometime after mid-1938. By then the last of the stolen State Department documents had been retyped on the machine and Chambers had defected.

THE FINAL VISIT

Whittaker Chambers said he made one last visit to the Hisses in 1938. On December 17 he had met with Herbert Solow, who urged Chambers to tell his full story. Chambers refused, according to a memo by Solow written later that day: "He also feels hesitant about breaking his story open because he does not wish to cause trouble to some agent whom he regards as a sincere and devoted person. He regrets having spoken to me of fighting fire with fire, feeling that his methods must be different than those of the CP and Moscow."[81]

When he next contacted Solow the following month, Chambers felt less reluctant. Sometime in late December 1938 he visited that "agent whom he regards as a sincere and devoted person" with results that apparently ended his reticence over full public disclosure.†

---

*For closer scrutiny of this point, see Chapter XI. The various "forgery by typewriter" theories are examined in detail in the Appendix.

†After the Hiss case broke, Chambers described visits made in December 1938 to the four underground sources within the government in whom he professed particular interest: George Silverman, Julian Wadleigh, Harry Dexter White, and Alger Hiss. Chambers said he warned the first three men that he would expose them unless they ceased working as agents. In the case of

"Happy New Year, and how!" Chambers wrote Solow in January 1939. "Remember I told you I didn't have stomach for it when I last saw you," he reminded Solow. "Since then I've seen two old friends: do you know that everything is going right along the way I left it? These encounters gave me back the necessary iron."[82]

In a letter sent that same month to Meyer Schapiro, Chambers described more fully his encounter with "the two I visited not long ago":

> We were very close indeed. Recently the wife told me that my occasional comments (the only form of letting off steam I dared risk) on the Soviet Union were "mental masturbation"—the rank obscenity of cultured women!* I was more shocked to hear her use such an expression than at the charge. Further, she said, she had just read over the minutes of the [Moscow] Trials and anybody who could doubt they were guilty.... The husband told me that the world is tottering on the verge of proletarian revolution.... Well, that's the type I meant. This same girl told me last year: "You taught us what the word Commissar means." One hardly knows which expression is more empty or in retrospect more sickening ... From such people such results....[83]

The "people" in question appear to have been the Hisses, although Chambers did not name them to Schapiro. In 1945, however, Chambers told the FBI about the visit:

> ... after he had broken with the Communist Party, he had made a special trip to [the] Hiss home in Georgetown, Washington, D.C., with the purpose of talking Hiss into breaking away from the Party. Chambers explained that when he arrived that Hiss's wife Priscilla was the only one there....
>
> When Hiss arrived, they had dinner together at his home and then [Chambers] talked with him all night long in an effort to persuade him to leave the Party. He stated that with tears streaming down his face, Hiss had refused to break with the Communists and had given as his reason for not breaking, his loyalty to his friends and principles. Chambers stated his reason in going to Hiss in order to get him to break away ... was that he personally thought an awful lot about Hiss and considered him an intelligent and decent young man whose better judgment should have led him to break with the Communist

---

Alger and Priscilla Hiss, who he said were friends, he described a tense visit that included dinner, much futile argument with them over the crimes of Stalinism, and an emotional leave-taking during which Hiss wept. Chambers told this story to the FBI in 1945. Julian Wadleigh later confirmed Chambers's account, recalling a meeting in January 1939 at which Chambers "told me two or three times that he had left the apparatus and the party." Wadleigh quotes Chambers as saying: "I deserted, that's all." And when they parted, the defector remarked: "'Well, now I'm going to become a bourgeois.' Then, patting me on the shoulder, he added: 'That's what you'll have to do, too.' I made no comment. I just said goodby." New York Post, July 17, 1949.

*In a 1948 pretrial deposition for Alger Hiss's slander suit, Chambers said of this last visit: "Mrs. Hiss was extremely unfriendly and referred to my doubts about Communism as mental masturbation." Baltimore Deposition, February 17, 1949, p. 1003.

movement. Chambers pointed out in his opinion, one of the strongest reason [sic] for Hiss's maintaining contact with the Communist Party was the fanatical loyalty to the Communist Party on the part of his wife.*[84]

For almost ten years after that visit Whittaker Chambers did not see either Alger or Priscilla Hiss again—and then encountered them only in committee rooms and courtrooms. Even during that decade, however, their lives and his intersected several times. By 1939 Chambers confronted an uncertain future as a fugitive from the Communist underground, while the Hisses may already have begun reflecting on the threat Chambers posed to their future by his special knowledge of their past.

---

*Hiss dismissed Chambers's claim to close friendship in a 1949 memo to his attorney, expressing particular irritation at his accuser's story of this final visit: "Chambers' personality and his history as we now know it indicate how likely it would be that I would regard him as a close friend. . . . The credibility of my being in tears is not likely to impress people who know me. I am not given to tears. . . . In making up a fictitious interview he may have ascribed to me action which he would have expected himself to take. . . . A rather far-fetched explanation of my alleged emotion." Hiss to Dr. Carl Binger, January 11, 1949, enclosing Hiss's "Analysis of Chambers's testimony as to 'intimacy' with me and my family," undated, Hiss Defense Files.

Part Three
CONCEALMENT

When you are judging the evidence, contrast this instinctive shrinking of the guilty, upon which these bands of blackmailers live, with the openness with which Mr. Wilde himself sought to have the charges investigated, the courage that brought him into the witness-box in this Court to face, once and for all, and, as he hopes and I hope, to dispose of the accusations which were being made against him. When a man comes forward with such letters as these and says 'I do not shrink from the judgment of the world upon these productions,' you cannot say that such a man is not to be believed. Has the defendant in this case not given the best proof of his innocence?

—*Sir Edward Clarke*, closing speech for the defendant in the second trial of Oscar Wilde

On the other side of the door, Chief Inspector Heat was saying to Mr. Verloc, the secret agent:

"*So your defence will be practically a full confession?*"

"*It will. I am going to tell the whole story.*"

"*You won't be believed as much as you fancy you will.*" . . .

"*Perhaps not. But it will upset many things. I have been a straight man, and I shall keep straight in this—*"

"*If they let you,*" *said the Chief Inspector, cynically.* . . .

—*Joseph Conrad*, The Secret Agent

VIII

PERJURY:
A QUESTION OF CANDOR

DECEMBER 4, 1948: ALGER HISS MEETS THE FBI

With the December 3 headlines of "pumpkin papers," "stolen typed documents," and "spy rings," the attention of press and public immediately focused again on the Hiss-Chambers case. Disclosure of the new evidence showed that, with or without Hiss, Chambers had engaged in espionage. Energized by the renewed publicity the various parties investigating the case—the FBI, the Justice Department, the Grand Jury, HUAC, and Hiss's attorneys—resumed their often-conflicting probes.

Only Chambers, in the storm's eye, appeared unruffled, doubtless pleased, and perhaps surprised. That same day the FBI interviewed Chambers and came away with an extensive statement: He described the documents, told how during the late thirties he had obtained them and from whom, supplied the names of others who he alleged had belonged to the espionage ring, and gave his purported reason for not previously mentioning either the stolen material or espionage—namely, "to try and preserve the human elements involved . . . shielding these people" who had acted with him.[1]

Next day the bureau conducted its oft-postponed interview with Alger Hiss in Baltimore. Accompanied by William Marbury, Hiss denied Chambers's latest charges, but acknowledged the apparent genuineness of the typed materials and agreed that documents "similar to these normally passed over my desk for perusal prior to being referred to Mr. Sayre." But Hiss had no "independent recollection of having seen any of these documents or the documents summarized while I was in the employ of the State Department." Moreover, he minimized their importance: "[T]hese do not appear to be documents of a very highly confidential nature and would not have been treated in the State Department with any special precautions at that time."*[2]

Nor, according to Hiss, had he seen the four handwritten memos, although "three of the four pages appear to be in my handwriting," while the fourth "does not look to me as if it were." Hiss said he did not give Chambers any of the

---

*Both former and current leading officials of the department disagreed with Hiss's assessment within the next few days

material—original documents for microfilming, typed copies, or handwritten memos. He had never met a Colonel Bykov or agreed to cooperate in espionage. He had not seen Chambers "at any time in the State Department," which Hiss joined in mid-1936: "I do not know whether Chambers personally obtained these documents from the State Department or whether he had some confederate who cooperated with him" in stealing them.

The agents pressed for Hiss's explanation of Chambers's motives for perpetrating such a fraud. Hiss and Marbury went into detail, although they preferred to omit these views from the signed statement itself. Hiss expressed his opinion, made after consulting Dr. Carl Binger, that Chambers was a homosexual. Asking that the agents arrange to have Chambers examined by Dr. Binger, Hiss cited the latter's argument that "homosexual behavior" was not inconsistent with expressing "real affection and admiration for another person" while still engaging in "actions to hurt that other person."

To support this diagnosis of Chambers's alleged homosexual jealousy toward Hiss, Marbury and his client offered the agents "some of their reasoning," which consisted primarily of the fact that Chambers had translated *Class Reunion,* whose story bore "a striking counterpart to the present Hiss-Chambers situation." The "accused" and his lawyer also suggested that "a possible reason for Chambers's fabrication involving Hiss [was] that the story was of assistance to Chambers in obtaining his present position with 'Time' magazine." Since Chambers had first told the story to Isaac Don Levine, they argued, and since most of those named by Chambers "were no longer in the Government employ" while Hiss "was advancing as a rather prominent official," without Hiss's name "in the exposé, the story would not be sufficiently sensational to attract the attention of *Time* magazine, a prospective employer of Chambers at the time."*

Both Hiss and Marbury suggested also "the possibility" that Chambers stole the State Department documents himself while working for the National Research Project early in 1938 at a building several blocks away. They reasoned that Chambers "might have gained access to the State Department through familiarity with other buildings in the general locality where he was employed." But the two men admitted that Chambers had left this job in February 1938, while the documents carried dates up to April 1, 1938. The FBI agents noted that the information provided by Hiss and Marbury "from their investigation and pre-trial deposition appears to be more generally of a personal nature involving

---

*This theory collapses over major factual problems. For one thing, Chambers did not tell Levine the names of government officials until their meeting with Adolf Berle in September 1939. By then Chambers had already been working for *Time* for five months. Second, he hid carefully for the next decade his involvement in espionage from his employers at *Time* and from his colleagues. Finally, most of those he named were still working for the government, and Hiss was then a middle-rank State Department bureaucrat without a notable reputation or immediate prospects for one.

[Chambers's] residences, employment, character, and associations with persons of ill repute, rather than with the Communist Party activities of Chambers." Hiss and his attorney pointed out that Chambers had not produced the documents "for patriotic reasons but only 'to save his neck in a libel suit,'" and assured the agents of a desire to cooperate "in every way in an effort to ascertain the true facts in this case."[3]

In the days ahead the FBI became caught in a cross fire between Justice Department officials and HUAC, owner of the only copies of the "pumpkin papers" microfilm. The bureau's December 3 interview with Chambers had been ordered by Alexander Campbell, who told FBI officials "confidentially" that Justice intended to bring Hiss—but not Chambers—before the grand jury on December 9: "They probably would not have Chambers actually appear before the Grand Jury," Campbell stated, "since an indictment against him for perjury was contemplated." In other words, even after revelation of the "pumpkin papers," and despite Campbell's promise of evenhandedness to Richard Cleveland that same day, Justice Department officials planned to let the "chips" fall only upon Chambers. Nor did departmental officials inform J. Edgar Hoover of their decision to interview Chambers immediately prior to indicting him. "I should have been advised of this *at the time*," Hoover wrote on a memo three days later.[4]

The interview with Hiss on December 4 also took place on Campbell's direct orders. And the following day the FBI's Louis B. Nichols—evidently monitoring the suggestions made by Hiss and Marbury—requested a bureau check "to know if there was anything in our files to show that Whittaker Chambers had been hospitalized in White Plains, New York [i.e., Bloomingdale], and whether he had been in an institution at Westminster, Maryland, when he was there and the nature of the institution." The FBI learned that Chambers had never been institutionalized, although he had suffered two severe heart attacks in 1942 and 1945.[5]

RICHARD NIXON'S "FIRST CRISIS" AND THE RETURN OF HUAC

As the grand jury prepared to hear testimony on December 7, the FBI–Justice Department probe continued to concentrate on the possibility of indicting only Chambers. At the same time Richard Nixon and others on HUAC worked vigorously to prevent Chambers's arrest and to mobilize public support instead for an indictment of Hiss. Hoover preferred putting both men on trial, but his superiors at Justice never sought his advice on the question, although they pressured him to obtain the microfilms from HUAC. He mediated quietly between Democratic Justice Department officials and Republican HUAC members while both groups battled behind the scenes and in the press for control of the Hiss-Chambers investigation.

In the earliest stage of this contest HUAC held most of the high cards. Two weeks of Justice Department and FBI fumbling had not yet determined the genuineness of the Baltimore documents. On December 3 a State Department official secretly delivered to the FBI copies of many of the original cables upon which the typed versions were based because he "wanted the Bureau to have copies of these documents just in case a 'freeze' was put on this material." Within hours the FBI had made photostats and returned the originals to the source at State.[6]

On December 5 Nixon returned from the Panama boat to Washington, and Mundt arrived from South Dakota on the 6th. Nixon and Stripling hastily arranged an executive session in New York on the evening of December 6. Before leaving Washington, the two men allowed reporters and photographers a first glimpse of the microfilmed State Department material.* One waiting newsreel photographer casually asked Stripling, "What's the emulsion figure on these films?" and explained that the numbers would reveal the year the films had been manufactured.[7]

Stripling and Nixon contacted an Eastman Kodak official, Keith B. Lewis, who phoned the company's Rochester headquarters and asked for the information regarding the Kodak strip. After holding the line open for a few minutes, Lewis hung up the phone, turned to the others, and announced: "This film was manufactured in 1945."

The news "jolted us into almost complete shock," Nixon later recalled. "This meant that Chambers was, after all, a liar." At that point Nixon's recollections and those of two other people in the room diverge. Nixon remembered maintaining tight self-control and ordering his secretary to contact Chambers in New York, where the latter was then testifying before the grand jury. With Chambers on the line, Nixon described the Eastman Kodak report and asked angrily for Chambers's reaction. "I can't understand it," he replied. "God must be against me." Nixon warned Chambers to come up with a better explanation by the time he faced committee questioning that evening and slammed down the receiver. "What'll we do now?" he said Stripling then asked, to which Nixon replied forthrightly that they would hold a press conference in thirty minutes and explain the situation. Nixon remembered thinking that it would be "the biggest crow-eating performance in the history of Capitol Hill, but I was ready to go through with it."[8]

Two others present, Stripling and Nicholas Vazzana, who had come to HUAC headquarters to watch the culmination of a drama he had helped stage, recalled a different scene. They said Nixon responded almost hysterically to Lewis's news

---

*One of those present, Willard Edwards of the Chicago *Tribune*, confirmed Stripling's recollection that early in December the paper's publisher, Colonel Robert L. McCormick, offered Stripling $10,000 for a copy of the entire "pumpkin papers," $5,000 for a single frame of the microfilm, which McCormick hoped to run on the *Tribune*'s front page.

of apparently forged microfilms. "Oh, my God," exclaimed Nixon, "this is the end of my political career." Nixon continued shouting, especially at Vazzana: "Well, you got us into this. This is all your fault." "Well, it's not my fault," Vazzana replied, "I didn't know there was any microfilm there."

Nixon continued to insist that Vazzana "do something," and his language (according to both onlookers) became "abusive." Finally, Nixon cried: "Get hold of Chambers! You'd better get hold of Chambers!" Vazzana then phoned Harold Medina's office in New York and arranged for Chambers to phone back. Stripling also reported shortly after the scene that, far from preparing to "eat crow," Nixon wanted no part of a press conference. Stripling, however, insisted on going through with it: "We'll tell them we were sold a bill of goods . . . that we were all wet."[9]

As it turned out, Nixon managed to avoid both eating crow and changing jobs. Just as he and Stripling prepared to face the press, a second call came from Eastman Kodak's Lewis. "I checked with Rochester after I got back to the office," he told Stripling, "and it seems we have made a little mistake." Microfilms with the same emulsion figure had been produced through 1938, then discontinued, and the same number used again in 1945. "I let out a Texas yell and leaped on Nixon's couch," Stripling recalled, shouting the news to those in the office while waltzing Nixon around the room. When the mood in the office quieted, Nixon, according to Stripling, had only one laconic observation: "Poor Chambers. Nobody ever believes him at first."[10]

In the midst of their celebration, neither Stripling nor Nixon apparently thought to call Chambers back and explain the mistake. Only later did Vazzana contact Medina with the information, and later that afternoon, when Chambers phoned Medina, he heard about the Eastman Kodak expert's clarification. Still, the events of those few days had taken their toll, and Chambers's thoughts returned—as they often did in times of stress—to suicide. He entered a Lower Manhattan seed store that afternoon and purchased a large can of cyanide compound. The corrected error only intensified the bleakness of his mood: "An error so burlesque, a comedy so gross in the midst of such catastrophe was a degradation of the spirit. . . . All the suffering of which I had been the cause and witness . . . all that pointless pain continued to roll me under in a drowning wave."[11]

The past weeks had exhausted Chambers both physically and emotionally. One evening early in December, at his mother's house in Lynbrook, he sat down and wrote farewell messages to his wife and children plus a note defending the truth of his testimony against Hiss and reiterating that, although he had not intended to injure any person while disclosing his evidence against Communism, "That I had been unable to do. But I could spare them the ultimate consequences of my actions and their own, by removing myself as a witness against them."

Then Chambers opened the cyanide tin, wrapped it inside towels as the fumes wafted out, and lay down on a bed. The suicide attempt failed; in the morning he awoke, vomiting and alive. Chambers made no further suicide try during this period.[12]

After listening to Chambers at the Commodore Hotel that evening, committee members returned to Washington on the afternoon of December 7 to hold a public session. Under gentle prodding by the FBI, Stripling and Mundt agreed to turn over a set of the microfilm's photostats (they had given some of the material to Thomas Donegan for the grand jury's use the previous evening). Since December 3 the "pumpkin papers" had been kept in a HUAC office safe under twenty-four-hour guard. When Donald Appell first brought in the film, Stripling ordered it sent to the Veterans Administration film laboratories for processing of the three undeveloped rolls. One proved blank, and prints were made from the other two. Understandably, both Justice and the FBI hungered for copies of these prints at the very least, or, if possible, for the microfilm itself.[13]

HUAC began its December 7 hearing by questioning Sumner Welles, under secretary of state from 1938 to 1945, and John Peurifoy, the State Department's leading security officer. Stripling had arranged Welles's appearance in order to stress the importance of the microfilmed papers. Welles read several of the cables contained on the microfilm and judged their publication to be "prejudicial to the nation's interest." Peurifoy supported Welles's caution against publishing the documents even in 1948. Committee members drew from Peurifoy an admission that persons in the department who passed such documents elsewhere or copied them for someone outside State would be breaking the law.[14]

On December 8 Isaac Don Levine told HUAC he had met Chambers first in 1939 (actually, November 1938) shortly after the latter's defection. Chambers had sought Levine's help in selling some articles on Soviet espionage. Levine described the efforts he and Chambers made in September 1939 to bring Communist espionage activities within the government to Adolf Berle's attention. He told of arranging the appointment with Berle and of the information given by Chambers at the time: "The names of Alger Hiss and Donald Hiss were among those which I recorded [as underground Communists] . . . upon my return to the hotel."[15]

Before concluding, Levine defended Chambers, evidently provoked by rumors of the *Time* editor's impending indictment for perjury: "I feel that there is altogether too much preoccupation and speculation as to why Chambers did not produce the documents in time, and that there is not enough concern about the persons who stole the papers."

Immediately Chambers's chief defender on the committee picked up the theme. "Technical crime" was Richard Nixon's euphemism for Chambers's earlier perjury, his denial to the grand jury in October that espionage had been committed or that he possessed documentary evidence. Nixon pointed out that "a collateral issue" had caught the imagination of public and press—namely, "why didn't Mr. Chambers turn over this information [earlier]?" To answer that question, Nixon read into the record a portion of Chambers's executive session testimony of the previous night:

> Every ex-Communist is faced at the moment of his break . . . by the question, "Shall I be an informer?" I faced this question very early, but I was reluctant to inform. [Chambers then described his decision to speak to Berle in 1939.] . . . Most of the men in the Communist underground apparatus were men of high type, some of them widely recognized for intelligence and ability. They had been my friends. I had been in their homes and knew their wives and children. . . . I desired to give these people an opportunity to make their own break, damaged as little as possible by me.[16]

Confronting the question most troubling HUAC, Nixon continued:

> The indication is at the present time that Mr. Chambers will certainly be indicted for perjury . . . probably before any of the other people involved . . . are indicted. I wish to point out to the Department of Justice to proceed along that line . . . that they will thereby have probably destroyed the only opportunity to obtain an indictment of the other individuals involved, because the star witness against the other individuals will have been an indicted and convicted perjurer.

Chambers's support among committee members seemed bipartisan, and one HUAC member asked Levine as the session closed what effect Chambers's indictment and conviction would have upon the possibility of obtaining leads from future informants, to which the witness replied: "I think it will make espionage safe."

THE HUAC-JUSTICE DEPARTMENT BATTLE

The committee, the Justice Department, and the FBI continued their uneasy tug-of-war, each acting primarily to protect its own interests. HUAC investigator Louis J. Russell (a former FBI agent) told the bureau on December 8 that "Nixon [is] out to embarrass the Bureau, if possible, in connection with this matter and . . . he also intends to do everything he can to get the Director before the Committee to testify."[17]

The prospect of embarrassment seemed to be Hoover's chief concern. Almost hourly reports flowed in from subordinates such as Ladd and Nichols recording new details of the conflict between Justice and HUAC, with the FBI caught squarely in the middle. Ladd told Hoover that several FBI agents had seen Nixon informally on December 8. Nixon was "extremely mad at the Attorney General and at Alex Campbell for not having more vigorously prosecuted this whole matter, but . . . [he] had nothing but praise for the Director and the Bureau. He voluntarily stated . . . that he had worked very close [sic] with the Bureau and with Mr. Nichols during the past year on this matter." Hoover remained unimpressed: "This fellow Nixon blows hot & cold. H," he wrote on the memo.[18]

The bureau's investigation of the case had moved well beyond HUAC's headline-hunting public sessions. By the time Nixon confided to FBI agents that he wished to obtain Hiss typing samples, Hoover had already ordered a search for such specimens, though both Alger and Priscilla Hiss had earlier told the FBI that they had disposed of the machine—make unknown—in 1938. Marked "URGENT," the crucial order went out under Hoover's signature on December 8:

> WASHINGTON FIELD [OFFICE] SHOULD MAKE IMMEDIATE AND EXHAUSTIVE EFFORTS TO LOCATE TYPEWRITER WHICH WAS DISPOSED OF BY MRS. HISS TO A SECOND-HAND TYPEWRITER DEALER OR SECOND-HAND STORE NEAR ONE OF THE HISS FAMILY ADDRESSES MENTIONED IN HISS STATEMENT DATED DECEMBER FOUR LAST SINCE POSSIBILITY EXISTS THAT THIS MACHINE MIGHT STILL BE IN EXISTENCE.[19]

Not only had the FBI begun searching for the machine that might have typed the Baltimore documents, but it had obtained a confession from a key witness in the probe, Henry Julian Wadleigh. After first denying all knowledge of Chambers and any participation in espionage, Wadleigh buckled under the pressure of perjuring himself and stated: "I'm not going to sign that statement." The FBI report on the incident continues: "Almost immediately thereafter . . . he announced rather dramatically that he was willing to give a statement and make a complete confession." Wadleigh then told the agents that he had served as a source of material from the State Department for a man he had known only as "Carl," but now identified as Chambers. His confession indirectly strengthened suspicions within the FBI and Justice that Hiss had been Chambers's second source at State. Two days after Wadleigh broke, the bureau began searching for Hiss's typewriter and for typing specimens that matched the stolen documents.[20]

On December 10 Whittaker Chambers resigned as a senior editor of *Time*. Chambers's departure was neither unexpected nor unwelcome to Henry Luce or to most other senior editors at the magazine. Although *Time* had provided legal support for him in October to help in defending against Hiss's lawsuit, Chambers's colleagues at the magazine learned only with the rest of the country—in early December—about his espionage activities. The "pumpkin papers" were a surprise and an embarrassment to them. Clare Boothe Luce later recalled having overheard a conversation between her husband and Chambers a few days after the "pumpkin papers" story broke. Luce complained to Chambers that the latter had never told him about being a Soviet spy, to which Chambers responded: "But you knew I was a Communist and all Communists were working for the Soviet Union. If a man of your sophistication didn't understand the nature of Communists and Communism, God help the country." Chambers's resignation presumably saved Luce the trouble of taking the initiative.[21]

Alger Hiss fared somewhat better at the hands of the Carnegie trustees that same month, although they too felt embarrassed by the unexpected results of Hiss's slander suit. Dulles, once his strongest supporter, had pulled away completely, and some of the other trustees remained chary of identifying closely with Hiss. But James Shotwell, the acting president, humane and without political responsibilities, remained a vigorous defender. "Frankly, it reminds me very forcibly of the way in which the Dreyfus case came about," Shotwell wrote the day the press first reported the "pumpkin papers." "I was in France as a student in those days and I know how bitterly public opinion was worked up. . . . I am afraid that we are on the way to having our Dreyfus case. . . . It is possible that as in the other case the treasonable agent may still be in the [State] Department or may be sheltered by prima-facie evidence against Hiss."[22]

When the Endowment trustees met on December 13, Hiss submitted his resignation. The trustees chose not to act on the offer, but instead voted Hiss a three-month leave of absence to devote full time to his defense. This represented a compromise plan favored by Henry Wriston, David Rockefeller, Philip Reed, and John W. Davis, who in Dulles's absence presided over the often-acrimonious debate. The three-month leave seemed to a majority the best of several unsatisfactory alternatives. "To accept his resignation and deprive him of the presidency instantly," Davis later wrote, "would be a pre-judgment of his case, and we had no right to do that."[23]

By the time Hiss received his leave from the Endowment, he had made six appearances before the grand jury between December 7 and 13. Even the normally confident Hiss began to recognize by the substance and tone of questions asked, both by jurors and by Justice Department officials, that he was in trouble. The Justice Department officials who joined in the grand jury's probe—Raymond Whearty, Alexander Campbell, and particularly Thomas Donegan—had all become increasingly skeptical of Hiss's testimony. They began steering the jurors' attention away from Chambers's self-confessed perjury toward an almost exclusive scrutiny of Alger Hiss.

THE GRAND JURY PROBE

The Justice Department's changed attitude reinforced Chambers's credibility. When U.S. Attorney John F. X. McGohey met with reporters on December 8, he spoke of "getting closer than we ever have been before to a final conclusion. We feel we are finally getting some real evidence." Still, McGohey and company faced a major hurdle: the difficulty in framing an indictment, even if the grand jury chose to land on either Hiss or Chambers. The microfilms and typed documents had been stolen during the late 1930s, and the statute of limitations ruled out prosecution for espionage or treason in peacetime after three years had elapsed. Justice Department prosecutors began examining the conspiracy and perjury laws for possible use in the case, although a conviction on either charge required significant corroboration beyond the documents themselves.[24]

A procession of familiar witnesses filed through the grand jury's room in the Federal Building at New York's Foley Square during mid-December: Chambers, Alger, Priscilla, and Donald Hiss, David Carpenter, Nathan I. Levine, Henry Collins, Hede Massing, Nixon, Robert Stripling, Adolf A. Berle, Henry Julian Wadleigh, William Ward Pigman, and A. George Siiverman. One witness changed his earlier testimony, although perhaps not sufficiently. Henry Collins now admitted having met Chambers "in Washington about '34 or '35," despite his earlier denials. "My impression is that someone brought him to a cocktail party I was giving," he wrote in reconstructing his grand jury testimony for Hiss's lawyers, "and I did see him on one or two other occasions subsequently either at my place or elsewhere in Washington. My acquaintance with him was casual, so casual that I have forgotten what name he was using at that time."[*][25]

The grand jury interrogated Priscilla Hiss on December 10 in a long and decidedly hostile session. The jurors questioned her at length about her recollections of "George Crosley" and his wife and baby. She said she had not been friendly with the couple, even when they stayed at the P Street home, and could recall nothing about her conversations with either "Crosley" or his wife: "I said something about their [P Street] visit really being a nuisance." She remembered having met Crosley only five or six times: "I said he dropped in—he was a 'dropper-inner.'"[26]

Priscilla Hiss also said that Noel Field, Pressman, Witt, and Abt had visited their house socially; she described Henry Collins as a close friend; and again she denied any involvement in Communist activities. Questioned persistently about her typewriter, Mrs. Hiss told the jurors that she "had no notion of how we disposed of it." As for Chambers's accusations against Mrs. Hiss and her husband— that Hiss had taken the documents from State and that she had typed them—"I said there was not a scrap of truth in [them]."

A more agile witness than his wife in a series of appearances before the grand jury beginning on December 7, Alger Hiss again told Whearty and Donegan that

---

*Collins told Hiss on the day of his grand jury appearance about a friend who knew a doctor who said he treated Chambers in the 1937–38 period in Manhattan "for gonorrhea, frigidity, shock and persecution complex." The "friend" turned out to be a director of the American-Russian Institute, which Collins headed, but, like many similar rumors before it and afterward, Collins's allegation remained unproven. Priscilla Hiss also had a friend who told her that same day that Chambers had been in a mental institution. Again, no corroboration emerged. See Alger Hiss's December 8, 1948, memo of a talk with Henry Collins and Hiss's dictated memo on Priscilla Hiss's conversation, December 8, 1948, both in the Hiss Defense Files.

he had written only three of the handwritten notes. The fourth one "still did not look to me like my handwriting." He denied any connection with the typed documents.[27]

The following day Hiss returned for a brief session. First came questions about his friendship with Noel Field. Donegan asked whether he knew a woman named Hede Massing or Hedda Gumperz, to which Hiss replied no. Whearty described Massing's account of her visit with Hiss at the Fields', but Hiss denied any knowledge of the occasion.

On December 9 Donegan arranged an encounter between Hiss and Hede Massing. According to Hiss, the woman "was completely unfamiliar to me." There was no conversation. Later that day Hiss underwent further questioning by Whearty about his knowledge of Hede Massing. Whearty also asked whether he knew Josephine Herbst and Hiss responded: "I said that I knew a writer who wrote under the name Josephine Herbst but I did not believe I had ever met her . . . I said that I knew of her only as an author. . . ." Hiss did not mention that his attorneys had already been in contact with friends of Herbst, or that Herbst claimed to have known Chambers as "Carl" and as a member of the Ware Group.

He met Hede Massing again the following day, at another encounter arranged by the FBI in the Federal Building. At that time Mrs. Massing "said she did not want to hurt me but only to help me." She asked Hiss if he recalled having had dinner with her at the Fields' apartment, but he did not. "She said that Noel Field also told her that he was deeply under my influence and that I had helped him to accept world socialism." Mrs. Massing remarked that she had met Hiss only on the one occasion at the Fields'. "Near the conclusion of the conversation, when I said that I had no recollection whatever of her or of the event she was describing, she said, 'Then it must have been another Alger Hiss.' I said that might be one possible explanation."[28]

On December 11 Hiss was asked by the grand jury if he had talked "with Mrs. Hiss about persons from whom we might have borrowed or bought typewriters?" The jurors and Donegan clearly had their minds on establishing a connection between Hiss's typewriter and Chambers's documents.

Further questioning of Hiss dealt mostly with the rug that Chambers claimed to have given him as a present from their Soviet intelligence contact. Hiss backed away slightly from an earlier assertion that the rug had been meant as partial payment for money he said Chambers owed on the apartment rental. When one juror asked whether the rug had been given by Chambers "in compensation" for this rent, Hiss noted: "I said nothing express [sic] had been said about it; it was just a gift." The witness also recalled receiving it at his P Street apartment (i.e., before June 1936), and he denied Chambers's testimony that the rug had been rolled and stored in a closet. (The government had not yet learned about the rug being kept in storage in 1937–38, and Hiss did not mention the fact.)

Julian Wadleigh proved nervous and loquacious in waiting-room conversation with Alger and Donald Hiss, and with Henry Collins on December 8. Alger's memo of the discussion that day described the extraordinary scene:

> I greeted Julian Wadleigh and he replied by saying, "My lawyer tells me I am not supposed to recognize you because I am going to have to refuse to answer on grounds that it might incriminate me whether I know you or not." He said this smilingly. . . . [Later] he said, "The F.B.I. came to see me and I got sort of panicky and told them that I had given some documents to Chambers. However, my lawyer tells me this may not be too bad to have said because I did not tell them whether the documents were restricted or not. Now my lawyer says I must not answer any questions or talk at all because one thing will lead to another and I will say too much."
>
> At this point Donald and I told him that he should realize that anything he told us we would have to repeat if asked about it before the Grand Jury where we would be testifying under oath. He then asked if we could not regard what he had told us as in confidence and we said we could not. He then said, "Couldn't you forget what I said so that it could be as if it hadn't been said?" and we again said we could not. He then went back to his own seat and sat there rather disconsolately for some time. . . . When he returned [from testifying] he said, "Now they want to talk to my lawyer but perhaps I shouldn't have told you even that. I don't know what to say and what not to say."[29]

Two days later Hiss described the conversation to the grand jury.

Vincent Reno, like Wadleigh, had denied Chambers's story at first, but on December 11 he walked into the FBI's Denver field office and confessed to agents that he had turned over materials from the Aberdeen Proving Grounds in 1937–38, as Chambers had testified earlier. Reno appeared before the grand jury in New York a few days later,* and his confession reinforced a belief growing steadily stronger among Justice Department and FBI officials that the core of Chambers's statements about Hiss was true. During its closing days the grand jury focused its inquiry almost entirely on Alger Hiss and not his accuser.[30]

In the race for headlines—and witnesses—between HUAC and the Justice Department, the FBI again found itself caught in the middle. Pressured by Justice to locate evidence that linked Hiss directly to the typed documents, bureau officials also heard regularly from Mundt and Nixon, exchanging information with them on their mutual interest in certain witnesses such as Reno.[31]

By that time even newspapers previously sympathetic to Hiss had begun raising questions about his involvement and the lack of cooperation among the investigating agencies. "Let's Have the Facts," *The Washington Post* editorialized

---

*HUAC failed in frantic efforts to obtain Reno and several other grand jury witnesses for its own hearings.

on December 9, denouncing what the paper termed "a four-ring circus" in operation since Chambers handed over the "pumpkin papers." "Four different investigations of the case are simultaneously in progress"—Hiss's slander-suit inquiry,
the HUAC probe, the Justice Department–grand jury inquiry, and a separate
investigation at State. The *Post* urged publication of all the stolen documents and
a greater effort to determine the facts, squarely criticizing the Truman administration's handling of the affair. Another important paper, the normally Democratic Atlanta *Constitution,* charged the attorney general, the Justice Department,
and the FBI with "dereliction of duty in its failure so far to follow up leads" on
espionage cases provided not only in the Hiss-Chambers controversy but in the
Canadian spy trials two years earlier. The *Constitution* demanded pursuit of those
at State responsible for stealing the documents, "vigorous investigation of the
espionage now known to have taken place, and full prosecution of the guilty."[32]

The extent to which many liberals had been shaken in their earlier belief in
Hiss's innocence emerged starkly in a December 14 FBI memo from Nichols to
Tolson reporting a conversation with J. Russell Wiggins, managing editor of the
Post, in which Wiggins passed along unverified rumors about Priscilla Hiss and
Timothy Hobson. In the months before Chambers turned over the documents,
a number of rumors unfavorable to Priscilla had circulated widely but, for the
most part, only among Alger's friends and lawyers: Few had reached the atten-
tion of the Justice Department.[33]

Increasingly, Hiss emphasized the psychiatric defense outlined earlier by
Rosenwald, Dr. Binger, and other advisers. "I said that I thought Chambers was
a person of unsound mind and not normal," Hiss wrote of his grand jury testimony, "that he had, for some reason which I did not pretend fully to understand,
acquired a grudge against me and was trying to destroy me. I said that I considered that he had deliberately tried to frame me." Throughout his appearances
before the grand jury, Hiss also argued that if the machine on which the stolen
documents had been typed turned out to have been his, then Chambers had
somehow obtained access to it during the late 1930s. "I said that I felt his use of
the typewriter, if the identity of the typed exhibits were established, was simply
a form of forgery less easily detected than an attempted forgery of handwriting
and was part of the pattern of attempting to frame me."[34]

Thus the essential elements of Hiss's later defense arguments—Chambers
as spurned homosexual, Chambers as unbalanced psychopath, and forgery by
typewriter—were first suggested by Alger Hiss himself in 1948 during the course
of the HUAC hearings, the slander-suit investigation, and the grand jury probe.

As the jury neared its final days, the question of whether or not Hiss would
be indicted centered increasingly on the issue of typewriter evidence. Could it be
shown that the stolen State Department material had been typed on Alger Hiss's
Woodstock? More important, could this be demonstrated before December 15,
the grand jury's final day?

THE WOODSTOCK COVER-UP

Hiss and Chambers were not the only figures in the case who feared indictment. HUAC's continued refusal to turn the microfilm over to the grand jury had angered Justice Department officials so much that they began considering the possibility of a contempt citation for Richard Nixon. Also, relations between the committee and the FBI remained uneasy. Hoover had sent Attorney General Clark a memo describing the rumor, passed along by HUAC investigator Louis Russell, that Nixon intended to "embarrass the Bureau and the Director" by forcing Hoover to testify. Clark jotted on the memo: "There will be no testimony." Nixon appeared before the grand jury on the 13th—Stripling had testified several days earlier—and again refused to turn over the microfilmed rolls and strips, although he offered to allow the grand jury to examine the material on request.[35]

A test of wills between Congress and the courts seemed inevitable when, after Nixon's appearance, the grand jury voted to demand the microfilm and issued a subpoena. Nixon "was then taken before a Federal Judge," Assistant Director Ladd reported to Hoover that same day, "and stated that he did not want to be abhorrent but would have to take it [the subpoena] back to the committee and then it [the microfilm] would be turned over to the FBI." HUAC, in short, persisted in its determination to deal directly only with the FBI—not with Justice— but Nixon promised "personally" to deliver the material to Ladd the following morning.

The committee met in executive session on the morning of the 14th and agreed to Nixon's arrangement. Once in possession of complete copies of the film, the FBI laboratory experts began the process of determining when the film had been manufactured, particularly the two State Department strips. HUAC's action in handing over the five rolls undercut the Justice Department's "case" against Nixon.[36]

The microfilm also intrigued the Communist press. *The Daily Worker* ran a series of news stories throughout December denouncing Chambers as a renegade liar and charging a frame-up involving faked microfilm. The CP had maintained an understandably lively interest in the Hiss-Chambers case from the beginning, attacking Chambers during the August HUAC hearings as "a police spy back in 1940 . . . after he had been a Trotskyite." The *Worker* had ridiculed Chambers's testimony "about 'rings' and 'cells' [as] . . . shabby hokum which these stooges for the profiteers and war-makers have dished up to help the Truman Democrats and the COP 'get off the hook' in front of the electorate." Truman's denunciation of the committee's probe as a "red herring" obviously caught the Communists by surprise, although the *Worker* gave the president's statement front-page coverage and—that same day—described Hiss's denial of Chambers's accusations this way: "His biting comments left the committee squirming for fear the whole spy scare they had carefully built up would explode in their faces."[37]

The newspaper continued to cover the HUAC hearings carefully in the weeks that followed. It headlined on August 26: "UN-AMERICANS PLOT TO 'GET' HISS ON PERJURY." The following day the *Worker* published a column, "The Key Problem in the Hiss Case," in which the writer took no position on the question of Hiss's truthfulness: "He says he didn't [belong to the CP] and that's convincing enough to me, although Heaven knows I wouldn't be one to hold it against him if it were true." The "key problem" turned out to be the change in American public mood since FDR's death:

> Here is a young man who, whatever one may think about his present enthusi-
> asm for the Marshall Plan, the Truman Doctrine, and the Cold War, performed
> a highly useful service for his country during the New Deal and particularly
> during the war. . . . Since 1945, Alger Hiss has lived under a cloud of fear, a
> deep sense of danger overhanging his job and his career. . . . What lies in store
> for him, only time can tell. Perhaps John Foster Dulles will boot him out of his
> job. Perhaps there will be an indictment for "perjury." In any event, the future
> is not bright. . . . But if this is the fate of such highly placed men as Alger Hiss,
> what about the hundreds of lesser government employees?

The commentary was a curious one, since Hiss himself had said nothing publicly about living under any "cloud of fear" since 1945 and had been at pains to deny that he ever considered the 1946 State Department–FBI investigation as anything but perfunctory and exonerating. After several articles denouncing the HUAC probe of J. Peters, the *Worker* suspended coverage of the case, although not before picking up the theme of Chambers's possible homosexuality in an unmistakable manner: The paper described him on August 31 as "a small, pudgy man with effeminate manners and shifty, colorless eyes."

The Communist attempt to discredit Whittaker Chambers on the eve of the Hiss trial went from the pages of *The Daily Worker* to plans laid by the then-head of the NKVD's virtually defunct agent network in the United States, Alexander Panyushkin. He cabled his superiors in Moscow in December 1948 with a bizarre proposal to launch a disinformation campaign "exposing" Chambers as a former Nazi—and not Communist—agent:

> As "Karl" [Chambers's main underground pseudonym while a Soviet agent] is
> of German origin, lived and studied for some time in Berlin [Panyushkin and
> presumably other Russians credited Chambers's excellent written and spoken
> German to ancestry and residence rather than to intensive studies, which was
> the case], "to find" in German archives "Karl's" file from which it would become
> clear that he is a German agent who by Gestapo instructions was carrying out
> espionage work in the U.S. and penetrated into the American Communist
> Party. If we claim it in our press and publish some "documents" which could
> be produced at home, the effect of this will be very big. This information will

be snatched not only by foreign communist parties but by the progressive press in all countries and, as a result, positions of the Committee on Un-American Activities, the Grand Jury [then considering testimony from Hiss, Chambers, and others on the matter] and other organs will be strongly undermined.

It can be also claimed that "Karl" as a Gestapo agent is well known to the Committee and Grand Jury and other American organs, but heads of these institutions being vehement haters of the USSR, the Communist Party and the progressive movement in general, presented the case as if "Karl" and others supposedly spied for the USSR and not for Germany.*

Panyushkin's proposal did not find support in Moscow and for perfectly sensible reasons outlined in an immediate response:

The station's proposal to produce and publish in our press "documents" stating that the traitor Chambers was a German agent [and] by Gestapo instructions carried out espionage work in the U.S. and by German instructions penetrated into the CPUS [Communist Party of the United States] can't be approved. Certainly publication of such "documents" will affect extremely negatively our former agents exposed by Chambers for knowing that they worked for us after "converting" [them] into German agents. [As a result] these people may go, for instance, to cooperate with authorities, giving frank testimonies and so forth. Besides, transformation of these individuals from supposed agents of the Soviet intelligence into determined agents of a country which fought against the U.S. by no means can help them from the juridical point of view.

Nonetheless, Moscow remained intrigued by another element in Panyushkin's plan: "The station's proposal about production and publication of documents exposing some leaders of the Committee on Un-American Activities and the federal jury as Gestapo agents must be carefully examined and weighed."†

After Chambers turned over the "pumpkin papers" in early December, *The Daily Worker* published a series of front-page stories questioning the genuineness of the documents. "HOUSE UN-AMERICANS PULL NEW 'SPY' HOAX OUT OF A PUMPKIN," the paper declared on December 6, labeling Chambers HUAC's "self-confessed stool pigeon." Articles on "the Pumpkin Hysteria" followed almost daily.[38]

While the Communist press focused on the microfilm, most of those concerned at firsthand with Chambers's new evidence were far more interested in the typed documents. After release of the "pumpkin papers," three sets of investigators— HUAC's, Hiss's, and the FBI's—began searching for the machine used to type the stolen State Department documents, and for samples of the Hisses' typing from that period. In late November, Alger and Priscilla Hiss could recall almost

---

*File #43173, Vol. 4, p. 479, KGB Archives.
†*Ibid.*, p. 203.

nothing about the typewriters they had owned during the 1930s. Six days after Chambers turned over the typed documents, McLean informed Marbury:

> I have been trying to get definite facts as to the Hiss family typewriters. I now understand that there may be some question as to whether they owned their present typewriter prior to 1939. Apparently they had another machine before they acquired their present one, but they do not recall at the moment just when or how they disposed of it. I think that specimens of the writing produced on the Hiss typewriter in 1938 should be examined promptly. I am wondering whether you have any letters from Alger during that period which could be used for this purpose.

Apparently McLean had no luck in questioning either Alger or Priscilla Hiss during the days that followed, since his extant files contain no memoranda on the subject until the press revealed on December 3 the existence not only of the "pumpkin papers" but of the Baltimore typed documents as well.[39]

In a chastening letter to Hiss that same day, Marbury said he was "troubled" by Hiss's inability to determine what became of the typewriter he owned in 1938, or to find specimens typed on the machine during the 1930s. From this point, after Chambers turned over the "pumpkin papers," events unfolded rapidly. The following day Hiss and Marbury met with FBI agents in Baltimore, where Hiss signed a statement characterized chiefly by its vagueness concerning the typewriter:

> During the period from 1936 to sometime after 1938, we had a typewriter in our home in Washington. This was an old-fashioned machine, possibly an Underwood, but I am not at all certain regarding the make. Mrs. Hiss, who is not a typist, used this machine somewhat as an amateur typist, but I never recall having used it. Possibly samples of Mrs. Hiss's typing on this machine are in existence, but I have not located any to date, but will endeavor to do so. Mrs. Hiss disposed of this typewriter to either a second-hand typewriter concern or a second-hand dealer in Washington, D.C., sometime subsequent to 1938, exact date or place unknown. The whereabouts of this typewriter is presently unknown to me. Prior to this typewriter coming into the possession of my immediate family, it was the property of Mr. Thomas Fansler, Mrs. Hiss's father, who was in the insurance business in Philadelphia.

Hiss had also indicated to the agents that the typewriter had been in his family's possession before they left New York City for Washington in May 1933, and that "he would make every effort to locate same as well as other specimens known to have been typed on the Hiss typewriter, especially during the period from 1933 to 1939."[40]

By the time Hiss and Marbury spoke to the FBI, McLean and Rosenwald had hired a documents examiner, J. Howard Haring, who identified the stolen

State Department papers as typed on a Woodstock. While Hiss spoke to the FBI on December 4, McLean and Rosenwald interrogated Mrs. Hiss and Timothy Hobson on the subject of typewriters.

Priscilla Hiss, like her husband, could remember owning only her father's machine prior to receiving their present typewriter, a Royal portable, as a gift from Donald Hiss's sister-in-law, Cynthia Jones, in 1942:

> Mrs. Hiss did not know where she disposed of the Fansler typewriter. She thought she must have sold it for a few dollars to some dealer in second-hand typewriters in Washington. She had no names of any of them. She also thought she might have given it to the Salvation Army because she frequently gave things to it.

Timothy Hobson, on the other hand, "very definitely recalled that between the time that they got rid of the Fansler typewriter and the time they acquired the Royal . . . they had a rickety portable which he thought was a Corona."[41]

Both Alger and Priscilla Hiss said at this time that the "Fansler machine," the office model, had been in the family's possession until sometime after 1938, when they disposed of it. (Later they would alter that date to 1937, which would have precluded either of the Hisses having typed the stolen State Department documents on it.)

Timothy Hobson found in the basement of the Hisses' home two specimens of typewriting, a 1939 Cub Scout menu and a list of Greek names. The Greek list turned out—according to Hiss's documents expert—to have been typed on the Corona portable Hobson had recalled. Otherwise, neither Mrs. Hiss nor Hobson proved of much help to the attorneys in identifying the Fansler machine.[42]

Priscilla Hiss told the FBI on December 6 that she knew nothing about the make of the typewriter, how long the family had owned it, or how they had disposed of it other than that it had probably been to some Washington-area junk or typewriter shop or to the Salvation Army—this sometime after the Hisses moved to Volta Place in 1938. Alger Hiss repeated his testimony on at least five occasions to the grand jury between December 7 and 15, while Priscilla Hiss stood by these assertions when she appeared as a grand jury witness on December 10.

Neither the FBI nor the grand jury—nor, for that matter, Hiss's own attorneys— knew at the time that during these weeks, when perjury indictments hung in the balance, Hiss withheld three critical pieces of information concerning the Fansler typewriter and one of its successors. He told only one of his lawyers the fact that as early as December 7, and perhaps earlier, he thought he knew who had been given the Fansler machine. Hiss also did not inform either the FBI or the grand jury that his own documents examiner had linked a specimen of Mrs. Hiss's typing to the same machine, a Woodstock, used to type the stolen State Department documents, despite frequent grand jury questions on this point. Finally, neither he nor Mrs. Hiss testified that the Royal portable they mentioned as their current typewriter had not been in their possession since 1946 and had been retrieved only weeks before from Cynthia Jones—presumably after Chambers turned over the Baltimore documents.

Through these efforts to conceal pivotal evidence from the government and from his own defense attorneys, Alger Hiss engaged in an extraordinary and extended cover-up during the first two weeks of December 1948.

It began with Cynthia Jones's Royal portable. "While testifying to the grand jury and to their attorneys that they had owned a Royal since 1942, the Hisses did not mention that, according to Cynthia Jones, they had returned the type-writer to her in 1946—the year the FBI conducted its probe of Hiss at State—and retrieved it only in late 1948. If the Hisses owned still another machine during those two years, they never referred to it.

None of this might have emerged, had not Cynthia Jones been named before the grand jury as a possible Communist in late December 1948 grand jury tes-timony that leaked to the press.* Harold Rosenwald then interviewed her and determined she had seen Hiss once or twice a month since he had been in New York with the Endowment. A conference took place at the Debevoise firm's office involving Rosenwald, McLean, Cynthia Jones, and Donald Hiss, all the more remarkable since the naming of Jones did not directly involve Alger Hiss. But, according to Rosenwald's memo of the meeting, Donald Hiss "and I discussed whether she should be advised by Mr. McLean or Hugh Cox [Donald's lawyer]. I thought that she should be represented by Hugh Cox. I consulted Mr. Debevoise and he was of the same opinion. Thereupon Donnie called Hugh Cox and he agreed to protect her interests. Although Miss Jones was in the office on that occasion, I deliberately refrained from asking her any questions whatsoever. The only problem that I dealt with was her representation by counsel."[43]

Rosenwald's and McLean's anxiety over Jones does not necessarily mean that they were aware of the passage back and forth of the Royal portable. But there is some evidence that the lawyers were concerned about their client's possible mis-representations involving Cynthia Jones and the typewriter. Alger Hiss's memos of his grand jury appearances that month suggest the nature of the problem. On December lo he could recall only vaguely the machine in question: "I said in answer to questions that I thought we had had one or more portables and that we had never bought a new typewriter, that one or more of the portables could have been purchased second-hand or could have been given or lent to us. I said that I had little interest in typewriters; I did not make use of them myself." (Hiss repeated consistently that he never typed material, only Mrs. Hiss typed, although there is evidence that some recovered specimens of the Hisses' typing from the 1930s were composed by Alger and not Priscilla.) Hiss told the grand

---

*The charges were never proved.

jury he could not recall anything about the portable typewriters his family had owned: "I was asked whether I had discussed with Mrs. Hiss last night the question of from whom we might have borrowed portable typewriters. I said that we had not discussed that. I was asked . . . to think and talk with Mrs. Hiss about persons from whom we might have borrowed or bought typewriters." He remembered telling the grand jury that he had talked "to other members of my family over the weekend about the typewriters that we had had. . . . I said that I thought that none of those that I had reached had actually lent us typewriters."[44]

Such cautious responses could not completely disguise Hiss's efforts to mislead the grand jury. On December 4 McLean phoned Cynthia Jones to check out the fact—which Mrs. Hiss had mentioned—that she "gave the Royal to Priscilla in 1942." Mrs. Hiss did nothing to correct McLean's impression that this machine had been owned by the Hiss family completely since that time, which was simply not the case.[45]

Cynthia Jones retained Hugh Cox as her counsel in time for three interviews with the FBI. She filed long memos of these interrogations with the Hiss defense in the course of which she described more precisely their dealings in connection with the Royal portable. She recalled first giving the Hisses the typewriter in Washington during the summer of 1942 when she was about to leave for a wartime assignment in California: "To my certain knowledge . . . they did not have a typewriter" at the time, she explained, although the Corona portable—according to Hiss—was still in his household. The FBI agents then "asked how long [the Royal portable] had been out of my possession and I said probably within the past two months or so. They asked me why I had given it back to Mr. Hiss and I said because his lawyer [Harold Rosenwald] or he had asked for it. . . . However, I told them that Mr. Hiss himself had asked me for the typewriter." Jones did not know why Hiss wanted the machine, and when the agents asked whether Hiss came for the Royal "at approximately the same time as the Woodstock typewriter began to figure in this case," she again said she didn't know.[46]

Apparently the machine had been a loan, not a "gift," from Cynthia Jones to the Hisses, since she told the FBI agents "that it had been bandied back and forth from about 1942 to 1946 when I returned here to New York and brought it here with me." An agent later renewed the question of why Hiss wanted the machine returned to him late in 1948. "I told him I did not know—I had not asked—but presumed he wanted to use it for writing up business matters. . . . 'Why,' he asked, 'would not Mr. Hiss use the typewriter belonging to his lawyers or at his office.' I said, I did not know."

Thus Hiss's repeated assertions to the grand jury that he could not recall how he had received the portable typewriters in his family's possession since the late 1930s were untrue. He visited Cynthia Jones in either October or November 1948 to recover one of the two machines, a typewriter that he now informed the grand jury and even his own lawyer, McLean, had been in his possession since 1942.

Did he retrieve it from Cynthia Jones to check on its vintage and perhaps, as McLean's November 23 letter to Marbury suggested, to claim that he had possessed the Royal continuously since the late 1930s? McLean's documents expert had identified the Baltimore typed material as the product of a Woodstock office model. But the Royal portable given to Hiss by Cynthia Jones in 1942 had not been built until after the State Department documents were stolen, so it could not be argued that the machine had been the only Hiss typewriter since the late 1930s. Besides, Timothy Hobson recalled definitely the existence of a Corona portable that the family had owned between (but not before) disposing of the Fansler machine and acquiring the Royal portable.

Whatever Hiss's intentions regarding use of the Royal, his real concern by early December had shifted to the Fansler typewriter. If it turned out to be a Woodstock, perhaps *the* Woodstock used to type the Baltimore documents, then his indictment and perhaps Priscilla's would be assured. Hiss told the FBI on December 4 that the machine was "possibly an Underwood," and Mrs. Hiss denied any knowledge of its make when she talked to bureau agents on both December 6 and 7.[47]

Yet on December 6 Hiss and his attorneys learned a great deal more about the Woodstock, information partially communicated to Mrs. Hiss by the following day. Moreover, Hiss himself displayed a familiarity with the Fansler typewriter's whereabouts that he failed to share with his chief attorney.

Hiss's handling of the typewriter question during the ten days beginning December 6 seems both secretive and improvised, as if he had not yet decided the best way to deal with certain uncomfortable and incriminating facts.

On December 6, two days after Hiss had told the FBI about his uncertainty concerning the Fansler machine's make, McLean suddenly remembered a batch of old family letters that Hiss had turned over to him in early September, two months before Chambers handed over the typed documents. The attorney showed one of the Hisses' typed letters—written to an insurance broker, signed by Hiss and dated January 30, 1933—to the defense's documents examiner, Haring (Hiss later identified the typist as Priscilla). Haring recognized at once that the letter had been composed on a Woodstock, the same machine he had previously told McLean had typed the stolen documents—and, after further analysis, Haring gave his "tentative conclusion" that the 1933 letter "was typed on the same machine as the Chambers Documents." McLean reported Haring's identification, which linked Hiss's typewriter and the stolen documents, to Hiss that same afternoon. Hiss told McLean to inform the FBI about the 1933 letter, but he did not instruct his counsel to say anything about the Haring identification.[48]

McLean followed his client's instructions precisely. He told an FBI agent later that day about the 1933 letter and that the Fansler typewriter had been identified as a Woodstock, but "I did not tell him the expert's opinion as to whether it was the identical Woodstock upon which the Chambers documents were typed."[49]

Haring's identification of the Fansler machine not only as a Woodstock but also, tentatively, as the machine on which the stolen documents had been typed either jogged Hiss's memory or forced his hand. Mrs. Hiss was still being interviewed by the FBI, whose agents had already told McLean about the massive search under way to find the Fansler machine and samples of the Hisses' typing from the 1930s. Although as late as December 4 Hiss could recall nothing about his disposition of the machine when interviewed by the FBI, he phoned John F. Davis three days later on December 7, the day after Haring's identification, to relay some startling news.* Davis was then directing Hiss's slander-suit investigation in the Washington area, and he described the telephone call in a letter later that month to McLean:

> Alger had called me on the first day public hearings were resumed before the Committee here [December 7] and asked [me to] check on an old machine which he remembers he gave to Pat, the son of Claudia Catlett who used to do washing for both his family and Don's. Don tells me that Mrs. Catlett's last known address, which is quite old, was 2728 P Street, N.W., and within the past year Pat was working in the Oak Hill Market. . . . Don's wife has seen him driving a delivery truck for another store more recently. Moreover she received a Christmas card, without any return address, from him this winter, I anticipate that he can be located without too much difficulty. However, I understood you to say over the telephone that you were checking on the whereabouts of the machine in some other way. If you wish me to do anything about it, let me know; otherwise I shall keep my hands off.

Hiss apparently did not tell McLean this news on December 7. When McLean offered that same day to send defense detectives searching for the machine and for typing samples in a joint investigation with the FBI agents—an offer that the bureau declined—he said nothing about the Catlett lead.[50]

Hiss failed to inform the FBI or McLean about the recollection that the "old machine" being sought had been given to his maid's family in Washington, not to some secondhand dealer, and on three separate occasions between December 10 and 15 he told the grand jury he had no knowledge of the typewriter's disposition. When asked by a juror if the machine had been sold or thrown away, Hiss replied: "I have not any recollection of its disposition at all," and he reiterated this answer on a number of other occasions to jurors during this period. When asked if he had ever made gifts to people other than his family, according to Hiss, he replied: "I said that I had not been able to recall anyone but after talking to Timmy and my wife, I remembered that we had given an old upright

---

*Why Hiss told even Davis—although not McLean or Marbury—about the Fansler machine being given to the Catletts remains unclear. He may have felt it best that Davis, who worked closely with Donald Hiss in his investigations, check on its whereabouts, if only to locate the typewriter before the FBI found it.

piano to Timmy's music teacher and a used radio to the son of our maid, Claudia Catlett"—but he mentioned no other gifts such as the Fansler Woodstock, which he had mentioned to Davis days earlier.[51]

That machine was the vital piece of missing evidence in the case. If the typewriter could be located, FBI experts could establish whether or not Chambers's stolen documents had been produced on it. Hiss would later assert that the defense first learned the whereabouts of the typewriter in late January 1949 when Donald Hiss was visited by Raymond (Mike) Catlett, one of Claudia Catlett's sons, who told Donald that the FBI had asked him several times earlier that month about the Hiss typewriter and he had denied all knowledge. Mike then told Donald that his family had in fact received the machine and he offered to help to find it. With the assistance of defense lawyers, Mike managed to do so a short time later.

Alger Hiss has always denied what the Davis letter shows to have been a fact: that he had an "independent recollection" of the Woodstock's whereabouts almost two months before Mike Catlett came calling on Donald Hiss. "I say I know [about the machine]," ran one of Alger Hiss's many statements on the point in 1949, only "from what the Catletts have told us."[52] He said also that he had not been informed by defense experts about the identification of his Woodstock typewriter as the one that typed the stolen documents, despite McLean's memo describing his conversation with Hiss about Haring's identification on December 6.[53] Throughout the critical last ten days of the grand jury's term in December 1948, however, Hiss withheld the significant piece of evidence that the Catletts had received his old Woodstock.

But was the "old machine" Hiss mentioned to John F. Davis on December 7 really the Fansler typewriter? Hiss's FBI and grand jury testimony that month resolved doubts about this. Both he and Mrs. Hiss told the FBI that the Fansler machine had been in their possession throughout the 1930s until sometime after 1938, when they acquired a Corona portable, although in December 1948 neither Alger nor Priscilla even mentioned the existence of that Corona—only Timothy Hobson had remembered it. Mrs. Hiss testified on December 10 that they had owned "an old office typewriter" throughout the 1930s: "My father had given it to me from his office when he retired." And Hiss pinned down the identification of this "old machine" more precisely on December 14 for the grand jury:

Q. How many typewriters did you have in your home over . . . that period of time . . . when you were changing from the Department of Justice to the Dept. of State [1936]?

A. I remember the old typewriter I have testified about before and you have examined me about.

Q. When you say the "old typewriter" you are referring to the typewriter—

A. That belonged to Mr. Fansler, my wife's father. . . . I think we had it from the early 30s for some period after that, some years after that.[54]

Nor did Hiss have much choice when he instructed McLean to inform the FBI about the 1933 letters, the lawyer having discovered another one dealing with insurance matters later that day. On December 4, in Marbury's presence, Hiss had promised the FBI agents to "make every effort to locate . . . specimens known to have been typed on the Hiss typewriter, especially during the period from 1933 to 1939," and Marbury had pressed him on this point in a December 3 letter, stressing the importance of Hiss's "voluntary production . . . of papers which were typed on that particular machine." Hiss's attorneys could not withhold the newly found 1933 letters from the FBI in the light of Marbury's advice, Hiss's own promise, and simple common sense. But it is worth recalling that Hiss insisted to McLean that *only* the letter be shown to the FBI. He did not ask that the bureau be advised about Haring's analysis of its relationship to the stolen documents, nor did he inform the FBI—as he told John F. Davis—about his recollection of having given the Fansler machine to the Catletts. Hiss spent that entire period pointedly hiding from the grand jury and the FBI any knowledge of the machine's disposal, leading the bureau in an extensive wild-goose chase through Washington-area junk, secondhand, and typewriter stores rather than looking for the Catletts, as Hiss's attorneys did the following month. Alger Hiss, in short, spent the critical part of December 1948 covering up his knowledge of the Woodstock typewriter's disposition, Haring's identification of the machine as the one that had typed the stolen documents, and Cynthia Jones's recent possession of his Royal portable.[55]

Priscilla Hiss proved no more helpful. When she met with the FBI on December 6, accompanied by McLean, she said she had received a typewriter from her father, Thomas Fansler, during the early 1930s. Beyond this, Mrs. Hiss could not go, as McLean's memo of the meeting indicates:

> [FBI Agent] O'Brien asked me directly whether I had obtained any information from the [Fansler] insurance office as to the typewriter. I told him that this afternoon, I had been informed by our investigator that he had found a man in the office . . . who said that he remembered that Mr. Fansler took a Woodstock Typewriter from the office and said that he was going to give it to Mrs. Hiss. . . . O'Brien asked whether Mrs. Hiss had any specimens of any typewriter [sic] done in her home. She said no. I felt it necessary to point out that this answer was incorrect.

McLean then mentioned the two specimens found by Timmy on December 4, "neither of them . . . done on a Woodstock," but said nothing until the following day about the January 1933 letter typed on a Woodstock that he had discussed with Haring and Alger Hiss earlier in the afternoon.[56]

Mrs. Hiss continued adamantly to deny all knowledge of the machine—despite learning from McLean on the 6th about her father's associate having told the Hiss investigator that Fansler gave her a Woodstock. McLean described her behavior during the December 7 FBI interview: "O'Brien showed her the carbon of the January 30th letter and asked her if she recognized it. She said she did not. He asked her whether she had typed it. She said she did not remember." Nor could Priscilla Hiss state "whether it looked like her typing or the type of her typewriter." O'Brien, "in some disgust," pointed out to McLean while Mrs. Hiss had left the room that unless she admitted the insurance letter had been typed on her machine, "the chain of evidence would still not be wholly completed even if it should develop that this was the typewriter which typed the Chambers documents." McLean could not tell whether O'Brien "thought that Mrs. Hiss was intentionally withholding this last link of evidence or not," adding in his memo of the encounter that when he had showed the same letter to Alger Hiss the previous day, "he said at once that he remembered the letter and the incident relating to his insurance to which the letter refers and that it must have been typed on the Hiss typewriter, undoubtedly by Mrs. Hiss, as he does not type that well."[57]

Three days later Priscilla Hiss continued to deny before the grand jury that she recalled the make of her father's machine, which had been in the Hiss household for at least six years, despite McLean's identification of the typewriter as a Woodstock during her FBI interview. When asked how she had disposed of it, Priscilla said: "I don't know whether we junked it, or what we did with it. . . . I think we may have given it to a junkman or may have given it to the Salvation Army, or something."*[58]

Until the defense recovered her father's typewriter in April 1949, Priscilla Hiss would continue to deny that she knew its make—despite the many public references by then to its being a Woodstock, despite Hiss's call to Davis, despite McLean's statement in her presence on December 6, and despite much other information with which she was undoubtedly familiar. Most significant in this connection were two letters Priscilla received from her brother, Thomas Fansler, which referred to the machine as a Woodstock. "I am sorry but I cannot recall anything definite about the Woodstock typewriter," Fansler wrote on December 26, 1948, answering Mrs. Hiss's inquiry on the question. Four days later he observed matter-of-factly about the machine: "Again, re how come the Chambers documents were copied on Father's Woodstock (if true)?"[59]

When did Alger Hiss first take up the question of "Father's Woodstock" with his wife? Did they refer to it during the critical days that followed Haring's December 6 identification of the typewriter as the one that had turned out the stolen documents? In 1949 Priscilla Hiss acknowledged in court having talked about the disposition of the typewriter with her husband "a day or two prior to my being in the grand jury" (on December 10)—in short, after Hiss told Davis the

---

*Mrs. Hiss later recalled the matter quite differently: "I most distinctly remember telling the grand jury . . . that the old typewriter was given to our housekeeper [Claudia Catlett]. Letter of Priscilla Hiss to the author, February 4, 1976.

machine had been given to the Catletts. Priscilla Hiss also later said she talked about the whereabouts of the "old machine" with her husband after his December 4 FBI interview but prior to her own December 7 statement.[60]

A possibility remains that while discussing the Woodstock's disposition with his wife during this period Hiss did not inform her about Haring's findings. Moreover, Priscilla Hiss had already heard about the report of McLean's investigator concerning a Woodstock during her December 6 meeting with the FBI, but she may have felt that the news from her father's former office was too imprecise to be conclusive. After being confronted by the FBI agents with the 1933 letter typed on the "old machine" on December 7, she denied having typed it (the following year she would admit this). Both to the FBI and to the grand jury three days later Priscilla said she did not know the make of the Fansler machine. Of course, she may have been so troubled by the case, or so forgetful, that she did not remember either the 1933 letter, the typewriter's make, or how she had disposed of it.

More likely, McLean and her husband both shielded her from knowledge of the damaging information in Haring's analysis of the January 1933 letter, at least while she underwent the FBI and grand jury interrogations. Hiss had insisted throughout this period that Priscilla and not he had typed all of the Hiss-family letters from the 1930s. Hiss's claim would have suggested, especially in the light of Haring's conclusions, that Priscilla had probably typed the stolen documents. Under the circumstances, both Hiss and McLean may have felt that the less Priscilla was told about the defense investigation on December 6 and 7, the better it would be for all. At the very least, Priscilla Hiss must have known more than she admitted about the family's typewriters when testifying to the FBI, to the grand jury, and even to her own attorneys.

But Alger Hiss certainly knew about the Fansler Woodstock. Donald Hiss, judging from Davis's December 28 letter, had been told about the typewriter and had begun searching for the Catlett family.* Donald's familiarity with the Catletts remains particularly fascinating in the light of a cryptic memo filed by Harold Rosenwald two days after Hiss's phone call to Davis: "Mr. Hugh Cox [Donald's lawyer] called me on the telephone at home early this morning. He said that 'they' had found the typewriter. He did not know anything more about it. He said that he received his information from 'down south.'" That same day a Woodstock Typewriter Company official in Chicago named Delmar DeWolff told the FBI about a phone call he had received earlier in the day from Hiss's chief investigator, Horace Schmahl, in which "Schmahl intimated that he knew [the] present location of [the] typewriter."[61]

---

*Yet when Donald Hiss phoned Harold Rosenwald to discuss the typewriter question on December 13—six days after Alger Hiss phoned John F. Davis about the Catletts—Donald Hiss stated (according to Rosenwald) that he "has no recollection of Alger's machine at all." Re Typewriters, December 13. 1948, Hiss Defense Files.

Did "down south" refer obliquely to the Catletts, who were African-Americans? Had Donald Hiss or another representative of his brother tracked down the Woodstock's location within the Catlett family's circle months before the defense went through this process openly to recover the machine? Or did Cox's phone call refer only to another of the rumors that the FBI had found the Hiss machine? If so, what reason did Cox have for his cryptic remarks about "they" finding the machine "down south"? Whatever the meaning of his call, both Horace Schmahl and the FBI agents continued their separate searches in Philadelphia and elsewhere for the Hiss machine, occasionally crossing wires, to the embarrassment of Schmahl and to the annoyance of the bureau.[62]

Both Schmahl and the FBI agents spent much of the week of December 7 checking on the Fansler Woodstock in Philadelphia, where Priscilla Hiss's father had run an insurance agency prior to his retirement in 1931. Fansler had taken on a junior partner in 1927 named Harry Martin, whom Schmahl located a day after the FBI. Martin seemed fuzzy on dates, whether about the year the Woodstock had been purchased or other matters.* Throughout its investigation in December, the question of dating the purchase also troubled the FBI, which remained uncertain about the exact year. But one memo from the Philadelphia office's special agent reported: "The Woodstock typewriter in question was obtained by the partnership at a later date, probably sometime in 1929, at which time the [firm's] Royal typewriter . . . was disposed of." A December 10 report from an agent named Boardman, who coordinated the search in Philadelphia, also asserted that Grady "sold the Woodstock to Fansler-Martin probably during 1929.[†63]

---

*Thus Martin told Schmahl inaccurately that Fansler took the Woodstock home in 1937—in fact, he acquired the machine upon retirement six years earlier—and that Fansler died in 1938 (he died in 1940). Although Martin informed Schmahl that he had purchased a new Woodstock for the firm in 1928 from a Philadelphia salesman named Thomas Grady, Martin had told the FBI the previous day that he bought the machine in 1927, and "that this typewriter was the only one in the partnership office during the entire [four-year] life of the partnership." But when FBI laboratory experts tested letters typed in the Fansler-Martin office in 1927, they found the material had been produced on a Royal, indicating that Martin's memory of a 1927 Woodstock purchase date was erroneous. Also, both Martin and Grady fixed the Woodstock purchase date to the presence at the firm of a stenographer named Anne Coyle, who started work there in the fall of 1928, which meant that the machine had been bought either late that year or in 1929. However, since Grady quit the Woodstock company in late 1927, a 1928 or 1929 purchase date would also have been puzzling.

†One theory favored by Grady held that two Woodstocks had been purchased by Fansler-Martin during this period, one in 1927 (or earlier) and another in 1929. But such suggestions proved impossible to verify by December 1948, since the Woodstock distributorship's records for the 1920s had apparently been destroyed by fire. Agent Boardman shifted his guess as to the machine's purchase date from 1929 to 1927 by December 20. The following year Boardman settled—erroneously, as it turned out—on a 1928 date. See Boardman to Director for December 10 (#200) and December 20 (#367), both 1948. The FBI laboratory was caught similarly between the results of its own analysis (which pointed to 1929 as the year) and the Grady-Martin testimony. "The standard in the laboratory's files which matches most closely the typewriting appearing on [the Baltimore documents]," concluded one December 30 report, "reflects that the "Woodstock Typewriter Company made such type in 1929."

But the Hiss defense investigator, Horace Schmahl, played no role in the FBI's obtaining letters typed by the Hisses on the Fansler Woodstock (McLean having previously delivered to agents in New York copies of the 1933 insurance correspondence he had found on December 6).[64] It was the bureau's receipt of additional Hiss typing—material dealing with Timothy Hobson's private-school education, which FBI laboratory experts concluded had been typed on the same machine that produced the stolen documents—that marked a decisive break in the case less than forty-eight hours before the Grand Jury ended its term.

INDICTMENT

What the FBI had located—or, more precisely, what Paul Banfield, the headmaster of the Landon School in Bethesda, Maryland, had given FBI agents—was a three-page typewritten "Description of Personal Characteristics of Timothy Hobson," which bore the date September 9, 1936. The Hisses were then trying to gain admission to Landon for young Hobson, and they prepared the description at the school's request, sending it as an enclosure to a handwritten letter to Banfield, also dated September 9, and signed by Alger Hiss.

The headmaster also supplied the FBI with a September 1 letter signed by Priscilla Hiss, again dealing with Timothy's application for admission that term, and a carbon of a letter sent by Banfield to Hiss on September 3, requesting the "written statement of your ideas of the boy" that Alger or Priscilla typed and sent out six days later. The headmaster had previously turned down requests from both Hiss's and Chambers's attorneys for such typewritten letters, and he stipulated when giving them to the bureau that under no circumstances was HUAC to receive copies; the FBI, he felt, "is the only agency entitled to this information."[65]

The FBI laboratory reported to an elated Hoover that the three pages had been typed on the same machine that turned out Chambers's stolen documents. Hoover informed the attorney general that same day and, in a general statement on the Hiss-Chambers situation, advised Clark that "over the week-end I had reviewed the material in our files on this case and felt we were entirely clear in this matter and had done everything that we possibly could." As usual, Hoover's major concern lay not in the investigation's outcome but in exonerating the bureau—and himself—from the recurrent charge of ineptitude for its earlier handling of the case.[66]

Positive identification of the still-missing Woodstock proved the crucial turning point in the probe. Thomas Donegan, the senior Justice Department official at the grand jury, later confirmed that the prospects for Hiss's indictment became overwhelming only after word spread on December 13 among jurors and departmental representatives in New York that the identification had been made. One

New York reporter who provided Hiss's attorneys with sometimes accurate inside information about the grand jury's actions, John Weiss of the New York *Star,* told Harold Rosenwald a few days later "that the critical evidence against Hiss concerned the typewriter and that an expert had testified before the Grand Jury that the Chambers documents were typed on the same machine as certain documents identified as having been written by the Hisses."[67]

That expert, FBI documents examiner Ramos Feehan, had supervised the analysis of Landon School materials and other "Hiss standard" letters being tested against the Chambers documents. Feehan told the grand jury on December 14 that the typing on the stolen material matched the three pages on Timothy Hobson and the January 1933 Hiss letter to a Massachusetts insurance broker. The FBI laboratory also identified another of the 1933 letters from Hiss to insurance agents, written on February 17, as a Woodstock production. Also tagged by the bureau's specialists as "Hiss standards" typed on the same machine (and matching the Chambers items) were two more letters, one a December 1931 note from Mrs. Hiss's sister, Daisy Fansler, to a Philadelphia physician; the second, Priscilla Hiss's May 1937 application for admission to a University of Maryland summer program.[68]

When Donegan confronted Hiss with the Landon School documents on December 14 for purposes of identification, Hiss stated, according to his memo of the grand jury appearance, "that I had no doubt Priscilla and I had jointly prepared [the "Description"] and that I had no doubt that it was typed at home, probably by Priscilla. I said that it would very probably have been typed on Mr. Fansler's old machine and that we had never had any other office-size or make machine except that machine." Donegan then stated "with great emphasis that positively the typewritten documents produced by Chambers on November 17 had been typed on the same machine that Timmy's application which had been shown to me had been typed on."

Hiss conceded finally that his own documents examiner had identified the Fansler machine as a Woodstock and had also established that the Chambers documents had been typed on a Woodstock, but Hiss insisted that he himself had not recalled the make of the Fansler machine. He still said nothing to Donegan to indicate that his own expert had also told McLean that a Hiss-family letter from the 1930s was typed on the same machine as the Chambers documents, one week before the FBI reached the same conclusion using another Hiss letter. Donegan and the jurors pressed Hiss about "the coincidence of the typing in the memorandum about Timmy and the Chambers documents."[69]

That morning the Justice Department dispatched from Washington to New York a "Mr. Kneif," whom the FBI's New York office called "allegedly the Department's indictment expert." Officials from Justice scheduled an evening strategy conference, although the New York FBI agent in charge of the case believed "that a possible indictment had already been drawn up against Alger Hiss, charging him with perjury." The Justice Department's major concern at this point was to disprove Hiss's claim that Chambers could have stolen the Woodstock or gained access to it to type the State Department documents, and departmental attorneys vainly pressed the FBI agents for positive identification of the Hisses' latent fingerprints on the documents, something the bureau said was impossible given the large number of people who had handled the material.

Justice Department representatives also wanted "Hiss standards" typed on the Woodstock even later than the 1936 Landon School "Description" in order to show that Hiss still owned the machine in 1937 and 1938. The agent in charge of the bureau's New York office reported that the department had considered seeking an indictment not only of Alger but Priscilla as well, "but they felt they did not have sufficient evidence against her." He also indicated that "there is no consideration being given to returning an indictment against Chambers now."[70]

During his December 14 grand jury appearance Hiss tried an unsuccessful counterattack, while barraged by questions from skeptical jurors about the "coincidence" in the fact that his family's Woodstock had produced both the Landon School correspondence and the stolen documents. According to Hiss's memo of the testimony, he reminded the jurors of his cooperativeness throughout the proceedings:

> I then told the Grand Jury that at noon today, Mr. Campbell had asked to speak to me and had told me that I would be indicted. I said that I wanted the jury to know that I realized the serious nature of the evidence that appeared to militate against me, that naturally I did not know all of the evidence which the jury had had but that I did know that much damaging evidence had been produced by my own direct efforts and had been turned over to the government officials at my direction. I said that I had never failed to answer any questions directed at me, had claimed no privileges and had cooperated as fully as possible in trying to get to the bottom of this matter. I said that I had testified as truthfully as I possibly could and would continue to do so. I said that whatever the evidence, I knew that I had done nothing that was a breach of trust or a dereliction of my duty, that I was proud of my years of government service. . . . [I told the jurors] Mr. Campbell said [yesterday] in practically these words, "The F.B.I. has cracked the case. You are in it up to your eyes. Your wife's in it. Why don't you go in there and tell the jury the truth?" I said that I had replied that I had continuously told the truth and that I will continue to do so. Mr. Campbell had then said, "'You are going to be indicted. I am not fooling. There're five witnesses against you." I said that I had replied that I was not fooling either. Mr. Campbell then said, "This is your government speaking." That concluded the very brief interview but later Mr. Campbell called me back in again and had said, "I want to make it plain, your wife will be included." I had replied that I understood that.
>
> The jurors seemed to be a little put out that Campbell had taken over their province and had concluded without any qualifications that they were going to indict.[71]

But the jurors continued questioning Hiss about how Chambers could have gained access to his typewriter in order to turn out copies of stolen documents. He speculated that Chambers did not do the typing in their house but took the machine and kept it elsewhere for a time "without our being aware of it." Hiss was asked whether his wife used the touch system of typing, but he denied any knowledge of her expertise (Priscilla disclaimed competence as a touch-system typist, though she had passed a typing course at Columbia during the 1920s). Whearty retorted: "You should know that Timmy testified that Mrs. Hiss used the touch system," which appeared to irritate Hiss. When Whearty went on to note that his stepson said also that he [Timmy] was a "rapid two-fingered man," Hiss volunteered an unnecessary correction: "I said that I knew that recently Timmy had actually taken a course in typing." But he said he did not know that Timmy's portable—acquired, according to his stepson, after disposition of the Woodstock—had been a Corona. Before dismissing him as a witness until the following day, Whearty [according to Hiss's memo] "on his own initiative . . . said something to the effect that it was still very much unsettled. He was affable and pleasant," in sharp contrast to Campbell's earlier reaction.

On December 15, the last day of the grand jury's term, Deputy Attorney General Peyton Ford phoned Assistant FBI Director Ladd to advise "that he thought it possible that an indictment might be returned against Hiss." Ladd asked Ford "if he had forgotten the charges of perjury against Chambers," to which Ford replied that "the Department wanted to see if they could obtain a conspiracy indictment for espionage first and thereafter they had in mind still considering perjury charges against Chambers."[72]

Uncertainty concerning the future of the Hiss-Chambers investigation, in short, persisted right up to the grand jury's final session, with both men still facing possible prosecution. A troubled Edward McLean wrote to William Marbury that morning: "I am very much afraid that Alger and Priscilla will be indicted today. I have done everything that I possibly can . . . to save them. I have urged Campbell to postpone any action for the new grand jury rather than to rush it through with this one. He has said that he will give consideration to that request but I am doubtful whether he will grant it."[73]

Arriving at the courthouse early, Hiss asked Donegan if he could appear before the grand jury "promptly this morning." Summoned soon after the session began, Hiss focused attention on Chambers's "background and . . . his strange disordered psychology." He told the assemblage, according to his memo: "One of the jurors yesterday had asked me if I didn't think my theory about how Chambers could have gotten access to our typewriter was fantastic and . . . I replied that I thought it was but that I thought Chambers was a fantastic person." Hiss pointed out that he had turned over information and material concerning the "psychological theory" of Chambers's motivation to Justice Department officials but he was not certain that "what seemed to me relevant information had reached the Grand Jury." He then began explaining the analysis of Chambers done by Dr. Binger—"an eminent psychiatrist whom we had been consulting"—to bring out "aspects of Mr. Chambers' strange and troubled life."

Even Hiss recognized that this effort fell flat. "Mr. Donegan promptly asked me if my psychiatrist had examined Chambers, obviously throwing cold water on my suggestion," noted Hiss's memo. Moreover, "the jurors did not indicate any very great interest in pursuing this although they listened to my statement with interest."

Once Hiss completed his statement, Whearty and Donegan resumed their questioning of when Hiss claimed to have seen Chambers for the last time. At one point "Whearty said he wanted to ask one question for the record. He said, 'You wouldn't be the first man who has testified falsely to shield his wife.' He said he was making no implication but that he wanted to ask me if I was shielding Mrs. Hiss. I replied that . . . I was not shielding my wife and that she needs no shielding in this matter." As for the Woodstock, "I had a visual memory of the machine being in the Volta Place house" in 1938. Hiss added that "Chambers might have bribed a maid [i.e., Claudia Catlett] to let him get access to the typewriter."[74]

The jurors also directed Hiss to repeat his explanation of Chambers's possession of four slips of paper summarizing State Department cables in Hiss's handwriting. Hiss thought it unlikely that Chambers came to State himself to filch the slips of paper, but suggested the possibility of some confederate, a cleaning person or another State Department employee who had access to Hiss's office.

By then Hiss had detected the decidedly unfriendly atmosphere in the jury room: "I got the impression that Mr. Donegan was himself favoring an indictment of me because I noticed on several occasions he would, after a reply of mine given to a question by a juror, ask a question . . . which tended to minimize the effect of my answer. Four or five of the jurors appeared very frankly to be completely skeptical of my testimony with respect to the possibility of Chambers having had access to the typewriter." Hiss stressed his belief that Chambers's use of his machine "was simply a form of forgery . . . and was part of the pattern of attempting to frame me," though he remained vague on his accuser's motives: "for some psychological reason that I did not understand, he was trying to destroy me." Evidently seeking some further explanation of the point, Whearty asked whether Hiss had had "any personal relations with Chambers" [presumably homosexual relations] or whether Chambers had engaged in an affair with Mrs. Hiss "which might have given him a motive for framing me. I said none whatever." But Hiss, according to later accounts by jurors, provoked outright laughter when he said: "Until the day I die, I shall wonder how Whittaker Chambers got into my house to use my typewriter."

The grand jury released Hiss as a witness early in the afternoon and handed down a two-count perjury indictment. The first, using Hiss's December 15 testimony, alleged that he had spoken falsely in denying that "in or about the months of February and March, 1938, [he] furnished, delivered and transmitted to one Jay David Whittaker Chambers, who was not then and there a person authorized to receive the same, copies of numerous secret, confidential and restricted documents, writings, notes and other papers, the originals of which had theretofore been removed and abstracted from the . . . Department of State." The second perjury count related to the first, charging that Hiss's testimony "was untrue in that the Defendant did in fact see and converse with the said Mr. Chambers in or about the months of February and March, 1938."[75]

Departmental lawyers had decided that it would be impossible to obtain an espionage indictment against Hiss, given the passage of a decade and the prewar circumstances involved. But the perjury indictment incorporated the broader assumption that, in meeting with Chambers in 1938 to hand over confidential State Department documents, Hiss had committed the crime of espionage.

Pleading not guilty to both counts, Hiss appeared shaken during his arraignment, according to the *New York Times* reporter covering the event:

> When he left the jury room shortly after the indictment was returned . . . he wore the same confident smile and polished manner that has characterized his demeanor in his brief but daily contacts with reporters during the grand jury hearings.
>
> Yesterday he appeared solemn, anxious and unhappy. He stared straight ahead with a grim and worried look, and had nothing to say. To observers it seemed obvious that he had not expected to be indicted, and that the action of the jury had come as a shock from which he had not yet recovered.

He was released on $5,000 bail. That same day, December 16, a new federal grand jury was sworn in at Foley Square.[76]

The indictment produced predictably variant reactions. Justice Department officials defended themselves against charges that the Truman administration had sought, as part of a "whitewash," to prevent Hiss's indictment. They took the unusual step of holding a press conference after the arraignment to announce that a sweeping FBI investigation of the case was continuing. Truman, for his part, refused to back down from his earlier opinions on the case and told a press conference that he stood by his view of the HUAC spy probe. "That's the President's story," Richard Nixon observed, "and he's stuck with it. Rather than the herring on the hook, I think that Mr. Truman is on the hook." HUAC and Justice continued their feud even after Hiss's indictment, as the press quoted "anonymous sources" who asserted untruthfully that bungling committee staff members had ruined one roll of microfilm by shining a flashlight on it.

The committee, in turn, treated Hiss's indictment as "vindication" of its earlier activities and publicly congratulated the grand jury, the FBI, and (suprisingly) the Justice Department. Also HUAC summoned additional witnesses connected with the case, and the Republican majority scheduled a final round of both executive and public sessions during the remaining weeks of December. Anticipating criticism, and perhaps a move to abolish HUAC by the Democratic-controlled 81st Congress when it convened in January, Nixon and Mundt announced recommendations for a "code of fair procedure" to govern future hearings and better protect the rights of witnesses.[77]

But HUAC was HUAC. On December 17 the committee resumed its headline-hunting pursuit of "highly important, highly valuable information" on Communist espionage with the first of a series of executive sessions held in New York. One witness was confessed ex-Communist Max Yergan, who, in the course of testimony, named Donald Hiss's sister-in-law Cynthia Jones as a Communist.[78]

J. Edgar Hoover and his aides were more concerned about locating the Woodstock. Hoover tried to arrange another interview with Mrs. Hiss to "seek her cooperation in coming to Washington to identify the second-hand store or dealer" that she said had been given the typewriter during the late 1930s.* McLean never agreed to a reinterview, so the bureau continued its search unaided by the Hisses. One FBI report suggested considering an immediate interview with Horace Schmahl and made it clear that the bureau had been keeping tabs on Schmahl's investigation:

> It is observed there has been no indication Schmahl is looking for a Woodstock typewriter but instead is attempting to secure specimens. No information has been received that Schmahl or any other Hiss representative has made inquiries in Georgetown area, Washington, D.C., where typewriter was disposed of, according to Hiss. Schmahl may know where typewriter is located. Schmahl's instructions from Hiss or Hiss's law firm would be of great interest as well as Schmahl's observation concerning results of his own investigation. He may have idea as to serial number of typewriter, where it was disposed of, when it was disposed of, if it was repaired, etc.[79]

The Hiss defense's apparent lack of interest in finding the Woodstock puzzled the FBI, considering its own ongoing, exhaustive, and fruitless search for the machine. But McLean's files indicate that Schmahl was not ordered to follow up Hiss's phone call to John F. Davis about the Catletts and the typewriter. Although McLean told Davis not to check on the matter himself—that he [McLean] was having it investigated—no defense lawyer contacted the Catletts until late January 1949. By then the FBI had already begun to question Claudia Catlett and her sons.

---

*An FBI memo the previous day to field offices in Washington, New York, and Baltimore noted that the Washington office "Presently has large number of agents attempting to locate Woodstock typewriter on which documents by Chambers to federal court in Baltimore were typed," that the "only information" furnished the FBI had come from the bureau's December 4 and 7 interviews with Alger and Priscilla Hiss, and that "in view of vastness of project of locating this typewriter" additional leads should be sought.

Worried at the time of his client's indictment about fund-raising for the defense or, as he described it in his December 15 letter to Marbury, "the sordid detail of money for investigations, etc.," McLean reported that Hugh Cox (Donald Hiss's lawyer, who had sent McLean more than $1,250 to cover investigative expenses in November) "says that he can give me no assurance that his principals will continue to contribute." Neither McLean nor Marbury ever indicated in their correspondence the identity of Cox's "principals." Also, Hiss could count on no further support, financial or moral, from the Carnegie trustees beyond their previous commitment to a three-month leave of absence. After the indictment, the trustees clearly anticipated a resignation at the end of the three months, if not sooner. Dulles objected even to Hiss's signature appearing on the 1948 president's report until Shotwell worked out a face-saving compromise.[80]

After returning from Paris in late December, Dulles quickly drafted a long statement for other trustees explaining both his and the Endowment's relationship with Hiss. He asserted that three people had turned down the post of president before Hiss was asked as "the next most available person," a claim challenged by John W. Davis in a December 30 letter to Dulles. Dulles's statement detailed his conversation with Hiss during the August 1948 HUAC hearings in which he urged Hiss's resignation from Carnegie, and mentioned the latter's request that this departure be deferred until after he had had a chance to fight the charges. It was clear by this time, with Dulles back in charge of Endowment affairs, that Hiss's few remaining supporters had abandoned hopes of saving his job.

Not that Hiss lacked for eminent adherents. "Personally," Eleanor Roosevelt wrote in her newspaper column on December 27, "I am going to believe in Alger Hiss's integrity until he is proved guilty. I know only too well how circumstantial evidence can be built up, and it is my conviction that the word of a man, who for many years has had a good record of service to his government, should not be too quickly disbelieved." What provoked Mrs. Roosevelt's anger was not only Hiss's indictment but also the fact that on the evening of December 20 Laurence Duggan fell to his death from the sixteenth floor of a Manhattan office building. Duggan's demise stirred an immediate public furor when Karl Mundt released HUAC testimony by Isaac Don Levine in which the latter accused Duggan of having been a Communist agent. Mundt also issued a callous and flippant statement in which he boasted that the committee would reveal the names of other figures in the probe "when they jumped out of the window."

Nixon had joined Mundt in "voting" to release Duggan's name and Levine's testimony, and he shared in the general criticism that came from Democrats and many Republicans. Even Hébert and Rankin denounced Mundt's release of Duggan's name, Hébert calling it "a blunder and a breach of confidence" while Rankin termed it simply a "mistake." There were far stronger attacks by liberal Democrats, who pointed out, as Nixon acknowledged, that Chambers had accused Duggan not of involvement in espionage but only of having been a "fellow traveler" with close ties to Communists during the thirties. Duggan had admitted such connections when interviewed by the FBI on December 10, substantially confirming Chambers's account.[81]

On December 24 Attorney General Clark issued a statement calling Duggan "a loyal employee of the United States Government," and both Nixon and Mundt backed away from earlier attacks to accept this verdict: Mundt called the incident "a closed book," although he and others had speculated earlier as to whether Duggan's death had any connection with the spy probes then in progress, especially considering Duggan's friendship with Hiss. "Here is a mystery that was still unsolved," Mundt observed. "A man had met a violent death. Perhaps it was homicide; perhaps it was suicide; perhaps it was accident. We didn't know and we still don't know." The police report described the death as an accident, a verdict Mrs. Duggan appeared to accept, although the deceased's insurance company understandably leaned toward suicide and opened an investigation.

A close friend of Duggan's, Sumner Welles, wired New York Mayor William O'Dwyer on December 21 that it was "impossible to believe" Duggan's death had been "self-inflicted." Welles urged an immediate and thorough probe, claiming to have received a letter from Duggan written the day of his death "in the best of spirits." Neither the police inquiry nor the FBI check turned up any evidence that Duggan had been murdered or planned a suicide. His post as president of the Institute for International Education had clearly been placed in jeopardy by the Bureau's interest in Duggan's earlier relationship with Hiss and Noel Field.[82]

On December 25, four days after sending his wire demanding an investigation into Duggan's death, Welles was found unconscious at his Virginia estate, almost frozen to death from exposure after an apparent heart attack. Helen Duggan later told Hiss's lawyers that she was "sure that Welles' . . . Christmas illness may have resulted from grief [at Duggan's death]." Edward McLean mused: "Some of the New York papers yesterday carried a story . . . that Laurence Duggan had told the FBI that he had been approached in the late 1930s by two people who asked him to join a Communist espionage ring. . . . This interesting revelation," McLean wrote Marbury on December 28, "together with Sumner Welles' mysterious heart attack on Christmas night, make me think that Duggan may well have known some things that we don't know and that very possibly Welles knows them too."[83]

At least four personal tragedies had been linked publicly, if indirectly, to the Hiss-Chambers probe: Harry Dexter White's fatal heart attack, W. Marvin Smith's suicide, Duggan's unexplained death, and Welles's heart attack. A fifth episode took place in December, shortly after Hiss's indictment, this one involving Esther Chambers.

She had been driving from Westminster to the Baltimore train station on the afternoon of December 17 to pick up her husband, who was returning from testifying before the new grand jury. Suddenly a seventy-year-old deaf woman stepped out from between two parked cars, and was hit by Mrs. Chambers's auto. The woman died in a hospital later that day. State police arrived in Westminster to escort Esther and Whittaker Chambers back to Baltimore, where she was booked and released on bail provided by attorney Richard Cleveland. Esther Chambers was later acquitted of manslaughter and reckless driving, and she settled out of court a civil suit brought by the victim's executors. But the incident scarred Mrs. Chambers emotionally as had none of her experiences in the Hiss case. "To my wife and me," Chambers later wrote, "this tragic episode seemed proof that there was no depth of the abyss that we were not to sound." Thus even Hiss's indictment and the grand jury's refusal to indict Chambers as well held little consolation for Chambers.[84]

All that lay ahead was struggle and stratagems. Once Hiss had been indicted, both the defense attorneys and the FBI dropped gentlemanly pretenses. Thus one bureau memo (already cited) proposed considering an interview with Hiss's investigator Horace Schmahl—who had already indicated a growing disbelief in his client's innocence—in order to determine what knowledge of the Hiss Woodstock the defense possessed and what moves its investigation had been making. The suggestion clearly envisioned making Schmahl a double agent on the Bureau's behalf. As for McLean, he had other tasks in mind for Schmahl, some of which skirted the edge of legality.

During the fall Schmahl had pretended to be interested in purchasing some antiques Laha Chambers, Whittaker's mother, wished to sell and also claimed to represent a relative interested in purchasing her home. Schmahl returned to Lynbrook on December 18 to check on a typewriter that he recalled having seen during the earlier visit. Apparently McLean hoped that the machine would turn out to be a Woodstock, so that the defense could argue Chambers also owned a typewriter of this make. But Schmahl reported on the 20th that he had "pursued the matter which we discussed and it proved to be a dud."[85]

Horace Schmahl's description of his visit indicates the lengths to which Hiss's investigators now felt impelled to go. After meeting Laha Chambers on December 18 "by pure accident" on a Lynbrook street, Schmahl made an appointment with Mrs. Chambers, who remained unsuspecting and cordial, to inspect her house for possible purchase. Later that day Schmahl and an associate toured the home with Mrs. Chambers and located the machine in question, an L. C. Smith. "The typewriter . . . was not a Woodstock but it had a sign on it saying that it had been repaired by a man named Woodward." Schmahl tried to take a typing sample, but found that "only a few keys worked" on the old machine, which Mrs. Chambers told him belonged to a neighborhood girl and was for sale. After a thorough, if covert, search of the house—"looking through the closets, attic and cellar"—Schmahl reported to McLean that he found no other typewriter or evidence that one had been recently moved. If only to prevent the trip from being a total loss, Schmahl found a desk used by Chambers during his visits to

Lynbrook; it was covered by manuscripts, and he "swiped two sheets of one of them for specimens."

The defense attorneys had begun to accumulate a file drawerful of damaging rumors concerning Chambers, in an attempt to substantiate their client's contention that he was an unbalanced, possibly homosexual paranoid who had set out to frame Hiss for malevolent personal reasons. The FBI sleuths had an almost equally implausible task ahead of them, that of ferreting out of the metropolitan Washington area a Woodstock typewriter that the Hisses said had been carted off to a junk store a decade earlier. As Louis Bender, the lawyer for Felix Inslerman, Chambers's underground photographer, told McLean in January 1949 while discussing the missing Woodstock, "the government's case would not be too strong if they do not have the typewriter and have to rely only on samples."[86]

Both McLean and Hiss knew this at the time and, therefore, they had little interest in sending Schmahl, John F. Davis, or other investigators to retrieve the Fansler Woodstock that Hiss recalled having given to the Catlett family. On the other hand, the FBI—misled in December 1948 by the Hisses about the Fansler machine's possible whereabouts—searched furiously in Washington's pawnshops, junk stores, and typewriter shops for the missing machine.

IX

THE DEFECTION OF "KARL"

THE ROOTS OF DEFECTION: "KARL" AND THE SOVIET PURGES

What makes someone raised in a Western democracy become a Communist? And why does that person decide to defect? The tangle of motives that produces political commitment to a revolutionary cause and, later, disillusionment, remains elusive. When Richard Crossman introduced *The God That Failed,* a collection of memoirs by six ex-Communists describing their journeys through the radical labyrinth of the 1930s and 1940s, he found few persuasive similarities of motive among the half-dozen:

> The only link, indeed, between these six very different personalities is that all of them—after tortured struggles of conscience—chose Communism because they had lost faith in democracy and were willing to sacrifice "bourgeois liberties" in order to defeat Fascism. Their conversion, in fact, was rooted in despair—a despair of Western values.... [One must recognize] the terrible loneliness experienced by the "premature anti-Fascists," the men and women who understood Fascism and tried to fight it before it was respectable to do so. It was that loneliness which opened their minds to the appeal of Communism.

Moving away from the Communist orbit in a process both extraordinarily painful and only partially successful, Crossman's subjects more easily rid themselves of belief than of loyalty:

> Not one . . . deserted Communism willingly or with a clear conscience. Not one would have hesitated to return, at any stage in the protracted process of withdrawal which each describes, if the Party had shown a gleam of understanding of his belief in human freedom and human dignity. But no! With relentless selectivity, the Communist machine has winnowed out the grain and retained only the chaff of Western culture.

Crossman's strictures apply directly to the ordeal of Whittaker Chambers. So does the ultimate question Crossman raises about the defector stripped of devotion to party: "What happens to the Communist convert when he renounces the faith?" Some, those who avoided intimate connection with the party's inner workings, managed to escape with their personalities relatively intact and, in any case, certainly "not molded" by the party. "Their withdrawal, therefore, though agonizing, did not permanently distort their natures." Others, however, could never completely transcend or escape from their identities as Communists:

"Their lives [were] always . . . lived inside its dialectic, and their battle against the Soviet Union . . . always a reflection of a searing inner struggle. The true ex-Communist can never again be a whole personality." This description fits Chambers, in whom, like Arthur Koestler (one of Crossman's subjects), "this inner struggle [became] the mainspring of his creative work."[1]

Chambers underwent a progressive alienation produced by three distinct sets of stresses: first, the pressure of events within the Soviet Union; second, conflicts within the Communist espionage network in the United States; and, finally, changing personal perceptions of "secret work." In his analysis of these changes, both during the Hiss case and subsequently in his memoir, *Witness,* Chambers mentioned all three dimensions of the experience but isolated the third—his growing ideological disagreement with Communism—as the pivotal element in his break. Given the anti-Communist climate of opinion during the late 1940s, Chambers's recollection that his doctrinal break with Communist ideology had figured most prominently in his decision to defect was understandable. "Karl's" declining faith in Marxist-Leninist theory and Stalinist practice certainly counted, but there is substantial evidence—some of which Chambers chose to omit or disregard a decade later and much of which he had apparently forgotten—that suggests another version of events.[2]

The motives that govern critical choices are always difficult to sort out, in retrospect, and, as Kenneth Burke, himself a committed radical during the 1930s, once wrote about such commitment:

> There were many for whom their political stand was interwoven with many strands not thus specifically political at all (except in the sense that one could reduce all human relations to politics). Yet the merging is so thorough, one would be hard put whether to say that it is or is not "deeply or religiously felt." . . . For some, politics had very definite sexual tie-ups (normal or perverted); for others, it meant the alternative to such involvements. For some it meant marriage, for some it meant divorce. . . . I am sure that there was a whole world of such motives operating somehow, in a tangle behind the tangle. . . .[3]

Some specifics of the "tangle behind the tangle" that led to Chambers's break: the impact of Stalin's purge trials on Russian intelligence agents abroad, the counterattack upon Stalinist influence in this country led by American Trotskyites and their supporters, and the emotional confusions of Chambers's bisexual life. In the end, however, when "Karl" went into hiding in April 1938, cutting all ties with former underground associates (and—according to his 1949 FBI deposition—ceasing to engage in brief homosexual affairs), he acted less as a recusant from Communist dogma than as a refugee from Stalinist reprisal. Chambers escaped, in short, for the most basic of reasons: self-preservation.

The roots of defection extended back to 1934 and the failure of his efforts—along with those of fellow agents John Sherman ("Charles Chase") and Maxim

Lieber—to establish the American Feature Writers Syndicate as a successful front for Soviet espionage in Japan. Sherman returned from Japan only to leave almost immediately for Moscow. There, Chambers told Herbert Solow, Sherman "got in bad . . . having fallen in with a group of malcontents including other secret agents [the Moscow purge trials had begun by then]. Finally, he [Sherman] talked himself out, got a sum of money to found a magazine in N Y (liberal), and when he got here, skipped. He contacted Chambers despite orders to the contrary, and told Chambers to tell the organization to leave him alone. They told Chambers they would, and the man vanished. He is now on the West Coast." Thus "Charles Chase," disillusioned with underground work by the time he returned from the Soviet Union in 1937, resumed his real name, John Sherman, and remained a member of the "open" Communist Party in California for years after he broke with the underground. Soviet agents in this country sought "Chase" without luck for months after his defection, but Chambers chose not to betray him, thereby provoking the anger and suspicion of his superior, Colonel Bykov.[4]

Eventually located in 1949 by FBI agents, Sherman remained mum, refusing to admit any of his underground activities, or to admit that he had ever known Chambers, or that he had ever met Alger Hiss (Chambers claimed later that he had introduced the two men). The photographer William Edward Crane, who had worked with both Sherman and Chambers in 1935–37, proved more cooperative in 1949. Crane confessed to the FBI his involvement in Communist espionage during the 1930s, confirmed a substantial portion of Chambers's story, and provided additional details of Soviet intelligence work during that decade. He had worked for a time with Bykov and could also corroborate the Russian's role in the network.

Before defecting, Chambers confided to Crane that he had become disillusioned with their activities:

> Crane advised that in the fall of 1937 [runs one of his FBI depositions in March 1949] Chambers told him that their work had fallen into the hands of the Nazis [Soviet and German intelligence services had begun cooperating in the United States at about this point, at the direct instructions of Moscow and long before the Nazi-Soviet Pact of August 1939] and that everyone seemed to be traitors. It was decided that Crane should return to the West Coast and get out of the work. Chambers told Crane that Sherman was living in Southern California, and warned him to stay away from Sherman and that everything would be all right.

Crane ran into Sherman in April 1940 in Los Angeles: "At this time Crane advised that Sherman was very bitter and stated that he had given his life to the Russians and that the wrong people were in power in Russia. . . . He described Sherman as a dangerous character with a cruel, sharp mind."[5]

John Sherman's successful flight from "secret work" undoubtedly served as a model for Chambers when he prepared for his own departure. The warning to Crane that he should leave the network and the similar indiscreet warning to Hideo Noda several years earlier suggested that "Karl" also nursed some discontent with "secret work." Further indication of his restlessness within the party came from one of Chambers's infrequent meetings with his friend Meyer Schapiro in December 1936. Schapiro had already begun working closely with other liberal and radical anti-Stalinists to rally support for a "Commission of Inquiry," headed by the philosopher John Dewey, that would investigate the Moscow trials and, specifically, Stalin's charge (widely believed among Communists) that Trotsky had collaborated with the Nazi regime to overthrow the Soviet government.

Although Schapiro himself had been close to the Communist Party earlier in the decade, he now actively opposed its work. He regretted having introduced the impressionable Hideo Noda to Chambers and had pleaded with Noda to abandon underground work and resume painting full-time. J. Peters was amused when Noda reported to their party superiors Chambers's favorable response to Schapiro's 1935 statement and denounced Chambers as a Trotskyite. Nevertheless, Noda's charge raised difficulties for Chambers, since it alerted his superiors to the fact that he had maintained contact with Schapiro, by then an avowed enemy of the CP. When Chambers visited the art historian in December 1936, the two men argued over the question of Stalinist repression, and Chambers stormed out of Schapiro's home. Now it was Chambers who castigated Schapiro as a Trotskyite and an enemy of the workers' revolution. The spy and the scholar did not meet again for a year.[6]

"Karl" soon learned the dangers of being denounced as a Trotskyite. Such episodes as the kidnapping of an American-born GPU operative in Greenwich Village, the gunning down of a high-ranking Russian agent in Switzerland, the execution in Moscow of the director of Fourth Branch Military Intelligence, and the decimation of several Soviet intelligence units abroad alerted even the most trusting. With a growing sense of helplessness, Chambers watched others in the underground, and finally himself, being drawn into the vortex of the Great Purge that swept over the Soviet Union and its secret outposts abroad. "Too late for all of them," Arthur Koestler wrote of the purges in *Darkness at Noon*.

> They were too deeply entangled in their own past, caught in the web they had spun themselves, according to the laws of their own twisted ethics and twisted logic; they were all guilty, although not of those deeds of which they accused themselves. There was no way back for them. Their exit from the stage happened strictly according to the rules of their strange game. . . . They had to act according to the text-book, and their part was the howling of wolves in the night.

By every rule of his own "strange game," Chambers should never have survived the purge, because in July 1937 he was called "home" to the Soviet Union.[7]

When Whittaker Chambers received the Moscow summons, five years to the month after joining the Soviet underground, he decided to stall. Agents had begun hearing rumors by late 1936 of massive purges within both GPU and military intelligence units. Charges of disloyalty were spreading, involving previously trusted operatives. Some agents disappeared; others were suddenly recalled to the Soviet Union for "reassignment" and never heard from again. None of the leading espionage agents in the United States familiar to Chambers wished to discuss these confusing developments. Peters, Colonel Bykov, and his other superiors silenced "Karl's" inquiries with brief comments about the importance of vigilance to detect and expose "Trotskyite wreckers" and "fascist hirelings" hidden in their ranks. Chambers, at first puzzled, became increasingly frightened.

He understood the significance of the order to Moscow. Chambers would later assert that his first doubts about Stalinist Russia had come even earlier, from reading the 1935 memoir of an escapee from a Siberian labor camp, *I Speak for the Silent*, although other anti-Bolshevik testaments were readily available to him in the United States. Chambers managed to delay his return to the Soviet Union for almost a year, while reflecting on the possibilities of a break. By the end of 1937 he had carefully prepared for his defection.[8]

In those months Chambers watched John Sherman detach himself from espionage work, while two other high-ranking Soviet agents in the United States proved less successful in avoiding the Stalinist web. The experiences of his former underground associates Juliette Poyntz and a man whom "Karl" knew as "Ewald" provided Chambers with object lessons in how not to escape from the GPU. He was determined to avoid similar entrapment.

The disappearance of Juliette Stuart Poyntz remains to this day an unsolved mystery in the files of the FBI and the New York City police. She had been a leading Communist since the mid-1920s and in 1934 had been recruited for espionage work by the GPU. An American-born Barnard College graduate, she had held important positions within the "open" CP—in 1928 she ran as the Communist candidate for attorney general of New York. Married to a German Communist doctor with connections within the German diplomatic community in the United States, Poyntz performed a number of counterintelligence jobs for the GPU and tried, as Chambers had, to recruit others for similar work. She was recalled to Moscow along with numerous other agents early in the purge, and managed to return to the United States. By 1936 she had become thoroughly and openly critical of the Soviet Union, avoiding both old underground associates and new assignments. Reports circulated among her non-Stalinist radical friends that she was writing her memoirs.[9]

On June 5, 1937, Juliette Poyntz left her room at the Women's Association Clubhouse in Manhattan. She was never seen again. Her clothes and books remained unpacked, indicating that she planned no trip. Not surprisingly, her

Communist Party associates did not report the disappearance to the police until December 1937, by which time anti-Stalinists such as the anarchist leader Carlo Tresca (a longtime friend of Poyntz's) and Herbert Solow had begun piecing together the circumstances surrounding the incident. Solow learned that a Russian GPU agent named Schachno Epstein, once reportedly Poyntz's lover, had arrived in New York City using a false passport only weeks before she dropped from sight. The two had been seen together several times, and Epstein left the country under another false passport soon after Poyntz disappeared. The evidence, although incomplete, suggested that she was either shanghaied aboard a Russian ship (a favorite GPU technique widely used in other countries during this period for retrieving recalcitrant agents) or murdered somewhere in the New York City area. "He thinks the GPU killed Poyntz," Solow quoted Chambers as stating in 1938.*

Shortly after Poyntz's disappearance was revealed, another agent known to Chambers, a man using a false American passport issued to one "Donald Robinson," was arrested in Moscow on suspicion of espionage. "Mrs. Robinson" was detained days later after complaining to American newsmen about her husband's arrest. Chambers had known "Robinson," a Latvian and a fellow Soviet agent who specialized in collecting false passports, under the pseudonyms "Ewald" and "Richard." "Ewald" had returned to Moscow after receiving orders from his superiors to make the trip.[10]

But when "Karl" was summoned back to the Soviet Union in July 1937, he temporized, while continuing to carry on his work as a courier. Chambers met his government sources in Washington regularly throughout 1937 and continued receiving documents from them, which he then had microfilmed and delivered to Bykov in New York. The following year, Chambers told Herbert Solow he "was on the carpet when [Meyer] Schapiro joined the Trotsky Defense Committee. . . . [Chambers] was once ordered to go on the Mar Cantabrico [a ship loading goods for the Soviet Union] as supercargo to watch the captain but got out of it." "Karl" had heard how easily Communist seamen could kidnap unwitting returnees, and he clung faithfully to his normal routine while reflecting on the possibilities of successful escape. "On two occasions in 1937," his friend Mike Intrator told the FBI in 1949, Chambers "had been requested to make a trip to Moscow, his passports having been prepared for him, but he managed to get out of those trips. He began to talk about breaking from the Communists and he was frightened as to what might happen to him after he made the break."[11]

His ascent from the underground, Chambers believed, had to be in slow and undetected stages. He began to reestablish a "visible identity," first persuading Peters and Bykov that this would facilitate his frequent appearances in

---

*During the 1940s, after he began working for *Time,* Chambers told others on the magazine that Poyntz had been killed and buried behind a brick wall in a Greenwich Village house.

Washington to collect material from government employees. Thus in November 1937, through Communist contacts in the New Deal, he obtained a temporary job working under his own name for the National Research Project. He purchased an automobile that same month, which, like the Maryland farm he had bought the previous March, he kept secret from the CP. Most important, he started in December 1937 to withhold some of the material he received from government sources instead of delivering it all to Bykov, squirreling it away for possible later use as a "life preserver," should he have to bargain with Communist superiors for his safety. Finally, in December, he approached several trusted anti-Stalinist friends—notably Schapiro, Intrator, and Cantwell—to ask their help in arranging for the flight. (It may not be entirely coincidental that on December 7, 1937, *The New York Times* and other papers printed an open letter by Walter Krivitsky revealing his defection and denouncing Stalinist terror.)[12]

Schapiro has described Chambers's December 1937 visit, his first since bitterly denouncing the art historian as a Trotskyite the previous year, and valuable confirmation of that meeting comes from Solow's 1938 memo: "I often saw Sidney Hook at that time, and he was intimate with my old friend Meyer Schapiro. . . . Sometime toward the end of the year 1937 Hook told me he had heard from Schapiro that Chambers was getting fed up with Stalinism. . . . I visited Schapiro several times, hoping he would open the subject . . . but he never did." Although skeptical of Chambers's seriousness about the break, Solow decided that a meeting might be useful for picking up information for his articles. He tried unsuccessfully to signal Chambers early in 1938 by writing several anti-Stalinist pieces for *The New Leader,* which he signed "W. C. Hambers" or "Walter Hambers," obviously playing on Chambers's name in hopes that the latter would contact him, "if only out of fright."

That effort failed, but in February 1938, shortly after *The New York Times* carried an interview with Carlo Tresca charging that the Communists had kidnapped Juliette Poyntz (an article that stirred a federal grand jury to subpoena Tresca), Chambers and Mike Intrator suddenly appeared on Solow's doorstep. Solow had friends in the apartment, so he shepherded the pair to a nearby restaurant. "Chambers said he had read the Tresca story," Solow wrote later that year, "and feared that Tresca, being in touch with me, might know Chambers's name and might give it to the Grand Jury. I asked him what he had to fear, whether he had anything to do with the Poyntz disappearance or the Rubens affair. He denied connection, said he had never heard of Rubens [later that year, after defecting, Chambers told Solow a more truthful story about his knowledge of Rubens], knew nothing about these matters, did not think much of my or Tresca's theories on such matters. But, he said, he had reasons for not wanting to be bothered with subpoenas." Solow assured Chambers that Tresca did not know his name and that they had not connected him with the Poyntz kidnapping. They began discussing politics, and Solow urged him to give up "all connection with his murderous CP friends," but Chambers remained "non-committal." They parted "in a friendly way" with Chambers promising to contact Solow again "in three weeks, after making a trip out of town."[13]

He had good reasons for holding back with Solow, who was a militant Totskyite and in whom he placed no particular trust. Meyer Schapiro had begun arranging with friends at Oxford University Press to obtain translating work for Chambers, who could not complete preparations for his break until he acquired an alternative source of income, preferably a translating job that would keep him out of sight. Chambers indicated to his friend the care with which he was planning his departure and, at the same time, tried to calm Schapiro's anxieties over possible Communist retribution against Chambers should the CP learn of his plans: "What I want is to finish off, and I will as soon as I see my way to do so—unless, of course, it is done for me, one way or another, in the meantime. . . . Briefly, I hope you will find some translation I can do: if I could be sure of two, I should feel well set up. If I could be sure of one, I should feel better than I do now. It will facilitate in every way what is bound to be a rather hard transition."[14]

Through his friend Philip Vaudrin, then a senior editor at Oxford, Schapiro learned that Paul Willert, Oxford's head in this country, wanted a translator for Martin Gumpert's German-language biography of the founder of the Red Cross, a book that later appeared as *Dunant—The Story of the Red Cross*. Chambers wrote Schapiro again in March 1938:

> Willert gave me the book on which to do a couple of chapters as an advance. If he is satisfied, then I can go ahead. . . . I've been working on the thing, and must confess that so far I do not find it insuperable. . . . I had a curious reaction to him [Willert], a man bristling with all those qualities which I ordinarily detest, yet I left with a feeling of his good-will, intelligence and an experience of things beyond the walls of a publisher's sanctum.* Thank you for your part . . . we both know what you have made possible for me. If you question what I intend to do . . . you must remember that whatever the hesitations in my life and their duration, they have usually ended in acts. . . . [A recent phone call from Esther Chambers to Schapiro] shows you clearly the taut wire of fear on which we balance. . . . I must confess that I have had to re-examine my position [as a Communist] as of 1929. I won't elaborate except in conversation.

---

*Willert was an Englishman who later served in British intelligence during the Second World War. When I interviewed him in London in 1975, he confirmed the essential elements in Chambers's account of their relationship. Willert had himself engaged in "secret work" for the underground *German* Communist Party earlier in the 1930s, performing courier missions inside Nazi Germany, and he maintained close connections with the American Communist Party in 1938. The Moscow trials and the experiences of friends such as writer Gustav Regler with Stalinist scheming during the Spanish Civil War had begun to alienate Willert from the CP, but he retained his ties in mid-February 1938, when he hired Chambers to translate the Dunant book.

Chambers's letter also mentioned that he had begun writing stories again—"about present circumstances"—and he sent them to Schapiro for criticism.[15]

"Karl" spent the next month translating the Dunant manuscript and frantically preparing for the move from Baltimore—and the Communist Party. Chambers collected his final materials from Alger Hiss and other government contacts in late March or early April, and dropped hints of his intentions to some contacts. Vincent Reno, for example, who saw Chambers for the last time "possibly early in 1938," told the FBI a decade later that "he had gathered the impression from Carl . . . that Carl planned either to go abroad or that Carl was pulling away from that type of activity." Esther Chambers withdrew their daughter from Baltimore's Park School, and the family moved from their Mount Royal Terrace apartment to another rented apartment on Baltimore's Old Court Road, which they had acquired as a "safe house."[16]

DEFECTION: THE REEMERGENCE OF WHITTAKER CHAMBERS

On or about April 10, 1938, Whittaker Chambers—alias "Karl," "David Breen," "Lloyd Cantwell," "Arthur Dwyer," "Harold Phillips," and other underground pseudonyms—became Jay David Whittaker Chambers again and disappeared again. A letter from Paul Willert to Chambers's Mount Royal Terrace apartment postmarked April 12 was returned undelivered with the postman's scrawl on the envelope: "GONE." Chambers wrote Willert from Florida on May 1 enclosing the first hundred pages of his translation, on which he had been working since late February: "Mail should be addressed to David Chambers, General Delivery, St. August., Florida. Quite unavoidable personal reasons have brought me here at a time when I should much rather have been nearer New York."[17]

Chambers returned to Baltimore with his family by the end of May and delivered the remainder of the Dunant manuscript. Not only was Willert pleased with the translation, but by then he had become fascinated by Chambers, to whom he wrote on May 23: "I have a novel for you to translate should you wish to do so. It is not for us, but for Longmans-Green, and it is a novel about the Spanish [Civil] War by Gustav Regler who was a Commissioner of the International Brigade. You will find it, I think, extremely exciting and sympathetic to you. . . ." (Regler, a close friend of Willert's and himself a Communist, criticized Stalinist behavior in Spain in *The Great Crusade*, which appeared in 1940.) Chambers, almost always flat broke during these months, gratefully accepted the commission, although other writing projects and a growing alienation from even anti-Stalinists Communists slowed his work on the Regler translation.[18]

Life as fugitives from the Party proved harrowing for the Chambers family. During the Florida stay they lived in a Daytona Beach bungalow, and Esther and Whittaker took turns on nighttime guard duty. Chambers worked on his translations with a loaded revolver beside him, nervously eyeing the many transients who passed through his neighborhood. Back in Baltimore, the Chamberses moved into their small Old Court Road apartment to begin a cautious but somewhat less secretive existence under their own name. They frequently patronized Center Street pawnshops, and, having no regular source of income except for his publisher's modest advances, the family lived close to poverty until Chambers began work for *Time* the following year. Still, aided by a $500 loan from his mother for use as a down payment, Chambers purchased a small house on St. Paul Street to which the family moved in June 1938. They remained there until November, when they moved to the Westminster farm acquired the previous year.[19]

Throughout the summer and fall of 1938 Whittaker and Esther lived in dread, waiting for an unannounced visit from an old associate in the underground. They believed correctly that Peters and Bykov had taken steps to locate him immediately after the disappearance. Three known attempts took place, and there were undoubtedly others.

Shortly before his defection Chambers had informed his brother-in-law, Reuben Shemitz, a Manhattan attorney, about his plans and indicated that he feared for his life. A month after Chambers broke, Shemitz was visited in his office by Grace Hutchins, a leading "open" CP member and former friend of Esther Chambers. Finding the lawyer out, Hutchins left the following note, which Shemitz retained: "Thursday, May 19, 1938. Dr. Mr. Shemitz, There is a *very* important message for your sister. If she or her husband will call either Steve [Alexander Stevens, alias J. Pesters] or me, we will have some important memos for them. Grace." Shemitz described the aftermath in a December 1948 interview with the FBI: "Later on that same day, upon Shemitz' return to his office, he made a telephone call to the previously mentioned number and talked with a woman he described as having a very 'intellectual and cultured voice,' who stated that if Shemitz would inform her of the whereabouts of Chambers, she would see to it that Chambers' wife and two children would have no harm done to them. . . . He did recall quite specifically that the woman indicated that it was a 'matter of life or death.'"

When Shemitz later arranged to meet Grace Hutchins at his office, she repeated the previous conversation and left another note, which Shemitz also retained. He, in turn, "agreed to get in touch with Mr. Chambers if he could." (Hutchins claimed in 1948 that she had merely been trying to collect money Chambers had borrowed from her.)[20]

By the time Shemitz reached him in June, Chambers had received a much fuller report of the party's efforts to locate him from Maxim Lieber, who was sent to Baltimore to trace his whereabouts. Within a few days after Chambers had left that city in April, his superiors had realized that their leading courier had either defected or been eliminated. "Bykov, the astute and experienced Russian," Chambers wryly observed in his memoir, "nursed the hope that I had merely been killed outright in an automobile accident, perhaps with my wife and children. Peters, the representative of the provincial American Communist Party, shook his head. 'He has deserted,' he said quietly. . . . Both chiefs agreed on one point: Paul [Lieber's pseudonym in *Witness*] must go to Baltimore at once and trace me. Paul had no choice. He had to go. But he made the trip reluctantly. . . . He did not want to find me."[21]

(The defection of "Karl" provoked grave concern not only in Bykov and among his subordinates, but also among Bykov's superiors in Moscow. During the fall of 1938 military-intelligence officials summoned Alexander Ulanovski to their headquarters for questioning. Ulanovski was interrogated about his knowledge of Chambers. Alexander's wife, Nadya, said in a 1977 interview that when her husband returned from Fourth Branch offices that day, he told her "the people in the office [say] that Chambers had been a German agent all along." The following year Ulanovski encountered Bykov in Moscow, the latter only recently returned from the United States: "Boris said that Chambers had turned traitor [the previous year] and had fled.")[22]

Lieber remembers his assignment vividly: "It was the [first] time I met Bykov. . . . They [Peters and Bykov] came to my office, and [Bykov] said, 'I want you to go and find Chambers.' Well, I knew that Chambers was no longer in Baltimore." Still, Lieber checked his friend's Mount Royal Terrace apartment, which he found vacated. "I went . . . because I realized that they might even put a tail on me and see whether I was going to Baltimore."

Lieber reported that Chambers had disappeared. Peters was unsurprised, but Bykov was furious and ordered Lieber to return to Baltimore and search again. Lieber does not recall making this trip, but he said that Chambers came to see him later in the year. The date remains vague, and although Chambers described several visits to Lieber while the latter remembered only one, their separate versions of the conversation matched.* Lieber told Chambers about his visit to Baltimore and its aftermath, while Chambers confirmed that he had broken and, in Lieber's words, "described the things he disliked about the Party. . . . We had lunch, and we walked down Fifth Avenue, up and down. And he pleaded with me. He said, 'Leave the Party, leave the Party.' I was sorry [he had left], but I wasn't influenced. It shows that I was more naïve than he was. You see, he had contacts with people that I never saw . . . with some of the Russian people here."[23]

---

*William Edward Crane told the FBI in 1949 that he had received a letter from Chambers in the spring of 1938—Chambers could not recall the document—in which the latter repeated his earlier comments to Crane that their work "was wasted because it had come into the hands of their worst enemy. . . ."

His meeting with Lieber was a milestone for Chambers, the first talk with any of his former underground or CP friends since defecting.* The argument with Lieber gave expression to Chambers's own growing uncertainty about Communist ideology. "Karl" had left the underground still a devoted Marxist; his basic quarrel—as in the cases of Ignatz Reiss, Krivitsky, and other agents who had fled virtual death sentences—had been with Stalinism. Now Chambers began cautiously to reexamine his entire worldview. A January 1938 letter to Schapiro briefly mentions the inner debate already in process. "My intellectual fingernails will have to be gnawed a good deal more," he wrote Schapiro in July. "Not to have a defined position is intolerable, especially for someone who has had one. Intellectually, I am much more catholic than protestant: heresy at my stage of life and experience means more than schism, it could only be postulated on the basis of negation, a position, or lack of one, difficult to maintain in one sixth or five sixths of the world. It deeply troubles me and continuously. . . ." The following month the "heretical" Chambers again visited Solow in Manhattan. Schapiro had served as a liaison between the two men during the intervening months, informing Solow about Chambers's break while telling Chambers, in turn, of Solow's advice to heed "what had happened to Reiss and to urge him immediately to make a public declaration such as Krivitsky and Barmine [another Russian defector] had made."[†24]

In September 1937, shortly after Reiss's murder, Trotsky had advised defectors from Stalinism to speak out immediately, in a widely publicized article called "A Tragic Lesson." Chambers initially balked, Schapiro informed Solow, but at an August 1938 meeting with Chambers in Hook's apartment, which Solow was then subleasing, the latter again urged candor. Solow's notarized memo in November described this meeting, which clearly indicated Chambers's state of mind:

> . . . I told him that, in my opinion, if he were really an ex-GPU agent who had broken with that organization, he must decide at once whether he would be "the American Reiss or the American Krivitsky." I urged him to make a public statement. He said this was impossible. I asked him whether he did not feel he had a duty to do so, and he said he was interested chiefly in getting clear of the CP, living out his life with his family, retiring to some remote neighborhood and going back to literary work. I said that he must nevertheless make a statement, in order that the GPU should cease to have any reason to want him out of the way. He said there were reasons why he could not make a public statement at this time, and anyway he felt he was safe from the GPU. He refused to

---

*A November 7, 1938, letter from Chambers to Solow indicated that the defector's last meeting with Lieber had taken place a few days earlier.

†Solow discussed at length with Sidney Hook all of his contacts with Chambers, past and future. Hook played a key advisory role in these dealings, although he never met Chambers at the time.

explain concretely what these "reasons" were. . . . He said he had really broken some months earlier, that the GPU could not find him, that he would not make a statement. I urged him at least to write out a statement and to deposit it with several people, not necessarily myself, and to inform the CP in some way that were anything to happen to him, the statement would be made public by the repositories. He said he would do this, that he had, in fact, written the statement and would soon inform the CP. . . . He refused, however, to tell me anything concrete about himself and his activities, merely suggesting that he had engaged in important secret work and could tell a story which would be terribly damaging to the GPU-CP.[25]

Chambers apparently distributed at least three copies of his statement to trusted associates. One went to Ludwig Lore, who had been expelled from the Communist Party years earlier and with whom Chambers had become friendly in 1936 and 1937.* Lore confirmed this to Solow in an October 1938 meeting. Lore told Solow in September that he had originally met their mutual friend, the defector, earlier in the thirties "when the man came with a letter from Ludwig C. K. Martens and Lore understood the man [Chambers] was a Russian who spoke remarkably good English and was the head of some secret organization here."† Solow told Chambers later that year about another Soviet operative named "Tina" whom Lore had mentioned to him. The name "Tina" seemed to startle Chambers, who replied: "That's a good reason for me to keep away from Lore, if he knows her." Sometime during the fall of 1938 Chambers confided to Solow that he had come to regard Lore "as untrustworthy, not out of malice but careless relations with some Stalinists. [Chambers] will not see him further.‡[26]

The "life preservers" changed hands sometime between September and November 1938. Not trusting Solow sufficiently and probably not wishing to involve Schapiro more deeply, Chambers transferred the material to Esther's young nephew, Nathan I. Levine, whom he had used previously that year as an

---

*Mrs. Lore provided additional details of the transaction in 1949 when interviewed by a Hiss defense lawyer. Her husband had told her "that Carl [Chambers] had asked him to keep some documents for him. For this purpose he had gotten a safety deposit box in a Bax Ridge [Brooklyn] bank. . . . After her husband's death, she went to the bank and looked into the box and found nothing there. She has no direct knowledge to the effect that her husband had deposited anything in this box. She can only say that he got the box in his name and that he told her that the arrangements were made in order that certain papers belonging to Chambers could be protected." Another Hiss defense memo noted that Mrs. Lore said "that these papers were to protect Chambers from the Russians and that arrangements had been made for their release in case of Chambers's death." Memoranda of conversations with Mrs. Lore, August 3 and 10, 1949, Hiss Defense Files. See also FBI Memo, September 8, 1949, #3932.

†Theodore Draper described Martens as "head of the Russian Soviet Government Bureau, the first official Soviet Agency in the United States." Theodore Draper, *American Communism and Soviet Russia* (New York: Viking, 1960), p. 175.

‡In 1940 Lore informed on Chambers to the FBI, the bureau's first tip concerning the latter's underground activities.

intermediary and mail drop in dealing with publishers over translations. Levine placed the brown envelope filled with documents, its contents unknown to him, in an unused dumbwaiter in his mother's Brooklyn home. His instructions from Chambers were identical to those Mrs. Lore had remembered—namely, to release the packet to government authorities in the event of his uncle's death. None of the three copies of the "statement" Chambers said he wrote at the time has ever surfaced. Neither Solow nor Schapiro received one. The two recipients other than Lore—if Chambers ever wrote the statement—were probably Mike Intrator and Reuben Shemitz.[27]

Maintaining this semi-secret life throughout the early fall,* Chambers translated and wrote at his Baltimore home, visited New York occasionally, and traveled once in August with his daughter, Ellen, for a visit to Meyer Schapiro in Vermont. Yet he remained convinced that the CP had not dropped its efforts to find him. "I myself am then more or less hard to locate—I hope," he wrote Schapiro in September, "[but] I have a terrible feeling in these last few days that we were being closed in on. . . . I imagine my fears, which have no visible justification, are the result of strains and stresses . . . but I woke up this morning with my first nightmare on this subject, and my heart pounding so that I thought it would burst open."[28]

The fears took visible shape within days of writing that letter, when Paul Willert phoned Schapiro to say that another publisher, Richard Childs of Modern Age Books, had asked for Chambers's address. Chambers later told Solow that Childs's call had been "on the pretext of giving him work," but Chambers felt that "Childs was inquiring for the GPU, although Childs may not be aware of that."

Reacting to Childs's inquiry, Chambers wrote to Schapiro displaying a mixture of fear and anger:

> . . . this is the first clash of the swords that were bound to clash. More and more I have convinced myself in these last five days that they must clash. Well, I hope they will be sorry, not we. For if we have to go to the limit, I am their man for that, but those fools can never see that . . . they infuriate me. I cannot speak for rage when I try to talk to E[sther] about such things, I swear that the first that

---

*Mark Van Doren later described a phone call from Chambers on September 1, 1938, in which the latter said "he must see me—alone, for he was in danger." When Chambers arrived at Van Doren's home, he recounted his defection from the CP, which, "because he had left it, and because he knew so many of its secrets—its plots, its murders, its misdeeds of every kind—was after him to kill him." Van Doren seemed incredulous when Chambers pleaded for his help in reestablishing a public identity, perhaps by obtaining a review for Chambers "in a reputable paper." But Van Doren remained persuaded for a time: "He was so mysterious about all this, and overstated things, I thought, so laughably in the old way, that I teased him a little, reminding him among other things that as a result of his dark life for a decade I knew nothing about him." In the end, Van Doren gave his former student a letter "recommending him to literary editors," after which Chambers slipped back into the night. *The Autobiography of Mark Van Doren,* pp. 218–19; Interview with Mark Van Doren, March 10, 1949, Hiss Defense Files.

steps within my range . . . will never leave that range in the same condition. . . . If I have to die [I will] take one or two of those bastards with me.

Chambers confided to Schapiro at this time that he had prepared for confronting his GPU pursuers in a shoot-out, if necessary. He had also determined to use his only real weapons against them: his signed "statement" and documents detailing his involvement and contacts in Soviet espionage.[29]

At this point Chambers dropped work on the Regler translation and on revising his own short stories and began to write the first drafts of several articles on the Communist underground in the United States. He spent most of October working on the pieces and, during the last week of that month, took the manuscripts to Solow in Brooklyn. "We talked all evening," Solow remembered, "[Carlo] Tresca joining us around 1 AM. We retired around 4, Chambers spending the night." Solow told Chambers he would show the articles to Isaac Don Levine, who was then helping Walter Krivitsky prepare his memoirs for serial publication in the *Saturday Evening Post*. Solow felt that Levine might find a magazine willing to purchase Chambers's articles. At Solow's suggestion, Chambers agreed to rewrite the articles to include more details about Soviet espionage projects and more names of Soviet agents.[30]

The following day Solow left his apartment early in the morning and returned after dinner to find Chambers still there. They were joined soon afterward by Tresca and his friend Margaret De Silver, another anti-Stalinist radical involved (like Solow and Tresca) with John Dewey's "Commission of Inquiry" into the Moscow trials. Solow, Tresca, and De Silver had planned to attend a party at the home of art historian Anita Brenner to celebrate the recent publication of the commission's final report. The trio impulsively invited Chambers to join them. Present were a number of Chambers's old friends and associates from Columbia and from his years as an "open party" journalist; the guests represented almost all shades of left-wing anti-Stalinist opinion. Only a few—notably Sidney Hook, Felix Morrow, and the journalist John Macdonald—knew prior to Brenner's party that Chambers had broken with the underground. Most assumed he was still a Communist, and Solow's memo described their reaction to his entrance. "I brought in Chambers. He met [Lionel] Trilling and several other people he knew . . . and one or two he had not known. There were about 65 people present, [Elliot] Cohen [later the editor of *Commentary*] and several others were annoyed by Chambers's presence and after half an hour I suggested to Chambers that he leave, which he did. He returned to [Solow's apartment], spent the night, and left early next day. Before leaving he gave me his address."[31]

But Trilling later recalled Chambers's visit as having been prearranged by Solow with the consent of Brenner's guests as a means of helping Chambers establish a public identity and thus deter potential reprisals by the GPU. In fact Chambers had no close friends left in this circle of New York anti-Stalinists except for Schapiro and Solow. A second, independent account of the Dewey Commission party, written by Sidney Hook, portrays more faithfully the emotional context into which Chambers was momentarily thrust. Hook, Herbert Solow's chief adviser during the latter's dealings with Chambers in 1938, realized that Chambers had indeed broken away and was not a Stalinist *agent provocateur* sent to disrupt the gathering. At the same time, Hook was aware of the damage that might be done to the commission, should its credibility be linked to the testimony of a single Communist defector such as Chambers. He counseled Solow, therefore, against pursuing Chambers's request for a meeting with Dewey. When Chambers appeared at the party, at which Dewey himself was expected momentarily, Hook's annoyance mounted:

> The atmosphere was unwontedly gay and relaxed. "When the festivities were at their height, in walked Whittaker Chambers. . . . A whisper, "Whittaker Chambers is here!," spread to every corner of the house. Even those to whom his name meant nothing were conscious of the sudden hush that fell on the assemblage. . . . The atmosphere became strained and awkward despite the efforts at animated conversation among the rest of us. Perhaps three-quarters-of-an-hour-later—it seemed much longer—Solow, red with fury and a sense of guilt, stalked out with Chambers in tow. Chambers left with the same fixed and sickly smile on his face with which he entered. . . .

Dewey had arrived by the time Chambers and Solow left, but the philosopher and the defector did not meet.[32]

The rebuff that Chambers experienced at Brenner's party reinforced his growing doubt in "rehabilitation" as an independent radical. Some suspected Chambers of trying to infiltrate their ranks to undermine the Dewey Commission report. Others felt that even if Chambers were a genuine renegade from the underground as claimed, he still deserved whatever punishment his former coworkers planned for him. This lack of compassion toward Chambers in the Dewey Commission circle can hardly have surprised Solow, considering the unremitting and often slanderous attacks then being leveled daily by CP members and sympathizers upon those American radicals who criticized the purge trials or any aspect of the Moscow line.

Returning to Baltimore, Chambers began revising the articles he had shown to Solow. He wrote to the latter proposing a meeting with Isaac Don Levine, whom he called "the arbiter," to discuss magazine outlets for the series. Recognizing Chambers's urgent need for money, Solow offered and made him a $200 loan. "In our position," wrote Chambers, "I cannot move at all when the ability to move quickly might mean everything."[33]

"Karl" possessed sound instincts in this respect. The CP had not abandoned its hunt, as a pair of unexpected phone calls from Schapiro and Willert showed in mid-November. Willert asked Schapiro for Chambers's telephone number to discuss an urgent matter. Schapiro gave him the number but phoned Chambers directly to alert him. Willert's call soon followed, but the publisher would say only that he had to see Chambers immediately. Chambers drove to New York, half expecting to be offered another translating job. Instead, Willert greeted him with the calm remark: "Ulrich is looking for you." Chambers thought he knew who "Ulrich" was but feigned ignorance, at which point the publisher said: "You know, Ulrich from Berlin."* Chambers then learned, for the first time, some of Willert's background: that he had worked for the Communist underground inside Germany, where he had met Ulrich; and that even now he continued to help American Communists ship anti-Nazi printed matter to Germany. Willert had dined with Ulrich a few nights earlier and had been asked to help find Chambers. Apparently the Englishman had refused, and when Chambers asked why Willert was warning him, the latter responded: "Because I admire what you have done, but I do not have the courage to do it myself."†34

Paul Willert identified "Ulrich" to the author not as a Russian (Chambers mistakenly believed him to be a GPU agent) but as a Czech who also used the names "Otto Katz," "Brader," and "André Simone," and was a high-ranking secret Comintern representative.‡ He had known Ulrich only casually in Berlin during the twenties and—through contacts in German Communist undercover work—in the thirties. Arthur Koestler was an intimate friend of the man, whose real name (not a pseudonym, as Willert suspected) was Otto Katz. In his autobiography, *The Invisible Writing*, Koestler describes Katz as having served throughout the 1920s as the "right-hand man" to the head of the German Comintern's secret organization, a flamboyant onetime publisher named Willi Muenzenberg. After the Nazi takeover of Germany, Katz helped prepare a widely read and influential exposé, *The Brown Book of the Hitler Terror*, and during the Spanish Civil War he played an important role in the preparation of foreign propaganda for the Republican government. Katz's close connections with Comintern intelligence agents made his presence in New York City in 1938 highly suspicious to Willert, who promptly warned Chambers about him.35

Despite Willert's warnings, Chambers narrowly missed running into Katz accidentally during these weeks, while visiting Maxim Lieber's literary agency. Presumably to warn Chambers, Lieber mentioned to his visitor that "Katz is

---

*This "Ulrich" is not to be confused with Alexander Ulanovski, whom Chambers had also known earlier in the 1930s under that pseudonym.

†Willert, who remains contemptuous of Chambers for having testified "indiscriminately" later against romantic idealists and professional agents alike, confirmed this account in a later interview.

‡The devious and peripatetic role of Otto Katz as a Soviet agent throughout Europe and the United States in the 1930s has been described thoroughly in Stephen Koch's *Double Lives: Spies and Writers in the Secret Soviet War of Ideas Against the West* (New York: Free Press, 1994), *passim*.

in the office." When Chambers asked for more information about him, Lieber replied: "You know who he is, he is a close friend of Willi Muenzenberg." Chambers left immediately, telling Lieber he still did not know Katz's identity. Like Willert, Lieber chose not to betray Chambers to the Comintern agent then hunting him, although he remained sufficiently loyal to the CP to refrain from telling Chambers the purpose of Katz's call.[36]

Returning to Baltimore, Chambers prepared for the possibly imminent arrival of Ulrich. At the same time, he took steps to launch a counterattack of his own against the CP. That a "Comintern man" should have been sent from Europe to find him indicated to Chambers either that Bykov and Peters had called for help in their search from the more experienced and ruthless GPU agents, or that GPU authorities in Moscow had simply decided to take charge of the hunt. For the first time, Chambers then considered telling American authorities his story. "I think there is no question about the visitor from abroad," he wrote Schapiro shortly after seeing Willert. We cannot move: we have not got a penny to move with [Solow's $200 apparently had either been spent or had not yet arrived] and nowhere to go. We are trapped exactly as they usually trap people . . . [but] morally I am equal to my fate, to the probable worst of it, at least I am ready to meet it. . . ."

Resuming their nightly vigil, gun at hand, Whittaker and Esther waited for visitors. But Chambers took an additional step this time to unnerve his former associates:

> I wrote them through Washington that Ulrich's hunt amused me [he informed Schapiro], that he is racing the U.S. and I shall be interested to see which gets there first, as I shall. I sent them some photographic copies of handwritten matters the appearance of which would seriously embarrass them, or so I should think, although one hardly knows. I said that at the first sign of monkey-business on their part, I would seek protection *bei einem amerikanischen Festungsgefaengnis, kostet was das persoenlich mag, denn wir haben eine Krise der Verzweiflung erreicht* [in an American prison, whatever the personal cost, given the crisis of despair involved]. I certainly mean what I said. They are sometimes such fools, it is possible that they cannot understand what a crisis of desperation means in a man's mind who is also the father of children.[37]

Chambers's reference to "photographic copies of handwritten matters" is a critical statement, since the only handwritten memos included in the packet he retrieved from Nathan Levine in 1948—apparently the only "documentary" proofs of espionage that he saved—were four memos later acknowledged by Alger Hiss to be in his handwriting and one memo in Harry Dexter White's handwriting. Whether Chambers sent copies of the memos directly to Bykov, Peters, or to some other underground figure remains unclear (Solow, according to Sidney Hook, had urged that Chambers write directly to Earl Browder, the head of the American Communist Party), but he now accepted Solow's earlier offer of assistance in contacting federal authorities.

First he wrote his friend a melancholic letter early in December 1938, enclosing a brief draft of some "essential points" that the journalist had offered to check with an attorney regarding Chambers's legal liabilities. Could he obtain, "and if so how, an unconditional pardon for past sins?" Chambers asked Solow to destroy the memo and his accompanying letter, stating: "I wonder if you really know how deep this water is." The letter closed on an even more pessimistic and confused note than usual:

> We have no right to ask, or reason to expect, that others will fly to our aid. . . . We ought to run, and run as fast as we can; we can't run . . . that is all we have left, and it is better to sit without hysteria, quietly and watchfully, and try to save ourselves, even though it seems foregone that we should fail. . . . So I am more apathetic about involving others [i.e., naming his underground coworkers, as Solow had urged], and still others who must suffer for us, than I was before. It is good, at every ultimate moment (I learned this at my brother's death) to have harmed no one needlessly, and takes more strength than the easy violent will ever know.[38]

But when he met Solow on November 26, Chambers talked at length about his underground work for the first time and named some of the "people involved in his work either as agents, fronts, sources or what not"* (Solow's characterization). Solow dutifully recorded these two days later:

> Maxim Lieber (literary agent) who has broken with the organization [actually not the case], Heda Gumpertz [sic] who was once recalled to Russia but returned and is rumored to have broken; John Abt . . . of the Dept. of Justice; Larry Duggan head of the Latin-American section of the State Dept. . . . Noel Field, formerly in State Dept., worked with Gumpertz [sic] . . . Chambers once tried to contact Larry Duggan, sending to him one of the Fields (Fdk Vanderbilt?), but Duggan excused himself on the grounds that he already had a connection. . . . Lore, Abt and others who have met him think he is a Russian.

Chambers also described in detail the failure of the American Feature Writers Syndicate ring in Japan, John Sherman's defection, and some other operations by Soviet agents within the United States.[39]

The extraordinary extent of the Russian spy networks described by Chambers led Solow to record and have notarized a detailed account of their talk (and

---

*But Chambers did not mention Alger Hiss to Solow. Even the following year, in his interview with Adolf Berle, Chambers seemed reluctant to bring in Hiss's name. Berle's notes recorded the names of Hiss, his wife, and his brother only at the very end of his memo on the meeting with Chambers.

previous ones) on November 28, a fifteen-page, single-spaced document that concluded with this description of their conversation two days earlier:

> Chambers has broken but fears he may be shot. He would like to deal the Comintern a body-blow as he feels it is a malevolent organization. He would like to make his knowledge public. But he fears the US government. . . . He wants to make a deal with the police. If he can't get a promise of executive clemency in advance, he will take his chances with the GPU, figuring that he can keep moving and escape them. If he gets a promise, he will tell all he knows and let the chips fall where they may. In the meantime, he refuses to make any public statement of repudiation of the CP; he claims that will only "anger" them and speed their work of pursuing him. He is moving from the Balto address [to the Westminster farm] and gives me no new address. . . . He has very few friends to trust, is in dire need [of money].[40]

Returning to New York again on December 2 in search of funds, Chambers handed Solow "15,000 words of MS. describing in general terms the methods of Soviet passport racketeers in the US." He asked Solow to show the material to Isaac Don Levine to determine whether Levine could sell the articles to the *Saturday Evening Post*. Chambers did not want Solow to leave the manuscript with Levine and, instead, waited at Solow's apartment while the latter took the articles to "the arbiter," who, after reading them, "expressed interest [but] suggested condensation."*[41]

On December 17 Chambers gave Solow disquieting news. He was revising his articles, "hoping to get the money from them for a trip across the border." The abrupt resignation of New York City's U.S. attorney, Lamar Hardy, who had just completed successful prosecution of a band of Nazi espionage agents, apparently inspired Chambers's sudden plan to flee. Reuben Shemitz had approached Hardy "on the suggestion of the newspaper people [from Scripps-Howard, with whom Shemitz—at Chambers's request—had discussed possible use of his story] to discuss immunity with him." Hardy's resignation was announced by President Roosevelt himself, and Chambers obviously feared that Hardy had passed word of his offer to high administration officials who—like the Communists he knew were operating within the government—might prove "a danger to him." Although Solow tried to offer reassurance, the weeks of awaiting Ulrich's appearance had clearly affected Chambers's nerves. "He heard the wind is up and would like to skip across the border," Solow wrote at the time about Chambers.

But Chambers's meetings in December 1938 with former underground contacts renewed his determination to do battle. He confided to Solow in January

---

*In *Eyewitness to History*, Levine placed this meeting in April 1939. But the Solow memo and postmarked letters from Chambers to Solow establish that the negotiations with Levine took place in November 1938.

1939 that he had instructed Schapiro to contact John Dewey so that the philoso-pher could arrange for a public statement by Chambers on his past, possibly to Roosevelt's newly appointed attorney general, Frank Murphy.[42]

He also took the bold step of warning the underground a second time not to bother him (a Westminster neighbor who tried to strike up a friendship with Chambers turned out to have close CP connections). The new letter was delivered by a friend of the defector's in mid-January to Felix Inslerman, with a request that he forward it to his CP superiors. Inslerman, who would break with the CP himself within months after this meeting, opened and read Chambers's letter before passing it along and made a copy of a portion of the document, which he gave to the FBI during the early 1950s.

Both Inslerman and his wife later told the bureau that they had read the letter and had been deeply moved by it. Moreover, according to the FBI's report of this interview, "it is [Mrs. Inslerman's] recollection that there was enclosed with the letter one or two strips of microfilm," further evidence that Chambers had taken documents with him when he defected in 1938. Subpoenaed by Senator Joseph McCarthy in February 1954, Inslerman described it as "a horrible letter. Death was mentioned there, but Bob [Chambers's pseudonym] was afraid of [sic] his life, and I imagine the life of his family." The portions of Chambers's letter pre-served by Inslerman duplicated sections of the letter he had sent to Schapiro the previous November when "Ulrich" (Otto Katz) appeared on the scene. There were some new touches, however, including mention of federal probes of the Communist underground:

> Do not imagine that F. Murphy [Attorney General Frank Murphy] is there wholly for the purpose of dampening all investigation or that the State Depart-ment can forever put the brakes on them. In fact, I should guess that the State Department is going to be sitting on some pretty hot coals in the near future. There is something brewing now, but from the calm way you are running around, you do not seem to know it.[43]

Whatever the precise meaning of his cryptic reference to an impending security probe of the State Department, he clearly meant to place Peters and Bykov on notice that he had initiated contacts with government intelligence agencies, an assertion that then contained more bluff than truth.

At the same time Chambers persisted in his quixotic effort to reach John Dewey through Schapiro and Solow, hoping that Dewey could be persuaded to plead with federal officials for immunity on his behalf.

But Dewey rejected a meeting on the grounds that Chambers might turn out to be a Stalinist *agent provocateur* or, if genuinely a defector, one who might tilt public opinion against the Dewey Commission report. Dewey also declined Chambers's request for another, more personal reason. Although acknowledging the horrors of the Soviet purges, he still had difficulty in bringing himself to believe that the

Russians operated a widespread espionage network within the United States, a feeling shared by many American liberals, then and later. Whittaker Chambers's story, Dewey informed Sidney Hook, sounded quite "odd."[44]

More knowledgeable anti-Stalinists—those who were aware of such underground activities—kept their distance chiefly for two reasons: first, principled objections to aiding a former practitioner of Stalinist "secret work," and, second, a personal distaste for Chambers himself, an abrasive and unaffable figure to most acquaintances even in the best of times. Chambers felt increasingly "isolated" from the anti-Stalinist left, and he complained to Schapiro at this time that Herbert Solow's "former affiliates," the New York City Trotskyists, "are so afraid of me that they would no doubt be relieved if a disaster befell and they were well rid of the ghost. Stupid bunch."*[45]

Once his hopes for support from these circles and from Dewey had faded by early 1939, Chambers devoted himself "to work and to rationalizing our life in such a way that I can work [despite] . . . the ever-present dangers . . . which it is useless to anticipate until they are close: otherwise nerves get taut." Whittaker and Esther made preparations at their Westminster farm during these months to plant a spring crop, a source of great satisfaction for the agent, who had often talked to other operatives during the 1930s about his desire to work the land. Chambers's mood lightened perceptibly as he plowed under his land, planting fruit trees and flowers as well as an extensive vegetable garden. He even invited Solow, then undergoing serious emotional problems that threatened a breakdown, to live with them on the farm and "share whatever we have, the best part of which is our family life." Still leery of new acquaintances, Chambers relaxed sufficiently so that on his occasional drives to New York City he began to seek out not only persons such as Solow and Schapiro but also new contacts like Isaac Don Levine, whom Solow had finally persuaded him to meet.[46]

---

*Several recently retrieved memoranda from the KGB archives by key operatives confirm the reality of and importance attached by Soviet intelligenc agents in the United States to Whittaker Chambers's [a.k.a. "Carl" or "Karl"] defection. In one of these, the head of Soviet networks in the United States at the time of Alger Hiss's first trial, Alexander Panyushkin, proposed to his superiors in Moscow that they launch a disinformation campaign against their former agent (Chambers) to undermine the credibility of his testimony against Hiss, by asserting falsely that "Karl" had actually been "a German agent who by Gestapo instructions was carrying out espionage work in the U.S. and penetrated into the American Communist Party." This curious suggestion is examined more fully on pages 251–52. Then, in March 1950, a leading, Soviet intelligence officer in the United States, Sergei Savchenko, distributed a memorandum to his underground colleagues reviewing the "serious blows [inflicted] at our agent network in the U.S." by several defections in earlier years— specifically those of Igor Gouzenko, Elizabeth Bentley (code-named "Myrna"), and a few others, including "Karl." Panyushkin also mentions "Karl" in an October 1950 memo complaining about the difficulties involved in recruiting agents in the current anti-Communist atmosphere. (See footnotes, p. 302, *passim.*)

On one trip Levine arranged a meeting between Chambers and Walter Krivitsky, who was also in hiding from possible Soviet retribution. Chambers and Krivitsky, at the start of this first encounter, viewed each other with great suspicion. Chambers's admission in *Witness* that he could not think "without revulsion [of] even ex-Communists" mirrored the reaction of many of art historian Anita Brenner's guests to him. As the evening wore on, however, Krivitsky and Chambers warmed to each other and talked through the night. Long after Levine had retired, he woke to find the pair still discussing their separate underground experiences and their former associates.[47]

The two defectors became close friends in the months that followed (Mrs. Krivitsky and her family would live in hiding at the Chambers farm for over a year after her husband's death). Even during their first meeting at Levine's apartment Krivitsky "said one or two things that were to take root in my mind and deeply influence my conduct, for they seemed to correspond to the reality of my position. . . . 'Looked at concretely [he quoted Krivitsky as observing], there are no ex-Communists. There are only revolutionists and counterrevolutionists.' He meant that, in the 20th century, all politics, national and international, is the politics of revolution. . . . In action there is no middle ground." Chambers was also struck by a remark of Krivitsky's on a more immediate dilemma: "'In our time, informing is a duty. . . . One does not come away from Stalin easily.' I knew [then] that, if the opportunity offered, I would inform."[48]

THE BERLE INTERVIEW

Shortly before his introduction to Krivitsky, Chambers landed a full-time job as a writer for Henry Luce's *Time*. During the next decade he became celebrated for waging "counter-revolutionary" interoffice battles with staff members whom he suspected of a Communist or pro-Communist slant in their writing. Robert Cantwell, who had helped support Chambers with loans and occasional freelance research jobs during the previous year, served as intermediary in obtaining him the $100-a-week post in April 1939. *Time* editor T. S. Matthews recalled that Cantwell had kept him posted on his friend's break with the CP and had shown him an earlier short story by Chambers that had impressed Matthews: "Something like Malraux: it was shot through with the same murky flashes of rather sinister brilliance." Cantwell arranged a meeting with Matthews, at which the latter made an offer Chambers accepted on the spot.[49]

Had it not been for the signing of the Nazi-Soviet Pact on August 23, 1939, Chambers might have remained at *Time*, limiting his "counter-revolutionary" activities to intramural attacks on more radical coworkers. The pact jolted loyal Communists and Russian sympathizers throughout the world and led to wholesale defections from the American Communist Party. Chambers received an unexpected and unwanted office visit several days later from Isaac Don Levine, who told him that Walter Krivitsky had begun informing American and British officials about Soviet agents who he knew had infiltrated both governments. Levine urged Chambers to take similar action immediately and to share his information about the Washington underground with American intelligence agencies.

Outraged, but not surprised,* by the pact and its consequences, Chambers agreed to cooperate on one condition: that he receive immunity from prosecution for his previous activities, something he had sought through Solow in 1938 without success. "How would you like to face a fifteen-to-twenty-year jail sentence if you were in my boots," Levine quotes his response, "with a wife and two children, and without any savings?" Levine agreed to explore the possibilities with friends in government, but Chambers went further and insisted that he would trust only President Roosevelt's personal promise of immunity. He agreed to tell his story to Roosevelt alone, if Levine could arrange for a White House audience.[50]

Although Levine took the proposal to Marvin H. McIntyre, Roosevelt's appointments secretary, McIntyre pointed out the impossibility of arranging a meeting on short notice and suggested, instead, that Levine and Chambers see Assistant Secretary of State Adolf A. Berle, Jr., the president's adviser on internal-security matters. Levine met Berle that same day, and after listening to the journalist sketch out the importance of Chambers's story, Berle agreed to meet both of them at his home on Saturday evening, September 2. (Levine, fearing leaks, never used Chambers's real name with Berle, either then or at their subsequent meeting, describing his informant only as an ex-agent named "Karl" who presently worked for *Time*.) Levine persuaded the reluctant Chambers to drop the notion of meeting Roosevelt personally and to trust the president's surrogate. Chambers agreed: "To me, Berle's word is as good as Roosevelt's."

Chambers arrived with Levine at Berle's estate at 8:00 PM, and after table talk over dinner about the German invasion of Poland, Mrs. Berle withdrew, leaving the three men to their discussion. Throughout the September evening they talked, seated first in chairs on the lawn and moving to Berle's study as the night grew cooler. Berle took extensive notes of Chambers's recollections and assured them that the information would go directly to Roosevelt and that Chambers would not be penalized for his willingness to cooperate. But he gave no assurance of immunity from prosecution.[51]

---

*Chambers had predicted an imminent German-Soviet alliance in one of his November 1938 articles on Russian espionage in the United States, partly because of his knowledge that Soviet underground agents in the United States had begun cooperating with their German counterparts the previous year.

Berle did not retire immediately. Instead, he transcribed his handwritten notes and memories of the conversation on an office typewriter; he titled the four-page memo "Underground Espionage Agent." Chambers dropped Levine at his hotel and drove back to Westminster, while Levine—still highly agitated after listening for the first time to Chambers's elaborate recital of his underground work and contacts—jotted down on his hotel stationery the names he remembered having been mentioned. Levine's list included the following names: "Duggan, Hiss [Donald, whose first name Levine forgot at the time], Alger Hiss, Field, Wadley [sic] . . . Vinc. Reno (Lance Clarke), Phil. Reno (Security), Sol Adler . . . Nat Witt, Pressman, Treasury—Frank Coe (A Gross), Mr. White, brother Coe, Marian Bachrach . . . John Abt, Jessica Smith, Peters, Lockwood Curry [Lauchlin Currie]."

Berle's memo on the visiting "Underground Espionage Agent" provided a full account of names and activities revealed by Chambers, including those of several individuals omitted from Levine's sketchy notes. Berle drafted his report carefully, proceeding name by name and department by department, until he had covered the essential information. Chambers clearly had stressed actual espionage rather than clandestine involvement with Communism. Terms such as "head of Underground Trade Union Group," "Underground connections," and "in 'Underground Apparatus'" recur in the notes, which described the alleged theft of Navy plans for new "Super-battleships" as well as Vincent Reno's work with "Aerial bomb sight Detectors." The Berle memo portrays "Peters," in a long passage on his activities, as "responsible for Washington Sector" and, "after 1929—head of CP Underground." Noel Field enters as one of Hedda Gumperz's contacts. Chambers described both Field and Laurence Duggan to Berle as CP members, although "Duggan's relationship was casual."[52]

Little of this would have surprised Herbert Solow, whose memo of the preceding November contained much that Chambers told Berle. But three new names, unmentioned by Chambers since his defection, conclude the document (except for a postscript on the theft of Loy Henderson's dispatches to the State Department concerning his interview with "Mrs. Rubens"): Donald, Alger, and Priscilla Hiss.*

Possibly because of a crowded schedule and many wartime responsibilities, Berle delayed checking the accuracy of "Mr. X's" charges concerning the

---

*Berle had difficulty explaining in 1948 why he had not sent his notes of the interview with Chambers to the FBI earlier than 1943, when the bureau finally requested them. Berle said "he did not feel free to divulge the contents of Chambers's conversation to the FBI inasmuch as Chambers had indicated that he did not so desire and had further indicated that he would not back up the story, and also did not desire the information furnished to the FBI, particularly if the source was to be revealed." More likely Chambers had asked simply that the information not be sent to the bureau until he had obtained immunity from prosecution, something Berle was asked to arrange but never followed up. His failure to check on any of Chambers's leads, not simply those involving the Hiss brothers, is particularly surprising, considering his role as Roosevelt's chief adviser on internal-security matters in 1939 and his energy and activity in other instances.

Hiss brothers until 1941. Then he talked to both Felix Frankfurter and Dean Acheson about the loyalties of Alger and Donald Hiss. Both Frankfurter and Acheson assured Berle, who knew the Hisses only slightly, that the charges were groundless.*

For over a year Levine tried doggedly to stir interest in Chambers's allegations among influential political figures. He told the story in March 1940 to Martin Dies and his aides on the then-temporary House Un-American Activities Committee, hoping "to interest them in employing a dozen ace investigators to obtain the evidence on the Communist espionage cells in Washington." The unpredictable Dies listened attentively and two days later called a press conference to announce that *he* was hot on the trail of several Soviet spy rings in the United States and would soon subpoena to testify before HUAC "the head of the Ogpu" in America. Dies used Levine's information not merely for publicity purposes but also, according to his aide Robert Stripling, to secure a hefty advance from *Cosmopolitan* to write an article on the subject, which he never produced.

Levine had no better luck elsewhere. Among those who listened to his recital of Chambers's activities in the underground were Loy Henderson, by then chief of the State Department's Russian Section; Republican Senator Warren R. Austin; Ambassador William Bullitt (who said he had heard the Hiss brothers called Soviet agents in 1939 by French counterintelligence officials); labor leader David Dubinsky; and gossip columnist Walter Winchell, who then broadcast an item about Soviet agents in the State Department. Bullitt, Dubinsky, and Winchell all brought the charges to Roosevelt's attention, according to Levine,† but the president continued to brush the story aside.[53]

After their initial encounter Chambers frequently met with Walter Krivitsky, and the latter's death left him especially shocked and stirred dormant fears of retribution in his own case. Krivitsky was discovered on February 10, 1941, in a hotel near Washington's Union Station, dead from a gunshot wound that police called self-inflicted. Krivitsky's friends doubted it was self-inflicted and challenged the official verdict of suicide, pointing out that he had been in good spirits over the preceding months. Krivitsky had returned recently from England, where information he supplied resulted in the exposure and arrest of a Soviet spy in the British cabinet's code room.[54]

Krivitsky's death persuaded Chambers that he should cease efforts to expose his former underground associates in the government. The talk with Berle convinced him that the effort would be futile and perhaps fatal.‡

---

*Berle also brought Chambers's information to the attention of Franklin Roosevelt—according to Levine—who scoffed at the charges of Soviet espionage rings within the government. Berle's diary does not mention this discussion.

†Winchell's posthumously published memoir confirms this in his case.

‡Krivitsky's death so alarmed Chambers that he left immediately for the South, where his family had been vacationing, to arrange for a hiding place for Esther, his children, and Krivitsky's

Once the United States had entered the war and become the Soviet Union's ally, Chambers's suspicion of the Roosevelt administration and of its intelligence services deepened. When Solow wrote him in 1942 asking for information about a man both had known during the thirties as a CP member and who was then being screened for a job in the OSS, Chambers responded bleakly:

> I should think that the Office of Strategic Services (whatever that is) would be an ideal place for him since, like most of the New Deal agencies, it is presumably packed with CP persons. There was a time when I was interested in cooperating with the Civil Service and the FBI in keeping CP's out of the gov't. Then I began to suspect, from the type of Civil Service and FBI agent sent around, that those agencies were incapable of doing anything to keep CPs out. The CPs under investigation regularly turned up in strategic agencies. Later still, I began to suspect that the New Deal was storing up data for a great Moscow Trial in which it would completely whitewash itself when public clamor forced it to. The sufferers in this purge would be people like you and me, other ex's and little no account CPs. But the big CPs would remain in control of the show; only then they would be completely disguised, having proved publicly that they are anti-CP. So I have become increasingly reluctant to have anything to do with this filth.[55]

By then Whittaker Chambers had become an editor at *Time*, had—after initially becoming an Episcopalian—joined a Quaker meeting, and had suffered the first attack of a heart disease that would eventually kill him. Little wonder that Solow's invitation to reopen the barely cauterized wounds of defection seemed so distasteful. Angry, bedeviled, and uncertain, Chambers now had no wish to relive in public his painful tale of bondage to and partial escape from the malevolent god that failed.

---

family. That accomplished, he returned in late February 1941, stopping off in Washington for a talk with Adolf Berle, who never mentioned this second visit during his 1948 testimony concerning Chambers. "Chambers returned from Florida and we—[Calvin] Fixx and I—met him at the Ritz Bar to hear of his talk with Berle," reads Robert Cantwell's February 28, 1941, journal entry. "Berle had said as he came in, 'I suppose you're here for protection.' Chambers pleased and reassured at the Government's knowledge." Berle, in turn, contacted the FBI about Chambers several times in the next month, telling one agent "that since we were not investigating Chambers, he was more worried about the matter than before, and he thought he knew who was . . . [namely] he was afraid that the Russian agencies were looking for him." Foxworth to Director, March 10, 1941, #1X2. Berle first contacted the bureau on February 28 offering information about Chambers, presumably his 1939 notes. Foxworth to Director, March 18, 1941, #1x3. Not for two years did the FBI ask for them. But this evidence of a second visit to Berle by Chambers in 1941 seriously undermined Berle's 1948 testimony that Chambers told him only about a "study group" with no espionage dimension.

X

ALGER AND WHITTAKER: THE FORGING OF CAREERS

THE JOURNALIST

"I served the Communist Party for seven years—the same length of time as Jacob tended Laban's sheep to win Rachel his daughter," wrote Arthur Koestler. "When the time was up . . . only the next morning did he discover that his ardors had been spent not on the lovely Rachel but on the ugly Leah." Unlike Arthur Koestler, Whittaker Chambers worked for only six years in the Communist underground before awakening in 1938 to find himself alongside a Stalinist Leah. For a year after defecting, Chambers continued searching for translating jobs and other work as a writer up to the moment he heard from Robert Cantwell of *Time*, Esther and Whittaker were penniless in April 1939 when they received a letter from Cantwell indicating that he could probably arrange a job for his friend. Cantwell had been among those urging Chambers to break with the CP and, in 1938, had given the defector small loans and occasional part-time research tasks to supplement his income. Interviewed and hired on a trial basis by one of the magazine's top editors, T. S. Matthews, Chambers began work soon after receiving Cantwell's letter. He quickly learned *Time* style and claimed in *Witness* that he had "always insisted that I was hired because I began a review of a war book with the line: 'One bomby day in June. . . .'"[1]

Of Chambers's earliest days at *Time*, Matthews later wrote that "although he told me almost nothing of himself and his circumstances, there was such an air of suppressed melodrama about him that I should not have been greatly surprised if one day a Communist gunman had shot him down in one of the office corridors. He may have had some such idea himself, for he always walked fast from the elevator to his office and, once inside, his door was shut and often locked. His suspiciousness soon became an office legend."[2]

The aura affected Chambers's associates at *Time*, even those who liked the man and admired his writing. A young journalist named Samuel Welles worked alongside Chambers in the magazine's Books department. Welles and Chambers became friends, and Welles—along with Cantwell and Matthews—was responsible for Chambers's brief conversion to Episcopalianism. It took a while, however, for Chambers to warm up to Welles, whom he considered naïve on the subject of Communism, an almost universal failing in Chambers's view. Welles invited his new colleague to lunch several times, each time without success, until finally Chambers—who generally skipped the meal—agreed to have a sandwich with him. Matthews describes the preparations for the Welles-Chambers "luncheon":

> First they took the subway to Herald Square, where they surfaced, Chambers leading the way, and dived into the ground floor of Macy's. . . . They walked rapidly to the nearest escalator, went up a floor, traversed its length to another escalator, went down, back into the subway, took a downtown train, got out at the second stop and came up again to the street. Chambers said, "I think it's all right now," and they went into a sandwich shop and had lunch.

Similar experiences, if not quite so extreme, were reported in the 1939–41 period by others on the magazine who later befriended the highly suspicious Chambers.[3]

Such respect as he enjoyed among his *Time* colleagues, even those whom he alienated with his odd and aloof mannerisms, came from their open admiration for his writing. Chambers worked fiercely: "*Time*," wrote the magazine's historian, Robert T. Elson, "not only offered him, at age thirty-eight, a better livelihood than he was likely to find again, but a kind of sanctuary. His depression was accentuated by loneliness; Chambers was aware that among his new associates he was an odd man out." A number of his colleagues, among them Cantwell and Robert Fitzgerald, who left the magazine for Harvard and greatness as a poet and translator, detected in Chambers this yearning to treat *Time* as a surrogate secular church to replace the Communist Party and to view anti-Communist journalism as a God-given opportunity to legitimize his break with the past. Matthews believed for a long time that Chambers was "definitely cracked on the subject of Communism" (he later changed this opinion), but he also was quick to admire a writer who successfully wrote a *Time* cover story—"not only creditably but with extraordinary style"—within his first or second week of work. A 1940 review of the movie version of John Steinbeck's novel *The Grapes of Wrath* brought Chambers to the attention of Henry Luce, who confessed admiringly that Chambers's review had explained not simply the movie's appeal but also the nature of the book to him for the first time.[4]

Chambers yearned to write for Foreign News, a department in which he felt his knowledge of Communism could be utilized, but this assignment eluded him for a half-decade. For most of his early years on *Time* he remained in the Books section. He exploited that department to its full potential because of his facility with languages, his wide knowledge of literature and history, and his broad range of cultural interests. So effectively did Chambers develop the section that Luce promoted him to senior editor during the summer of 1942 and placed him in charge of every "back-of-the-book" department except Business.[5]

Among his earlier friends, those whom he knew from the twenties or thirties, only Cantwell remained, and even this relationship became strained during the war years. Chambers appeared intent upon separating himself emotionally from every salient aspect of that past: his Communist associates, naturally, and his various homosexual contacts, but, along with these, even the non-Stalinist friends who had remained faithful during the agony of defection. These included Cantwell, Herbert Solow (whom he saw occasionally since Solow found a job at the neighboring Luce publication, *Fortune*, but otherwise did not meet socially), Mike Intrator, and Meyer Schapiro (whose letters and visits from Chambers were rare after he began work at *Time*).[6] He tried to explain this attitude toward his old friends in a 1943 letter to Solow:

> I have not seen you in a long while. I've been told that you say I am an anti-semite. I hope you do not though I believe I understand why you might. These have been years of deep change and strain for us. I have worked very hard. I have had much malicious (CP & left liberal) opposition [at *Time*] to make my life harder. But hardest of all I have had to transform my whole way of life and thought. In this process I have thrown off many-year-old influences. It happened that they were almost completely semitic [presumably a reference to Chambers's many Jewish friends at Columbia and later within the Communist Party]. There is no question of blaming these influences. Rather I should blame my own susceptibility to them. My break with CP was accompanied by a religious experience which I have never gone into, I think, with you, and do not need to go into in detail now. But it became essential if I was to go on living at all, that I find a peace in the Christian experience for myself and for my family. It was difficult for all the reasons that made one reject the established churches in the first place. Now I have reason to believe that the change has effected itself naturally and with a minimum of trial and error. In the last year I have become a Quaker and have taken my family into the Meeting with me. . . . In the "gathered meeting" I have found the experience that I have been seeking all my life. To sit in the deep silence with my children beside me and our friends about me is perhaps more than I had any right to expect in life. And yet I have always wanted goodness, never evil.[7]

But Chambers's work at *Time* allowed him little opportunity to pause for such reflections on times past. He told his new friends that he viewed the Books section as the magazine's editorial page, because "no one could comment on books without at the same time commenting on the whole range of views and news." Chambers's editorial "policy" had one obsessive concern, an attack upon Communist influences both within American society and abroad. There were then a number of Communists and close sympathizers at the magazine (enough to issue a newsletter tagged *High Time* that intermittently appeared on the desk of every staff member, with the subheading "Published by the Communists at Time Inc."). Chambers quickly alienated all of them—along with many New Deal liberals, whom he was prone to lump together with the Communists, at least insofar as their judgment of political questions was concerned. "I wrote under a barrage from [the Communists] and their unwitting friends," Chambers recalled in his memoir. "But it was no longer a massacre; it had become an artillery duel. 'Every week,' said one of my amused friends, 'that mortar goes off in the last five pages of *Time*.'" Chambers conducted a number of such "counter-revolutionary" campaigns in the Books section, and at least one had repercussions that entered into the Hiss case more than a half-decade later.[8]

During his first years at *Time* he remained fearful about Communist efforts either to embarrass him or, perhaps, even to assault him physically. He announced to some coworkers that he had a loaded revolver in his office. Welles, however, who worked more closely with Chambers during the 1939–42 period than any other writer at *Time*, told the author that Chambers locked his door only (if at all) when he worked all night in the deserted building, a normal precaution, and that his door was generally open to daytime visitors.

Once he became friendly with Welles, Matthews, and others on the staff, Chambers often regaled his new intimates with stories of his days as a Communist courier. Most of them knew at least some of the details that he had given to Berle in 1939. As word spread among the magazine's Communists and fellow travelers that Chambers was a defector, their hostility surfaced in everyday contacts, and he in turn made no effort to hide his contempt for radicals and left-liberals on the staff.[9]

Few things frightened Chambers more than his brief contacts with others who had broken recently with the CP. In 1940 a journalist named Howard Rushmore who had left the party days earlier walked unannounced into his office and pleaded with Chambers to help him get a job at *Time*. Chambers's response, although understandable, was harsh: "That a man of whom I had never heard, a day or two out of the Communist Party, should know who I was and exactly where to find me, filled me with instant cold rage which is one of the forms that alarm takes." He declined to assist Rushmore: "I thought [he] was lying." Joseph Freeman, a former colleague on *The New Masses*, experienced a similar rejection two years later.[10]

Chambers wrote a long and critical piece for the January 6, 1941, issue of the Books section on "The Revolt of the Intellectuals" concerning such writers as Granville Hicks, Newton Arvin, Waldo Frank, Lewis Mumford, Malcolm Cowley, and Archibald MacLeish, who had broken their links to the Communist Party's "Popular Front" in reaction to events of the previous few years: "Stalin's Purge, the Nazi-Soviet Pact, Russia's grab of half of Poland, . . . the attack on Finland, the seizure of part of Rumania, and all of the Baltic States." Because of this, Chambers explained, "fellow travelers began to jump off the train ["The Red Express"]." At one point in the article he observed: "Malcolm Cowley, writing a book 'to clarify my mind,' craved only to be left in peace to lick his spiritual wounds." The following year Chambers reviewed a new book of Cowley's poems, *The Dry Season*, although not in Books but, surprisingly, in the National Affairs section.

By then the United States had entered the war and Cowley, formerly literary edi-tor of *The New Republic,* held a post in Washington as "chief information analyst of the Office of Facts and Figures." Chambers denounced several of Cowley's poems as pesudo-Communist agitprop and pointedly quoted HUAC Chairman Martin Dies's recent charge that Cowley had "seventy-two connections . . . with the Communist Party and its front organizations."[11]

While Chambers was researching "The Revolt of the Intellectuals," he met Cowley once in December 1940. Cowley captioned his memo of the meeting "Counter Revolutionary," observing that Chambers had reviewed his CP history and his work in the underground: "He resigned about 1937 [Chambers appar-ently gave all of his *Time* associates this break date as a means of establishing his earlier anti-Communist credentials], and threats were made that he would be assassinated. Maybe they weren't idle threats, considering the disappearance of Juliette Poyntz and Rubens. . . . He gave me a lot of dope on the Communist underground. He said that it had its people all through the government service and that Nathan Witt of the Labor Board is the only one who has so far been forced to resign." Chambers told Cowley that "there were two complete underground apparatuses, entirely distinct from and without knowledge of each other."[12]

All of this would have been familiar to Solow, Berle, and others to whom Chambers had unburdened himself after defecting. One sentence in Cowley's account of the talk, however, was new. "Sayre, the high commissioner to the Phil-ippines, is also connected with the underground movement." Former Assistant Secretary of State Francis B. Sayre, Alger Hiss's superior from 1936 to 1939, had left that post for the Philippines assignment. But nowhere else did Chambers ever refer to Sayre as "connected" in any way with the underground or with the charges he leveled against Hiss. Only through Hiss, according to Chambers, had Sayre been "connected" to Communist espionage.

A friend of Cowley's who worked closely with Hiss's lawyers, A. J. Liebling of *The New Yorker,* put Cowley in touch with the Hiss defense in 1948, and he testi-fied about the 1940 meeting at Hiss's first trial. Chambers denied having impli-cated Sayre in his conversation with Cowley and countered by asserting that he might "quite possibly have told Cowley that a member of Mr. Sayre's department [i.e., Alger Hiss] was a member of the Communist underground." Chambers also claimed that Cowley had had "quite a few" drinks at their meeting, a fact Cowley challenged. Chambers's friend Ludwig Lore had apparently confused the Sayre story in this fashion when he told the FBI in 1941 that Chambers said two girls who were "private secretaries" to assistant secretaries of state had given him information. But Cowley stated in 1948 that Chambers had indeed mentioned Sayre—and not Hiss—twice in their 1940 talk.[13]

Malcolm Cowley had good reason for being angry at Chambers, consider-ing the unfavorable review of his book in 1942 and the critical remarks on his radical politics there and in the earlier article on ex-fellow travelers: "He paid for the luncheon, nearly $4 worth," Cowley wrote in his notes on the meeting with Chambers. "It will cost me a great deal more when the article comes out."

Had Cowley ever taken part in action designed to attack Chambers? He mentioned none in 1948, but Cowley seems to have played a minor role in such action.* The episode opened with a letter to Cowley from a young writer and apparent radical named Maus Darling. Darling wrote on March 19, 1942, expressing his dismay at the *Time* review of *The Dry Season* and stating: "From your description, I have guessed that the writer of that story was Whittaker Chambers, one of the 'tar babies' of this world. . . . I would like to do something about Chambers, but don't quite know how to go about it." Darling was about to join the Navy, but he informed Cowley: "I cherish the hope that [before being called up for naval duty] . . . I will be able to somehow settle the Chambers account. I have a good many able assistants for this task, some of whom now work for *Time*, some of whom did work for *Time* but were bounced thru Chambers's efforts." Cowley must have responded immediately—and positively—because on March 25 Darling wrote back: "Thanks for your letter, and [for] being on our side."[14]

Cowley had suggested, among other things, writing a "frank and full" letter to Henry Luce, a course of action Darling rejected on grounds that Luce was one of Chambers's sponsors by then. Darling also was "no longer interested in reprimanding *Time* privately. I'm after something that will hurt." Again he asked for Cowley's help, in researching or writing an article on Chambers for another magazine.

Cowley also offered to contribute information he had collected—or would collect—on Chambers, because on April 1 another letter from Darling said that "the job was unravelling by degrees" with the assistance of two other radicals on *Time*, Felice Swados and Tabitha Petran, plus a third enemy of Chambers at the magazine, Carolyn Marx. "Felice Swados [sister of the late novelist-critic Harvey Swados] will tackle the stories," Darling wrote, and later that day he would "see Ella Winter, who says over the phone, 'There is a much bigger story to this whole thing, and Chambers is only part of it.'" Darling pointedly reminded Cowley: "I think your material should go to [Tabitha Petran] and be lumped in with the rest." Nothing came of the project.[15]

So suspicious was Chambers of his Communist and pro-Communist adversaries at *Time* that he rarely bothered to distinguish between those who felt real malice toward him and others who—in those wartime days of Soviet-American entente—were politically aligned with the liberal left, whether as New Dealers, non-Stalinist radicals, or even fellow travelers, but without particular animus

---

*This emerges from letters in Cowley's papers at the Newberry Library, written to Cowley by a former associate of Chambers's on *Time*, Maus V. Darling, who later corresponded with Hiss in 1948 and served as a link between the Hiss defense and those hostile to Chambers at the magazine, including several former Communists.

toward him. John Osborne recalled his relations with Chambers at a time when Osborne wrote on labor affairs for the news magazine. At some point Chambers decided erroneously that Osborne was probably a secret Communist and so informed his superiors at *Time*. Osborne thought that the incident that triggered the defector's suspicion occurred when Chambers appeared at his office door one day to introduce himself. While they talked, Osborne mentioned having been invited to a cocktail party honoring a new folk opera by Marc Blitzstein, *The Cradle Will Rock*, "a musical darling of the Left." When Osborne invited Chambers to accompany him, the effect upon his visitor was "unforgettable": "He stiffened. The little blood below the skin of his pale face drained away. He truly 'went white.' Without a word he whirled and *ran* from my office."[16]

Such fear in the face of any contact with those associated, however slightly, with the left in New York led even some of Chambers's friends on the magazine—particularly those without radical political pasts—to consider him (in T. S. Matthews's phrase) "definitely cracked on the subject of Communism." Matthews considered his obsessive anti-Communism a bothersome "quirk" editorially, since it meant that on "any subject that touched on Russia or Communism he seemed to me so biased that he could not be trusted to write fairly. . . . [W]henever Chambers referred to Stalin or the Soviets, he made them out to be not friendly allies but cynical and treacherous enemies." For this reason, during the early years of World War II Chambers's editors at *Time* rebuffed his persistent efforts to shift from book reviewing, at which he excelled, to the Foreign News department. After an early tryout in that section, the Foreign News editor, Frank Norris, complained to Managing Editor Manfred Gottfried about Chambers's anti-Communist polemics: "He evidently thinks that having changed sides, he has to play capitalist and denounce Communists." According to Gottfried, Chambers felt his colleagues at *Time* were hopelessly naïve on the subject: "He thought capitalists were innocents, not aware of the conspirators who were about to overthrow them." Subsequently, Chambers was reassigned to the back-of-the-book departments.[17]

It was while working on *Time*'s cultural departments that Chambers suffered a physical collapse. For three years Esther Chambers had run their farm, assisted by a hired man and his children, with Whittaker commuting each weekend to Westminster, where he invariably used a good portion of his time to assist in chores on the farm rather than to rest. The accumulation of physical and emotional strains took its toll, and in November 1942 he began suffering intense pains in his chest, which a family physician diagnosed as angina pectoris. Chambers went home, remaining in bed or on a restricted work schedule for the next eight months, returning to *Time* only in the summer of 1943.[18]

The pattern of events that led up to Chambers's physical collapse resembled, in some ways, the earlier period of trauma that preceded his brother's suicide in 1926 and the following months spent immobilized and recuperating. Then it had been the accumulation of family tensions—fights with his father, efforts to deflect Richard's earlier suicide attempts, and refusal to join the latter's proposal for a joint death—that had worn him down. This time, in addition to the grueling schedule and the battles with the *Time* radicals, two things happened that may have contributed a psychosomatic aspect to his physical collapse: a visit to his office by FBI agents in May 1942, and the breakdown of his assistant and closest friend on the magazine, Calvin Fixx, a fellow anti-Communist, whose nervous system gave way only a few weeks before Chambers's attack.[19]

For many reasons Chambers did not welcome the arrival of the two FBI agents. The Soviet-American alliance was in effect, and he distrusted the Roosevelt administration more than ever. He still lacked immunity from prosecution. As a result, the interview unsettled him profoundly by stirring up again his fear of government action and by reviving his suppressed memories of the underground years. All of this stress undoubtedly contributed to bringing on his angina attack.

When the FBI first learned about Chambers's earlier work as a CP operative in 1940 from his old friend and confidant Ludwig Lore, the latter described Chambers as a former GPU agent "who has more material than you could ever hope to get by running around for a year. The man is bigger and more important than the whole American [Communist] hierarchy." Lore then blurted out additional details, sometimes inaccurate or exaggerated, about Chambers's activities, gained from conversations during the period surrounding the latter's defection. He pointed out that his friend, whose name he did not mention at first, was still fearful of possible prosecution for his previous underground activities. "If he could get a promise of immunity he would reveal the whole GPU set-up in this country."[20]

When the two agents visited Chambers at *Time* in May 1942, they had been checking into his background for several months without learning a great deal. Chambers suspected the agents' motives in coming to see him and later wrote to Herbert Solow that his questioners apparently were probing to learn if Chambers had anything to do with the death of Walter Krivitsky. Before answering their questions, Chambers told the agents about his 1939 meeting with Adolf Berle. He assumed incorrectly that Berle had informed the FBI about their talk long before, and he phoned Berle on the spot to ask permission to repeat his story to the FBI agents. (Chambers's letters to Solow indicate his deep suspicion of the bureau at this time, especially because the fact that he still lacked a promise of immunity from prosecution for past activities weighed heavily on him.) Presumably for this reason, Chambers not only avoided all mention of espionage (the country, after all, was then at war) but he distorted his real role in Soviet intelligence and even claimed that he had left the party a year earlier—in the spring of 1937, not 1938. According to the FBI agents' report, "Chambers further stated that he was not directly connected with the OGPU, but that on the contrary his real position was with the Underground Movement of the Communist Party, U.S.A." (which was technically correct up to a point, because of his continuing ties to the head of that movement, J. Peters). Throughout the interview, however, Chambers sprinkled broad hints of his actual situation during the 1930s. He described, for example, the parallel networks organized in Washington to separate secret government contacts of particular interest: "such [a] person is segregated from the Party proper and becomes a member of the OGPU."'[21]

To the FBI, Chambers repeated his earlier description of the underground organization—names and activities—given in 1939 to Berle, although he did not stress the critical espionage component as he had done three years earlier. Again he named Alger and Donald Hiss as underground Communists, although without singling them out for special mention any more than he had done with Berle (only three sentences of the agents' eight-page, single-spaced report dealt with Alger Hiss). Apparently Chambers's fear of assassination had lessened by then, since he observed when discussing the GPU's "terror squads" that "they knew he had talked and that they would have nothing to gain by liquidating him now."

The FBI's New York office sent a special eight-page report of the interview directly to Hoover. The director dismissed the detailed description of individuals involved in espionage provided by Chambers, concluding that "most of his information is either history, hypothesis, or deduction."[22]

The bureau's casual and haphazard follow-up on its 1942 interview with Chambers reflected its general ineptitude in dealing with Soviet espionage during the Second World War. Hoover may have felt inhibited by the wartime alliance between the United States and Russia, but it is extraordinary that the FBI deemed Chambers unworthy of a follow-up interview for the next three years, or that among those whom he had named, only J. Peters received even a cursory investigation by the New York field office. A December 1 report by agents confirmed Peters's prominence within the Communist Party but since the bureau had identified Peters as an important figure in the "open" party it simply set up a separate case file on him and announced, without further explanation, that "the instant case regarding Whittaker Chambers is being closed at this time."*[23]

Once separated from the stresses of *Time*, Chambers began a slow process of recovery at Westminster. His health repaired and his spirits restored to a state of normal melancholy, Chambers returned to the magazine during the summer of 1943. Some of his closest friends were no longer on the scene: Calvin Fixx was still recovering from his collapse, and Sam Welles had taken a leave of absence to

---

*FBI agents conducted a five-minute interview with Chambers at his Westminster farm on March 5, 1943, where he identified a photograph of Peters under his current pseudonym, "Alexander Stevens."

work in the State Department's public-information section. Welles's unexpected departure provoked the first of several convergences prior to 1948 of the very separate and distant worlds of Whittaker Chambers and Alger Hiss. Chambers was acutely conscious of Welles's possible future contacts with his former underground friend: "The minute I told Whit I was going to the State Department," Welles recalled, "he warned me specifically and by name against Alger Hiss. To repeat, this was in December 1942. Whit added that nothing had still come of what he had told Adolf Berle in 1939, and that Hiss had continued to move up in the State Department."[24]

Welles did not meet Hiss during the war, serving in London as an assistant to American Ambassador John Winant. He returned to Washington in January 1945 to become special assistant to the director of the Office of European Affairs, H. Freeman Matthews, and spent a weekend with Chambers at Westminster. Rumors concerning Hiss's alleged Communist ties had been circulating through the State Department by then as a result of Chambers's 1942 FBI interview, the 1939 Berle memo, which reached the FBI in 1943, and other sources.

Soon after Welles arrived in Washington, Raymond Murphy, a special assistant in the Office of European Affairs who concentrated on security matters, asked him about Chambers, who he had heard "knows something about Communists in Washington." Welles mentioned Chambers's previous statements to Berle and to the FBI. Murphy appeared to know about these, although he complained he could not obtain copies. Welles agreed to try to arrange a meeting with Chambers. On March 20, 1945, Chambers talked to Murphy at Westminster. When Murphy returned, he approached Welles again to ask if Chambers had ever told him about Alger Hiss, the only State Department official whom Chambers had mentioned (Hiss had just taken part in the February 1945 Yalta Conference and was then helping to organize the April UN founding meeting at San Francisco). Welles repeated Chambers's 1942 warning about Hiss and asked Murphy what he planned to do with the information. "Ray Murphy looked at me, and said: 'What can I do? Hiss outranks me in the Department.'"[25]

By the time he met with Murphy in 1945 Chambers had achieved his ambition to edit Foreign News at *Time*. Shortly after returning to the magazine in mid-1943, he had been assigned again to the back-of-the-book, with the work now divided more reasonably between himself and another senior editor. When John Osborne, the then Foreign News editor, left for Europe in the summer of 1944, Chambers argued successfully for assignment to the post. He and Henry Luce shared not only a passion for the magazine but similar views on the postwar dangers of Communism, and Chambers wrote his employer soon after receiving the new assignment:

> I should like to edit Foreign News for a long time to come.... It is my first choice my second and my third.... I have spent some 15 years of my life

actively preparing for FN. Some of those years were spent close to the central dynamo that powers the politics of our time. In fact, I can say: I was there, I saw it, at least in a small way, I did it. . . . In dealing with international affairs, I feel like a man in a dark but familiar room: I may bump against the furniture, but I'm usually sure where the door and the windows are. . . . I want to sit here and figure out history.[26]

The Foreign News section soon reflected his strident anti-Communism, and Chambers was strongly criticized by many of his colleagues. But he retained the support of Luce and most of his fellow senior editors. Chambers's familiar distrust of all those on the magazine, liberals and radicals alike, who did not share his "counter-revolutionary"' beliefs caused splits within *Time*. He "infuriated" a chief researcher in his section, according to Robert Elson, by passing along "deliberately inaccurate lists of scheduled stories so that she wouldn't know what he was up to. . . . He often rewrote stories without explanation to his writers and rode roughshod over the objections of researchers. His chief adversaries were among the foreign correspondents."

Time's senior correspondents abroad were among the most impressive group of writers on the magazine, yet Chambers, they complained, mercilessly butchered, deformed, or discarded their dispatches. Such reporters as Osborne, C. D. Jackson, Charles Wertenbaker, and Walter Graebner in Europe, John Hersey in Moscow, and Annalee Jacoby and Theodore H. White in China protested angrily and often to Luce and the other New York editors about Chambers's determination to rewrite their reports in order to project an anti-Soviet editorial line within the Foreign News department. Fillmore Calhoun, the cable editor for *Life*, complained by memorandum after an overseas tour: "Hell, I read the incoming cables and week after week I am amazed to see how they are either misinterpreted, left unprinted or weaseled around to one man's way of thinking. I like Whit and I admire his slickness, but I wouldn't trust him with any set of facts concerning Russia any more than I would trust John L. Lewis to ask for less wages for his coal miners."[27]

So insistent and widespread had the protests become by late 1944 that Luce, though still agreeing with Chambers's anti-Communist line, finally had to intervene. In a January 1945 memo, distributed to his New York editors and the magazine's senior correspondents, Luce praised both Chambers and the correspondents for doing a "fine job," but supported Chambers's judgment on the central question of the Soviet Union's postwar behavior and intentions: "If Chambers's editing has suggested that he doubts Russia's desire for peace then he has been guilty, as perhaps indeed he has, of unclarity. For far from disbelieving in Russia's desire for peace, our view is that Russia is, if anything, over-exploiting her own and the world's desire for peace." Luce reprimanded Chambers for not distinguishing carefully enough between "the general revolutionary, leftist, or simply chaotic trends [in the world] and, on the other hand, the specifically Communist politics in various countries." But on the basic question of the Soviet Union's character as a society Luce toyed sardonically with those of his correspondents and editors flushed with the military successes of the wartime Grand Alliance. He, like Chambers, anticipated no sudden evolution toward democracy in Russia or in any territories under Russian control. "I have just been told, in a highly confidential manner," he parried, "that Stalin is, after all, a Communist. . . . A good Foreign News Editor, while guarding against the prejudices arising from his own convictions, will not ignore the circumstance that the Pope is a Christian and Stalin a Communist and Hersey [John Hersey, a leader in the protest against Chambers], God bless him, a Democrat."[28]

Despite his genial defense of Chambers, Luce moved to curb his authority over handling foreign news. Chambers would remain as Foreign News editor, but the department's overemphasis on the Soviet Union called for creating a new section called "International," which, as Elson later wrote, had "as its scope diplomacy on a world scale" and would "be free to take over all stories on international relations from both the U.S. at War and the Foreign News sections." Luce quickly passed the word down through his editors that many areas about which Chambers had written in Foreign News would henceforth be channeled through the new International department, which, to achieve even greater balance, would have John Osborne as its head.

Chambers clearly had won the battle for Luce's approval, but had lost the war for control of *Time*'s foreign-news output. Osborne wrote subsequently: "I took the job only when I got Luce's promise, relayed to me through managing editor T. S. Matthews, that Chambers would never again replace me in any job or that he never again would be put in a position to misuse and distort the reports of *Time*'s foreign correspondents." But Chambers had already devised his own strategy for circumventing Luce's decision and, at the same time, commenting forcefully on the February 1945 Yalta Conference, which was then being widely hailed as the forerunner of an international era of understanding.[29]

Shortly after the last meeting of Churchill, Roosevelt, and Stalin disbanded, Chambers appeared at Matthews's office with the draft of a political satire he had written about the event in the form of a fable that he called "The Ghosts on the Roof." His tale—which predicted a postwar era of Soviet expansionism and confrontation between the wartime allies—was told through the figures of the murdered Czar Nicholas and his family, whose shades peered down from the roof of their onetime palace at Yalta at the meeting between the Big Three leaders. Most of the cynical and caustic assessments of Stalin's intentions are rendered by Nicholas himself (clearly Chambers's surrogate in the piece), who comments approvingly on Stalin's ruthlessness on behalf of Russian imperialism, the Czar having converted to Marxism after his death with the Czarina's approval. "Even peace," she says at one point, "may be only a tactic of struggle." The royal ghosts are joined in discussion by the Muse of History, and the fable concludes with

Nicholas first intoning: "What makes Stalin great . . . is that he understands how to adapt revolutionary tactics to the whirling spirals of history. . . . We Marxists believe that in the years of peace Britain and the U.S. will fall apart." To which "History" responds, à la Chambers: "More is at stake than economic and political systems. Two faiths are at issue. It is just that problem which these gentlemen below are trying to work out in practical terms. But if they fail, I foresee more wars, more revolutions, greater proscriptions, bloodshed and human misery. . . . [But] I never permit my foreknowledge to interfere with human folly, if only because I never expect human folly to learn much from history."[30]

Controversy swirled around "The Ghosts on the Roof" from the moment Chambers submitted the article. Matthews "was visited by an unofficial delegation from the staffs of both *Time* and *Life,* urging me strongly not to print the piece: it would drive a wedge between the Allies, it was biased and bitter, irresponsible journalism, etc. I was sufficiently shaken to postpone publication for a week. Then I sent it to press." Chambers believed that one of those responsible for the staff protest was John Osborne. But Osborne later wrote that he "sent my carbon to Matthews with a note to the effect that it was a brilliant piece and should be run as written." Letters to the Editor after the printing of "The Ghosts on the Roof" were, in Elson's words, "almost wholly adverse," and Chambers rode out the storm for the next few months, but again was felled by illness, this time a serious heart attack. Returning to New York to begin his week's work in August 1945, Chambers suddenly passed out on the train and, after a physical examination, received confirmation of his heart condition.[51]

Once more, as in 1942, Chambers's sudden collapse took place while he was unwinding from a long period of intense physical and emotional pressure. The year-long struggle over control of Foreign News at the magazine had ended inconclusively but with Chambers's apparent demotion. The tempest over "The Ghosts on the Roof" had obscured briefly that temporary eclipse of his anti-Soviet opinions at the magazine, and was probably viewed by Chambers as a diversionary move, but one that had no real impact upon the journal's coverage of international affairs. Alger Hiss's presence at Yalta may well have been an inspiration for Chambers's decision to write "The Ghosts on the Roof." Osborne later recalled that in 1945 Chambers had "cited as evidence of Communist influence on *Time* the fact that I had edited and published a favorable story about Hiss in his role as secretary general of the founding United Nations conference. . . . Chambers didn't know that Henry Luce, who attended the conference, was impressed by Hiss and ordered me to have the story written and printed. Luce was furious with me when I killed the first story submitted to me because it was poorly done and severely cut a second version that he had approved."[32]

Actually, both FBI and State Department counterintelligence officials had begun earlier in 1945 to scan Chambers's depositions and the Berle memo, reacting uneasily to the rise of Alger Hiss. In March 1945, after Hiss had already been

chosen to head the San Francisco conference, the FBI belatedly dispatched copies of Chambers's 1942 interview with bureau agents to State Department security officers. Raymond Murphy visited Chambers at Westminster, and the latter
named Hiss as a secret Communist and leader of a cell within the Ware Group.
"The top leaders of the underground," Murphy wrote in his notes of the meeting,
"were 1. Harold Ware. 2. Lee Pressman. 3. Alger Hiss. In the order of their importance." Chambers told Murphy, inaccurately, that he broke at the "end of 1937"
and described "several conversations with Alger Hiss in the early part of 1938
during which Hiss was adamant against the plan of breaking with the Party."
Among the others he named as party members were Donald Hiss and Henry
Collins. Noel Field "was described as a member at large of the Party, [Laurence]
Duggan was not. Neither was connected with the underground." Harry Dexter
White was called "a member at large but rather timid," who assigned members
of the underground group as assistants in the Treasury Department. Nathan Witt,
John Abt, and Jessica Smith were listed as members of the underground.[33]

Distributed widely among departmental security officers, Murphy's information left them shaken and somewhat at a loss over how to proceed. Hiss was
known within State as a correct, slightly conservative, hardworking, extremely
efficient "paper pusher," a bureaucrat's bureaucrat and a rising policy maker in
the field of international organizations. Prior to receipt of Chambers's information there had been no hints of possible disloyalty, and he had a record of almost
a decade's service with only a vague 1942 FBI security probe tainting an otherwise perfect loyalty record. Hiss, moreover, was a protégé and special favorite
of Secretary Stettinius as well as a friend of Dean Acheson and other leading
departmental officials.

Despite Murphy's troubling inquiry, therefore, Hiss's place in the Department
appeared secure as long as Stettinius remained Secretary. Neither Murphy nor
any other State Department security officer questioned him about Chambers's
accusations in March 1945, although one departmental intelligence agent (perhaps Murphy) did file a "top secret" report on Hiss on March 26 which incorporated Chambers's statements and Hiss's 1942 denial of Communist affiliations
to the FBI. The report described at tedious length the CP links of the International Juridical Association, to which Hiss had belonged early in the 1930s, and
repeated some gossip by former employees of the AAA about Hiss's ties to Communists and fellow travelers within the agency. But apparently it made no recommendations concerning future investigation, and Hiss did not learn about the
departmental probe before leaving for San Francisco.[34]

But Hoover and other leading FBI counterintelligence officials had begun to
fret considerably about Hiss. Not only did they send the bureau's file on Hiss
and the Berle memo to State, but Hoover ordered Chambers interviewed again.
Hiss's more prominent role within State inspired the director's concern. Two FBI

agents spent over eight hours with Chambers at his *Time* office on May 10, 1945, probing for details of Communist underground involvement that the journalist had omitted in 1942. Chambers provided the agents with enough material—much of it new—to fill a twenty-two-page, single-spaced report.[35]

Although the FBI did not immediately send copies of Chambers's interview to State, certain bureau officials, including Hoover's close aide William C. Sullivan, leaked those portions regarding Hiss to a few members of Congress and to Father John Cronin. Hiss figured prominently in Cronin's report for the bishops, completed in November 1945. The priest displayed evident familiarity with Chambers's FBI interviews, although his report never mentioned them by name. Cronin's report did mention Hiss as a Communist four times.[36]

Past sorrows and present disorder combined to strike Chambers down again. His financial position had become comfortable and less dependent upon any income Esther, his children, and the hired hand might extract from the Westminster farm. His *Time* salary had increased to almost $15,000 plus benefits (he began working for $5,200 a year in 1939 and was making $21,000 when he left the magazine in 1948). Chambers's involvements over the previous half-decade were reflected also in a group-insurance application he took out in December 1945 shortly after returning to *Time* in which, should Esther and his two children die before him, three beneficiaries would share his insurance proceeds equally: the Pipe Creek Monthly Meeting of the Society of Friends, his handyman (described as "Donald Pennington, friend"), and his close friend on *Time*, James Agee.[37]

When Chambers recovered from his heart attack during the late autumn of 1945, he reversed an earlier decision to leave the *Time* office for good and write book reviews from Westminster. He "asked for his job back, but [according to Robert Elson] Matthews, who had seen Chambers work himself into two physical collapses, was determined to put him on a less exacting schedule, and by that time he had assigned the section to another editor." John Osborne presented a different version of this decision to deny Chambers any further role in foreign coverage. Matthews informed Osborne soon after Chambers's recovery "from what all of us had assumed to be a permanently disabling illness . . . that he was again to replace me as foreign editor." Osborne then reminded Matthews of his (and Luce's) earlier promise that Chambers would never again replace him on a Time assignment and "insisted that it be honored":

> Matthews begged me to skip it and spare him the task of telling Luce that Chambers, who then was still a favorite of his, could not have back a job that he desperately wanted. Matthews pleaded that the promise would not have been made if he and Luce had not thought at the time that Chambers would never again be able to swing a full-time job [actually, Matthews had made the promise *before* Chambers's 1945 heart attack]. . . . Matthews finally went to Luce and Luce honored his promise.[38]

Matthews reckoned correctly the depth of Chambers's disappointment. He accepted the official explanation for the transfer, however, and after returning briefly to the Books section with no reduction in either salary or rank, "was assigned as an editor-at-large on Special Projects and given a substantial increase in salary." During the next two and a half years, until the Hiss case broke in August 1948, Chambers turned out for both *Life* and *Time* some of their best writing on historical and theological topics: long articles for *Life* on "Medieval Man," "The Venetian Republic," "The Age of Exploration," "The Enlightenment," and "The Devil"; insightful essays (often cover stories) for *Time* on such themes as "The Story of Religion" and on such figures as Reinhold Niebuhr, Albert Einstein (a biography of whom Chambers had once planned to translate in 1939 before joining the magazine), Arnold Toynbee, and Marian Anderson.[39]

A brooding hostility toward Communism and an equally anguished belief in the rapid decline of the West emerged clearly in some of these essays. But he rarely had the opportunity again to influence the magazine's weekly news coverage of developments in the Communist world or the evolving Soviet-American Cold War confrontation. Occasionally Chambers did manage a brief toehold on more contemporary reporting at *Time*, as when he replaced the vacationing editor of the Foreign News section in July 1946. But even then memories of earlier battles with correspondents in the field lingered at *Time*, and Matthews felt it necessary to dispatch a memorandum warning against future quarrels: "The news of your grey imminence has not been well received. . . . The situation affects both me and you. I expect that there may be difficulties . . . but I also expect to take a hand in them, if they occur . . . and I shall expect you to do as you would be done by. . . . I do insist on good behavior, on both sides."[40]

But Matthews need not have worried. Chambers's tenure as a substitute Foreign News editor was brief and uneventful. He returned to his Special Projects assignment—a department shared with James Agee—apparently willing to avoid abrasive and physically debilitating confrontations with those on *Time* who did not share his passionate anti-Communist beliefs. Not that he had changed any of the beliefs that provoked the conflicts. Reviewing Rebecca West's *The Meaning of Treason* for a *Time* cover story in December 1947, Chambers wrote: "Other ages have had their individual traitors—men who from faint-heartedness or hope of gain sold out their causes. But in the 20th century, for the first time, men banded together in millions, in movements like Fascism and Communism, dedicated to the purpose of betraying the institutions they lived under. In the 20th century, treason became a vocation whose modern form was specifically the treason of ideas."[41]

That same year Chambers's thoughts of treason turned closer to home. When Arthur Schlesinger, Jr., came to see him while researching a *Life* article on Communism in 1947, he told Schlesinger about those he had known as Communists within the federal government during the 1930s, including Alger Hiss. Yet when

HUAC sent several staff members to interview him at Westminster in March 1948, Chambers turned down their request that he testify before the committee. He pleaded that the committee not summon him as a witness. At that point he had no desire to relive in public either his turbulent experiences as a Communist or his painful escape.[42]

THE BUREAUCRAT

Alger Hiss continued to serve as Francis B. Sayre's assistant until Sayre became United States high commissioner to the Philippines in the summer of 1939, when Hiss transferred to the office of Stanley K. Hornbeck, political adviser to the department's Far Eastern Division. At Sayre's request, Hiss recommended two people for the Philippines post of assistant to Sayre. One of these was a State Department employee named Claude Buss, who eventually got the job. But Hiss first urged Sayre to hire Noel Field, who had left the department in 1936 to join the League of Nations. Because Field's name had been linked to Communist causes in testimony before the Dies Committee, officials at the State Department conducted an intensive investigation of the Field recommendation, with a number of departmental officers writing either on his behalf or in opposition. Curiously, Adolf Berle monitored the entire controversy but did not inform anyone at State that Chambers had mentioned Field as an undercover Communist months earlier. Hiss's reasons for recommending a former official at State with only European experience—Noel Field—for a sensitive post in the Philippines with Sayre have never been satisfactorily explained.* Field, Hiss wrote Sayre (about a person he knew only for months prior to entering State), "is an expert draftsman and has a brilliant and flexible mind."[43]

From 1939, Hiss served as Hornbeck's personal aide in a two-man office, supplemented by several secretaries, similar to the earlier arrangement with Sayre. Hornbeck, like Sayre, had only the highest praise for Hiss's performance as an assistant, both at the time and in later years: "Alger had my full confidence," he told Hiss's lawyer in January 1949, "and saw everything that I saw." (Hornbeck did point out in 1949 that it was not part of Hiss's duties to read or summarize cables "in the fashion similar to the handwritten summaries in this case" that had come from Sayre's office.) Hornbeck's esteem for Hiss's character

---

*Although, in 1948, Hiss minimized the importance of the Field recommendation and linked it with his suggestion of the more conservative Buss, the actual sequence of events was quite different. After writing Sayre that the few possible assistants within the department requested by Sayre were—for one reason or another—not available, Hiss urged his former superior to hire Noel Field. Only after considerable opposition within the department—including Sayre's—was the Buss nomination first raised. State Department files document the uproar over Hiss's recommendation of Field in 1940.

and trustworthiness remained high, even after being confronted with disturbing rumors about his new assistant early in their relationship.[44]

Ambassador to France William C. Bullitt visited his old friend Hornbeck at State. Hiss came into the office briefly, and afterward, when Hornbeck identified him, Bullitt seemed startled. Hornbeck's and Bullitt's later accounts of what followed varied considerably. Bullitt thought the visit took place in 1939, while Hornbeck placed it during the period of American involvement in the war, perhaps 1941 or 1943. The ambassador later declared publicly he had told Hornbeck at the time that French Premier Edouard Daladier had warned him shortly before his departure from France (this would have placed the conversation with Hornbeck prior to German occupation of France in mid-1940) about "two brothers named Hiss," both in the State Department, who were "Soviet agents." Daladier, according to Bullitt, attributed his information to French intelligence sources. When he encountered Alger Hiss accidentally in Hornbeck's office, Bullitt later recalled advising his friend to open an immediate investigation into Daladier's charges.*[45]

According to Hornbeck, however, Bullitt called the Hiss brothers not Communists but "fellow travelers" and said nothing about their being Russian spies. Hiss's recollection squared with Bullitt's. In 1946 Hiss informed the FBI that "Hornbeck told him that someone, name unknown to Hiss, had stated that Hiss was a 'red.'" Nor did Hornbeck later confirm Bullitt's having named Daladier as his source, saying that he only cited a "high official of the French Foreign Office."[46]

Whatever the source, Hornbeck was clearly disturbed.† After Bullitt's departure he confronted Hiss: "I came right out and asked point-blank what did he know about Communism or Communists, what contacts had he had with personnel

---

*Bullitt's reference to Daladier came from April 8, 1952, testimony before the Senate Internal Security Subcommittee. In October 1949, however, Bullitt told the FBI that he had heard the charge "from a Frenchman, whose identity Mr. Bullitt could not recall." FBI Report. October 7, 1949, #4049.

†In 1946, acting on a trip from State Department security officer Fred B. Lyons, the FBI interviewed a former Soviet diplomat named Alexander Gregory-Graff Barmine, who defected in 1937 in Athens. Barmine told the FBI in 1946 he did not know the identity of any Soviet agents in the United States, but he was not questioned directly about Hiss. Interviewed by the bureau again on December 14, 1948, Barmine was asked specifically about his knowledge of Hiss. He said "that he had heard Alger Hiss referred to as being an agent of Soviet Military Intelligence." "In explanation of this," a February 4, 1949, FBI report noted, "he said that in the early part of 1938 after his own defection from the Soviet Diplomatic Service he had visited Walter Krivitsky in the latter's hotel in Paris, France. . . . In an attempt to establish the reliability of the man, Barmine said he . . . asked Krivitsky to name some of the individuals who were working for the Soviet Military Intelligence in America. According to Barmine, Krivitsky then named about ten persons, including Alger Hiss, George Mink and Harry Dexter White." Either Barmine or Krivitsky may have been the source to French intelligence coming upon the names of the Hiss brothers during the late 1930s.

or organizations oriented toward the Left." To all these questions "Alger gave replies which ran counter to the idea that he was or could be a 'fellow-traveler.'" Even after Hiss's conviction in 1950, Hornbeck refused to believe that he had ever stolen departmental documents for Chambers: "But, that Alger committed perjury [in testifying about his lack of familiarity with Chambers] there was ample and conclusive proof."[47]

In 1942 an FBI agent questioned Hornbeck about the Hiss brothers. The bureau's files show that its initial investigation of Alger Hiss was set off not by Chambers or Bullitt but through an erroneous tip from HUAC, then a temporary committee chaired by Martin Dies. The Texas Democrat sent to Attorney General Francis Biddle on October 17, 1941, a list of 1,124 alleged "Communists, fellow travelers and Communist sympathizers" employed by the federal government. Alger and Donald Hiss were on this list—but only as alleged members of a radical group called the Washington Committee for Democratic Action. As it turned out, their wives were members briefly; but neither man had joined.

After checking with several of Alger Hiss's former or present associates in the government, an FBI Washington field agent met with him on February 4, 1942, and confronted him with the accusation. Hiss denied membership in the group, denied past or present membership in the Communist Party, and argued forcefully for his loyalty: "There is only one government that I want to overthrow and that is Hitler's." The bureau made no further effort to investigate Hiss during the war years.[48]

Serving as Hornbeck's aide until May 1944, Hiss then became special assistant to the director of the department's newly created Office of Special Political Affairs, a policymaking post under the supervision of an economist, Leo Pasvolsky. But for the next two and a half years Hiss worked directly with a series of secretaries and under secretaries of state. Without formally bypassing Pasvolsky, Hiss rose in stature within the department as a result of his regular and almost unrestricted access to its leading officials. He described the situation this way to his lawyers in 1948:

> During the whole period from May 1944 until the end of the first meeting of the [UN General] Assembly my immediate superior was Dr. Leo Pasvolsky. However, I worked directly and regularly with Mr. Stettinius [who was then under secretary and became secretary in November 1944] from just about this date right on through the first session of the General Assembly and subsequently after his return to this country as our representative before the Security Council. The United Nations was clearly his first interest and he devoted far more time to them than to any other topic. I saw him practically daily in this period and received direct instructions from him continuously. . . . After [Pasvolsky's] resignation I reported directly to [Under Secretary] Dean Acheson or to Mr. [Secretary] Byrnes and from the summer of 1946 on continued to do so. As

Mr. Byrnes was away from the city attending conferences during a good part of this time most of my contacts were with Dean Acheson. I attended regularly the 9:30 morning meeting of Directors of Offices in his office during this period.[49]

From the spring of 1944 Hiss's major responsibility involved postwar planning for international organization. By the year's end he was deputy director of the Office of Special Political Affairs and in March 1945 became its director. Such rapid advancement for a junior departmental officer was unusual, but, in addition to his obvious talents, able staff work, and administrative skill, Hiss had two admiring sponsors in State's hierarchy, Stettinius and Acheson. Hiss and Stettinius remained "Alger" and "Ed" to each other throughout the latter's period as secretary.

After Hiss's service as executive secretary of the four-power Dumbarton Oaks Conference that laid plans for the United Nations, Stettinius wrote praising his "splendid cooperation" that "contributed to the foundation of an international peace." The two shared, among other things, a belief that postwar difficulties for the United States were at least as likely to come from a resurgent Great Britain intent upon protecting a revived empire as from the Soviet Union. Letters written by Hiss both at Dumbarton Oaks and, the following February, after the Yalta Conference in the Crimea indicate his belief that the Soviet Union would remain a postwar American ally, a position common within the department at the time. "The Soviet group has impressed all of us quite favorably and has definitely pulled its full weight in the work at Dumbarton Oaks," Hiss wrote in September 1944.[50]

The last year of Franklin Roosevelt's administration—and of the war—was perhaps the most exciting in Hiss's career. After Dumbarton Oaks he joined other State Department officials in a series of speaking engagements around the country to explain the proposals for postwar international organization. Roosevelt and his diplomatic advisers were determined to avoid the mistakes made by Wilson after the First World War in negotiating a peace settlement without keeping the American public and leading politicians informed. At the same time, Hiss and other officials involved in postwar planning worked hard to prepare for the Yalta Conference. In January Stettinius and a small group of advisers—including Hiss—stopped at Marrakesh, Morocco, for briefings concerning American proposals and strategy for the upcoming conference. The group then flew to Naples for additional conferences with Roosevelt's personal adviser on foreign policy, Harry Hopkins, and Charles Bohlen, the department's leading Russian specialist.[51]

At Yalta, Hiss's involvement was greatest in connection with decisions taken on the United Nations. The American delegation was an imposing one, and Hiss was far from being the most prominent or most influential member. Roosevelt's advisers included General George C. Marshall, Admirals William D. Leahy and Ernest F. King, James F. Byrnes, ambassador to Russia Averell Harriman, Hopkins, and Bohlen. Hiss described his role at the meeting this way:

I was primarily responsible for the United Nations topics which were rather numerous and of considerable importance. The most important objective was to obtain agreement on voting procedure in the Security Council [the veto]. Other topics were fixing the date and place of the United Nations Conference and determining the governments to be invited. . . . The determination of nations to be invited was of particular importance to us as we wanted all of the Latin-American countries to be invited; the Russians on the other hand wanted only nations actually at war with the Axis. On each of these points the full objectives of the United States delegation were obtained. (We, however, did not succeed in preventing any of the Soviet Republics from being invited.) . . . The United Nations questions, once agreement was reached on the date and place of the Conference and the nations to be invited, were not of great interest to the other participants in the Conference. I had to keep pressing to see that the remaining details, like the Conference of Jurists, the principles of the Trusteeship System, and the form of the invitation, were covered.

Hiss had also "participated in meetings in the Department of State before we left when we were preparing our draft" of the Declaration of Liberated Europe, the crucial negotiations with the Russians over the future of Eastern European governments. As Hiss recalled this aspect of his work in 1948, "the final text [of the declaration] was very close to the United States draft," although critics of Yalta felt that the Americans had made a number of damaging concessions to the Russians.[52]

Considering his recent rise, relative youth (forty-one), and middle-rank status within the department, Hiss played a surprisingly important role at the meeting, partly because of his considerable bureaucratic abilities. Again in Hiss's own words:

Stettinius put me in charge of assembling all the background papers and documentation of the State Department group before we left Washington. On the trip I was in charge of receiving and dispatching reports from and to the Department. Many things, of course, were referred to the Secretary of State that had nothing to do with the Conference. In addition to these duties I was also to be responsible for any general matters that might come up relating to the Far East or the Near East and had talked to the Far Eastern and Near Eastern Divisions before I left. . . . Before leaving Washington I also was given by Mr. [Green] Hackworth [another departmental official] papers relating to a possible agreement on the trial of war criminals.

Hiss was thus privy to most of the department's documents used at Yalta, even those outside his special field of interest, and to the range of policy debates that preceded the decisions taken at the Crimea conference.

Nor did his importance end there:

Stettinius, Matthews, Foote and I returned in Stettinius' plane over the long route during which Stettinius made a number of official calls, Moscow, Cairo, Dakar,

Monrovia, Rio de Janeiro, Trinidad and Mexico City. We arrived in Mexico City in time for the Chapultepec [Inter-American] Conference which began on February 21. I remained but a few days, returning to Washington to carry on with the arrangements for the San Francisco [United Nations] Conference. From this time until the day before the Conference when I flew to San Francisco I was fully occupied in helping with the preparation of the United States policies for the Conference and with the setting up of the mechanical arrangements. I was appointed Director of the Office of Special Political Affairs during this period (the formal date is March 19 but my recollection is that Stettinius sent word back from Yalta that the appointment was to be made promptly and that I began to discharge these duties as soon as I returned to Washington).[53]

While "en route from Moscow to Cairo" on Stettinius's plane after the Crimea conference ended, Hiss conveyed his "personal and private" assessment of Yalta to his nominal superior, Leo Pasvolsky. The report went to great lengths to flatter Stettinius as the guiding spirit of the conference—a role that few other observers at the time or scholars since have accorded him—but its tone indicates that Hiss approached Pasvolsky not as a subordinate submitting an overdue report but as someone stealing time from a busy schedule to brief a concerned colleague of equal rank. Stettinius is referred to as "Ed [who] crowded in his consultations with Doc, Chip and me," and Pasvolsky is cautioned at the end: "As the Secretary naturally wants all the details, color, etc., kept absolutely to the fewest possible individuals, please show this only to Mr. Grew and Mr. Dunn."

At the time Hiss wrote this letter, Stettinius had already decided to promote him to the directorship of the Office of Special Political Affairs (a position he assumed in March 1945). By then Pasvolsky had been made a department "special assistant" in the field of international organizations. Particularly interesting is Hiss's assessment of the two other delegations' performance at the conference: "The Associated Nations question [i.e., Latin American membership in the United Nations] caused a lot more trouble and our British friends were definitely not helpful. The Russians on this, as on almost all other issues, were surprisingly cooperative and conciliatory." Hiss's view of the Russians would have found few supporters among the American delegation, who saw the positive results at Yalta as the product of hard bargaining with both the British and the Russians.[54]

Considering Hiss's familiarity with the background of international organizational planning from Dumbarton Oaks to Yalta, and in view of his close relationship to Stettinius, he was the logical choice to serve as Temporary Secretary-General of the United Nations's organizing conference at San Francisco in April 1945.*[55]

---

*Hiss's selection to organize the U.N. Conference remains puzzling in one respect, since the State Department already had a Division of International Conferences to carry out such

After returning from the San Francisco meeting and delivering a copy of the United Nations charter directly to President Truman, who praised his work, Hiss settled into his new responsibilities as director of the Office of Special Political Affairs. He helped prepare departmental officials for the Senate hearings on American membership in the United Nations that took place in July and, according to Hiss's 1948 memo, "simultaneously helped in preparing instructions to our delegation to the Preparatory Commission that was held in London beginning August 16 and continuing right up to December 2–3. Our delegation was headed by Stettinius." Hiss attended the first meeting of the UN General Assembly, held in London in January and February 1946. He served as "principal adviser (chief of staff) to the delegation."[56]

By that time the American wartime policy of cooperation with the Soviet Union had already faded. Truman and his new secretary of state, James F. Byrnes, were both far more suspicious of postwar Soviet intentions than their predecessors. The Potsdam Conference in July 1945, in which Hiss did not participate, was a far less amicable meeting than Yalta, and the hopes for postwar cooperation seemed to be fast disappearing.

Despite these changes, Hiss's promotion within State to more important policymaking roles was assured. Although Stettinius had departed in July 1945, Dean Acheson was Byrnes's under secretary. Before Stettinius gave up the secretaryship, he wrote Hiss an extremely warm letter, expressing his "heartfelt thanks for the magnificent support you have so loyally given me. At Dumbarton Oaks, at Yalta, in Washington, and again at San Francisco your advice and assistance have been invaluable to me. I shall always remember our association as one of the happiest of my life, and I hope that it will continue in the future. With affectionate regards, Faithfully. . . ."[57]

Hiss's close and daily ties to Stettinius were to have a fateful impact within months of receiving this letter. In September 1945 Igor Gouzenko, a Russian code clerk at the Soviet Embassy in Ottawa, Canada, defected, taking with him

---

responsibilities. In his 1949 book on the department, Graham H. Stuart termed "inexplicable" Stettinius's decision to bypass the division in favor of Hiss's *ad hoc* staff for such an important undertaking. The result was administrative confusion, according to Stuart, including a "very unsatisfactory distribution of tickets and . . . bitter complaints regarding housing." But Stettinius's diaries indicate that the assignment came from FDR himself while at Yalta: "He gave a signal to me that Alger Hiss and I should handle this entirely ourselves," the secretary wrote on February 8, 1945. Hiss's subordinate in the Office of Special Political Affairs, Joseph C. Green, opposed a proposal by General Donovan of the OSS that the agency be available for "research work" assisting Stettinius at San Francisco, briefing him on the background of delegates and issues: "Hiss vigorously endorsed Green's views in a note to Stettinius, and American intelligence work at the conference was sharply limited." Graham H. Stuart, *The Department of State* (New York, 1949), p. 419; Thomas M. Campbell and George C. Herring. eds., *The Diaries of Edward R. Stettinius, Jr., 1943–1946* (New York, 1975), pp. 249, 302–03.

hundreds of documents that proved the existence of a large Russian espionage network in Canada and the United States. Questioned in October by Canadian security officials and by a representative of the FBI, Gouzenko stated (according to a bureau memorandum the following month): "That he had been informed by Lieutenant Kulakov in the office of the Soviet military attaché that the Soviets had an agent in the United States in May 1945 who was an assistant to the then Secretary of State, Edward R. Stettinius." When this was linked by the FBI to Whittaker Chambers's earlier statements and to information from other recent informants, the bureau decided finally that Gouzenko's statement could only refer to Alger Hiss.*[58]

Allegations of Hiss's Communist activities received independent reinforcement in 1945 from *two* additional informants, in fact, neither of whom knew Whittaker Chambers. The new testimony provoked consternation at the State Department and caused both its security officers and the FBI to start a searching but secret inquiry into Alger Hiss's loyalty.

Igor Gouzenko's statement about the Russian agent close to Stettinius reached the FBI in October 1945 at almost the same time that Elizabeth Bentley provided the bureau with a related accusation. Bentley had worked through a leading Russian agent in this country named Jacob Golos, who was her lover. Several years after Golos's death, Bentley defected. Among many details, she told the FBI about an effort she had made while a Soviet courier to arrange for the return to her group of a government contact named Harold Glasser, whose role in the underground had also been noted by Chambers and who had been transferred to a different secret network. Another member of Bentley's group, Charles Kramer, an associate of Hiss's in AAA, told Bentley:

That the person who had originally taken Glasser away . . . and turned him over to a Russian was a man named Hiss, who was employed in the Department of State. Miss Bentley subsequently was advised by her Russian contact named Jack that he had learned of the identity of Hiss. Miss Bentley indicated that the Hiss in question was an advisor to Dean Acheson of the Department of State named Eugene [sic] Hiss. Subsequent inquiry pointed to the individual referred to as being Alger Hiss.[59]

---

*Canadian Prime Minister Mackenzie King, reflecting on Gouzenko's statement, noted its apparent reference to Hiss in this February 5, 1946, diary entry: "Suspicions are directed right up to the top of the treasury [in the United States], naming a person; also . . . [they are] directed against another person who was very close to Stettinius at San Francisco and who took a prominent part in matters there. I said in regard to the latter I was not particularly surprised. I confess I was surprised when I said the particular person he mentioned filling the position he did." Cited in James Barros, "Alger Hiss and Harry Dexter White: The Canada Connection," *Orbis*, vol. 21, no. 3, 1977.

EASING HISS OUT

In November 1945 Hoover asked Attorney General Tom Clark to allow the bureau to "install a technical surveillance" in Alger Hiss's Washington home. After the Gouzenko and Bentley statements, Hoover no longer dismissed Chambers's information. Clark agreed to the plan early in December. The investigation involved not only phone taps but also, judging from the bureau's memos, a mail cover, physical surveillance (tailing of Hiss and his wife), and the use of either a friend's or a maid's services to keep tabs on the Hisses' daily movements.*

This intense surveillance lasted throughout Hiss's final twelve months at State.[60]

When Gouzenko's information first came to his attention, Byrnes had assigned Acheson to discuss the Canadian espionage case with Hoover, and the under secretary asked the FBI director whether he had any information on the identity of the State Department aide whom Gouzenko had in mind. Hoover acknowledged that the bureau had not been able to identify the man positively. When Acheson asked if Hoover suspected anyone, the director replied that the FBI considered one person a possible suspect, "although there was no direct evidence to sustain this suspicion." Hoover then mentioned Alger Hiss's name, but cautioned Acheson "that he did not feel it was the time to make any accusations as he lacked direct proof." Acheson observed he would not mention Hiss's name to Byrnes because he assumed that Hoover intended to, but Hoover said he preferred not to name Hiss "at that time because of the vagueness of the suspicion." Their exchange suggests both the FBI's uncertainty over the reliability of evidence and the respect that Hiss enjoyed within the State Department. Once Elizabeth Bentley added her independent statement to the bureau, however, Hoover shed any residual hesitancy about labeling Hiss as a security risk.[61]

In an extended report to President Truman summarizing available FBI information on "Soviet Espionage in the United States" on November 27, Hoover devoted several pages to discussing Hiss. The director gave Secretary Byrnes and State Department security officials a summary of these sections the following week, the first of several similar FBI memos that labeled Hiss a Russian operative. These memos reached Truman, Byrnes, and Clark as well as other leading government officials from January to March 1946.[62]

True or not, the repeated charges had clearly made Hiss an embarrassment to his superiors. Because of his past record, his influential defenders, and the FBI's lack of conclusive documentary evidence, the question of how to handle the situation created considerable vexation. Hiss was in England throughout January

---

*The exact person is unclear after the bureau's excisions from the released file.

and most of February 1946 attending a UN conference. But the situation came to
a head in March, when a special assistant to Byrnes advised a bureau agent

> that Alger Hiss was on the secretary of state's "pending" list, and that Hiss was
> to be given no further consideration for promotion or assignment of respon-
> sible duties in the State Department, and that a study should be made of his
> case to determine if he could be dismissed summarily under Civil Service
> regulations.

Similar information reached Hoover on March 19 from Attorney General
Clark, who told the FBI that Byrnes wished to dismiss Hiss but had learned that
a Civil Service hearing would be mandatory. Hoover advised Clark that "he did
not think a hearing would be wise as the material against Hiss was confidential
and if it were not used there would not be enough evidence against him." He recommended that Clark tell Byrnes to move Hiss to "an innocuous position where
he would understand the situation and resign."*[63]

Byrnes then proposed summoning Hiss and informing him, without disclosing the source, that complaints against his loyalty had been lodged. Hoover
argued that this would alert Hiss to the nature of the information possessed by
the FBI, and pointed out that Byrnes could—after listening to Hiss—decide to
reject any further investigation as unwarranted. Any interview Byrnes held with
Hiss would "alert him and ruin an important espionage investigation." Hoover
proposed instead that he "contact several key men in the House and Senate and
explain his predicament to them," so that both the FBI director and Byrnes could
avoid future criticism from "the Hill," while the secretary could tell Hiss that
Congress was the source of adverse comment about him. Byrnes considered this
an appropriate way to proceed and agreed to phone some legislators himself.
Throughout these negotiations Hoover played skillfully on the fears shared by
Byrnes and Clark of unfavorable political repercussions if the FBI turned up evidence proving conclusively that Hiss was indeed a Soviet agent.[64]

Byrnes informed Hiss on March 21 that "two separate committees 'on the
Hill'" were accusing him of Communist ties. Hiss swore he had never belonged
to any subversive organization or been in any way disloyal. The secretary suggested that Hiss contact Hoover directly to clear the matter up. Byrnes then
informed Hoover of this conversation, and the director left orders with Assistant Director Ladd that if Hiss phoned for an interview, Ladd (but not Hoover)
should give him one, but that he should not "disclose information on current
cases" to Hiss, nor mention the name of Whittaker Chambers. "He [Hiss] was

---

*So determined was Hoover in later years to show that he had taken every appropriate step
to try and warn Byrnes and Clark about Hiss that the FBI director collected the relevant 1946
memos of his conversations with the two cabinet officers. These he placed in a separate "Official
and Confidential" (or "do not file") file, the only such file he has been shown to have maintained
privately on the Hiss case.

going to do the talking," Hoover told Clark that same day, "and we would do the listening."

Hiss appeared at FBI headquarters on March 25 for a long discussion with Ladd. He denied membership in any Communist or Communist-front organizations, and speculated as to the sources of such rumors about him. Byrnes had asked Hiss about his association with Lee Pressman. "Hiss stated that he told Mr. Byrnes," according to Ladd's report, "that he used to know Pressman very well but had had no contacts with him recently." Hiss acknowledged belonging "for a period of five or six months" in the early thirties to the International Juridical Association, "which he characterized as a small group interested in labor law." He mentioned Chambers's old contact Isaac Don Levine, who had written an article in July 1945 for the *Reader's Digest* "claiming that at the Yalta Conference, Hiss had persuaded the late President Roosevelt to agree to the admission of the Ukraine and Byelorussia to the United Nations [as independent voting members] at a meeting where Roosevelt, Hiss, and Stalin were present. Hiss said this was a fabrication because he had never met with Roosevelt and Stalin alone, and besides he does not speak the Russian language."[65]

The next day a State Department security officer, Robert Bannerman, sent a comprehensive secret report to Donald Russell, assistant secretary of state for administration, outlining the negative information, Chambers's and Bentley's, accumulated by the FBI against Hiss. In his new post as director of the Office of Special Political Affairs, Bannerman pointed out, not only did Hiss have responsibility for initiating and coordinating policy "in the fields of international security and organization, and dependent area affairs," but, more important: "In his position, he has access to all top secret material that comes to the Office of Special Political Affairs for action, and participates in top secret discussions and negotiations with other offices and divisions of the Department and with representatives of other governments. He is also in constant contact with ranking officers of the Department, of the War and Navy Departments as well as other governmental agencies and departments, and of the American delegation to the United Nations Organization." In short, if the charges leveled against him were true, Hiss was an ideal Soviet "agent-in-place."[66]

But were the charges true? However deeply involved in the Communist underground Hiss may have been during the 1930s when he knew Chambers, was he also a Soviet spy after the latter's defection? And, if so, what kind of agent? Was his primary function to steal documents, "mess up policy," provide information on departmental policymaking—or all three? The answer is not readily apparent, but certain aspects of the evidence remain intriguing.

Whittaker Chambers's testimony, if accurate, placed Hiss within the CP as late as Christmas 1938. Walter Krivitsky's comments to Barmine, if accurate, corroborated Hiss's place on the rolls of Soviet intelligence agents during the thirties, but not beyond. Other ex-Communists, including Louis Budenz, later asserted that high party leaders had discussed Hiss as a secret CP member. But Budenz offered no proof for this hearsay, nor could the FBI corroborate the testimony of either Ralph de Sola or George Hewitt—both confessed former Communists—of having seen Hiss at party gatherings.[*67] Nor does it prove Hiss's complicity in espionage to observe his continuing close friendship with Henry Collins, who was apparently involved in Soviet spying throughout this period, nor do Hiss's earlier contacts with others—some noted during the 1946–48 FBI probe–whom Bentley and Chambers had linked to the Soviet underground.[†]

Most of Hiss's State Department associates and superiors—fervent anti-Communists such as Charles Bohlen, Dean Acheson, Leo Pasvolsky, and Stanley K. Hornbeck—found no evidence of disloyalty. Yet one colleague at State, Erle R. Dickover, speculated on this possibility in a September 28, 1948, memo to security officer Frederick B. Lyons:[‡]

> . . . If the recommendations of this Committee . . . were conveyed to the Russians, it would explain some later occurrences. For example, the Committee recommended that South Sakhalin and the southern group of the Kuriles be retained by Japan. . . . Likewise, it was recommended that Manchuria be handed back, in toto, to the Chinese. If the Russians knew our thinking on these subjects [as presumably they did if the accusations against Hiss are substantiated] they were in a very advantageous position at Yalta and other conferences. They

---

[*]Even before the files of Russian intelligence began to be opened to Western scholars, two significant bits of "informed hearsay" deserve mention. One concerns a tantalizing set of references to a group of Soviet operatives in the United States made by the leading British double agent, Harold Kim Philby, after his defection. Philby had served Soviet intelligence loyally from the mid-1930s until he fled to Russia in 1963. He has sometimes been called the "British Hiss," referring to his extraordinary rise to a position of influence within British intelligence during the 1940s, although this title might best be reserved for Philby's opposite number in the British Foreign Office—and in Russian intelligence work—Donald Maclean. In his 1968 memoir, My Secret War, written in Moscow and therefore with the approval of his KGB superiors, Philby observed at one point about the spy hunt in postwar America: "It was also the era of Hiss, Coplon, Fuchs, Gold, Greenglass, and the brave Rosenbergs—not to mention others who are still nameless." A reference to Hiss in context of a passage praising people who Philby evidently either knew or believed were Soviet agents is suggestive, but again hardly constitutes usable proof. My Silent War, p. 164. Also, Professor Karel Kaplan said, when I interviewed him, that Noel and Herta Field's interrogations with Hungarian and Czech security officers all mentioned Hiss as a fellow member of the Soviet underground within the State Department during the mid-thirties, a fact confirmed by Professor Maria Schmidt's research in Hungarian secret police files, previously cited. Field, naturally, had no firsthand information about Hiss's possible secret activities during the 1940s.

[†]Although various FBI informants at this time mentioned either having seen Hiss at party meetings or having heard of his involvement within Communist circles, such information remains useless without corroboration, and such confirmation does not appear in the FBI files.

[‡]Dickover and Hiss were among a small group of officials at State who served on an Inter-Divisional Area Committee planning postwar American policy proposals for the Far East. Hiss represented Stanley Hornbeck on the committee.

knew what we hoped to do and could make their plans accordingly. Hence, perhaps, their insistence upon their claims as their price upon entry into the war against Japan (return of South Sakhalin to the Soviets, handing over of all the Kuriles, restoration of most of the Czarist rights in Manchuria, etc.). They perhaps would not have made these claims had they not known the disposition which we hoped to make of these territories.

But, as Dickover conceded, none of this had been proved, even by the methodical State Department probe of Hiss's behavior in 1946.[68]

Security officers at State, however, did not know of one extraordinary piece of information about Hiss. It emerged during a conversation held by Secretary of State Stettinius with Soviet Ambassador to the United Nations Andrei Gromyko in London on September 7, 1945. In a wide-ranging discussion of postwar international organizations, Gromyko urged that the United Nations be located permanently in the United States, not Europe, after which Stettinius pursued a still-unsettled problem:

> I inquired as to whether his government had given any thought to a person who would take the position of [U.N.] secretary general [Stettinius wrote in his diary later that evening]. He [Gromyko] said he had not given this matter a thought. . . .
>
> He volunteered however that if the constituent assembly were held in the United States this autumn, and we were not in a position to select [before then] the permanent secretary general, he would be very happy to see Alger Hiss appointed temporary secretary general as he had a very high regard for Alger Hiss, particularly for his fairness and his impartiality.

The endorsement of a leading American official by the Russians remains practically unique in the annals of Soviet-American diplomacy at this time. Although it does not provide evidence that Hiss had been or remained a formal undercover agent for the Russians in 1945, it indicates the extent to which they appreciated his usefulness. But security officers at State never learned, from either Stettinius or anyone else, about the curious exchange with Gromyko.[69]

Stranger still were portions of a wide-ranging request for top-secret files from the Office of Strategic Services made by Hiss in February 1945 to the OSS's Liaison Office at State. Hiss himself acknowledged in 1948 that from mid-1944 until after the Yalta Conference, he "worked exclusively on United Nations affairs." Yet he submitted a request in early 1945 for confidential studies prepared by the OSS's Research and Analysis Branch (popularly known as R & A) unusual for its breadth and for its specific concerns, given his UN responsibilities at the Office of Special Political Affairs. In addition, this extensive request for highly classified intelligence data, which vacuumed the R & A inventory, might have been expected to come from Hiss's superior and director of OSPA, Leo Pasvolsky, and not from the deputy director, Alger Hiss.

The OSS liaison officer at State, Paul L. Ward, informed his associates in a February 5, 1945, memo that in future distribution of R & A studies Hiss's request should "be taken into account":

> Mr. Hiss had expressed a wish to receive R & A Studies on the following subjects:
>
> 1) British, Soviet, French, and Chinese policies in relation to world organization and world security *and also in relation to the internal security of these countries themselves* to the extent that such policies have a bearing on the problems of world security.
> 2) Latin American reactions on problems of Hemispheric security, world security, and world organization.
> 3) *Policy developments of importance in the Far East or directly related to the Far East.* (Mr. Hiss explained when he made this request that in his office there was no one charged with following the implications for world organization of developments in the Far East) [italics added].[70]

Although Hiss asserted vaguely in his 1948 memo that he was "responsible for any general matters that might come up [at Yalta] relating to the Far East or the Near East," he never asked the OSS for documents on the Near East. His request was submitted too late, in any event, for the materials in question to be used at Yalta; they reached him only upon his return. By that time, Hiss had become director of the OSPA and was evaluating, along with other officials at State, one of the most controversial issues related to Far Eastern diplomacy: the territorial and political price in that region to be paid by the United States in exchange for Russian entrance into the war against Japan. As for OSS memos relating to "the internal security" of England, the Soviet Union, France, and China, there were no guidelines available to assist R & A Branch officials responsible for separating out only those internal security memos with a "bearing on the problems of world security." Whether or not this request related to Hiss's legitimate work at State on the UN in 1945 and 1946, it seems evident that he sought almost total access at war's end to the highly sensitive intelligence files that dealt with the "internal security" of America's major allies—including the Soviet Union.

Hiss also lobbied within State, following the San Francisco Conference, to gain for the Office of Special Political Affairs a far-reaching role in overseeing American foreign and military policies, both within the department and elsewhere. Thus, on September 7, 1945, Hiss proposed "Creation of [the] Post of Special Assistant for Military Affairs," a job linked closely to OSPA. Since State had not "yet reached the stage of establishing the post of Assistant Secretary for Security Affairs, in charge of SPA and another Office of Military Affairs," Hiss wrote, he suggested instead a special assistant who would serve as chairman of one of the government's most important policymaking bodies—the State, War and Navy Coordinating Committee (SWNCC). Such an officer would routinely receive information on all aspects of U.S. military, diplomatic, and security policies; and Hiss strongly recommended that "SPA should be represented upon each of the subcommittees of the State, War and Navy Coordinating Committee."

These subcommittees handled, among other matters, captured enemy archives, "technical information security control," "rearmament," and UN "security functions." Whatever Hiss's motives in making this suggestion, his proposals at State in 1945 and '46 clearly envisioned transforming the Office of Special Political Affairs into a clearinghouse for U.S. foreign policymaking. Hiss spelled out his view of OSPA's proper jurisdiction: "1. REGULATION OF ARMAMENTS . . . 2. CONTROL OF ATOMIC WEAPONS . . . 3. COOPERATION TO MAINTAIN INTERNATIONAL PEACE AND SECURITY . . . 4. SPECIAL AGREEMENTS TO PROVIDE FORCES . . . 5. INTER-AMERICAN REGIONAL SECURITY ARRANGEMENTS . . . ," plus fourteen additional areas—all to be made concerns of the expanded office.

Nor did Alger Hiss's range of interests stop there. FBI surveillance in 1946 and 1947 indicated that Hiss had also developed a keen interest in atomic energy matters that went well beyond the responsibilities in the area of atomic diplomacy at the UN to which his duties at OSPA confined him. Only once in Hiss's 1948 memo did he even mention any involvement in this area and then only in passing, as part of his general concern for "the most significant" UN issues of 1946—"Iran, Greece, Albania, atomic energy, and Spain." Yet the FBI's wiretaps and monitoring of his movements showed Hiss constantly attentive to the subject, both while at State and afterward. Thus, in May 1946, while discussing the need for an "atomic energy man" to represent State on the high-level interagency commissions that dealt with nuclear policy questions, Hiss indicated that his office was

> well organized to take care of the "procedural needs," but that he felt this still did not give them "any break into the substance; it doesn't use the procedure as a means of breaking into substance." Hiss stated he felt it was necessary to get somebody who knows something about atomic energy subsidy question as part of the general disarmament picture.

Even after leaving State, Hiss maintained this concern for atomic energy policy, informing an associate, whose name was blacked out of the FBI report, in February 1947 that "he had contacted [name blacked out] in Baltimore, regarding him as a possible deputy to [name blacked out] on Atomic Energy and Disarmament, but [blacked out] indicated he did not want the position." Phoning a former government colleague earlier in the day, a woman "who is going to be working on atomic energy," Hiss "thanked her for telling him how she was getting along and said he would see [name blacked out] and her as he is following atomic energy very definitely."[71]

That same month, a British Embassy official, Donald Maclean, also a Russian agent and later a defector to the Soviet Union, was appointed to serve as his government's representative on the super-secret Combined Policy Committee, a group composed of American, British, and Canadian representatives that dealt with atomic energy issues. At no time has Alger Hiss ever mentioned either seeing or knowing Maclean. Yet on September 14, 1946, Hiss's desk calendar (monitored later that year by State Department security officers for the August–October 1946 period) recorded a meeting with "McLean [sic], British Emb." None of the State Department records on Hiss's work nor the 1945–46 files of the Office of Special Political Affairs refer to a meeting with Maclean or any departmental business that would have led Hiss to arrange one. Maclean did not work on U.N. matters, nor was he Hiss's counterpart in British policy making on "special political affairs." Since the FBI did not conduct physical surveillance of Hiss during the month of September 1946, knowledge of the encounter ends with the single unexplained entry on Alger Hiss's desk calendar.[72]

On March 26, 1946, Bannerman wrote Russell that his office had taken into consideration Hiss's stellar record within the department, but still he concluded unfavorably: "In view of the seriousness of the above information [Chambers's FBI reports and Gouzenko's statement], it is recommended that immediate action be taken to terminate Mr. Hiss's services with the Department." Bannerman suggested that he be informed "that his connection with the Department is embarrassing to the Department and that Mr. Hiss should be given an opportunity to resign." If he failed to resign, however, "his services should be terminated by an order of the Secretary." Considering Hiss's prominence, the difficulties in confirming the Chambers-Bentley charges, and Hiss's many supporters within the department, it is not surprising that Russell took no immediate action on Bannerman's proposal.[73]

Although Hiss may have believed that he had successfully quashed the charges that Byrnes told him were being leveled against him "on the Hill," both FBI and State Department security officers continued their probe. The bureau's phone taps and scrutiny of his business appointments turned up information—possibly harmless in itself but undoubtedly damaging to him in the eyes of his superiors—that Hiss had met and exchanged letters at various points with several individuals accused by Chambers, Bentley, or other FBI informants of prior involvement in Communist espionage.

Henry Collins, for example, was a regular visitor and, according to one March 1946 bureau report: "Michael Greenberg, another individual mentioned by Miss Bentley as being connected with the espionage ring which she has described, addressed a letter to Alger Hiss, setting forth his qualifications [for a UN post] and stating, 'I expect to be in New York City next week and would appreciate any suggestions you might make. If it be possible to put me in touch with principal UNO people, I would appreciate it duly.'"* In a related FBI reference: "On December 30, 1946, it was determined . . . that [name blacked out], also mentioned by [Bentley] as being involved in the spy ring reported by her, spent three hours at the office of Alger Hiss in the Department of State."[74]

Declassified State Department memos show that by the spring of 1946 almost all of the department's security staff thought Hiss had been involved in some form of undercover Communist work. Not only was his future at State placed in a departmental holding pattern—with consideration for promotion or for confidential assignments ruled out by orders from Secretary Byrnes's office—but Hiss's daily work and associates came under the closest scrutiny. By August, even his desk calendar was being monitored, its appointments list duly noted for future investigation. His personnel recommendations and handling of secret documents also received careful study, and Byrnes placed restrictions on Hiss's access to confidential departmental documents.[75]

All of this was done without any formal charges being leveled against Hiss, who later said he thought the rumors of Communist ties had been laid to rest with his FBI interview. Given the thoroughgoing nature of the probe revealed by release of the State Department security memos, an extensive and ongoing investigation during the summer and fall of 1946, it is difficult to believe Hiss remained ignorant of it, especially considering his close ties to Acheson and his many other friends within the department. One of them, Joseph Green, whose contacts with Hiss went back to Nye Committee days, told Hiss in 1946 he had heard rumors of Hiss's alleged Communist associations. Hiss replied casually that he, too, had been aware of the rumors.

The State Department soon found itself under attack from several conservative congressmen. Byrnes was asked during a July 26 press-conference broadcast about congressional reports that Hiss was among those State Department officials who had received "adverse reports on security." The secretary defended Hiss but hedged in his answer. He denied that his security committee had reported adversely on Hiss (which was technically true), but said he was not familiar with all such personnel matters, and he never mentioned the FBI and State Department investigations then in progress. Byrnes denounced those who carelessly charged individuals with disloyalty to the government; they could "destroy that man for life [and] ruin a man's reputation in a few minutes." But he carefully backed away from defending Hiss. In any department, he avowed, a security probe "must be a matter that is discreetly and wisely done."[76]

---

*Hiss evaded answering the questions of Robert Stripling at the HUAC hearings that dealt with Greenberg suggesting that he knew the man only "as a State Department official." HUAC I, p. 654.

Byrnes, like Hoover, appreciated the hearsay nature of the Gouzenko-Bentley testimony concerning Hiss, and that Chambers then claimed to have no documentary proof against him.* Throughout the year, therefore, and with FBI approval, Byrnes allowed Hiss to continue as director of the department's Office of Special Political Affairs with responsibility for UN business. But Hiss complained to an associate at one point (a conversation recorded in the FBI files) that he "had been having trouble" getting the appointments of particular people through, "trouble [that] seemed to center around [State's] . . . Security Investigations Department."[77]

Decades after Alger Hiss had left government, new evidence would emerge from both Soviet and U.S. intelligence sources that reinforced the likelihood that he had maintained a link with Soviet Military Intelligence operatives beyond the 1930s and throughout World War II. The first such inside report came from Colonel Oleg Gordievsky, a high-ranking KGB official who had "doubled" as a British intelligence informant from the mid-1970s before defecting to the West in 1985. Five years later, in Gordievsky's memoir and history of the KGB, he and his coauthor, British scholar Christopher Andrew, wrote that although most Soviet agents in Washington during World War II "belonged to the Silvermaster and Perlo networks [described elsewhere in this book], a handful of the most important agents were run individually. Among them was Alger Hiss (code-named ALES) . . . [whose] wartime controller was the leading NKVD illegal in the United States, Ishak Abdulovich Akhmerov."†

"ALES" was identified more recently as "probably Alger Hiss" when the National Security Agency released in 1996 thousands of intercepted and decoded Soviet intelligence cables from the World War II years, gathered together in the legendary but (until now) top secret "VENONA" project. The VENONA cable in question was sent on March 30, 1945, a month after Hiss's participation in the Yalta Conference and subsequent flight home, with Deputy Secretary of State Stettinius's party, stopping—(among other places)—in Moscow. What provoked Moscow's apparent interest at the time—*if* "ALES" was Hiss—was his appointment that month *both* as director of State's potentially influential Office of Special Political Affairs and his designation as temporary secretary general of the United Nations organizing conference scheduled for San Francisco in April.

The message from the Ministry of State Security's (MGB) Washington "Resident," Anatolij Borisovich Gromov, to his Moscow superiors refers to an earlier

---

*Hiss was on vacation at the time, but a friend at State, J. C. Ross, wrote him the next day to report what Ross termed Byrnes's "very spirited" defense of Hiss. If nothing else, Ross's letter indicates that Hiss was aware of the continuing complaints concerning his "loyalty" as late as midsummer 1946. Ross to Hiss, July 27, 1946, Hiss Defense Files.

†Christopher Andrew and Oleg Gordievsky, *KGB: The Inside Story* (New York: HarperCollins, 1990), pp. 285, 286.

telegram on "ALES" and states that as a result of [undecipherable person's alias] chat with 'ALES' the following has been ascertained:

1. ALES has been working with the NEIGHBORS [i.e., a normal NKVD/MGB designation for the GRU or Soviet Military Intelligence] continuously since 1935 [the year Chambers testified that Hiss first began working with him on gathering intelligence for the GRU].

2. For some years past he has been the leader of a small group of the NEIGH-BORS' probationers, for the most part consisting of his relations [Priscilla Hiss? Donald Hiss?].

3. The group and ALES himself work on obtaining military information only. Materials on the "'BANK" [i.e., the State Department] allegedly interest the NEIGHBORS very little and he does not produce them regularly.

4. All the last few years ALES has been working with "POL," who also meets other members of the group occasionally.*

5. Recently ALES and his whole group were awarded Soviet decorations.

6. After the YALTA Conference, when he had gone on to Moscow, a Soviet personage in a very responsible position (ALES gave to understand that it was Comrade VYSHINSKI) [then Deputy Soviet Foreign Minister] allegedly got in touch with ALES and at the behest of the Military NEIGHBORS passed on to him their gratitude and so on.

Of the four U.S. officials including Stettinius who traveled on to Moscow after Yalta, only Hiss had ever been identified at any point with known Communist agents such as Chambers or any others.

Only once does Hiss's name appear directly in any of the VENONA intercepts, this as part of a September 28, 1943, memorandum to Moscow from a Soviet vice consul in New York that states, after identifying the real names of various individuals known to Moscow by their aliases: "The NEIGHBOR [i.e., GRU] has reported that [here a phrase has not been decrypted] from the State Department by the name of HISS. [Alger Hiss was then assistant political advisor for the Far East at State.]†

The KGB archives themselves contain this tantalizing, previously undisclosed description of "ALES" in a cable sent that same month, March 5, 1945, by Anatoly Gorsky, who had been "controller" in London for the "Cambridge Five" ring of Soviet agents that included Harold "Kim" Philby, Donald Maclean, and Guy Burgess. When Maclean was posted to Washington as first secretary of the British Embassy in 1944—an unexpected information bonanza for the

---

*"POL" probably referred to "PAL," the code name for Nathan Gregory Silvermaster, another alleged Soviet agent in the U.S. government at the time.

†Document No. 1822, Washington to Moscow by VADIM, March 30, 1945; Document No. 1579, New York to Moscow, MOL'ER to DIRECTOR, September 28, 1943; both in the VENONA file collection.

Soviets—Gorsky's superiors in Moscow sent him there also to continue supervising Maclean. In time, Gorsky was assigned also to reorganize the American agents who had reported previously to another Russian operative, Jacob Golos, who had died recently. Golos left behind a network that included an especially bereaved agent, his lover, Elizabeth Bentley, who would soon turn her irritation at Gorsky and others who tried to replace Golos into covert cooperation with the FBI.

The same month as Hiss's announced promotions and the intercepted VENONA cable on "ALES," on March 5, 1945, Gorsky cabled Moscow to report on the State Department employee known as "ALES" from whom *his* network now expressed an interest in gaining cooperation and information. Gorsky's source was another American agent for the Soviets, a Treasury Department official code-named "RUBLE":

> Concerning "ALES" we spoke with "RUBLE" several times [Gorsky informed Moscow]. As we have already written, "RUBLE" gives to "ALES" an exceptionally good political reference as to a member of the Communist Party. "RUBLE" informs [me] that "ALES" is a strong, determined man with a firm and resolute character who is aware that he is a Communist with the illegal status with all consequences. Unfortunately, he evidently understands the rules of security [*konspiratsia*] on his own as all local Communists.

"ALES," in short, declined to work directly with "RUBLE," leading Gorsky to speculate with Moscow that "ALES" had another direct connection to Moscow through yet another Soviet controller, of whom there were several in the United States at this time.

The links between "RUBLE" and "ALES" (Alger Hiss) served as the basis for another internal NKVD memorandum the following month, when a leading Soviet intelligence official in the United States, Pavel Fitin, wrote to Vsevolod Merkulov, then the organization's head (i.e., "People's Commissar for State Security") in April 1945:

> Our agent RUBLE, drawn to work for the Soviet Union in May 1937, passed (with short breaks caused by official trips) initially through the military "neighbors" and then through our station valuable information on political and economic issues. . . . To our work RUBLE gives much attention and energy [and] is a devoted and disciplined agent.
>
> According to the data from VADIM [i.e., Anatolij Gromov, Fitin's colleague who sent the March 30, 1945, cable intercepted and translated in the VENONA files, previously cited] the group of agents of the "military" neighbors whose part RUBLE was earlier, recently was decorated with orders of the USSR. RUBLE learned about this fact from his friend ALES, who is the head of the mentioned group. Taking into account RUBLE's devoted work for the USSR for eight years and the fact that, as a result of transfer to our station, RUBLE was

not decorated together with other members of the ALES group, [we] consider [it] expedient to put him forward for a decoration of the Order of the Red Star. Ask for your consent.*

The interrelationships linked to the new evidence on "ALES"—from Gordievsky, the VENONA files, and the KGB archives—are compelling in pointing toward Alger Hiss when viewed within the framework of existing information on him during this period, much of it reviewed previously in these pages:

1. An American official in the State Department who moonlighted for Soviet Military Intelligence and flew to Moscow after the Yalta Conference aboard Secretary Stettinius's plane, on a flight that (as Hiss himself later noted) had only four such State Department passengers—Stettinius, himself, and two lesser officials, both free of either influence or suspicion;

2. Elizabeth Bentley's identification in October 1945 of a Treasury official— among all the Soviet agents whom she named—having discussed existing espionage networks with Alger Hiss earlier that year blends into Anatoly Gorsky's March 1945 cable to Moscow recounting a similar conversation with "RUBLE" about the State Department agent code-named "ALES";

3. In Canada, that same year, Igor Gouzenko provides the FBI in October 1945 with information, given to him by an official of the GRU (according to Gouzenko), that "the Soviets had an agent . . . in May 1945 who was an assistant to the then [Under] Secretary of State Edward R. Stettinius."

Fortunately for Alger Hiss, it proved far more difficult at the time to piece together compelling evidence of his complicity with the Soviets, while under investigation by U.S. security officials in 1945 and 1946, than in recent years.

Even after six months of thorough checking and the accumulation of additional adverse hearsay reports concerning Hiss, both the FBI's and State's security inquiries proved inconclusive, turning up little concrete evidence. Raymond Murphy visited Chambers a second time on August 28, but he got no new material except an assertion that Hiss had been a leading underground Communist whose task "was never to make converts. His job was to mess up policy." Chambers continued to insist that Hiss's underground unit "was not a spy ring."[78]

Although Hoover had persuaded Byrnes to tell Hiss that the rumors of Communist ties came from unfriendly congressmen, and although Hoover resisted taking personal responsibility for recommending Hiss's dismissal, he was apparently dismayed when Byrnes failed to act. Thus, when complaints from Congress did not persuade the secretary to fire Hiss—and when Byrnes chose instead merely to insulate Hiss for further investigation within the department—Hoover

---

*File #43072, Vol. 1, pp. 96–97, KGB Archives.

began a calculated campaign of leaks to his own supporters in Congress and the press. Walter Winchell, the FBI director's most intimate journalistic confidant, broadcast a clear reference to Hiss on September 29: "It can be categorically stated that the question of the loyalty and integrity of one high American official has been called to the attention of the President." Hoover kept up a steady flow of memos about Hiss throughout the year to Truman, Clark, and Byrnes. By late autumn Hiss had made arrangements to leave the department for a position that might have attracted him under normal conditions.[79]

"This afternoon Mr. Dulles asked me if I would be interested in succeeding Nicholas Miraculous Butler as President of the Carnegie Endowment at $15,000 to $17,000 a year!" Hiss had written Priscilla from the *Queen Elizabeth* on January 4, 1946, while en route to the UN meeting in London. "He [Dulles], of course, as a cautious New York lawyer said he was only one of the trustees and could only recommend me, etc. . . . I am not, of course, seriously tempted but it indicates we can still, as of today's prices even, earn a living in some lines of work." Among those recommending Hiss to Dulles for the post were several reporters on board ship to whom Dulles had mentioned the opening, including Bert Andrews, chief of the New York *Herald Tribune*'s Washington bureau, and James Reston of *The New York Times*. Although Hiss dismissed Dulles's inquiry flippantly in this January 1946 letter, he developed more interest in the post as the year progressed.[80]

Dulles had checked with Byrnes prior to the FBI probe, and the secretary had urged him to delay any appointment of Hiss until the following December—should Hiss prove interested in the job—since the State Department (in Dulles's words) "did not want to lose Hiss at that time." Dulles raised the question again, according to Hiss, "once or twice, in May or June," but Hiss "was not prepared to leave the Department because of the conversation I had with Mr. Byrnes in March, which might make it look as though I were leaving under fire." Hiss did not tell Dulles about his precise reasons for postponing a decision. At no time before he was selected by the Carnegie Endowment trustees as their new president in December did he inform them of the charges of Communist ties, or about his March discussions with Byrnes, or about his subsequent FBI interview.

In November, Hiss contacted Dulles again. By then, he later claimed—a curious assertion in light of his January 1946 letter to Priscilla—"I felt warranted in assuming that the matter had blown over and I felt free to pursue my intentions of some long standing to return to private life." He had expressed such an intention to William Marbury during the spring of 1945 shortly after Roosevelt's death. Marbury, then a member of a committee recruiting new faculty for the Harvard Law School, later remembered Hiss saying "that he was not in the least interested in teaching." But Hiss indicated he expected to resign from State in the near future to enter private law practice.[81]

Now Hiss told Dulles that he was "very much interested" in considering the Endowment post; he would talk to his superiors to see if he could leave "without injury to the work of the Department." Hiss asked Dean Acheson to check with Byrnes and determine "whether he did not think that I would no longer be in the position of resigning under fire." Acheson's response apparently satisfied Hiss, because he resigned from the department on December 10, one day after the Endowment trustees elected him president. He remained with State clearing up his work until January 15, 1947, and assumed control of the Endowment's New York headquarters on February 1.

But Hiss never spoke to Byrnes directly throughout the entire resignation process. Acheson handled the leave-taking and announced Hiss's departure to the press with a statement lauding his labors at State. A "Dear Alger" letter from Byrnes also expressed "regret" at Hiss's leaving and commended his contribution to the department, although in more restrained terms. "I welcomed the news that he had been offered a position elsewhere and had accepted it," Byrnes wrote in a *Look* article several years later. His exact words, Byrnes told the FBI, were "That's wonderful," and "his exuberance over this information was based on the fact that Alger Hiss was actually leaving the State Department." Byrnes said also that it was Acheson who had written the farewell letter sent to Hiss in December 1946, and that he (Byrnes) had only "hastily skimmed through" it before signing it. Undoubtedly the secretary had felt trapped by this time between his anxieties over departmental security on the one hand and his unwillingness to condemn Hiss solely on the basis of undocumented allegations. In that same *Look* article Byrnes wrote that after his March 1946 interview with Hiss "I directed that certain matters of importance in our foreign relations were not to go to Hiss's office."[82]

More significantly, Hiss's assertion that when he accepted the Carnegie presidency he believed that the probe of his possible Communist ties "had blown over" was contradicted by the one person in a position to know the details. Dean Acheson told a different version of Hiss's leave-taking in a January 1949 appearance before the Senate Foreign Relations Committee. Hiss came to see him, according to Acheson, to tell him about the Endowment's offer, stating

> that he did not want to leave the government while he was subject to this criticism. He thought that ought to be cleared up, and did I have any advice for him.
>
> I said yes, I had. I said, "My advice to you is to take this job. This is the kind of thing which rarely, if ever, gets cleared up. The Government has to protect its sources of information; there is no way of having any final adjudication of this matter. People will continue to raise these doubts about you so long as you are in a position where you are subject to this sort of attack, and if I were you, I would just leave and go to New York."
>
> He followed that advice.[83]

HOLDING THE PAST AT BAY

The Carnegie Endowment's new president had not even arrived in New York when Dulles, chairman of its board, received the first of several complaints about his alleged Communist involvements. The accusation came from Alfred Kohlberg, a wealthy importer who financed the right-wing anti-Communist monthly *Plain Talk* (edited by Isaac Don Levine) and who would later help bankroll the China Lobby. Dulles, like Byrnes, understandably insisted on tangible proof before acting against Hiss, and Kohtberg dropped the matter. As he wrote Dulles, "the information while first-hand is uncorroborated except, I am informed, by the files of the FBI." Dulles then phoned Hiss to ask him about the reports of past CP associations. According to a 1948 Dulles memo on the discussion, "Hiss replied that there had been some rumors which, however, he had completely set to rest at Washington. . . . I do not recall that Hiss then mentioned the FBI but he might have done so, although I recall he treated the matter very lightly." Kohlberg raised the question again in May, this time claiming a new informant, but again he backed away from a full airing of the charge. Although Dulles now wrote Kohlberg, "I told Mr. Hiss [presumably in May] that I . . . had heard from two or three quarters that he was inclined to be communistic in his thinking," the rumors were still vague and he dismissed them.[84]

Dulles had no way of knowing that the FBI had not dropped its investigation of Hiss. Finally, on June 2, agents conducted simultaneous interviews with Alger and Priscilla Hiss, Alger's at the Endowment's Washington office and his wife's at their Greenwich Village apartment. For the first time the Hisses were confronted with the name of Whittaker Chambers. Each denied knowing him and having been involved in any way with the Communist Party or its espionage underground, although Alger provided the agents with a fuller portrait of his earlier radical contacts and organizational ties than he had before. Hiss said of his former associates in the International Juridical Association that he had "heard a number of individuals state the belief since my association with them that Lee Pressman and Nathan Witt were Communists. I have also heard allegations that [Shad] Polier was a Communist." (Polier was not.) But Hiss insisted "that he was not acquainted with an individual by the name of Whittaker Chambers," the agents' report noted at one point, largely reiterating his signed statement: "He said at least he could recall no one by that name being one of his acquaintances. He further stated that as far as he can recall no individual by that name has ever visited his home on any occasion."[85]

Mrs. Hiss was questioned directly about Alger's possible involvement with espionage, in the most candid avowal of the FBI's views on the subject up to that point:

[She] was informed that the Bureau had information to the effect that her husband, Alger Hiss, had, while employed by the Federal Government, collected and secured information from the files of the government agency and turned this information over to a third party who was not authorized to receive same. She was also informed that her husband was allegedly a member of a ring which was formed for the purpose of . . . delivering such information through appropriate channels to the Soviet Union. Mrs. Hiss immediately commented that the aforementioned allegation was "absolutely false."

Priscilla Hiss was also asked about Chambers in a far from cursory manner:

Mrs. Hiss was questioned at length concerning Whittaker Chambers. She immediately denied ever hearing of the name and elaborated by saying that she "knows no such person." It was pointed out to her that Chambers was a former member of the Communist Party who renounced his affiliation and subsequently entered the newspaper field and that Chambers was well known. It was also mentioned that Chambers allegedly knew Mr. and Mrs. Hiss intimately and on occasion was a guest in the Hiss home. Mrs. Hiss steadfastly denied being acquainted with him or knowing his identity.[86]

The Hisses encountered Chambers's name in connection with the same charges twice more during the months that followed their 1947 FBI interviews. One of Hiss's friends, a State Department official named Edward Miller, heard a fellow dinner guest mention Chambers's accusations against Hiss one evening early in 1948. Miller promptly challenged the speaker, Barbara Kerr, either to substantiate or to retract her statements. Mrs. Kerr had recently interviewed Chambers for a *Life* article on Communism by Arthur Schlesinger, Jr., that she had helped research. Lacking any additional information, she withdrew her charge. Miller informed Hiss, however, who later testified at his first trial that he learned then, in February 1948, that Chambers "was connected with *Time*." Yet Hiss made no move to contact his accuser to question him about the basis of his allegations.

Both Alger and Priscilla Hiss were subpoenaed the following month to appear before a federal grand jury that had been empaneled the previous year to investigate charges of Communist espionage in the government. Alger was asked once more whether he knew "an individual by the name of Whittaker Chambers," and he responded: "No. I have been asked that question before but I do not know Mr. Chambers."*[87]

Still a third Hiss family member learned of Chambers's accusations early in 1948. According to a December 1948 memo, a friend of Donald Hiss was at the

---

*Alger Hiss testified at his first trial that he had not "connected" the "Chambers" about whom Edward Miller had informed him a few weeks earlier with the man mentioned during his grand jury testimony.

same party attended by Edward Miller and heard the identical story. Donald described the incident for his brother's lawyers while reviewing his own grand jury testimony in December 1948. A Justice Department official had asked Donald Hiss when he had first heard of Whittaker Chambers, and, according to Donald's memo, he replied: "Sometime in the spring of 1947 my brother came to my office in Washington and said that he had been interviewed by two representatives of the FBI in which he had been asked whether he knew a number of people. He came to me stating that he thought he would probably need [legal] counsel. I said that certainly he did not need counsel." It would be illogical to assume that Alger and Donald Hiss did not exchange stories about their friend's argument with Barbara Kerr in February 1948, and Alger's comments to Donald the previous year indicate that the name Whittaker Chambers had become firmly fixed in his mind. Furthermore, Alger's statement to Donald that "he would probably need counsel" indicates he recognized the gravity of Chambers's accusations against him, especially in view of his troubles at State in 1946 and the 1947 FBI interviews with himself and Mrs. Hiss. It is just as unlikely, then, that Hiss, as he testified at his first trial, failed to connect the "Chambers" about whom Miller had told him in February 1948 with the man mentioned during the grand jury testimony, particularly in the light of the FBI's extended discussion with Mrs. Hiss the previous year.[88]

On the same day in March 1948 that Hiss appeared before the grand jury, Dulles asked him about still another letter charging him with Communist ties. For the first time Hiss spelled out in vague terms for Dulles some of his radical associations during the 1930s, minimizing their importance. "In searching for a basis for the stories concerning him he had in mind that when he came from Harvard Law School to Cotton & Franklin in 1933 [sic], he and a few others, including Lee Pressman, had for a year or two edited a small publication about labor law and labor decisions." (Hiss had previously told the FBI that his contact with the International Juridical Association extended barely half a year.) "He also said," according to Dulles's memo of the meeting, "that when he was in the Department of Agriculture there were there some persons who might have had some Communist sympathy, but he had with them only casual acquaintance."* He mentioned his grand jury appearance earlier that day, claiming that "no embarrassing questions had been put to him," and "that he had been asked questions about a few people, most of whom he did not know." That was the closest Alger Hiss ever came to telling Dulles about Whittaker Chambers's charges.[89]

Before responding to this latest complaint about Hiss, which had come from the conservative Congressman Walter Judd, Dulles contacted State Department

---

*Hiss did not mention Pressman's presence there along with Abt and Witt, with all of whom he was quite friendly.

security chief John Peurifoy, a friend of Hiss's (the 1947 FBI files claimed, apparently on the basis of phone taps, that Hiss had exerted influence to obtain the post for Peurifoy). The latter, in turn, assured Dulles that "while he thought Hiss might be mentioned in some of the FBI files, he, himself, was absolutely satisfied as to the complete loyalty of Hiss, and that he knew of no evidence of any kind which cast any doubt on the matter." Given the extensive security probe at State in 1946, Peurifoy's comments remain inexplicable. Apparently he had been less positive in talking to Judd, because Dulles wrote the congressman later in March that "if he [Peurifoy] seemed to you to suggest otherwise, this was a misunderstanding. I shall keep alert, but so far have not changed my judgment."[90]

Later that year, in appearing before HUAC, Hiss claimed to have heard the name "Whittaker Chambers" initially during his June 1947 FBI interview, although he said it had not made much of an impression on him. Chambers, Hiss asserted, had been only one out of some thirty or forty people about whom the agents asked. "That was all there was to the reference to him," he later informed his own lawyers. Hiss did not mention, either to HUAC or to his attorneys, that the agents had also asked whether Chambers had stayed in his house or that Mrs. Hiss had been questioned closely about the alleged "intimacy" between Chambers and the Hisses. (When Hiss had been asked about Chambers by the grand jury in March 1948, he did recall the earlier FBI questioning.) Also, Edward Miller's report the previous month and Donald Hiss's identical statement had alerted Hiss to the fact that "a man named Whittaker Chambers" seemed to be the source of the recurrent charges of Communist involvement that had been plaguing his career.*[91]

Although Chambers was the only person who had leveled a firsthand accusation of Communist involvement against Hiss, the latter made no effort to confront Chambers and question him prior to the HUAC hearings. "When asked to explain this strange indifference at his first trial for perjury, Hiss commented:

> The same person [presumably Edward Miller] who told me that Chambers' name had come into a dinner conversation told me he had checked and told me he had been assured either that the person who spoke to him was talking through her hat or that Chambers had not said what he was said to have said, or in any event he certainly was not saying it anymore.

But Miller had not spoken to Chambers, nor did he tell Hiss he had done so. Edward Miller merely extracted from Barbara Kerr the obvious admission that her only source for the allegation was Chambers. She had therefore agreed—in

*Priscilla Hiss's memory of these incidents failed her even more acutely than her husband's under questioning at his first trial. She testified then that she did not think she had ever heard the name of Whittaker Chambers prior to August 1948. She recalled neither the FBI questioning nor the grand jury's similar inquiry about that name.

the absence of additional proof—to retract her original assertion that Hiss was a Soviet agent; nothing else. And Hiss, as his earlier statements to HUAC concerning the incident showed, clearly understood this.[92]

Whittaker Chambers would soon demonstrate his willingness to repeat the accusations against Hiss in public forums, first before HUAC in August 1948 and later that month on *Meet the Press*. At that point the question of Alger Hiss's alleged Communist involvement, which had been simmering below the surface for a decade, "suddenly" emerged as a full-blown mystery.

As a Johns Hopkins undergraduate, Class of '26, Hiss (first row, third from left) was prominent in a number of student groups, including The Cane Club.

Chambers in 1931, before he joined the Communist underground.

Hiss, sitting behind Secretary Stettinius and President Roosevelt, attended the February 1945 Yalta Conference as an important American staff assistant. Other statesmen seated around the table include Stalin, Churchill, Molotov, Eden, and Gromyko. Gromyko would later recommend Hiss to Stettinius for the post of Temporary Secretary General of the United Nations.

Hiss, chief organizer of the U.N.'s founding conference at San Francisco in April 1945, shakes hands with President Truman after the latter's speech to the delegates. At right is Stettinius and behind them is Major General Harry Vaughan.

During the HUAC hearings, Hiss studied the two 1935 photographs of Chambers which displays the poor and missing teeth which Hiss had associated with the man he claimed to have known as "George Crosley"; but Hiss testified that he did not recognize "Crosley" in these pictures. Standing over Hiss as he examines them is HUAC staff director Robert Stripling.

Hiss's handwritten notes, which Chambers turned over in November 1948, concerned mainly military or intelligence matters. Hiss acknowledged that he had written the notes, but denied giving any of them to Chambers.

Austria, Germany

Feb. 16. Wiley, U.S. charge at Vienna, cabled the cabinet changes
approved by Miklas the preceding night, adding that he was informed
through official sources that the German Government had demanded
action on its requests by midnight and had staged an impressive
military demonstration along the frontier.

Feb. 14. Gilbert, U.S. charge at Berlin, cabled that Hemmen, former
German counsellor of Embassy at Buenos Aires and the negotiator
of the Canadian-German commercial agreement of 1935 and the
German-French agreement of 1937 and now in the economic section of
the Foreign Office, was being sent to the United States. He would
travel around securing economic information and would be available
after the signature of the U.S. - British trade agreement to
discuss possibilities of negotiating a trade agreement between
Germany and the United States.

Feb. 17, Phillips cabled from Rome that Ciano said that while the
inclusion of Seyss-Inquart in the cabinet meant "a pronounced increase
of German influence in Austria he nevertheless felt that it was far
better to have cooperation between the two governments since any
increase of Austrian opposition or hostility to Germany might of
itself be an invitation to Hitler to take some drastic step. Ciano
also told me that there would be very much closer cooperation between
the German and Austrian armies and that during the next year there
would be an exchange of high ranking officers between the two
armies."

Feb. 18. Gilbert, U.S. charge at Berlin:
        "The Military Attache reports that as a result of numerous
conversations and discussions with army sources he is convinced that
the agreement reached with Austria as a result of the Hitler-
Schuschnigg conversations contains military clauses providing for
the gradual & assimilation" of the Austrian army into the German.
        "Presumably this military agreement covers: (one) unification
of tactical doctrine through adoption of similar text books,
(two) Austrian adoption of German military organization, (three) gradual introduction of uniform weapons, (four) coordination
of war plans.
        "The Military Attache believes that within the relatively
near future there will be evidence of a military alliance through
the appointment of standing military missions by each country
to the other country.
        "As a corollary of the foregoing it is believed here that
further changes in the Austrian Government will be announced
shortly which will include the appointment of a "pro-German" Chief
of Staff of the Austrian army."

Chambers's cache included sixty-four pages of retyped 1938 State Department documents,
all of which were later identified by defense and FBI experts as having been typed on Hiss's
Woodstock in early 1938. The page above summarizes incoming cables at State dealing with
the major international crisis of the day, Hitler's campaign to seize control of Austria.

Secretary of State,
Washington.

110, February 14, 6 p.m.
Embassy's 104, February 11, 5 p.m.

One. Passenger trains on the Peiping Hankow Railway have not
left or arrived at Peiping yesterday and today except for service be4w
tween Peiping and Changhsintien, a few miles south of Peiping.
This partially substantiates widespread but unconfirmed reports
of activities of Chinese irregulars at Paoting and points along
the railway south thereof.
Two. Press reports of Japanese advance southward in Southern
Hopei have not been confirmed. An American reports that several
tens of thousands of Japanese troops have moved during the last
few days from Shihkiachuang in the direction of Taiyuan. With
large numbers of Japanese troops already in Shansi and in Southern
Hopei and Northern Honan, it is doubtful whether irregulars to
the north of them can seriously hamper their movements unless the
irregulars are supported strongly by the National Government.
        Repeated to Hankow. By mail to Tokyo.
                LOCKHART

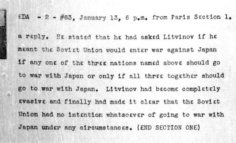

EDA - 2 - #63, January 13, 6 p.m. from Paris Section 1.

a reply. He stated that he had asked Litvinov if he
meant the Soviet Union would enter war against Japan
if any one of the three nations named above should go
to war with Japan or only if all three together should
go to war with Japan. Litvinov had become completely
evasive and finally had made it clear that the Soviet
Union had no intention whatsoever of going to war with
Japan under any circumstances. (END SECTION ONE)

                        BULLITT

EDA
This telegram must be
closely paraphrased
before being communi-
cated to anyone (D)

PARIS
Dated January 13, 1938
Received 3:15 p.m.

Secretary of State

Washington

63, January 13, 6 p.m. (SECTION ONE).

STRICTLY CONFIDENTIAL FOR THE SECRETARY.

Dr. Tingfu Tsiang recently resigned as Chinese
Ambassador in Moscow and will return to China next week
via Singapore to become Secretary to the Cabinet called
on me this morning and made a number of statements which
seemed to me important.

He said that he was convinced that the Soviet
Union would refuse to enter the Sino-Japanese conflict
under any and all conditions. He believed that
internal difficulties in the Soviet Union were such
at the present time that the Russians would be afraid
to attack the Japanese even if the Japanese army should
be greatly weakened by a prolonged Chinese resistance.

He said that Litvinov had stated to him repeatedly
that the Soviet Union would declare war at once on
Japan if England, France and the United States should
declare war on Japan. He said that he did not believe
that this was true and that in his final conversation
with Litvinov he had pinned down Litvinov and compelled
                a reply

The two strips of microfilmed
State Department material
turned over by Chambers
in December 1948 contained
several cables initialed by
Hiss, including a "strictly
confidential" message for
Secretary Hull (at bottom
and right) concerning the
Sino-Japanese War then in
progress. Also shown is a
typed summary of a cable
dealing with Japanese troop
movements.

When Chambers handed over the "pumpkin papers" microfilm to HUAC staffers in December 1948, he brought the Committee—and Richard Nixon—briefly back into the limelight. *At left:* Nixon and Stripling examine the microfilm.

Below: A HUAC hearing that month (to Nixon's left are John E. Rankin and John McDowell).

HENRY JULIAN WADLEIGH

WILLIAM ROSEN

FRANCIS B. SAYRE

EDWARD CRANE

FELIX A. INSLERMAN

MEYER CHAPIRO

ISAAC DON LEVINE

HEDWIG MASSING

NATHAN WITT

LEE PRESSMAN

ADOLPH A. BERLE

ELIZABETH BENTLEY

Many of those who figured in the Hiss-Chambers case testified to a Federal Grand Jury impaneled in New York City in December 1948 immediately following Hiss's indictment. One of the jurors made these sketches of witnesses.

At both trials, Edward McLean (shown with Hiss, left) directed investigative work for the defense and Prosecutor Thomas Murphy (right) represented the government.

Esther and Whittaker Chambers wait outside the courtroom in mid-1949 to testify at Hiss's first trial.

Outside Manhattan Federal Court House, Donald and Alger Hiss before testifying to the Grand Jury in December of 1948, prior to Alger's indictment (left) and Priscilla Hiss in 1950 (right).

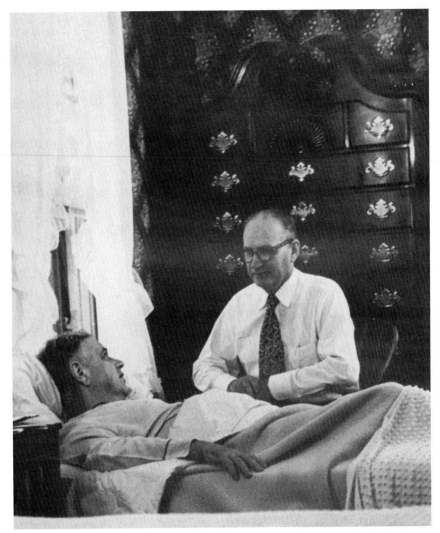

Chambers talks to a friend at Westminster while recuperating from a 1953 heart attack.

Handcuffed to another prisoner, Hiss leaves for Lewisburg Penitentiary in March 1951, several months after both the Court of Appeals and the Supreme Court denied his appeal to overturn his perjury conviction.

Alger Hiss in the fall of 1977.

Part Four

DISCLOSURE

I remember that as I was sitting in the dock on the occasion of my last trial listening to Lockwood's appalling denunciation of me—like a thing out of Tacitus, like a passage in Dante, like one of Savonarola's indictments of the Popes of Rome—and being sickened with horror at what I heard, suddenly it occurred to me, how splendid it would be if I was saying all this about myself. I saw then at once that what is said of a man is nothing. The point is, who says it. A man's very highest moment is, I have no doubt at all, when he kneels in the dust, and he beats his breast, and tells all the sins of his life.

—Oscar Wilde, De Profundis

Whether they knew it or not, the interest that drew them there was purely psychological—the expectation of some essential disclosure as to the strength, the power, the horror, of human emotions. Naturally nothing of the kind could be disclosed. The examination . . . was beating futilely round the well-known fact, and the play of questions upon it was as instructive as the tapping with a hammer on an iron box, where the object is to find out what's inside. However, an official inquiry could not be any other thing. Its object was not the fundamental why, but the superficial how, of this affair.

—Joseph Conrad, Lord Jim

XI

RUMORS AND WHISPERS: THE PURSUIT OF EVIDENCE

THE HISS DEFENSE

From the moment HUAC opened its August 1948 hearings, Alger Hiss faced a situation unique among those at the time accused of Communist activities. Many of the accused had difficulty obtaining competent legal counsel, but Hiss enjoyed an abundance of advice from attorneys of the first rank. His lawyers often disagreed on strategy: before HUAC, in mounting a slander suit against Chambers, and during the December 1948 grand jury hearings. The roster of legal talent devoting time to the case by December 1948 included: in New York City, Edward McLean, his young associate Robert von Mehren, and their colleagues at Debevoise, Plimpton and McLean; also in New York City, Harold Rosenwald; in Baltimore, William Marbury and his juniors at Marbury, Miller, and Evans; in Washington, John F. Davis, Hugh Cox (Donald Hiss's attorney), and Donald Hiss's firm, Covington, Burling. Once Alger Hiss had been indicted, his many attorneys recognized the need to coordinate efforts and to obtain a first-rate "barrister" for the trial.

The decision to hire Lloyd Paul Stryker, according to von Mehren, "was made by Alger's friends in Washington," specifically such figures as "Acheson and Frankfurter to some extent." Few of these men, von Mehren later noted, "had [any] experience with criminal cases." Stryker appealed to some of Hiss's advisers because of his wide background in criminal cases. He had been recommended initially by William Marbury's friend, ex-Secretary of War Robert Patterson.[1]

Short and stately, with closely cropped white hair, Stryker had a reputation for dynamic speaking and mastery of courtroom rhetoric. Marbury, McLean, and Rosenwald had already laid down the basic lines of defense when Stryker and his two assistants, Harold Shapero and Harold Wolfram, entered the case. Stryker apparently never disputed any of the previously made strategy decisions. McLean, Rosenwald, John F. Davis, and von Mehren continued to maintain basic responsibility for the pretrial investigation, assisted by Horace Schmahl and other private detectives.

Hiss's lawyers hoped to demonstrate three essential points to the jury in order to obtain an acquittal: that their client's character and reputation made him an unlikely candidate for the role of espionage agent; conversely, that a man of Chambers's disreputable personal and political background had "means, motive, and opportunity" to devise a frame-up against Alger Hiss, either consciously or for hidden psychological reasons; and, finally, that the documents turned over by Chambers could have been obtained from others in government.

After discussing the case with Stryker, Marbury wrote Acheson on March 24 that the barrister had "gotten to the heart of the case in a surprisingly short time. He feels, as do I, that the question of character is basic, and he intends to bend every effort to see that Alger has the full benefit of the unblemished reputation which was his prior to last August." Stryker would emphasize testimony concerning Hiss's character—and the contrast with Chambers's—as central to his defense, recognizing that the Supreme Court had held (in *Michelson v. United States*) that "such testimony alone, in some circumstances, may be enough to raise reasonable doubt of guilt and that in the federal courts a jury in a proper case should be so instructed."[2]

Thanks to the efforts of Stryker and Hiss's other attorneys, many distinguished Americans agreed to attest publicly to Hiss's excellent reputation at the trial, either by direct trial testimony or through depositions. They included John W. Davis, President Isaiah Bowman of Johns Hopkins, Judge Charles Wyzanski, Jr., Judge Calvert Magruder, diplomats Charles Fahy and Philip C. Jessup, Governor Adlai E. Stevenson of Illinois, and two Supreme Court Justices, Felix Frankfurter and Stanley M. Reed.

Not all of those approached by Hiss's lawyers—John Dickey, for example—volunteered to help. Among the hesitant witnesses was Francis B. Sayre, who expressed faith in Hiss's innocence but raised a number of questions about the documentary evidence against the accused in pretrial meetings with Marbury, McLean, and Hiss. Also, Sayre would not corroborate Hiss's version of his office procedures while working at State during the 1936–39 period.[3]

Other old associates who were uncooperative or questioned Hiss's character included James F. Byrnes, onetime Nye Committee chief-of-staff Stephen Raushenbush, former AAA administrator Chester C. Davis, Senator Gerald Nye, John Foster Dulles, and Charles Dollard, president of the Carnegie Corporation. Dollard's reservations probably reflected those held by many of Hiss's friends and associates: "[H]e does not believe Alger stole the documents but he also does not believe that Alger has told all he knows about his relations with Chambers. He thinks that Alger should be reminded that other people are involved to some extent in his fate and that his conviction will reflect unfavorably upon men like Acheson and Dulles as well as upon the Carnegie Corporation."[4]

Even Marbury and McLean shared Dollard's uncertainties. They seemed half convinced that Hiss might be covering up for his wife: "The file clerk in the Carnegie Corporation," McLean wrote Marbury, "a Miss Ballard, who has been there for years, told Dollard last summer when this [rumor] started that, of course, everyone knew that Priscilla was a Communist. She did not have any real information. She had known Priscilla by reason of the fact that Priscilla wrote the book which the Carnegie Corporation published [in 1934]."

Coordinating the defense probe, McLean collected all of Marbury's files in New York, received almost daily letters from John F. Davis which outlined the Washington end of the investigation, and read regular reports from Schmahl and other detectives hired by the defense. Angered at the prosecution's refusal to allow the defense access to papers on the case in government possession, "even the Chambers documents that we turned over to it," McLean filed successful motions to obtain such material—including the several typewritten letters from the Hisses found by the FBI, copies of the "pumpkin papers" microfilm, and "any and all typewriters formerly owned or possessed by Mr. or Mrs. Hiss, now in the possession of the government."[5]

Horace Schmahl's reports indicated some progress on locating witnesses, many of them Communists, willing to testify to Chambers's homosexuality. He told McLean in January he had just spent "three more nights looking at files in Forest Hills made available by Licht. These are files of the Daily Worker and one folder of the New Masses. They contain bills, correspondence, pieces of manu-script. Nothing by or concerning Chambers." "Licht," not further identified, was evidently a CP official of sufficient influence to obtain the back files of these jour-nals (including correspondence) for inspection by the Hiss defense. McLean's memo continues: "Licht says that he has had a talk with Lieber who says that he does know Hiss but does not propose to admit it." McLean could only have been relieved, since any testimony by Maxim Lieber at the forthcoming trial that cor-roborated Chambers's account of a meeting between the two men while Priscilla Hiss was allegedly visiting Lieber's Pennsylvania farm would have devastated the Hiss defense.[6]

The Hiss defense lawyers had become thoroughly absorbed in the task of destroying Chambers's credibility. Harold Rosenwald outlined part of their favorite psychiatric theory as it applied to *Class Reunion*, the novel Chambers had translated, in a December 23, 1948, memo for Professor Edmund Morgan, a legal scholar being consulted on the problem of admissible evidence. The memo outlined defense trial strategy, other than showing Hiss's good character—namely, to introduce into evidence those of Chambers's writings and translations that supported the theory* to summon Dr. Carl Binger as a witness to interpret the writings; to request a court-appointed psychiatrist "to testify concerning

---

*Rosenwald also pointed out a mite exuberantly that in another book Chambers translated during the 1920s "there appears a banana stuffed with poison which may have furnished the explanation for the pumpkin stuffed with poisonous evidence in the form of microfilm."

Chambers' motives" (the Hiss attorneys apparently abandoned this notion); and to demonstrate "if we can develop the evidence in provable form, that Chambers is homosexual."*[7]

As the chief architect of the psychiatric theory among Hiss's lawyers, Rosenwald submitted a second memorandum before the trial that analyzed with remarkable astuteness and pitiless candor problems inherent in the two conflicting defense theories of Chambers's behavior, which he called those of "conscious" and "unconscious" motivation.[8]

The theory of "conscious motivation" held that before defecting Chambers had tucked away government documents "to authenticate his stories concerning his experiences as a Communist espionage agent." Later, first through Isaac Don Levine and then on *Time*, Chambers had "tried to capitalize upon his experiences as a Communist." Chambers had selected Hiss as "a perfect target for . . . attack in the summer of 1948" in order to help elect Thomas E. Dewey, Henry Luce's choice for president. Hiss "was big enough but not too big . . . [and] had been associated with the phases of the Roosevelt foreign policy which were the obvious objects of right-wing attack"—Dumbarton Oaks, Yalta, and the UN. Chambers held back the microfilm, but, "under pressure in the libel action, he manufactured the typewritten Baltimore papers from pictures on the films. Later he produced the films, or what remained of them after cutting off those containing the Baltimore typewritten papers."

But Rosenwald recognized the obvious problems with this scenario. For one thing, "as in the case of the psychiatric theory, [it] does not prove that Hiss did not give Government papers to Chambers. Hiss could have given Chambers papers and Chambers might have wanted to write truthfully about his experiences." For another, it "fails to suggest any method by which Chambers might have secured the handwritten or typewritten papers [and] assumes, without any proof at this time, that the typewritten papers were written last summer." Here, as elsewhere, Rosenwald clearly preferred the psychiatric theory as "far superior": "Under the plan set forth in *Class Reunion,* we can suggest a method by which Chambers might have secured the documents and might have forged both the handwriting and typewriting of Alger and Priscilla Hiss."

Most important, the theory of "conscious motivation," Rosenwald went on, "utterly fails to explain the coincidence of Chambers' prior acquaintance with Hiss and Chambers' acquisition of papers that emanated from Hiss. This inadequacy is particularly acute in the case of the handwritten documents of Alger

---

*Even the normally cautious McLean had joined by then in the avid pursuit of psychiatric "evidence" against Chambers by Hiss's attorneys, filing a memo about "passages of interest in 'The Scorpion,' another book translated by Chambers. These involve selling silverware and putting it back again before the loss is discovered." McLean Memo, December 31, 1948, Hiss Defense Files.

Hiss." Rosenwald noted that proponents of "conscious motivation" among the Hiss defense lawyers simply avoided the problem, thereby leaving themselves vulnerable to Chambers's corroborated testimony of close association with Hiss.

Although the argument that Chambers hoped to elect Dewey might reasonably explain "the production of the documents," Rosenwald argued, "the basic question in this case is the acquisition of the documents by Chambers." A HUAC-*Time*-Republican conspiracy during the summer of 1948 did not offer much help. If it turned out that Hiss's old Woodstock typed the Baltimore documents (apparently Rosenwald still harbored hopes that it had not, despite Haring's unfavorable judgment the previous December), then "we will get no help from the theory of conscious motivation in explaining this fact."

Rosenwald criticized Stryker's overreliance on a defense by reputation, matching Hiss's purportedly excellent character against Chambers's alleged malevolence. "An excellent character is not inconsistent with the charges made in this case," he pointed out. "There have been people who have betrayed their country because of a loyalty to something more important to them. The current case of Judith Coplon is also in point." Moreover, although the grand jury undoubtedly received "a better impression" of Hiss's character, "this was not enough to upset the damaging documentary evidence which Chambers produced."

Instead Rosenwald plumped for the psychiatric theory and defended it against criticism that "it will seem like a red herring, calculated to divert the jury from the real issues." After all, jurors might also view the conscious motivation argument in this light, believing that defense efforts to stress the election of 1948 were "intended to take their minds away from the documents."

The heart of Rosenwald's argument was brutal but, in view of the many weaknesses in his client's story, highly realistic:

> The psychiatric theory has been criticized because it may be regarded as an unjustified smear of Chambers as a homosexual. Surely we intend to smear Chambers in any event. I have no objection to such smearing and hope that it will be very thoroughly and effectively done. But I see little difference between smearing Chambers as a homosexual and smearing him as a liar, a thief and a scoundrel.

Besides, "there is no evidence that supports the theory of conscious motivation. . . . ."

A more serious objection to the psychiatric-theory approach, he granted, was that "it will smear Alger because it will be believed by some jurors that he is a homosexual." Acknowledging the problem, Rosenwald pointed out that "the fundamental basis" of his theory was "that Hiss rejected Chambers's abnormal advances," and though "incidental smearing will be unfortunate," use of the argument for "unconscious motivation" would prove "extremely helpful" in obtaining an acquittal. But Rosenwald conceded that the theory could "boomerang since it will tend to show a motive not only why Chambers should have received papers from Hiss but why Hiss should have given them to him," especially if jurors believe that the men had been homosexual lovers. Despite the risks, which "with skillful handling . . . can be met," Rosenwald felt that there were even graver risks "which cannot be avoided by dodging the main issue in the case . . . Chambers' reasons for framing Hiss . . . [and] only a psychiatrist can explain those reasons."

No government prosecutor could have improved on Rosenwald's dissection of the difficulties confronted by the Hiss defense. His arguments apparently swayed other, more skeptical lawyers on the defense team, since the months preceding Hiss's perjury trial brought a flurry of activity designed to provide both factual and theoretical support for the theory of Chambers's unconscious motivation. Rosenwald, Dr. Binger, and Dr. Viola Bernard all contributed extensive psychoanalytic studies of Chambers's life and motivation bolstering their arguments with evidence drawn from the biographical details provided by Chambers himself. A handwriting expert, Dr. Meta Steiner, analyzed specimens of Chambers's writing during the 1923–26 period (preceding his brother's suicide) and concluded that the subject's scribblings, among many other things, displayed "marked narcissism," "self-love," a drive to dominate his environment, and "extreme egocentricity." But even Dr. Steiner carefully hedged her analysis: "There is no indication in the writing of the presence of a break with reality."[9]

Early in January, Harold Rosenwald met with Carol Weiss King, the lawyer for J. Peters. She berated Rosenwald both for the disorganized nature of Hiss's defense efforts and for Hiss's earlier cooperation with the government. Rosenwald had come for information from Peters, but Mrs. King parried his request by pointing out that a "liaison had been established between the proper persons and Hiss's attorneys" that might eventually produce some items from Peters. A puzzled Rosenwald could not draw Mrs. King out more specifically as to the name of that "liaison," although McLean's private detective Horace Schmahl apparently served as the link between Hiss's lawyers and the Communist Party described by King.[10]

During the weeks that followed Rosenwald's interview with King, several important Communist officials who had known Whittaker and Esther Chambers during the 1920s and 1930s agreed to see Schmahl or McLean. All of them provided derogatory information about Chambers, but none could offer proof. Grace Hutchins claimed that her former friend Esther Shemitz had told her "years ago, that Whittaker Chambers had spent time in the Westchester Division of Bloomingdale Hospital for Mental Diseases," an oft-repeated rumor. Under further questioning by Schmahl, however, Hutchins "changed her story" and cited as her source a third party who, when located by the detective, denied having given Hutchins such data.*

"It was common knowledge," Grace Hutchins also told Schmahl, "that Chambers had been a sex pervert when he was employed by the 'Daily Worker.' She does not know the name of any person who might shed more light on this statement nor does she know the identity of anyone with whom Chambers might have had association along the lines mentioned." During this same period much similarly unverified information reached the Hiss lawyers from both Lee Pressman and Henry Collins.[†][11]

Pressman, according to McLean, undertook to investigate the Hiss case's possible connection with the 1945 Amerasia affair (which also involved allegedly stolen State Department documents) and to collect information on Hede Massing, A. George Silverman, David Carpenter, and Frederick Vanderbilt Field. Pressman told McLean that he had also "heard many rumors about Chambers' residence at Bloomingdale . . . [and] will try to find out something specific about them. . . . Pressman was most cooperative and seemed sincerely anxious to help in every way possible." Harold Rosenwald filed a memo several weeks later about a progress report Pressman gave "sometime ago." The memo included not only references by Pressman to the individuals discussed with McLean in January but also comments on Ward Pigman and the Reno brothers as well as on others who figured in Chambers's testimony about the Communist underground.[12]

Nathan Witt kept in touch with the Hiss defense through Pressman and through Cynthia Jones, who had given Alger and Priscilla Hiss their Corona portable. Jones heard about Witt "because of an amusing story that Donald [Hiss] first told me about Nat," and she had met Witt in 1948 through a mutual friend. She told Donald Hiss's attorney, Hugh Cox, that she had seen Witt "one or two times on his initiative. She says that he asked to see her so he could inquire what was happening in the affairs of Alger Hiss."[13]

But most of the information reaching the Hiss defense about Chambers's Communist past came either from Rosenwald's interviews or from Horace Schmahl's investigation. Schmahl informed McLean in late January that "through a very confidential contact" he had learned that A. B. Magill, former editor of *The Daily Worker,* "knew the identity of a man with whom Chambers is said to have had an extensive affair in his younger days." Schmahl interviewed Magill, who described Chambers's affair with Ida Dales and strongly implied that she and other women had been lesbians when Chambers took up with them.

---

*At first Hutchins also told Schmahl that she had no CP connections, but then "qualified that by saying: 'I don't want any part of anyone who breaks with the Party'" as an explanation for why she broke off relations with the Chambers couple during the late 1930s.

[†]Collins regularly passed along uncorroborated rumors of Chambers's alleged incarceration in mental hospitals.

Magill also said "that Chambers had an affair with a good-looking young boy, nicknamed 'Bub' ... when Chambers was employed on the staff of The Daily Worker." Magill reiterated a theme that characterized the CP line on Chambers by this time and the unofficial comments of those Communists who volunteered information: "Chambers was in the habit of showing Magill his manuscripts for perusal before publication. According to Mr. Magill, 'some of those manuscripts would turn your stomach.' They were, said Mr. Magill, 'dripping with perversities, violence and weird plots.'"[14]

Sender Garlin, once of The Daily Worker, also tagged Chambers as a homosexual during the 1920s when interviewed by McLean: "It is his [Garlin's] opinion that the relationship between Chambers and [Mike] Intrator was homosexual [this rumor recurred among Communist friends of both men]. ... All of Chambers' friends were very much surprised when Chambers and Esther married." Garlin, who spent a summer in Long Beach during the mid-twenties, recalled Chambers living in a tent there "with a boy named Bub whom Chambers went around with continually. Garlin thinks that was a homosexual relationship. He does not know where Bub is or what his full name was."

But Garlin also acknowledged Chambers's interest in women, mentioned his companion Ida Dales, and thought "that Chambers had other mistresses." Garlin also referred to Chambers's passion for "mystification" (in Meyer Schapiro's word) even before going underground: "He was always very mysterious and secretive. While working on the Daily Worker, he would be away for several days at a stretch and would tell Garlin that he could not say where he had been." Garlin also confirmed the reasons for Chambers's abrupt departure from The New Masses: "It is true that Chambers disappeared from New York in 1933. Garlin understood that he had gone 'underground.' He was told that Chambers was working in Washington."[15]

Both Garlin and another radical writer, Paul Peters, told Hiss's investigators the same story about a man to whom Chambers allegedly made homosexual advances in 1932. Garlin brought the person, Leon Herald Srabian, to see McLean the same day, February 8, that the attorney interviewed Garlin himself. According to McLean's memo, Srabian (who used the last name Herald) "was a Communist for many years but left the Party around 1937."

Herald told McLean that he had known Chambers at the New York Public Library during the mid-twenties and met him again during the winter of 1932 in Chicago, when both were delegates to the national convention of John Reed writers' clubs. Chambers asked if Herald would find him a room, which the latter located in his own rooming house. He awoke in the middle of the night, according to Herald, to discover Chambers "in his bed assaulting him in a homosexual way. Herald repulsed him and would not participate. Chambers remained in Herald's room for over an hour pleading with him to agree to homosexual intercourse. Herald refused. Chambers finally left the room." Herald claimed never to have seen Chambers again after the Chicago incident. The Hiss investigators found it impossible to identify "Bub" more fully or to obtain corroboration of Chambers's alleged homosexuality. As for Leon Herald, the defense decided against using him as a witness. Cross-examination might have brought out the link to Garlin.*[16]

Defense lawyers realized that any effort to identify Chambers as a homosexual involved a clear possibility that the tactic would backfire. As Rosenwald had pointed out, the prosecution might try to "smear" Hiss himself. Also, the FBI knew about Timothy Hobson's alleged homosexuality, and Hobson's activities were widely known among Hiss's friends and associates, a number of whom speculated unhelpfully for the defense lawyers about the problem.[†] Hobson's role in the case troubled the Hiss attorneys and clearly entered into their debates over mounting a full-scale attack on Chambers's "perversions." Even before Hiss's indictment, Charles Wyzanski had written to William Marbury in mid-October 1948:

> Sitting next to John Cowles at the [Harvard] Overseers' meeting Monday, we fell into some talk about Alger's case. I think you might be interested in what John says the working newspaper men [Cowles was head of Cowles Publications] give as an explanation of the Hiss-Chambers controversy. Most of them are inclined to believe that Alger is shielding Priscilla. Others have the notion that Alger had a homosexual relationship with Chambers.

Wyzanski ridiculed the notion to Cowles as a "canard," pointing out that he knew "too many girls who are fond of Alger for it to be possible for his inclinations to run in the direction of the male sex."

But all three rumors—Alger's shielding Priscilla[‡] and the possibility of either a Hobson-Chambers or a Hiss-Chambers affair—had reached Marbury and McLean often enough to disturb them both. "I have already heard from a number of sources the suggestions which John Cowles made to you," Marbury wrote Wyzanski several days later. "I think that they are both wholly unfounded, but

---

*"When confronted by the FBI with Herald's story, Chambers denied having attended the John Reed convention during the winter of 1932. By that" time Chambers had already joined the Communist underground and disappeared from the *New Masses* office, making such an open appearance a thousand miles from his New York base of operations unlikely. No other Communist interviewed by the Hiss defense said anything about seeing him there. The fact that the FBI had heard about Herald's claims, however, indicates good intelligence within either the Hiss defense camp or the Communist Party.

†When the FBI interviewed Hiss's friends, acquaintances, and former associates, a number of them would provide Hiss and his attorneys with full accounts of the interrogations.

‡McLean's assistant at Debevoise, attorney Robert von Mehren, told me that McLean always felt Priscilla Hiss (but not Alger) was guilty of Chambers's charges—"this was always his view." Marbury also apparently leaned toward this view, as did other lawyers and friends of Alger, and von Mehren himself believed that at the very least "she knew more than she told about the relationship of the [two] families." Interview, Robert von Mehren, December 11, 1974.

the suggestion about Chambers and Alger would readily occur, I think, to those who knew Chambers well."[17]

Yet the fingers continued pointing, even among friends and supporters. Thus Charles Dollard told McLean that he "has talked about the case with various psychiatrists who all advocate the homosexual theory, sometimes involving Timothy, sometimes Alger. They think that Alger's insistence upon Chambers's teeth was significant in this connection."[18]

The basic difficulty for the defense in attacking Chambers as a homosexual remained: Once opened, this line of questioning would spill over in all directions. Witnesses might speculate over Hobson and over the rumors concerning Hiss. Should this happen, as Rosenwald suggested, the homosexual argument might easily boomerang and end by reinforcing Chambers's credibility as a witness, thus strengthening the case against Alger Hiss. McLean also remained concerned over prosecution scrutiny of the Hisses' private lives as close as the defense study of Chambers.[19]

Before the trial Hiss received volunteer help from many people who knew him only slightly but believed in his innocence. Walter Lippmann, for example, proposed a novel approach to Carl Binger. Lippmann suggested that since the "gravest charge against [Hiss] has to do with espionage," then "as public evidence of his good faith . . . [he should] have his lawyers announce that he is prepared to waive the statute of limitations" so that he could be tried on espionage charges. Whatever Hiss may have thought of Lippmann's suggestion, he never pursued it.[20]

Most of those who helped the Hiss defense were private citizens unfettered by government involvement. That status no longer applied to Dean Acheson after January 7, 1949, when he replaced George Marshall as secretary of state. Conservative congressmen denounced Acheson's appointment, both because he had been labeled (unfairly) as the leader of a faction at State during World War II that had opposed a tough policy toward the Soviet Union and because of his ties to Alger Hiss. A tough confirmation fight loomed in the Senate.

The Senate Foreign Relations Committee opened hearings on the appointment on January 13. Acheson discussed his relationship with both Hisses, but because of the close ties of friendship and law partnership, was more protective of Donald.[21]

Republican Senator Arthur Vandenberg of Michigan, who had worked with Hiss in organizing the initial meeting of the UN, expressed sympathy for Acheson's dilemma, but criticized him. Although Vandenberg agreed that it would have been improper for Acheson to comment on Hiss's guilt or innocence with the case still pending, he did not agree that Acheson could not "comment in any way" on the Hiss case. Friendly toward Acheson, Vandenberg suggested that he make a stronger statement about "the appalling dangers to national security in the State Department leaks, not a speculative question requiring suspension of judgment pending court decisions."

Acheson disagreed with Vandenberg's statement that Hiss withheld facts from Secretary Byrnes: "The whole situation is one of complete perplexity to a person who is a friend of Alger Hiss's. . . . If you start with the assumption that [he] was guilty of the things with which he is charged, then he has behaved in a way which leads you to doubt his sanity . . . [and] his subsequent conduct is little short of insane." In that statement and others, Acheson seemed undecided over some aspects of the case.* "One has a feeling that there is something here that one does not understand," he told the senators. "For myself, I cannot believe that this fellow has done any of these things. It seems to me there must be something which has not yet been brought out, that there is some other fact in this situation which we do not yet know." Acheson's suspicions became a bit clearer when he evaded giving direct answers to several questions about the possibility that Priscilla Hiss had stolen the papers. He would say only: "That theory has been expressed."[22]

His contacts with Hiss had been largely professional, Acheson stressed: "We were never close at all. He seemed to me to be a man of character. . . . Throughout this thing he has conducted himself, I think, foolishly as a lawyer. His attitude has been technical, and sometimes almost pedantic in the way he has proceeded, but he has also conducted himself with calm and dignity and not at all in the way of a person who has been caught in a really terrible crime. . . . He was, and he is—not a close friend, but I am not going to abandon him and throw rocks at him when he is in trouble. If it is proved that I have been misled . . . I shall be glad to say so at that time, but I am not willing to say so now."

But Acheson seemed more supportive of Donald Hiss: "Donald had a very mediocre record in the law school [by contrast with Alger]. He came along as a 'C' man, something in that area, and he was always somewhat under the shadow of his brother's brilliance." Disingenuously, considering his cooperation with Hiss's defense from the first HUAC hearings, Acheson stressed to the committee that his "involvement with the whole Alger Hiss business came from Berle. If it had not been for Berle [and his testimony about Acheson vouching for Hiss in 1941], I would have had nothing to do with Alger Hiss at all."[†]

He denied that the endorsement of Hiss had been "unqualified": "There was a very unqualified endorsement of Donald Hiss and then a very restrained and very careful statement about Alger Hiss" followed by "a complete demonstration . . . that I never had anything to do with him in the State Department in any way"—a misleading statement, given his role in arranging for Hiss's departure.

---

*According to a close friend of the journalist Joseph Alsop, Acheson advised Alsop at this time not to open a campaign in his columns on Hiss's behalf when Alsop indicated an intention to do so.

†Neither Acheson nor Justice Felix Frankfurter commented publicly on their discussions of the Hiss case, which probably served as a regular subject of conversation during their daily morning walks at this time.

Before it voted on Acheson's nomination, the secretary-designate read into the record a two-sentence summary of an earlier statement denouncing Communism. The committee then unanimously recommended approval of the nomination, and four days later the full Senate confirmed Acheson's appointment by an 83-to-6 vote.

Hiss's attorneys failed shortly thereafter in an effort to gain Acheson's agreement to testify as a character witness, but they had far more important concerns at the time.[23] Although still interested in recovering Alger Hiss's "old machine," the lawyers approached the task with surprising slowness. Defense documents examiner J. Howard Haring and the FBI laboratory expert had both identified the Fansler Woodstock as the machine on which the stolen documents had been typed. Hiss had told John F. Davis the previous December 7 that he recalled giving the machine to Pat Catlett, but McLean did not learn this news until December 28 when speaking to Davis. Even then, only days after Horace Schmahl had entered the Lynbrook home of Chambers's mother to check on a typewriter there, McLean and other defense lawyers did almost nothing about Davis's information, despite the fact that the "old machine" in question was undoubtedly the office Woodstock they had been seeking.

Although McLean told Davis during their December 28 conversation that he was "checking on the whereabouts of the machine in some other way," making contact with the Catletts ranked low on the agenda of defense detectives and lawyers at this time. During December 1948 the Catletts were mentioned in extant defense files only in a brief notation by McLean at the bottom of a list of things for Schmahl to do. Donald Hiss had indicated to Davis that month that he had seen Pat Catlett around Washington and could assist in locating him. Despite the fact that Davis had evidently told him about the Catletts having received Alger's old typewriter, Donald phoned Harold Rosenwald on December 12 and stated that he had "no recollection of Alger's machine at all."

Not until late January did defense attorneys begin searching intensely for the Woodstock. As late as January 21 McLean compiled still another list for "further investigation by Schmahl," including as one of seven suggestions on the hunt for the typewriter: "Pat Catlett, 17th St., S.W., Washington," which showed that the defense had at least learned Catlett's approximate address.[24] But in late January and early February the FBI also reached members of the Catlett family, not primarily to question them about the typewriter but to seek corroboration of Chambers's claim that he had met Claudia Catlett at Hiss's home several times. Bureau agents conducted interviews with Claudia Catlett and her eldest sons, Perry M. (Pat) and Raymond Sylvester (Mike).*

---

*How the FBI first obtained information about the Catletts' whereabouts remains difficult to determine from the files.

To the FBI the Catletts said they knew nothing about typewriters owned by the Hisses, but in private Mike and Pat both said they had received the old office machine from Alger and Priscilla Hiss. Several months later Mike explained to bureau agents his lack of candor: "The Hisses, and particularly Alger, had been good to him in the providing of odd jobs, the furnish[ing] of clothing, and the affording of employment for his mother," the agents wrote in their report of the interview. "Raymond indicated he felt indebted to Alger Hiss for this kindness." Also, "apparently Priscilla brought him hot soup when he was sick." Moreover, the Catletts felt a similar loyalty and for similar reasons to Donald Hiss, and they all believed Hiss innocent of the charges.[25]

Thus Mike Catlett was more candid with Alger Hiss's attorneys than with the government's. While under FBI questioning in late January, he visited Donald Hiss to tell him about the interrogations.* Mike informed him that the Catletts had received the typewriter during the late 1930s, and he offered to help locate it.[26]

Edward McLean spent several days in Washington during this period, having come specifically to question the Catletts. His memorandum of these interviews provides a far more thorough and accurate portrayal of events than either Donald's or the Catletts' later testimony. McLean had known about the Catletts' possession of the Woodstock since late December, but he had held off further inquiry until the FBI forced his hand by finding the Catlett family.

Although the memo does not describe McLean's reasons for taking personal command of the inquiry, he had probably concluded—as when Marbury turned over the Baltimore documents—that Alger Hiss's interests would best be served if the defense (and not the FBI) located the machine. One of the Catletts might reveal that Hiss had withheld information earlier from the FBI and from the grand jury when asked about the typewriter. McLean's memo indicates that he kept Hiss informed about his dealings with the Catletts, although the few comments by Alger at the memo's conclusion did not take issue with any of its statements:

> I interviewed Mike Catlett at Donald Hiss's house on the evening of Monday, January 31; Mike and Clytie at Donald Hiss's on the evening of February 1; Mike and Clytie again at Donald Hiss's on the evening of February 2; and Pat at his house on Howard Road on the morning of February 3. I have not seen Buckie [James Catlett], Mary or Burnetta.
>
> Clytie, Mike and Pat all agree that at a time when the Hisses were moving from one house to another, they gave the Catlett family certain property, consisting of clothing, books and an old, high, worn-out typewriter. They are

---

*Donald Hiss's account of the sequence is questionable, since neither his memo of this episode nor his subsequent trial testimony mentions earlier discussions with John F. Daws about locating Pat Catlett. Instead, Donald put forth a story that claimed inaccurately that he and others in the defense had no knowledge of the Catletts' connection with the machine until Mike Catlett came to see him in late January 1949.

vague as to when this occurred but are positive that it took place at the time of a move. Inasmuch as Clytie stopped working for the Hisses in September 1938, when they were living at Volta Place . . . it seems likely that the typewriter was given to the Catletts on the move from 30th Street to Volta Place at the end of 1937. [The previous December the Hisses had told the grand jury that they had disposed of the Woodstock "after 1938" and Hiss had a "visual recollection" of the machine at Volta Place. Perry Catlett signed a statement for the FBI in February 1949 that he had received the machine in 1938, after the Hisses moved to Volta Place.]

Neither Clytie nor Mike remembered what kind of a typewriter it was. Pat, however, was sure that it was a Woodstock. He is more interested in typewriters than the others and can type himself. . . . He remembers taking the typewriter to a repair shop on K Street, S.E. [a shop that opened late in 1938]. . . .

A year or two after his marriage . . . Pat gave the typewriter to his sister, Burnetta, who wanted to use it for her high school work. . . . Burnetta did not live with the other Catletts but lived and "was brought up by" a Dr. Easton [Easter] . . .

Burnetta lived with Dr. Easton until he died . . . [and] almost immediately after the doctor's death, Burnetta and her husband moved to Detroit. . . . Clytie is sure she did not have the typewriter with her and did not take it to Detroit . . . because she has visited Burnetta in Detroit and says that the typewriter is not there.

The man who either owned Dr. Easton's house during the doctor's lifetime or bought it after his death is a Mr. Marlow, colored. We interviewed Mr. Marlow at his house. He said that he knew nothing about any property of Burnetta's because it had all been cleaned out before he moved in . . . [by] a boy whom he "had brought up" named Vernon. . . . We interviewed [Vernon]. He was partially intoxicated and his memory was not in good condition. He said that he remembered nothing about it. . . . The most likely supposition is that Burnetta gave away the typewriter or threw it away when she moved to Detroit. All the Catletts are positive that she did not give it to any of them.

Pat's memory of the typewriter is clear and definite. . . . Mike remembers seeing it around the house at P Street before it was given to Burnetta. Clytie remembers it clearly. . . .

Pat, Mike, Clytie and Buckie have all been interviewed by the FBI and have all told the FBI that they know nothing about the Hiss typewriters. They claim that they have not signed any written statement to that effect. . . .[27]

Neither McLean nor any of the other Hiss lawyers revealed anything about this interview to the FBI in the months that followed, nor did McLean advise the Catletts to correct their false testimony about the machine.

The Catletts contradicted the Hisses' grand jury testimony on several major points when talking to McLean. Claudia Catlett recalled seeing Priscilla Hiss recently: "[T]he last time was a few years ago shortly before the Hisses moved to New York [in the late summer of 1947] when they lived at their last P Street Residence." James (Bucky) Catlett said to the FBI that he had never told Mrs. Hiss in 1946 that his mother was dead, and Claudia Catlett's statement showed that Priscilla knew Claudia was alive and well as late as the 1946–47 period.* Mrs. Catlett also described more fully to McLean her memory of having seen Chambers once at the Hisses' P Street house during the fall of 1936: "She remembers that he stopped in late in the afternoon and Mrs. Hiss offered him tea but he said he could not stop long enough to take it."[28]

Although McLean interviewed Claudia, Mike, and Pat after their talks with FBI agents, the bureau had apparently learned nothing from the Catletts about the Hiss Woodstock. That, for the moment, left the defense a clear field in trying to locate the machine with the Catletts' help.

Neither the two eldest Catlett brothers nor their mother told the FBI that Burnetta had been in possession of the Woodstock as late as 1945. "As far as we know," McLean wrote after his round of Washington conferences with the Catletts, "they [the FBI] do not know of her existence." Harold Rosenwald flew to Detroit on February 6 to interview Mrs. Burnetta Fisher, who said her brother Pat had given her the machine while she was in high school: "[I]t worked fairly well when she first got it but . . . she and her sister Mary gave it quite a beating. She never had the typewriter repaired."[†] Burnetta and her husband had moved to Detroit—without the Woodstock—in January 1945.[29]

When she left Washington, Dr. Easter was already in the hospital and dying. A man named Vernon Marlow who seemed to be running the household refused to allow her "to take her things with her. . . . The typewriter was left behind." According to Burnetta, "Vernon may have sold the typewriter for junk. There is no one else who might have taken it."

Even before Rosenwald's interview with Burnetta Fisher, the trail led to Vernon Marlow. In early February, probably after Rosenwald's interview with Burnetta, Mike Catlett again contacted Vernon, who now admitted having removed the typewriter from Dr. Easter's home when John Marlow evicted him. Vernon could not recall how he had disposed of the machine until Catlett offered him $50 to help locate it. Then Marlow suddenly remembered lending the machine to someone named "Bill," who, when contacted, "disclaimed any knowledge of the

---

*Further confirmation that Priscilla Hiss had more than vague reports about Claudia Catlett in 1946 came from Mike, who told McLean that he called on Mrs. Hiss to ask for work "probably [in] 1946" when he got out of the Army. His brother Pat (whose 1941 wedding Alger had attended) apparently kept in touch as well, since he listed both Priscilla Hiss and Mrs. Donald Hiss on a December 27, 1946, job application form as current references.

†Alger and Priscilla Hiss both testified that they had given the typewriter to the Catletts four years earlier because it no longer worked well.

present whereabouts of the typewriter." "Bill" turned out to be Ernest (Bill) Bell, Vernon Marlow's stepson. From Bell, Mike Catlett then learned that "it was his [Bell's] understanding that the typewriter was in the possession of Ira Lockey," a Washington trucker and junk dealer. According to Bell, who later told the story to the FBI, "Lockey had moved the personal belongings of Vernon Marlow . . . when his former house was condemned, and as a result of the move, received the typewriter and a washing machine in payment." Catlett later conceded having offered Bell $50 if he could lead him to the machine. At that point Mike Catlett contacted Donald Hiss, who drove both Mike and Bill to Ira Lockey's house.[30]

Lockey was ill at the time, but a "Mrs. Hall" who lived with him told the two visitors (Donald Hiss remained in the car) that Lockey had junked the typewriter and washing machine. Catlett checked a nearby dealer, found the washing machine and another typewriter, a Royal, which he bought at Donald Hiss's request. Catlett returned to the Lockey house, but Mrs. Hall repeated that Lockey had junked the machine. According to Donald Hiss, Mike Catlett then told him that "Lockey was still too sick to talk and wanted absolutely nothing to do with the typewriter."[31]

Apparently Mike believed that Mrs. Hall had lied to him, but still, according to his later testimony, Catlett claimed to have made no other move to interview Lockey for the next two months. This mysterious pause in the intensive defense hunt for the Hiss Woodstock seems even stranger considering McLean's earlier four days spent interviewing the Catlett family and Rosenwald's flight to Detroit on February 7.

Although by mid-February the Woodstock had been traced to Ira Lockey's household, Donald Hiss and Mike Catlett—both of whom said they made no further effort to talk to Lockey until April—kept McLean and other Hiss lawyers in the dark about this crucial development until McLean returned in mid-April to begin another round of questioning about the typewriter.* When he arrived in Washington, McLean still knew nothing about Ira Lockey. He had come to search John Marlow's basement and attic, where Burnetta Fisher told Rosenwald she had left the typewriter in 1945. Accompanied by Charles Houston, a black attorney who had joined the Hiss defense team specifically to assist in finding the typewriter, McLean searched Marlow's home in mid-April, but found no machine.[32]

---

*Mike Catlett did admit to Hiss investigator Maurice de F. Lockwood in 1950 "that he learned of Lockey's possession of the typewriter about a month before it was recovered," actually two months. Also, he "could not recall" to Lockwood "after which visit to Lockey . . . he phoned Donald Hiss concerning the typewriter." Rosenwald had pursued his interest in the search in March by arranging for a Detroit attorney to contact Burnetta Fisher and "try to induce her to go to Washington to look for the typewriter, clear-cut evidence that Rosenwald also had *not* been informed by Donald Hiss that Mike had already traced the machine to Lockey.

John Marlow again suggested that McLean talk to Vernon Marlow about the Woodstock, after which the two attorneys visited the latter's home. Vernon again played dumb. Next, McLean and Houston "interviewed Louise [Marlow, Vernon's wife] at her mother's house. . . ." From Mrs. Marlow, and not from Donald Hiss and Mike Catlett, who had learned of this two months earlier, McLean first heard about Ira Lockey:

> She [Louise] remembers that the typewriter was in her front yard . . . after Dr. Easter's death. She remembers that she engaged a truckman, Ira Lockey, to move certain furniture and other belongings to Louise's mother's house [also in Washington, in 1945]. . . . She remembers that she gave the typewriter to Lockey as part payment for his charges in moving.

The following month Louise Bell Marlow—like her husband and the Catletts before her—would conceal these facts from the FBI.[33]

Once McLean finally learned from Louise Marlow about Ira Lockey's involvement, Mike Catlett took McLean to see Lockey, who proved extremely cooperative:

> Lockey also says that he got the typewriter at that time and in that fashion. He says he took it in payment of a debt Vernon owed him. . . . The typewriter has been in the possession or under the control of Ira Lockey ever since February 1945 until I purchased it from him on April 16, 1949. I obtained a bill of sale from him [for $15] identifying it by number, Model 5n No. N230099. He told me on April 16 that in recent months it had been in his son's house. . . . Neither Vernon nor Louise nor Bill Bell nor Lockey ever saw or heard of the Hisses.[34]

The most puzzling aspect of the transaction is that Lockey parted with the machine for only $15. Mike Catlett had told Mrs. Lockey (Mrs. Hall) in January that "it would be worth quite a bit of money to him if he could find it," and Catlett had offered others from $15 to $50 for their help. Lockey's willingness to accept only $15 for the machine from McLean raises a serious and inevitable question about his own role in the affair, Mike Catlett's and perhaps Donald Hiss's. Did Lockey hand over the Hiss Woodstock or perhaps some other machine? Why did he sell the machine for only $15? Had all the fuss and "sleuthing" regarding the typewriter given it the appearance of being a dangerously "hot" item?*

---

*The lack of candor among the Catletts and their associates was contagious. Lockey later told the FBI that he gave the typewriter to his son, Ira Lockey, Jr., in February shortly after Mike Catlett first asked Mrs. Hall about its whereabouts. The son, in turn, told the bureau "that he borrowed it for the use of his daughter, who was starting junior high school. But the machine "didn't work well," so he placed it in a closet, where it supposedly remained for two months until his father asked him to return it.

Vernon Marlow, in an FBI interview, denied knowing the typewriter's current whereabouts, which contradicted his statement to McLean. Raymond and Perry Catlett, when reinterviewed

Although McLean had obtained the Woodstock, the FBI did not come away empty-handed. The bureau received an important new specimen of typing from the machine once it had been found, and significant information about the Woodstock itself. They learned that it had been in good working order even after 1945. Lockey said (and his daughter, Mrs. Stafford McQueen, confirmed the fact) that although he received the typewriter in poor condition, he cleaned it up and inserted a new ribbon, and it proved serviceable for several years. From Stafford McQueen, Lockey's son-in-law, the FBI learned that his July 29, 1947, typewritten application for federal employment on a standard Civil Service Commission form had been typed on Woodstock N230099. On May 23, after analyzing the form, the FBI laboratory concluded that it had been typed "on the same machine that was used to type Documents Q–6 through Q–69, and commonly known as the Baltimore papers."[35]

The Hiss Woodstock, in short, the machine on which the stolen State Department documents had been typed, was given to the Catletts in the late 1930s and eventually ended up in the Lockey household, where it was used to type McQueen's 1947 application. More impressionistic but still significant corroboration of this fact came from the Catlett family itself when McLean confronted them with Woodstock N230099 on April 16: "The handle which is used to turn up the paper was broken [when the Catletts received it], so that it was necessary to turn the roller by using the knob on the right," McLean noted in his May 18 memo. "Also, part of the knob on the left side of the roller was missing. Pat, Mike and Buckey each identified the typewriter which I purchased on April 16 as the Hiss typewriter on the basis of these features."[36]

The Catlett family's loyalty to the Alger Hisses varied according to the extent of their earlier associations with the couple. The youngest children—James (Bucky), Burnetta, and Mary—who had not known the Hisses well, gave straightforward and apparently truthful depositions to both the defense lawyers and the FBI. The two eldest sons, Raymond and Perry, and their mother, Claudia, had worked for the Hisses for years and they preserved feelings of obligation and gratitude that led all three Catletts to withhold, distort, or (in Raymond's and Perry's cases, by their own later confessions) fabricate important details.[37]

But even loyalty had its limits. When McLean came to Washington and recovered the Hiss Woodstock, he interviewed the Catletts extensively on their recollections of receiving the machine. Mike, the son who had helped Donald Hiss look for the typewriter, continued to insist that Priscilla Hiss had delivered the

by the FBI in May 1949 after the Hiss Woodstock had been found, at first denied that they had discussed the matter with Hiss's attorneys, but then revised their story to match approximately the one told by Donald Hiss—that *they* had come to Donald in late January after the FBI first contacted them. Neither the Hiss lawyers nor Donald Hiss informed the FBI that Alger Hiss had first recalled the typewriter's whereabouts early in December 1948, when he phoned John F. Davis. FBI Report, May 18, 1949, #3173.

machine to the Catletts, according to McLean's memo, "at the end of 1937, along with some other property . . . at the time the Hisses moved from 30th Street to Volta Place." This fitted in with the Hisses' own revised account of the transaction. Pat Catlett, on the other hand, the son most knowledgeable about typewriters, the one to whom in December 1948 Hiss told Davis he had given the machine—and also the one most chary about involving himself in the hunt for the Woodstock—now proved less helpful to the defense:

> Pat Catlett says he remembers getting the typewriter from Volta Place [McLean wrote]. He says he was working there one day "cleaning up," that he saw the typewriter in the "upstairs study," that Priscilla told him it was no good and that he could have it, that he personally carried it in his hands from the Volta Place house to the Catlett house on P Street. He is vague as to when this occurred. He said it was in the spring of the year, "about this time of year," i.e., April. . . . He thinks it was before Clytie ceased to work regularly for the Hisses . . . that would make it April 1938.

Thus Pat Catlett fixed the date he received the typewriter as the same month Whittaker Chambers defected from the Communist Party.[38]

His brother Mike, according to McLean, "tried to argue Pat out of it," but Pat stuck to his story in the face of strong pressure from other family members and the anxious queries of Hiss's attorney. When Pat saw the FBI again on May 28, he signed a statement that waffled completely on the question of the date the Hisses gave him the Woodstock: "I can't remember whether they gave it to me before they moved or after they had moved to Volta Place. They could have lived on Volta Place for several months before they gave it to me."[39]

Even Hiss's attorney found it difficult to place much confidence in Mike Catlett's version of events, if only because of his curious entrepreneurial role and shifting assertions during the hunt for the Woodstock. The lawyers, of course, did not know that Mike and Donald Hiss had withheld news of Lockey's possession of the machine for two months, which might have made them still leerier of Mike. After interviewing Mike Catlett in 1950, Manice de F. Lockwood pointed out that he "did not impress me as being at all reliable; he said that he could not remember the sequence of events or dates and months when various events took place. He contradicted himself frequently during the interview, and later remembered events that he said he could not recall during the first part of the interview"—all while being questioned by a presumably friendly attorney. Apparently Mike Catlett found it difficult to keep his stories straight, even among Hiss's associates.[40]

Alger Hiss himself expressed a degree of uneasiness about using the Catletts as witnesses in a cogent but surprising intervention into the investigation on May 9, 1949, after the Woodstock had been recovered but before the start of the trial. Hiss's May 9 memo reveals familiarity with McLean's April 13–16 interview with the Catletts (and even with later questioning of the family by Donald Hiss), although McLean did not prepare a memo of these interviews until May 18. The Hiss memorandum was candidly titled: "Catlett Variations and Aids to Recollection (Need for reconciliation and final form joint version). (Hope that Mr. Houston can get Cleide [sic], Pat and Mike together)." Hiss outlined the story told by each of the Catletts about receiving the Woodstock and was reasonably content with the measure of agreement between Claudia and Mike. The difficulty—and the basic reason for the memo—remained:

> Pat: (1) Originally agreed with Mike's version: i.e., he and Mike apparently jointly remembered the details of (1) [carrying the typewriter away from the house with other items in their little wagon at the time the Hisses moved to Volta Place] . . .
>
> (2) Pat later remembered receiving typewriter at Volta Place and getting it from upstairs room off sun porch.
>
> (3) Still later, he told Donie version (1) again [presumably after McLean left Washington in mid-April].

Hiss then questioned whether Pat had carried the typewriter all the way to the Catlett home, "a good 6 or 7 blocks away," as Pat claimed. He then noted—for the first time—"as Tim and Priscilla remember definitely, a small second-hand radio that had been . . . kept [in Volta Place] in very room Pat says he got typewriter from. . . . Could he be confusing gift of radio from Volta Place in same room he describes with earlier gift of typewriter?"[41]

But if Pat stuck to his story of having received the typewriter from Hiss's study the same month Chambers defected, Hiss had prepared another line of defense that implicated the maid's family more directly in the case: Chambers had somehow received the machine from the Catletts. "Important to recheck Catletts on boarders and frequent visits of friends to their house," Hiss wrote McLean. "Also that their house was kept unlocked and all Catletts were often away while boarders and friends were present."[42]

At the same time, McLean began preparing an argument, also relying on the malleable memories of the Catlett family, that the Hisses had acquired their second typewriter, a portable, even before disposing of the Woodstock. McLean noted that Claudia Catlett now remembered the Hisses having a portable machine at their 30th Street home, where "Timmy played with it when he was laid up with his broken leg"—Pat and Mike could recall only "seeing the portable at Volta Place." (Claudia Catlett said nothing about the portable in any of her depositions to the FBI, and in her earliest statement, in February, she disclaimed any knowledge of typewriters whatsoever.) McLean pointed out in May that the latest known specimen of typing—other than the stolen documents—done by the Hisses on their Woodstock was Priscilla's Bryn Mawr club presidential report in

May 1937: "It looks as though the Woodstock had not been used after that time for correspondence."[43]

If it could be established that the Hisses had the portable in 1937, this would indicate that Alger and Priscilla Hiss "would have been much more liable to use the portable for any typing after the summer of 1937 than they would have been to use the Woodstock. Probably with the portable, they might not even notice the absence of the Woodstock. This may lend some plausibility to the theory that Chambers obtained the Woodstock in 1937 and returned it later." McLean even theorized that the Hisses could have left it for a time at the Westminster farm that Chambers later purchased, but conceded that "this seems a remote possibility." Some of McLean's speculations were extreme: "Conceivably, he could have borrowed it from Timmy without either Alger or Priscilla's knowledge," although acceptance of this theory would have meant accepting as factual the rumors that Timmy (then still a child) and Chambers were seeing one another privately. That McLean should even have considered this grotesque possibility indicated the depth of his concern over disassociating the Hisses from their Woodstock typewriter no later than mid-1937.[44]

Both Hiss and McLean had good reason for concern. By May 1949 two leading documents examiners hired by the defense had both certified that the stolen Baltimore papers were typed on the same machine as the "Hiss standards" from the 1930s. The second of these experts had studied Woodstock N230099 itself and concluded that the Baltimore documents had been typed on the Hiss machine. (Later in the year FBI lab experts took twenty-one pages of typewritten specimens from N230099 and confirmed the conclusions of defense examiners: that the same typewriter had turned out the copies of stolen State Department cables.)[45]

Defense expert J. Howard Haring had stated in December 1948 that the 1933 insurance letters signed by Hiss had probably been typed on the same Woodstock that produced the Baltimore documents. In January Rosenwald sent Haring a large batch of typing and handwriting specimens of both Alger Hiss and Whittaker Chambers, asking him to determine: (1) whether Hiss or Chambers wrote the four handwritten notes (especially the Mary Martin cable, which Rosenwald termed a possible imitation of Hiss's handwriting); (2) who had composed the handwritten corrections on the Baltimore typed documents; and (3) who had done the typing. Haring's conclusions were unhelpful. The four handwritten notes were written "by the person whose writing was submitted to me as being written by A.H." As for the interlinear corrections on the typed documents, "I am inclined to the opinion that the A.H. corrections more closely resemble the questioned writing, than do the writings of W.C." Haring could not establish the identity of the typist on the basis of photostats and suggested examining the originals (the defense hoped that Chambers could be identified this way).[46]

Several months later, after the defense had already hired a new expert, Haring gave his "final opinion" about the documents: "The Baltimore typed papers were typed on the identical Woodstock which typed the Hiss standards." Haring thought the Woodstock had been manufactured between 1925 and 1928 because both "the Baltimore papers and the Hiss samples contain a figure 6 of a type which was used only on typewriters manufactured during those years." (The next Hiss expert would disagree.) As for the typist, Haring still could not say definitely, but he did note that "the only pronounced difference between the known Hiss samples and the Baltimore papers is that the Baltimore papers are all single spaced whereas most of the Hiss samples are double spaced. Priscilla says that she always double spaces. However, the 1933 letters . . . contain single spacing." Haring left behind one final disturbing point: "the Baltimore papers are on a thin paper which is similar to the paper used in the Bryn Mawr report [typed by Priscilla], although it is not exactly the same kind."[47]

In March, Priscilla Hiss had copied a few pages of the typed stolen documents for Edwin H. Fearon, a new defense expert, on a Woodstock rented by Hiss's lawyers. Mrs. Hiss managed a top speed of only 12.7 words per minute in the test runs, although years earlier she had passed a typing proficiency test while applying at the Columbia School of Journalism and had typed the greater part of her manuscript on the fine arts in America. McLean asked the newly appointed prosecutor in the case, Thomas F. Murphy, to allow Fearon to examine the original Baltimore documents. Murphy agreed and sent a representative from his office and an FBI agent along with the documents to Fearon's Pittsburgh laboratory, where Fearon had typing samples taken from N230099. Fearon did not share Haring's belief that the Woodstock on which the stolen documents and Hiss standards had been typed was produced sometime between 1925 and 1928. His speculations ranged over a longer period: The machine had been "manufactured between 1919 and 1938," which made it possible for N230099—built in 1929—to have typed all of the material.[48]

His report to Lloyd Paul Stryker came as a major blow to the Hiss attorneys: "I regret that I am compelled to report that it is my opinion that the questioned typing . . . was typed on Woodstock typewriter #N230099." Fearon also judged "that the person who typed the standards did not type the questioned exhibits," and that Hiss had done the four handwritten memos. His final report to the defense attorneys stated that the Baltimore documents had been typed on a 1928 Woodstock, and that, despite "points of similarity" between Mrs. Hiss's typing and the stolen documents, he could reach no positive conclusion about the typist. "I did hope that my report of this typewriting would be in favor of your client," Fearon admitted to Stryker. "I am positive it is not. . . . I cannot discover anything to help us."[49]

Stymied in their efforts to obtain favorable opinions about Hiss's handwriting on the notes or the typing of the stolen material, McLean and Stryker had only one reasonable course of action open to them: They decided not to summon as a trial witness either Haring or Fearon, although Fearon specifically declined to testify.* Now that Fearon had examined Woodstock N230099, the defense had lost the option of declining to introduce the machine into evidence at the trial. Although McLean did not inform the FBI or the prosecutors prior to the trial about having located the Hiss Woodstock, Stryker and the other lawyers planned a strategy of candor. They would introduce the Hiss Woodstock into evidence as if the defense, having produced the machine, had nothing to hide in connection with it.[50]

At the same time, defense lawyers began to shift the tactical emphasis away from the typewritten evidence to an effort at demonstrating that others at the State Department might have stolen the documents. When Robert von Mehren prepared to visit State to examine originals of the typed documents in June, McLean wrote him: "We want to prove two things: 1. That many of the documents were so widely distributed that anyone could have procured them. 2. That those documents which were not so widely distributed could also have been stolen or procured by someone else, presumably by Wadleigh." Despite the unfavorable typewriter evidence, McLean and Stryker still hoped to obtain an acquittal by demonstrating the easy accessibility of the stolen documents, their client's good character, and the contrasting poor character of his accuser.[51]

The defense's final pretrial effort to increase its knowledge of Whittaker Chambers came in mid-February, when McLean questioned him in a Baltimore deposition nominally requested for later use in the slander suit. Both Chambers and the government objected futilely to the two-day interrogation, which allowed the defense an opportunity almost unique in major criminal cases to probe for weak spots in the testimony to be given by the prosecution's star witness. On February 17 and 18 Chambers underwent exhaustive questioning in Baltimore by McLean (Marbury and Rosenwald were also on hand) while his own counsel, Richard Cleveland and William D. Macmillan, and Raymond Whearty of the Justice Department observed.[52]

Much of the interrogation covered familiar ground as McLean sought contradictions and inconsistencies in testimony already given by Chambers. McLean pressed Chambers for details on when and where he had received each of the documents, photostats of which he displayed to the witness. Chambers made no pretense of recalling the precise circumstances—time, words spoken, and other minutiae—in which he obtained each document, and the questioning soon

---

*Not only had the FBI laboratory experts confirmed the facts by May 1949, using for comparison five separate "standards" typed on Woodstock N230099 between 1931 and 1947, but unknown to the Hiss defense, a leading documents expert hired by *Time*, Ordway Hilton, had compared several of the FBI specimens—somehow obtained by HUAC investigators—with the Baltimore documents. Hilton reached the identical conclusion: They had all been typed on the same Woodstock.

dissolved into a sparring match between lawyer and witness. Chambers testified that he gave the material to Nathan Levine "probably, but not certainly, [in] May or June of 1938," a month or two after he defected, which meant that it might have been in other hands (such as Ludwig Lore's) briefly.

Probing repeatedly for Chambers's knowledge of the four handwritten notes, McLean elicited from the witness an estimate that Hiss had passed perhaps a dozen such notes to him in 1937 and early 1938 on confidential government documents. As for the typed material, Chambers reiterated that he had never seen Priscilla Hiss type the pages but had learned in conversation with the Hisses that she did the typing. The witness did not recall having seen a typewriter in the various Hiss households.

Chambers said he did not make handwritten corrections on the typed documents. After the typewritten materials he received from Hiss had been microfilmed, he simply destroyed them. Unlike the photographed State Department originals, the typed documents were never returned to Hiss. As for the documents he had saved, Chambers said that all of the microfilming would have been done by Felix Inslerman and that he had stopped collecting material shortly before his break, so that those typed documents he had received in March 1938 might not have been given to Inslerman but immediately hidden away.

What kind of typewriter had Chambers used in 1937? McLean asked. He said he had owned only a Remington portable. (All of Chambers's letters and articles that have surfaced from that period were typed on a Remington.) He had disposed of it in a strange manner, by leaving it "on a street car or subway . . . deliberately," claiming that it had reminded him too much of his earlier experiences as a Communist. Never, Chambers said, had he used a Woodstock typewriter.

As for the microfilm, the witness believed "that the photographer for the undeveloped film was probably [his underground associate] David Carpenter, and that the developed film [the two State Department rolls] was developed by Felix [Inslerman]." Chambers displayed a clear knowledge of the technical procedures used in film development. But he changed one important piece of earlier testimony, stating that he now believed the trade-agreement documents on the microfilm had come from Hiss and not Wadleigh, because "the film is completed with cables from Bullitt. Such cables would never have come from Wadleigh. They would have come from Alger Hiss."[53]

Before testifying in Baltimore, Chambers had taken one precaution unknown to the defense lawyers. On February 15, after concluding a long interview with the FBI in New York, Chambers gave one of the agents an envelope, asking that its contents be read after his departure. Inevitably, reports concerning the months of investigation by Hiss's lawyers and detectives about his alleged homosexuality had reached Chambers. Confronted by the prospect that Hiss's attorneys might question him on this point the following day, Chambers—taking a page out of Hiss's book of candor—decided to confess his past homosexual activities to the FBI first, apparently assuming that the entire matter would be aired thoroughly by the defense at the trial.

When the agent opened Chambers's letter, he found a handwritten statement and a covering note:[54]

> We have now reached a point in my testimony where I must testify to certain facts which should be told only to a priest. Therefore, to save embarrassment to myself, and possibly to others, I have attached a general statement of these facts which may be used as a basis for specific questions.
>
> As a special courtesy, I should like to have only one agent present during this interview. For some reason the presence of a second agent makes the ordeal more difficult.

The statement itself reviewed Whittaker Chambers's homosexual involvements. Chambers acknowledged having been a homosexual and explained his basic reason for disclosing the facts only at that point:

> Alger Hiss's defense obviously intends to press the charge that I have had homosexual relations with certain individuals. With the resumption of pretrial deposition, it is necessary to face this issue since my answer or refusal to answer certain questions must have a direct bearing on the case. I am for stating the facts.

He then narrated his version of past homosexual experiences: the intense psychological intimacy with Lewis Green during the 1920s and the procession of one-night stands in parks and cut-rate hotels during the 1930s. Chambers denied specifically any homosexual relations with Alger Hiss or with other underground associates, adding that he had "conquered" his "affliction" after breaking with the CP:

> This does not mean that I am completely immune to such stimuli. It does mean that my self-control is complete and that for years I have lived a blameless and devoted life as husband and father.
>
> The Hiss forces, of course, will seek to prove that my weakness entered into my relations with Alger Hiss and possibly others. This is completely untrue. At no time, did I have such relations, or even the thought of such relations with Hiss or with anybody else in the Communist Party or connected with Communist work of any kind. I kept my secret as jealously from my associates in the C.P. as I did from everyone else. I tell it now only because, in this case, I stand for truth. Having testified mercilessly against others, it has become my function to testify mercilessly against myself. I have said before that I am consciously destroying myself. This is not from love of self-destruction but because only if we are consciously prepared to destroy ourselves in the struggle can the thing we are fighting be destroyed.

Chambers had no way of knowing that Hiss's investigators had not been able to corroborate his past homosexuality sufficiently to raise the issue at the depositions or at the trial. Presumably it came as a surprise that McLean failed to interrogate him on the subject and only tangentially inquired about the possibility of alleged psychiatric problems.

But Chambers's reaction was minimal compared to the shock and consternation that spread among FBI and Justice Department officials, especially those investigating and prosecuting the Hiss case, when they learned that their star witness had confessed to many homosexual involvements during the same years he had been meeting with Hiss. When the FBI agents began questioning Chambers the following day, they demanded a complete personal history of his tormented bisexual existence.

THE FBI PROBE

Whittaker Chambers's admission of a homosexual past did not completely surprise FBI agents assigned to the Hiss investigation. They were acquainted with the many rumors floating in the defense camp, the earliest of them spread by Hiss himself. The bureau received reports in February from persons familiar with Chambers's earlier association with Lewis Green. Hoover directed his agents, once they finished interrogating Chambers, to begin inquiries among his associates "relative to their knowledge of Chambers particularly as to his credulity and moral character." Presumably the many rumors of homosexuality helped strengthen Chambers's resolve to confess to the bureau before submitting to questioning by Hiss's attorneys in Baltimore.[55]

Although Chambers's confession did not necessarily conflict with his earlier statements about Hiss, the FBI feared defense exploitation of the facts, should they become public knowledge. Hoover ordered agents in New York to pass the disquieting news "informally" to Thomas Donegan, then organizing the government's case against Hiss.

But Hoover delayed informing Attorney General Clark for two weeks, despite the FBI's interrogation of Chambers on February 17. The director also ordered an extensive investigation of persons known to have associated with Chambers, presumably to gather additional facts on the touchy question.[56]

During the pretrial period the FBI also investigated Timothy Hobson's background. Hoover wired the special agent in charge of the New York office in early June:

> A confidential source advised that according to an existing rumor, Alger Hiss plans on using as a defense in connection with his trial in answer to the question as to how Chambers happened to use the Hiss typewriter that Chambers, an admitted pervert, was in the Hiss household having relations with Hiss's stepson, Timothy Hobson. This source made the observation that Chambers

had admitted to him that he had been a pervert since he was 18 years of age. The informant also made the comment that this showed Hiss's character in that he was ready to sacrifice his stepson in order to defeat the charges of perjury which had been brought against him.[57]

The bureau knew that Hobson had been discharged from the Navy in 1945 on emotional grounds related to homosexuality. As FBI agents checked with Hobson's acquaintances and former Navy superiors, supposedly for specimens of his typing, they also gathered information on homosexuality. The agents seemed particularly interested in questioning former medical officers or psychiatrists whom Hobson had consulted and who could hardly have provided 1937–38 Woodstock specimens. According to Hobson, the bureau agents mentioned some of his homosexual friends while interviewing him, making it clear that the subject would surface at the trial if he should testify.[58]

Eventually the prosecutors decided to sit back, well prepared, and let the defense raise the Chambers homosexual issue if it dared. A New York agent wired Hoover in late April 1949 about discussions between prosecutors Donegan and Murphy on "the desirability of having Chambers sign the lengthy statement which has been in preparation for some months" concerning his underground activities. Both men believed that Chambers should not sign. The agent, apparently alluding to the homosexuality issue and perhaps to other information helpful to the defense, explained that "if Chambers did sign it, the fact of the signed statement's existence might be brought out during the course of the trial, and . . . there was a possibility that the judge might allow the defense attys to read this statement."

Donegan feared "complications"—that defense lawyers "might use some of the material therein to at least cloud the issue." He suggested, despite conflicts with standard FBI practice, that Chambers sign the statement after the trial. Unless Hoover directed to the contrary, the agent intended to comply with the prosecutor's request. Thus Chambers, the government's star witness, clearly remained a distasteful personality to Hoover and to the chief Justice Department officials involved. Hoover and other FBI officials, moreover, were convinced that Chambers was leaking data to Nixon and others on HUAC. The bureau remained extraordinarily defensive throughout this investigation, considering Hiss guilty (but with high-placed friends in the Truman administration) while viewing Chambers as a potential embarrassment even before his confession of homosexuality.[59]

One possible lead in the Hiss case that the FBI flubbed, despite its extensive probing, involved the apparently unrelated case of a Justice Department clerk named Judith Coplon. The FBI arrested Coplon and a Russian employed at the United

Nations, Valentin A. Gubitchev, on March 4, 1949, charging the pair with conspiracy to commit espionage.*

Judith Coplon began working for Justice in New York City in 1943 and transferred to Washington two years later to become a political analyst in the department's Foreign Agents Registration Section. In October 1948 she joined the Internal Security Section, assigned to examine all FBI reports dealing with Russian agents or domestic Communists. Coplon's superior, William E. Foley, head of both the Foreign Agents Registration and Internal Security sections, became suspicious when she began discussing reports concerning certain Russian agents and asked several times to see a particularly top secret report. Despite Coplon's protests, Foley assigned another employee to perform her duties. Her successor reported that Coplon visited her office and continued to look through the FBI reports, removing several of them. A few days later Coplon returned again and asked to see reports relating to foreign embassies, especially those marked "internal Security-R." She obtained about fifty such reports.[60]

The FBI began tailing Coplon in January 1949, following a trip to New York, where she met Gubitchev. On February 18, once more under FBI surveillance, Coplon passed some material from her purse to Gubitchev. Coplon told Foley on March 3 that she planned another trip to New York the following day. Apparently with the FBI's approval, Foley allowed Coplon to see specially prepared memos dealing with the Soviet government's trading company, Amtorg, reports marked "STRICTLY CONFIDENTIAL" and dealing with the firm's efforts to obtain atomic information. FBI agents observed Coplon and Gubitchev together on March 4 in New York City engaging in a series of apparent efforts to avoid detection—meeting, separating, and meeting again over a period of hours.

Finally, agents arrested the couple that evening, searched Coplon's purse, and discovered thirty "data slips"—"memoranda of information contained in FBI reports on file in the Department of Justice"—along with a four-page memo she had typed that included this paragraph:

> I have not been able (and don't think I will) to get the top secret FBI report which I described to Michael on Soviet & Communist Intelligence Activities in the US. . . . When I saw the report, for a minute, I breezed through it rapidly, remember very little. It was about 115 pages in length; summarized first Soviet "intelligence" activities, including Martens, Lore, Poyntz, Altschuler, Silvermaster et al. . . .

Also, Coplon was carrying a two-page handwritten memo in which she described the contents of Amtorg memoranda that Foley had shown her the previous day.[61]

---

*Coplon's activities for Soviet intelligence are discussed in Klehr et al., *Secret World of American Communism,* pp. 294–95. The VERONA files also contain a significant body of information dealing with the Coplon case.

Several data slips on FBI files in Coplon's handbag related to the Hiss investigation. Her interest in the data was difficult to explain except on the grounds that someone outside the government had asked her to search for information on one individual. They concerned only John Loomis Sherman, who then lived in California and had broken with the underground—but not with the CP—during the late 1930s. Sherman would not discuss his past with FBI agents when approached in 1946 and in January 1948. After Chambers named Sherman as a coconspirator in January 1949, the bureau renewed its interest and spent months trying to locate him. William Edward Crane had known Sherman well during the 1930s and described him to the FBI.

Although prosecutors in the Hiss case did not plan to subpoena Sherman, presumably because he appeared as hostile to the government as to the Russians, the FBI prepared summary reports on Chambers's testimony concerning the man. One of these reports on Sherman carried the date March 3, 1949, Judith Coplon's last day at work in Washington, and it was presumably this report to which one of her data slips referred when it was seized in her purse the following day. Some of the FBI data slips later found in her apartment also concerned Sherman. Since he was of interest to the bureau only in connection with the Hiss investigation then in progress, and since only a few trusted underground CP leaders would even have known of Sherman's existence by then, Coplon's possession of those slips may have related to worry in the Communist Party's secret ranks about Sherman turning informer as Chambers had done. Chambers told the bureau that Sherman met Hiss once; Sherman denied the claim in his testimony before HUAC, but if he had confirmed it, the case against Hiss would have been immeasurably strengthened.[62]

Her interest in Sherman helps explain another puzzling aspect of the material Coplon labored so hard to inspect in March 1949. Her typewritten memo on the top-secret FBI report on Soviet intelligence in the United States specifically mentions (among a very few names) two other figures then directly connected with the Hiss-Chambers case—and with no other matter conceivably related to current Communist underground work: Ludwig Lore, who had first told the FBI about Chambers, and Juliette Poyntz, the Communist agent whose kidnapping in New York in 1936 had so disturbed Chambers. Moreover, one of the FBI's wiretaps on Coplon also disclosed that on February 24, 1949, she engaged in another inquiry possibly linked to the Hiss investigation. The wiretap log reads:

4:03 PM. Coplon received call from Anderson at State Dep't. [Walter Anderson later testified as a government witness identifying departmental documents at the Hiss trial.] He stated that her request was very complicated and very sticky and he was unable to give her the information. Anderson said that if the original requestor would direct a written letter to Douglas Heck at State Dep't telling why and what information was wanted the information may be given out. Anderson said this was true only on this individual and could give out information on other persons. Coplon said we probably could ask the FBI to do it for us or they may already have information on him. Coplon said she would tell the fellow about the needed written request and leave it up to him.[63]

At her trial Coplon failed to explain to the jury's satisfaction her interest in the FBI material. She was found guilty, but an appeals court later overturned the conviction because the government had obtained evidence illegally.[64] Coplon had enjoyed normal access since 1945 to the Justice Department's copies of FBI files on internal-security investigations (the bureau began its probe of Alger Hiss in November 1945), but it is impossible to determine how many other FBI reports on suspected Communist agents alerted those under investigation because of her efforts during the four years prior to her arrest.

Several key witnesses misled the FBI in its Hiss-Chambers probe. The Catletts—Claudia, Raymond, and Perry—were only the most glaring examples. Josephine Herbst told FBI agents she knew nothing of espionage activities engaged in by her husband, Harold Ware, Chambers, or others in Washington in 1934. Yet she had given a full account of these activities earlier to Hiss's lawyers. Nor did she mention having been told by Ware, Herrmann, and Chambers about the latter meeting Hiss in mid-1934, important corroboration for Chambers's story of their relationship. Herbst sent John Herrmann a letter warning her former husband about the FBI's interest in him and describing the false story she gave the agents. When the bureau finally traced him to Mexico, Herrmann denied having known Chambers or having taken part in Communist underground work.[65]

Maxim Lieber refused to cooperate with the FBI, despite having provided Hiss's lawyers earlier with some information about past activities. Lieber, in some haste, took his family to Mexico: "The Party said, 'Get the hell out of here; get the hell out of here. Do you want to go to jail?' They were afraid that I was involved too much because of the Chambers thing. So I went to Mexico. . . . My files were destroyed when I went to Mexico by the Party." According to Lieber, FBI agents had intimidated his clients after the Hiss case broke, threatening that the writers would not be able to find publishers if they continued to use Lieber as an authors' representative. Lieber told the author that A. B. Magill, who provided information on Chambers to the Hiss defense, was the representative of the American Communist Party who helped him make contacts in Mexico with Eastern European embassies (Lieber and his family, after several years in Mexico, settled in Poland).[66]

The Justice Department had hoped for a change in heart from one important but uncooperative witness, J. Peters, then facing deportation. But the FBI's informants within the CP agreed that Peters would remain a loyal Communist and never cooperate with the government. So on April 13 Justice announced that a deportation order had been issued against Peters, a curious step considering the fact that he was a potentially significant witness—even if he remained silent—in several pending cases, including the perjury prosecution of Alger Hiss.*[67]

Throughout the pretrial investigation the FBI and its director fretted over press coverage. Even many Americans normally sympathetic toward the bureau wondered why it had failed to turn up evidence concerning Hiss's Communist ties years earlier. Chambers's decision to hand over one batch of stolen documents to Hiss's attorneys in November 1948 and another to HUAC the following month left the FBI looking foolish, and its failure to find the Woodstock typewriter before the defense—despite the Catletts' shaky testimony—made the bureau's strenuous investigation seem either haphazard or inept. In these circumstances, Hoover and his top aides monitored press coverage minutely and suspiciously.[68]

In the months preceding Hiss's trial more than three hundred agents worked on the probe, fanning out across the country. The mass of material they filed became sufficiently unwieldy by February for Hoover to complain: "I think we should have one overall memo which will include everything. It should be most carefully prepared & indexed." The report, written by agents in the New York office and ready by April 5, summarized "the available evidence to date," including information on potential government witnesses. Although the FBI did not scale down its investigation, the report became the basic source book—along with the grand jury minutes and HUAC testimony—from which prosecutors prepared their case.[†69]

The most embarrassing moment for Hoover came in May 1949, when he learned that defense lawyers had found the Woodstock. Once more the many men

---

*Even some of those who cooperated with the bureau were not useful for purposes of testifying at Hiss's trial. Thus William Edward Crane, closely questioned by FBI agents during this period, proved an invaluable background witness. He confirmed having worked with Boris Bykov and John Loomis Sherman. Yet Crane knew nothing "usable" about the government sources who furnished secret material and, like Wadleigh and Reno, could corroborate only Chambers's general account of Communist underground activity. He offered no confirmation of Alger Hiss's involvement in the ring. Crane's one attempt at specificity degenerated into a protean mass of hearsay:

That Chambers had mentioned some persons in the younger set at the State Department [notes one of Crane's FBI reports], including the names of Alger Hiss, Laurence Duggan, Dean Acheson, Adolpf [sic] Berle, and also the late Harry Dexter White. He [Crane] stated that these conversations may have been with Colonel Bykov, and it was his impression that material was to be expected from some of these people or that some of them were considered as possible sources of material.

Chambers did charge, later, that "some of them"—Hiss, White, and possibly Duggan—were CP agents. Ladd to Hoover, FBI Report, February 16, 1949, #2236.

†The bureau's mass of evidence created an inescapable impression that occasionally it had trouble separating fact from opinion. Thus Chambers was sometimes described in agents' reports (following Hoover) as a "pervert," and defense psychiatrist Dr. Carl Binger, whose few minor involvements in radical causes received inordinate investigation, was categorized this way in one "synopsis of fact": "Informant advises that Binger belongs to Freudian school of psychiatrists and thus is anti-God in his beliefs." FBI Report, June 13, 1949, #3362.

of the FBI had been trumped by a few investigators with limited resources. The bureau's discovery that Hiss's lawyers had located the machine came almost accidentally in the course of a routine questioning of Claudia Catlett on May 13 about other matters. This time Mrs. Catlett said "that the Hisses had made a gift of an old typewriter to her sons." The excited agents probed further, but her statements remained muddled. Mrs. Catlett said she remembered the machine only after meeting with Hiss's attorneys, and that her sons—when they brought it home— told her they "had found it in trash" (owners unknown), and in June 1936![70]

But Claudia Catlett's confused memory of the machine contained a hard grain of disconcerting fact for the agents: that Hiss's attorneys had shown her the Woodstock about three weeks before. The defense's recovery of the typewriter led Hoover to order the immediate and tough requestioning of Mrs. Catlett's sons, Raymond and Perry, both of whom began by denying any contacts with Hiss's attorneys or with Donald Hiss, only to change their statements at subsequent interviews. Through talks with the Catlett brothers and with others involved in the defense's hunt for the Woodstock—including Ira Lockey—the agents began to piece together the machine's history from the time it had left the Hisses' hands to the present.[71]

News that the recovered Woodstock bore the serial number N230099, indicating that it had been produced in the late summer or early fall of 1929, might have been expected to please the bureau since it had learned from its laboratory the previous December (only to discount the finding) that "the standard in the Laboratory's files which matches most closely the typewriting appearing on [the stolen documents] reflects that the Woodstock Typewriter Company made such type in 1929." But Hoover, irritated that agents had spent five months on a wild-goose chase in search of 1928 or earlier-model Woodstocks (mainly because of the interviews with Harry Martin and Thomas Grady), ordered a thorough and immediate postmortem "to determine [the] history" [of] this typewriter since its manufacture including sale, resale and repair."[72]

When the FBI first learned about Hiss's lawyers finding Woodstock N230099, it reacted in fear—fear that the defense might be trying to palm off a phony machine that had not been used to type the stolen documents.* Had the defense found the wrong Woodstock, whether deliberately or inadvertently? Special Agent Boardman of the Philadelphia field office thought so. He wired Hoover on May 17, noting about Woodstock N230099, "allegedly" owned at one time by the Hisses, "in the event this has not previously been considered, that the definite possibility exists this typewriter is not the one received by Priscilla Hiss from her

---

*Agents filed long reports attempting to justify their failure to locate the Woodstock. Several of these correctly pointed out that the Catletts had deliberately withheld information about the machine from the FBI until after it was found, and that even now the Catletts seemed to be less than candid about the matter, in order to protect their former employers.

father Thomas Fansler. The investigation to date has established that the Fansler-Martin partnership purchased a Woodstock typewriter in 1927." Boardman's memo reiterated the claims made by Martin and Grady about the 1927 purchase date and pointed out also that, although N230099 had been found through the Catlett family, Priscilla Hiss had claimed she disposed of her typewriter to a secondhand dealer. Boardman's analysis, in short, indicated the annoyance and suspiciousness with which FBI field agents involved in the search for the typewriter viewed this unexpected turn of events.[73]

Was the defense trying to gain vindication through a ruse? Even some leading bureau agents believed this was a definite possibility and outlined their fears in a May 24 memo to Assistant Director Ladd, pointing out that the Fansler-Martin partnership had kept no records, and those of the Woodstock Company concerning the sale of typewriters during that period had been destroyed. The earliest document definitely identified as having been composed on the "identical" machine that typed the Chambers documents was a December 6, 1931, letter by Daisy Fansler, Priscilla's sister, prepared after her father's retirement. That the Hisses acquired the typewriter in 1932 while they lived in New York seemed evident from the fact that the next available specimen identified was a January 30, 1933, letter by Hiss to an insurance company written from New York (and a companion letter written in February 1933 and signed by Hiss). The memo, by agent H. B. Fletcher, suggested possible defense complicity in "alter[ing] its characteristics" once the Woodstock had been found.

But Fletcher also reported one piece of good news—the discovery and identification of Stafford McQueen's 1947 government job-application form, done on N230099 in 1947, as typed on the same machine used to type the stolen documents. Because of this identification—and despite his mistrust of Hiss's lawyers—Fletcher concluded "that the defense attorneys have in fact recovered the typewriter which was originally in the possession of Alger and Priscilla Hiss."[74]

However, the FBI lab findings did not put to rest completely the bureau's fear that the Hiss defense had planted a phony machine, because they left unexplained the discrepancy of Harry Martin's and Thomas Grady's earlier testimony about a 1927 (or '28) typewriter. Hoover ordered agents to reinterview the two men immediately. Martin's memory about the machine's purchase appeared even less reliable than when FBI agents first saw him in December 1948, if that were possible. Now Martin linked a complimentary letter he had received from Fansler to the 1928 acquisition date. But when the FBI found the letter several months later, it turned out to have been written in July 1929.

And Martin stood firm in his belief that he bought the machine from Grady, who, he had told Schmahl the previous December, had left Philadelphia under a cloud—"gone out of business, apparently disappeared some time ago . . . with something of a bad reputation."

In his interviews with FBI and defense investigators Martin wavered between 1927 and 1928 purchase dates. But Thomas Grady entertained no doubts. Nor, without opening himself to a charge of larceny, could he have, since Grady had resigned as a Woodstock salesman in December 1927. On reinterview in 1949, Grady stuck to his memory of a 1927 sale date, despite the conflict between that date and the two circumstances to which he had tied the transaction in his earlier FBI interviews—the hiring of a new secretary (who actually started work in 1928) and the application of his commission to a new life-insurance policy (which he actually took out in 1930). The only new twist in Grady's June 7 statement was his suggestion that Fansler-Martin might have bought *his* Woodstock in 1927 and then traded it in for a second Woodstock—N230099—two years later. Martin, however, denied having made such a trade-in.[75]

Later that year both the FBI and a third defense examiner, Harry E. Cassidy, took samples from Woodstock N230099 and confirmed, after extensive testing, Fearon's earlier conclusion that the stolen State Department documents had been typed on that machine.* The Catletts had recognized the typewriter immediately when McLean produced it because of Woodstock N230099's distinctive damaged features. And the FBI laboratory had identified the typeface of the stolen documents and Hiss standards as most closely resembling a 1929 Woodstock, long before there was any controversy over dating the machine so exactly. Moreover, the numerous specimens of Fansler-Martin typing collected by the FBI showed that the firm did not use a Woodstock until mid-1929.[76]

What explains, then, the only two flaws in this overwhelmingly solid pattern of identification: Harry Martin's statements that the machine had been purchased (alternately) in 1927 or 1928, and Thomas Grady's insistence that he sold the typewriter to Martin in 1927? The recollections of both men on these dates proved understandably fallible after two decades, as seen in their numerous changes of testimony and conflicting statements to the FBI and to defense investigators. Did they both simply misremember the purchase date by a year?

At the time, Hiss, McLean, and the other defense lawyers never questioned the fact that Woodstock N230099 was the machine that had typed the stolen documents. Instead, they directed their attention toward demonstrating, through the Catletts' testimony, that the machine had left the Hisses' possession in late 1937 so that neither Alger nor Priscilla Hiss could have typed the stolen documents. Much later the Hiss defense would propose the theory that they had found—or been led to—the wrong Woodstock.

---

*Letters written on the machine over a sixteen-year period, 1931 to 1947, confirmed Woodstock N230099's chain of ownership: Fansler-Martin to Daisy Fansler, to Alger and Priscilla Hiss, to the Catletts, to Ira Lockey, and, finally, to Edward McLean in April 1949. See FBI Laboratory Report, October 27, 1949, and Edwin Fearon's defense reports for April 5 and 23, 1949.

But all theories that assume a conspiracy to frame Hiss using a substituted Woodstock N230099 run into problems. First, the prime candidates for the role of conspirators are Mike Catlett and Donald Hiss. Only they, among the many defense or government investigators, knew the location of the Hiss Woodstock from early February to mid-April 1949. Edward McLean heard the name Ira Lockey for the first time in mid-April, and the FBI learned about Lockey the following month. Thus, if Lockey had somehow participated in a plot to switch typewriters on the Hiss defense, he did so not at the behest of FBI agents, whom the Catletts had deceived, but at the urging of someone connected with Alger Hiss.

In December 1948, Hiss told the FBI and the grand jury that he had no "independent recollection" of how he had disposed of the machine. But Hiss had already informed John F. Davis that the typewriter had gone to the Catletts. Also, he had surreptitiously retrieved Cynthia Jones's Royal portable, although he gave his own attorneys and government agents the impression that the machine had never left his possession. Then, beginning in late January, the Catletts played their false part. McLean, Rosenwald, and Donald Hiss knew this and used the Catletts' information to begin their independent search for the machine. By mid-February Donald Hiss and Mike Catlett learned that Ira Lockey had the machine. They, in turn, withheld this information from McLean and the other Hiss lawyers for over two months, a cover-up within a cover-up.

Is the explanation of Woodstock N230099's 1929 origin, therefore, to be found in the realm of faulty memory, rather than in conspiracy? Both Harry Martin and Thomas Grady were proved wrong on a number of points related to dating the Woodstock's sale to Fansler-Martin: Grady on linking the event to Anne Coyle's presence and to purchasing an insurance policy from Martin; the latter on the question of when Fansler retired and took the machine home, as well as on other dates. Both men appear to have been wrong about a 1927 sale, if only because Martin's secretary, who worked for the firm until mid-1928, said she used only a Royal typewriter, a statement supported by the FBI laboratory analysis of many Fansler-Martin letters.

Had Martin, the firm's junior partner, purchased a machine with Grady serving as a middleman who arranged the sale through his former associates at Woodstock? Grady certainly had no wish to admit such a transaction years later, yet Martin described Grady's reputation, both to the Hiss attorneys and to the FBI, as poor. Or had Fansler-Martin exchanged its earlier Woodstock for another machine from the same company in 1929, as Grady suspected? The "second Woodstock" theory—a machine sold perhaps to Thomas Fansler without his partner's knowledge and taken home by Fansler upon his retirement—is wispy, and no evidence supports it.

Another possibility remains: that Woodstock N230099 was indeed the wrong machine, given to Ira Lockey along with hush money in exchange for Lockey's machine (the "real Hiss machine," perhaps a 1928 model) and for Lockey's silence. But it is not likely that three separate defense documents examiners, the FBI laboratory experts, and the documents authority hired by *Time*—all of whom concluded independently that various standards of typing done on the Hiss Woodstock between 1931 and 1947 matched the typing on the stolen documents—were all wrong.

The crucial identification came from comparison of the standards of Hiss typing during the 1930s with Chambers's documents, not from Woodstock N230099. Moreover, Hiss understood the dangers of allowing the government to retrieve the real Woodstock. For over five months, from December 1948 to April 1949, aided by his brother and by the Catletts, he tried to keep the FBI from finding his old typewriter. Any problems that remain regarding the genuineness of the machine found by McLean are directly linked, therefore, not to the FBI's unsuccessful pursuit of that machine, but to Hiss's calculated cover-up.

In this situation J. Edgar Hoover did what came naturally: He looked for scapegoats. He was particularly furious at the Catletts for having lied to the bureau. Hoover exploded when he learned that one of those approached by Mike Catlett during his search for the Woodstock, a Mrs. Booth, signed a statement asserting that Mike had come to her apartment late at night "stating that he was working for the FBI, and advising her not to mention [the] visit to anyone." Hoover scrawled on the memo: "If possible I would like to see prosecution for impersonation here."[77]

Of more immediate concern than the Catletts at this time, both to the FBI and to Hiss's prosecutors, was the possibility that defense documents examiners might give trial testimony contradicting the findings of the FBI laboratory. The clearest evidence that the government knew nothing about the unfavorable findings of Haring and Fearon comes from a request made by Donegan and Murphy that the bureau obtain copies of the two defense experts' tax returns for the past five years. The prosecutors had learned about Fearon and Haring because both men had examined government documents in the case at the request of defense attorneys. "Tax returns desired for possible impeachment use," the New York field office wired Hoover. Separately, on May 17, the prosecutors requested "any readily available information re Fearon has been proved wrong in any of his expert appearances."[78]

In requesting the tax returns of possible defense witnesses, the prosecutors exceeded the bounds of propriety and legality. But their other request, for a general check on Fearon's professional reputation, was logical and legitimate. After searching the files, Hoover's agent wired back that FBI data on Fearon "was favorable as to his reputation and professional standing." Still, the prosecutors appeared to be in luck: "His appearance as a witness is poor," Hoover noted; "his voice is rather squeaky and uninteresting and he rambles on in incoherent style." As it turned out, the FBI check proved unnecessary, since Fearon declined to appear as a defense witness because of his findings.[79]

Donegan also inquired, on May 24, whether the bureau believed it "desirable to obtain from Hiss's attorneys samples of typewriting" taken from Woodstock N230099. "Mr. Donegan indicated he did not desire to do it but he would if the Bureau believed it necessary." Although later that year the FBI obtained such samples, Ladd directed that Donegan be told that the FBI laboratory had just identified a 1947 letter [the Stafford McQueen application] as having been typed on the same machine as the Chambers documents. In view of this new identification, "the Bureau has no suggestion to offer and would leave it to the judgment of Mr. Donegan as to whether or not specimens should be obtained at this time from the typewriter." Donegan, as uncertain as Ladd about the genuineness of the machine recovered by the defense, exercised caution. He decided not to request typing samples.[80]

But Hoover remained obsessed with criticisms, real or imagined, concerning the failure of the FBI's search for the Hiss Woodstock, especially when the speaker happened to be the government's prosecutor in the case. Thus when Hiss's trial finally got under way in June, the director complained to subordinates that Thomas F. Murphy "in his opening statements . . . reflected rather unfavorably upon the Bureau, particularly in pointing out that a large squad of Bureau Agents had unsuccessfully looked for the Hiss typewriter." Refracted through Hoover's mental prism, the prosecutor's statement of fact became a declaration of enmity. He instructed his underlings to determine whether Murphy's past record indicated that he "has been unfriendly to the Bureau." Apparently Ladd handled the delicate assignment of checking on a government prosecutor's past in the midst of a major trial, only to assure Hoover that Murphy was "clean" and bore no apparent ill will toward the FBI.[81]

Nor were the prosecutors any happier than Hoover about the defense having located the Woodstock. This development raised the specter that Hiss's attorneys would attempt to prove that their machine could not have typed the stolen documents. Donegan and Murphy had no intention of assisting the defense by introducing Harry Martin or Thomas Grady as a witness to a 1927 or 1928 purchase date, any more than Lloyd Paul Stryker planned to allow his documents examiners, Haring and Fearon, to testify. Thus on both sides the typewriter evidence proved embarrassing in at least some respects. When the trial opened on May 31, neither the government nor the Hiss defense wished to tell all that it knew about the search for Woodstock N230099.

XII

DEADLOCK: THE FIRST TRIAL

Alger Hiss received a fair but not a speedy first trial. Five and a half months elapsed between his indictment and the start *of U.S. v. Hiss* on May 31 at the Federal Courthouse in Manhattan's Foley Square. Directly below, on the first floor, Judge Harold Medina (father of the lawyer assigned to Chambers by *Time*) presided over the trial of eleven Communist Party leaders charged with conspiracy to advocate the overthrow of the U.S. government.[1]

The defendant entered the courtroom impeccably dressed (according to *Time* correspondent James Bell) in a "light grey herringbone suit, soft shirt, brown shoes, plain blue tie and narrow brimmed brown hat," with Priscilla Hiss at his side: "a plain woman with short grey hair, taut lips and an upturned nose." Alger Hiss's fingernails, according to Bell, "were filed down near the quick. His face was youthful, unlined. He looked less than his 44 years. Mrs. Hiss looked more like his older sister than she did his wife. He sported a new haircut."[2]

Under Judge Samuel H. Kaufman's direction, jury selection moved rapidly, almost amicably, and was completed by early afternoon. Questioning dealt mainly with two sets of concerns: whether prospective jurors had any links, personally or through relatives, to *Time* or to the government, and whether they considered themselves prejudiced against testimony by Communists, ex-Communists, or those accused of Communist ties. The twelve jurors empaneled included two women and a plethora of middle-level businessmen plus two female alternates. An auto-company credit manager, Hubert E. James, served as foreman. None of the twelve jurors had displayed discernible political views during questioning by Kaufman, although they seemed to represent a cross section of middle-class white America.[3]

The following morning Assistant U.S. Attorney Thomas Murphy, a strapping, round-faced six-footer with a walrus mustache and straight muscular torso (the picture of "a conscientious British guards officer," thought Alistair Cooke), began his crisp and unhistrionic opening statement while standing almost at attention at a lectern facing the jury box. He plunged immediately into the issue at hand: "The Government charges that this defendant lied when he testified before the grand jury on December 15, 1948 . . . that he lied twice. . . . He lied the first time when he said that he never gave any documents to Whittaker Chambers, State Department documents . . . this defendant [also] lied . . . when he said that he never saw or conversed with Whittaker Chambers after January 1, 1937," Hiss had lied "deliberately" on both counts, Murphy charged, laying out in summary the case to be presented by the prosecution.[4]

"How are we going to prove that?" asked the prosecutor. Chambers's testimony and the stolen documents themselves were the heart of the government's case: "We are not going to give you photographs of the man lying. We are going to prove it the same way as you would prove it in your family life or business." Hiss, Murphy said, handed over secret documents to Chambers "in wholesale fashion. . . . The documents were all secret. In fact, one of them is secret to such an extent that we are going to have the Judge not to permit you to see it. We are going to show you all of the others."

In reviewing the history of Chambers's statements concerning his dealings with Hiss and the facts about how the stolen documents had come to light the previous year during Hiss's slander suit, Murphy described the defendant's statements about the Fansler typewriter and the FBI's search for the machine, in that tone which Hoover found so objectionable: The bureau "shook down the City of Washington to a fare-thee-well. Approximately 25 to 30 agents scoured the City but could not find it." But Murphy pointed out that the FBI had found specimens of Hiss typing for comparison with the stolen documents. With Chambers's testimony about receiving the documents, plus proof that they were typed on a machine in Hiss's "possession or control," plus proof that the material (some of it from Hiss's office) came from State, "I daresay that you will be convinced that Hiss lied in the grand jury."

FBI experts would testify not only about typewriter specimens but about the four manuscript notes written by Hiss: "[W]e will corroborate Chambers's testimony by the typewriting and by the handwriting." But also they would hear Chambers's "complete story . . . to really test his credibility." Murphy reminded the jury that, because of Chambers's HUAC testimony, the Hiss defense had come thoroughly prepared and fully familiar "almost to the nth degree" with what Chambers would say in court. He stressed his chief witness's reliability as much as the documents themselves: "I want you to examine Chambers. I want you to listen attentively; watch his conduct on the stand . . . because if you don't believe Chambers then we have no case under the federal perjury rule . . . where you need one witness plus corroboration, and if one of the props goes, out goes the case." He warned the jury to be alert for Stryker's "searching cross-examination," which the prosecution "actually welcomes." Afterward, "examine what motive he would have for lying, and I daresay you will be convinced as I am that he is telling the truth and that what Mr. Hiss told the grand jury were lies."

Standing in front of the box and staring directly at the jurors, Stryker spoke without notes for an hour. He began quietly, expressing pleasure that his client had finally reached "a dignified, calm and quiet and fair court of justice" so that "the days of the Klieg lights, the television, and all the paraphernalia, the propaganda which surrounded the beginning of this story are over." Murphy had stated "quite fairly" the trial's central issue: "Did Hiss testify truthfully that he did not give or hand restricted documents to Chambers?" Both perjury counts boiled down to that question about the relationship between the two men in 1937–38, at the time the documents were allegedly passed.[5]

How could the jury decide that question fairly? "Mr. Murphy has also told you that if you do not believe Chambers the Government has no case. So . . . what you here are going to determine is whether or not you believe Chambers." Stryker then began developing the central theme of his opening argument: the contrast in "character" between the accuser and the accused. He began with Hiss. "Who is he? What is he? What is his life? What has he done?" He reviewed Hiss's record of achievements—Johns Hopkins to Harvard Law, the Holmes clerkship to the New Deal posts—dwelling on the defendant's reputation for reliability and truthfulness: "[E]veryone had believed him; everyone had trusted him." In the State Department—at Yalta, the UN Conference, and afterward—Stryker pointed out that "his integrity, his honor and his veracity" were never questioned. Nor were they questioned by the Carnegie Endowment trustees. "I will take Alger Hiss by the hand, and I will lead him before you from the date of his birth to this hour even," Stryker said, "though I would go into the valley of the shadow of death I will fear no evil, because there is no blot or blemish on him."

Abruptly Stryker shifted from eulogizing Hiss to excoriating Chambers: "Now who is the accuser? He is a man who now styles himself as J. Whittaker Chambers. He began changing his names early. I think the name given him was J. Vivian Chambers. . . . Now who and what is this man, this accuser of ours? Who is he? What is he?"

Stryker turned to Chambers's early membership in the Communist Party and denounced the CP as an organization "that believed that wrong was right . . . that it [was] right to commit any crime, and here I see you will be interested, especially lying—lying." The defense counsel called the roll of the many aliases Chambers had used. The accuser, cried Stryker, his voice rising with emotion, "was a member of this low-down, nefarious, filthy conspiracy . . . [for] twelve long years . . . a voluntary conspirator against the land that I love and you love. He got his bread from the band of criminals with whom he confederated and conspired."

Above all else, Stryker insisted, Chambers had been a criminal for years: lying, filing no tax returns, and "how many crimes he committed during that period I don't know." Not only a criminal but an atheist, although Chambers's "criminal propensities," Stryker quickly pointed out, had been developed before he became a Communist. Even before then "he had been a confirmed liar . . . [and] a blasphemer . . . [having] written a filthy, despicable play about Jesus Christ when he was in Columbia." In short, Chambers's life had been characterized by "atheism, destruction of religion, lies, stealing." This was the man who, "out of the blue" in August 1948, had accused Alger Hiss: "Whittaker Chambers, a Communist, conspirator, and thug."

After outlining contradictions between Chambers's HUAC testimony about Hiss and his later claim that Hiss had committed espionage, Stryker shifted suddenly to his client again. What was Hiss's reaction to Chambers's charges? "It was the conduct of an honest man and a straightforward man. . . . Now, did he skulk?. . . . He telegraphed the chairman of that Committee. . . . And he went and he testified and he denied the charge. He went even without taking the time and without any thought of a lawyer; it was the instantaneous and spontaneous reaction of an honest man."

Pointing out that Hiss had defended his integrity by filing suit for slander, Stryker reviewed the history of how Chambers turned over the documents in November 1948, reminding the jurors that before then Chambers had denied involvement in espionage "sixteen times" to HUAC, the grand jury, and Hiss's lawyers. It was at Hiss's insistence, Stryker noted, that the Baltimore documents were brought to the government's attention: "Is that the conduct of a guilty man?" Hiss's lawyers, not the FBI, found the typewriter. Yet "we will consent . . . to let these FBI eyes who could not find it come down and look at it all they want. Now, I ask you again, is that the conduct of a guilty man?"

When the two men met, Stryker reminded the jurors, Hiss found Chambers "a glib and interesting talker . . . another Jack London." He agreed that the accuser was not only that but also "a very able man . . . a writer, a dramatic writer. No one was there to warn him about this man, as I now am warning you. In the warm southern countries, you know, where they have leprosy, sometimes you will hear on the streets perhaps among the lepers a man crying down the street, 'Unclean, unclean' at the approach of a leper. I say the same to you at the approach of this moral leper."

Surprisingly, neither Murphy nor Kaufman interrupted Stryker with objections either to his perfervid language or to the manner in which he strayed from "opening" to closing argument. "Jurors, spectators and some newsmen expected some sort of monster to crawl to the witness stand," Jim Bell informed his editor. "[Stryker] had keyed the jury to expect a witness whom you couldn't believe even if God were holding his right hand."[6]

Whittaker Chambers entered the courtroom, neatly dressed and displaying no emotion. Through most of Murphy's questioning the witness remained expressionless, his hands clasped and held closely to his lap, his eyes often staring impassively at the ceiling as the words flowed out. Murphy stood a long distance away from Chambers, close to the jury box, and both he and his witness spoke in flat, precise tones. Chambers's voice often became inaudible.

Murphy's opening questions elicited the first of two extraordinary autobiographical narrations—Hiss's being the other—that formed the heart of the trial.

Murphy took Chambers through the bare details of his childhood in Lynbrook and subsequent college years at Columbia. Chambers described "drifting" for several years in Europe and in the States. When Stryker objected to this recital (and was sustained by Kaufman), Murphy defended the elaboration of Chambers's youth as relevant in view of the defense attorney's announced intention of "baring" Chambers's life, "starting with this man's birth . . . and continuing right down to the present . . . for the purpose of affecting his credibility." Clearly, Murphy hoped to preempt the Hiss defense by having Chambers himself admit the worst of his experiences prior to defecting from Communism.[7]

Even at that point, parts of Chambers's testimony were in error. He recalled joining the CP in January 1924 (it was actually a year later), and he blurred over his various early links to organized religion—Quakerism, in particular—with the half-truth: "I had had no religious upbringing." Presumably hoping to throw the witness off balance, Stryker regularly raised objections, but he succeeded only in nettling Murphy.

After Kaufman recessed the trial until the following day and dismissed the jury, Murphy urged the judge to allow Chambers to continue portraying his experiences as a Communist prior to meeting Hiss and thereafter up to his defection. Only that way, the prosecutor argued, could Chambers's credibility, "of prime importance in this case," be fairly tested. But Kaufman ruled that such testimony seemed inadmissible and would "confuse the issue in this case, which is a very simple one . . . you are concerned not with the charge of espionage but with the charge of perjury. That is the only thing we are concerned with here." Murphy disagreed vehemently: "I think it is so inextricably united that you could never separate [the two charges] at all. Doesn't it come down, your Honor, to a rather simple rule of law, and that is whether in proving one crime and you thereby happen to prove a dozen others, that that is just unfortunate?"

When Stryker supported the judge's position, he drew both Kaufman's and Murphy's wrath by suggesting that the prosecutor wished to introduce testimony about Chambers's CP background "just because the Government thinks it is fun to put it in." Stryker apologized, then reversed himself, acknowledging that he thought Murphy had "a right to introduce his witness as a Communist and a reasonable amount of that." Kaufman took the issue under advisement.

The defense attorney asked Kaufman for permission to bring a psychiatrist into court the following day to observe Chambers from the audience. Murphy protested, but the judge decided to allow it. At that point Stryker asked approval for telling the press about the psychiatrist, possibly to convey to the public, and perhaps to the jury, that the defense believed Chambers mentally unstable, but Kaufman rejected that request.

The following morning, in chambers, Murphy brought to the attention of Kaufman and Stryker an FBI communication he had received a few hours earlier. The bureau reported an incident that occurred the previous evening at a New

Jersey convalescent home. An informant had been visiting a patient at the home, and several other people joined their discussion, including a "Mrs. James [who] said she was the wife of the foreman of the jury that was trying Alger Hiss and that he was sympathetic for the defendant Alger Hiss and that he would use his influence to convey that sympathy to the other jurors." Since neither Murphy nor the FBI had yet checked out the report, the prosecutor raised the matter tentatively, cautioning the judge that "if we find there is such a person and she is the wife of the foreman I think we have a very delicate situation. I do not know just how to handle it." Both Murphy and Stryker agreed with Kaufman's description of James as being a very able, level-headed gentleman. Murphy suggested investigating the report further. Both Stryker and Kaufman agreed.*[8]

Soon after Chambers's testimony resumed, now dealing with his CP underground years, a tall, bald-headed man entered the courtroom and sat directly behind the defense lawyers' table. Stryker turned to greet the new arrival, and Murphy asked: "May I have this gentleman identified for the record? I don't think I met him." Stryker explained: "This is the gentleman whom I mentioned to your Honor at the bench with Mr. Murphy." Kaufman: "Do you know who he is now, Mr. Murphy?" "Yes, sir." Kaufman: "We will not go any further on that subject. Proceed."

Dr. Carl Binger's entrance had been carefully staged by Stryker and drew the attention of everyone in the courtroom. Binger slipped on a pair of thick glasses, opened a stenographer's pad, and began staring intently at Chambers, often pausing to make notations. The press—and presumably the jury—soon learned that the man was a psychiatrist, Hiss's chief expert on the matter of Whittaker Chambers's purported mental instability.[9]

After Chambers testified that Hiss began passing to him confidential State Department documents at approximately ten-day intervals "in February of 1937," he reviewed the procedures used for microfilming and returning the

---

*Foreman Hubert James later voted to acquit Hiss. What neither Murphy nor Kaufman knew was that James was related by marriage to a man who would soon become an adviser to Hiss: New York prison reformer Austin MacCormick, a New Deal acquaintance of the defendant, counseled Hiss in 1951 on appropriate behavior during his forthcoming period in jail. "Austin MacCormick's brother-in-law was foreman of the jury," Claude Cross, Hiss's second-trial lawyer, told me in 1974 during an interview shortly before Cross's death, "and he kept that jury hung." Cross continued: "Austin MacCormick was head of corrections in New York City. He was very much mixed up [in the case] at the time. . . . Someone told me at the second trial that [James, the first-trial foreman] was an executive in some big corporation, and he stood on his own feet and held out for an acquittal." John Chabot Smith, who was also present at the interview with Cross, then asked: "Do you know whether Stryker was surprised with the hung jury?" Cross replied only: "I didn't know it was Austin MacCormick until afterwards." Knowledge by Kaufman and Murphy of the relationship between James and MacCormick might have resulted in a mistrial. Interview, Claude B. Cross, July 15, 1974. The following 1949 FBI reports describe the bureau's investigation of the charges against James: July 11, 1949, #3662; July 12, 1949, #3641; June 2, 1949, #3226; and two reports for June 3, 1948, #3228 and #3330.

material. The witness mentioned his own role and that of his underground photographers, Inslerman and Crane. He described Bykov's proposal that Hiss bring home files nightly for typing in his home so that the documents could be delivered to Chambers along with original files on the days he picked up Hiss's cache. Both the originals and the typed copies would be photographed before delivery to Bykov.

Until Chambers began talking about his break with Communism, Stryker allowed him to proceed almost uninterrupted. But when Murphy asked the witness to tell "the facts . . . that caused you to break in April 1938," Stryker objected on grounds that such testimony was both immaterial and irrelevant. Kaufman sustained the objection, ordering Chambers to give, in Murphy's words, "just the bald statement that he broke." He spoke about retaining the "life preservers"—typed documents, microfilm, and handwritten notes, some of which came from Hiss—and told how he sequestered the material with Nathan Levine in May 1938.

After identifying the stolen documents themselves, Chambers again said Hiss had given him all of the material at the latter's Volta Place home. His last encounter with Hiss was the Christmas 1938 visit to Volta Place, at which he urged Hiss to break with the CP. Murphy tried unsuccessfully to introduce testimony concerning Chambers's reasons for not mentioning espionage or documentary evidence prior to November 1948, but Kaufman again sustained objections. The prosecutor did manage to ask Chambers if he had told Adolf Berle about Alger Hiss in 1939. "I named him as a member of the Communist Party." "And did you name others?" "Yes, I did." Abruptly, and presumably to Stryker's surprise, Murphy concluded his questioning.

Stryker waded in: "Mr. Chambers, do you know what an oath is?" "I suppose I do." ". . . Well, what is your definition of an oath?" "I would say that an oath is that declaration which a man makes when he promises to tell the truth." "And in our country," Stryker persisted, "in our courts, and elsewhere, it is an affirmation made by a man who calls on Almighty God to witness the truth of what he says, is that right?" "That is right."

Producing a photostat of Chambers's application for employment on the National Research Project, Stryker commented:

> STRYKER: Then we have your answer that in . . . October 1937, you were an underhanded enemy of your country, doing what you could against its interests in favor of a foreign country, is that right?
>
> MURPHY: I object to the form of the question.
>
> KAUFMAN: I will allow it. . . . This is cross examination.

Chambers acknowledged that in October 1937 he had been everything Stryker charged and that—"of course" he had sworn falsely while applying for the job. But Stryker pursued his point that the witness had perjured himself "in order to deceive and cheat the United States Government into giving you a job."

The defense lawyer peppered Chambers with questions designed to illustrate his view of the witness's defective character. He asked about *A Play for Puppets,* Chambers's Columbia *cause célèbre,* dubbed by Stryker "an offensive treatment of Christ." Next came Chambers's 1924 letter to Mark Van Doren in which he told about gaining Dean Hawkes's permission to reenter Columbia by lying and telling the dean he wanted to teach history. Stryker had Chambers read aloud the passage and observed: "In other words, lying came easy to you, Mr. Chambers?" "I don't believe so," came the response.

The next day, Stryker began with a series of questions about the aims and practices of the Communist Party. Chambers acknowledged that the CP demanded absolute obedience from its members, that it "may order [them] to lie, to steal, to rob, and to go out into the streets and fight," and that "every Communist during your time was a potential spy and saboteur and was actually an enemy of our system of government." Disloyalty to the American government, Chambers agreed, was "a matter of principle" with Communists, including himself while he remained a member of the party. "And for some fourteen years," Stryker asked, "you were an enemy and traitor of the United States of America?" "That is right," Chambers responded.

Piety, or the lack of it, became the next element to be explored. Chambers admitted having held "anti-religious" views even before joining the CP. To pin that down, Stryker had the witness read portions of the 1922 *Play for Puppets.* Having established Chambers's youthful atheism, Stryker asked if he lived in a New Orleans "dive" at one time with a prostitute named "One-Eyed Annie." Chambers's denial provoked Stryker's next query: "Did there come a time when you lived with a prostitute named Ida Dales?" "Ida Dales was not a prostitute," Chambers rejoined, while agreeing that during the late twenties he had lived with Dales for about a year, part of that time at his mother's home—"at my mother's suggestion" because, after Richard's suicide, Laha "did not want to lose another" son.

Once Stryker had drawn Chambers's acknowledgment that he had refused his brother's request to enter into a suicide pact, there followed this exchange about Ida Dales's residence in Lynbrook:

> STRYKER: Lest I leave any unjust aspersion on anyone, your mother is a respectable and decent woman, is that not true?
> CHAMBERS: I need scarcely answer that.
> STRYXER: I am glad to state it for you.
> KAUFMAN: Please, Mr. Stryker.
> STRYKER: All right. Tell me . . . do you not think it was a lowdown, scoundrel thing for you to bring a woman not your wife in and foist her in your mother's home?

After Kaufman sustained Murphy's objection, Stryker returned to the theme of Chambers as a Communist conspirator and "if not an actual perjurer a potential perjurer during more than half of your [adult] life." But, Stryker noted wryly, Chambers "repented and reformed and became a God-fearing citizen. . . . What month?" Chambers preferred not to set a precise date on this process, but finally cited April 1938, the month he broke with the CP. "Has it been completed now, do you think?" "Well, it never stopped, it never is in any man's life, is it?"

But Stryker lingered on the subject of repentance and reformation: "There came a time then in April . . . 1938 when you became an honest man who no longer believed in lying, cheating or stealing, is that right?" Chambers agreed. "So, you became a God-fearing Christian, is that right?" "That is right." Kaufman rebuked Stryker for arguing with the witness at one point after the lawyer had snapped angrily at Chambers: "Find me rather amusing?"

When Chambers was questioned about the 1939 conference with Adolf Berle, he admitted not mentioning either Colonel Bykov or the fact of Alger Hiss having turned over secret State Department papers. Stryker's underlying purpose was to show that Chambers had continued to lie about his Communist past even to HUAC as late as August 1948. The witness said that he had "suppressed facts" before the committee, but noted that he had "told various parts of the [complete] story to various people" over the preceding decade.

He had not mentioned spying to the FBI in his pre-1948 interviews, however, or to Raymond Murphy of the State Department in 1945 and 1946. More important still, Chambers said he had lied to the grand jury in October 1948 about this question and agreed with Stryker that he had "testified falsely and committed perjury before the grand jury in this building."

Before Chambers returned to the stand on Monday, June 6, the attorneys argued in Kaufman's chambers over crucial points: Foreman Hubert James's reportedly prejudicial statements favorable to Hiss; news stories leaked by HUAC about executive-session testimony derogatory to Hiss; other weekend news accounts that alleged Judge Kaufman was biased in favor of Hiss; and, finally, Dr. Binger's continued courtroom presence. Murphy produced an FBI memorandum dealing with a witness to the conversation with Hubert James's wife, who claimed that she had said "in substance that if they knew his sympathies they would not have picked him [as a juror]. If it was up to him, Hiss will get away with it."[10]

Kaufman minimized the report, remarking curiously that it "sounds like the story of a disappointed wife." Murphy, continuing the spousal theme, argued that "a juror should be like Caesar's wife, above suspicion." He urged Kaufman to question James privately. The judge declined, insisting that James's wife's remarks were only "her version of his sympathy," whereas Murphy argued that "it is probably more than her version, because she might be expressing what he had previously told her." Kaufman dismissed this as sheer speculation on the prosecutor's part, but offered a mistrial. Murphy turned it down categorically: "The Government is not moving for a mistrial in words, substance, effect, or inference." Nor would Murphy move that the juror be disqualified, only that the matter be probed further by Kaufman.

After urging retention of James, Stryker suggested that Murphy and Donegan had played a role in planting "adverse" news stories about Hiss. Murphy reminded Kaufman he had originally urged that the judge instruct the jurors to avoid newspaper or radio accounts of the trial, and he denounced as "vicious" some news reports stating "that the Government still might indict Chambers for perjury."

Kaufman appreciated the nonjudicial aspects of the case. He complained about reports in a weekend paper suggesting that he could not conduct a fair trial, "that I had been put on this case because I am a New Dealer and because Hiss was one of the New Dealers." Stryker expressed sympathy, but, like Murphy, opposed any move for a mistrial.

As for Dr. Binger's role, his public display of "psyching out" Chambers disturbed Murphy: "I think it has reached almost Hollywood proportions now with that doctor sitting right there in the courtroom, and I think it is an insult to every lawyer and the Court. Furthermore it intimidates the witness, and it is an inference before the jury that perhaps there was something mentally wrong with this witness which is not observable to anybody else." Kaufman demurred, citing a memorandum of law by Stryker in support of his position. Binger could not be barred from the courtroom despite the defense's intention to summon him as a witness. (Priscilla Hiss was the only other defense witness allowed to remain in court other than the defendant.) The judge's rationale: "Defense Counsel states he [Binger] is necessary to help him in connection with this examination of his of Mr. Chambers."

Proceedings had been moved to a smaller thirteenth-floor courtroom on June 6, and Chambers's testimony resumed against the backdrop of a massive demonstration in Foley Square protesting the trial of CP leaders. Stryker pointed out continuously that Bykov, espionage, and documents had not figured in Chambers's August discussions with HUAC. "I intended to suppress the fact of espionage," Chambers reiterated. "You became quite a prominent personage?" snapped back Stryker. "Unfortunately," replied Chambers. Kaufman had to caution Stryker several times to stop arguing with the witness. Chambers agreed he had committed perjury in omitting mention of espionage to the committee. Stryker shifted to the matter of Hiss's alleged $400 loan to Chambers in 1937 to buy a car, confronting the witness with Esther's testimony at the Baltimore deposition that (although she had no personal knowledge of this) the funds had probably come from Chambers's mother, but Chambers stuck to his story.

That day Stryker's cross-examination lacked the moral outrage that had pervaded Friday's questioning. At moments he appeared to be lost in the details of the case. Sometimes he asked associates at the defense table—and, once, even a juror—to help him catch Chambers in contradictions. Keeping on the attack, however, Stryker ridiculed the witness's testimony about his postdefection experiences: Chambers's fear of being "ambushed," by which Chambers meant "kidnapped or assassinated"; his claim to have spent a year beginning in April 1938 living secretively with a gun always in easy reach; Chambers's failure to use a pseudonym during this period of hiding; and his trips to New York to see publishers. ("Did you go up in an armored car?" "Must I answer such a question?" Chambers asked Kaufman. "Answer the question." "'No, I did not come up in an armored car. . . . The facts that you are presenting are a little absurd.") Clarifying the general subject, Chambers said: "I did not hide in any secretive place [in 1938, but] I was extremely careful in my movements."

On June 7 Kaufman opened the proceedings by announcing his determination that Chambers's grand jury testimony of October 14–15 (containing denials of espionage) had been "inconsistent" with his trial testimony and that all the material be released to the defense because of "19 very substantial discrepancies." But Kaufman found only "minor discrepancies" in Chambers's grand jury testimony in December 1948, and he ordered only portions of those pages turned over to Stryker. Murphy felt that Kaufman had exercised undue discretion in releasing the material before Stryker had laid a proper foundation in questioning Chambers: "I think you are wrong on the law," complained the prosecutor, "but . . . I have no remedy."[11]

Then Chambers admitted to Stryker that his initial HUAC testimony had come in the midst of the 1948 presidential campaign (a stab by Stryker at applying Rosenwald's theory of "conscious motivation"), and that in his opening statement to the committee he had linked Hiss to the record of Democratic foreign-policy making—"coupled . . . in the same paragraph with your statement that Mr. Hiss you said was a member of some Communist group." What was Chambers's "purpose in joining those two statements together?" Stryker wished to know. "For the [sole] purpose of identifying Mr. Hiss, I suppose," the witness stated unconvincingly, and in such a soft voice that Stryker asked him to repeat the answer. Hadn't Chambers been trying to be helpful to the Republicans by linking Hiss to Yalta, a 1948 campaign issue? He denied this.

Visibly angry, Stryker returned to the querulous tone of his earliest crossexamination, arguing with Chambers constantly:

STRYKER: You became quite a figure there in this Washington hearing, didn't you?

CHAMBERS: I am afraid so.

STRYKER: You know you were referred to repeatedly by members of the Committee as star witness? You remember that?

CHAMBERS: No, as a matter of fact I do not. . . . I remember one member of the Committee stating that there is no Committee witness.

STRYKER: . . . All right. But at all events, you were televised, weren't you?

CHAMBERS: YES.

STRYKER: And you were on the radio, weren't you?

CHAMBERS: That is right.

STRYKER: So you would think it would be a reasonably fair statement, wouldn't you, Mr. Chambers, that you were widely publicized indeed during the very middle of that political campaign.

CHAMBERS: That is true.

As for Chambers's claim to have fought Communism for the entire decade that followed his defection, Stryker wanted to know why, if this was true, he had not protested the favorable stories about Alger Hiss that appeared in *Time* and *Life* in 1945 after the UN Conference. Why had he not contacted the secretary of state or the president or the Justice Department "or anyone and [said], 'Watch out. This man should not be trusted with that important post. He was in a conspiracy with me to get papers from the State Department and turn them over to some Russian fellow by the name of Bykov out in Prospect Park, or anything like that?' Did you communicate any such thing to your Government then? Yes or no." "I did not. . . . I didn't think it was possible." Chambers's voice again dropped to a whisper, and Stryker complained that the answer was inaudible. Kaufman interrupted: "You didn't think it was possible to do what?" The witness replied: "I didn't think it was possible to interest anybody in the subject." Tension rose in the courtroom as Stryker pressed: "Did you tell *Time,* your magazine, about that before they published this article about Alger Hiss? Yes or no." "No." "Well, you preferred to wait with your attack on Alger Hiss, and, incidentally, the Yalta Conference and perhaps President Roosevelt until you got a sitting before a House Committee which you attended with the intention of committing perjury, and knowing that you would not be cross-examined and exposed as you have been right in this courtroom?"

Although Kaufman sustained Murphy's objection to the question as "argumentative," the prosecutor—as furious as Stryker—had not finished. "And ask counsel to apologize to the Court and to me, and as to the claque back here I am getting tired of it." Stryker and Kaufman both protested Murphy's reference to the spectators sitting in the section reserved for those holding defense passes who, not infrequently, laughed or indicated approval of Stryker's sallies.

Now Stryker returned to *Time*'s 1945 coverage of Hiss and read from a May 28 story:

> In a class by himself was young, handsome Alger Hiss, a U.S. State Department career man functioning as international secretary general. Relaxed and alert amid innumerable annoyances, Hiss was master of the incredibly complicated Conference machinery. The wheels turned. A charter of world organization was taking shape.

"You remember that?" Stryker asked. "I believe I wrote that," responded Chambers.

Taken aback for a moment, Stryker became confused briefly and changed the subject: "Mr. Chambers, you never wanted to be indicted in this matter, did you?" Over Murphy's disallowed objection, Chambers agreed that he did not wish to be indicted for perjury or any other charge connected with his past activities. The witness said he had talked to Richard Nixon about the possibility of such an indictment, but insisted: "I don't fear indictment." Stryker tried to insert into the proceedings Nixon's statements that urged immunity for Chambers, but Kaufman sustained Murphy's inevitable objection.

By then Stryker had almost run out of questions. He probed for details of Chambers's alleged 1938 visits to Hiss's Volta Place home—to collect documents—time of day, number, and procedures for gaining entrance (Chambers remembered having a key). Stryker skimmed quickly through the few newly released segments of Chambers's grand jury testimony, searching for inconsistencies, and came up with some minor ones that the witness ascribed to mistaken recollection: "The intention was not to lie." A dubious Stryker retorted: "If that is your testimony we won't chalk that up as another perjury," drawing an objection from Murphy and a reprimand from Kaufman for injecting "a gratuitous statement." After some desultory questions Stryker demanded to know: "Which version of those facts is correct, the one that you swore to in this trial or the one that you swore to before the grand jury?" "The one in this trial," came Chambers's answer.

Stryker had concluded his three-and-a-half-day cross-examination, but Murphy was not yet through with the witness. "Mr. Chambers, did you tell the grand jury in the month of December, 1948, why you hadn't told them before about Mr. Hiss and the documents?" Stryker objected, and Kaufman warned that Murphy might "open the door . . . to an inspection of those minutes," but the prosecutor replied laconically: "Your Honor, I wouldn't care now who looked at the grand jury minutes." Kaufman allowed the question, and Chambers finally got to repeat the explanation he had given of the "perjuries" earlier in 1948 for which Stryker had berated him:

> I told [the grand jury] that in testifying from August on I had had two purposes: one was to disclose in part and to paralyze the Communist conspiracy; the other purpose was to preserve from injury in so far as I could all individuals involved in the past in that conspiracy. . . . I was particularly anxious not to injure Mr. Hiss any more than necessary out of grounds of past friendship and because he is by widespread consent a very able man. Therefore, I chose to jeopardize myself rather than reveal the full extent of his activities and those of others.

Chambers reiterated the time factor in breaking with Communism: "My own break was not a precipitous thing but developed over a period of time. I sought to give those people whom I had last known within the Communist Party, or on its fringes, an equal opportunity with me to find the strength necessary for such a break."

At Baltimore, Chambers said, he had answered all questions put to him by Hiss's attorneys, had even given them permission to examine his hospital records and insurance policies, and had withheld no facts from them concerning his past "that I am aware of." Murphy evidently hoped to impress the jury with the irony that Stryker's cross-examination depended to a major extent upon accepting the candor of this alleged "perjurer."

The prosecutor turned to the question of Chambers's 1937 application for government employment, which Stryker had used against the witness skillfully: "My purpose . . . was twofold: my more important purpose was to establish an identity for myself . . . because at this time I was already beginning to think actively of breaking with the Communist Party. . . . My second and lesser purpose was to obtain extra funds whereby I might finance my break."

Whittaker Chambers's fifth day in the witness chair began with a question by Murphy directed squarely at the defense's psychiatric theories: "Mr. Chambers, at any time since February 1934 have you had treatment or observation in a clinic, health resort, hospital, or sanitarium?" "No, I have not," Chambers said, except for two days in a New York hospital "for streptococcus sore throat." Chambers denied that he had ever been treated in any sanitorium or hospital either in New York or Virginia, nor had he ever consulted a psychiatrist or had a psychiatric examination, nor been treated for a mental illness, in or out of a mental institution. Murphy's questions suggested there would be little if any "objective" evidence of mental instability available to Hiss's lawyers. He then introduced photostats of Chambers's insurance records, further evidence that outside investigators had turned up no proof of mental illness in his background.

In answering questions about his relations with Julian Wadleigh, Chambers stressed two points: first, that Wadleigh had left the country in March 1938, before the last of the typed documents had been stolen; second, and more important, that Wadleigh had not given Chambers any of the material introduced in the Hiss trial: "None whatsoever." "*That* you are certain of?" Murphy asked. "Absolutely." "From whom did you get those?" "From Mr. Hiss." Chambers based his new certainty about the microfilm in particular on the fact that "the documents are photographed on two separate strips of film. Part of the long document, the German trade agreement, runs over or fills one strip and then continues on to the second strip. The rest of that strip is filled but with cables from Bullitt and other people, material of the kind that never came from Mr. Wadleigh but came from Mr. Hiss." Moreover, Wadleigh had not given him typewritten or handwritten items—only Hiss and Harry Dexter White among his government sources had done so.

On recross-examination, Chambers admitted he had not made a "full disclosure" to Adolf Berle in 1939, especially with regard to Alger Hiss's alleged espionage activities. He had not told Berle about Hiss's meeting with Bykov and other details contained in a portion of the Baltimore deposition that the defense lawyer instructed Chambers to read.

Stryker turned again to the witness's testimony about the reasons for not trying harder to expose Hiss prior to 1948: "As a matter of fact, you went down there to Washington in the hot summer of last year really to take part in a political campaign?" Stryker exclaimed, but Murphy's objection was sustained. As "proof," Stryker cited the fact that at the Commodore Hotel confrontation, when Hiss asked to hear his voice again, Chambers had read a *Newsweek* story which stated that Truman was "hoping or planning to make the greatest possible political capital out of the appointment" of a new secretary of labor. Chambers remained unflappable: "I simply don't recall what I read."

To Stryker's demand that he restate his reasons for not exposing Hiss's espionage or producing the documents until December 1948, Chambers replied: "I would say that I was led by a strong belief that I should not do any more injury than necessary to any of the members of that group." Partly because of his former friendship with Hiss, he had "a Christian duty" to commit perjury in his earlier testimony about espionage, a duty that "outweighed" his oath to tell the complete truth. Stryker emphasized what he felt was the witness's hypocrisy in professing friendship toward Hiss while having testified against him to HUAC. "Don't you recognize," he taunted, "that your explanation for your silence for these ten years on the ground of friendship is another piece of perjury, is a sham, and a fraud . . . ?"

After another day of desultory questioning by both attorneys, Whittaker Chambers finally left the witness chair. Despite Stryker's assault, his testimony had not been impaired substantially by cross-examination.

The following day Esther Chambers—small, slim-boned, plain-faced— walked through the courtroom, passing the Hisses without glancing in their direction, and took the stand. She spoke quietly, but so nervously that she misstated the date of her 1931 marriage. Judge Kaufman strained to hear her almost-whispered answers until Murphy interrupted to suggest that Kaufman sit in the court clerk's chair only a few feet away from the witness.[12]

At the start, the prosecutor established Esther's credentials as wife, mother, and solid citizen: The marriage to Chambers was her "first and only" one; she had a twelve-year-old boy and fifteen-year-old girl; she lived on a farm where each day for the past decade "I milk 18 cows and take care of some 40 head of cattle, dairy cattle, and take care also of some six beef cattle, plus some chickens." At the time she met her husband, Mrs. Chambers said, she had herself been "sympathetic" toward the CP but "never a member." She had followed Chambers, however, from residence to residence during his period in the underground.

And her relationship with the Hisses? "I met Alger Hiss for the first time at St. Paul Street [in Baltimore in 1934]." Chambers, she testified, had brought Hiss home one day. Mrs. Chambers had a great deal of difficulty with dates in her testimony. Rarely was she precise as to a month, and she generally used her children's ages and other personal events as milestones to measure her connections with the Hisses.

Her next meeting with Hiss came when Alger and Priscilla had dinner at her house. After these initial meetings "there were many occasions on which I met Mr. and Mrs. Hiss," and she listed some. Mrs. Chambers remembered the Hisses giving them the apartment at 28th Street almost completely furnished, since the Chambers family had almost no furniture at the time except for "the baby's things." She lived at the apartment for about two months, during which time she saw Mrs. Hiss for lunch and once when Priscilla took her and the baby for a drive to Washington's Hains Point. Also, "Mrs. Hiss and I both went to visit Dr. Nicholson about Timmy together, at which time Dr. Nicholson examined my baby, and we went to Mt. Vernon together."

She recounted the Chamberses' move to New York City later in 1935, when the couple stayed at Meyer Schapiro's home: "Mr. and Mrs. Hiss both brought [our] belongings . . . in their car to . . . West 4th Street. . . ." Next came the Chambers family's residence at Maxim Lieber's cottage at Smithtown, where, Esther said, Priscilla had visited them for ten days, with Alger joining them "at the close . . . to bring her back to Washington." Priscilla had come to visit, according to Mrs. Chambers, to help care for the baby while Esther painted. Then the Chamberses had stayed three to five days at the Hisses' P Street home, an event both couples acknowledged had taken place, after which they had moved to Eutaw Place in Baltimore, where Esther "frequently saw Mr. and Mrs. Hiss."

One incident in particular stuck in Esther's mind. She and Priscilla Hiss had taken Ellen Chambers to a nearby square. She also remembered Mrs. Hiss "bringing us a rug, which we still now have." Once Priscilla met her in the dining room of Hutzler's, a Baltimore department store. And she recalled receiving from the Hisses books, toys, and other articles of furniture—including a dining-room table, a table, a chair, and a chest of drawers.

Esther Chambers said she painted a landscape at the Smithtown cottage that she gave to Mrs. Hiss and later saw in the Hisses' 30th Street house. She was confused over the dates of her visits there but provided a thorough description of the home. Esther remembered calling "Alger Hilly and Priscilla Pros," nicknames she believed the couple used with each other. She recalled going to the 30th Street house twice, the second time fixed in her mind "because my [younger] baby wet the floor and Priscilla gave me a lovely old linen towel to use as a diaper."

The witness also said she had visited Volta Place, this time for a "New Year's Eve party" on January 1, 1937 (Mrs. Chambers turned out to be off by a year on dates again, since the Hisses moved to Volta Place on December 27, 1937). She described the Volta Place house carefully, indicating considerable knowledge of its interior room divisions and furnishings. That was the last time she recalled seeing Alger or Priscilla Hiss.

Still fuzzy about dates, Esther testified to an earlier visit the Hisses had made to the Chamberses' Mount Royal Terrace apartment in Baltimore to celebrate the former's wedding anniversary in December 1937. Alger and Priscilla, the witness said, "brought a bottle of champagne" on that occasion. Continuing this backward train of reminiscences, Mrs. Chambers described an occasion in 1936 when she and Mrs. Hiss took Ellen Chambers to the Baltimore Zoo at Druid Hill Park. Also, "twice we were with Mr. and Mrs. Hiss, my husband, the baby, Ellen, and myself on trips on the Potomac" to Great Falls in 1935.

At one point Kaufman asked the last name by which they were known:

ESTHER CHAMBERS: We never had a last name to them. . . . They always called us by the names either Carl or Liza.

KAUFMAN: Now, Mr. Chambers testified that you were known by the Hisses as Crosley.

MURPHY: Oh, no, your Honor, I don't think—why, that is not the testimony at all.

STRKER: Your Honor is practically correct. The witness said that probably or possibly the name Crosley was used. Your Honor's memory is correct.

KAUFMAN: Do you say, Mrs. Chambers, that they did not know your last name?

ESTHER CHAMBERS: That is correct. . . . they didn't know us as Chambers.

KAUFMAN: They knew you by a name other than Chambers, is that correct?

ESTHER CHAMBERS: They knew us by the names and referred to us and spoke to us each as Carl and Liza in my presence.

Kaufman appeared confused, and his face flushed as he tried to back away from his initial—and crucial—error in questioning Mrs. Chambers about the name "Crosley." Murphy asked Esther whether she recalled her husband ever using that name, and Esther replied. "No. That name means nothing to me at all," although she remembered Chambers's other underground pseudonyms.

Lloyd Stryker challenged one verifiable (and vulnerable) detail of Esther Chambers's story—her recollection that Alger Hiss had been trying a case in the U.S. Supreme Court at the time she visited Priscilla Hiss at P Street to pick up the key to the 28th Street apartment. Stryker probed for precise details on this visit until the irritated witness said quietly: "I think you are making a great deal of nothing," a remark Kaufman ordered stricken from the record. Stryker's point then emerged: that the only case Hiss tried before the Court was in March 1936, not the previous year when Esther picked up the key. Had Chambers been an underground Communist in October 1937, Stryker asked, when they applied to enroll their daughter in Baltimore's Park School? Again Esther could not handle the subject: "Well, sir, I don't know about dates, and if that is . . . within the period in which he was in the underground, that was the period in which he was in the underground. I don't know why you are trying to stump me on dates." Kaufman interrupted: "Now, Mrs. Chambers, no one is attempting to stump you at all—" "Well, it is very easy," Esther responded. To which the judge retorted: "—and the Court resents any such implication, and I am certain that the jury does. Nobody here is attempting to stump anybody. . . . We are here attempting to get the facts . . . and it comes with very bad grace for you to indicare that anyone is attempting to stump you. . . . Now we don't want any more of these insinuations."

Finally Esther confessed that she did not know the exact date Whittaker Chambers had broken with the CP. Over Murphy's objection to the question's form, Kaufman allowed Stryker to ask Mrs. Chambers: "Now, wouldn't you as the man's wife know when you got out of this underground criminal conspiracy known as the American Communist Party? As his wife wouldn't you know when he started to reform from that criminal activity?" Even before Esther could reply, Kaufman prodded her: "Can't you answer that question, Mrs. Chambers?" To which Esther replied: "Oh, I didn't know there was any question." Esther's answer finally came after more bickering between Murphy and Kaufman: "It was a long time in coming and thought out very thoroughly and suffered through, and he finally broke. That particular moment of the breaking has been unimportant in my life and I have long since forgotten it." When the precise moment came, the witness could not recall: " '38 or '37, I have forgotten."

Esther Chambers returned to the stand on June 13, but not before judge and prosecutor renewed their argument in chambers over Kaufman's belief that Whittaker Chambers had testified that the Hisses knew him as "Crosley." Kaufman now attempted to retreat gracefully from his earlier erroneous statements on the point. But when Murphy pointed out that Chambers had said only that he had "no definite recollection" of ever using "Crosley" among his pseudonyms, the judge commented: "Yes, that is right, but he studiously avoided testifying in any place that the Hisses knew him as Chambers." Murphy rebuked the jurist: "I don't know what you mean by 'studiously.' I think he testified unequivocally Hiss did not know him as Chambers." Neither man could satisfy the other on his interpretation of Chambers's testimony, but Kaufman agreed to clarify the statement in his final charge to the jury.

Again Stryker broached the subject of Esther Chambers's radical past "as a warm sympathizer with the Communist movement . . . a fellow traveler with them," a characterization that the witness accepted. He ran Mrs. Chambers through a recital of her Communist involvements during the 1920s. Esther said she knew about her husband's work as a Communist after their marriage in 1931 and that, in Stryker's words, "every piece of bread" she and Whittaker had eaten from 1931 to his defection had been given them "by Communist conspirators."

Berating Esther Chambers for having given her young child the same alias she and her husband were using at any given moment during those years, Stryker exclaimed: "Now, did that not shock you as a mother? Did you not think that psychologically that was a dreadful thing to do, to take a little girl and teach her to cheat and deceive by using a false name?" "Well, it did worry us," came the measured response. "Then you had some conscience?" Stryker asked next. Mrs. Chambers, calmer that day than on the previous Friday, turned to Kaufman: "Do I have to answer that?" The judge sustained Murphy's objection.

When had Chambers first begun thinking of "repenting" and breaking with Communism? Here Esther Chambers provided some new insight into the background of that decision. She traced it back to the spring of 1937, noting that her husband had not talked much about this with her, struggling privately with the matter: "I myself was concerned with the details of housekeeping and raising two babies, and so the problem wasn't so much with me as it was with him. He was actively working in the underground movement." Stryker confessed puzzlement that the couple had not discussed the matter more, but Esther remained insistent. She had not helped Chambers to decide: "He himself made [his mind] up."*

The purpose behind Stryker's line of questioning became apparent. If the Chamberses had put lying behind them by April 1937 (something Esther Chambers had not testified), then why had she lied in her application to the Park School in October about Chambers's line of work? The answer was obvious—with her husband still in the underground—but, to Stryker, irrelevant. Mrs. Chambers conceded her lies to the school. Stryker asked whether the witness did not have a "pang of conscience" after having "misrepresented facts" to the school. He observed caustically that she apparently "didn't think it was very much of a misrepresentation to present your husband to this school as a decent citizen whereas he was—"

Esther Chambers shouted back for the first time in two days: "I resent that. My husband is a decent citizen, a great man." "Mrs. Chambers," Kaufman interjected dryly, "it is your province to answer questions." But Stryker picked up the line: "Was he a great, decent citizen in October, 1937?" "Yes, and always," came an equally angry cry from the witness. Stryker was unmoved: "And so that the jury will understand your conception: It is your idea that a man who was plotting and conspiring by any and all means to overthrow the Government of his country, who had been sneaking around for twelve years under false names,

---

*Alger Hiss told me in 1974 that he rarely discussed major decisions in *his* career with his wife. Thus, Hiss asserted, the decision to sue Chambers for slander had been his own. As for Priscilla Hiss's reaction: "It was none of her business. . . . We—Priscilla and I—discussed Timmy, Tony, houses, family matters. But I never talked about the U.N., for example, and in this case I didn't discuss the libel [sic] suit." Interview, Alger Hiss, September 20, 1974.

that is your conception of the great decent citizen, is that right?" "No," replied Mrs. Chambers, her voice choked with emotion, "but if he then believed that is the right thing to do at the moment I believe that is a great man, who lives up to his beliefs. His beliefs may change, as they did."

But Stryker continued his efforts to persuade Esther Chambers that she had confused testimony about the "New Year's Eve" party at Volta Place with the "wedding anniversary" party at Mount Royal Terrace. The witness, however, held firm. Both Esther and Whittaker had apparently mixed up their memories of several different parties with the Hisses, but Stryker's incessant questioning on the point did not clarify matters. He renewed his attempt to expose inconsistencies in Mrs. Chambers's description of the Hisses' Volta Place and 30th Street homes: she recalled the latter painted white outside (it turned out to have been yellow) and remained confused as to whether Volta Place had had a porch during the 1930s (it had not). "Now, wasn't the FBI sufficiently alert to advise you that this structure [the porch] . . . was not built until the year 1943?" Stryker shouted. Kaufman sustained Murphy's objection, but defense counsel held to the point: "Will you not admit that your testimony about going to Volta Place is wholly untrue? Come, Mrs. Chambers, will you?" " No."

Turning to her family's assets—farm, stock, equipment, and personal funds—Stryker said, "Mr. Chambers has told us that sometime he became judgment proof." Murphy objected, but to no avail, though Stryker's next question backfired when Esther Chambers said that her husband had not transferred any of his assets to her at the time of Hiss's slander suit. All of their property was held in both their names "and always has been." Shortly afterward Mrs. Chambers stepped down from the stand. To the last, she had remained more indignant at Stryker's criticisms of her husband than at his challenges to her own veracity.

Henry Julian Wadleigh, a slim, brown-haired man wearing horn-rimmed glasses, slightly disheveled in appearance, answered Murphy's questions in an accent that bespoke his graduate training in economics at Oxford and the University of London. Dubbing himself a former CP "sympathizer," Wadleigh recounted the story he had previously told the FBI about handing over documents to David Carpenter and to Chambers (whom he had known as "Carl Carlson") during the 1936–38 period while Wadleigh worked for State's Trade Agreements Section.[13]

He had not passed to Chambers any typed documents and, only rarely, a handwritten one (Chambers recalled none). Murphy showed Wadleigh the microfilmed material and asked if he had given it to Chambers or anyone else. Wadleigh responded carefully. There was a "possibility" that he had done so, but he thought it "most improbable," since he did not remember seeing those particular items, nor had he worked on the German trade agreements "at the time when these documents were prepared." Also, Wadleigh pointed out that the cables that completed the microfilm run were copies of cables sent to Sayre's office but not to Trade Agreements; hence he would not have had access to them. Wadleigh said that he left Washington for Turkey on March 9, 1938, and had neither seen Chambers nor delivered any documents to him for some weeks prior to departure.

Noticeably calmer than when he had questioned Whittaker and Esther Chambers, Stryker asked whether the witness had been "in quest of any rich finds" (Wadleigh's phrase) to hand over to Chambers. Wadleigh agreed with the description, after which Stryker asked if he had wandered into the offices of colleagues at State in search of such "rich finds." The witness retorted: "I never did anything so foolish." Stryker argued the point, but could not shake Wadleigh's insistence that he had not even taken such "rich finds" from the office of his superior at Trade Agreements, Harry Hawkins: "I just did not do it." He stole only from the papers that came to his desk and from nowhere else: "It just never occurred to me."[14]

He had been in Sayre's office at times but only on official business and never alone. Wadleigh displayed no anxiety over Stryker's questioning, and his rejoinders often deflected the lawyer's probe. Stryker hoped to implant in the jury the idea that Wadleigh might have stolen from Hiss's office the materials—at least the handwritten and microfilmed documents—that Chambers turned over a decade later. Several times he referred sarcastically to Wadleigh's British accent and background—"I realize you have the benefit of—what was it? London University and Oxford, too?"—but his tactic lacked substance.

Judge Kaufman refused to allow Murphy to call two other government witnesses: Hede Massing, whose testimony placed Alger Hiss in Noel Field's home in 1935 discussing Communist "secret work,"[15] and William Rosen, who had signed the Ford title transfer. After hearing in chambers Stryker's objection that the prosecutor's real purpose in summoning these witnesses was to encourage "the rawest form of prejudice" against Hiss and not to confirm facts in the case, Kaufman excluded both Massing and Rosen. Nor would the judge allow Murphy on rebuttal to summon an official of the Cherner Motor Company "to prove the purchase and sale" of Hiss's Ford in 1936.

Even more important to the government's case than Massing and Rosen, neither of whom could speak directly to the two perjury charges against Hiss, was a string of witnesses who offered testimony relating to stolen State Department microfilmed, typed, and handwritten documents. By the time Murphy and Donegan had finished with these witnesses, they had shown that all but one of the stolen papers had come from State Department originals; that Hiss's account of working procedures in Assistant Secretary Francis B. Sayre's office in 1937–38 differed from the recollections of Sayre's secretary; and that FBI laboratory analysis identified the stolen typed documents as having been turned out on the Woodstock owned by the Hisses during the 1930s.

Nathan I. Levine told of Chambers's visit to Brooklyn in November 1948 to collect the packet he had left behind a decade earlier. Donald T. Appell of HUAC described how he and William Wheeler had retrieved the "pumpkin papers" from Chambers on December 2, and he outlined procedures for handling the microfilm after it came into his possession. Du Pont and Eastman Kodak officials identified the State Department microfilm strips, and an FBI lab expert brought out evidence that they had been photographed by Felix Inslerman's Leica.[16]

One of the government's most important witnesses testified to the contents of each stolen document, while another traced the operation of Francis B. Sayre's office at State. Walter H. Anderson, chief of the department's Records Branch, explained the nature and distribution of each document—sixty-five typed and four handwritten, plus the two strips of microfilm—that Chambers claimed to have received from Alger Hiss. Anderson described departmental methods in 1937 and 1938 for handling incoming cables. He detailed the manner in which one "action copy" on yellow paper—"the permanent record for the Department files"—and additional "information copies" on white paper for distribution to the appropriate divisions and officials within State were run off on mimeographed stencils. Only the "action copies" were preserved; the others would eventually reach the Records Branch from the individual offices concerned. Then all "information copies" would be destroyed. The branch always kept records of what had gone where. Officials could tell the degree of secrecy of a message by noting both the color and letter codes listed on its face: either gray or the more confidential green, and letters A through D (the latter being State's most confidential classification).[17]

After the prosecutor produced photostats of the original State Department documents from which the materials turned over by Chambers had been taken, Anderson identified each document and described its routing. Stryker had proposed privately that all the documents be introduced at once, thereby saving time. But Murphy rejected the idea, as he explained to reporters. "If I did what they want," Jim Bell quoted Murphy, "the jury would forget all about the importance of these documents. I'm going to keep reading and keep reading. I'm going to pile it up. If I bore them, they will remember how much there was during this part of the case." The jury and the spectators could hardly forget, since Anderson remained on the stand for the better part of two days.

Beginning with the first of the handwritten documents, the Mary Martin cable, and running down the distribution list, Anderson mentioned Francis Sayre's office as a recipient of an information copy. Next came the other three handwritten notes, also routed to Sayre, but with Stryker gaining Murphy's acknowledgment that Section 2 of the March 2, 1938, cable from Paris—which contained information of possible interest to the Soviet Union—had not been recopied on Hiss's note.[18]

After finishing with the original cables from which Hiss had transcribed handwritten notes, Murphy turned to the typed documents. When he came to the January 12, 1938, War Department report, the one document not typed on a Woodstock (and also not routed to Sayre's office), the prosecutor made the best of the situation. He had his witness concede the obvious: that he could not tell "other than that one stamp [Far Eastern Division] who in the Department had it."

In cross-examining Anderson, Edward McLean tried to demonstrate that many people had the opportunity to read departmental "information copies" during the late 1930s, bringing out the fact that "as a general rule some fifteen information copies of each cable were distributed," often many more. These, according to the witness, were "retained in the code room for an indefinite period and then they were destroyed by burning." Anderson clarified his idea of an "indefinite period"— generally from two to three weeks, or "until they were certain no further copies would be needed." Nor could Anderson tell McLean how many of these information copies were kept in the code room, although he conceded that they were stored in unlocked cabinets during working hours. McLean pointed out that thirty or thirty-five people had access to documents in the code room over a normal twenty-four-hour period.

There were guards, to be sure, but McLean showed skillfully that security regulations at State at the time were lax, almost nonexistent, in contrast with those in effect by 1949. Outside the courtroom during a brief recess Jim Bell overheard another reporter, Edwin Lahey of the Chicago *Daily News*, remark that a "Strictly Confidential" State Department cable in 1938—which McLean showed that more than a hundred people could have read—appeared to have been as private as "one of those street toilets in Paris where everyone can see your head and feet."[19]

Francis Sayre's private secretary, Eunice A. Lincoln, described the "physical layout" and procedures in Sayre's office, with herself, Sayre, Hiss, a messenger, and Anna Belle Newcomb, Hiss's secretary, as its five occupants. Newcomb was responsible for sorting incoming mail into appropriate categories for Sayre and Hiss. Someone was always present in the outer office, thereby limiting the possibility that an outsider could examine or steal materials. As for both "action" and "information" copies of departmental memos, Lincoln evinced a skilled secretary's pride in handling them carefully—placing the documents in envelopes until they were picked up and sent elsewhere for burning. But—and this seemed important to Murphy—she never pestered either Sayre or Hiss for such copies. She collected them weekly for disposal and simply waited "until I got them from the men," since the items could be burned the following week."[20]

Eunice Lincoln knew Julian Wadleigh from his "infrequent" business visits to Sayre's office, always in the company of other officials; she did not recall Wadleigh ever having been in the office alone. Since she and Newcomb alternated lunch hours, "there was always one of us there," minimizing further Wadleigh's (or anyone's) chances of sneaking in unobserved.

She said both Hiss and Sayre took departmental documents home to work on, but she did not recall Hiss frequently making handwritten memos of cables. She identified the writing on the four handwritten exhibits as Hiss's, although she had not seen any of them before. After reading the Mary Martin cable, she testified she would have placed it in the category of documents that Sayre did not have to read, an "information" category of material "which he was not interested in, but which he should have knowledge of." Lincoln agreed that the other three handwritten notes by Hiss—or the documents from which they came—would have been placed in the same category.

Under cross-examination, the witness added an important piece of testimony. Hawkins and Darlington—other departmental officials—had, as a "general practice," included with original memos sent to Sayre a carbon copy, in the event Sayre wished to keep it while sending the original elsewhere. Although Murphy did not press the point further, he evidently meant to suggest that a few of the documents contained in Chambers's cache that did not bear Sayre's date stamp might be explained in this way. Eunice Lincoln stepped down, walked directly to Alger Hiss, smiled, and shook his hand before leaving the courtroom.[21]

Several prosecution witnesses took the stand to introduce in evidence material that had been typed on Alger and Priscilla Hiss's Woodstock during the mid-thirties, preliminary to demonstrating that the stolen State Department papers had been turned out on the same machine. Paul Banfield, headmaster of the Landon School, submitted the 1936 application letters from Hiss that the FBI laboratory had used in identifying the Chambers documents as having been typed on the Hiss Woodstock. Stryker turned Banfield into a character witness for Hiss—the two men were friends—over Murphy's objections.[22]

Marie Abbott, president of the Washington Bryn Mawr Alumnae Association the year following Priscilla Hiss's term in office, introduced the president's report for 1936–37, which the government found had also been typed on the Woodstock. Again Stryker converted the witness into a reference for the Hisses—Mrs. Abbott's husband had worked with Hiss at State, and she agreed that his reputation "was that of a person of the highest caliber."[23]

The most important testimony about the stolen documents came from FBI laboratory expert Ramos C. Feehan, an individual whose talents included considerable skill as a witness. Feehan had served as a bureau documents examiner for eleven years, analyzing "questioned handwriting, hand printing, [and] typewriting. . . ." He spoke while standing on a platform beyond the witness chair, using a pointer to illustrate his comments upon photographic enlargements mounted on two stands behind him; one held the typed documents (Exhibits 5 to

47), and the other, known standards of Mrs. Hiss's typing. Murphy questioned Feehan about the Baltimore documents, all of which he had analyzed and compared with the "Hiss standards." First came the four handwritten notes, but before Murphy could ask whether these matched Alger Hiss's known handwriting, Stryker interrupted to concede the point: "They are in the handwriting of Mrs. Hiss." Stryker claimed to have stated that in the opening, but Kaufman reminded him that he had expressed some doubt about the Mary Martin note.[24]

As for the typed material, "Baltimore 5 to 47," Feehan noted that he had compared them to four specimens submitted for FBI analysis: Daisy Fansler's 1931 letter, the 1936 Landon School documents, Priscilla Hiss's 1936–37 president's report, and Mrs. Hiss's 1937 application for admission to the University of Maryland at Baltimore. Photographic copies of all four documents had been mounted on one of the stands. What conclusion, Murphy asked, had Feehan reached after comparing the documents? "I reached the conclusion that Government's Exhibits 5 through 9 and 11 through 47, that the typewriting on those specimens was typed by the same machine which typed the four known standards which were submitted to me for comparison purposes." Government Exhibit 10, the War Department document, had been typed on a different machine.

The expert began his real performance when Murphy asked him "to explain the basis for his conclusions, especially about all but Government Exhibit 10."

Feehan described the similarities between the Baltimore documents and the Hiss standards. Specific letters became important elements in his presentation: lowercase "g" and the terminating stroke of lowercase "e," for example, had "characteristics . . . [that] are shown in all these known standards." Murphy passed out photostatic copies of the Baltimore documents to jurors so that they could follow the presentation more easily. Next came similarities in several other lowercase letters—"i," "o," "u," "d," "a," "r," and "I." Feehan explained that, inevitably, there were variations in the striking of each letter that depended upon such things as the amount of dirt on a ribbon and the quality of paper used. But if the observable similarities—including common defects in typing a letter—far outweighed minor variations, this showed the "tendency of the machine." Stryker, who had asked Feehan for some clarifications while Murphy questioned the witness, did not cross-examine.

When the trial resumed on Monday, June 20, Kaufman began by denying defense motions for dismissal as "a strictly legal matter" that did not prejudge the innocence or guilt of the defendant, "but simply acknowledged that there are sufficient facts to go to the jury."[25]

The defense lawyers pursued four main lines of testimony in defending their client. They summoned witnesses to suggest, first, that Chambers was mentally unstable; second, that Hiss's Woodstock had been given to the Catletts before the stolen documents had been typed on it; third, that Hiss had described his working habits at State accurately—thereby accounting for the four handwritten notes; and, fourth, that Hiss's reputation precluded his having engaged in the activities described by his accuser. Although Alger and Priscilla Hiss both testified, their attorneys bolstered the defense case with an array of supporting witnesses.

Several described bizarre behavior on Chambers's part, although Kaufman did not allow one of them—Dr. Carl Binger—to testify fully. The first of these "poor character" witnesses, journalist and literary critic Malcolm Cowley, described his luncheon with Chambers on December 13, 1940, at which—according to Cowley—Chambers named Francis B. Sayre as one of the underground Communists he had known in the government. Although Kaufman had previously excluded government attempts to question Chambers about his underground associates other than Hiss, he permitted the defense to use Cowley's evidence. The witness was certain that Chambers had named Sayre, and he introduced a journal entry written at the time to support his recollection. He remembered being "shocked" and asking Chambers: "'Not Woodrow Wilson's son-in-law?' and he said, 'Yes.' And I said to Chambers again, 'The High Commissioner to the Philippines?' and he said, 'Not merely that, but he's the head of a Communist apparatus in the State Department.'"[26]

Cowley's personal distaste for Chambers emerged clearly in his testimony. He described Chambers at their luncheon meeting as looking "as if he had slept on a park bench the night before. His clothes were old, unpressed and rather dirty. His linen was not clean. He would never look me in the eyes, but kept glancing suspiciously around the restaurant." Laughter erupted in the courtroom when Cowley described one of Chambers's teeth as "nothing but a piece of metal, evidently a bridge from which the enamel had been chipped." Jim Bell recorded counsel's reaction: "'Oh,' said Stryker, as though he were describing the monster Dr. Frankenstein created, 'a metal prong, eh?'" Cowley said that Chambers did not mention the name of Alger Hiss as a Communist.*[27]

Conceding that he had not told anyone about the conversation until A. J. Liebling approached him in the fall of 1948, Cowley omitted mentioning his exchange of letters with Maus Darling about Chambers during the war.† He testified that he had voted Communist during the 1930s and registered as a Communist in the 1936 election (Cowley broke with the CP after the Nazi-Soviet Pact of 1939).‡ Also, although Cowley testified that Chambers told him Sayre was

---

*Cowley had told Hiss's attorneys the previous October only that he "did not recall" whether Chambers had mentioned Hiss. "Memorandum re Malcolm Cowley," October 29, 1948, Hiss Defense Files.

†At Hiss's second trial, but not this time, Cowley said Libeling had contacted several other people for information in connection with an article he planned on Chambers, specifically "Maus Darling [and] Matthew Josephson." Transcript, Second Trial, p. 1770.

‡Cowley never actually joined the party.

head of a Communist apparatus at State, his memo noted only: "Sayre, the High Commissioner to the Philippines, is also connected with the underground movement." Murphy suggested that Cowley had somehow misunderstood an oblique reference by Chambers to Sayre's "connection" to the CP through his assistant, Alger Hiss, but Cowley held to his testimony.

Although Kaufman had previously discussed with opposing counsel "informally and . . . no part of the record at any time" the fact that he intended to exclude Dr. Carl Binger as a witness, nevertheless the judge allowed Stryker to summon the psychiatrist to the stand. Binger had spent many days at the trial, watching not only Esther and Whittaker Chambers but other witnesses as well. Kaufman rejected Murphy's request that Stryker first prove—with the jury excluded—the relevance of Binger's testimony. Instead the judge allowed Stryker to question the witness so that "a foundation should be laid for the objection that you talked about."[28]

Binger had frequently talked to reporters and conveyed his views about Chambers's mental condition. Shortly before he took the stand, Jim Bell observed him in the hall outside court:

> He slapped newsmen on the back; introduced [a friend] to the *Herald Tribune's* John Chabot Smith as "an honest reporter," a remark which caused the Baltimore *Sun's* Tom O'Neill to determine then and there to misspell his name. He was like a bench athlete warming up to go in the game.
>
> "What do you think of Whittaker Chambers' personality?" he asked an unidentified . . . newsman.
>
> "I'm not qualified to say, sir," the character said.
>
> "You're qualified to have your leg pulled, aren't you?" Doctor Binger said, and strolled away with his lady.[29]

A graduate of Harvard Medical School in 1914, Binger had studied several fields including psychiatry. He testified that he "will not accept compensation in this case." He said he had watched Chambers testify on June 2, 3, 6, 7, and 8. Stryker read a hypothetical question for Binger—"Now, Doctor, assume that the following facts are true"—that took thirty-five minutes to complete.[30]

This device allowed defense counsel to summarize for the jurors every aspect of Chambers's life that might conceivably mark Hiss's accuser as somehow strange or deviant. Stryker went through the entire litany: Chambers's high-school behavior, his troubles prior to joining the CP, his Columbia years, his brother's suicide, "Tandaradei," *Class Reunion,* his work as a Communist during the twenties, Ida Dales, his use of pseudonyms in the thirties, his break with the underground, his visit to Berle and subsequent work on *Time,* his HUAC testimony, his production of the documents at the Hiss slander suit, the "pumpkin papers," his health problems in 1942 and 1945, his meeting with Cowley in 1940, and dozens of other incidents.

"Now, Dr. Binger," Stryker finally asked, more than a half-hour later, "assuming the facts as stated in the question to be true, and taking into account your observations of Chambers on the witness stand, and knowledge of his writings and translations, have you as a psychiatrist an opinion within the bounds of reasonable certainty as to the mental condition of Whittaker Chambers?"

Even while Stryker was reading the elongated question-statement, Murphy had objected several times. He had again asked Kaufman to exclude the jury while defense counsel read the question, but once more the judge had refused: "The defendant has the right to make this record." Kaufman offered a rather puzzling rationale, arguing that "in view of the great uncertainty as to the admissibility of this testimony, [defense] is entitled to make its record" and to make it before the jury. Stryker insisted that the material he read consisted only of "statements of fact" previously entered as trial testimony. Once defense counsel had finished, Murphy objected to the question. He said that Stryker's reading, "a summation of Mr. Chambers' testimony before the time of summations," was "a grave injustice to the Government and one on which we have no right of appeal." Murphy then made *his* appeal to jurors with a brief countersummation:

> And of course it is not a complete summary of the witness' testimony here by a long shot; he left out his marriage to his wife; his only wife; he left out the fact that the man is now a member of the Quaker religion and has been for many years; he left out the fact that he is the father of a boy and a girl; he left out other writings, particularly the child's book "Bambi," and innumerable things, so I think the question is not a fair summary upon which the doctor could base his opinion. But, however, the damage is done.[31]

Murphy demanded that Kaufman instruct the jury to disregard Stryker's question. The judge complied, although somewhat obliquely. He announced his decision to exclude the psychiatric testimony only "because I think that the record is sufficiently clear for the jury . . . to appraise the testimony of all of the witnesses." With that, the silent Dr. Binger stepped down.[32]

Defense strategy rested heavily on an attempt to show that the Hisses had not possessed the Woodstock at the time the stolen documents were typed on it. Five witnesses—three of them Catletts—presented the defense's version of how the Hisses had disposed of the machine and then, a decade later, recovered it. Claudia Catlett said she saw Chambers only once during the 1930s at the P Street house, where Priscilla Hiss served him tea (Alger Hiss was not at home at the time, according to the witness). When she met Chambers at P Street, "he called his name Crosby" (an allusion to Hiss's assertion that he knew Chambers as George Crosley).[33]

Had the Hisses ever given her family things? McLean asked. Claudia Catlett recalled a chair, "one of them old kind Victrolas, and some clothes . . . some pictures and them little things." "Anything else?" "And they gave the children an old typewriter." "The children" meant her now adult sons Raymond (Mike) and Perry (Pat) Catlett. Claudia Catlett thought that she had received the machine "when they [the Hisses] moved from P Street . . . to 30th Street" in June 1936. Since Mrs. Hiss's Bryn Mawr report and University of Maryland application had been typed on the Woodstock the following year, the witness's testimony on the point seemed improbable. McLean tried to get Mrs. Catlett to recall seeing "a portable typewriter" at 30th Street, but she answered only: "They had one, but I don't know what kind it was . . . I don't remember no typewriters at all."

McLean referred gingerly to Claudia Catlett's contacts with Hiss's attorneys, not correcting her when she placed their first meeting in March or April instead of two months earlier. Mrs. Catlett also said she had not recalled at the time—or when she first spoke to McLean and Donald Hiss—either the Hisses having given her boys a typewriter or the machine's make. (Actually, Mrs. Catlett told McLean and Donald Hiss then that she remembered receiving the typewriter.)

On another significant point Claudia Catlett admitted that, except for "Crosby," she did not know the names of any friends or callers who visited the Hisses, no matter how frequently, during her four years in the household in the 1930s: "Some Washington people. I don't remember." When she saw Chambers, however, she knew him immediately as "Crosby." But Murphy confronted the witness with her signed statement to the FBI on February 10, in which Mrs. Catlett described meeting Chambers, but not remembering what name he used during their P Street encounter. The witness promptly disavowed the statement: "I put there what they told me to put."[*]

Claudia Catlett seemed both frightened and confused by Murphy's lengthy cross-examination, and she revised portions of her earlier testimony. Now Mrs. Catlett claimed to have recalled the typewriter only after her son Raymond reminded her earlier in 1949 that the family had received the machine from Hiss. But she insisted that this discussion had not yet been held when she signed a statement for the FBI on February 10 disclaiming all knowledge of any Hiss typewriter.[†] She placed the discussion with Raymond "just before they found it," implying deceptively that she had not known anything about having received the Woodstock until late March or April 1949.

The cross-examination exposed many inconsistencies in Claudia Catlett's version of the evidence, and McLean tried to restore some credibility to this critical defense witness on redirect questioning. He brought out the fact that Mrs. Catlett had been questioned by the FBI "seven or eight times" and had signed several statements written by the agents. McLean noted she had told him at their first

---

[*]Mrs. Catlett also denied telling the FBI that she had not recalled "Crosby's" name until Hiss's lawyer suggested it.

[†]Claudia Catlett and her sons talked several times with Donald Hiss and Edward McLean beginning in January 1949.

meeting that her daughter Burnetta "had the big typewriter that Pat gave her, the one Mr. Hiss gave him." (Again McLean made no effort to clarify the date of this meeting, so that Murphy could not know that it had taken place weeks before Mrs. Catlett's February 10 interview with the FBI.)

Twenty-seven-year-old Raymond (Mike) Catlett had been the major intermediary between the Hiss attorneys and people in Washington's black community who had knowledge of the Woodstock. McLean asked him the crucial question: Did the Hisses at the time of a move—either from P Street to 30th Street or from there to Volta Place—give him something? "Yes, sir. They gave us some clothes, books, and a typewriter. . . . A Woodstock." In what condition? "It was broke . . . the keys would jam up on you and it would not work good. You could not do any typing hardly with it." Any other defects? McLean asked. "The wheel and the ribbons would not work." McLean returned to the defense table and with the help of his colleagues pulled an old Woodstock typewriter out of a carton under the table. A murmur ran through the courtroom as he walked to the witness stand and showed the machine to Catlett. The witness pushed on a few keys, examined the roller, and replied: "This is it." McLean offered the machine in evidence.[34]

When had the witness first talked to McLean and Donald Hiss? Catlett settled on a February 1949 date. He described his offer at that time to help find the Hiss typewriter and his subsequent inquiries in Washington, a process he described as "traveling around," which took him about a month. Once Catlett stumbled deftly out of a question by McLean that threatened to reveal the two-month gap:

MCLEAN: Now, did you find it, Mike?
CATLETT: Did I find it?
MCLEAN: Yes.
CATLETT: Well, I didn't. I mean it was found but I didn't. I wasn't the man that, you know, to go and pick it up. . . . I mean it was located. I mean you may get it. I didn't get it.
MCLEAN: That is a simple question, Mike. Did you find it at that time or not?
CATLETT: No, sir. I didn't find it at that time.*[35]

This last bit of direct questioning drew from the witness a startling reversal of earlier testimony. McLean had skimmed over the exact Hiss household move during which the Catletts had acquired the Woodstock. Now Judge Kaufman returned to that subject and asked when Mike received the typewriter. Catlett's

---

*The entire cover-up nearly emerged in Mike's testimony at the second trial as well, through another slip of his tongue. Hiss's lawyer asked Mike if he could fix the number of months after his first FBI interview—which Catlett agreed had been either in December 1948 or January 1949—he had found the Woodstock. "It was a little while—" Mike responded, cutting himself short before continuing, "let us see, when they first come down [presumably a reference either to the FBI's or McLean's first visit]—it was a good while afterwards." Transcript, Second Trial, p. 1593.

answer: "It was in the moving. . . . They was moving from the house." Kaufman persisted: "Now what house were they moving from at the time that they gave you this typewriter?" And Catlett responded: "I can't recall what moving it was. It was so long ago." Alger Hiss's "aids to recollection" had evidently not helped align the various Catlett stories.* Apparently the defense had decided to let the date remain vague, if possible, although McLean had suggested earlier that Catlett typed on the machine "in 1937."

Had it not been for Kaufman's unexpected intervention, McLean might have succeeded. But Murphy picked up the scent after the witness had indicated his hostility toward the prosecutor. Catlett's mother had raised no objections to being called "Clytie" by both McLean and Murphy, but Catlett repudiated this patronizing first-name approach that most African-Americans of his mother's generation had accepted, unquestioningly, from whites:

MURPHY: Now, may I call you Mike?
CATLETT: —Sir?
MURPHY: Did you want to say something?
CATLETT: What did you start to say?
MURPHY: Can I call you Mike?
CATLETT: My name is Raymond Sylvester Catlett.
MURPHY: All right, Raymond Sylvester Catlett, will you tell us . . . when it was that you received the typewriter?
CATLETT: Sir? You ask did I tell them the date?
MURPHY: Yes. Did you tell them what day it was, what year?
CATLETT: No, I didn't tell them.

Mike Catlett's aggressiveness abruptly collapsed, and, although still angry, he responded almost incoherently to the question of when he had received the Hiss Woodstock: "It has been so long ago, and you come right back and you ask me the same thing. . . . I mean you are getting me all balled up here. . . . You ask me the same questions over and over again." He could not pinpoint the specific move during which the Hisses brought him the Woodstock. He now told Murphy he had no knowledge of that fact as vehemently as he had insisted a month earlier to others in the Catlett family and to McLean that the Volta Place move had produced the gift: "No sir, I couldn't really—I couldn't hardly say." Nor could Catlett now recall (unlike his earlier interviews with McLean) whether Alger or Priscilla Hiss had given him the machine: "It could have been the maid."† Nor

---

*At the second trial Mike was more precise but less helpful to Hiss. He fixed the date he received the Woodstock as June 1936, during the Hisses' "move from P Street to 30th Street," although he admitted under questioning by Hiss's lawyer that it could have been during the later move to Volta Place. Not only was the 1936 date useless to the defense, it was patently inaccurate, given the 1937 "Hiss standards" typed by Priscilla Hiss and found by the government.

†By "the maid" Catlett presumably meant Claudia Catlett's successor in mid-1938, although this would have undermined the claim that he got the machine in 1937 or even earlier.

did he remember if he had picked it up at the Hiss residence or if someone had brought it to him: "I know I got the typewriter, that is all I remember about it."* Mike Catlett's apparent fear of being trapped into some provable perjury on these questions made him a thoroughly muddled witness.

While claiming he had first talked to Donald Hiss about locating the machine in January, "two or three weeks" before seeing McLean early in February, Catlett acknowledged another critical point—his close contact with the Hiss family in recent months. He had gone to see Donald Hiss to ask him for work "sometime between July of 1948 and January 1949." Catlett also met Donald Hiss in January after FBI questioning about a typewriter, and had not told the bureau about the Hiss machine.

Murphy asked if he had had the Woodstock fixed after receiving it from the Hisses. Although the Catlett brothers had told McLean about this, Mike now denied knowing anything about such repairs. He also remained evasive about the sequence of events after he had traced the machine to Ira Lockey. He said that the search "took me about a month's good work" and admitted having promised Lockey (among others) $50 for the machine (although Lockey settled for only $15 from McLean).

During McLean's brief redirect examination Catlett said that after the machine had been found, an FBI agent questioning him "told me it was worth $200 or more, saying he would give me $200 or more if I got this typewriter for him." Murphy jumped to his feet: "What agent told you that?" Catlett identified him as "Jones" and he stuck to his testimony about the cash offer, although he could not recall how much later he had told McLean the story.

In contrast, Perry (Pat) Catlett, quieter and more cheerful than Mike, stated crisply and precisely that he and his brother had received the Hiss Woodstock "when they were moving from 30th Street to Volta Place" in December 1937. (The two brothers had evidently reversed roles at the trials, with Pat's earlier belief that he had been given the machine later—in 1938—now unmentioned, while Mike's previous certainty about getting it on the Volta Place move had completely dissolved.) Pat Catlett said that the Woodstock was in "fair condition, pretty bad condition," when he received it, and he testified that he carried the machine to a typewriter shop at "K Street and Connecticut Avenue to have it repaired." In identifying the machine shown him as the Hiss Woodstock, Pat cited the same defects mentioned earlier by Mike. Although Pat Catlett had told Hiss's attorneys previously that his wife (to whom he was then engaged) had used the machine to do homework, he now denied that it had been workable enough for her to type on it.[36]

---

*By the second trial Mike Catlett had become "quite sure it was brought down in the car . . . by Mrs. Hiss," whereas Priscilla continued to insist that the Catlett boys had picked up the typewriter along with other gifts in their wagon. Transcript, Second Trial, pp. 1585, 1631–34.

Although Mike Catlett had placed the Woodstock in the "den" of his family's P Street home, Pat insisted that it had been kept mainly in a closet except for the time he took it down to be repaired. Pat, also, could not recall if the Hisses had brought the machine to them, or if he and Mike had carried it back. Nor did he remember which of the Hisses, Alger or Priscilla, had made the present. But he remained "positive" that very soon after receiving the Woodstock he took it to the typewriter repair shop at K Street just off Connecticut Avenue.*

He had not told the FBI about the typewriter when asked about it in January. Murphy then showed Pat a statement he had signed for the bureau asserting that the Hisses "could have lived on Volta Place for several months before they gave it to me."

Initially, in mid-May, Catlett had denied talking to Hiss's lawyers about the machine, only to correct that point in a second May interview with the agents. He now persisted in his original denial of the earlier meetings with McLean. Had he spoken to any lawyers "about where the typewriter was" before its recovery? Murphy asked. "I have not." "You never did?" "No, sir . . . I have not discussed any typewriter with the Hisses' lawyers." (Pat had met several times with those attorneys since January 1949.) "Between January, when the FBI agent saw you, and that day Mr. McLean brought it to your house," Murphy persisted, "you did not talk to a soul about it?" "That is right." Pat went so far as to deny talking to Mike during these months about the Woodstock: "No, sir, never did." "Not once?" "No, sir."

Murphy then startled the witness: "Supposing I tell you that the Woodstock repair shop at Connecticut and K did not come into existence until September of 1938? Would that cause you to fix the time after September when you took it there?" "I don't know, sir." The prosecution thus, through the witness's own recollection of the specific repair shop, undermined Catlett's testimony about receiving the Woodstock at some point before the stolen documents had been typed.

Altering his earlier testimony to Murphy, Pat now admitted that he had spoken to McLean about the typewriter "two or three" months before its recovery in mid-April. The attorney had asked Mike Catlett similar questions, if only because defense counsel may have detected in Murphy's inquiries an interest in later perjury charges against the Catlett brothers—and perhaps anyone else who shielded their distortions. Like his brother before him, Pat Catlett left the stand badly discredited by his contradictory testimony.

Ira Lockey, who followed Catlett as a witness, said he had sold Woodstock N230099 to McLean on April 16. Then came the Washington attorney Charles

---

*At the second trial Pat Catlett backed away from this precise recollection, stating only that the repair shop to which he took the Woodstock was right in [the] neighborhood" of Connecticut Avenue and K Street. Transcript, Second Trial, p. 1727.

Houston, who described how he and McLean had made the contacts necessary to find the machine. But Houston's account remained fuzzy and confusing: "The next day, and final day, Mr. Lockey called me and I called you and then I got another call from you and you met me at the Catletts'. . . . There was a typewriter there present at the time when I came in." Houston never said how McLean had finally acquired the machine from Lockey.[37]

Among Murphy's five rebuttal witnesses, each challenging aspects of the Catletts' testimony, was Claudia Catlett's daughter Burnetta Fisher, who had received the Woodstock from Pat while she was in high school. She had used the machine frequently, indicating that it had been in workable condition years after it left the Hisses' possession, having been repaired.[38]

The FBI agent whom Mike Catlett had accused of offering him a $200 bribe to deliver the Woodstock to the government, Courtland J. Jones, denied making such an offer: "The only thing mentioned concerning money was the fact that he [Mike Catlett] told me he had received $40 from Donald Hiss to assist him in locating the Woodstock typewriter."[39]

Stryker berated the FBI agents, including Jones, for intimidating the Catletts. Had not Jones quickly determined that Mike Catlett was "an ignorant colored boy," asked Stryker, that both brothers were "uneducated colored boys"? "Yes," came the response, "I thought he did not receive much education."* But Jones denied asking Catlett why he had not sold the Woodstock to the FBI "or something like that": "I asked why he had not told the agents in January he had received the typewriter from Mr. Hiss."

Harry C. Hawkins, chief of State's Trade Agreements Section from 1936 to 1943, an office that Francis Sayre supervised, said that his department had sent to Sayre the original of the microfilmed "Darlington report" without a carbon copy (Ramos Feehan had testified that the microfilming had been done from a carbon copy). But Hawkins said that carbons of the document had been sent to other divisions within State. He also contradicted Eunice Lincoln's testimony by recalling times he had gone into Hiss's office on business when the latter was not present, without anyone stopping him from entering. Hawkins acknowledged to Murphy he had "no specific recollection" of any instance in which he had been in Hiss's office alone, only an assumption that while waiting for Sayre at times he

---

*Mike Catlett's story fell apart at the second trial, when he changed his testimony. There he said that Jones had not offered him $200 to get the Woodstock—a point on which he insisted at the first trial—but only that "Mr. Jones said that he would have given me $200 for the typewriter. He said I would have." Also at the second trial, Army Sergeant George Roulhac, who boarded with the Catletts in 1938, testified that he first saw a typewriter in the home "about three months after we lived there," or sometime in April or May 1938, not earlier as the Catletts had avowed. Cross made no effort to contradict Roulhac. Transcript, Second Trial, pp. 1660, 2965–71.

might have wandered in and sat there. Nor could Hawkins say definitely that his secretary had not attached carbons to the original ribbon copy of the Darlington memorandum when sending it to Sayre's office, a practice previous witnesses had described as normal at the time.[40]

Two other State Department witnesses called by the defense, Charles Darlington and Frank Duvall, did not prove especially helpful to Hiss. Darlington tried to implicate Julian Wadleigh in snooping within their offices at the Trade Agreements Section, but he could provide no evidence for this suspicion. Duvall, billed as an expert witness on documents routing within State in 1937–38, proved to have little expertise on that question beyond a general knowledge of departmental procedures at the time. Although McLean showed through Duvall's testimony that departmental security had unquestionably been lax during the late 1930s, suggesting that many people might have read—and taken—the documents later turned over by Chambers, the idea did not necessarily exonerate Hiss. Quite the contrary, since a trusted departmental employee such as Hiss would have found it easy to obtain access to duplicates of "information copies," even of cables not routed to Sayre's office, which later appeared on the typed and microfilmed exhibits.[41]

A bevy of character witnesses attested to Alger Hiss's reputation for "integrity, loyalty and veracity," either by taking the stand or filing depositions. They included two Supreme Court justices, several other jurists, an admiral, a former solicitor general, a onetime Democratic presidential nominee and a future one, and a handful of State Department officials.

The testimony of the Supreme Court justices was unprecedented. On June 22, after shaking Judge Kaufman's hand, Felix Frankfurter described his early relationship with Hiss, primarily during the period he selected the young Harvard Law graduate to serve as Justice Holmes's secretary. Frankfurter called Hiss's reputation "excellent": "I never heard it called into question."[*][42]

Opening his cross-examination, Murphy challenged that remark and asked whether Judge Jerome Frank had not complained to Frankfurter about Hiss's role in the AAA purge. Frankfurter recalled the incident vaguely, but insisted it did not involve any question of Hiss's loyalty as an American. Had the incident not raised a question about Hiss's loyalty to his superior, Judge Frank? Frankfurter, apparently nettled, denied any knowledge of this or any "independent recollection" that he had even recommended Hiss to Frank, although

---

*Apparently Frankfurter had forgotten writing to John Lord O'Brian in 1938 after receiving one such challenge—which concerned him deeply at the time—to Hiss's integrity. See Frankfurter to of O'Brian, March 10, 1938, and O'Brian to Frankfurter, March 12, 1938, Frankfurter MSS, Library of Congress.

he thought that likely. "Did you recommend Lee Pressman?" asked Murphy. Kaufman sustained Stryker's objection to the query as "immaterial," but, despite Kaufman's ruling, Frankfurter persisted in his answer: "I should say it is highly unlikely."

Justice Stanley Reed outlined Hiss's work at the Justice Department in 1935–36 and agreed that his reputation for "integrity, loyalty and veracity" was good "as far as I know." Reed, who was not well acquainted with Hiss, endorsed the defendant's reputation in less categorical terms than Frankfurter: "I have never heard it questioned until these matters came up."[43]

Several Hiss character witnesses received sharp cross-examination. Thus, John W. Davis, the 1924 Democratic candidate for president and one of Hiss's most faithful supporters among Carnegie Endowment trustees, said he had come to know Hiss well since Hiss became the Endowment's president. But Davis conceded to Murphy that he had first met Hiss only in mid-1948 and had learned of him before then only in connection with his "various public offices." Moreover, according to Davis, he had not received reports prior to the summer of 1948 that Hiss was a Communist.*[44]

Testifying to Hiss's pro-British sentiments at the time of the Nazi-Soviet Pact (when Communists opposed American aid to England), Stanley K. Hornbeck related his knowledge of his former assistant. Hornbeck also said Hiss had favored aiding only the Nationalist government in China and not the Communist insurgents during the war, a dubious argument since the Soviet government took much the same position at the time toward Chiang Kai-shek's regime, its wartime ally. Hornbeck recalled Hiss making handwritten notes to summarize documents for him, the practice Hiss said had been followed with Sayre as well.[45]

But Hornbeck agreed that Hiss had "summarized" only lengthy cables, not brief two-line documents such as the Mary Martin telegram. Moreover, he could not recall Hiss composing handwritten summaries of documents when he (Hornbeck) was away from Washington. Murphy's main concern was whether Hornbeck had heard "reports concerning the loyalty of the defendant." Neither the prosecutor nor the witness mentioned William C. Bullitt's name, although obviously both were familiar with his evidence, and Hornbeck replied: "A close personal friend of mine came to see me on one occasion and said he had heard . . . that Mr. Hiss was a fellow traveler."

---

*Dean Acheson told a conflicting story to a Senate Foreign Relations Committee hearing in January 1949, saying there that "Mr. John Davis spoke to me about the matter in the early part of 1947 and I told him . . . that there had been these rumors about [Hiss] . . . and that I did not take any stock in these rumors." But Murphy knew nothing about this executive-session testimony. Dean Acheson, Executive Session Testimony, *Senate Foreign Relations Committee (Historical Series)*, January 14, 1949.

Others who avowed a knowledge of Alger Hiss's exemplary reputation included retired Admiral Arthur J. Hepburn, who had worked with Hiss at Dumbarton Oaks and the San Francisco U.N. Conference; Calvert Magruder, chief judge of the U.S. Court of Appeals for the First Circuit (Boston), who had taught Hiss at Harvard Law and become friendly with him later in Washington; Judge Charles E. Wyzanski, Jr., a friend since Harvard days; corporation lawyer Gerard Swope, Jr., who had worked with Hiss at the New York firm of Wright, Gordon in 1932–33; Philip C. Jessup, Carnegie Endowment trustee and State Department "ambassador at large," who had known Hiss and served with him both at State and at the Endowment; Governor Adlai Stevenson of Illinois, who knew Hiss first in AAA's Legal Division and a decade later when Stevenson attended the San Francisco UN meeting; and former Solicitor General Charles Fahy, a Washington friend.[46]

The prosecutor could do nothing to counter the effect of this procession of eminent defense witnesses except to bring out in cross-examination that all of them— Hornbeck excepted—knew little about the events that had led to Hiss's indictment for perjury. But Murphy did subpoena as a rebuttal witness John Foster Dulles, whose testimony did not enhance Hiss's reputation for "integrity, loyalty and veracity."

Reviewing his relations with Hiss at the Carnegie Endowment since first offering him the post of president in late 1946, Dulles described his conversations with Hiss in 1947–48 about rumors of the latter's Communist ties. A critical element in Dulles's testimony was his statement that Hiss told him in 1947 he had "satisfied the FBI or some such language" (Hiss denied making such a statement to Dulles). Stryker objected repeatedly to Murphy's questioning on the grounds that none of Dulles's testimony contradicted any of Hiss's earlier statements. Murphy pointed to one obvious discrepancy between Dulles's version of events and Hiss's. Dulles had talked to Hiss on August 18, 1948, before he left for Europe, explaining the embarrassment involved for the Endowment in the charges against Hiss. He said he had obtained from Hiss a firm commitment to resign "at a fairly early date," probably "sometime in September," once the HUAC hearings had been concluded. Hiss had previously denied this. But Dulles could not remember whether, in Stryker's words, Hiss had "made a definite, flat, binding promise that he would resign in September." Rather, defense counsel suggested, "it was merely discussed as a possible date."[47]

Alger Hiss took the stand on June 23:

> STRYKER: Mr. Hiss, are you now or have you ever been a member of the Communist Party?
> HISS: I am not and I never have been.
> STRYKER: Or a fellow traveler or a sympathizer?
> HISS: No, Mr. Stryker, I never have.

Hiss acknowledged authorship of the four handwritten notes turned over by Chambers. But he denied having furnished Chambers any "unauthorized" government information—handwritten, typed, or microfilmed.[48]

Those specifics attended to, Stryker moved to review his client's life. He dwelt on Hiss's year with Justice Holmes, pointing out that the defendant had dealt discreetly with much "secret and confidential" material as Holmes's clerk. He reiterated the point in connection with all of Hiss's subsequent jobs: that he had handled without challenge or suspicion at every stage of his career "confidential, secret information."

Hiss detailed his work in preparing a security system for the Dumbarton Oaks Conference ("I was in charge of it"), his help in making arrangements for President Roosevelt's schedule at Yalta ("I was privy to and participated in a very small way"), and his greater role in organizing the UN San Francisco conference, easily his finest achievement as a government official. He described his service as principal adviser to the U.S. delegation at the first UN General Assembly early in 1946, and his subsequent post at the Carnegie Endowment. Concerning his departure from that position, Hiss said only that he had submitted his resignation in December 1948 but that the trustees had declined to accept it "and I continued to serve out my full term." (Hiss omitted mentioning the three-month leave of absence.)

When Stryker raised the question of Hiss's relations with Chambers during the 1930s, the witness repeated earlier testimony. He denied that he and Priscilla had become friendly with the Crowleys/Chamberses or that the families had seen each other regularly after the initial contacts in "the winter of 1935–36." He placed his last meeting with "Crosley" sometime in May or June of 1936 and reiterated that these final encounters involved efforts by Crosley to borrow money. Hiss agreed that he had given Crosley his old Ford and that he received an Oriental rug from him, both in 1936. Asked by Stryker if he had handed over to Chambers any of the typewritten, handwritten, or microfilmed documents in evidence, Hiss replied emphatically: "I certainly did not."

More denials followed. His wife had not typed documents for Chambers, he had not met Colonel Bykov, and Chambers had never visited him in 1937–38 at his 30th Street or Volta Place residence. Nor had he loaned Chambers $400 to buy a car. And during their Commodore Hotel confrontation, according to Hiss, he had identified Chambers as Crosley "without hesitation."

Stressing his cooperation with the FBI and Justice Department in early December—"I was as interested in trying to find out the real facts in this matter as they could possibly be"—Hiss noted he had told McLean to hand over the insurance-company letters found to have been typed on his "old machine," whose "name or the make" he did not then remember. Since that time his "impression" had changed and he recalled its make. "What has changed it?" asked Stryker. "The information discovered by my counsel with respect to the Catletts." He said he had instructed his lawyers to locate the machine, and when it was found by McLean in mid-April, he had told Stryker "to offer it to the Government for their inspection."

Questioning centered on when Hiss purchased a portable typewriter. His "best recollection" was "in the fall of 1937," when, Stryker would later argue, Hiss had disposed of the Woodstock to the Catletts. But Hiss could not say how he had got rid of the Corona portable in 1942: "Mrs. Hiss did the disposing." Did the family then purchase another portable? "We were given by a friend a second portable, which we now have I might add," responded Hiss, not alluding either to the frequent transfer of the portable between his family and Cynthia Jones or to the fact that he had recovered the machine from her only the previous fall after Chambers turned over the documents.*

Shifting to the Nye Committee period, Hiss said he had never given Chambers "any furniture or books" such as those described by Esther and Whittaker.† In conclusion, Stryker led Hiss through a description of his handling by HUAC at the public confrontation on August 25, with the defendant noting that, even earlier, "members of the Committee by statements indicated an [unfriendly] attitude toward me." After Hiss's lengthy and scathing portrayal of HUAC's behavior, Stryker concluded by asking: "And in truth and in fact are you not guilty?" The defendant answered: "I am not guilty."

While Murphy's cross-examination moved rapidly in seemingly unfocused fashion from subject to subject, seldom bearing down on major points, Hiss remained almost unflappable. "Mr. Witness," Murphy began, "do you want to amplify or change any of your testimony that you have given us so far the last three days?" "No, Mr. Murphy." The prosecutor then reviewed the dozen or more occasions on which Hiss agreed that he had seen Chambers. When Hiss challenged a characterization of Chambers as "particularly shabby" on his first visit, Murphy alluded to Malcolm Cowley's testimony: "You did not notice his linen to be pretty bad, did you, in any of those twelve times you talked to him?" "I would not notice linen unless it was very offensive," came the response.

Murphy challenged the witness's memory of the various dates on which he saw Chambers, much as Stryker had done with both Whittaker and Esther

---

*Three months previously, before Mike Catlett began telling McLean that his family had received the Woodstock in 1937, perhaps earlier, Hiss had been far less definite about the portable. Questioned by Stryker and Harold Shapero on March 8, 1949, he said only that "at some time we definitely had in addition [to the Woodstock] an old portable typewriter." "Did you remember the make?" he was then asked. "I do not and I do not remember when we got it." "Statement of Alger Hiss," Hiss Defense Files, p. 66.

†To Stryker and Shapero on March 8, 1949, Hiss responded differently: "There was at the 28th Street house an old rug which had been patched in part, and a broken sofa which Priscilla had left for the superintendent . . . perhaps an old wing chair. . . . Apparently Chambers appropriated the rug and the sofa & chair, and that appropriation accounts for his testimony. . . ." "Statement of Alger Hiss," p. 60.

Chambers. Hiss testified that Chambers had borrowed his Ford "for a period of about two months" during the fall of 1935. But he pleaded ignorance as to what use Chambers made of the vehicle on the occasions that he "borrowed" it. Murphy brought out the fact that Hiss had only one car when he loaned his Ford to Chambers: "Yes, but I was shopping for another one at that very time." Hiss said Chambers took "the title certificate at the same time . . . as evidence he was in lawful possession of the car." Murphy seemed amused by the claim, since possession of the title certificate—without some accompanying paper explaining the transaction—would indicate "if a policeman stopped him" that the bearer was Alger Hiss. Why had he given Chambers the title to the Ford in 1936—*signed* over this time—despite the latter's purported unpaid debts and continued requests for money? To fulfill an earlier promise, Hiss responded.

Did Hiss type? "I do not," came the response. "I don't think I have typed a half page since" college. The prosecutor then questioned him about his recollection of family typewriters. A "second-hand portable," the Corona, had been purchased by Mrs. Hiss, said the witness, "sometime in the fall of 1937." Hiss gave a careful response to Murphy's inquiry concerning the Woodstock: "I remember what I now know to be a Woodstock typewriter brought from—I remember the old office machine that Mr. Fansler gave Mrs. Hiss." At first Hiss denied Murphy's claim that he had informed the FBI in December 1948 that the Fansler machine had been in his home "until after 1938." He said he had told the agents "sometime in 1938," but Murphy refreshed the witness's recollection by reading a portion of Hiss's signed December 4 statement containing the phrase "sometime subsequent to 1938."

Agreeing that Priscilla Hiss "typed some," her husband still "would not" categorize her "as a proficient typist." He called her, instead, "a careful one and one who when she did type was very neat" (too neat, presumably, to have made all the errors requiring interlinear corrections on the typed documents).

Although Hiss had told Stryker that he first heard of Chambers's charges in August 1948, Murphy got him to agree that he had learned about the accusations the previous February from Edward Miller. As for his 1947 FBI interview, at which Whittaker Chambers's name had been mentioned, it was one of "40 or 50 names." And the 1946 "congressional rumors" of CP ties? Hiss said he had met with Byrnes about them, but indicated that the decision to contact the FBI for an interview had been his and not Byrnes's: "What did I do after I spoke to [Secretary Byrnes]? I went immediately to my own office and put in a call for Mr. J. Edgar Hoover." (Later in the cross-examination Hiss noted, after Murphy's challenge, that the idea had come from Byrnes.) He informed the FBI agents about the organizations he had belonged to: "I told them of a small editorial group that I had written for during the winter of 1932–33 here in New York as the, I think, International Judicature—I am not sure of the exact name—Society which got out notes on current cases. It specialized, as I recall it, in labor law."

Confronting Hiss with his contradictory statements to HUAC about the Ford gift, Murphy read from his testimony: "I sold him an automobile. I had an old Ford that I threw in with the apartment. . . . I let him have it along with the rent." Hiss admitted making the statements: "That was my best recollection at the time." Murphy stressed the point, citing additional HUAC testimony by Hiss: "[I] charged the rent and threw the car in at the same time. . . . We were using the other car." Despite Hiss's admission that his earlier statement had been inaccurate, Kaufman interrupted to comment on Murphy's questioning: "I don't think that any [HUAC] testimony you have read is inconsistent with the [trial] testimony he has given thus far."

Inquiring about the defense's documents examiners, Murphy asked if the government exhibits offered as standard comparisons to the stolen typed documents had all been produced on the Fansler Woodstock. Kaufman allowed these questions, and Hiss proved less than candid in answering. He falsely denied knowing when his attorneys had first hired such experts, and on the question of whether or not he knew that the experts had identified the "Hiss standards" as typed on the same machine that turned out the Baltimore documents, the witness also lacked candor: "I have no knowledge as to whether the experts said specifically that the standard or the questioned documents were typed on a particular machine. I do know that I was told that they said they were typed on a Woodstock. I was not told more."

When had Hiss learned of the recovery of Woodstock N230099? "I knew the day it was located . . . the next business day when Mr. McLean returned from his house in Darien with the typewriter." Hiss then backed away from an earlier claim made by his counsel. When had he instructed Stryker to make the machine available to the government? "To make it known to the Government? I knew the Government knew about it before. . . . The Catletts told us that they had informed the FBI [in May] that the typewriter had been found." (Only a month after its recovery did the bureau learn inadvertently from Claudia Catlett about the Woodstock's discovery, or even that the Catletts knew anything about it.) Hiss conceded that McLean had rented a Woodstock typewriter earlier that year for "a couple of days I think" (actually several months) to help identify his own machine. "Is that the only reason your counsel got that machine?" Murphy asked. "The only reason that was given to me, Mr. Murphy," stated Hiss, not mentioning the typing samples taken from his wife.

He claimed to have had no precise knowledge about the Woodstock's whereabouts in December 1948 except that Priscilla had given the machine away: "I did not know the details." Only through his conversations with McLean had he learned that the Catletts received it: "I had not talked to the Catletts." "That is the reason for your present knowledge?" Murphy inquired. "Yes, sir." Moments later Hiss added: "I did not have any independent recollection of the disposal of the typewriter, quite frankly. I have never had any independent personal recollection." The prosecutor persisted: "So that you do not know of your own knowledge whether or not that typewriter was given to the Catletts, or not, is that correct?" " In the sense of my recollection it is correct." Thus Hiss in carefully phrased denials circumvented having to admit that he had known the facts since the previous December.

Next Murphy raised the subject of Hiss's 1946 FBI interview. Had Hiss mentioned his earlier relationship with Lee Pressman? Yes, and the witness repeated the "substance" of those 1946 statements. He could not recall telling the FBI that Pressman might have been involved in selecting him for the AAA (Hiss had described the FBI interview to Stryker in detail during pretrial questioning in March). Murphy also confronted Hiss with the fact that not only had he heard the name Whittaker Chambers from the FBI in 1947 and from a friend in February 1948, but he had been questioned about Chambers before the grand jury in March 1948. Hiss could not recall the episode.

The prosecutor reminded Hiss that in December 1948 he had told the grand jury about gifts made to the Catlett family but had not mentioned giving them a typewriter. Hiss agreed and added: "I thought Mrs. Catlett was dead at that time." He said he had not remembered giving the Catletts a typewriter when he testified the previous December (an assertion contradicted by John F. Davis's letter describing this recollection). Moreover, Hiss conceded that when testifying before HUAC in August he had mentioned the names of a maid, Martha Pope, who had worked previous to Claudia Catlett, and another maid employed at Volta Place after Mrs. Catlett's illness, but that he had not named Claudia Catlett.

Changing his previous testimony that the Oriental rug that Chambers gave him had been on the floor constantly at P Street and 30th Street (Mrs. Catlett said that the rug had been rolled up in a closet at 30th Street in 1937), Hiss now remembered "trying" the rug in various rooms at both residences but "not the whole time." Aligning his recollections with Mrs. Catlett's testimony about 30th Street, he avowed: "I know we did not use it there continuously."

What about the $400 car loan? Hiss admitted having borrowed $300 in December 1937, a month after withdrawing the $400 supposedly to purchase items for the Volta Place home with cash. The $400 in November had been "to take care of these items that we bought by check or bought on charge account." Hiss had said earlier that all of these transactions were necessary because the Volta Place home was considerably bigger than his 30th Street residence, but Murphy read into the record a statement Hiss made to the grand jury on December 14 describing Volta Place as "a slightly larger detached house."

The prosecutor suggested that Hiss's belated story about acquiring a portable typewriter in the fall of 1937 also differed significantly from his grand jury testimony. At that time the witness had been uncertain whether or not he had owned both machines at once. Furthermore, he had remembered nothing in December 1948 about buying the portable: "'I frankly do not recall it at all."

Now Hiss agreed that he had received State Department documents while working for the Nye Committee—"copies" but not "originals"—thus revising his earlier testimony on the matter. Still, he insisted inaccurately: "I personally had little to do with that. The flow of those documents started after I had left the committee." (Not so. Hiss left the committee only near the end, after almost all such State Department materials had been sent over. Hiss dealt directly with Joseph C. Green of the State Department in receiving such documents.)

Murphy returned to Hiss's involvement in the International Juridical Association. He asked whether the witness had known Carol Weiss King, and Hiss replied carefully: "I think I met her once, perhaps twice, during that period." Murphy persisted: "My question is, did you know her?" Hiss's response: "I cannot answer that yes or no." (Mrs. King had told Harold Rosenwald in January that she "knew Alger and Priscilla Hiss and liked them very much.") Nor could he recall composing any articles for the group, although he "probably wrote one or two"—yet another instance of Hiss's fuzzy memory on the stand but precise recollections elsewhere (Hiss had spent a considerable amount of time working on IJA research projects, evenings and weekends, while living in New York).

Cross-examination turned up additional examples of inconsistencies between Hiss's trial testimony and his earlier statements. Murphy showed that his grand jury comments about Chambers's gift of a rug had been far less exact than his trial statements, to the point that the previous December he could not recall whether Chambers or Mrs. Hiss had been present at the time. Nor was there any mention in the earlier account of a conversation with Chambers about the alleged "gift" from "a wealthy patron." Murphy read into the record both HUAC and grand jury excerpts contradicting various aspects of Hiss's testimony, the most telling of which concerned his earlier denial that he had written the Mary Martin cable: "It just doesn't look like my idea of my handwriting." Hiss agreed that he had recommended Noel Field to Sayre in 1939 for a possible job in the Philippines, again with little clear explanation as to why.

The prosecutor returned to Hiss's numerous grand jury statements in December 1948 in which he had denied knowledge of how the Fansler Woodstock had been disposed of. "I am sure," the witness agreed, "that I said [to the grand jury] I did not independently, of my own recollection, definitely recall." One statement to the grand jury remains particularly damning in the light of Hiss's December 7, 1948, phone call to John F. Davis. When a grand juror asked, "How did you dispose of the typewriter?" Hiss responded, "I frankly have no idea."

Regarding what Hiss had told Dulles about his 1946 interview with the FBI, he dated his "telephone" conversation with Dulles on the subject in December 1946, before assuming the Endowment's presidency. But Murphy, evidently aware of

Dulles's memos, corrected the witness and noted that the discussion had taken place in February 1948. Hiss could not remember the conversation. Had Dulles asked Hiss at some point during the HUAC hearings to resign "voluntarily," "out of consideration for the Endowment?" Hiss responded: "He did not." (Later Hiss retracted that statement and recalled the conversation.) Nor, according to Hiss, had he asked Dulles to delay the matter of resignation until after the committee hearings ended. (Again, Hiss would later admit having done so.)

At that point Murphy read into the record Hiss's March 16, 1948, grand jury testimony when asked if he knew "an individual by the name of Whittaker Chambers." Hiss had then responded: "No, I have been asked that question before but I do not know Mr. Chambers." Earlier in trial testimony Hiss had denied having made any connection between the 1947 FBI questions about Chambers and the February 1948 account of the latter's charges by his friend Edward Miller (Donald Hiss's later memo contradicts his brother's denial).

When Murphy concluded, Stryker rose to demand access to all the grand jury minutes "from parts of which Mr. Murphy has read and referred to." Over Murphy's objection, Kaufman ruled that the defense was "entitled to the [entire] testimony of the witness on the days from which you read parts of the testimony." Stryker also wanted the March 25, 1946, FBI interview with Hiss, and Kaufman ordered that produced as well. The prosecutor offered to place in evidence the entire grand jury transcript, but now it was Stryker's turn to object, and Kaufman took the decision under advisement.

Alger Hiss left the stand a bit battered by Murphy's relentless comparison of his earlier statements with his contradictory trial evidence. But, like Chambers, he had held firmly to his basic story.

Priscilla Hiss was a gentle-faced, small, well-tailored woman wearing white gloves and a fixed smile. She chose, in Quaker fashion, to "affirm" rather than "swear" her oath. Initially her voice, like those of both Esther and Whittaker Chambers, proved too soft for the courtroom, and Stryker asked that she speak louder.[49]

After the standard autobiographical review, Stryker asked how she had met George Crosley. The answer stirred murmurs in the audience, since Stryker had berated Esther Chambers for a similar response. "I expect my husband said, 'This is my wife.'" As for Mrs. Chambers, she "was introduced [to me] as Mrs. Crosley." "Did you ever call her by her first name . . . [or] by the name of Liza . . . ? "No." "Did she at any time ever address you as Pros or Prossy?" "She did not, Mr. Stryker."

The defense counsel had difficulty in framing questions for Mrs. Hiss—he labored to place sufficient detail in his question to elicit an obvious answer, and this brought repeated objections from Murphy, some of which Kaufman sustained. He got the witness to deny Esther Chambers's story about receiving "a very fine old linen towel" to help clean her baby. Mrs. Hiss also said that the Chambers couple had never visited Volta Place for a party—wedding anniversary, New Year's Eve, or any other kind.

Then came the critical question: "Did you ever hand Exhibits 1 to 47, which include the four handwritten notes and the typewritten notes, to Mr. Chambers at any time?" "I certainly did not." "Did you ever agree in the summer of 1937 to make typewritten . . . copies of State Department papers for the purpose of transmitting them to Mr. Chambers?" "No, Mr. Stryker, I didn't." "Did your husband ever ask you to do that?" "No."

Asked about Claudia Catlett, Mrs. Hiss said she had worked for the Hisses full-time from 1934 to 1938: "Clidie [sic] came and got breakfast . . . about eight o'clock . . . she was a full-time maid and stayed through dinner."

When had Mrs. Hiss received her father's Woodstock? "I think 1932 is just about right." Was the typewriter exhibited at the trial, Woodstock N230099, the machine Mr. Fansler gave her? "Yes, I am sure it is the machine." When had she acquired a portable? "I am pretty sure it was in the fall of 1937." And when had it been disposed of? "In the fall of 1943." Did the Hisses acquire another portable at that time? "Yes." "And have you still got that?" "Yes."

She conceded having told the grand jury that she believed the Fansler Woodstock had been at Volta Place and also that she had disposed of it either to a junk dealer or to the Salvation Army. Now, however, Mrs. Hiss believed it had been the portable that went to the Salvation Army in 1943. How had her recollection been refreshed about the manner in which she got rid of the Woodstock? "Because of the Catlett boy's description of the gift of the typewriter and several other things that I also remember giving him."

Denying that she gave Chambers the $400 withdrawn from her savings account at Riggs National in November 1937, Priscilla Hiss agreed with her husband that the money was used to buy household furnishings for the Volta Place home. After some last-minute questions ending with the witness's account of a missing pocketbook at Volta Place (it held a house key and car key, according to Priscilla), Stryker sat down. This left an excited courtroom audience speculating over this latest example of Stryker's stagecraft: Had Chambers somehow stolen Mrs. Hiss's purse and, using her key, entered Volta Place and typed the documents? (Priscilla Hiss later conceded that the theft had not been reported to the police.)

Murphy returned to the subject of the witness's Riggs National checking account. Mrs. Hiss said she had maintained a checking account and a number of Washington charge accounts in 1937, but still insisted she had spent the withdrawn $400 by the time—forty days later—the Hisses moved into Volta Place on December 29, 1937. The prosecutor reviewed every purchase the witness said she had made, asking where each had been bought, how it had been delivered, and the precise purchase amount. (The FBI had gone to Washington antique and furniture stores before the trial trying unsuccessfully to locate records of such purchases by Priscilla Hiss in November or December 1937.)

In the midst of questions concerning Mrs. Hiss's New York residences in the early 1930s, Murphy asked suddenly: "And during that time were you a member of the Socialist Party?" "I do not think so," came the response. Hadn't she registered as a member of the Socialist Party? "I don't think so. I voted for Norman Thomas." Murphy produced a New York City voter-roll page that included Priscilla Hiss's 1932 Socialist registration. The witness challenged the point: "I was not a member of the Socialist Party and I assume that I was indicating that I was going to vote for Mr. Thomas." "Mrs. Hiss, don't you know that the records of the Socialist Party, Morningside branch, list you in 1932 as a member?" "I certainly do not know that," she replied. Priscilla Hiss also denied knowing the chairman of that branch in 1932, Mrs. Corliss Lamont, or her husband, a Columbia University philosophy professor. (Norman Thomas told Victor Lasky in 1949 that the Lamonts informed him they had known Mrs. Hiss well in 1932.)[50]

After obtaining Priscilla Hiss's admission that she had typed the four "Hiss standards" used by the FBI lab to identify the Fansler machine as the one on which the Chambers documents had been typed, Murphy turned to her reasons for giving the machine away. Mechanical defects had already appeared in the Woodstock, Mrs. Hiss said, by 1936 or '37, even earlier. She described these defects, when pressed further, as a ribbon that "puckered like a fold of cloth" and keys that sometimes stuck. Apart from the defects, she conceded moments later, "nothing happened to [the machine] that prompted me to give it to [the Catletts]." (But Priscilla Hiss had testified to the grand jury in December 1948 that she did not know whether any keys on the old office typewriter—the Woodstock—had stuck improperly: "I don't recall any.") Murphy asked, almost casually, if she had had "occasion to write the exhibits in evidence," the stolen typed documents. "Certainly not," Mrs. Hiss responded angrily. "I did not type them."

As for disposing of the Woodstock, the Catletts had come to the Hisses' 30th Street house in late December 1937 "with their little express wagon," into which they loaded an old wind-up Victrola, some clothes, and the typewriter. (In Alger Hiss's earlier account, Priscilla herself had driven to the Catletts' home with the machine. When talking to McLean about the incident in April, the Catlett brothers recalled it both ways.)

Although Mrs. Hiss said the Catletts took the gifts to their P Street home, Murphy noted that—according to their lease—the Catlett family had moved to P Street on January 17, 1938, or a month or so after the Hisses claimed to have given the machine away. Priscilla remained skeptical: "I would think it most unlikely, from my knowledge of Georgetown and people like the Catletts, if there was some such thing as a lease it in no way affected their residence in the house." Murphy asked whether Mrs. Hiss had met Claudia Catlett in Georgetown in

1946. "No, I did not recall it. I am sure since she said it happened, I am sure she is right and it did happen."

In the case of the portable Corona, Priscilla Hiss said she bought it during the fall of 1937 for use by her son Timothy, then eleven years old.

After the witness stated she had first met Chambers at 28th Street "when he came to see the apartment," Murphy read some conflicting and highly damaging statements from the transcript of Priscilla Hiss's grand jury appearance. There she testified she "must have seen [Crosley] two or three times I imagine before he and his wife came to look at our apartment . . . to see if she would think it would do for subletting." These visits, Priscilla Hiss told the grand jury, had been at 28th Street:

> QUESTION: What was he doing at your house on those two or three occasions?
> MRS. HISS: He was simply calling.
> QUESTION: Upon whom?
> MRS. HISS: Upon my husband. . . .
> QUESTION: You don't remember what they talked about at all?
> MRS. HISS: No.
> QUESTION: Were they purely social calls?
> MRS. HISS: I think so, yes.

"Which is correct," Murphy demanded of the witness, "what you told the grand jury in December or what you told these ladies and gentlemen today?" Priscilla Hiss challenged his assumption: "Well, I don't think they are very inconsistent." Murphy then read a strangely unexplained and plainly "inconsistent" portion of Mrs. Hiss's Grand Jury testimony in which she said of Crosley's visits:

> QUESTION: Those first two or three visits that you spoke of. Had you invited Crosley to come to the house?
> MRS. HISS: No. I think he simply dropped in. I think he is a dropper-inner.
> QUESTION: Did he drop in alone?
> MRS. HISS: Yes.
> QUESTION: And the first time that you saw his wife I take it was the time that the two of them came to look at your apartment?
> MRS. HISS: That's right. . . .

In another of her statements to the grand jury Murphy noted, Priscilla Hiss had said she and her husband "may" have disposed of the Fansler machine as late as 1943, when they moved out of Volta Place. Nor, when asked by grand jurors, could she recall when or how the Corona portable had been purchased, nor anything about its make, nor when or how she had disposed of it. Murphy also confronted Mrs. Hiss with an assertion she had made to the grand jury that proved embarrassing in view of her contradictory trial testimony. The previous December Mrs. Hiss had said flatly: "I am just not a typist, and I don't type."

After some desultory questioning by Stryker, the witness stepped down. Priscilla Hiss's trial testimony had conflicted so regularly with her previous statements to the grand jury or with material collected during the FBI investigation that it seriously damaged her husband's claims.

Her evident nervousness did not end when she left the witness chair. "Prossy 'went into a panic,'" her son Anthony wrote, "as Al[ger] describes it now. 'At first [when the case began] she was stunned in a way I'd never seen before. . . . Then as soon as we were alone she reacted with great anxiety. . . .' Prossy remained this way almost continuously, and [for the next two years] . . . [nothing] could ever stop her from being overanxious and on occasion hysterical for more than an hour or two at a time." Anthony Hiss quoted his father's 1977 postmortem on the 1949 situation:

> I, myself, was not frightened. As Helen Buttenwieser said to me once, "Alger, you know, you don't terrorize easily." But Prosy did go into a type of collapse. I tried to impart courage to her. I didn't catch fear from her. I'd always known that she frightened easily. . . . God, it was burdensome to go over her anxieties at length [in private with her]. Every day seemed a new wound to her. One blow after another. . . . And, by God, the last thing I wanted to do after a long day with the lawyers was a long anxious talk session with Prossy, when I would have enjoyed sleeping or reading or being loving. . . . But Prossy got into a near paranoid state, I guess I'd call it. She believed the walls of our apartment were bugged. . . . She was dependent on me and I had to support her. It was on my mind all the time.[51]

Although Alger Hiss did not describe the reasons for his wife's strained emotions at the time, her testimony made it clear that Priscilla found it more difficult than did her husband to maintain their story of earlier casual knowledge of Chambers—particularly with respect to her Woodstock typewriter and the stolen material that had been typed on it.

Both sides rested their cases on the morning of July 6. Stryker began his summation by pointing out that the prosecutor had to show to the jury's satisfaction, "and beyond a reasonable doubt, that Mr. Hiss furnished, transmitted, and delivered these papers to Chambers." The burden of proof, he reiterated, was on Murphy "to establish beyond a reasonable doubt that Whittaker Chambers told the truth about this matter." And Chambers was the only witness to this transaction, Stryker reminded the jurors, quoting Murphy's opening statement that "if you don't believe Chambers then we have no case under the federal perjury rule."[52]

Before describing Chambers, Stryker announced that he wished "to acquit" J. Parnell Thomas and the other HUAC members from knowledge of Chambers's intention "to commit perjury" before the committee. Not that HUAC had been faultless in the matter of his testimony: "It was a good deal as though a distributor of milk had filled several bottles from the gutter . . . and sent them out as Grade A certified milk . . . he should not have certified it."

Then he turned to the dissection of the government's chief witness: "He began life with trickery and deceit. . . . [W]e find the pattern of an unusual personality. I am only a layman . . . [but] I observe in his life strange incidents, strange patterns in them." Stryker then rehearsed a selective account of Chambers's past, closely following his "hypothetical question" to Dr. Binger. As for Chambers's credibility, "I would not believe him if the FBI erected a stack of Bibles as high as the building . . . this man on whose sole word they are asking you to destroy Alger Hiss, this man had no respect for God."

Dwelling on Chambers's having lived in his mother's house with Ida Dales, Stryker asked: "Can [you] think of a lower, filthier, more scoundrel piece of conduct in the world?" The lawyer denounced Chambers for "psychopathic . . . sadism, enjoyment in the creation of suffering by a filthy act. . . . A man who is an enemy of the republic, a blasphemer of Christ, a disbeliever in God, with no respect either for matrimony or for motherhood . . . there is not one decent thing that I can think of that Whittaker Chambers has not shown himself against."

He reminded the jury of Malcolm Cowley's testimony about Chambers naming Sayre as a Communist. Julian Wadleigh became, in Stryker's words, Chambers's "fellow thief and confederate in crime . . . an acknowledged thief and rogue on his own testimony." He suggested that Chambers had testified before HUAC mainly to influence the 1948 presidential election, to curry favor with the Republicans and "those who did not like the New Deal." He reiterated Truman's "red herring" description of Chambers's charges and argued that the *Time* editor had hoped to become influential if Republicans emerged as "the successful party. But, you see, he guessed wrong on that." And he guessed wrong, according to Stryker, because Alger Hiss fought back. (Thus did Stryker entangle Chambers in an argument combining elements of both the "conscious" and "unconscious" theories of motivation laid out earlier by Harold Rosenwald.)

As for Hiss, Stryker called him "an honest and maligned and falsely accused gentleman." He came to Chambers's statement at the Baltimore hearing on November 17, 1948, that he had withheld knowledge of Hiss's espionage and of the stolen documents in order not to injure a former friend, while still describing Hiss as "the concealed enemy," and Stryker harped on the contradiction. The audience broke into laughter when the defense counsel observed: "You know, that reminds me of the lady who picked up a shotgun and let her husband have both barrels in the head, you know, taking right off the top of his head. She was asked about it afterwards and she said, 'Well, I pulled the trigger sort of soft because I had been very fond of him.'"

Suggesting that Chambers had somehow manufactured the documents and slipped them into the envelope at Nathan Levine's home in order to protect himself against the slander-suit judgment, Stryker contrasted this with Hiss's instruction that Marbury hand the material immediately to the Justice Department. And the hollowed-out pumpkin in which the microfilms were briefly stored: "[W]ithout benefit of psychiatry, what [do] you think of the normality and mentality of a man" who does such a thing? Was that "the act of a rational normal man?"

He ridiculed the notion that Whittaker and Esther Chambers could have become friends of the Hisses when Alger Hiss, like Wadleigh, was allegedly a coconspirator: "It is as though Benedict Arnold had gone around with [Major] André all over the place, gone to New York to cocktail parties, and came back and forth and said 'Here we are together.' It is absurd." And since Alger Hiss was not "an idiot or a stupid man . . . had he been in this thing as Chambers' stories [sic], would he not have acted as Wadleigh acted?" He scoffed also at the testimony of government witnesses, accusing the FBI of having coached them: "The F.B.I. have been all over this thing."

And Claudia Catlett? "An utterly truthful, not at all educated Negro woman from the deep South who was telling the complete truth"—and who said she had never seen Chambers either at 30th Street or at Volta Place. Was she not more credible than Chambers? He tried to get her in the FBI office to remember him "by saying 'You made mashed potatoes.' Can't you see Clidi there on the stand? It reminded me of the picture of Aunt Jemima. 'Did anybody make mashed potatoes?'"

"Now, on the question of this now famous typewriter," Stryker observed, the FBI had not accepted the defense's offer to examine the machine despite the fact that, in Murphy's words, it "had shaken down Washington to find this typewriter." Instead the bureau sent Ramos Feehan—"who said he was an expert"—to testify that the Hiss standards had been typed on the same machine that produced the stolen documents. Why hadn't Stryker cross-examined Feehan? "Because I know . . . that we did not have that typewriter in our possession at the time of the dates of these documents, namely in February and March of 1938. Whether in fact those are on that typewriter or not I don't know . . . [and] I don't care. In my opinion, the evidence does not come anywhere near establishing that they were." (Either Stryker misspoke or he had not been told about the analysis of Woodstock N230099 by defense expert Edwin Fearon, which confirmed that the stolen documents had been typed on that machine.) As for the Hiss Woodstock, "that typewriter left our possession on a move either to Volta Place or a prior move."

Quickly correcting himself, Stryker acknowledged that the 1937 "Hiss standards" showed that the machine had remained in the Hiss household at least until the Volta Place move. Moreover, "the uncontradicted evidence in the case is that in the fall somewhere . . . a portable typewriter was acquired by the Hiss family." How did defense counsel know the Hisses had disposed of the

Woodstock in December 1937? "You heard testimony of Pat and Mike, undoubtedly very ignorant colored boys but honest. . . . Now, I say to you, ladies and gentlemen, that the corroboration is perfect and complete, that testimony of all the Catletts. . . ."

One of Stryker's best points was that the FBI could not find a letter typed by Mrs. Hiss on the Woodstock after May 25, 1937, which—for Stryker—confirmed the fact that the machine had not been used after that prior to being given to the Catletts. As for Chambers's story that he feared an "ambush" when he visited the Hisses in December 1938 after defecting, Stryker called it "the most preposterous bit of testimony that I have ever heard in a court." Esther Chambers? "I don't believe a fair-minded man or woman, and we have twelve who will go into that court room, could believe a word that woman said." Moreover, Chambers had probably "suborned perjury" on his wife's part in connection with her testimony about Hiss's appearance before the Supreme Court: "I would not exclude Chambers from any immoral, indecent, illicit or criminal act in the world."

And Alger Hiss? "Was there a flaw or blemish in that man? . . . This case comes down to this: Who is telling the truth? Alger Hiss or Chambers? . . . Alger Hiss . . . everywhere he has gone and everything he has done and every trail he has left behind is pure, wholesome, sound, clean, decent, strong, fine. Now think of it, Alger Hiss, imagine his prostituting a great career, a great background and a great future. For what? A rug?"

Stryker concluded:

Ladies and gentlemen, I have been called florid-faced. They tell me I have grey hair. Alas, I am afraid it is true. It seems only a moment when people . . . were commenting on my extreme youth . . . but with all my faults if I have offended any one of you in any way, hold it against me, not against Alger Hiss . . .

Ladies and gentlemen, the case will be in your hands. I beg you, I pray you to search your consciences and have no fear, "Yea, though I have walked to the valley of the shadow of death," in this case. Alger Hiss, this long nightmare is drawing to a close. Rest well. Your case, your life, your liberty are in good hands. Thank you. . . .

After a luncheon recess, Murphy began by talking directly to the twelve jurors before turning to his lectern, which had been placed immediately in front of the box. He suggested, clearly with Stryker in mind, that they approach the case "in a cool, analytical fashion without emotion" and "apply your reason to these facts." Murphy then offered some "uncontradicted" facts: "That Mr. Chambers had in his possession copies of original State Department documents," that these documents "were all dated in the first three months of 1938," and "that they were all copies, of course except the handwritten documents, but the typewritten documents were all copied, except No. 10, on the Hiss typewriter." From these "uncontradicted" facts, Murphy submitted, "only one inference can be drawn, only one, and that is that that defendant, that smart, intelligent, American-born man gave them to Chambers." As for "proof" of perjury in federal courts, Murphy noted that there were two ways to determine this: "By two witnesses, or by one witness and corroborating evidence . . . we fit into the second class. . . ."[53]

No match for Stryker's in rhetorical effects, Murphy's summation offered only the analogy of a child caught with jam on his face but who denied having taken jam from the pantry: "Admitted you did not see him." But one's "normal, everyday intelligence . . . tells you that the boy is lying. Why? Why, there is the jam on his face." The jam on Hiss's face, Murphy contended, was "the typewritten documents typed on . . . the Hiss typewriter."

The jurors, Murphy said, would have to set aside certain "emotional factors," one being "that this defendant is a clean-cut, handsome, intelligent American-born male" whereas "Mr. Chambers is short and fat and he had bad teeth." Similarly, "Mrs. Chambers is plain and severe" while "Mrs. Hiss is demure and attractive, and intelligent to boot. Very intelligent." Another "emotional factor" Murphy then raised concerned Stryker's opening remarks that he intended summoning as a witness for Hiss "the shade of Oliver Wendell Holmes." If defense counsel could call "the ghost of that revered Justice" as a character witness, "there are a couple of shades that I would like to call here," two in particular: "One man's name was Judas Iscariot and the other Major General Benedict Arnold."

The prosecutor then tackled Stryker's denunciation of Chambers: "If Mr. Stryker calls Mr. Chambers a moral leper, what is the defendant Hiss? What is the name of an employee of this Government who takes Government papers and gives them to a Communist espionage agent? . . . Very simply, Alger Hiss was a traitor, a traitor to this country, another Benedict Arnold, another Judas Iscariot . . ." If roses that fester "stink worse than weeds," Murphy avowed, "a brilliant man like this man who betrays his trust stinks. Inside of that smiling face that heart is black and cancerous. He is a traitor."

He tore into Stryker's habit of misstating testimony for effect while questioning witnesses—as when defense counsel asked Chambers whether he had lived with a prostitute in New Orleans, knowing that the witness himself had testified at the Baltimore deposition only to having lived in a house where another tenant had been a prostitute, or, later, when Stryker asked the witness: "Were you living with a prostitute named Ida Dales?" Murphy dismissed such innuendo: "Does a man who is married to one woman for 18 years, who is the father of her two children, have no regard for womankind?" As for Chambers's other alleged iniquities, was he the only student ever to have stolen books from his college?

What was Chambers's motive, Murphy asked, in having perjured himself about Hiss as Stryker alleged? To lose a $30,000-a-year job as senior editor of *Time*? Or perhaps "it was because he did not pay back that $135. . . . Let's forget about the rug. $150 and they broke off relations with that debt hanging in mid-air," the prosecutor scoffed. But Stryker had mentioned Chambers injecting himself into the 1948 campaign for "some political advantage," noting that he had read a *Newsweek* story critical of Truman during the August 17 confrontation scene: "The only thing bad about that entire argument is that that confrontation at the Ambassador [sic] was an executive session." In short, "no motive [for perjury by Chambers] has been proved." Chambers came forward with the documents because his story was true: "That motive was not touched upon—truth. Mr. Chambers desired the truth."

Reminding the jurors that Esther and Whittaker Chambers had given the defense most of its information about them at the Baltimore depositions, Murphy argued: "There was not a blessed thing that the defense did not know before this trial commenced . . . they [even] had these documents. . . . They also had the standards of four typewritten letters that the [FBI] expert used as a standard of comparison. They knew everything. They even had the typewriter." "Armed" with this knowledge, Murphy contended, "this defense was conceived. It is not a true defense; it was conceived to avoid the facts." Only the $400 loan had come as a surprise and, to hear Murphy tell it, Stryker "fumbled . . . dropped the ball on that one."

How could the jurors determine whether or not Chambers told the truth about his relationship with the Hisses? Pointing out that the Hisses had testified that neither of the Chamberses had been at the 30th Street house or the one in Volta Place, Murphy mentioned the elaborate descriptions Esther and Whittaker Chambers had provided of both homes, even allowing for a small number of inaccuracies (which Murphy did not acknowledge as such): "Is it possible . . . for two people to describe two houses in such detail and not to have been there? Is it humanly possible?"

Lingering over the Commodore Hotel confrontation scene, Murphy came close to reenacting it. Hiss had not tried to confront Chambers after learning his name, his location, and his charges. As for the Ford transfer, the prosecutor asked the jurors: "When was the last time you gave your car away?"

Now Murphy's ridicule reached a high point:

This Harvard man, a brilliant law student, then a lawyer . . . permitted a man whom he did not know too well, did not know where he worked, did not know where he could reach him, permitted him to become a sub-tenant of his without a written lease, without demanding the money in advance, and then, to clinch the bargain in 1935, to clinch it, gave him a Ford.

Later Hiss changed that testimony to state that he gave Chambers "the use" of the Ford, a detail that Murphy found revealing: "That is Mr. Hiss's forte. He is able to distinguish, to combine truth with half-truth, a little bit to color it, a little bit more to testify and then, if placed in a corner, to rely upon the truthful part, and you have to be pretty good to do that, and he is pretty good."

The prosecutor seemed to derive special pleasure in spoofing Stryker's portrayal of Hiss's yearning for full disclosure, as when he instructed Marbury to turn over the stolen documents to the Justice Department the previous November: "They wanted to run in first. 'I want to be first.' You don't suppose that Mr. Chambers's lawyers . . . were going to dig a hole and hide it? No, but they thought that if they got there first that would prove they were innocent. They wanted to be the first to yell 'Cop.'" As for Hiss's appearance before HUAC on August 5, "what else could he do if he did not deny it immediately? . . . This was a man in high places. . . . He only had two choices, he could call up the chairman and say, 'Well you got me at last,' or deny it."

Mrs. Hiss proved similarly "helpful," Murphy pointed out, in telling the grand jury that Claudia Catlett was dead. That way the bureau "could just eliminate her from the list of people to see." Moreover, Mrs. Hiss recalled very little in her grand jury testimony about the typewriter: "You can see this mad desire to help."

How had Hiss's lawyers found the Woodstock? Murphy asked. By seeing the Catlett sons, who proceeded to deny knowing about the machine when questioned by the FBI in January 1949. Murphy suggested a scenario for understanding Hiss's relation to the Catletts and the typewriter, which "formed a connecting link between Chambers and they." After the latter's defection, the prosecutor argued, the Hisses had not sold the machine—since a record of that could be traced—but had given it to the Catletts, assuming it would "fall into disuse and get banged around . . . disintegrate and finally end up in some ashcan" but, in any event, "never be traceable." (Murphy failed to explain why the Hisses had not simply thrown away the machine.) When Chambers turned over the documents, Hiss had then phoned one of the Catlett sons and said, according to Murphy, something like the following: "If the FBI ever come looking for a typewriter, don't telephone me but tell my brother Donald." On the other hand, "if the agents did not find the Catletts, all well and good."

As for Mrs. Hiss's testimony about the $400 loan, Murphy asked "the ladies on the jury, is that the way you do it when you have a checking account and a charge account, and you have not moved in? Do you take the $400 out in one lump? Do you go around and buy curtains and items for the house to be delivered later and pay for them in cash? Is that $400 explanation reasonable to you or is it just another lie . . . ?"

The prosecutor interjected a word about Hiss's slander suit against Chambers: "He had to bring the lawsuit. If he didn't . . . he would have been laughed at from here to Borneo, laughed out of town. In self-defense he had to bring the lawsuit." Turning to the stolen documents, Murphy drew the jurors' attention to the first handwritten note, the Mary Martin cable—a verbatim copy, he reminded them, adding wryly: "And that is a summary of an important trade agreement matter." He practically shouted at the jury: "Ladies and gentlemen, forget about the typewriter, forget about it. Just confine yourselves to these handwritten documents. Those are the things he [Hiss] has no explanation for. That is the jam on his face."

He concluded with a word of caution for the twelve jurors, or at least for one of them: "You are not bound by one another . . . you are all independent jurors. The foreman, for instance, is here by virtue of chance. . . . He has no authority other than to announce the verdict. You are all individual jurors." Hubert James had blushed (according to Jim Bell) as the prosecutor stared straight into the eyes of the man whose wife had allegedly proclaimed his pro-Hiss sympathies. Murphy continued: "Or assuming that you told your wife, Mr. Foreman, or anybody, that you thought so-and-so was lying, today is the day . . . I ask you as a representative of the United States Government to come back and put the lie in that man's face. Thank you." And with that curious ending, Murphy took his seat.

Judge Kaufman's charge to the jury was an elaborate amalgam of defense and prosecution suggestions with some of his own. Kaufman instructed the jurors that if they found Hiss not guilty of passing the documents to Chambers (Count One), they "must" also find him not guilty on the second count of meeting with Chambers after January 1, 1937. On the other hand, if the jurors found him guilty of the first count, they "may" find him guilty on Count Two. The judge explained at some length the legal meaning of the term "reasonable doubt." The jury's own "recollection of the evidence is controlling as to all questions of fact in the case," whereas counsel's closing statements "simply presented their versions of the facts." Kaufman's comments on how the jury might evaluate Chambers's testimony dwelt on the witness's previous "inconsistencies" prior to turning over the documents and accusing Hiss of espionage. He directed the jury to find Hiss not guilty on both counts if it did not believe Chambers's testimony "beyond a reasonable doubt." If, on the other hand, the jurors believed Chambers, then they had to consider all the evidence produced at the trial for its corroborative value.[54]

The jury retired to deliberate and, minutes later, sent a note asking to see the exhibits, a copy of the indictment, the typewriter, and all the typing standards used by the prosecution. Six hours later, at 10:39 PM, Kaufman asked the jurors if they anticipated a verdict that evening. Foreman James saw "no immediate verdict," and the judge let them adjourn for the night.[55]

No longer smiling, Alger Hiss remained in his seat or in the defense's anteroom much of the next day, July 7, while his wife chatted with friends in the corridor outside court. At 4:55 PM Kaufman announced: "I have another note from the jury which reads as follows: 'The jury is unable to agree at a verdict.'" The case had taken almost six weeks to try, and the judge asked with some impatience if Murphy had any suggestions. Murphy recommended taking the jurors at their word and discharging them, but he declined Kaufman's invitation to move formally for discharge: "I don't know whether the burden should be put on me." Besides, if the prosecutor made such a motion, Murphy reminded him, that "might possibly raise some basis for a question of double jeopardy," assuming the government wished a retrial. Stryker also preferred to leave matters in Kaufman's hands.

The judge urged the jury to make one more effort to reach a verdict. The jurors filed out, only to return in two hours. Foreman James agreed with Kaufman that the jury was deadlocked, but one juror requested additional time. Once more they retired, and at 8:55 PM Kaufman read another note from the foreman: "The jury find it impossible to reach a verdict," the third such communication that day.[56]

Again Kaufman ordered the jury into court. Foreman James saw no chance of unanimity, and the judge discharged the dozen glum jurors "with the thanks of the Court." Murphy moved to impound the typewriter. Meanwhile, Edward McLean approached the jury box and asked about the vote. "Eight to four for conviction," came a juror's response. Word of the tally spread quickly through the courtroom, even before the clerk of the court realized—and announced— that the impounded Woodstock was still in the jury room. Appearing somewhat dazed as well as disappointed, Stryker said a final "Good night, sir" to Kaufman, who responded "Good night," as the first trial of Alger Hiss ended.[57]

The defendant sat expressionless for a moment while spectators and reporters crowded around him. Tears filled Priscilla Hiss's eyes, but, like her husband, she gazed ahead reflectively without speaking. Finally, Hiss rose and, with Mrs. Hiss on his arm, moved briskly through the encircling spectators. He deflected questioners with a single word—"Please"—as the couple left the courtroom.

Would the case be retried? reporters asked U.S. Attorney McGohey, Murphy's superior. "We'll put it back on the calendar," McGohey said. "When judges are available we'll try it again. And Tom Murphy will try it. He has done a magnificent job." Murphy refused all comment, but mentioned the eight-to-four vote for conviction with some satisfaction. When reporters approached Stryker asking if he would defend Hiss again, the response seemed unequivocal: "I'll defend this fellow forever—if he asks me to."[58]

Surrounded by pursuing newsmen, Alger and Priscilla Hiss walked down the Foley Square courthouse steps. A solitary supporter clapped several times as photographers snapped their pictures. Hiss refused to make a statement and helped his wife into the back seat of a waiting car in front of the courthouse. Photographers who reached the automobile before it drove off found Hiss blocking his face and his wife's from their cameras with a magazine.

Hiss's lawyers and friends recognized the increased peril of a second trial. Two-thirds of the jury considered him guilty despite Chambers's admitted earlier perjuries and Stryker's prestigious character witnesses.*[59]

---

*Of these, only five would reappear at the second trial. Missing were the most eminent, Supreme Court justices Reed and Frankfurter.

In the weeks following the jury's deadlock, Judge Kaufman felt the lash of public criticism from those who believed Alger Hiss guilty. The New York *Journal-American* published a misleading story the day after the trial ended, stating that Kaufman had refused Murphy's request early in the proceeding to excuse Foreman James for prejudicial statements supporting Hiss.

The jurors began to talk to newsmen from the moment Kaufman discharged them, with five of those who voted to convict Hiss expressing their belief that the judge had been biased in favor of the defendant. Foreman James had "no comment at all." Three jurors who favored acquittal—Louis Hill, Arthur L. Pawlinger, and Louise Torian—all spoke at length to Hiss's attorneys in the weeks that followed, providing detailed descriptions of the jury's deliberations. A number of jurors who voted for conviction submitted to similar interviews with the FBI. Probably the most outspoken of these, Helen Sweatt, argued publicly that if James had not been foreman, the other three jurors might have voted to convict: "He led the fight to support the defense." Still another "guilty" vote, juror James F. Hanrahan, denounced all four dissenters: "The foreman was emotional, two were blockheads, and one was a dope." Most jurors told the press—and, privately, the FBI or defense attorneys—that the key split had come over the Woodstock typewriter. Eight had been persuaded that Mrs. Hiss typed the stolen documents on the machine; the four voting for acquittal lacked a firm alternative theory, but thought someone else had composed the papers on Woodstock N230099.[60]

Shortly after the trial deadlocked, several reporters—among them Victor Lasky of the New York *World-Telegram*—published verbatim transcripts of the session in Kaufman's chambers when he rejected Murphy's request to use Hede Massing as a witness. One juror who voted to acquit, Arthur L. Pawlinger, claimed he had received a series of threatening phone calls after the trial and demanded that the FBI investigate. At the same time, outraged Republicans in Congress, including Richard Nixon,* pilloried Kaufman for alleged bias and demanded a House inquiry into the judge's fitness to serve on the federal bench. (Democrats in Congress, like the new HUAC chairman, John Wood of Georgia, and Senate Judiciary Committee Chairman Pat McCarran, although anti-administration, rejected the demands for a legislative probe of Kaufman.)[61]

The judge's critics denounced not only the fact that his rulings on questions of law and admissible evidence usually favored the defense, but also his action in

---

*Nixon maintained informal contact with Murphy through Victor Lasky, who wrote the prosecutor during the first trial: "As you probably realize Dick has a heck of a lot at stake in the outcome. Anyway, I got a couple of things which he thought you should [sic] like to know, based on his many dealings with our boy, Alger, in the House committee." Lasky listed a variety of points on which Nixon felt Murphy should question Hiss, and Nixon later supplied Lasky (who, in turn, sent the material to Murphy) with two lengthy sets of questions about contradictions in Hiss's previous testimony. The information on Nixon and Lasky is contained in Justice Department files on the case released in 1977.

stepping down from the bench to greet and shake hands with Justices Reed and Frankfurter, behavior that Representative Keefe of Wisconsin termed "an act of bias on the part of the judge for the defendant . . . [and] degrading to the dignity of the bench." President Truman took the unusual step of defending Kaufman publicly on July 14 as "a good judge. I appointed him." Judge Kaufman, proclaimed the president, "acted all right" during the Hiss trial.* But few observers expected the judge to preside at the retrial of Alger Hiss that the government promptly scheduled for the fall.[62]

---

*A person who traveled to Europe on the same ship as Kaufman shortly after the first trial wrote to Alger Hiss in 1975. Kaufman had discussed the trial, asserted Mrs. Alma W. Meyer of St. Louis, and had told her "that if he had been on the jury he would have voted you innocent." Alma W. Meyer to Alger Hiss, March 13, 1975; letter courtesy of Mr. Hiss.

XIII

CONVICTION: THE SECOND TRIAL

The American mood had altered dramatically in the four-month interval between the deadlock at Alger Hiss's first trial and the opening of his second. During this period the Cold War heated up within the United States and abroad. Congress approved the NATO treaty, and Truman announced on September 22 that the Soviet Union had exploded an atomic bomb, thereby breaking the American nuclear monopoly. "This is now a different world," commented Arthur Vandenberg. Mao Tse-tung's Red Army continued taking over China's mainland while remnants of Chiang Kai-shek's forces retreated to the island of Formosa. A State Department "White Paper" defended administration policies toward China, arguing that the civil war there had been "beyond the control" of United States actions. But Republicans and conservative Democrats in the "China Lobby" denounced the White Paper as a whitewash and demanded continued military aid to Chiang. HUAC probed alleged Russian espionage in the wartime atomic-energy program, while opinion polls revealed a hardening of public sentiment toward the treatment of domestic Communists. In this charged setting the second trial of Alger Hiss began on November 17, 1949.[1]

Although Thomas F. Murphy again led the prosecution, the defense team was now headed by Claude B. Cross, wry and diffident, a transplanted Southerner long resident in Boston and senior partner in one of the city's prominent law firms. Cross had solid control of defense strategy for the retrial. "Mr. Stryker is completely out of the case," McLean wrote Marbury on October 3, "and although my firm will remain as attorneys of record, I do not expect to devote much personal time to the second trial." On the prosecution side, John F. X. McGohey had been named a federal judge, and Irving H. Saypol, Murphy's immediate superior, succeeded him as U.S. Attorney for the Southern District. The circuit's second senior judge, Henry W. Goddard, a crisp, tough jurist, had replaced Samuel Kaufman on the bench.[2]

Before the opening of the trial, the courts had disposed quickly of two pretrial defense motions, one for a change in venue to Rutland, Vermont, and the other for access to passport records that might shed light on whether Chambers had obtained such documents during the 1930s under assumed names.[3]

McLean argued for Vermont on the grounds that because of the "unprecedented volume" and "extraordinary virulence" of press coverage at the first trial, it was now impossible for the defendant to receive "a fair and impartial" trial in New York City. Hiss's attorney had received positive reports from Vermont lawyers on the general character of jurors in the state—"definitely better than New York blue ribbon juries," ran one such assessment, since "the members are prosperous farmers, small town bankers and merchants and retired people." Moreover, Vermont had only "two Roman Catholics out of twelve" (at the first trial, most Catholic jurors had voted to convict Hiss), "probably . . . no Jews," and few "prejudices against New Dealers." Claude Cross had been hired in anticipation of this change of venue.[4]

The defense stressed several things about New York's press coverage: publication of evidence that had been excluded from the trial, editorials criticizing defense character witnesses (especially Justices Reed and Frankfurter), numerous interviews with jurors at the first trial, wide publicity given to newspaper and congressional attacks on Judge Kaufman, and posttrial publication by the New York *Post* of Julian Wadleigh's series of articles on his underground experiences. Finally, McLean introduced affidavits and exhibits from three jurors who had voted to acquit Hiss and subsequently received threatening mail and phone calls.[5]

But the prosecution argued that trial coverage had been mostly fair and that some press coverage had clearly favored the defendant. "The Court's attention is called particularly," Murphy wrote, "to all of the stories in the New York *Herald Tribune* by John Chabot Smith." Murphy's analysis of news stories during the trial found "68.5 percent to be completely factual; 8.3 percent pro-Hiss; 6.1 percent anti-Chambers; and 17.1 percent pro and anti the trial judge." Moreover, the prosecution had hired its own survey-research analyst, who challenged the defense pollster's assessment of the data as grounded "on such a narrow statistical basis and [containing] so many contradictions of his own arguments as to have no . . . factual basis in a court of law" other than "the rather mealy-mouthed conclusion" that New Yorkers were more likely to have made up their minds already than people in Rutland. Finally, Murphy asked "Why Vermont?" noting that Hiss had specifically asked for transfer of the case there and not to any other district, despite the fact that the federal district judge in Vermont had died recently and had not yet been replaced. Here the prosecutor raised an obvious but telling point: "Oddly enough, no mention is made [in the defense motion] of the fact that the defendant Hiss has spent all of his summers since 1938 at Peacham, Vermont." On October 14 Judge Alfred C. Coxe denied the motion for a change in venue.

But the second pretrial motion succeeded. Hiss forced release of Passport Office records on Chambers (the defense was particularly interested in obtaining one made out to "David Breen" in 1935).

Jury selection was again an easy process. The eight women and four men included seven housewives, three businessmen, and two professionals. Goddard warned the jurors and alternates that they were "not to talk with anybody about this case or allow anyone to talk to you about it. You are not to read or listen to any comments on the trial."*[6]

Both in substance and tone, Murphy's opening statement differed from his first trial comments. No longer did he stress that without belief in Chambers's story, "the Government has no case," a strategy that had made the prosecution and its star witness vulnerable to Stryker's assault on Chambers. Instead, he emphasized the issue of *Hiss's* credibility—"Did this defendant lie?"—and suggested that juries in normal trials "are asked to draw an inference from" the story they would confront in this case: "You see, we do not always have direct proof." How would the government then "prove" Hiss's alleged perjuries to the grand jury? "We are going to prove it by the immutable documents themselves, documents that just can't change There they are, the documents."[7]

The prosecutor tackled the issue of Chambers's acknowledged perjuries. Murphy asked jurors to project back into the 1930s, when many intellectuals such as Chambers believed that Russia was "the most active [force] against Nazism and Fascism" in order to understand how he—and, by inference, Hiss—could have remained Communists for so long. Murphy evidently had more confidence in Judge Goddard than in his predecessor, since he urged the jury to allow the judge to explain "all technical questions" and to think only about the facts: "Where does the truth lie?" Murphy admitted that Chambers had lied prior to November 1948 about Hiss's involvement in espionage, and he detailed the record of his previous misstatements, a record sure to be stressed by Claude Cross. After turning over the papers, however, Chambers had bared his personal

---

*The second trial jury also became enmeshed in controversy. The prosecutors informed Goddard early in the trial—and he, in turn, told the defense—that the wife of the bailiff in Judge Coxe's court was a jury member (Coxe had denied the motion for a change in venue). The Hiss defense waived its right to dismiss a woman from the jury, not wishing a mistrial. Whether or not Claude Cross would have responded similarly had he known about the affiliations of several other jury members remains problematic. Hiss's appeals lawyer, Chester Lane, learned after the trial that one woman on the jury was a member of the church in which Judge Goddard served as a vestryman (a fact that might or might not have led to her exclusion from the jury had it been known before the trial). Also, an FBI report filed four days after the trial began reported that two jury members had distant relatives working for the bureau: one, the wife of an agent's second cousin; the second, the mother of a former clerical employee who had resigned. Whether the exposure of such tangential associations indirectly linked to the trial, had they been known, would have led even to removal of the jurors, much less a mistrial, remains uncertain. Cross's response to the news about Judge Coxes bailiff's wife suggests that the Hiss defense might have been prepared to proceed, as Murphy had done when confronted with reports of Foreman James's wife's statements at the first trial. In legal efforts long after Hiss's conviction, however, Alger Hiss and his lawyers raised complaints about jury bias at the second trial, although without mentioning the pivotal role played by Austin MacCormick's brother-in-law, Hubert James, in obtaining a hung jury for Hiss at the first trial. Interview, Claude B. Cross, July 15, 1974; Tony Hiss, *Laughing Last,* p. 134.

history to Hiss's lawyers, the prosecutor insisted, in the slander-suit deposition of 1,300 pages. So had Mrs. Chambers.

As for lying about Hiss, Murphy repeated Chambers's explanation: that he did not wish to inflict harm upon his former friend until Hiss's slander suit forced him to do so in self-protection. But "the ultimate question in this case," Murphy concluded, was not the testimony of Whittaker Chambers alone but a related one: "Does the documentary proof . . . in this case prove beyond a reasonable doubt . . . that Whittaker Chambers is telling the gospel truth from that chair?"

Claude Cross's opening remarks proved equally cogent and unmarred by Stryker's rhetorical excesses. He also stressed the documents as the "one issue in the case": "If Hiss did not turn over copies or originals of State Department papers to Chambers in February and March [1938], then there should be an acquittal." Murphy objected when Cross reminded the jurors of the prosecutor's opening at the first trial—"if you do not believe Whittaker Chambers the Government has no case"—and Goddard agreed that the statement "is not evidence." Cross compared Hiss's life and achievements with Chambers's admitted record of perjuries while a Communist and before, reworking familiar ground but with one new detail that he developed effectively—that Chambers had obtained a false passport in 1935 in the name of "David Breen," a "ghoulish" act since the real David Breen had died in 1900 as an infant. Using none of Stryker's soaring imagery but with more coherence and logic—as if the first trial's opening defense statement had been run through a computer for substance alone—Cross reviewed the familiar contrast between Hiss's reputation and that of his accuser.[8]

The only major new element in the defense argument was Cross's suggestion that Chambers's two "pipelines" at State, the persons who actually turned over all of the government's typed and microfilmed exhibits, had been Julian Wadleigh and some unknown confederate in its Far Eastern Division (where the one non-Woodstock-typed document had been sent). All of the State Department materials in question, Cross argued, had been sent either to Wadleigh's Trade Agreements Section or to the Far Eastern Division. Cross did not try to explain in his opening how Hiss's initials happened to be on many of the documents sent to Sayre's office, nor did he try to explain how Wadleigh or his unidentified confederate typed the documents on Hiss's Woodstock. He said that several of the typed cables had not been sent to Sayre's office and that the filmstrips—made on one photographic run—included a carbon of the German trade agreement sent to Wadleigh's office, along with the three cables that bore Hiss's initials. Clearly, Julian Wadleigh would figure prominently at the second trial.

Yet Cross conceded a significant point: the defense had not cross-examined the prosecution "witness at the first trial who said in his opinion [the typing] was done on the Woodstock." Ramos Feehan had testified, in fact, that the stolen documents and the "Hiss standards" had been typed on the same machine. Cross made another damaging admission: "I tell you, in frankness, that we have consulted some experts and they say that in their opinion it [the typed documents] was typed on the Woodstock typewriter. That is an opinion. What the fact is as to who actually typed it only the person who typed it knows." (Cross did not reveal the opinion of Harry E. Cassidy, the latest Hiss examiner, prior to the second trial, that Priscilla Hiss had been the typist.) "And it is our contention that either Whittaker Chambers or his confederate typed those Baltimore documents . . . at some period subsequent to April 1, 1938. We don't know when it was, except Whittaker Chambers." In short, Hiss's new defense counsel argued that Chambers had obtained the Hiss Woodstock after defecting and then had typed the documents received from Wadleigh and from another unknown State Department confederate, sometime between April 1938 and November 1948.

The character of the trial, more professionally managed and less flamboyant on both sides than its predecessor, became set from the moment Chambers took the stand as the government's first major witness. Judicial decorum prevailed. Preliminary decisions by Goddard overruled Cross's objections to Murphy's use of "background testimony," suggesting that the judge intended to define "admissible evidence" more liberally than had Kaufman. At the same time, it seemed apparent that Cross had no intention of behaving like a "correct" version of Stryker. Rarely, if ever, would he try to goad the prosecutor, one of Stryker's recurrent tactics. Opposing counsel at the second trial remained unfailingly polite.[9]

Most of Chambers's testimony reviewed ground covered at the first trial, although Murphy raised some new points. One involved the Westminster farm, optioned in 1935 by Alger Hiss, who then withdrew from the arrangement only to have the property bought in 1937 by Chambers: "I saw the farm [first] in the company of Alger Hiss."[10]

Chambers offered an explanation for having placed the microfilms in a pumpkin before leaving for Washington on December 2: "People who represented themselves to be investigators for Mr. Hiss," he avowed, "had been in and out of my farm and the neighborhood for some time." Most important of all the new information, because of Judge Goddard's apparent intention to give both sides great latitude in introducing evidence they considered relevant, was Chambers's testimony about the Ford. He told his version of the car transfer, involving Hiss's desire to donate it to a poor Communist organizer over Chambers's protests about this violation of normal underground procedure.

The contrast between Chambers's manner at the second trial and his earlier behavior under Stryker's cross-examination emerged vividly in his responses to Cross's questions. Although an effective interrogator in his own right, Cross's technique as a cross-examiner was distinctly mild in comparison to his predecessor's. He rarely emulated Stryker's studied expressions of indignation and shock at Chambers's testimony. The witness, in turn, seemed far more relaxed and confident. His voice rarely dropped and, normally, he stared directly at Cross when responding and not at the ceiling, as he had done with Stryker. He made a far more effective witness now that the preacher of "moral leprosy" had departed the scene.

In dealing with the "David Breen" passport issue, Cross brought out a fact that neither prosecution nor defense had previously mentioned. Chambers applied for the passport in late May 1935, and, according to the photo he used, he then had a mustache. Neither Alger nor Priscilla Hiss had mentioned any mustache in their descriptions of "George Crosley," although most of their acknowledged meetings with the man had taken place in mid-1935. (Photographs of Chambers in 1936 and 1937 showed that by that time he had removed the mustache.)

Reviewing the inconsistencies between Chambers's earlier version of events and his testimony after turning over the documents in November 1948, Cross asked why the witness had mentioned Julian Wadleigh to Berle in 1939 but not to Raymond Murphy or to the FBI until 1948.* He questioned Chambers at length about his relations with Wadleigh in the underground. Goddard anticipated his later ruling on the admissibility of Dr. Binger's testimony by allowing Cross, over Murphy's objections, to ask Chambers questions about his brother's suicide to lay the "foundation for psychiatric testimony."

After failing to weaken any aspect of Chambers's story, Cross returned the witness to Murphy, who questioned him about the stolen documents, once more calling the jury's attention to his "immutable witnesses." The prosecutor also read into the record Raymond Murphy's two interviews with Chambers and introduced as an exhibit Adolf Berle's notes of his talk with Chambers in 1939. Murphy evidently gambled that a juror's uneasiness about inconsistencies between Chambers's earlier accounts and his late-1948 testimony could be offset by evidence that he had named Hiss as an underground Communist in 1939, 1942, 1945, and 1946. Meanwhile, Chambers said—for the first time—that the Hisses probably had known him as "David Breen" as well as "Carl," a dubious score for the defense since Hiss claimed to have learned about the "Breen" name only through an anonymous call in 1948.

Esther Chambers, like her husband, was better prepared and less flustered with Lloyd Stryker no longer on the scene. Although she added almost nothing to her previous testimony, she presented it far more effectively. She did not appear perturbed by Cross's efforts to quote inconsistencies from her earlier testimony or his attempts to indicate that some reminiscences appeared now for the

---

*The matter was never satisfactorily resolved. Isaac Don Levine recalled receiving a phone call from Chambers in late 1948 asking for the name of the "other" State Department employee—Wadleigh—mentioned to Berle. Chambers had forgotten it during the intervening decade, or so he claimed.

first time: "Yes. There is a new recollection, yes. I will probably keep on recollecting for the rest of my days—too late perhaps for the trial."[11]

At the first trial Esther had said the Hisses had never been given her last name, but she now corroborated Chambers's belated recollection that Alger and Priscilla Hiss had known them in 1935 as the "Breens." Cross spent much of his time reading portions of Esther Chambers's statements at the Baltimore deposition and the first trial, often not to demonstrate inconsistencies but to put into the record her admission that she had told falsehoods during the 1930s. Murphy pointed out on cross-examination that Whittaker Chambers had never shown his wife the birth certificates of "David and Ursula Breen" nor talked to her about them. Esther saw these first in court.

The FBI documents expert, Ramos C. Feehan, reviewed his earlier testimony with few changes. Murphy slipped into redirect questioning of Feehan the fact that defense experts had already examined the typed documents, planting in the jurors' minds an inevitable question as to whether those experts would be summoned to contradict Feehan's testimony.[12]

Julian Wadleigh denied having worked on the German *aide-memoire* found in the microfilmed documents or having given these documents to Chambers. Wadleigh said it was barely "conceivable" he had supplied these particular items, but unlikely. As for the cables with Hiss's initials, Wadleigh was certain he had not supplied them, nor had he been responsible for the typewritten material. Murphy again paraded his "immutable witnesses" before the jury, handing Wadleigh each typed document and asking if he had seen it before, producing a denial in every case. Wadleigh also said he had not stolen Hiss's four handwritten notes nor, for that matter, had he been in Sayre's office unaccompanied by either Hiss or Sayre.[13]

After an almost perfunctory cross-examination of Julian Wadleigh at the first trial, Lloyd Paul Stryker had told newsmen that he had been gentle because he "felt sorry" for him, "a poor thing, laying there bleeding," a confessed espionage agent. Claude Cross proved more dogged in his questioning. Raising doubts in the jurors' minds about Wadleigh's extracurricular spying lay at the heart of his defense strategy. Cross lingered on the witness's confessed violation of the espionage laws and of his government oath, on Wadleigh's previous Communist sympathies, and on his inability to recall the contents of perhaps "four or five hundred" documents he admitted having stolen from the State Department in 1937–38. This latter point seemed crucial, since, if Wadleigh's memory proved fallible on his acknowledged thefts, how could he state so confidently that he had not given Chambers the microfilmed materials critical to the government's case against Hiss?

Had Wadleigh known he was violating the espionage laws? "What I knew," the witness responded, "was that I was acting illegally." But Cross could not shake Wadleigh's testimony concerning his lack of culpability for the specific documents turned over by Chambers. The most Wadleigh would concede, as he had done at the first trial, was that among the typed documents "there were a few that I might possibly have seen and given to Chambers," if only because this small batch had also been sent to Trade Agreements. But the concession remained a pyrrhic victory, useless to the defense without an explanation of how these documents came to be typed on the Hiss Woodstock if Wadleigh had provided them. Cross knew this, returning in the end to his suggestion that Wadleigh had somehow stolen the microfilmed cables ("an unusually rich find") from Sayre's office.

But Wadleigh declined the nomination, and Murphy reminded the jurors that the cables from Ambassador Bullitt had not been sent to Trade Agreements. The prosecutor also quashed Cross's assumption that Wadleigh had somehow managed to steal—on four different occasions—the four Hiss handwritten notes as well, then return to Sayre's office to take the microfilmed cables, and, at still other times, come back for a number of the typewritten documents. In this connection, Murphy emphasized the fourth handwritten note's date, March 11. Wadleigh left Washington on March 9 for New York City, and his ship sailed for Turkey on the 11th.

While reading excerpts from Wadleigh's New York *Post* articles into the record, Murphy cited one with potential importance for jurors concerned over Hiss's inability to recognize "George Crosley" immediately during the HUAC hearings' initial weeks. "Except for the now repaired tooth and a considerable gain in weight," Wadleigh wrote on July 13, "Chambers' appearance does not seem to me to have changed perceptibly since the day I first met him some 13 years ago."

Hede Massing, whom Kaufman had prevented from testifying at the first trial, was the only person to corroborate Chambers's story of having met Hiss as an underground Communist. She ran through her account of a 1935 meeting at the home of Noel Field. Cross brought out the fact that Massing's memory for certain persons, dates, and events seemed fuzzy, and that she had lied in testifying during her husband's citizenship hearings. An admitted former Soviet agent, the witness stuck to her story about having met Hiss in Field's company.[14]

But Cross caught Massing unprepared—and more than a bit flustered—when he asked if she had met a man named Henrikas Rabinavicius one night at the home of her friend, *Reader's Digest* editor Eugene Lyons. She could not recall such an encounter. Cross went on to ask if, as apparently Rabinavicius remembered, she had been questioned that evening about her meeting with Hiss, turning to Lyons and asking: "What happened next?" Lyons then allegedly said, "You ought to know better than I." Massing did not recall that "exactly," but described it "in a manner of a joke" if it occurred.

By the time Massing testified, Noel and Herta Field had vanished in Eastern Europe. But Murphy quashed the implication left by Cross, that only because of the Fields' disappearance had Massing come forth, by eliciting testimony that she had first told the FBI about Hiss in December 1948—before the Fields had left public view. The couple could have returned, in short, to contradict Hede Massing.*

The defense later brought to the witness stand Henrikas Rabinavicius, formerly a Lithuanian diplomat, who repeated testimony previously mentioned by Cross. He admitted having told his story only to Hiss's lawyers and not to the FBI. The witness also confessed strong sympathy for Alger Hiss and said that if he was convicted, it should be on the basis of "real proof and not just the testimony of two former Russian spies in this country [Chambers and Massing]." Rabinavicius's testimony, offered reluctantly and only after strong pressure from Hiss's attorneys, cast some doubt upon the firmness of Massing's memory.[15]

Through a series of supporting witnesses, summoned mainly for rebuttal, Murphy presented the final pieces of his evidentiary puzzle. There were last strands of testimony that uncovered more than a few surprises, as well as some new and significant information. The Hisses' pediatrician, Dr. Margaret Nicholson, badly undermined Alger and Priscilla Hiss's claim that Mrs. Hiss had been in Chappaqua, New York, with Timothy over the 1937–38 New Year's period, when Chambers and his wife recalled visiting the Hisses for a party. The doctor's records show that Mrs. Hiss and Timothy had returned to Washington at least by January 2—not a week later, as Mrs. Hiss testified—since Dr. Nicholson had paid house calls on the sick boy on January 2, 3, and 6.[16]

Socialist Party official August Claessens produced Priscilla Hiss's registration card in the Morningside Heights Socialist Party, which showed that she had joined the branch as early as March 23, 1930 (Mrs. Hiss testified that she had never been a member of the party).[17]

Murphy instructed an FBI agent to type on the Hiss Woodstock an entire page from the stolen typed documents, which the prosecutor then offered as an exhibit. This suggested two important points for the jurors: first, they could compare for themselves the two versions of the same document, and second, that the Woodstock was still in reasonable working order if repaired, despite its known defects.[18]

---

*Noel and Herta Field in their interrogations by Hungarian and Czech security officers in 1949 (according to Professor Karel Kaplan, who read the dossiers) both named Alger Hiss as a Soviet agent in the State Department during the 1930s. Interviews, Professor Karel Kaplan, March 27 and April 19, 1977. Professor Maria Schmidt, who read the same files in the 1990s, has also confirmed the naming of Hiss by Field as a Soviet agent, as do NKVD records opened to the author. See Chapter VI, pp. 178–82.

The prosecutor then threw into doubt Hiss's claim to have arranged rental of the Volta Place residence by mid-November 1937, hence the $400 savings-bank withdrawal on November 17, supposedly to purchase furnishings for the new home. After introducing several ads from Washington newspapers that showed the Volta Place home offered for rental first in late October and for the last time on December 5, 1937, Murphy called Mrs. Gladys Tally to the stand. Mrs. Tally, who had placed the last ad and whose mother owned the house, confirmed that two parties were interested in Volta Place early in December and she rented the residence to the Hisses at that time. Whatever the date on which Hiss made his final rental arrangement with the realtor, Mrs. Tally recalled that this could not have occurred before the first week in December. Otherwise, she would not have placed the December 5 ad. Cross did not challenge the witness on these points, which apparently confirmed that a $400 withdrawal by the Hisses on November 17 to buy furnishings for Volta Place was premature.[19]

The most damaging rebuttal witness was Edith Murray, who had worked as a maid for the Chambers family at two Baltimore houses in 1935–36 (when he used the pseudonym "Lloyd Cantwell"). She said the "Cantwells" had had "only two visitors that I know of," one several times, a lady who said "she lived in Washington" and whom Mrs. Murray had called "Miss Priscilla," and—on one occasion—her husband. Mrs. Murray pointed to Alger and Priscilla Hiss and identified them as the visitors.[20]

Challenging the reliability of Edith Murray's memory, Cross suggested that she had been coached extensively by the FBI. Mrs. Murray admitted having suffered a "nervous breakdown" in 1942 but, despite repeated questions, insisted that she had not kept up on the details of the case and rarely read newspapers. Cross brought out the fact that the first time the FBI showed Edith Murray a photo of Priscilla Hiss, she had said something to the effect that Mrs. Hiss looked "like an actress." The witness tried to clarify this point: "No, when I first saw the picture I said it looks like somebody I seen in the movies. I knew I had seen the woman but just couldn't recall where I had seen her. I just saw the side of the face." But she retained her composure under extensive cross-examination, and Cross never addressed Edith Murray's subsequent identification in New York while Mrs. Hiss was one of a number of people emerging from an elevator. Soon after Mrs. Murray stepped down, Murphy rested the government's case.

Seven present and former State Department officials led the lineup of defense witnesses, most of them holdovers from the first trial. Stanley K. Hornbeck took the stand again, noting that Hiss had scribbled memos for him similar to the four handwritten exhibits. Hornbeck said, however, that the handwritten "chits" he sometimes received from Hiss clipped to memos were always initialed (unlike the four exhibits in the case) and that he (Hornbeck) would never have asked for or received an exact handwritten copy of a cable such as the Mary Martin wire.[21]

Francis B. Sayre, whose failure to appear as a witness at the first trial may have hurt the defense seriously, testified now at the urging of Hiss and his attorneys. He was then U.S. representative on the U.N. Trusteeship Council and throughout the year had cooperated with the FBI in a number of interviews, a fact known to Hiss and his lawyers. Reviewing Hiss's duties in the 1936–39 period, Sayre described himself as interested not only in trade agreements and other purely commercial matters but also in Philippine policy and in neutrality issues. Hiss had been his "right hand man" during those years, "an outstanding man," who regularly combed through cables looking for those that should be brought to Sayre's personal attention. He said Hiss would sometimes send him handwritten summaries or notations attached to departmental cables on small sheets of paper, although usually a "brief penciled comment, saying 'Agree' or 'This won't hold water'" or some similar remark. Obviously, such memos did not resemble the summaries introduced in evidence, but Cross passed over that fact, since Sayre had "no specific recollection" as to whether Hiss ever prepared memoranda like the handwritten exhibits for use in briefing him."[22]

"There are some who believe absolutely in the integrity of his character . . . there are others who do not," observed Francis Sayre, thereby qualifying significantly his own character evidence for Hiss. "It is difficult to give a sweeping answer because there is such a divided opinion about it." The witness would attest to his own belief in Hiss only up to the previous August, when he had written him a letter of support during the HUAC hearings.

In cross-examining, Murphy pointed out that neutrality legislation did not fall within Sayre's "immediate problems" at State in 1937–38. Nor could the witness remember seeing any of the four specific handwritten notes or the three January 14, 1938, cables initialed "AH" and contained on the microfilm. As for the Mary Martin memo or the original cable, it "meant nothing to me. I did not remember what it was about." Sayre agreed with the prosecutor that two handwritten memos, introduced by the defense as evidence that Hiss wrote such notes, "differ markedly" from the four turned over by Chambers in that "they are comments on memoranda" rather than summaries or digests of incoming cables. Nor did Sayre have any knowledge of the military information contained on Hiss's handwritten notes such as the nature of the French "Potez-63" airplane. Murphy noted that Sayre had hired Hiss primarily because of his knowledge of trade-agreements legislation and had not known at the time about the AAA controversy or much about Hiss's personal background. Murphy asked if Sayre had ever told anyone he did not understand why he was on the distribution list for the Mary Martin cable—a comment recorded during an FBI interview. The witness recalled only the possibility that he told that to the grand jury.

Sayre's testimony had not helped the defense. Cross never questioned the witness about the German trade-agreement documents on the microfilm because Sayre had told Hiss's attorneys "that he cannot say that Exhibit 48, or any other of the documents in this group, did not come to [his] office at some point." The most that could be said was that Sayre honored a moral obligation to appear on behalf of his former assistant.

Even character witnesses, Cross discovered, could sometimes prove unhelpful. Thus a partner in Hiss's old Boston law firm, John L. Hall of Choate, Hall and Stewart, testified to the defendant's "excellent" reputation, but, in the course of his comments, denied having invited Hiss to return to the firm in 1946. Hiss had testified that he planned to leave State to return to Choate.[23]

William Marbury, Hiss's first lawyer, reviewed his close personal relationship with Alger and his involvement in the case. Cross tried to use the witness to contradict Mrs. Chambers on a major point. Marbury denied she had testified to any visits to the Hisses' 30th Street home during her deposition at Baltimore. The attempt backfired when Marbury acknowledged to Murphy that he had not specifically asked Esther Chambers that question. Murphy also drew the interesting admission that Robert Patterson, formerly secretary of war, had told Marbury in 1947 about rumors that Hiss was a Communist. Both Marbury and Patterson had dismissed the rumors as ridiculous, but the incident showed that the Baltimore attorney was not entirely unprepared for the events which began unfolding in August 1948.[24]

During Donald Hiss's brief appearance Cross did not ask him about his and Mike Catlett's efforts to recover the Woodstock typewriter, nor had Donald talked about that at the first trial. But Cross obtained firm denials from him that he had ever been an espionage agent, a Communist, or a fellow traveler. Donald said he had never turned over government documents to Chambers or even seen the man until the grand jury hearing in December 1948. Nor had he discussed the Harry Bridges case or his move from the Labor Department to State with anyone but his superiors. He specifically denied having worked on the Bridges case.*[25]

When Alger Hiss took the stand, Cross led him, as Stryker had previously done, through that same meticulous tabulation of achievements and honors that comprised his public record. Cross also asked a curious question: "Was your mother very domineering?" "No," Hiss replied, although not only Chambers but some of the defendant's closest friends told another story."[26]

Almost all of what followed—the familiar story of Hiss's relationship with "George Crosley"—repeated testimony given at the first trial, although Hiss added a few twists. He confirmed Chambers's account of a New York meeting with a flamboyant soldier of fortune, Colonel Dean Ivan Lamb. According to Hiss, however, the meeting was arranged not to obtain Lamb's cooperation in Communist underground work involved with defense information—Lamb was known as an anti-Communist—but rather, at the instructions of the Nye

---

*The exchange of letters between Secretary Frances Perkins and Francis Sayre in 1938 contradicts Donald Hiss directly on this crucial point. The letter appears on p. 196.

Committee's staff director, to determine if Lamb had anything useful to contribute. Lamb had nothing, Hiss recalled, and he had not seen him again. Oddly, given Hiss's statements disclaiming any but the briefest association with the man, Cross introduced into evidence a copy of Lamb's autobiography, *The Incurable Filibuster,* inscribed "To Alger Hiss With All Best Wishes of Dean Ivan Lamb." Lamb, when interviewed by the FBI in 1949, confirmed the substance of Chambers's version of his relationship with Hiss and contradicted the latter's claim of a single innocuous meeting.[27]

Except for that single episode, however, Hiss made a blanket denial of Chambers's account of alleged secret meetings, trips taken by the families, and visits to each other's houses other than those already acknowledged. On the Ford car, Hiss now recalled definitely that "Crosley" had "picked it up some time in the spring of 1936." He could not remember whether his auto trip to New York with Chambers sometime in 1935 had been to interview Lamb, although he did not discount the possibility. Also, Hiss said that he met "Mrs. Crosley" only once, while the Crosley family stayed at the Hisses' P Street home for two or three days.

Introducing a letter he mailed from Washington to Mrs. Hiss on December 30, 1937, the witness tried to rebut Chambers's story about a December 31 New Year's Eve party with the Hisses that year. At the time Mrs. Hiss was in Chappaqua, New York, with Timothy Hobson, visiting her brother's family. Timothy had contracted chicken pox on the trip. When did they return to Washington? Cross inquired. "Some time after New Year's Day," replied Hiss (although Dr. Nicholson's testimony showed that they had returned by January 2). He denied having known anything about possible Communist involvement by Lee Pressman, Nathan Witt, John Abt, or Noel Field when he associated with these men during the thirties. Nor was he deaf in one ear, as Chambers had claimed (but a letter from John F. Davis confirmed a serious hearing loss in one ear).

How Chambers had acquired the typed materials or microfilmed documents remained a mystery to Hiss, and Cross used his client—rather than Sayre—to explain at length the link between the microfilmed German *aide-mémoire* and the Trade Agreements Section. He then read into the record a portion of Hiss's December 4 FBI interview to suggest the defendant's altered recollection about when he disposed of the Woodstock— from "sometime after 1938" to December 1937—only to discover that the statement also denied knowledge of the typewriter's make ("possibly an Underwood"). Murphy pointed up this inconsistency with Hiss's earlier testimony that he had told the FBI the machine was a Woodstock, but Cross still had not recognized that he had confused Hiss's statement with Mrs. Hiss's FBI interview.

Cross-examination also followed the lines laid out at the first trial, with a few exceptions. Murphy put Hiss through a series of questions designed to alert the jury to the improbable aspects of emptying one's savings for anticipated purchases at a time when the Hisses had a checking account and charge privileges in leading Washington stores. He brought out the fact that Hiss said he had saved his check stubs only beginning in November 1937, thus could not produce the August 1937 stubs that might have shed light on earlier alleged dealings with "Crosley" such as the Peterborough trip. The witness claimed that when he and his wife moved to New York in September 1947, they decided to keep checks for exactly a ten-year period, splitting the 1937 checks and keeping only the last two months. All the previous checks, Hiss testified, had been thrown out in the move.*

The prosecutor subjected Hiss to a scathing interrogation on his apartment rental to "Crosley." He ridiculed the witness's assertion that he offered, without a lease and at minimum rent to a purportedly casual acquaintance (for whom he had no address or references), a furnished apartment for two months, utilities free, with an automobile tossed in. Had Hiss tried to check up on "Crosley" among other newsmen when the rent money remained unpaid? He had not. Nor, since, according to the Hisses' account, they left the 28th Street apartment furnished except for kitchen supplies and linens, did the story of the P Street visit by the Chambers family sound persuasive.

Turning to the mysterious Ford, Hiss had claimed he disposed of the car to Chambers, for all practical purposes, after purchasing his new Plymouth in August 1935. But he acknowledged that he probably continued paying insurance on both cars until July 1936, when he transferred title on the Ford. Moreover, Hiss now remembered having started up the car on Georgetown streets during the winter of 1935–36.

Hiss failed to clear up an equally mysterious point. How, Murphy asked, had he known that there existed a 1935 passport made out to one "David Breen"? Hiss said only that one of his lawyers, Harold Rosenwald, "had received a tip during the summer [of 1949]" that Chambers had traveled abroad several times during the 1930s, once under the name of David Breen. "Who was the source of that tip?" the prosecutor continued. "That I don't know. I wasn't told that." Nor, it turned out, had he inquired. "It wasn't you, Mr. Hiss, was it?" "It was not." (Hiss himself had been the recipient of a similar anonymous "tip" in 1948, according to his own defense memo, that first revealed Chambers's use of the name "David Breen.") After a luncheon recess Murphy restated the question, but Hiss proved remarkably uncurious about the matter. "Did Mr. Rosenwald tell you during lunch who the informer was?" "No, sir." "Did you ask him?" "No, I did not." Nor had he by the following day when Murphy renewed his question.

Changing his earlier version of the August 1948 talk with Dulles about resigning, Hiss now acknowledged that he had offered to quit at any time Dulles

---

*In fact, check stubs for December 1935 and April 1936 were available in the Hiss Defense Files when I examined them.

thought it seemed sensible, and that he had been prepared to resign after the HUAC hearings ended. Essentially, this had been Dulles's testimony.

A previously unknown and puzzling fact about the Bokhara rug also emerged in cross-examination: that Hiss had written a check for forty-eight cents each month from September 1937 to December 1938 to a Washington storage company that held the rug for that period. The witness could not "recall the exact reason why it stayed so long." Although Mrs. Hiss had testified that the rug had been in use both at 30th Street and at Volta Place, the storage episode tended to confirm Claudia Catlett's initial statement that she found the rug rolled up and unused at 30th Street (presumably before it was placed in storage).

Reading into the record Hiss's entire March 16, 1948, grand jury testimony, Murphy weakened the defendant's repeated claim that he had been asked at that time about a long list of people, perhaps some forty or so names. The grand jury queried Hiss only about his knowledge of the following fourteen names: Charles Kramer, Harold Ware, Henry Collins, Marian (Abt) Bachrach, Victor Perlo, Harold Glasser, A. George Silverman, Helen Silvermaster, Ludwig Ullman, Earl Browder, Lee Pressman, John Abt, Donald Hiss, and Whittaker Chambers. Murphy tried to anticipate Dr. Carl Binger's expected testimony by reading into the record the December 15, 1948, grand jury proceedings in which Hiss pleaded with the jurors to hear Binger as a witness on the question of Chambers's "motives." One juror asked at that time: "Is your psychiatrist in any position to offer any information . . . [explaining] how it came about that the documents . . . which Chambers turned over to his attorneys . . . [were] written on the [Hiss] typewriter?" No, Hiss acknowledged, Binger could not do that. By the time he left the witness stand, it had become clear that, despite contradictions brought out by the prosecutor, Hiss intended to hold fast to his fundamental account of George Crosley as told to HUAC sixteen months earlier.

Priscilla Hiss's testimony also rarely deviated from her version of the facts given at the first trial. Concerning her Socialist activities in New York, she said these had been limited to voting for Norman Thomas in 1932 and contributing to a Morningside Heights "feeding station," where at times she "made sandwiches and coffee and dispensed them" during "the winter of '31–32." She had never attended a Socialist meeting or participated in any Socialist activities except for her feeding-station work. (Priscilla's membership in the American Labor Associates, however, would certainly qualify her as a socialist activist.)[28]

The witness repeated her earlier testimony about the Hisses' contacts with the "Crosleys." At one point, while denying Chambers's version of the December 1937 New Year's Eve party, Mrs. Hiss supported her husband's version of her stay at Chappaqua, New York, for "a week or ten days" after Christmas, while her son Timothy recovered from chicken pox—indeed, for at least a week after receiving Alger Hiss's December 30 letter. (Dr. Nicholson had not yet testified to Mrs. Hiss's and Timothy's presence in Washington on January 2.)

Turning to typewriters, Priscilla Hiss recalled "rather vaguely" that the Hisses had acquired a Corona portable in the fall of 1937. She was more definite about the disposal of the Woodstock, which she placed during the move to Volta Place. She insisted that the Catlett brothers had come for the machine and other items with their "pull wagon." She acknowledged having told the grand jury that she remembered having the Woodstock at Volta Place, but claimed that McLean's conversations with the Catletts "and his retracing its history" had refreshed her memory. As for giving a machine to the Salvation Army, that had been the Corona portable during their move from Volta Place in 1943. Did she own a typewriter now? Yes, a Royal portable. "How long have you had that?" "Since about 1942."

Goading the witness because of her apparent ability to turn up helpful 1936 and 1937 letters while, at the same time, declaring that her check stubs and other potentially significant evidence for those years had been thrown away, Murphy asked: "Mrs. Hiss, isn't a fact that you have thrown away very, very little of anything since the time you were first married?" Priscilla Hiss denied the suggestion.

Claude Cross had saved the heart of his case until the Hisses finished testifying. Murphy objected to Dr. Carl Binger's appearance on the witness stand, but was overruled. During his earlier career Binger had concentrated on such fields as epidemic research and physiology, but by the 1930s he had shined his concern to psychiatry.[29]

After Dr. Binger confirmed having watched Chambers testify at both trials and having read through his writings ("specifically . . . *Class Reunion*"), Cross began reading an even lengthier version of the "hypothetical question" posed by Stryker at the first trial. It began, "Now, Doctor, assume that the following facts are true"—whereupon Cross recited every actual or potentially damaging fact known to the defense about Chambers. Sixty-five minutes later, after completing his presentation, Cross asked whether Binger, "as a psychiatrist, [had] an opinion within the bounds of reasonable certainty as to the mental condition of Whittaker Chambers." Dr. Binger responded in the affirmative: "I think Mr. Chambers is suffering from a condition known as psychopathic personality, which is a disorder of character, of which the outstanding features are behavior of what we call an amoral or an asocial and delinquent nature." Moreover, Binger asserted that his category of "psychopathic personality'" was "a recognized mental disease."[30]

Asked to outline "some of the symptoms of a psychopathic personality," the psychiatrist described them as "quite variegated":

> They include chronic, persistent and repetitive lying; they include stealing . . .
> acts of deception and misrepresentation . . . alcoholism and drug addiction;
> abnormal sexuality; vagabondage; panhandling; inability to form stable attach-
> ments, and a tendency to make false accusations.

Binger stressed that he meant not what "the layman" thought of as lying but "a peculiar kind . . . known as pathological lying, and a peculiar kind of tendency to make false accusations known as pathological accusations, which are frequently found in the psychopathic personality." He apparently believed that "pathological lying" involved much more than not telling the truth.

Cross led the witness through the terms that defined his view of Chambers's "illness"—"particular fantasy," "paranoid thinking," "bizarre behavior and impulsive acts," "a kind of middle ground between the psychotic and the neurotic," which, he insisted, was a personality disorder that began early and "always [lasts] throughout life." Psychopaths like Chambers, asserted Binger, "act as if a situation were true which, in fact, is true only in their imaginations," and were "amazingly isolated and egocentric," incapable of establishing rapport with others and insensitive to the feelings of others. But "perhaps the most outstanding characteristic is what we call a defect in the formation of conscience . . . so that the psychopath . . . very frequently acts impulsively and frequently in a destructive manner." Binger began to illustrate his argument by quoting from a standard psychiatric text and with such relish in citing passages potentially applicable to Chambers that Murphy objected. Judge Goddard chided him: "Doctor, you are here as a witness, not as an advocate." Chambers possessed all the marks of the classic psychopathic personality, Binger avowed, "with the exception of two, alcoholism and drug addiction."

Breaking down Chambers's actions into these symptoms, the psychiatrist tallied them: common "lying"; "stealing" (the Columbia Library and Public Library books as a youth, and the documents from Julian Wadleigh); "withholding truth" (Chambers's partial testimony to Berle, HUAC, and the grand jury before November 1948); "insensitivity'" (the *Play for Puppets*, and living in his mother's house with Ida Dales—"I have never heard anyone else tell me he lived in an illicit relationship in his mother's house"); "pathological lying" (Chambers's use of pseudonyms from his earliest adult years, and his testimony about Alger Hiss); "bizarre and impulsive acts" (sending strange letters to a one-day Williams College roommate, disposing of his typewriter on a New York subway, and hiding the microfilms in a pumpkin—"definitely bizarre behavior," also fearing assassination by "ambush" when he visited the Hisses at Christmastime 1938); "vagabondage" (Chambers's New Orleans experience as a youth, plus his unkempt appearance and foul teeth during the 1930s); "panhandling" (his small borrowings from Hiss and, later, from Wadleigh); "abnormal emotionality" (immobility after his brother's death). Moreover, according to Binger, Chambers's writings also revealed him as a "psychopathic personality." As for the latter's "fear of being persecuted" in 1938 after defecting from the underground, the psychiatrist saw that as only more "evidence of paranoid thinking."

Extracting from Binger the admission that his testimony had not explained Chambers's possession of the stolen documents, Murphy began his cross-examination. He subjected the psychiatrist to a probing series of questions designed to nail down more precisely, if possible, Binger's definition of a psychopathic personality as a "character . . . disorder involving the mental and emotional life."

The prosecutor uncovered some embarrassing facts about Binger's credentials as an expert that the latter had omitted in his review for Cross. He had been certified as a psychiatrist only in 1946, and on more than one occasion his admission to the American Psychiatric Association had been deferred because of insufficient training. Binger said he did not consider Whittaker Chambers a psychotic or technically "insane" and that no one could be committed to a New York mental institution on evidence of a "psychopathic personality" alone.

"Doctor," Murphy asked, "would it be a fair statement to say that a great many sinners and saints have psychopathic personalities?" Binger pleaded ignorance, not knowing the "life patterns" of many such people. But he did know Chambers's "life pattern"? Murphy asked. "That is right." "Starting, as you did, from almost the time he graduated from high school?" "Correct." And "with that paucity of information concerning his early childhood and adolescence . . . you have the basis to form the opinion that you gave us?" Indeed he had, Binger argued, because his diagnosis was "based on behavior over a long period of time." Had not the former head of the American Psychiatric Association, Dr. A. A. Brill, called Abraham Lincoln "a schizophrenic"? inquired the prosecutor. Binger disassociated himself from the diagnosis and claimed to "have no use" for "that kind of amateur, armchair analysis." "You go more or less for the studied analysis, do you?" asked Murphy. "I try to find out as many facts as I can. . . . Not the number of facts; the quality of them. . . ."

Did Binger believe that someone who had "a psychopathic personality would never tell the truth at any time?" No, he could tell the truth "if his particular emotions were not involved." Binger agreed that a "psychopathic personality's" egocentric features did not necessarily apply to those with monastic tendencies. As for "anti-social" qualities, the prosecutor asked if Chambers had ever been arrested. "Not to my knowledge." Was there any evidence that Chambers had "deliberately and vengefully hurt a friend?" Binger's reply: "I don't recall his mentioning any friend except he said Hiss was his friend." (Chambers had cited Meyer Schapiro, Robert Cantwell, Mike Intrator, and Maxim Lieber among his friends during the 1930s, and an entire circle of acquaintances at Columbia and in the CP during the 1920s.)

But Binger would concede almost nothing benign about Chambers's personality. Holding down a steady job at *Time* for ten years "could or could not be consistent with psychopathic personally." Working around the clock for forty-eight hours, as Chambers often did, "is usually a sign of an emotional disturbance." Murphy parodied Cross's hypothetical question with this exchange:

MURPHY: Let us assume further, Doctor, that a man was married to the same woman for 19 years and was the father of her two children; would you say that there perhaps was some evidence of a stability of attachment? . . .

BINGER: It could be. It depends on the nature and character of the attachment.

According to the psychiatrist, he and his wife had known the Hisses since 1947. Mrs. Binger, like Priscilla Hiss, had graduated from Bryn Mawr—and he had declined a fee for his services as an expert. "Can we say, Doctor, that your opinion as an expert is in some way measured . . . by your friendship with Mr. or Mrs. Hiss?" Murphy asked. Binger: "In no way."

In a crucial concession, the witness agreed that most psychiatrists considered the term "psychopathic personality" a vague analytic category at best, although Binger disagreed with Murphy's categorization of the phrase as a catch-all, "a wastepaper basket classification of a lot of symptoms." The prosecutor read from a recent psychiatric monograph criticizing the concept of psychopathic personality as "highly unsatisfactory" and "useless in psychiatric research." Binger had not read the book in question but, curiously, "agreed with every word" of the passage Murphy read, including the sentence: "It serves as a scrapbasket to which is relegated a group of otherwise unclassified personality disorders and problems." Murphy had obviously been coached carefully by his own psychiatric adviser and he questioned Binger about a number of passages dealing with "psychopathic personalities" that seemed to challenge the witness's testimony: "What I am trying to prove," Murphy concluded, ". . . is that the basis for your expert opinion is not a warranted basis for an expert opinion . . . that you don't have enough information to form an honest, intelligent psychiatric opinion."

Ridiculing the "symptoms" Binger had used in defining his key concept, Murphy began with the notion of lying. The courtroom audience laughed at one point when he asked if telling children that the stork brought babies constituted "a symptom of psychopathic personality." Binger replied: "Well, if the parents believed it I would think it might." Often, the doctor pointed out, psychopaths have a "malign purpose" in lying. What about "lying to your wife?" "Pretty normal." What about prisoners of war? Also normal.

The prosecutor's point was that it remained critical to understand the "specific purpose" of a lie to determine whether it was normal or not. Thus Chambers's lie to Dean Hawkes, which Binger had stressed, had been told so that he could reenter Columbia, and had been promptly confessed to Mark Van Doren.

Whenever Murphy caught Binger in an inconsistency, the latter generally dismissed the point as having "no bearing" on his overall analysis of Chambers. Thus when Chambers lied while a Communist during the 1930s, Murphy asked, was he not simply "acting as a soldier in a cause that he believed in?" Binger disagreed: "It is evidence to me only of another lie in a series of lies." Binger was equally firm about Chambers's use of the "Charles Whittaker" alias in his father's office, even when Murphy pointed out that Jay Chambers had told his son to do this. "If I ordered my son to change his name," the witness responded, "I doubt very much whether he would do it." By Murphy's count, Binger had mentioned only twenty lies told by Chambers in his first thirty-six years. "What would par be?" he asked the psychiatrist. "How many lies is the normal person entitled to have in 36 years?" When Binger responded, "Well, you have had more experience at that than I," Murphy demanded and received an apology: "I meant you had more experience with liars than I, naturally."

But defining "par" for a "normal person" proved impossible for Binger, and he conceded that it "is much easier to define a sick person than a normal person." At one point Murphy caught the witness in another amusing trap of his own making. Binger had testified on direct examination that there existed "certain confirmatory things" by which to detect a psychopathic personality and mentioned, as one of them, Chambers's tendency on the witness chair to gaze up at the ceiling frequently. One of Murphy's assistants had counted Binger staring in that direction fifty times in fifty-nine minutes, and the prosecutor asked if this constituted such symptoms as the doctor ascribed to Chambers. "Not alone," came the irritated response.

Murphy read into the record an August 17, 1948, *New York Times* interview with Binger at an international conference on mental health, which contained this passage:

> Professor Binger pointed to the "bugaboo of communism," which he said was now spreading a state of "neurotic anxiety" throughout the United States. Fanned largely by "big business and by the vote-getters, this "neurosis," Professor Binger added, has become confused in public minds with the "legitimate fears" of Russia and, under such conditions, he asserted, not only the people of the United States but also its leaders and policymakers are in danger of losing a rational, objective approach to world problems.

Agreeing that he had made the statement, Binger insisted in equally sweeping terms to Murphy that all of the lies told by Chambers revealed him to be a "psychopathic personality": "I include the lies told while he was a Communist even if under orders and even with the collaboration and help of his friends as lies."

As for Binger's other "symptoms," Murphy asked if he considered one known episode as a youth, stealing the library books, adequate evidence of a propensity toward theft on Chambers's part. That, plus receiving stolen documents from government officials during the late 1930s, came the response. Binger admitted that his analysis of Chambers's "insensitivity" depended on only two incidents: his having written *A Play for Puppets* and his period of residence with Ida Dales at his mother's house. As for "bizarre behavior," Murphy ridiculed the Williams College story and drew Binger's acknowledgment that it is not necessarily bizarre for a person to discard something (even a typewriter) that reminds him of the past.

The pumpkin incident was another "symptom" examined. Did Binger know about the episode of hiding the Connecticut Charter from the British in an oak tree? Was that bizarre? No, because "that was a very primitive community and in olden times . . . but I still regard hollowing out a pumpkin and putting microfilms in it as sufficiently bizarre . . . because it is not the way a modern Twentieth Century human being . . . usually behaves." Even if it had been done to hide the documents from intruders on the day Chambers turned them over to HUAC? Even then, avowed the witness. Was it bizarre for Major André to have hidden the plans for West Point he received from Benedict Arnold in the sole of his boot? "No, I wouldn't say so." "Well, how about the mother of Moses hiding the little child in the bullrushes? Was that bizarre?" "Well," Binger replied, "she could hardly put it in a safe deposit box."

But had Chambers's fear of assassination after his defection been "bizarre," as Binger had labeled it? The witness had "no comment" on that: "I don't know the practices of the Communist underground and no idea whether there was any reasonable basis for the fear or not." Was it "fair" to assume that Chambers, "a paid [CP] functionary for many years, would have a normal, healthy fear of reprisal?" Binger agreed to this, and the prosecutor pinned down the point by mentioning the fate of Trotsky and Krivitsky. Murphy also argued at length with the witness about whether Chambers's grief-stricken reaction to Richard's suicide had been that of a "normal" or an "abnormal" personality, with neither man budging from his position. He criticized Binger for having taken one passage from Chambers's 1948 *Life* article "The Devil" out of context to argue that the man was psychopathic, and Murphy had the court reporter read the entire piece. Binger agreed that it was "a brilliant article" but still "the work of a man who was psychopathic." He described Chambers as an "extraordinarily creative" person but frustrated because "he has created so pathetically little in his life in the way of literary productions except hack work and translations and a few poems."

Binger defended the *Class Reunion* analogy to the Hiss case, with Chambers as the manipulative Sebastian and Alger Hiss as the victimized Adler. But he apparently had read only Harold Rosenwald's memo on the book, since he asserted in describing the plot: "[Adler] comes back 25 years later, and is seen by Sebastian," while in fact the novel ends with Sebastian's recognition that he has made a mistake and the man he thought was the Adler he knew as a youth turns out to be someone else. Murphy made the obvious points: Had Chambers modeled himself after any character in the many other books that he translated? Did Binger "draw any analogies from the translation of the book 'Bambi'?" No, the witness acknowledged, nor had he read this translation in preparing for his appearance in court. Indeed, he had not made a thorough study of all of Chambers's writings: "I browsed through some of them." Thus he had read the *Life* piece on

"The Devil" but not the *Time* cover story on Marian Anderson or the article on Albert Einstein.

Even if Chambers's fears about CP reprisals had been justified, Binger testified as Murphy returned to the subject, his words and actions in responding to these fears would still have labeled him as a "psychopathic personality." "Doctor, could it be paranoid thinking if what he was thinking about was true and the facts if they existed in reality—could that be paranoid thinking?" "The way it is put," said Binger, "sounds like it."

The prosecutor challenged Binger's few examples of Chambers's alleged vagabondage" and "untidiness," asking the witness whether such celebrated figures as Albert Einstein, Will Rogers, Thomas Edison, Howard Hughes, and Bing Crosby (all sloppy dressers normally indifferent to their appearance) were also pathological. As for Binger's last category, "unstable attachments," Murphy brought up once more Chambers's nineteen-year marriage and two children. Was all this not "cogent evidence of a real stable attachment?" Binger conceded no such thing. Was not Chambers's successful ten-year career at *Time* similar evidence? "In that particular instance, yes." The witness acknowledged that his evidence of Chambers's alleged "instability" had been drawn mainly from his youth and his experiences in the CP.

Having countered each category used by Binger in his analysis, Murphy returned to his basic question. Did the psychiatrist still believe that Chambers was a psychopathic personality? "Most certainly," Binger responded, and with that comment Murphy turned the witness back to Cross, who tried to refurbish Binger's credentials, left battered by Murphy's scathing cross-examination. Cross had Binger review his career as a psychiatric consultant and writer, his personal psychoanalysis by Carl Jung, and his relationship to the Hisses. Before the witness stepped down, Murphy, in turn, elicited from Binger the admission that Harold Rosenwald had first invited him into the case.

The next defense expert, Dr. Henry A. Murray, a psychologist at the Harvard Medical School, had been approached by the Hiss attorneys shortly before the second trial to serve as a back-up for Binger's testimony. As it turned out, Murray—who had worked extensively on assessments of OSS recruits during the Second World War, had helped devise a number of standard psychological tests (including the Thematic Apperception Test, or TAT), and had written one of the OSS's psychological profiles of Adolf Hitler—proved a far more adept witness in most respects.[31]

He had read a number of Chambers's writings in preparation for testifying, and on the basis of having analyzed those writings alone, and with no courtroom observation, Murray claimed that Chambers "has been suffering from a mental ailment known as psychopathic personality without symptoms of psychosis or insanity." Much of what followed repeated Binger's review of "psychopathic personality"' as it related to Chambers's life (Murray had not been in court while Binger testified), although he drew also on his previous experiences evaluating OSS candidates and analyzing Hitler.

While questioning Murray, Cross did not dwell on specific illustrations drawn from Chambers's life, if only because Murphy's cross-examination of Binger had possibly reduced many of these examples to absurdities in the minds of the jurors. But he asked if Murray believed in the notion that "psychopathic personality" was a "scrapbasket" category. Not wholly, the witness replied, although his answer trailed off at this point. He observed that there was a "common saying among psychiatrists, 'once a psychopath always a psychopath,'" and that the "general view is that they are incurable." Murphy objected to this answer as unresponsive. The best Murray could offer by way of clarification was to suggest that the concept of psychopathic personality was "the unifying principle that explained a great many of these different kinds of behaviors. . . ."

The prosecutor scored strongly on the psychologist's random sample of Chambers's writings. Dr. Murray agreed he had read nothing written by Chambers for *Time* from 1939 to 1948, and nothing written during the thirties. He admitted having read (in Murphy's words) only "a rather meagre part of a man's writing"—in the psychologist's own words, "a small sample"—yet on it he based largely his diagnosis of Chambers's psychopathic personality: "I have not read anything except what was given to me. . . ."

Had Murray read Chambers's *Time* cover stories on Arnold Toynbee, Reinhold Niebuhr, Albert Einstein, or Pope Pius XII? "No." His *Life* articles in the "History of Civilization" series? "No." *Bambi* or most of his dozen other translations? "No." "And hundreds of stories in *Time* from 1939 on, cinema, religion, international news—you read none of those?" "No." Murray pointed out that, often, *Time* stories were reputedly written by a number of people, not one, and hence his disinterest in reading those allegedly done by Chambers. In that case, the prosecutor countered, how did Murray know that the *Life* article "The Devil," on which the doctor had "placed so much reliance," was not also the product of joint authorship and editing?

Yet Murphy was not above his own bit of deviousness, as when he asked Murray whether the psychologist wished to accuse Chambers of "abnormal sexuality" on the basis of imagery in the poem "Tandaradei." Murray backed away from that charge.

Despite the fact that "the subject" had worked for a decade at *Time* and completed two decades of marriage and family life, Murray, like Binger, still diagnosed Chambers as a psychopathic personality who lacked stable attachments. He added a new and even sillier touch, describing Chambers's abandonment of the Episcopalian church for Quakerism as yet another example of the man's instability. Nor would Murray credit long-lasting friendships such as Chambers's relationship with Meyer Schapiro or the more recent ones with people at *Time* as instances of "stability," since even psychopathic personalities "all have friends of various degrees of steadiness."

Asserting that he had not formed any opinion of Chambers's writings until he read them and "brooded," Murray said that by Christmas he had become persuaded of his analysis. But, under Murphy's questioning, the witness acknowledged having interviewed one of Chambers's *Time* colleagues on November 26 and having asked him for confirmation of the various symptoms of Chambers's psychopathology. But Murray denied Murphy's suggestion that he had been already "prejudiced at the time" and had already developed "a preconceived bias." He said that a friend, Lewis Mumford, had directed him to the *Time* employee. Murphy asked if Dr. Murray had told the person at *Time* "that Mr. Chambers was a pathological liar." "I might have," came the response. Finally, Murray conceded that he had said to his informant at the magazine: "Oh, you are just whitewashing Mr. Chambers."*

Because of the increased roster of witnesses and because Judge Goddard allowed opposing counsel great scope in questioning witnesses, the second trial proved longer than the first. Beginning on November 17, 1949, it lasted two months. In summing up on January 19, 1950, Cross attacked Chambers's admitted "perjuries" and noted the absence of proof for much of the story told by Hiss's accuser about their personal friendship.[32]

Recognizing that Murphy had based his case this time on "the immutable proof of the documents" and not primarily on Chambers's word, Cross zeroed in on Julian Wadleigh, "the real thief," and he stressed the fact that several of the typed documents had not been sent to Sayre's office. He speculated that Chambers had kept files on possible victims within the government—including one on Hiss and another on Francis Sayre. Moreover, Wadleigh (and not Hiss), according to Cross, had stolen "every one of those [microfilmed] papers." As for the handwritten memos, Chambers or some confederate took these from Hiss's office, perhaps from a wastebasket.

The most ingenious addition to the defense argument concerned the notion of Chambers's other confederate at State, purportedly a "second Wadleigh" either in Trade Agreements or in the Far Eastern Division, whom Cross credited with

---

*The *Time* figure, unnamed at the trial, related the story of Dr. Murray's visit to James Agee, a good friend of Chambers, who passed it along to Murphy. Agee also told FBI agents that when Hiss's picture had appeared in *Time* during the San Francisco UN meeting, Chambers had said to him: "Yes, he [Hiss] is a very able man and at one time he was my best friend . . . [but] Alger Hiss was a Communist." Agee said that after the HUAC hearings began in August 1948, Chambers told him "he could not understand how Alger Hiss could deny that he was a Communist . . . since he must well know that he, Chambers, knew that Hiss was not only a Communist but that he had done some terrible things. . . . This statement was made prior to the time that the microfilms were found in the pumpkin at Westminster, Maryland." FBI Summary Report, January 4, 1950, #4454.

responsibility for stealing the documents turned over by Chambers for which Wadleigh could not be held accountable. The defense attorney suggested several candidates for the role of "second Wadleigh": Leander Lovell, whom Chambers had named as an underground Communist (but not a source of material) in the Berle memo, and possibly even Hiss's onetime superior Leo Pasvolsky, whose office had received copies of a number of the stolen documents, but whose integrity had never been questioned prior to Cross's summation.

He agreed that the stolen documents had been typed on Hiss's Woodstock: "But it is not the question of what typewriter was used but who the typist was. That is the question." Cross said nothing about the conclusions of defense examiners that Mrs. Hiss had probably typed the material. He suggested an alternative nominee for the typist—namely, Whittaker Chambers or a confederate who sneaked into the Catlett home at some point to transcribe the material for his "file" on Alger Hiss. The defendant claimed he had not seen Chambers since mid-1936, but Cross did not explain how, if this was true, Chambers learned that the Catletts had been given the machine by Hiss in early 1938.

Chambers's motive in producing the documents from his "files" in 1948 was simple. He meant to protect himself, according to defense counsel, against an unfavorable slander-suit judgment. Considering the amount of time spent with Doctors Binger and Murray on the witness stand, Cross said surprisingly little about Chambers's "psychopathic personality." Murphy's cross-examination of the two analysts had apparently destroyed Hiss's "psychiatric defense" for the moment. To explain Chambers's actions against Hiss, Cross relied more on the notion of Chambers's desperation in November 1948 than on an alleged yearning for vengeance. Moreover, he insisted that Hiss's behavior, from the earliest denials to HUAC up to his conduct at the trials, could only be explained as that of an innocent man: "If Alger Hiss knew that those documents existed the man was crazy."[33]

Again, once Cross had finished, Murphy pleaded with jurors to put emotions aside, although he admitted of the protagonists: "One is handsome and tall and the other is pudgy and small; one went to Harvard and one to Columbia; Mrs. Hiss went to a party with Mrs. Dean Acheson. Mrs. Chambers's mother and father came from Russia." Murphy turned then to his high cards: "The facts would be proved by the documents, and there, ladies and gentlemen, are the documents [indicating]. They do not change. . . . Nobody has altered them . . . you will always come back to the documents in applying reason to this case."[34]

And Hiss had great advantages in preparing his case: "The defendant is a lawyer. He told us that he has nine lawyers . . . eminent in their field. . . . He has been able to cross-examine the principal Government witness before trial. Have you ever heard of that?" Hiss summoned nineteen character witnesses, "more than one-third the number of his total witnesses," to attest to his reputation. But "what kind of reputation did a good spy have? Of course it must be good. The fox barks not when he goes to steal the lamb. . . . we are not concerned with reputations. Poppycock." Murphy reminded the jurors of his cross-examination of the two doctors—"they wanted to help a friend."

Repeating parts of Chambers's testimony that the prosecution said proved his close association with Hiss—the apartment rental, the Ford car, the three-day stopover at the Hisses' home ("that P Street shelter for wandering subtenants"), the rug gift, and others—Murphy stressed those aspects which could not have been learned except through friendship with the defendant: among them Hiss's meeting with Colonel Lamb while at the Nye Committee, the unusual nickname of a friend of the Hisses named "Plum" Fountain (whom Chambers claimed to have met once), Mrs. Hiss's Socialist involvement, the $400 car loan, and Mrs. Hiss's summer course in 1937.

The prosecutor tackled directly the question of Hiss's reputation, suggesting that some jurors might be asking, "How could a man like Mr. Hiss do these things? You hear it all over." He reminded the jury that Julian Wadleigh was the son of an Episcopalian minister, well educated (like Hiss) and with a fine career. "Now if Wadleigh can do it, Hiss can do it. . . . The analogy is there." As for Hiss's motives in fighting Chambers's charges, Murphy remained unimpressed: "He had to admit or deny . . . fish or cut bait. If he admitted—bang. Everything crumbles at once, the job to boot. So you deny, you accuse, accuse the other guy, yell cop."

Murphy had special fun with the Commodore Hotel confrontation scene, illustrating it with a story about a giraffe (Hiss) and a hippopotamus (Chambers):

> . . . the giraffe says to the hippopotamus, "I don't remember you at all."
> The hippopotamus says, "You must remember me. We were in the jungle together, the two of us; we were friends."
> He says, "No, I don't remember you."
> But he says, "You must. We lived together. We ate together."
> "No."
> So the giraffe says, "Let me see your teeth."
> So he looks and he says, "Oh, George Crosley. I know you."
> George Crosley my aunt.

Murphy pointed out that others confronted with Chambers—Claudia Catlett and Edith Murray, for example—had recognized Chambers immediately.

After ridiculing Hiss's initial inability to remember the Woodstock typewriter, Priscilla Hiss's statement to the grand jury that Mrs. Catlett was dead, and the Hisses' failure to recall Chambers having a mustache in 1935 (as he had on the David Breen passport), Murphy pointed to the Catlett brothers' contradictory testimony on which move had brought them the typewriter. The Hisses, he observed with some amusement, are stuck with the Catletts. That is their choice." As for Priscilla Hiss's denial of skill with a typewriter, Murphy could hardly contain himself: "Three typewriters in ten years for a woman who was a long-hander, a longhander."

Why had the Hisses given the Catletts the typewriter? Murphy had an answer for this: "When Chambers . . . broke with the Party they realized, 'Well, we haven't got the—we got the rug stored away. The only thing remaining to get us into trouble other than his word is the typewriter. If they find those instruments [sic] we are sunk.' So what do they do? If they sold the typewriter they might be traced. If they . . . dropped it in the Potomac, somebody might see them. Guilty knowledge. So they give it to their trusted maid's children, knowing full well that they didn't type, that it would be put to abuse and gradually disintegrate, gradually."

Charging that the Hisses had told the Catletts to contact Donald Hiss if the FBI came looking for the machine late in 1948, Murphy asked: "Don't you think that was by prearrangement?" No matter; the Woodstock was found "after it became, for all practical purposes, useless to us. We had the specimens, we had the very letters Mr. Feehan could compare with the documents, so that the actual typewriter didn't mean anything. But we have it here to prove that it wasn't a wreck. The girl, Burnetta Fisher, used it in school, and Mrs. McQueen used it, and the man from the FBI used it. No trouble."

The prosecutor heaped scorn on Hiss's argument (and Cross's) that others had stolen the documents for Chambers: "But what does he say? Who did it? 'Wadleigh did it. X did it. Y did it. Anybody but me. Blame anybody.'" He reminded the jury that defense counsel had suggested three other sources within State for the stolen material—Wadleigh, Lovell, and Pasvolsky ("this sounds Russian, let's use that one"). Murphy also denounced Cross for suggesting that the FBI had schemed to frame Hiss.

Murphy concluded by reiterating his point about the "immutable" evidence, "the documentary proof": "Each of these documents, the typewritten documents, and the handwritten documents, each has the same message. . . . And what is that message? 'Alger Hiss, you were the traitor. Alger Hiss, your feathers are but borrowed and you can't change those documents.' . . . Why? Why did he do it? Because he was in love with their philosophy, not ours. We were not at war then. He was concerned with their philosophy. . . . Take them with you to the jury room, those photographs; take the machine, the instruments. What do they prove? Ladies and gentlemen, it proves treason, and that is the traitor."

The jury took less than twenty-four hours. After Judge Goddard's charge, which, like Kaufman's at the first trial, wove together points submitted by opposing counsel, it retired at 3:10 PM on January 20. Later that day the jurors asked to examine portions of testimony by major witnesses and the crucial stolen documents. The next day they returned with a verdict after lunch. The forewoman read: "We find the defendant guilty on the first count and guilty on the second."[35]

Alger and Priscilla Hiss sat quietly, both pale, as the jurors were polled. Crowded on all sides, the defendant and his wife moved slowly out of the courtroom through a throng of lawyers, newsmen, and spectators. Before dismissing the jurors, Goddard thanked them for having rendered "a just verdict" and cautioned against talking to the press.[36]

On January 25 Claude Cross moved for a new trial or for an "arrest of judgment" on a number of grounds, mainly connected with the judge's alleged errors. Goddard denied the motions. Cross then made a plea that the defendant not be sent to jail, stressing Hiss's sufferings up to that point and his earlier contributions as a public official. Murphy recommended a five-year sentence "on each count to run concurrently," and Goddard reiterated his belief that Hiss had received "an eminently fair trial."[37]

The judge instructed Hiss to rise, but before Goddard imposed sentence, Cross asked if the defendant could make "a very brief statement." Goddard consented, and Alger Hiss approached the bench:

> I would like to thank your Honor for this opportunity again to deny the charges that have been made against me. I want only to add that I am confident that in the future the full facts of how Whittaker Chambers was able to carry out forgery by typewriter will be disclosed. Thank you, sir.

Goddard, accepting Murphy's recommendation, sentenced Hiss to five years in prison on each count, "sentences to run concurrently."[38]

Once convicted, Hiss quickly mobilized an almost entirely fresh group of lawyers to handle the appeal. Heading the new defense team was Chester Lane, another Harvard Law School classmate of Hiss's and a New York lawyer in private practice. Lane had apparently begun preliminary discussions with his client about managing the appeal even before the second trial concluded. His assistants numbered only one original defense lawyer, Harold Rosenwald. Also on board were Helen Buttenwieser, a friend of the family (the Hisses stayed at Mrs. Buttenwieser's apartment for a time after the jury verdict came down), and Robert Benjamin, whom Hiss had met initially when Benjamin clerked for Justice Holmes, and who wrote most of the appeal brief. Claude Cross returned to Boston without taking part in posttrial legal maneuvers, while Edward McLean's firm—Debevoise, Plimpton and McLean—which had served as Hiss's attorneys of record during the slander suit and the two trials, withdrew from the case. McLean severed himself completely from the defense after the second trial, presenting the reasons for this rupture in a blunt letter to Hiss, copies of which McLean sent to Cross, Marbury, John F. Davis, and Richard H. Field, the Harvard Law School professor who headed up Hiss's defense-fund appeal.[39]

Hiss and McLean parted company in a February 2 conversation, two weeks after conviction, and the following day McLean wrote to "confirm" their talk:

Whitney Debevoise and I stated that our firm was prepared to represent you on your appeal, on condition that we have an undivided responsibility and final authority to decide, in our best judgment, as to how the case should be briefed and argued. We point out that there have been a number of occasions in the past on which you have preferred to follow other people's advice rather than ours . . . which has hampered us in our efforts to help you and which we felt should not continue if we were to stay in the case.

You said, in substance, that you did not wish us to undertake the appeal on the basis which we proposed, and that you desired to select new counsel who you believed would be more sympathetic to your views as to how the case should be handled.[40]

Although he offered assistance in helping to familiarize the "new counsel" with the case's record, McLean clearly did not wish to place the Debevoise firm in the same position as during the trials: "The firm's name was being used," Robert von Mehren recalled of McLean's decision to withdraw, "but it wasn't in a position to have its advice fully effective." Moreover, according to Von Mehren, McLean and others at the firm complained not only that "Hiss rejected its advice at critical junctures in both trials," but also that "a number of emphases [were] wrong." Von Mehren mentioned specifically the stress on psychiatric testimony and on the "forgery by typewriter" theory that "we never felt . . . was more than a theory." At neither trial did Cross or Stryker raise the "forgery by typewriter" thesis—which Alger Hiss mentioned first in his closing statement before Goddard—suggesting that McLean left the case partly because of an unwillingness to lend his name and services to an appeal process that would prepare arguments and evidence trying to sustain this wispy theory.[41]

Chester Lane harbored no such objections, and his two-pronged strategy unfolded from the moment Hiss assigned him complete control of the case in February. Lane intended to prepare the appeal motion while undertaking fresh investigative work and a careful review of available records.[42]

Lane had been only a casual acquaintance of Hiss's at Harvard, but had come to know him better while both worked in Washington. In the winter of 1940–41, and at the suggestion of Justice William O. Douglas, Hiss asked whether Lane, general counsel of the Securities and Exchange Commission, would have any interest in accompanying Francis Sayre to the Philippines as a legal adviser. Hiss had previously—but unsuccessfully—nominated Noel Field for the position, as well as several other friends. But Lane declined.[43]

During the war years he worked with others in government whom Chambers accused of Communist ties—Harry Dexter White, Sol Adler, and Harold Glasser among them—and Lane believed firmly that none of these men had been a Communist. As for Hiss, Lane's faith in his client's innocence never wavered, unlike that of earlier attorneys such as McLean and Marbury, both of whom expressed concern that either Alger or Priscilla Hiss (or both) had not been completely candid with them. Under the circumstances, replacing McLean with the far less skeptical Lane seemed a logical step for Hiss.

Financing the appeal posed problems. Substantial amounts were needed, not only for researching the brief but for simultaneous investigations toward a motion for a retrial. Richard Field sent a "report to contributors" on February 17, appealing for funds and sketching out "the magnitude of the financial problem that lies ahead." Hiss and his family had themselves largely financed the first trial, aided by several thousands in "unsolicited gifts from friends," according to Field, spending a total of over $50,000. With Hiss's own money exhausted, Field and other supporters had undertaken the job of raising funds for the second trial, receiving over $31,000 from almost three hundred contributors. Most of this had gone toward attorneys' fees, although none of Hiss's many lawyers—Marbury, Stryker, Cross, McLean, Rosenwald, Davis, and the others—had ever received more than modest sums for their work. Now Field asked donors to contribute at least another $30,000 to subsidize the appeal process. As it turned out, much more was required.[44]

The major shift in American public mood on the question of Communism in government accelerated during the months Hiss and his lawyers labored on their appeal brief. The verdict accounted for part of that change. Far more significant were the outbreak of the Korean War in June 1950 and Senator Joseph McCarthy's rise to notoriety, and power. But, judging from the appeal brief Lane and his associates completed in September 1950, regardless of the climate of public opinion, there seemed no compelling basis for the court of appeals to overturn the jury's verdict.

Much of the material in the brief dealt with unfavorable rulings by trial judges Kaufman and Goddard. Thus the argument began by rehabilitating the defense contention that a judgment of acquittal should have been ordered in the case because: (1) Chambers's charges lacked sufficient documentary corroboration under the federal perjury rules; (2) those charges had been disproven by showing Chambers himself to be an unreliable perjurer.[45]

The brief also argued at length that Judge Goddard should not have allowed four witnesses to testify: William Rosen, Felix Inslerman, Hede Massing, and Edith Murray. Hiss's lawyers claimed that Rosen's avowed intention to plead self-incrimination made his very appearance prejudicial to the defendant. As for Inslerman, demonstrating that his Leica produced the "pumpkin" microfilm provided only "pseudo-corroboration," to use Hiss's later term, for the charge that the defendant had given the materials to Chambers for microfilming. "It is this tendency," Hiss later wrote, "which is ridiculed in the popular saying: 'George Washington slept in that bed. If you don't believe it, there's the bed.'" Hede Massing's appearance also seemed unjustified to the defense, and Edith Murray should have been introduced not as a rebuttal witness, but earlier, to allow the defense full opportunity to prepare cross-examination.[46]

Most of the other points dealt with Thomas Murphy's alleged misconduct, citing numerous examples of what the defense considered the prosecutor's "inflammatory and prejudicial questioning of witnesses and argument to the jury." It was further alleged that Judge Goddard had been biased against the defense, both in conducting the trial and in his charge to the jury. Although Claude Cross had not accused Goddard of partiality during the trial itself (as Murphy had repeatedly done with Kaufman at the first trial, if only to build a record), Robert Benjamin and Hiss made that subject a pivotal one in the appeal brief, contrasting Goddard's supposed prejudice with Samuel Kaufman's purportedly model decorum during the previous trial.*

The court of appeals affirmed Hiss's conviction on December 7, 1950, rejecting each point made in Robert Benjamin's appeal brief. Judge Harriet B. Chase, who wrote the opinion for the three-man court, held that the government had been within its rights in summoning Rosen and Inslerman as witnesses, pointing out that whenever Rosen did not plead the First Amendment but answered questions, he "testified favorably to Mr. Hiss in that he denied that he knew him." Chase also found Hede Massing's testimony admissible and Edith Murray's role as a rebuttal witness for the prosecution, rather than as an initial witness, well within Goddard's discretion to allow.[47]

Defense complaints about Murphy's misconduct seemed unwarranted to Chase: "There was nothing in his [Murphy's] general conduct which can justify reversal." Similarly, Goddard's charge—about which Hiss's appeal brief complained—seemed to the court of appeals "clear and comprehensive," with all of the defense requests concerning that charge "which should have been granted . . . adequately covered. We find no error in it."[48]

The defendant, if not his attorneys, would later discern political bias in Judge Chase's decision. Hiss noted in his memoir that Chase had also spoken for the court in William Rosen's appeal from a contempt-of-Congress conviction and therefore knew a great deal about the HUAC hearings, too much for Hiss's taste (the court of appeals, however, had reversed Rosen's conviction). According to Hiss, even in disposing of his appeal "the pervasive influence of the Committee played a major and unjustified role." Hiss attacked Judge Chase for accepting "uncritically" HUAC's version of the case, but Chase's two colleagues, Judges Augustus N. Hand and Thomas Swan, joined in affirming the verdict.[49]

Richard Field's letter to defense-fund contributors had indicated that if the court of appeals rejected the defense brief, Hiss would seek U.S. Supreme Court review under a petition for a writ of certiorari. Chester Lane requested a writ on January 27, largely on the same grounds that had been used in seeking to

---

*In a chapter titled "Conduct of Prosecutor and Judge—Appeal," Hiss nicely summarizes the defense's complaints concerning Murphy and Goddard as presented in the appeal brief. *In the Court of Public Opinion,* pp. 329–55.

persuade the Court of Appeals to overturn the verdict. By a four-to-two margin, the Supreme Court denied certiorari on March 12. Justices Douglas and Black voted to grant review, but Chief Justice Fred Vinson, joined by Justices Burton, Jackson, and Murphy, rejected certiorari. Three members of the high court disqualified themselves: Tom Clark, who had been attorney general at the time of Hiss's indictment, and Frankfurter and Reed, who had appeared as character witnesses for the defendant. Had Frankfurter and Reed not testified, it seems probable that both would have favored reviewing the case (only four justices were needed for review). But it seems just as likely that, even had "cert" been granted, the same three justices would have disqualified themselves from voting because of prior associations with Hiss or the case, and the Supreme Court would have split four-to-two against Hiss.[50]

On March 22 Hiss surrendered himself at the Foley Square courthouse. A reporter on the scene found him displaying "no particular emotion, though he did smile a time or two" as federal marshals led him off to the House of Detention, handcuffed to another prisoner.[51]

At the Lewisburg, Pennsylvania, federal penitentiary Hiss began his five-year sentence for perjury. Despite his removal from the scene, and even while Chester Lane and his associates continued their efforts to produce fresh evidence and move for a new trial, the symbol of Alger Hiss continued to ignite controversy within political and cultural circles. For the moment, the Hiss case had terminated in the courts, but its hold on the American imagination grew steadily.

Part Five

CONSEQUENCES

*In Paris, society wrangled interminably about the Affair. Finding them-
selves unable to agree on the question of Dreyfus' guilt, once-loving sisters and brothers, parents and children stopped speaking to one another;
betrothals were abruptly broken off by parents who could not see eye
to eye on the affair with their prospective in-laws; bitter arguments dissolved long-standing business associations, fashionable hostesses invited
their friends to dinner with the assurance that "the Dreyfus case will
positively not be discussed. . . ."*

—*Betty Schechter,* The Dreyfus Affair: A National Scandal

*Those who can forget their own history are rewarded by having it forgot-
ten by pretty much everyone else.*

—*Murray Kempton*

XIV

COLD WAR ICONOGRAPY I: ALGER HISS AS MYTH AND SYMBOL

"The Hiss Case was an epitomizing drama," Whittaker Chambers wrote shortly before his death. "It epitomized a basic conflict. And Alger Hiss and I were archetypes. That is, of course, what made the Hiss Case. . . . What gave the peculiar intensity to the struggle."

Two incidents that occurred less than a month after Hiss's conviction illustrated the case's "peculiar intensity" and dramatized the symbolic firestorm that swirled around it. The first took place the day of Alger Hiss's sentencing, January 25, 1950, generating a controversy that nearly unseated Secretary of State Dean Acheson. That morning Acheson, still a friend of Donald Hiss's and a supporter of Alger, held a press conference. Acheson had been involved in defense efforts from the day Alger Hiss first appeared before HUAC. Two years before that, Acheson had helped ease Hiss out of the State Department despite continuing security inquiries. Now Hiss stood as a convicted perjurer. Homer Bigart of the New York *Herald Tribune* asked the inevitable question: "Mr. Secretary, do you have any comment on the Alger Hiss case?"[1]

Acheson had brooded about the case, and especially about the verdict. He wrote his daughter later on the 25th: "Here is stark tragedy—whatever the reasonably probable facts may be." Despite the obvious political repercussions, Acheson had determined to speak his mind and tell reporters, who caught the scent of a major story, "what one really meant—forgetting the yelping pack at one's heels—saying no more and no less than one truly believed."[2]

The secretary began his answer to Bigart by disavowing as "highly improper" any comment on the trial itself, then on appeal. But Acheson went on to say:

> I should like to make it clear to you that whatever the outcome of any appeal which Mr. Hiss or his lawyers may take in this case I do not intend to turn my back on Alger Hiss. I think every person who has known Alger Hiss or has served with him at any time has upon his conscience the very serious task of deciding what his attitude is and what his conduct should be. . . . For me, there is very little doubt about those standards or those principles. I think they were stated for us a very long time ago. They were stated on the Mount of Olives and

if you are interested in seeing them you will find them in the 25th Chapter of the Gospel according to St. Matthew beginning with verse 34.

Reporters in the unsaintly assemblage who checked the King James Bible found the chapter and verse: "For I was hungered, and ye gave me meat: . . . I was a stranger, and ye took me in: Naked, and ye clothed me: I was sick, and ye visited me: I was in prison, and ye came unto me. . . . Verily I say unto you, inasmuch as you have done it unto one of the least of these my brethren, ye have done it unto me."[3]

Not only Acheson but other top administration officials were deluged by mail in the days following publication of the secretary's statement. Most newspapers had reported the press conference in bold headlines comparable to *The Washington Post*'s: "ACHESON NOT TO TURN BACK ON HISS/CITES BIBLE VERSES/MUNDT ASKS PROBE OF CONVICTED MAN'S 'INFLU-ENCE' WITHIN STATE DEPARTMENT." Complaints from those troubled by Acheson's public defense of a convicted perjurer and apparent Russian espionage agent left the secretary unperturbed. Acheson recognized that he had to satisfy only one potential critic, Harry S. Truman, who himself had doubts about Hiss's guilt. More to the point, Truman nursed a grudge toward Whittaker Chambers's HUAC supporters. Nothing helped Acheson so much with the president as Republican reaction to his press conference: Karl Mundt's blast at Hiss's alleged "influence" at State, or GOP demands for Acheson's resignation, or Richard Nixon's labeling of Acheson's statement as "disgust-ing." The secretary wrote his daughter that Truman told him shortly after the press conference "that one who had gone to the funeral of a friendless old man just out of the penitentiary had no trouble in knowing what I meant and in approving it."*[4]

Major moderate-to-liberal dailies divided editorially in their assessment of Acheson's remarks. *The Washington Post* deplored the secretary's judgment, but Acheson drew support from the New York *Herald Tribune* and from the New York *Post,* whose editor, James Wechsler, had come reluctantly, like many anti-Stalinist liberals, to believe Hiss guilty. Old New Dealers also rose to Acheson's defense. Thurman Arnold, Paul A. Porter, Joseph L. Rauh, Jr., and other signers of a letter to *The Washington Post* complained about the paper's editorial criticism of Acheson: "Whether Alger Hiss is innocent or guilty, we believe that Secre-tary Acheson has reaffirmed with great simplicity and magnificent restraint the fundamental principle . . . that in a Christian and democratic society men may extend compassionate sympathy to their fellow men even though they may be ultimately persuaded of his [sic] guilt before the law."[5]

---

*Truman in 1945, while vice president, had drawn similar fire from press and public for attending the funeral of his friend and political mentor, a convicted felon and the onetime Demo-cratic boss of Kansas City, Thomas J. Pendergast.

The second incident occurred on February 9, a few hundred miles from the Capitol, where a then-obscure senator voiced a less favorable view of Acheson's statement and of Hiss's conviction. The Republican women of Wheeling, West Virginia, had invited as their Lincoln Day speaker Joseph R. McCarthy, a first-termer from Wisconsin. McCarthy had arrived in Washington during the 1946 Republican congressional sweep and, like many of his freshman colleagues, was worried about the impending 1952 reelection campaign. He needed an issue and finally seated on the "Reds in government" theme.

Hiss's conviction made the Truman administration extremely vulnerable for its alleged "softness" toward Communists in government. The State Department, especially after Acheson defended Hiss, provided a prime target for such criticism.

By then, as McCarthy and his advisers recognized, Truman had become a hostage to the internal-security monster. On the heels of Hiss's conviction came the president's order to proceed on a hydrogen-bomb project and the British announcement that one of its top atomic scientists, Klaus Fuchs, had confessed to spying for the Russians from 1943 to 1947. (One London reporter described Fuchs in terms now familiar to Americans because of the Hiss case as "the last man in the world you would expect to be a spy.") McCarthy had already departed for Wheeling on February 9 when Homer Capehart of Indiana, another Republican arch-conservative, drew strong applause from fellow senators and spectators when he demanded to know: "How much more are we going to have to take? Fuchs and Acheson and Hiss and hydrogen bombs threatening outside and New Dealism eating away the vitals of the nation. In the name of Heaven, is this the best America can do?"[6]

Although McCarthy's speech at Wheeling went largely unnoticed, talks elsewhere that month by the Wisconsin Republican established him as the new master of the anti-Communist stump speech. The most often quoted portion of McCarthy's maiden effort at Wheeling concerned his extraordinary and ludicrous accusation that the State Department under Dean Acheson remained "thoroughly infested with Communists"—205, to be precise. Although McCarthy later revised his number downward, the Wheeling oration seems most notable for the central role assigned in his demonology to Alger Hiss, "who is important not as an individual any more, but rather because he is so representative of a group in the State Department. It is unnecessary to go over the sordid events showing how he sold out the nation which had given him so much. Those are rather fresh in all of our minds."

More than any other factor, Alger Hiss's conviction gave McCarthy and his supporters the essential touch of credibility making their charges of Communist involvement against other officials headline copy instead of back-page filler. "If Alger Hiss, why not others?" ran the argument of those who, thanks to McCarthy's fulminations, believed that the State Department harbored a multitude of radicals. So fretful had departmental officials themselves become as a result of Hiss's conviction, Acheson's defense, and McCarthy's assault that on February 13 State released a summary of its loyalty-security investigations since 1947 to reassure the public. In the three years of Truman's Loyalty Program the FBI had investigated over 16,000 employees at State, of whom the department had removed only two as security risks. An additional 202 employees whose security situation appeared uncertain had either resigned or left because of departmental cuts during this same period; and State declared that "it knows of no Communists who are presently employed."[7]

From the beginning of the case, both Hiss and Chambers manipulated its symbolic resonance as best they could. Lloyd Paul Stryker focused attention during the first trial on Chambers's opening statement to HUAC, in which he had linked Hiss closely to the Roosevelt-Truman record in domestic and foreign policies. Alger Hiss used every formal statement to the committee in August 1948 as an occasion to associate himself with those same New Deal and international-ist policies, rallying behind him both Truman liberals and Wallace Progressives. Chambers, in turn, drew his support largely from the administration's Republi-can opposition and other conservative forces in the American press and elector-ate. The partisan battle lines had therefore been formed even before Alger Hiss first went to trial. But there were numerous individual "deserters"—mainly anti-Communist liberals gradually persuaded of Hiss's guilt—who moved quietly across the line that separated the opposing camps.

"Ours is an era of 'cases,'" the critic Diana Trilling wrote, reflecting on the Hiss-Chambers conflict. She suggested that such controversial and well-publicized cases provoked within their society a basic "confrontation between opposing social principles."[8] The Hiss case dramatized, not simply for Dean Acheson and Joseph McCarthy but for millions of Americans, the emerging political and cul-tural implications of the Cold War. Inevitably, the complex disputes over evi-dence became reduced to compelling images of the total event. Almost from the moment the "facts" began to emerge in 1948, they congealed in partisan accounts, each side serving up a simple morality tale. Alger Hiss and Whittaker Chambers and their supporting casts achieved even before Hiss had gone to prison the status of icons in the demonologies and hagiographies of the opposing camps. Contemporary arguments by politicians and intellectuals alike over the "mean-ing" of the Hiss case, more than the evidence itself, set the direction and limits of subsequent historical investigation.

The Hiss case provoked feverish debate over the nature of alleged internal Communist "subversion" in the United States: "As 1949 wore on," wrote Eric Goldman, "the color and drama of the trials gave way to a different type of impact. Whittaker Chambers receded into the background, the specific testimony was less and less discussed. Even the figure of Alger Hiss the individual blurred.

Everything was turning into Alger Hiss "the symbol." The question of whether or not Hiss had perjured himself, whether or not he had spied for the Russians, and whether or not he had been a Communist Party member became enmeshed in a broader set of public issues: the meaning and validity of the Cold War, the treatment of domestic Communists whose leaders were themselves undergoing Smith Act conspiracy trials that generally resulted in convictions, the response of intellectuals to their own radical pasts, the true extent of Communist infiltration into government during the New Deal, and the proper role of congressional committees in investigating subversion. In sum, concern for the facts that would establish Alger Hiss's legal guilt or innocence blended into an even larger quest for the meaning of the Hiss case itself. Invariably, analysts began by assuming the existence of a single perjurer: that one man's story of their relationship was essentially truthful and the other's a tissue of lies.[9]

The Hiss case figured prominently in American political debate in the years that followed the verdict, with Republicans invoking Hiss's presumed treachery to indict the Democratic Party for tolerating traitors. Hiss's conviction soon "revolutionized public opinion" on the question of Communism in American government. "Without the Alger Hiss case," notes Earl Latham, the leading scholar of the McCarthy era's spy probes, "the six-year controversy that followed might have been a much tamer affair, and the Communist issue somewhat more tractable."[10]

Undeniably, HUAC's probe of the case restored in part the committee's tarnished public reputation. "The great lesson which should be learned from the Alger Hiss case," Richard Nixon said, "is that we are not just dealing with espionage agents who got 30 pieces of silver to obtain the blueprint of a new weapon ... but this is a far more sinister type of activity, because it permits the enemy to guide and shape our policy." Nixon's role as Hiss's chief pursuer on the committee paid off immediately with election to the Senate in 1950, after a viciously fought campaign against Democrat Helen Gahagan Douglas, a liberal anti-Communist whom Nixonites dubbed "the Pink Lady." Two years later Nixon was given the Republican vice-presidential nomination, winning as part of the Eisenhower ticket.[11]

Nor was Nixon the only GOP orator to exploit the Hiss case. Denunciations of Democratic opponents, linking them somehow to the misdeeds of Alger Hiss, became a staple of conservative Republican rhetoric during the congressional campaigns of 1950. Meanwhile Republican congressmen concentrated during 1950–52 on a related theme, excoriating the Truman administration for its responsibility for the Yalta Conference agreements. The question, although posed in a variety of ways by Republicans and anti-administration Democrats, related to the charge that Alger Hiss had "subverted" the controversial conference, "selling out" U.S. interests to the Soviet Union not only at Yalta but at the first UN conference. McCarthy and his supporters dwelt repeatedly on Hiss's alleged influence upon a "physically tired and mentally sick Roosevelt."[12]

To hear McCarthy tell it—or, for that matter, according to Nixon, Mundt, and other Republican stalwarts—Hiss practically lived at FDR's side during the Crimean conference, playing the crucial advisory role to the president. But there was little truth to the notion that Alger Hiss shaped the course of postwar policy-making at Yalta, the oft-repeated claim that dominated Republican speechmaking on that conference during the closing years of the Truman administration. "Hiss's conviction," wrote Athan Theoharis, "enabled the 'extremists' and 'partisans' to use Hiss and Yalta as symbols that justified the revision of some decisions and the repudiation of others. They insisted that certain policies reflected Communist influence or communistic ideas."

In the imagery of Republican partisans, Hiss became the linchpin in a "Communist conspiracy" to take over the American government under Roosevelt and Truman. Thus Nixon called a press conference in January 1950 to crow over Hiss's conviction and to describe the Red "master plot": "This conspiracy would have come to light long since had there not been a definite . . . effort on the part of certain high officials in two Administrations to keep the public from knowing the facts."[13]

Karl Mundt, like Nixon, met the press frequently that month to claim his own credit for exposing the man who had exerted "pro-Communist" influence at Yalta over Roosevelt. Because of ill health, according to Mundt, Roosevelt could not "think things through himself." Mundt reprinted thousands of copies of his Senate speech on the case—"What the Hiss Trial Actually Means"—a jeremiad whose subtitles indicated the symbolic uses to which Republicans would put the case: "Hiss's Job Was to Pervert Policy" . . . "White House Obstructed Investigation" . . . "Alger Hiss and the Yalta Conference" . . . "Alger Hiss and Our China Policy: Today's Political Plotters Must Be Stopped."

The theme of national betrayal reached its fullest expression in the hands of McCarthy. The likes of Alger Hiss and Dean Acheson, according to McCarthy, had led the United States into a worldwide Communist trap: "We know that since Yalta the leaders of this Government by design or ignorance have continued to betray us. . . . We also know that the same men who betrayed America are still leading America. The traitors must no longer lead the betrayed." McCarthy's and Nixon's indictment of the Democratic Party for presiding over "twenty years of treason" would have been far less effective had it not been possible for the Republican right to "validate" their claims by pointing to Alger Hiss's conviction.[14]

Republican exploitation of the Hiss case peaked (or dragged bottom) during the 1952 presidential campaign in speeches by McCarthy, Nixon, and others. The focus of most of the Republican attacks was on the character deposition given for Hiss at his trials by then-Governor Adlai E. Stevenson, the 1952 Democratic presidential nominee. During a nationwide television speech in October, Nixon discussed the Hiss case and denounced the Stevenson deposition as "going down the line for the arch traitor of our generation." Nixon insisted that he did not doubt Stevenson's "loyalty." "The question is one as to his judgment, and it is a very grave question." But Nixon remained defensive about the case, blaming it for what he believed to be the implacable hostility toward him of Democrats and newsmen. Robert Stripling, the former HUAC counsel, then working in the Eisenhower campaign, visited Nixon's New York hotel suite in the campaign's closing days. "Strip, those sons of bitches are out to get me," said the man who had spent the preceding months denouncing Adlai Stevenson, Dean Acheson, and Felix Frankfurter because of their personal support for Alger Hiss. "They got Mr. [J. Parnell] Thomas, they tried to get me, and they'll try to get anybody that had anything to do with the Hiss case."

Throughout the campaign GOP orators accused the Democratic candidate of "softness" on domestic Communism. Even Eisenhower joined in the chorus of Republican voices attacking and repudiating the Yalta agreements. McCarthy, like Nixon, made a nationally televised speech toward the end of the campaign in which the Hiss case's relationship to Stevenson figured prominently. His slanderous oration referred to the Acheson-Hiss-[Owen] Lattimore group, which, he charged, had (along with Stevenson) given "aid to the Communist cause." Promising to provide "the coldly documented history" of these charges, McCarthy warned: "Now these facts, my good friends, cannot be answered—cannot be answered by screams of smears and lies. And we call upon Adlai of Illinois to so answer those facts."[15]

The "facts" turned out to be the relationship between some of Stevenson's advisers—Arthur Schlesinger, Jr., among them—and Americans for Democratic Action, a liberal anti-Communist group that was a favorite McCarthy target despite the ADA's antipathy toward Communism, foreign and domestic. "Strangely Alger—I mean Adlai—Adlai in 1952," McCarthy interjected and cackled at his little joke, "now that he's running for President, says, I will dig out the Communists using as my weapon the loyalty program which my campaign manager damns and condemns." McCarthy pointed out that Hiss—"a convicted traitor"—had recommended Stevenson for a wartime conference post, and he suggested broadly that the candidate shared Hiss's political sympathies.

Neither Eisenhower nor any of his staff protested McCarthy's effort—or those by Nixon and other Republicans—to smear Stevenson as a fellow traveler or possibly worse. The Democratic candidate and his advisers became so concerned over the effectiveness of this Republican attack that Stevenson devoted speeches to explaining and attempting to minimize his involvement with Alger Hiss and the case. Stevenson defended his character deposition as an obligation imposed on any citizen when summoned by the courts, although Stevenson had volunteered the deposition. In earlier speeches the candidate, while denouncing McCarthy's rhetorical excesses, had defended his own anti-Communist credentials, praised the FBI and J. Edgar Hoover, and promised that as president he would "smash the [Communist] conspiracy beyond repair."[16]

As for Alger Hiss, Stevenson now asserted, less candidly than usual, that he had known Hiss "briefly . . . he never entered my house and I never entered his." Nor had he deposed, as Nixon charged, that Hiss's reputation had been "very good," only "good so far as I had heard from others." Moreover, Stevenson noted correctly, if irrelevantly, that his opponent, Dwight Eisenhower, and the Republican secretary of state-apparent, John Foster Dulles, had both expressed confidence in Hiss while serving as Carnegie Endowment trustees. Finally, Stevenson avowed that he "never doubted the verdict of the jury." Thus the Democratic candidate buckled slightly under Republican attack, trimming and qualifying his unqualified 1949 endorsement of Hiss's reputation.

Some Democratic campaigners such as Eleanor Roosevelt continued to express confidence in Hiss's innocence. But the majority of Democratic liberals had long since followed the lead of their most prominent spokesmen and periodicals in accepting the jury's verdict, however reluctantly. Anti-Stalinist contributors to *The New Leader*, veteran radicals who had struggled against the Communist Party as early as the "Popular Front" period of the thirties, had been persuaded of Hiss's guilt almost from the start of the case. Other liberals, disgusted by HUAC's "trial by publicity" and by the antics of committee Red-baiters, withheld judgment. *The Progressive*, the house organ of Midwestern La Follette liberalism, for example, wavered throughout the trials, agreeing that the circumstantial case against Hiss seemed strong, but retaining doubts about Chambers's credibility and "stability."[17]

The flap over the "pumpkin papers" and the Woodstock typewriter bemused some commentators. "If my hope of staying out of jail depended on my remembering correctly what I did with a typewriter I owned twelve years ago," said radio commentator Elmer Davis, "I think I'd wind up behind the bars." Accepting Chambers's word as "proof" of Hiss's guilt seemed the major stumbling block; journalists such as Richard Rovere, James Wechsler, and Bruce Bliven agreed that the government had produced sufficient corroboration to persuade them of Hiss's guilt.[18]

Not all liberal political voices were persuaded, however, if only because of the growing national hysteria surrounding the case. Attacks by Nixon and other conservatives on Judge Samuel Kaufman for his conduct of the first trial offended leading liberal newspapers and magazines. Even after Hiss's conviction the doubts remained for a few papers like the Chicago *Sun-Times*, which editorialized that "even if the verdict is sustained there remain important factors that are yet to come out." The St. Louis *Post-Dispatch* challenged the verdict directly and argued the Hiss defense's position that the evidence was so meager, the case should never have been brought to trial.

Some influential liberal writers—A. J. Liebling in *The New Yorker,* Robert Bendiner in *The Nation,* and Merle Miller in *The New Republic*—adopted positions similar to Dean Acheson's. They urged compassion for the defendant on grounds that he had acted from legitimate antifascist beliefs during the 1930s, not from an unpatriotic intention of injuring the American government. Others, like Marquis Childs and Max Lerner, questioned whether Hiss *could* have demonstrated his innocence, given the climate of public opinion. "There will be a persistent doubt," wrote Childs, "whether Hiss received a fair trial in the present atmosphere when guilty accusers seek to unload their burden of guilt by public accusation." Nor could liberals be pleased by the manner in which such men as Nixon and McCarthy rode to prominence on the coattails of the case, or the degree to which congressional committees such as HUAC and the Senate Internal Security Subcommittee had regained a measure of respectability because of the jury verdict on Hiss.[19]

However credible the case for Alger Hiss's involvement, these observers viewed his conviction as a disaster for American liberalism. The guilty verdict left all liberals exposed to right-wing assault, having supported and thus linked their fortunes—through character depositions, financial aid, press columns, editorials, and in every other conceivable manner—to a man who stood convicted of perjury related to espionage. If Hiss was indeed guilty, wrote Alistair Cooke, "what he owed to the United States and the people who had stood by him was a dreadful debt of honor." Liberals who believed in Hiss and had defended his innocence found themselves now on the defensive as he was converted into a symbol of the New Deal's treachery, particularly in the State Department."[20]

Radicals had less difficulty in dealing with Hiss's conviction. They saw it as additional evidence (in line with the Smith Act convictions of Communist leaders) of America's turn toward reaction and incipient fascism. Newspapers like the New York *Star* and its successor, the *Compass,* weeklies such as the *National Guardian,* and the Communist Party's *Daily Worker* agreed in assessing the meaning and symbolism of the case. "There is a new way to spell Franklin D. Roosevelt. Now they spell it H-I-S-S," editorialized the *Worker* on January 24, 1950. "In going after the youthful New Dealer Alger Hiss, they are out to drive their daggers into the reputation of Roosevelt's four administrations":

> Hiss is just a fall guy for much bigger game. The Hearst press tipped the hand of the men who launched this obscene spectacle with the disgusting Whittaker Chambers as their finger-man. . . . The theory of the Hiss indictment was that the New Deal was "Communist" and that the Communists are "spies and, therefore, the New Deal was itself a program of "pro-Russian espionage." . . . The middle-class jury performed as expected. . . . In the fear-laden atmosphere of

the "Cold War" blackmail, the jury is no less on trial than the particular victim. . . . Will our country let itself be tricked into police state suppression of all
opposition to the "Cold War" conspiracy? Will we let the confessed perjurer
Whittaker Chambers be the Judas goat to lead the nation into the same trap
into which the dope fiend and degenerate Van der Lubbe helped Hitler push
the German nation? . . .*[21]

But the notion of a government-sponsored anti-Communist "conspiracy" to
frame Hiss held sway during the 1950s mainly among Communists and others
on the far left. Even Hiss's lawyers argued only that HUAC, the FBI, or some outside agency had helped Whittaker Chambers in what the defense then believed
had probably been a "plot" against Hiss devised mainly by his accuser.

Had Hiss been framed? And, if so, how and by whom? Most liberals who
believed Hiss an innocent victim of perjured testimony and concocted evidence
pointed the finger squarely at Chambers. Yet the assault on Hiss, these defenders
recognized, foreshadowed the effort already begun by Republicans to discredit
New Deal liberalism and bipartisan internationalism. And the Hiss case's rever-
beration extended beyond the political stage. It stirred a fervent response among
American intellectuals, many of whom had not been so profoundly disturbed
by a public event since the Nazi-Soviet Pact of 1939. They had engaged in the
quarrels of the late thirties between those who supported an antifascist Popular
Front coalition (often led by Communists), on the one hand, and other antifascist
left-liberals who had opposed such alliances with the CP.

Propelled by the Hiss case, many liberal and radical intellectuals resumed this
internecine warfare between "Popular Fronters" and "anti-Stalinists." The latter
generally accepted Chambers's account of events, often with no attempt to hide
their distaste for Chambers himself, and dismissed Hiss as a classic representative of what Leslie Fiedler called "the Popular Front mind at bay." The Hiss case
offered anti-Communist intellectuals on the liberal left a unique opportunity to
reargue the pitfalls of political innocence for a new, postwar generation unfamiliar with, and unaccustomed to, the radical factionalism of the thirties.[22]

A significant number of anti-Communist intellectuals seemed less concerned
with Hiss's guilt, in fact, than with determining whether they could confront
their own personal belief in his guilt. The case represented for them a rite of
passage from a more activist past into a reflective present, a test of their ability
to face up to the cruel realities of the Cold War. Men and women who had been
wedded firmly, in Emerson's phrase, to the "party of hope" during the 1930s
and 1940s saw, in the mirror of the Hiss case, their faces now reflecting instead
the "party of memory," and they mused on the failures and lessons of radical
involvement. One such figure, literary critic Lionel Trilling, appropriately called

---

*A reference to the deranged Dutchman arrested by the Nazis for supposedly setting the
Reichstag fire in 1933.

his 1947 novel, with a major character modeled after Whittaker Chambers, *The Middle of the Journey.*

Those who doubted Whittaker Chambers even after Hiss's conviction were in a clear minority among commentators when they questioned his charges against Hiss as well as the aggressive anti-Communism of Chambers's intellectual adherents. With Hiss in jail, the latter group felt no compunctions over pounding home the apparent lessons taught by the case. They frequently appealed to Hiss himself to remove the lingering doubts (and perhaps their own) by confessing his guilt. "If he had told the Committee," the sociologist David Riesman mused, ". . . how it happened that a more or less idealistic and successful young lawyer could get involved with the Communist Party, he would have contributed to clarification instead of mystification. . . ."[23]

"Come clean, Alger Hiss," one law professor writing in *The Progressive* titled his discussion of the trials. Leslie Fiedler observed: "Had [Hiss] been willing to say, 'Yes, I did these things'—things it is now possible to call 'treason'—'not for money or prestige, but out of a higher allegiance than patriotism'—had he only confessed . . . then he need not even have gone to prison. Why did he lie?"[24]

For anti-Communists of the liberal left, accepting Hiss's guilt implied renouncing one's own earlier hopes concerning the Soviet Union, the American Communist Party, and the benefits that Communism supposedly held out for American society. "The anti-Hiss liberal," admitted Diana Trilling, "thinks 'There but for the grace of God go I.' But by 'there' he means Chambers as well as Hiss. And he refers, if he was ever close to the Communist movement, not to a mysterious possibility in his emotional and ideological life but to a choice fully confronted." Diana Trilling and others in the close-knit circle of New York intellectuals—many of them former radicals, although usually of the anti-Stalinist variety—either asserted or implied, in effect, that "Alger went to jail for all our sins."[25]

A burden of guilt over past radical associations and beliefs hung plainly on the shoulders of many of Hiss's critics in the literary and scholarly communities. To them the case dramatized the failure of their own previous radical CP affiliations or flirtations with Stalinism. Their essays revealed the deep uncertainties of a penitential liberalism, the emergence of a new self-questioning ethos that surfaced in many ways: Arthur Schlesinger urging that Chambers study Reinhold Niebuhr (about whom Chambers had actually written a *Time* cover story) in order to temper his anti-Communist extremism; James Wechsler and other ex-Communists describing the "god that trailed"; Lionel Trilling's tormented protagonist in *The Middle of the Journey* measuring the conceits and illusions of his fellow-traveling friends.

Anti-Communists of the liberal left now proclaimed publicly that earlier in their lives they too had trusted self-proclaimed "'idealists" who in retrospect appeared treacherously similar to Alger Hiss. "It is not necessary that we liberals be self-flagellants," Leslie Fiedler insisted, in a passage reminiscent of T. S. Eliot's *Four Quartets,* an influential work within this group:

> We have desired good, and we have done some! But we have also done great evil. The confession in itself is nothing, but without the confession there can be no understanding, and without the understanding of what the Hiss case tries desperately to declare, we will not be able to move from a liberalism of innocence to a liberalism of responsibility.[26]

For Fiedler and other liberal intellectuals, the emergence of postwar anti-Communism in American politics coincided dramatically with their own efforts to convince others like themselves of the essential symbolic meaning of Alger Hiss's conviction: not alone the "end of innocence" proclaimed by Fiedler's essay, but, in a practically religious sense, the shame of gullibility. The historian and poet Peter Viereck, although more conservative than the liberal-left analysts of the Hiss case, expressed their general assessment of the case's meaning:

> To whitewash Hiss and to blacken Chambers (whose only real sin is his maudlin prose style) has become a compulsive defense mechanism for all liberals who once fellow-traveled with Stalinism. During 1930–47, they befriended its fronts, parroted its poppycock, but lacked Hiss's guts for logically translating a criminal ideology into criminal action. . . . The Hiss case is the bad conscience of all America's political *demi-vierges.* In future decades, Hiss may become an "epic figure," the mythic national symbol of the whole guilty 1930's. The guilt is "tragic," in the true sense of the word, by being intermingled with the noble social idealism of the 1930's, which inspired the heroes of the antifascist resistance movements and some parts of the New Deal.[27]

The most ardent defenders of Hiss or of Chambers often proclaimed that "mere" evidence alone could never shake an essential belief in their man's truthfulness. The episode became, for many, an article of faith. Thus Walter Lippmann told Richard Rovere during a 1949 conversation: "I know Alger Hiss. He couldn't be guilty of treason." Some of Chambers's closest friends at *Time* argued with equal implacability on his behalf, inevitably, Hiss's supporters appeared the more beleaguered. Thus a Columbia philosophy professor and summer neighbor of Hiss's at Peacham insisted, according to Sidney Hook, when asked what evidence would convince him that Chambers told the truth: "Even if Hiss himself were to confess his guilt, I wouldn't believe it."[28]

But defenders of Alger Hiss were a small and uneasy band at the height of the Cold War during the 1950s. They had neither adequate evidence to prove Hiss innocent nor a climate of public opinion receptive to a "reversal" of judgment without new evidence. In addition, those who defended Hiss publicly after 1950—by involving themselves in his legal efforts, contributing to his defense fund, or publishing articles or books arguing his innocence—ran the risk of stirring FBI interest in their own careers and ideas. J. Edgar Hoover kept close tabs on those who touched too closely on the Hiss case, and many of them found they were subjected to FBI investigation.[29]

Although the bureau tended to lump together in a single category all those who maintained belief in Hiss's innocence, such belief stemmed from widely different political and personal motives. Nor did all of Hiss's supporters accept the notion of a conspiracy. The faithful ranged across a spectrum from Communist scholars like Herbert Aptheker, who wrote a widely distributed *Masses and Mainstream* article on Hiss's "frame-up," to staid Baltimoreans and Bostonians unpersuaded that "Alger" could have been guilty of anything Whittaker Chambers claimed he had done.[30]

The pages of some liberal journals—*The New Leader, The New Republic, Partisan Review,* and *Commentary* among them—were closed to pro-Hiss articles during the years that followed the trials. Only *The Nation* persisted in trying to stir public interest in the unresolved questions of evidence that remained, and in keeping alive the hope that Alger Hiss could be proved innocent. Links between *The Nation* and the Hiss defense had been close from the beginning of the case. Frieda Kirchwey, its publisher during the time of trial and a friend of Hiss, advised the defendant and his lawyers throughout the trials.* Kirchwey's successor as publisher of the magazine, George Kirstein, was married to Elinor Ferry, a writer who worked closely with Helen Buttenwieser on research for Hiss's retrial motion.

The most devoted believer in Hiss's innocence on *The Nation* entered the case even later. Carey McWilliams, a respected author, investigative journalist, and liberal activist, then editor of the magazine, opened its pages to a steady stream of editorials, articles, and reviews dealing with the Hiss case between 1952 and 1962—twenty-seven in all, including two special issues given over completely to the case. They were all favorable to Hiss and most argued his innocence on the grounds of a frame-up. McWilliams commissioned reporter Fred J. Cook to conduct a fresh investigation of the case, and maintained close contact with defense lawyers.† His concern about the case stemmed partly from sensitivity to its symbolism—especially his belief that establishing Hiss's innocence was somehow pivotal to reinvigorating American liberalism. In his role as Hiss's chief journalistic advocate during the first quarter-century after his conviction, McWilliams served as Zola for "the American Dreyfus."[31]

Whittaker Chambers had his own loyal band of partisans during the years that followed Hiss's conviction. Chambers's viewpoint on the evidence and symbolism of the case was most often reflected in the columns of a new journal founded in 1955 by conservative William F. Buckley, Jr. Buckley's *National Review,* to which Chambers himself contributed, became the anti-Hiss equivalent of Carey McWilliams's *Nation,* and the magazine's articles and the editors' books

---

*Hiss told the author that it was Kirchwey who recommended Claude Cross as his counsel.
†Cook's findings are described in the Appendix.

continued to revere Chambers and to defend him from liberal attack. Scholars of post–World War II American conservatism agree, in George Van Dusen's words, that "the Hiss-Chambers case occurred at the right time to fill the void in conservative thought" and that Chambers, personally, became "to the modern conservative what Achilles was to the Greeks in the Trojan War—simply put, a hero."[32]

Never in American history had a self-confessed "informer," a man deeply ambivalent about his role in this respect, been so sympathetically received by such a broad segment of American opinion makers and the public. In this process, contributors to the *National Review*—respected conservative analysts such as Buckley, Ralph de Toledano, James Burnham, John Chamberlain, John Dos Passos, and Arthur Koestler—provided Chambers with his most responsive and uncritical circle of supporters. Buckley and de Toledano became Chambers's most intimate friends in the decade that followed the trials.[33]

By the time the Hiss case broke, Chambers's hostility toward and contempt for American liberalism had become as intense as his bitterness toward Communism, and his relations with older friends from the 1930s such as Schapiro, Cantwell, and Solow had become strained or had ruptured completely. Chambers blamed these former radicals, many of whom maintained a commitment to liberal ideals, for playing a major role in having enticed him to Communism and "atheistic modernism." Crediting his youthful excesses partially to the influence of these Columbia friends and those whom he met later as Communists, Chambers constructed a portrait of his early years in his autobiography, *Witness*, and in later writings, that often left the facts far behind.[34]

Essays on the case written by liberal scholars particularly angered him. Thus he wrote de Toledano in August 1951, after reading Leslie Fiedler's *Commentary* article "Hiss, Chambers, and the Age of Innocence," that "the piece is dishonest":

> Its purpose is to hose out that Augean stable, the Liberal mind, by getting rid of *both* Hiss and Chambers—the first of whom makes them feel guilty, and the second of whom makes them feel—an even less forgiveable sin—small. . . . To achieve their triumph, it has been necessary to denigrate Chambers even more than Hiss.[35]

Thoroughly alienated by this time from left-liberal friends, Chambers turned increasingly to former *Time* associates like Duncan Norton-Taylor and to younger men like Buckley and de Toledano, none of whom had known him during his formative years as a writer and Communist. Such people could respond more approvingly to his conservative rebirth as a self-professed "counterrevolutionary" anti-Communist. Thus Buckley provided him with a journalistic forum, while de Toledano—who marshaled evidence supporting Chambers's veracity in *Seeds of Treason*—constructed arguments on his behalf against pro-Hiss critics.

If Chambers felt uneasy with former left-liberal friends and associates, including those who believed his testimony concerning Hiss, they in turn were no less uncomfortable with his conservative doctrines and arguments. Sidney Hook spoke for anti-Communist centrist liberals in criticizing this aspect of Chambers as it emerged from the pages of *Witness:*

> He recklessly lumps Socialists, progressives, liberals and men of good will together with the Communists. All are bound according to him by the same faith; but only the Communists have the gumption and guts to live by it and pay the price. . . . Chambers does not consider the possibility that the opposition of genuine American liberals to the cultural and physical terror of the Kremlin was deeper and more sustained than that of any other group because it was fed by a passion for freedom, and an opposition to all forms of authoritarianism. . . . The logic by which he now classifies liberals and humanists with the Communists is not unlike the logic by which, when a Communist, he classified them with Fascists.

Hook, although sympathetic to Chambers's "great honesty" and "magnificent courage," found this "self-declared mystic" and opponent of secular humanism to be quite incapable of analyzing systematically the complex interrelationships between different political groups in American society.[36]

The same factors that made *Witness* a bible for American political conservatives in the 1950s made both book and author appear flawed and unpalatable to American liberals, even those who accepted most of Chambers's claims concerning Alger Hiss and the Communist underground. One of the central issues confronting such liberals with radical backgrounds during the 1950s involved the question of whether one's repudiation of Communism and fellow-traveling implied an obligation to inform on others who were part of those circles. Although Chambers provided the extreme example, since it included testifying not simply about membership in radical groups but about alleged espionage, his behavior during the Hiss case and his subsequent description of that behavior in *Witness* disturbed many liberals.

Many "professional" informers were then parading before anti-Communist congressional inquisitors such as the McCarthy Committee and HUAC. Hannah Arendt, writing in *Commonweal,* drew a distinction between "ex-Communists," for whom "Communism has remained the chief issue in their lives . . . on which they base present careers and ambitions," and "former Communists," determined not to exploit their past or distort it for present advantage. Arendt viewed Chambers as the model and chief culprit of her first group, the "ex-Communists," who tried to "form a solid political group" and engage in "the public humiliation of a spectacular confession." Arendt erred in thinking that this had led in Chambers's case to the "compensation" "of an unbroken public career." Such "ex-Communists," Arendt argued in terms not unlike Hook's analysis of Chambers's thought processes, closely resembled Communists in being "unsqueamish in their means [because] . . . they think of themselves as the makers of history."[37]

In his memoirs Chambers had quoted an aphorism by the Italian writer Ignazio Silone, another former Communist: "The final conflict will be between the Cornmunists and the ex-Communists." He also cited the "lesson" learned from Soviet defector General Walter Krivitsky that "in our time, informing is a duty." But centrists like Hook and Arendt challenged Chambers's sharp and unrealistic division of political forces in a democratic society—a "plurality of forces"—into two opposing camps, participants in a Manichean morality play.

Describing the "ex-Communists" not as former Communists but as "Communists 'turned upside down'" for whom only two groups mattered, Communists and themselves, Arendt concluded: "Ultimately, others don't count; we are only bystanders in the great battle of history being fought out by these two protagonists. Surely they need allies. . . . [but] the same contempt which the Communists used to have for their supporters and allies, the ex-Communists announce for theirs." Arendt, Hook, and others recognized that American liberals were trapped conceptually in Chambers's analysis: once considered by Communists "unconscious and therefore stupid or cowardly helpers of capitalism; they now have become those who are too stupid or too cowardly to think their own tenets through and find that it naturally leads them into Communism." In short, both Communists and "ex-Communists," argued Arendt, "respect only their real opponents"—each other.[38]

Writing shortly after Hiss's conviction on this same question, "the complex issue of the ex-Communists," Arthur Koestler quoted an anonymous correspondent who made some of Arendt's points in more personal terms:

> Reading about Alger Hiss I always think: there but for the grace of God and the Communist Party, stand I. . . . I was one of those who, had the party only asked for [this], would have spied on God Almighty without the least bit of a bad conscience. . . . [Later] I changed my mind about our "Religion." . . . I only know of the Hiss case what I have read. . . . Could not this trial be brought around to the real issue: even if he did steal the documents, what were his [decent] motives? Probably . . . when Alger Hiss changed his mind as so many did who had been Communists in good faith, he was in no position to announce that change. . . . Whittaker Chambers is the real villain because he didn't keep his mouth shut about things past and done with.

Koestler disagreed, defended Chambers, but recognized wearily the unpopularity of his pro-Chambers position as a "psychological fact" among liberal intellectuals. "In short, people don't mind if you betray humanity in the name of some particular cause; but if you betray your club or party they will turn from you in contempt. . . . I think one must accept the fact that Chambers and Kravchenko and the rest of us who have once borne allegiance to the 'God that Failed' will always be looked upon somewhat like defrocked priests regardless of each individual's history and motives."[39]

But Chambers's suggestions that the New Deal was somehow inherently linked to Communist influence and that New Dealers, failing to recognize this fact, had been duped did not sit well with most American liberals. Chambers "errs," wrote Arthur Schlesinger, Jr., in reviewing *Witness*,

> when he identifies the Popular Front mind, which was a psychosis of the New York intellectual, with the New Deal mind, which was essentially concerned with trying to hold the American system together against economic crisis. The New Deal mind had its Popular Front version. . . . But this was a consequence, not of the corruption of the New Deal, but of its innocence. Preoccupied with the day-to-day necessities of keeping the nation afloat, the New Dealers had little time for the intricacies of Soviet conspiracy. . . . Nor does Mr. Chambers' contention that the New Dealers were psychologically disabled from opposing Communists have more than a fragment of validity. . . .

Schlesinger criticized the writings and arguments of Whittaker Chambers during the 1950s for their moral "arrogance" in dividing the "real" world only into "atheistic Communists" and messianic "Christian anti-Communists." He reminded Chambers that religious belief had been instrumental in making Quakers such as Noel and Herta Field (and perhaps Priscilla Hiss) Communists during the 1930s, and that Chambers's "narrow view . . . would welcome such believers as General Franco and the Grand Inquisitor and Ivan the Terrible into the community of freedom, but would bar many decent, humble people who have no pretensions to certainty about the absolute."[40]

Nor was Chambers's Columbia classmate Lionel Trilling any more impressed by the quality of mind displayed in his writings: "He [Chambers] had a sensibility which was all too accessible to large solemnities and to the more facile paradoxes of spirituality, and a mind which, though certainly not without force, was but little trained to discrimination and all too easily seduced into equating portentous utterance with truth."[41]

Supporters of both Hiss and Chambers found it incongruous that the one first-rate work of fiction on the case had been written several years prior to the 1948 HUAC hearings and published in 1947.* Trilling's *The Middle of the Journey* became a source book for those interested in the psychological dimensions of the episode. Not that Trilling's novel, in which Chambers figured as the Communist defector "Gifford Maxim," clarified in any way the evidence against Alger Hiss (although some readers detected strong similarity between the Hisses and a fellow-traveling couple in the novel, "Nancy and Arthur Croom"). A drama of

---

*The only other possibility, also written before the case, was Eleanor Clark's 1946 novel *The Bitter Box*, one of whose major characters bore more than passing resemblance to Whittaker Chambers. Clark, a friend of Herbert Solow's, had known Chambers slightly during the thirties.

ideas, *The Middle of the Journey* juxtaposes its major characters in bitterly complex arguments about their loyalties and beliefs: Maxim, a "counter-revolutionary" anti-Communist; the Crooms, innocently destructive radicals; and "John Laskell" (Trilling), a liberal humanist sympathetic toward both sides but disgusted ultimately by their moral arrogance and intolerant posturing.[42]

Trilling portrayed Nancy and Arthur Croom as devoted to "radical chic" of the thirties, "a modern couple," in Irving Howe's words, "glinting with 'progressive' opinions—people generous in their private lives but rigid in their doctrinaire attachment, not so much to the Communist Party, as to the political and cultural styles created within its ambience." And, opposing them, Gifford Maxim: "[Y]esterday their Stalinist guardian, now repudiated by them as a backslider into reaction and religion. . . . Infatuated with visions of apocalypse, wantonly yielding himself to a new absolutism."[43]

Before his death Trilling acknowledged that Chambers had been the model for Gifford Maxim, but denied having patterned the Crooms after Alger and Priscilla Hiss, whom Trilling did not know, calling such a comparison between "the fictive and the actual couples . . . wholly fortuitous." Trilling had known Chambers at Columbia but insisted in later years that he "had never been a friend." Trilling knew the details of Chambers's defection and subsequent struggle to establish himself as a writer at *Time,* probably through conversations with their mutual friend Meyer Schapiro, but he encountered Chambers only casually during the mid-1940s while writing *The Middle of the Journey.*[44]

The notoriety of that novel in 1948, therefore, when both the Hiss defense and the FBI read it as history and not fiction, caught Trilling unprepared: "To me as the author of the novel there was attributed a knowledge of the events behind the case which of course I did not have. All I actually knew that bore upon what the trial disclosed was Whittaker Chambers' personality and the fact that he had joined, and then defected from, a secret branch of the Communist Party."

After the two Hiss trials, despite doctrinal and temperamental differences, Trilling continued to believe in Chambers and to defend him publicly as "a man of honor." Describing his support as rooted "in principle and not in friendship," Trilling remained sensitive to the personal dilemma of a Maxim/Chambers:

> The obloquy that fell upon him with the Hiss case went far beyond what he had hitherto borne, and there was no way in which he could meet it, he could only bear it, which he did until he died. The educated, progressive middle class, especially in its upper reaches, rallied to the cause and person of Alger Hiss, confident of his perfect innocence, deeply stirred by the pathos of what they never doubted was the injustice being visited upon him. By this same class Whittaker Chambers was regarded with loathing—the word is not too strong—as one who had resolved, for some perverse reason, to destroy a former friend.[45]

And Chambers's "credibility" problem with the "educated, progressive middle class," Trilling noted correctly, became even worse after Hiss's conviction: "If anything was needed to assure that Chambers would be held in bitter and contemptuous memory by many people, it was that his destiny should have been linked with that of Richard Nixon. . . . As the dislike of Nixon grew concomitantly with his prominence, it served to substantiate the odium in which Chambers stood" among those who detested Nixon's political recklessness, including many who believed Chambers's trial testimony against Alger Hiss.

In the years that followed the trials, the believers did not find Chambers any more admirable for having spoken truthfully, nor Hiss less deserving of their sympathy despite his lack of candor.

XV

ALGER AND WHITTAKER: THE VIGIL AND THE DEATH WATCH

Personal wishes aside, after the two perjury trials neither Alger Hiss nor Whittaker Chambers could return to a "normal" existence removed from the symbolism of the case. Hiss served three years and eight months in Lewisburg Penitentiary, leaving in 1954 to pick up the threads of a shattered life that offered neither job nor prospects. Chambers could not resume his career at *Time* and, like Hiss, failed to fully reconstruct a life apart from the case during the years that followed.

Not that either man altered his public demeanor following Hiss's conviction. Chambers, even in triumph, remained a brooding and angrily tormented figure. Hiss, even in adversity, retained his familiar courteous and cool serenity.

Both avowed futile intentions to live as individuals rather than symbols; but this proved impossible. In fact, the protagonists had recognized their appropriate symbolic roles almost from the moment the case broke. At the outset, Chambers announced himself an incipient martyr for the Christian virtues of Western civilization, "bearing witness" for American culture as it stood in mortal Cold War battle. From start to finish of his life, Chambers's moral vision would remain Manichean.

Hiss proved as immodest, symbolically, as his melodramatic accuser. Basically, Alger Hiss avowed himself an innocent victim of public "hysteria" and upheld his claim of absolute rectitude. Shortly after the Supreme Court had denied certiorari in March 1951, but prior to entering prison, Hiss—the beneficiary of nine first-rate attorneys' services, hundreds of thousands of dollars in past and present contributions to legal expenses, two dozen eminent character witnesses, and countless additional well-known supporters in government and the press—issued a plea of innocence that offered this version of the case's legal history:

> The efforts of the Committee on Un-American Activities, vociferously supported by like-minded elements in the press, succeeded in making a fair jury trial impossible in the present atmosphere of public opinion. Due to these efforts, prejudice, fear and perjury prevailed to produce a verdict. But the wrong will surely be righted. My attorneys and friends will continue to search

for the facts which will show how Chambers fabricated the evidence against me. Today as formerly I am proud of my 15 years of public service and with a clear conscience I continue to look forward to the time of my vindication.[1]

"Vindication." The word best characterizes Hiss's dream from the moment he entered Lewisburg in 1951 up to his death, just as it could be employed also to describe Chambers's obsession with public response to his efforts after the trials.

But neither man ever acknowledged clearly the price their confrontation exacted from others, or the suffering it engendered among those whose lives became entwined in the case. "I'm sorry," Gifford Maxim tells a surprised Arthur Croom in *The Middle of the Journey*, "but we must go hand in hand. Let it be our open secret. . . . We will hate each other and we will make the new world. And when we've made it and it has done its work, then maybe we will resurrect John Laskell."[2]

Sometimes, however, it proved impossible to resurrect the "John Laskells" trapped in the Hiss-Chambers web. Laurence Duggan's fall to his death in December 1948, for example, might conceivably have been averted had he not been subjected to months of intense pressure by the FBI and the defense. The arrests of Noel and Herta Field in Eastern Europe in 1949 may have been linked to the case. In 1956, after their release from prison, a newsman quoted Field as stating that he and his wife could not return to the United States because of the Hiss case. Although Field denied this in a letter to Hiss, he remained in Budapest until his death. Maxim Lieber lost many of his clients, closed his literary agency, gave up his files, and, under pressure from both the FBI and his Communist associates, chose exile, first in Mexico and later in Poland. Returning in retirement to this country, Lieber was subjected to gratuitous harassment by local FBI agents. Felix Inslerman lost his job for refusing to testify at the time of the case, while William Edward Crane lost his despite having cooperated with the bureau. Julian Wadleigh became a salesman for a time, his career as a government economist ended. William Rosen disposed of his dry-cleaning business and fled Washington, pursued by FBI and HUAC investigators. He was convicted in 1949 on contempt-of-Congress charges for refusing to testify about the Ford car, although an appeals court overturned that verdict. Invariably, these and less celebrated victims of the case, swept by its momentum briefly and dangerously into the public eye, found no network of supporters similar to that enjoyed by the two protagonists.

In 1951 Alger Hiss prepared to enter prison in his customarily methodical manner. He discussed his impending incarceration with experts on jailhouse life, including the prison reformer Austin H. MacCormick, director of the Osborne Association, who counseled Hiss on appropriate behavior inside the walls. Hiss's appeal lawyers maintained contact with MacCormick and exchanged information on the parole board that dealt with their client's successive applications for early release. Ken McCormick, editor-in-chief of Doubleday, who would later publish the first book that argued Hiss's innocence (by the British jurist Lord Jowitt), told Meyer Zeligs about a conversation with Alger and Priscilla Hiss in his office shortly before Alger entered Lewisburg. They discussed a book Hiss might prepare while in prison, and McCormick recalled that "the fact that he was going to prison seemed to exhilarate him and excite her." The editor may have sensed the nervous anticipation that inevitably surrounds a major change in life, even so distasteful a change as the one confronting Hiss.[3]

Inside Lewisburg, Hiss found his normal mannerisms intrinsically self-protective. He remained, as he had been on the "outside," polite yet aloof, cooperative and unfailingly helpful to others. He worked in the prison warehouse as a stock clerk, and in his spare time assisted less-educated inmates in need: helping to teach a few to read and write, discussing personal problems with others, and preparing letters for those who asked. Hiss was careful never to present himself as a "favored" prisoner. He made no special requests of authorities and followed punctiliously the inmates' normal routine. As a result, he gained the respect of certain groups within the inmate population: Mafia members, conscientious objectors, and "white collar" criminals. One conscientious objector, Arthur Bergdoll, became a favorite of Hiss's, and the two men exchanged ideas at a time that Hiss later described as one of profound "self-examination": "Well, I can tell you what my mind was like in those days," he once told an interviewer. "I was toying with the philosophical question of free will, decision, and so on. And I came to the conclusion—it's really the Bentham, Stuart Mill, utilitarian theory—that one decides what one wants to do. I remember having discussions [on this] with Bergdoll. Bergdoll said he was ambiguous. I said I've never been ambiguous in my life."[4]

At Lewisburg, Hiss conversed with the top Communist leaders as politely as with other prisoners. Although Hiss apparently exchanged ideas on parole strategy with one of the CP convicts, Carl Winter, there was no intimacy with the Smith Act violators. More than any other single group, he seems to have gained the friendship of mobsters, the one circle that Austin MacCormick had predicted Hiss would cultivate. "They're the most stable group in prison," Hiss later told a journalist. He compared them "to prisoners-of-war captured by an enemy society. They have the most wonderful family relationships. . . . Once you find a common ground—and it has to be a real interest, nothing egregious—they're wonderful people." Hiss, after his release, also described the Mafiosi as "the healthiest inmates of the prison. They had absolutely no sense of guilt."[5]

Timothy Hobson and others close to Alger Hiss feel that his relations at Lewisburg with a variety of other prisoners, but especially those in organized crime, served as a turning point in his life, stimulating self-assessment, strengthening his ego ("one decides what one wants to do"), and reducing an obsessive altruism. Hobson viewed his stepfather as a severely repressed and morally rigid person prior to his imprisonment, a man capable of inflicting great suffering upon himself in order to protect others at all costs: "Prison changed him. He could never have left Priscilla before he went to prison, nor could he have sustained [another] relationship of [that] sort . . . before then." Moreover, asserts Hobson, "until then, Alger had no sense of evil."[6]

Not that the prison years seemed, either at the time or since, particularly happy ones for Hiss. Yet he managed the difficult task of maintaining his dignity and equanimity under the depressing and submissive circumstances of daily life in a federal prison. That a convicted perjurer and alleged Communist should acquire "affection and respect" from Lewisburg's often unstable inmates at the height of the Second Red Scare may seem logical, considering Hiss's personality—but only in retrospect. Another convicted perjurer, William Remington, named by Elizabeth Bentley as a former CP member and imprisoned during the same period at Lewisburg, was murdered by a fellow prisoner whom he caught one night in the act of robbing his cell. But Hiss's friendships with Mafia inmates may have protected him against such assaults, and when he left Lewisburg on November 27, 1954, shortly after his fiftieth birthday, some prisoners cheered him from their cell windows.[7]

While in jail Hiss participated as actively as possible in Chester Lane's preparations to file a motion for a new trial. Lane kept his client informed of the investigation's progress in 1951 and 1952, either by correspondence or through visits to Lewisburg. Eventually he filed three motions (the last two supplemental) between January and April 1952. On May 1, shortly after reading the last of Lane's affidavits, which Hiss considered "superb," he wrote Priscilla in hopeful but cautious terms:

> No wonder Chester is so delighted with the results of his brilliantly conceived and executed investigation. There is little that is more cruelly disheartening than disappointment in great hopes and the last thing I would want to do is to raise thy hopes and Tony's unjustifiably. I know the bitter winds that are blowing in this loveless and causeless era and I know that the dust they raise can obscure reality and values for the time being. So I make no predictions, and honestly abstain from judgment in my own mind, as to the near term outcome. But this I *know*—that Chester's work has exposed the fabricated story and documents for all who in a calmer time will care to examine the record for themselves. And *that* is a great and stirring accomplishment.

Hiss correctly gauged the outcome. After reading Lane's briefs and the government's rebuttal (and Lane's response to the rebuttal), Judge Goddard heard arguments on the motion, but on July 22 he denied a new trial. The same three-judge panel that earlier had refused Hiss's appeal now heard the arguments for a new trial and sustained Goddard's decision on January 30, 1953. Three months later, on April 27, the Supreme Court declined to review.[8]

Shortly after leaving prison in 1954, Hiss underwent major gallbladder surgery. Upon recovery, he worked determinedly on his *apologia*—Chambers's had already appeared—a book that he called *In the Court of Public Opinion,* which Knopf published in 1957. Choosing not to counter the confessional autobiography written by Chambers, Hiss prepared instead a meticulous brief for the defense, thorough yet spare and restrained. "The book was written as a lawyer's brief," he later told an interviewer, "and it says all I have to say about the case. I'm not going to write an autobiography—nothing that interesting about my life, anyway—just as I'm not going to write about my time in prison—because I hold certain strong views about privacy."* [9]

Throughout the mid-1950s Hiss spent much time pursuing job possibilities, none of which seemed to work out. Hiram Haydn, then an editor at Random House, described a visit from Hiss arranged by a mutual friend:

> He was looking for any kind of freelance editorial work, and even if I had none at hand, [my friend thought] it would be good for his morale to be accorded serious consideration. . . . I was, of course, curious about the man. . . . For the first ten minutes of our meeting, I was much impressed. . . . He was quiet, dignified, and—most of all—bore himself with no trace of either defensiveness or aggressiveness.
>
> More than an hour later, I was bewildered. Mask succeeded mask, role role, personality personality. There was a half hour during which our actual situation was reversed, as though *he* had granted *me* an interview. He asked me many questions about my work, suggested improved methods in running the editorial department, etc. All, no doubt, with an eye for how he might fit into the Random House structure. But the authority with which he spoke suggested that he was *in charge.*
>
> Suddenly something brought this phase to an end, and he became gamin-like, elusive, answering my questions with the manner of a shrewd, precocious boy who was playing games and admiring his skill at them.
>
> Another shift, and he seemed abruptly defensive. There were fear and suspicion in his expression, and he answered me in guarded monosyllables. This attitude passed like a summer storm, and he reverted to his original personality. We concluded our talk pleasantly, no hint at his (unconscious) other impersonations remaining. [10]

Hiss's first public appearance after his release was on April 26, 1956, at Princeton. The Whig-Cliosophic debating society's invitation unleashed protests from many alumni and others upset at Hiss's being accorded so respected a forum for his maiden speech after emerging from jail. Hiss later called the occasion his "initial opportunity to break out of Coventry." Newsmen crowded into Princeton for the event. "The administration fears passion," wrote Murray Kempton, "and the reporters seek it." Hiss spoke to a limited-admission audience of two hundred

---

*Hiss's charges of conspiracy in his "lawyer's brief" are analyzed in the Appendix.

students and fifty reporters, restricted by Whig-Clio itself to minimize possible violence or an unpleasant incident.

Under the circumstances, the talk seemed anticlimactic: "A gaunt figure with trembling hands spoke in a flat monotone to the tense audience. . . . A reporter groused, 'The story ended when he walked in the front door.'"[11]

Having "broken out of Coventry" and into national headlines because of the Princeton talk, Hiss took pains to avoid a repetition of the Whig-Clio circus. But it had helped create an expectant (if largely disappointed) audience for his book when it was published the following May. Claude Cross invited Hiss in June 1957 to debate Sidney Hook on the case in Boston's Ford Hall Forum, but Hiss declined. "I have followed a policy," he avowed to Cross, "of avoiding, rather than seeking personal publicity and the topic is one that would necessarily involve me personally almost as much as if I were to talk on my experiences or on my book." By then Hiss had begun work at a small company called Feathercombs: "I now have a job which I like and sensational publicity would also be likely not to be in the interests of my employers. Therefore I feel I should not take steps, unless some important issue is involved, that invite publicity [such as] a debate—especially with someone like Hook. . . ." Hiss suggested instead that Cross contact for possible speakers his friend and defense researcher Elinor Ferry, "secretary of the Emergency Committee for Civil Liberties [which is] making a special study of the investigating committees."[12]

The late fifties and early sixties were difficult years for Hiss, involving a series of readjustments in his private and business lives. He exhausted himself reorganizing the Feathercombs company from 1957 to 1959, ludicrously underpaid for his efforts at $6,000 a year. So deeply involved with the company's fortunes did Hiss become that he loaned to its president, R. Andrew Smith, $3,500 of a $15,000 bequest received on his mother's death in 1958 for use in a patent fight essential to Feathercombs's survival. During these two years Hiss seemed preoccupied with business matters, making only rare public appearances.[13]

At intervals throughout his postprison years Alger Hiss maintained involvement in the continuing defense efforts. He sanctioned and engaged quietly in several private investigative efforts related to the pursuit of new evidence, efforts that included the use of undercover agents and possibly wiretapping. In the late 1950s and early 1960s he cooperated with (among other writers) a friendly psychoanalyst who wrote a treatise on the case based upon many hours of interviews with Hiss in which, despite a professed concern for privacy, he intimately described his family and his own psychological attitudes.*

---

*Meyer Zeligs, *Friendship and Fratricide* (New York, 1967). Another friendly biographer elicited additional intimate details from Hiss, but a memoir by Hiss's son "scooped" all previous books with "revelations" about his parents' sex lives and most intimate moments. John Chabot Smith, *Alger Hiss: The True Story* (New York, 1976); Anthony Hiss, *Laughing Last* (New York, 1977).

On at least one occasion in the mid-sixties, Hiss opened a major new investigative move. It involved efforts in 1965–66, first, to locate his former private detective Horace Schmahl (now suspected by Hiss of having conspired against him) and, second, to extract information from a Bessie A. Meade (Mrs. Adam Kunze) of the Kunze Typewriter Company, which (in the opinion of some of Hiss's friends) may have fabricated the Woodstock typewriter. More than a dozen memos by a woman operative working for the Hiss defense, who met with Bessie Meade while disguising the true reason for their meetings, detailed the frustrating history of this inquiry. It yielded little in the way of tangible results, even though Hiss's letters in the defense files contain indications that he tried to obtain the services of a wiretapper to tape the conversations between his investigator and Bessie Meade.*[14]

Books that argued Hiss's innocence (but differed in their versions of the "frame-up" he now insisted had convicted him) appeared until the mid-1970s at roughly half-decade intervals. Although Hiss's defense files show that he endorsed warmly each successive project, even when its premises contradicted previous friendly studies, they also indicate that Hiss kept his detachment and a measure of distance from each writer.[†]

Rarely did he remove the veil from his personal values or provide any useful hints about the aspects of his character that puzzled friends and made even many persuaded of his innocence considered him an enigma. One such insight emerged during Hiss's talk with Hiram Haydn in 1954: "I can't understand people who tell me they are ashamed about something," Hiss told Haydn. "I have never done anything of which I am ashamed. I always mean to do what I do."[‡]

In 1959 Hiss's fortunes sank to a low point. He came to an amicable leave-taking from Andrew Smith and Feathercombs, starting five months of unemployment before finding work again—as a stationery salesman for the Manhattan firm of Davison-Bluth in February 1960. He also left Priscilla and arranged for a legal separation. The failure of his marriage and his business chances, coming almost simultaneously, deeply affected Hiss for a time. The case seemed moribund, and for the moment his ambitions appeared more private. Although he had already acquired a hundred new customers for Davison-Bluth within months, Hiss described the position in 1960—a job he held full-time until the mid-1970s—as "only something temporary." He mentioned three types of jobs that he would find more attractive because of his abilities: teaching, working with an emergent African nation "as an adviser," or publishing—"there are some hopes that I might find something of that sort soon."[15]

---

*The Hiss defense probe of Horace Schmahl's role in the case is described in Chapter XVI and in the Appendix.

†See the Appendix.

‡During one of our interviews Hiss confirmed having made the statement to Haydn.

But the case continued to have a public life outside of the law, and in 1962 Hiss became involved in two brief but controversial incidents, both related to the career of Richard Nixon. Defeated in 1960 for the presidency, Nixon published his memoir, *Six Crises,* as he began preparations to contest California's governorship in 1962. The book began with a long, embroidered chapter on Nixon's involvement with Hiss. Its original edition stated that the FBI had found the Woodstock typewriter in December 1948 and brought it to New York, where samples from it were typed for the grand jury, which promptly indicted Hiss. Immediately Hiss and his lawyers picked up this apparent confusion in Nixon's mind between the Woodstock typewriter and the samples of Mrs. Hiss's typing, which the FBI did find and display to the grand jury. The story made the case front-page news once again. Nixon attributed the statement to a "researcher's error" and corrected it in later editions of *Six Crises.*[16]

Alger Hiss, not Nixon, provoked the second flap in 1962 when ABC ran a television news special following Nixon's defeat in the California gubernatorial election. The program, titled "The Political Obituary of Richard M. Nixon" and narrated by Howard K. Smith, reviewed Nixon's rapid ascent to political prominence and his two major defeats. Both friends and enemies were interviewed, and among the latter was Alger Hiss. Nixon protested, and thousands of viewers telephoned or wired CBS complaining about Hiss's presence. Several stations would not show the program, and elsewhere, network studios were picketed.

But even some fervent anti-Communists like Robert Stripling defended the Smith program. "As far as I'm personally concerned," the former HUAC investigator told an AP reporter on November 14, "I want everybody who is an American citizen always to have the opportunity to be heard." Stripling had little respect for either man, considering Hiss a perjurer about his relations with Chambers, and Nixon a liar about his role in the case. "Mr. Hiss was convicted, and Mr. Nixon was defeated, and they both seem a little bitter."[17]

That Alger Hiss's public fortunes were inextricably tied to those of Richard Nixon's, as the latter's had once been to Hiss's, became still clearer in 1968. Nixon's presidential victory occurred at the height of anti–Vietnam War protests, and it brought a marked revival of interest in Hiss as a campus speaker and television personality.

Under the pressures of opposition to the war and growing hostility toward the Nixon administration, the symbol of Alger Hiss had begun enjoying a public revival independent of the facts in his case. To sympathetic listeners Hiss seemed an embodiment of what McCarthyism could do, and a nostalgic talisman of the pre–Cold War Roosevelt era. Gradually Hiss built up a new clientele in the 1960s and 1970s among college audiences, faculty and students, both in this country and in England. He became a steady, if unspectacular, fixture on the university lecture circuit, and with each brief burst of renewed interest in the case he reiterated his polite but firm claim of innocence.

A new generation had reached maturity by then, detached from earlier Cold War emotionalism and far more familiar with—and interested in—Hiss's symbolism than his evidentiary claims. Inevitably, when his nemesis on HUAC reached the White House in 1969, Richard Nixon's success revived concern for a person whom many Americans had come to regard as Nixon's first "victim."

Thus, by dint of survival, Hiss had managed—as had his chief remaining adversary, Nixon—the transition from the political world of the fifties to a far different America in the seventies. Both men displayed in the process a combination of good luck, cautious self-projection, and enormous resiliency. Above all, both had managed to endure and to maintain devoted followings against great odds and stiff opposition.

Paralleling the illusion of a "new Nixon" was that of a "new Hiss." Neither image had substance. Mainly there were newer audiences, or more forgetful older ones. Robert Alan Aurthur, himself strongly sympathetic to Hiss's drive for vindication, described the scene at a 1972 birthday party on Manhattan's West Side:

> I edge closer to where Alger sits on a couch. People here are all politically oriented, most of an age to have been formed during the Depression . . . and Alger Hiss was there. When in conversation he says, "And then Franklin said to me. . . ." he means F.D.R., and when he talks of Yalta there is instant recall of those photos of Roosevelt, Churchill and Stalin with Hiss poised at their shoulders. They are posing; he is working.
>
> And so at parties where Alger is present there is a tendency to gather around, waiting for—what? . . .
>
> . . . Accused, trapped, pilloried, vilified, jailed, stripped of career and honors, reduced nearly to pauper, Alger Hiss today, at sixty-seven, sees hope. You listen, and recognizing the brilliance as well as the courage and determination, you are almost ready to go along.[18]

Hiss had reason to be celebrating that evening in 1972, since he had just won a court decision that restored his $80-a-month government pension. "What cheers Alger Hiss tonight," wrote Aurthur, "is his belief that this court victory is one more step toward his ultimate goal of vindication." Harper and Row reissued *In the Court of Public Opinion* in 1972 with a new preface by Hiss describing that republication as "part of my effort for the full vindication I have at all times anticipated." Hiss noted that he and his lawyers had "continued to seek further evidence" during the fifteen years since the book's original publication, although the reissue added no new material to the original text.

This renewed public attention left Hiss in an ebullient mood when interviewed in April 1972 by Thomas Moore for *Life*. Harper and Row "thinks there may be a good market for [Hiss's book] on college campuses," Moore noted, and Hiss was nearing completion of his personal history of the New Deal, "tentatively entitled *The Beginning of My Love Affair with America*."* Relaxed and mellowed in his pronouncements—"Good wine, good food, Havana cigars—I have a depraved taste for them—and good thought go together"—Hiss met Moore for lunch at Rocco's, a favorite Greenwich Village restaurant where waiters greet him as "Professor." Insisting that he held "no personal bitterness" toward Richard Nixon, Hiss seemed confident about the case: "'By the time I am 80,' he says, lighting up a pipe given him by actor Zero Mostel, who was once blacklisted for left-wing activities, 'I expect to be respected and venerated. Fortunately, whatever other virtues I may lack, patience is not one of them.'"[19]

By contrast to the relaxed and amiable Hiss, Whittaker Chambers "bore witness" to his version of events after the trials with a mixture of public discomfort and private despair. Alger Hiss's conviction brought no feeling of relief to Chambers; it meant for him only a deepening sense of anguish over the consequences of his own actions. When he wrote Ralph and Nora de Toledano in late January 1950 to thank them for assistance during the trials, Chambers described his mood at their conclusion:

> I have an all but incurable wound. My good, intuitive friend, Marjorie K. Rawlings [author of *The Yearling*], wrote during the first trial: "When this is over, I believe that you are planning to kill yourself." In the literal sense, this was not true, but it was so close to my feeling from the beginning that I have never trusted myself to answer her. At the end of that day of turmoil in which I decided to put the Baltimore papers in evidence, I thought: "Because of Esther and the children, I cannot pray to God to let me die, but I cannot keep from hoping that He will." Now this feeling dogs me through these beautiful, unseasonable days and in the hours of the night when I wake. . . .

"Add to this the feeling that it was all for nothing," he concluded, "that nothing has been gained except the misery of others."[20]

Chambers would dispatch such letters, more often than not, in hopes of gaining solace. His friends invariably responded with words of encouragement. In subsequent letters to friends Chambers returned to the theme of protecting one's offspring, speculating that the Hisses' denial of his charges had been "inspired by a desperate hope to save something for the child [Anthony Hiss] they had so longed for [as they used to tell me]. . . . True, they would have sacrificed my children for that child and have thought it a good deed. But who, being desperate, would not kill for his children if there was no choice." His own two children, Ellen and John, both approaching adulthood, were obviously instrumental

---

*Hiss's study of the New Deal never appeared.

in repressing thoughts of suicide. "I must live until [the children] have reached their majority, at least," he wrote Buckley, "so that they . . . would be their own man and woman." His teenage son took over many of the farm chores alongside Esther during the two years it took Chambers to write *Witness*. "Esther has fixed me up a very good writing room in the basement of our middle farm— 'Medfield,'" he wrote de Toledano in February 1950. "It is about a quarter mile from the home place, & out of sight & sound of almost anything. . . . I do not visit every part of [Pipe Creek farm] daily as I used to do, for it has been alienated by the last year's experiences and may not be entered upon again until I have mastered the meaning of those experiences."[21]

While writing his autobiography slowly and unhappily, staring out upon the "alienated" acres, Chambers composed bleak poetry filled with images of death and decay, similar in theme to his student verse of the 1920s. But life imposed its lighter moments as well. There was one memorable Westminster Quaker meeting when Chambers sat in silence for an hour surrounded by a circle of Friends. Finally the Spirit moved one Quaker matron directly facing Chambers to break silence and ask: "Does thee feel that Dean Acheson must go?"[22]

One of the most difficult aspects of Chambers's post-trial existence was his relationship with former colleagues on *Time*. He retained close friendships with T. S. Matthews, Duncan Norton-Taylor, and—except for a short period early in 1950—with Henry Luce.

The brief moment of bitterness toward Luce resulted from an episode following Hiss's conviction. Pierrepont I. Prentice, editor and publisher of *Architectural Forum*, a Luce publication, proposed that Chambers be offered a post on the magazine. With Luce's approval, Prentice sent an invitation to Westminster. Swept along by this magnanimous spirit toward his friend and former employee, Luce—with the approval of Matthews—decided to invite Chambers to return to *Time* itself and summoned him to New York. But before Chambers's arrival the publisher had reversed himself on both offers, deferring to the complaints of other company executives that Chambers remained too controversial a figure to be brought back.[23]

By the time Chambers reached the magazine's offices, Luce had fled, leaving an unhappy Matthews to inform his friend of the decision. "Harry, I've seen Whit," Matthews wrote his employer later that day, "and told him it was a no go. I did *not* go into the various reasons; it wasn't necessary. It was apparently not much of a surprise to him: he'd been thinking it over too, and was in some doubts about whether he should take such a job at all—let alone come back to *Time*. . . ."[24]

Chambers's disappointment remained private until he received a note from Henry Luce in February. The latter's decision to veto Chambers's return had in effect sentenced his former senior editor to an emotional prison of his own making at Westminster, more comfortable and familial than Hiss's at Lewisburg, but a prison of the mind nonetheless. Distraught but disingenuous, Luce now suggested to "Whit" that the company's position was not final and that, in any case, Matthews and not Luce had decided: "I'm not sure whether Tom and you did arrive at the right answer in this sense. I had thought it was best for Tom to take up the question with you personally since your working relationship had been mostly with him and he is now editor of TIME. . . . However, I guess for my part I will not be satisfied that a right decision is made unless I have an opportunity to talk with you myself."[25]

Luce probably never realized how sorely his earlier reversal had wounded Chambers, who had viewed *Time*'s welcoming him back as an omen of redemption and as a sign that national opinion accepted his role in the Hiss case. Chambers finally responded a month later:

> Never, even as a child, did I believe in the happy ending. And to that extent, I never could wholly believe in the American Dream, to which the happy ending is the essential tag.
>
> You are the only person who has ever made me believe in the happy ending, and that only for a few hours. . . . Then, quite suddenly, my sense of the world took over again, and I said "No, it is not true." Thus, I was quite prepared for Tom's reversal of his offer. That did not spare me hours of a bitterness such as I trust life will spare you—a bitterness that I cannot wholly shake off. . . .
>
> But why should we worry it with talk? I recently wrote Tom in this connection: "Our enemies can never do these things to us. Only our friends can drive the knife quite through our vitals." But I do not think that we are then required to turn the knife in the wound. And that, it seems to me, is what a talk between us would amount to.
>
> Surely, my last letter to you said all that was needed: for your many kindnesses, I am grateful; we shall not meet again. I am very tired.
>
> Faithfully, Whittaker

The harsh letter to Luce proved "purgative" to Chambers, and within two months the relationship had been restored.[26]

Witness became an immediate best-seller despite its eight-hundred-page length and the density of its prose style. It was the Book-of-the-Month Club selection for May 1952, relieving Chambers of future financial worries. Just as pleasing to its author, he received more than a thousand—largely sympathetic— letters about the book.

Reviewers from all parts of the political spectrum responded predictably. Centrist liberals such as Arthur Schlesinger, Jr., and Sidney Hook praised Chambers's personal courage and accepted his version of the facts regarding Alger Hiss. At the same time, they criticized both his slapdash equation of "liberalism" and "socialism," and his "messianic" Christian anti-Communism. Critics on the left like I. F. Stone complained about the proliferation in America of well-paid "memoirs of informers, spies, and Communist renegades."

Noting that Chambers had received a reported $75,000 for serial rights from *The Saturday Evening Post*, Stone carped: "No martyrdom was ever more lavishly buttered. This man so suffocatingly ostentatious in his new-found Christianity is the kind of martyr familiar in its early annals—the kind who threw others to the lions and retired to a villa." *Time*'s reviewer pronounced: "Its depth and penetration make *Witness* the best book about Communism ever written on this continent. It ranks with the best books on the subject written anywhere."[27]

More satisfying to Chambers was the response of leading European ex-Communists like Arthur Koestler and André Malraux, the latter writing: "You have not come back from hell with empty hands." But he also cherished Henry Luce's exuberant reaction to the book: "A great deal of the book is written with great beauty and skill. If you could write 'fiction' as well as you can write history—and maybe you could!—you would be one of the great novelists. . . . I salute you, as of old, as a great writer. I salute you, too, as a great warrior of the spirit—and as a friend."[28]

At this time Chambers confided to Luce that he was writing an article on St. Benedict. He had become intrigued with the image of himself as a "Hildebrand," a farmer-monk—albeit in Westminster—striving to preserve Christian civilization against the inroads of a Communist "dark age." After four years of living under enormous emotional pressure—first during the case and later while writing *Witness*—Chambers turned briefly to farming, persuaded (as always) both of his messianic purpose and of his failure. That domestic peace lasted only two months. In November 1952 Chambers suffered his third heart attack, both previous ones also having followed long periods of intense physical labor and emotional pressure.[29]

While in the hospital and when he was back at Westminster early in 1953, Chambers's thoughts remained bleak and unsparing. "Do you think I care whether I get out of this bed again or not?" he wrote de Toledano in March 1953. "I would like to see my children started in life, and they are close to the line [John would enroll at Kenyon College in a few years]. But I know that we cannot take care for all such matters and must leave an unfinished job, sooner or later, in any case. We never really know what is best."[30]

Also in March 1953 Senator Joseph R. McCarthy and his future wife, Jean Kerr, appeared in Westminster with results predictable to those few who knew Chambers well. McCarthy wanted to consult with Chambers about an attempt to block President Eisenhower's nomination of Charles Bohlen as ambassador to the Soviet Union. "McCarthy looked very tired," Chambers wrote a friend several days later. "He was in his most mock hearty mood, which, for some reason, perhaps because I've been sick, particularly irritated me as being a false note. I thought: 'Why doesn't the man act natural?'"[31]

Chambers, then recovering from the heart attack, asked McCarthy what evidence he had against Bohlen: "'Is it security or is it something else?' I meant homosexualism [sic], which I suspected was the chief difficulty. Both, said McCarthy, but he was pretty vague." It soon emerged that McCarthy had no evidence at all but objected merely to Bohlen's earlier relationship with, in Chambers's words, "leftists and morning glories." Chambers remained unimpressed and told McCarthy bluntly "that he had lost the fight against Bohlen's confirmation," urging him to abandon the struggle. McCarthy wanted Bohlen to take a "painless" lie-detector test, but Chambers objected, observing realistically "that it might be painless but a stigma was attached and that it was impossible to send anywhere as an ambassador a man who had been subjected to the test." McCarthy expressed his displeasure at Chambers's attitude, but dropped the subject and remained as an overnight guest.

The following morning Chambers learned the real purpose of McCarthy's unexpected appearance. A reporter from *The Washington Post* phoned asking for the senator. McCarthy had tipped off newsmen that he was going to visit Whittaker Chambers, intimating that he had gone to question the man who had testified against Alger Hiss because Chambers had important, unrevealed, and damaging information against Charles Bohlen. After McCarthy left, reporters telephoned Chambers for several days demanding to know what he had told McCarthy. Finally Chambers issued a statement to the press disavowing any suggestion that he could link Bohlen to Communism, but calling Bohlen's nomination a "poor choice" because of his role as an adviser at Yalta. Had he not talked to the press, Chambers explained to a friend, he would have been left "in the position of the man whose silence was itself an indictment of Bohlen. McCarthy, of course, took the great chance that, for the sake of the cause, I would go along with him and play his game. [Then] . . . McCarthy would have had me where he wanted, as an accomplice, ever after. That's the way he plays."[32]

Next year, when McCarthy complained about the supposedly "unfriendly" portrait of him in a generally sympathetic book, *McCarthy and His Enemies*, by William F. Buckley, Jr., and L. Brent Bozell, Chambers defended the book to its publisher, Henry Regnery, pointing out that the fatal flaw in McCarthy's demagoguery was that "the senator is a bore":

> The Senator is not, like Truman, a swift jabber who does his dirty work with a glee that is infectiously impish; or, like F. D. Roosevelt, an artful and experienced ringmaster whose techniques may be studied again and again and again. . . . [He] is a heavy-handed slugger who telegraphs his fouls in advance. . . . it is repetitious and unartful, and with time, the repeated dull thud of the low blow may prove to be the real factor in his undoing. Not necessarily because the blow is low, or because he lacks heart and purpose, but because he lacks variety and, in the end, puts the audience to sleep.[33]

Unlike many ex-Communist informants of the period, who booked themselves solidly on the government witness circuit during the early and middle fifties, Chambers showed little interest in continuing to testify about past experiences in exchange for headlines and per-diem expense accounts. He appeared only infrequently as a witness before HUAC and the Senate Internal Security Subcommittee and, despite repeated requests, declined any involvement with Joe McCarthy's investigative road show.

After 1950 Chambers weighed his political activities against a single yardstick of how they might affect public response to his earlier role in helping to convict Alger Hiss. "The Hiss Case," he wrote Buckley in 1954, "is a permanent war. . . . I am not really a free agent and scarcely even an individual man. I am the witness on whom, to a great degree, it still swings. . . . My reactions are a kind of public trust. They call for the most vigilant intelligence and careful judgment." Privately, in correspondence with friends like Buckley, Chambers labeled McCarthy a witless primitive whose antics endangered the entire anti-Communist movement, as in the Bohlen episode.[34]

But that incident came three years too late to undo Chambers's own role in an earlier and sordid case of government witch-hunting: the Oliver Edmund Clubb affair. Chambers had seen a news photograph of Clubb in 1950 shortly after the latter returned from China, where he had been a consular official during the Communists' takeover of the mainland. Vaguely Chambers recalled—to HUAC staffers, the FBI, Senate Red-hunters, and Loyalty Board probers—having met Clubb at *The New Masses* in 1932, though he misremembered his name as "Chubb" and, far more important, misstated the innocent circumstances of the visit. Then a young State Department official back from China, Clubb had brought a letter of introduction from his friend, the radical writer Agnes Smedley, to *New Masses* editor Walt Carmon. For that single 1932 visit—during which he had talked to Chambers briefly—Clubb endured FBI interrogations, appearances before congressional investigating committees, and an extensive Loyalty Board hearing (which, without any significant evidence, declared him a "poor security risk") until he finally resigned from State in 1952. Thus Chambers's careless mention of the 1932 incident grievously victimized a respected government official entangled accidentally in the emotional backwash of the Hiss case.[35]

Richard Nixon came to disappoint Chambers, and the two men seldom met during the 1950s. Although retaining sympathy for Nixon born of gratitude for his role in the case, Chambers described his disillusionment in a March 1960 letter to Buckley shortly after Nixon had visited Westminster to talk about his presidential ambitions: "I came away with a most unhappy feeling. I suppose the sum of it was: we have really nothing to say to each other." Chambers went on to describe Nixon to Buckley as personally inadequate for the "awful burden" of the presidency.[36]

Thus Whittaker Chambers proved far from generous or tolerant during the 1950s toward would-be allies like Nixon or McCarthy, or imagined opponents like Clubb. Chambers reserved his amity for family and close friends during his final decade, although he occasionally professed compassion toward Alger and Priscilla Hiss. "To me and to my wife they remain essentially what they were," he wrote Buckley; "the friends for whom our feeling never changes, but whom history forced me to make suffer." Still, he mixed this with a nagging bitterness toward his foe: "I understand, as few others can, the rules of war that Alger fought under.... but I found myself thinking: Nevertheless, if you take your eyes off those peculiar rules for an instant, there is nothing left to say but that Alger behaved like a complete swine. Not a very bright swine, either."

When Hiss got out of prison in 1954, still proclaiming his innocence, Chambers complained to Buckley that Alger had regained the offensive: "As a tactician (and a lawyer), he is trying for the advantage of surprise and the initiative." Describing what he believed Hiss meant by vindication, Chambers wrote: "It is the moment when one of the most respectable old ladies (gentlemen) in Hartford (Conn.) says to another of the most respectable old ladies (gentlemen): 'Really, I don't see how Alger Hiss could brazen it out that way unless he really was innocent.' Multiply Hartford by every other American community. For the CP, that is victory.... And all that Alger has to do for this victory is to persist in his denials."[37]

The appearance of *In the Court of Public Opinion* in 1957 revived Chambers's gloomy reflections on the case. He responded favorably to a proposal by Duncan Norton-Taylor that they try to persuade *Time* to release Jim Bell's colorful narrative of the two trials for publication as the "weapon" (Norton-Taylor's word) with which to "counter-attack" Hiss's book.

The "witness" of Westminster believed correctly that Hiss had seen his *apologia* as a "tactic" for beginning the "re-habilitation of his case, which is rather a feat.... Alger's first big problem was to make a noise, any kind of a noise in order to bring a crowd, [and] the press was his." As in the case of Lord Jowitt's previous book, however, Chambers refused to respond directly. "My tactic hinged on not playing this game," he wrote a friend, reasoning "that, if I shut up and stayed strictly out of the hassle, the press would have nothing to work on but a book, which I believed could not possibly succeed because . . . no man can sustain a lie for the length of a book—not successfully. . . . the hubbub would soon wear itself out. . . . The big thing was not to let myself be provoked into action in any form and so feed the fire. . . . I think it was the right tactic, that the upshot proves it so. I think the war is over and Alger is finished."[38]

But within a month Chambers decided that he had been mistaken and that what he termed the "classic battle of annihilation" between himself and Hiss, as so often in the past and future history of the case, had ended inconclusively. By then *Time* had decided not to release Bell's trial reports, leaving the "tactician" with neither a new "weapon" for the publishers nor—had one been available—the will to deploy it. For a time Chambers still seemed hopeful. His antagonist's troops appeared routed, to judge from the various critical and skeptical reviews of Hiss's book even by liberal "deserters," apparently leaving as the opposing forces only a skeletal company of academics: "Clumps of pro-Hiss professors at this and that campus."* But the defection of previous Hiss supporters in the press pleased him.[39]

Fulfilling his need for companionship and intellectual stimulation mainly through correspondence with friends and through their infrequent visits to Westminster, Chambers accepted an offer from William F. Buckley, Jr., in 1957 to join *National Review* against the advice of both his doctor and Esther, and began a weekly schedule of two-day working trips to New York reminiscent of his earlier schedule at *Time.* The visits seemed spurred more by the prospect of frequent talks with Buckley, John Chamberlain, James Burnham, and others on the staff than by the requirements of his infrequent contributions to the journal. Chambers's writing proceeded slowly, whether on short articles which—to Buckley's chagrin—he often burned rather than submit, or on his opus, "The Third Rome," a philosophical work that dealt with his principal subject—the decline of the West.[40]

Obsessed with the theme of the case as he saw it, Chambers believed he had voluntarily sacrificed career and privacy to rally American resistance to Communism. Thus he regarded his final years not only as a living martyrdom on behalf of the "Christian West," which he felt to be losing its death struggle with a "Communist East," but as a neglected martyrdom to boot.

His heart pains persisted and worsened in 1958 until Chambers was forced to cut the weekly trips to New York in half and restrict the work schedule even in Westminster. Late that year he suffered another heart seizure and spent a month in bed, recuperating slowly until the following summer, when he and Esther left on a long-postponed vacation trip to Europe, which included a meeting with Arthur Koestler in Austria.

The trip proved to be the emotional highlight of his final years. Since the Hiss trials Chambers had taken refuge from his obsession with the case in a romanticized portrayal of his own experiences as a Communist—not unlike Alger Hiss's penchant in later years for describing the early New Deal period as a "Golden Age" for himself and others interested in basic social reforms. Chambers had

---

*Chambers apparently never learned about Sidney Hook's suggestion to *Life,* which the magazine rejected, that Chambers be invited to review Hiss's book: "Hook thought of it as no mere antic of journalism, but as a serious analysis by a man peculiarly qualified to comment on the completeness (or incompleteness) of the author's recollections." Bill Furth to Robert Elson, January 30, 1957, Time Inc. Archives.

begun associating his own past with a revolutionary tradition of greater stature, represented by the Koestlers, Malrauxs, and Silones—generational peers and "exes" for whom the god of Communism had failed. Although he had been only a routine underground agent and courier in the United States—albeit an important one—Chambers now claimed a place for himself among international Communism's former *haute noblesse*—an American Arthur Koestler, perhaps. The effort reached a climax of sorts in his visit to Koestler. Also present at their encounter was Greta Buber-Neumann, Martin Buber's daughter-in-law and a survivor of seven years in Russian and Nazi concentration camps. Their discussions, recorded by Chambers in letters to Buckley, are deeply moving, and his imaginative use of the talks emerges in this passage: "Then, we realized that, of our particular breed, the old activists, we are almost the only survivors, the old activists who were articulate, consequent revolutionists, and not merely agents. Of the latter there are some around." Chambers ended in July 1961 comparing himself with Malraux's fictional revolutionary Katov, who walked willingly to martyrdom after having first divided his cyanide "with those comrades less able to bear man's fate."[41]

Throughout the 1950s Whittaker Chambers had toyed with the idea of suicide. His self-destructive broodings intruded even into otherwise lighthearted letters to friends. Retaining to the end a deep pessimism, Chambers believed Communism's ultimate triumph inevitable and tried often to divert his thought and energy from this overwhelming sense off impending doom by such activities as his occasional flyers in the stock market or his European trip. Always, however, Chambers returned—unrefreshed—to his private war with the Marxist laws of history, dogmas that he held accountable for most off the world's modern tragedies.

In his imagination, history and Alger Hiss seemed locked in satanic embrace, with Chambers despairing of ever being able to rout their combined forces. Believing himself rejected by most Americans, despite his self-pronounced martyrdom in the Hiss case, Chambers ransacked the Western tradition for appropriate literary and religious analogues to his own status. A small company of such messianic figures marched across the pages of his essays and writings during the fifties: Chambers as Jonah, as Katov, as Camus's Sisyphus, as a doomed Russian revolutionary *narodik*, as Kafka's Hunter Gracchus, and just before his death (in the last letter he wrote) as the Oedipus who reached Colonnus—after the fall.

Chambers was forced to shorten his 1959 European tour because of recurrent heart pains and after his return he resigned from *National Review*. Although personally fond of Buckley and others on the magazine, Chambers viewed them as "conservatives" while he "at heart [was] a counterrevolutionist. . . . [My] primary interest is to win a war rather than to defend a position." The difference in tactics emerged from the positions he took that often surprised his colleagues at *National Review:* Chambers opposed McCarthy, supported the 1956 Polish and

Hungarian uprisings, and even defended Alger Hiss's right to a passport,* all the while urging a Republican version of Tory radicalism to counteract Democratic Party "socialism," this despite a waning faith in his nominee for the role of an American Disraeli—Richard Nixon.[42]

But the major reason for Chambers's resignation from *National Review* was that he had returned to school, enrolling as an undergraduate at Western Maryland College near his Westminster farm. For the next two years Chambers carried a full-time student's load in hopes of obtaining the B.A. degree he had repudiated thirty-five years earlier.

Despite an exhausting round of reading assignments and tests at Western Maryland, there as well his thoughts turned invariably to the case: "Even the facts of the fathers are unknown to the sons, who find the past generation almost entirely baffling," he wrote James Rorty in July 1960:

> "Papa, who was Mussolini?" my daughter asked me mid-way of her career at Smith. Then I knew. . . . The campus generation that I am so curiously embedded in also does not know who Mussolini was—except as a name. . . . of [his history] they know nothing; least of all that it still bears on this world and on them.
>
> Last semester, I would often hear, coming from somewhere on campus, a strong unself-conscious whistling: Mack The Knife. Those whistlers would have been astonished (and, I think, in some curious way, angered) if any one had told them that Mack The Knife was written by a Communist, who was a friend of several friends of the old man in their midst.[43]

The happiest personal moment in Chambers's last years came in his final weeks when, on June 8, 1961, he attended the wedding of his son, John, in Washington. A month later he died. "I hope you have my obit ready," he had written de Toledano in 1956. "What fun the yappy little dogs will have. I don't even begrudge it them, rest seems so welcome."[44]

When his fatal heart attack came on July 9, 1961, the ensuing mystery would probably have neither displeased nor surprised Whittaker Chambers. His passing was shrouded in secrecy, the news released to the press only after his body had been cremated and his oversedated widow taken to the hospital. Supporters of Alger Hiss mused about a double "suicide pact," and Meyer Zeligs, a stranger to modest, later speculated to Hiss and Timothy Hobson that his research for *Friendship and Fratricide* may have provoked Chambers's death.[†] More likely, Chambers's heart finally gave out, as he himself had hoped it would. With his

---

*Granting Hiss a passport in 1959 for a European trip briefly rekindled popular feeling about the case. The CIA monitored Hiss's movements throughout the trip. See James Angleton to J. Edgar Hoover, April 14, 1959, CIA Files.

†Zeligs theorized in his book that Chambers somehow schemed a double suicide with his wife. Zeligs, Hiss's psychobiographer, "had the goods on Chambers," according to Timothy Hobson, who believes that fear of exposure drove Chambers to suicide. Zeligs, *op. cit.*, pp. 427–33;

children grown and married, a natural death may have seemed welcome and not to be fought against. Only Esther Chambers knew for certain, and she—whether by accident or design—nearly took her knowledge to the grave hours later. In the end, Whittaker Chambers, who had yearned intermittently for death since his unhappy Lynbrook beginnings, was dead.

Both Esther Chambers and Priscilla Hiss had lost their husbands by 1961. Esther adjusted to widowhood by maintaining her normal routine in Westminster, once she emerged from the hospital after Chambers's death: family visits, farm work, friends, painting, and Quaker meetings helped fill the void. Priscilla, jolted by her husband's departure in 1959 and his association soon afterward with another woman, also continued her schedule but with some changes. Before separating from Alger, Priscilla Hiss had worked as a bookstore saleswoman and then as a children's book editor. An avid museum visitor and concertgoer, she became involved during the 1960s in a number of community projects in Greenwich Village and for a time served as a member of the local planning board. A spirited activist, she took pride in her continued commitments to New York City and its political and cultural life.

Both wives worked themselves to exhaustion during the 1950s: Priscilla, to support herself and her teenage son, Anthony, in New York while Alger was in prison and after he emerged to extended periods of unemployment or low-salaried jobs; Esther, to manage the Westminster farm while Whittaker devoted himself largely to writing or to recovering from his several heart attacks.

Personal loss came hard for both women, especially after their children were grown. John and Ellen Chambers had both married. John followed in his father's and grandfather's tradition, leaving his small town for life as a journalist. Like his father, John would later return to run a farm in upper Maryland, commuting between work as a newsman in Washington and his rural retreat. Timothy Hobson studied medicine, married, and settled in California with his family. Anthony Hiss graduated from Harvard and soon afterward became a staff writer for *The New Yorker*.[45]

Neither Esther Chambers nor Priscilla Hiss ever deviated publicly from her trial testimony. Mrs. Hiss continued to defend her husband's innocence, despite their separation, and Mrs. Chambers remained as devoted to Whittaker's memory as she was to him. Only one startling 1968 incident in Priscilla Hiss's life intruded momentarily into this pattern of loyalty.

Neither Esther Chambers nor Priscilla Hiss involved herself in the arguments of their husbands' respective partisans. Both women tried to avoid discussing the

---

interview with Timothy Hobson, August 16, 1974; interview with Alger Hiss, June 21, 1975; Smith, *op. cit.,* pp. 435–36.

case, each having made a separate and private peace with the anguish it brought into their lives. Just as Priscilla Hiss refused to be drawn into the campaign to vindicate Alger (a refusal that provoked a rupture with her younger son in the mid-seventies), so Esther Chambers shunned all contact with those probing the controversy, even sympathizers.

Mrs. Chambers's one brief encounter with a researcher on the case who was *un*sympathetic to her husband left her profoundly shaken and determined to avoid any repetition. The incident that apparently triggered Esther Chambers's unwillingness to move beyond the protective shell of family and trusted friends in the Westminster area occurred in May 1962, almost a year after her husband's death. Meyer Zeligs, then researching his psychobiography, visited the Pipe Creek farm accompanied by a local minister familiar to Esther Chambers. Zeligs acknowledged that the visit "was unexpected and was understandably a surprise to Mrs. Chambers." He had spoken earlier to her on the phone and written "some months earlier and received no reply." Despite that, he appeared on her doorstep with the minister. Mrs. Chambers, according to Zeligs, spoke to them "in a cordial but guarded manner," and asked: "Are you the doctor from California who is writing about my husband?"

After several minutes, Zeligs says, the pair was invited to sit in the living room, where Esther "spoke poignantly and reverently" about Chambers. Despite her suspiciousness, Esther Chambers (according to Zeligs) then took the pair on a tour of the farm. "Her loneliness and sense of bereavement were clearly apparent as we walked about the grounds. . . . Tears welled in her eyes. . . . We drove back to Westminster, moved by the afternoon visit."[46]

Esther Chambers described a less cordial encounter. Shortly after Zeligs appeared at her home, he interviewed Herbert Solow in New York. Solow phoned Esther and wrote immediately about the psychiatrist, receiving this reply:

Thank you for your notes and comments on Dr. Zeligs. Whit was quite right wasn't he, they never quit and this is a field in which they can muddy the waters endlessly.

One thing I wanted to make clear. Dr. Z. had never previously contacted Whittaker or me before his phone call from San Francisco. Upon receiving his "letter of identification" as he called it, I refused to have anything to do with him or to be involved in any way with his project. He then forced his way into the house here accompanied by a brother of a friend (or acquaintance) of his, Dr. Kirk, a minister in Westminster, who I imagine did not realize he was being used. . . . Please I would be grateful if more develops, to learn about him. Yours gratefully, Esther.[47]

From then on, Esther Chambers shielded herself from all contacts that threatened to revive the past, enlisting family and local friends to help protect her

Westminster world against unwanted intruders.* Letters from those associated with the case, even from former friends like Robert Cantwell and Meyer Schapiro, went unanswered. Negotiations between Esther and John Chambers with Buckley and de Toledano for a published edition of Whittaker Chambers's letters to his two friends dragged on for months until Buckley, risking an invasion-of-privacy suit by the family, finally published in 1969. The episode further embittered and alienated Esther and her children from those who, like Buckley, esteemed Chambers but breached his family's insistence on privacy. United and fiercely determined on the subject, the Chambers family insulated itself from the pressures caused by involvement in the case, pressures that brought its patriarch such persistent anguish.[48]

Priscilla Hiss, like Esther Chambers, continued to live in the last residence she had shared with her departed husband, a Greenwich Village apartment. She also lived surrounded by mementoes of her marriage, including the complete file of several hundred letters exchanged between the Hisses while Alger served his sentence at Lewisburg. Mrs. Hiss maintained as much contact with her husband during his forty-four months at the prison as regulations allowed: three letters each week and one monthly visit, often accompanied by Tony. Throughout Hiss's years at Lewisburg, Priscilla believed herself to be "carrying the flag for the family," working to support Tony and herself while keeping in touch with family, friends, and supporters.[49]

Both Alger and Priscilla Hiss proved reluctant to discuss publicly the reasons for their marital breakup five years after Hiss's release from prison. Shortly after their separation, Meyer Zeligs, who interviewed Hiss, offered only this spare and tactful account of the experience:

> During the two-year period in which Hiss was taken up with the organizational and legal problems of rescuing Feathercombs [1957–59] . . . his life with Priscilla was going through a deepening estrangement. The belated recognition of this marital breach came neither as surprise nor shock. It was the ultimate emergence of a subliminal fact: for many years, he then saw, their marital partnership had been wearing thin, and in his opinion they were left with a paucity of the essential ingredients of a good marriage. Chambers's accusations against them had the salutary effect of drawing them together in a protective alliance. . . .
>
> As an extension of their having been drawn together, after his return from prison, Hiss lived in hopeful expectation of a closer or more meaningful marriage. But the painful vicissitudes of separation, the emotional stresses of rehabilitation following his release, weighed heavily on a marriage that had

---

*In the years after Chambers's death the FBI paid Mrs. Chambers and her children occasional—and unwanted—visits, leading the family to surmise that the bureau intended keeping it under observation.

been sustained but had not been consolidated through the years. A collapse of this kind, explained Hiss, has early beginnings and does not build up like a sudden storm.[50]

But Priscilla Hiss found Zeligs's account of the breakup ungenerous and unfair to her, and she sent a researcher a review of Zeligs's book by another analyst, Dr. John A. P. Millet (whom Mrs. Hiss had consulted for a time), which in her opinion offered a more balanced portrait:

> Dr. Zeligs has so little to say about Priscilla Hiss [complained Dr. Millet], whose complete devotion and loyalty to her husband throughout the years of his imprisonment and whose unaided dedication to the education and welfare of their son, Tony, made possible for Hiss a return to a welcoming family [sic]. Her patient acceptance of the situation in which she found herself, which included a state of enforced isolation from the opportunities for employment and for the sort of social acceptance to which her personality, her education, and her experience entitled her, exhibited a spiritual courage which was the best proof of the integrity which had been so cruelly questioned during the trials.[51]

Having sacrificed her independent ambitions to those of her husband in the 1930s, and after living vicariously for two decades through the rise and fall of Alger's career, Priscilla Hiss found herself thrown completely upon her own resources. She survived, not happily, perhaps, but effectively, turning Hiss's "abandonment" into still another variant of self-sacrifice. She refused to give Hiss a divorce (according to her husband) so that he could marry the woman he loved, despite the intercession of once-mutual friends. For a long time Priscilla apparently persuaded herself that Alger would "come to his senses" and return to her, a hope that Hiss never encouraged. Both Timothy Hobson and Anthony Hiss have talked to interviewers or written at length about the often-strained relations that existed between Priscilla and those for whom she proudly "carried the flag." "Pros is tough," Hobson commented to an interviewer. "While she is answering your questions politely, she might be inwardly thinking: 'Thee is a son-of-a-bitch.'"[52]

Priscilla Hiss's "toughness," her strength to survive a solitary life detached not only from her husband but from the case, overrode even her tendency in conversation to refer to Whittaker Chambers as "that monster" or "the monstrous man," never by his name. To interviewers she asserted an inability to recall the case or its details, a reaction reminiscent of Esther Chambers's similar attitude. "A curtain has descended, and I don't remember the period," Priscilla said in 1975. "I don't want to remember it, and I can't therefore be of any help to you. Living alone and being forced on my own resources has done this to me."[53]

The "curtain" rose briefly and painfully only once, in 1968, shortly after publication of Zeligs's book left Mrs. Hiss embittered over the author's treatment of her. Priscilla was visiting family members in Chicago that year when, according to a guest of the family, someone made a "tactless remark" about the case over dinner one night at her sister's house. Priscilla exploded and, according to another guest: "Pros announced that she was sick of all the lies and coverups—or whatever it was that she said. Jane didn't remember the words but immediately remembered the painful tension between Pros and her sister-in-law, each being fairly polite and 'covering up' intense dislike and animosity. Jane remembers that the party blew up and Prossy was the cause. . . . by 1968 Pros no longer talked of 'the case,' in fact for years now she has avoided it entirely."[54]

In public, however, Priscilla Hiss continued to maintain her husband's innocence and to inveigh against Whittaker Chambers, while insisting upon her right (as did Mrs. Chambers) to draw the curtain upon her knowledge of the episode. Esther Chambers and Priscilla Hiss chose, in short, to distance themselves from the case. Unlike their husbands, whose interlocked pursuit of vindication turned into a pair of obsessive vocations in themselves, both women defended their privacy against all those—however friendly—who tried to involve them once again in the unending Hiss-Chambers saga.

Priscilla Hiss died in October 1984. Esther Chambers died in August 1986.

XVI

COLD WAR ICONOGRAPHY II: FROM WATERGATE TO RED SQUARE

The Watergate crisis of the mid-1970s revived public interest in Alger Hiss's plight and in his assertion that government officials had conspired against him. For many Americans, the symbolism of the Hiss case underwent rapid if temporary transformation during Watergate. For a time, Hiss and his defenders enjoyed once again, as during the trials, an interested and minimally ambivalent media. Those who accepted Chambers's story and the jury verdict against Hiss, on the other hand, often found themselves now on the defensive, much as Hiss's advocates had been during the McCarthy era.

Even without Watergate, 1972 would have been a watershed year in Alger Hiss's campaign for vindication. In March he won a landmark federal court victory that restored his government pension. Later that year, the American Civil Liberties Union—Hiss's attorneys in the pension case—returned to federal court, filing a suit on behalf of the author demanding that the FBI's Hiss-Chambers file be opened immediately for historical research.[1]

But it was again Hiss's link to Richard Nixon—and the latter's rapid decline in popular esteem after his landslide 1972 reelection victory—that drew the convicted perjurer back into the headlines. Nothing did more to restore a measure of public support for Alger Hiss than Nixon's disgrace and downfall. "Watergate" remains both a specific designation of the terminal drama in Nixon's presidency and a code word that summarized revelations during the mid-1970s of two generations of abuse of power by the FBI, the CIA, and presidents of both parties. Beginning in late 1972 the trail of deception, lies, and "stonewalling" engaged in by Nixon and his aides sapped his administration's credibility as journalists and federal judge John Sirica unraveled the cover-up's several layers. Thus, when Nixon assured reporters at an October 1972 press conference that the internal review of Watergate culpability by his aides had been so thorough it made his 1948 investigation of Hiss seem a "Sunday School exercise" by comparison, the effect was to strengthen suspicions of a cover-up in the earlier case as well.

Writing of the Rosenberg spy case in terms applicable to Hiss, Daniel Yergin observed that the Watergate crisis corrupted our faith in the sanctity and essential goodness of our institutions. One refuge of those troubled by this case has always been the assumption that the government would not lie, that law enforcement agencies would not fabricate evidence; we can no longer accept such assumptions. [Recently] a whole torrent of disturbing information about FBI practices has come out: its agents, it seems, have not shied away from forging letters, faking death threats, planting informers who functioned as agents provocateurs, even kidnapping in the "interests of national security." How much further would the bureau have moved into illegality and fabrication when the spy mania was at its height and J. Edgar Hoover was in total control?[2]

The evidence shows that Hoover and the FBI had never been "in total control" during the Hiss-Chambers probe; indeed, often the bureau had been blatantly uninformed about basic matters of evidence from Chambers's revelations of the typed documents and handwritten notes (which he delivered to Hiss's attorneys) to the microfilms (given to HUAC investigators) to discovery of the Hiss Woodstock (by Hiss's own lawyers). Nevertheless, supporters of Alger Hiss alleged an apparent connection between that case and the more widely recognized abuses by intelligence agencies during the preceding decades. Hiss himself drew the media's attention to the analogy in a series of 1973 interviews, claiming that "they [the U.S. government] did the same thing to me that the [Nixon] administration did to Watergate." Thus Hiss-Chambers again became "Nixon v. Hiss," with the latter now taking the offensive.

The *New York Times* op-ed page published in 1973 a provocative article by Alger Hiss entitled "My Six Parallels," the title modeled on Nixon's *Six Crises*. Hiss drew a series of explicit comparisons between his case and subsequent ones—Daniel Ellsberg, the Berrigans, and the Watergate break-in—suggesting that Nixon's actions and those of other government officials in the 1948–50 period foreshadowed their behavior during the late 1960s and the Watergate crisis. Hiss's "parallels" included "tapping of telephones and bugging of dwellings . . . using as principal witness an unstable informer beholden to the prosecution [an analogy between Chambers and the chief prosecution witness in the Berrigan trial, Boyd Douglas] . . . tendentious and prejudicial press stories based on official leaks or statements . . . delay in producing Government records as ordered by the court . . . forgery by typewriter [Howard Hunt's efforts to forge a telegram implicating President Kennedy in the assassination of Ngo Dinh Diem] [and] . . . attempts to influence the trial judge [apparently a misdirected reference to the posttrial attacks on Judge Samuel Kaufman]."[3]

Urging speedy action by the courts to release FBI files in his case, Hiss avowed that his "hopes, as they have always been, are for vindication." Although he disclaimed any special pleasure at Nixon's discomfort in the Watergate affair—"I am not interested in seeing the Biter Bitten"—Hiss's article ascribed four of his six Hiss case "parallels" to unethical or illegal actions by Congressman Richard Nixon.

He had discussed an ironic indebtedness to Nixon two months later. In September 1973 his son Tony interviewed Hiss for *Rolling Stone*. When Tony asked whether Nixon's "very presence" did not constitute "one of the few elements of continuity from 25 years ago . . . [focusing] a certain amount of attention on you," Alger replied: "Well, I welcome the fact of that public attention. In that sense, Mr. Nixon is sort of a press agent for me. I now have a chance to state my own position simply because of the fact that Nixon was one of my initial tormentors." But Hiss went on to describe "the whole atmosphere of Watergate [as] more conducive to truth telling than anything we've had at any time since my trial. The people who know about the dirty tricks in my case will now come forward."[4]

The parallel between past and present, between the case and Watergate, remained uppermost in Hiss's mind and in his public presentation as he suggested appropriate questions for his son to ask:

> Some of the same things have happened in the Ellsberg case, in the Berrigan case, in the Camden 28 case, in the Gainesville 8 trial that's on now. And that's why you're interviewing me about it. . . . [But] when the same kind of cases are brought now, they don't succeed.

"Talk has been going around Washington recently," Tony commented, "that all the recent political trials, beginning with the 'Hiss' case, were fixed." "Yeah," his father replied, "and that there's a certain unpleasant similarity about all of them—that they're all contrived for political purposes. But the big difference, I think, is the difference in public opinion, so the juries now aren't led by the nose. At the time when my case came up, the Cold War was already well under way, there was a great deal of hysteria, it was a case of the blind leading the blind, or, worse than that, of madmen leading the blind. . . . That hasn't been working today."

Identifying himself personally with the political "cases" of the seventies, Hiss spoke at an antiwar seminar in Harrisburg, Pennsylvania, called to support defendants in the Berrigan or "Harrisburg 7" case then in progress. "Nothing good can happen in this country," he declared, "until the war is over." To a correspondent inquiring about an "*ad hoc* off-the-cuff comparison" Hiss made at the time between his case and the Ellsberg trial, he replied: "I certainly didn't mean to stress it. I find far greater similarity with the Berrigan case. But I had chiefly in mind the maze of disclosures growing out of the Watergate incident in recent weeks, including the Ellsberg case disclosures."[5]

Thus Nixon's involvement remained crucial to encouraging a belief in Hiss's innocence, and the president's undoing was pivotal in the campaign during the 1970s to vindicate Alger Hiss. "Unraveling" the Ellsberg burglary, wrote philosopher Richard Popkin, "will unravel what was involved in Richard M. Nixon's whole career: fraud, fakery, framing of innocent victims. . . . His whole public career is based on fraudulent activities. When we know more about how the Ellsberg case was plotted, we will know how the Hiss case itself was constructed. . . . The Hiss case may turn out to be the American Dreyfus case."[6]

In no segment of American society did Alger Hiss benefit personally more than among university audiences, faculty, and students, and particularly those who protested America's continuing involvement during the Nixon presidency in Vietnam, Cambodia, and Laos. Not only New Left "revisionist" scholars such as Popkin but many liberals and moderates began to view Hiss in their own terms, as a direct ancestor of the Ellsbergs, Berrigans, Spocks, and Coffins who fought government harassment and illegality in politically motivated trials during the 1970s. As antiwar sentiment converged with popular outrage over Watergate, Hiss found himself transformed from a symbol of deception into one of injured innocence. Watergate and more responsive media brought Hiss for a time a renewed measure of public acceptance if not instant vindication, although for some it brought that as well. Articles asserting his innocence began to appear again in both liberal and radical journals, provoking a counterattack from defenders of Chambers.[7]

Once more, as had happened two decades earlier and as would occur again briefly in the early 1990s, Americans debated the guilt or innocence of Alger Hiss and the meaning of the case. Now, however, earlier roles were reversed. "Hares" of the McCarthy era, who defended Hiss as a victim of a Cold War frame-up, reemerged as the "hounds" of the Watergate era, arguing (*post hoc ergo propter hoc*) the plausibility of a government-sponsored conspiracy against Hiss. Similarly, the anti-Stalinist "hounds" of the fifties—either recanted earlier positions (as in the case of Leslie Fiedler), remained silent, or found themselves increasingly on the defensive when arguing that the evidence demonstrated Alger Hiss's guilt. Encouraged by sympathetic news media, Watergate helped create a new generation of believers in Hiss's innocence. The cultural verdict of the previous quarter-century and the jury's verdict at Hiss's second trial were abruptly brought into question, often by younger Americans unfamiliar with the complex facts and history of the case.

Epitomizing the controversy and the continuing role of intellectual survivors from the earlier battle over symbols and meaning was a dispute involving Lionel Trilling, Diana Trilling, and Lillian Hellman. Because of the renewed interest in Hiss-Chambers, Lionel Trilling's publishers reissued *The Middle of the Journey*, with a new introduction reiterating Trilling's belief in Chambers's integrity, which *The New York Review of Books* reprinted in April 1975.[8]

Reading Trilling's piece at her Martha's Vineyard home, playwright Lillian Hellman brooded over the Hiss case while she prepared the manuscript of

Scoundrel Time, her memoir of the McCarthy era. Hellman, a friend both of the Trillings and of Alger Hiss, recalled in this memoir spending an afternoon "asking myself how Diana and Lionel Trilling, old, respected friends, could have come out of the same age and time with such different political and social views from my own."[9]

Sections of *Scoundrel Time* took up the argument for Hiss's innocence and his frame-up, with Hellman observing, "Facts are facts . . . and there had never been a chance that, as Trilling continues to claim . . . Chambers was a man of honor." Hellman offered three major sets of "facts" to support her belief in Alger Hiss's innocence: that Chambers hid his microfilms in a pumpkin for a long period of time (every news account in 1948 and all subsequent books on the case pointed out that Chambers placed the films in the pumpkin the morning of the day he turned them over to HUAC); that "most of the frames [of the five rolls of microfilm] were unreadable" (also well publicized was the fact that only one roll was illegible, while the two strips of State Department documents were perfectly "readable"); and that the "pumpkin papers"—finally released to Hiss and other researchers in 1973—were found "to contain nothing secret, nothing confidential" (which applied only to the non-State Department rolls). Hellman's insistence that she "wasn't a historian" was thus amply vindicated.*[10]

Soon after the appearance of Hellman's book, Hilton Kramer in a *New York Times* article denounced the "cultural chic" represented by *Scoundrel Time* and similar recent works: "A new wave of movies, books and television shows is assiduously turning the terrors and controversies of the late 1940s and 1950s into the entertainments and best-sellers of the 1970s." The aim of all these post-Watergate productions, argued Kramer, was "to persuade us that the Cold War was somehow a malevolent conspiracy of the Western democracies to undermine the benign intentions of the Soviet Union. . . . The point, it seems, is to acquit 60's radicalism of all malevolent consequence, and to do so by portraying 30's radicalism as similarly innocent, a phenomenon wholly benign, altruistic and admirable. . . . the myth of total innocence must be upheld even where it is contravened by the acknowledged facts."[11]

But Kramer despaired of combating the New Symbolism, one that dispensed an artful neo-Stalinism—including even *apologias* for earlier support of Communist purges and political prisons—with casual self-exoneration. Kramer recognized

---

*Lionel Trilling died in 1975. His wife, literary critic Diana Trilling, commented on *Scoundrel Time* in a collection of essays. Trilling's publisher, Little, Brown, which had previously brought out Lillian Hellman's book, asked for deletion of several passages that criticized Hellman and her arguments (Arthur Thornhill, the firm's president, described Hellman as "one of our leading successful authors"). When Trilling refused, Little, Brown canceled her contract, and the dispute drew front-page notice. Trilling's book, when published elsewhere, retained the comments. See *We Must March My Darlings* (New York: Harcourt Brace Jovanovich, 1977), pp. 41–66, "Liberal Anti-Communism Revisited," for Trilling's analysis of that subject. Diana Trilling died in 1996.

that liberal anti-Communists like himself had been placed on the defensive cul-
turally in the aftermath of Vietnam and Watergate. "What has been swamped
in the new wave of revisionism about both the 60's and the 30's is the liberal
view that regarded *both* Stalinism and the blacklist as threats to democracy—the
view that looked upon both the conduct of the House Un-American Activities
Committee and the values of the Communist Party as plagues to be resisted."
Instead, the popularity of books such as *Scoundrel Time* and the rehabilitation
of such once-moribund "Popular Front" causes as the Hiss case represented for
Kramer a cultural "climate of amnesia" regarding the facts and symbolism of
earlier struggles between "anti-Stalinist" and "Popular Front" intellectuals. He
lamented the fact that the combined impact of Watergate, Vietnam, and the Nixon
presidency had restored to an honored place the fellow-traveling arguments and
spokesmen repudiated by most American intellectuals a generation earlier.

As one expression of this "climate of amnesia," Alger Hiss was well on the
way in the mid-1970s toward restoring public respect for himself and refurbishing his older conspiracy claims. The case's symbolic dimension, as during the
early 1950s, had again become controlling for many Americans who—because
of the Nixon connection—now considered Hiss exonerated without knowing the
evidence, vindicated without the inconvenience of first demonstrating himself
innocent.

But while Hiss campaigned actively for vindication beginning in 1972, his
beleaguered adversary brooded constantly about the case from his White House
"bunker":

> There will be time, there will be time
> To prepare a face to meet the faces that you meet. . . .
> And indeed there will be time
> To wonder, "Do I dare?" and, "Do I dare?"

"P" [President Nixon], whose fretful psyche emerged from the White House
tapes, might just as easily have stood for "Prufrock" as for "president," so anxious and uncertain did Nixon appear at most times. Rarely did "P" speak with
authority to the coterie of schemers who surrounded him. But on the Hiss case, if
not on Watergate, "P" remained self-assured, unwavering, and knowledgeable.
Just as Nixon's presidential adventurism served as Alger Hiss's springboard to
renewed public attention, so the Hiss case remained central to Nixon's understanding of how best to handle crisis situations, even those of an embattled president and leader of the free world.

Early in his political career Nixon had translated experiences gained in the
Hiss-Chambers probe into a political *code duello* against enemies. He came to
believe that successful political action requires sustained hatred toward all those
who disagree or try to block one's efforts. This "killer's code," to use Garry
Wills's term, served Nixon effectively, for the most part, in a quarter-century of

politics following the 1948 HUAC hearings. But it consumed him during his last crisis—Watergate.[12]

In *Six Crises,* Nixon pointed out that the Hiss case taught him "some valuable lessons in crisis-conduct—the necessity for thorough preparation for battle" and, especially, "the need for handling a crisis with coolness, confidence and decisiveness." When high administration officials set out in 1971 and 1972 to destroy their political and other presumed "enemies"—Ellsberg, McGovern, Lawrence O'Brien, various other high-ranking Democrats, antiwar activists, and just plain folks—Nixon frequently exhorted his captains to utilize the old battle strategy: "Go back and read the first chapter of *Six Crises.*" Clausewitz on War; Nixon on Hiss.

The president hectored even those aides who assured him that they had indeed read his memoirs to do it again. "Warm up to it, and it makes fascinating reading," Nixon told Bob Haldeman (already a *Six Crises* buff). "I want you to reread it." Charles Colson claimed to have read the book no less than fourteen times, a record even for the Nixon White House.[13]

Nixon's concern was frankly sentimental. The White House tapes revealed that he yearned to participate personally in the Watergate cover-up even while recognizing the need to keep a distance from that effort. With a staff apparently lacking the skill and cleverness required, Nixon tried to foist the first chapter of *Six Crises* on his aides as a handbook and case study of crisis management (although, as John Dean later noted, Nixon's experiences in the Hiss case led him to an ironic identification with the investigators and not with those—like himself—being investigated). He raised the case no less than three times in a February 28, 1973, conversation with Dean.

Judging from the White House tapes, the Hiss case rarely left Richard Nixon's thoughts during his last months as president. Almost any kind of major domestic problem he encountered that related to internal security found itself transmuted instantly into grist for his rehash of the Hiss case. Thus when the Pentagon Papers case became an administration dilemma, Nixon instructed the "plumber" charged with nailing Daniel Ellsberg, Egil Krogh, to read the Hiss case chapter. Nixon, no less than Hiss, equated the Ellsberg affair with the earlier case, at least in its ramifications. "It could become another Alger Hiss case," Charles Colson— mimicking "the boss"—observed to E. Howard Hunt in 1971, "where the guy [Ellsberg] is exposed, other people were operating with him, and this may be the way to . . . discredit the New Left."[14]

Nixon's obsession with Hiss had deep personal roots. "By feeling the need to reenact his life's high moments, mixed as they were with bitterness," Garry Wills theorized, "Nixon remained the underdog fighting power—even when he had all the power he could wish. He lived always with what he felt were prior aggressions against him, and felt a license to fight back with any means at hand. . . . Everything was, for him, The Story of Nixon . . . always a tale of

Nixon's mistreatment at the hands of others. . . . Nixon's absorption in himself became a literal act of self-consumption by the end."[15]

In the 1970s Nixon's alleged role in the case twice became news. The first instance involved a February 28, 1973, conversation with John Dean—one of the key Watergate tapes—that contained this passage in the version released by the White House:

> P: . . . F.B.I., Hoover, himself, who's a friend of mine, said "I am sorry I have been ordered not to cooperate with you" and they didn't give us one [adjective omitted] thing. I conducted that investigation with two [characterization omitted] committee investigators—that stupid—they were tenacious. We got it done.
>
> Then we worked that thing. We then got the evidence, we got the typewriter, we got the Pumpkin Papers. We got all of that ourselves. The FBI did not cooperate. The Justice Department did not cooperate. . . . [16]

Nixon distorted a number of facts about the Hiss case in this and other taped White House conversations. Hoover, far from being a "friend" of Nixon's in 1948, did not even know the young congressman and considered him an opportunist potentially harmful to FBI interests. Nor was HUAC's probe of the Hiss case, as Nixon fantasized, the model of judicious decorum. It was marred by frequent leaks to the press, badgering of witnesses, and devious behavior on Nixon's part—as in scheduling the Commodore Hotel session, or not informing fellow committee members about his prior information concerning Hiss.

But Hiss and his supporters picked up on Nixon's apparent claim that HUAC "found" the Woodstock. "WILL NIXON EXONERATE HISS?" began a long article on the question by Carey McWilliams in *The Nation,* and *The New York Times* carried an interview with Hiss on May 3, 1974, under the headline: "ALGER HISS SEES 4 WORDS IN NIXON TRANSCRIPTS AS CHANCE FOR EXONERATION." Despite the fact that Nixon's assertion explicitly "exonerated" the FBI, which Hiss and associates had previously charged with responsibility for the "forgery by typewriter," Hiss was enthusiastic about the turn of events. "I think it is very important," he told the *Times* reporter. "The implication is that he [Mr. Nixon] found it; and nobody knew he found, it."[17]

Neither Hiss nor his supporters, however, called attention to the later transcription of that same February 28 conversation prepared by the House Judiciary Committee's staff and generally acknowledged to be more accurate than Nixon's doctored White House rendition. On the Judiciary Committee's transcript, made by more objective transcribers using superior equipment, Nixon babbles: "But we broke that thing . . . without any help. The FBI then got the evidence which eventually—See, we got Piper who—We got the, the, the, oh, the Pumpkin Papers, for instance. We, we got all of that ourselves. . . . The FBI did not cooperate." There is no mention of HUAC finding the Woodstock typewriter, and "Piper" (which may have thrown off the White House transcriber) may have been a reference to Hiss's attorney at the time Chambers turned over the stolen documents, William Marbury, later of the Baltimore firm of Piper and Marbury[18]

The controversy over Nixon's role in any "forgery by typewriter" surfaced yet again in 1976 with the release of excerpts from John Dean's memoir, *Blind Ambition*, in which Nixon's former counsel quoted a conversation with Charles W. Colson. Colson had just seen the president in March 1972 in the course of discussing how best to contact Dita Beard, an ITT official, and persuade her to repudiate her embarrassing memo as a "forgery." Dean quotes Colson's alleged version of the president's response. "'The typewriters are always the key,' the President told Chuck. 'We built one in the Hiss case.'" But even Alger Hiss seemed unpersuaded when contacted by the press. "Presumably, Dean wasn't even present," Hiss observed. "It becomes hearsay, second-hand hearsay."*[19]

Several days later Charles Colson claimed "no recollection" of Nixon having suggested that the Hiss typewriter had been "phonied": "If Nixon had made such a remark, Colson said, he believes the former President would have meant that the case against Hiss was built on the evidence of the typewriter." Colson did recall "extensive conversations with Mr. Nixon regarding the typewriter analysis, its reliability and the great length to which the FBI went to verify its analysis." He denied conveying "any other impression to Mr. Dean," but, as in all such instances, the denials received far less attention from the press than the charges.[20]

Although Dean stuck by his story and said that his "notes" suggested the conversation did take place, he did not identify the date and acknowledged that the talk had not been recorded. Moreover, Dean's literary agent insisted somewhat contradictorily that his client believed "nothing in the book . . . would lead you to [the] conclusion" that evidence in the Hiss case had been doctored. FBI documents expert Ramos Feehan, who had testified at Hiss's trials, declared from retirement that "forgery by typewriter is impossible" and, as for the Hiss Woodstock, "not only could the typewriter not have been forged, but it was not as far as I know."[21]

Nixon made no public comment on the uproar over Dean's book, but from San Clemente he answered an inquiry from Sidney Hook about Dean's claim:†

> The statement I was alleged to have made with regard to "having built a typewriter" in the Hiss Case is totally false.
>
>   This, as you know, was a thesis Hiss and his lawyers put forward 25 years ago—that Chambers, the F.B.I. or others involved in the Hiss prosecution had

---

*ITT hired Pearl Tytell as a documents analyst to determine the Beard memo's genuineness; Pearl's husband, Martin, had built a fake Woodstock to support Chester Lane's motion for a new trial two decades earlier. See the Appendix and also *Blind Ambition*, pp. 56–57.

†Printed here for the first time.

built a typewriter. Even his most ardent supporters could not swallow such a ridiculous charge. A typewriter is, as you know, almost the same as a finger- print. It is impossible, according to experts in the field, to duplicate exactly the characteristics of one typewriter by manufacturing another one.

What I said after Hiss was convicted, and have consistently said since that time whenever I discussed the case, was that "the typewriter evidence was a major factor in leading to the Hiss conviction." I have never in any conversa- tion at any time said or implied that "we built a typewriter in the Hiss case."[22]

But Nixon's obsession with the Hiss case during Watergate led him to credit other "ridiculous charges" first raised at the time of the HUAC hearings. Thus at the height of the impeachment crisis a congressman who spent an evening sail- ing down the Potomac with Nixon on the presidential yacht said later that Nixon had told him "the true story of the Hiss case." The congressman was highly amused: "I didn't know those two guys were queers." Others close to Nixon con- firmed his use of this analysis: that a homosexual relationship between Hiss and Chambers caused Hiss to steal the documents. Thus Nixon, in adversity, turned to "explaining" the complex Hiss case with an unproved rumor, a persistent one during the 1948 HUAC hearings, thereby revealing far more about himself under pressure than about the case.[23]

Nixon remained incapable of confronting the realities of that experience. He emerged from the Hiss-Chambers drama, aided by Robert Stripling at the crucial moment in December 1948, billing himself as "cool, confident, and decisive." Except for those on the inside like Stripling, few Americans then recognized the combination of accident, good luck, inside information, fear, and panic that marked Richard Nixon's first encounter with political crisis. Whether Nixon eventually came to believe his own distorted version remains unclear even today. But it seems probable that, like Hiss and Chambers, he found it more satisfying in later years to nourish his own myths about the affair rather than to accept the more complex and sometimes embarrassing facts.

During the 1980s, aided by a series of published memoirs and foreign-policy books, Nixon combined extensive foreign travel with a self-designed role as informal counselor to Presidents Reagan, Bush, and Clinton. His access to world leaders and the collapse of the Soviet empire converged to serve as an inter- national setting against which Nixon worked diligently—and with much suc- cess—to restore his public reputation. He died in 1994.

Although Alger Hiss continued to work as a salesman for Davison-Bluth, demands for his services as a speaker increased during the Watergate years. He lectured and held seminars at several dozen American and English universities, including Virginia, Princeton, the New England College of Law, Columbia, and his two alma maters, Johns Hopkins and Harvard.[24]

For the first time since his conviction Hiss appeared to enjoy a reasonably comfortable financial status. In addition to high lecture fees and his salary at Davison-Bluth, he also received a government pension and a trust fund that yielded more than $5,000 yearly. He maintained an apartment in Manhattan, and in 1973 he purchased a summer home in East Hampton, Long Island.

In the 1950s and 1960s Hiss had refused to appear on television shows and lecture platforms to argue his innocence, on grounds that this violated his privacy. "I am not a public freak," he told Brock Brower in 1960. But he showed no similar hesitation beginning in the 1970s and subsequently. He also continued to meet socially with many old friends from the New Deal and the State Department years, although, increasingly, he described himself to reporters as an ex-New Deal liberal who had become "radicalized" by events since the 1950s. In this connection, Hiss made no effort by the 1970s to disguise his contacts with Old Left friends, including those once accused of membership in the Ware Group (he had minimized his associations with people in this circle at the time of the case). Thus he told an interviewer in 1975 that he, John Abt, Nathan Witt, Jessica Smith, and Telford Taylor (the one liberal in the group)—all but Smith former AAA staffers along with Hiss—had met a short time earlier for a "reunion," and that he also had visited Abt and Jessica Smith at their summer home.[25]

If Hiss had seemed more comfortable with radical friends of an earlier generation than when he described them to interrogators in the 1948–50 period, they, in turn, remained protective. Those once accused of Ware Group membership normally declined to be interviewed about the case. Nathan Witt told historian David Caute, when asked if Hiss had been a Communist or had known Chambers, "If I did know, I would not want to involve others."[26]

Those of Hiss's old friends willing to comment publicly on the case since 1950 generally expressed a belief in Priscilla's—but not Alger's—possible culpability or insisted simply (as did Robert von Mehren) that "Alger would not have put his friends and others through what they went through for him if he was guilty. He is not that type of individual." Still, von Mehren acknowledged, "no convincing defense alternative explanation of the case emerged at either trial." Journalist Philip Nobile and others who remain persuaded of Hiss's innocence expressed similar views, arguing that, despite the damaging evidence, Hiss could not have been guilty and maintained so serenely his insistence upon his innocence for a quarter-century: "To inflict such gratuitous suffering [on himself and those close to him] for the sake of a known false cause is crazy," Nobile concluded. "But Hiss is not crazy."[27]

Although Hiss's friends and lawyers have challenged Chambers's sanity ever since the case began, Nobile has pointed out that no one ever questioned Hiss's. Still, Nobile admitted that, in retrospect, Hiss might have been both sane and untruthful, at least in relation to the facts under dispute.

To an interviewer in 1975 Hiss confided that he had considered bringing suit against William Manchester when *The Glory and the Dream* restated the arguments for Hiss's guilt. Also, several months after a *Commentary* article by Cornell law professor Irving Younger appeared in August 1975 analyzing the evidence for his culpability, Hiss said to the author: "I can't but assume that it was commissioned.... For a professor ... suddenly to bang this out.... My speculation is that he was asked to write it."[28]

But neither Manchester nor Younger had much impact upon the growing support Hiss received during the Nixon-Ford years. The symbolic tides ran as strongly during the Watergate seventies as they did during the Cold War fifties. When Nixon resigned the presidency, Hiss was vacationing in France. He issued a statement applauding "the beginning of a new era of justice in our country." Whether guilty or innocent, Hiss made "good copy" so long as Richard Nixon remained on the public stage.[29]

Attorney General Elliot Richardson's decision in August 1973 to allow release to "qualified historical researchers" of FBI and Justice Department material more than fifteen years old began the process of opening the key files on the case to the author and other scholars, files that Hiss had repeatedly asserted would vindicate him. After Congress passed amendments strengthening the Freedom of Information Act in late 1974, allowing all Americans to petition for previously classified intelligence files, Hiss filed a request to examine the most dramatic piece of evidence against him, the five rolls of "pumpkin papers" microfilm, including the two with State Department records. Attorney General Edward Levi released the material to Hiss and his attorneys in August 1975, and Hiss held a news conference along with three other researchers who had also requested FBI files on the case.

The press's reception of Hiss's statements at that conference illustrated the degree to which his claims had become almost immune from its close scrutiny, despite the tough investigative journalism that helped unseat Richard Nixon. Hiss began with a summary of the case, presumably designed to brief those reporters present who were too young to have lived through the events:

> In 1948, a man named Whittaker Chambers swore that he had been a Communist spy, and that I, a State Department official, had given him Government papers in 1938. I never gave him secret papers. But largely because a young Congressman named Nixon said he believed Chambers, I was convicted of perjury when I denied the charge and went to jail for 44 months.

Apart from the intriguing distinction Hiss drew between having handed over "secret papers" and having been accused of giving Chambers "Government papers"—about which no reporter questioned him—his prepared "statement of fact" was remarkable for its distortion and oversimplification.[30]

Nor did the press examine closely the assertions made by Hiss about the "pumpkin papers" themselves. According to Hiss, he learned only after receiving the five rolls of microfilm from the Justice Department in 1975 that much of the photographed material consisted of apparently innocuous Navy Department technical data that would have been, in his words, "useless for espionage." William H. Reuben, Hiss's co-plaintiff in a suit for FBI records, termed the rolls "totally useless espionage material. Total garbage." The reporters present seemed to agree, and their stories the next day simply recorded Hiss's assertions as fact. "The evidence against [him]," said the Boston *Globe* editorially," . . . appeared fishy at the time, and no less so today."[31]

To stir public belief in his innocence, Hiss dwelt on Nixon's tactics in publicizing the "pumpkin papers" and argued that even the two rolls of State Department film "in no way supported Chambers' charge that I had been a Soviet spy. [The others] don't either. But all five helped to convict me because almost every newspaper carried pictures of Nixon peering at these strips of film through a magnifying glass. The message intended and conveyed was that microfilm and spies go together." The "message intended and conveyed" by Alger Hiss at the press conference was that *faked* microfilms and Richard Nixon went together, at least in his case. Did Hiss believe that Nixon had framed him? asked one reporter. Hiss responded obliquely: "I didn't come here to bury Caesar or to praise him. He was an opportunistic politician."[32]

Throughout the press conference Hiss asserted that only then, in 1975, had he learned about the contents of the three non-State Department rolls of microfilm. Actually, Hiss and his attorneys were aware of their contents within weeks of his 1948 indictment, both because of press stories that detailed them and because of an interview Edward McLean held on January 17, 1949, with Richard Nixon. "Nixon says that of the five rolls of microfilm," McLean's memo noted, "two were developed and three were not. Of the latter, one was completely blank and illegible. The other two contained partial photographs of documents containing information from the Bureau of Standards for use of the Navy. These rolls have no State Department papers." Nixon offered to send McLean not only copies of all these Navy Department documents but also copies of the originals from which they were taken, an offer Hiss's counsel accepted.*[33]

At the time, Nixon volunteered also a broad range of information to McLean about the type of film used on the five rolls, the nature of the State Department documents, and Francis Sayre's still-secret executive-session HUAC testimony about the stolen materials. McLean's memo ended with this report (he

---

*Some of the news accounts in 1975 overlooked completely the existence of the State Department microfilm strips, suggesting somehow that all five rolls had been from the Bureau of Standards, an impression Hiss did nothing to correct at the press conference.

interviewed Nixon a second time soon afterward): "Nixon several times said that if he found out anything which tended to absolve Hiss, he would let me know."[34]

Alger Hiss, in short, achieved a media coup in 1975, offering as new revelations old material that had been well known to himself and to his lawyers at the time of the trials. Hiss's arguments demonstrated only that Chambers had better luck getting top-quality documents from his State Department sources than from his contacts at the Bureau of Standards.

After more than twenty thousand pages of FBI documents on the case had been released in 1975 and 1976, Hiss charged at another press conference that the files showed, among other things: that the FBI knew the Catlett family held possession of his Woodstock typewriter months before the final stolen documents had been retyped on it (the files merely reported the contradictory evidence given by Claudia, Raymond, and Perry Catlett on the various dates they claimed to have received the machine); that one of Hiss's defense documents examiners had changed his analysis of the typing after the bureau began looking into his tax returns (the expert's unfavorable conclusions had actually been delivered to Hiss's lawyers prior to the FBI's scrutiny of his tax returns, and his analysis remained unchanged); and that one of his defense investigators, Horace Schmahl, had been a "double agent" working for the bureau (in fact it was Hiss's own lawyer Edward McLean who first offered Schmahl's cooperation to the FBI but was refused).*[35]

When other FBI documents showed that the Woodstock salesman Thomas Grady and Harry Martin (partner of Hiss's father-in-law) recalled the sale of that machine not in 1929 but in either 1927 or 1928—both men remained fuzzy about the precise date—Hiss revived the charge of conspiracy: this time, an FBI-sponsored "forgery by typewriter" frame-up. But Hiss failed to inform newsmen that he and his attorneys had got most of this information about Grady's and Martin's opinions concerning the Woodstock's date of purchase long before the trials, from their own investigation. Along with Hiss's other "new" evidence, these assertions received wide, sympathetic, and uncritical coverage in the nation's news media.[36]

From the 1950s to the present, Alger Hiss and his advocates have argued a number of older and mutually exclusive conspiracy theories: the notion that Chambers was (in Hiss's words) a "spurned homosexual who testified . . . out of jealousy and resentment," which was Hiss's response to the FBI's release of Chambers's confession of homosexuality ("I have a vague impression of boastful kinds of sexual exploits but no hint of unnatural sex interests," Hiss had written McLean in September 1948); the J. Edgar Hoover-FBI conspiracy; the idea of Chambers as a "psychopath" who acted alone against Hiss to avenge alleged

---

*Schmahl's complicated role in the case and Hiss's subsequent investigation of his investigator are discussed in the Appendix and in Chapters VII, XI, and X-V, *passim.*

slights; the belief that Horace Schmahl had built a phony Woodstock for an assortment of right-wingers to use against Hiss at the appropriate moment; the assertion that Nixon directed a plot by HUAC staffers to concoct the incriminating evidence; the notion that journalist Isaac Don Levine organized a cabal against Hiss; the claim that top OSS officials led by General William "Wild Bill" Donovan had invented all of the phony evidence to stir public support for creation of the CIA; and even the argument that Henry Luce and other "China Lobby" anti-Communists had managed to concoct Chambers's "false" testimony.*[37]

All of the theories have depended for public acceptance less on any supporting evidence than on the credulousness of younger generations unfamiliar with the basic facts in the case, yet drawn strongly to the notion that somehow Alger Hiss was done in by Richard Nixon or "The Friends of Richard Nixon." Discussions of the "McCarthy era," Michael Kinsley and Arthur Lubow noted (in the October 1975 *Washington Monthly*), are often based on "three Watergate-induced delusions":

1. Every victim of McCarthyism was a victim of Nixon and the extreme right.
2. Everyone ever attacked by Nixon was by definition innocent.
3. Innocence can be established—perhaps can only be established—by secret tapes, transcripts, etc. This is the smoking gun fallacy.[38]

Solidly grounded in a supportive post-Watergate media mentality conditioned to the emergence of "smoking guns" (single pieces of evidence that appear to establish guilt or innocence conclusively), Hiss's continuous campaign for vindication from the 1960s until his death in 1996 took three closely related directions: rehabilitation in the news media and, therefore, in the public mind; restoration of his right to practice law; and reversal of his conviction in the courts. During the 1970s, Hiss achieved some success in the first objective, full success in the second, and failure only in the third. Watergate brought Hiss renewed acceptance in the press, while efforts by his former counsel, the late Claude Cross, were largely responsible for his readmission to the Massachusetts Bar in August 1975, only days after his celebrated "pumpkin papers" press conference.

Cross had organized and lobbied quietly before his death in 1974 for Hiss's petition to be readmitted to the bar, and his firm served as Hiss's representatives throughout the proceedings. A report to the Supreme Judicial Court by the counsel to the state Board of Bar Overseers had opposed the petition, but Hiss and his supporting witnesses made a decidedly favorable impression on the justices during a hearing. Even opposing counsel acknowledged that Hiss had led "a modest, decent life" and been "'a credit to society'" since his release from prison, but Justice Paul Reardon raised a critical question in challenging the assertion

---

*These and an assortment of other conspiracy theories receive extended analysis in the Appendix.

that Hiss lacked "repentance": "Is it appropriate to ask here where juries make mistakes?" Chief Justice Joseph Tauro later asked the Board of Bar Overseers' counsel whether "anything inside or outside the record of the past 25 years" supported "the thesis that Mr. Hiss was actually guilty of espionage," receiving the curious assurance that no such evidence had emerged from a study of Hiss's *post*-conviction life. Forcing Hiss to admit guilt as the price of readmission to the bar when he "believes" he is innocent, Tauro concluded, "would be to force a man to forgo the last vestige of human dignity."[39]

The Massachusetts Supreme Judicial Court approved Hiss's readmission unanimously in August 1975. The court rejected the Board of Bar Overseers' negative judgment while responding instead to what that board had termed its "personal sympathy for Mr. Hiss, his upright and persuasive bearing, humility and reasonableness."* As for the board's conclusion that it could not recommend reinstatement so long as Hiss asserted his innocence, the court found that position "harsh" and "unforgiving," "foreign to our system of reasonable, merciful justice." An admission of guilt as a prerequisite for readmission would have placed Hiss in a "cruel quandary," Judge Tauro wrote on behalf of the seven-member court: "Simple fairness and fundamental justice demand that the person who believes he is innocent though convicted should not be required to confess guilt to a criminal act he honestly believes he did not commit." Alger Hiss "has the moral qualifications, competency and learning in law required" for readmission, and his return "will not be detrimental to the integrity and standing of the bar, the administration of justice or to the public interest."[40]

Hiss's exemplary life since prison turned the scales in his favor with the justices, and he was the first lawyer ever readmitted to the Massachusetts Bar following a major criminal conviction. Tauro's decision took note of that verdict, stating that "Hiss comes before us now as a convicted perjurer, whose crime . . . is further tainted by the breach of confidence and trust which underlay his conviction." Moreover, "nothing we have said here should be construed as detract-

---

*"Some members of the high court may have reached their decision even before the Bar Overseers had presented their unfavorable recommendation on April 4 or before the hearing on Hiss's petition was held the following month." That, at least, is what (according to Hiss) Judge Charles Wyzanski—not himself a member of the Massachusetts Supreme Judicial Court—told Hiss's former attorney Harold Rosenwald. "Charlie telephoned to Harold Rosenwald," Hiss stated to me in a taped interview, "and he said, 'Harold, I think you've won the Hiss case.' And Harold said, 'What do you mean?' And he said, 'Well, I've talked to a couple of the judges.'" Wyzanski denies categorically that any justice "intimated to me his or his colleagues' views or when they arrived at them," though he concedes that "it is possible—*although I do not recall it*—that before the opinion was announced I may have predicted how I, on the basis of general impressions of his earlier opinions, would expect a justice to vote." He further denies having discussed any judge's possible vote on the question with Harold Rosenwald. Interview with Judge Wyzanski, April 3, 1975, and with Alger Hiss, June 21, 1975. Judge Charles E. Wyzanski, Jr., to the author, April 11, 1978.

ing one iota from the fact that in considering Hiss's petition we consider him to be guilty as charged."[41]

But both the timing of the decision's release by the Massachusetts high court—five days after Hiss's "pumpkin papers" press conference—and the innocence, in short, helped to persuade Judge Tauro and his colleagues that he merited the restoration of his right to practice law.[42]

The petitioner did not always state the facts precisely at the May 1975 hearing on his readmission. Hiss was asked by the chairman of the Bar Association's hearing board, Robert W. Meserve, whether he had "made any attempt to contact for purpose of criticism or otherwise any of the people who were active in your prosecution or sat on a jury or in any way participated except on your side of the case." He replied: "My counsel Chester Lane . . . did get in touch—it was the other way around. She [an alternate juror] got in touch with him. We thought it was improper for us to talk to individual jurors." Hiss failed to mention that, shortly after his first trial ended, Lloyd Paul Stryker's assistant counsel, Harold Shapero, and another Hiss lawyer interviewed the three jurors other than Foreman Hubert James who voted for acquittal.[43]

Nor did Hiss inform Meserve that he and some close associates, including Maurice de F. Lockwood, had been engaged for years in efforts to obtain information from Horace Schmahl, his private detective before the trials who subsequently became an FBI informant. These efforts included approaching Schmahl for information about the case under false pretenses that involved suggestions of possible business deals, watching Schmahl surreptitiously from a panel truck parked outside his Fort Lauderdale home, and approaching third parties (one of whom, according to Hiss, was author Jim Bishop) to gain their help in questioning Schmahl secretly. None of these extraordinary means employed over the past decade in pursuit of Hiss's vindicatory "end" emerged at the Bar Association's public hearing in May 1975.[44]

Release of the Hiss-Chambers case's essential FBI file, containing over thirty thousand pages of bureau records, coincided with Alger Hiss's readmission to the Massachusetts Bar in 1975. In the years immediately following, Hiss's attorneys returned to federal court, armed now with the FBI and Justice Department documents on the case, seeking to overturn the 1950 jury verdict in a *coram nobis* petition on grounds that Hiss had not received a fair trial under federal court standards that prevailed in 1949–50.*

---

*The account of Hiss's *coram nobis* petition, which follows, draws upon the relevant documentation for that appeal and on a variety of secondary commentaries including—perhaps most helpfully—John W. Berresford, Whittaker Chambers and Alger Hiss: The Courts Decide, *Federal Bar News & Journal*, February 1993, pp. 102–03. For a summary of Alger Hiss's perspective on the matter, see William A. Reuben, *Footnote on an Historic Case: in re Alger Hiss* . . . (New York: Nation Institute, 1983).

Hiss's 1978 writ of *coram nobis* was filed in the U.S. District Court for the Southern District of New York, where he had been tried and convicted. As John Berresford noted in his article on the legal evolution of the Hiss-Chambers ease, the writ "is used rarely, and only to re-open old cases because of factual errors not apparent in the record." Moreover, since "it requires a new trial of an old case if it is granted, it imposes a heavy burden of proof on the petitioner."

The use of a *coram nobis* writ proved an ingenious if eventually unsuccessful strategy by Alger Hiss and his supporters to maintain public focus on the case and on his assertion of innocence absent a new trial, which Chambers's death (among many other impediments) precluded. Acceptance by the federal courts of Hiss's arguments in the *coram nobis* appeal turned *only* on the issue of whether or not he had received an adequately fair trial by 1949–50 standards, not on the question of whether or not Chambers had testified accurately regarding their relationship in the Communist underground or Hiss's having passed on government documents to his accuser. Moreover, quite understandably, the voluminous 1978 Hiss legal brief focused only on its allegations of governmental pretrial and trial abuses, omitting any mention of the type of investigative excesses engaged in by the defense that—along with those committed by the prosecution—have been cited throughout this book.

Almost all the major strands of documentary material that Hiss's attorneys collected for their *coram nobis* petition have been described in the pages of *Perjury:* The FBI kept a mail cover and phone tap on Hiss prior to, possibly during, and certainly after his two trials. In addition, the bureau withheld from defense lawyers Whittaker Chambers's confession of homosexuality, knowledge of which might have been exploited by Hiss's attorneys to impeach Chambers's credibility with a jury in that less tolerant era (though at the price of besmirching the reputation as well of Hiss and possibly others). During the trials, moreover, the FBI occasionally used the services of an informant, the private detective Horace Schmahl, who had formerly worked for the Hiss defense lawyers but left their employ after telling various witnesses in the case that he believed Hiss guilty. Schmahl later provided minor aid to the government side though in the *coram nobis* brief he served as the centerpiece of alleged prosecutorial misconduct during the Hiss trials. (The activities of Horace Schmahl are described in detail throughout *Perjury,* and his alleged role as a conspirator against Hiss is evaluated in the Appendix.) The FBI also monitored the tax returns of several defense witnesses and took other actions that are abuses of civil liberties by current standards, and possibly even by those prevailing in federal law enforcement at the time.

All these facts appear in the book, in context, and often with greater clarity than in the *coram nobis* petition. (Readers might find it instructive in this connection to contrast the *coram nobis* account of the FBI's search for and evaluation of Woodstock N230099, the controversial Hiss typewriter, with the analysis of the same evidence in this book.) But the *coram nobis* petition, understandably, does not attempt to undermine far more germane and damaging evidence described in *Perjury*, including the identification of the stolen typed materials with samples of Mrs. Hiss's typing, the four Hiss handwritten notes turned over by Chambers which dealt with confidential State Department matters, and the depositions provided by three of the defense's own expert examiners on the stolen documents.

There exists evidence also of questionable behavior on the part of the defense itself, duty recorded in *Perjury*. Alger Hiss and his lawyers sometimes resorted to tactics they deemed vital to the achievement of their aims at the time of the trials. Thus Edward McLean, Hiss's chief pretrial investigative lawyer, employed Horace Schmahl (among other tasks) to attempt to find a Woodstock typewriter in the home of Whittaker Chambers's mother, where Schmahl and an associate conducted an unsuccessful search under false pretenses. The author's research into defense files also turned up previously unpublished memoranda in which a leading defense lawyer argued the necessity of "smearing" Chambers by any means available at Hiss's first trial, including an attack upon the former's past homosexuality which the defense suspected but could not then prove and which, in any event, was patently irrelevant to the validity of his accusations against Hiss. Perhaps more serious from a legal standpoint, defense lawyers withheld from the FBI their knowledge of lies told the bureau by key witnesses in the case: In February 1949, three members of the family of Alger Hiss's former maid—the maid herself, Claudia Catlett, and her two sons, Raymond and Perry—confessed to Edward McLean, Donald Hiss, and others in the defense team that they had failed to give the FBI, during earlier interviews, crucial facts concerning what they knew of the disposition of the Hiss Woodstock typewriter. The Catletts, in FBI interviews in May 1949 admitted their earlier misstatements, as they did later at Hiss's first trial for perjury.

Both sides exercised little restraint in scrutinizing jury members. The FBI interviewed members of the hung jury at Hiss's first trial who had voted for conviction, and in the second trial, there were tangential connections between officers of the court and several jurors. On the question of possible jury tampering, the FBI's mid-trial investigation of the foreman at Hiss's first trial, who subsequently voted for acquittal, was handicapped by ignorance of the link between this individual and an acquaintance of Hiss's—a link about which the author was informed by Claude Cross, who represented Hiss at his second trial. Moreover, at Hiss's Massachusetts Bar Association hearing in 1975, he misspoke in claiming that neither he nor his lawyers had contacted jurors at his trials: In fact, they had interviewed three of the four jurors who voted for acquittal at the first trial, exempting only the foreman from their inquiries.

Nor did such questionable behavior cease with the trials. The FBI continued to investigate Hiss and his closest supporters well into the mid-1970s. For his part, Hiss, along with some associates, sporadically pursued various alleged conspirators against him during the 1960s and '70s, a campaign that included an intense investigation of Horace Schmahl, his former private detective turned FBI informant (investigators working for Hiss approached Schmahl under false pretenses), and there were similar efforts against other supposed "enemies," including discussions of wiretapping, described in the concluding chapters of this book and in the Appendix. Such possible violations of personal privacy might be expected from Hoover's FBI or Nixon's HUAC, but appear somewhat untoward on the part of friends of Alger Hiss.

The record of procedural abuse by both prosecution and defense before, during, and after Alger Hiss's two trials, in short, seems remarkably mixed in retrospect, studded with examples of both sides acting with far more zeal than fairness in pursuit of their respective ends.

Judge Richard Owen's 1982 ruling rejected decisively Alger Hiss's various claims that he had not received a fair trial at the time. Reviewing the evolution of the case and the evidence offered against the defendant at the trials, Owens concluded: "The jury verdict rendered in 1950 was amply supported by the evidence—the most damaging aspects of which were admitted by Hiss—and nothing presented in these papers, extensive though they are, places that verdict under any cloud." Neither Horace Schmahl's few discussions with the FBI (at first, while working for the Hiss defense and encouraged by them) nor lack of defense access to Chambers's confession of homosexuality to the bureau nor any of the other assertions in the *coram nobis* writ, Owen ruled, established credibly Hiss's claim that he had been denied "effective counsel" during the trials. As for the conspiracy argument underlying the *coram nobis* brief, that the FBI had hidden definite knowledge that Woodstock N230099 was not the machine on which the stolen documents had been typed (a point examined in some detail in the Appendix), Owen concluded, correctly, that the FBI's behavior on the matter revealed a "sea of confusion" and not involvement in any conspiracy against Alger Hiss.

Subsequently, the U.S. Court of Appeals for the Second Circuit affirmed the lower court's decision to reject Hiss's brief without additional comment and, similarly, the Supreme Court denied certiorari on October 11, 1983. Thus ended the three-and-a-half decades of legal efforts related to the Hiss-Chambers case. As for *coram nobis,* legal analyst John W. Berresford wrote in the *Federal Bar News & Journal* that Judge Owen brushed aside various Hiss "arguments as frivolous and denied his . . . petition in unusually strong terms. Although the judge did not say so, he clearly believed that Hiss was guilty, and was wasting the court's time with trivialities that cast no real doubt on the fairness or outcome of the second trial."

The *coram nobis* arguments survived for a time mainly in nonlegal media. One of Alger Hiss's most loyal supporters since the trials themselves, Rutgers University law professor John Lowenthal, produced a documentary film, *The Trials of Alger Hiss,* that incorporated the defense perspectives denied by Judge Owen and his colleagues. Moreover, portions of a British-produced miniseries on the case, *Concealed Enemies,* also absorbed much if not all of the *coram nobis* argument. Neither documentary film nor television series, however, aroused any public demand for further reopening or scrutiny of the case.

It would be a decade after the failure of his *coram nobis* writ before Alger Hiss and his case would again attract national interest. "The 1980's brought a resuscitation of the reputation of Mr. Chambers," *The New York Times* later wrote. President Ronald Reagan honored Whittaker Chambers in 1984 with the White House presentation—attended by Chambers's family and friends—of a posthumous Medal of Freedom. Four years later, in 1988, the Reagan administration assigned to Chambers's now-famous Westminster farm, site of the "pumpkin papers" episode, the status of a national historic landmark.*

During the eighties, also, Richard Nixon reemerged from self-imposed public silence and San Clemente exile to a set of new careers as memoirist, author of foreign-policy books, and occasional private counselor to Reagan and administration officials. Nixon opened a new office in Manhattan and took up residence in New Jersey, provoking occasional media comment that both Hiss and his HUAC pursuer shared the same urban setting in their retirement years. Nixon played no further visible role in the Hiss-Chambers saga other than delivering private remarks and an occasional talk reaffirming his well-known views on the case. He emerged as a champion of Boris Yeltsin's post-Communist Russia during the early 1990s after the collapse of the Soviet Union. Nixon died in April 1994, enjoying by then a fuller measure of public respect than might have been anticipated when he left Washington in disgrace two decades earlier.

Alger Hiss celebrated his eightieth birthday in 1984, but Hiss's earlier prediction that by the time he reached eighty *he* would be widely "respected and venerated" remained accurate mainly for his friends, family, and circle of faithful supporters.

Hiss remarried after the death of Priscilla Hiss in 1984. "In the Hamptons and in New York," David Remnick wrote in a 1986 *Washington Post* profile that described his subject's two residences, "Hiss is a fixture on a certain level of the social circuit. His friends are editors, artists, musicians, civil liberties attorneys." Remnick's sketch of Hiss captured shrewdly what he called "the triumph of Alger Hiss's dotage":

> His persistence gives him the *possibility* of martyrdom, even if he is probably not one. It has helped him win friends, loyal defenders. It has made him more

---

*For one unsympathetic visitor's caustic narrative of an attempt to locate the landmark on a trip to Westminster, see Jon Wiener, *The Nation,* Nov. 18, 1996, pp. 6–7.

important than he ever could have been, either as a loyal servant to Franklin Roosevelt or to the Communist Party. Ambiguity has been a savior to him.*

Briefly, in 1992, that ambiguity was replaced by triumphant headlines and news broadcasts throughout the world, which proclaimed Alger Hiss's complete innocence upon highest Russian authority. In a half-century-old drama notable for its sharp twists and unexpected turns, none proved more remarkable than the sudden entry into the Hiss-Chambers case in November 1992 of General Dimitri A. Volkogonov—military historian and adviser on Soviet-era archives to President Boris Yeltsin of Russia.

As Volkogonov recounted the story later that year, his interest in the case began in August 1992, when he received a letter from Alger Hiss asking that he search for any KGB archives that might mention Hiss or his case. "Hiss wrote that he was 88 and would like to die peacefully, that he wanted to prove that he was never a paid, contracted spy," Volkogonov told *The New York Times* in mid-December 1992. (Assuming Volkogonov's description of Hiss's letter is correct, it should be noted that not even Whittaker Chambers had ever claimed Hiss to be a "paid [and] contracted" Soviet agent.)

Later in August, after getting Hiss's letter, Volkogonov received a visit in Moscow from John Lowenthal, Hiss's longtime friend and supporter, former law professor, and producer of the documentary *The Trials of Alger Hiss.* "His attorney, Lowenthal," Volkogonov informed *The New York Times* in mid-December, "pushed me hard to say things of which I was not fully convinced."

Whether or not "fully convinced," in the months during which—according to Hiss supporters—he was supposedly deeply absorbed in KGB file research concerning Hiss, Volkogonov had spent most of his time and energy on a different assignment, according to the September 18, 1992, *Moscow Times.* In that period, as co-chairman of a joint U.S.-Russian commission on the subject, preparing for a visit by its American members, Volkogonov "had been devoting the majority of his time to research in the presidential archives for information on the issue [of American MIAs and POW's possibly brought to the Soviet Union]."

Volkogonov later acknowledged that he spent only "two days swallowing dust" looking at KGB files potentially relevant to Americans such as Alger Hiss who may have worked for the Soviets during the 1930s and 1940s. (The actual KGB archives for this period contain tens of thousands of pages, much of which has been used by the author and a Russian colleague doing research for another book.) Despite his scant attention to the bulk of KGB files on U.S. agents for

---

*David Remnick, "Alger Hiss: Unforgiving and Unforgiven," *The Washington Post Magazine,* October 12, 1986, pp. 29, 30.

this period, Volkogonov agreed to the Hiss-Lowenthal request that he provide a letter of exoneration "primarily [on] humanitarian grounds."

The general gave Lowenthal such a letter for Alger Hiss on October 14 and, the following day, videotaped remarks later used by Hiss and Lowenthal at a New York City news conference, in which Volkogonov said this about his two days of "swallowing dust": "Not a single document, and a great amount of material [has] been studied, substantiates the allegation that Mr. A. Hiss collaborated with the intelligence services of the Soviet Union." Moreover, the general continued, Hiss was "never a spy for the Soviet Union. . . . The fact that he was convicted in the 50s was a result of either false information or judicial error. You can tell Alger Hiss [Volkogonov concluded in his communication with John Lowenthal] that the heavy weight should be lifted from his heart." Not content with those sweeping assertions, Volkogonov went on to assert also that, in his two days of archive rummaging, he had found no evidence of Whittaker Chambers's involvement in espionage (despite voluminous evidence to the contrary documented in these pages, including Soviet NKVD files from the period). Rather, according to the general, "I found only that he was [a] member of the Communist Party, the American Communist Party."

At late-October 1992 press conferences and interviews, surrounded by family and friends, Alger Hiss basked in Volkogonov's apparent "vindication." Newspaper headlines of the announcement provided the basic story: "RUSSIAN FILES: HISS NEVER SPIED" (*USA Today*); "AFTER 40 YEARS, A POSTSCRIPT ON HISS: RUSSIAN OFFICIAL CALLS HIM INNOCENT" (*The New York Times*); "HISS WELCOMES RUSSIAN VINDICATION/HIS NEXT GOAL: TO BE CLEARED HERE" (*Baltimore Sun*).

Predictably, those persuaded of Hiss's innocence prior to the Volkogonov announcement reveled in its decisiveness while those who believed Hiss guilty questioned the media's instant rush to positive judgment. Many American newspaper and magazine stories on the matter, followed in this by virtually all television newscasts, tended to accept the general's statement as conclusive.

Then came the backlash. Criticisms of Volkogonov's statement came initially from American scholars of Soviet history, many of whom knew at first hand the disorganized and lamentably incomplete condition of government files in that country. Also, at a Moscow meeting with the author shortly after news broke of Volkogonov's statement, Director Yvgeny Primakov of the Russian Intelligence Service (SVR) noted that the SVR (keeper of all KGB files) and military intelligence (i.e., the GRU, in whose service Chambers always asserted that he and Hiss had worked, not the civilian NKVD) maintained entirely distinct archives. Volkogonov's two-day search had been entirely in KGB records maintained by the SVR and not (to Primakov's knowledge) in military intelligence files.

Volkogonov later conceded this crucial point, telling *The New York Times* in December 1992:

> I was not properly understood. The Ministry of Defense also has an intelligence service, which is totally different, and many documents have been destroyed. I only looked through what the KGB had. All I said was that I saw no evidence.

Volkogonov's memory, however, played tricks with him in December. He had written to Alger Hiss in mid-October that "Mr. A. Hiss had never and nowhere been recruited as an agent of the intelligence services of the U.S.S.R.," a sweeping assertion that obviously included military intelligence agencies (at whose files Volkogonov had not even glanced) as well as service with the KGB.

Barely a month after providing Hiss and Lowenthal with his dramatic statement of vindication, Volkogonov retracted. He did so first in a letter to the *Nezavisimaya Gazeta* (Independent Newspaper) newspaper of Moscow, in which he insisted that his earlier statement had been made only under prompting by "Hiss and his lawyer" because of a "humanitarian" concern on his part about the aging Hiss, who "only wanted to die peacefully."

The general repeated his recantation to a *New York Times* reporter in mid-December, acknowledging that his brief and limited scrutiny of only selected KGB documents meant "that he was in no position to fully clear Mr. Hiss and that perhaps no one ever can." Volkogonov acknowledged that even if he had "scoured all the voluminous archives of the KGB, the Defense Ministry and the Communist Party there were also untold files that were destroyed in the upheavals after Stalin's death."

None of the U.S. television networks and virtually no major newspapers— except for *The New York Times, The Washington Post,* and the *Washington Times*— considered worthy of coverage this crucial retraction of the earlier front-page story of Hiss's supposed exoneration.

Nor has Volkogonov's retraction caught up completely with his earlier "vindication" of Alger Hiss in popular and even academic sources. Thus the entry on Hiss that users of Microsoft's Windows 95 software find, drawn from the 1995 edition of *The Concise Columbia Encyclopedia,* a widely used resource guide for researchers and students, concludes simply: "In 1992 a high-ranking Russian official said he had found no evidence in the archives of the former USSR that Hiss had been a spy." Similarly, the Associated Press's initial story on Hiss's death in 1996, perhaps the single most important source of information distributed worldwide and used by print and electronic media in preparing Hiss obituary stories, noted that Hiss "proclaimed that [vindication] had come finally in 1992, at age eighty-seven, when a Russian general in charge of Soviet intelligence archives declared that Hiss had never been a spy, but rather a victim of

Cold War hysteria and the McCarthy Red-hunting era." For many unfamiliar with the complex evidence and history of the Hiss-Chambers case, therefore, Volkogonov's later retracted *ex cathedra* declaration of vindication will remain the last word on the case.*

As the Hiss-Chambers case approached its half-century mark, two additional documentary bombshells gained public attention during the mid-1990s after the Volkogonov episode. Unlike the initial impact of the latter's retracted "vindication," these documents appeared to confirm Chambers's account of Hiss's deep involvement in espionage activity for the Soviets. Although both would be challenged vigorously by Hiss and his defenders, the documents in question—if taken at face value—linked Hiss to another key Soviet agent in Washington during the 1930s (as Chambers had alleged) and to Soviet military intelligence spying during—World War II, years after Chambers's defection.

The first concerned Noel Field, a State Department official during the New Deal and close friend of Alger Hiss. Field later acknowledged his involvement in "secret work" for the party. He fled the United States for Eastern Europe at the time of the Hiss case, was arrested apparently at Soviet instructions in Prague (many of Field's former colleagues in the underground such as Hede Massing had defected, presumably throwing his own reliability into question), and jailed in Hungary. There, prior to his release from prison in 1954 (coincidentally, on the same day Alger Hiss was released from prison in the United States), Field's captors interrogated him about his activities and associates in the Communist underground—including Alger Hiss.

Field remained in Hungary after his release from prison and died there in 1970. An anti-Communist government came to power peacefully in that country two decades later and began opening to scholars and journalists a number of previously restricted archives. One Hungarian historian, Maria Schmidt, while researching a book on the Hungarian secret police in February 1992, "came upon a stack of aging documents among the restricted files of the Interior Ministry in Budapest," among them the 1954 interrogations of Noel Field prior to his release

---

*General Volkogonov's initial statements, released by Hiss and his supporters, and early commentary can be found in the following: *The New York Times,* October 29, 1992; *The Washington Post,* October 31, 1992; *USA Today,* October 30–Nov 1, 1992, and *Newsweek*, November 9, 1992. Volkogonov's statements clarifying and retracting his initial assertions on the case are chronicled in *The New York Times,* December 17, 1992; the Washington *Times,* December 18, 1992; and in George F. Will's January 11, 1993, *Newsweek* column, which also cites Volkogonov's late-November 1992 statements of clarification to Moscow's *Nezavisimaya Gazeta*. See also Allen Weinstein, "Reopening a Cold War Mystery," *The Washington Post,* November 4, 1992; Michael Wines, "Hiss Case's Bogymen Are Still Not at Rest," *The New York Times,* December 13, 1992; and Jacob Cohen, "Innocent After All?", and Amos Perlmutter, "Soviet Historiography: Western Journalism," in *National Review,* January 18, 1993.

from prison. If Field told the truth in those interviews—which confirmed, among other points, Hede Massing's testimony at Hiss's trial that Field discussed their joint involvement in Soviet espionage with Hiss—then Chambers's biographer Sam Tanenhaus's description of the Schmidt findings as an evidentiary "smoking gun" in the Hiss case is valid.

Among the papers she turned up in the Interior Ministry archives, Schmidt states that she discovered several earlier drafts of the well-publicized 1957 letter from Field to Hiss in which he supports Hiss's innocence of Chambers's charges. Those early drafts suggest that Field was coached by Communist intelligence officials and encouraged to send his supportive letter. Some Hiss advocates have argued that Field's interrogations reveal similar coaching by Hungarian intelligence agents to portray Hiss as a genuine Soviet operative, although why Communist authorities would wish an easily checked falsehood from a prisoner under custody remains puzzling and unpersuasive.

Professor Schmidt presented her findings first in an October 1993 paper delivered at New York University's Center for European Studies. She linked the "false testimony" issue to another argument of Hiss supporters on Field's confirmation of Hiss's involvement in Soviet espionage, that the files in question may have been fabricated to malign Hiss ("forgery by interrogation"?): "As for the Soviets fabricating the documents," Schmidt pointed out, "remember that at the time of Field's confession, the Soviets were conducting a massive public campaign protesting that Hiss was innocent. They had nothing to gain by creating documents that would undermine their effort to keep the truth from getting out." Hiss's more responsible defenders accept the Field interrogations as genuine, however, especially since Schmidt has provided detailed file citations for the still-unreleased documents. What remains at issue is the unresolvable question of whether—for whatever weird reason—Noel Field was encouraged in his 1954 questioning to bear false witness from prison against his old and still-cherished friend, Alger Hiss. No credible explanation for such belated perjury has yet to emerge, and newly available NKVD files confirm the Hiss-Field underground link.*

The second recent documentary revelation addressed directly the question of whether Alger Hiss remained a covert agent working (as he had done during the 1930s in cooperation with Whittaker Chambers and others) for the Soviet Union's military intelligence service (GRU). In 1995 and 1996, the Central Intelligence Agency and National Security Agency released thousands of intercepted and decoded transmissions from Soviet agents in the United States to Moscow during the Second World War—the so-called VENONA files. A number of Americans who worked for the Soviets during these years were identified in the

---

*For an informed analysis of the Volkogonov episode and Field interrogations that revived the Hiss case in 1992–93, see Jeffrey A. Frank, "Unending Trial of Alger Hiss," *The Washington Post*, October 29, 1993. See also Chapter VI, pp. 178–82.

transmissions, and, since the VENONA material was released in several installments, it provoked periodic news headlines.*

VENONA documents showed that leaders of the "open" American Communist Party, including its head, Earl Browder, led double lives as Soviet spies. Even those inclined to question the complicity of Americans in such espionage were confronted (quoting Walter and Miriam Schneir in *The Nation*) with "so much amazing, sad, disturbing material, [that] one hardly knows where to begin." The Schneirs had long argued that Julius and Ethel Rosenberg were innocent victims of perjured testimony but now shifted ground at least in the case of Julius: "What these messages show, briefly, is that Julius Rosenberg was the head of a spy ring gathering and passing nonatomic defense information." (The Schneirs continue to believe Ethel Rosenberg "was not a Soviet agent" and that the couple did not engage in *atomic* espionage.)[†]

One VENONA transcript, Number 1822 in the series, dated March 30, 1945—from "VADIM" (Anatoli Gromov, Soviet station chief in Washington at the time) to Moscow—has become the object of sustained debate among those interested in the Hiss case. The cable describes a "chat" with a Soviet agent, code-named "ALES," who (according to the text) "has been working with the NEIGHBORS continuously since 1935." "The NEIGHBORS," in NKVD agent parlance, traditionally referred to the GRU.

From the message, it is evident that "ALES" had been a trusted agent, "leader of a small group of the NEIGHBORS's probationers, for the most part consisting of his relations." Whether Priscilla and/or Donald Hiss were among "his relations" cannot be determined from the cable itself. "ALES" and his group (according to "VADIM") "work on obtaining military information only. Materials on the 'BANK' [i.e., the State Department], where "ALES" evidently worked allegedly interest the NEIGHBORS very little and he does not produce them regularly." Moreover, "all the last few years 'ALES' has been working with 'POL' [also identified as "PAUL"] who also meets other members of the group occasionally."

The CIA and NSA considered "POL" an "unidentified cover-name." Most likely, the alias referred to a U.S. government official who led a major Soviet espionage ring within the U.S. government during these years—identified as such throughout the VENONA traffic and in the existing secondary literature—Nathan Gregory Silvermaster, whom his Soviet overseers called "PAL." (The author's research in KGB files for his book on Soviet espionage in the United States, *The Haunted Wood*, confirms Silvermaster's alias, "PAL," used throughout this period.)

---

*A sampling of the VENONA cables has been published in Robert Louis Benson and Michael Warner, eds., *VENONA: Soviet Espionage and the American Response, 1939–1957* (Washington, D.C.: National Security Agency & Central Intelligence Agency, 1996).

[†]Walter Schneir and Miriam Schneir, "Coptic Answers," *The Nation,* August 14/21, 1995, p. 152.

The cable's concluding comments retain the capacity to startle even today:

5. Recently ALES and his whole group were awarded Soviet decorations.
6. After the YALTA Conference, when he [ALES] had gone on to MOSCOW, a Soviet personage in a very responsible position (ALES gave [us] to understand that it was Comrade VYSHINSKIJ) allegedly got in touch with ALES and at the behest of the Military NEIGHBORS passed on to him their gratitude and so on.

                                                                VADIM

"Comrade Vyshinskij" referred to the then-foreign minister of the Soviet Union.

We know—and have reviewed details of this episode in connection with "ALES" elsewhere in the book—-that Alger Hiss attended the 1945 Yalta Conference as an adviser to then-Secretary of State Edward J. Stettinius. After the conference, Hiss and Stettinius and two lesser State Department functionaries flew on Stettinius's plane back to the United States, stopping at various cities, including Moscow, where Stettinius held official meetings. Alger Hiss's Moscow schedule and activities cannot be reconstructed today in the absence of firsthand accounts or documents.

A convergence of collateral evidence, however, supports the presumption that Alger Hiss was "ALES." How else to account for Oleg Gordievsky's identification in 1988, over a half-decade before the decoded VENONA cable was made public, of Hiss's Soviet alias as "ALES"? How else do we explain why Soviet code clerk Igor Gouzenko, in debriefings with the Canadian prime minister and that country's intelligence officials after his 1945 defection in Ottawa, asserted that he had been told by a Soviet military attaché that the GRU had an agent who was an assistant to a leading State Department official, an individual whom Prime Minister Mackenzie King and others warned U.S. officials later that year was undoubtedly Alger Hiss? KGB files cited elsewhere in this book, moreover, reveal additional discussions by "RUBLE," another alleged Soviet agent in the United States, with "ALES" and reinforce the probability that Alger Hiss was the individual in question.

A brief flurry of debate over the "ALES" identification absorbed the American media after Cable Number 1822 was released.* In the absence of further materials regarding "ALES," however, that agent's identification as Hiss remains persuasive but not conclusive. But this single document does not alter the extensive underlying fabric of evidence outlined throughout this book, which demonstrates the credibility of Chambers's charges against Hiss and the latter's culpability as

---

*See, for example, the following March 6, 1996, news accounts: *The New York Times, The Washington Post, Baltimore Sun,* and the Washington *Times.* Most skeptical of the Hiss-ALES link is Tim Weiner's *New York Times* account. See also Eric Breindel, "New Evidence in the Hiss Case, *The Wall Street Journal,* March 14, 1996. See also Chapter X, pp. 324–27.

a Soviet agent. If accurate, the "ALES" identification proves that Hiss not only worked for the Soviets from 1935 to 1938, when Chambers defected, but that he remained a valued agent through 1945, during his period as a leading State Department policymaker. In the war years, Hiss had access to the widest range of Roosevelt administration secrets and policy decisions.

Strangely, the media and others interested in the Hiss-Chambers case neglected a *second* VENONA cable that mentions Alger Hiss directly though obliquely. In a September 28, 1943, dispatch to Moscow from "MOLIERE" (identified in VENONA notes as Pavel P. Mikhajlov, Soviet vice-consul in New York), the following information is conveyed in a cable, most of which could not be decoded: "2. The NEIGHBOR [i.e., military intelligence or GRU] has reported that [words unrecovered] from the State Department by the name of HISS . . . [end of recovered wording]." Why a GRU agent mentioned Hiss to the Soviet vice-consul in New York in 1943 will remain a mystery in the absence of a more fully deciphered cable.

Although the documentary revelations of Noel Field's interrogations and VENONA's "ALES" cable derailed Hiss's continuing pursuit of vindication in the court of public opinion, he was helped by Oliver Stone's 1995 film biography, *Nixon*. The movie provided viewers with a brief profile of a patently innocent Hiss in the early days of Richard Nixon's career, hounded by the latter's cynical ambition and by faked evidence. Neither a film produced by Hiss nor by one of his lawyerly advocates could have improved on the image that Stone's "Alger Hiss" presented to audiences around the world.

Even though he was ninety-two years old, Hiss's death in New York City's Lenox Hill Hospital on November 15, 1996, caught the media and the American public by surprise. Presumably he would have been pleased by the long front-page obituary articles that filled the country's newspapers on November 16 and by the prominence given to his death on America's major television network news shows.* A number referred to Volkogonov's "vindication" without reference to the Russian general's subsequent recantation. One television anchor,

---

*Virtually every major U.S. newspaper, radio newscast, and television news broadcast reported Alger Hiss's death. The initial Associated Press report stated that "in 1992 . . . a Russian general in charge of Soviet intelligence archives declared that Hiss had never been a spy but rather a victim of Cold War hysteria and the McCarthy Red-hunting era." Only in later AP wires on Hiss's death did the news service refer to Volkogonov's later clarifications and retractions. Comprehensive obituaries of Alger Hiss can be found in the November 16, 1996, *New York Times*, *Washington Post*, *Boston Globe*, and most other major U.S. papers. For a sampling of the commentary surrounding Hiss's death, see the following: Christopher Matthews (the Washington *Times*, December 23, 1996); Robert D. Novak (*The Washington Post*, November 21, 1996); Victor Navasky (*The Nation*, December 9, 1996): Evan Thomas (*Newsweek*, November 25, 1996); George F. Will (*The Washington Post*, November 21, 1996); and *The Economist* (November 30, 1996). Alger Hiss's son, Tony Hiss, published a tribute to his father in *The New Yorker* (December 2, 1996).

apparently taking as his source an erroneous foreign news-agency dispatch, asserted that Russian President Boris Yeltsin *personally* had announced in 1995 that Alger Hiss had never been a Soviet agent! Hiss's death came on the same day, November 15, that forty-eight years earlier, Whittaker Chambers handed to his attorneys for transmission to Hiss's lawyers and the Justice Department the typed documents and handwritten notes that would seal Alger Hiss's fate before a jury of his peers. His passing, preceded by that of Richard Nixon and much earlier by those of Whittaker and Esther Chambers and Priscilla Hiss, brought closure for the case's principals. Future debate over its facts and meaning is now in the hands of surrogates.

From the beginning of the case, Alger Hiss had apparently persuaded himself that Whittaker Chambers's testimony could not hurt him or, ultimately, would not prevail either against his own word in front of a jury or in the court of public opinion. Events since then proved him wrong on both counts. "Like any human being caught in a complex difficulty, in which forces and people beyond his control are at work," wrote Elizabeth Drew about Richard Nixon's Watergate actions, "the President may not have [had] a strategy other than taking it day by day, getting through each dangerous passage as best he can, and hoping for the best." Such expedient stonewalling served neither Hiss nor Nixon well in their respective endgame crises.[45]

Future historians undoubtedly will provide more complete accounts of the case itself than this report on its occasionally contradictory and sometimes spotty pattern of evidence. "More often than not," Robert Griffith aptly observed about major Cold War internal-security dramas such as this one, "the 'cases' twisted back through a gray area of fact and fantasy, of judgment, opinion, and prejudice."[46]

Despite compelling evidence that Alger Hiss stole the documents in question and that Whittaker Chambers told the truth about their relationship, the case will not close. Alger Hiss died professing his innocence, and the underlying symbolism of the episode remains compelling to Americans even today. The Hiss-Chambers case has been transformed over the past several decades by those on both sides who have argued its imagery, as well as its facts. If only for them, the case's symbolic elements have increased the burden of personal anguish. Its continuous revival merely confirms the imminence of further grief for any still living who were deeply involved.

The case has ended for both Whittaker Chambers and Alger Hiss, but their drama continues. Although arguments will persist in the court of public opinion, the body of available evidence proves that Hiss perjured himself when describing his secret dealings with Chambers, so that the jurors in his second trial made no mistake in finding Alger Hiss guilty as charged.

Part Six
MEMORY

Moment by moment the whole fabric of events dissolves into ruins and melts into the past; and all that survives of the thing done passes into the custody of a shifting, capricious, imperfect, human memory . . . the facts work loose; they are detached from their roots in time and space and shaped into a story. The story is molded and remolded by imagination, by passion and prejudice, by religious preconception or aesthetic instinct, by the delight of marvelous, by the itch for the moral, by the love of a good story; and the thing becomes a legend. A few irreducible facts will remain; no more, perhaps, than the names of persons and places. . . .

—*F. M. Cornford,* Thucydides Mythistoricus (1907)

A NOTE TO THE READER ON THE THIRD EDITION

The framework of a historical study often cannot accommodate the starker shadings of personality and moral insight in a chronicle devoted to the dispassionate evaluation of evidence. Specifically, a number of supposedly minor characters in the tale, people whose role as "witnesses" to the lives and interplay of Alger Hiss and Whittaker Chambers, required only brief description by the historian. Not that the protagonists themselves—Hiss, Chambers, Richard Nixon, and those close to them—were dull figures. Even in their lives, however, episodes and observations that might best reveal the dimension of character sometimes had no appropriate place in a factual analysis of the "Case." Instead, such episodes were often consigned to the status of "outtakes" to be boxed and stored along with other raw research material.

The Hiss-Chambers case's deeper meaning, like other contested dramas in the American past, contains a rich blend of extraordinary situations and characters. A number of people, some of them prominent figures, had their lives changed profoundly by the "Case," often for the worse.

I offer the following profiles of persons and places on three continents—most largely undescribed in *Perjury*'s factual narrative as such examples. Many more are available for the diligent researcher; interested in pursuing the Hiss-Chambers world beyond the boundaries of *Perjury* developed by the current author.

Welcome to the Hiss-Chambers Case!
[December 2012]

XVII

THE HISS LABYRINTH: SIX PROFILES

SAN CLEMENTE, 1975: A VISIT TO ELBA

The former president lived a half-mile beyond the gate with its insistent sign: "NO SIGHTSEERS BEYOND THIS POINT: COAST GUARD STATION." As a young congressman, he had built his career upon public belief that he had "trapped" Alger Hiss into apparent perjuries during House committee hearings covered generously on every front page in the country. Richard Nixon had often said (and written) that his pursuit of Hiss had taught him lessons of cool behavior in times of crisis, lessons that served him well on his accelerated rise to high office. A quarter-century later, in the months before resigning as president, his own tapes and the accounts of his subordinates showed him returning incessantly in conversation to the themes of his earlier triumph—the Hiss Case—as if this earlier experience contained some unique insight, some iconographic epiphany, capable of rescuing him and his counselors from their end-game crisis.

Nixon returned to his Western White House in disgrace and encouraged friends' perception of the situation as an American Elba while working on a set of memoirs that would become a credible *apologia*. (What other "Case" in the country's history can match this one in the grandiosity of its protagonists' illusions: The former president confronting defeat unrepentant on his Pacific ramparts; Hiss a self-proclaimed "American Dreyfus," and Whittaker Chambers, Hiss's now-deceased accuser, an anti-Communist St. Benedict, a farmer-monk bleakly counting the days before the West lapsed into his predicted decline and fall?)

In exile, some of Nixon's former legislative aides had not been kind to him. Robert Stripling, for example, told me a far different and less complimentary version of his behavior under stress during the Case than the one that brought him fame. In his account, Nixon had been fearful and indecisive at critical moments during the committee hearings and afterwards, not the cool and confident investigator of his memoirs. I came to meet with Nixon in 1975, seeking either confirmation or denial of these allegations. Would Nixon meet with me? Perhaps, said his chief assistant-in-exile, Frank Gannon, when I phoned, but first I should come to San Clemente to discuss the material with him. Once past the Secret Service's scrutiny, I drove through the compound and walked from a nearly deserted parking lot to the aide's office, straining for a first impression: buildings in disrepair, meteoric holes in the ground where once stood White House communications gear and Quonset huts filled with presidential staff, brittle and unkempt lawns— yet all of this on a bluff commanding a magnificent view of the Pacific. "He isn't seeing people of your ilk yet," Gannon began with a laugh, and we proceeded to his office in one of the few "temporary" buildings still in operation to discuss the Case. "I will listen to you, ask the obvious questions, and brief him. Perhaps later, he will agree to talk to you." Well-educated, candid, and genial, Gannon had followed his leader into exile from an earlier post at the White House. After our conversation ended, he led me on a walk through the ghost town past the former president's walled home, and I could only wonder if I had been placed on display for an unseen curious occupant inside.

The assistant suggested dinner before I drove back to Los Angeles and, to my surprise, we went not to a local restaurant but to his nearby beachfront apartment, joined there by another aide, Diane Sawyer, also at that time a former White House staff assistant. The meal was simple and satisfying—pasta and good wine—and I watched this attractive pair relaxed as would not have been possible during their last months in the White House bunker. Nixon obviously remained a great man to them, worthy of their evident protectiveness. Only when conversation turned to his fall did they seem curt and defensive.

Walking down the ocean-front boulevard toward my car after our farewells—no promise of a return visit to meet the boss—I thought it was remarkable how quickly even these two latecomers to Richard Nixon's embattled life appeared to have managed to internalize for the moment his life-long sense of grievance. (A decade later, at a Chinese Embassy reception in Washington, Nixon walked up to me, arm-in-arm with the ambassador, while leaving the party. I stuck my hand out and introduced myself. He smiled, threw his arm around me for a photograph and, turning to my wife, said "Gutsy fellow, your husband. It took courage to write that book." We posed for pictures. A first and last meeting.)*

---

*An earlier version of this vignette appeared in the November 1975 issue of *Esquire.*

BUDAPEST, 1975: THE ALLEGED SPYMASTER

"The toilet has problems." The sullen chambermaid at Budapest's Duna Inter-
continental Hotel knocked on the door to announce that difficulty only five minutes before Josef Peters, alleged handler of Soviet agents in the United States
during the 1930s, was due to arrive. Only two minutes earlier, I had used the
suddenly injured instrument without incident. The maid nodded, first left and
then right, at the pair of husky "plumbers" in work clothes on either side. "They
will fix—stop toilet shaking." The two specialists in commode technology smiled
and began hammering at the bowl while I returned to writing postcards. After a
minute, they both stood looking over my shoulder and announced, "Is good. All
fix," at which point they turned and left. As if on cue, Peters quietly walked past
the door that the "plumbers" had neglected to close and entered the room.

He was far more imposing than the quarter-century-old photographs of him
that made front pages throughout the United States, the ones of a short, stocky
man with a look midway between a smile and a wince, handcuffed visibly to a
pair of tall, stolid FBI agents who looked remarkably like the pair of "plumbers"
who had just completed their mission. At eighty, Peters remained a handsome
figure with flowing white hair and an appearance that—in what seemed a norm
for many figures in the Hiss case—made him look decades younger. He wore a
well-cut German suit, a far better fit than the one he had worn in the 1949 wire
service photographs taken prior to his deportation from the United States. Since
then, the alleged spymaster had edited international journals and become a leading figure in the Hungarian Communist Party.

"So you have arrived," he had begun his phone conversation with me the
previous evening. Earlier Peters had written urging me not to come to see him,
though finally relenting and agreeing to meet. Not last night, however: "I am
busy day and night—everyone is—with the Party Congress. I have kept tomorrow free for you. Someone else from America is visiting me right now." The year
was 1975. When I had arrived at the Budapest airport, it was crowded with sol-
diers carrying automatic weapons. My commercial flight had circled for a half
hour while General Secretary Leonid Brezhnev's flight and those carrying the
Eastern European leadership landed. My hotel, I found, was overrun by German
businessmen—West as well as East—many strolling along the balconies to watch
the magnificent sunset over the Danube and to strain for a better glimpse of the
imperial castle that dominates the city's Buda section across the river.

Peters and I spent the next several hours sipping coffee and talking in my
room—presumably the "plumbers" got their money's worth—before leaving to
have lunch. He stared at me coldly and steadily, apparently measuring both my
sympathies and my knowledge of the events I had come to discuss. "You are
wasting your time," he began. "I have nothing of consequence to tell you about

those absurd charges of espionage. I was in organization work—always—for the open Party in America."

"Others disagreed," I noted as politely as possible, and there was much corroborative evidence (and many credible witnesses) on the record about his "secret work."

"Lying bastards! The FBI planted two guys in the building where I lived and tapped my phone for years. Yet they never brought charges against me—only deportation."

Had he ever met Hiss's accuser, Whittaker Chambers, I asked, who once described Peters (as had a number of others) to the FBI as the leading American Communist Party link to the Soviet underground throughout the 1930s? "Never—except perhaps once while he was still a writer for *New Masses*—before his so-called 'underground' work."

Had he ever been to Washington, where Lee Pressman (later) and other former underground members of the Communist Party had placed him during the New Deal years? "Only to help lead the Bonus March in 1932—not after. My work was in New York." Not ever during the New Deal? No.

The questions and denials continued, until we shifted to other subjects: his view of American Communist Party leaders ("Earl Browder was a disaster"), his attitude toward an acknowledged Soviet agent, American Noel Field, who was arrested in Hungary during Stalin's post–World War II purges ("a Quaker fanatic"), the 1956 Hungarian uprising ("a counter-revolution, very anti-Semitic, a pogrom for Jews before it was crushed; you knew that, didn't you?—thousands of Jews fled"), and American officials ("J. Edgar Hoover was a homosexual. So was Roosevelt. That whole crowd around him was—Hopkins, I think.").

How could he speak of an "open party" for which he worked, I asked, while denying that there existed a "secret party"? His smile broadened, but no response came. Did he object to my requesting his FBI files under the Freedom of Information Act? A moment's pause: "I think it would be unwise . . . other people were involved. I was in hiding for a time . . . I don't think it is wise."

He was suddenly nervous and irritable. No longer smiling and with his eyes fixed upon me, he cautioned: "No involvement of my name in your book should involve the American Communist Party in this case. That's all they need, those poor guys. Be very careful. I am here and nothing can happen to me. Be very careful that the party shall in no way be hurt by your book."

After lunch, we walked through Vaci Street's crowded section of shops, the best in Eastern Europe, and he posed for pictures. All of the accounts by former members of the party who knew him described Peters as gentle and urbane: "It disturbs me that all those bastards liked me," he said, though without apparent conviction.

Had he ever thought of returning to the United States, I asked. "Once. The fellows in the party wanted to throw me an eightieth birthday dinner. I went to the American consulate and began filling out the application for a visa. Then I came to a question on the form about whether I had ever used an alias and, if so, to list all aliases." Peters chuckled for the first time that day: "I put down the form and walked out."

"Tell me something," he said in farewell. "Was it worth it, this trip to Budapest?" Of course, I responded. I had never expected him to "confess." He laughed a second and final time. My later notes record only one final exchange before he turned to leave: "Hiss made a great mistake in suing for libel." I agreed. Then: "Use all of this wisely . . . ," a final handshake, and he was gone.

On an impulse and at a comfortable distance behind, I followed him down the street. He entered the back seat of a car that had been parked on the next block, his driver swung a U-turn through the crowded downtown traffic, and drove off.

GUADALAJARA, 1975: SYLVIA

Air France from New York to Guadalajara. A 1947 Studebaker taxi to the village on nearby Lake Chapala. From the square, dead-center in the village with its six thousand Mexicans and its three thousand expatriates, I asked for Sylvia: first by name, then by profession ("the photographer"), and finally, recognition when someone in the small crowd that has gathered asks you in turn by reputation ("You mean the *loca gringa* who shouts?").

Sylvia Salmi, the *loca gringa,* had made her home in the village since her husband Herbert Solow, a noted American journalist, died in 1961. Almost all of the other Americans who lived on the Lake had built homes in the hills overlooking the largely Mexican central "lowland" portion of the village. From their overlooks, they had separated themselves further from the daily dramas of life among a poor Mexican village by their high walls, security systems, and protective servants. Not Sylvia.

Sylvia had taken all of her late husband's files with her to Mexico after Solow's death. He had once been a leading anti-Stalinist radical journalist, a friend of Whittaker Chambers since the latter's college days, and a dogged investigative journalist at the time—the mid-1930s—especially in relation to Soviet espionage in the United States. When Chambers defected from the Communist underground in 1938, he came to Solow and to a few others on the anti-Stalinist left, seeking money to help support his family and to apologize for his activities while still a party operative. Through old friends of Sylvia, Professor Meyer Schapiro and Dr. Lillian Schapiro, I learned that Solow's widow had gone to Mexico, and I gambled the cost of an airline ticket for a chance to examine whatever files her late husband might have kept on the Hiss-Chambers case.

Sylvia had spent years restoring a small "inner village" block of run-down houses into a wildly elegant villa crammed with outlandish art works from several continents, which she had acquired during a long career spent photographing celebrities and world leaders for *Life* and other magazines.

After Solow's death, Sylvia moved to Lake Chapala where she rebuilt the interior of her villa while mothering a procession of visiting American friends. In a studio across the street from her home, Sylvia displayed for tourists some of the thousands of photographs that she had taken during her career and that also lined the walls of her villa: rare shots, some of them—of Péron, Nehru, Tito, Eleanor Roosevelt—taken mainly on her periodic excursions away from the Connecticut home she had shared with Solow, then an editor of a national business magazine: "Herbert would say goodbye, never knowing where I was headed, and then we began our game. One year (to show you how it worked) I flew to London, caught a plane for Oslo, and left immediately for Stockholm. I swear that, until I landed in Sweden, I hadn't the foggiest idea where I would be that evening—I was due in Paris for an assignment the next day—but there in my Stockholm hotel room (booked from the airport) was a telegram from Herbert and a bunch of flowers. God knows how he did it, but almost every time, he managed to track me down."

Sylvia had been a beautiful young woman, and the pictures others had taken of her that filled the house showed the smiling profile, full figure, and superb complexion of a young Finnish-American. The aging Sylvia who met me at the door, however, had become pudgy and wrinkled. Only her eyes and skin displayed any residue of a rapidly fading sensuality. Until that day, we had corresponded but never met, so the nature of her welcome took me by surprise.

When I reached the village, a party she had organized, apparently on my behalf, was already in progress. Sylvia grabbed my arm as I walked into the house and dragged me from guest to guest shouting my name at each one: "Allen's here to read Herbert's papers about 'the Case.' I think he has *sisoo*. (The word, I learned later, was Finnish—as Sylvia was—and her favorite descriptive, translating roughly as Scandinavian *chutzpah*.)

I managed to get to Herbert Solow's files at 3 AM, thirteen hours and at least that many margaritas after my arrival. Sylvia's party—still going strong—was attended by an unending procession of resident *Norteamericanos:* a former Hollywood film producer and his wife, who ran amateur theatricals in the town while waiting for that elusive next film project to emerge; a retired screen actor with his still-boyish face, whose most unforgettable role had been his first when, as a young man, he had played opposite Marlene Dietrich in *The Blue Angel;* a pair of childless New York executives who escaped from Manhattan to this Mexican fantasy life every weekend; Sylvia's beautiful young secretary who (she said) had traded marriage to a wife-beating author of pornographic novels for a life of managing Sylvia's volatile moods and mercurial Mexican lovers; and Lake Chapala's own former private investigator who had turned his case file into a profitable second career writing detective stories. Through the door they came, along with dozens more, each a part of Sylvia's adopted "post-Herbert" family to be put on display for her visitor.

My notes for that day show that, finally, I declined another drink and retired to the top-floor guest apartment overlooking Lake Chapala, rooms that housed Solow's personal papers. I removed the contents of four file drawers and, while urgently chugging down mug after mug of coffee, began reading through the yellowing pages. It was immediately clear that Herbert's files were invaluable for an understanding of the case. Struggling for sobriety, I read through folder after folder on Soviet espionage activity in the United States collected by Sylvia's methodological late husband through numerous interviews with Communist defectors, anti-Stalinist radicals, labor leaders, and other sources. Solow's card file on possible Soviet agents in America was far more detailed (and cautious in its conclusions) than the material I had received earlier that year from the

FBI's archivists after winning my Freedom of Information Act lawsuit against the bureau for its files on the case.

The most stunning "find" in Solow's papers was a systematic record he had kept of his friend Chambers' defection from the Communist Party, a scholar's bonanza: affidavits notarized at the time of Herbert's contacts and conversations with Chambers, two unpublished articles on Soviet espionage in the United States during the late-1930s written by Chambers that Solow had tried—unsuccessfully—to sell to popular magazines, letters from Chambers to Solow while in hiding about the fearful process of breaking with the Soviet underground (Solow, considerately for my purposes, had even saved the envelopes, which allowed precise dating), and much more.

I read and took notes until dawn, when I came downstairs and shook Sylvia awake, asking somewhat plaintively if there was a xerox machine in town? "Of course," came her sleepy response. "Do you think we're hicks or something?"

As it turned out, there were several duplicating machines in the offices of brokerage firms and banks that serviced the wealthy American community on Lake Chapala, and I spent the morning reproducing those irreplaceable documents that Solow had saved bearing on the case. Why, I asked Sylvia, had he not come forward during Hiss's two trials with this material? Herbert, she speculated, although no longer either a radical or even a friend of Chambers, probably feared for his privacy and even (given the climate of opinion at the time) for his job once he became involved in the case. Others had been ruined by even innocent association with either principal, much less such deep and unique knowledge of a critical, disputed moment in the affair. Instead, Solow simply filed everything away for some future book on the case that, at the time of his death, he had just begun writing.

I stayed with Sylvia several days longer, enjoying her company but restless at my inability to return home to my study and put this new data together with other research. She had kept me there by hinting of still-undisclosed files but, finally, said: "You have it all and should probably leave. Herbert never stopped me when I left. It was what kept us together so long, when all of his friends wondered how he put up with a loon like me."

Sylvia called a taxi to take us to Guadalajara Airport—she had never learned to drive, even in Mexico, and planned to hitchhike back. She took some photographs of me before I boarded my plane but said, "I won't send them to you unless they make you look handsome, which you are not!"

I never received them. Instead she sent me a packet of photographs as rare and memorable in its way as Herbert's files, among them a picture of Solow and Leon Trotsky in Mexico during the 1937 Dewey Commission hearings investigating the Moscow Trials, another of John Dewey with Solow outside Trotsky's home, and a third of Eleanor Roosevelt taken shortly before her death, a beautifully withered woman whose anguished eyes stare back at me as I write this.

The following year, Sylvia was hospitalized after a terrible fall. She never recovered and died several days before I was to return to Lake Chapala to visit and to remove Solow's papers for safekeeping in an American university archive. Sylvia had agreed to part with the collection—her last link to Herbert—only on condition that they be stored in nearby California and that she receive a xeroxed set to put back into the file drawers.

There were three telephones in the village, none in her home, and we talked on one of these—for the last time, it turned out—shortly before her death. Sylvia promised me another party when I came, not only with my "old friends" (as she considered those who had shared margaritas and spicy tortilla chips with me last time), but with many who had not managed to come to the earlier party. Considering the crowd, I told her, I doubted that she could turn up a fresh cast of characters. "Wait and see," she said, and hung up. Days later, a phone call brought news of her death. The next day, I collected material on her life and career, phoned *The New York Times* obituary desk, and suggested that the paper run a death notice. The person to whom I spoke, however, had heard neither of Sylvia Salmi nor of Herbert Solow—nor, when I asked, of "*sisoo*"—and suggested instead a memorial advertisement.

LONDON, 1974: THE EXPATRIATES

Their Hamstead home had once belonged to Ramsay Macdonald, the British prime minister. The books, paintings, sculptures, poster art, and artifacts jammed into every corner of the house told their own story of a lifetime's friendships with both artists and political activists.

I had come to see the lady of the house, Ella Winter, a self-described rebel girl for five decades, but I found her husband waiting to greet me at the door. A cheerful man with a failing memory, Donald Ogden Stewart had been one of Hollywood's most successful screenwriters and humorists in the 1930s and '40s until a House Un-American Activities Committee investigation sent this gentle "fellow traveler," as the term was then used, into permanent British exile. Winter, born in England, had accompanied him, her career already crowded with political and literary involvements on four continents that dated back to the First World War. At the Versailles Peace Conference in 1919, she had met and later married her first husband, Lincoln Steffens, then America's most popular muckraking journalist, a marriage that lasted until his death during the Thirties. At seventy, Ella Winter had supported revolutionary governments first in the Soviet Union after the Bolshevik Revolution and then in China, Africa, and elsewhere.

She bustled through the house, displaying for my benefit its extraordinary trophies, the accumulation of a life spent amidst many of the century's great artists and noted revolutionaries. Original Picassos and Modiglianis—personal gifts from the painters—hung above prized Chinese statuary acquired during the Communist takeover period (Mao and his colleagues were also counted among her friends), modern Nigerian paintings, and an occasional long-forgotten landmark of vividly dramatic American "proletarian art."

"Did I know [Chambers] during his Communist days in the Thirties?" she began. "Of course I did! That bastard tried without success to get me to spy for him, but a friend on *The Daily Worker* warned me off. He tried several times. Once he even asked me to filch papers in Washington from the desk of my friend Bill Bullitt, whom Roosevelt had just appointed our first ambassador to the Soviet Union. Naturally I refused." (Her first husband, Steffens, had praised Chambers in the mid-1930s for some short stories he published in *The New Masses* as America's best young "proletarian writer" and had visited him in New York.)

Ella Winter had never joined the Communist Party but avowed: "I'm fairly well known as a 'Red.'" Old friendships, however, and not politics absorbed her recollections that day. She described her work during the Thirties in the United States as a fundraiser and publicist for radical causes, recalling at one point a millionaire friend and supporter. He had once invited England's Edward VII and Wallis Simpson, Winter recalled, to spend their wedding night at his country home in France, where he watched their love-making through a one-way mirror.

Was this story really true, I asked? Who knows, she responded, but the millionaire had once asked her to make love in front of such a one-way mirror in his Manhattan apartment. "Did you?" She smiled but never responded, since at that moment, her husband entered the room and launched into his own prolonged account of a lost girlfriend early in the century. Don Stewart had driven up to Northampton from New Haven, a newly minted Yalie, only to be thrown out of a Smith College prom for kissing a young woman in public. Ella Winter flashed an annoyed glance in his direction and interrupted his story: "Thank you, dear, but our guest came to talk to *me*."

CONNECTICUT, 1975: THE LITERARY AGENT

Months after my Budapest meeting with Josef Peters, I mentioned the encounter to an old acquaintance of his, Maxim Lieber, an elderly and ailing figure who had been perhaps the most prominent authors' agent for young radical writers in the United States during the 1930s and '40s—and, also, close to the Communist Party. Lieber's life, both personal and professional, had been tragically altered by his peripheral involvement in the Hiss-Chambers case. He was perhaps its foremost victim on the American Left except, of course, for Alger Hiss himself.

Lieber described his experiences reluctantly when I came to visit him at his home near Hartford, displaying the inevitable hesitation that besets a memory jolted by two severe strokes. Unlike so many characters in the case whom I had met, he looked his age, although atop a weakened body was a ravaged face that could not quite restrain a cheerful glint when talking about earlier, happier times. Lieber would pause in mid-sentence occasionally when the effort to sustain reminiscence became too difficult and, irritated, would start again until he gained control of the memory.

"The only thing I bore against Chambers," he observed sadly of his former friend, whose allegations against Hiss had begun the drama, "was that he exposed a lot of honest, decent, dedicated people." For years, the two "agents"—one in the publishing world and the other in a more covert realm—had shared common interest in writers, artists, music, and chess.

When the case broke in 1948, Lieber was harassed with inquiries for information both from FBI agents and from defense lawyers. J. Edgar Hoover's men inflicted immediate damage upon him, warning his clients—including some who had become famous by then—to expect constant questioning themselves if they continued to be represented by their uncooperative agent. Once Hiss was convicted, life became even more difficult: "The party said, 'Get the hell out of here; get the hell out of here. Do you want to go to jail?' They were afraid that I was involved. . . . So I closed my agency and took my family to Mexico." And, from Mexico to Poland. The literary agent's wife and daughter, now sole support of the family, hovered protectively as we talked, presumably fearful that somehow even this interview conducted a quarter-century after the case might add to their burdens. They had some justification. Local FBI agents had brought Lieber to their office only a few years earlier, after his return from Poland—and decades after Hiss's conviction—urging him even then to "talk." The former literary agent seemed nonetheless pleased to have a visitor and to talk about the period before his crippling strokes.

What had happened to his agency's records, I asked, an extraordinary file of American literary radicalism seen through the careers of such writers as Erskine Caldwell, Jack Conroy, Albert Halper, Joseph Freeman, Josephine Herbst, and

Grace Lumpkin—all clients of Lieber's? (For a time, at least until friends of a special new client discovered Lieber's links to the Communist Party, he had even represented Leon Trotsky!) "My files were destroyed by the party when we went to Mexico. . . . The American Communist Party had a representative in Mexico. . . . He lives in New York now and is very wealthy. He sent me to the Czech Embassy, and they had me fill out the application forms for residence. They discovered that I had been born in Poland. 'You should go to Poland, then,' they told me. That's how I went to Poland." In Poland, the literary agent and his family lived as honored guests for over a decade, until the Six Day War in 1967 again shattered his life. He watched anxiously as the Polish government sponsored anti-Semitic protests after Israel defeated the Arab armies. Eventually the persecution of Polish Jews touched his own life. Friends avoided him, his children—grown by then—suffered ostracism, and he decided to return to the United States: "All of my adult life since the Twenties, I had been a loyal Communist, remaining in the party when many of my friends left—some because of Trotsky's assassination, some because of the Moscow Trials and the Nazi-Soviet Pact, some because of the Russian invasion of Hungary in 1956. As for myself, I rationalized everything. . . . We were naive, so naive. Communism-socialism was my Eden. I believed everyone should have enough to eat, good shelter, be happy. Then, the Six-Day War comes and suddenly, I'm nothing but a Jew to the Poles. Not an old-timer Communist—a Jew."

Was he still a Communist, I asked? He laughed: "We learned about the New Class for ourselves in Poland in the 1960s. The people were treated like dirt, while Brezhnev had his dachas and his five limousines. You had to see it for yourself."

JERUSALEM, 1977: NADYA

The daughter, Maya, had met me in downtown Jerusalem for the hour-long bus ride to her apartment in a housing project for Russian immigrants outside the city. Her mother, Nadya Ulanovskaya, and I had corresponded, but this would be our first meeting.

When Maya opened the apartment door and I caught my first glimpse of the spymaster's wife, I restrained an impulse to laugh. Either all Jewish grandmothers of that generation looked alike—or my own "bubba" had a twin sister! My parents and my mother's mother had come to America from Czarist Russia early in the twentieth century, and my late grandmother had the same quiet smile, pursed lips, and melancholic expression as the tiny, chain-smoking seventy-three-year-old who stubbed out her cigarette and rose to greet me.

Nadya's late husband, Alexander Ulanovski, had directed Soviet Military Intelligence (GRU) operations in the United States from 1931 to 1934 while the couple lived in New York City. Nadya shared Alexander's underground assignments, and one of the young American Communist agents whose work they directed was Whittaker Chambers. I had come to Jerusalem to meet with Nadya to discuss details of Soviet "secret work" in the United States during the 1930s but, long after I had exhausted her memory of that subject, I returned to visit in order to learn more about Nadya's remarkable life and those of her family members.

Both she and Alexander, although Jews, had begun separate careers as revolutionaries long before the Russian Revolution itself. Alexander spent several years in a Siberian penal colony early in the century where he came to know—and dislike—an abrasive Georgian named Joseph Djugashvili—"Stalin," to use his underground name.

Despite the fact that Alexander was a Menshevik—not a Bolshevik—and that neither he nor his wife ever joined the Communist Party, after the revolution they were assigned—because of years spent fighting in the Red Army during the civil wars that consolidated Bolshevik rule—to its newly created "Fourth Branch," the military intelligence unit. They worked underground during the 1920s in China, Germany, and Argentina before coming to the United States in 1931: "If you had worn a sign saying 'I AM A SPY' in America at that time," Nadya laughed, "you might still not get arrested."

Nadya and Alexander returned to the Soviet Union and inexplicably managed to survive the "Great Terror" of 1936–39, the purge years that caused so many of their friends to disappear into labor camps or death. The Nazi invasion of the Soviet Union restored for them, although bitter and alienated from the Communist Party, and many other Russians a semblance of allegiance to the regime.

Alexander served as a combat officer while Nadya found work as a translator in Moscow for American and British correspondents.

She came to know and share confidences with a number of them— C. S. Sulzberger, Walter Kerr, Drew Middleton, Larry LaSueur, and others for whom she was a highly reliable source in a secretive capital. One of them, an Australian friend named Geoffrey Blunden, told her life story (and Alexander's) in a thinly disguised 1947 novel, *A Room on the Route,* whose readership included officials of the state security services (then called the NKVD). Nadya was jailed on charges of passing state secrets to a foreigner.

First came months of solitary confinement in Moscow and, then, a fifteen-year term at hard labor, eight of which she served in several Siberian camps. Women imprisoned with Nadya later shared with Soviet scholar and dissident Vitaly Rubin descriptions of Nadya's selflessness and courage under the rigors of labor camp life. She spent much of her time bolstering the spirits of weaker inmates, and when officials at one camp threatened her with severe punishment unless she informed on other prisoners, Nadya simply refused.

After his wife's arrest in 1947, Alexander—Old Menshevik to the last—wrote to Stalin demanding Nadya's immediate release and (for good measure) sending back all of the medals he had been awarded since the revolution. The action cost him his own freedom and a ten-year sentence at hard labor. Their daughter Maya, then fifteen, nearly starved to death. A child of convicted "enemies of the state," she wandered through Moscow seeking shelter and food at friends' homes and, almost always, was turned away. Maya was herself arrested in 1951 and sent to Siberian labor camps for a twenty-five year term.

When Stalin died in 1953, the Gulag's prisons and labor camps began slowly opening their doors and releasing the wronged. It would not be until three years later, however, within weeks of one another, that Nadya, Alexander, and Maya all straggled into Moscow and found one another. In the years that followed, the family's apartment became a meeting place for dissidents (Maya had married one of their leaders). Often Nadya translated works from English and French authors for younger "oppositionists," books such as Robert Conquest's *The Great Terror,* after completing which Alexander said: "Now I can die in peace. The story is known, and it will survive."

Their roster of friends included an honor roll of the Soviet Union's "democratic movement": Sinyavsky, Daniel, Grigorenko, Bukovsky, and many less prominent figures. Nadya introduced Solzhenitsyn to some of the characters whom he would later describe in his *Gulag Archipelago.* At one point, the KGB brought her in for questioning, and she told the obviously discomfited agents: "You can't hurt me any longer."

Nadya and Alexander's grandson, Maya's child, became a Zionist at an early age—his grandparents having long ago abandoned the religion of their ancestor—and eventually persuaded his mother to emigrate with him to Israel in 1973. Nadya remained behind until her husband's death two years later, when she too left her homeland for exile in Jerusalem.

"Do you think the American government will allow me back into the country if I came with Maya to visit?" Nadya asked me at one point. "After all, I am a confessed major Soviet agent." I stared incredulously at the old woman who sat across from me, before reflecting with some embarrassment upon the provisions in our once-generous immigration laws that now barred even Marxist writers and scholars (much less underground agents) from the United States as dangerous "subversives." I recalled my conversation years earlier in Budapest with Josef Peters and replied finally: "Of course you will be allowed into the States but, first, you must list all of your aliases."*

---

*An earlier version of this essay appeared in *Encounter* magazine in June 1977.

APPENDIX

"FORGERY BY TYPEWRITER": THE PURSUIT OF CONSPIRACY, 1948–1997

[For over six decades the Hiss-Chambers case has been both a drama and a dispute. Not only must the story of the case be fully told, but the arguments concerning Hiss's guilt or innocence require thorough and careful scrutiny. Rather than injecting lengthy assessments of the different theories of conspiracy at separate points in the narrative, however, I have deferred examination of the major ones to this Appendix.—A.W.]

THE TRIALS

None of Alger Hiss's attorneys had claimed, throughout the two-year pretrial and trial period, that their client had been framed in a conspiracy that involved anyone other than Whittaker Chambers. Nor did they assert at the time that the incriminating documents were anything but genuine. Two of Hiss's lawyers, William Marbury and Edward McLean, had become persuaded that Alger could not answer many questions satisfactorily because he was probably shielding Priscilla. Although at the trials Lloyd Paul Stryker and Claude B. Cross both suggested the possibility of the FBI's having unethically coached some government witnesses—notably the Chamberses, Julian Wadleigh, and Edith Murray—they and the other Hiss attorneys accepted the genuineness of the handwritten, typed, and microfilmed State Department documents turned over by Chambers—what Thomas Murphy called his "immutable witnesses." Claude Cross, therefore, though continuing to believe Hiss innocent, told me that "it came as a great surprise" to him when, upon conviction in 1950, Hiss made his "forgery by typewriter" charge against Chambers.

In the end, the documents proved decisive in obtaining Hiss's conviction, and at neither trial was their authenticity challenged. Alger Hiss's lawyers did not dispute the evidence that he had written the notes, that the cables on the microfilm contained his initials, and that the typed documents had been produced by the Hisses' Woodstock machine (except for a single War Department document). Nor did the defense challenge the lone FBI documents examiner, Ramos Feehan, who testified at both trials that errors and similarities on all but one of the Baltimore documents (the War Department one), when compared to acknowl-edged samples of Priscilla Hiss's typing, established her Woodstock (N230099) as their source. Fearful that Feehan would identify Priscilla Hiss as the typist and not simply peg Woodstock N230099 as the typewriter, neither Stryker nor Cross questioned him on that crucial matter. Two of the defense documents examiners had named Priscilla as the probable typist after having obtained samples of her typing from another Woodstock, and the Hiss attorneys did not know that the bureau's experts had been more cautious on this point, if only because they lacked comparable recent samples.

Instead Alger Hiss's lawyers argued that the Hisses had given their Woodstock to the Catletts in December 1937, before the documents were typed between January and April 1938. But the Catletts, when talking candidly with McLean and other defense lawyers, said that they had most likely received the typewriter after April 1938. Moreover, unknown to the defense lawyers, Mike Catlett and Donald Hiss had located *the* Woodstock at Ira Lockey's home by February 1949, two months before Edward McLean, in an independent search, tracked the machine down, no thanks to Catlett or Alger's brother.

Defense lawyers, therefore, tried to explain away the "immutable witnesses" in several ways. One argument ran: Hiss's attorneys, not Chambers, had submitted the handwritten and typed material to the Justice Department in November 1948 and had retrieved the Woodstock after a long search, hardly the acts (the defense attorneys avowed) of a guilty person. Chambers's possession of the documents, therefore, had an explanation different from the obvious one: Either he managed somehow to obtain Woodstock N230099 after the Hisses had disposed of it; or he had somehow used the machine even while it remained in Hiss's home but without the latter's knowledge; or he received the State Department records from his other source at the department—Julian Wadleigh, aided by some still-unknown "Mr. X" in the Far Eastern Division.

Although various possible conspiratorial explanations for the documents were broached during 1948–49, most came directly from Alger Hiss and were either rejected by his lawyers or disproved by the facts. Thus in December 1948 Henry Collins sent Tabitha Petran to McLean with the suggestion that the documents might have come from "German sources," specifically the files of a Baron von Weizaeker. "She implied," wrote McLean on December 30, "that her informant was a German spy." (Petran had been one of Maus Darling's associates at *Time,* mentioned several times in Darling's letters to Cowley, in the abortive 1942 effort to attack Chambers.) Hiss, aided by Telford Taylor, a friend from AAA days and a prosecutor at the Nuremberg war-crimes trials, put John F. Davis on the Weizaeker lead. (The following 1949 letters in the defense files describe the process: Hiss to Davis, January 19 and January 27; Davis to Hiss, January 25 and February 25; Davis to Taylor, January 24.)

In late 1948 Hiss suggested a second alternative explanation for the documents: "Hiss told me some time ago," McLean wrote on January 17, 1949, "that he was at the San Francisco Conference in 1945 when the Amerasia scandal broke and that Stettinius told him that he had seen some of the papers taken from [Philip] Jaffe [who then edited the magazine *Amerasia*, in whose offices scores of classified government documents were seized] and that they included papers from Stettinius's office and from Hiss's office. I have asked Hiss to find out all he can about this and I have asked John Davis to try and find out from the House Committee whether it has any record of the documents which were involved." McLean interviewed Jaffe and others involved in the affair, while Davis probed in Washington. Both men satisfied themselves that Chambers's documents could not have come from the batch seized at *Amerasia* (which would have assumed government complicity in a plot against Hiss), and Davis's inquiries into the Baron von Weizaeker possibility proved similarly fruitless.

Thus Hiss had failed to show that the documents had come from tainted sources. But he then began arguing that Chambers had plotted to frame him with the material, an assertion Hiss made even during his December 1948 appearances before the FBI and the grand jury. There he first raised a forerunner of the "forgery by typewriter" theory. On December 15, indictment day, Hiss theorized that Chambers had sneaked into his home and typed the incriminating material on his machine, a notion that bemused the jurors. In defense memos the following year Hiss continued to raise the possibility. His attorneys decided, however, to pursue other strategies.

THE MOTION FOR A NEW TRIAL

Not until Chester Lane entered the case in January 1950, after Hiss's conviction, did the charge of a conspiracy become central to defense arguments. John F. Davis had suggested to McLean the previous year, in a September 8 letter, that the defense hire a technician to construct a Woodstock identical to N230099, prior to the second trial. Davis's letter outlined the "forgery by typewriter" theory: that someone constructed a phony machine using samples of Priscilla Hiss's typing from the 1930s, after which the incriminating Baltimore documents were typed in imitation of her personal typing. Both McLean and Cross rejected Davis's plan, and it was left to Chester Lane to implement the strategy.

In 1951, while preparing his motion for a new trial, Lane not only engaged new experts to examine the Baltimore documents but, at the same time, hired Martin Tytell, an authority on typewriter analysis, to construct a replica of Woodstock N230099. It took Tytell well over a year to build a machine that came close to matching the specimens turned out by N230099 but still not exactly. The one

professional documents examiner hired by Lane, Elizabeth McCarthy, acknowledged: "I am not prepared to say that the duplication between the two machines
is even yet complete to the highest degree of accuracy and in fact I know that
there are still a small number of characters sufficiently dissimilar so that in the
light of the careful observation I have had occasion to give to samples from the
two machines during the progress of the experiment I should myself find it possible to distinguish between the product of the two machines." Still, McCarthy
argued that an expert—in the end—"would find it difficult if not impossible to
distinguish" between samples from the two machines and that, in any event, FBI
examiner Ramos Feehan's trial testimony, identifying the machine on the basis
of only ten characters in the two sets of documents [the Baltimore stolen ones
and the 'Hiss standards'] is absolutely worthless." (Feehan showed in a subsequent affidavit, however, that at the trial he had been asked to testify only about
"some of the evidence"—that is, ten characters—but had actually tested *every*
letter prior to completing his analysis, a defense mistake in the motion for a new
trial that Judge Henry Goddard termed proceeding "on an erroneous elementary
assumption.")

Nor did Chester Lane and his associates describe precisely in their brief and
accompanying affidavits the background of Martin Tytell's experiment. Both
Lane and Tytell asserted that only "after many months" and numerous rejec-
tions by other experts did Lane manage to hire Elizabeth McCarthy, and the latter's January 22, 1952, affidavit pinned this date down: "In the earlier part of
this year I was consulted by Chester T. Lane" about the typewriter construction.
But Claude Cross had written to Lane early in the previous year, on February 1,
1951: "I telephoned to Miss Elizabeth McCarthy . . . who said that she would be
glad to work on the matter. She could not come over until Sunday. . . . I gave
her your name, address, and telephone number." After months spent working
with Tytell to improve the samples turned out by the phony machine (Manice de
F. Lockwood, who also labored on the project, said that Tytell went "font blind"
at one point because of the difficulties), Lane wrote McCarthy on December 18,
1951, enclosing a check "in partial payment of your recent bill."

Thus the Tytell machine failed to match exactly the specimens from Woodstock N230099, but not for lack of time or expert effort. McCarthy acknowledged
as much in a later interview: "She only came into the case some five or six months
after Mr. Tytell began working," runs the summary of the interview, confirming a
March–April 1951 date for this. "She went to Lane's office to examine the results
of his efforts—it took her only fifteen minutes to decide that the results were no
good at all. She didn't even need to magnify the typing to see all the differences
from the original. From then on she went almost weekly down to New York to
work with Tytell. She is sure that she is the only expert who could tell the final
results from the original, and that only because she was so intimately involved
for so long." Yet even McCarthy's final affidavit acknowledged the differences

between the two sets of samples, and the FBI documents examiners found many others neglected by McCarthy and the second Hiss expert, Evelyn Ehrlich, who specialized not in documents analysis but in art forgeries.

Lane's experts also claimed that spectroscopic and internal analysis of the Baltimore documents showed, first, that they were the product of several different typists other than Mrs. Hiss and, second, that they could not have been kept for ten years in a dumbwaiter-shaft package as Chambers claimed. An analysis of the soldering and internal construction of the machine also revealed, to one defense expert, that Woodstock N230099 was a fake, painstakingly constructed at some later date, and that the Baltimore documents might not have been typed even on this fake machine. But government analysts showed that paint stains on the envelope in which the documents had been kept matched those taken from inside the dumbwaiter, and other tests disputed almost every defense contention in the motion for a new trial. A Woodstock factory manager, for example, criticized the defense expert's understanding of Woodstock manufacturing procedures and stated that the characteristics found on N230099 were "not abnormal" but in line with established production methods at the time. An FBI laboratory examiner challenged the defense's spectroscopic evaluation of the typing paper, and pointed out also that claims for more than one typist were based upon an assumption that the typing displayed (in McCarthy's words) the characteristics of "two typists, whose work varied sharply in evenness of pressure, typing skill, mechanical understanding and control of the machine, style habits, and other similar respects." Although this might be true of an experienced typist, one who regularly transcribed significant amounts of material, the FBI affidavit noted that "these [factors] certainly cannot be applied to an inexperienced typist who is copying documents," or to a person who typed irregularly, where variations would be greater. Also, an FBI lab study showed soldering done on N230099 to be normal and similar to that on the machine rented by the defense early in 1949.

Government attorneys also asked how Chambers could have produced by himself in several months (i.e., between August and November 1948) a phony typewriter and the entire array of doctored evidence when it had taken Hiss's experts, working full-time, well over a year to construct only a typewriter that was not a perfect copy.

Lane's motion for a new trial touched also on other aspects of the case. He produced an affidavit by Paul Willert of Oxford University Press, for example, pointing out that Chambers had begun working on the translation of *Dunant* in February 1938 and, therefore, presumably must have broken with the CP underground by then. If this was true, how could he have continued collecting government documents from Hiss and others through April 1938? Only with later evidence that Chambers obtained the translation while preparing for his break (this material is described at length in Chapter IX) has this puzzling question finally been resolved.

But the heart of the motion lay in its assertion of "forgery by typewriter," illustrated by Tytell's machine and the accompanying affidavits. Arguments on both sides, defense and government, turned often on questions of intention and strategy: for example, if a fake had been produced to turn out the documents, why plant it deliberately where the defense might find (and presumably examine) it? Hiss later reasserted the "forgery by typewriter" argument, concluding *In the Court of Public Opinion* with a chapter summarizing Lane's appeal briefs. Subsequent writers—Fred J. Cook (*The Unfinished Story of Alger Hiss*), William Reuben (*The Honorable Mr. Nixon and the Alger Hiss Case*), and Meyer Zeligs (*Friendship and Fratricide*)—also recapitulated the theory, while effective rebuttals of the "forgery by typewriter" hypothesis appeared in works by Earl Latham (*The Communist Controversy in Washington*), and Herbert L. Packer (*Ex-Communist Witnesses*). None of these writers knew, of course, that Donald Hiss and Mike Catlett had traced the Hiss Woodstock two months before the defense lawyers independently located the machine and three months before the FBI first learned of its whereabouts. The material presented in Chapters VIII and XI concerning the "Woodstock cover-up" suggests that there were only two persons in a position to replace the Hiss machine with another Woodstock—whether one specially manufactured or simply a substitute—at a time when both defense and FBI investigators were still searching for it: Alger Hiss's brother and Mike Catlett.

In the end, Judge Goddard found the government's brief and its experts' affidavits far more compelling than those of the defense. He rejected the appeal for a new trial on July 22, 1952. Ridiculing the notion that Chambers somehow turned out a phony Woodstock on which to type the State Department documents, Goddard noted that "there is not a trace of any evidence that Chambers had the mechanical skill, tools, equipment, or material for such a difficult task. It is quite unlikely that Communist friends constructed it or provided the material, etc., for Chambers, as the defense suggests, because at that time his relationship with them was far from friendly." (One writer on the case, Ronald Seth, even suggested in *The Sleeping Truth* that the KGB had manufactured the Woodstock and other evidence for Chambers so that the latter, presumably still a KGB agent in 1948–49, could sow discord in the United States by falsely accusing Alger Hiss.)

The judge noted another major discrepancy in Lane's argument: "If Chambers had constructed a duplicate machine how would he have known where to plant it so that it would be found by Hiss? In planting a duplicate typewriter he would subject himself to the risk of the real Hiss machine being found and his entire case being destroyed. . . . In the absence of any proof and in view of the many improbabilities in the theory of the defense, a jury could not reasonably find that Chambers constructed a duplicate typewriter or that #230099 is not the Hiss machine." Those interested in evaluating the persuasiveness of Goddard's conclusions should read not only Chester Lane's motion briefs and affidavits but also those prepared by the government attorney in the case at this time, Miles J. Lane, from which Goddard drew liberally.

In moving for a new trial, neither Chester Lane nor Hiss's other lawyers spent much time challenging the genuineness of either the handwritten notes or the microfilm. Thus even if the "phony typewriter" argument had been accepted, Murphy's other "immutable witnesses" would have remained to be disposed of. Lane's entire effort, however ingenious, smacked of "alternative pleading" since, as Professor Irving Younger of the Cornell Law School pointed out: "Nothing would have been changed had the Woodstock never been found. It was by comparison with Mrs. Hiss's concededly authentic alumnae report [and a half-dozen other samples of her typing, as well as one typing sample by Stafford McQueen and another by Daisy Fansler], not by comparison with the machine McLean brought to court, that the authenticity of the State Department documents was established." Younger also reiterated a point made earlier by Goddard: "To leave the counterfeit Woodstock lying about for the defense to pick up and examine would serve only to expose the whole scheme to the risk of discovery—and for no reason. An FBI bright enough to forge typewritten documents is bright enough to destroy the instrument of forgery as soon as it has done its work."

At least two of the lawyers associated with Hiss's motion for a new trial agreed with this assessment. Thus Richard Field wrote to Helen Buttenwieser on February 8, 1952, that, although "very much impressed by the way Chester [Lane] marshalled his material," he remained "pessimistic" about the outcome because he did not consider that the information produced the "very potent evidence" needed to persuade Goddard to reopen the case. Field explained his skepticism in a later interview: "They built the new typewriter, which I thought was foolish. It was going to cost ten or eleven thousand dollars to do, and I said that what this expert essentially is saying is that . . . given samples of the work done on the original, it is possible to manufacture a typewriter that's virtually impossible to distinguish from the original. He can testify to that right now."

Nor, once Goddard had denied Lane's motion, did the attorney who prepared the earlier appeal brief, Robert M. Benjamin, think much of pursuing the "forgery by typewriter" argument. In a set of notes for Lane concerning their appeal of Goddard's denial of a new trial, apparently written (though undated) in August 1952, Benjamin pointed out that "in view of the fact that our experts say that they can still distinguish the product of Tytell's machine from the product of No. N230099, I do not think that we can make effective use, on any appeal, of the Government's failure to accept our challenge [for a comparison testing of the two machines] . . . since the defense experts themselves concede that we have not succeeded in making a true duplicate." Moreover, Benjamin's letter suggested the confusion in Lane's argument over which machine—N230099 (presumably a phony) or the original typewriter—had actually produced the stolen documents.

"It is quite possible that the Baltimore documents were typed on the Hisses' own machine, and that that was still in Chambers's possession or that he had thrown it away at whatever time No. N230099 was fabricated."

Not for nothing had it proved difficult for Lane to obtain qualified experts to construct the "perfect" phony Woodstock. Prior to hiring McCarthy as a typewriter analyst, the defense had tried to employ the services of several other respected documents examiners. Those who turned down the invitation to simulate or study N230099 were such leading figures in the profession as Albert Osborne, Donald Doud, and Ordway Hilton, whose later standard study, *Scientific Examination of Questioned Documents,* gave Tytell's "forgery by typewriter" efforts roughly the same critical rating that subsequent courses in trial examination at leading law schools would afford Dr. Carl Binger's testimony under cross-examination.

SIX CONSPIRACIES IN SEARCH OF AN AUTHOR, 1948–1996

For the past 60 years, those disposed to believe Hiss innocent have generally relied on conspiracy theories, most of which made the transition from the era of McCarthy to the era of Watergate to the present roughly intact. Some of the theories are inconsistent or contradictory but have an underlying theme: that Whittaker Chambers perjured himself. Beyond that, the conspiracy scripts alternate between named and nameless plotters who not only concocted phony microfilm to stuff into Chambers's hollowed-out pumpkin, but also constructed a forged Woodstock typewriter on which to produce stolen documents. Although such scenarios have been received skeptically by most Americans, those who believed in Alger Hiss continue to launch, discard, and occasionally repeat variations on these basic plot themes. Those accused of complicity in Hiss's frame-up (other than Chambers) included J. Edgar Hoover, the FBI, Richard Nixon, the House Committee on Un-American Activities, the CIA, the KGB, Henry Luce, Isaac Don Levine, General William ("Wild Bill") Donovan of the OSS, the "China Lobby," and Horace Schmahl.

More than a dozen full-fledged conspiracy theories have been suggested. Some have proved too improbable to sustain interest even among defense loyalists. Thus Ronald Seth's "sleeping truth"—namely, that Chambers framed Hiss at the behest of the nefarious Russian agents of SMERSH [sic], who provided the necessary documents under the direction of a Kremlin agent named Mikhail Shpigelglas—was not well received. Suggestions made originally by Earl Browder and other Communists interviewed by the Hiss defense during the trials—and pursued later by one defense investigator who worked with Chester Lane—that the "Trotskyists" provided the stolen documents from a special "stolen-documents center" they kept for such purposes during the 1930s in collaboration with the Gestapo, also never took wing. (The first allegation of such a misalliance was presented during Stalin's purge trials, as an explanation of Trotsky's "perfidy.") Comparable theories over the past sixty years that the trail of skulduggery led directly to the door of the American Communist Party, the OSS, or the CLA also fell flat.

Occasionally commentators have raised unanswered questions about the case, but without arguing in favor of conspiracy. My own 1971 article in *The American Scholar* fits this category, and Richard Morris's chapter on the Hiss case in his 1952 book, *Fair Trial,* expressed in balanced fashion the writer's skepticism concerning Hiss's guilt, although Morris received assistance from the defense lawyers: "My colleague, Robert Benjamin, had considerable contact with Morris during the preparation of the book," Chester Lane wrote in October 1952.

In 1953 Earl Jowitt published *The Strange Case of Alger Hiss.* Jowitt, formerly lord chancellor and attorney general of Great Britain, reviewed numerous questions about the fairness of Hiss's trial and about unexplained aspects of the evidence. Before Doubleday published the book in the United States, it requested a number of excisions and changes in the text of the original English edition to ensure greater accuracy, after receiving complaints from friends or supporters of Whittaker Chambers concerning Jowitt's bias and his research. Rebecca West had pointed out thirty misquotations from Chambers's *Witness* and perhaps as many as one hundred factual errors in Jowitt's original edition. Jowitt, like Alistair Cooke in *A Generation on Trial,* had criticized many aspects of the American legal system, including the freedom allowed the press in reporting trials, the prosecutors' domination of grand jury actions, and the functioning of trial juries. But at the heart of Jowitt's analysis were the same doubts Hiss and his lawyers had worked to keep alive in their appeal and in Lane's motion for a new trial. The English jurist inferred strongly that the FBI sought to obtain from Chambers perjured testimony (and perhaps faked documents) in order to frame Hiss.

Despite Jowitt's assertion of "absolute impartiality," there is evidence that he received help in his project from Hiss's lawyers and shared their views. Defense researcher Elinor Ferry wrote Helen Buttenwieser from London on October 8, 1952: "Yesterday, Lord Jowitt invited me to lunch at Middle Temple. . . . From the record of the second trial, he has concluded that on the evidence, AH should not have been convicted. Moreover, he believes AH to be innocent and asked some quite penetrating questions. . . . P.S. Jowitt was extremely happy to have the House hearings—And sends his thanks."

Like Jowitt, subsequent writers such as William Reuben, Dr. Meyer Zeligs, Fred J. Cook, and John Chabot Smith received cooperation from Alger Hiss and his lawyers while developing their own conspiracy theories which, in all cases, built upon arguments first made by Hiss and his attorneys between 1948 and

1952. There have been few original theories of conspiracy since then—mainly, instead, extensive elaborations of the durable older models using newer bits of "evidence."

Hiss himself rarely shied away, either in his own volume on the case or subsequently, from suggesting the plausibility of several competing theories at once. Thus, at a May 1, 1959, meeting with historian C. Vann Woodward and others, Hiss again presented the "forgery by typewriter" argument, pointing the finger at "not more than three people" who devised the plot, particularly Chambers and Isaac Don Levine. Although Hiss specifically excluded the FBI from complicity in the scheme, he asserted (according to Woodward's notes of the meeting) that they knew of the phony Woodstock and, also, "suborned every witness in this case." Elsewhere, during the 1950s and more often in later years, Hiss assigned the bureau a more active role, either in helping to build a fake machine or in substituting one with Ira Lockey in time for the defense to "find" it.

Woodward's notes contain an intriguing passage in which Hiss described his notion of confronting Chambers at Westminster that year, something he said his lawyers had dissuaded him from doing: "I planned to go out to his farm and walk in on him and simply say . . . Why did you do it? Not that I expected much to come from that, but it would have been some satisfaction, I think. My lawyers . . . thought it was very dangerous. The man might murder me. . . . In the second place my lawyers thought that the public would construe my visit as evidence of a deep attachment. . . ."

For almost a half-century, Hiss placed great stress in lectures, radio and television appearances, and press conferences on such a "deep attachment" on Chambers's part as an explanation for the latter's supposed actions. In this version, Chambers framed Hiss because of a frustrated and unrequited homosexual passion for his adversary, something Hiss in 1949 conferences with Stryker explicitly denied having had any awareness of at the time, a denial he repeated to Woodward. But throughout the past sixty years several conspiracy theories of the case have usually been put forth at the same time, the most frequent or important of which deserve separate analysis.

1. The "Faked" or "Substituted" Woodstock: Hoover and the FBI

"As you know," Chester Lane wrote Hugh Cox in February 1951 while preparing his appeal motion, "we have been developing leads recently which indicate the possibility that the FBI did find, and now has, a different machine from ours, and that the one they have is the real Hiss machine—the machine found in Lockey's possession being a synthetic one planted on us by Chambers." To Lane, the FBI seemed the likeliest candidate for the role of coconspirator with Chambers in faking a Woodstock, if only because that agency had the technical resources to accomplish such a project. That same theme became central to Fred J. Cook's view of the Hiss case, offered in *The Unfinished Story of Alger Hiss* (1958) and in four articles written for *The Nation* between 1957 and 1973. Critics of the "forgery by typewriter" theory such as Herbert Packer and Earl Latham ridiculed the notion that Chambers had produced unaided a phony typewriter and tainted documents, but they skirted the more serious charge of FBI complicity. Yet Hiss's advocates have yet to uncover from 40,000 pages of FBI files any evidence of bureau involvement with Chambers prior to Hiss's indictment, except for widely separated interviews between 1942 and 1948. Therefore, the Hiss defenders have concentrated, from Cook's arguments to those made by John Lowenthal (*The Nation*, June 26, 1976) and Robert Sherrill (*The New York Times Book Review*, April 25, 1976), not on trying to prove without evidence that the FBI built a fake Woodstock, but on showing that the bureau had possession of the original Woodstock before Hiss's attorneys found N230099—a substituted and perhaps faked machine—or were led to it. Even if this were so, and it has never been demonstrated, it would not prove that the FBI provided the evidence to substantiate Chambers's story (a point made effectively by Packer), only that the bureau *could* have done so.

Defense supporters have relied chiefly for their view of FBI complicity upon a series of scattered reports that the FBI had "found" the typewriter, one of them in the first edition of Nixon's *Six Crises* (1962), later removed as a "researcher's error." Other such reports came from Representative John McDowell; from an official 1951 HUAC report on Soviet espionage in the United States; allegedly from the manager of the Woodstock factory (who later denied having so informed a Hiss investigator); and from FBI Assistant Director William C. Sullivan (who also later denied the assertion).

But, as I hope I have made abundantly clear, the FBI suffered from uncertainty about the Woodstock's serial number throughout its six-month search for the typewriter, and the Catletts' evasiveness during interviews with bureau agents did not simplify the task of locating N230099. No evidence has thus far surfaced from any source to show that the bureau aided, abetted, or had knowledge of "forgery by typewriter," substituted "the wrong machine," or engaged in any similar chicanery involving typewriters.

The FBI collected hundreds of Woodstocks, production dates ranging from the early 1920s to the early 1930s, but not the Hiss machine. When Hoover learned after the May 1949 interview with Claudia Catlett that defense lawyers had recovered the machine, he was furious and demanded an explanation for this further "embarrassment" to the bureau, which added to the humiliation of Chambers's having turned over the vital stolen documents not to the FBI but first to Hiss's attorneys and then to HUAC.

Both Sherrill's and Lowenthal's "substituted Woodstock" theories place great reliance upon a memo by FBI agent Boardman (described in Chapter XI) in which the latter states as a "definite possibility" that N230099 might not be the Hiss Woodstock. The FBI's initial confusion concerning the purchase date of Fansler's Woodstock (N230099)—bureau laboratory tests in December 1948 correctly determined from the typeface on documents sampled that the machine was manufactured in 1929—stemmed mainly from the testimony of Thomas Grady and Harry Martin, whose confused memories of the true purchase date, familiar both to defense and FBI investigators at the time, have been described (Chapters VIII and XI). Largely because of the Grady-Martin testimony (whose inaccuracies, when discovered, pointed to a 1929 purchase), FBI agents concluded that the Woodstock had probably been manufactured in 1928, the differences in typeface between 1928 and 1929 machines being negligible.

This minor mistake in the bureau's investigation became the starting point later for reviving the "phony Woodstock" theory by Sherrill, Lowenthal (one of Hiss's lawyers), and others. What these writers neglected to mention is the FBI's overriding concern at the time that the Hiss defense might deliberately try to produce the *wrong* Woodstock at the forthcoming perjury trial, one that tests would show had not typed the stolen documents. The bureau's fears proved groundless. When its documents examiners took typing samples from Woodstock N230099 in October 1949, five months after the memo by Boardman, the tests confirmed conclusions reached independently by earlier FBI laboratory tests and by the defense documents examiners: that the machine in question (N230099), although made in 1929, had indeed produced both Mrs. Hiss's letters from the 1930s and the typed documents turned over by Chambers. Stafford McQueen's government application form, also typed on N230099 in 1947 and tested in the FBI lab in 1949, added more weight to that conclusion.

As I wrote in a 1976 article, the FBI's pursuit of the Hiss Woodstock "leaves the Bureau reasonably open to a charge of failure (or ineptitude) rather than malevolence." And if there existed any persons with means, motive, and opportunity to "substitute" a different Woodstock for the Hiss machine in the months after Alger Hiss's indictment, the evidence offered in Chapters V, VIII, and XI indicates the possible conspirators, Mike Catlett and Donald Hiss, who for two months withheld knowledge from Alger's lawyers that the typewriter had been traced to Ira Lockey.

2. Richard Nixon, HUAC, and the "Phony Microfilm"

"[Largely] because of a young Congressman named Nixon said he believed Chambers," Alger Hiss began his statement to the press on July 31, 1975, in announcing his receipt of the "pumpkin papers" microfilm, "I was convicted of perjury when I denied the charges, and went to jail for 44 months." Nixon's role, though hardly so conclusive as Hiss alleged, was a critical one during the 1948

HUAC investigation in ways that both Nixon and Hiss distorted for their separate purposes over the years. Following Watergate, Nixon figured even more prominently in the case, rallying support for Alger Hiss among the many Americans who harbored political or personal aversions to Nixon. Hiss's advocates have argued for six decades that *somehow* Nixon's involvement "explained" the incriminating evidence against Hiss, especially the "pumpkin papers" turned over to HUAC by Chambers in December 1948 (Chapters XIV and XVI elaborate on the theme of Nixon, Hiss, and the liberal imagination).

Alger Hiss was often asked, in both public and private appearances, whether he believed that Nixon played a direct role in helping to frame him. Generally, Hiss avoided making so explicit a charge, if only because of the total absence of evidence to support it, and contented himself with a caustic dismissal of Nixon's exploitation of the case as a young and "opportunistic" politician. Still, Nixon's occasional statements helped revive interest in the case, ranging from the 1962 "researcher's error" in *Six Crises* about the FBI's having found the Woodstock, to the remark made on the Watergate tapes about HUAC's having found the typewriter (contradicting the *Six Crises* avowal but still useful to Hiss), to a statement in 1976 by John Dean. Dean asserted that Charles Colson told him Nixon said he (presumably aided by HUAC staffers and the FBI) had "built" the phony Woodstock, a claim that conflicted with *both* their earlier statements about Nixon or the FBI having "found" the machine. Alger Hiss dismissed Dean's assertion as second-hand hearsay.

But some of Hiss's supporters have been less cautious in their charges and theories about a conspiratorial role for Nixon. Thus Fred Cook in *The Nation* (April 7 and May 12, 1962) and, in 1976, Robert Sherrill in *The New York Times Book Review* reopened the argument for Nixon's possible complicity in concocting evidence against Hiss, both writers stressing the notion that Nixon had been privy to inside facts about locating the typewriter. More seriously, at a press conference in June 1975 announcing a lawsuit by Hiss and three researchers for the "pumpkin papers"—and at the subsequent July 31 press conference once the Justice Department released the microfilms—Hiss and his supporters emphasized the possibility that those documents had been fabricated. Hiss concluded his June 5, 1975, statement: "Watergate and the recent disclosure that the FBI has typed and sent faked letters designed to ruin people's careers have not lessened my eagerness to know what is contained in those files."

In an accompanying "Fact Sheet on Microfilms" distributed at the same press conference, Stephen W. Salant (litigant in a companion suit and one of the three researchers) revived charges that the initial misdating of the Eastman Kodak film by a company representative in December 1948 (see Chapter VIII) "would have meant that at least part of Chambers' evidence was fabricated." Noting that for two years he had been trying "to ascertain the production dates of those three Kodak films," Salant strongly suggested that the films would be proved forgeries.

Salant had pinned down his belief in a February 19, 1974, letter to me: "In brief, I believe that at least one of the 3 undeveloped rolls of film was produced in the 1940s, that Nixon discovered it, realized that it would discredit Chambers' story and 'lightstruck' it." Salant's theory avoids one inconvenient chronological certainty: that the three undeveloped rolls and two developed strips of film— including the one found to be "lightstruck"—were analyzed (and the lightstruck one discovered) by Veterans Administration laboratory experts the day after Chambers turned them over, and two days before Nixon returned to Washington and first saw the films.

The rumor that the microfilmed documents might have been faked spread in 1949 after publication of Stripling's book describing the initial Eastman Kodak misdating (curious candor on Stripling's part if he had been an accomplice to Nixon's chicanery or even privy to it). Further check of the company's records— and later those of Du Pont, which manufactured the remaining film—showed the overwhelming probability that all of the film had been produced in either 1937 or 1938. HUAC retained possession of the microfilm for months, mainly for political leverage against the Truman administration and not—as Salant suggests—to hide its complicity in "lightstriking" the film. Despite strenuous efforts by both the FBI and the Justice Department to acquire the microfilm, the committee relinquished the material only in May 1949, shortly before Hiss's first trial. By then FBI tests had already confirmed the genuineness of the material (Chapters VIII and XI). Efforts made by the bureau to construct a thorough chronology of the microfilm's whereabouts—and who had come into contact with it—from the moment Chambers turned it over were aimed at forestalling accusations that the film had been tampered with.

Harold Rosenwald consulted in 1949 with both Du Pont and Eastman Kodak experts and received the same information provided to the FBI months earlier. Rosenwald also learned from the Du Pont official that the microfilm "could have been preserved in a dumbwaiter under the conditions described by Chambers for as long as ten years if it had been developed before storage there," as the two State Department strips had been. Rosenwald concluded, after visiting Eastman Kodak, that there was (except for possible careless exposure) "no basis at this time for any challenge to the accuracy of Chambers's story on any technical grounds in connection with the pumpkin films."

When another Hiss attorney, Helen L. Buttenwieser, tried in 1952 to track down the original story about the misdated microfilm, M. K. Robinson, Eastman Kodak's general counsel, explained Keith B. Lewis's initial mistake:

> I have now had an opportunity to talk with the gentleman here in Rochester who received the original telephone call from . . . Washington regarding the marking on the film used in the Hiss case. . . . After he gave the young lady the original information over the phone, which turned out to be in error, he thought about the matter some more and a doubt rose in his mind as to whether

the information he had given was correct. To verify this, he called the people at Kodak Park where the original records are kept, and found that his doubt was justified, and the correct year of manufacture of the film, as indicated by the small square, was 1937. He immediately called either Mr. Lewis or his secretary and advised them of the error and of the correct year.

Robert Stripling's version of the episode, however, was incorrect in one respect. Only Du Pont—not Eastman Kodak—had used identical code markings on their film for two different years. The Eastman Kodak marking for films produced in 1944 and 1945, according to Robinson, differed from the 1937 markings: "The symbols used showing time of manufacture and slitting for the year 1944 [were] a small triangle followed by a small square; for the year 1945, a small square followed by a small circle. . . ." The actual markings on the Eastman Kodak strip of State Department microfilm, when I inspected it at the Justice Department in 1976, showed neither of the above markings, but rather that of film produced by the company in 1937, a small square—without a circle or a triangle.

As for Nixon's role in the case, the FBI files confirmed my earlier interviews with Stripling and Nicholas Vazzana, described in Chapters V and VIII. Nixon, who never admitted this fact, was told in advance by both men about Chambers's having turned over stolen typed documents to Hiss's attorneys. Not waiting to see what a HUAC subpoena for additional documents might uncover, the cautious Nixon fled Washington on a cruise-ship vacation. Once HUAC staff members had obtained the microfilm and determined its importance, Nixon hurried back to steal the headlines and to claim credit for the coup: "opportunistic" behavior surely, but hardly conspiratorial.

3. The Radical Right: Isaac Don Levine and the "Cabal"

Until his death, Alger Hiss argued the notion that the incriminating evidence against him had been manufactured under the auspices of a far-ranging conspiracy of "right-wing anti-Communists" mobilized by the journalist Isaac Don Levine. Hiss first mentioned Levine as the source of earlier charges of Communist involvement against him in an interview with the FBI several years before the case broke, and he returned to the theme in his 1959 conversation with historian C. Vann Woodward. On that occasion, according to Woodward's notes, Hiss named Levine as the chief culprit, along with Chambers, in having forged a Woodstock typewriter: "I have a theory here and a good deal of evidence to support it though nothing conclusive." Levine, according to Hiss, "was known to have visited Chambers," which was true, "and was also known to have been associated with several cases involving forged or suspicious documents."

Later, Peter H. Irons expounded on the theory of Levine's possible culpability as part of a more broadly based plot against Hiss. Irons's analysis emerged in a series of letters and articles—mainly unpublished, but copies went into the Hiss defense files and also appeared in the December 1975 letters column of *Commentary*. There Irons noted "the assertion by a former private investigator hired by Hiss's lawyers in 1948 . . . that he had been hired [earlier] by a high OSS official to arrange the fabrication of a forged typewriter in the Hiss case." The detective in question, Horace Schmahl, allegedly made that claim only to one Hiss investigator, Manice de F. Lockwood, whose letters record an assertion Schmahl later denied. (Conspiracy Theory Number 5, in the pages that follow, examines the tangled role of Horace Schmahl in the Hiss case.)

In 1974 letters to Hiss (on April 26, May 24, and May 20, the latter enclosing Irons's "tentative . . . hypotheses for future exploration" in the form of "Notes on the Origins of the Hiss Case") and in letters and conversations with me in the mid-1970s, Irons described the outlines of what appeared to be a far less "tentative" theory, one he elaborated in greater detail in a twenty-five-page essay titled "Pumpkin Papers and Watergate Tapes" and in fifteen pages of "Notes on the Roles of Horace W. Schmahl, Adam Kunze and William J. Donovan in the Hiss Case." Briefly—since the plot is intricate and the conspirators many—Irons speculated that Schmahl and perhaps others had been hired by General William Donovan, former head of the OSS, between the end of World War II and the August 1948 HUAC hearings to build the phony Woodstock for later use against Hiss. The documents used in the scheme, Irons theorized, might have come from the *Amerasia* papers (a return to an older theory), and the general purpose of the plot—in which purported "China Lobby" and other right-wing elements figured—was to stir anti-Communist sentiment by destroying the career of Hiss, who supposedly had been identified in the public mind as a symbol of both New Deal social reform and a policy of Soviet-American friendship culminating in the Yalta "sellout."

Robert Sherrill's 1976 review picked up on some but not all of Irons's cast of possible conspirators: Schmahl, Donovan, Adam Kunze (an allegedly pro-Nazi typewriter-store owner), Isaac Don Levine, HUAC staff member Ben Mandel, several "reactionary" security officers at State, and various China Lobby and other right-wing anti-Communists—all of whom were potential actors in the plot to frame Alger Hiss. Sherrill carried Irons's "tentative . . . hypotheses" even further, implicating in the scheme Chambers, Nixon, Hoover, Henry Luce, the FBI, HUAC, *Time,* and the Communist Party. The absence of any evidence encouraged, rather than restrained, the "conspiracy fever" of both writers. Neither Irons nor Sherrill has produced a comprehensive study of the Hiss case. Irons's views have been made known largely through writings deposited in the Hiss defense files, in a brief law-journal paper on the FBI files, and in the letters columns of several magazines. In the November 1976 issue of *Law Library Journal* Irons retreated a bit from his conspiracy theory, at least in this erroneous but suggestive passage:

The FBI and State Department files also demonstrate conclusively that the impetus for the charges against Hiss, and for Chambers' August 1948 appearance before the House Un-American Activities Committee, came from the leaders of the China Lobby. In fact, the leading forces behind Chambers' testimony were China Lobby leaders on the staffs of the Un-American Activities Committee and the National Catholic Welfare Conference, both [sic] of whom were close associates of both Congressman Nixon and informants of the FBI. This historical evidence does not, of course, bear on Hiss' guilt or innocence, but it does illuminate the genesis of the campaign against Hiss, which was based on his role at Yalta and in formulating Far Eastern policy in the State Department during the war, a policy perceived as a sell-out by the China Lobby.

Irons was wrong about the "genesis" of the HUAC hearings (see Chapters I and X). Also, several times in 1948–49 Hiss described himself as a strong supporter of the Nationalist Chinese government while serving as Hornbeck's adviser during the war, and he disassociated himself from any connection with those advisers inside China who urged a coalition government including the Communists. Under the circumstances, he made a curious target for General Donovan and the many others whom Irons termed "China Lobby leaders."

4. Chambers as Paranoid: The Revenge Motif

"Was there any evidence of homosexuality involving Chambers?" Alger Hiss was asked at the 1959 gathering recorded by C. Vann Woodward's notes. "Very definitely yes," he replied. "In fact my lawyers had witnesses who were fully prepared to testify to Chambers's advances to them which they repulsed. But the lawyers decided not to introduce this evidence for fear of the jury reaction and public relations." Hiss's reply distorts the circumstances under which McLean and Stryker decided not to use the one witness who would testify to this effect, an ex-Communist whose motives might have been thought suspect by jurors. Most important, Hiss's attorneys in 1949 worried about the inevitable prosecution counterassault, which might have placed Timothy Hobson on the stand. For those reasons, and for those reasons only, did the defense lawyers and analysts reluctantly abandon Rosenwald's proposal to make homosexuality a major issue in their attack on Chambers's credibility.

Hiss's hostess at the 1959 reception pursued her inquiry into the theme: "Did Chambers have any homosexual impulses toward you?" "Chambers never made any homosexual advances to me. His attitude toward me, however, and his relations were strange and I did not understand them. There were many evidences of his identifying himself with me. . . . My guess is that he had some obscure kind of love attachment . . . about me, and he came to hate my wife." "Then how would he come to wish to injure and ruin you?" asked his questioner, raising the theme of Chambers's alleged motivation for having perjured himself about Hiss, a question that had surfaced first in the inquiries of HUAC members eleven years earlier. "That is something I have never understood. . . . It may have been because of his feeling of rejection and exclusion. . . . Perhaps the psychoanalyst could find some evidence of a transfer of guilt to me, guilt of his own in connection with his brother [Richard's suicide]. . . ."

At the time of the trials Hiss and some of his attorneys explored a variety of rumors concerning the state of Chambers's psyche in order to "explain" his testimony. Ultimately, they rejected the unproved tales of alcoholism and plain lunacy, also deferring use of the half-supported allegations of homosexuality in favor of an elaborate and somewhat Gothic tale of family instability, suicidal tendencies, and paranoid revenge. In this version, offered by Dr. Binger at the second trial and described earlier in Harold Rosenwald's memos on "unconscious motivation," Chambers had schemed his revenge against Hiss since the time in the 1930s when the latter allegedly rejected his overtures. Hiss's lawyers spread through the records of both trials a detailed—if highly selective—account of Chambers's purported psychopathology. The prosecution ridiculed these maneuvers, effectively so far as the jury was concerned, but the psychoanalytic theories themselves have survived in subsequent accounts of the case.

They received elaborate restatement in 1967 in an "objective psychobiography" by Dr. Meyer Zeligs, *Friendship and Fratricide*. Zeligs was criticized by several reviewers, notably in the February 23, 1967, *New York Review of Books* by Professor Meyer Schapiro, Chambers's friend but also one of the world's leading scholars on the subject of psychoanalysis and artistic personality. Both Zeligs and his mentor, Dr. Binger, drew sweeping conclusions about Chambers's adult personality largely from a carefully culled account of childhood experiences.

The Binger-Zeligs analysis underwent refurbishing with publication of John Chabot Smith's *Alger Hiss: The True Story* (1976), which restated the earlier analytic themes. Chambers's, in Smith's words (quoting Binger), was a "psychopathic personality" (see Chapter XIII for the colloquy between Murphy and Binger on the impreciseness of that term) prone to "extraordinary fantasies," a "nobody from nowhere" who nursed "a sense of personal resentment and desire for revenge" against Hiss for having slighted overtures toward friendship in 1935 and 1936. In this view, Chambers had "a mind deranged by tragic and destructive experiences throughout his early life." Neither the two psychiatrists nor Smith went into Hiss's own traumatic youth as having possibly induced distortions of normal personality growth such as those they detected in Chambers. Thus, in Hiss's case, the fact that his father slit his throat when Alger was three, that his mother may have neglected him, that Hiss's older and revered brother died after a wasted youth, and that his favorite sister poisoned herself—all of this, according to Binger and Zeligs, produced a splendid character strengthened by adversity, while, by contrast, bizarre family experiences in Chambers's case purportedly unhinged the latter's moral sensibilities.

"Having appointed myself the biographer of such a unique pair of adversaries, Zeligs told his readers in the Preface, "it was incumbent on me to maintain careful analytic neutrality toward them." In a May 19, 1960, letter to Helen Buttenwieser the psychoanalyst wrote "on the advice of Alger Hiss," whom he had first seen several weeks earlier, requesting copies of the trial transcripts and announcing the plan for his "careful clinical and factual psychoanalytic investigation." The following year he wrote Claude B. Cross (on March 13): "I can readily appreciate your strong sentiments about Mr. Hiss's innocence and must say that I share the same conviction." Yet, in a May 11, 1962, interview with Herbert Solow, transcribed verbatim by Solow's secretary, we find this passage:

SOLOW: Hiss surely is aware you think he is innocent.
ZELIGS: I think he is so convinced of his own innocence that he is convinced that anybody who approaches this psychologically must also be convinced.

Release by the FBI in 1976 of Chambers's voluntary 1949 statement concerning his past homosexual experiences (described in Chapter XI) revived interest in the Binger-Zeligs "revenge motif," and John Chabot Smith used their psychoanalytic conclusions in his own book, also researched in close cooperation with Alger Hiss. (Philip Nobile provided a description of the manner in which Smith replaced Alden Whitman as Hiss's biographer in the June 1976 issue of *More*.) Once again in 1976 Hiss himself returned to the theme, claiming that Chambers was "a spurned homosexual who testified . . . out of jealousy and resentment. (In September 1948 Hiss had written to McLean about Chambers: "I have a vague impression of boastful kinds of sexual exploits but no hint of any unnatural sex interests.") But attempting to "smear" Chambers as a homosexual today, Rosenwald's strategy of 1949, may prove less persuasive to Hiss's sympathizers today than sixty years ago.

5. The Double Agent: Horace Schmahl, Mystery Man

Horace Schmahl, whose activities on behalf of Edward McLean are chronicled in Chapters V, VIII, and XI, worked for McLean from October 1948 to sometime in February 1949 (evidence in the defense files contradicts Hiss's assertion that Schmahl worked without written directives from McLean). Beginning in December 1948, Schmahl told several people whom he interviewed—including Harry Martin, Martin's lawyer, and Grace Lumpkin—that (in Martin's words) "there is some doubt in his [Schmahl's] mind as to Hiss's innocence since . . . Hiss's story concerning the typewriter and 'several other points' has been found to be inaccurate. . . . Schmahl did state that if Hiss were proven wrong on 'one more thing' his firm would withdraw from the case." That same month, December 1948, McLean at least twice offered the bureau Schmahl's services in the search for the Hiss typewriter and samples of Priscilla's typing. FBI agents turned down this offer of cooperation. Encouraged by McLean, however, Schmahl made direct offers of such assistance to FBI agents in Philadelphia, where his well-publicized "investigation" crossed paths several times with the more discreet bureau inquiries, but again the FBI kept him at arm's length.

In January and February 1949 Schmahl spent most of his time not searching for the Woodstock (as Hiss and his supporters later claimed) but (as the defense files document) pursuing leads on McLean's behalf concerning Chambers's alleged homosexuality. Schmahl then left McLean's employ, he told FBI agent J. T. Hilsbos on February 15, because "there was insufficient money involved . . . he did not believe in the case, and differences with [the detective agency head] on other investigative matters." Schmahl admitted to Hilsbos "that actually [he] has no papers reflecting his investigations other than copies of his expense accounts. . . ." But he offered to furnish the bureau "any information within the bounds of ethics." But Hilsbos advised his superiors against accepting Schmahl's offer, "as it is not believed that he can furnish any information" except possibly news concerning defense pretrial strategy. Moreover, alluding to the FBI's problems with Schmahl the previous December, Hilsbos noted that "at no time has he volunteered any information of value." New York FBI Field Office Director Belmont agreed with Hilsbos in a marginal notation to this February 16 memo:

> We should not encourage him [Schmahl] in any way in this case. The defense attorneys could charge us with unethical tactics. He has no info of value from what we know.

Although bureau agents avoided Schmahl, he again offered his help the following month, conceding that his information "was not too important." Schmahl had phoned on March 22 to state that McLean had asked him to undertake one final, routine assignment, but the agent with whom he dealt observed that Schmahl had not been "pressed to disclose anything concerning his relations with McLean." Prosecutor Thomas Murphy proved less fastidious. He interviewed Schmahl in June, at which time the detective told him about the Hiss lawyers' rental of a Woodstock from the Kunze typewriter firm earlier in the year. (Had Schmahl and Kunze conspired to frame Hiss, as one conspiracy theory asserts, Schmahl's action in volunteering this tidbit would have been supreme folly.) On September 22, an FBI memo described this minor item as "the most significant information revealed by Schmahl," stark corroboration of the man's insignificance as a government informant.

In 1950 Harold Rosenwald and Manice de F. Lockwood, both assisting Chester Lane on his motion for a new trial, tried to obtain from Schmahl an affidavit stating that Harry Martin told him the Fansler Woodstock had been purchased in 1928. Schmahl was reluctant to sign the affidavit and told Rosenwald that all of his reports on the case were in the custody of "Steve" Broady, whose detective firm had employed him at the time. Rosenwald returned the next month and Schmahl reported the visit to the FBI on December 7, 1950. According to Schmahl, when he again declined to sign the affidavit, Rosenwald said "that they might get rough with him, also indicating that Hiss had some very important people backing [him], and mentioned that Senator Lehman was interested."

While Chester Lane prepared his motion for a new trial, he recorded a memo on January 29, 1952, about a telephone call he had received earlier that day from a man who identified himself only as "Morrow" (not Chambers's friend Felix Morrow). The man said he was passing along information on behalf of someone else "who is anxious for you to have these facts." According to "Morrow," Horace Schmahl had made a deal with the FBI shortly after he began working for the defense. In return for dropping pending charges against him for impersonating an FBI agent (Schmahl actually had never been indicted for such an offense), "he agreed to turn over his investigative reports in the Hiss case to them. In fact, every report he made to the defense was turned over by him to the FBI." Also, more ominously, "Morrow" continued: "I think if you look into this you will find that Schmahl was implicated with the typewriter."

The report of Lane's anonymous informant remained in the Hiss defense files, unexplored for over a decade. Then, in the "mid-1960s," according to a September 12, 1973, unsigned memo in those files, "a retired investigator named Bretnall said he had been on Broady's staff assigned to the Hiss investigations. He reported that he found that his colleague, Schmahl, was helping the other side and so he [Bretnall] got out of the assignment. Bretnall said he had learned that the fake typewriter [i.e., the one found by McLean in April 1949] had been produced in Adam Kunze's shop and he claimed Schmahl had helped." But "Bretnall" remained as elusive a figure as "Morrow'" had been, and his supposed allegations were unsupported by any documentation, so that not even an affidavit or separate memo on the "interview" with "Bretnall" appeared in any of the Hiss defense files I examined.

The September 12, 1973, memo continued: "Kunze's widow . . . reported to a representative of Hiss's that the FBI had 'found' the typewriter in her husband's shop." The assertion referred to a report by undercover investigator Elizabeth Grey Hamilton, who conducted more than a dozen interviews under false pretenses with Bessie Meade (Mrs. Adam Kunze) while an investigator for Hiss and Manice de F. Lockwood in 1965. The results of Hamilton's interviews with Meade, outlined in her reports, fail to provide even the clear-cut hearsay referred to in the 1973 memo, as Hamilton herself acknowledged.

But the unsigned September 12, 1973, memo continued "documenting" the case against Horace Schmahl: "In the latter part of August of this year,

Schmahl spent some hours with a Hiss representative, was affable and friendly and talked at length. He now lives in Port Everglades, Florida." Schmahl ran a boatyard there and, though the memo does not mention this fact, the "Hiss representative," Lockwood, visited Schmahl several times under the pretext of conducting business connected with the boatyard (Lockwood sent reports of these 1973 interviews to Hiss on August 10, August 12, and October 5). According to Lockwood's account, summarized in the September 12 memo, Schmahl told this story (subsequently Schmahl broke off contact with Lockwood and denied the tale):

> He said he had been a "consultant" on Kunze's fabrication of a Woodstock typewriter. He said OSS had framed Hiss and that Donovan and Leisure [the law firm of General William Donovan] had ordered the Kunze job. He didn't know if it was completed because Kunze went "font blind." He said he had found the real Woodstock that was produced at the trial. He expressed surprise when told that the serial number did not correspond to the machine Hiss had owned. He said Chambers, not HUAC, had framed Hiss. . . . He claimed to have "monitored" Chambers in 1946 for OSS. . . . He expressed some interest in writing a book or a magazine article about his career.

(General Donovan's only known contact with the Hiss case came in October 1949 when Claude B. Cross interviewed him about Noel Field, who had been an OSS agent briefly; nor has any evidence linked his firm to Kunze or Hiss.)

One of Schmahl's other comments to Lockwood at their initial 1973 meeting was less helpful to Hiss, according to Lockwood's account. Schmahl said that the owner of the Smithtown house rented by Chambers, who claimed that Hiss had visited there, told Schmahl "that he had a picture of the Hiss's [sic] and Chambers's [sic] together" (see Chapter VI). Hiss denied making this visit.

By the time Lockwood visited Schmahl in October 1973, the latter's story had become even more muddled. Thus Lockwood's memo noted: "I asked again for the date of Kunze's work and he replied it was at about the same time he had Chambers's farm under surveillance, when he saw all the 'government cars' going in and out prior to the discovery of the 'Pumpkin.'" (Chambers had told HUAC investigators in December 1948 that he handed over the microfilms partly because he thought his farm was being watched.) Schmahl then avowed that the date was "probably later than [1946]," his earlier claim. As to the reason Donovan's firm wanted a Woodstock manufactured in 1946, Schmahl said he knew only that it had been "an experiment." Lockwood, however, sensed his host's deepening suspiciousness: "Schmahl asked me why I was so interested in the Hiss case now and I replied that it seemed highly topical in view of the present headlines from Washington. We parted on what seemed to be a less friendly tone than last time. No lunch offered. My efforts to interest him in a German yacht broker from North Carolina . . . did not seem to elicit more discussion of

Horace's business. I will follow up with him but may need more background material such as could be supplied by the G2 man. M. Lockwood." The reference to the "G2 man" remains unexplained, unless it referred to some other under-cover operative working for Hiss.

Lockwood had suggested to Schmahl that the latter should have a professional writer prepare his story, obviously with the Hiss case information prominently featured. After considering a most unlikely candidate—Hannah Arendt—the two men settled on *New Yorker* writer Thomas Whiteside, whose meeting with Lockwood to discuss the Schmahl story was recorded in a November 12, 1973, letter from Lockwood to Hiss. Whiteside apparently left unconvinced that Schmahl's alleged statements had any merit, and the story idea lay dormant until 1976, when (according to Hiss) he persuaded Jim Bishop—who had met Schmahl as an insurance adjuster assessing damages on Bishop's sunken boat—to question Schmahl about his alleged role in the Hiss case (both Hiss and Peter Irons told me they prepared questions for Bishop to use).

The pursuit of Horace Schmahl entailed considerable effort by supporters of Alger Hiss. Lockwood's contacts with Schmahl were under the guise of conduct-ing legitimate business—"Lockwood was talking business with the man," Hiss noted in an interview on June 21, 1975, "and he showed Lockwood his books"—and that same year Lockwood told me that Schrnahl was being watched by investigators operating from a panel truck outside his home. Several attempts by journalists to approach Schmahl, including Jim Bishop's alleged effort, were made in cooperation with the Hiss defense since the mid-1970s, all presumably in the hope of finding some usable evidence for the notion that Donovan ordered Alger Hiss "framed" through construction of a phony Woodstock two years before the HUAC hearings opened.

More than one thousand pages of released FBI material on Schmahl's role in the Hiss case and on his subsequent activities contain no hints of such a plot, nor do any of the reports by Schmahl in 1948–49, or those about Schmahl since that time. All we know is that Schmahl conducted a short but thorough investigation for Edward McLean. The evidence also shows that Schmahl became persuaded of Hiss's guilt and quit the investigation. After that, he passed information on the defense efforts to the FBI.

6. The "True Story": A Composite Conspiracy

Without the complicity of Whittaker Chambers, all the other alleged plotters would have lacked the vehicle to achieve their purposes. Explaining Chambers's motivation, therefore, has usually required a reliance upon the theory of "uncon-scious motivation"—that is, of paranoid revenge. But only in 1976 did virtually the entire spectrum of conspiracy theories find expression within a single volume, John Chabot Smith's *Alger Hiss: The True Story*. Because Smith adopted elements from at least six previous theories, it became possible for the first time to blend favorite bits of conspiratoriana.

Conspiracy Number 1, for Smith, is the view of a leading Communist official who claimed that Chambers was an imposter, a Stalinist Walter Mitty creating fantasies of underground Soviet espionage cells in Washington where none had existed or, if they had existed, Chambers had never participated in them. In Conspiracy Number 2, Smith appears to accept the "fantasy" as fact, arguing that Chambers was involved in such activities, but not with Hiss. Others within the State Department—that is, Julian Wadleigh—actually stole the material, Smith suggests (adopting the Stryker-Cross theory, by sneaking into Hiss's office while he was away from his desk (pp. 410–419).

Meanwhile—Conspiracies Numbers 3, 4, and 5—Smith speculates that someone helped Chambers to construct a phony Woodstock similar to Hiss's in order to type documents in Priscilla Hiss's style and then to frame her husband a decade later. For Smith, Chambers's possible collaborators in "forging" the typewriter were, variously, the FBI, HUAC (led by Nixon), and the Communist Party (pp. 429–432 and 482–483, for example). He suspects many public figures, ranging from former Secretary of State James Byrnes to financier Bernard Baruch, of minor complicity. Each one, Smith argues, had reasons to assist in the undoing of Alger Hiss (this despite the fact that Byrnes kept Hiss at State and refused to fire him in 1946 against all of Hoover's considerable pressure).

In the end, Smith puts together his own scenario (Conspiracy Number 6). He believes that Chambers stole the Hisses' Woodstock sometime during 1935 or 1936 when the latter knew Chambers as "George Crosley." After "Crosley" stole the "real" Woodstock, he substituted in its place a similar machine. The Hisses, unaware of the exchange, later gave the substituted Woodstock to the Catletts. This, then, became the typewriter recovered by Hiss's lawyers in 1949.

Chambers, according to Smith, collected the documents in 1937 and 1938 both from confederates at State other than Hiss and by going on periodic snooping trips himself to the department's Division of Communications and Records. There he salvaged memos that were about to be burned. Of course he preferred those with Alger Hiss's initials on them. Smith's theory is that Chambers was able to enter the department, and to walk unnoticed through its corridors, by using a government identification card he had acquired while working as a clerk at the National Research Project several blocks away. The fact that Chambers left this job several months before the dates on the final group of State Department documents in question adds to the implausibility of Smith's theory. He also does not confront the likelihood that a trusted employee at State such as Hiss might have found it easier than any outsider to search for documents inside the department.

Smith believes that Chambers, once he obtained the documents, either had them microfilmed by his underground associates (real spies this time and not those who, like Chambers, were living "fantasy" lives) or retyped them himself on the stolen Woodstock. The papers, of course, included notational corrections in handwriting later identified by Hiss's own experts as Alger or Priscilla Hiss's.

Once satisfied that Chambers had the "means" and "opportunity" to frame Hiss, Smith proceeds to the problem of "motive." Why did Chambers construct such an elaborate frame-up of Alger Hiss, then do nothing with it on the off chance that he might one day have use for it? Smith's answer depends upon a painfully literal rendition of the Rosenwald-Binger-Zeligs theory of "unconscious motivation," the view of Chambers as a "pathological" psychopath seeking revenge against Hiss for having slighted his overtures of friendship in 1935 and 1936. Among Chambers's "fantasies" Smith includes his apparent belief "at the time [i.e., the mid-1930s] that Hiss was a Communist, and he acted on this belief as though it were true."

Release of the FBI files inevitably focused the attention of Alger Hiss's defenders, including Smith, on the possibility of a bureau plot. But for Smith, the notion of an FBI-sponsored scheme would preclude his own favored conspiracy version: Chambers acting alone for revenge. Therefore, in his 1977 "Afterword" to the paperback edition of his book he reviewed the Boardman memo and other purported "new evidence" for FBI foreknowledge or tampering (described earlier in this Appendix) as well as information on the manner in which Woodstock N230099 passed from the Catletts eventually to Ira Lockey (but without mentioning Donald Hiss's and Mike Catlett's covert role in recovering the machine). Then Smith concludes as diffusely as in his original analysis: "The rambling story lends color to speculation that Chambers in 1938 or an agent of HUAC or [the] FBI in 1948 might have switched No. 230099 for the machine the Hisses gave the Catletts." But his next sentence states: "No evidence has been found that anything of the sort ever happened, or that Chambers, HUAC or the FBI knew anything about what happened to the typewriter before the FBI's interview with Claudia Catlett on May 13, 1949. But the record isn't complete." In any event, having devoted his "Afterword" to the supposed "new evidence" that emerged from the FBI files, Smith retreats to his original formulation: "None of these discrepancies in the evidence affects the grounds stated in this book for concluding that Hiss was innocent. . . . They concern the very different subject of the way the trial was conducted."

As for the conspiracy theories themselves, we may expect that newer and perhaps more ingenious defenses of Hiss may emerge, if only because none of the many theories raised during the past six decades has proved persuasive. There has yet to appear, however, from any source, a coherent body of evidence that seriously undermines the credibility of the evidence against Alger Hiss.

A NOTE ON DOCUMENTATION

The endnotes and bibliography that follow, along with the footnotes included in the text, aim at providing adequate documentation without becoming too cumbersome for the interested reader. References in the text to endnotes have been organized by passages, not sentences, in order to minimize the proliferation of citations, especially with regard to testimony at the HUAC hearings and the Hiss trials. For the most part, sources have been cited in full only when they first appear, similarly in the interests of rendering the notes more usable. Only the books consulted most frequently or helpfully have been listed in the Bibliography. Articles important to an understanding of the case have been cited in the text, footnotes, endnotes, and Appendix. When *Perjury*'s original edition was published in 1978, my intention was to deposit the 60,000 pages of material used in preparing the book at the Harry S. Truman Library. A lawsuit apparently encouraged by supporters of Alger Hiss against the author, his publisher, and *The New Republic* magazine—subsequently settled without trial—made it advisable to maintain the files accumulated through personal research. The author has deposited the FBI files used in his research at the Truman Library. Also, various scholars, including Sam Tanenhaus in his biography of Whittaker Chambers published in 1997, have made extensive use of the author's personal research files with permission.

NOTES

The title and author of secondary works are usually provided at first mention. Subsequently, only the author's name is cited, unless more than a single work by the same author is in question. The following abbreviations for manuscripts and other basic sources used in the book apply throughout the endnotes, with full citations available in the Bibliography:

BALTIMORE: depositions taken in Alger Hiss's slander suit at Baltimore, Maryland

CIA: CIA files

COLUMBIA: Oral History Collection, Columbia University

COURT: Alger Hiss, *In the Court of Public Opinion*

FBI: FBI files, normally citing the last names of the person sending and the person receiving the document, the date, and the file number when available

FIRST: transcript of Alger Hiss's first trial for perjury

HISS: Hiss Defense Files (no attempt has been made to distinguish among copies of particular files that I examined in the offices of Hiss attorneys Helen Buttenwieser, Claude Cross, William Marbury, or Robert von Mehren)

HUAC I: the August–September 1948 HUAC hearings

HUAC II: the December 1948 HUAC hearings

INS: Immigration and Naturalization Service files

INTERVIEW: the author's interviews of figures in the case

JUSTICE: Justice Department records

LC: all collections held at the Library of Congress

NYT: *The New York Times*

POST: *The Washington Post*

SECOND: Transcript of Alger Hiss's second trial for perjury

SIX: Richard Nixon, *Six Crises*

SOLOW: Herbert Solow Papers, at the Hoover Institution (Stanford University)

STATE: State Department files

TIME: *Time* Magazine Archive

TRUMAN: Harry S. Truman Library

WITNESS: Whittaker Chambers, *Witness*

CHAPTER I

1. The shrewdest and liveliest analysis of HUAC's entire history is Walter Goodman's *The Committee*. On the 1947–48 period, see Goodman, pp. 190–271. See also Frank J. Donner, *The Un-Americans*.

2. On HUAC's Hollywood hearings, see Goodman, pp. 202–25; Murray Kempton, *Part of Our Time*, pp. 181–210; Stefan Kanfer, *A Journal of the Plague Years*, pp. 39–80; and House Committee on Un-American Activities, 80th Cong., Hearings Regarding Communist Infiltration of the Motion-Picture Industry, Oct. 20–24, 27–30, 1947.

3. J. Parnell Thomas to Karl Mundt, July 26, 1948, and Mundt to Thomas, July 27, 1948, both in Mundt MSS (Madison, S.D.). On Bentley's testimony and her background, see Goodman, pp. 244–49; Elizabeth Bentley, *Out of Bondage;* Herbert L. Packer, *Ex-Communist Witnesses,* pp. 52–120. Assistant FBI Director D. M. Ladd reviewed the voluminous bureau file on Elizabeth Bentley beginning with her first appearance at the FBI's New York office on November 7, 1945, in the course of summarizing the bureau's probe of Alger Hiss. Ladd to Hoover, Feb. 4, 1949, #2058. For Bentley's July 31 testimony, see HUAC I, pp. 503–62.

4. HUAC I, *ibid.* On HUAC's interest in pursuing the leads, see SIX, p. 2; Robert E. Stripling, *The Red Plot Against America,* pp. 89–94; and F. Edward Hébert, *Last of the Titans . . . ,*" pp. 272–319.

5. The basic source for Congressman Mundt's involvement in the case is the Mundt papers at the Karl E. Mundt Memorial Library (Madison, S.D.), which contain numerous HUAC files and other data on the Hiss-Chambers investigation. Mrs. Mary Mundt kindly shared additional information and documents on her late husband's role in the case with my researcher, Ms. Kathleen McCarthy, in a 1975 interview. See especially "What the Hiss Trial Actually Means," private reprint of Mundt's Jan. 25, 1950, Senate speech, and his 1962 CBS-TV interview with Paul Niven that dealt in part with the Hiss case. On Chambers's reluctance to testify, see Stripling, p. 96.

6. SIX, p. 2; Stripling, p. 100.

7. HUAC I, pp. 564–66, for Chambers's prepared statement.

8. Thus, the Aug. 4 NYT head included this statement: "Ex-Communist Names Alger Hiss, Then in State Department."

9. HUAC I, pp. 563–86, for Chambers's testimony.

10. SIX, pp. 2–4. Nixon's previous knowledge of the charges against Alger Hiss is summarized in Allen Weinstein, "Nixon vs. Hiss," *Esquire,* Nov. 1975. See also INTERVIEW, Father John Cronin, Nov. 27, 1975; Bela Kornitzer, *The Real Nixon,* pp. 172–75; and Garry Wills, *Nixon Agonistes,* pp. 34–38. In his statements from 1948 until his death in 1994, Nixon consistently denied any prior knowledge of Chambers's charges against Hiss.

11. Hiss to Dulles, Aug. 3 and Aug. 5, 1948, HISS; INTERVIEW, Alger Hiss, Sept. 20, 1974.

12. Edmund F. Soule to Alden Whitman, April 24, 1974, and Aug. 2, 1974, courtesy of Mr. Whitman.

13. HUAC I, pp. 585–611, for Silvermaster's testimony and Bentley's rebuttal.

14. *Ibid.,* pp. 620–22.

15. Marbury to Alger Hiss, Aug. 4, 1948, enclosing Marbury to Donald Hiss, Aug. 4, 1948; for a typical supporting letter, see Robert P. Patterson (former Secretary of War) to Alger Hiss, Aug. 4, 1948; Hiss to Dulles, Aug. 5, 1948, HISS. INTERVIEW, William L. Marbury, Feb. 24, 1975.

16. HUAC I, pp. 633–42; INTERVIEW, Robert E. Stripling, April 2–8, 1975.

17. HUAC I, pp. 642–43, for Hiss's opening statement; pp. 642–59 for Hiss's Aug. 5 testimony.

18. INTERVIEW, Alger Hiss, Sept. 20, 1974.

19. "Statement of Alger Hiss, March 8, 1949, at the office of Lloyd Paul Stryker . . . ,"

p. 102, HISS; FBI, June 2, 1947, statement of Alger Hiss.

20. FBI, March 25, 1946, interview with Alger Hiss. For a review of the FBI's investigation of Hiss prior to 1948, see D. M. Ladd to Hoover, Jan. 28, 1949, #2058, pp. 1–11, FBI.

21. HUAC I, pp. 650–52.

22. SIX, pp. 9–10. On the aftermath of Hiss's testimony, see also Stripling, pp. 115–16.

23. NYT, Aug. 6, 1948. On the origins of Truman's use of the "red herring" phrase, see also Charles G. Ross to Norman R. Anderson, May 26, 1950, and Anderson to Ross, May 25, 1950, TRUMAN. Donald Hiss to Karl E. Mundt, Aug. 5, 1948, Mundt MSS; Joseph F. Johnston to John Foster Dulles, Aug. 10, 1948, Dulles MSS, Princeton University. See also Frank McNaughton (*Time* Washington bureau chief) to Don Bermingham, "Communists . . . ," Aug. 7, 1948, McNaughton MSS, TRUMAN.

24. SIX, pp. 10–12; Stripling, pp. 116–17; Hébert, *op. cit.* According to Hébert's account, Stripling supported the move to send all evidence to Justice and cease the HUAC probe of Hiss-Chambers. Stripling denied this version and recalled supporting Nixon's proposal. INTERVIEW, Robert Stripling, April 28, 1975. Nixon recalled Stripling's strong support at the time.

25. Nixon to Dulles, Sept. 7, 1948, Dulles MSS. Bruce Mazlish, *In Search of Nixon*, pp. 41–42; SIX, p. 7 and *passim.*

26. INTERVIEWS, Robert Stripling, March 12, 1975, and April 28, 1975.

27. William Marbury to John Foster Dulles, Aug. 5, 1948; Joseph F. Johnston to Dulles, Aug. 10, 1948; HISS. Hiss to Dulles, Aug. 5, 1948; Philip C. Jessup to John Foster Dulles, Aug. 6, 1948, and Dulles to Jessup, Aug. 9, 1948, Dulles MSS.

28. WITNESS, pp. 549–50, 558; for Chambers's Aug. 7 testimony, see HUAC I, pp. 661–72.

29. WITNESS, pp. 545–46; Richard Nixon, "Memorandum on the Hiss-Chambers Case," ca. Feb. 1949, p. 3, Ralph de Toledano MSS, Hoover Institution.

30. On the prothonotary warbler, HUAC I, p. 666. See also Nixon, "Memorandum," *op. cit.*

31. HUAC I, pp. 666–67, 671.

32. Transcript, CBS-TV interview with Paul Niven, n.d. 1962, Mundt MSS.

33. Perlo's testimony: HUAC I, pp. 677–86, 692–701; Bentley's testimony: pp. 687–93, 810–16. See also Frank McNaughton to David Hulburd, Aug. 9, 1948, McNaughton MSS, TRUMAN.

34. Silverman's testimony: HUAC I, pp. 835–50. See also interviews with A. George Silverman, March 21, 1949, and April 26, 1949, and the Jan. 12, 1949, interview with his lawyer, Bernard Jaffe, HISS.

35. HUAC I, pp. 877–906, for White's testimony.

36. Collins's testimony: *ibid.,* pp. 802–10.

37. For Collins's denials, *ibid.,* pp. 805, 809; for Duggan's statement about Collins, interview with Laurence Duggan (New York office), Dec. 10, 1948, FBI.

38. Donald Hiss's testimony: HUAC I, pp. 928–35. Testifying also on Aug. 13 was Lauchlin Currie, a former assistant to President Roosevelt, who denied Elizabeth Bentley's charges that he had been peripherally involved in underground CP activities. Dean Acheson, who declined a similar request from Alger Hiss on Aug. 13, accompanied Currie to the hearing in a conspicuous show of support.

39. Nixon, "Memorandum," *op. cit.;* see also SIX, pp. 14–22.

40. *Ibid.,* pp. 22–23; see also interview with Allen Dulles, John Foster Dulles Oral History Project, pp. 53–58, interview

with Richard M. Nixon, J. F. Dulles Oral
History, Project, pp. 1–4, and J. F. Dulles to
Herbert Brownell, Aug. 20, 1948, all Dulles
MSS. Karl Mundt to Herbert Brownell,
Aug. 13, 1948, Mundt MSS. See also Mundt
to Harold O. Lovre, Aug. 9, 1948, *ibid.*,
containing this passage: "Frankly, this is
more the work for a Sherlock Holmes than
a member of Congress but somebody has
to do it so we have the bit in our teeth."
When Mundt told newsmen that Truman
would have to eat his "red herring" statement "word by word" before HUAC's
probe had ended, the president confirmed
his assessment that the inquiry "was a
red herring of the strongest type you can
smell." New York *Herald Tribune,* Aug. 13,
1948.

41. Interview with Richard M. Nixon
and interview with Allen Dulles, Dulles
MSS, *op. cit.* See also Nixon to Dulles,
Sept. 7, 1948, and Dulles to Nixon, Sept. 9,
1948, Dulles MSS.

42. James David Barber, *The Presidential
Character,* pp. 347–417. INTERVIEW, Robert
Stripling, April 28, 1975.

43. SIX, pp. 23–25.

44. Hiss to Marbury, Aug. 31, 1948,
HISS; COURT, pp. 14–15. On being
"unrepresented," see *ibid.*, pp. 20–21.

45. Hiss's Aug. 16 testimony: HUAC I,
pp. 935–74.

46. *Ibid.*, pp. 948–49.

47. *Ibid.*, pp. 953–55. In Dec. 1948 both
Priscilla and Alger Hiss would tell a New
York grand jury that Claudia Catlett was
dead, although Mrs. Catlett later told the
FBI that she had met Mrs. Hiss in Wash-
ington in 1946. For the full story of the
Catletts and the case, see Chapters XI and
XII, *passim.*

48. Interview with Claudia Catlett,
Feb. 1, 1949, FBI.

49. HUAC I, pp. 955–7, for the details
that follow.

50. *Ibid.*, pp. 961–62.

51. Mazlish, pp. 70–74, offers the best
analysis of this feature of Nixon's personality. See also SIX, pp. 12–13, 33–34.

52. *Ibid.*, pp. 31–33; INTERVIEW,
Robert E. Stripling, April 28, 1975;
COURT, p. 37.

53. COURT, pp. 77–82.

54. For the Aug. 17 Commodore Hotel
confrontation testimony, see HUAC I,
pp. 975–1001.

55. *Ibid.*, pp. 984–85, for the exchange.

56. *Ibid.*, pp. 985–86.

57. *Ibid.*, pp. 988–92, 1001. Nixon's
account was the most thorough of the
rushed reports: NYT, Aug. 18, 1948;
McDowell's came over the news wires
first in an International News Service
story on the evening of Aug. 17.

58. INTERVIEW, Donald Appell,
Aug. 29, 1974.

59. HUAC I, pp. 1004–5. Among those
recognizing Chambers immediately after
a decade were Sender Garlin, Josephine
Herbst, Julian Wadleigh, William Edward
Crane, and Maxim Lieber.

60. SIX, pp. 40–42; Mazlish, pp. 90–91;
HUAC I, pp. 1011–13, for Priscilla Hiss's
testimony.

61. Hiss to Thomas, Aug. 18, 1948,
HISS.

62. New York *Herald Tribune,* Aug. 20,
1948. For the testimony by Pressman, Witt,
and Abt, see HUAC I, pp. 1015–33.

63. *Ibid.*, p. 1050. For Martha Pope's
testimony, see *ibid.*, pp. 1043–52.

64. For Cherner's, Mensh's, and
Gertler's testimony, see *ibid.*, pp. 1052–71.

65. Smith's testimony: *ibid.*, pp. 1071–74.

66. Alger Hiss to J. Parnell Thomas,
Aug. 24, 1948, HISS.

67. HUAC I, p. 1076. For the entire
Aug. 25 testimony, *ibid.*, pp. 1075–1206.

68. *Ibid.*, pp. 1088–89, for the Nixon-
Hiss exchange.

69. On Samuel Roth and "George Crosley," see Roth's affidavit summarizing his statements, Sept. 3, 1948, HISS. See also Leo Hamalian, ". . . Samuel Roth and the Underside of Modern Letters," *Journal of Modern Literature,* April 1974, pp. 910–12, and Roth to Dr. Meyer Zeligs, Oct. 2, 1963, HISS, which gives a behind-the-scenes glimpse of his role in the Hiss case. Hiss told of several "anonymous" phone calls and letters identifying people who allegedly knew Chambers as "Crosley," although none of the letters have been preserved in the defense files. See memo "Re: George Crosley," n.d., HISS.

70. Beverly Smith, "Voice from the Bleachers [Senator Gerald D. Nye]," May 1935, and General Hugh Johnson, "Talks About the Tools of War," April 1935, both *American Magazine.*

71. HUAC I, p. 1095. Testimony about the Ford transaction: *ibid.,* pp. 1093–95, 1097–1116, 1118–26.

72. *Ibid.,* pp. 1124–26, for Nixon's summary.

73. *Ibid.,* pp. 1132–35. Dulles to Herbert Brownell, Jr., Sept. 14, 1948, "Supplement to August 20, 1948, memorandum [Dulles to Brownell], Re: Alger Hiss," Dulles MSS.

74. Dulles to Judd, March 22, 1948; see also Dulles to Judd, Feb. 2, 1948; "Memorandum for Confidential Files," John Foster Dulles, March 18, 1948; *ibid.* See also FBI interviews with Alger Hiss, March 25, 1946, and June 2, 1947.

75. Hébert: HUAC I, pp. 1139–40; Mundt: *ibid.,* pp. 1157–60.

76. *Ibid.,* pp. 1160, 1166–67.

77. For Chambers's Aug. 25 testimony, see *ibid.,* pp. 1176–1206.

78. *Ibid.,* pp. 1191, 1204.

79. William Rosen's Aug. 26 testimony: *ibid.,* pp. 1207–22; Farrell's Sept. 8 testimony: *ibid.,* pp. 1316–19.

80. Addie Rosen's testimony: *ibid.,* pp. 1301–12. Rosen's Sept. 9 testimony: *ibid.,* pp. 1329–41. The committee later cited Rosen for contempt because of his refusal to discuss the Ford transfer. The following year he was convicted and sentenced to six months in jail, but the U.S. Court of Appeals overturned the conviction.

81. Edward C. McLean, "Memorandum re William Rosen: Conference with Emmanuel Bloch, Rosen's Attorney, Today," March 9, 1949, HISS. The memo appeared publicly for the first time in Allen Weinstein, "Was Hiss Framed? The New Evidence," *The New York Review of Books,* April 1, 1976.

82. Baltimore *News-Post,* Aug. 27 and 28, 1948. HUAC I, pp. 1255–60, 1263–65, for Chambers's testimony about the farm purchase. Among the many FBI reports dealing with the transaction, the following two summarize most of the information collected: Sept. 10, 1948 (Baltimore, Md.), and Nov. 19, 1948, #4269, FBI.

83. HUAC I, pp. 1257, 1263. Edward Case, the realtor, summarized his knowledge of the entire set of negotiations, first with Hiss and then with Chambers, in an interview with FBI agents, included in their Sept. 10, 1948, report.

84. "Westminster Story," n.d., ca. Aug.–Sept. 1948, HISS.

85. The Sept. 10, 1948, FBI report reprints the entire correspondence involving realtor Edward Case and the Hisses and the Chamberses, including these letters.

86. *Ibid.* See also John F. Davis to Edward C. McLean, Sept. 17, 1948, HISS.

87. "Memorandum on Trip to Westminster," John F. Davis, Oct. 11, 1948 (Davis accompanied the Hisses on their visit), HISS.

88. HUAC I, pp. 1347–57.

89. For the Gallup Poll, see POST, Sept. 5, 1948. Also see "The Confrontation," New York *Herald Tribune*, Aug. 26, 1948; "Washington Drama," NYT *Week in Review*, Aug. 29, 1977; and "Smoked Herring," New York *Daily Mirror*, Sept. 1, 1948, the latter for a view from the Right.

90. The show's transcript was reprinted as "Whittaker Chambers Meets the Press," *The American Mercury*, Feb. 1949, from which this and subsequent quotes have been taken.

91. The deportation files on "J. Peters," released at my request by the Immigration and Naturalization Service, contain several hundred pages that present a persuasive case for Peters's background as an underground Communist leader as well as an "open" CP functionary. Perhaps the most curious memo in the file is a handwritten one sent three days before Peters testified to HUAC: "Memo for File; 3:40 PM, Aug. 27, 1948. Mr. Noto [a leading INS official] phoned from Washington. Said C.O. [Commanding Officer?] instructs that Whittaker Chambers is to be interviewed but *NOT* to be used as witness unless his testimony is the *only* testimony that can save Government's case. E. P. Emanuel." Both "NOT" and "only" had been underlined several times.

92. INTERVIEW, Joszef Peters, March 20, 1975. For the testimony of "Alexander Stevens," see HUAC I, pp. 1267–77.

93. For Chambers's Aug. 30 testimony about Peters's career, *ibid.*, pp. 1271, 1277–90.

94. Peters's INS deportation file is the most extensive source for information about his career in the American Communist underground. *Passim.*

95. David Y. Dallin, *Soviet Espionage*, pp. 412–13; INTERVIEW, Joszef Peters, Mar. 20, 1975. My long talk with Peters in Budapest was his first with a non-Communist Western scholar since his 1949 deportation and included his first public comments on the Hiss-Chambers case. Peters smiled once during our talk when I suggested that his frequent use of the terms "open" and "secret" Communist parties when describing the division in American CP ranks indicated an awareness of that second realm that most Party "functionaries" would deny having possessed.

96. See Chapters III and IV for further examination of these points.

97. Berle's testimony: HUAC I, pp. 1291–1300. The visit is described in greater detail in Chapter IX.

98. Berle's notes became a government exhibit at Hiss's second trial and a copy can be found in Volume VI of the transcript, attached to p. 3325. On the Berle notes, see H. B. Fletcher to D. M. Ladd, Feb. 11, 1949, #2228, and Fletcher to Ladd, Feb. 9, 1949, #2227, also Ladd to Tolson, Feb. 24, 1950, #4532, all FBI.

99. The diary entry is reprinted in Adolf Berle's collected papers, edited by Beatrice Bishop Berle and Travis Beal Jacobs as *Navigating the Rapids, 1918–1971*, pp. 249–50. See also INTERVIEWS, Isaac Don Levine, Sept. 16 and 17, 1974; and Isaac Don Levine, *Eyewitness to History*, pp. 193–95.

100. Adolf Berle to Jerome Frank, Frank MSS, Yale University.

101. Adolf Berle, Diary File, Sept. 3, 1948, Berle MSS, FDR Library (Hyde Park). See also the Diary File entries on Hiss-Chambers for Aug. 9 and Aug. 18, 1948.

102. Alger Hiss, "Memorandum re Acquaintanceship with Mr. A. A. Berle," ca. Sept. 1948, HISS. See also Hiss, "Memorandum re Mr. A. A. Berle's Testimony of August 30, 1948," ca. Sept. 1948, HISS.

103. Marbury to Bruce, Nov. 4, 1948; Bruce to Warren, Nov. 9, 1948; Warren to Bruce, Nov. 16, 1948; HISS. See also

Warren to Berle, Nov. 16, 1948, and Berle to Warren, Nov. 23, 1948, Berle MSS, FDR Library "Memorandum re Acquaintanceship with Mr. A. A. Berle," *op. cit.*

104. For a full description of these efforts, see Chapters V, VIII, and XI, *passim.*

105. "Interview with Mrs. Carol Weiss King . . . ," Jan. 7, 1949, HISS.

106. The full text of the letter can be found in the Hiss Defense Files. See especially pp. 8–10.

CHAPTER II

1. "Autobiographical Notes: Alger Hiss," n.d., HISS. Information on Alger Hiss in this chapter has been drawn from a variety of sources, including the following: Hiss's own statements in the Defense Files; my interviews with Alger Hiss, Priscilla Hiss, William Marbury, Dr. Timothy Hobson, Judge Charles E. Wyzanski, Jr.; my researcher Catherine Brown's interview with Richard Field; transcripts of the first and second Hiss perjury trials; Hiss's March 8, 1949, statement to Lloyd Paul Stryker, previously cited; and three books that contain much useful personal data on his early years: Tony Hiss, *Laughing Last;* John Chabot Smith, *Alger Hiss: The True Story;* and Meyer A. Zeligs, *Friendship and Fratricide.*

2. Zeligs, pp. 142–43.

3. HUAC I, p. 669, for Chambers's comments; for Hiss's retort, Alger Hiss to Carl Binger, Jan. 11, 1949, enclosing "Analysis of Chambers' Testimony as to 'Intimacy' with Me and My Family," p. 7, HISS. Alger Hiss's childhood reminiscences: "Autobiographical Notes," *ibid.*

4. "Autobiographical Notes," *ibid.*

5. *Ibid.;* INTERVIEW, William Marbury, Feb. 24, 1975.

6. Smith, pp. 55–56. INTERVIEW, William Marbury, *op. cit.* See also "The Hiss Case," a memoir by William Marbury, privately distributed and sent to me by Mr. Marbury, p. 5.

7. "Biographical Notes: Priscilla Hiss," n.d., HISS; Smith, pp. 55, 62–63.

8. Hiss to Frankfurter, Feb. 27, 1930, Frankfurter MSS, LC; Smith, p. 56; Zeligs, p. 173. Several years later, while clerking for Holmes, Hiss told the Justice and a visitor the "Rheinhart legend" tale of his Harvard years. According to the visitor, Hiss described a Harvard student "who knew no one but who hoped to gain friends and make a favorable impression by calling out his own name under his dormitory window. Of course, other students discovered him in the act, and poor Rheinhart soon became a laughing-stock." "And when may this legend have happened?" Holmes asked. Hiss flushed slightly, the visitor recalled, and replied: "Oh, all of twenty years ago, sir!" But Alger Hiss had none of Rheinhart's problems while at Harvard. John Knox, "A Luncheon with Justice Oliver Wendell Holmes and Alger Hiss," *The Brief Phi Delta Phi Quarterly,* Winter 1975–6, p. 103.

9. Kempton, p. 20.

10. Zeligs, p. 167.

11. *Ibid.,* pp. 168–69, 175; Smith, p. 65.

12. Hiss to Frankfurter, Oct. 14, 1929, Frankfurter MSS, LC.

13. Smith, pp. 68–69.

14. Compare William Marbury's recollection on this point: "Alger told me that he had to go back to work for Justice Holmes immediately, since in getting married during his clerkship he was really violating one of the conditions of his employment. Under the circumstances he said that he and Priscilla were planning to be married

by a Justice of the Peace and that no one would be asked to the wedding—not even the members of their immediate families. Largely at my instigation he finally decided that the immediate families and a few friends should be invited. . . ." Marbury, "The Hiss Case," *op. cit.*

15. Hiss to Frankfurter, Dec. 13, 1929, Frankfurter MSS, LC. In 1948 Hiss asserted that he knew nothing about Chambers's charges against him until the latter's initial testimony before HUAC, despite unmistakable mentions of Chambers in this connection by the FBI and a grand jury over the past two years (described in Chapter X). Hiss told me in 1975, in another illustration of the point, that he did not realize his stepson, Timothy Hobson, had become a homosexual during the mid-1940s until confronted with the situation when Hobson was detained while serving in the Navy. INTERVIEW, Alger Hiss, June 21, 1975.

16. Smith, p. 66. Priscilla naturally wanted no one else to know about it," John Chabot Smith wrote, "and Alger kept her secret for thirty-five years or more—over forty-five, according to Priscilla, who says she told him about it when they were first married; as Alger recalls it she didn't tell him until they had been married at least ten years." *Ibid.*, pp. 70–71. Priscilla told me in 1975 that she could not believe that Smith had learned from Alger Hiss the facts about William Brown Meloney and about her abortion, although Hiss himself told me that he had described the episode to Smith. Hiss also described the facts to me and to Alden Whitman in a Sept. 11, 1974, interview.

17. Smith, pp. 66, 68. "There was a great deal of the knight-errant in [Alger Hiss's] makeup," William Marbury wrote later, "and the girls to whom he attached himself from time to time were almost always in

some sort of difficulty. His friends were at times quite concerned for fear that he would involve himself with someone who was unstable in order to rescue her from her troubles. Priscilla Hiss was clearly in trouble, although apparently not unstable. . . . She was, therefore, clearly a damsel in distress, and that Alger Hiss should come to her rescue was strictly in character." "The Hiss Case," pp. 4–5.

18. Smith, p. 69; INTERVIEW, William Marbury, Feb. 24, 1975; INTERVIEW, Alger Hiss, Sept. 20, 1974. Hugh Cox, Donald Hiss's attorney, reported in 1948 "that Donald had always had an inferiority complex because his brother always did everything a little better than he did. [Donald] was particularly affected by the fact that Alger made the *Law Review* and he did not. According to Cox [reporting to one of Alger Hiss's attorneys]; this has brooded on his [Donald's] mind all his life." Conference with Hugh Cox, Dec. 8, 1948, HISS.

19. INTERVIEW, Alger Hiss, Sept. 20, 1974.

20. Hiss to Frankfurter, Feb. 27, 1930, and March 20, 1930, Frankfurter MSS, LC. Hiss's concern to avoid offending Field was understandable, as Field would recall in a later interview with Catherine Brown: "He was probably my closest friend in law school. We were classmates and we worked together and we studied together and we played together and it was a very close relationship. In fact, when I was to be married in Minneapolis, in the spring of 1930, and he was just winding up his year as law clerk to Justice Holmes, I asked him to be my best man. And he couldn't do it, because he frankly couldn't afford the trip. . . . I'm telling this merely to indicate how close we were." INTERVIEW, Richard Field, July 16, 1974. For Hiss's rejection of the offer, see Hiss to Frankfurter, March 24, 1930, Frankfurter MSS, LC.

21. INTERVIEW, Alger Hiss, Sept. 20, 1974. Hiss to Frankfurter, April 8, 1930; Frankfurter to O'Brian, April 1, 1930; Frankfurter to O'Brian, March 10, 1938; O'Brian to Frankfurter, March 18, 1938; Frankfurter MSS, LC.

22. INTERVIEW, William Marbury, Feb. 24, 1975; INTERVIEW, Alger Hiss, Sept. 20, 1974.

23. "Personal History of Whittaker Chambers," in FBI Summary Report, May 11, 1949, #3220, p. 151, FBI; WITNESS, p. 91.

24. WITNESS, pp. 91–92.

25. "Personal History . . . , op. cit., pp. 154–55. Information on Whittaker Chambers in this chapter has been drawn from a variety of sources, including the following: Chambers's summary "Personal History" to the FBI and a variety of other statements he gave to the bureau's agents in the 1948–49 period; WITNESS; FBI interviews with a number of his former associates, some of which are incorporated into the bureau's April 6, 1949, Summary Report, "Background and Personal History of Whittaker Chambers," #3059; interviews with many of these same people found in the Hiss Defense Files; and my own interviews of Jacob and Esther Burck, John Chambers, Sam Krieger, Maxim Lieber, and Meyer and Lillian Schapiro.

26. "Personal History . . . ," #3220, p. 155.

27. Ibid., pp. 153–55.

28. WITNESS, p. 97; "Personal History . . . ," p. 154.

29. WITNESS, pp. 120, 124.

30. "Personal History," p. 155.

31. WITNESS, p. 105.

32. See, for example, his recollection of attending a performance of Maurice Maeterlinck's The Bluebird. Ibid., p. 108.

33. Ibid., pp. 134–35.

34. "Personal History," pp. 152, 156–57; WITNESS, pp. 148–49.

35. Ibid., pp. 157–60. See also E. B. White, "Noontime of an Advertising Man," The New Yorker, June 25, 1949, and "Personal History," pp. 159–60. Chambers's one-day Williams roommate, Karl D. Helfrich, testified at Alger Hiss's perjury trials that he received a few strange letters from Chambers after his departure, although the letters never surfaced and the story could not be corroborated.

36. WITNESS, pp. 160–63. See also Chambers's posthumously published essay on those years, "Morningside," in Cold Friday, Duncan Norton-Taylor, ed., pp. 89–144.

37. "Morningside," pp. 124–25; "Personal History," pp. 160–61.

38. "Morningside," p. 114; "Memorandum of Conversation with Prof. Mark Van Doren," Nov. 15, 1948, HISS; FBI interview with Clifton Fadiman, March 22, 1949, in "Background and Personal History . . . ," April 6, 1949, #3059, p. 58.

39. A Play for Puppets, The Morningside, Nov. 1922.

40. "The Damn Fool," ibid., March 1922.

41. Journalist Charles Wagner's recollections of the incident can be found in an undated clipping in the Hiss-Chambers folder in Herbert Solow's papers.

42. "Personal History," pp. 165, 173; WITNESS, p. 166; "Memorandum of Conference with Sendor [sic] Garlin," Feb. 3, 1949, HISS; interview with Sender Garlin by Alden Whitman, July 24, 1974, courtesy of Mr. Whitman.

43. "Personal History," pp. 166–67. On these ruminations, see WITNESS, pp. 191–97.

44. "Personal History," pp. 167–68, 174; Chambers to Schapiro, "Summer 1924," n.d., courtesy of Prof. Schapiro; Chambers

to Van Doren, Sept. 15, 1924, reprinted as a trial exhibit in SECOND, p. 3669.

45. INTERVIEWS, Meyer Schapiro, May 7 and Aug. 9, 1975.

46. "Personal History," pp. 171–72.

47. *Ibid.*, p. 170; WITNESS, pp. 173–74.

48. *Ibid.*, pp. 174–78; "Personal History," pp. 170–73.

49. Chambers to Van Doren, March 8, 1925; SECOND, p. 3671.

50. Zeligs, p. 184; interview with Harvey Bundy, COLUMBIA.

51. "Autobiographical Notes: Alger Hiss," HISS; INTERVIEW, Richard Field, July 16, 1974; Zeligs, pp. 184–87; Marbury, "The Hiss Case," pp. 7–8.

52. Smith, pp. 72–74. Priscilla Hiss's 1932 Socialist Party registration and her Socialist Party membership, 1930–32, were both confirmed in testimony and documents at Alger Hiss's perjury trials. See Chapter XII, p. 482, and Chapter XIII, p. 509.

53. For Hiss's account of his relationship to the International Juridical Association, see Alger Hiss to Edward McLean, n.d. (ca. Sept. 1948), HISS.

54. Interview with Jerome R. Hellerstein, April 5, 1949, *ibid.*

55. Interview with Carol Weiss King, Jan. 6, 1949, *ibid.*

56. Information on the American Labor Associates and on Priscilla Hiss's involvement in the group comes from Corliss Lamont to Sidney Hook, June 16, 1932, enclosing William L. Nunn (Chairman, American Labor Associates) to Corliss Lamont, May 23, 1932, and "NEXT STEPS IN RADICALISM: AN OUTLINE for discussion at A.L.A. meeting, Wednesday, June 15, 1932," all courtesy of Prof. Hook.

57. "NEXT STEPS . . . ," *ibid.*

58. Lamont to Hook, *ibid.*

59. FBI Summary Report, May 11, 1949, #3220, pp. 4–5. Krieger discussed his

relationship with Chambers with me in an interview, the first time he spoke about the subject to anyone writing on the case. INTERVIEW, Sam Krieger, Aug. 9, 1974.

60. *Ibid.* On the Nearing study group, see Stephen J. Whitfield, *Scott Nearing*, p. 145.

61. "Personal History," p. 168; "Poem" (April 7, 1926) and "Lathrop, Montana" (June 30, 1926), both in *The Nation.*

62. "Personal History," p. 169. See also Scheidt to Hoover, March 28, 1949, #2746, FBI.

63. "Personal History," p. 176. On Chambers's confession to the FBI and "Lewis Green," see Chambers's Feb. 15, 1949, confessional letter and Hoover to Attorney General Clark, March 1, 1949, enclosing the transcripts of the subsequent Feb. 18 interview with FBI agents on the subject, #2152, FBI; for "Green's" own statement on the subject, see his interview with FBI agents, March 22, 1949, incorporated into the Summary Report "Background and Personal History of Whittaker Chambers," April 6, 1949, #3059, pp. 23–28, FBI.

64. The poem's lovemaking proceeds toward either healing or exhaustion, or both, in nine stanzas such as this one: "All that I can have at all / Is your body; all I can feel, As our bodies precipitate and fall, / Is the stretch of your body, I would kneel / If I could touch more than the small / Back of the head of the heavy face you conceal. . . ." "Tandaradei," *Two Worlds,* June 1926.

65. "Personal History," pp. 175–76.

66. Chambers to Schapiro, Nov. 3, 1926, courtesy of Prof. Schapiro.

67. INTERVIEW, Sam Krieger, *op. cit.;* "Personal History," p. 174; Chambers to Schapiro, Dec. 15, 1926, courtesy of Prof. Schapiro. See also Chambers to Schapiro, Dec. 16, 1926.

68. FBI interview with "Lewis Green," March 22, 1949, *op. cit.*

69. *Ibid.* See also Chambers's Feb. 18, 1949, interview with the FBI about his homosexual experiences, *op. cit.*, and the March 29, 1949, FBI interview with Ida Dales, reprinted in the April 6, 1949, "Background and Personal History . . ." report, #3059, especially p. 32, *op. cit.*

70. See the various FBI interviews cited in notes 68 and 69.

71. *Ibid.*, especially interview with "Lewis Green"; "Personal History," p. 177. Chambers told the FBI in 1949 that he believed Mrs. Hutchinson, who had died by that time, had "in her possession a number of letters written to her by Chambers in which he discusses the relationship and association between her, Chambers and [Lewis Green]. . . ." FBI report, March 28, 1949, #2746.

72. "Personal History," pp. 177–78; WITNESS, p. 239.

73. Chambers to Schapiro, Feb. (n.d.) 1927, courtesy of Prof. Schapiro.

74. Chambers to Schapiro, April 24, 1927, courtesy of Prof. Schapiro; also see "Personal History," pp. 176–78; FBI Summary Report, May 11, 1949, #3220, pp. 6–12.

75. *Ibid.*, p. 13; "Personal History," p. 178; INTERVIEW, Jacob and Esther Burck, Dec. 30, 1974.

76. "Personal History," p. 177; FBI interview with Ida Dales, March 29, 1949, *op. cit.* "Personal History," p. 178. Ida Dales saw Chambers only once more, in 1936,

accidentally, in Washington, where she lived at the time: "One evening while on her way home from work, she stopped for dinner in a tea room and sat alone. . . . While sitting there, she happened to look up and was surprised to see Chambers walking past her table. He looked at her and 'through her,' ignoring her, saying nothing, and going off to another table to sit down alone. Dailes [sic] was embarrassed, finished her meal quickly and left the tea room. She saw no one join Chambers at his table while she was there. She had no idea what he was doing in Washington and had not known he was there." FBI interview with Ida Dales.

77. *Ibid.*

78. INTERVIEW, Jacob and Esther Burck, *op. cit.*; FBI interview with Michael Intrator, March 16, 1949, in Summary Report, April 6, 1949, #3059, pp. 39–42; "Personal History," pp. 172–73.

79. *Ibid.*; WITNESS, pp. 262–63; Summary Report, #3220, pp. 20–24.

80. *Ibid.*, pp. 20–21; "Personal History," pp. 205–06 (for Esther Chambers's background); see also the FBI interviews with Michael Intrator and Grace Lumpkin, in Summary Report, #3059, *op. cit.*, pp. 39–55; and INTERVIEW, Jacob and Esther Burck, *op. cit.*

81. *Ibid.*; "Personal History," p. 180.

82. Smith, p. 74; Robert Cruise McManus to Alger Hiss, Oct. 18, 1948, HISS.

83. Bertolt Brecht, "To Posterity."

CHAPTER III

1. WITNESS, pp. 277–79; Summary Report, May 11, 1949, #3220, p. 26.

2. *Ibid.*; WITNESS, pp. 275–76. Southerners in the antebellum period referred to slavery as "the peculiar institution."

3. "Ulrich's" wife, Nadya Ulanovskaya, confirmed this portion of Chambers's story for me in an interview on Jan. 3, 1977. See also Summary Report, pp. 27–30.

4. Chambers was asked about his reasons for accepting the underground assignment by Hiss's lawyers at a 1948 pretrial slander-suit deposition. See also INTERVIEW, Jacob and Esther Burck, *op. cit.*

5. INTERVIEW, Ella Winter, March 6, 1975; INTERVIEW, Maxim Lieber, May 10, 1975.

6. Simon E. Gerson, cited in Alden Whitman's notes of a July 24, 1974, conversation with Sender Garlin, courtesy of Mr. Whitman; INTERVIEW, Ella Winter, *op. cit.* Similar references to Chambers's ostentatious self-dramatization of his new role as a "secret agent" recur in the journals of Robert Cantwell, and in recollections of the time by Chambers's friends Meyer and Lillian Schapiro, David Zabladowsky, Mike Intrator, Grace Lumpkin, and Herbert Solow.

7. See, for example, INTERVIEW, Meyer and Lillian Schapiro, Oct. 7, Oct. 19, and Nov. 17, 1974; INTERVIEW, Robert Cantwell, Nov. 12, 1974; and Cantwell's journal entries for March 17, 1934 (a Chambers visit in Boston accompanied by Joseph North of *The Daily Worker*); April 30, 1934 (a Chambers visit in New York City accompanied by John Sherman); and May 7, 1934 (another New York City visit), courtesy of Mr. Cantwell.

8. Notarized memorandum by Herbert Solow on his relations with Whittaker Chambers, Nov. 12, 1938, p. 4, Solow MSS, Hoover Institution; hereafter referred to as Solow Memo; INTERVIEW, Meyer Schapiro, Oct. 7, 1974; Intrator and Lumpkin interviews, in "Background and Personal History of Whittaker Chambers," April 6, 1949, #3059, FBI, pp. 39–55.

9. Both cards were shown to me and copies provided through the courtesy of Prof. Schapiro. See also INTERVIEW, Meyer Schapiro, Oct. 7, 1974; INTERVIEW, Jacob and Esther Burck, Dec. 30, 1974.

10. *The New Republic,* July 19, 1933. Another journalist, John Osborne, later a colleague of Chambers at *Time* but not a friend, recalled this related occasion: "Some years later, when I was the foreign editor of *Time* [in 1944], another episode made it believable that he'd [Chambers] been more deeply involved in Soviet-Communist activity than any of us then knew. He came to my office with a carbon copy of a story about wartime Russia. It included a few lines describing a feature of Odessa. He said flatly that the description was incorrect; the street or section or building or whatever the lines described looked so-and-so. I said, 'Oh, you've been there?' Again he went rigid and unusually pale, stammered that he'd never been to Russia, and ran from my office. After Chambers disclosed that he'd been a working Soviet spy, another ex-Communist told me that Whit had been secretly to Russia at least once. It was never established that he had." *The New Republic,* April 17, 1976.

11. Reprinted in "Background and Personal History," #3059, pp. 72–74.

12. Solow Memo, p. 14; INTERVIEW, Meyer Schapiro, Oct. 7, 1974; for Wadleigh's recollection, New York *Post,* July 14, 1949. Chambers later denied that he read or spoke Russian, a language in which close friends report that he was fluent. Meyer Schapiro, however, had the copy of the introductory Russian primer used by Chambers to learn the language early in the 1930s, a copy that contains marginal notations in Chambers's handwriting. Yet Chambers insisted, even to the FBI, that he had only a "slight knowledge of Russian words and [did] not understand the Russian language." On his general ability as a linguist, his son confirmed in a later interview his father's lifelong interest in learning new ones, even in the years

shortly before his death. INTERVIEW, John Chambers, July 12, 1977.

13. Esther Chambers's testimony about their years in the underground emerged most fully during Alger Hiss's two perjury trials. See Chapter XII, pp. 451–456, and Chapter XIII, p. 500.

14. H. B. Fletcher to D. M. Ladd, Feb. 18, 1949, #2238, FBI, enclosing Chambers's Feb. 15 letter from which the excerpt is drawn.

15. Hoover to Clark, March 1, 1949, enclosing the transcript of Chambers's Feb. 18, 1949, interview with FBI agents that produced this statement. #2152, FBI.

16. *Ibid.* The Hiss case intruded only once into Chambers's 1949 confession of homosexual encounters to the FBI and then only tangentially. William Edward Crane, a member of his underground network and an FBI informant in 1949, told the bureau that Chambers had once confided that "Dave" (David Carpenter), a third member of the ring, had suggested Chambers "making a connection on a homosexual basis for the apparatus with [name deleted—identified privately as a leading United States Senator], but that Chambers turned this suggestion down." Chambers told the FBI that he had not recalled the proposal until then, but that Crane "refreshed his recollection": "He [Chambers] stated that as a matter of fact this was information that he had at one time probably told to Crane. According to Chambers, while he was seeing Donald Hiss in Washington, D.C., the latter on one occasion told him about [Senator X] who had made homosexual advances to Donald Hiss. Hiss in turn told Chambers about this and suggested the possibility of approaching [Senator X] not necessarily by Donald Hiss himself, on homosexual basis in order to secure information. Chambers stated that he vetoed this suggestion and

nothing further was ever said or done about it." Special Agent in Charge, New York, to Director, n.d. (summarizing interviews with Crane, Feb. 8–16, 1949), #2446, p. 21, FBI (released subsequently after initially being withheld under a Freedom of Information Act b-7-C exemption).

17. Summary Report, p. 31.

18. *Ibid.*, pp. 33–35, 39. For the Osman case, see Dallin, pp. 398–400.

19. *Ibid.*, p. 49. For Chambers's description of its various activities, *ibid.*, pp. 37–51. See also interviews with Clayton B. Darrow, May 2 and July 3, 1934, summarized in FBI report, Jan. 27, 1949, #1720. Chambers recalled Darrow's last name and described him to the bureau early in 1949: Summary Report, p. 49. Chambers also described the Electric Boat operation and similar underground ventures to his friends during meetings in the 1933–35 period. See INTERVIEW, Meyer Schapiro, Oct. 7, 1974; INTERVIEW, Felix Morrow, May 13, 1975; and Solow Memo, pp. 4–5. Thus Solow recalled in 1938 that in early 1933 Chambers "mentioned to me a trip to New London, which sounded to me like more of the secret work. Then or later . . . I heard there was some sort of naval base there." *Ibid.*, p. 5.

20. Summary Report, p. 53.

21. *Ibid.*, pp. 32, 57.

22. INTERVIEWS, Nadya Ulanovskaya, Jan. 3–6, 1977. Ulanovskaya had an extraordinary and adventurous career, both before and after the period in which she and her husband, Alexander ("Ulrich") Ulanovski, served in the United States. He had known Stalin and other major revolutionary leaders during pre-1917 Siberian exile, from which Alexander escaped. After the Revolution he and Nadya became secret agents—"world revolutionaries"— in Germany, Argentina, China, the United States, Denmark, and elsewhere (the

famous Russian agent Richard Sorge's first assignment was as an aide to Ulanovski in China during the late 1920s). Nadya worked during the Second World War as a translator for Western correspondents including C. S. Sulzberger, Drew Middleton, and Walter Kerr. After the war Nadya, Alexander, and their daughter, Maya, all served long periods at hard labor in Siberia. Released in 1956, the family reunited in Moscow and quickly became important figures in the dissident world. After Alexander's death Nadya left the Soviet Union to join Maya and her family in Israel. For a fuller account of their lives, see Allen Weinstein, "Nadya: A Spy Story," *Encounter,* June 1977.

23. INTERVIEWS, Nadya Ulanovskaya, *op. cit.* Ulanovskaya also provided a unique updating of the later lives of those in Ulrich's American network. Joshua Tarner and his wife migrated to Moscow, where they managed to survive unharmed the purges of the late 1930s. Another Moscow expatriate, Dr. Philip Rosenbliett, proved less fortunate, and he disappeared in 1937 during the "great terror." "Charley" (real name: Leon Minster) also died in the Soviet Union, but his wife later returned to the United States as an emigrant. Dr. Isadore Hiller, a physician when not engaged in secret work, delivered Nadya's baby in New York's St. Luke's Hospital on Oct. 10, 1932. Ulrich and Nadya used the last name "Jurotovitch" while living in the U.S., and their baby's birth certificate was in the name of May Jurotovitch. Now Maya Ulanovskaya, she went into exile with her mother in Israel. See also "Nadya: A Spy Story," *op. cit.*

24. INTERVIEW, Ella Winter, *op. cit.* During this period both Ella Winter and Robert Cantwell met another "Harold Phillips," whom Cantwell identified as John Sherman. Chambers simply borrowed

his friend Sherman's alias during his encounter with Winter. INTERVIEW, Robert Cantwell, *op. cit.;* Cantwell, Journal, April 30, 1934, courtesy of Mr. Cantwell.

25. INTERVIEW, Ella Winter, *op. cit.*

26. *Ibid.* Cantwell was then working closely with Lincoln Steffens and Ella Winter on the Filene biography and refused Sherman's offer. The Filene connection may have made Cantwell appear to the CP a credible prospect for acceptance by the Du Ponts, if only as a "businessman's biographer." Chambers later appropriated Cantwell's name, with permission, as one of his aliases—something Lloyd Robert Cantwell (he had dropped his legal first name) observed personally during a 1937 visit to "Lloyd Cantwell" at Chambers's Baltimore apartment.

27. INTERVIEW, Ella Winter, *op. cit.* Nadya Ulanovskaya also recalled her husband's having met Winter on one occasion to urge her, unsuccessfully, to assist the CP's "secret work." INTERVIEWS, Nadya Ulanovskaya, *op. cit.*

28. See, for example, Diana Trilling's account of one such request for "letter drop" aid. *Encounter,* June 1976, p. 94.

29. Subcommittee on Internal Security, Senate Judiciary Committee, "Activities of United States Citizens Employed by the United Nations," Hearings, Oct. 24, 1952, pp. 151–53. INTERVIEW, David Zabladowsky (with Mrs. Elizabeth Lenneberg), Nov. 1, 1975.

30. Solow Memo, p. 4; INTERVIEW, Robert Cantwell, *op. cit.* Felix Morrow and Meyer Schapiro heard similar tales from Chambers of counterespionage work directed against Japanese agents. INTERVIEW, Felix Morrow, *op. cit.;* INTERVIE'W, Meyer Schapiro, Oct. 7, 1974.

31. WITNESS, pp. 309–10; Summary Report, p. 60.

32. Summary Report, pp. 61–62.

33. *Ibid.*, pp. 70–71.

34. *Ibid.*, pp. 63–66, for details of establishing the syndicate. Confirmation of the American Feature Writers Syndicate's underground operations came from FBI interviews with two of Lieber's secretaries and from testimony to the bureau by a brother of one secretary, a seaman, whom Chambers had tried to recruit as an espionage courier. The FBI also located the syndicate's bank records. Finally, Maxim Lieber corroborated the entire story in my interviews with him. Lieber said that he expected his willingness to aid the CP's secret apparatus in setting up dummy organizations in Japan and England would not only prove his devotion as an antifascist but, at the same time, extend his business operations in a significant and potentially profitable manner. See the related 1949 FBI memos on the following dates: June 6, #3377; July 13, #3650; Aug. 24, #4027; and Nov. 4, #4144.

35. After giving up his valuable agent-client files as a precaution recommended by leading officials of the American Communist Party, Lieber migrated with his family first to Mexico, in the early fifties, and later to Poland. He then lived in retirement in Connecticut, where he suffered occasional harassment by visiting FBI agents. Chambers remained fond of Lieber long after his defection, a process in which Lieber briefly played a supporting role described in Chapter IX. Lieber also figured in *Witness* as "Paul," to whom Chambers appealed to step forward and confirm his story. WITNESS, pp. 44–48.

36. INTERVIEWS, Maxim Lieber, May 10 and 13, 1975.

37. *Ibid;* Summary Report, p. 65.

38. Summary Report, pp. 65–66; INTERVIEWS, Meyer Schapiro, Oct. 7 and 19, 1974.

39. Solow Memo, Supplement 1, Dec. 3, 1938.

40. Summary Report, p. 72.

41. *Ibid.*, pp. 72–75; Solow Memo, p. 15; INTERVIEW, Meyer Schapiro, Oct. 19, 1974.

CHAPTER IV

1. On Frank and the AAA, see Arthur M. Schlesinger, Jr., *The Coming of the New Deal,* pp. 40–84.

2. Hiss's claim not to have known that Pressman and Frank were associated in the same law firm in 1932 conflicted with William Marbury's recollection of Hiss's New York years: "During this time [1932–33] Alger sent me a letter introducing Lee Pressman, who planned to file a stockholders' suit in Maryland against a large holding company. Pressman came to see me and explained what he had in mind." Smith, p. 11; INTERVIEW, Alger Hiss, June 21, 1975; Marbury, "The Hiss Case," p. 8.

3. Frank to Pressman, April 10, 1933; Pressman to Frank, April 12, 1933, Frank MSS, Yale University.

4. On Pressman's 1950 testimony, see Chapter I, p. 51 and *n.;* also Frankfurter to Frank, June 6, 1933, Frank MSS, *op. cit.*

5. Beverly Smith, "Uncle Sam Grows Younger," *American Magazine,* Feb. 1934, p. 124; Schlesinger, pp. 50–51.

6. Earl Latham, *The Communist Controversy in Washington,* pp. 102–03.

7. "The excitement of the emergency, the tremendous hurry to get things done, the existence of a common enemy to the right, all gave them protective coloration. Their superiors found them useful on the

job and were not aware of their private reservations, their division of loyalty, their shrouded evening meetings, or their secret scorn and contempt. And, indeed, the presence of Communists in AAA had its own futilities. While the cell [the Ware Group] was no doubt constantly trying to figure out ways to help the cause, the nature of the farm problem was such that it did not lend itself, except in the most general and long-run way, to Communist purposes. . . . [N]othing of importance took place in AAA as a result of their presence that the AAA liberals would not have done anyway. For the Communist Party, the AAA group was a staging area for personnel, not a fulcrum for policy." Schlesinger, p. 54.

8. Interviews with Lee Pressman, Aug. 30 and 31, 1950, in FBI report, Oct. 2, 1950, #4651.

9. For Weyl's testimony, see Guy Hottel to Director, Nov. 27, 1950, #4670, FBI; for Herbst, see "Memorandum to Mr. McLean; Paraphrase of Interview with Miss Josephine Herbst on January 7, 1949," Jan. 8, 1949, HISS.

10. Interviews with Lee Pressman, Summary Report, Jan. 31, 1949, #1515, FBI.

11. The following material on Weyl is drawn from his Nov. 27, 1950, FBI interview, *op. cit.*; INTERVIEW, Nathaniel Weyl (by telephone), Oct. 28, 1974; Senate Internal Security Subcommittee, Hearings, "Institute of Pacific Relations," Feb. 19, 1952, and *ibid.*, Hearings, "Subversive Influence in the Educational Process," March 30, 1953, both "Testimony of Nathaniel Weyl"; and Weyl, "I Was in a Communist Unit with Hiss," *U.S. News and World Report*, Jan. 9, 1953.

12. *Ibid.* On Weyl's departure from Washington, see also John L. Shover, *Cornbelt Rebellion*, p. 175, and Nathaniel Weyl to the author, April 14, 1978. Shover provides an excellent sketch of the efforts made by Harold Ware and other CP militants to take over the nonpartisan Farm Holiday Movement.

13. Weyl's testimony about Hiss: Hottel to Director, Nov. 27, 1950, *op. cit.*

14. For Herbst's FBI interviews, see the reports of Feb. 8, 1949, #1820, and Nov. 19, 1949, #4329; for Herrmann's interview, see Director, FBI, to SAC, New York, June 13, 1949, #3391, FBI.

15. Josephine Herbst's testimony in this and the following paragraphs comes primarily from three interviews with defense lawyers, held on the following dates in 1949: Jan. 7 (Jan. 8 memo), April 10 (April 13 memo), and Nov. 25 (Nov. 26 memo), HISS.

16. These unpublished letters exchanged between Herrmann and Herbst are in Josephine Herbst's papers at Yale, to which the writer was allowed access thanks to the generosity of Herbst's literary executor, Hilton Kramer. They not only confirm Herbst's account of Chambers's relationship to the Ware Group but also provide a more intimate glimpse into that group's activities than any previously known source. I am in Hilton Kramer's debt and in debt also to Elinor Langer, the biographer of Josephine Herbst, for sharing with me their knowledge of Herbst. On the Ware Group, see also Latham, pp. 101–23.

17. Herrmann to Herbst, March 9, 1935, Herbst MSS, Yale. The Duggan mention is in an undated letter.

18. Herrmann to Herbst, June (n.d.) 1934. For references in the correspondence to either Chambers or Ware, see the Herrmann-Herbst letters on the following 1934 dates: Sept. 19, Sept. 24, Oct. 4, Nov. 15, Dec. 7, Dec. 12, Dec. 13. At one point Chambers urged Herrmann to abandon his underground work for farming and a return to writing. Herrmann to Herbst, Dec. 12, 1934.

19. Interview with Josephine Herbst, April 10, 1949, HISS.

20. McManus to Hiss, Aug. 5, 1948; Hiss to McManus, Aug. 6, 1948; and Hiss's annotations to McManus's memo, "Agricultural Purge," HISS.

21. Summary Report, May 11, 1949, #3220, FBI, pp. 72–80, for Chambers's account in these paragraphs of the Ware Group and the establishment of a "second apparatus."

22. For Hiss's version of the transfer to the Nye Committee, see Hiss to Marbury Oct. 25, 1948, HISS, and INTERVIEW, Alger Hiss, June 21, 1975; for Frank's, see Jerome Frank, Oral History, Frank MSS, Yale; for Gardner Jackson's, see Jackson's Oral History, Columbia University, pp. 468–69.

23. *Ibid.* See also Alger Hiss, "Memorandum re Acquaintanceship with Gardner Jackson," n.d., HISS.

24. Summary Report, #3220, FBI, pp. 81–82.

25. Hiss to Malcolm Mason, Dec. 8, 1934; Hiss to Abe Fortas, Dec. 8, 1934; Mason to Hiss, n.d.; "Memorandum," Hiss to Mason, n.d.; HISS.

26. For Chambers's accusations, see the FBI Summary Report, #3220, pp. 83–84; for Hiss's denials, see INTERVIEW, Alger Hiss, June 21, 1975, and "Memorandum re Conference with Joseph C. Green," Oct. 25, 1949, HISS.

27. Nye Committee's Preliminary Report, "Mr. Hiss, Copy #11," HISS; John E. Wiltz, *In Search of Peace: The Senate Munitions Inquiry, 1934–1936,* pp. 52–53, 58–60.

28. WITNESS, pp. 349–50. Chambers did not meet Herbst again after 1935, so it is unlikely that he drew upon her memories when recalling this meeting.

29. These observations by Hiss can be found in his "Account of Contacts with George Crosley," contained in his "Autobiographical Notes," ca. Aug.–Sept 1948, HISS.

30. *Ibid.* The various aspects of Chambers's story that the Hisses agreed had occurred are described at length in Chapters I, VIII, XII, and XIII, *passim.*

31. For Chambers's account of his personal relationship with the Hisses, see Summary Report, #3220, FBI, pp. 108–110, 126–30, 181–83, and *passim.*

32. *Ibid.,* p. 129; FBI teletypes, Feb. 15, 1949, #1899, and Mar. 1, 1949, #2272, deal with the Nicholson matter. See also John F. Davis to William Marbury, Nov. 29, 1948, and Davis to Alger Hiss, Nov. 19, 1948, HISS. Davis's letter to Marbury contains this passage: "Dr. Nicholson politely refuses to disclose any information from her records without a request from Mrs. Chambers." See also Chambers's Nov. 4, 1948, testimony, and "Alger Hiss, Plaintiff, vs. Whittaker Chambers, Defendant, Civil No. 4176, in the United States District Court for the District of Maryland, Baltimore, Maryland, November 4, 1948," p. 600, for Mrs. Chambers's first testimony on this point in Nov. 1948. Citations for this and subsequent depositions hereafter given as BALTIMORE.

33. BALTIMORE, p. 1128; INTERVIEW, Alger Hiss, June 21, 1975.

34. For Chambers's version of Hiss's visit to Smithtown, see Summary Report, #3220, p. 128. Among the many FBI memos dealing with Smithtown, the following deserve special mention: Nov. 9, 1949, #4160; Jan. 4, 1950, #4425; Nov. 18, 1949, #4249 INC; Jan. 31, 1949, #1517; and Feb. 3, 1949, #1587. During the Smithtown period Chambers obtained both British and French visas on a passport he had taken out in May 1935 under the name "David Breen," indicating that his Russian

superior "Bill" still had plans then for an English network involving him.

35. See the interviews with Lieber in the Hiss Defense Files on the following dates: Oct. 11, 1948; Oct. 29, 1948; and Nov. 12, 1948 (the last also with Lieber's lawyer, Joseph H. Crown). For the comment by "Licht," see "Oral Report from Mr. [Horace] Schmahl Today," Jan. 21, 1949, HISS.

36. "Memorandum re Maxim Lieber," Nov. 12, 1948, HISS; Robert Alan Aurthur, "Hanging Out," Esquire, July 1972; INTERVIEW, Maxim Lieber, May 10 and 13, 1975.

37. Among the numerous FBI memos on the search for "Edith," see the following: Sept. 20, 1949, #3886; Sept. 22, 1949, #3885; Sept. 29, 1949, #3920; and Oct. 3, 1949, #4028.

38. For Edith Murray's signed statement, see FBI report, Oct. 3, 1949, #4028, pp. 4–7.

39. For Edith Murray's identification of Priscilla Hiss, see the following 1949 FBI reports: Oct. 10, #4114; Oct. 17, #4087; Nov. 17, #4184; and Nov. 19, #4226. See also SECOND, p. 3032, and "How the FBI Trapped Hiss," The American Weekly, Aug. 6, 1950.

40. SAC, Philadelphia, to Director, Jan. 21, 1949, #1692, FBI.

41. Davis to Hiss, Oct. 18, 1948; Hiss to Marbury, Nov.1, 1948, HISS.

42. For Hiss's explanation of the friendship, see Hiss, Jan. 11, 1949, to Dr. Carl Binger, enclosing a ten-page "Analysis of Chambers' Testimony as to 'Intimacy' with Me and My Family," HISS.

43. For accounts of the AAA "purge," see Schlesinger, pp. 74–83; David E. Conrad, The Forgotten Farmers, especially pp. 136–53; Dwight Macdonald, Henry Wallace: The Man amid the Myth, pp. 45–58; E. L. and F. H. Schapsmeier, Henry A. Wallace of Iowa: The Agrarian

Years, 1910–1940, pp. 201–05; and Gardner Jackson, "Henry Wallace: A Divided Mind," The Atlantic Monthly, Sept. 1948, p. 28.

44. Macdonald, pp. 54–55.

45. For Hiss's version, see his "Memorandum on Circumstances Attending the AAA 'Purge'" (n.d., ca. Sept. 1948), his "Memorandum re Acquaintanceship with Gardner Jackson" (n.d., ca. Sept. 1948), and his "Memorandum of Conversation with . . . Telford Taylor, October 29, 1948," HISS. Frank's unpublished handwritten "Memorandum Concerning the Legal Opinion Dated February 4, 1935 . . ." accompanies a covering letter to Chester Davis (n.d., ca. Feb. 1935), Frank MSS, Yale. See also Frank's Oral History interview for details of the purge, ibid., especially pp. 178, 186, and POST, Feb. 6 and 7, 1935.

46. Oral History, p. 186, Frank MSS, Yale. The Frank papers contain an excellent file of memoranda related to the cotton-sharecropper decision and the background of the AAA purge.

47. Ibid.

48. For Hiss's version, see "Memorandum on Circumstances Attending the AAA 'Purge,'" op. cit. For the Wallace-Davis press conference and its aftermath, see Conrad, pp. 149–51.

49. For Davis's refusal, see Chester C. Davis to William L. Marbury, March 31, 1949; for Wenschel's, see John F. Davis to Claude B. Cross, Dec. 20, 1949; HISS.

50. Whittaker Chambers, Lee Pressman, and Nathaniel Weyl all testified later to Perlo's membership in the Ware Group. For the assertion that Perlo headed the group after Harold Ware's death, see Chambers's account in WITNESS, pp. 378–79. On the "Perlo Group," see the summary in Latham, pp. 159–67.

51. On Mrs. Perlo's letter, see the following 1949 FBI memos: Mar. 10, #2291; April 21, #2928; and March 3, #2126.

Katherine Wills Perlo suffered an apparent emotional breakdown in 1949, according to FBI records. Hottel to Director, April 21, 1949, #2928. Hope Hale Davis to the author, April 27, 1978.

52. Summary Report, May 11, 1949, #3220, pp. 83–84, 88.

53. A number of FBI memos summarize these facts. See, for example, D. M. Ladd to Director, Feb. 16, 1949, #2236.

CHAPTER V

1. Alan R. McCracken, Acting Assistant Director, CIA, "Memorandum for the Secretary of State," Sept. 21, 1948, CIA; Washington *Times-Herald*, Sept. 26, 1948.

2. POST, Sept. 28, 1948; NYT, Sept. 28, 1948.

3. *Ibid.*, Oct. 9, 1948; POST, Oct. 26, 1948.

4. NYT, Oct. 13, 1948.

5. Hiss to Marbury, Aug. 31, 1948, HISS. William Marbury's files on the case contain the fullest record of debates among Alger Hiss's friends and lawyers on the advisability of filing a lawsuit against Chambers. Marbury interviewed both Alger and Priscilla Hiss at their apartment prior to filing suit, and both assured him that "there were [no] skeletons in the closet of either one of them. . . . However, I found my interview with Priscilla somewhat mystifying. I had asked to see her alone after Alger had left for the office, and we talked for nearly an hour. I got the impression that she felt that in some way she was responsible for the troubles which had come to Alger. However, she stoutly supported Alger's story of his association with 'George Crosley' and insisted that neither of them had ever been connected with the Communist Party." Marbury, "The Hiss Case," pp. 32–33.

6. Davis to McLean, Sept. 10, 1948; McLean to Davis, Sept. 13, 1948; HISS.

7. Marbury to Grenville Clark, Sept. 15, 1948, *ibid.*

8. Charles E. Wyzanski, Jr., to Charles A. Horsky, Sept. 1, 1948; Clark to Marbury, Sept. 18, 1948, *ibid.*

9. *Ibid.;* Marbury to Hiss, Sept. 22, 1948; Marbury to Clark, Sept. 22, 1948 (copy to President James B. Conant); Clark to Marbury; Sept. 24, 1948; Marbury to Joseph F. Johnson, Sept. 29, 1948; *ibid.*

10. On the Hiss suit and the Carnegie Endowment, see the following 1948 letters: Marbury to John F. Davis, Sept. 29; Marbury to John W. Davis (copies to Arthur Ballantine and John Foster Dulles), Sept. 29; Marbury to Hiss, Sept. 29; Davis to Marbury, Sept. 30; *ibid.* Dulles to Ballantine, Sept. 10; James T. Shotwell to Dulles, Sept. 16; Hiss to Dulles, Sept. 27; Dulles to Hiss, Oct. 1; Shotwell to Dulles, Oct. 20; Dulles MSS, Princeton. See also William Harbaugh, *Lawyer's Lawyer*, pp. 448–49.

11. Alger Hiss, "Memorandum of Conversation with Clarence Pickett . . . September 21, 1948 . . . ," HISS.

12. The original Hiss private investigators filed a summary report in mid-fall 1948 under the title, "Re: Jay Vivian Chambers . . . History of the Case," incorporating many of their daily reports to Edward McLean. For the statement of objectives, see p. 4 of the report.

13. On Chambers's alleged mental illness, see *ibid.*, pp. 19–28. On the homosexuality probe, see Harold Rosenwald, "Memorandum . . . ," Oct. 25, 1948. By Oct. 1948, rumors of a homosexual relationship between Hiss and Chambers began to spread, and Hiss's friends worked to quash the reports. Charles E. Wyzanski, Jr., to William Marbury,

Oct. 14, 1948; see also John F. Davis to Edward McLean, Sept. 3, 1948, and McLean to Marbury, Oct. 19, 1948; HISS.

14. "Re: Jay Vivian Chambers . . . ," *op. cit.*; Alger Hiss to Donald Hiss, Oct. 20, 1948, *ibid.*

15. Memo, "Information from Mr. Collins," Sept. 22, 1948. See also "Re: Jay Vivian Chambers . . . ," and Davis to McLean, Sept. 3, 1948, *op. cit.*

16. "Memorandum of Conversation with Prof. Mark Van Doren," Nov. 15, 1948. See also the memo of Rosenwald's March 10, 1949, conference with Van Doren, and Rosenwald's Oct. 7, 1948, memo of a conference with Liebling; HISS.

17. Marbury to Johnston, Sept. 22, 1948. See also Davis to McLean, Oct. 12, 1948. *Ibid.*

18. Marbury to Hiss, Oct. 25, 1948, and Nov. 3, 1948. *Ibid.*

19. Hiss to Marbury, Oct. 18, 1948. *Ibid.*

20. The correspondence exchanged among Hiss's lawyers during this period is voluminous. See the following important 1948 letters: Hiss to Richard Field, Nov. 1; Hiss to Marbury, Nov. 3; Field to Hiss, Oct. 29; Field to Marbury, Nov. 17; Marbury to Field, Nov. 22; Donald Hiss to Marbury, Oct. 23; Marbury to Donald Hiss, Oct. 25; Donald Hiss to Marbury, Oct. 30; Spencer Gordon to Marbury, Nov. 17; Hugh B. Cox to Marbury, Nov. 19. *Ibid.*

21. McLean to Marbury, Nov. 1, 1948. *Ibid.*

22. For Chambers's Nov. 4, 1948, testimony, see BALTIMORE, pp. 1–209.

23. *Ibid.*, p. 208.

24. *Ibid.*, pp. 211–14. For Chambers's Nov. 5 testimony, see pp. 210–440.

25. *Ibid.*, pp. 312–17.

26. Marbury to Robert Proctor, Nov. 11, 1948, HISS.

27. WITNESS, p. 730.

28. *Ibid.*, p. 735; FBI teletype, May 27, 1949, #3188, for the mysterious telegram received by Levine that bureau agents located in the files of Western Union.

29. FBI Summary Report, May 11, 1949, #3220, pp. 135–36.

30. SAC, Baltimore, to Director, Nov. 25, 1948, #317.

31. FBI Summary Report, #3220, *op. cit.*, p. 136.

32. For Esther Chambers's Nov. 16, 1948, testimony, see BALTIMORE, pp. 441–640.

33. For Esther Chambers's Nov. 17, 1948, testimony, see BALTIMORE, pp. 641–715.

34. *Ibid.*, pp. 698, 713–15.

35. *Ibid.*, pp. 717–19. For Chambers's Nov. 17, 1948, testimony, see *ibid.*, pp. 716–829.

36. For these exchanges, *ibid.*, pp. 719–20.

37. *Ibid.*, pp. 739–42.

38. *Ibid.*, p. 743.

39. The testimony was quoted at Hiss's second trial for perjury, pp. 350–51.

40. SIX, p. 49.

41. SAC, Baltimore, to Director, Nov. 25, 1948, *op. cit.* See also Marbury, "The Hiss Case," pp. 48–49.

42. SAC, Baltimore, to Director, *op. cit.*; D. M. Ladd to Director, Nov. 23, 1948, #221; Alexander M. Campbell to Director, "Subject: Testimony of Whittaker Chambers Before Grand Jury," Nov. 23, 1948, #57L, FBI.

43. *Ibid.*; POST, Nov. 19, 1948; FBI memo, Dec. 5, 1948, #52. Clark had made a similar inquiry in August, and the FBI informed him at that time that there was no evidence Chambers had ever been in a mental institution. F. L. Jones to H. B. Fletcher, Dec. 5, 1948, #52, FBI.

44. D. M. Ladd to Director, Nov. 23, 1948, *op. cit.*

45. D. M. Ladd to Director, Dec. 13, 1948, enclosing Ladd to Director, Dec. 10, 1948, #1479. See also Ladd to Hoover, Sept. 8, 1948, #12X.

46. Among the many 1948 FBI memos dealing with the renewed pursuit of its Hiss-Chambers probe at this time, see especially the following: Director to SAC, Baltimore, Nov. 24, 1948, *op. cit.;* Hoover to Campbell, Nov. 30, #96; and Director to SAC, Washington Field, Dec. 1, #18.

47. See the following 1948 FBI memos: L. Whitson to D. M. Ladd, Nov. 24, #93; H. B. Fletcher to D. M. Ladd, Nov. 26, #94; L. L. Laughlin to H. B. Fletcher, Nov. 29, #94; M. W. McFarlin to Director, Nov. 29, #317; Director to Campbell, Nov. 30, #96; Director to SAC, New York, Nov. 26, #317X; and H. B. Fletcher to D. M. Ladd, Dec. 1, #97 Hoover repeated his earlier gratuitous yet pointed comment at the bottom of the Dec. 1 Fletcher-Ladd memo dealing with the bureau's probe of Chambers: "Give this matter careful & meticulous attention. Collaterally I can't understand why such effort is being made to indict Chambers to exclusion of Hiss." Throughout this period Hoover clearly favored indicting both men.

48. On the hiring of Broady's firm and Schmahl's services, see the following 1948 letters and memos: "Memorandum for File," Oct. 28; McLean to Marbury, Nov. 10; bill for services, John G. Broady, Nov. 19; Marbury to McLean, Nov. 22; Cox to Marbury, Dec. 2; Marbury to Hiss, Dec. 3; HISS.

49. For Schmahl's investigation during this period, see his summary report, Nov. 1, 1948, and Marbury to Hiss, Dec. 3, 1948, HISS.

50. INTERVIEW, Dr. Viola Bernard, June 23, 1975.

51. Harold Rosenwald, "Memorandum . . . ," Oct. 25, 1948, HISS.

52. INTERVIEW, Alger Hiss, March 15, 1975; Harold Rosenwald, "Memorandum re 'Class Reunion,'" Nov. 23, 1948, HISS.

53. Franz Werfel, *Class Reunion,* pp. 202–03. "Chambers stated that if he was asked to remember one line of the story 'Class Reunion' he would be unable to do so [and] . . . that regardless of the book's contents, nothing in his association with Alger Hiss was motivated by or had the remotest connection with any thing set forth in that book." SAC, New York, to Director, March 15, 1949, #2715, FBI.

54. Harold Rosenwald, "Memorandum for Professor Morgan," Dec. 23, 1948, HISS.

55. McLean to Marbury, Nov. 29, 1948; Marbury to McLean, Dec. 3, 1948; *ibid.* INTERVIEW, William Marbury, Feb. 24, 1975.

56. *Ibid.* See also Marbury, "The Hiss Case," p. 52; Marbury to Hiss, Dec. 3, 1948; HISS.

57. The most thorough description of the circumstances under which Chambers turned over the microfilm and its subsequent handling in Dec. 1948 can be found in "Chronology of So-called 'Pumpkin Papers' . . . ," March 3, 1949, FBI, and in FBI Summary Report, May 11, 1949, #3220, pp. 137–39.

58. *Ibid.* The note read: "Karl—If you have given up playing around with my girl friend, she wishes you would take your stuff out of her closet, so she can use it for her clothes instead of yours. H." Chambers insisted that "stuff" referred to his "photographic equipment" and that the memo was a coded warning by some underground colleague—perhaps Henry Collins or John Herrmann, but *not* Alger Hiss. Whitson to Fletcher, March 28, 1949, #3102, FBI.

59. On Nixon's phone call warning the bureau about the new documents, see Nichols to Tolson, Dec. 2, 1948, #101. On the Justice Department's handling of the probe, see Laughlin to Fletcher, Dec. 2, 1948, #99, and Fletcher to Ladd, Dec. 2, 1948, #98; FBI.

60. Fletcher to Ladd, Dec. 4, 1948, #46. See also the following: Dec. 3, 1948, Fletcher to Ladd, FBI memos #21, #103, and #104.

61. Fletcher to Ladd, Dec. 4, 1948, *op. cit.*

62. Ladd to Director, Dec. 4, 1948, #106; Nichols to Tolson, Dec. 2, 1948, *op. cit.*; Nichols to Tolson, Dec. 2, 1948, #102.

63. POST and Washington *Daily News,* both Dec. 1, 1948. See also NYT, Dec. 2, 1948, "Hiss Inquiry Lagging."

64. The following paragraphs draw substantially on my interviews with Robert Stripling and Nicholas Vazzana, several by telephone but especially those in person on April 28, 1975 (Stripling), and June 30, 1975 (Vazzana). They had not seen each other since the Dec. 1948 events described, but after I traced each man, they told virtually identical stories of the events in question. See also Allen Weinstein, "Nixon vs. Hiss," *Esquire,* Nov. 1975.

65. SIX, pp. 50–51.

66. INTERVIEW, Robert Stripling, June 30, 1975.

67. Bert Andrews and Peter Andrews, *A Tragedy of History,* pp. 175–76.

68. Nichols to Tolson, Dec. 2, 1948, *op. cit.*

69. SIX, p. 51; INTERVIEW, Robert Stripling, June 30, 1975.

70. *Ibid.;* Andrews to Dulles, Dec. 2, 1948, Dulles MSS, Princeton.

71. INTERVIEW, Robert Stripling, *op. cit.;* WITNESS, pp. 752–54; "Chronology of So-called 'Pumpkin Papers' . . . ," March 3, 1949, FBI, p. 2.

72. *Ibid.,* p. 3; INTERVIEW, Donald Appell, Aug. 29, 1974.

73. In 1975, at the Justice Department, I placed 65 sheets of onionskin paper, four folded memo sheets comparable to the handwritten notes, and the actual three canisters and two rolls of microfilm in an envelope identical in size to the one turned over by Chambers (which I had measured while inspecting Hiss trial exhibits in the U.S. Attorney's office in Manhattan). The package was bulky but easily closed and sealed.

74. Testimony of Nathan I. Levine, HUAC II, p. 1456, Dec. 10, 1948. Levine's entire testimony: pp. 1451–65.

75. Summary Report, Mar. 30, 1949, #3221, p. 130.

76. HUAC II, p. 1454; Ladd to Director, Dec. 7, 1948, #62.

77. INTERVIEWS, Meyer and Lillian Schapiro, Nov. 17, 1974, and Aug. 9, 1975.

78. SIX, p. 52; Andrews and Andrews, pp. 172–73; Stripling, pp. 147–48.

79. For Stripling's statements and the fast-breaking events of early Dec. 1948, see NYT, Dec. 3, 4, and 5.

80. *Ibid.,* Dec. 3, 1948.

81. McLean to Marbury, Dec. 3, 1948, HISS.

CHAPTER VI

1. For Browder's statements about Hiss and Chambers, see the following: Alger Hiss, "Memorandum of a Conversation with John Weiss of the New York *Star,*" Dec. 31, 1948" (memo dated Jan. 4, 1949), HISS; FBI memo, March 11, 1949, #2457, and Director to SAC, New York, Feb. 25, 1949, enclosing the Director's Feb. 21,

1949, teletype, #2432, FBI; Philip J. Jaffe, *The Rise and Fall of American Communism,* p. 175.

2. One of Browder's former CP associates later became more candid, if still only in private conversation. An influential Communist leader who left the Party in 1956, he confided to Philip Jaffe, himself once close to the CP and an intimate of Browder's, that Chambers had told the truth about Hiss. INTERVIEW, Philip J. Jaffe, Sept. 17, 1975.

3. Dallin, pp. 403–04. The leading Soviet agent in this country in 1932–34, whom Chambers had known as "Herman," "Herbert," and "Oscar" (later identified as Valentin Markin), Ulrich's enemy, was found with his head bashed in in 1934 in a New York City hallway. Walter Krivitsky's memoirs quoted the chief of the GPU's Foreign Section as telling him in 1937 that Markin had been murdered by "Trotskyists" in his own network. Most of his replacements proved equally unimaginative, though more productive. Hede Massing, for example, spent a good deal of time on assignment as an agent in 1936 and 1937 shadowing another GPU operative, Ludwig Lore, who later befriended Chambers and whom Massing's superiors suspected of disloyalty. Summary Report, May 11, 1949, #3220, pp. 53–57; Hede Massing, *This Deception,* pp. 156–62, 201–05.

4. Irving Howe and Lewis Coser, *The American Communist Party,* pp. 319–55; Daniel Bell, *Marxian Socialism in the United States,* pp. 143–44; Arthur M. Schlesinger, Jr., *The Politics of Upheaval,* pp. 563–70. Herbert Solow wrote in 1938 that his last meeting with Chambers prior to the latter's defection had been a shouting match in 1935 over the merits of the Franco-Soviet Pact. Solow, a militant anti-Stalinist radical by then, denounced the agreement as a betrayal of revolutionary principles, while Chambers defended the pact as necessary because of Germany's remilitarization. Solow Memo, Nov. 12, 1938, p. 6.

5. Alexander Orlov, *Handbook of Intelligence and Guerrilla Warfare,* pp. 108–09.

6. Noel Field, "Hitching Our Wagon to a Star," *Mainstream,* Jan. 1961.

7. Information in this section comes from several sources, notably Flora Lewis, *Red Pawn;* Hede Massing, *This Deception,* especially pp. 163–80; Stewart Steven, *Operation Splinter Factor;* Karel Kaplan, "Triplo gioco per Stalin," *Panorama,* May 24, 1977; and from my interviews with the following people: Hermann Field, March 24, 1975; Prof. Karel Kaplan, March 27 and April 19, 1977; and Hede Massing, Nov. 11, 1974. Not only did Prof. Kaplan describe Field's comments to Hungarian and Czech secret-police interrogators about Alger Hiss's role in the CP underground and Field's own career as an agent, but he placed at my disposal his thoroughly researched manuscript on the Czechoslovakian purge trials (an English translation of which I received through the courtesy of Stewart Steven), as well as other previously unavailable Czech studies of the Field case. On Prof. Kaplan's importance as an archivist and historian, see Steven, pp. 232–33 and *Time,* May 9, 1977, p. 38.

8. INTERVIEWS, Prof. Karel Kaplan, *op. cit.*

9. Massing, pp. 274–78.

10. INTERVIEWS, Prof. Karel Kaplan, *op. cit.;* Lewis, *passim.*

11. Although Stewart Steven does not provide persuasive evidence to support his intriguing thesis that Field's arrest in Czechoslovakia in 1949 and his subsequent role in the Eastern European purge trials were orchestrated by an undercover CIA agent in Polish intelligence, his book contains a number of shrewd observations

about the Soviet reaction to Field during this period. *Passim.*

12. For Duggan's statement, see the Dec. 10, 1948, FBI memo of the interview, and Hoover to Campbell, Dec. 10, 1948; FBI. For Massing's charges against Duggan, see her Dec. 7 and 8, 1948, FBI interviews, and Scheidt to Hoover, Feb. 9, 1949, #2029.

13. Lewis, pp. 57–58.

14. The general dilemma is well described in David Caute's chapter on "The Popular Front Era" in *The Fellow-Travellers,* pp. 132–84. After the Second World War the contradictions in Field's life surfaced once again. He sought a new role as a journalist to combine both aspects of his "dual life," but the result proved tragic for himself and his family. Field disappeared in Eastern Europe, Herta followed him to an identical fate, and it later emerged that both had been arrested by Czech and Hungarian secret police, tried as American agents, and convicted. They served prison terms until their release in 1956. Field's brother and foster daughter suffered similar arrest and imprisonment when they went in search of him. Lewis, *passim;* Steven, *passim.* INTERVIEW, Hermann Field, *op. cit.;* INTERVIEWS, Prof. Karel Kaplan, *op. cit.*

15. FBI interviews with Hede Massing, Dec. 7 and 8, 1948, *op. cit.;* Massing, p. 174.

16. For Detzer's recollections, see FBI report, Jan. 10, 1949, #1124.

17. Alger Hiss, "Memorandum Relating to Noel Field . . . ," Oct. 18, 1948, HISS.

18. *Ibid.,* p. 1. On allegations of Field's Communist ties, Hiss wrote only that "Mr. Field ran afoul of narrow prejudices," p. 3. See also Field to Hiss, July 21, 1957, and Hiss to Field, Feb. 15, 1958; HISS.

19. Priscilla Hiss, "Memorandum of Grand Jury Appearance," Dec. 10, 1948, p. 12, HISS.

20. Dr. Wilhelm Staehelin, "Interview with Mrs. Noel Field," July 25, 1949; see also Staehelin to Robert von Mehren, Aug. 4, 1949, *ibid.*

21. INTERVIEWS, Prof. Karel Kaplan, *op. cit.*

22. FBI interview with Laurence Duggan, Dec. 10, 1948, *op. cit.*

23. See, for example, the following 1948 letters: Field to Duggan, April 19; Hiss to Field, May 7; Field to Hiss, May 12; Hiss to Field, Oct. 19; Field to Hiss, Nov. 2; Hiss to Marbury, Nov. 12; HISS.

24. "Memorandum of Interview with Mrs. Helen Duggan," Jan. 24, 1949, *ibid.* Hermann Field speculated that Hiss may have been forced since the opening of the case in 1948 into an unnecessary form of role playing—"pushed into a corner"—because of his effort to repudiate or minimize most earlier connections on the left during the 1930s, including those with Noel Field. Although Hermann Field had no personal knowledge of the relationship between Hiss and Chambers, he thought that Hiss's effort at the time of the case to obscure earlier associations with antifascist radicals demeaned the "fibre of the generation" whose essential ethos Hermann Field—himself imprisoned in Poland for five years—continued to defend. INTERVIEW, Hermann Field, *op. cit.*

25. Priscilla Hiss pointed this out in describing her appearance before the grand jury in 1948:

They asked me if I knew Mr. and Mrs. Harold Ware? My answer was no. [But, according to Alger Hiss, Priscilla and Jessica Smith Ware had known each other since the 1920s.]

Had Mr. and Mrs. Witt been to the house? Mr. Witt had been there. Pressman, Abt? Yes for both.

Henry Collins? Certainly he had been. He was always welcome. He was there a number of times.

Priscilla Hiss, "Memorandum . . . ," Dec. 10, 1948, *op. cit.*

26. Henry Collins, "Digest from Memory of My Appearance Before the Grand Jury 12/3/48." On Collins's background, see "Further Information from Mr. Collins," Oct. 6, 1948, HISS.

27. Herrmann to Herbst, March 9, 1935, Herbst MSS, Yale. "Interview with Josephine Herbst," April 10, 1949, HISS.

28. Kim Philby, *My Secret War,* p. 214; Rebecca West, *The New Meaning of Treason,* p. 187.

29. Philby, p. 21; Field, "Hitching Our Wagon to a Star," *op. cit.*

30. Smith, pp. 83–84.

31. "Statement of Alger Hiss" for Lloyd Paul Stryker, March 8, 1949, p. 14, HISS.

32. Smith, p. 96; Hiss to Marbury, June 13, 1935, HISS.

33. Marbury to Hiss on the following 1935 dates: Aug. 7, Aug. 22, and Nov. 16. *Ibid.*

34. On Hiss's transfer to State from Justice, see the following memoranda by Alger Hiss: "Department of Justice," "Department of State," and "Memorandum on Acquaintanceship with John S. Dickey," n.d.; HISS. See also Francis B. Sayre to Secretary Hull, April 28, 1936, and "Memorandum of Interview on . . . January 15, 1949 with John S. Dickey," *ibid.*

35. Interview with Francis B. Sayre, Oct. 27, 1949, HISS.

36. Alger Hiss, "Memorandum on . . . John S. Dickey," *op. cit.;* "Memorandum of Interview . . . with John S. Dickey," *op. cit.*

37. For Chambers's account of Bykov's "arrival and the rug incident, see FBI Summary Report, May 11, 1949, #3220, pp. 91–95.

38. *Ibid.,* p. 95.

39. "Statement of Alger Hiss," March 8, 1949, *op. cit.* The Hisses provided at least three different versions of how Chambers delivered the rug. When questioned by the grand jury on Dec. 13, 1948, Hiss said that he "was not sure" if Chambers had delivered it personally, "and I was not sure that I was home when it was received." In a memo to his attorneys on the appearance, moreover, Hiss said he told the grand jury that Chambers "had said that he got it from a wealthy patron." But the actual grand jury testimony, cited at Hiss's first trial, mentions no such patron. At the first trial, his recollection of the rug was more precise. Hiss testified that he and probably Mrs. Hiss had been at home when Chambers delivered it (Hiss did not recall Priscilla's presence when testifying before the grand jury). When she testified at the trial, Mrs. Hiss said she had been present for the delivery. Alger Hiss, "Memorandum of Grand Jury Appearance," Alger Hiss, Dec. 13, 1948, HISS; FIRST, pp. 2202, 2204.

40. Harry Dexter White's widow told her lawyer only "that she received a rug not later than the fall of 1937." In 1949 the FBI located A. George Silverman's former maid, Florence Tomkins, who recalled three Oriental rugs—not four— having been delivered to Silverman's Washington home "in the fall or winter of 1936" (but, in any event, before the spring of 1937 when the Silvermans moved). One of Silverman's neighbors in the apartment building during 1937–38 to which Silverman moved, a man who "had a nodding acquaintance with Alger Hiss . . . remembered taking Hiss up on the manually operated elevator and letting him out on the third floor [Silverman's], but he did not know which apartment Hiss entered."

Interview with A. George Silverman, April 26, 1949, and memorandum re Mrs. Harry White, March 11, 1949; HISS. See also FBI reports on the Bokhara rug question in 1949 for the following dates: April 26, #2938; May 20; March 9, #2284; and also one for Nov. 16, 1950.

41. At Hiss's first trial in 1949 Mrs. Catlett confirmed that the rug had been rolled up at 30th Street, but she repudiated her earlier deposition to the FBI about Mrs. Hiss's response. Answering a question put by Hiss's attorney, she acknowledged having questioned Priscilla Hiss about the rolled-up rug's ownership, but insisted now that Mrs. Hiss "didn't say anything about it." At Hiss's second trial Mrs. Catlett also changed her earlier testimony about when the Hisses received the rug, stating that although it had been rolled up—"on the wrong side, you know"—at 30th Street, "I know it is the same rug that was in the back room on P Street [in 1935]." However, at least on the question of whether the rug had been rolled up at 30th Street in the basement closet—as Chambers recalled and Hiss denied—Mrs. Catlett's memory did not deviate during the pretrial and trial periods. See FBI deposition by Claudia Catlett, Feb. 10, 1949; FIRST, p. 16–28; SECOND, p. 1575.

42. The above transactions were confirmed by Schapiro and Touloukian in FIRST, pp. 767–77, in the Feb. 3, 1949, FBI interview with Schapiro, #1583, and in my interviews with Schapiro.

43. At his first trial in 1949 Hiss was "not sure of the exact time," but placed it in "the late spring of 1936." Later, he told John Chabot Smith, however, that the rug was acquired in late 1935. Smith, p. 91. Julian Wadleigh identified "Harold Wilson" through FBI photographs as a CP associate of Chambers named David Zimmerman (alias David Carpenter),

Wadleigh's contact man with the underground and the person who introduced him to Chambers. FBI report, Feb. 9, 1949, #1910.

44. Mrs. Catlett stated on several occasions that she had no knowledge of whether the rug had been in the Hiss household on P Street, where the Hisses had lived until June 1936, but at Hiss's second trial she testified to remembering the rug there.

45. Identifying the Bokhara more exactly is impossible, considering the distinctive qualities of each handmade rug. Edward Touloukian, who sold the rugs to Schapiro in Dec. 1936, told Hiss's lawyer in March 1949 "quite positively that he could not identify the rug in the possession of the Hiss family as one of the rugs which he sold to Schapiro. He also stated that no one else could make this identification. He said there was no way to determine when the rug was sold or manufactured. The only thing that could be determined is that the rug is a Bokhara. . . ." Harold Rosenwald, "Chambers' Rugs," March 9, 1949, HISS. But a rug expert who inspected Hiss's Bokhara for the defense in 1949 declared that its "dimensions were for all intensive [sic] purposes the same as those indicated on the sales slip [which Meyer Schapiro had received for the four rugs purchased in Dec. 1936]." "Memorandum of Conversation with Harold Shapero," Oct. 1, 1949, ibid.

46. BALTIMORE, pp. 602–03.

47. FIRST, pp. 280–81; COURT, pp. 234–35.

48. Priscilla Hiss to W. M. Hillegeist, May 25, 1937, reprinted as Government Exhibit 34, SECOND. See also Mrs. Hiss's testimony at the first trial, pp. 2322–24, and Hiss to Marbury, Nov. 11, 1948, HISS.

49. For Sister Celeste's letter to Mrs. Hiss, SECOND, pp. 3859–60. See

also BALTIMORE, p. 280, and Alger Hiss, "Biographical Notes: Priscilla Hiss," *op. cit.*

50. Among the many FBI reports in 1949 that dealt with its probe of the Peterborough trip, see especially the following: Feb. 25, 1949, #2255; Jan. 27, 1949, #2175; March 4, 1949; March 2, 1949, #2367; and March 21, 1949. The FBI reports prove, at least, that Chambers did not add what Hiss later termed "the Thomaston embroidery . . . only in the second trial, when Mr. Cross [Claude Cross, Hiss's attorney] was emphasizing the distance between Washington and Peterborough." Chambers told the FBI about the Thomaston visit even before the first trial during his earliest statements about the Peterborough trip. See also FIRST, pp. 209–10; SECOND, pp. 1688–99; and COURT, pp. 231—33.

51. Memorandum re Mrs. Harry Dexter White, March 11, 1949, *op. cit.* For Dorothy Detzer's testimony about Alma White's friend, see FBI report, Oct. 26, 1950, #4660, and Hoover's Nov. 30, 1950, memo, #4665.

52. The FBI had sought "Evelyn" unsuccessfully during Hiss's two perjury trials, but only after Hiss's conviction did Chambers find papers in his files that identified her last name. She still lived in Baltimore when FBI agents located her in 1952. See the FBI reports for Feb. 15, 1952, #4913, and Feb. 16, 1952, #5053.

53. The best account of the political impact of the Bridges case can be found in George Martin, *Madame Secretary: Frances Perkins*, pp. 407–19.

54. Donald Hiss, "Memorandum re Testimony . . . Before the Grand Jury," Dec. 9, 1948. On Donald Hiss's background and his attitudes toward Alger and Priscilla Hiss, see the revealing memo by McLean of his "Conference with Hugh Cox [Donald Hiss's lawyer and friend]," Dec. 8, 1948; HISS.

55. Donald Hiss, "Memorandum re Testimony . . . ," *op. cit.*

56. Frances Perkins to Francis Sayre, April 22, 1938, HISS.

57. J. L. Houghteling to Edward G. Cahill, April 15, 1938, *ibid.* On Donald Hiss and the Bridges case, see also SECOND, pp. 1703–06, for Donald Hiss's testimony. His attorney, Hugh Cox, obtained a statement for Alger Hiss's attorneys in 1948 from Gerard Reilly concerning "the events that preceded the resignation of Donald Hiss from the Labor Department." Reilly's initial recollection squared with Perkins's letter to Sayre in remembering complaints that Donald Hiss's departure would deprive Labor of its chief expert on the Bridges case just before the scheduled deportation hearing. Cox to Marbury, Oct. 25, 1948, HISS.

58. BALTIMORE, pp. 674–75; COURT, p. 240.

59. The FBI report for Dec. 5, 1949, #4319, outlines the bureau's handling of these records from the outset.

60. FBI report, Feb. 14, 1949, #2354.

61. FBI report, Dec. 5, 1949, #4319.

62. Hiss remembered acquiring several sets of glassware in Nov. 1937 for use in entertaining colleagues because of his "position in the State Department," although his maid, Claudia Catlett, "didn't remember any quantity of new glassware being bought at this time." FIRST, p. 2777; "Memorandum re Catletts," Oct. 31, 1949; and "Things Bought by Cash for 3415 Volta Place," n.d., HISS.

63. FIRST, p. 2775.

64. FBI report, Aug. 25, 1949, #3926.

65. Testimony of Gladys F. Tally, SECOND, pp. 3058–70, FBI reports for Oct. 10, 1949, #4042, and Oct. 20, 1949, #4146.

66. See note 65.

67. FBI reports for Sept. 30, 1949, #4037, and Oct. 27, 1949, #4109.

68. The record of Mrs. Hiss's and Timothy Hobson's visits to Dr. Nicholson is reprinted as a trial exhibit of the latter's Account Book. SECOND, p. 3882.

69. INTERVIEW, Claude B. Cross, July 15, 1974; INTERVIEW, Alger Hiss, June 21, 1975.

CHAPTER VII

1. This and subsequent information on the 1939 meeting comes from interviews with Nadya Ulanovskaya, Jan. 3–6, 1977.

2. Wadleigh's description of Bykov, whom he knew as "Sasha," matched up to those provided by Chambers, Crane, and Maxim Lieber except in one distinctive particular: The man Wadleigh remembered meeting appeared to have only one arm. He told the FBI on Jan. 18, 1949, that "the man was armless on his right side and that the sleeve hung loose on the right." See also Wadleigh's New York *Post* article of July 15, 1949, for a similar description. Yet Wadleigh's description of "Sasha's" demeanor and remarks fits the portraits provided by Chambers and Crane of their Russian contact. Wadleigh's one-armed "Sasha" remains puzzling, unless Bykov was attempting a crude disguise to prevent future identification. Chambers recalled that Bykov "invariably carried his right hand inside his jacket or overcoat (Napoleon style)," which might be the simplest explanation for Wadleigh's observation. Nadya Ulanovskaya confirmed the fact that Boris Bykov had not lost an arm. See also Walter Krivitsky's mention of Bykov as "chief of the Soviet Military Intelligence in this country since 1936" in Krivitsky's Oct. 13, 1939, testimony before Chairman Martin Dies's House Special Committee on Un-American Activities, the earliest public identification of Bykov. Both Wadleigh and Crane recalled Bykov's appearing in the U.S. a full year earlier than Chambers testified. Harvey R.

Kornberg, although accepting Chambers's essential story of Hiss's involvement in the spy ring, theorizes that Chambers distorted some aspects of his relationship with Bykov in an effort to strengthen his case against Hiss. Harvey R. Kornberg, "Bykov, Chambers, and Hiss: New Revelations About an Odd Relationship," unpublished, 1977, courtesy of the author.

3. FBI report, Jan. 28, 1949, #2540.

4. Sorge's comments are quoted in Ralph de Toledano, *Spies, Dupes, and Diplomats*, p. 80. See also Dallin, p. 414.

5. For Chambers's account of the Bykov-Hiss meeting, see Summary Report, May 11, 1949, #3220, pp. 95–98.

6. New York *Post*, July 15, 1949.

7. For Chambers's account of his espionage work in 1937–38 and his government sources, see Summary Report, *op. cit.*, pp. 99–127.

8. "The Faking of Americans: 1. The Soviet Passport Racket," *op. cit.*, SOLOW, pp. 26–27. Ewald would soon play a prominent role in the relations between Hiss and Chambers because of two false passports he traveled under in 1938 bearing the names "Robinson" and "Rubens." See pp. 245–46 and notes.

9. *Ibid.*, pp. 14–16. See also Part II of the unpublished article "Welcome, Soviet Spies!," *passim.* The passages that follow are drawn from these two 1938 articles.

10. On J. Peters and his work ("Sandor"), *ibid.*, pp. 21–23.

11. For Inslerman's underground career, see the following: Testimony of

Felix Inslerman, "Subversion and Espionage in Defense Establishments and Industry," Hearings, Permanent Subcommittee on Investigations, Senate Committee on Government Operations, 83rd Cong., 2nd Sess., Pt. 2, Feb. 19–20, 1954, pp. 98–110; Memo, "Re: Felix Inslerman (Interview with Attorney Louis Bender)," Jan. 21, 1949, HISS; SAC, Albany, to Director, March 9, 1949, #2370; and FBI report (Albany, N.Y.), May 14, 1954.

12. Testimony of Felix Inslerman, *op. cit.*, pp. 105–06.

13. FBI report for March 12, 1949, #2446, and the undated summary (SAC, New York, to Director) of Crane's Feb. 9, 10, 11, 14, and 16, 1949, interviews with the bureau, #2446.

14. On David Carpenter, see especially FBI Summary: Report, #3220, pp. 87, 100–05; and FBI reports (interviews with Julian Wadleigh), Dec. 7, 1948, *op. cit.*, and Jan. 28, 1949, #2540.

15. The material in these paragraphs draws upon Wadleigh's statement to the FBI on December 6, 1948, cited in the Dec. 7 report on Wadleigh, *op. cit.*

16. *Ibid.* See also FBI report, Feb. 9, 1949, #1910.

17. The discussion of Franklin Victor Reno's involvement in underground activities draws upon a voluminous batch of FBI reports. The bureau conducted a far more extensive probe of Reno, who was still working with technical data, than it did of either Wadleigh or Crane, the other two confessed members of the Washington spy ring who corroborated Chambers's story. For Reno, see especially the following FBI reports: Director to Attorney General, Dec. 15, 1948, #138; Jan. 28, 1949, #1791; Feb. 11, 1949, #1981; and April 6, 1949, #3057. Hoover's Dec. 15 memo to Clark enclosed the Dec. 12 report on Reno's confession the previous day.

18. FBI Summary Report, May 11, 1949, #3220, pp. 113–15, for Chambers's statements concerning Reno. Enjoyment of the adventure and mysteriousness of such "secret work" should not be discounted as a possible motive for Reno's involvement and that of others among Chambers's government contacts. Reno corrected some details of his initial statements to the FBI in later accounts but confirmed the essential story. A Feb. 12, 1949, FBI report described him as being in "poor physical, mental, and highly neurotic condition . . . [with] evidence of paranoia." Reno was indicted for perjury in 1951 for concealing CP membership while answering a 1948 loyalty questionnaire at Aberdeen prior to his confession. He pleaded guilty in 1952 and served two and a half years in prison. See especially his statements of Dec. 12, 1948, and Feb. 11 and March 28, 1949, in the FBI's massive Reno file.

19. The handwritten White memo is reprinted in David Rees, *Harry Dexter White: A Study in Paradox*, pp. 432–35.

20. Director, FBI, to (Attorney General?), "Re: Whittaker Chambers," June 26, 1945. Although Chambers said he told the FBI about White's activities in 1942, the transcript of the interview does not mention him. But State Department security officer Raymond Murphy recorded this statement by Chambers in March 1945: "Harry White if [sic] the Treasury was described as a [CP] member at large but rather timid. He put on as assistants in the Treasury Glaser a member of the underground group and an Adler or Odler another Party member. The two Coe brothers, also Party members, were also put on by White." Raymond Murphy, "Memorandum of Conversation . . . March 20, 1945, Westminster, Md.," STATE.

21. Bentley, *Out of Bondage*, pp. 164–65. Rees, pp. 196–220. For Chambers's

relations with White, see FBI Summary Report, #3220, pp. 106–10.

22. Rees, pp. 432–35.

23. White had ordered Edgar Snow's *Red Star over China* for the Treasury Department library. FBI report, May 31, 1949, #3213.

24. FBI report, June 9, 1949, #3349. For the FBI's identification of White's handwriting as that of the memo's author, see FBI report, Dec. 7, 1948, #109. For the VA's identification, done for HUAC, see the March 2, 1949, report by handwriting expert Harold Gesell, reprinted in Rees, pp. 435–36.

25. Rees, p. 425. Rees evaluates the four-page memo more thoroughly on pp. 76–97.

26. FBI teletype, March 4, 1949, #2318. See also FBI Summary Report, *op. cit.*, pp. 103–05, for Chambers's account of his relations with Ward Pigman in the underground.

27. FBI report, Jan. 31, 1949, #2107. For a complete listing of the Navy Department documents, see FBI report, March 15, 1949. Chambers proved precise in recalling his complex arrangements with CP photographers a decade earlier. He said that his chief photographers, Carpenter and Inslerman, did not know of each other's existence for reasons of security. Moreover, for similar reasons, Chambers used Inslerman's services almost exclusively to photograph materials received from White and Hiss, while Carpenter handled Pigman's and Wadleigh's documents. The only exception to this rule seemed to be Reno, whom Carpenter had introduced to Chambers but whose document transmissions, according to Chambers, sometimes went to Inslerman.

28. On Ward Pigman, see the following: FBI reports for Feb. 8, 1949, #2347, and Feb. 15, 1949, #2394. See also Alger Hiss's

Dec. 11, 1948, memo of a talk with Pigman in the grand jury waiting room, and "Memorandum re William Ward Pigman," Dec. 21, 1948; HISS.

29. Chambers's descriptions of these procedures remained virtually identical in all of his numerous post-Dec. 1948 statements on the matter, whether to the FBI, in trial testimony, or in pretrial depositions for Hiss's slander suit. See, for example, his Dec. 3, 1948, signed statement for the FBI, and the May 11, 1949, FBI Summary Report, *op. cit.*, pp. 101–02, 127.

30. *Ibid.*; WITNESS, pp. 428–29.

31. *Ibid.*, p. 429; Chambers to Schapiro n.d. (ca. mid-Nov. 1938), courtesy of Prof. Schapiro.

32. The handwritten, typed, and microfilmed documents taken from the State Department and turned over by Chambers in 1948 were reproduced in the printed transcript of Alger Hiss's second trial, Volumes VII–IX. Accompanying the documents themselves in Volume VII were copies of the original State Department documents from which they had been drawn, in Volumes VIII and IX, all hereafter cited as SECOND with the appropriate volume numbers.

33. SECOND, VII, 3435; VIII, 3537.

34. *Ibid.* The March 2 and March 3 notes both began with brief notations in blue ink that Hiss, judging from the black ink used to write the second part of both memos, rewrote more carefully at some later moment. The imprint at the top of the memo pad used for two of the four notes—"Department of State/Assistant Secretary"—had been removed in both cases.

35. *Ibid.*, VII, 3437; VIII, 3539.

36. *Ibid.*, VII, 3439; VIII, 3541.

37. *Ibid.*, VII, 3433; VIII, 3535.

38. On the so-called Robinson-Rubens case, see NYT for the following 1937 dates:

Dec. 10–17 and Dec. 28–31; and the following 1938 dates: Jan. 25, Feb. 6, and Feb. 11. See also the following material in Herbert Solow's papers: Solow, "Stalin's American Passport Mill," *The American Mercury,* July 1939; Solow's memorandum of his relations with Whittaker Chambers, Nov. 12, 1938; and the correspondence exchanged between Solow and Loy Henderson, especially Henderson to Solow, July 8, 1939; SOLOW. The Robinson-Rubens case left an ironic sidelight related to the Hiss case. Hede and Paul Massing, like Ewald, had been summoned back to Moscow in 1937. Hermann Field, whom Paul Massing had recruited for courier work during the mid-1930s, recalled that the Massings stopped to visit him in England before proceeding on to Russia. Paul Massing, whom Field remembered appearing "scared stiff," asked Field to keep sending him postcards. Field told me he believed that this was an attempt by Massing to make the Russians recognize that the couple's presence in the Soviet Union was known to Western friends and, thereby, to help forestall their disappearance.

Once in Moscow, the Massings were questioned repeatedly by the GPU but allowed to remain free. They lived at the Metropole Hotel, where the Rubenses had also stayed until their arrest. Mrs. Massing credited the latter's case with having made it more difficult for the Russians to deal with her husband and herself in a similar manner: "The Metropole was swarming with newspapermen; they were on the alert, hoping for a scoop. . . . I took advantage of [the commotion]," fraternizing with newsmen and making herself highly visible to American acquaintances in Moscow. It was at the Metropole that Hede Massing ran into Noel and Herta Field, from whose room she bluffed GPU officials into returning passports and exit visas for herself and

her husband. Massing, p. 281; INTERVIEW, Hermann Field, March 4, 1975.

39. When the FBI interviewed Mary Martin in 1949, the woman who had sent the telegram that Henderson cabled to Hull a decade earlier turned out to be an improbable figure: a fanatical anti-Semite who exaggerated her claims to expertise on the Communist underground. It is not even certain that her identification of Rubens as the Soviet agent she had known earlier in Latvia was correct. Although Mrs. Rubens had confirmed that her husband was a Latvian, State Department security officers in 1938 placed "little confidence" in Mary Martin's identification of Rubens. (See FBI report, April 19, 1949, #3050.)

But the accuracy of Mary Martin's information or the significance of her telegram to Henderson does not depend either upon her mental condition in 1949 or upon her deficiencies as an informant on Communist espionage. The crucial element remains Hiss's transcription of Loy Henderson's confidential "Mary Martin" cable to Hull in Jan. 1938, a handwritten memo that Chambers retained and turned over ten years later.

40. On Ewald, see "The Faking of Americans . . . ," *op. cit.,* pp. 2–12, 23–29, 32–35. See also Solow's Nov. 12, 1938, memorandum, *op. cit.,* p. 15.

41. "The Faking of Americans . . . ," pp. 9–10. Chambers's article, at that point, had mentioned the public uproar in the United States over Mrs. Rubens's imprisonment and the reluctance of Soviet officials to allow Henderson to see her:

The interview took place in the Butkuri Prison in the presence of a Red Army Intelligence officer. By then Mrs. Rubens' will had been destroyed; during the interview she seldom took her eyes from the Red Army man.

The Americans were especially interested in positively identifying Mrs. Rubens as an American citizen, but had had difficulty in finding any of her former friends or connections. A woman employee of the American legation at Riga, Latvia, however, had identified Rubens in a code telegram from the Riga Legation to the American Embassy in Moscow. This woman was the widow of a former American official in eastern Europe. But when the American asked Mrs. Rubens if she remembered her, the Intelligence officer instantly forbed [sic] her to answer their question. *He had been waiting for this question since he had read the telegram on which it was based, and which said (this is a literal quotation): "Remember well Rubens from my work with Hugh (her late husband). Be strict if necessary."* [My italics.] There followed a reference to something in the Library of Congress that the Soviet Intelligence never understood.

In the end, Mrs. Rubens requested the American Government to leave her to her fate.

After this second visit, Mr. Loy Henderson wrote a detailed confidential report of the interview to the State Department in which he gave it as his opinion that Mrs. Rubens and her husband were agents of the Communist International caught in the Purge. This was not strictly accurate, but close enough to satisfy the Soviet Government that there would be passivity in Mr. Rubens' case in Washington. *For like the rest of Mr. Henderson's official correspondence, this report also found its way to the Soviet Military Intelligence.* [My italics.]

42. Compare pp. 1 and 4–6 of Loy Henderson's classified report on the Feb. 10 interview with Mrs. Rubens, Henderson to Hull, Feb. 10, 1938, STATE. See also the following 1938 documents from the State Department's Robinson-Rubens file: "Confidential—for Staff Use

Only," Jan. 20; Hull to Henderson, Jan. 28; Hull to Henderson, Feb. 8; Henderson to Hull, Feb. 9; Welles to Henderson, June 18; Hull to Henderson, Sept. 15. See also Chipman to Hull, July 6, 1939; Moore to Steinhardt, Aug. 14, 1939; and Steinhardt to Hull, Nov. 17, 1939; *ibid.* The State Department declassified these and related documents in response to my request under the Freedom of Information Act.

43. Sizoo to Harbo, Nov. 30, 1948, #320, FBI; J. Howard Haring to Harold Rosenwald, Jan. 26, 1949, HISS.

44. "Statement of Alger Hiss," March 8, 1949, *op. cit.,* pp. 79–80.

45. For the defense attorneys' difficulties with Francis B. Sayre, see the following memos of their interviews with Sayre: Dec. 27, 1948; Jan. 18, 1949; Feb. 5, 1949; Oct. 27, 1949; HISS. See also the following FBI reports on interviews with Sayre: Nov. 7, 1949, #4143, and Jan. 4, 1950, #4454.

46. Interviews with Francis B. Sayre, Jan. 18 and Oct. 2–7, 1949, *op. cit.;* Ralph de Toledano, *Seeds of Treason,* 1962 edition, p. 233. Although Sayre had managed to resolve partially his doubts about Hiss's version of the handwritten notes by the time he testified as a defense witness at the second trial, he still would not state that Hiss had ever used such notes to brief him orally, and his testimony remained ambiguous. Thus he never conceded any interest in the Robinson-Rubens case and could not fathom "especially" why Hiss had made an exact copy of the Mary Martin cable. For Sayre's testimony, SECOND, pp. 1472–1524.

47. Memoranda of interviews with Anna Belle Newcomb, Jan. 19 and Oct. 25, 1949, HISS.

48. Memorandum of interview with Eunice A. Lincoln, March 15, 1949, *ibid.*

49. Memorandum of interview with Francis B. Sayre, Feb. 5, 1949, *ibid.*

50. Interview with John S. Dickey, Jan. 17, 1949, *ibid.*

51. For copies of the microfilmed documents, see SECOND, VII, 3521–33, and enclosed reproductions.

52. But the marking "A-S" on the side of the July 21, 1937, "Aide-Mémoire" linked that document to Sayre's office, although identifying the recipients of specific items from the German trade-agreement memos remains almost impossible. They passed from office to office within the various divisions of State—Sayre's, Hawkins's, and others—concerned with international economic policy. See FBI report, May 26, 1949, #3191, and interview with Francis B. Sayre, Oct. 27, 1949, HISS.

53. Interview with Sayre, Oct. 27, 1949.

54. See Wadleigh's testimony on the point at Hiss's first trial, pp. 1340–42. For Hiss's denial that he stole the German trade documents, see SECOND, p. 1115.

55. FBI report, March 22, 1949, #2720.

56. COURT, p. 251; interviews with Anna Belle Newcomb (Jan. 19, 1949), Eunice A. Lincoln (March 15, 1949), and Francis B. Sayre (Jan. 18, 1949), HISS; FBI report, Jan. 4, 1950, #4454. Sayre's Jan. 14, 1938, diary entry contains the notation "Lve. with E.E.S.," and diary entries for Jan. 15 and 16 indicate that he had left the previous day for the weekend with his wife, whose initials were "E.E.S."

57. For copies of the three cables, see SECOND, VII, 3531–33.

58. Memorandum, "Sayre's Office," Dec. 7, 1948, HISS.

59. Interviews with Anna Belle Newcomb and Eunice A. Lincoln, *op. cit.*, especially the March 15, 1949, interview with Lincoln.

60. Hiss's account of the manner in which Chambers acquired the three cables with his initials remained substantially unchanged from Dec. 1948 on. See, for example, Memorandum, "Sayre's Office," *op. cit.*; COURT, pp. 259–60; and FBI interview with Alger Hiss, Dec. 4, 1948.

61. Among the numerous FBI reports involved in analyzing the microfilm and its contents, see the following: Hoover to Attorney General, Dec. 22, 1948; May 19, 1949, #3277; June 15, 1949, #3582; Laboratory Report, Feb. 23, 1949; and "Chronology of So-called 'Pumpkin Papers,' " March 3, 1949, #3018.

62. FBI report, June 15, 1949, #3582. See also Hoover to Attorney General, Dec. 22, 1948.

63. D. M. Ladd to Director, Feb. 23, 1949, and the related Laboratory Report for that day, *ibid.* See also the following 1949 FBI reports: Feb. 2, #1736; March 23, #3018; March 4, #2266; March 30, #2752; and April 8, #3038.

64. Efforts by Hiss's attorneys to show that the microfilm might have been faked, both prior to his trials and afterward, proved totally unsuccessful. Thus Harold Rosenwald concluded, after discussions with Eastman Kodak and Du Pont officials, that, except for possible careless exposure, there was "no basis at this time for any challenge of the accuracy of Chambers's story on any technical grounds in connection with the pumpkin films." Rosenwald, "Interview with Officials of Eastman Kodak . . . January 25, 1949." See also Rosenwald, "Interview with Officials of Dupont [sic] Company on April 7, 1949"; M. K. Robinson (Eastman Kodak) to Helen Buttenwieser, Sept. 29, 1952; Robinson to Buttenwieser, Sept. 4, 1952, and Sept. 15, 1952; and Clarence Wynd (Eastman Kodak) to Buttenwieser, Aug. 4, 1952; HISS.

65. FBI statement, Dec. 3, 1948.

66. For copies of the typed documents, see SECOND, VII, 3441–3519. For the originals of these, see *ibid.*, VIII–IX, 3543–362–9.

67. Among the many FBI reports comparing the typed stolen documents with hundreds of sample letters collected, the following distill the conclusions by bureau experts that certain "Hiss standard" letters from the 1930s and other material collected had been typed on Woodstock N230099 along with the State Department documents Hottel to Director, June 9, 1949, #3381, summarizing the Woodstock's history by year and by letters identified as having been typed on it; Director to Attorney General, Dec. 13, 1948; and Laboratory Reports for Dec. 14 and 15, 1948. For 1949 identifications, see these FBI memos: Feb. 5, #1616; March 3, #2147; May 24, #3195; Oct. 27, #4124; Nov. 3, #4163; Nov. 4, #4150; and Nov. 4, #4162. For comparable conclusions by documents examiners hired by the defense, see the following: "Memorandum re [J. Howard] Haring's Opinion," Dec. 13, 1948; "Typewriter," April 6, 1949 (on Haring's opinion); Edwin H. Fearon to Lloyd Paul Stryker, April 23, 1949. By the time the defense lawyers hired a new expert prior to Hiss's second trial, so persuaded did they appear that the stolen documents had been typed on Woodstock N230099 that Harry E. Cassidy, the new examiner, was not instructed to deal with that question. Instead he was told to assess—among other things—whether or not Priscilla Hiss had typed the State Department memos. Cassidy concluded that she probably had. See his Nov. 21, 1949, report to Harold Rosenwald; HISS.

68. On the War Department document, see COURT, pp. 276–77, and "Government Documents—Distribution," March 2, 1949 ("Our Exhibit No. 10"), HISS. This long memo summarizes, document by document, the distribution within the State Department of all the material turned over by Chambers. The comparable FBI document is a Jan. 4, 1949, report, #2121.

69. COURT, p. 277; "Government Documents—Distribution" ("Our Exhibit No. 10"), op. cit.

70. Smith, pp. 414–20. On the casual, practically nonexistent security procedures at the State Department in 1937–38, see interview with Assistant Secretary of State G. Howland Shaw, Oct. 24, 1949, HISS.

71. Edward McLean, "Documents Produced by Chambers . . . ," Jan. 7, 1949, ibid.

72. "Government Documents—Distribution" ("Our Exhibit No. 14"), ibid.

73. SECOND, VII, 3607, for the Hurban memo.

74. "Government Documents—Distribution" ("The Manchukuo Report and Accompanying Documents"), HISS.

75. "Our Exhibit No. 46," ibid.

76. Interview with Francis B. Sayre, Jan. 18, 1949, ibid. See also FBI interview with Sayre, Jan. 4, 1950, #4454.

77. See note 67 above.

78. One of Hiss's examiners said that Mrs. Hiss made the interlinear corrections, while two others believed that these resembled Hiss's handwriting more closely than Chambers's. The FBI analysts came to no firm conclusion about the interlinear corrections. The three defense experts agreed that Hiss had penned the four handwritten notes, including the "Mary Martin" cable, which he disavowed. On the interlinear Corrections, see J. Howard Haring to Harold Rosenwald, Jan. 26, 1949; Edward Fearon, "Report . . . ," May 2, 1949; Harry E. Cassidy, "In re: Hiss . . . ," Nov. 21, 1949, all HISS; and FBI Laboratory Report, Jan. 21, 1949. On Priscilla Hiss as the possible typist: Cassidy, op. cit.; E. C. McLean, "Typewriter," April 6, 1949, on Haring's conclusions; and Fearon's report, "To Whom it May Concern . . . ," April 5, 1949, HISS. Fearon could arrive at no

firm conclusion as to the typist; Cassidy thought it was definitely Priscilla, and Haring leaned strongly in that direction.

79. E. C. McLean, "Typewriter," April 6, 1949, *ibid.* See also Herbert L. Packer, "A Tale of Two Typewriters," *Stanford Law Review,* vol. 10, No. 3 (May 1958).

80. Why the Hisses did not simply toss the machine into the Potomac River or destroy it in some fashion, rather than giving it away, remains a mystery.

81. Solow Memo, Supplement 3, Dec. 17, 1938, SOLOW.

82. Chambers to Solow, n.d. (ca. Jan. 1939), *ibid.*

83. Chambers to Schapiro, n.d. (ca. Feb. 1938), courtesy of Prof. Schapiro.

84. FBI interview, June 26, 1945, pp. 11–12.

CHAPTER VIII

1. FBI interview, Chambers, Dec. 3, 1948.

2. FBI interview, Hiss, Dec. 4, 1948. Material in the following paragraphs is drawn from both Hiss's signed statement and the FBI agents' notes on their discussion with Hiss and William Marbury.

3. *Ibid.* Thus John Chabot Smith's notion of Chambers pirating State Department documents out with an expired identity card from the National Research Project had its genesis in Hiss's Dec. 4, 1948, interview with the FBI. Like almost all of the conspiracy theories, it arose first in the comments or assertions of Alger Hiss at the time of the case.

4. Fletcher to Ladd, Dec. 3, 1948, #104; Fletcher to Ladd, Dec. 6, 1948, #110, FBI.

5. Jones to Fletcher, Dec. 5, 1948, #52, *ibid.*

6. Fletcher to Ladd, Dec. 3, 1948, #30, *ibid.*

7. Stripling, *The Red Plot Against America, op. cit.,* pp. 148–50, for Stripling's "official" version of this episode at the time. See also INTERVIEWS, Robert Stripling, April 28 and June 30, 1975, for a fuller account.

8. SIX, pp. 58–60.

9. INTERVIEWS, Robert Stripling, *op. cit.;* INTERVIEW, Nicholas Vazzana, June 30, 1975.

10. Stripling, p. 150.

11. INTERVIEW, Nicholas Vazzana, *op. cit.;* WITNESS, pp. 768–71.

12. *Ibid.,* pp. 773–75.

13. *Ibid.,* pp. 771–73; "Chronology of So-called 'Pumpkin Papers,'" March 23, 1949, #3018, FBI.

14. Welles's testimony, pp. 1386–91; Peurifoy's testimony, pp. 1391–97, HUAC II. Other witnesses before the Committee in this brief resumption of public hearings on the Hiss-Chambers case between Dec. 7 and 14 included Julian Wadleigh, Keith B. Lewis, and Nathan I. Levine.

15. For Isaac Don Levine's testimony, see *ibid.,* pp. 1399–1428. Levine allowed me to inspect these notes, mainly the names of those mentioned by Chambers along with Levine's subsequent telegrams checking out some of the names.

16. *Ibid.,* pp. 1419–2.

17. Hottel to Director, Dec. 8, 1948, #136, FBI.

18. Ladd to Director, Dec. 9, 1948, #157.

19. FBI teletype, Dec. 8, 1948, #87.

20. Interview with Julian Wadleigh, Dec. 7, 1948, *ibid.*

21. Robert T. Elson, *The World of Time Inc.: Volume Two, 1941–1960,* pp. 241–42. For Chambers's letter of resignation, see Chambers to James A. Linen (publisher of *Time*), Dec. 9, 1948, TIME. For public response to the resignation, see the following 1948 material from that archive:

"Notations on Whittaker Chambers's Resignation, n.d. (ca. Dec. 11); Margaret McConnell to James Linen, Dec. 10; Boyce Price to Bernard Barnes, Dec. 15; Margaret McConnell to James Linen, Dec. 17; *ibid.*

22. James T. Shotwell to Geoffrey Parsons, Dec. 4, 1948, Dulles MSS, Princeton.

23. Harbaugh, *Lawyer's Lawyer,* pp. 448–51. See also Richard D. Challener, "New Light on a Turning Point in U.S. History," *University: A Princeton Quarterly,* Spring 1973, pp. 30–31.

24. New York *Herald Tribune,* Dec. 8, 1948.

25. *The Washington Post,* New York *Herald Tribune,* and *The New York Times* kept close tabs on the grand jury probe during Dec. 1948, with daily accounts of those who appeared at Foley Square to testify. For Collins's testimony, see his "Digest from Memory of My Appearance . . . ," Dec. 8, 1948, HISS.

26. Priscilla Hiss, " . . . Appearance Before the Grand Jury," Dec. 10, 1948, *ibid.*

27. "Alger Hiss, "Appearance Before Grand Jury," Dec. 7, 1948, *ibid.* The paragraphs that follow are drawn from similar memos by Hiss about his grand jury testimony on Dec. 8, 9, 10, 11, 13, 14, and 15, where appropriate and except where indicated. Beginning in 1975, I became the first researcher to request access to the grand jury files for December 1948 on the Hiss-Chambers investigation. Although grand jury records are normally closed forever and under seal, the Department of Justice indicated no opposition to opening these because of the widespread historical interest in the case. At the time the second edition of this book went into production, the files remained closed.

28. Hiss, "Memorandum of Conversation with Hetty [sic] Massing," Dec. 10, 1948, *ibid.*

29. The colloquy with Wadleigh can be found in Hiss's Dec. 8 memo of his grand jury appearance, *ibid.* Campbell noted that Wadleigh "would make the second witness to prove the perjury case of Hiss." Fletcher to Ladd, Dec. 9, 1948, #131, FBI.

30. Director to Attorney General, Dec. 15, 1948, enclosing the report on Reno's confession four days earlier.

31. Among the most important in this flurry of Dec. 1948 FBI reports dealing with these exchanges among bureau officials, HUAC members or staff, and Justice Department officials, see the following: Director to Attorney General, Dec. 8, #91; Director to Attorney General, Dec. 9, #89; Whitson to Fletcher, Dec. 9, #150; Ladd to Director, Dec. 7, #92; Nichols to Tolson, Dec. 7, #134; Nichols to Tolson, Dec. 7, #91; Nichols to Tolson, Dec. 8, #125; Ladd to Director, Dec. 8, #48; Nichols to Tolson, Dec. 8, #127; Ladd to Director, Dec. 8, #89; Nichols to Tolson, Dec. 9, #181; Ladd to Director, Dec. 9; Nichols to Tolson, Dec. 9, #163; Nichols to Tolson, Dec. 9, #180; Nichols to Tolson, Dec: 9, #179; Nichols to Tolson, Dec. 10, #213; Ladd to Director, Dec. 10, #72; Ladd to Director, Dec. 9, #78; and Ladd to Director, Dec. 10, #74.

32. POST, Dec. 9, 1948; Atlanta *Constitution,* Dec. 11, 1948.

33. Nichols to Tolson, Dec. 14, 1948, #261, FBI.

34. Alger Hiss, memoranda of grand jury appearances, Dec. 14 and 15, 1948, HISS.

35. Ladd to Hoover, Dec. 11, 1948, #75, FBI.

36. Ladd to Hoover, Dec. 13, 1948, #224; Ladd to Hoover, Dec. 14, 1948, #263; Ladd to Fletcher, Dec. 14, 1948, #264; *ibid.* On the threat to indict Nixon for contempt, see Alexander Campbell's comments in Ladd to Hoover, Dec. 14, 1948, #249; *ibid.*

37. *The Daily Worker,* Aug. 5 and Aug. 6, 1948. Dates for other issues of the paper cited in the following paragraphs are provided in the text.

38. *Ibid.,* Dec. 7, 8, 9, 10, 12, 14, 15, 16, 17; all 1948.

39. McLean to Marbury, Nov. 23, 1948, HISS.

40. Marbury to Hiss, Dec. 3, 1948, *ibid.;* interview with Alger Hiss, Dec. 4, 1948, #418, FBI.

41. The interview was recorded by McLean three days later: "Hiss Typewriters,'" Dec. 7, 1948, HISS. At one point, after McLean's departure—this portion of the memo was added by Harold Rosenwald, who was also present on the 4th—Mrs. Hiss telephoned her sister, Daisy Fansler, to ask whether she recalled the make of their father's old machine. "Miss Fansler said that the father's typewriter was an L. C. Smith or Remington." Rosenwald's memo noted, "When I finally suggested to Mrs. Hiss that she inquire whether it might have been a Woodstock, the reply by Miss Fansler was that it might have been a Woodstock." Rosenwald's comment indicates that defense attorneys may already have been advised by their documents examiner, J. Howard Haring, that the Baltimore documents handed over by Chambers on Nov. 17 were typed on a Woodstock.

42. *Ibid.*

43. Cynthia Jones was named in testimony by a former employer and acknowledged ex-Communist, Max Yergan. Harold Rosenwald, "Interview with Cynthia Jones," Feb. 7, 1949, *ibid.* See also Rosenwald's "Memorandum of Conference with Cynthia Arden Jones on December 23, 1948," Dec. 24, 1948, *ibid.*

44. Alger Hiss, "Appearance Before the Grand Jury Today," Dec. 10, 1948, *ibid.*

45. McLean, "Hiss Typewriters," *op. cit.*

46. Cynthia Jones, "Memorandum of interview . . . [with] Messrs. Sullivan and Schnell of the FBI on 4 Jan. 1949," Jan. 7, 1949, HISS. See also Cynthia Jones's Jan. 7, 1949, memo on a Dec. 30, 1948, interview with the same FBI agents, and her Jan. 26, 1949, memo of Jan. 11 and 17 interviews with the agents. *Ibid.*

47. FBI interviews: Alger Hiss, Dec. 4, 1948; Priscilla Hiss, Dec. 6–7, 1948.

48. Edward C. McLean, "Letter of January, 30, 1933, Dec. 8, 1948, HISS. See also another Dec. 7 memo by McLean, "Haring's Opinion on Typewriting of Relevant Documents," *ibid.*

49. McLean, "Letter of January 30, 1933," *op. cit.*

50. *Ibid.;* John F. Davis to Edward McLean, Dec. 28, 1948, HISS.

51. FIRST, p. 2217, quoting Hiss's Dec. 10 grand jury testimony. Not once in Dec. 1948 testimony did Hiss acknowledge knowing anything whatsoever about the disposition of the "old machine," his Woodstock office typewriter, despite his Dec. 7 phone call to John F. Davis about the Catletts having received the machine. See, for example, Hiss's memo of his Dec. 15 grand jury appearance, where he discussed the question of "gifts" without mentioning the typewriter given to the Catletts. See also his Dec. comments to the grand jury when asked how he disposed of the typewriter, a passage quoted verbatim at his first trial: "I frankly have no idea." *Ibid.,* p. 834. On a number of occasions Hiss reiterated his basic contention concerning disposition of the Woodstock: "I am sure that I said I did not independently, of my own recollection, definitely recall" its disposition. Moreover, "I thought Mrs. Hiss had disposed of it to either the Salvation

Army, a junkman, or in some such way."
Ibid., p. 2216.

52. On Hiss's insistence that he learned about the typewriter's whereabouts only from what the Catletts had told him, see *ibid.*, pp. 2064 and 2339; also COURT, pp. 271–72.

53. *Ibid.*, p. 2058: "I have no knowledge as to whether the experts said specifically that the standard or the questioned documents were typed on a particular machine. I do know that I was told that they said they were typed on a Woodstock. I was not told more."

54. For Priscilla Hiss's testimony, *ibid.*, p. 2424; for Alger Hiss's testimony, *ibid.*, p. 2058. Portions of grand jury, testimony were introduced by the prosecutor into both of Hiss's trials and, along with memos on grand jury appearances in the Hiss Defense Files, constitute the best available sources for this testimony until the complete grand jury transcript is released.

55. FBI interview, Alger Hiss, Dec. 4, 1948, "Details . . . Not included in Signed Statement"; Marbury to Hiss, Dec. 3, 1948, HISS.

56. Edward McLean, "Memorandum of Interview with FBI," Dec. 6, 1948, *ibid.* See also "Letter of January 30, 1933," *op cit.*

57. *Ibid.*

58. Her grand jury testimony is quoted in FIRST, pp. 2423–26.

59. Thomas Fansler to Priscilla Hiss, Dec. 26 and 30, 1948, HISS.

60. SECOND, p. 2511.

61. Rosenwald, memo, Dec. 9, 1948, HISS; FBI teletype, Dec. 9, 1948, #168.

62. Schmahl found the cupboard bare closer to home. When he searched the basement storage room of Alger Hiss's apartment for typing samples done on the Woodstock during the 1930s, he reported to McLean "that he found vast quantities

of letters written to the Hisses by various people over a period of many years but no copies of letters from the Hisses to anyone. There was nothing which served as a specimen of typing." The only typing samples the Hisses provided were the two insurance letters accidentally turned up by McLean. "Typewriter," Dec. 31, 1948, HISS.

63. The FBI's probe of Grady and Martin in Dec. 1948 was extensive, and the following memos detail the frustrating inquiry: Dec. 9, #168; Dec. 7, #40; Dec. 9, #295; Dec. 13, #225; Dec. 7, #127; Dec. 11, #215; Dec. 8, #131; Dec. 8, #143; Dec. 15, #276; Dec. 14, #253; Dec. 7, #117; Dec. 10, #197; Dec. 18, #343; Dec. 16, #336; and Dec. 16, #240. During this period Schmahl proved a decided irritant to the FBI agents, who declined his various offers to share or trade information. For the 1929 dating of the machine's manufacture, see SAC, Philadelphia, to Director, Dec. 9, 1948, #295. See also McLean's Dec. 7 and 8 memos of Schmahl's reports on Grady-Martin, HISS.

64. Schmahl told both Harry Martin and Grace Lumpkin during this period that he had begun to doubt Hiss's innocence since "Hiss's story concerning the typewriter and 'several other points' has been found to be inaccurate . . . [and] if Hiss were proven wrong on 'one more thing' his firm would withdraw from the case." FBI report, Dec. 8, 1948, #143; Grace Lumpkin to Thomas Murphy, Jan. 2, 1950, JUSTICE.

65. Hoover to Campbell, Dec. 13, 1948, #229.

66. *Ibid.*; Hoover to Tolson and Ladd, Dec. 13, 1948, #414 (reviewing his conversation with Clark).

67. INTERVIEW, Thomas Donegan, Nov. 11, 1974; Harold Rosenwald, memo, Dec. 17, 1948, HISS.

68. For Feehan's testimony and the other FBI identifications of "Hiss

standards" that matched the typing on the Baltimore documents, see the following FBI memos: Sizoo to Harbo, Dec. 15, 1948, #281; Fletcher to Whitson, Dec. 15, 1948, #279; and Whitson to Fletcher, March 2, 1949, #2135.

69. Alger Hiss, "Memo of Appearance Before Grand Jury," Dec. 14, *op. cit.*

70. Milnes to Fletcher, Dec. 14, 1948, #258; Milnes to Fletcher, Dec. 15, 1948, #283; Ladd to Fletcher, Dec. 17, 1947 #308; FBI.

71. Hiss, "Appearance . . . ," *op cit.*

72. Ladd to Fletcher, *op cit.*

73. McLean to Marbury, Dec. 15, 1948, HISS. Alger Hiss later recalled McLean having been surprised at the indictment, as Hiss claimed to have been. But Marbury, as well as McLean, had advised Hiss in the days preceding his indictment to expect this turn of events. INTERVIEW; Alger Hiss, Sept. 20, 1974; INTERVIEW, William Marbury, Feb. 24, 1975.

74. Alger Hiss, "Memo of Appearance Before Grand Jury," Dec. 15, *op. cit.*

75. For the text of the indictment, Fletcher to Ladd, Dec. 15, 1948, #76, FBI. Hiss later claimed—and John Chabot Smith repeats the assertion—that the vote to indict was by "only one more than a bare majority" and that the jurors had been persuaded, presumably by Justice Department officials, not to indict Chambers at the same time. Hiss cites a grand juror's statement to his lawyers as the source of this information. Yet Richard Nixon asserted in *Six Crises* that "all nineteen members voted to indict Hiss." Hiss's normal source for grand jury scuttlebutt, John Weiss of the New York *Star,* told Harold Rosenwald on Dec. 17 only that the vote to indict Hiss "was not unanimous. He [Weiss] does not know how many voted against the indictment." Since Weiss's statement to

Rosenwald was apparently the source for the rumors about Justice officials quashing a Chambers indictment, Hiss may have exaggerated his claim of a closely divided jury. Without the grand jury minutes themselves, there can be no accurate determination of the matter. Rosenwald, memo, Dec. 17, 1948, HISS; COURT, p. 197; Smith, p. 270; SIX, p. 65.

76. NYT, Dec. 17, 1948.

77. For HUAC's pronouncements: *ibid.,* Dec. 15, 1948, and POST, Dec. 16, 1948. The "code of fair procedure" had been discussed throughout the 1948 hearings. For Truman's continued attack on the Committee: New York *Herald Tribune,* Dec. 17, 1948. On moves to abolish HUAC in the new Congress: POST and NYT, both Dec. 10, 1948; also Clark Clifford, "Memorandum for the President," Dec. 21, 1948, Clifford Files, TRUMAN. For the FBI's relations with HUAC, see Ladd to Hoover, Dec. 17, 1948, #308, FBI.

78. NYT, Dec. 18, 1948; Ladd to Fletcher, Dec. 21, 1948, #375, FBI.

79. Hoover teletype, Dec. 20, 1948, #403; Hoover teletype, Dec. 22, 1948, #399; Hottel to Director, Dec. 22, 1948, #481; *ibid.*

80. McLean to Marbury, Dec. 15, 1948, HISS. Allen Dulles to John Foster Dulles (Marconigram), Dec. 18, 1948; "Comment by Dr. Shotwell," Dec. 22, 1948; Dulles's Dec. 27, 1948, "Draft Statement," and John Foster Dulles to John W. Davis, Dec. 30, 1948, Dulles MSS, Princeton.

81. Eleanor Roosevelt, Chicago *Sun,* Dec. 27, 1948; POST, Dec. 22, 1948. The FBI opened an investigation into the circumstances surrounding Duggan's death that proved inconclusive. Duggan's insurance company sent investigators to the bureau seeking cooperation; but these efforts went nowhere.

82. New York *Herald Tribune,* Dec. 23, 1948; NYT, Dec. 24, 1948. The Mundt

papers at Madison, S.D., contain an extensive collection of letters and press clippings that deal with Duggan's death. Mundt remained understandably defensive about his behavior in the affair.

83. POST, Dec. 26, 1948; McLean, interview with Mrs. Helen Duggan, Jan. 24, 1949, and McLean to Marbury, Dec. 28, 1948, HISS.

84. WITNESS, pp. 777–80.

85. Edward McLean, "Memorandum for File," Dec. 20, 1948, HISS.

86. McLean, "Re: Felix Inslerman," Jan. 21, 1949, *ibid.*

CHAPTER IX

1. Richard Crossman, ed., *The God That Failed*, pp. 4–5, 10–11.

2. WITNESS, pp. 25–26, 75–76; FBI Summary Memo, May 11, 1949, #3220, pp. 123–24.

3. Quoted in Daniel Aaron's essay "The Treachery of Recollection," in Robert H. Bremner, ed., *Essays on History and Literature*, p. 23.

4. Solow Memo, Nov. 12, 1938: Supplement 1, Dec. 3; SOLOW.

5. For Crane's comments, see the enclosure, Hoover to Peyton Ford, March 12, 1949, #2708. On Crane, see also: Ladd to Director, Feb. 16, 1949, #2236; Hood to Director, March 4, 1949, #2706; and SAC, New York, to Director, Sept. 22, 1949, #3862, FBI.

6. Solow Memo, *op. cit.*, p. 6; INTERVIEWS, Meyer Schapiro, Oct. 7 and 19, 1974.

7. On Reiss and his murder, see his wife's memoir: Elizabeth K. Poretsky, *Our Own People*. On the Poyntz case, see Solow Memo, *op. cit.*, pp. 8, 13; also Solow's unpublished article "The Communist Lady Vanishes," SOLOW. Arthur Koestler, *Darkness at Noon*, p. 180.

8. WITNESS, pp. 79–80. On the Soviet purges of the 1930s, see Robert Conquest, *The Great Terror*. For the impact of the purges upon Party activists and the Russian intelligence services, see Conquest, *passim*, and also Roy A. Medvedev, *Let His-tory Judge*, pp. 214–18, and Adam B. Ulam, *Stalin*, pp. 440–42, 459–62, 471–74.

9. Solow, "The Communist Lady Vanishes," *op. cit.*, for these paragraphs on Poyntz's disappearance.

10. For the "Robinson" case, see Chapter VII, pp. 218–21 and notes. See also Walter Krivitsky, *I Was Stalin's Agent*, pp. 191–92.

11. Solow Memo, *op. cit.*, pp. 13, 15; Intrator interview, March 16, 1949, reprinted in "Personal History," April 6, 1949, #3059, p. 41, FBI.

12. #3059; Solow Memo, *op. cit.*, pp. 6–7; INTERVIEW, Meyer Schapiro, Oct. 7, 1974; INTERVIEW, Robert Cantwell, Nov. 11, 1974; Summary Report, May 11, 1949, *op. cit.*, pp. 124–28. For George Silverman's role in arranging the National Research Project job for Chambers, see the March 21, 1949, and April 26, 1949, interviews with Silverman, HISS.

13. Solow Memo, *op. cit.*, pp. 6–9.

14. Chambers to Schapiro, n.d. (ca. Jan. 1938), courtesy of Prof. Schapiro; INTERVIEWS, Meyer Schapiro, Oct. 7, Oct. 19, and Nov. 18, 1974.

15. See note 14; Chambers to Schapiro, n.d. (ca. March 1938), courtesy of Prof. Schapiro.

16. For these moves, see WITNESS, pp. 37–42; Summary Report, May 11, 1949, *op. cit.*, p. 131; and FBI interview with Vincent Reno, Dec. 12, 1948, *op. cit.*

17. Chambers's 1938 correspondence with Oxford University Press was collected in 1951 for use in Hiss's appeal for a new trial and much of it reprinted as Appendices to William A. Reuben, *The Honorable Mr. Nixon and the Alger Hiss Case.* See Appendix 46 for Chambers's May 1 letter to Willert, and Appendix 47 for Willert's May 4 response.

18. Willert to Chambers, May 25, 1938, HISS.

19. WITNESS, pp. 42–44, 56–63; Summary Report, *op. cit.*, p. 131.

20. For Shemitz's story, see Summary Report, pp. 133–34, and Director to Attorney General, Dec. 21, 1948, FBI. For Hutchins's version, see Horace Schmahl's Jan. 27, 1949, report on several interviews with her; HISS.

21. WITNESS, pp. 44–48, for Lieber's search for Chambers in 1938.

22. INTERVIEWS, Nadya Ulanovskaya, Jan. 3–6, 1977.

23. INTERVIEWS, Maxim Lieber, May 10 and 13, 1975.

24. Chambers to Schapiro, n.d. (ca. July 1938), courtesy of Prof. Schapiro; Solow Memo, pp. 9–11.

25. *Ibid.*, pp. 10–11.

26. *Ibid.*, pp. 11–12, 14, and Supplement 2, Dec. 6, 1938.

27. For Levine's testimony, HUAC II, pp. 1452–54. Chambers's correspondence in 1938 shows that he made regular use of Levine's services as an intermediary in contacts with publishers and others.

28. Chambers to Schapiro, n.d. (ca. Sept. 1938), courtesy of Prof. Schapiro. Several other letters from Chambers to Schapiro during this period attest to his state of mind. Not only did Prof. Schapiro prove helpful in dating the correspondence, but Chambers's letters to Herbert Solow from fall 1938 to spring 1939 contained sufficient references to the Schapiro letters (and vice versa) to allow more precise dating. Solow, moreover, retained the postmarked envelopes in most cases.

29. See Chambers's two letters to Schapiro during Oct. 1938 and one to Solow, all n.d. Also see Chambers to Solow, Nov. 2 and 7, 1938.

30. Chambers to Solow, Nov. 2 and 7, 1938. Solow Memo, p. 12.

31. Solow Memo, p. 12.

32. Lionel Trilling, "Whittaker Chambers and 'The Middle of the Journey,' " *The New York Review of Books,* April 17, 1975; pp. 21–22; Sidney Hook, "The Strange Case of Whittaker Chambers," *op. cit.*, pp. 86–87.

33. Chambers to Solow on the following 1938 dates: Nov. 2, Nov. 7, and two undated letters filed by Solow along with these two and, from their contents, Nov. 1938. That Solow met often with Chambers in Nov. and Dec. 1938 is confirmed by his memo, pp. 12–15, and Supplements, SOLOW.

34. Chambers's letters to Solow and Schapiro in Oct. 1938 (see note 29 above) describe his visit to Willert and his concern over "Ulrich." See also INTERVIEW, Meyer Schapiro, Oct. 7, 1974; WITNESS, pp. 51–55; Solow memo, p. 15; and Summary Report, May 11, 1949, *op. cit.*, pp. 132–33.

35. INTERVIEW, Paul Willert, March 17, 1975. On the career of Otto Katz, see also Theodore Draper, "The Man Who Wanted to Hang," *The Reporter,* Jan. 6, 1953; David Caute, *The Fellow Travellers,* esp. pp. 133–35; and Theodore Draper to the author, Jan. 8, 1977. One reliable description of Katz's career during the 1920s and 1930s can be found in Arthur Koestler's memoir, *The Invisible Writing.* Koestler and Katz maintained a friendship throughout this period.

36. Summary Report, May 11, 1949, *op. cit.*, p. 134. Lieber was Katz's American literary agent.

37. Chambers to Schapiro, n.d. (ca. Oct. 1938), courtesy of Prof. Schapiro.

38. Chambers to Solow, n.d. (ca. Dec. 1938), enclosing a memo titled "The Attorney," SOLOW.

39. Solow Memo, pp. 12–15.

40. *Ibid.*, p. 15.

41. *Ibid.*, Supplement 1, Dec. 3.

42. *Ibid.*, Supplement 3, Dec. 17; Chambers to Solow n.d. (ca. Jan. 1939)—the letter opens: "Happy New Year, and how!"

43. Inslerman quoted the letter in his 1954 testimony. Hearings, Permanent Subcommittee on Investigations . . . Feb. 19–20, 1954, *op. cit.*, pp. 108–09. For Inslerman's interview with the bureau, see FBI report, Albany, N.Y., May 14, 1954.

44. Hook, *op. cit.*, pp. 84–87; INTERVIEW, Sidney Hook, April 30, 1975.

45. Chambers to Schapiro, n.d. (ca. Feb. 1938), courtesy of Prof. Schapiro. David Dallin describes a similarly unproductive encounter during these months between Chambers and Jay Lovestone, presumably arranged by their mutual friend Mike Intrator, a follower of Lovestone at the time. Dallin, p. 418. See also Chambers to Solow, n.d. (ca. Jan. 1938), SOLOW.

46. Chambers to Solow, n.d. (ca. Jan. 1938), SOLOW.

47. WITNESS, pp. 459–63; Levine, *Eyewitness to History*, pp. 190–91.

48. WITNESS, pp. 462–63.

49. INTERVIEW, Robert Cantwell, Nov. 11, 1974; INTERVIEW, T. S. Matthews, March 22, 1975. Matthews's comment is from his unpublished memoir of Whittaker Chambers, courtesy of Mr. Matthews. Cantwell's daily journal for 1939–41 contains a number of entries concerning Chambers's work on *Time* and effectively undermines the theory among some supporters of Hiss that Chambers received his position through personal intervention by Henry Luce.

50. Levine, *op. cit.*, pp. 191–93; INTERVIEWS, Isaac Don Levine, Sept. 16 and Oct. 18, 1974; WITNESS, pp. 463–71.

51. Levine, *op. cit.*, pp. 193–5; INTERVIEW, Isaac Don Levine, Sept. 16, 1974.

52. Berle's notes of the visit are reprinted in the FBI Summary Report, May 11, 1949, *op. cit.*, pp. 2255–34, with accompanying analysis by Chambers. On the visit itself, see also Chapter I, pp. 55–59.

53. Levine, *op. cit.*, pp. 197–99; INTERVIEW, Robert Stripling, April 28, 1975.

54. Levine, *op. cit.*, pp. 195–97, 199–200; WITNESS, pp. 485–87.

55. Chambers to Solow, n.d. (ca. 1943).

CHAPTER X

1. Arthur Koestler, in *The God That Failed*, p. 75; WITNESS, pp. 85–86; INTERVIEW, Robert Cantwell, Nov. 11, 1974; INTERVIEW, T. S. Matthews, March 22, 1975.

2. T. S. Matthews, unpublished memoir of Whittaker Chambers, *op. cit.*; Elson, p. 103.

3. Matthews, *op. cit.*; INTERVIEW, Samuel Welles (with Elizabeth Lenneberg), Nov. 6, 1975.

4. Elson, pp. 103–04; INTERVIEW, Robert Cantwell, *op. cit.*

5. Elson, pp. 104–05. Robert Elson describes Chambers as "an almost demonic worker . . . often [working]

thirty-six hours at a stretch, catnapping in his office . . . a superb technician, particularly skilled at the mosaic art of putting a *Time* section together. He enjoyed not only the confidence of his managing editor and editor-in-chief but had as well some loyal friends among his peers." One of these, Duncan Norton-Taylor, felt that Chambers "yearned for companionship." Within a few years after joining the magazine, he had acquired a circle of friends and supporters, including Matthews, Cantwell, Norton-Taylor, Welles, the film critic James Agee (who worked for a time with Chambers in Books), Henry Grunwald (who rose from copy boy to managing editor and was a protégé of Chambers in his earliest days at *Time*), John K. Jessup, and Calvin Fixx.

6. INTERVIEW, Robert Cantwell, *op. cit.* Cantwell's journal entries of 1939–43 record the changes in his old friend's temperament and attitude toward past associates.

7. Chambers to Solow, n.d. (ca. 1943), SOLOW.

8. WTNESS, pp. 480–81,493–94; Elson, p. 104.

9. INTERVIEW, Samuel Welles, *op. cit.;* INTERVIEW, T. S. Matthews, *op. cit.;* WITNESS, pp. 473–76, 501–02.

10. Allen Weinstein, "The Hiss Case Revisited," *The American Scholar,* Winter 1971–72, p. 125; Whittaker Chambers, *Cold Friday,* pp. 273–78; and Joseph Freeman to Daniel Aaron, July 6, 1958, courtesy of Prof. Aaron.

11. *Time,* Jan. 6, 1941, and Feb. 16, 1942.

12. Malcolm Cowley, "Friday, Dec. 13, 1940. Counter Revolutionary," HISS. Chambers had written a review for *The New Republic* in 1933 as "Hugh Jones" while his friend Robert Cantwell briefly substituted for Cowley as its book editor.

Both Cowley and Chambers recalled Cantwell being present at the 1940 luncheon, although Cowley insisted that Cantwell left early in the meeting. Cantwell does not remember being present. INTERVIEW, Robert Cantwell, Aug. 1, 1977. See Chapter III for "Hugh Jones."

13. See the following 1948 memos on talks with Cowley in the Hiss Defense Files: Oct. 29, Nov. 24, and Dec. 13, HISS. For Cowley's trial testimony, see Chapter XII, pp. 462–463.

14. Maus Darling to Malcolm Cowley, March 19 and 25, 1942, Cowley MSS, Newberry Library.

15. Darling to Cowley, April 1 and May 9, 1942, *ibid.* None of Cowley's letters to Darling are in Cowley's papers, so his responses are known only through Darling's comments on them. See also Darling to Alger Hiss, Dec. 15, 1948, HISS.

16. John Osborne, *The New Republic,* April 17, 1976.

17. T. S. Matthews, *op. cit.;* Elson, p. 104; INTERVIEW, Robert Cantwell, Feb. 10, 1975. Cantwell's journal records an even earlier brief period at *Foreign News* when Chambers replaced the vacationing Cantwell in that section in October 1939 with predictable results. The furor occasioned among others in the section because of Chambers's stern anti-Communism landed on Cantwell when he returned.

18. Elson, p. 105; WITNESS, pp. 494–96. See also Chambers to Luce: Sept. 11, 1942; n.d. (early Dec. 1942), two letters; Luce to Chambers, Dec. 7, 1942; and Luce to "Writers in Mr. Chambers's Division," Nov. 24, 1942; TIME.

19. WITNESS, *op. cit.*

20. See the following interviews with Lore and FBI efforts to confirm his information: Oct. 2 1941; Oct. 13, 1941, #10;

Jan. 9, 1942, #18; and Dec. 1, 1942, #25. See also Hoover's Jan. 26, 1949, memo, #1725.

21. Chambers to Solow, n.d. (ca. late 1942 or early 1943), SOLOW. See also the May 14, 1942, FBI report on the interview with Chambers held on May 13, FBI.

22. *Ibid.*, pp. 2–3, 8.

23. FBI report, Dec. 1, 1942, #25.

24. Chambers to Solow, n.d. (ca. 1943), *op. cit.*; INTERVIEW, Samuel Welles, *op. cit.*; Welles to Chambers, Nov. 26, 1949, files of prosecutor Thomas Murphy, JUSTICE.

25. Welles to Chambers, Nov. 26, 1949, JUSTICE; Raymond Murphy, "Memorandum of Conversation, Tuesday, March 20, 1945, Westminster, Md." SECOND, p. 3323.

26. Elson, p. 105; WITNESS, p. 497; Chambers to Luce, Sept. 18, 1944, and Matthews to Luce, Sept. 28, 1944, TIME.

27. Elson, pp. 105–07; WITNESS, pp. 498–500; and the following interoffice *Time* memos: Allen Grover to Luce, Oct. 31, 1944; Luce to Chambers, Jan. 17, 1945; Fillmore Calhoun to Luce, Nov. 14, 1944; and Grover to Luce, Nov. 29, 1944.

28. Elson, pp. 107–09; John Billings to Charles Wertenbaker, Jan. 15, 1945, TIME.

29. Elson, pp. 109–10; John Osborne, *The New Republic, op. cit.*; Chambers to Luce, Nov. 4, 1945, and "1/45," and Calhoun to Grover, Feb. 6, 1945, TIME.

30. *Time*, March 5, 1945.

31. Elson, pp. 114–16; Osborne, *op. cit.*; INTERVIEW, T, S. Matthews, *op. cit.*; WITNESS, pp. 500–01.

32. *Ibid.*, pp. 503–04; Osborne, *op. cit.* Visits by Raymond Murphy in March 1945 and by another team of FBI agents at his *Time* office in May had revived Chambers's dormant memories of his underground past, from which he was now removed by seven crowded personal and professional years. Chambers had also been approached apparently by intermediaries acting for the Catholic priest Father John Cronin, who

was then preparing a confidential report on Communist activities in the United States for the Catholic bishops. According to that report, issued in 1946, Chambers had stated that he would publicly expose Alger Hiss if Hiss were elected permanent secretary general of the United Nations (Hiss had served as temporary, presiding officer at its organizing meeting at San Francisco in April 1945). See pp. 7–8.

33. Raymond Murphy, "Memorandum of Conversation . . . March 20, 1945," *op. cit.*; see also Murphy's Aug. 28, 1946, memo on a second talk with Chambers, SECOND, *ibid.*

34. The March 26, 1945, unsigned report on Hiss was one of dozens of such reports filed by State Department security officers in 1945 and 1946, released to me in response to a Freedom of Information Act request.

35. The May 10, 1945, interview with Chambers was sent to Hoover by the SAC in New York seven weeks later on June 26, 1945. The reason for this long delay remains difficult to determine from the FBI files.

36. Rev. John F. Cronin, *The Problem of American Communism in 1945: Facts and Recommendations,* typescript, Francis P. Matthews MSS, TRUMAN, pp. 16, 37, 49–50, for references to Alger Hiss. See also INTERVIEW, Father John F. Cronin, Nov. 26, 1975.

37. The Hiss investigators collected information from insurance companies that had dealt with Chambers, and these records can be found in the Defense Files.

38. Osborne, *op. cit.* Elson, p. 115; Matthews to Chambers, Nov. 10 and 21, 1945, and Chambers to Luce, June 24, 1946; TIME.

39. WITNESS, pp. 504–09.

40. Elson, pp. 115–16.

41. WITNESS, p. 524.

42. On Chambers's meeting with Schlesinger and his research assistant, Mrs. Barbara Kerr, see pp. 369–70. Arthur Schlesinger, Jr. confirmed these facts for me.

43. State Department correspondence on the Field recommendation is voluminous. See the following items, declassified and released by the FBI with State Department approval in response to my Freedom of Information Act request: Hiss to American Consul (Geneva), Oct. 24, 1940; Hiss to Fletcher Warren, Nov. 1, 1940; Hiss to Sayre, Nov. 18, 1940; Breckenridge Long to Hiss, Nov. 12, 1940; Berle to Long, Nov. 6, 1940; Llewellyn Thompson to Warren, Nov. 1, 1940; Laurence Duggan, "Mr. Noel Field," Nov. 4, 1940; and Berle (?) to Long, Nov. 5, 1940; STATE.

44. Interview with Stanley K. Hornbeck, Jan. 18, 1949, HISS.

45. NYT, April 8, 1952; FBI reports, Oct. 7, 1949, #4049, and #4039 (two reports).

46. Alger Hiss, FBI interview, March 25, 1946, p. 1.

47. Memorandum on Alger Hiss, n.d. (ca. 1951), Stanley K. Hornbeck MSS, Hoover Institution.

48. Statement of Alger Hiss, Feb. 14, 1942, FBI. See also "Alger Hiss," Jan. 27, 1949, #1724, *ibid.*; and G. Howland Shaw (Asst. Secretary of State for Security) to J. Edgar Hoover, March 26, 1942, STATE.

49. Alger Hiss, "Memorandum of Duties in the Department of State, 1944 Until January 15, 1947," ca. Sept. 1948, HISS.

50. Stettinius to Hiss, Oct. 6, 1944; Hiss to J. M. Maury, Sept. 15, 1944; HISS.

51. Hiss, "Memorandum . . . ," *op. cit.*

52. *Ibid.*, p. 2.

53. *Ibid.*, p. 3.

54. Hiss to Pasvolsky, Feb. 14, 1945, Leo Pasvolsky MSS, LC.

55. Hiss, "Memorandum . . . ," *op. cit.*

56. *Ibid.*, pp. 3–4.

57. Stettinius to Hiss, July 3, 1945, HISS.

58. For Gouzenko's statement, see FBI report, Nov. 27, 1945, "Soviet Espionage in the United States," p. 67. For the reports on Hiss, see pp. 16–17, 66–67 of that report. See also Ladd to Hoover, Jan. 27, 1950, #4511, FBI.

59. For a summary of Bentley's 1945 statements to the FBI, see Ladd to Director, Jan. 28, 1949, #2058, pp. 4–5.

60. *Ibid.*, pp. 5–11. The extensive FBI phone tap, mail cover, and surveillance of Alger and Priscilla Hiss can be seen in the reports filed as part of the bureau's investigation of Nathan Gregory Silvermaster (code-named "Gregory"), and released as a separate filing section of the Hiss-Chambers file entitled "Silvermaster (Hiss Related Material)," hereafter cited as FBI, SILVERMASTER.

61. Hoover compiled several Summary Reports in 1948 and 1949, once the Hiss-Chambers case broke, of his earlier efforts to alert White House, State Department, and Justice Department officials to the damaging information about Hiss, and these reports represent the most convenient summaries of the bureau's 1945–48 memoranda on the matter. For the conversation with Acheson, see Hoover's Jan. 27, 1949, memo, "Alger Hiss," #1724, pp. 2–3, citing their Oct. 11, 1945, meeting. See also Ladd to Director, Dec. 28, 1948, #1480, enclosing a Dec. 10 Summary Report on this and other conversations between Hoover and high State Department officials about Hiss in the previous years.

62. *Ibid.*, pp. 1–3; Hoover, "Alger Hiss," *op. cit.*, p. 3; FBI report, Nov. 27, 1945, *op. cit.*, pp. 16–17, 66–67.

63. FBI Summary, Report, Dec. 10, 1948, #1480, *op. cit.*, pp. 3–4.

64. *Ibid.*, pp. 4–5. See also Director to Attorney General, Jan. 17, 1949, #1921.

65. For Hiss's FBI interview, see Ladd's memorandum to Hoover, March 25, 1946, FBI.

66. Bannerman to Russell, March 22, 1946, STATE.

67. De Sola's charge received particularly extensive but inconclusive investigation. Among the dozens of 1949 FBI reports filed, see the following: Feb. 5, #1772; Feb. 23, #2160; and March 3, #2426.

68. Earl R. Dickover to Frederick B. Lyon, Sept. 28, 1948, STATE.

69. The conversation is recorded in Thomas M. Campbell and George C. Herring, eds., *The Diaries of Edward R. Stettinius, Jr., 1943–1946*, p. 416.

70. Hiss, "Memorandum . . . ," *op. cit.*; Richard Hartsborne to Division, Subdivision, and Section Chiefs, Office of Strategic Services, Feb. 5, 1945, CIA.

71. FBI surveillance logs, May 16–31, 1946, p. 53, #1364; Feb. 1–28, 1947, p. 15, #2326; FBI, SILVERMASTER. See also the following logs on Hiss's interests in the atomic-energy field: pp. 44–45, #1210; p. 50, #1359; pp. 51–52, #1364; p. 59, #1447; pp. 39–41, #2294. "Henry Hill Collins, Jr. in contact with Alger Hiss," reads the "Synopsis of Facts" heading on a Sept. 1, 1946, report dealing with Aug. 1946 surveillance. "He [Collins] is allegedly requesting records, information, and reports at the State Department not directly concerned with his work." #1673. For his proposals to enlarge the scope of OSPA, see Hiss to Pasvolsky, Sept. 7, 1945, and Hiss to Rothwell, Nov. 29, 1945, OSPA files, NA.

72. "Notes Taken from Desk Calendar of A. Hiss on 11 October 1946," Document #23, STATE. See also Bruce Page, David Leitch, and Phillip Knightley, *The Philby Conspiracy*, pp. 183–92.

73. Bannerman to Russell, March 26, 1946, STATE.

74. Ladd to Hoover, Jan. 28, 1949, #2058, pp. 5–6. See also FBI, SILVERMASTER, *passim*.

75. See, for example, the following 1946 State Department memos: Bannerman to Russell, May 10; Counsel, ACOPS, to Security Officer (for Director, CON), Sept. 4 and Sept. 13; Klaus to Panuch, Sept. 4 and Oct. 1; and Bannerman to Allen, Oct. 11; STATE. Two of Hiss's colleagues at State—Ernest Gross, deputy assistant secretary for occupied areas, and Loy Henderson, director of the Office of Near Eastern and African Affairs—were among those who received orders in early 1946 from leading department officials to withhold confidential information from him. James Barros, "Alger Hiss and Harry Dexter White: The Canadian Connection," *Orbis*, vol. 21, No. 3, 1977.

76. "Excerpts from Secretary Byrnes' Press . . . Conference," July 26, 1946, HISS. For Joseph C. Green's conversation with Hiss, see the deposition given by Green for prosecutors at the second trial, Nov. 25, 1949, JUSTICE.

77. Nov. 16, 1946, FBI, SILVERMASTER, #2294, p. 40. See also the 1949 FBI interviews with Byrnes: Scheidt to Director, Sept. 15, #3860; June 29, #3454, #3455, and #3457; and Aug. 29, #3927.

78. Raymond Murphy, "Memorandum . . ." Aug. 28, 1946, *op. cit.*

79. FBI Summary Report, Dec. 10, 1948, #1480, *op. cit.*, pp. 3–5.

80. Alger Hiss to Priscilla Hiss, Jan. 4, 1946, HISS; John Foster Dulles to John W. Davis and Arthur Ballantine, Jan. 7, 1946, Dulles MSS, Princeton.

81. On the background of Hiss's negotiations with Dulles and his subsequent career at the Endowment, see the following: Chapter I, pp. 42–43; INTERVIEW, William Marbury, Feb. 4, 1975; Richard D. Challener, "New Light on a Turning Point

in U.S. History," *op. cit.;* and the following 1948 letters from the Dulles papers: Dulles to Walter Judd, Feb. 2 and March 22; Dulles, "Memorandum for Confidential Files," March 18; and Dulles to Herbert Brownell, Jr., Aug. 20. Alger Hiss insisted from the time of the case to his death that he felt the FBI's interest in him had ended—and that, in effect, he had been "cleared"—long before he entered into serious discussions with Dulles over the post of Carnegie Endowment president. See especially Hiss's statements to HUAC on Aug. 25, 1948, substantially repeated during his two trials. HUAC I, pp. 1133–35; see also FIRST, pp. 2153–56.

82. "Statement by Acting Secretary Dean Acheson," Dec. 10, 1946, N1. 892; Byrnes to Hiss, Dec. 20, 1946; STATE. See also the FBI interview with Byrnes, Sept. 15, 1949, #3860, p. 5; also James C. Byrnes, "Yalta and Hiss and the Atomic Bomb," *Look,* Oct. 14, 1958; and Alger Hiss, "Discussions with Secretary Byrnes Prior to Accepting the Carnegie Endowment Job," n.d. (ca. Nov.–Dec. 1948), HISS.

83. Testimony of Dean Acheson, Jan. 14, 1949, *Executive Sessions of the Senate Foreign Relations Committee* (Historical Series), Vol. II,

81st Cong., 1st and 2nd Sess., 1949–50, "Made Public July 1976," pp. 11–12.

84. Kohlberg to Dulles, Feb. 24 and May 19, 1947; Dulles to Kohlberg, May 21, 1947; Dulles to Brownell, Aug. 20, 1948, "Supplement" of Sept. 14, 1948; Dulles MSS, Princeton.

85. Interview with Alger Hiss and Hiss's signed statement, June 2, 1947, FBI.

86. Interview with Priscilla Hiss, June 2, 1947, FBI.

87. The grand jury testimony was introduced at the first trial. See FIRST, pp. 2224–25; also *ibid.,* pp. 2016–18, and INTERVIEW, Alger Hiss, Sept. 20, 1974.

88. Donald Hiss, "Memorandum re Testimony . . . Before the Grand Jury," Dec. 9, 1948, p. 9.

89. Dulles, "Memorandum for Confidential Files," March 18, 1948, *op. cit.*

90. *Ibid.;* see also Dulles to Judd, Feb. 2 and March 22, 1948, *op. cit.*

91. "Statement of Alger Hiss," March 8, 1949 (to Lloyd Paul Stryker), p. 102; FIRST, pp. 2089–90, 2016–18, 2224–25. For Priscilla Hiss's failure of recollection on the first mention of Chambers, see *ibid.,* pp. 2370–71.

92. *Ibid.,* p. 2017.

CHAPTER XI

1. INTERVIEW, Robert von Mehren, Dec. 11, 1974.

2. Marbury to McLean, Feb. 4, 1949, HISS; Stryker to William De W. Mitchell, Dec. 16, 1949, Laurence M. Hyde MSS, Western Historical MSS. Collection, University of Missouri, courtesy of William Leuchtenburg.

3. For Sayre's reservations, see Chapter VII, p. 229.

4. Memorandum of conference with Charles Dollard, Jan. 21, 1949. See also McLean to Marbury, Jan. 17, 1949; HISS.

5. Debevoise, Plimpton & McLean to Alexander Campbell, Jan. 8, 1949; *ibid.* Edward McLean's investigative files and John F. Davis's daily reports to McLean together comprise the most important archive on the Hiss defense investigations.

6. "Oral Report from Mr. Schmahl Today," Jan. 21, 1949, *ibid.*

7. "Memorandum for Professor Morgan," Dec. 23, 1948, *ibid.*

8. The paragraphs that follow draw from Harold Rosenwald's "Memorandum

re Chambers' Motivation," March 15, 1949, *ibid.*

9. Edward McLean, "Conference with Psychiatrists," May 5, 1949, *ibid.*

10. Harold Rosenwald, interview with Carol Weiss King, Jan. 6, 1949, *ibid.*

11. Horace Schmahl, "Miss Grace Hutchins," Jan. 27, 1949; on Nathan Witt's involvement, see "Memorandum re William Rosen," March 29, 1949; on Pressman's (and Witt's), see "Re Lee Pressman," March 7, 1949; *ibid.*

12. Interviews with Lee Pressman, memos, Jan. 17 and Feb. 7, 1949, *ibid.*

13. Memorandum, interview with Cynthia Jones, Jan. 7, 1949, *ibid.*

14. Horace Schmahl, "Mr. A. B. Magill," Jan. 31, 1949, *ibid.*

15. Edward McLean, "Memorandum of Conference with Sendor [sic] Garlin," Feb. 8, 1949, *ibid.*

16. Edward McLean, "Memorandum of Conference with Leon Herald Srabian," Feb. 8, 1949; Harold Rosenwald, memo (on Paul Peters); Nov. 19, 1948; Horace Schmahl, "Mr. Paul Peters," Jan. 27, 1949; *ibid.* See also Zeligs, p. 126, for Srabian's later—and racier—version of the encounter with Chambers.

17. Wyzanski to Marbury, Oct. 14, 1948, and Marbury to Wyzanski, Oct. 19, 1948, *ibid.*

18. "Memorandum of Conference with Charles Dollard . . . ," Jan. 21, 1949; see also "Memorandum of Interview with Mrs. Helen Duggan," Jan. 24, 1949; *ibid.*

19. See, for example, McLean's "Memorandum re Conversation with Mrs. Jean [Kenneth] Walser," Jan. 24, 1949, *ibid.*

20. Walter Lippmann to Dr. Carl Binger, Dec. 24, 1948; see also Alger Hiss, "Memorandum of Telephone Conversation with Miss Gertrude Samuels . . . ," March 2, 1949; *ibid.*

21. For Acheson's Jan. 14, 1949, testimony, see *Executive Sessions of the Senate Foreign Relations Committee* (Historical Series), *op. cit.*, pp. 3–38.

22. For Acheson's comments about Alger and Donald Hiss, see *ibid.*, pp. 4–21, *passim.*

23. Marbury to Acheson, Jan. 14 and March 24, 1949; Acheson to Marbury, Jan. 19 and March 30 1949; Acheson to Stryker, March 30, 1949; *ibid.* State Department security officers confided their fears to FBI officials later that year about Acheson's having possibly leaked confidential departmental documents to Hiss's lawyers. That Acheson maintained close and possibly indiscreet ties to the Hiss defense can be seen from his having confided the substance of his Jan. 13 executive-session testimony to Donald Hiss. Fletcher to Ladd, Nov. 14, 1949, #4186, FBI; Edward McLean, "Dean Acheson," Jan. 25, 1949, HISS.

24. See McLean's memo "Oral Report from Mr. Schmahl Today," Jan. 21, 1949; also Rosenwald's memo "Re Typewriters," Dec. 13, 1948, HISS.

25. Among the numerous 1949 FBI interviews and reports on Claudia Catlett and her sons Raymond and Perry, the following provide summaries of their initial statements concerning the typewriter and later revised versions: May 18, #3173, pp. 1–18; Fletcher to Ladd, July 8, #3606; Oct: 31, #4225, pp. 72–122; March 1, #2653, pp. 9–21; and May 16, #3172; FBI.

26. Manice de F. Lockwood, "Memorandum of Conversation with Donald Hiss re Search for Typewriter," Dec. 20, 1951, HISS.

27. Edward McLean, "The Catlett Family," Feb. 4, 1949, *ibid.*

28. *Ibid.*, pp. 5–6; FBI report, Oct. 31, 1949, #4225, pp. 108–09.

29. Harold Rosenwald, "Conference with Pauline Burnetta Catlett Fisher . . . ," Feb. 7, 1949, HISS.

30. Mike Catlett's inquiries about the typewriter in January and February emerge from FBI interviews in May 1949 with Vernon Marlow, Ernest Bell, Vernelle Bell, John Marlow, Mary Lockey, and Ira Lockey, among others, summarized in two extensive reports, May 18, #3173, and May 26, #3273. Additional facts come from the following defense memos: Manice de F. Lockwood, "Memorandum re: Woodstock. Interview with Raymond Catlett and Ira Lockey, Nov. 3, 1950"; Lockwood, memo of interviews with Raymond Catlett and Ira Lockey, Nov. 8, 1950; Lockwood, "Memorandum of Conversation with Donald Hiss re Search for Typewriter," *op. cit.;* and Edward McLean, "Catlett Family: Additional Information Obtained April 13–16, 1949"; HISS.

31. Lockwood, ". . . Conversation with Donald Hiss . . . ," *op. cit.,* p. 3. Mike Catlett remembered receiving $40 from Donald Hiss for "taxi money" during his swing around the Catlett-Marlow-Bell-Lockey circle, which took place between late Jan. and mid-Feb. 1949. Donald Hiss said he gave Mike Catlett more money once the typewriter had been found, which—along with the "taxi money"—came to about $65 or $70. *Ibid.,* p. 4. See also FBI report, May 18, 1949, #3173, interview with Raymond (Mike) Catlett.

32. McLean, "Catlett Family: Additional Information Obtained April 13–16, 1949," *op. cit.* "Excerpts" from two letters by Donald Hiss to Alger Hiss (dated Feb. 4 and 5, 1949), although not the originals or copies of the complete letters, were given to McLean at the time and later deposited in the Defense Files. The excerpts were typed on the Hiss machine of the moment,

apparently by either Alger or Priscilla. They show that the two brothers kept in close touch during the crucial months when defense and FBI investigators hunted for the Woodstock. They reveal, also, that Donald remained active on his brother's behalf in Washington, monitoring the FBI probe through talks with friends and former servants of the Alger Hisses who had undergone questioning by bureau agents. They also reinforce the probability that Donald informed Alger immediately about Mike's having followed the trail of the Hisses' old Woodstock to Ira Lockey's home. "The sky has definitely brightened," Donald wrote on Feb. 5. "Hope everything goes well in New York."

33. FBI report, May 18, 1949, #3173, pp. 22–24, 30–32; McLean, "Catlett Family . . . ," *op. cit.,* p. 4.

34. *Ibid.,* p. 5.

35. FBI Laboratory Report, May 23, 1949, #3196, and Director to Attorney General, May 24, 1949, #3161; FBI.

36. McLean, "Catlett Family . . . ," *op. cit.,* p. 2.

37. See the FBI reports cited in note 25 above for the tangled testimony of the three Catletts.

38. McLean, "Catlett Family . . . ," *op. cit.,* p. 1.

39. FBI report, Oct. 31, 1949, #4225, p. 114.

40. Lockwood, interview with Raymond Catlett, Nov. 8, 1950, *op. cit.,* p. 4.

41. Alger Hiss, "Catlett Variations and Aids to Memory," May 9, 1949, HISS.

42. *Ibid.,* pp. 2–3.

43. McLean, "Catlett Family . . . ," *op. cit.,* pp. 9–10.

44. *Ibid.*

45. For a summary of these conclusions by defense and FBI documents examiners, see Chapter VII, note 67. For the FBI's

testing of the 21 specimens typed on the Woodstock, see Laboratory Report, Oct. 27, 1949, FBI.

46. J. Howard Haring to Harold Rosenwald, Jan. 26, 1949, HISS.

47. E. C. McLean, "Typewriter," April 6, 1949, HISS.

48. Edwin H. Fearon to Lloyd Stryker, April 23, 1949, HISS. Laughlin to Fletcher, March 30, 1949, #2704, and Scheidt to Director and SAC, April 14, 1949, #2925, FBI.

49. Fearon to Stryker, April 23, 1949, HISS. See also Fearon's report, "To Whom It May Concern . . . ," April 5, 1949, HISS.

50. Fearon to Stryker, *op. cit.*

51. McLean to von Mehren, June 27, 1949, HISS.

52. For Chambers's Feb. 17–18 testimony, see BALTIMORE, pp. 830–1290. Chambers also deposed in the slander suit on March 25, 1949. For the testimony, see BALTIMORE, pp. 1291–1382.

53. For the Wadleigh-Hiss change, *ibid.*, pp. 1047–48.

54. For the text of Chambers's Feb. 15 covering letter and his statement, see Fletcher to Ladd, Feb. 15, 1949, and enclosures. For a photostat of Chambers's original letter and statement, see FBI, #2237.

55. For Hoover's order, FBI teletype, Feb. 9, 1949, #1758. For rumors of Chambers's homosexuality that reached the FBI, Fletcher to Jones, Feb. 25, 1949, #2247; (blacked out) to Hoover, Feb. 11, 1949, #2323; and Gleason to Hoover, April 20, 1949, #2948.

56. Director to Attorney General, March 1, 1949, #2152; Ladd to Director, March 1, 1949; FBI memo, Feb. 16, 1949, #2237.

57. Director to SAC, New York, June 7, 1949, #3389. See also "Memorandum for Mr. Tolson," June 1, 1949, #3389, and Director to Campbell, June 7, 1949, #3266.

58. For the FBI's interview with Hobson, see their Feb. 9, 1949, report, #1829. See also Director to SAC, New York, Nov. 1, 1949, #4130; Director to Washington and New York, Feb. 3, 1949, #2707; FBI teletype, Feb. 8, 1949, #1465; FBI report, Feb. 3, 1949; and INTERVIEW, Dr. Timothy Hobson, Aug. 16, 1974.

59. Scheidt to Director, April 27, 1949, #2971, FBI.

60. The best published summaries of the facts in the Coplon case can be found in Dallin, pp. 478–92, and in Sanche de Gramont, *The Secret War*, pp. 66–108.

61. Quoted in Dallin, pp. 482–83. See also NYT, April 28 and May 1, 1949, which reprint many of the memos found on Coplon. John Fox examined all of the data slips and other trial exhibits on my behalf, retrieving them from storage under a Freedom of Information request made to the Department of Justice.

62. On the FBI's interest in Sherman and Crane's description, see Whitson to Fletcher, Aug. 16, 1949, #3715. At the time Coplon took the data slips on Sherman, the FBI had not yet interviewed him. See also NYT, May 1, 1949, and Dallin, pp. 482—85.

63. NYT, May 1, 1949; FBI transcript of phone taps of Judith Coplon, Feb. 24, 1949, Court Records, JUSTICE.

64. Dallin, pp. 486–92; De Gramont, pp. 99–108; 191 *Federal Reporter*, 2nd Series, pp. 750–54; John Fox, "Background Memo, Coplon Case," personal files.

65. See the following FBI interviews: Feb. 8, 1949, #1820 (Herbst); Nov. 19, 1949, #4239 (Herbst); and Director to SAC, New York, June 13, 1949, #3391 (Herrmann).

66. INTERVIEWS, Maxim Lieber, May 10 and 13, 1975.

67. FBI report, Feb. 7, 1949, #1873.

68. For Hoover and the press, see the following 1949 FBI memos: Nichols to Tolson, March 30, #2766; Nichols to Tolson, Feb. 9, #1879; Nichols to Tolson, Jan. 25, #1485; and Ladd to Director, April 7, #2769.

69. See Hoover's handwritten orders on the cover (distribution) page of an undated FBI memo, #1478, and Connelly to Director, Feb. 14, 1949, #2050. The Summary Report itself was prepared by Special Agent Joseph M. Kelly of the New York field office: March 30, 1949, #3221 (446 pages).

70. FBI report, May 16, 1949, #3172.

71. FBI report, May 14, 1949, #3148.

72. FBI Laboratory Report, Dec. 30, 1948; FBI report, May 14, 1949, #3106. Thousands of pages of FBI reports document the bureau's unsuccessful pursuit of the Hiss Woodstock. A 120-page Summary Report on the hunt on January 28, 1949, indicates the scope and intensity of that search. Subsequent letters confirm an ongoing investigation for the machine. See, for example, Fletcher to Ladd, Feb. 23, 1949, #2241, and Director to SAC, Washington Field, March 1, 1949, #2234.

73. Boardman to Director and SACs, May 17, 1949, #3114, *ibid.* For an analysis of the Boardman memo and other FBI documents of this period as interpreted by a lawyer for Alger Hiss and from the defense perspective, see John Lowenthal, "Woodstock N230099: What the FBI Knew But Hid from Hiss and the Court," *The Nation*, June 26, 1976, pp. 776–82. Lowenthal's analysis omits the relevant FBI reports cited in this section and earlier that explain Boardman's chagrin and suspiciousness when confronted with the defense's recovery of an allegedly genuine Hiss Woodstock.

74. Fletcher to Ladd, May 24, 1949, #3162 INC, *ibid.*, and FBI Laboratory Report, May 23, 1949, #3169. The Fletcher memo sets out the background information concerning recovery of the Hiss Woodstock to the extent that the FBI knew that information. See also Hottel to Director and SAC, May 14, 1949, #3148, one of several memos during this period urging an intensive bureau investigation to determine whether the machine recovered by the Hiss defense was actually the typewriter used to turn out the Baltimore documents and not a defense "plant."

75. For Martin's re-interviews in 1949, see the following FBI reports: May 28, #3198; May 28, #3325; June 9, #3257; June 30, #3552. For Grady's: May 25, #3233; June 7, #3322; June 13, #3584: For their Dec. 1948 interviews, see Chapter VIII, p. 262 and *n.*

76. FBI Laboratory Report, Oct. 27, 1949; FBI Laboratory' Report, Dec. 30, 1948; Harry E. Cassidy to Harold Rosenwald, Nov. 21, 1949, HISS. For the bureau's Summary Memo tracing the history of Woodstock N230099 from 1929 to 1949, see Hottel to Director, June 9, 1949, #3381. See also note 75.

77. Hoover's handwritten comments can be found on Hottel to Director, June 24, 1949, #3424, FBI. See also Fletcher to Ladd, June 29, 1949, #3419.

78. Scheidt to Washington, May 17, 1949, #3111; Scheidt to Director, n.d. (ca. May 1949), #3208; FBI.

79. Hoover to Communications Section, May 18, 1949 (document number omitted). See also FBI report, May 17, 1949, #3111.

80. Fletcher to Ladd, May 24, 1949, #3165; FBI Laboratory Report, Oct. 27, 1949; FBI.

81. Ladd to Hoover, June 2, 1949, #3250; Ladd to Hoover, June 6, 1949, #3249; FBI.

CHAPTER XII

1. *United States of America vs. Alger Hiss, Defendant,* United States District Court, Southern District of New York, C. 128–402, hereafter cited as FIRST with the appropriate page numbers. The transcripts of the first Hiss trial and the Baltimore depositions were lent to me through the courtesy of Mrs. Helen Buttenwieser. The best published account of Hiss's two trials for perjury; is in Alistair Cooke, *A Generation on Trial,* pp. 98–335.

2. James Bell to Robert T. Elson, June 1, 1949, Yale University Library (donated by Henry Luce). Bell's detailed daily reports to Luce (via Elson) on the two Hiss trials were retyped after each trial in manuscript form; copies can be found at Yale and in TIME. They remain a superb source, if tilted toward Chambers, for the dramatic background of the trials. *Ibid.,* pp. 1, 6.

3. *Ibid.,* pp. 2–6; Cooke, pp. 101–03.

4. *Ibid.,* p. 109; FIRST, pp. 12–25, for Murphy's opening remarks.

5. FIRST, pp. 25–54, for Stryker's opening remarks.

6. Bell, p. 14.

7. Whittaker Chambers's testimony: FIRST, pp. 96–116, 135–302, 317–445, 462–684, 696–726. To avoid unnecessarily cluttering the narrative of the two trials with hundreds of references, for each specific citation from trial testimony, only the pages for each witness's testimony will be cited at the first reference to that witness.

8. *Ibid.,* pp. 127–31.

9. Bell, p. 22; Cooke, pp. 139–40.

10. FIRST, pp. 303–316a, for these exchanges in Kaufman's chambers.

11. *Ibid.,* pp. 446–62, for these exchanges in chambers and Kaufman's decision.

12. Esther Chambers's testimony: *ibid.,* pp. 841–908, 914–1043.

13. Julian Wadleigh's testimony; *ibid.,* pp. 1332–64.

14. Bell, pp. 145, 150.

15. For Massing's testimony at the second trial, see Chapter XIII, pp. 425–26.

16. See the following trial testimony: Nathan I. Levine, pp. 807–11; Donald T. Appell, pp. 686–95; Henry T. Ireland, pp. 756–58; George Hunter, pp. 758–61.

17. Walter H. Anderson's testimony: pp. 1057–1141, 1153–1240.

18. For an analysis of the handwritten, typed, and microfilmed documents turned over by Chambers in Nov. and Dec. 1948, see Chapter VII.

19. Bell, p. 130.

20. Eunice A. Lincoln's testimony: FIRST, pp. 1240–67.

21. Bell, p. 134.

22. Paul Banfield's testimony: FIRST, pp. 738–47.

23. Marie Wilcox Abbott's testimony: *ibid.,* pp. 761–66.

24. Ramos C. Feehan's testimony: *ibid.,* pp. 1290–1332.

25. *Ibid.,* p. 1428.

26. Malcolm Cowley's testimony: *ibid.,* pp. 1811–38. See also Edward E. Edstrom's testimony: *ibid.,* pp. 2397–2408.

27. Bell, p. 194.

28. FIRST, p. 2446.

29. Bell, p. 274.

30. Dr. Carl Binger's appearance: FIRST, pp. 2446–76.

31. *Ibid.,* pp. 2473–74.

32. *Ibid.,* pp. 2474–76.

33. Claudia Catlett's testimony: *ibid.,* pp. 1600–78.

34. Raymond (Mike) Catlett's testimony: *ibid.,* pp. 1679–1757.

35. *Ibid.*, p. 1697.

36. Perry (Pat) Catlett's testimony: *ibid.*, pp. 1758–79.

37. Ira Lockey's testimony: *ibid.*, pp. 1791–95; Charles H. Houston's testimony: *ibid.*, pp. 1795–1801.

38. Burnetta Catlett Fisher's testimony: *ibid.*, pp. 2477–81. See also testimony by Marguerite McQueen, pp. 2482–85; Stafford J. McQueen, pp. 2485–88; and Henri P. Henry, pp. 2489–97; *ibid.*

39. Courtland J. Jones's testimony: *ibid.*, pp. 2497–2550.

40. Harry C. Hawkins's testimony: *ibid.*, pp. 1429–39.

41. Charles F. Darlington's testimony: pp. 1439–56; Frank E. Duvall's testimony: pp. 1525–43; *ibid.*

42. Bell, pp. 166–72; Cooke; pp. 180–82; Justice Felix Frankfurter's testimony: FIRST, pp. 1566–81.

43. Justice Stanley Reed's testimony: FIRST, pp. 1581–87.

44. John W. Davis's testimony: *ibid.*, pp. 1268–75.

45. Stanley K. Hornbeck's testimony: *ibid.*, pp. 1276–90.

46. See the following testimony (or depositions, where indicated): Admiral Arthur J. Hepburn, pp. 2440–42; Judge Calvert Magruder, pp. 1588–92; Judge Charles E. Wyzanski, Jr., pp. 1945–54; Ambassador Philip C. Jessup (deposition), pp. 1544–51; Governor Adlai E. Stevenson (deposition), pp. 1559–65; and Charles Fahy, pp. 1806–10; *ibid.*

47. John Foster Dulles's testimony: *ibid.*, pp. 2551–67.

48. Alger Hiss's testimony: *ibid.*, pp. 1875–1944, 1960–2116, 2126–2250.

49. Priscilla Hiss's testimony: *ibid.*, pp. 2251–2396, 2412–39, 2443–45.

50. For the Norman Thomas-Lasky exchange, see Victor Lasky to Thomas Murphy, n.d. (ca. June 1949), JUSTICE.

51. Tony Hiss, Laughing Last, pp. 137–40.

52. Lloyd Paul Stryker's summation: FIRST, pp. 2724–2843.

53. Thomas F. Murphy's summation: *ibid.*, pp. 2845–2910.

54. Judge Samuel H. Kaufman's charge: *ibid.*, pp. 2911–41.

55. *Ibid.*, pp. 2942–44.

56. *Ibid.*, pp. 2945–62; Bell, pp. 336–40.

57. Bell, pp. 341–42; FIRST, pp. 2962–64; Cooke, pp. 271–77.

58. Bell, *op. cit.* On the Hisses' response to the verdict, see also POST, July 9, 1949.

59. "I appreciate your remarks about our handling of the case," Edward McLean wrote William Marbury. "Frankly, I was not excessively disappointed at the outcome, but naturally, I hope that we will have better luck next time." McLean to Marbury, Aug. 22, 1949, HISS.

60. On the jurors' statements to the press, see the following: New York *Journal-American*, July 9 and 12, 1949, and New York *Herald Tribune*, July 12, 1949. On the interviews by Hiss's attorneys with jurors who voted for acquittal, see the memos on those with Hill (July 13, 1949), Pawlinger (July 13, 1949), and Tourian (July 12, 1949), HISS. On the FBI's interviews with those jurors who voted for conviction, see Belmont to Ladd, July 20, 1949, #3887, FBI.

61. For Lasky's transcript: New York *World-Telegram*, July 12, 1949; for Pawlinger's complaint NYT, July 23, 1949; for the attack on Kaufman: Baltimore *Sun*, July 13, 1949; New York *Herald Tribune*, July 12 and 18, 1949; and New York *Journal-American*, July 10, 1949.

62. POST, July 15, 1949.

CHAPTER XIII

1. Vandenberg is quoted in Walter LaFeber, *America, Russia, and the Cold War, 1945–1971*, p. 79. LaFeber's chapter "New Coalitions, 1948–1950" provides a useful summary of the global context of American affairs for those years. *Ibid.*, pp. 66–94.

2. McLean to Marbury, Oct. 3, 1949, HISS; *United States of America vs. Alger Hiss, Defendant*, United States District Court, Southern District of New York, C. 128–142, hereafter cited as SECOND with the appropriate page numbers. The "Transcript of Record" for Hiss's second trial was reprinted as part of his appeal record for the U.S. Court of Appeals for the Second District, including all trial exhibits. Prof. John F. Davis of the University of Maryland Law School kindly allowed me to use his copy of the ten-volume transcript.

3. For the pretrial motions, affidavits, and exhibits, see SECOND, pp. 93–161.

4. Edward McLean, "Conversation with Clarke Smith," Sept. 8, 1949; see also R. Clarke Smith to Edward McLean, Sept. 10, 1949; HISS.

5. SECOND, pp. 93–161, *passim*, for the pretrial arguments and evidence.

6. *Ibid.*, p. 162; Cooke, pp. 281–84.

7. Thomas F. Murphy's opening statement: SECOND, pp. 163–78.

8. Claude B. Cross's opening statement: *ibid.*, pp. 178–201.

9. See, for example, the exchange on pp. 229–32, *ibid.*

10. Whittaker Chambers's testimony: *ibid.*, pp. 218–302, 312–322, 327–558, 562–686.

11. Esther Chambers's testimony: *ibid.*, pp. 954–1071.

12. Ramos C. Feehan's testimony: *ibid.*, pp. 1071–1106.

13. Julian Wadleigh's testimony: *ibid.*, pp. 1107–53, 1164–1256.

14. Hede Massing's testimony: *ibid.*, pp. 1261–1301.

15. Henrikas Rabinavicius's testimony: *ibid.*, pp. 2639–63. For the Hiss lawyers' contacts—and problems—with Rabinavicius, see the following 1949 defense documents: "Interview with . . . Rabinavicius," Oct. 11; "Memorandum re Hede Massing," Dec. 11; Rabinavicius to McLean, Dec. 15; "Statement Concerning . . . Rabinavicius," Dec. 19; and "Memorandum for Mr. Rosenwald," Feb. 14, 1950; HISS.

16. Dr. Margaret Mary Nicholson's testimony: SECOND, pp. 2553–58.

17. August Claessen's testimony: *ibid.*, pp. 3007–09.

18. For the typing performance, see FBI agent John S. McCool's testimony: *ibid.*, p. 3019.

19. Gladys F. Tally's testimony: *ibid.*, pp. 3058–71.

20. Edith Murray's testimony: *ibid.*, pp. 3023–58.

21. Stanley K. Hornbeck's testimony: *ibid.*, pp. 1348–82.

22. Francis B. Sayre's testimony: *ibid.*, pp. 1472–1524. Sayre's personal papers at the Library of Congress, although extensive, contain no items dealing with Alger Hiss or with the case, such material apparently having been culled out prior to deposit. For testimony by other State Department officials, see the following pages: G. Howland Shaw, pp. 1322–31; Harry C. Hawkins, pp. 1331–48; Frank E. Duvall, pp. 1385–1427; Charles F. Darlington (first-trial testimony read in lieu of deposition), pp. 1438–51; Joseph C. Green (deposition), pp. 1451–71; and Clyde Eagleton, pp. 2415–22; *ibid.*

23. Testimony of John L. Hall, *ibid.*, pp. 1553–56.

24. Testimony of William L. Marbury, *ibid.*, 2444–82.

25. Testimony of Donald Hiss, *ibid.*, pp. 1700–08.

26. Testimony of Alger Hiss, *ibid.*, pp. 1801–2117, 2125–63, 2178–2257, 2259–69.

27. According to Lamb, Hiss contacted him on several occasions between Oct. and Dec. 1934, asking that Lamb collect military information from various companies and private sources for use by the Nye Committee. Lamb remembered delivering to Hiss a quantity of material on guns and cannon manufactured by the Sperry Ordnance Company—to which Hiss had referred him—and on airplane sales to Russia, information supplied by journalists and others knowledgeable about the sales. The president of Sperry agreed in an FBI interview that "it is very probable" he had seen Lamb, but denied supplying any information. Other sources interviewed by bureau agents confirmed the negotiations on the sale of American planes to Russia at the time, which had fallen through, but the FBI learned that Lamb—though involved in such inquiries—tended to exaggerate his role in the events. Lamb said that Hiss paid him about $500 over the few months for his work, but that Hiss became angry, when Lamb reminded him about an initial offer to find him a post on the Nye Committee's staff. Hiss "promptly advised me that I was never on the Nye Committee [payroll] but rather I was working directly for Mr. Hiss . . . [with] money that he took out of his own expenses. . . ." After this meeting, sometime around Christmas 1934, Hiss broke off contact with him, according to Lamb. As for Chambers, Lamb said they had met about 1936 or 1937, but he could not verify earlier meetings. FBI reports for

March 20, 1949, #2787, and May 17, 1949, #3024, pp. 9–35.

28. Priscilla Hiss's testimony: SECOND, pp. 2282–2326, 2336–2414, 2423–28, 2483–2514.

29. Murphy's objections to the psychiatric evidence and Judge Goddard's response: *ibid.*, pp. 2516–18.

30. Dr. Carl Binger's testimony: *ibid.*, pp. 2519–53, 2558–2633, 2663–2791.

31. Dr. Henry A. Murray's testimony: *ibid.*, pp. 2792–2833, 2846–2950.

32. Claude B. Cross's summation: *ibid.*, pp. 3091–3175.

33. New insights into Cross's difficulties in defending his client emerged from a later interview with Dr. Henry Murray, who apparently spent time at the trial analyzing not only Whittaker Chambers but Alger Hiss as well. "Hiss is just too much a goody-goody," Murray told Mrs. Elizabeth Lenneberg, whose notes record the discussion: "Hiss, as he [Dr. Murray] sees him, has such an 'ideal image of himself as unspotted by the world' that he can't give it up. And his ideal image is not one of self-honesty. As Dr. Murray explained it, jokingly, the honest man is the man who can look into himself and see and name all the horrors he finds there. . . . Not Alger Hiss. In fact, as Dr. Murray read the testimony being given by Hiss during the trial—and especially after he listened to one newspaper reporter griping about Hiss as such a 'boy scout that there's no story'— he went to Cross and said, 'Look, you have to do something to make this man human.' [Murray] felt that the testimony, which talked about nothing but Hiss's successes, his morality, his intelligence, etc., was doing him a great disservice. He suggested to Cross that the lawyer ask Hiss about things in his life where he'd failed, things where he hadn't always acted like the knight in shining armor, the fair-haired

boy. As he [Dr. Murray] put it, no jury could find for someone so inhumanly perfect as Hiss. Cross was impressed by this line of reasoning, and suggested its adoption to Hiss. Hiss refused. He would have absolutely no part in discussing any aspects of himself that made him seem less than perfect. Perhaps he couldn't recognize [Murray speculated] that there were any such aspects. It's not that Murray doesn't see Hiss as basically a good man—he thinks he is. He noted [however] Hiss's 'excessive gallantry toward women,' which he thinks has possibly led him into 'a conflict of allegiances.'" Interview with Dr. Henry Murray by Mrs. Elizabeth Lenneberg, Nov. 4, 1975.

34. Thomas F. Murphy's summation: SECOND, pp. 3213–62.

35. For Judge Goddard's charge and the jury's verdict, see *ibid.*, pp. 3263–96.

36. *Ibid.*, p. 3295; NYT, Jan. 22, 1950.

37. SECOND, pp. 3297–3304.

38. *Ibid.*, p. 3302.

39. Chester Lane to John F. Davis, March 10, 1950; Edward McLean to Alger Hiss, Feb. 3, 1950; HISS.

40. *Ibid.*

41. INTERVIEW, Robert von Mehren, Dec. 11, 1974; INTERVIEW, Claude B. Cross, July 15, 1974.

42. On the new investigators, see the following: Chester T. Lane, "To Whom It May Concern" (introducing Manice de F. Lockwood 3rd), April 11, 1950; Elinor Ferry to Helen Buttenwieser, Aug. 15, 1950; Lockwood to John F. Davis, Feb. 23, 1950; Davis to Lane, March 15, 1950; *ibid.*

43. Chester T. Lane, Oral History Memoir, Columbia University.

44. Richard H. Field, "Report to Contributors . . . ," Feb. 17, 1950, HISS; INTERVIEW, Richard H. Field, July 16, 1974.

45. United States Court of Appeals for the Second Circuit, No. 78—October Term, 1950, Docket No. 21800, *United States of America, Appellee, v. Alger Hiss, Appellant,* hereafter cited as APPEAL. Copies of the opposing briefs and of the Dec. 7, 1950, decision can be found both in Justice Department and Hiss Defense Files.

46. COURT, p. 328.

47. APPEAL, pp. 256–59.

48. *Ibid.*, pp. 258, 260.

49. COURT, pp. 355–62.

50. NYT, Jan. 28, 1951; POST, March 3, 1951. Justice William O. Douglas's *Go East, Young Man . . . ,* pp. 377–79, reprints the Supreme Court tally sheet on the vote.

51. NYT, March 16, 1951; POST, March 23 and 29, 1951.

CHAPTER XIV

1. Whittaker Chambers to James Rorty, n.d. (ca. July 1960), courtesy of Duncan Norton-Taylor; POST, Jan. 26, 1950.

2. Dean Acheson, *Present at the Creation,* pp. 359–60.

3. *Ibid.*, p. 360.

4. *Ibid.*, pp. 360–61; Alonzo L. Hamby, *Beyond the New Deal,* pp. 377, 385, 394. Acheson's papers at the Truman Library contain boxes of mail he received following his statement about Hiss, many

hundreds of letters all sent within the next few weeks. An informal sampling of the correspondence indicated that the great majority of those writing criticized his position.

5. POST, Jan. 30, 1950, for the letter.

6. Eric F. Goldman, *The Crucial Decade and After,* pp. 137–44.

7. The literature on McCarthy's career and what came to be called "McCarthyism" is extensive. Earl Latham, ed., *The Meaning*

of McCarthyism, offers a useful compendium of conflicting perspectives on both the man and the "ism." For McCarthy's sudden emergence to prominence, see any of the following: William Manchester, *The Glory and the Dream,* pp. 512, 520–27; Goldman, pp. 137–45; or Hamby, pp. 390–93. On McCarthy's life and career, see the following two critical works: Robert Griffith, *The Politics of Fear,* and Richard Rovere, *Senator Joe McCarthy.* For a favorable view, see William F. Buckley, Jr., and L. Brent Bozell, *McCarthy and His Enemies.* For an even more favorable view, see Joseph R. McCarthy, *McCarthyism: The Fight for America.* See also POST, Feb. 14, 1950.

8. Quoted in Allen Weinstein, "The Symbolism of Subversion: Notes on Some Cold War Icons," *Journal of American Studies,* Aug. 1972, on which many of the themes in this chapter draw.

9. Goldman, pp. 103–04. See also the chapter on "The Hiss Case: An Ideal Tarnished" in Joseph Goulden, *The Best Years, 1945–1950,* especially pp. 339–40.

10. Latham, *The Communist Controversy in Washington,* p. 10 and *passim.*

11. Nixon spoke on the "lessons" of the Hiss case in a House speech soon after Hiss's conviction. *Congressional Record,* Jan. 26, 1950, pp. 999–1007.

12. For the pivotal role played by Alger Hiss and the Hiss case in the demonology of those who raised the Yalta Conference as a campaign issue, see Athan Theoharis, *The Yalta Myths,* pp. 91–93 and *passim.* See also Jim Bishop, *FDR's Last Year, passim,* for a more accurate version of Hiss's role— important in staff work but hardly critical in policymaking—at the conference.

13. Theoharis, p. 91; Manchester, p. 521.

14. Theoharis, pp. 92–93.

15. *Ibid.,* pp. 130–53; LaFeber, pp. 137–38; Manchester, pp. 627–28; INTERVIEW, Robert Stripling, April 28, 1975.

16. Hamby, pp. 497–98. For Republican attacks on Stevenson's deposition for Hiss, see NYT for the following 195 2 dates: Aug. 10, Aug. 19 (Dirksen), Aug. 22, Sept. 20, Sept. 21 (McCarthy), Sept. 24 (Nixon), Oct. 6 (Stassen), Oct. 14 (Nixon), Oct. 18 (Nixon), Oct. 25 (Dulles), and Oct. 28 (McCarthy). For Stevenson's defense of his actions and his retreat from his unqualified endorsement of Hiss in 1949, see *ibid.,* Aug. 10 and Oct. 24.

17. Hamby, pp. 383–84. See also Weinstein, "Symbolism of Subversion," *op. cit.,* and Norbert Muhlen, "The Hysteria of the Hisslings . . . ," *The New Leader,* May 13, 1950.

18. Hamby, pp. 384–86.

19. *Ibid.* See, for example, Merle Miller's "The Second Hiss Trial," *The New Republic,* Feb. 6, 1950; Marquis Childs, "The Hiss Case and the American Intellectual," *The Reporter,* Sept. 26, 1950; and Goulden, p. 339.

20. Goulden, p. 339.

21. *The Daily Worker,* Jan. 24, 1950; I. F. Stone, *The Truman Era,* pp. 182–90.

22. Weinstein, "Symbolism of Subversion," *op. cit.*

23. David Riesman, *Individualism Reconsidered . . .* (Glencoe, Ill.: Free Press, 1954), p. 129.

24. Fred Rodell, "Come Clean, Alger Hiss," *The Progressive,* June 1950; Leslie Fiedler, "Hiss, Chambers, and the Age of Innocence . . . ," *Commentary,* Aug. 1951.

25. Diana Trilling, "A Memorandum on the Hiss Case," *Partisan Review,* May 1950.

26. Fiedler, *op. cit.*

27. Peter Viereck, "Symbols: Hiss and Pound," *Commonweal,* March 28, 1952.

28. Richard H. Rovere, "Walter Lippmann," *The American Scholar,* Autumn 1975, pp. 601–02 Sidney Hook, "The Strange Case of Whittaker Chambers," p. 78.

29. One of the more lamentable results of Hiss's conviction was Hoover's decision, apparently on the basis of scant (if any) consultation with his nominal superiors at the Justice Department, to continue a full-scale monitoring of the Hiss case. Over the next two decades this produced mail covers and surveillance of Hiss and his closest friends and supporters as well as the use of informants to keep tabs on their movements. In the process, it generated hundreds of FBI reports, regularly submitted, by a small cohort of agents assigned to the "Hiss beat." Not the least irony of this shameful abuse of the FBI's investigative powers—none of Hiss's friends or supporters was ever suspected of a single "crime" except the (to Hoover) crime of continued belief in Alger Hiss's innocence—was the fact that it resulted in the creation of a bureau "file" on the Hiss case almost as large *after* the trials as before and during them.

30. Herbert Aptheker, "Behind the Hiss Frameup," *Masses & Mainstream,* Oct. 1953.

31. Fred J. Cook, "New Perspectives on the Strangest Case of Our Time," *The Nation,* Sept. 21, 1957. McWilliams gave over almost the entire issue, pp. 141–80, to Cook's article. The magazine's persistent advocacy of Hiss's innocence and of a frame-up in the case can be traced in the following articles: George T. Altman, "The Added Witness," Oct. 1, 1960; Fred J. Cook, Nixon Kicks a Hole in the Hiss Case," April 7, 1962; Fred J. Cook, "The Ghost of a Typewriter," May 12, 1962; Raymond A. Werchen and Fred J. Cook, "New Light on the Hiss Case," May 28, 1973; Carey McWilliams, "Will Nixon Exonerate Hiss?," Sept. 20, 1975; and John Lowenthal, "Woodstock N23099 . . . ," June 26, 1976, *op. cit.*

32. George Van Dusen, "The Continuing Hiss: Whittaker Chambers, Alger Hiss, and *National Review* Conservatism," *Cithara,* Nov. 1971. See also John Diggins, *Up from Communism,* and George Nash, *The Conservative Intellectual Movement in America since 1945.* For Chambers's relationship to the magazine, see Chapter XV, pp. 478–79; also William F. Buckley, Jr., ed., *Odyssey of a Friend, passim.*

33. For the Buckley-Chambers friendship, *ibid.* See also Buckley, "The End of Whittaker Chambers," *Esquire,* Sept. 1962. On de Toledano and Chambers, see the massive unpublished correspondence in de Toledano's papers at the Hoover Institution, Stanford University; also see Ralph de Toledano, *Lament for a Generation,* pp. 104–45.

34. INTERVIEWS, Meyer Schapiro, Oct. 19 and Nov. 18, 1974; INTERVIEW, Robert Cantwell, Nov. 11, 1974.

35. Chambers to de Toledano, Aug. 17, 1951, de Toledano MSS, Hoover.

36. Sidney Hook, "The Faiths of Whittaker Chambers," *The New York Times Book Review,* May 25, 1952.

37. Hannah Arendt, "The Ex-Communists," *Commonweal,* March 20, 1953.

38. *Ibid.*

39. Arthur Koestler, "The Complex Issue of the Ex-Communist," *The New York Times Magazine,* Feb. 19, 1950.

40. Arthur Schlesinger, Jr., "Whittaker Chambers and His 'Witness,'" *Saturday Review,* May 24, 1952.

41. Lionel Trilling, "Whittaker Chambers and 'The Middle of the Journey,'" *The New York Review of Books,* April 17, 1975.

42. Lionel Trilling, *The Middle of the Journey* (New York: Doubleday / Anchor, 1957).

43. Irving Howe, "On 'The Middle of the Journey,'" *The New York Times Book Review,* Aug. 22, 1976.

44. Trilling, "Whittaker Chambers . . . ," *op. cit.* On the extent to which the two men met during the 1930s, see the exchange of letters between Sidney Hook and Diana Trilling, "Remembering Whittaker Chambers," *Encounter,* June 1975. See also INTERVIEW, Sidney Hook, April 30, 1975, and INTERVIEW, Meyer Schapiro, Oct. 19, 1974.

45. Trilling, "Whittaker Chambers. . . ." See also Trilling to Herbert Solow, July 23, 1962, and Trilling to William F. Buckley, Jr., July 20, 1962, SOLOW.

CHAPTER XV

1. Alger Hiss, "Statement Released to Press March 12, 1951 . . . ," HISS.

2. Trilling, *The Middle of the Journey,* p. 345.

3. Zeligs, pp. 392–93; Tony Hiss, pp. 145–47; INTERVIEW, Dr. Timothy Hobson, Aug. 16, 1974.

4. *Ibid.;* INTERVIEW, Alger Hiss, Oct. 4, 1975; Zeligs, pp. 393–401; Tony Hiss, pp. 147–63; Brock Brower, "Hiss Without the Case," *Esquire,* Dec. 1960.

5. C. Vann Woodward, notes of a conversation with Alger Hiss, May 3, 1959, courtesy of Prof. Woodward; see also Brower, *op. cit.* For Hiss's talks with Winter, see Robert M. Benjamin to Austin H. MacCormick, July 24, 1953, HISS.

6. INTERVIEW, Dr. Timothy Hobson, Aug. 16, 1974. See also INTERVIEW, Dr. Viola Bernard, June 2–3, 1975, and INTERVIEW, Alger Hiss, Oct. 4, 1975.

7. Zeligs, p. 416.

8. COURT, pp. 363–419, "The New Evidence of Fraud and Forgery," for Hiss's own summary of Lane's briefs and the motion for a new trial.

9. Brower, *op. cit.*

10. Hiram Haydn, *Words and Faces,* p. 290.

11. The best account of the Whig-Clio incident is John D. Fox's "The Hiss Hassle Revisited," *Princeton Alumni Weekly,* May 3, 1976. Richard Nixon chose the day of Hiss's appearance to announce his decision to seek renomination as vice president on the Republican ticket.

12. Alger Hiss to Claude B. Cross, June 28, 1957, HISS.

13. Brower, *op. cit.;* Zeligs, pp. 408–10.

14. Several investigators, apparently volunteers, may have participated. Memos were signed variously as "Liz," "Phyl" (?), and "E.G.H." See memos on meetings with Bessie A. Meade or investigations elsewhere of Horace Schmahl on the following 1965 dates: Aug. 25, Sept. 4 (a letter to "My dear Chip," Manice de F. Lockwood's nickname), Oct. 21 ("Report No. 4"), Oct. 30, Nov. 12 ("My dear Chip"), Nov. 11, Nov. 12 ("My dear Chip"), Dec. 13, Dec. 14, Dec. 15, Dec. 16, Dec. 17, Dec. 22; also Oct. 12, 1966. See also Alger Hiss to "Dear Chip" (Lockwood?), Nov. 26 and Nov. 30, 1966?, in which arrangements for "the mechanical man" are discussed in detail, although in carefully evasive language.

15. Brower, *op. cit.* On the background of the Hisses' separation, see the following: INTERVIEW, Dr. Timothy Hobson, Aug. 16, 1974; INTERVIEW, Dr. Viola Bernard, June 23, 1975; INTERVIEW, Alger Hiss, Oct. 4, 1975; Zeligs, p. 411; Tony Hiss, pp. 183–86.

16. Fred J. Cook, "Nixon Kicks a Hole in the Hiss Case," April 7, 1962, and "The Ghost of a Typewriter," May 12, 1962, both in *The Nation.* Nixon remained more than slightly concerned with Hiss at this point. Interviewed by Lord Altrincham in late 1962, he remarked in answer to a question about Hiss: "He [Hiss] had 'gone to bits

completely.' . . . And had he shown any overt sign of being a Communist since he came out of prison? Mr. Nixon thought that he [Hiss] had recently attended a Communist meeting, but could not give chapter and verse." Lord Altrincham, "Mr. Nixon at Home," *The Times* (London), Dec. 4, 1962.

17. Howard K. Smith to Robert Stripling, Nov. 20, 1962, and San Angelo *Standard-Times*, Nov. 14, 1962, both courtesy of Mr. Stripling.

18. Robert Alan Aurthur, "Hanging Out," *Esquire*, July 1972.

19. *Life*, April 7, 1972. See also Alger Hiss, "Notes on Hiss Act Case" (sic), n.d. (ca. 1972), HISS.

20. Whittaker Chambers to Ralph de Toledano, Jan. 26, 1950, de Toledano MSS, Hoover Institution.

21. Chambers to de Toledano, Feb. 1, 1950, *ibid;* Buckley, "The End of Whittaker Chambers," *op. cit.*

22. See the poems "Exercises" and "Spring Rain" in de Toledano's papers, *op. cit.*

23. INTERVIEW, T. S. Matthews, March 22, 1975. Prentice to Luce, Jan. 24, 1950, and Luce to Prentice, Jan. 27, 1950, TIME.

24. Matthews to Luce, n.d. (ca. early Feb. 1950), *ibid.;* INTERVIEW, T. S. Matthews, March 22, 1975, Elson, *op. cit.*, pp. 242–43.

25. Luce to Chambers, Feb. 21, 1950, TIME.

26. Chambers to Luce, March 25, 1950, *ibid.* See also Chambers to Luce, March 21 and July 31, 1952; Luce to Chambers, July 18, 1952; *ibid.* Also Chambers to Luce, Sept. 2, 1952, courtesy of Duncan Norton-Taylor.

27. For Hook and Schlesinger, see Chapter XIV, notes 36 and 40. I. F. Stone, *The Truman Era*, pp. 182–85; Elson, pp. 243–44.

28. Luce to Chambers, July 18, 1952, *op. cit.;* Buckley, *Odyssey of a Friend*, p. 78.

For Chambers's publisher's view of the man and of *Witness*, see Bennett Cerf, *At Random*, pp. 242–44.

29. Chambers to Luce, March 21, 1952, *op. cit.* See also Esther Chambers to Luce, Nov. 11, 1952; Buckley, "The End of . . ."; and Chambers to Henry Regnery, Dec. 3, 1951, courtesy of Duncan Norton-Taylor.

30. Chambers to de Toledano, Mar. 19, 1953, de Toledano MSS, *op. cit.*

31. Chambers to Duncan Norton-Taylor, March 23, 1953, courtesy of Mr. Norton-Taylor.

32. *Ibid.*

33. Chambers to Henry Regnery, Jan. 14, 1954, reprinted in Buckley, *Odyssey* . . . , pp. 47–49.

34. *Ibid.*, p. 50. On Chambers's view of McCarthy, see also pp. 47–53 and 100–04.

35. On the details of Clubb's ordeal, see the following: O. Edmund Clubb, *The Witness and I;* E. J. Kahn, Jr., *The China Hands,* pp. 226–31 and *passim;* and Goodman, *The Committee*, pp. 310–11.

36. Buckley, *Odyssey* . . . , pp. 284–85.

37. *Ibid.*, pp. 55–56, 86–88.

38. Chambers to Norton-Taylor, May 21, 1957; Norton-Taylor to Chambers, May 19 and 28, 1957; courtesy of Mr. Norton-Taylor. On Chambers's reaction to Jowitt's book, see Chambers to de Toledano, March 19, 1953, de Toledano MSS, *op. cit.*

39. Chambers to Norton-Taylor, "June 2, 3, 4, ?, 1957, Sun., pm, anyway," courtesy of Mr. Norton-Taylor.

40. Buckley, "The End of. . . ."

41. For descriptions of the trip and for Chambers's "Old Bolshevik" imagery, see the following: *ibid.;* Buckley, *Odyssey* . . . , pp. 248–57, 271–72, 291–93. Conspirator to the last, Chambers preferred to have the CIA arrange for his passport rather than apply through normal channels. CIA documents released in response to my request

under the Freedom of Information Act show that fact and, also, that the agency monitored Hiss's movements during *his* European trip in the late fifties (and perhaps on subsequent trips).

42. For an analysis of these themes in Chambers's last years, see my review of Buckley's *Odyssey of a Friend in Commentary,* June 1970. See also Buckley, "The End of . . ."; INTERVIEW, John Chambers, Aug. 5, 1975; and Chambers, *Cold Friday, passim.*

43. Chambers to James Rorty, n.d. (ca. July 1960), courtesy of Duncan Norton-Taylor.

44. Ralph de Toledano, "Let Only a Few Speak for Him," *National Review,* July 29, 1961. That issue of the magazine offered a number of tributes to Chambers. His former employer proved less effusive. Contrast *Time*'s somewhat niggardly obituary with *Life*'s more generous words of praise. Elson, *op. cit.,* p. 244.

45. Information on the two families after the trials comes in part from the following sources: the books on Alger Hiss and the Hiss case by Zeligs, Smith, and Tony Hiss; Buckley's collection of letters by Chambers and his *Esquire* article; Brower's *Esquire* article; and from my interviews of Dr. Viola Bernard, John Chambers, Ralph de Toledano, Alger Hiss, Priscilla Hiss, Dr. Timothy Hobson, Manice de F. Lockwood, T. S. Matthews, Meyer and Lillian Schapiro, and Alden Whitman.

46. Zeligs, p. 434.

47. Esther Chambers to Herbert Solow, May 28, 1962, and Solow to Esther Chambers, June 25, 1962, SOLOW. See also the verbatim transcription by Solow's secretary of his May 11, 1962, discussion with Dr. Zeligs, and their subsequent exchanges of correspondence on the case.

48. Buckley's and de Toledano's difficulties with the Chambers family

emerge from their correspondence in de Toledano's MSS, *op. cit.* INTERVIEW, Ralph de Toledano, July 19, 1977; INTERVIEW, John Chambers, May 20, 1975.

49. Smith, p. 433. When Tony Hiss requested the file to use in a magazine article several years ago, his mother declined to turn it over as a matter of privacy. While Alger was still at Lewisburg, Mrs. Manice de F. Lockwood accompanied Priscilla on one of her regular visits (according to Alger) and raised discreet questions—at Chester Lane's request—about a rumored love affair between Mrs. Hiss and Henry Collins during the 1930s that might account for the stolen documents. Priscilla Hiss indignantly denied the rumors. INTERVIEWS, Alger Hiss, June 21 and Oct. 4, 1975; INTERVIEW, Dr. Timothy Hobson, Aug. 16, 1974; INTERVIEW, Claude Cross, July 15, 1974; INTERVIEW, Dr. Viola Bernard, June 23, 1975.

50. Zeligs, p. 411. See also INTERVIEWS, Priscilla Hiss, June 24 and Nov. 11, 1974; Tony Hiss, pp. 175–77, 183–87; INTERVIEW, Alger Hiss, June 21, 1975. Alger Hiss talked freely about the separation, among others to John Chabot Smith and Tony Hiss. Both offer intimate glimpses of Hiss's version of the breakup in their books.

51. John A. P. Millet, "The Power of the Accuser," *Psychiatry and Social Science Review,* April 1967.

52. INTERVIEW, Dr. Timothy Hobson, Aug. 16, 1974; Tony Hiss, *op. cit.*

53. INTERVIEWS, Priscilla Hiss, June 24 and Nov. 11, 1974; June 24 and Sept. 3, 1975.

54. Abbott Millspaugh to the author, Nov. 18, 1973; Roberta Fansler to Alden Whitman, Dec. 7, 1974, courtesy of Mr. Whitman.

CHAPTER XVI

1. For the ACLU lawsuit, see the briefs in *Weinstein v. Kleindienst, Gray, et al.* On Hiss in 1972, see *Life,* April 7, 1972. See also NYT, March 4, 1972, on Hiss's pension suit.

2. Daniel Yergin, "Were the Rosenbergs Framed?," *New Times,* May 16, 1975.

3. Alger Hiss, "My Six Parallels," NYT, July 23, 1973. See also "Alger Hiss Says Trials Similar to McCarthy Era," Boston *Globe,* March 29, 1972, and "Hiss Case Is Ruled No Longer an Equal-Time Issue," NYT, Aug. 2, 1973.

4. Tony Hiss, "I Call on Alger," *Rolling Stone,* Sept. 13, 1973. See also "Nixon Campaign Letter Asks Alger Hiss to Help; PS . . . He Won't," Boston *Globe,* April 9, 1972.

5. Boston *Globe,* March 29, 1972; Alger Hiss to "Mr. Peck," May 8, 1973, HISS.

6. Richard H. Popkin, "Hiss Story Repeats Itself," *University Review,* April 1974.

7. For a sampling, see the following: Popkin, *op. cit.; Boston Phoenix,* Aug. 12, 1975; *The Nation,* May 28, 1973; and 1973 newspaper columns by William F. Buckley, Jr. ("The Revisionists at Work"—Nov. 26), George Frazier ("Let's Hear It for Alger Hiss"—Nov. 2), James J. Kirkpatrick ("Giving Witness for Whittaker Chambers"—June 15), and William A. Rusher ("Liberals Do Recover Their Wounded—Even Hiss"—Nov. 26).

8. Chapter XIV, note 41.

9. Lillian Hellman, *Scoundrel Time,* pp. 83–84.

10. *Ibid.;* see also p. 39n. Lillian Hellman continued to take an interest in the Hiss case, according to Alger Hiss, who said that Hellman told him at a party in the 1970s about having tried unsuccessfully in 1948 to track down one of the many rumors that Chambers had been institutionalized at a mental hospital. INTERVIEW, Alger Hiss, June 21, 1975.

11. Hilton Kramer, "The Blacklist and the Cold War," *The New York Times Arts and Leisure Section,* Oct. 3, 1976. See also Diana Trilling, "Liberal Anti-Communism Revisited," in *We Must March My Darlings,* pp. 41–66.

12. The best analysis of Nixon's use of the Hiss case is Garry Wills's "The Hiss Connection Through Nixon's Life," *The New York Times Magazine,* Aug. 25, 1974. See also my article "Nixon vs. Hiss," *Esquire,* Nov. 1975, and John W. Dean III, *Blind Ambition,* pp. 57, 139, 186–87.

13. Wills, *op. cit.*

14. *Ibid.* See also House Judiciary Committee, *Transcripts of Eight Recorded Presidential Conversations,* 93rd Cong., 2nd Sess., May–June 1974, p. 200 (April 16, 1973).

15. Wills, *op. cit.*

16. For the White House's transcription of this conversation, see NYT, May 1, 1974.

17. *The Nation,* Sept. 20, 1974; NYT, May 3, 1974.

18. *Transcripts . . . , op. cit.,* p. 21.

19. Dean, pp. 56–57; *The Los Angeles Times,* Oct. 9, 1976; New York *Post,* Oct. 8, 1976.

20. *Los Angeles Times,* Oct. 12, 1976.

21. *Ibid.* For Feehan's comments, see *Los Angeles Times,* Oct. 11, 1976.

22. Richard Nixon to Sidney Hook, Nov. 24, 1976, courtesy of Prof. Hook.

23. Weinstein, "Nixon vs. Hiss," *op. cit.*

24. Hiss told James Reston, Jr., shortly after beginning a lecture tour of universities in the fall of 1976 to raise money for a new defense fund to reopen litigation on his case, that he commanded a $2,500 fee for each appearance. Much of

the information on Hiss's lecture-circuit travels during these years and on the details of his personal life come from the "Reinstatement Questionnaire," which he completed for the Massachusetts Board of Bar Overseers as part of his application for reinstatement as a lawyer: In Re: Alger Hiss, No. J 74–151 CIV. This and other documents connected with his application were supplied to me through the courtesy of Mrs. Manice de F. Lockwood.

25. Brower, *op. cit.;* Woodward notes, *op. cit.;* INTERVIEWS, Alger Hiss, June 21 and Oct. 4, 1975; Deborah Davis, "Alger Hiss Remembers . . . ," *The Village Voice,* Nov. 10, 1975; Dave O'Brian, "Alger Hiss: Battling On in Changing Times," *Boston Phoenix,* Aug. 12, 1975.

26. David Caute, *The Great Fear,* pp. 566–67. "Are you hung up on the truth?" one of Hiss's lawyers asked writer Elinor Langer, who inquired about the case. INTERVIEW, Elinor Langer, Dec. 28, 1974.

27. INTERVIEW, Robert von Mehren, Dec. 11, 1974; Philip Nobile, "The State of the Art of Alger Hiss," *Harper's,* April 1976.

28. INTERVIEW, Alger Hiss, Oct. 4, 1975; Irving Younger, "Was Alger Hiss Guilty?" *Commentary,* Aug. 1975; Manchester, pp. 502–12.

29. During Watergate, the NYT op-ed page not only published Hiss's "My Six Parallels," but also allotted space to reprint Richard Nixon's favorable review of Whittaker Chambers's *Witness* alongside a critical one written at the same time by Nixon's Watergate attorney, Charles Alan Wright, who believed Hiss innocent. Oct. 26, 1973.

30. NYT, Aug. 1, 1975; POST, Aug. 1, 1975; *Time,* Aug. 11, 1975; *Newsweek,* Aug. 11, 1975.

31. POST, Aug. 1, 1975; Boston *Globe,* April 14, 1975.

32. Alger Hiss's opening statement, July 31, 1975, HISS. See also POST, Sept. 12, 1975, and Hiss's interview with Orr Kelly, Washington *Star,* Sept. 12, 1975. Two skeptical writers later observed of that opening statement: "While it fits nicely into our current mood, Hiss's suggestion that Richard Nixon single-handedly sent him to jail on the basis of no evidence at all simply is not true. The evidence was wide-ranging and included important inconsistencies in his own story. To believe in his innocence requires acceptance of a string of improbabilities—the most spectacular involving an enemy's reconstruction of his wife's typewriter—to which no one but an enemy of Nixon would be entitled." Michael Kinsley and Arthur Lubow, "Alger Hiss and the Smoking Gun Fallacy," *Washington Monthly,* Oct. 1975. On conspiracy mania in the United States during the mid-1970s, see also Mordecai Richler, "It's a Plot!" *Playboy,* May 1975; Jacob Cohen, "Conspiracy Fever," *Commentary,* Oct. 1975; and Joseph Epstein, "A Conspiracy of Silence," *Harper's,* November 1977.

33. Edward C. McLean, memorandum, "Un-American Activities Committee: Conference with Mr. Nixon on Wednesday, January 12, 1949," Jan. 17, 1949, HISS.

34. *Ibid.* See also "Mr. Patch to Mr. McLean," "Digest of Interview with Hon. Richard M. Nixon . . . January 12, 1949," Jan. 13, 1949, HISS. Patch was an investigator working for the Hiss defense. A February 1949 memo by McLean shows that Thomas Donegan also allowed him to examine prints of the microfilm in question ("Government Documents Microfilm," Feb. 20 1949, HISS).

35. NYT, March 18 and 19, 1976. See, especially, Hiss's opening prepared statement at his March 18, 1976, press conference.

36. See Chapters VIII and XI, *passim,* for the Martin-Grady information, recorded in a number of defense memos at the time of the case.

37. Hiss generally expressed interest in several conspiracy theories simultaneously. INTERVIEWS, March 27 and June 21, 1975; Woodward notes, *op. cit.* See also Smith, pp. 363–64, and the Afterword to the paperback edition of his book, pp. 443–52, for an argument that the FBI files confirm a conspiracy against Hiss; also John Lowenthal, "Woodstock N230099 . . . ," *op. cit.,* and David Levin, "In the Court of Historical Criticism: Alger Hiss's Narrative," *The Virginia Quarterly Review,* Winter 1976. For critiques of the various conspiracy theories, see the Appendix and my articles: "Nixon vs. Hiss," *op. cit.;* "F.B.I.'s Hiss Files Show Bumbling, Not Malice," *The New York Times Week in Review,* Feb. 1, 1976; "The Hiss and Rosenberg Files," *The New Republic,* Feb. 14, 1976; and "Was Alger Hiss Framed?" *The New York Review of Books,* April 1, 1976, plus exchanges with my critics in the May 27, 1976, and Sept. 16, 1976, issues of that journal.

38. Kinsley and Lubow, *op. cit.*

39. INTERVIEW, Claude Cross, July 15, 1974; Supreme Judicial Court for the Commonwealth (of Massachusetts), *In the Matter of Alger Hiss,* No. 269. The various briefs, reports, transcript of the January 7, 1975, hearing, and the court's Aug. 5, 1975, "Opinion on Reinstatement" were given to me through the courtesy of Mrs. Manice

de F. Lockwood. See also Boston *Globe,* Jan. 8, 1975, and NYT, May 10, 1975.

40. For Tauro's comments, see "Opinion on Reinstatement . . . ," *op. cit.*

41. *Ibid.,* pp. 4–7, 20. See also Vern Countryman, "One Small Step for Alger Hiss," *The New Republic,* Aug. 30, 1975.

42. *Ibid.,* pp. 17–20; NYT, Aug. 6, 1975; Boston *Globe,* Aug. 6, 1975.

43. Readmission Hearing, Jan. 7, 1975, *op. cit.,* pp. 140–41; for the defense interviews with those jurors who voted for acquittal, see Chapter XII, note 60.

44. For the investigation of Schmahl, see the Appendix and the following: Chapter XV, note 14; INTERVIEWS, Alger Hiss, Sept. 11, 1974, March 27 and June 21, 1975; INTERVIEW, Manice de F. Lockwood, May 1, 1975; INTERVIEWS, Peter Irons, Feb. 17 and Mar. 13, 1975. The pursuit of Horace Schmahl by Hiss and his associates emerges also in memos and letters found in the Defense Files. Curiously, Fred J. Cook's article, "Alger Hiss and the Smoking Typewriter" (*New Times,* Oct. 14, 1977), which argues for the "double agent" theory, never mentions this intensive defense scrutiny of Schmahl. In the 1949 interviews with the three pro-Hiss jurors, they described jury deliberations and made recommendations and suggestions for defense strategy at the second trial.

45. Elizabeth Drew, *Washington Journal* (New York: Random House, 1975), p. 185.

46. Robert Griffith, *The Politics of Fear,* p. 35.

BIBLIOGRAPHY

INTERVIEWS

A Note on the Interview Listing: I have limited this list mainly to those whom I interviewed who provided important or helpful information concerning the case, occasionally by telephone. A dozen of these interviews were conducted by my extremely capable then research assistants, Catherine Brown, Elizabeth Lenneberg, and John Fox. Almost all of the myriad interviews I held by telephone during my research as well as several additional personal interviews that I conducted have been omitted, either to protect the privacy of the people who provided "background" material or because the interviews did not produce significant information. Those who either declined my request for an interview or never answered my letters, other than those mentioned in the Introduction, included Ralph de Sola, Loy Henderson, Jay Lovestone, Joseph North, Horace Schmahl, Mrs. Reuben Shemitz, and William C. Sullivan. Many of those with intimate knowledge of the case died prior to publication of this book's original edition in 1978: Whittaker Chambers, Dean Acheson, Dr. Carl Binger, Karl Mundt, Judge Samuel Kaufman, Lee Pressman, Henry Collins, Noel Field, Josephine Herbst, and John Herrmann. Principals in the case who have died between then and the appearance of this edition include Alger Hiss, Richard Nixon, Priscilla Hiss, Esther Chambers, and Thomas Murphy. I would like to express my appreciation to all those who did agree to be interviewed.

Donald T. Appell: Aug. 29, 1974.

Dr. Viola Bernard: June 23, 1975.

Jacob and Esther Burck: Dec. 30, 1974.

Robert Cantwell: Nov. 11, 1974; Feb. 10, 1975; Aug. 1, 1977.

John Chamberlain: Aug. 4, 1976 (John Fox).

John Chambers: April 25, 1975; May 20, 1975; Aug. 5, 1975 (telephone); July 12, 1977.

O. Edmund Clubb: Nov. 20, 1975 (Elizabeth Lenneberg).

Rev. John Cronin: Nov. 26, 1975.

Claude B. Cross: July 15, 1974.

John F. Davis: Aug. 29, 1974.

Ralph de Toledano: July 19, 1977.

Judge Thomas Donegan: Nov. 11, 1974.

Willard Edwards: June 23, 1975.

Robert Elson: Aug. 5, 1976 (John Fox).

Hermann Field: March 4, 1975.

Prof. Richard Field: July 16, 1974 (Catherine Brown).

Robert Fitzgerald: Aug. 20, 1976 (John Fox).

Dr. Frank Gannon: July 9, 1975.

Alger Hiss: Sept. 11, 1974; Sept. 20, 1974; Nov. 7, 1974; March 27, 1975; June 21, 1975; Oct. 4, 1975; March 10, 1976.

Donald Hiss: Sept. 29, 1975.

Priscilla Hiss: Nov. 11, 1974; June 24, 1975; Sept. 3, 1975; Sept. 16, 1975; Aug. 23, 1977 (all luncheon meetings).

Dr. Timothy Hobson: Aug. 16 and 17, 1974.

Prof. Sidney Hook: April 30, 1975.

Dr. Peter Irons: Feb. 17, 1975 (telephone); March 13, 1975.

Philip J. Jaffe: Sept. 17, 1975.

Matthew Josephson: Dec. 9, 1974.

Prof. Karel Kaplan: March 27 and April 19, 1977.

Sam Krieger: Aug. 16 and 18, 1974.

Persis Lane: Nov. 5, 1975 (Elizabeth Lenneberg).

Elinor Langer: Dec. 28, 1974.

Isaac Don Levine: Sept. 16, 1974; Oct. 18, 1974.

Maxim Lieber: May 10 and 13, 1975.

Manice de F. Lockwood III: May 1, 1975.

Elizabeth McCarthy: Nov. 19, 1975 (Elizabeth Lenneberg).

William Marbury: Feb. 24, 1975; March 10, 1975; Dec. 27, 1976.

Hede Massing: Nov. 11, 1974.

T. S. Matthews: March 22, 1975.

Harold Medina, Jr.: Aug. 6, 1976 (John Fox).

Felix Morrow: May 13, 1975.

Dr. Henry Murray: Nov. 4, 1975 (Elizabeth Lenneberg).

Duncan Norton-Taylor, July 17–19, 1976 (John Fox).

Joszef Peters: March 20, 1975.

June Reno: Dec. 30, 1974.

Prof. Meyer and Dr. Lillian Schapiro: Oct. 7, 1974; Oct. 19, 1974; Nov. 18, 1974; May 7, 1975; Aug. 9, 1975; Oct. 4, 1975.

Robert Stripling: April 28, 1975; June 30, 1975.

Martin and Pearl Tytell: Nov. 2, 1975 (Elizabeth Lenneberg).

Nadya Ulanovskaya: Jan. 3–6, 1977.

Nicholas Vazzana: June 30, 1975.

Robert von Mehren: Dec. 11, 1974.

Samuel G. Welles: Nov. 6, 1975 (Elizabeth Lenneberg).

Nathaniel Weyl: Oct. 28, 1974 (telephone).

Alden Whitman: March 21, April 17, July 24, Sept. 11, Oct. 15, Nov. 6, and Dec. 10—all 1974.

Paul Willert: March 17, 1975.

Ella Winter: March 16, 1975.

Judge Charles E. Wyzanski, Jr.: April 3, 1975.

David Zabladowsky: Nov. 1, 1975 (Elizabeth Lenneberg).

MANUSCRIPT COLLECTIONS CONSULTED
PRIVATE COLLECTIONS OR DOCUMENTS

Alger Hiss's Defense Files as of 1977:

1. Attorney Helen Buttenwieser's files (the main body of Hiss Defense Files were kept in her Manhattan offices).

2. Attorney Claude B. Cross's files (dealing mainly with the second trial and pretrial investigations).

3. Attorney William Marbury's files (extraordinarily well organized and rich in the early details of the case from August to December 1948).

4. Attorney Robert von Mehren's files (the crucial Edward McLean investigative records and strategy memos for the two trials are contained in this small but invaluable batch of materials).

(A Note on the Hiss Defense Files: There is a great deal of overlap among the separate collections, with the same letter or memo often turning up in two, three, or all four places. Also, Mr. Hiss apparently kept to the practice of adding materials to the files in Mrs. Buttenwieser's office, which contained a great many letters and other items dealing with the ongoing defense probe added between 1950 and when I examined the material in the 1970s. My researcher Mrs. Elizabeth Lenneberg and I last used the Buttenwieser files in 1975, when they were being stored in an unused floor of offices being rented by the firm to a company that had no awareness of the material's historical importance. The company had strewn the files over the floor of a large storage closet in order to retrieve the boxes for other purposes. Painstakingly, over a two-day period, Mrs. Lenneberg and I restored the files as carefully as possible to their original order.)

Sidney Hook: personal letters.

Isaac Don Levine: notes of Chambers's interview with A. A. Berle.

William Marbury: "The Hiss Case," a privately distributed memoir, 1977.

Mrs. Mary Mundt: memorabilia of the Hiss case (given to my researcher Ms. Kathleen McCarthy).

Prof. Meyer Schapiro: letters from Whittaker Chambers.

Herbert Solow: letters from Whittaker Chambers; two unpublished articles by Chambers on Soviet espionage written in 1938; Solow's notarized memo on his talks with Chambers in 1938; and many other valuable items on Soviet underground work in the United States during the 1930s (courtesy of the late Mrs. Sylvia Salmi Solow). After Mrs. Solow's death, the material was given to the Hoover Institution (Stanford).

Russian Intelligence Service (SVR) files, Moscow, reviewed from 1994–97 in cooperation with Alexander Vassiliev, my coauthor on *The Haunted Wood: Soviet Espionage in America.*

Robert Stripling: letters and other memorabilia of the case.

Time Inc. Archive: files on Whittaker Chambers's service on *Time,* on the Hiss-Chambers case, and on Chambers's later contacts with the magazine.

Alden Whitman: letters dealing with the case, notes of two interviews with Communist officials, and several important leads.

C. Vann Woodward: memo on his 1959 meeting with Alger Hiss.

MANUSCRIPT DEPOSITORIES

(As in the case of interviews, I have included only depositories and collections that produced material of importance or help to the book. Stray items garnered from other depositories have been omitted.)

Columbia University (1) Oral History Collection—transcripts of the memoirs of Harvey Bundy, Chester T. Lane, Gardner Jackson, Max Schactman, and Lee Pressman; (2) Carnegie Endowment MSS, 1947–49; (3) Random House MSS, 1950–59 (letters from Whittaker Chambers).

Franklin D. Roosevelt Library, Hyde Park, N.Y.: Adolf A. Berle MSS.

Harvard Law Library: letters of Charles E. Wyzanski, Jr.; letters connected with Hiss Defense Fund efforts.

Hoover Institution, Stanford University: Stanley K. Hornbeck MSS; Ralph de Toledano MSS.

Library of Congress: Felix Frankfurter MSS; Leo Pasvolsky MSS; Francis Sayre MSS.

Karl E. Mundt Library, Dakota State College, Madison, S.D.: Mundt MSS (including files of the House Committee on Un-American Activities for 1946–48).

National Archives: Agricultural Adjustment Administration records; Nye Committee records; Office of Special Political

Affairs, Department of State, records,
1945–47.

Newbery Library (Chicago): Malcolm
Cowley MSS.

New York Public Library: David Dallin
MSS.

Princeton University: John Foster
Dulles MSS; John Foster Dulles Oral History Project—memoirs of Allen Dulles and
Richard M. Nixon; Harry Dexter White
MSS.

Harry S. Truman Library, Independence,
MO: Dean Acheson MSS; Democratic
National Committee files; Francis Matthews
MSS; J. Howard McGrath MSS; John F. X.
McGohey MSS; Frank McNaughton MSS;
Harry S. Truman presidential files, and the

files of the following Truman aides—Clark
Clifford, George Elsey, Martin Friedman,
David D. Lloyd, Charles Murphy, and
Stephen J. Springarn; Oral History Interviews—Jack L. Belt, Edward T. Folliard,
Martin Friedman, Donald Hansen, Stephen
J. Spingarn, Richard L. Strout, and Robert
K. Walsh.

Yale University: (1) Beinecke Rare Book
Library: Josephine Herbst MSS (with the
permission of Hilton Kramer); (2) Historical Manuscripts Division: Jerome Frank
MSS (with the permission of Mrs. Jerome
Frank), including a copy of Frank's Oral
History Memoir; V. J. Jerome MSS; James
Bell's reports for *Time* on Alger Hiss's
perjury trials (two bound volumes).

GOVERNMENT DOCUMENTS

(A note on the government documents:
At the time of publication of the second
edition of this book, the FBI files on Hiss-
Chambers had reached more than 40,000
pages released. Depositions taken during
the spring and summer of 1977 led directly
to review of the entire Hiss-Chambers
file and to release of several thousand
additional portions of pages previously
withheld under claimed exemptions. Material from every other government agency
listed below was also obtained in response
to my requests under the Freedom of Information Act.)

Federal Bureau of Investigation: Alger
Hiss–Whittaker Chambers and Hiss-
Chambers case files; Noel Field files; Joszef
Peter files.

Central Intelligence Agency: Alger Hiss
and Hiss-Chambers case files (including
records from the Office of Strategic Services on Alger Hiss); Noel Field files.

Department of Justice, Washington:
Hiss-Chambers case files, trial exhibits

(notably the original "pumpkin papers"
microfilm).

Department of Justice, Immigration
and Naturalization Service: J. Peters
(a.k.a. Alexander Stevens) deportation
files.

Department of Justice, U.S. Attorney's
Office, Southern District of New York:
Hiss-Chambers case files, trial exhibits,
records of both trials.

Department of the Navy, Naval Intelligence Command: Hiss-Chambers case
records (almost nothing released except
newspaper clippings, although Chambers
had given information to Robert Morris,
then working for Naval Intelligence during
the Second World War. The records had not
been located at the time of publication of
the second edition).

Department of State: Alger Hiss's personnel records; files on the Department's
1945–47 investigation of Alger Hiss; later
files on the Hiss-Chambers case; Noel Field
files.

PRIMARY PRINTED OR TYPESCRIPT RECORDS

Baltimore Depositions, October 1948–March 1949 (copy in possession of Hiss Defense Files, Attorney Helen Buttenwieser, New York City). See complete citation below.

Communist Party of U.S. vs. Subversive Activities Control Board. 81 S. Ct. 1357 (1961). Contains history of litigation involving Communist Party.

Fund for the Republic. Digest of the Public Record of Communism in the United States. New York, 1953.

———. Bibliography on the Communist Problem in the United States. New York, 1955.

Hearings of the Special Committee on Un-American Activities, "Investigation of Un-American Propaganda Activities in the United States," Vol. II. Washington: Government Printing Office, 1939.

House Committee on Un-American Activities. Annual Report to the United States House of Representatives. December 31, 1948.

U.S. Congress, Senate, Committee on the Judiciary. Cumulative Index to Published Hearings and Reports of the Internal Security Subcommittee, 1951–1955. Washington: Government Printing Office, 1957.

U.S. Congress, House of Representatives, Committee on the Judiciary Transcripts of Eight Recorded Presidential Conversations. Washington: Government Printing Office, 1974.

U.S. Congress, House, Committee on Un-American Activities. Hearings Regarding Communism in the United States Government, August–September 1950, Part 2. Washington: Government Printing Office, 1950.

U.S. Congress, House, Committee on Un-American Activities. Hearings Regarding Communist Espionage,

November–December 1949, February–March 1950. Washington: Government Printing Office, 1951.

U.S. Congress, House, Committee on Un-American Activities. Hearings Regarding Communist Espionage in the United States Government, July–September 1948. Washington Government Printing Office, 1948.

U.S. Congress, House, Committee on Un-American Activities. Hearings Regarding Communist Espionage in the United States Government, Part 2, December 1948. Washington: Government Printing Office, 1949.

U.S. Congress, House, Committee on Un-American Activities. The Shameful Years: Thirty Years of Soviet Espionage in the United States. Washington: Government Printing Office, 1952.

U.S. Congress, House, Committee on Un-American Activities. Soviet Espionage Within the United States Government. Washington: Government Printing Office, 1949.

U.S. Congress, Senate, Committee on Foreign Relations. Executive Sessions . . . (Historical Series), Vol. II, 81st Cong., 1st & 2nd Sess., 1949–1950.

U.S. Congress, Senate, Committee on Government Operations. Congressional Investigations of Communism and Subversive Activities. Washington: Government Printing Office, 1956.

U.S. Congress, Senate, Committee on the Judiciary. Hearings Before the Internal Security Subcommittee on the Institute of Pacific Relations, August 1951. Washington: Government Printing Office, 1951.

U.S. Congress, Senate, Committee on the Judiciary. Hearing on Interlocking Subversion in Government Departments,

May 26, 1953, Part 10. Washington: Government Printing Office, 1953.

U.S. Congress, Senate, Committee on the Judiciary. Hearings on Interlocking Subversion in Government Departments, November and December 1953. Washington: Government Printing Office, 1954.

U.S. Congress, Senate, Committee on the Judiciary. Institute of Pacific Relations (Hearings), July and August 1951, Part 1. Washington: Government Printing Office, 1951.

U.S. Congress, Senate, Committee on the Judiciary Institute of Pacific Relations (Hearings), January and February 1952, Part 8. Washington: Government Printing Office, 1952.

Senate Internal Security Subcommittee of the Committee on the Judiciary. Hearings to Investigate the Administration of the Internal Security Laws. 82nd Cong., 2nd Sess., October 23, 1952.

U.S. Congress, Senate, Committee on the Judiciary. Internal Security Report for 1957. Washington: Government Printing Office, 1958.

United States Court of Appeals for the Second Circuit; No. 78. October Term, 1950. United States of America against Alger Hiss; appeal from a judgment of the District Court of the United States for the Southern District of New York. Affirmed. Transcript of Record (Second Trial), vols. I–X. On appeal from the District Court of the United States for the Southern District of New York. Brief for the Appellant.

United States District Court, for the District of Maryland, Baltimore, Md. (Civil #4176). Deposition of Whittaker Chambers and Esther Chambers in the case of Alger Hiss (plaintiff) vs. Whittaker Chambers (defendant), November 6–7, 1948, February 17–18, 1949, March 25, 1949.

United States District Court, Southern District of New York: United States of America against Alger Hiss. Transcript of Record (First Trial), May 31–July 8, 1949.

United States District Court, Southern District of New York: United States of America against Alger Hiss. Affidavit submitted in opposition to the motion of defendant for a third trial. Memorandum in support of defendant's motion for a new trial under Rule 33 on the ground of newly discovered evidence. Motion for a new trial based on the ground of newly discovered evidence, January 24, 1952. Supplemental affidavits in support of motion for a new trial. Federal Supplement, 1952, Vol. 107.

United States Supreme Court; October Term, 1952; No. 629. Alger Hiss against the United States of America. Petition for a writ of certiorari to the United States Court of Appeals for the Second Circuit, March 1953.

NEWSPAPERS

A variety of newspapers consulted during the research for this book have been cited in the text. Those used most frequently included *The New York Times, The Washington Post,* the New York *Herald Tribune,* and the Baltimore *Sun.* Excellent clipping files of articles dealing with the Hiss-Chambers case can be found in the Hiss Defense Files (Buttenwieser Archive), the Democratic National Committee records at the Truman Library, and the Karl Mundt MSS.

MEMOIRS AND PERSONAL ACCOUNTS

Abell, Tyler, ed. *Drew Pearson: Diaries, 1949–1959.* New York: Holt, Rinehart and Winston, 1974.

Abt, John. *Advocate and Activist: Memoirs of an American Communist Lawyer.* Urbana, Ill.: University of Illinois Press, 1993.

Acheson, Dean. *Present at the Creation.* New York: Norton, 1969.

Beal, Fred. *Proletarian Journey.* New York: Da Capo, 1971.

Bentley, Elizabeth. *Out of Bondage: The Story of Elizabeth Bentley.* New York: Ballantine, 1988 ed., with Afterword by Hayden Peake.

Berle, Beatrice B., and Travis B. Jacobs, eds. *Navigating the Rapids, 1918–1971: From the Papers of Adolf A. Berle.* New York: Harcourt Brace Jovanovich, 1973.

Bohlen, Charles E. *Witness to History, 1929–1969.* New York: Norton, 1973.

Browder, Earl. "The American Communist Party in the Thirties," in *As We Saw the Thirties,* Rita J. Simon, ed., 1967.

———. *Communism in the United States.* 1935. Urbana, Ill.: University of Illinois Press, 1967.

———. *People's Front.* 1938.

Budenz, Louis F. *This Is My Story.* Dublin: Browne and Nolan, 1948.

Byrnes, James F. *All in One Lifetime.* New York: Harper, 1958.

———. *Speaking Frankly.* New York: Harper, 1947.

Chambers, Whittaker. "Before the End." *News Magazine Supplement,* July 9, 1947.

———. "Braun." *The Morningside,* Dec. 1924.

———. *Can You Hear Their Voices?* International Pamphlets, 1932.

———. "Can You Make Out Their Voices?" *The New Masses,* March 1931.

———. *Cold Friday* (Duncan Norton-Taylor, ed.). New York: Random House, 1964.

———. "The Damn Fool." *The Morningside,* March 1922.

———. "The Death of the Communists." *The New Masses,* Dec. 1931.

———. "Deep River." *Time,* Dec. 18, 1945.

———. "The Devil." *Life,* Feb. 2, 1948.

———. "End of a Dark Age Ushers in New Dangers." *Life,* April 30, 1956.

———. "The Ghosts on the Roof." *Time,* March 5, 1945.

———. *Ghosts on the Roof: Selected Journalism of. . . .* Washington, D.C.: Regnery Gateway, 1989.

———. "The Herring and the Thing." *Look,* Dec. 29, 1953.

———. "The Hissiad: A Correction." *National Review,* May 9, 1959.

———. "Lathrop, Montana." *The Nation,* June 30, 1926.

———. "October 21st, 1926." *Poetry,* Feb. 1931.

———. *Odyssey of a Friend* (William F. Buckley, Jr., ed.). New York: Putnam, 1969.

———. "Our Comrade Munn." *The New Masses,* Oct. 1931.

———. "A Play for Puppets." *The Morningside,* Nov. 1922.

———. "Poems." *The Nation,* April 7, 1926.

———. "Quag Hole." *The Nation,* Dec. 31, 1924.

———. "Rosedale Trestle." *The Morningside,* Dec. 1924.

———. "Sanity of St. Benedict," excerpt from "Saints for Now," ed. by C. B. Luce. *Commonweal,* Sept. 19, 1952.

———. "Tandaradei." *Two Worlds,* June 1926.

———. "What Is a Communist?" *Look,* July 28, 1953.

———. *Witness.* New York: Random House, 1952.

———. "You Have Seen the Heads." *The New Masses,* April 1931.

———. "Whittaker Chambers Meets the Press." *The American Mercury,* Feb. 1949.

Davis, Hope Hale. *Great Day Coming: A Memoir of the 1930s.* South Royalton, Vt.: Steerforth Press, 1994.

Dean, John. *Blind Ambition,* New York: Simon and Schuster, 1976.

Gitlow, Benjamin. *The Whole of Their Lives.* New York: Scribner's, 1948.

Grunwald, Henry. *One Man's America.* New York: Doubleday, 1997.

Halper, Albert. *Goodbye, Union Square.* Chicago: Quadrangle, 1970.

Haydn, Hiram. *Words and Faces.* New York: Harcourt Brace Jovanovich, 1974.

Hébert, F. Edward. "*Last of the Titans. . . .* " Lafayette, La.: Center for Louisiana Studies, 1976.

Hellman, Lillian. *Scoundrel Time.* Boston: Little, Brown, 1976.

Hicks, Granville. *Part of the Truth.* New York: Harcourt, Brace and World, 1965.

Hiss, Alger. "Basic Questions in the Great Debate." *The New York Times Magazine,* Nov. 16, 1947.

———. *In the Court of Public Opinion.* New York: Knopf, 1957.

———. "My Six Parallels." *The New York Times,* July 23, 1975.

———. "The General Assembly of the United Nations." *Illinois Law Review,* Jan–Feb. 1947.

———. *Recollections of a Life.* New York: Seaver Books/Henry Holt, 1988.

———. "Two Essential Elements for European Reconstruction." *Christian Register,* March 1948.

———. "Yalta: Modern American Myth." *Pocket Book Magazine,* Nov. 1955.

Hiss, Tony. "I Call on Alger." *Rolling Stone,* Sept. 13, 1973.

———. *Laughing Last.* Boston: Houghton Mifflin, 1977.

Hull, Cordell. *The Memoirs of Cordell Hull,* Vol. I. New York: Macmillan, 1948.

Koestler, Arthur. *The Invisible Writing.* London: Collins, 1954.

Krivitsky, Walter. *I Was Stalin's Agent.* Bristol, England: Right Book Club, 1940.

Lamphere, Robert J., and Tom Schachtman. *The FBI-KGB War: A Special Agent's Story.* New York: Random House, 1986.

Lattimore, Owen. *Ordeal by Slander.* Boston: Little, Brown, 1950.

Levine, Isaac Don. *Eyewitness to History.* New York: Hawthorn, 1973.

Massing, Hede. *This Deception.* New York: Duell, Sloan & Pearce, 1951.

Matthews, T. S. *Name and Address.* New York: Simon and Schuster, 1960.

Murrow, Edward R., and Fred Friendly. Columbia record ML 4261: "I Can Hear It Now—Chambers and Hiss Appearance Before HUAC. August 25, 1948."

Nixon, Richard M. *RN. The Memoirs of Richard Nixon.* New York: Warner Books, 1979.

———. *Six Crises.* New York: Pocket Books, 1962.

Philby, Kim. *My Silent War.* New York: Grove, 1968.

Poretsky, Elizabeth. *Our Own People.* Ann Arbor: University of Michigan Press, 1969.

Rusher, William. *Special Counsel.* New Rochelle, N.Y.: Arlington House, 1968.

Steffens, Lincoln. *The Letters of Lincoln Steffens.* New York: Harcourt, Brace, 1938.

Stettinius, Edward R., Jr. *Roosevelt and the Russians.* Garden City, N.Y.: Doubleday, 1949.

———. *The Diaries of Edward R. Stettinius, Jr., 1943–1946.* Thomas M. Campbell and George C. Herring, eds. New York: New Viewpoints, 1975.

Stripling, Robert. *The Red Plot Against America.* Robert Considine, ed. Drexel Hill, Pa.: Bell, 1949.

Sudoplatov, Pavel, with Anatoli Sudoplatov, Jerrold L. Schechter, and Leona P. Schechter. *Special Tasks: Memoirs of an Unwanted Witness—A Soviet Spymaster.* New York: Little, Brown, 1994.

Trilling, Diana. *The Beginning of the Journey.* New York: Harcourt, 1993.

Ulanovskaya, Nadezhda, and Maya Ulanovskaya. *Istoriia Odnoi Semyi* [The Story of One Family]. Benson, Vt.: Chalidze, 1982.

Van Doren, Mark. *The Autobiography of Mark Van Doren.* New York: Harcourt, Brace, 1958.

Wadleigh, Julian. "Why I Spied for the Communists." New York *Post,* July 12–24, 1949.

Wechsler, James A. *The Age of Suspicion.* New York: Random House, 1953.

———. *Reflections of an Angry, Middle Aged Editor.* New York: Random House, 1960.

Winter, Ella. *And Not to Yield.* New York: Harcourt, Brace and World, 1963.

BOOKS

Aaron, Daniel, ed. *America in Crisis.* New York: Knopf, 1952.

———. *Writers on the Left.* New York: Avon, 1961.

Abrahamsen, David. *Nixon vs. Nixon—A Psychoanalytic Inquest.* New York: Farrar, Straus and Giroux, 1977.

Ambrose, Stephen E. *Nixon: The Education of a Politician, 1913–1962.* New York: Simon and Schuster, 1987.

Andrew, Christopher, and Oleg Gordievsky. *KGB: The Inside Story.* New York: HarperCollins, 1990.

Andrews, Bert, and Peter Andrews. *A Tragedy of History.* Washington: Robert B. Luce, 1962.

Aptheker, Herbert. *History and Really.* New York: Cameron Associates, 1955.

Ascoli, Max, ed. *Our Times: The Best from The Reporter.* New York: Farrar, Straus and Cudahy, 1960.

Auerbach, Jerold S. *Labor and Liberty: The La Follette Committee and the New Deal.* Indianapolis: Bobbs-Merrill, 1966.

Barber, James David. *The Presidential Character.* Englewood Cliffs, N.J.: Prentice-Hall, 1972.

Barron, John. *KGB: The Secret Work of Soviet Secret Agents.* New York: Dutton, 1974.

Barros, James. *No Sense of Evil: The Espionage Case of E. Herbert Norma.* New York: Ballantine Books, 1987.

Barth, Alan. *Government by Investigation.* New York: Viking, 1955.

———. *The Loyalty of Free Men.* New York: Viking, 1952.

Belfrage, Cedric. *The American Inquisition 1945–1960.* Indianapolis: Bobbs-Merrill, 1973.

Bell, Daniel. *Marxian Socialism in the United States.* Princeton: Princeton University Press, 1967.

———, ed. *The New American Right.* New York: Criterion, 1955.

Benson, Robert Louis, and Michael Warner. *VENONA: Soviet Espionage and the American Response, 1939–1957.* Washington,

D.C.: National Security Agency & Central Intelligence Agency, 1996.

Bishop, Jim. *FDR's Last Year*. New York: Morrow, 1974.

Blum, John Morton. *From the Morgenthau Diaries . . . 1938–1941*. Boston: Houghton Mifflin, 1965.

———. *V Was for Victory*. New York: Harcourt Brace Jovanovich, 1976.

Blum, Richard H. *Surveillance and Espionage in a Free Society*. New York: Praeger, 1972.

Bontecou, Eleanor. *The Federal Loyalty and Security Programs*. Ithaca: Cornell University Press, 1953.

Boveri, Margret. *Treason in the Twentieth Century*. New York: Putnam, 1963.

Bremner, Robert H., ed. *Essays on History and Literature*. Columbus: Ohio State University Press, 1966.

Brower, Brock. *Other Loyalties*. New York: Atheneum, 1968.

Brown, Ralph. *Loyalty and Security*. New Haven: Yale University Press, 1958.

Brown, Stuart G. *Conscience and Politics—Adlai E. Stevenson in the 1950's*. Syracuse: Syracuse University Press, 1961.

Buckholder, Roger Glen. "Whittaker Chambers: The Need to Believe." Bowdoin Prize, Harvard University, 1965. Thesis filed in Harvard Library.

Buckley, William F. (and the editors of the *National Review*). *The Committee and Its Critics: A Calm Review of the House Committee on Un-American Activities*. New York: Putnam, 1962.

Buckley, William F., and L. Brent Bozell. *McCarthy and His Enemies*. Chicago: Regnery, 1954.

Bullitt, William Marshall. *A Factual Review of the Whittaker Chambers—Alger Hiss Controversy*. New York: privately printed, 1949.

Burnham, James. *The Web of Subversion: Underground Networks in the U.S.*

Government. New York: John Day and Co., 1954.

Busch, Francis X. *Guilty or Not Guilty?* Indianapolis: Bobbs-Merrill, 1952.

Campbell, Thomas M. *Masquerade Peace: America's UN Policy, 1944–1945*. Tallahassee: Florida State University Press, 1973.

Carr, Robert Kenneth. *The House Committee on Un-American Activities, 1945–1950*. Ithaca: Cornell University Press, 1952.

Caute, David. *The Fellow-Travellers*. New York: Macmillan, 1973.

Chase, Harold. *Security and Liberty: The Problem of Native Communists*. Garden City, N.Y.: Doubleday, 1955.

Chastellain, J. *L'Espionage Soviétique aux Etats-Unis: L'Affaire Alger Hiss*. Lausanne: Impr. Jaunin, 1950.

Chollet, Laurence B. "The Hiss-Chambers Affair: An Evaluation of the Case and Its Effect on American Intellectuals." A senior thesis submitted to the History Department of Princeton University for the degree of Bachelor of Arts, April 18, 1973.

Clark, Eleanor. *The Bitter Box*. Garden City, N.Y.: Doubleday, 1946.

Clubb, O. Edmund. *The Witness and I*. New York: Columbia University Press, 1974.

Cole, Wayne S. *Senator Gerald P. Nye and American Foreign Relations*. Minneapolis: University of Minnesota Press, 1962.

Conquest, Robert. *The Great Terror: Stalin's Purge of the Thirties*. London: Macmillan, 1968.

Conrad, David Eugene. *The Forgotten Farmers: The Story of Sharecroppers in the New Deal*. Urbana: University of Illinois Press, 1965.

Cook, Fred J. *The FBI Nobody Knows*. New York: Pyramid, 1965.

———. *The Unfinished Story of Alger Hiss*. New York: Morrow, 1958.

Cooke, Alistair. *A Generation on Trial.* Baltimore: Penguin, 1952.

Costello, John, and Oleg Tsarev. *Deadly Illusions.* New York: Crown, 1993.

Cronin, Rev. John F. *Communism, a World Menace.* Washington: National Catholic Welfare Conference, 1947.

Crossman, Richard, ed. *The God That Failed.* New York: Bantam, 1954.

Dallin, David Y. *Soviet Espionage.* New Haven: Yale University Press, 1955.

Deacon, Richard. *The Chinese Secret Service.* New York: Taplinger, 1972.

———. *A History of the Russian Secret Service.* New York: Taplinger, 1972.

Demaris, Ovid. *The Director.* New York: Harper's Magazine Press, 1975.

Deriabin, Peter, and Frank Gibney. *The Secret World.* Garden City, N.Y.: Doubleday, 1959.

de Toledano, Ralph. *Lament for a Generation.* New York: Farrar, Straus and Cudahy, 1960.

de Toledano, Ralph, and Victor Lasky. *Seeds of Treason.* New York: Funk and Wagnalls, 1950. Revised and updated by de Toledano. Chicago: Regnery 1962.

———. *Spies, Dupes, and Diplomats.* New Rochelle, N.Y.: Arlington House, 1967.

Detzer, Dorothy. *Appointment on the Hill.* New York: Holt, 1948.

Deutscher, Isaac. *The Prophet Outcast.* London: Oxford University Press, 1963.

Diamond, Sander A. *The Nazi Movement in the United States, 1924–1941.* Ithaca: Cornell University Press, 1974.

Dies, Martin. *Trojan Horse in America.* New York: Dodd, Mead, 1940.

Diggins, John P. *Mussolini and Fascism: The View from America.* Princeton: Princeton University Press, 1972.

———. *Up from Communism: Conservative Odysseys in American Intellectual History.* New York: Harper & Row, 1975.

Donner, Frank J. *The Un-Americans.* New York: Ballantine, 1961.

Douglas, William O. *Go East, Young Man . . .* New York: Random House, 1974.

Draper, Theodore. *American Communism and Soviet Russia.* New York: Viking, 1960.

———. *The Roots of American Communism.* New York: Viking, 1957.

Dulles, Allen. *The Craft of Intelligence.* New York: Harper & Row, 1963.

Eastman, Max. *Love and Revolution.* New York: Random House, 1964.

Elson, Robert T. *The World of Time Inc.: Volume Two, 1941–1960.* New York: Atheneum, 1973.

Ernst, Morris L., and David Loth. *Report on the American Communist.* New York: Holt, 1952.

Fiedler, Leslie. *An End to Innocence: Essays on Culture and Politics.* Boston: Beacon, 1955.

Freeland, Richard M. *The Truman Doctrine and the Origins of McCarthyism.* New York: Knopf 1972.

Gaddis, John Lewis. *The United States and the Origins of the Cold War.* New York: Columbia University Press, 1972

Gilbert, James Burkhart. *Writers and Partisans.* New York: Wiley, 1968.

Gilder, Peggy Allen. "American Intellectuals and the Moscow Trials." Smith College thesis, 1960.

Goffman, Erving. *Strategic Interaction.* Philadelphia: University of Pennsylvania Press, 1969.

Goldman, Eric F. *The Crucial Decade and After: America, 1945–1960.* New York: Vintage, 1960.

Goodman, Walter. *The Committee.* New York: Farrar, Straus and Giroux, 1968.

Goulden, Joseph C. *The Best Years, 1945–1950.* New York: Atheneum, 1976.

Gramont, Sanche de. *The Secret War.* New York: Putnam, 1962.

Griffith, Robert. *The Politics of Fear: Joseph McCarthy and the Senate.* Lexington: University of Kentucky Press, 1970.

Griffith, Thomas. *Harry and Teddy.* New York: Random House, 1995.

Guttmann, Allen. *The Wound in the Heart.* New York: Free Press of Glencoe, 1962.

Gwynn, Beatrice V. *The Discrepancy in the Evidence.* Privately printed pamphlet on behalf of Hiss, March 1972.

———. *Whittaker Chambers: The Discrepancy in the Evidence.* London: Mazzard, 1993.

Halsey, Margaret. *The Pseudo-Ethic.* New York: Simon and Schuster, 1963.

Hamby, Alonzo L. *Beyond the New Deal: Harry S. Truman and American Liberalism.* New York: Columbia University Press, 1973.

———, ed. *Harry S. Truman and the Fair Deal.* Lexington, Mass.: Heath, 1974.

Harbaugh, William H. *Lawyer's Lawyer: The Life of John W. Davis.* New York: Oxford University Press, 1973.

Harney, Malachi L., and John C. Cross. *The Informer in Law Enforcement.* Springfield, Ill.: Charles C. Thomas, 1960.

Harper, Alan D. *The Politics of Loyalty: The White House and the Communist Issue, 1946–1952.* Westport, Conn.: Greenwood, 1969.

Hinchley, Vernon. *Spies Who Never Were.* New York: Dodd, Mead, 1965.

Hirsch, Richard. *The Soviet Spies.* New York: Duell, Sloan, and Pearce, 1974.

Hook, Sidney. *Heresy, Yes—Conspiracy, No!* New York: John Day and Co., 1953.

Hoover, J. Edgar. *Masters of Deceit.* New York: Holt, 1958.

Howe, Irving. *Politics and the Novel.* Cleveland: World, 1962.

Howe, Irving, and Lewis Coser. *The American Communist Party.* New York: Praeger, 1962.

Hyde, H. Montgomery. *Room 3603.* New York: Farrar, Straus, 1962.

Isserman, Maurice. *Which Side Were You On?: The American Communist Party During the Second World War.* Champaign: University of Illinois Press, 1993.

Jaffe, Philip J. *The Rise and Fall of American Communism.* New York: Horizon, 1975.

Jazunski, Grzegorz. *Sxpiedxy.* Warsaw: Czytelnik, 1969 (also available in a Russian edition published subsequently).

Jowitt, William Allen, 1st Earl. *The Strange Case of Alger Hiss.* Garden City; N.Y.: Doubleday, 1953.

Kahn, David. *The Codebreakers.* New York: Macmillan, 1967.

Kahn, E. J., Jr. *The China Hands.* New York: Viking, 1975.

Kanfer, Stefan. *A Journal of the Plague Years.* New York: Antheneum, 1973.

Keeley, Joseph. *The China Lobby Man.* New Rochelle, N.Y.: Arlington House, 1969.

Kempton, Murray. *Part of Our Time: Some Monuments and Ruins of the Thirties.* New York: Dell, 1967.

Kirkendall, Richard S., ed. *The Truman Period as a Research Field.* Columbia: University of Missouri Press, 1967.

Klehr, Harvey. *The Heyday of American Communism: The Depression Decade.* New York: Basic Books, 1984.

Klehr, Harvey, and John Earl Haynes, with Fridrikh Igorevich Firsov. *The Secret World of American Communism.* New Haven: Yale University Press, 1995.

Klehr, Harvey, and Ronald Radosh. *The Amerasia Spy Case: Prelude to McCarthyism.* Chapel Hill: University of North Carolina Press, 1996.

Koch, Stephen. *Double Lives: Spies and Writers in the Secret Soviet War of Ideas Against the West.* New York: Free Press, 1994.

Koen, Ross Y. *The China Lobby in American Politics.* New York: Macmillan, 1960.

Koestler, Arthur. *Darkness at Noon.* New York: Macmillan, 1941; Signet ed., 1950.

Kornitzer, Bela. *The Real Nixon.* New York: Rand-McNally, 1960.

LaFeber, Walter. *America, Russia, and the Cold War, 1945–1971.* 2nd ed. New York: Wiley, 1972.

Latham, Earl. *The Communist Controversy in Washington.* New York: Atheneum, 1966.

———, ed. *The Meaning of McCarthyism.* Lexington, Mass.: Heath, 1973.

Lawson, R. Alan. *The Failure of Independent Liberalism, 1930–1941.* New York: Putnam, 1971.

Leuchtenburg, William E. *Franklin D. Roosevelt and the New Deal.* New York: Harper & Row, 1963.

Levine, Isaac Don. *The Mind of an Assassin.* New York: New American Library, 1960.

Levitt, Morton. *A Tissue of Lies: Nixon vs. Hiss.* New York: McGraw-Hill, 1979.

Lewis, Flora. *Red Pawn: The Story of Noel Field.* Garden City, N.Y.: Doubleday, 1965.

Liebling, A. J. *The Press.* Rev. ed. New York: Ballantine, 1964.

Lowenthal, Max. *The Federal Bureau of Investigation.* New York: Harcourt, Brace, 1950.

McCoy, Donald. *Angry Voices: Left-of-Center Politics in the New Deal Era.* Lawrence: University of Kansas Press, 1958.

Macdonald, Dwight. *Henry Wallace: The Man and the Myth.* New York: Vanguard, 1947.

McWilliams, Carey. *Witch Hunt: The Revival of Heresy.* Boston: Little, Brown, 1950.

Mairowitz, David Zane. *The Radical Soap Opera.* London: Wildwood House, 1974.

Manchester, William. *The Glory and the Dream.* Boston: Little, Brown, 1973.

Martin, George. *Madam Secretary: Frances Perkins.* Boston: Houghton Mifflin, 1976.

Mazlish, Bruce. *In Search of Nixon: A Psychohistorical Inquiry.* New York: Basic Books, 1972.

Mazo, Earl. *Richard Nixon.* New York: Harper, 1959.

Miller, Douglas T., and Marion Nowak. *The Fifties: The Way We Really Were.* Garden City, N.Y.: Doubleday, 1977.

Miller, Merle. *The Judges and the Judged: Report for the American Civil Liberties Union.* Garden City, N.Y.: Doubleday, 1952.

Mitchell, Broadus. *Depression Decade.* New York: Harper & Row, 1947.

Morris, Richard B. "The Case of Alger Hiss," in *Fair Trial.* New York: Knopf, 1953.

Morris, Robert. *No Wonder We Are Losing.* New York: Bookmailer, 1958.

Morris, Roger. *Richard Milhous Nixon: The Rise of an American Politician.* New York: Holt, 1990.

Nash, George. *The Conservative Intellectual Movement in America Since 1945.* New York: Basic Books, 1975.

Newton, Verne W. *The Cambridge Spies: The Untold Story of McLean, Philby and Burgess in America.* Lanham, N.Y.: Madison Books, 1991.

O'Brian, John L. *National Security and Individual Freedom.* Cambridge: Harvard University Press, 1955.

Oeste, Bob. *The Last Pumpkin Paper: A Novel.* New York: Random House, 1996.

Orlov, Alexander. *Handbook of Intelligence and Guerrilla Warfare.* Ann Arbor: University of Michigan Press, 1965.

Packer, Herbert L. *Ex-Communist Witnesses.* Stanford: Stanford University Press, 1962.

Page, Bruce, David Leitch, and Phillip Knightley. *The Philby Conspiracy.* Garden City, N.Y.: Doubleday, 1968.

Parmet, Herbert S. *Richard Nixon and His America*. Boston: Little, Brown, 1990.

Paterson, Thomas G., ed. *The Origins of the Cold War*. 2nd ed. Lexington, Mass.: Heath, 1974.

Pells, Richard H. *Radical Visions and American Dreams*. New York: Harper & Row, 1973.

Pilat, Oliver. *The Atom Spies*. New York: Putnam, 1952.

Polenberg, Richard. *War and Society: The United States, 1941–1945*. Philadelphia: Lippincott, 1972.

Powers, Richard Gid. *The Life of Edgar Hoover*. New York: Free Press, 1987.

Pritt, D. N. *Spies and Informers in the Witness Box*. London: Bernard Harison, 1958.

Radosh, Ronald, and Joyce Milton. *The Rosenberg File*. New York: Holt, Rinehart & Winston, 1983.

Rappaport, Doreen. *The Alger Hiss Trial*. New York: HarperCollins, 1993.

Rees, David. *Harry Dexter White: A Study in Paradox*. New York: Coward, McCann & Geoghegan, 1973.

Reuben, William A. *The Atom Spy Hoax*. New York: Action Books, 1960.

———. *Footnote on an Historic Case: In re Alger Hiss. . . .* New York: Nation Institute, 1983.

———. *The Honorable Mr. Nixon and the Alger Hiss Case*. New York: Action Books, 1956; revised ed., i158.

Rogin, Michael Paul. *The Intellectuals and McCarthy: The Radical Specter*. Cambridge: MIT Press, 1967.

Rorty, James, and Moshe Decter. *McCarthy and the Communists*. Boston: Beacon Press, 1954.

Ross, Irwin. *The Loneliest Campaign*. New York: New American Library, 1968.

Rovere, Richard H. *The American Establishment and Other Reports, Opinions, and Speculations*. New York: Harcourt, Brace & World, 1962.

———. *Senator Joe McCarthy*. Cleveland: World, 1960. Meridian edition.

Saposs, David Joseph. *Communism in American Politics*. Washington: Public Affairs Press, 1960.

Schaar, John H. *Loyalty in America*. Berkeley: University of California Press, 1957.

Schapsmeier, E. L. and F. H. *Henry A. Wallace of Iowa: The Agrarian Years, 1910–1940*. Ames: Iowa State University Press, 1968.

Schechter, Betty. *The Dreyfus Affair: A National Scandal*. Boston: Houghton Mifflin, 1965.

Schlesinger, Arthur M., Jr. *The Coming of the New Deal*. Boston: Houghton Mifflin, 1959.

———. *Crisis of the Old Order*. Boston: Houghton Mifflin, 1956.

———. *The Politics of Upheaval*. Boston: Houghton Mifflin, 1960.

Schneir, Walter and Miriam. *Invitation to an Inquest*. Garden City, N.Y.: Doubleday, 1965.

Seale, Patrick, and Maureen McConville. *Philby: The Long Road to Moscow*. New York: Simon and Schuster, 1973.

Service, John S. *The Amerasia Papers: Some Problems in the History of US-China Relations*. Berkeley: University of California Press, 1971.

Seth, Ronald. *The Sleeping Truth*. New York: Hart, 1968.

———. *Unmasked! The Story of Soviet Espionage*. New York: Hawthorn, 1965.

Shannon, David A. *The Decline of American Communism*. New York: Harcourt, Brace, 1959.

Sherwin, Martin J. *A World Destroyed*. New York: Knopf, 1975.

Sherwood, Robert E. *Roosevelt and Hopkins.* New York: Harper, 1948.

Shils, Edward Albert. *The Torment of Secrecy: The Background and Consequences of American Security Policies.* Glencoe, Ill: Free Press, 1956.

Shover, John L. *Cornbelt Rebellion.* Urbana: University of Illinois Press, 1965.

Slesinger, Tess. *The Unpossessed.* New York: Avon, 1934.

Smith, Geoffrey S. *To Save a Nation.* New York: Basic Books, 1973.

Smith, John Chabot. *Alger Hiss: The True Story.* New York: Holt, Rinehart and Winston, 1976. The paperback Penguin edition (1977) contains a new Afterword.

Smith, R. Harris. *OSS: The Secret History of America's First Central Intelligence Agency.* Berkeley: University of California Press, 1972.

Sommerville, John. *The Communist Trials and the American Tradition.* New York: Cameron Associates, 1956.

Starobin, Joseph R. *American Communism in Crisis, 1943–1957.* Cambridge: Harvard University. Press, 1972.

Steven, Stewart. *Operation Splinter Factor.* Philadelphia: Lippincott, 1974.

Stewart, William J. *The Era of Franklin D. Roosevelt: A Selected Bibliography.* Washington: National Archives and Records Service, 1971.

Stone, I. F. *The Truman Era.* New York: Vintage, 1973.

Stott, William. *Documentary Expression and Thirties America.* New York: Oxford University Press, 1973.

Stuart, Graham H. *The Department of State.* New York: Macmillan, 1949.

Swanberg, W. A. *Luce and His Empire.* New York: Scribner's, 1972.

Tanenhaus, Sam. *Whittaker Chambers: A Biography.* New York: Random House, 1997.

Taylor, Telford. *Grand Inquest.* New York: Ballatine, 1961.

Theoharis, Athan G. *Seeds of Repression.* Chicago: Quadrangle, 1971.

———. *The Yalta Myths.* Columbia: University of Missouri Press, 1970.

———, ed. *Beyond the Hiss Case: The FBI, Congress and the Cold War.* Philadelphia: Temple University Press, 1982.

Theoharis, Athan G., and Robert Griffith, eds. *The Specter: Original Essays on the Cold War and McCarthyism.* New York: Watts, 1974.

Thomas, John N. *The Institute of Pacific Relations.* Seattle: University of Washington Press, 1974.

Tiger, Edith, ed. *In re Alger Hiss . . . Petition for a Writ of Error Coram Nobis.* New York: Hill & Wang, 1979.

Trilling, Diana. *We Must March My Darlings.* New York: Harcourt Brace Jovanovich, 1977.

Trilling, Lionel. *The Middle of the Journey.* Garden City, N.Y.: Doubleday, 1957.

Ulam, Adam B. *Stalin.* New York: Viking, 1973.

Ungar, Sanford J. *FBI.* Boston: Little, Brown, 1975.

Ward, Estolv E. *Harry Bridges on Trial.* New York: Modern Age, 1940.

Warren, Frank A., III. *Liberals and Communism.* Bloomington: Indiana University Press, 1946.

Werfel, Franz. *Class Reunion.* New York: Simon and Schuster, 1929 (trans. of *Der Abituriententag,* Berlin: Zsolnay, 1928).

Wertenbaker, Charles. *The Death of Kings.* New York: Random House, 1954.

West, Rebecca. *The New Meaning of Treason.* New York: Viking, 1967.

Weyl, Nathaniel. *The Battle Against Disloyalty.* New York: Crowell, 1951.

————. *Treason: The Story of Disloyalty and Betrayal in American History.* Washington: Public Affairs Press, 1950.

White, Nathan I. *Harry Dexter White, Loyal American.* Waban, Mass.: 1956.

Whitehead, Don. *The FBI Story.* New York: Random House, 1956.

Whitfield, Stephen J. *Scott Nearing: Apostle of American Radicalism.* New York: Columbia University Press, 1974.

Wills, Garry. *Nixon Agonistes.* New York: New American Library, 1970.

Wiltz, John E. *In Search of Peace: The Senate Munitions Inquiry, 1934–36.* Baton Rouge: Louisiana State University Press, 1963.

Wise, David. *The American Police State.* New York: Random House, 1976.

Wise, David, and Thomas B. Ross. *The Espionage Establishment.* New York: Random House, 1967.

Wolin, Simon, and Robert M. Slusser, eds. *The Soviet Secret Police.* New York: Praeger, 1957.

Worth, E. J. *Whittaker Chambers: The Secret Confession.* London: Mazzard, 1993.

Yarnell, Allen. *Democrats and Progressives.* Berkeley: University of California Press, 1974.

Zeligs, Meyer A. *Friendship and Fratricide.* New York: Viking, 1967.

ARTICLES

The file of published articles on the Hiss-Chambers case from 1948 to the 1990s is voluminous. Many of those of particular importance to an understanding of the case are cited in the text, footnotes, endnotes, and Appendix.

ABOUT THE AUTHOR

Allen Weinstein served as The Archivist of the United States from 2005–2009. From 1985 to 2003, he served as President of The Center for Democracy, a Washington-based nonprofit foundation that he helped found. He was a founding director of The United States Institute of Peace (USIP) from 1985–1999. Weinstein has held professorships at Georgetown, Boston University, and Smith College among other posts. He received a BA from The City College (New York) and an MA and PhD from Yale University. Weinstein's awards include the United Nations Peace Medal in 1986, The Council of Europe's Silver Medal twice, in 1990 and 1996, and the Edgar Allan Poe Special Award from the Mystery Writers of America for *Perjury: The Hiss-Chambers Case*. In addition to *Perjury* (third edition, 2013), Weinstein's previous books include *The Story of America* (with David Rubel), *Freedom and Crisis: An American History, Prelude to Populism,* and *The Haunted Wood: Soviet Espionage in America—The Stalin Era* (with Alexander Vassiliev). Weinstein is currently a member of the USIP's International Advisory Council and a board member of the DC Arts and Humanities Education Collaborative.

INDEX

CREDITS FOR PHOTOGRAPHS
IN INSERT FOLLOWING PAGE 396